Gardening 1-2-3®

Meredith® Books
Des Moines, Iowa

Gardening 1-2-3®
Table of contents

Chapter 1 GETTING STARTED 4

Chapter 2 UNDERSTANDING YOUR GROWING CONDITIONS 18

Chapter 3 DESIGN AND PLANNING BASICS 44

Chapter 4 SPECIALTY GARDENING 102

Chapter 5 PREPARATION, PLANTING, AND PROPAGATION 134

Chapter 6 MAINTENANCE 170

Chapter 7 LAWNS 224

Chapter 8 VEGETABLES, HERBS, FRUITS, AND OTHER GARDEN EDIBLES 248

Chapter 9 CONTAINER GARDENING 268

Chapter 10 HOUSEPLANTS 282

PLANT ENCYCLOPEDIA 292

Getting Started

Thomas Jefferson said, "But though an old man, I am but a young gardener."

What Jefferson meant is that gardening is a process. No one creates a beautiful garden overnight. Instead each gardener gradually learns the basics: How to grow plants, how to place them, soil basics, peculiarities of climate, how to cope with the inevitable diseases and pests, and how to create a garden that reflects your personal lifestyle and

your personal preferences.

In this book you'll learn all that and more. And in this chapter you'll find information on design fundamentals, how to find your personal garden style, how to build good soil, and how to understand the microclimate of your region and even your own garden.

So pour youself a cup of coffee, pull out your paper, sharpen your pencil, and get planning!

Chapter 1 Getting Started

Features in This Book

Gardening 1-2-3 is from the gardening experts at the Home Depot. In this book you'll find almost everything you need to get you started on the garden of your dreams.

First you will learn the importance of climate and ways to cope with climate fluctuations. Then you will learn how to design, prepare, plant, and maintain your landscape. You'll also find ideas for specialized kinds of gardens. Finally the Plant Encyclopedia provides precise information on the most popular plants for all areas of North America.

The Plant Encyclopedia

Starting on page 292, you'll find a Plant Encyclopedia that has a detailed entry for each plant. Each description includes light and soil needs, mature size, special features, and care and selection information for the most commonly grown plants in North America. It also includes zones in which the plant thrives (see page 26). However, zone information should be used as a rough guide. Local conditions are the real test for what grows well in each area.

Daisy, Shasta
Daphne
Date Palm
Datura; Angel's Trumpet
Davallia fejeensis
Dawn Redwood
Daylily
Dead Nettle, Spotted

Special Features for Quick Reference

Every project tells you how easy or difficult the project is and how long it might take to do it. It also includes a list of tools and materials you'll need to get the job done right.

Clear step-by-step directions make garden projects easy.

PROJECT DETAILS

SKILLS: Digging
PROJECT: Digging up bulbs in fall that would die if left to winter outdoors

TIME TO COMPLETE

EXPERIENCED: 1 hour for a few dozen bulbs
HANDY: 1 to 2 hours
NOVICE: 2 to 3 hours

STUFF YOU'LL NEED

TOOLS: Spading fork or spade, soft brush (optional), hand pruners
MATERIALS: Storage box, newspaper, material such as sawdust in which to store bulbs

Digging and Storing Bulbs

1 After fall frost has blackened the bulb foliage, dig up bulbs carefully to avoid injuring them. A spading fork is less likely to do damage than a spade. Cut off the dead foliage for easier handling.

2 Shake or rub the soil from the bulbs, using a soft brush if necessary. Then spread the bulbs to dry for a few days on newspapers in a shady but dry and breezy spot, such as a porch or a garage with the door left open.

3 Store the dried bulbs in a cardboard box or paper bag. Avoid plastic because it promotes mold. Fill the box or bag with slightly damp sawdust or other packing material, and label it. Store in a cool to moderate—35 to 75°F (7 to 23°C)—room. Check every month or so, and remove any shriveled, moldy bulbs.

A CLOSER LOOK

WHAT IS A BULB?

Some flowers we commonly think of as bulbs really aren't bulbs at all. True bulbs look a little like an onion, with many layers. Lilies, hyacinths, amaryllis, and daffodils, for example, are true bulbs. Others are actually corms, tubers, or rhizomes (see page 160 for planting information). Don't let the terminology throw you, though. They're not treated any differently. Just follow the label directions.

TYPES OF BULBS

Tulip bulb
Crocus corm
Iris rhizome
Anemone tuber
Dahlia tuber
Giant ranunculus tuberous root

Learn more about specific topics with tidbits of extra information.

Plant lists get you started with specific plants. Common and botanical names are provided, as well as zones in which the plant will thrive best.

Good Shrubs for Foundation Plantings

Common Name	Botanical Name	Zones
Alpine currant	*Ribes alpinum* spp.	2-7
Amur privet	*Ligustrum amurense*	3-7
Azalea, various	*Rhododendron* spp.	xx-xx
Boxwood, lower growing	*Buxus* spp.	4-11
Burning bush, dwarf	*Euonymus alatus* 'Compacta'	xx-xx
Bush cinquefoil	*Potentilla fruticosa*	2-7
Carefree Beauty rose	*Rosa* 'Carefree Beauty'	4-8
Cherry laurel	*Prunus laurocerasus* 'Otto Luyken'	6-8
Chinese hibiscus	*Hibiscus rosa-sinensis*	9-10
Common witch hazel	*Hamamelis virginiana*	3-8
Compact American cranberrybush	*Viburnum trilobum* 'Alfredo'	2-7
Compact Japanese holly	*Ilex crenata* 'Compacta'	5-8
Cornelian cherry	*Cornus mas*	4-8
Dwarf balsam fir	*Abies balsamea* 'Nana'	3-6
Dwarf Norway spruce	*Picea abies* 'Pumila'	3-8
Emerald arborvitae	*Thuja occidentalis* 'Emerald'	2-7
Gardenia	*Gardenia jasminoides*	8-10
Glossy abelia	*Abelia* × *grandiflora*	x-9
Golden Vicary privet	*Ligustrum* × *vicaryi*	5-8
Gray dogwood	*Cornus racemosa*	4-7
Holly, lower-growing types	*Ilex* spp.	xx-xx
Hydrangea	*Hydrangea* spp.	xx-xx
Indian hawthorn	*Rhaphiolepis indica*	8-10
Japanese aucuba	*Aucuba japonica*	7-10
Japanese barberry	*Berberis thunbergii*	4-8

Gardening Where You Live

ROSES FOR THE PACIFIC NORTHWEST

Some roses do better than others in the cool, misty Pacific Northwest. In general, pink roses are more resistant to the region's fungal diseases, and yellow and red roses do not fade in the afternoon sun as they do elsewhere. Roses with fewer petals do better than those with many petals, because they don't ball up and rot as easily after days of rain. Any of the rugosa roses also do well. Other top rose performers include 'Bonica', 'Flower Carpet', 'Peace', 'Queen Elizabeth', and 'The Fairy'.

You'll benefit from this information targeted specifically at a particular region of North America.

GOOD IDEA!

THE STICK TEST

What's the easiest way to see how dry soil is? Feel it! Wiggle your finger or poke a stick 2 to 3 inches into the ground. If it's bone dry at that depth, it's time to water.

Smart ideas that make gardening simpler or easier are given throughout.

DESIGN TIP

WRITE IT DOWN

When visiting local public gardens or going on a garden tour to see what does well in your area, bring a camera and/or a notebook so you can record plants that are doing well in your climate. Also take note of plant combinations, colors, and heights that appeal to you. If possible, visit that spot several times during the year so you can see how a plant performs over time and can see plants that peak at different times of the year.

You'll find lots of design tips to help you skillfully lay out your landscape.

TOOL TIP

POWER EDGERS

If you have a large area to edge, or you'll be edging fairly frequently, consider renting or purchasing a power edger.

This nifty tool is ideal for creating crisp, fast, neat turf edges around beds and borders, edging around walks and drives, or digging quick, perfect mini trenches for installing plastic, metal, and other narrow edging.

See page 15 for more information on power edgers.

Having the right tool and knowing how to use it makes gardening more efficient.

BUYER'S GUIDE

LAWN TRACTOR, YARD TRACTOR, OR GARDEN TRACTOR?

They all sound similar, but they're each different.

A lawn tractor is made specifically for cutting grass, though it also can haul some light accessories, such as a small trailer.

Yard or garden tractors are more powerful and more general purpose. They can cut grass, but they also have the power to pull plows, rakes, and harrows and pull larger trailers carrying heavier loads.

Save money with tips on buying plants and supplies.

WORK SMARTER

THE ROSE EXPERTS

The American Rose Society (ARS) sponsors a toll-free rose hotline for gardeners to pose questions to rose experts. Call 800-637-6534 with your rose questions. Also check out the ARS's extensive website, which has rose recommendations and growing information: www.ars.org.

Learn to work more effectively.

Garden Knowledge Basics

The Golden Rules of Gardening

Follow these fundamental rules in your garden and you'll be well on your way to having a beautiful landscape:

1 Invest in your soil. Before planting, spend time and money on improving your soil. Loose, rich, well-drained soil reduces watering, makes weeding easier, fights diseases, and helps plants grow bigger and better in a way that no chemicals can.

The no-fail way is to work in plenty of compost—it's almost impossible to add too much—and to keep adding it year after year. See page 136 for more details on enriching your soil.

2 Put the right plant in the right place. Choose plants that are well-suited to your climate—they will require minimal attention, watering, sprays, altered pH, staking, or digging up each year. See page 60 for other ways to work with nature rather than against it.

3 Look at your garden every day. Spend a little time in the morning before work, or steal a few moments each evening. Make it a treat (this is fun, remember?) by having a cup of coffee or a cold drink in your hand. You'll enjoy your garden, get ideas, and spot problems while they're small and can be remedied easily.

4 Learn and plan. Read and research plants and gardening techniques. Look through mail-order catalogs and gardening magazines. Browse the Internet. Visit public gardens. Look at neighborhood gardens and ask lots of questions. Go to garden shows and attend garden tours. (Bring a camera and notebook!) You'll get ideas that will help you garden better and more efficiently. See page 46 for more planning ideas—planning is a good way to spend the winter!

5 Read the instructions. Whether they're on a plant label or a seed packet, read the directions and follow them exactly. You'll save time and money.

6 Kill a few plants. Gardening is all about experimenting. It's OK if there are a few plant casualties along the way. Even the most experienced gardeners kill plants, because even they, too, are learning as they go and are always trying new things. You don't have a brown thumb if a plant dies; consider it a learning experience and move on.

7 Have patience. Gardening is a gradual process. It takes time—often years—to master techniques, and it takes time for gardens to reach their potential. Learning to appreciate nature's pace is actually one of gardening's most valuable lessons.

8 Have confidence. This is not rocket science. In gardening, there's seldom one hard and fast "proper" way to do things, rather there are often various ways to get the same or slightly different results. Just do it!

9 Remember that a garden is a work in progress. A bed and a garden change over the days, the weeks, the months, and even the years. This change is an integral part of gardening and believe it or not, is all part of the pleasure of gardening.

10 Have fun! Working in your garden provides welcome relief from the trials and stresses of everyday life. Why fuss about whether things are perfect or fret about what the neighbors think? Personal fulfillment, enjoyment, and satisfaction are what gardening is all about, so enjoy!

The Name of the Game

What's up with those Latin names?

Most plants have at least two names—a common name and a botanical (Latin) name. The common name is the one that most people use when they talk about a plant. The botanical name is assigned to each plant by botanists for accurate identification.

Common names are easy to remember and often charming (Johnny-jump-up, love-lies-bleeding, lady's mantle), but common names can vary widely by region. And two or three different plants might share the same common name, as in the case of African daisy (which refers to both *Arctotis* and *Dimorphotheca).* Botanical names can be hard to remember and may be tongue twisters, but each plant usually has only one botanical name.

That's why, in the Plant Encyclopedia starting on page 292, most plants are also listed by their botanical names. It's the most reliable way to help you find the right plant for your garden.

Also refer to the general index in the back of this book to search for specific information on gardening techniques and methods.

What's What?

Even if you know the difference between an annual and a perennial, you'll find that a perennial sometimes can act like an annual—and sometimes like a groundcover. Here's how to sort it all out:

ANNUAL

A plant that sets seed and dies in just one year or less. It can be a little confusing, however, because sometimes plants that technically are perennials or even shrubs are treated as annuals in colder climates and labels aren't always detailed enough to explain this. If in doubt, ask your Home Depot garden associate.

EVERGREEN

A plant that keeps fresh-looking leaves all year, even in winter. Includes not only needle-leaved plants such as pines and spruces (also called conifers), but also broad-leaved evergreens such as rhododendrons and boxwood.

DECIDUOUS

Has woody stems and sheds its leaves as it goes through a yearly period of dormancy. Oaks, elms, and lilacs are examples.

PERENNIAL

A plant that grows year after year. Some perennials die back to the ground in the winter; others are evergreen.

TREE

A woody plant with one or more main trunks. Usually grows to at least the height of an adult person. Some plants, such as certain dogwoods and magnolias, could be classified as either tall shrubs or small trees. A tree can be evergreen or deciduous. Many palms are considered trees.

SHRUB

Can be evergreen or deciduous and vary in height from just a few inches to several feet. Usually has woody stems, though sometimes some plants that technically are perennials, such as peonies, are thought of as shrubs.

GROUNDCOVER

Any plant that is used in a mass planting to cover the ground. Can be a low shrub, perennial, vine, ornamental grass, or annual as long as a number of them are planted together to carpet the ground.

Creating a Garden with a Sense of Place

A garden in Seattle shouldn't look like a garden in Atlanta or even a garden in Maine. The best, most interesting gardens have a strong sense of place—that is, they reflect the region in which they grow. The American desert garden shown here is a perfect example.

Here's how to create a garden that celebrates regional style and substance:

- Use native plants. Plants that evolved locally strongly suggest a garden's regionality. What would a prairie garden be without purple coneflowers? Or a California mountain garden without brilliant golden California poppies? When striving for regionality, it's also smart to avoid a lot of anything that isn't well-suited to the region, such as a large expanse of lawn in a desert garden, or tall, moisture-loving delphiniums in arid, windy western Nebraska.
- Use local hardscaping materials whenever possible. Giant lava boulders can look out of place in, say, Illinois. Local stone, such as limestone, seems more a part of that landscape.
- Keep a region's style in mind. Southern gardens have a rich tradition of formal, symmetrical beds separated by brick paths. Western gardens tend to be more casual and rambling. Brightly painted Mexican clay pots might look out of place on an urban rooftop garden, but they're right at home in a Southwestern garden.
- Attend local garden tours and visit local public gardens. You'll get good ideas and find nifty plants, and you'll collect tips on what makes gardens in your area distinctive.
- When traveling beyond your area, visit as many gardens as you can. Sometimes the best way to determine your region's garden style is to see other regions, so you'll have a basis for comparison.

Keeping Track

One of the best ways to save money and time in the garden is to keep a garden record. It doesn't have to be fancy—maybe just a shoebox that you tuck labels and receipts and notes into—but it is invaluable for planning.

You may want to keep a beautiful garden journal in a hardcover book especially for that purpose. Or you may be happier with a plain spiral notebook or a binder with pockets for receipts, labels, and clipped magazine articles. Perhaps you'll want to keep records on your computer. Whatever you decide to do, here are suggestions for some of the information you'll want to keep track of:

Receipts

Many garden centers will refund a plant only if you have the receipt. Or you may need to return a tool or other garden item. That can be hard to do without the receipt.

Also, keeping receipts helps you keep tabs on your garden spending. (Some gardeners like to keep a running account of their garden expenditures to stay within a budget.)

Bloom Times

Nearly everybody wants color in the garden year-round. That's easy to do if you keep a list of your plants and their bloom times. Each year, write down a chronological list of what blooms when. Note what's going on in your own garden, of course, but also include plants you've seen blooming or at peak interest in your neighborhood and local public gardens. You'll create a list of the plants you need in your own garden to have something in bloom or beautiful every week of the year.

Plant Labels

Trying to remember the name of that rose? Or exactly what type of juniper that is? Keeping plant labels will jog your memory, especially because many of them include a photo of the mature plant.

Gardening Reminders

If you have a professional garden plan, keep it handy so you always know where to find it—for your reference and perhaps to bring with you to the garden center.

A garden record-keeping system is also the perfect way to keep track of miscellaneous gardening notes—such as a reminder to add some fall-blooming perennials to the back of your flower garden next spring. And when it comes time to plant spring-blooming bulbs in fall, did you want to remember to add some late-blooming pink tulips in front of the peony?

Magazine Articles and Notes

Why not organize your collection of clipped garden articles with all those gorgeous pictures? Keep them in one spot where you can refer to them or even bring them along to the garden center for reference.

A garden record-keeping system is also the perfect place for you to tuck notes to yourself, such as the name of that splendid Japanese maple you saw on a garden tour last year.

Fun Stuff

Garden record-keeping can be enjoyable. Have fun tucking in photos of your beautiful results or favorite plants. Press a few flowers in a book and include them. Or buy a handsome fabric-covered box to hold all your plant labels.

Saving Time In the Garden

You can create a beautiful garden if you have unlimited time. But of course, no one has unlimited time. Those who tend large gardens do so with smart time management. Here's how you also can have a beautiful landscape, even with limited time.

- Research your plant and landscape decisions. Take a few minutes to read up on your next garden project. You'll make better choices that will save you from having to redo the project later.
- Block out time for gardening. Some gardeners like to do a 10-minute weed and deadhead session before work each morning. Others make Saturday mornings their time for puttering in the garden.
- Get organized. Devote a corner of the garage or a shed to gardening supplies, and keep them in good working order. You'll save hours of trying to find the right tool. In the garden, put all the small tools and supplies you need often into one basket or organizer so they'll always be handy.
- Look at your garden every day. Take a minute or two each day to walk through your yard. It will give you a jump on small problems before they become big ones.
- Keep a garden journal or notebook. Centralize all those magazine articles, seed packets, and notes to yourself in one location.
- Plant in large groups. As a rule, planting a large group of the same type of plant is more efficient, because you spend the same amount of preparation time regardless of the size of the planting. Larger plantings mean fewer sessions of preparation time. You spend the same amount of time getting out tools and supplies and preparing the site.
- Group plants according to their needs. Put all acid-loving plants in the same area so you can acidify the soil more efficiently. Keep all moisture-loving plants together so you can water more efficiently.
- Mulch! Mulching saves water, suppresses weeds, and inhibits many soilborne diseases.
- Avoid exotics. Choose low-maintenance plants that don't require staking, spraying, excessive feeding, protection, or digging up each fall.
- Choose plants that do well naturally in your area. Yes, you can grow delphiniums in a desert, but they'll take lots of time, effort, and water. If you're determined to have a bumper crop of blueberries in alkaline soil, you can spend lots of effort on building raised beds and acidifying the soil regularly—but is it worth it? Appreciate what grows easily in your area. Those plants will practically take care of themselves.
- Experiment with flowering shrubs. Excellent timesavers compared to many perennials and annuals, they require little more than a bit of pruning once a year, if at all. In return, they give you abundant flowers and, often, fragrance.

WORK SMARTER

KEEP A GARDEN-CENTER LIST

Right next to your grocery list or tacked to the wall in the garage, keep a list of what you need at your Home Depot garden center. That way, you'll be sure to get everything you need in one stop.

BUYER'S GUIDE

BE FLEXIBLE

Have a good idea of what you need when you go to the garden center, but also be open to new plants and ideas. Let the garden staff guide you to the best choices available. Rather than spending time trying to track down difficult-to-find plants, you may discover a new favorite in the process.

Organizing small garden supplies into a handy caddy saves time looking for them.

The Well-Equipped Garden Shed

Gardening goes easier and takes less time and toll on your body when you have the right tools for the job. Here are the basic tools that every gardener should have:

Working the Soil and More

Round-point shovels are the best choice for digging holes, mixing soil, and planting trees or shrubs. Handles come in wood or fiberglass. Brightly colored fiberglass makes the tool easy to spot if you forget where you left it.

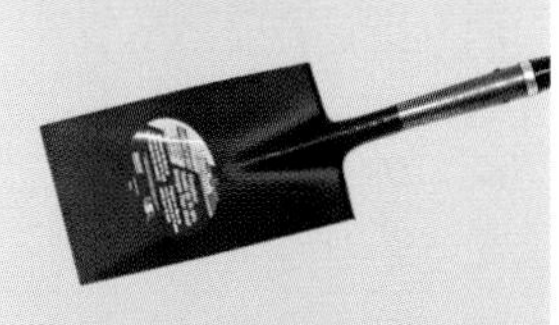

Flat-edge spades are designed for scraping and moving material, and edging beds and walks. A D-handle makes it easy to hang the tool on a wall.

A **hand trowel** is essential. Look for one with an ergonomic handle for added comfort.

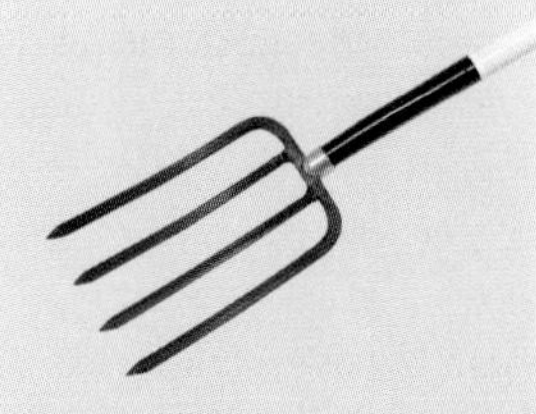

Garden forks, also called spading forks, are sturdy and versatile. They can be used for turning compost, loosening soil, and digging delicate bulbs or vegetables.

A **bow or ground rake** is an essential tool for making planting beds and combing soil to remove rocks, roots, and clumps of earth prior to planting. It also helps you work the soil's surface to the correct height and proper slope for good drainage.

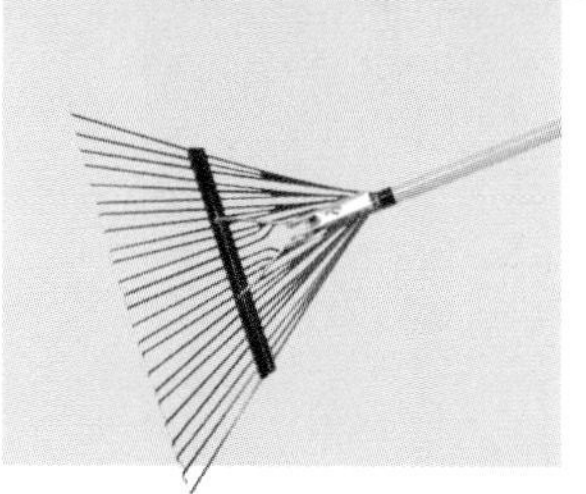

A **leaf rake** is useful for raking up autumn leaves, bits of grass, and lawn litter, as well as loose winter mulch from flower beds in spring.

A **broad hoe** is a multiuse tool for your garden. Use it for weeding, turning soil, mixing compost, chopping mulch, and more.

A **warren hoe** has a pointed end that allows for tighter, more accurate weeding than some other hoes—an important feature for flower beds and borders.

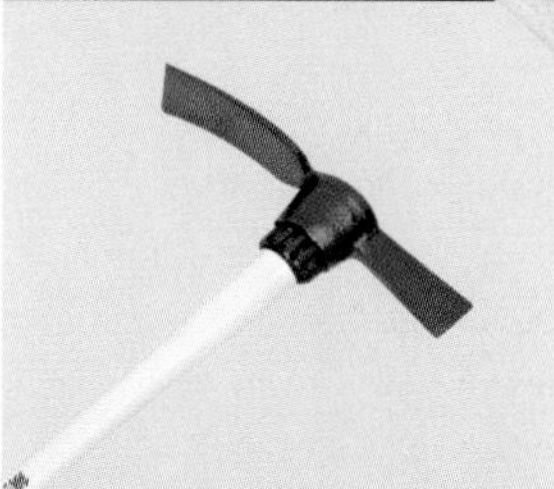

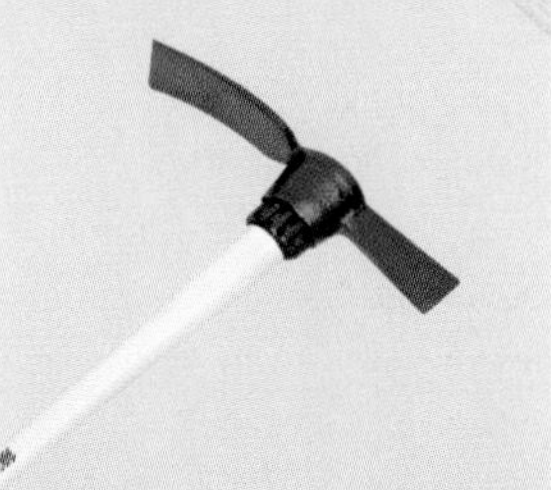

A **mattock** is good for chopping and digging in root-laden or hardpan soil. Use the ax-head end to chop away roots and the flat end to dig like a hoe. A pick mattock has a sharp, pointed end instead of an ax head for use in rocky soils.

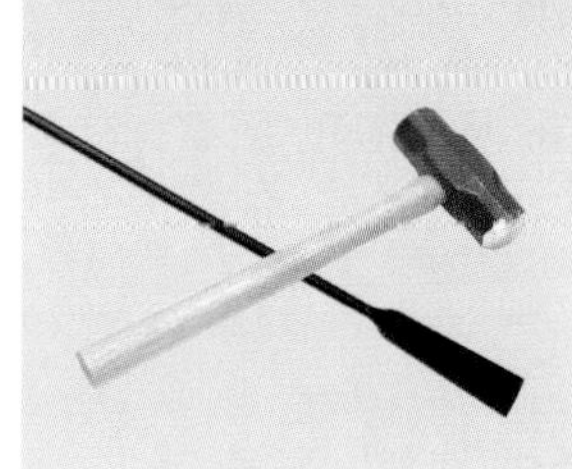

A **sledgehammer** and **digging bar** are invaluable in rocky, compacted, or heavy clay soils. The weight of the digging bar makes it easy to drive into resistant soil. The sledgehammer breaks up rocks and roots with ease.

Pruning and Cutting

Bypass hand pruners are essential. They work like scissors, with both blades moving. They make cleaner cuts than anvil pruners, which have one fixed edge and one moving cutting blade.

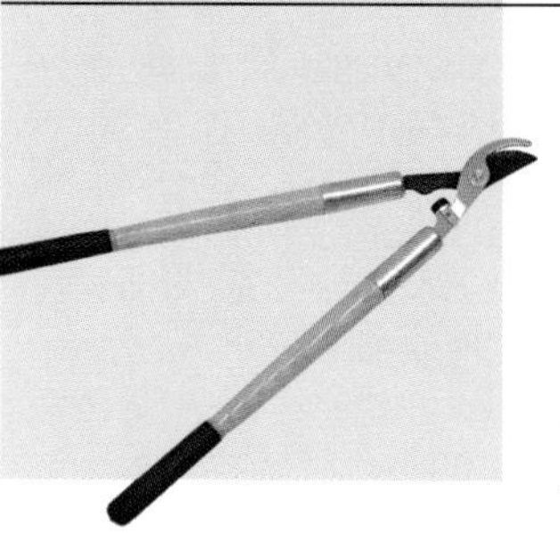

Bypass loppers have long handles for leverage and bigger blades than hand pruners. They're necessary for cutting branches that are thicker than a pencil; using hand pruners on a large stem can strain your hand and make a jagged cut, which invites disease.

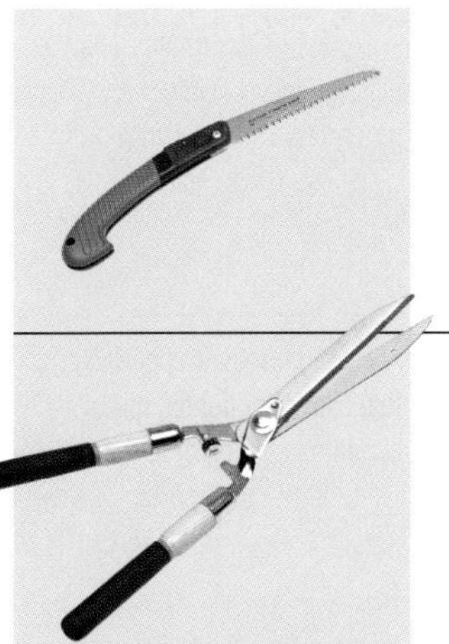

A **pruning saw** is needed for removing large branches that are too big for loppers to cut. The small, serrated blade is strong enough to cut into green wood but light enough for easy handling.

Hedge trimmers have long blades and handles. They are designed for cutting along the surfaces of shrubs to trim, maintain, and shape them. Power versions are available.

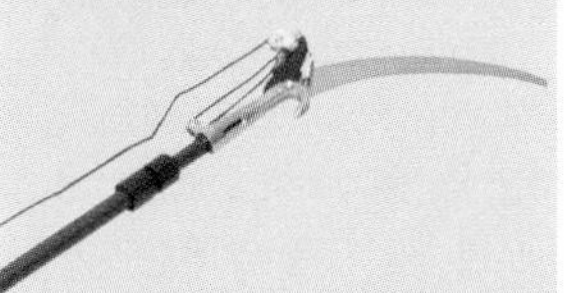

A **pole pruner** easily removes overhead branches. Wear eye protection when you're working above your head.

A **hand ax** is invaluable when dividing the root ball of perennials with tough roots, such as daylilies and peonies. It's also good for chopping through small tree roots when working the soil or digging up a small tree or shrub.

Watering

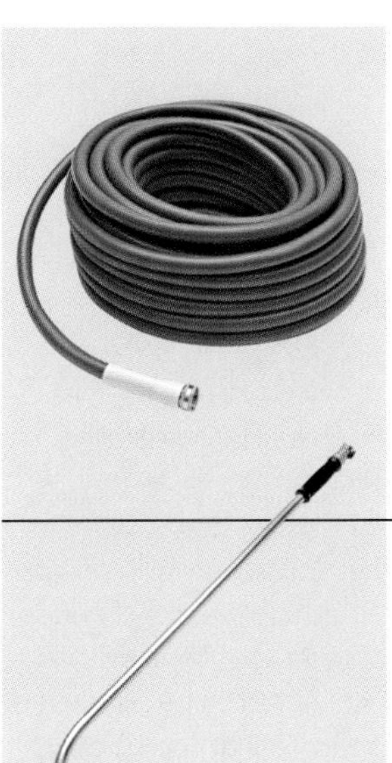

A good-quality **garden hose** is a sound investment. The extra expense is worthwhile if the hose kinks less and lasts longer. Look for a hose that has no visible veining and features a long brass nozzle and brass screw ends. Even if you have a sprinkler system, you'll need a garden hose for supplying water to freshly planted trees and shrubs.

A **watering wand** attaches to the end of a hose. Its long handle makes it easy to water hard-to-reach corners of beds as well as containers and hanging baskets. The wand head showers plants like raindrops instead of blasting them with a hard stream of water.

A **watering can** always comes in handy. Choose one with a large head to disperse water gently. A rounded handle makes the can easy to grip when it's full.

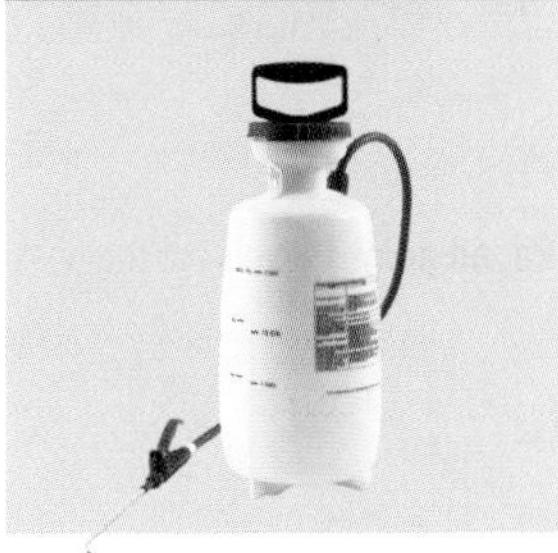

A sprayer is useful for a variety of tasks, including foliar feeding as well as spraying for pests, diseases, and weeds. However, be sure to use a separate sprayer for weed killers so you don't get any residue when spraying other garden plants.

Other Good Stuff

Knee pads or a kneeling pad is ideal for cushioning when weeding or doing other tasks. It also keeps pants clean and dry.

Leather gloves are necessary for heavy-duty landscaping projects and hauling stone and concrete. They protect your hands against thorns, sharp branches, and tools. Look for gloves that tighten at the wrist to keep out dirt.

A **garden hat** protects your face from the sun. Open-weave material breathes to keep you from overheating. Use a sun hat and sunscreen when you're working outdoors.

A **wheelbarrow** is the landscaping workhorse, saving time and your back when you're transplanting trees and shrubs, or moving soil, amendments, mulch, and tools. The more you spend on a new wheelbarrow, the longer you can expect it to last. Store your wheelbarrow hanging up to keep it from resting on its tire. Keep a replacement tire handy.

Power Tools

Power tools make the job go faster and easier, so much so that sometimes investing in a power tool can save you from having to hire a pro.

If you're not ready to buy one of these powerful devices, check into renting them. (Many Home Depots now offer power tool rental.) Rental may be the most cost-effective way to tackle a single project or two.

On these pages are some of the most popular power tools for gardeners, with tips on what to consider when shopping for one.

String Trimmer

The perfect complement to a mower, a string trimmer usually is used for cutting grass in places that mowers can't, such as around or under fences or other tight spots. More powerful string trimmers can cut large weeds or even light brush.

What to look for:

- Gas, corded electric, or cordless? Gas-powered trimmers usually are the most powerful, but they are also usually the heaviest, weighing between 10 and 13 pounds. Corded electric models are quieter and lighter (usually around 5 to 7 pounds), but of course there's the cord to deal with. Battery-powered electric models are convenient, but they're also the least powerful and therefore usually work only with relatively short grass. A charge lasts 20 to 30 minutes, and models can weigh up to 12 pounds.

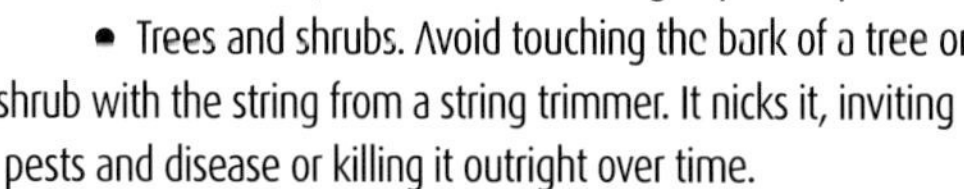

- Trees and shrubs. Avoid touching the bark of a tree or shrub with the string from a string trimmer. It nicks it, inviting pests and disease or killing it outright over time.
- Look for attachments that convert the trimmer into a power blower, edger, or pole saw.

Chipper-Shredder

These machines are ideal for shredding branches, leaves, and all manner of yard waste. They can turn a mountain of leaves into a small pile. And because they cut up material finely, they're perfect for serious composters who want to create better compost faster (see page 182).

Shopping pointers:

- The more powerful the machine, the more and larger the material that it can shred. Small chipper-shredders start at around 5 hp and can handle limbs up to 3 inches in diameter. Midrange tools have about 6 to 10 horsepower (hp) and can handle limbs from $2\frac{1}{2}$ to $3\frac{1}{2}$ inches. The most powerful are 10 hp-plus and can handle limbs 4 inches and larger.
- Choose from gas or electric models. Gas, as a rule, is more powerful, but electric is quieter and does not create fumes.
- Consider weight and portability. Make sure you can maneuver the machine around your yard or into your garage as easily as needed. Electric models tend to be lighter.
- Check service needs. Some chipper-shredders need annual tune-ups and sharpening. If you won't be doing these tasks yourself, check the cost of having them done and the transportability of your machine.
- Shredding only leaves? A power vacuum with a shredder and bagger may be a better alternative.

Tiller

Tillers make short work of creating new beds and borders and turning over vegetable gardens each spring. They're also ideal for working in soil amendments, such as compost or peat moss, over large areas.

When considering purchasing a tiller, keep the following in mind:

- Weight and horsepower. Large, powerful tillers (those with 6 hp and up) are ideal for tilling large gardens—with more than 5,000 square feet. However, they can weigh as much as 200 pounds and often need a trailer to be transported any distance. Also, the largest tillers require a lot of strength to handle well.

A garden under 5,000 square feet should do fine with a 4- to 6-hp machine, which is lighter and easier to handle.

Then there are the smallest, so-called "mini" tillers or cultivators that you can lift with one hand. These are best for keeping down weeds between rows and other light tilling rather than creating new beds.

- Rear tine vs. front tine. Rear-tine tillers are increasingly popular because the motor powers the wheels in front, which pull the tiller forward. They are powerful and a good choice for hardpan and stony soils. Front-tine tillers have rear-mounted wheels, which allow you to easily push the machine from one location to another.
- Tilling depth and width. Check the tines to see how deep the machine can till. If you're creating shrub or perennial borders, you'll want to till several inches deep, at least. Working in soil amendments or turning over a vegetable garden requires less depth. Also check how wide a swath the tiller covers; wide swaths mean fewer passes to cover an area.
- Gas or electric? Gas engines tend to be more powerful but trickier to

start. (Look for an electric starter.) Electric tillers are quiet and light but tend to be far less powerful and have a cord to deal with.

- Your soil. Tillers work best in soil that is at least moderately soft when moist and free from large stones.

Power Hedge Trimmer

If you have a hedge you want to keep tidy, or more than only a few shrubs or evergreen trees you want to keep trimmed tightly, a power hedge trimmer is an excellent investment. Some can be adjusted to be used as a lightweight edger.

Some features to keep in mind when shopping:

- Gas vs. corded electric vs. battery powered. Gas-powered hedge trimmers have ample power but can weigh 10 to 15 pounds. Corded electric models are quiet and usually weigh less than 10 pounds, but the cord can limit how far from the power source you can trim, and the cord could get sliced along with the branches. Battery-powered electric models are quiet and light (less than 10 pounds) but less powerful—a problem for heavy-duty trimming. Charge time is usually around a half hour.
- Double edge vs. single edge. Double-edged blades are the most common and have teeth on both sides, allowing you to make cuts as you pass the machine back and forth.
- Blade length/pole design. Long blades are good for straight cuts along hedges. Short blades are better for shaping small shrubs. Also consider pole hedge trimmers, which have long polelike handles that make them excellent for cutting high hedges without a ladder.
- Blade angle. Many hedge trimmers allow you to set the blade at different angles or articulate the blade so you can reach the top of tall hedges and awkward spots.

Chain Saw

Chain saws aren't only for property owners with large, wooded lots. Small, less expensive models are ideal for gardeners with small suburban lots and only a few trees. They make quick work of a small tree or an overgrown shrub.

Features to consider include:

- Gas vs. electric. Gas models are heavier but more powerful; electric models are lighter and quieter but have a cumbersome cord.
- Power. The higher the rpm (revolutions per minute), the faster and smoother (with less vibration) the saw will cut. That means it's less likely to kick back and is therefore safer. In general, the larger the material, the larger the saw you'll need. Also note a machine's bhp (brake horsepower) or kilowatts (kW). Some manufacturers calculate a power-to-weight ratio, kW/kg (kilowatts per kilogram), expressed as a percent. In all these cases, the higher the number, the more powerful the machine.
- Weight. Lift the machine and estimate how easily you could handle it for a half hour to an hour.
- Blade length. A 16-inch bar may be able to cut small branches, but a professional-grade 32-inch bar will let you cut without bending over, a major back saver.
- Safety features. Look for antikickback devices on small saws. Also look for a chain brake, which stops a moving chain if it breaks; a throttle trigger lock, which locks the throttle trigger while the saw is idling to prevent the accidental opening of the throttle; and a chain catcher, which catches a broken or jumping chain.

Leaf Blower

Leaf blowers and leaf blower-vacuums can make short work of fallen leaves and other light garden debris. When shopping for one, keep in mind the following:

- Vacuum or not? Some leaf blowers also have a built-in vacuum-mulching function to suck up leaves and shred them. Still others have an optional kit that converts them to vacuums.
- Gas or electric? Gas is considerably more noisy than electric, so much so some cities have rules about how noisy they can be. Gas models are also usually heavier. Also, emissions from gas leaf blowers have been a concern. However, gas blowers don't have a cord the way equally powerful electric types do.
- Weight. The lightest battery-operated leaf blowers weigh in at around 6 pounds. Heavier types can weigh more than 15 pounds and are strapped on your back for better weight distribution.
- Cordless electric types are convenient but not as powerful as other types. Cordless electric is best for sidewalks and drives rather than lawns and gardens.

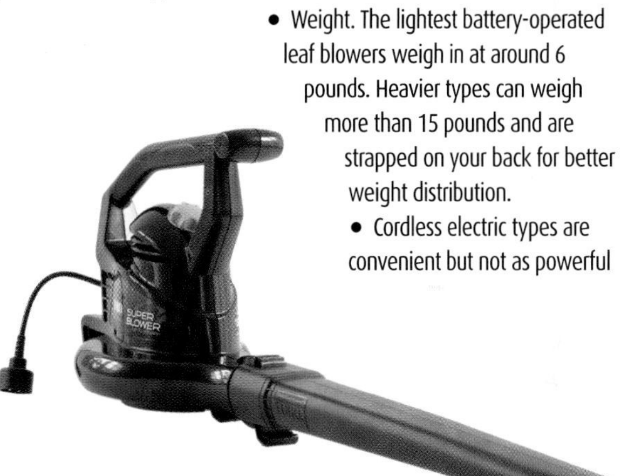

- Power. With electric models, compare amps. With gas types, compare horsepower, expressed as hp. More power means easier, faster cleanup.

Power Tool Basics

When using power tools, safety is important. With noisy engines, wear ear plugs. Protect hands with heavy gloves to prevent cuts, injuries, and fatigue from vibrations. Safety glasses protect eyes from flying debris. Don't wear loose clothing that might get caught in moving parts. Sturdy shoes prevent injury from falling limbs and sharp moving parts.

It's also important to take proper care of your power tools. Keep them clean and dry to prevent rust and undue wear. Over the winter, remove gasoline from the engine to prevent damaging the tool. Use an oil-gasoline mix when necessary. Check the owner's manual for recommended care to prolong the tool's life and performance.

Smart Spending

Money alone doesn't make a good garden. Sure, it helps, but few gardeners have an unlimited budget. Stretch your hard-earned garden dollar with smart shopping and clever landscaping. Here's how:

- Visit your home and garden center often. Garden centers offer different plants and supplies throughout the year. If you stop by often, you'll get the best plants at the best price at the best time. You're also more likely to see the plants at their peak or in bloom.
- Ask! Your garden center associates know a lot, so use them. If possible, go on a nonweekend day when the staff have more time to give you full attention. Bring in photos (on a digital camera is ideal) or drawings of your garden or a map so they can better envision what you need.
- Try a plant by buying only one. If you like an expensive perennial, buy one and see how it looks in your garden. The only way to know is to give it a try.
- Know your light. This is fundamental to making the right plant choices and avoiding losing a lot of expensive plants. (See page 24.)
- Learn to propagate your own plants. Starting plants from seed (page 166) or from cuttings (page 169) is easy and can give you dozens of plants for only a few dollars, even if you have to invest in start-up equipment such as a potting medium and a good grow-light.
- Share plants. Give your friends, family, and neighbors divisions of your favorite plants. They're likely to return the favor.
- Split costs. If you've been yearning for a chipper-shredder but are unable to afford it or justify its limited use in one yard, go in with a trusted neighbor or family member and share it.
- Consider renting. If a tool isn't in your budget, renting it occasionally might do the trick.
- Grow plants that do double duty. A cherry tree, for example, has gorgeous flowers in spring and delicious fruit in summer. A hedge of lilacs creates privacy and provides armloads of flowers. You get twice the pleasure for the same amount of work.

BUYER'S GUIDE

INVEST IN YOUR SOIL

There's an old garden saying about putting a $5 plant into a $15 hole. It's good advice. What it means is to spend money on improving your soil, so the money for plants will be well-spent.

So be sure to amend the soil (page 138) or build raised beds (page 143) or whatever it takes. You'll be rewarded with better results and fewer ailing plants.

Learning to start plants from seed is a good way to spend your garden dollars wisely. You'll get dozens of plants for only a few dollars spent on seeds and supplies.

Hiring a Pro

There are times when you need to call in the professionals.

A landscape professional can give you good ideas for the general layout of your garden as well as create a design for a specific portion of your yard. Some charge a fee and some will do the design for free, with the expectation that you'll buy most of the plants through them or at the store they're associated with.

Help the process along by thinking through some general landscaping issues (see "How You Use Your Landscape" and "Deciding on Your Garden's Style," on pages 48 and 49 respectively).

Also keep a file of landscapes and plants you love. Clip pictures from magazines and catalogs, and take photographs of elements in gardens you've seen that you like, such as arbors or paths or raised beds. Pictures will help you communicate with the designer more clearly.

Installing a landscape can be expensive, and you don't have to do it all at once. Instead talk to the professional about creating a landscape that can be installed in stages as you have the funds to realize the landscape of your dreams.

Working with a professional to design your landscape assures you better results faster. A professional can create a beautiful, flowing design, recommend the best plants, and tell you exactly where to position them.

A CLOSER LOOK

EXPERT QUALIFICATIONS

Hiring a pro can save you time and money by preventing costly mistakes in building structures and choosing plants. No matter who you hire, ask for references, visit their sites in progress, and see completed jobs before you negotiate a contract. Show the person the landscapes you like. Set a budget and stick to it, and avoid paying the entire fee up front.

Associates at home and garden centers often offer informal design advice as part of their service. They can be expert gardeners.

Garden designers might not be licensed, but they often are very qualified and can offer advice on planning and preparing your landscape. They charge fees for design services.

Landscape architects are professionals licensed to prepare plans and guide planting, grading, and landscape construction. Expect a licensed architect to charge a higher fee.

Landscape contractors often provide free design services if they're hired to do the work as well.

GOOD IDEA!

PLAN BEFORE YOU REMODEL

If you're planning a construction project, talk with a landscape professional before or during the planning, instead of after the remodeling is completed.

Landscapers and architects may differ in their approach. Where a contractor might suggest a sidewalk against the house, a landscape professional might draw a curving sidewalk farther out that allows for plantings along an entryway.

Landscape professionals also have good ideas for decks, patios, outdoor living areas, and positioning doors and windows in ways that take advantage of current or potential garden features.

Understanding Your Growing Conditions

All gardening, to put a twist on the old saying, is like all politics—it's local. Even after years of working in a yard, an experienced gardener continues to learn about the region's climate as well as the microclimates of soil, temperature, moisture, and light in that particular garden. What thrives for your neighbor may not do well in your garden, and vice versa. But you can learn what works best—and what works less well—in your region and your backyard. Determine the types of microclimates you garden in. Find what region you're in, and read up on it, but also look at other regions so you have a basis for comparison.

Chapter 2 Understanding Your Growing Conditions

Gardening Smart Wherever You Live

DESIGN TIP

WRITE IT DOWN

When visiting local public gardens or going on a garden tour to see what does well in your area, bring a camera and/or a notebook so you can record plants that are doing well in your climate. Also take note of plant combinations, colors, and heights that appeal to you. If possible, visit that spot several times during the year so you can see how a plant performs over time and can see plants that peak at different times of the year.

Understanding your climate is a key to successful gardening.

Take notice of how much rain you get and when, the average low and high temperatures, the type of winds, and the nature of winters, springs, summers, and autumns in your area. Read up on your climate in the local newspaper, and browse the Internet. Ask local experienced gardeners as well as your Home Depot garden center associates about specifics of your weather. With this information, you can orchestrate a garden that's beautiful and healthy. Here's how:

Invest in a Rain Gauge

Keep track of rainfall. Most plants do well with an inch of water a week, so a rain gauge is critical for figuring out how much watering you'll need to do. It also helps you see patterns, so you can decide which plants are best for your garden, when you'll need to do the most watering, and how you can plan ahead with strategies for soil amending and watering.

Check the Weather Page

Look in the newspaper or browse the Internet for regional weather information (also check out the zone map on page 26). Look for information on record rainfalls and droughts, cold snaps and heat waves, winds, snows, and spells of foul or fair weather. Then you'll know what to expect and be prepared. Use this information to guide plant buying and planting. If you know that temperatures in your area regularly dip below -20°F (-30°C), you won't be tempted to buy a shrub that's hardy only to -10°F (-24°C).

Compare Other World Climates

If you live in Southern California, you'll find that your climate is fairly similar to that of many regions of the Mediterranean. Parts of the upper Midwest have climates similar to those of Siberia. The botanical names of potential plants for your garden may give you some ideas. For example, if the Latin name has the word *sibirica* in it and you live in Minnesota, you're probably making a good choice.

Be Aware of Microclimates

In mountainous regions, growing conditions can vary

You can have a beautiful garden no matter where you live. It's all a matter of choosing the right plants for your soil, rainfall, and lifestyle.

according to elevation and which side of a mountain or slope you live on. In the Great Lakes area, they can vary according to your proximity to the water. Talk to neighbors and your Home Depot associate about your yard's location and what plants might work best for you.

Chilling Out

In very warm climates, some plants won't do well if it's too hot. Some plants, especially fruits, have a chilling requirement and need a certain number of days below a certain temperature. Others stop blooming, die back, or suffer severely when temperatures stay high for an extended period of time. Again check with your Home Depot associate if in doubt.

Hot and Cold

Cold air tends to flow from higher areas to lower. That means frost-cold air, when it happens, tends to roll down hills and can settle in lower-lying areas.

Conversely, stone and concrete, especially dark stone and concrete, absorb the sun's rays during the day and then release it at night. This can help plants ward off damaging cold during cold nights.

Look at Plants in Untended Places

Take notice of flowers and other plants thriving in local untended lots, in alleys and cemeteries, along railroad tracks, or around abandoned houses. They'll also do well for you in your more cultivated garden.

Choose Star Plants

Once you find a plant that performs well, look for others that share similar characteristics. Silver- and hairy-leaved plants, for example, tend to resist drought. Hostas with thick, dense leaves fend off slugs better than hostas with thin leaves. Roses with single petals shed water easily and may thrive in wet-climate gardens better than roses with many tightly packed petals.

Microclimates in Your Yard

Even within your own yard, you have still more specific microclimates. Plants that might languish in one part of your yard might do very well in another part.

As you can see in this illustration, the north and east sides of the house and other buildings tend to be shadier, cooler, and moister than the south and west sides of the house, where heat- and drought-tolerant plants are more likely to thrive. The way the land rises or falls also plays a role, as does the way you landscape with stone, water, and trees.

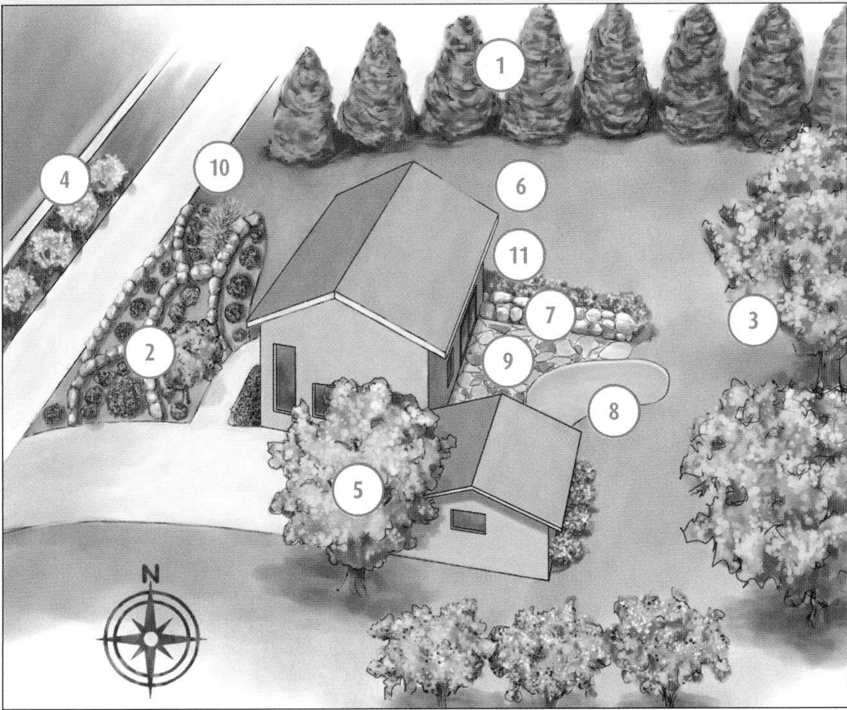

1 A hedge of evergreen trees diffuses north winds, protecting both the house and plantings from extreme cold and drying winds.

2 Stone terraces on a slope create an extremely well-drained area, perfect for plants that don't like wet feet (especially in the winter), such as lavender, thymes, tulips, daffodils, crocuses. It's also a good place to plant many alpines, natives of well-drained mountainsides.

3 Large shade trees to the east create a cool spot. When breezes blow on a hot day, they are cooled in this area and move toward the patio area—nature's own air conditioning.

4 The strip between the street and sidewalk is usually hot and baked and difficult to water well. Also, city rules also usually dictate that plants don't grow taller than a foot or two. Fill such areas with drought-tolerant low-growing perennials (see page 116).

5 Deciduous shade trees on the south side of the house keep the house cooler in summer. In winter, they drop their leaves allowing sunlight to warm the house and melt ice on pavement.

6 An open lawn area to the north allows for snow, in colder regions, to reflect light into the house.

7 A low, south-facing stone wall creates a valuable warm pocket in colder regions. In spring, this area will warm up quickly, giving as much as a week's head start on early bloomers such as daffodils. In summer, however, it can be quite warm and should be planted with heat-tolerant plants.

8 A large water feature, especially if it has a spray or fountain, positioned next to a sitting area is cooling when breezes blow over it.

9 East is the ideal side of the house on which to locate porches, patios, and decks. The area receives warming sun in the cool of the morning and cooling shade in the heat of the late afternoon.

10 At the bottom of a slope, avoid placing a fence or wall. In cold weather, cold air flows down slopes and if obstructed, will pool to create a problematic cold air pocket.

11 The north side of walls, fences, and buildings is always shaded for at least a foot or two out. Plant shade-lovers closest to the structure.

Understanding Your Soil

The best way to know your soil is to simply get out there and grow things in it. Plant a small grouping of annuals and see how they do. Dig up a handful of soil at various times throughout the year to see how the soil feels when it's wet, dry, hot, and cold. Following are some things you can do to get a better idea of what kind of soil you have and which plants will grow best in it:

Analyze Soil Structure

Ideal soil is loose and crumbly but still holds together when you squeeze it in your hand. This texture allows water, air, and nutrients to percolate easily down to plant roots, making plants healthy and vigorous. Dig holes about 18 to 24 inches deep in several places in your yard. If the soil is dark and crumbly and you haven't hit rock, quietly give thanks, because your soil is probably in pretty good shape.

Most gardeners, however, aren't that blessed. They have soil that's riddled with clay, filled with rock, has a shallow layer above a concrete-hard sheath of hardpan, or is sandy and holds water poorly.

To find out more about the texture of the soil in your garden, do this easy soil test: Grab a handful when the soil is moderately moist. Squeeze it into a ball in your hand. If it crumbles, it's sandy soil. If it's a tight ball and slick, it's clay. If it forms a loose ball that's easy to break apart, it's loam—the ideal soil.

TOOL TIP

A HANDY PH METER

A pH meter, available in garden centers for about $20 and up, can instantly measure soil pH. Simply insert the probe into the soil and check the reading. Because it's so fast, you can test several areas of your garden in just minutes.

A pH meter is not as accurate as a soil test from a lab or the extension service (see pages 540 to 541), but it will give you a general idea—instantly.

What Kind of Soil Do You Have?

Sandy soil is crumbly and fails to hold its shape when squeezed.

Loam, the ideal soil, holds together somewhat when squeezed but crumbles easily.

When slightly damp, clay soil forms a tight clump when squeezed.

Test the Drainage

Further analyze your soil by testing the drainage. Fill an 18-inch-deep hole with water. If it drains within a half hour, you have well-drained soil, which will support a wide variety of garden plants. If it takes more than an hour to drain, your soil does not drain well. You'll either need to install drainage tiles—a time-consuming but sometimes worthwhile process (see page 56)—or build raised beds, a more practical alternative (see page 143).

If the hole won't fill with water at all, your soil is quick-draining and you need to work in compost, sphagnum peat moss, and other soil amendments to improve its ability to retain moisture (see page 138).

Analyze Your Soil's pH

It's also a good idea to know the pH of your soil—that is, how acidic or alkaline it is. A pH test kit, a pH meter, or a test conducted through your county extension service can tell you more precisely. Ideal soil is neutral, with a pH between 6.0 and 7.5. A high (alkaline) reading (above 7.5) or low (acidic) reading (below 6.0) will limit what you can grow successfully—though many plants actually prefer alkaline or acidic soil.

Soil pH is determined by many factors, but acidic soil is common in the East and Pacific Northwest. Alkaline soil is common in the dry West, in the Southwest, and in some parts of the Midwest.

You can alter the pH somewhat by digging in soil amendments to raise or lower the pH (see page 138).

Once you know what type of soil you have, you can take measures to amend and thereby improve it. This sandy soil is getting a liberal addition of sphagnum peat moss, which will help it retain moisture better.

Understanding Sun and Shade

Knowing what type of sun and shade you have in your garden is critical to choosing plants that will survive and thrive.

Sun and Shade Are Moving Targets

Understanding a landscape's light really well is something that takes a few years and some trial and error. Even experienced gardeners who have gardened for several years in their yard are always learning something new about the kind of light different spots get. Further complicating things is that light changes over the years as trees grow or are removed.

But simply doing some basic observation will help you figure roughly how much sun different spots in your garden get. Take note of the light in your garden all through the day. Light falls differently in the morning, at noon, and in the late afternoon and early evening.

Also take note of how light falls in different seasons. The sun changes position in the sky over the course of a year. Also, how much shade a spot gets can be affected by whether mature trees have fully leafed out. Daffodils, which need full sun, often do well under an oak tree in March before the tree leafs out, but late tulips might not do well if they bloom in mid-May when the oak leaves have emerged.

Which Side of the House?

The type of light that an area receives also depends on where it is in relation to the house, garage, or other buildings.

Anything within a few feet of the north side of a building will be in shade. The east side of a house catches the soft morning light and avoids the harsher afternoon light. The south and west side gets the most light and the most intense light.

Light-colored surfaces also affect light exposure. A concrete driveway or broad sidewalk will reflect a surprising amount of light.

Regional Considerations

Light also varies according to where you live on the globe. A plant guide or label may list a plant as doing well in part sun, but experienced gardeners in Canada and the northern United States know that their light is less direct. So in northern climates, this "part sun" plant is more likely to do well in full sun.

Gardeners in the southern third of the United States, which gets more direct light, know that if a plant is listed as needing full sun, it will probably be happier in an area that receives a little afternoon shade.

Dry Shade

It's important to consider soil conditions when selecting plants, especially shade-loving plants.

If the soil is black, crumbly, and well drained but also moisture retaining, plants probably can tolerate more shade than if the soil were heavy and wet or hard and dry.

Roots from pines, some types of maples, and other trees can draw moisture away from plants, making it difficult to grow much of anything under those trees. (See pages 114 to 117 for lists of plants that tolerate dry conditions.)

Sun, Shade, and Everything in Between

Full sun

6 hours or more of full, undappled light a day

A wide variety of colorful plants will thrive in full sun. In Canada and the northern third of the United States, full sun is a blessing, ensuring that many different plants can be grown. In the southern third of the United States, however, full sun can bake some plants. So position them to receive a little afternoon shade—a real boon to most plants.

Part sun, part shade, partial shade, partial sun

4 to 6 hours of full, undappled light or several hours of lightly dappled sun a day

There are several terms for this kind of light, but they all mean the same thing: partly shady/partly sunny. Many plants thrive in this type of light, especially in hot Southern climates. Also, plants that may dry out quickly in full sun stay moister longer when they get a little shade. See page 110 for a list of plants that thrive in somewhat shady conditions.

Full shade

4 hours or fewer of sunlight a day

There are few plants that thrive in full shade and fewer still that are colorful; the notable exceptions being impatiens, bleeding heart, and astilbe. If the full shade is under a tree, you may also have dry shade, which is especially challenging. Still, if you design a shady area well, it can be exceptionally beautiful and peaceful looking. See page 110 for a list of plants that thrive in full shade.

A CLOSER LOOK

TOO MUCH SUN, TOO MUCH SHADE

Plants can't talk, but they will tell you when something is wrong. Look for signs that plants aren't getting the right kind of light.

If a plant gets too much sun, leaves wilt even shortly after watering. If the plant has far too much sun, leaves may even turn brown and crisp, as though they've been fried.

If a plant has too much shade, growth is tall, weak, and spindly; stems and leaves tilt toward the light, as shown here. Foliage and flowers are sparse. The plant may also have more disease problems than expected, especially fungal diseases such as mildew.

A CLOSER LOOK

A TEST TO DETERMINE SUN AND SHADE

If you're unsure how much sun or shade an area gets, try this trick. Plant an impatiens, a red salvia, and a marigold next to one another in the same light. After a couple of months, take note which plant is growing the best.

If it's the marigold, you probably have full sun. If it's the salvia, you most likely have part sun. If the impatiens does best with little wilting, even though it can take a considerable amount of sun, you most likely have full shade.

A CLOSER LOOK

CHECK THE LABEL

On most plant labels, the supplier specifies what light conditions the plant needs. Often you'll see simply a sun symbol.

A full yellow or white sun or circle means full sun; a half black/half yellow or white sun or circle means part shade; a fully black sun means full shade.

U.S.D.A. Zone Map

Regardless of where you live, it's important to know approximately what climate zone you live in. The U.S. Department of Agriculture has divided the country into zones based on lowest average temperatures to help gardeners decide which plants do best in which regions. (More specific information on zones is often available on the Internet.)

Because these zones are based on winter temperatures, they serve as a rough guide to tell you which plants are most likely to last through the winter, but they can't tell you whether they'll be happy in the soil, the rainfall, or the heat of that region.

U.S.D.A. zones, categorized from 1 to 11 in North America, are often listed on plant labels. For instance, the label may tell you that a specific plant does best in Zones 4 to 11. The lower the number, the colder the region the plant will tolerate. So a plant that can be grown in Zone 4 is cold-hardy, whereas a plant that can be grown as a perennial only to Zone 8 is less cold-hardy.

Other groups have developed their own zoning systems, but these are not the official government zones found on most plant labels and in most garden books.

In the past several years, for example, "heat zones" have been developed to help gardeners decide how much heat a plant can tolerate—a huge help to gardeners in the southern third of the United States.

In the West, gardening publishers have developed yet another set of zones—from 1 to 24. They're more specific but are not the official government zones mentioned on plant labels.

Range of Average Annual Minimum Temperatures for Each Zone

Zone 1: Below -50° F (below-45.6° C)
Zone 2: -50 to -40° F (-45.5 to -40° C)
Zone 3: -40 to -30° F (-39.9 to -34.5° C)
Zone 4: -30 to -20° F (-34.4 to -28.9° C)
Zone 5: -20 to -10° F (-28.8 to -23.4° C)
Zone 6: -10 to 0° F (-23.3 to -17.8° C)
Zone 7: 0 to 10° F (-17.7 to -12.3° C)
Zone 8: 10 to 20° F (-12.2 to -6.7° C)
Zone 9: 20 to 30° F (-6.6 to -1.2° C)
Zone 10: 30 to 40° F (-1.1 to -4.4° C)
Zone 11: Above 40° F (above 4.5° C)

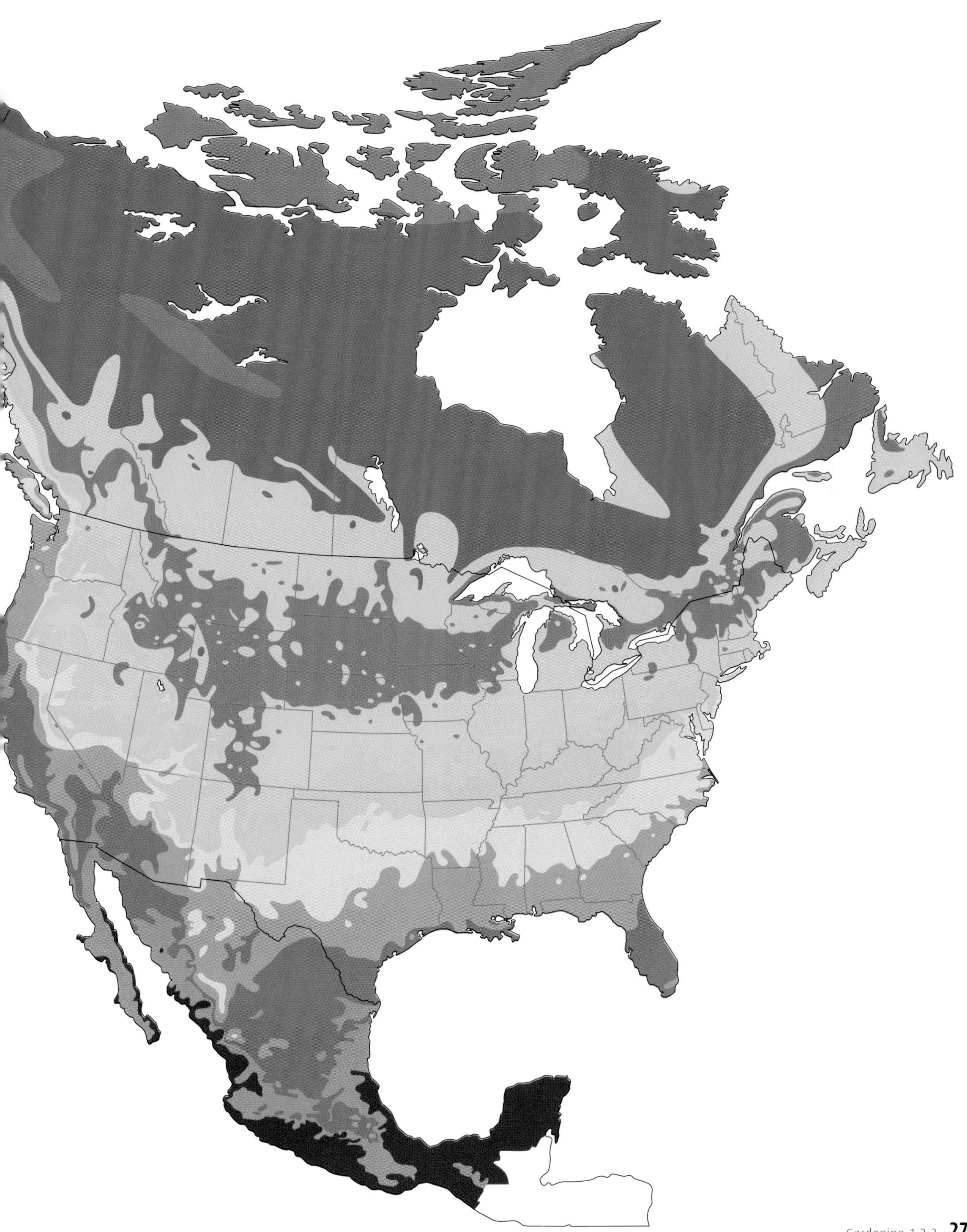

Precipitation Map

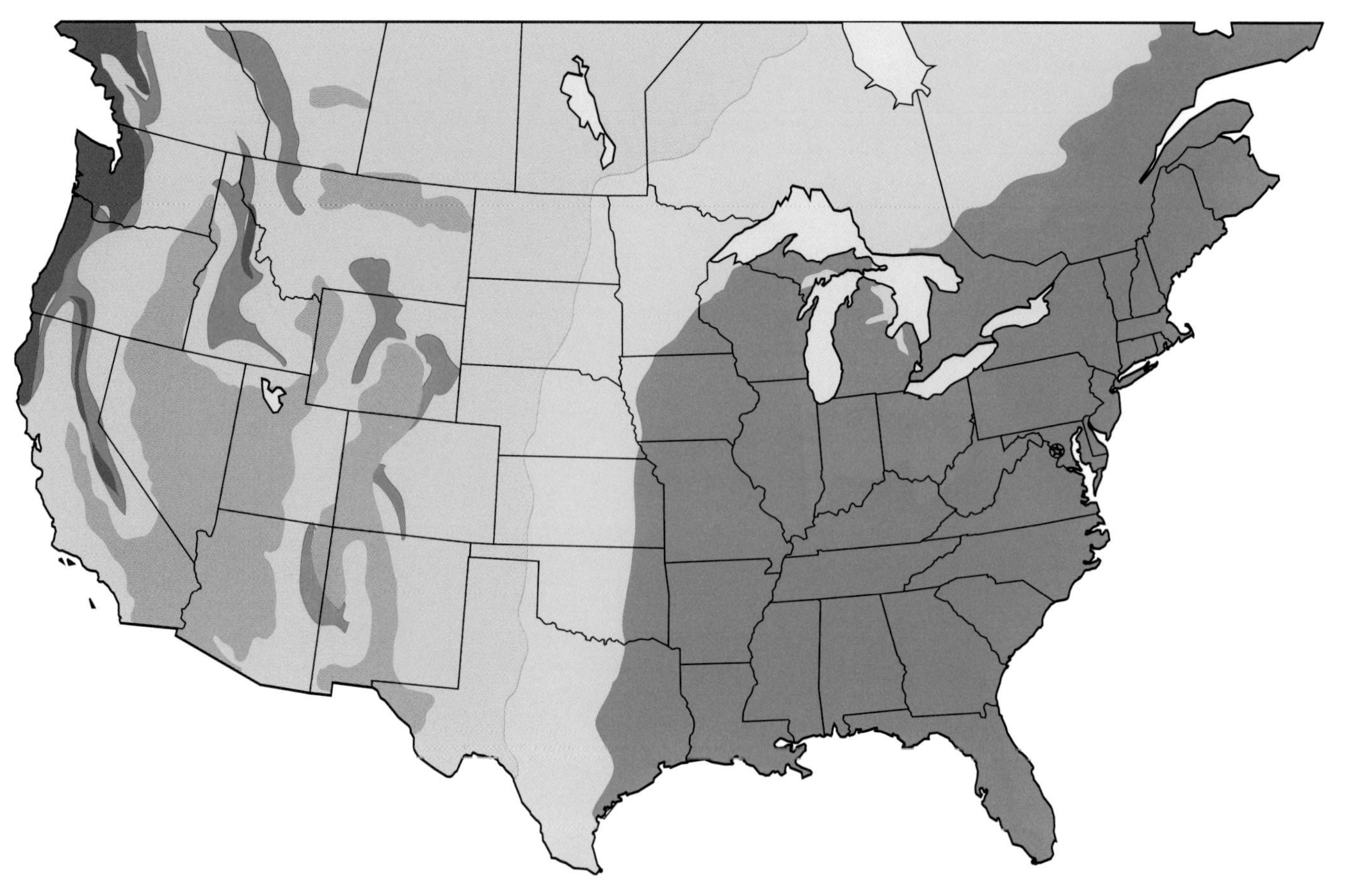

Average Annual Precipitation

- 70 to 100 inches
- 30 to 70 inches
- 20 to 30 inches
- 12 to 20 inches
- Less than 12 inches

This map is a rough interpretation of source material from the Canadian Department of Transport, 1931 to 1960 data and the U.S. National Climatic Data Center, 1961-1990.

Average Frost Dates

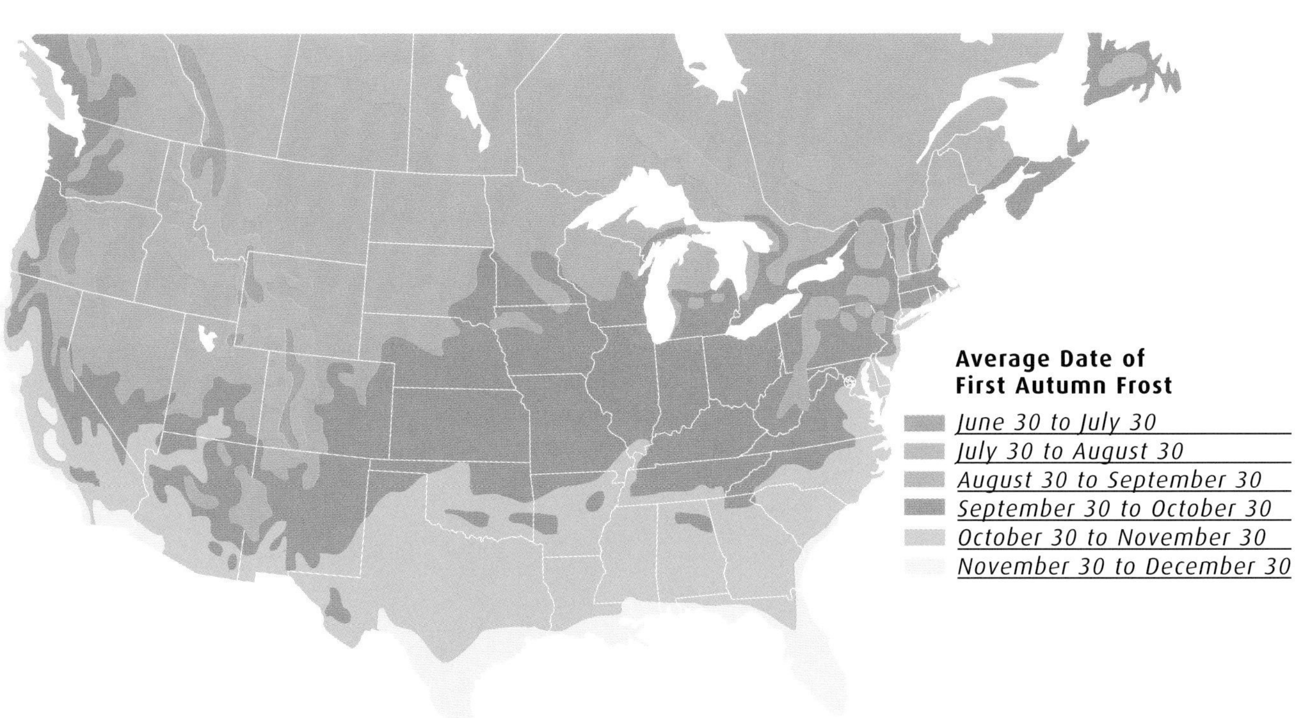

Gardening in The Northeast

In the Northeast, cold winters and often-stony soils are a challenge. The cold may prevent you from planting some flowers, though it allows others to thrive. The following tips will help you make the most of your climate.

Extend the Season

- Plant cool-season annuals. Unlike heat-loving, warm-season annuals, these plants like it on the cool side. They will often bloom even with a bit of snow around them. They include stock, kale, dianthus, snapdragons, pansies, lobelia, violas, and calendula. Plant in spring four to six weeks before your region's last frost date (see page 29). Cool-season annuals bloom until temperatures regularly hit the 80s, then stop blooming. In cold climates, if cut back, they'll often start blooming again in early autumn.
- Cover up. Cold frames (page 31) are ideal for starting plants such as cosmos or marigolds from seed, six to eight weeks earlier than they usually are planted directly in the garden. And porous landscape fabric is ideal for covering favorite plants in autumn when frost threatens to fell them. It lets in sunlight and rain but protects from frost. Cloches made from milk jugs with the bottoms cut out are good for protecting small, individual plants.
- Add winter interest. Plants such as sedums, ornamental grasses, and shrubs with bright bark or berries look attractive even with snow and ice on them.

Preventing Winter Losses

Another challenge of cold-climate gardening is preventing plants from dying out in winter. Here's how to minimize winter loss or damage:

- Choose hardy plants. Know your U.S.D.A. zone (see page 26). Read plant labels carefully and skeptically. If you want a plant to survive the winter, make sure you're at least one zone warmer than the coldest zone the plant will take. If you're in Zone 5, for example, buy plants listed as hardy to Zone 4.
- Mulch intelligently. Perennials and small shrubs need light mulch to protect them during the winter. Cover them with pine boughs, or rake chopped autumn leaves right onto the beds. Remove mulch in early spring once the plants show signs of new growth.
- Take advantage of your site. Plants on the south side of a building, fence, hedge, or other protection are less likely to be damaged by north winds. Protected sites with a southern exposure may cause early bloomers to come on too soon, then be nipped by a late frost. Plant early bloomers on the north or east side of structures.

Cope with Problem Soil

- Raised beds are the rocky soil gardener's friend, especially because all those stones often are the perfect material for stacking around the beds to hold in the soil. See page 143 for tips on building raised beds.
- Even if you don't create raised beds, prepare the soil to provide good drainage. Plants don't like wet feet during the winter.

Must-Have Plants for the Northeast

Common Name	Botanical Name	Zones
Black-eyed Susan	*Rudbeckia* spp.	3-10
Boxwood	*Buxus* spp.	(5) 6-8
Butterflybush	*Buddliea* spp.	5-10
Coneflower, purple	*Echinacea purpurea*	3-9
Daffodils	*Narcissus* spp.	3-8
Daylily	*Hemerocallis* spp.	3-10
Iris, German bearded	*Iris* spp.	3-10
Hollies	*Ilex* spp.	Variable
Hosta	*Hosta* spp.	3-8
Hydrangeas	*Hydrangea* spp.	Variable
Lilac	*Syringa* spp.	3-7
Grasses, ornamental	Various	Variable
Peony	*Paeonia* spp.	2-8
Rhododendrons; azaleas	*Rhododendron* spp.	Variable
Roses, rugosa hybrids	*Rosa rugosa*	4-10
Maple, Sugar	*Acer saccharum*	4-8
Coreopsis	*Coreopsis* spp.	4-9

The cool, moist climate of a Northeastern woodlands has ideal growing conditions for hostas, tiarella, primulas, and a few woodland phlox.

Gardening in The Midwest

This Midwestern front yard is filled with ornamental grasses and prairie natives, including goldenrod and Joe-pye weed.

Gardening in the Midwest is about gardening with extremes.

Because the Midwest is between two mountain ranges, the weather fluctuates, not only from year to year but from day to day. One year may be wet; another dry. A plant may be in the sun and warmth one fine spring afternoon and dusted with frost the next morning. One year may be exceptionally warm, another have record cold.

It's tempting to buy drought-tolerant plants during a dry year, but do so with caution. During a wet year, these plants may rot where they stand. Instead, consider native plants, which have adapted naturally to these extremes and usually are low maintenance as a result.

Also work on creating a sheltered landscape. If you live in the country, plant windbreaks that protect your landscape from the extremes of wind and cold. Even in a city, a hedge or fence on the north side of the garden will minimize winter losses.

Many landscapes in the Midwest, especially those in former prairie or flat wooded areas, are blessed with rich, dark, deep soil from years of grasses and leaves breaking down. If your yard is not so endowed, work on improving your soil or building raised beds (see page 143). Good drainage prevents winter losses caused by wet, frozen roots.

Much of the Midwest also is lucky enough to receive steady, ample rainfall, which allows for a rich variety of plants with minimal upkeep.

Because of sufficient rainfall, gardens in most of the Midwest can do without irrigation systems. However, irrigation systems are useful in landscapes with large lawns. And in the western and southern reaches of the Midwest, an irrigation system can make watering in the dry months of late summer and early autumn easier and more efficient.

Must-Have Plants for the Midwest

Common Name	Botanical Name	Zones
Black-eyed Susan	*Rudbeckia* spp.	3–10
Coneflower, purple	*Echinacea purpurea*	3–9
Crabapple	*Malus* spp.	4–8
Daylily	*Hemerocallis* spp.	3–10
Iris, German bearded	*Iris* spp.	3–10
Grasses, ornamental	Various	Variable
Hollyhock	*Alcea rosa*	3–7
Lilac	*Syringa* spp.	3–7
Oak	*Quercus* spp.	Variable
Peony	*Paeonia* spp.	2–8
Redbud	*Cercis canadensis*	3–9
Spirea, Bridalwreath	*Spiraea prunifolia*	5–8
Sunflower, annual	*Helianthus annuus*	Annual

Gardening in The South

DESIGN TIP

GIVE PLANTS ROOM

Consider a plant's size at maturity when positioning it in the garden. Use flour or landscaping spray paint to mark the mature size before you dig the hole. Plant annuals for color, or use containers to fill in the gaps while your first choices are reaching maturity.

With a rich gardening tradition, the South is home to many beautiful gardens. The long growing season is a plus, but Southern gardeners have to cope with clay soils as well as summer heat and humidity.

Also, because most regions of the South have extended periods of frost-free days, bugs and pests are more numerous. Despite these sometimes tough conditions, however, it's possible to have a superb garden in the South. Here's how:

Take a Soil Test

Many Southern soils are acidic—that is, they have a low pH. Test your soil with a pH kit or meter. Then choose plants that do well in that pH range and/or amend the soil as needed to raise the pH (see pages 136 to 139).

- Good drainage is essential. Many Southern soils have a high clay composition, which absorbs poorly and bakes into a brick in dry weather. Adding organic matter will improve the drainage and composition of these soils (see pages 136 to 139).

Pay Attention to your Light

The South is blessed with many species of trees. If you have large trees in your landscape that provide dappled or partial shade, take advantage of them.

- Use larger trees to protect smaller plants. Large trees can provide welcome shade to plants that take a limited amount of full sun—that is, plants that need moister, cooler conditions or that prefer partial shade. Shade is especially useful when it can provide relief from the beating afternoon sun, which can kill plants.
- Learn from nature. Southern woodlands are home to some of the world's most beautiful plants. Create a gorgeous, shady Southern garden by carving out paths among the trees

Formal gardens defined by brick hardscaping and filled with boxwood and ivy are a favorite for Southern gardeners.

and using shade-loving plants suited to woodlands (see page 123).

Provide for Good Air Circulation

Because humidity creates a perfect environment for fungal and other diseases, be sure to leave ample space around susceptible plants.

Water Wisely

- Irrigate deeply. During periods of low rainfall, water deeply and less frequently rather than shallowly and often. If your clay soil absorbs water slowly, water it enough to allow the water to puddle, then let it soak in for an hour or two. Then water again to ensure that the water goes down deep to the roots.
- Water the soil, not the plants. Avoid wetting the leaves, which encourages fungal diseases. (See page 172 for more watering tips.)

Choose Plants Carefully

Choose plants that are suited to your local growing conditions. Consider cold-hardiness and tolerance for heat and humidity (see the U.S.D.A. map on page 26).

- Use native plants. These plants are well-acclimated to conditions in the South. Ask your Home Depot garden associate to direct you to various native plants currently in the garden center.
- Plant for all seasons. By choosing plants carefully, you can have flowers almost all year long, even in winter. For best results, seek out cool-season annuals (see page 148) and perennials that thrive in the cooler temperatures of late autumn, winter, and early spring.

Group Plants According to their Needs

Group sun-loving plants together in one spot and shade-loving plants in another area. Do the same for thirsty plants and drought-tolerant plants. Every Southern garden should include the latter to save on irrigation costs and conserve water.

Visit Regional Gardens

There are beautiful public gardens throughout the South, and many will have climate and soil conditions similar to those in your garden. Visit them, take notes, talk to gardeners who work there, and get ideas for creating your own paradise right at home. Visit these sites during difficult growing times, such as the heat of late summer, to get a sense of the problems you may face in your garden.

Because they are so beautiful and thrive despite the heat and the acidic clay soils of the South, azaleas are one of the most popular plants throughout the region.

Must-Have Plants For Southern Gardens

Common Name	Botanical Name	Zones
Black-eyed Susan	*Rudbeckia*	3–10
Camellia	*Camellia* spp.	7–11
Christmas rose	*Helleborus* spp.	4–9
Coneflower, purple	*Echinacea purpurea*	3–9
Crape Myrtle	*Lagerstroemia indica*	7–9
Daylily	*Hemerocallis* spp.	3–10
Dogwood, various	*Cornus* spp.	Variable
Fringe tree, Chinesse	*Chionathus retuses*	6–8
Gardenia	*Gardenia jasminoides*	8–10
Goldenstar	*Chrysogonum virginianum*	5–8
Holly, various	*Ilex* spp.	Variable
Hosta	*Hosta* spp.	3–9
Hydrangeas	*Hydrangea* spp.	Variable
Jasmines	*Jasminum* spp.	Variable
Lantana	*Lantana camara*	8–10
Lilyturf	*Liriope muscari*	7–10
Pentas	*Pentas lanceolata*	3–11
Phlox, creeping	*Phlox divaricata*	2–8
Phlox, garden	*Phlox paniculata*	4–8
Pieris	*Pieris* spp.	Variable
Pinks; 'Bath's Pink'	*Dianthus* spp.	4–9
Magnolia	*Magnolia* spp.	Variable
Maple, red	*Acer rubrum*	3–9
Oak, various, but especially willow, water, and live oak		Variable
Rhododendrons; azaleas	*Rhododendron* spp.	Variable
Roses, various, but especially 'Knockout'		Variable
Salvia	*Salvia* spp.	Variable
Verbena, moss	*Verbena tenuisecta*	8–10
Viola	*Viola* spp.	6–9
Yarrow	*Achillea* spp.	3–9

Gardening in the Pacific Northwest

With mild, moist winters and drier, moderate summers, the Pacific Northwest has a climate that helps a tremendous variety of plants thrive. From unusual species of rhododendrons, azaleas, and dogwoods to brilliantly blooming rock garden and alpine plants, the Pacific Northwest is a gardener's paradise.

Here's how to maximize your gardening efforts in this region:

The cool, moist, cool-summer, mild-winter climate of the coastal Pacific Northwest is a near-perfect home for rhododendrons and azaleas of all kinds. Shown here are Rhododendrons 'Relaxation' (front), 'Elizabeth' (red), and 'Seisime' (lavender).

Capitalize on the Long Growing Season

Spring starts as early as February in the Pacific Northwest, with hardy primroses and minor bulbs breaking forth beneath the protection of tall evergreens. Plant these in fall to ensure that colorful and early spring blooms start the season as soon as possible.

- Underplant. Midspring explodes with blooms from rhododendrons and azaleas. Underplant them with shade-tolerant blooming groundcovers such as ajuga, lamium, and lungwort, which will provide color later in the season after the shrubs have faded.
- Cut back. For summer bloom, extend perennials' flowering season by cutting back faded flowers in spring. Phlox, hollyhocks, and foxgloves, for example, will bloom a second time if you cut them back. This second bloom can be encouraged further with an application of fertilizer at the same time you cut them back.
- Use the seasons. Fall is like a second spring in the Northwest, with annuals such as begonias and impatiens continuing to bloom until the first hard frost in midautumn. Pansies, snapdragons, dusty miller, and stock also thrive in fall.

The Cold Facts

Along the coast, where a heavy freeze is rare, winter rains cause more damage than cold weather. Canna, dahlia, and gladiola bulbs rot before they freeze. Dig and store them in a dry spot indoors (see page 205). Sun-loving perennials such as lavender, Russian sage, and artemisias also can drown in the wet. Raised beds (see page 143) and quick-draining soil (achieved by amending with sand, gravel, or other grit) are insurance against losing plants in wet winters.

- Clean up in fall. Blights, molds, and mildews (see pages 217–218) thrive in the cool, damp winter season. Fall cleanup of dead foliage (especially that of peonies, irises, and roses) prevents fungi from making it through the winter and reviving in spring.
- Install nonslip pathways. In winter, patios and paths of gravel or cedar chips are much preferred to those of brick and tile or soggy grass, which become slippery with moss and rain.

Shade Specifics

- Provide filtered shade. Evergreen trees provide the filtered shade that's ideal for rhododendrons, camellias, azaleas, and small-leaved Japanese maples.
- Go shade tolerant. Shade-tolerant perennials such as astilbe, corydalis, hostas, and coral bells bloom well beneath the skirts of understory trees and shrubs such as vine maple and dogwood.
- Go native. The Pacific Northwest has many native shade lovers. Plant small bulbs such as scilla and snowdrop, as well as wildflowers such as trilliums, violets, skunk cabbage, piggyback plant, hardy cyclamen, and primroses.
- Slug the slugs. Shady gardens require a vigilant watch against slugs. Pick slugs off one by one, use environmentally safe slug bait, or set up barriers of wood ashes or copper strips around slug magnets such as hostas.

In the Pacific Northwest, the moderating influence of ocean, bay, and sound extends far inland to the coastal mountains.

Gardening Where You Live

ROSES FOR THE PACIFIC NORTHWEST

Some roses do better than others in the cool, misty Pacific Northwest. In general, pink roses are more resistant to the region's fungal diseases, and yellow and red roses do not fade in the afternoon sun as they do elsewhere. Roses with fewer petals do better than those with many petals, because they don't ball up and rot as easily after days of rain. Any of the rugosa roses also do well. Other top rose performers include 'Bonica', 'Flower Carpet', 'Peace', 'Queen Elizabeth', and 'The Fairy'.

Must-Have Plants for the Pacific Northwest

Common Name	Botanical Name	Zones
Astilbe	*Astilbe* spp.	3-8
Begonia	*Begonia* spp.	Annuals
Boxwood	*Buxus* spp.	5-8
Camellia	*Camellia* spp.	7-11
Candytuft	*Iberis sempervirens*	4-8
Clematis	*Clematis* spp.	4-9
Coral bells	*Heuchera sanguinea*	3-9
Cosmos	*Cosmos* spp.	N/A
Daffodils	*Narcissus* spp.	3-8
Dogwood, kousa	*Cornus kousa*	5-8
Ferns, various	Various	Variable
Fuchsia (hardy types)	*Fuchsia* spp.	8-10
Geranium, hardy	*Geranium* spp.	3-8
Honeysuckle	*Lonicera* spp.	Variable
Hydrangea	*Hydrangea* spp.	Variable
Lady's mantle	*Alchemilla* spp.	3-8
Leyland cypress	*×Cupressocyparis leylandii*	6-9
Leucothoe	*Leucothoe* spp.	5-8
Lobelia, edging	*Lobelia erinus*	Annual
Mahonia; Oregon grape-holly	*Mahonia aquifolium*	5-9
Manzanitas, esp. Bearberry	*Arctostphylos uva-ursi*	2-7
Maple, Japanese	*Acer palmatum*	5-8
Nandina	*Nandina domestica*	6-9
Pieris	*Pieris* spp.	Variable
Primroses	*Primula* spp.	5-8
Pulmonaria	*Pulmonaria* spp.	3-8
Rhododendrons; azaleas	*Rhododendron* spp.	Various
Staghorn sumac	*Rhus typhina* 'Lacinata'	3-8
Sweet woodruff	*Galium odoratum*	4-8
Viburnum	*Viburnum* spp.	Variable
Wisteria	*Wisteria* spp.	5-9

Gardening in the Arid West and Southwest

You can have color from flowers and foliage in this region all year if you select native and drought-tolerant species and plant them in the dappled shade of lacy-leaved desert trees.

Here are other tips for gardening in this hot, arid climate:

Conserve Water

Average rainfall ranges from 4 to 16 inches per year in the desert Southwest, but some years only half the average may fall, and the next year it might be double. In El Paso, rain is most likely to occur in late summer; in Southern California and similar climates, rain comes in winter; and in Phoenix, the rainy season is divided between summer and winter. Talk to neighbors and your Home Depot garden center associates about specific rainfall patterns. Then make the most of limited rainfall by doing the following:

- Minimize your lawn. Wrap your flower garden around a covered patio or a small lawn of drought-tolerant buffalograss and blue gramagrass.
- Install drip irrigation. And water when the sun is down to keep evaporation at a minimum.
- Create swales and berms. Low spots and high spots capture water from roofs, driveways, and patios.
- Position plants on the south edge of a slight hollow to trap water and shade their roots.
- Make walls. Enclose gardens with masonry walls to hold in water, cast shade, and lessen evaporation.
- Mulch. Use crushed stone or decomposed granite to deter weeds and conserve moisture.

Choose Drought-Tolerant Plants

Plants native to desert areas are drought-tolerant and are becoming more widely available.

- Low-growing native flowering shrubs will provide bright spots of color.
- Plant bunchgrasses, such as Mexican feather grass, deergrass, bamboo muhly, or pink muhly, for soft accents.
- Plant reseeders. Tie everything together with reseeding desert flowers such as California poppy, desert marigold, butter daisy, fragrant evening primrose, and globe mallow.

DESIGN TIP

GO FOR STRUCTURE

Seek out plants that will provide structure (sometimes called "architecture") for your garden year-round. Yuccas, agaves, cactus, and other succulent evergreens and many others will create focal points when other plants aren't blooming.

Even in arid regions, a highly drought-tolerant garden can be beautiful. This one is filled with cacti, succulents, a bougainvillea scaling the wall, and euphorbia.

Organpipe and barrel cactus, occotillo, mesquite, and bougainvillea complement the southwestern theme of this Phoenix home's Spanish architecture..

Must-Have Plants for The Arid West and Southwest

Common Name	Botanical Name	Zones
Agave	*Agave* spp.	8-11
Aloe	*Aloe* spp.	8-11
Bougainvillea	*Bougainvillea* spp.	9-10
Bouvardia	*B. longiflora* 'Albatross'	9-10
Bunny ears; prickly pear cactus	*Opuntia* spp.	Variable
Butter daisy	*Melampodium* spp.	annual
Butterfly vine	*Muscagnia macroptera*	9-10
Cypress, Arizona	*Cupressus arizonica*	7-9
Desert willow	*Chilopsis linearis*	8-9
Evening Primrose	*Oenothera speciosa*	3-9
Four-O-Clock	*Mirabilis jalapa*	8-11
Golden barrel cactus	*Echinocactus grusonii*	8-11
Grass, feather	*Stipa* spp.	8-11
Mesquite	*Prosopis glandulosa*	10-11
Mexican false heather	*Cuphea hyssopifolia*	10-11
Mexican sunflower	*Tithonia rotundifolia*	Annual
Moss rose	*Portulaca grandiflora*	Annual
Oleander	*Nerium oleander*	8-10
Palms, date	*Phoenix* spp.	9-10
Palm, Mexican fan	*Washingtonia robusta*	9-10
Palm, pindo	*Butia capitata*	8-10
Palo verde	*Cercidium texanum*	9-10
Penstemon	*Penstemon* spp.	3-8
Potentilla, shrubby	*P. fruticosa*	2-7
Sages	*Salvia* spp.	Variable
Santolina	*chamaecyparissus*	6-9
Texas ranger	*Leucophyllum frutescens* 'Silverado'	8-10
Verbena, moss,	*Verbena pulchella*	8-10
Vinca, annual	*Catharanthus* spp.	Annual
Yucca	*Yucca* spp.	Variable

CLOSER LOOK

GARDENING WHERE YOU LIVE

In the Southwest, elevation is everything—so much so that planting dates are determined not only by the calendar but by how high the garden is.

In Arizona, for example, tomatoes in the desert at 1,000 to 2,000 feet can be planted as early as mid-January, whereas at 2,000 to 3,000 feet gardeners should wait until at least mid-March, and at 3,000 feet, until early May.

Also coming into play are valleys. Cold air sinks and can collect in valleys or other frost pockets at the base of hills and mountains. In these cold pockets, temperatures can be 5 to 10°F (3 to 6°C) colder than in areas only a house or two away. These valleys are more prone to late-spring and early-fall frosts, which shorten the growing season and limit the ability of residents to grow frost-sensitive fruit trees.

Gardening in California

California climates are as diverse as the people who live there. California has four of the five major climate zones found in the world—Mediterranean, semi-arid, desert, and alpine. Tropical is the only major climate not found in this state.

On the same day, the northern part of the state may be in the low 60s and cloudy, while deserts surrounding Bakersfield, in Southern California, may be above 100°F (38°C). Along California's northwest coast, annual rainfall can be as much as 110 inches, whereas Bakersfield receives just 10 inches. The northwest coast has a climate much like that of southern Ireland, whereas the climate in the southwest corner resembles that of the northern Sahara desert.

Even in the same city in California, climates from one yard to another can vary depending on elevation and distance from the ocean. What grows in your garden depends not only on your region but on your neighborhood. A California gardener needs to be a master of the microclimate (see page 21). The best information will come from your neighbors and garden center staff who understand your garden's unique climate.

Know your garden's specific needs for soil and rainfall. If your area gets frost, know the last frost date in spring and the first frost date in fall. Track weather patterns in your local paper. Watch for articles that address your area's weather.

Arid California

- Buy drought-tolerant plants. Your local garden center will highlight plants that use minimal water, or simply ask your Home Depot garden associate.
- Group plants according to water needs. Create a small oasis of plants with higher water needs near the house—and the outdoor faucet—to make watering easier, and put plants with lower water needs together farther away from the house.

Must-Have Plants for Arid California

Common Name	Botanical Name	Zones
Abelia, glossy	*Abelia ×grandiflora*	6-9
African lily	*Agapanthus* spp.	8-10
Bougainvillea	*Bougainvillea glabra*	9-10
California poppy	*Eschscholzia californica*	Annual
Citrus, various	*Citrus* spp.	8-11
Fuchsia	*Fuchsia* spp.	8-10
Gazania	*Gazania* spp.	8-10
Geranium	*Pelargonium* spp.	8-11
Ice plant	*Malephora crocea*	9-11
Lavender	*Lavandula* spp.	Variable
Palm	Various	Variable
Passionflower vine	*Passiflora* spp.	7-10
Salvia, various	*Salvia* spp.	Variable
Trumpet tree	*Tabebuia* spp.	10-11

- Improve the soil. Low rainfall can make soil more alkaline. In general, avoid adding lime to the soil, because it raises the pH further. Instead, work in organic matter, such as well-rotted organic matter, including compost, dry leaves, and grass clippings. In many arid California soils, working in gypsum can help leach salts (see below), lower pH, and improve soil drainage.
- Think salt. Coastal gardens are vulnerable to salty ocean spray. Low rainfall also contributes to high salt concentration in the soil—a problem for many plants even far inland. If salt is a problem, talk to your garden center staff about choosing salt-tolerant plants and soil amendments for your garden.
- Install an irrigation system. Water is a natural resource that should not be wasted, and it's expensive to purchase from a municipality. An irrigation system will pay for itself.
- Create shade. Many plants will do better in hot, dry regions if they have light shade. Acacia, palo verde, and desert willow cast the dappled light shade that plants like best. Position a tree so it gives afternoon shade.
- Mulch! Whether you use crushed stone or wood chips, mulch keeps soil cooler and moister—and it deters weeds.

Mountainous California

- Know when spring normally arrives. Spring in the mountains is notoriously fickle, with balmy weather one day and snow the next. Keep track of your last spring frost dates, or talk to people who know.
- Make the most of a short growing season. Look for perennials that thrive in cooler temperatures, and familiarize yourself with cool-season annuals (see page 148). Many spring-blooming bulbs (see page 101) also do well in the cool temperatures and excellent drainage found in some mountain areas.
- Garden at an angle. Gardening on a slope (see page 118 for information on rock gardening) involves disturbing the least amount of soil when planting or weeding, to prevent erosion. Build low, informal terraces to retain water and slow erosion. Plant moisture lovers at the lower part of a slope and drought-tolerant plants at the top.
- Outsmart the critters. Mountain living often includes a glimpse of deer, rabbits, woodchucks, raccoons, and other wildlife that love your garden too. Buy plants that wildlife are less likely to eat (see page 222), and consider installing a deer fence.
- Realize that the sun is brighter. Gardens at 3,000 feet and higher receive 20 percent more light than those at sea level. If a plant likes part shade at sea level, you will want to give it a little more shade at higher altitudes.

Northern California

- Plant in the fall. Get a head start on early spring by planting perennials and shrubs in autumn.
- Choose roses wisely. Thickly petaled roses tend to ball up and rot in steady rain and mist. Choose single or double roses, which have fewer petals. As a rule, pink roses are more resistant to the region's fungal diseases. Rugosa roses also perform well.
- Take advantage of the cool, moist winter by planting cool-season annuals that will provide winter color (see page 148).

Even with limited water, this arid California garden blooms with color year-round.

Must-Have Flowers For Mountainous California

Common Name	Botanical Name	Zones
Blanket flower	*Gaillardia ×grandiflora*	2–10
California poppy	*Eschscholzia californica*	Annual
Crocus	*Crocus* spp.	3-8
Cosmos	*Cosmos* spp.	Annual
Daffodils	*Narcissus* spp.	3-8
Gazania	*Gazania* spp.	8-10
Larkspur	*Consolida ambigua*	Annual
Lupine	*Lupinus* hybrids	4-6
Oriental poppy	*Papaver orientale*	3-8
Pansy	*Viola* spp.	Annual
Poppies, annual types	*Papaver* spp.	Annual
Potentilla, shrubby	*Potentilla fruticosa*	2-7
Lavender cotton	*Santolina chamaecyparissus*	6-9
Shasta daisy	*Leucanthemum ×superbum*	4-9
Snapdragon	*Antirrhinum majus*	Annual

Must-Have Flowers for Northern California

Common Name	Botanical Name	Zones
California poppy	*Eschscholzia californica*	Annual
Camellia	*Camellia* spp.	7-11
Clematis	*Clematis* spp.	3-9
Coral bells	*Heuchera sanguinea*	3-9
Cypress, various	*Cupressus* spp.	6-10
Daphne, winter	*Daphne odorata*	7-9
Lobelia, edging	*Lobelia erinus*	Annual
Ferns	Various	Variable
Foxglove	*Digitalis purpurea*	4-8
Fuchsia	*Fuchsia* spp.	8-10
Hydrangea	*Hydrangea* spp.	Variable
Nasturtium	*Tropaeolum majus*	Annual
Palms	Various	Variable
Pansy	*Viola* spp.	Annual
Rhododendrons, azaleas	*Rhododendron* spp.	Variable
Snapdragon	*Antirrhinum majus*	Annual

Gardening in the Mountain West

With the possibility of snow at the highest elevations in any season, flower gardening in the mountains can be a risky business. But a look at nature's own high-altitude gardens demonstrates that it is possible to grow flowers in glorious profusion in the mountains.

Take Note of Key Elements

- Heat. During the growing season, take advantage of any heat that comes your way. Use south-facing exposures, or place tender plants near large rocks, boulders, or stone walls, which absorb heat during the day and release it slowly at night.
- Light. Full-sun areas at elevations of 3,000 feet and higher receive 20 percent more light than full-sun areas at sea level. Although some plants thrive in this excessive light, others need some shade protection.
- Water. If you garden on a slope, terrace your plants to slow rainwater runoff. Use groundcovers such as creeping juniper to further prevent eroding soils. Use mulch to conserve soil moisture. Irrigate plants during dry months by watering deeply and seldom rather than shallowly and often, encouraging the plants to develop deep roots.
- Soil. Most mountainous soils are rocky and shallow, so adding organic matter to the soil is a necessity. Add compost, well-rotted manure, leaf litter, or other organic materials to enhance the nutrient value and composition of the soil.

Be Ready to Spring In Spring

- As soon as you can work the soil, start digging and enriching it so you can garden in earnest as soon as warm weather arrives.
- Gardeners at high altitudes should have plants ready to put in the ground as soon as warm temperatures seem ready to stay. Starting plants from seed indoors can extend the growing and blooming season by several weeks. Grow enough seedlings for several successive plantings. The first time you plant, keep back some of your seedlings in case the first ones are nipped by a late frost.

Use Cold, Bright Days

Sunny days in winter are ideal for gardening chores, including pruning trees and shrubs. (If you prune spring-blooming shrubs in winter, you risk trimming off buds with the branches. Wait until right after they bloom to prune these shrubs. See pages 190–192 for more information on pruning trees and shrubs.) Also be on the lookout for frost-heaved perennials and small shrubs. If you see exposed roots, press the plant back in the ground and pat soil around the base of the plant to protect the roots.

Choose Plants Wisely

Because mountainous areas have fewer frost-free days than other gardening regions, it's important to choose plants that bloom quickly.

If you live at an extremely high elevation, include flowers such as violas, pansies, lobelia, and calendula. These are tolerant of cooler temperatures. (See page 148 for a list of cool-season annuals that thrive in cooler temperatures.)

The short growing season of higher elevations doesn't have to get in the way of a beautiful garden. This one is filled with columbine, delphiniums, salvias, irises, snapdragons, and sweet alyssum.

Must-Have Plants For the Mountain West

Common Name	Botanical Name	Zones
Annuals/Perennials		
Bee balm	*Monarda didyma*	4-8
Bellflower	*Campanula* spp.	4-9
Blanket flower	*Gaillardia* spp.	2-10
Bleeding heart	*Dicentra* spp.	2-9
Cardinal flower	*Lobelia cardinalis*	2-9
Catmint	*Nepeta* spp.	4-9
Columbine	*Aquilegia* spp.	3-9
Coreopsis	*Coreopsis* spp.	4-9
Delphinium	*Delphinium elatum*	2-7
Larkspur	*Consolida ambigua*	Annual
Lupines, Russell	*Lupinus* Russell hybrids	4-6
Oriental poppy	*Papaver orientale*	3-7
Pansy	*Viola* spp.	Annual
Rugosa roses	*Rosa rugosa*	3-9
Shasta daisy	*Leucanthemum* ×*superbum*	4-9
Snapdragons	*Antirrhinum majus*	Annual
Violet	*Viola* spp.	Variable
Yarrow	*Achillea* spp.	3-9
Trees and Shrubs		
Arborvitae, giant	*Thuja plicata*	5-7
Barberry, Japanese	*Berberis thunbergii*	4-8
Potentilla, shrubby	*Potentilla fruticosa*	2-7
Juniper, various	*Juniperus* spp.	Variable
Lilac	*Syringa* spp.	3-7
Pine, various but especially mugo	*Pinus* spp.	2-7
Spirea	*Spiraea* spp.	Variable
Spruce, various	*Picea* spp.	Variable

Gardening in Florida And the Gulf Coast

Gardening successfully in Florida and the Gulf Coast means gardening in a way that is very different from that in the rest of the country. Seasons are upside down, so you'll need to become an expert at adapting information and observing what works best in your own garden. Here's how to have a good garden in this region.

A Long Growing Season

- Enjoy color year-round. Blooms are spread over a long period of the year. However, the impact is seldom as intense as in cooler climates, because not everything blooms at the same time.
- Timing is vital. Although there is seldom the same pressure as in other parts of the country to plant, prune, and maintain the garden in a narrow window of time, it's still important to do the right task at the right time.
- Plants perform differently here from those in the rest of the country. Many plants, such as petunias and nasturtiums, grow well from fall until spring but die out in the heat of summer. Some plants, such as impatiens and peppers, are annuals elsewhere but may be perennials here. Still others that are perennial in most of the country, such as delphinium, thyme, and yarrow, are best treated as annuals in Florida, because the summer heat often kills them. Peonies and lilacs may not grow at all. However, for every plant that doesn't grow here, 10 more exotics well-suited to the region will thrive beautifully.

The Highs and the Lows

- The highs. An increased interest in gardening in desert and subtropical regions has led plant merchants to include information about heat tolerance on plant labels.
- The lows. Plants grow more slowly in winter. With its short days and different sun and shade patterns, winter dramatically slows the growth of plants. Reduce watering and feeding accordingly.
- Frost can still happen. Keep a list of your cold-sensitive plants and be ready to cover them, move them, or take cuttings to renew them whenever frost is predicted. Good maintenance and abundant compost in the soil can give you a few extra degrees of protection.

In central and southern Florida, group together frost-sensitive annual flowers. That way you can throw a sheet or burlap over the whole group when the temperature dips and avoid costly replacements.

Thriving areca palms and elephant ears capture the tropical luxuriance of the southern Florida coast.

Must-Have Plants For Florida and the Gulf Coast

Common Name	Botanical Name	Zones
Annuals/Perennials		
Butter daisy	*Melampodium paludosum*	Annual
Calla lily	*Zantedeschia* spp.	8–11
Canna lily	*Canna* spp.	8–11
Impatiens	*Impatiens* spp.	Annual
Ferns	Various	Variable
Lantana	*Lantana camara*	8–10
Pentas	*Pentas lanceolata*	10–11
Petunia	*Petunia* spp.	Annual
Salvia	*Salvia* spp.	Variable
Snapdragon	*Antirrhinum majus*	Annual
Sweet alyssum	*Lobularia maritima*	Annual
Viola and pansy	*Viola* spp.	Annual
Wishbone flower	*Torenia fournieri*	Annual
Shrubs/Vines		
Allamanda	*Allamanda cathartica*	10–11
Aucuba	*Aucuba japonica*	7–10
Azalea	*Rhododendron* spp.	Variable
Bird of Paradise	*Strelitzia* spp.	9–11
Bougainvillea	*Bougainvillea glabra*	9–11
Camellia	*Camellia* spp.	7–11
Crepe myrtle	*Lagerstroemia indica*	7–9
Datura	*Brugmansia* spp.	9–11
Gardenia	*Gardenia jasminoides*	8–10
Hibiscus, Chinese	*Hibiscus rosa-sinensis*	9–10
Jasmine	*Jasminum* spp.	Variable
Ixora	*Ixora coccinea*	10–11
Plumbago	*Ceratostigma plumbaginoides*	5–9
Sweet olive	*Osmanthus fragrans*	8–9
Trees		
Banana	*Musa* spp.	8–11
Citrus, various	*Citrus* spp.	8–11
Magnolia	*Magnolia* spp.	Variable
Oak, southern live	*Quercus virginiana*	8–10
Palms	Various	Variable

Gardening In Texas

Texas is a state of climatic extremes: East Texas is hot, wet, and muggy; West Texas is hot and dry; northern Texas has constant wind, gruelingly hot summers, and frigid winters. Soil types range from clay to thin dust on top of rock.

Cope with Extremes

- Grow native and naturalized plants. Pamper them with extra water and fertilizer. Also consider time-tested heirlooms such as milk-and-water lilies and four-o-clocks. Look at ditches and abandoned farmsteads for thriving remnants of long-abandoned gardens; these plants thrive with little attention.
- Take advantage of the seasons. In central and southern Texas, winter, spring, and autumn are the best times to garden. In the Panhandle, the best times are autumn and spring. Plant annuals such as pansies, sweet peas, and snapdragons in autumn for winter and spring color.
- Include ornamental grasses. Consider those with attractive flowers such as gulf muhly or Mexican feather grass.
- Plant in microclimates—those little niches in the garden that are protected from extremes of sun, wind, and weather. Otherwise, buy one each of several different plants and test them in different areas to see what works where.

A casually designed garden filled with drought-tolerant plants perfectly complements this rustic Texas home.

Whack Away

Digging is hard work in the clay-laden and rocky soils often found in Texas. Instead of using a spade, try a pick mattock, which has a pointed blade at one end and a flat blade at the other. Swing it as you would an ax—carefully—and remember to be fully focused on the task at hand.

Must-Have Plants for Texas Gardens

Common Name	Botanical Name	Zones
Annuals/Perennials		
Agave	*Agave* spp.	8-11
Blanket flower	*Gaillardia pulchella*	Annual
Blazing star	*Liatris* spp.	3-9
Sages	*Salvia* spp.	Variable
Butter daisy	*Melampodium paludosum*	Annual
Flowering tobacco	*Nicotiana alata*	Annual
Four-o-clock	*Mirabilis jalapa*	8-11
Mexican false heather	*Cuphea hyssopifolia*	10-11
Paper-white narcissus	*Narcissus papyraceus*	7-9
Evening primrose, showy	*Oenothera speciosa*	3-9
Lupine: Texas bluebonnet	*Lupinus texensis*	6-8
Lantana	*Lantana camara*	8-10
Texas ranger	*Leucophyllum frutescens*	8-10
Grasses		
Gulf muhly	*Muhlenbergia capillaris*	7-10
Lindheimer muhly	*Muhlenbergia lindheimeri*	7-10
Mexican feather grass	*Stipa tenuissima*	8-11
Shrubs and Trees		
Beautyberry	*Callicarpa dichtoma*	5-8
Butterfly bush	*Buddleia* spp.	5-10
Crape myrtle	*Lagerstroemia indica*	7-9
Holly, Yaupon	*Ilex vomitoria*	7-10
Junipers	Various	Variable
Magnolia, sweet bay	*Magnolia virginiana*	5-9
Magnolia, southern	*Magnolia grandiflora*	6-10
Nandina	*Nandina domestica*	6-9
Oak, laurel	*Quercus laurifolia*	7-10
Oak, southern live	*Quercus virginiana*	8-10
Oak, willow	*Quercus phellos*	4-8
Roses	*Rosa* spp.	Variable

Special Considerations When Gardening on The Seashore

When gardening near the sea, it's important to understand the special soils and conditions created by beach microclimates.

In coastal regions, microclimates can change significantly from one neighborhood to the next. Take note of what does well in your area and compare the selection to that in other areas even a few blocks away.

Observe, too, what plants thrive in relation to their distance from the water, salt tolerance, temperature highs and lows, light levels, soil and rock composition, and wind patterns.

Choose the Right Plants

- Seek out salt-tolerant plants. A handful of plants copes with salty conditions (soil or spray) better than most. They aren't salt-proof, but they will thrive in moderately salty conditions. Keep in mind that salt spray travels a tremendous distance, blowing several miles inland in some areas.
- Cope with environmental realities. Beaches and the land near them are environmentally fragile areas and should be gardened with great care. Some garden plants can be invasive, crowding out important local plants. The role of some plants, such as American beach grass and sea oats, is so critical that some states prohibit their destruction.
- Let the plant name guide you. Many plants well-suited to coastal conditions have "sea" or "beach" in their names.
- Check out plants with fewer petals. Choose roses and other flowers with less complex blooms. The fog and dew common to most coastal areas make thickly petaled flowers rot and fall before they open.

Cope with Wind

- Choose low growers. Unlike vertical plants, ground-hugging plants do not require staking.
- Choose strong rooters. Strong, deep roots anchor plants in sandy soil and strong winds, and help them find moisture far into the soil. Flowering shrubs usually do better than annuals, which have shallow root systems.
- Watch wind patterns. Winter winds can rapidly dry out and otherwise damage many plants. Plant in protected areas alongside the house, garage, or other buildings.

Even a low wall can protect flowers from salt spray and relentless coastal winds.

Improve Sandy Soil

- Add plenty of compost, sphagnum peat moss, commercial soil conditioner, and other moisture-retaining soil amendments. They improve the soil's ability to hold water.
- Plant in pots. For roses and prized perennials, use large (5-gallon plus) pots with a drainage hole, and sink them directly into the sandy soil. Fill with a mixture of compost, potting soil, and a soilless potting mix. This gives flowering plants the rich soil they prefer, and the soil won't wash away. You can also recycle plastic containers, such as old garbage cans (add a drainage hole), to create these buried gardens in the sand.
- Build raised beds. Use wood, stone, or other materials (see page 143) for the sides. If you'll be growing relatively shallow-rooted plants in the raised bed, line the bottom with porous landscape fabric to prevent the soil from washing into the sand. Then fill with a mixture of high-quality topsoil and compost.

Must-Have Plants for Seashore Gardens

Common Name	Botanical Name	Zones
Annuals/Perennials		
Black-eyed Susan	*Rudbeckia* spp.	3–10
Blanket flower	*Gaillardia* spp.	2–10
Cape plumbago	*Plumbago auriculata*	8–11
Catmint	*Nepeta* spp.	4–9
Coreopsis	*Coreopsis* spp.	3–9
Dusty miller	*Centaurea cineraria*	6–11
Morning glory, dwarf	*Convolvulus tricolor*	Annual
Gazania	*Gazania rigens*	8–10
Geranium	*Pelargonium* spp.	Annual
Grasses, ornamental	Various	Variable
Lavender	*Lavandula* spp.	5–8
Moss rose	*Portulaca grandiflora*	Annual
Russian sage	*Perovskia atriplicifolia*	3–9
Santolina	*Santolina chamaecyparissus*	6–9
Statice; Sea lavender	*Limonium latifolium*	3–9
Vinca, annual	*Catharanthus roseus*	Annual
Yarrow	*Achillea* spp.	3–9
Shrubs and Trees		
Bush cinquefoil	*Potentilla fruticosa*	2–7
Butterfly bush	*Buddleia* spp.	5–10
Ceanothus	*Ceanothus* spp.	8–10
Hydrangea	*Hydrangea* spp.	Variable
Rose, rugosa	*Rosa rugosa* hybrids	3–9
Rosemary	*Rosmarinus officinalis*	7–11
Palms	Various	Variable

Design and Planning Basics

Doing a little garden planning is the best way to save time and money. With some research and plotting, you'll have more success with less work. And it's fun! What could be more enjoyable than developing garden plans and thinking grand thoughts about how to achieve the garden of your dreams?

Chapter 3 Design and Planning Basics

Planning Basics

Whether you have a yard that's bare except for the sod the builder left, or a landscape that seems like an overgrown jungle, the starting point is the same—gathering ideas.

It's best to live in your house a full year before plunging into any major landscape projects. This allows you to get an idea of soil, sun and shade exposure, local climate, and pests. During that time, go on garden tours, visit local public gardens, and browse through magazines and books. Put all your favorite photos and lists of your favorite plants into one folder or notebook.

There are various ways to plan a garden. Some wonderful gardens have been created with the gardener never having developed a plan on paper. Some gardeners prefer to work with the real thing. But this advice will serve you well: Lay out a garden hose where you want the edges of your flower beds and borders. Or take photos of the site and sketch in new beds and borders with a grease pencil. Or lay a piece of tracing paper over the photo and draw your ideas on that with a regular pencil.

A number of gardening software programs are available. If you enjoy playing on the computer, these programs can be a fun way to plan your dream garden.

Planning on paper is a tried-and-true method. Do rough sketches of what you're envisioning, or lay it all out on graph paper—an ideal project for a cold, dreary winter day.

Hiring a professional garden designer is an increasingly popular option. Many garden centers, including some Home Depots, have designers available to come to your home and draw up a landscape plan, usually for a reasonable flat fee.

No matter how you choose to plan your garden, start slowly, planting a small area or two at a time. Gorgeous gardens don't happen in a year or two. They evolve over time, one of the pleasures of gardening.

PROJECT DETAILS

SKILLS: Measuring, drawing, basic plant knowledge
PROJECT: Drawing a landscape plan to scale

TIME TO COMPLETE

EXPERIENCED: A few hours off and on, depending on the level of detail
HANDY: Several hours
NOVICE: Several hours

STUFF YOU'LL NEED

TOOLS: Measuring tape, pencils
MATERIALS: Wooden stakes, ¼-inch-grid tracing paper, straightedge, compass

Sketching a Garden Plan

1 Measure the distances between fixed elements in your garden landscape. Your garden design will be limited by the fixed points in your landscape, which you can't change, such as mature trees, structural elements, and walkways. Measure accurately, and locate these benchmarks on your garden plan.

2 Using grid paper, position the fixed points on your plan. It is useful to prepare an underlay of only the portions of your garden design that will not change. Then design your garden on a tracing paper overlay. That way, you have to redraw only the things that are changeable as you experiment with garden designs.

What Do I Want in My Garden?

As you plan your garden, ask yourself some basic questions:

- How much time do I want to spend gardening? Figure an average of about a half hour a week during the growing season to maintain a 5×20-foot flower bed. And figure about one half to one hour a week for every 50×100-foot stretch of lawn.
- What's my budget? Plants, tools, and supplies can add up quickly. Make a budget and stick to it.
- What are my growing conditions? How much sun and shade fall on various parts of my yard? What's my soil like? How wet or dry is the climate at various times of year? What are record temperature lows and highs?
- What look do I want? Formal, country, English cottage, native, manicured, eclectic?
- What's my region's style? What sort of gardens and hardscape materials look at home in my part of the country? Drought-tolerant native plants? Lush, tropical plants? Prairie natives? Mountain wildflowers? Weathered wood? Bluestone? Granite? Brick?
- What's my lifestyle? How do I want to use my garden? As a retreat? As a place for entertaining? Will children play there? Will pets have access?
- From what angles do I most often view my garden? From the patio? From a particular window overlooking the backyard? From the sidewalk leading from the garage to the back door?
- What are my favorite colors? Will the flowers and plants look good with the existing structures, such as house, fences, and garage?
- What animals do I want to attract or deter? Birds, butterflies, and hummingbirds (page 132) are usually welcome guests, whereas deer and rabbits (page 222) are usually not.

3 Fill in with plantings and accessories. Take into consideration the mature heights and widths of your plantings, the color of the blooms, seasonal progression of blooms, and soil type, as well as the light and water requirements of plants. You might try several garden layouts before you find one you like.

The Right Order

When undertaking a major landscaping project, you can save money and time by doing big-ticket items in a certain order to prevent having to tear up or redo previous projects. Here's the rough order:

1. Make sure you know the exact property lines and setbacks. Have them surveyed if necessary. This could save you costly moving of fences, beds, and more. Then create or commission a master plan.
2. Remove structures and plants you don't want.
3. If necessary, grade the property for improved drainage and esthetics. Install any drain system needed.
4. Build any walls or fences you want along the property line or setback.
5. Install walks, drives, and decks. Be sure to run ¾-1-inch PVC sleeving under any concrete, including driveways, to allow for future irrigation, electrical, or other wiring work.
6. Build garden structures, such as a gazebo or pond. Build any permanent planters and raised beds.
7. If you haven't already done so, plan where you will do any future planting of trees, shrubs, and flowers. Then prepare beds and planting areas, and install an irrigation system according to that plan.
8. Plant large trees and shrubs.
9. Sod or seed the lawn.
10. Plant perennials, groundcovers, and annuals.

DESIGN TIP

DESIGNING ON THE SPOT

Use powdered lime, gypsum, flour, landscape spray paint, or a garden hose to mark future beds and borders. Look at them for a day or two to make sure you like their shapes and positioning.

DESIGN TIP

GARDENS EVOLVE OVER TIME

It's important to realize that gardens change not only with the weeks and months but also over the years. Light changes as trees grow or die; some plants thrive far more than you thought and others don't survive at all. Also, as you learn more about gardening, your preferences and needs will change and you'll move things around. The everchanging garden is part of the cycle of nature and something experienced gardeners learn to celebrate.

TOOL TIP

TAKE A PICTURE

A camera is a valuable landscaping tool. Snapshots can give you an objective perspective. You might be surprised at what you've become used to seeing. Take photographs from across the street and from different angles to get different views. Take a sequence of photos that can be taped together to form a panoramic view by holding the camera steady and pivoting slightly as you shoot. (Panoramic cameras make this job easier.) And take your photos shopping with you. They're a helpful tool for communicating with sales associates.

How You Use Your Landscape

A guiding factor in developing a landscape design is determining how you use your landscape.

The exterior area around your house can be broadly divided into two categories—public and private. Most landscapes also have some areas that are in between.

A CLOSER LOOK

LANDSCAPING FOR PETS

A pet and a beautiful landscape can be compatible. Here's how to create a peaceful coexistence:

- Install a gravel path or patio and designate it as the area where your dog does its business. Train your dog to use it. The more the pet goes there, the more it will want to return there, saving your turf and shrubs from damage and dead spots.
- If dogs tend to romp through or dig up your flower beds, install a decorative edging several inches high around the beds. Depending on the dog's size and personality, the edging may be enough to deter it.
- For bigger or multiple dogs, use fencing to separate the dog from the garden. Create a small play yard for the dogs with fencing, or put flowers and more delicate trees and shrubs in a fenced-in area of their own.
- Invisible fencing keeps dogs within property boundaries, but you can also use it to confine pets to a certain area of the landscape or to keep them out of beds and borders.

Public Spaces

Public spaces are the parts of your yard that you present to guests and the public, including passersby. For many people, these public areas are a top priority, because this portion of the landscape is seen by the most people.

Making public areas your first landscaping priority is a practical decision too. A well-designed landscape welcomes people, gives them a place to park, and provides clear access to the house. It also adds value to your home by providing curb appeal. In fact, most builders will spend the entire landscape allowance on the front yard because that's what helps sell the house.

But you don't have to automatically concentrate on the front yard if you'd rather begin by working on more private family areas (see "Private Spaces," at right). Put your efforts where they're most important to *you.*

If you do choose to work on the public area, make it welcoming by including a wide, inviting, well-lit walkway close to the area where people get out of their cars or approach from public sidewalks. (Consider creating separate guest parking.) Add pots of brightly colored flowers and an attractive welcome mat. Put extra effort into keeping the landscape colorful and well groomed around the door that you'd like guests to use. If a front entry looks as though no one uses it, no one will.

You might need to block views of your private entry area to make the public space more appealing. If visitors are bypassing the front door and instead entering your house through a garage strewn with toys and tools, it's time to rethink your landscape. It's directing traffic the wrong way.

Block views of doors that you don't want people to use. A vine-covered trellis or artfully arranged trees and shrubs keep family entries from becoming magnets for guests.

Private Spaces

Private spaces have different functions. Some areas are for quiet activities, such as low-key entertaining and visiting, sitting, reading, talking, or snoozing in the fresh air. Active private spaces include children's play areas, cooking areas, and places for growing vegetables or favorite flowers. Plan for each of these places that you want in your overall landscape plan.

How you landscape your yard dramatically affects how you use it and how you interact with neighbors and passersby.

Also plan for utility areas, which are also private—or should be. There's no need for neighbors (or even you) to view garbage cans, dog runs, and storage spots.

Most backyards and some side yards are private spaces. If you don't enjoy being in your backyard, or feel you're on display when you sit there, make some changes. Common backyard problems you can fix include a lack of focus, poor views, no privacy, drainage problems, too little or too much shade, and unattractive plants.

If some of these descriptions sound like your backyard, working on it might be more important than working on the public spaces. Let family members have a say. The landscape is part of your home and should meet everyone's needs—including those of your pets.

Deciding On Your Garden's Style

The best advice on garden style is to have one. The most successful gardens are unified with a particular style; everything makes sense in relation to everything else. It's tempting to choose garden structures, accessories, and plants based on what appeals to you at the moment, but, in the long run, clear and unified choices are far more satisfying.

Garden styles are as individual as the gardeners themselves, yet they still reflect personal taste and the environment they exist in. The choices are limited only by your imagination: an Asian-inspired tropical garden, a garden featuring a collection of birdhouses, a wildflower garden outside a New England saltbox, a landscape showcasing a daylily collection, a formal brick-and-boxwood garden surrounding a traditional pillared Southern home, a garden surrounded by woods that welcomes wildlife, or a garden of roses enclosed by a picket fence surrounding a bungalow.

Here's what to consider when you're planning a garden:

Your Home's Architecture

Your house is part of your garden too. When designing your garden, take cues from the architecture and the building materials of your home.

A brick home looks good with brick paths. A simple wood ranch calls for simple wood structures in the yard. A '30s clapboard bungalow is complemented by a charming picket fence.

What's Already There

Work with existing features. A wooded lot calls for a woodland garden. A tiny urban yard, hemmed in by tall buildings, is a natural for a courtyard garden.

Landscapes and structures visible from the garden must also be taken into account. Be sure to look at the big picture while you're planning, so you won't be surprised later.

Formal vs. Informal

Formal gardens tend to have straight and geometric lines, such as a garden divided into four or six or eight squares or rectangles. They can also be circular or a perfect oval, perhaps with straight or curving paths running off the circle or oval.

Many formal gardens include a central axis—a long, straight path that runs through the center of the planting beds, giving a feeling of depth.

Formal gardens don't have to look stuffy. True, traditional formal gardens have tightly clipped hedges, symmetric plantings, and strict themes, such as a rose garden. But even a wildflower garden could be formal if the paths you cut through it are in a geometric pattern.

Informal gardens are more free in form. Beds and borders are usually abstract, flowing shapes. Their layouts are unpredictable, and paths may curve and make many turns. A bird's-eye view would reveal that the garden is not symmetrical in the way that formal gardens often are.

The casual cottage style of this garden works well with the small homes in this neighborhood. French doors bring the outdoors in and also expand limited living space.

Hardscape Materials

What you use for your paths, fences, patios, porches, decks, and other hardscape in the garden affects the garden's style as well.

Paths can be constructed from any of various materials. Wood chips set a casual tone, whereas brick is formal. Pea gravel edged with brick is somewhere in between.

Strive to unify the hardscape. A white wood arbor works well with a white wood bench. Brick paths may look out of place with a flagstone patio.

Region and Neighborhood

Although your garden doesn't need to be a copy of the other landscapes in your neighborhood, it should fit in.

A grand, lush, water-thirsty garden with a large lawn and high-maintenance annuals would look out of place in a modest neighborhood in the desert Southwest. Use some of the same type of fencing or the same trees you see in the neighborhood. This is especially important in the public spaces, such as your front yard, where your garden will be on display to passersby.

Personality

Let your personality shine through in your garden. After all, personal expression is a big part of why you're spending all this time and money. Use your favorite colors. If you love purple, use lots of it. Let your garden look like *your* garden.

DESIGN TIP

PAPER GARDENS

As you're deciding which garden style is best for you, do what interior designers recommend to their clients: Clip photos of gardens you love from magazines, newspapers, and fliers, and file them in a folder. After you have a large collection of photos, go through them and note what they have in common. An abundance of yellow flowers? A formal layout? An English cottage look? Use this information to guide you to a unified garden style all your own.

Designing with Decks, Porches, and Patios

Gardening Where You Live

YOU SAY VERANDA; I SAY PORCH
The popularity of outdoor spaces is regional. In the chilly North, homeowners might make do with a small porch, but in the South, they're more likely to have a large porch and dub it a veranda.

Enclosed sunrooms and three-season rooms are understandably most popular in the North, where long winters and iffy springs and falls make them a sunny retreat during cool weather.

Decks started out as the quintessential California space but are now probably most popular in the Midwest; patios and porches have again regained popularity on the West Coast.

Some regions have spaces so specific that they're named after the area. In Florida, so-called Florida rooms are large, sturdily screened-in spaces—sometimes even with a swimming pool—which keep out the big, problematic insects that thrive in the subtropical climate.

One of the easiest ways to expand your living space is by creating an outdoor room.

These come in many variations: decks, porches, patios, three-season rooms, and sunrooms. All do the same thing: provide a living space closely connected to the surrounding landscape.

Whether you're considering building such a space, remodeling it, or simply enjoying the space you already have, here are some guiding principles and factors to consider in creating an outdoor living space:

- Exposure. In general, an east-facing outdoor room is ideal. It gets warming morning light and avoids beating afternoon sun. (If necessary, add curtains, blinds, or awnings on the west side to cool things down.) However, a north-facing space can be welcomingly cool in hot climates, and a south-facing space can be toasty warm in cold climates.
- Interface with the outdoors. Make the space serve as a seamless transition from indoors to out. Avoid perching a deck up high, detached from the landscape. Design a sunroom with big French doors, which can be left open in fine weather. With a stone or paver patio, leave pockets for planting against the house and in spots around the perimeter.
- Enough room. If you're building, consider that you'll probably want to eat in the space as well as sit there. Be sure to include enough space for a table and chairs as well as comfortable furniture for lounging.
- Insects and weather. In rainy climates, a roof is a must. And in all but the mildest, driest climates, screens add months of enjoyment to spaces when mosquitoes would otherwise drive you indoors.
- Heating and cooling. A ceiling fan can make a space seem 10 degrees cooler, even on an open porch. An electric baseboard heater in an enclosed area can make the space more useful during more months of the year.
- Consider professional help. Many Home Depots have design and installation services to offer.

A well-designed deck can be one of the most popular, restful areas of your home.

Designing with Walks and Paths

Many gardeners think that sidewalks and paths are purely functional, that their only role in the landscape is to get you from one point to another.

But paths also play an important visual role. They draw a major line (or two or three) across your yard. So it's important that you design your paths with looks and function in mind.

For help, consult your Home Depot garden center. Many centers offer design and installation services to help you get the best designed, best built space possible.

Materials

Paths can be made of various materials: brick, pine needles, wood chip mulch, crushed seashells, crushed stone, turf, poured concrete, bluestone, limestone, flagstone, wood, concrete or stone pavers, and more.

Of course, the more often a path is used, the sturdier it should be. A front path should be made of a material that is smooth and easy for people of all agility levels to navigate. Poured concrete and brick are the most popular options. Paths in cold-winter climates need to be solid enough to make snow and ice removal easy. Crushed stone would be difficult to shovel.

Take your cue for paths from the materials and style of your home as well as other materials in the garden. If your home is brick, a path using brick would make sense. If you have flagstone edging around a garden pool, a flagstone path would blend in nicely.

You can also combine materials. A simple poured concrete walk has more visual interest when edged with brick. A wood chip path is more durable when topped with pavers. Wood or brick edging on crushed stone paths is decorative and keeps the stone in place.

Pattern

Keep in mind that paths are a design element. A path doesn't have to stretch straight from point A to point B just because it's the most direct route; consider a path with a graceful curve to add beauty to the landscape.

Paths in backyards are also important. They can be useful in pulling visitors (and you) into the garden rather than taking in the landscape from the back door. Watch how visitors move through your yard and how you would like to move through your yard, and use that as your cue to where to lay out paths.

In the backyard of homes with small children, many gardeners create solid-surface paths that make a loop. Loops encourage fun with trikes, wagons, and other riding toys.

This stone path and steps not only is practical in keeping feet high and dry in wet weather, it also adds a striking visual element that makes the area even more beautiful.

Regardless of what type of path you create, be sure to think through how plantings will fit with the path. A front walk should be spaced away from the house to leave a pocket for planting tubs and flowers, and perhaps future plantings of trees, beds, and borders.

DESIGN TIP

HOW WIDE?

Paths and walks should be different widths depending on their use. A walkway to a front door should be 48 to 60 inches wide, to allow two people to approach side by side. This width also helps balance the size of the house when viewed from the street.

In the back and sides of the house, paths can be narrower: 24 to 36 inches.

Access paths, those rough paths that cut through vegetable gardens and large flower beds to allow you access to working the bed, can be as narrow as 18 inches. Just be sure you can get a wheelbarrow down the path, and make a spot to turn it around easily.

GOOD IDEA

CHILDREN AND PATHS

Well-designed paths are key to creating a child-friendly landscape. Children naturally follow paths (rather than walking through flower beds), so if you find that small children are wandering all over beds and borders, make sure that they can clearly determine where they *should* be walking.

A bonus: For children, walking along paths is like a little journey. Adding paths behind shrubs and through flower beds makes your garden more fun.

Designing with Arbors and Trellises

Arbors are old-fashioned favorites that have become popular once again.

An arbor can be large, with a grid overhead and enough space for a sitting area. Sometimes arbors are long and narrow, designed to follow a path. And sometimes they are only wide enough to accommodate a bench or porch swing or other modest seating.

The most common type of arbor looks like a little doorway. And that's exactly what it is—an attractive entry to place at the beginning or end of a path or even to straddle a path somewhere along its middle.

Avoid the common mistake of plunking one of these doorwaylike arbors in the middle of the garden. That would be like putting a door in the middle of a room.

Arbor Materials

Arbors are made of a variety of materials: wood timbers, lumber, metal, and vinyl. Wood is a favorite, and an excellent material, but it presents a maintenance problem, because an arbor, with its intricate design, can be a bear to paint.

Many gardeners leave the wood unpainted, perhaps treating new wood with a deck sealer. Others add a traditional coat of paint, or use a stain to give the wood color while preventing the peeling problems that occur with paint.

Erecting an Arbor

Large arbors need to be securely mounted in concrete to prevent settling. Small arbors can benefit from being seated on concrete pilings, too, though the concrete can contribute to rot problems with wood structures.

Kits are available that secure the arbor to the ground with chains and ground screws. One of the easiest ways to secure a wood arbor so it doesn't settle or blow over is to screw two sturdy flat steel strips or stakes a couple of feet long onto each of the four corner legs and insert the stakes securely into the soil.

Popular Vines for Arbors and Trellises

When planting on an arbor or trellis, choose a vine that will stay within bounds, or it can quickly overwhelm and even topple the structure. Below are vines that grow between 6 and 20 feet, good sizes for arbors.

Common Name	Botanical Name	Zones
Black-eyed Susan vine	*Thunbergia alata*	Annual
Chocolate vine	*Akebia quinata*	5–9
Clematis, large flowered	*Clematis* spp.	3–9
Jessamine, Carolina	*Gelsemium sempervirens*	7–9
Morning glory	*Ipomoea tricolor*	Annual
Moonflower	*Ipomoea alba*	Annual
Passion flower	*Passiflora* spp.	7–10
Roses, smaller climbing types	*Rosa* spp.	Variety
Jasmine, star	*Trachelospermum jasminoides*	8–10
Sweet pea	*Lathyrus odoratus*	Annual
Trumpet honeysuckle	*Lonicera sempervirens*	4–9

Arbors lend storybook charm to front entries, backyards, and just about any spot they're added.

Designing with Other Structural Elements

Fences and Hedges

Good fences may make good neighbors, but they also make for good landscapes. Fences offer a sense of enclosure and are an attractive backdrop for plantings. They also keep children and pets in designated areas.

Chain link fence is one of the most popular types of fencing because of its low cost. However, wood fencing adds infinitely more warmth and character to a landscape, will pay for itself with years of enjoyment, and adds to the easier resale of your home.

If you are installing a privacy fence, consider adding lattice or other openwork at the top. Fences higher than 4 feet in a modest-size yard can feel oppressive and confining if they are made from solid wood.

Hedges are an excellent alternative for providing privacy and backdrop in a yard. Evergreens are the plant of choice, because they offer greenery and privacy year-round. Some hedging plants grow faster than others, however, so check growth rates (see page 57).

Also check sun and shade tolerance. Hedges often continue from a shady area to a sunny area. If plants aren't chosen carefully, the hedge may be shorter and sparser in the shady area and taller and fuller in the sunny area.

A rustic picket fence perfectly complements a casual planting of reseeding flowers.

A cut stone retaining wall is a durable, beautiful addition to the landscape and creates an excellent raised bed.

Retaining Walls

Retaining walls can be 8 feet high or just a few inches high. It all depends on your landscape design and how the landscape is used.

Low retaining walls made from stones or pavers stacked just a foot or so high (see page 58) are an ideal way to reduce erosion and create interesting pockets for planting.

Retaining walls 1 to 3 feet high are good projects for the experienced do-it-yourselfer. Anything higher than 3 feet probably should be left to professionals, because of the amount of soil moving involved and the importance of building secure, safe walls that will last for decades.

Edging

Edging around beds and borders adds pleasing visual definition, creating a landscape that looks tidy year-round. Edging also helps keep plants in bounds and keeps lawn grasses from spreading into flower beds.

Edging can be made of a variety of materials. Brick edging (see page 146 for how to install) is popular, as is black plastic edging. Edging can also be made from small boulders, cut stone, stacked flagstone, wood, and even large seashells.

Whatever edging you choose, take your cues from other materials used in the landscape so your yard has a unified appearance.

Limestone edging keeps grass out of the flowerbed and prevents creeping plants from growing into the lawn.

Good garden lighting not only makes a landscape safer, it also allows you to enjoy it into the evening hours.

Lighting

Evenings are often when the yard is most enjoyable. Temperatures are lower, the wind has often died down, and after sunset many insects slow their activity.

Lighting your landscape, then, is an excellent way to enjoy it longer. Yard lights and light fixtures attached to the outside of your house and garage add bright task lighting to make sure that you and your visitors can walk safely, and to make sure that you can see the grill or the pool.

Low-voltage lighting is more for mood. Granted, low-voltage lighting installed along a path makes it more safe, but it also adds a pretty glow. Lighting for water features is increasingly popular, also, and allows you to enjoy your pool or waterfall after work and into the evening with friends.

Installing low-voltage lighting—an easy do-it-yourself project—has another advantage. When you look out a window or door at night, your landscape will look lovely accented by the soft light. For extra-easy installation, check out solar-powered lights and lighting kits.

Designing for Outdoor Living

Create spaces for outdoor living—pleasant spots to sit and read a book, share a meal with family and friends, entertain company, or simply relax.

These outdoor spaces greatly expand your living area. Many homeowners have marveled at how adding an outdoor living area to their landscape is like adding a whole new room to their home—at a fraction of the cost.

Areas for Sitting and Lounging

Group a few chairs and low tables in a comfortable spot. Porches, patios, and decks are the obvious places to create a sitting area. However, it's also a nice idea to tuck a few chairs into a far corner of the yard. They invite visitors (and you!) to view the landscape from a refreshingly different angle. They also heighten the sense of getting away from it all, even if it's only 40 feet away.

Choose seating that is large and inviting and has arms. Small, hard, straight chairs seldom encourage people to sit for any length of time.

One large chair, chaise, or hammock is fine if you are the primary user. Two chairs are more companionable. For entertaining, place four or more seats together. For convenience, include at least one low table for drinks and snacks.

Comfort in outdoor areas is paramount. Screen for insects with one of the portable screen tents now available. Make sure chairs have weather-resistant cushions. Consider an outdoor fireplace (either portable or permanent), a fire pit, or a chiminea to ward off evening chills in spring and fall.

Dining Areas

All you need is a table and some sturdy chairs, and you have an outdoor dining area. Set them up on a porch or patio, or place them on the lawn for a romantic English effect. Purchase new patio furniture, or use a coat of paint to spruce up garage sale and flea market finds. Even a card table can be put into service if you cover it with a water-resistant vinyl tablecloth. Picnic tables are a dining classic.

Move dining furniture around to suit the seasons. It's pleasant to have it in a sunny spot for lunch on a balmy spring day, but better to move it under a tree in summer when temperatures mount. Be cautious in setting up close to shrubs and flowers that attract bees so you don't invite stings.

Outdoor kitchens have been gaining in popularity in recent years. Create an inexpensive version by building a small roof off the wall of the garage or a side of the house. Set up a grill with an attached gas burner or two. Add a small dorm fridge, with a ground fault circuit interrupter (GFCI) outlet to prevent shocks, along with a roll-away cabinet to hold paper or plastic plates and cups.

A simple table and chairs turn nearly any area into a haven for outdoor dining and enjoyment.

Designing with Garden Accessories

Garden accessories add character and personality to a garden. Chosen carefully, they create focal points, drawing attention to certain areas of the garden.

Functional vs. Decorative

Garden accessories fall into one of two categories: functional or decorative. Functional accessories do double duty. They're pleasant to look at but also serve a purpose. They include benches, birdhouses, butterfly houses, birdbaths, accent lighting, and sundials. Functional accessories look as though they belong in the garden. Purely decorative accessories, such as plaques, statues, fountains, gazing balls, or figurines, can beautify a garden, too, but they need to be used with caution and restraint. Too many can make a garden look busy.

Garden Style

Garden accessories should fit in with your overall garden style. Rustic, country accents are perfect for a rustic, country garden but may not look right in a formal garden. And the accessories should be compatible. They don't have to match, but they do need to harmonize with one another. If in doubt, place all your garden accessories together and see if they look good as a group.

A Focal Point

If you have a lot of accessories, you can prevent a cluttered look by having one clear, large focal point, such as a striking fountain, an arbor, or a fence. A focal point, to which all accessories should be secondary, directs the eye and makes a yard with several accessories look less confusing.

Garden accessories look most at home when they're functional, such as this bird feeder.

DESIGN TIP

PRACTICE RESTRAINT
Garden accessories are most effective when they don't clutter the garden. It's tempting to accumulate nifty items whenever you see them, but too many accents in a garden can look kitschy rather than cute.

Cluster garden-inspired collections, such as these birdhouses, to achieve maximum impact and prevent a cluttered look.

Coping with Poor Drainage

Even though plants need consistent watering, once the water hits the soil it needs to drain away freely. Granted, enough of it needs to stay next to the roots so they can absorb it, but if the soil stays too wet, much-needed oxygen fails to reach the plant roots, and rot and fungal problems can set in. Amending the soil can help prevent drainage on the top foot or so of the soil; in more serious cases, consider installing drainage pipe.

Wet Spots

Some gardens have spots that are low-lying and chronically wet. These areas can be ideal for moisture-loving perennials that otherwise would need huge amounts of water, such as astilbe and ligularia. Or consider planting shrubs that like wet conditions (see page 76) or trees that thrive in wet soil (see page 68).

Install Drainage

If the soil doesn't drain at least reasonably well (see "How to Test Your Soil for Drainage," at right), you may want to consider installing drainage pipe in beds and borders to divert water elsewhere.

Drainage pipe is not a good idea in extremely heavy clay soils. They hold the water, not allowing it to percolate down to the drainage pipe.

Some slope is needed when installing drainage pipe. After all, the pipe needs to drain somewhere. If the area is perfectly flat or is so low that gravity cannot pull the water away from the area, the pipe will not solve the problem.

Raised Beds

An excellent solution for chronically wet soils is a raised bed (see pages 143 to 144 for building instructions). A raised bed provides excellent drainage and, if the soil is problematic (as in heavy clay), creates an ideal planting bed with top-notch soil.

WORK SMARTER

HOW TO TEST YOUR SOIL FOR DRAINAGE

Here's an easy test to see how well your soil drains. Dig an 18-inch-deep hole and fill it with water. If it drains within an hour, the soil is well-drained and will support a variety of plants. If it takes more than an hour to drain, the soil doesn't drain well. If it takes more than 4 hours to drain, you have very poorly draining soil.

PROJECT DETAILS

PROJECT DETAILS: Laying drainage pipe to direct water away from a planting bed
SKILLS: Digging
PROJECT: Creating soil drainage

TIME TO COMPLETE

EXPERIENCED: An hour for a small area
HANDY: 1 1/2 hours
NOVICE: 2 hours

STUFF YOU'LL NEED

TOOLS: Spade, gloves, hoe
MATERIALS: Perforated (must have drainage holes) flexible drainage pipe, coarse gravel or road rock, gloves, a spade, and a silt sock or landscape fabric to prevent soil from washing into the pipe (optional).

How to Install Drainage in the Garden

1 Along the front or back of the planting bed or any other poorly draining portion of the bed, dig a trench several inches to 1 foot deep, depending on the ease of digging your soil.

2 Fill the bottom of the trench with an inch or two of coarse gravel or road rock. This is what allows water to quickly drain to the area surrounding the drainage pipe.

3 If desired, wrap the perforated drainage pipe in a silt sock or landscape fabric to prevent silt from clogging holes and slowing the pipe. Top an inch or two more of rock. Cover with soil and plant.

Planting For Privacy

Few gardens have pretty views in every direction. Most landscapes have unappealing garbage cans or air conditioners to deal with. Views of ugly signs, unkempt alleyways, or your neighbor's messy garage can spoil your time outdoors. The beauty of landscaping is that you can avoid looking at anything unattractive. Make unwanted views disappear behind plantings.

Evergreens vs. Deciduous Plants

Evergreen plants are often used as screens because they retain their foliage year-round. Some are so dense that they form screens like living walls.

Deciduous plants can also be used for screening. Look for plants with a rapid growth rate or ones that are described as good choices for informal hedges.

Plant Shape and Height

Some screening plants such as privet and arborvitae are green from top to bottom and create a solid screen. Others, such as a redbud or crabapple, create a screen higher up. If the unfortunate view is the top half of your neighbor's peeling garage as seen over your fence, for example, one or two of these small trees will serve nicely.

Consider Vines

If you have a chain link or other openwork fence between you and the unpleasant view, plant it with fast-growing annual vines, such as morning glory, or a perennial vine. A perennial vine won't cover the fence as quickly, but it will offer more screening in the long run.

Other Ideas

- A planting that screens can be something other than a long row of plants that are all the same. A deciduous tree with a couple of evergreens, a few shrubs, and some perennials would work well.
- Build a berm (see page 145). Berms instantly block out the lower portion of a view with soil. They also make even newly planted trees and shrubs seem taller by elevating them.

This hedge of upright yew is dense and thick, a perfect backdrop for plants. It also creates less of an enclosed feeling than a fence would.

Good Trees for Privacy Plantings

* Growth rate: S=Slow , M=Medium, R=Rapid

Common Name	Botanical Name	Zones	Growth*
Evergreen Trees			
Arborvitae, American	*Thuja occidentalis*	3–7	M-R
Cedar, blue atlas	*Cedrus libani* 'Glauca'	6–9	S
Cedar, deodar	*Cedrus deodara*	6–9	M
Cedar, eastern red	*Juniperus virginiana*	3–9	M
Cypress, Arizona	*Cupressus arizonica*	7–9	R
Cypress, Leyland	*×Cupressocyparis leylandii*	6–9	R
Fir, bristlecone	*Abies bracteata*	7–8	S
Fir, Douglas	*Pseudotsuga menziesii*	4–6	M
Fir, Frasier	*Abies fraseri*	4–7	S
Fir, white	*Abies concolor*	3–7	M
Hemlock, Canada	*Tsuga canadensis*	3–7	M
Holly, blue	*Ilex ×meserveae*	5–8	S
Holly, lusterleaf	*Ilex latifolia*	7–9	S
Holly, Savannah	*Ilex ×attenuata* 'Savannah'	5–9	S
Holly, Yaupon	*Ilex vomitoria*	7–10	R
Incense cedar, California	*Calocedrus decurrens*	4–8	M
Juniper, Hollywood	*Juniperus chinensis* 'Torulosa'	4–9	M
Juniper, skyrocket	*Juniperus scopulorum* 'Skyrocket'	4–8	S
Magnolia, southern	*Magnolia grandiflora*	6–10	S
Magnolia, sweet bay	*Magnolia virginiana*	5–9	M
Myrtle, Pacific wax	*Myrica cerifera*	7–9	R
Pine, eastern white	*Pinus strobus*	3–8	R
Pine, Japanese black	*Pinus thunbergii*	5–7	M
Spruce, Colorado blue	*Picea pungens glauca*	2–7	S
Spruce, Norway	*Picea abies*	2–7	M
Spruce, Serbian	*Picea omorika*	4–7	S
Spruce, white	*Picea glauca*	2–6	M
Yew, Japanese upright	*Taxus cuspidata* 'Capitata'	4–7	S
Deciduous Trees			
Ash, green	*Fraxinus pennsylvanica*	3–9	R
Bald cypress	*Taxodium distichum*	4–10	M-R
Birch, river	*Betula nigra*	4–9	R
Chaste tree	*Vitex agnus-castus*	6–10	M
Crabapple	*Malus* spp.	4–8	M
Crape myrtle	*Lagerstroemia indica*	7–9	R
Elm, Chinese	*Ulmus parvifolia*	5–9	R
Magnolia, saucer	*Magnolia × soulangiana*	5–9	M
Maple, red	*Acer rubrum*	3–9	M
Oak, Willow	*Quercus phellos*	4–8	M
Pagoda tree, Japanese	*Sophora japonica*	6–8	R
Pear, Callery	*Pyrus calleryana*	4–8	R
Plum, purple-leaf	*Prunus cerasifera* 'Atropurpurea'	4–8	R
Privet	*Ligustrum* spp.	3–9	R
Redbud	*Cercis canadensis*	3–9	M
Zelkova, Japanese	*Zelkova serrata*	5–9	M

Taming A Slope

A slope presents a landscape challenge and an opportunity.

The challenge is in preventing erosion and designing attractive plantings on a site where turf is difficult to grow. Water often drains too quickly from a slope, so grass receives too little moisture, or the erosion problem is bad enough that grass fails to establish.

The opportunity is that a slope can make an attractive planting site when terraced with low retaining walls and planted with a variety of perennials and shrubs, and even perhaps a few small trees. (The roots of large trees would become exposed over time as the soil washes downward.)

Low retaining walls, such as the one shown here, are relatively easy for the do-it-yourselfer. Retaining walls taller than 3 feet are better left to the pros. Tall walls, if not meticulously designed and executed, can become unstable and a safety hazard.

On a slope where grass is nearly impossible to grow, this planting in spring explodes with color from soft pink heather, white creeping phlox, white candytuft, and an assortment of red, pink, and white azaleas.

PROJECT DETAILS

PROJECT DETAILS: Digging terraces, laying wall block or stone, backfilling
SKILLS: Digging, laying stone or block evenly, backfilling
PROJECT: Creating a low terrace

TIME TO COMPLETE

EXPERIENCED: 1 to 2 days
HANDY: 3 to 4 days
NOVICE: 4 to 5 days

STUFF YOU'LL NEED

TOOLS: Spade, level, wheelbarrow
MATERIALS: Wall block or cut stone, coarse sand, coarse gravel/road base, landscape fabric

Laying a Low Retaining Wall

1 Dig out terraces, making sure they tilt backward a bit to allow for the addition of sand and crushed stone.

2 Add a layer of coarse sand, topped with crushed stone or road base. This allows for better placement of the stone and good drainage to prevent them from dislodging.

3 Position the stones, nearly burying the first course. (This terrace has three courses of pavers.) Stone should run horizontally level; use a builder's level to check. Stones should also tip very slightly backward to allow for settling. And they should overlap backward slightly as you lay them, so the first course is slightly farther forward than the second, and so on.

4 Cut a strip of landscape fabric and position it behind the stone to prevent soil from washing forward. Fill behind the stone wall with good quality topsoil or a combination of topsoil and compost.

Gardening in A Small Space

Although some gardeners dream of gardens that stretch over acres, many gardeners create perfect little jewel boxes of plants on apartment balconies, in condo courtyards, and in handkerchief-size backyards.

Creating a tiny garden is a challenge, but it's immensely rewarding when done well. Here's how:

- Containerize! Use every bit of space creatively with containers. Have a flat stretch of concrete? Fill it with a collection of large pots, or build a large planter to fill the space. Faced with a brick wall? Line the base with a series of window boxes inserted with trellises, and plant them with ivies or other vines. A fence can be dressed up with window boxes along its top or pots hung from special rings or other supports.
- Go for immediate size and color. Splurge on big, gorgeous plants that will transform a small space with color. Tiny plants take a while to mature and bloom. They're an economical option when you have large spaces to fill, but in tight quarters you need quick drama.
- Make the space come to life. Maximize the gardening experience in minimal spaces by appealing to all the senses. Add a small tabletop or container water feature for the soothing sound of water. Choose fragrant plants whenever possible to appeal to your sense of smell. Include intriguing or highly textured plants, such as wooly creeping thyme (see page 521) or lamb's-ears (see page 421). This packs a lot of activity and interest into a small amount of square footage.

Even a an apartment balcony can be turned into a restful garden retreat with the addition of simple seating and container plants.

- Keep the garden immaculate. In a tiny garden, even a few browning leaves or one dying plant make the whole space look less appealing. Spend a few minutes every day watering, deadheading, and grooming plants so the space always looks inviting. Bring in fresh plants immediately if a current planting is flagging.

This pergola is an excellent example of how much color and charm you can pack into even the smallest space.

GOOD IDEA

TASTY TREATS

In a small garden, it's especially rewarding to grow a few edibles. Many lettuces, tomatoes, and herbs do beautifully in small spaces and containers. (See pages 258–259 for specifics on growing edibles in containers.) And nothing is more rewarding than snipping a few fresh herbs for dinner or harvesting a beautiful ripe tomato—a pleasure that's the same whether you garden in 3 acres or 3 square yards.

The Right Plant In the Right Place

Situate a plant where it's well-suited to the sun, soil, and moisture, and it will thrive, rewarding you with vigorous growth and good performance. Put it in a place not suited to its needs and you may well end up with an ailing or dying plant. Learning a plant's needs takes a little time and patience, but it's well worth the effort.

Here's how:

Know A Plant's Needs

Read the plant label carefully; it gives basic information. But also ask about the plant at your Home Depot garden center, and read up on it in the Plant Encyclopedia, starting on page 292. That way, if the plant is a sun lover, you can avoid putting it in the shade, where it will perhaps live but grow spindly and weak. Know its light and moisture needs, its soil and drainage needs, its ultimate height and width, and what regions of the country it's most likely to do well in.

Experiment with Containers and Annuals

The best way to find out more about your garden's growing conditions is just to get growing. Grow plants in containers and move them around your garden to see where they do best. Move them to a brighter or shadier spot as needed.

Annuals are a good, inexpensive way to find out more about soils and conditions. When planted in the ground, annuals will give you clues on how hot and dry or dark and damp a spot is, as well as an idea of what pests and diseases you need to be aware of before investing in more permanent and expensive perennials.

GOOD IDEA!

PLANTS ARE LIKE FURNITURE

You'll hear many experienced gardeners say that they treat their plants a little like their living room furniture—they keep moving them around until they find just the right spots for them.

Granted, you can't move a mature tree easily, and there's a right way to do these things (see "Move Plants Around" on the opposite page), but small shrubs, small trees, and perennials can generally be moved to another spot where they might thrive or at least look better.

If a plant such as this yarrow isn't thriving, move it to another spot better-suited to its light, soil, or moisture requirements.

Some plants thrive only with excellent drainage and a sunny exposure. This rock garden is the ideal place for such plants. Plants that need moist soil and cooler, shadier conditions would bake in this location.

Watch the Sun

Putting a plant in a spot with too little sun is a common mistake. What may seem at first like full sun in a section of your yard might actually be part shade. Full sun is direct, unfiltered light for at least six hours a day. Observe the patterns of light and shadow in your garden at different times of the day as well as at different times of the year.

Being aware of the patterns of light and shadow in your garden is a learning experience. By experimenting with growing different plants in different spots you'll learn about the sun and shade levels in your landscape. You might plant a chrysanthemum in a spot that seems like full sun, only to watch the stems grow at an angle as they stretch toward the sunnier portion of the yard. Or you may think you have a beautifully shady spot and plant a hosta there, only to watch portions of the leaves turn beige, then brown with sunscald. (See page 24 for more information on determining sun and shade.)

Move Plants Around

If a plant is still struggling in a spot after a year or two, consider relocating it. Moving a plant only a few yards can make a big difference. One gardener watched the astilbe on the northwest side of her house struggle for years. She moved it 3 feet to the east and was rewarded with vigorous foliage and flowers a few weeks later.

Within reason and with care, you can move most perennials and small shrubs. The best time is in spring or fall. Most important, make sure the plant is not in bloom when you move it.

Choose a cloudy, overcast day—avoid hot, sunny, windy days. Dig up as much of the root ball as possible, and keep the plant well watered in its new home for the next two to four weeks.

Know When to Say Good-bye

Some plants will fail to do well in your garden no matter how much attention you lavish on them or how many times you move them around. These are the plants that simply limp along, year after year, looking unhappy, contributing what one gardener calls "negative ornamental value." They are plants that, for whatever reason, are not suited to your climate, your yard, or your personal gardening style. Tough as it is to do, dig them up, discard them or pass them on to a gardening friend, and write them off as a learning experience.

For more information on plant selection and positioning, check out microclimates on page 20.

A CLOSER LOOK

TOP 10 SIGNS THAT A PLANT IS FAILING TO THRIVE

10. Chronic yellowing or dropping leaves, especially on the bottom portion of the plant
9. Failure to bloom or poor, sparse blooms
8. Slow to restart growth in spring, especially roses
7. Chronic disease or insect problems
6. Pale, spindly new growth
5. Overall leggy plant growth
4. Wilting between waterings, even when soil seems somewhat moist
3. Pale or white spots on shade-loving plants that may be a sign of sunscald
2. Overall small size and lack of fullness
1. And finally . . . it's dying!

Color in Your Landscape

You can have a garden that has color from one plant or another all year long with a little know-how and a little planning. Try these ideas:

Seek Out Plants with Four-Season Appeal

Some plants look good all year long. Tall sedums are fresh looking in spring and summer, develop attractive brick red flowers in fall, and, if left standing, lend interest to the winter garden. Red-osier dogwoods have flowers in spring, foliage in summer, and in fall and winter attractive red stems that stand out against the snow. Use four-season plants such as these as much as possible.

Look for Color from Foliage

Gardeners often think that color comes just from flowers. But foliage comes in many colors too—deep purples, variegated greens and whites, yellows, and blue-greens. Use a variety of foliage colors to keep your garden interesting.

Choose Long-Blooming Perennials

Some perennials bloom for only a few days, whereas others bloom for months. Plant as many of the long bloomers as possible (see page 93). A good long-blooming perennial will bloom for two to even three months.

Deadhead to Extend Bloom Time

Deadheading (page 206) keeps your garden tidy and encourages plants to bloom longer.

Some plants respond better to deadheading than others. And some, such as coreopsis, have so many sprawling blooms that it's best to cut or shear them back all at once—taking a little of the plant's foliage with them—to clean up the plant and encourage a new flush of bloom.

Cut back plants with long, bare stalks, such as irises and daylilies, to the base of the stalk.

A Year of Bloom from Perennials and Roses

Daffodil *Narcissus* spp. | Tulip *Tulipa* spp. | Columbine *Aquilegia* spp. | Siberian iris *Iris sibirica* | Peony *Paeonia* spp. | Shrub rose *Rosa* spp.

Seek Early- Through Late-Season Bloomers

Some tulips will bloom while snow is on the ground, others are midseason cultivars, and still others will bloom with the earliest roses. Each type may bloom for only two to three weeks, but planted together they will extend tulip time to more than two months. Plant a variety of plant times for longer bloom of favorite plants.

Seek Repeat Bloomers

Some plants will bloom in flushes, with a first, heavy flowering. If you're diligent in deadheading or cutting back the plant slightly (page 206), they'll often respond with a second, third, or even continual series of blooms. Hardy geraniums are a good example of this, as are many roses. Repeat bloomers extend the bloom time in your garden.

DESIGN TIP

PLAN FOR WINTER INTEREST

No matter what your climate, you can have a beautiful garden, even in winter. In warm climates, seek out evergreen plants that bloom in winter. In colder climates, use tall sedums, ornamental grasses, berries, shrubs, and trees with colorful barks to create visual interest even in the deepest snow.

Visit local public gardens and neighborhood gardens, and chat with garden center staff even in winter to learn more about these useful off-season plants.

BUYER'S GUIDE

KEEP THE BLOOMS COMING

Visit your garden center throughout the growing season for ideas on what's blooming when. Nurseries usually highlight plants that are at their peak.

In August, for example, you'll spot some beauties that flower during that difficult time of the year. However, peak bloom is usually not the ideal time to plant. Consult your garden center staff on the best time for planting your choice.

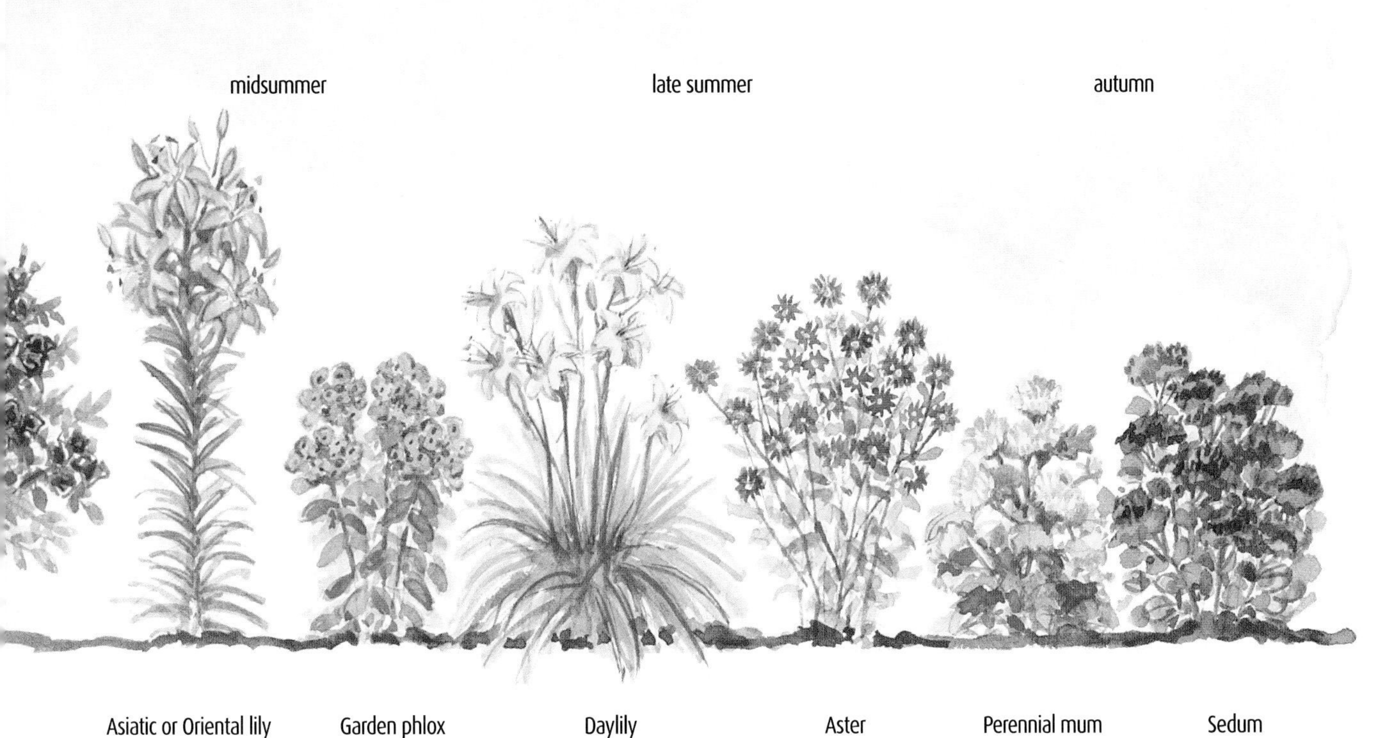

How to Choose and Design With Trees

Trees impact your property perhaps more than any other landscape design element. They help determine sun and shade and overall planting and usage patterns. It's important to design around trees you already have, and to position any new trees carefully.

A CLOSER LOOK

WHAT TREES CAN DO FOR YOU

A well-chosen, well-positioned tree is an asset to any landscape. Here's what a tree can do for you:

- Add privacy
- Cool your home and landscape with shade
- Protect shade-loving plants from excess sun, especially in hot climates
- Keep your home warmer in winter by deflecting wind
- Establish a background for your garden
- Provide fruits or nuts
- Provide flowers
- Provide fragrance
- Create a nesting area and provide fruits for birds
- Clean the air
- Muffle traffic noise

Incorporating Existing Trees

Assess the trees you already have. Are they properly pruned? Do they look healthy throughout the growing season? Are they reasonably well-positioned? Are they growing into the sides or roof of houses or other buildings? Are they a good size for the landscape? Are they attractive and free from problems—for example, do they litter excessively or have shallow roots that make other planting problematic?

If a tree fails to work well in its current position, consider removing it—a major expense but perhaps a good move for your landscape in the long run, especially if the tree isn't very large.

What Do You Want in a New Tree?

Would you prefer a tree that keeps its foliage year-round (evergreen) or one that sheds its leaves once a year (deciduous)? Evergreen trees offer more privacy year-round. Deciduous trees are usually the top choices for providing summer shade, and some also flower.

Trees are key to good plantings. At this new home, they add greenery and shade and create a more established feel.

Keep in mind that the right plant in the right place is critical to success. Before adding a tree to your yard, you need to know its ultimate size and how long it will take to reach maturity. That way, you can avoid having to prune a tall, stately tree severely because you failed to take telephone or power lines into account at planting. Pruning a tree drastically to control size is never a good idea. It is labor-intensive to work against nature, and it's often difficult to maintain a tree's lovely overall shape.

Knowing how big a tree will grow also helps you avoid the common problem of planting a tree that will grow large too close to your house, where its roots could damage the foundation.

Ask or read up on a tree's root system (check the Plant Encyclopedia, starting on page 292, for specifics). Trees with a large root system can buckle paving and are poor choices for planting next to patios, sidewalks, parking areas, or streets. These areas need trees that have well-behaved roots. The trees should also be able to thrive next to the reflected heat of paving. (Always check easements and right-of-way restrictions before planting.)

Also check on whether a tree has invasive roots, so you can avoid planting it around septic and drainage systems.

Other questions to ask about a tree:

- What sort of litter does it produce? Does it drop fruits, the way some crabapples do, that can produce a hazard on sidewalks and a mess otherwise? Does it shed lots of small broken branches, as some weeping willows do? This is especially important in areas around swimming pools.
- If a tree drops its leaves, how does it do it and when? Some trees drop all their leaves at once in autumn, making for heavy but one-time leaf removal. Others shed their leaves gradually. And some, such as scarlet oak, hold on to their leaves almost all winter and are a bit unsightly in early spring when bulbs are blooming but the tree is still covered in brown.
- What diseases is it prone to? If the diseases are severe in your region of the country, you may want to choose another tree.
- Is it prone to splitting or breaking? Bradford pears and some arborvitae trees are lovely, but once mature, they tend to split down the middle in some climates, especially in areas with heavy snowfall or ice storms.
- Does it have spring flowers or other interest? Does it have fall color or other interest such as berries?
- Is it a tree that wildlife enjoy? (Trees for wildlife usually produce berries or have flowers with nectar.)
- Is it prone to winter-kill or injury? If so, be prepared to wrap it, at least for the first few winters.
- How attractive is it to deer and rabbits? If these animals are a problem in your area and you can provide protection for the tree (see page 220), fine. Otherwise, you should reconsider.

Position a Tree Correctly

When positioned with care, trees can beneficially affect the climate around your home.

Trees suitable for use as windbreaks can be positioned to deflect harsh northwest winter winds. Deciduous trees planted along the south and southeast sides of your home offer cooling shade during the warm seasons. Then they shed their leaves, allowing winter rays to light and warm your home. Trees known for providing leafy shade can be positioned to block hot afternoon summer sun coming from the west.

VISUALIZE YOUR SPACE

Here's an easy way to make sure you choose or position a new tree correctly: If the mature tree will have a spread of, say, 15 feet, use a garden hose or a handful or two of white flour to mark the perimeter. That way you'll see whether the mature tree's canopy will touch your house or overwhelm other plantings or nearby trees.

3 Design and Planning Basics

Choose the Right-Size Tree

These trees looked fine with first planted, but 20 years later they are way out of scale with the modest-sized house. They overwhelm the structure rather than complement it.

These trees are at their mature height but work with the scale of the house rather than against it. They soften corners but don't overwhelm.

How to Choose and Design with Trees *continued*

BUYER'S GUIDE

TAKING A TREE HOME
When toting your tree home, be sure that the leaves are sheltered from the wind. Zipping down the road with your tree hanging out the window may strip most of the leaves off the branches. So tuck the tree into the vehicle completely or slip a large bag or tarp over the branches and fasten it securely. (Ask your garden center for help as needed.)

With pyramid-shape evergreens, be careful to avoid breaking off the top tip, or the tree may develop a forked top, ruining its pleasing conical shape.

Planting trees adds shade, privacy, and pleasure to the landscape.

Buy the Tree You Want

Informed, thoughtful selection of a tree is more important than easy availability. Decide what type of tree you want before you go to the garden center; avoid buying whatever is on sale or looks good that day. If the store doesn't have the tree you want, talk to a garden associate about other options, or see if the garden center will be getting in the tree you want or can order it for you.

Shapes of Trees

VASE SHAPE

WEEPING

PYRAMIDAL OR CONICAL

UPRIGHT

SPREADING

Trees For Your Landscape

Spring-Flowering Trees

Common Name	Botanical Name	Zones
Acacia, Bailey	*Acacia baileyana*	8–10
Cherry, Kwanzan	*Prunus serrulata* 'Kwanzan'	5–8
Cherry, Sargent	*Prunus sargentii*	4–7
Cherry, weeping Higan	*Prunus subhirtella* 'Pendula'	4–8
Cherry, Yoshino	*Prunus ×yedoensis*	5–8
Chokecherry, Amur	*Prunus maackii*	2–6
Crabapple	*Malus* spp.	5–8
Crimson bottlebrush	*Callistemon citrinus*	8–11
Desert willow	*Chilopsis linearis*	8–9
Dogwood, flowering	*Cornus florida*	5–9
Dogwood, Kousa	*Cornus kousa*	5–8
Fringe tree, Chinese	*Chionanthus retusus*	6–8
Hawthorn, thornless cockspur	*Crataegus crus-galli* 'Inermis'	4–7
Hawthorn, Washington	*Crataegus phaenopyrum*	3–9
Magnolia, saucer	*Magnolia ×soulangiana*	5–9
Magnolia, star	*Magnolia stellata*	5–9
Magnolia, sweet bay	*Magnolia virginiana*	5–9
Maple, red	*Acer rubrum*	3–9
Mayday tree	*Prunus padus commutata*	3–6
Mesquite	*Prosopis glandulosa*	10–11
Mountain ash, European	*Sorbus aucuparia*	3–6
Palo verde, Texas	*Cercidium texanum*	9–10
Pear, callery	*Pyrus calleryana*	4–8
Plum, Newport	*Prunus cerasifera* 'Newport'	4–8
Plum, purple-leaf	*Prunus cerasifera* 'Atropurpurea'	4–8
Redbud	*Cercis canadensis*	3–9
Russian olive	*Elaeagnus angustifolia*	3–8
Sea grape	*Coccoloba uvifera*	10–11
Serviceberry, Allegheny	*Amelanchier laevis*	4–8
Serviceberry, downy	*Amelanchier arborea*	4–9
Serviceberry, shadblow	*Amelanchier canadensis*	3–8
Snowbell, Japanese	*Styrax japonicus*	5–8
Trumpet tree	*Tabebuia chrysotricha*	10–11
Yellowwood, American	*Cladrastis kentukea*	6–8

Flowering dogwood

Trees with Good Autumn Color

Common Name	Botanical Name	Zones
Ash, green	*Fraxinus pennsylvanica*	3–9
Beech, American	*Fagus grandifolia*	3–9
Birch, European white	*Betula pendula*	2–7
Birch, paper	*Betula papyrifera*	2–5
Birch, whitespire	*Betula platyphylla* 'Whitespire'	4–7
Cherry, Kwanzan	*Prunus serrulata* 'Kwanzan'	5–8
Cherry, Sargent	*Prunus sargentii*	4–7
Cherry, weeping Higan	*Prunus subhirtella* 'Pendula'	4–8
Chokecherry, Amur	*Prunus maackii*	2–6
Crabapple	*Malus* spp.	4–8
Crape myrtle	*Lagerstroemia indica*	7–9
Dogwood, flowering	*Cornus florida*	5–9
Dogwood, Kousa	*Cornus kousa*	5–8
Elm, Chinese	*Ulmus parvifolia*	5–9
Ginkgo	*Ginkgo biloba*	3–9
Hawthorn, cockspur	*Crataegus crus-galli* 'Inermis'	4–7
Hawthorn, Washington	*Crataegus phaenopyrum*	3–9
Honeylocust, thornless	*Gleditsia triacanthos inermis*	3–8
Hornbeam, American	*Carpinus caroliniana*	3–9
Katsura tree	*Cercidiphyllum japonicum*	4–8
Linden, littleleaf	*Tilia cordata*	3–7
Maple, Amur	*Acer tataricum ginnala*	2–6
Maple, Japanese	*Acer palmatum*	5–8
Maple, paperbark	*Acer griseum*	4–8
Maple, red	*Acer rubrum*	3–9
Maple, sugar	*Acer saccharum*	4–8
Maple, trident	*Acer buergerianum*	4–8
Mayday tree	*Prunus padus commutata*	3–6
Mountain ash, European	*Sorbus aucuparia*	4–7
Oak, northern red	*Quercus rubra*	4–7
Oak, pin	*Quercus palustris*	4–8
Oak, scarlet	*Quercus coccinea*	4–9
Oak, Shumard	*Quercus shumardii*	5–9
Oak, white	*Quercus alba*	4–9
Pear, callery	*Pyrus calleryana*	4–8
Pistachio, Chinese	*Pistacia chinensis*	6–9
Possumhaw	*Ilex decidua*	3–9
Quaking aspen	*Populus tremuloides*	2–6
Redbud	*Cercis canadensis*	3–9
Serviceberry, downy	*Amelanchier arborea*	4–9
Serviceberry, shadblow	*Amelanchier canadensis*	3–8
Smoke tree	*Cotinus coggyria*	4–8
Snowbell, Japanese	*Styrax japonicum*	5–8
Stewartia, Japanese	*Stewartia pseudocamellia*	5–7
Sweet gum	*Liquidambar styraciflua* 'Rotundiloba'	5–9
Yellowwood	*Cladrastis lutea*	6–8

Trees *continued*

Common Name	Botanical Name	Zones
Fast-Growing Trees		
Acacia, Bailey	*Acacia baileyana*	10
Ash, green	*Fraxinus pennsylvanica*	3–9
Bald cypress	*Taxodium distichum*	4–10
Birch, European white	*Betula pendula*	2–7
Birch, paper	*Betula papyrifera*	2–7
Birch, river	*Betula nigra*	4–9
Birch, whitespire	*Betula platyphylla* 'Whitespire'	4–7
Bird-of-paradise, Mexican	*Caesalpinia mexicana*	10
Bottlebrush, crimson	*Callistemon citrinus*	9–10
Chaste tree	*Vitex agnus-castus*	6–10
Chokecherry, Amur	*Prunus maackii*	2–6
Crape myrtle	*Lagerstroemia indica*	7–9
Cypress, Arizona	*Cupressus arizonica*	7–9
Cypress, Leyland	×*Cupressocyparis leylandii*	6–9
Dawn redwood	*Metasequoia glyptostroboides*	4–8
Desert willow	*Chilopsis linearis*	8–10
Elm, Chinese	*Ulmus parvifolia*	5–9
Fir, Veitch	*Abies veitchii*	3–6
Holly, yaupon	*Ilex vomitoria*	7–10
Honeylocust, thornless	*Gleditsia triacanthos inermis*	3–9
Magnolia, saucer	*Magnolia* ×*soulangiana*	5–9
Maple, red	*Acer rubrum*	3–9
Mesquite	*Prosopis glandulosa*	10
Myrtle, Pacific wax	*Myrica cerifera*	7–9
Oak, laurel	*Quercus laurifolia*	7–10
Oak, northern red	*Quercus rubra*	4–7
Oak, pin	*Quercus palustris*	4–8
Oak, scarlet	*Quercus coccinea*	4–9
Oak, shumard	*Quercus shumardii*	5–9
Oak, willow	*Quercus phellos*	4–8
Pagoda tree, Japanese	*Sophora japonica*	6–8
Palm, Washington	*Washingtonia robusta*	9–10
Pear, Bradford	*Pyrus calleryana* 'Bradford'	4–8
Pine, white	*Pinus strobus*	3–8
Plum, Newport	*Prunus cerasifera* 'Newport'	4–8
Plum, purple-leaf	*Prunus cerasifera* 'Atropurpurea'	4–8
Possumhaw	*Ilex decidua*	3–9
Quaking aspen	*Populus tremuloides*	2–6
Redbud	*Cercis canadensis*	3–9
Russian olive	*Elaeagnus angustifolia*	2–7
Spruce, Norway	*Picea abies*	2–7
Willow, corkscrew	*Salix* 'Golden Curls'	4–8
Willow, golden weeping	*Salix alba* 'Tristis'	3–8
Willow, weeping	*Salix babylonica*	4–9
Zelkova, Japanese	*Zelkova serrata*	5–9

Ash

Common Name	Botanical Name	Zones
Trees for Wet Conditions		
Bald cypress	*Taxodium distichum*	4–10
Birch, river	*Betula nigra*	4–9
Hornbeam, American	*Carpinus caroliniana*	3–9
Magnolia, sweet bay	*Magnolia virginiana*	5–9
Maple, red	*Acer rubrum*	3–9
Oak, willow	*Quercus phellos*	4–8
Possumhaw	*Ilex decidua*	3–9
Serviceberry, shadblow	*Amelanchier canadensis*	3–8
Sugarberry; hackberry	*Celtis laevigata*	5–9
Sycamores	*Platanus* spp.	5–9
Willow, golden weeping	*Salix alba* 'Tristis'	3–8
Willow, French pussy	*Salix caprea* 'Kilmarnock'	4–8

River birch

Common Name	Botanical Name	Zone
Trees That Thrive in Light Shade		
Ash, green	*Fraxinus pennsylvanica*	3–9
Bird-of-paradise, Mexican	*Caesalpinia mexicana*	10–11
Buckeye, Ohio	*Aesculus glabra*	3–7
Cherry, sargent	*Prunus sargentii*	4–7
Fringe tree, Chinese	*Chionanthus retusus*	6–8
Dogwood, flowering	*Cornus florida*	5–9
Honeylocust, thornless	*Gleditsia triacanthos inermis*	3–8
Horsechestnut, Common	*Aesculus hippocastanum*	3–7
Linden, littleleaf	*Tilia cordata*	3–7
Loquat	*Eriobotrya japonica*	8–10
Magnolia, saucer	*Magnolia ×soulangiana*	5–9
Maple, Norway	*Acer platanoides*	3–7
Maple, red	*Acer rubrum*	3–9
Maple, silver	*Acer saccharinum*	3–9
Maple, sugar	*Acer saccharum*	4–8
Maple, trident	*Acer buergerianum*	3–8
Mesquite	*Prosopis glandulosa*	9–11
Oak, bur	*Quercus macrocarpa*	2–8
Oak, coast live	*Quercus agrifolia*	7–10
Oak, laurel	*Quercus laurifolia*	7–10
Oak, northern red	*Quercus rubra*	4–7
Oak, pin	*Quercus palustris*	4–8
Oak, scarlet	*Quercus coccinea*	4–9
Oak, shumard	*Quercus shumardii*	5–9
Oak, southern live	*Quercus virginiana*	8–10
Oak, white	*Quercus alba*	4–9
Oak, willow	*Quercus phellos*	4–8
Olive	*Olea europaea*	8–10
Pagoda tree, Japanese	*Sophora japonica*	6–8
Palo verde, Texas	*Cercidium texanum*	8–10
Pecan	*Carya illinoinensis*	5–9
Redbud	*Cercis canadensis*	3–9
Sea grape	*Coccoloba uvifera*	10–11
Spruce, white	*Picea glauca*	2–6
Sweet gum, fruitless	*Liquidambar styraciflua* 'Rotundiloba'	5–9
Yellowwood	*Cladrastis lutea*	6–8
Zelkova, Japanese	*Zelkova serrata*	5–9

Redbud

Common Name	Botanical Name	
Small Trees		
Crabapples	*Malus* spp.	4–8
Crape myrtle	*Lagerstroemia indica*	7–9
Holly, blue	*Ilex ×meserveae*	5–8
Juniper, skyrocket	*Juniperus scopulorum* 'Skyrocket'	4–8
Magnolia, saucer	*Magnolia ×soulangiana*	5–9
Magnolia, star	*Magnolia stellata*	5–9
Magnolia, sweet bay	*Magnolia virginiana*	5–9
Maple, Amur	*Acer tataricum ginnala*	2–6
Maple, Japanese	*Acer palmatum*	5–8
Redbud	*Cercis canadensis*	3–9
Russian olive	*Elaeagnus angustifolia*	3–8
Serviceberry	*Amelanchier* spp.	3–8
Wax myrtle, Pacific	*Myrica cerifera*	7–9

Japanese maple

These are trees that when not positioned carefully might cause problems with shallow roots, broken twigs and tree litter, or have a habit of reseeding to the point of being a weed.

Common Name	Botanical Name
Trees to Use with Caution	
Cottonwoods	*Populus* spp.
Eucalyptus	*Eucalyptus* spp.
Maple, silver	*Acer saccharinum*
Mulberries	*Morus* spp.
Poplars	*Populus* spp.
Willows	*Salix* spp.

How to Choose and Design with Shrubs

3

Design and Planning Basics

The number of shrubs to choose from these days is staggering. Often, gardeners stroll through a garden center and pick up one that looks good in that pot on that day. It's smarter to read up on the subject in advance so you can choose the right shrub for your intended use.

Some questions to ask when choosing a shrub:

- What is the mature size and spread of the shrub? Have I measured the space where I'd like to put it, both lengthwise and vertically? Many shrubs quickly outgrow their allocated space because of poor planning.
- Does the shrub do well in sun, shade, or a little of both? (See page 24 for an explanation.)
- Does it have spring flowers or berries? What does it look like in autumn? Does it have interesting or brightly colored bark?
- Does it attract birds or butterflies?
- Are deer or rabbits attracted to it? If so, am I willing to put up chicken wire or other protection for the next few years? (See page 220.)
- Is it fragrant? Does it have an odor that I might not like? Some viburnums, for example, produce berries that when ripe smell as though a dog has been doing its business nearby. Others are beautifully fragrant.
- What kind of soil does it like? Some shrubs do well only in neutral to alkaline soil, whereas a number of others need acidic soil (see page 23).
- What are its water needs? Some shrubs are choosy and need soil on the dry side. Many others need soil that is so constantly moist as to be almost boggy.

Using Shrubs as Groundcovers

Many shrubs make a perfect groundcover. If the shrub is low and spreading, it can probably be planted in large groupings on slopes and other areas where you want widespread coverage.

Common Name	Botanical Name	Zones
Bearberry	*Arctostaphylos uva-ursi*	2–7
Blueberry, lowbush	*Vaccinium angustifolium*	4–9
Candytuft	*Iberis sempervirens*	4–8
Cotoneaster, bearberry	*Cotoneaster dammeri*	6–9
Cotoneaster, cranberry	*Cotoneaster apiculata*	5–8
Euonymus, wintercreeper	*Euonymus fortunei*	4–8
Heather	*Calluna vulgaris*	3–8
Junipers, low spreading	*Juniperus* spp.	3–9
Lantana	*Lantana* spp.	8–10
Roses, low spreading	*Rosa* spp.	Varies
St. Johnswort	*Hypericum calycinum*	5–9

A CLOSER LOOK

IS IT A TREE OR A SHRUB?
Sometimes it's hard to decide whether a plant is a tree or a shrub. Many trees, such as saucer magnolias, look like shrubs; they may have several trunks and grow to just 10 to 15 feet—about the same height as a mature common lilac. Likewise, many Japanese maples look like shrubs.

The point is not to rely on terminology. Just research the plant's mature size and growth habit, and make your design—and purchasing—decisions accordingly.

Sometimes it can be hard to tell if something is a small tree or a large shrub. This spring-blooming kousa dogwood could be classified as either.

Without the shrubs in this foundation planting, the house and its landscape would look stark and bare.

Foundation Shrubs

A foundation planting is the combination of trees, shrubs, perennials, annuals, and groundcovers right in front of a home.

A foundation planting helps the house blend into the landscape around it and gives it a softer, more established look. It's a good way to add value to your home because it improves curb appeal dramatically.

Foundation plantings can be as simple as a row of matching shrubs on either side of the front door. Some homeowners add small trees at each end of the house to soften the corners. Or they put a small vertical evergreen on either side of the front door to accent it.

These formulas are tried and true, but foundation plantings can be as straightforward or as creative, as simple or as elaborate, as you want them to be.

Shrubs are the backbone of most foundation plantings. They should be pruned to a good height—large enough to have an impact but not so high as to block windows.

Characteristics to look for in foundation shrubs (and most other foundation plants):

- Attractive four seasons of the year. For this reason, many foundation plantings are evergreens. But many deciduous shrubs that offer interesting bark, a pleasing shape or spring flowers have their place in foundation plantings.
- Neat growth habit. Because these shrubs will be viewed up close, and they're not behind other plantings, foundation plants should be fairly compact and tidy looking. Avoid plants that have a tendency to get rangy, such as forsythia or mockorange. They're excellent in natural settings but can look untended up close.
- Complement other plantings. Foundation shrubs should work well with other nearby plantings, in terms of texture, color, and shape.

Good Shrubs for Foundation Plantings

Common Name	Botanical Name	Zones
Abelia, glossy	*Abelia × grandiflora*	6-9
Arborvitae, Emerald	*Thuja occidentalis* 'Emerald'	3-8
Arborvitae, Little Giant	*Thuja occidentalis* 'Little Giant'	3-7
Aucuba, Japanese	*Aucuba japonica*	7-10
Barberry, Japanese	*Berberis thunbergii*	4-8
Bayberry, northern	*Myrica pensylvanica*	2-6
Boxwoods	*Buxus* spp.	6-9
Burning bush, dwarf	*Euonymus alatus* 'Compacta'	3-8
Camellia, sasanqua	*Camellia sasanqua*	7-9
Currant, alpine	*Ribes alpinum*	2-7
Dogwood, cornelianchberry	*Cornus mas*	4-8
Dogwood, gray	*Cornus racemosa*	4-7
Fir, dwarf balsam	*Abies balsamea* 'Nana'	3-6
Fothergilla	*Fothergilla* spp.	4-8
Gardenia	*Gardenia jasminoides*	8-10
Hibiscus, Chinese	*Hibiscus rosa-sinensis*	9-10
Holly, compact Japanese	*Ilex crenata* 'Compacta'	5-8
Holly, lower-growing types	*Ilex* spp.	varies
Hydrangeas	*Hydrangea* spp.	varies
Indian hawthorn	*Rhaphiolepis indica*	8-10
Junipers	*Juniperus* spp.	4-8
Laurel, cherry	*Prunus laurocerasus* 'Otto Luyken'	6-8
Lilac, Korean	*Syringia patula*	3-7
Mountain laurel	*Kalmia latifolia*	4-9
Pittosporum, variegated	*Pittosporum tobira* 'Variegata'	8-10
Potentilla, shrubby	*Potentilla fruticosa*	2-7
Privet, Amur	*Ligustrum amurense*	3-7
Privet, golden vicary	*Ligustrum ×vicaryi*	5-8
Rhododendrons, azaleas	*Rhododendron* spp.	Varies
Spirea, Limemound	*Spiraea japonica* 'Limemound'	4-9
Spruce, dwarf Norway	*Picea abies* 'Pumila'	3-8
Viburnum, compact American cranberrybush	*Viburnum trilobum* 'Alfredo'	2-7
Viburnum, Korean spice	*Viburnum carlesii*	4-8
Viburnum, Mohican	*Viburnum lantana* 'Mohican'	4-8
Witch hazel, common	*Hamamelis virginiana*	3-8
Yew, lower-growing types	*Taxus × media*	4-7

How to Choose and Design with Shrubs *continued*

BUYER'S GUIDE

MEASURE TWICE, BUY ONCE

When designing a hedge, it's important to measure the length of the area so you can calculate how many shrubs you'll need to fill it.

As a rule, if a shrub's mature width is 4 feet, you'll want to plant individuals 4 feet "on center"—that is, the center of each shrub is 4 feet from the center of its neighbor.

Also remember to measure the area's width. Persian lilac, for example, may be a perfect height (4 to 8 feet) for the hedge you've been wanting, but once you check out the width (5 to 10 feet), you may find that you simply lack the space.

Hedges

Hedges are good problem solvers. They can add privacy to an open area, screen views that are less than ideal, provide a sense of enclosure, and serve as an attractive background for the rest of your landscape.

Here are some pointers to keep in mind when designing a hedge:

• Evergreen or deciduous? Evergreen shrubs are attractive all year long, but deciduous shrubs can offer variety, such as spring flowers.

• One type of plant or several? Hedges can be all of one type of plant, as in the classic privet hedge, or they can be a mix of evergreen and deciduous, tall and short, and all sorts of characteristics. When mixing several types of shrubs, it's best to make the hedge wider and design it more like a wide mixed border rather than a simple, straight row of plants.

• Make the hedge the right length. Most hedges should stretch from one logical point to another—say, the back of the garage to the back end of your property.

Often, homeowners plant only a few shrubs to serve the purpose at hand (maybe screening a view of the neighbor's back patio) and fail to keep in mind that the hedge might be more attractive and logical if it stretched a bit farther.

• Consider varying sun and shade. Hedges often are designed to extend from a sunny area into a shady area. If that's the case, be sure to choose a shrub that will thrive in both, or you may have low, sparse shrubs in the shady area and larger, fuller shrubs in the sunny spots.

• To trim or not—and how often? Choose plants carefully according to whether they should be trimmed. Some homeowners plant a bridalwreath spirea hedge, then prune it tightly, destroying the shrub's natural arching shape as well as many of the developing flower buds. On the other hand, evergreens such as yew and boxwood grow thicker with regular pruning.

If you do decide to trim, be aware of how often you'll need to do it. Yew and boxwood do well with trims just a couple of times a year; other shrubs grow more rapidly and may need pruning four to six times a year to stay neat looking.

This mixed hedge of several shrubs looks far less austere than a fence and is more casual than a hedge of all one type of shrub. It's also easier to maintain than a pruned hedge and serves as a haven for birds and butterflies.

Good Shrubs for Hedges

When choosing a shrub for a hedge, remember that some hedges are all of one type and tightly clipped, others are all of one type and grow loose and natural, and still others are part of a mixed hedge of different types, sizes, and colors.

Common Name	Botanical Name	Zones
Abelia, glossy	*Abelia × grandiflora*	6-9
Arborvitae, Emerald	*Thuja occidentalis* 'Emerald'	3-8
Azaleas, Exbury	*Rhododendron* Exbury hybrids	4-8
Azalea, Northern Lights	*Rhododendron* 'Northern Lights'	4-7
Barberry, Japanese	*Berberis thunbergii*	4-8
Bayberry, northern	*Myrica pensylvanica*	2-6
Boxwood, edging	*Buxus sempervirens* 'Suffruticosa'	6-8
Boxwood, Green Beauty	*Buxus microphylla* 'Green Beauty'	5-9
Boxwood, Japanese	*Buxus microphylla japonica*	6-9
Boxwood, Korean	*Buxus microphylla koreana*	5-9
Boxwood, Wintergreen	*Buxus microphylla* 'Wintergreen'	4-6

Zigzagging Boxwood

Common Name	Botanical Name	Zones
Camellia, sasanqua	*Camellia sasanqua*	7-9
Cape honeysuckle	*Tecomaria capensis*	10-11
Coralberry	*Symphoricarpos orbiculatus*	4-7
Currant, Green Mound alpine	*Ribes alpinum* 'Green Mound'	2-7
Dogwood, corneliancherry	*Cornus mas*	4-8
Dogwood, gray	*Cornus racemosa*	4-7
Euonymus, Manhattan spreading	*Euonymus kiautschovicus* 'Manhattan'	4-8
Firethorn, scarlet	*Pyracantha coccinea*	6-8
Firethorn, Yukon Belle	*Pyracantha angustifolia* 'Yukon Belle'	5-9
Forsythia, border	*Forsythia × intermedia*	6-9
Hawthorn, Indian	*Rhaphiolepis indica*	8-10
Hibiscus, Chinese	*Hibiscus rosa-sinensis*	9-10
Holly, dwarf Burford	*Ilex cornuta* 'Bufordii Nana'	6-9
Holly, dwarf Yaupon	*Ilex vomitoria* 'Nana'	7-10
Holly, Green Lustre Japanese	*Ilex crenata* 'Green Lustre'	4-6
Holly, winterberry	*Ilex verticillata*	3-9
Honeysuckles	*Lonicera* spp.	Varies
Ixora; jungle geranium	*Ixora coccinea*	10-11
Jasmine, downy	*Jasminum multiflorum*	9-10
Juniper, Parson's	*Juniperus chinensis* 'Parsonii'	3-9
Juniper, tam	*Juniperus sabina* 'Tamariscifolia'	3-7
Laurel, cherry	*Prunus caroliniana*	6-9
Lilac, common	*Syringa vulgaris*	3-7
Lilac, cutleaf	*Syringa × laciniata*	4-8
Lilac, Miss Kim	*Syringa patula* 'Miss Kim'	3-7
Lilac, Persian	*Syringa × persica*	3-7
Oleander	*Nerium oleander*	8-10
Photinia, redtip	*Photinia* x *fraseri*	6-9
Pieris, Japanese	*Pieris japonica*	5-8
Pieris, mountain	*Pieris floribunda*	4-8
Pittosporum, variegated Japanese	*Pittosporum tobira* 'Variegata'	8-10
Privet, Amur	*Ligustrum amurense*	3-7
Potentilla, shrubby	*Potentilla fruticosa*	2-7
Privet, Chinese variegated	*Ligustrum sinense* 'Variegatum'	7-10
Privet, golden vicary	*Ligustrum × vicaryi*	5-8
Privet, wax-leaf	*Ligustrum lucidum*	7-10
Rock rose, White	*Cistus × hybridus*	8-10
Rose, Adelaide Hoodless	*Rosa* 'Adelaide Hoodless'	3-9
Rose, Betty Prior	*Rosa* 'Betty Prior'	4-9
Rose, Carefree Beauty	*Rosa* 'Carefree Beauty'	4-8
Rose, Country Dancer	*Rosa* 'Country Dancer'	4-9
Rose, Frau Dagmar Hartopp	*Rosa* 'Frau Dagmar Hartopp'	4-9
Rose, Graham Thomas	*Rosa* 'Graham Thomas'	5-9
Rose, Gruss an Aachen	*Rosa* 'Gruss an Aachen'	5-9
Rose, Henry Kelsey	*Rosa* 'Henry Kelsey'	4-9
Rose, Iceberg	*Rosa* 'Iceberg'	4-9
Rose, Margo Koster	*Rosa* 'Margo Koster'	5-8
Rose, Morden Centennial	*Rosa* 'Morden Centennial'	3-9
Rose, Peace	*Rosa* 'Peace'	5-8
Rose, Pink Meidiland	*Rosa* Pink Meidiland	5-8
Rose, redleaf	*Rosa rubrifolia*	4-9
Rose, Sir Thomas Lipton	*Rosa* 'Sir Thomas Lipton'	2-7
Serviceberry	*Amelanchier alnifolia*	4-5
Silverberry	*Elaeagnus pungens*	7-9
Spirea, baby's breath	*Spiraea thunbergii*	2-8
Spirea, bridalwreath	*Spiraea prunifolia*	5-8
Spirea, Vanhoutte	*Spiraea × vanhouttei*	3-8
Spruce, dwarf Alberta	*Picea glauca* 'Conica'	3-8
Spruce, dwarf Norway	*Picea abies* 'Pumila'	3-8
Texas ranger	*Leucophyllum frutescens* 'Silverado'	8-10
Viburnum, arrowwood	*Viburnum dentatum*	3-8
Yew, Hick's upright	*Taxus × media* 'Hicksii'	4-7
Viburnum, compact American cranberrybush	*Viburnum trilobum* 'Alfredo'	2-7
Viburnum, sweet	*Viburnum odoratissimum*	8-10
Yew, Anglo-Japanese	*Taxus ×media* 'Densiformis'	4-7

How to Choose and Design with Shrubs *continued*

Flowering Shrubs

Flowering shrubs are workhorses. They provide foliage throughout the growing season and, almost as a bonus, they burst into color for a few to several weeks.

Most flowering shrubs bloom in spring, with a number also blooming in summer. There are few shrubs that have flowers in fall (summersweet is one of them), but many flowering shrubs have foliage that turns red or gold during that time, flowers that dry right on the shrub, such as some hydrangeas, or attractive berries or fruits.

Only a few flowering shrubs—such as rhododendrons, mountain laurel, heaths, and heathers—are evergreen.

Choosing Flowering Shrubs

When choosing a flowering shrub, ask yourself the same questions you would when choosing any other type of shrub (see page 70). But also consider the flower:

- What color is it? Even on shrubs renowned for being a certain color, such as lilacs, there is a great variety: pale lavender, deep purple, white, and now even pink.
- How long does it bloom? Often gardeners expect a flowering shrub to bloom all growing season long. But most flowering shrubs bloom for only a couple of weeks.

Fragrant Flowering Shrubs

* Not all types are fragrant. Refer to the Plant Encyclopedia, starting on page 292, for specifics, and check the plant label.

Common Name	Botanical Name	Zones
Bouvardia	*Bouvardia longiflora* 'Albatross'	9–10
Witch hazel, common	*Hamamelis virginiana*	3–8
Daphne	*Daphne* spp.	Varies
Gardenia	*Gardenia jasminoides*	8–10
Honeysuckle*	*Lonicera* spp.	3–9
Viburnum, Korean spice	*Viburnum carlesii*	4–8
Fothergilla	*Fothergilla* spp.	4–8
Lilacs*	*Syringa* spp.	Varies*
Northern Lights azalea	*Rhododendron* 'Northern Lights'	4–7
Purple-leaf sand cherry	*Prunus × cistena*	2–8
Silverberry	*Elaeagnus pungens*	7–9
Skimmia, Japanese	*Skimmia japonica*	6–9
Summersweet	*Clethra alnifolia*	3–9
Sweetshrub	*Calycanthus floridus*	4–9
Sweet olive	*Osmanthus fragrans*	8–9
Sweet viburnum	*Viburnum odoratissimum*	8–10
Roses*	*Rosa* spp.	Varies*
Variegated Japanese pittosporum	*Pittosporum tobira* 'Variegata'	8–10
White forsythia	*Abeliophyllum distichum*	4–8

In early spring, the brilliant yellow of forsythia lights up the landscape.

- When does it bloom? For a garden with the most interest for the greatest amount of time, choose flowering shrubs that are at their peak at different times of the year. Many shrubs bloom in late winter or early spring, with the daffodils, and add much to the garden when few other plants have hit their stride. Among them are azaleas, camellias, quince, Korean spice viburnum, daphne, witch hazel, forsythia, flowering cherry, and heath.
- Are the flowers fragrant? Many shrubs have fragrant flowers. It's fun to choose some that have scent while in bloom.
- Are the flowers good for cutting? One of the great pleasures of planting flowers is cutting them to bring indoors. Some shrubs, such as hydrangeas, are outstanding for cut flowers; others, such as some azaleas, are so fragile they tend to shatter before or shortly after you get them arranged.

Designing with Flowering Shrubs

Flowering shrubs work almost anywhere in the landscape, but fragrant types are especially pleasing near porches, patios, and other sitting areas.

Near front entries, shrubs with a neat, tidy growth habit and foliage that looks good all four seasons tend to work best because they're under close scrutiny year-round. These include most hydrangeas, azaleas, rhododendrons, heaths, heathers, spireas, daphnes, compact varieties of lilacs, and potentillas.

In the backyard or in more casual, naturalistic plantings, you can choose larger shrubs with a looser, wilder growth habit, such as forsythia, mockorange, large rhododendrons, kerria, witch hazel, large fothergilla, and broom.

Accent Shrubs

An accent shrub is any shrub or small grouping of shrubs used to add flourish to the landscape. It's used much in the way that jewelry or a scarf is used to accent an outfit. The purpose is to embellish and brighten.

An accent planting of shrubs might consist of a few azaleas planted at the base of a large tree to draw attention to the thick trunk. Or it could be a brilliant yellow forsythia planted in an empty corner of the backyard to add a burst of color in late winter or early spring. Or it could be a burning bush at the corner of a foundation planting to add color in autumn.

Another way to use shrubs as an accent is to mix them into a large flower bed. Five or so small spruce shrubs planted at regular intervals throughout a large bed of perennials and annuals add rhythm, regularity, and structure to the planting.

Specimen Shrubs

A specimen shrub is one that is planted all by itself to show off its particular beauty.

A specimen shrub needs to be glorious, worthy of the spotlight. Specimen shrubs, for that reason, are usually large. A single lilac, rhododendron, smoke tree, Japanese maple, or burning bush is often a favorite for specimen planting.

Shrub Borders

A border of only shrubs is beautiful, and it's usually low-maintenance, especially if you lay down landscape fabric and top it with mulch (see page 184).

When planting shrub borders, use the same principles you'd use in other plantings. Select a mix of foliage color, leaf size, plant shape and height, bloom time, and interest from bark and berries.

Scale the shrub border to be in keeping with the size of the property. In most cases, a shrub bed or border should be several feet across to allow for an interesting mix of plants. On larger properties, shrub borders can be 10, 15, or even 20 feet or more long to add maximum interest and variety to the landscape.

Background Shrubs

Background shrubs do just what the name implies: they stay quietly in the background, screening views and providing a neutral backdrop for more showy plantings.

An evergreen hedge backing a flower bed is a good example. But it could also be a planting of privet or holly or any other shrub that's not particularly showy that creates a screen of foliage so you can better appreciate what's planted in front of it, even if it's just an expanse of green lawn.

A flowering plum tree is set off with boxwood, barberry, and azaleas, as well as grape hyacinths and creeping phlox.

DESIGN TIP

MIXING UP OR NOT?

When planting a number of shrubs for a hedge, in a border, or any other purpose, consider whether you want to mix shrub types or use just one type.

Planting a number of the same type of shrub adds unity and order to a landscape, giving it a sweeping, clean look.

Mixing a variety of shrubs gives a landscape a look that is more complex, varied, and—when well-done—filled with garden charm. The mix can be of a number of completely different shrubs, such as a forsythia and a hydrangea and a burning bush. Or it can be the same type of shrub, such as a lilac, but with different flower colors or slightly different, but somewhat overlapping, bloom times.

3

Design and Planning Basics

Shrubs for Shade

These shrubs do well in 6 hours or less of sun a day.

Common Name	Botanical Name	Zones
Azalea, Cornell Pink	*Rhododendron mucronulatum* 'Cornell Pink'	4-7
Azaleas, Glen Dale hybrids	*Rhododendron* Glen Dale hybrids	6-9
Azalea, Northern Lights	*Rhododendron* 'Northern Lights'	4-7
Azalea, Southern Indica hybrids	*Rhododendron* Southern Indica hybrids	8-10
Camellia	*Camellia* spp.	7-11
Laurel, cherry	*Prunus caroliniana*	6-9
Chokeberry, black	*Aronia melanocarpa*	4-9
Coralberry	*Symphoricarpos orbiculatus*	4-7
Cranberrybush, European	*Viburnum opulus* 'Roseum'	3-8
Daphne, Carol Mackie	*Daphne* × *burkwoodii*	5-7
Dogwood, yellow-twig	*Cornus stolonifera* 'Flaviramea'	3-8
Forsythia, border	*Forsythia* × *intermedia*	6-9
Forsythia, Vermont Sun	*Forsythia mandshurica* 'Vermont Sun'	4-8
Forsythia, white	*Abeliophyllum distichum*	4-8
Fothergilla	*Fothergilla* spp.	4-8
Fuchsias	*Fuchsia* spp.	8-10
Hydrangea, Annabelle	*Hydrangea arborescens* 'Annabelle'	3-9
Hydrangea, oakleaf	*Hydrangea quercifolia*	5-9
Hydrangea, peegee	*Hydrangea paniculata* 'Grandiflora'	3-8
Jasmine, showy	*Jasminum floridum*	7-9
Leucothoe, drooping	*Leucothoe fontanesiana*	5-8
Leucothoe, dwarf	*Leucothoe axillaris*	5-9
Mahonias	*Mahonia* spp.	Varies
Mountain laurel	*Kalmia latifolia*	4-9
Pieris, Japanese	*Pieris japonica*	5-8
Pieris, mountain	*Pieris floribunda*	4-8
Rhododendrons	*Rhododendron* spp.	Varies
Serviceberry	*Amelanchier alnifolia*	4-5
Silverberry	*Elaeagnus pungens*	7-9
Skimmia, Japanese	*Skimmia japonica* spp.	6-9
Snowberry	*Symphoricarpos albus*	3-7
Spirea, Vanhoutte	*Spiraea* × *vanhouttei*	3-8
Summersweet	*Clethra alnifolia*	4-9
Sweet shrub	*Calycanthus floridus*	4-9
Viburnum, arrowwood	*Viburnum dentatum*	3-8
Viburnum, blackhaw	*Viburnum prunifolium*	3-9
Viburnum, compact American cranberrybush	*Viburnum trilobum* 'Alfredo'	3-7
Viburnum, double-file	*Viburnum plicatum* f. *tomentosum*	4-8
Viburnum, Korean spice	*Viburnum carlesii*	4-8
Viburnum, Mohican	*Viburnum lantana* 'Mohican'	4-8
Witch hazel, common	*Hamamelis virginiana*	4-9

Shrubs for Wet, Boggy Areas

These shrubs are good choices for areas where water often collects or in climates that receive large amounts of rain.

Common Name	Botanical Name	Zones
Bayberry, Northern	*Myrica pensylvanica*	2-6
Beautyberry, Chinese	*Callicarpa dichotoma*	5-8
Blueberry	*Vaccinium* spp.	4-9
Chokeberry, red	*Aronia arbutifolia*	4-9
Dogwood, Red-osier	*Cornus stolonifera*	2-8
Fringe Tree, Chinese	*Chionanthus retusus*	6-8
Holly, winterberry	*Ilex verticillata*	3-9
Hydrangeas	*Hydrangea* spp.	Varies
Inkberry	*Ilex glabra 'Compacta'*	3-9
Possumhaw	*Ilex decidua*	3-9
Summersweet	*Clethra alnifolia*	4-9
Sweet Shrub	*Calycanthus floridus*	4-9
Viburnum, American cranberrybush	*Viburnum trilobum*	2-7
Viburnum, European cranberrybush	*Viburnum opulus*	3-8
Willow, French pussy	*Salix caprea*	4-8

Bigleaf Hydrangea

Shrubs for Light, Poor Soil

These shrubs thrive even in poor, dry, light, or sandy/rocky soils.

Common Name	Botanical Name	Zones
Bayberry, northern	*Myrica pensylvanica*	2-6
Bearberry	*Arctostaphylos uva-ursi*	2-7
Bluebeard	*Caryopteris ×clandonensis*	5-8
Brooms	*Genista* spp., *Cytisus* spp.	4 (6)-8
Burning bush	*Euonymus alatus*	3-8
Ceanothus	*Ceanothus* spp.	8-10
Junipers	*Juniperus* spp.	Varies
Lavender	*Lavandula* spp.	5-8
Nandina	*Nandina domestica*	6-9
Oleander	*Nerium oleander*	8-10
Pine, Japanese black	*Pinus thunbergii*	5-7
Pine, Mugo	*Pinus mugo mugo*	2-7
Possumhaw	*Ilex decidua*	3-9
Potentilla, shrubby	*Potentilla fruitcosa*	2-7
Rose, rugosa	*Rosa rugosa*	3-9
Rosemary	*Rosmarinus officinalis*	7-10
Russian olive	*Elaeagnus angustifolia*	3-8
St. Johnswort	*Hypericum* spp.	5-9
Sweet olive	*Osmanthus fragrans*	8-9
Weigela	*Weigela florida*	4-9
Yucca	*Yucca filamentosa*	4-10

'Frau Dagmar Hartopp', a rugosa rose

Drought-tolerant Shrubs

These shrubs, once established, do well with minimal moisture, especially in arid regions of the Western third of the United States and Canada.

Common Name	Botanical Name	Zones
Abelia, glossy	*Abelia ×grandiflora*	6-9
Barberry	*Berberis* spp.	4-8
Bayberry, northern	*Myrica pensylvanica*	2-6
Bluebeard	*Caryopteris ×clandonensis*	5-8
Brooms	*Genista* spp., *Cytisus* spp.	4 (6)-8
Butterfly bush	*Buddleia* spp.	5-10
Ceanothus	*Ceanothus* spp.	8-10
Chaste tree	*Vitex agnus-castus*	6-10
Currant, alpine	*Ribes alpinum*	2-7
Honeysuckles	*Lonicera* spp.	Varies
Mahonia	*Mahonia* spp.	Varies
Manzanita	*Arctostaphylos* spp.	Varies
Mockorange	*Philadelphus* spp.	4-8
Oleander	*Nerium oleander*	8-10
Potentilla, shrubby	*Potentilla fruticosa*	2-7
Rose-of-Sharon	*Hibiscus syriacus*	5-9
Rose, rugosa	*Rosa rugosa*	3-9
Snowberry	*Symphoricarpos albus*	3-7
Staghorn sumac	*Rhus typhina*	3-8

Glossy abelia

Shrubs for Acid Soil

These shrubs are good for soil with a low pH (less than 6.0), especially often found in the South, portions of the Northeast, and the Pacific Northwest

Common Name	Botanical Name	Zones
Blueberry	*Vaccinium* spp.	4-9
Camellia	*Camellia* spp.	7-11
Fothergilla	*Fothergilla* spp.	4-8
Gardenia	*Gardenia jasminoides*	8-10
Heath	*Erica* spp.	4-8
Heather, Scotch	*Calluna vulgaris*	3-8
Holly	*Ilex* spp.	Varies

Common Name	Botanical Name	Zones
Hydrangea	*Hydrangea* spp.	Varies
Leucothoe, drooping	*Leucothoe fontanesiana*	5-8
Mountain laurel	*Kalmia latifolia*	4-9
Pieris	*Pieris* spp.	4-8
Rhododendrons and azaleas	*Rhododendron* spp.	Varies
Skimmia, Japanese	*Skimmia japonica*	6-9
Summersweet	*Clethra alnifolia*	4-9

How to Choose and Design with Roses

This arrangement demonstrates the many colors and forms found among roses.

WORK SMARTER

THE ROSE EXPERTS
The American Rose Society (ARS) sponsors a toll-free rose hotline for gardeners to pose questions to rose experts. Call 800-637-6534 with your rose questions. Also check out the ARS's extensive website, which has rose recommendations and growing information: www.ars.org.

BUYER'S GUIDE

A ROSE BY ANY OTHER NAME
So what's a landscape rose? A shrub rose? A low-maintenance rose?

These are similar terms for a rose that is easy-care and disease- and pest-resistant, has a fairly long bloom time, and has a compact, shrubby growth habit that looks good in the landscape.

Roses have a reputation for being fussy. But if you choose a low-maintenance rose and provide good growing conditions, you'll see how ill-deserved that reputation is.

Choosing the Site

- Bring on the rays. Roses are sun lovers. Plant them where they will get at least six hours of direct, unfiltered light a day. Less light invites pest and disease problems and results in fewer blooms.
- Provide good drainage. Although roses like moist soil, they dislike soggy soil. Choose a well-drained site (see page 56 on drainage) and work in plenty of organic matter (pages 136 to 139).
- Let them breathe. Many disease problems can be prevented by placing roses where air can circulate freely around them.
- Position for easy irrigation. In arid climates, most roses need regular watering of the soil, not the foliage. A drip, bubbler, or microsprinkler system should be part of the landscape design.

Choosing the Rose

- Know your area's climate and gardening zone. Many roses die out in winter in cold climates, suffer from mildew and molds in high humidity, or wither and die from drought in arid climates. There are hundreds of different roses. Choose the right rose for your region. (Refer to the section on regional gardening, starting on page 18, for specifics on types of roses recommended for your part of the country.)
- Choose the right size. Roses can grow from 1 foot tall and 1 foot across to 30 feet tall and 10 feet across. Read labels carefully.
- Consider form. Roses can be tall, sprawling climbers or neat shrubs. Some have elegant "vase" shapes; others are groundcovers. Know what you're getting and use it accordingly.

  Also check flower form. Some roses are single—only a simple row of petals. Some are many-petaled with a cabbage-rose look. Hybrid teas have elegant oval, pointed buds that open into a classic rose shape.
- Consider bloom patterns. Roses may bloom only once

in June or in flushes throughout the season. Read the label to know what you're getting.

- Check for fragrance. Roses range from no scent to lightly fragrant to intensely fragrant. Give a sniff when the rose is in bloom. Otherwise, read the label.

Using Roses in the Landscape

Roses can play a variety of roles in the garden. These wonderful shrubs come in a variety of sizes and shapes with different flower colors, forms, bloom times, and different fragrances (or no fragrance at all). Get started with enjoying roses in your landscape with these ideas:

- Roses in a mixed border. Roses are compatible with annuals, perennials, herbs, other shrubs, even vegetables. A nice aspect of this amiability with other plants is that underplanting roses—especially hybrid teas, which tend to be leggy—with other flowers makes the roses even more attractive. (See page 80 for more information on roses in mixed borders.)
- The rose garden. If you love roses, a whole garden of them is a treat. But even a rose garden can stand a little variety. As mentioned above, consider interplanting them with complementary perennials, such as lavender, campanula, and hardy geraniums—just not as many or as large as you would in a mixed border. Additional plants add another dimension to the garden even when the roses aren't blooming and are thought to prevent rose diseases and pests. (See page 81 for more information on rose gardens.)
- Hedges. Why limit your hedge choices to evergreens or plain old privet? Any vigorous, tall rose makes a good choice for an informal flowering hedge. The roses can be powerfully fragrant, and the thorns make the hedge impenetrable. (See page 82.)
- Roses for cutting. You don't need to have a special cutting garden to gather armloads of roses from your yard. Roses like being cut (it's a form of deadheading, after all), so even a few shrubs—especially repeat bloomers—will provide a bounty of flowers. Hybrid teas, especially, make superb cut flowers because of their long stems and long vase life. (See page 83 for more information on roses for cutting.)
- Climbing. One of the joy of roses is being surrounded with them. Climbing roses scramble over arbors or pillars and rambling roses are even more vigorous, covering whole walls or large pergolas. (See page 84 for more information on climbing and rambling roses.)
- As a miniature. In recent decades breeding advances have created a whole line of downsized roses that grow just several inches high. The roses, the leaves—everything—have been beautifully miniaturized. (See page 85 for information on miniatures.)
- As a groundcover. Low, sprawling roses are good for planting on slopes or in other areas where a casual, flowering groundcover is needed. (See page 85 for information on groundcover roses.)
- As a standard. Trained into a lollipop shape, rose standards can be just a couple to 6 feet high. They're excellent for vertical accents in flower beds and beautiful in containers as well. (See page 85 for more information on rose standards.)

A CLOSER LOOK

WHAT'S AN ANTIQUE OR OLD GARDEN ROSE?

Technically an old garden rose is any rose introduced prior to 1864, when the first modern hybrid tea rose was introduced. Some of these antique roses, such as the gallica rose, alba rose, and damask rose, were grown in Biblical times.

Old garden roses are valued for their history and lore and for their rich fragrance. They usually have large, abundant berrylike rose hips (fruits) in late summer and autumn.

Most bloom heavily, just once a year in June or so, with old-fashioned-looking flowers crowded with petals.

Categories of old roses include the following: Bourbon and hybrid perpetual roses were favorites of the Victorians; China and tea roses were imported from China two centuries ago; and moss roses were so named for their fascinating mossy twigs, leaves, and flower buds.

Well-sited and properly supported, a climbing rose makes an attractive backdrop for garden accessories and other flowers.

Popular Low-Maintenance Roses

Name	Zones
Low-Maintenance Types	
David Austin roses	5-11
Meidiland roses	5-10
Rugosa roses	3-9
Low-Maintenance Cultivars	
'Abraham Darby'	5-11
'Ballerina'	5-10
'Belle Story'	5-11
'Betty Prior'	5-10
'BlueGirl'	5-10
'Bonica'	5-10
'Carefree Beauty'	4-10
'Carefree Wonder'	5-10
'Constance Spry'	5-10
'Flower Carpet'	5-10
'Graham Thomas'	5-11
'Hansa'	4-9
'John F. Kennedy'	5-10
'Knock Out'	5-10
'Lady Banks'	8-10
'Linda Campbell'	4-10
'Madame Hardy'	4-10
'Nearly Wild'	4-10
'Mary Rose'	5-11
'Queen Elizabeth'	5-11
'Roseraie de l'Hay'	5-10
'Royal Bonica'	5-10
'Simplicity'	5-10
'The Fairy'	4-10

Popular Fragrant Roses

Name	Zones
'Angel Face'	5-9
'Autumn Damask'	5-11
'Constance Spry'	4-9
'Double Delight'	6-10
'Fair Bianca'	5-9
'Fragrant Cloud'	5-10
'Mme Isaac Periere'	6-10
'Mister Lincoln'	5-10
'Othello'	5-10
'Royal Highness'	5-10
'Sheer Bliss'	6-10
'Souvenir de la Malmaison'	6-9
'Zephirine Drouhin'	5-9

How to Use Roses

In a Mixed Bed

Many gardeners like to grow their roses in mixed beds, that is, flower beds or borders that are mixture of different types of plants: Small shrubs, perennials, annuals, herbs, bulbs, and more.

Roses, especially those with long bloom times, work well in mixed borders. But just about any type of rose, actually, will work in a mixed border.

Taller roses are good in the back. Medium-sized roses work well closer to the front and groundcover, miniature, and other low-growing roses work well in the front.

When planting roses in a mixed border, make sure they have plenty of room to breathe and to take up nutrients and water. Don't plant them too close to other shrubs and make sure any surrounding perennials don't shadow them or cover or brush their foliage. Competition from other plants could stunt growth or encourage disease.

Take into account a rose's color when considering it for the flower bed. It should look good with the other flower colors. Pink, yellow, and white roses work well with most other colors. Orange, brighter yellow, brighter pink, and red roses can be more tricky, so incorporate those into your design with care.

Great Roses for Mixed Beds

Name	Zone
'Amber Queen'	5–10
'Angel Face'	5–9
'Astride Lindgren'	4–9
'Betty Boop'	5–10
'Betty Prior'	4–9
'Bill Warriner'	5–10
'First Light'	5–9
'Intrigue'	5–10
'Margaret Merril'	5–11
'Nearly Wild'	4–9
'Pillow Fight'	4–9
'Singin' in the Rain'	5–11
'Sun Flare'	5–10
'The Fairy'	4–10

'Six Hills Giant' catmint makes an excellent companion with 'Lavender Lassie' climbing rose in a mixed planting.

In A Rose Garden

Whether you want just a bed devoted to roses or a whole garden area, rose gardens are a long-time favorite.

Rose gardens allow you to display a rose collection in style. (You'll want to label your roses to keep them all straight.) They also make care easier since you can water, prune, control problems, and fertilize all in the same space. And when a rose garden is in bloom, the fragrance multiplies and is all the more heavenly.

When planning a rose garden, it's important to remember that roses grow in different shapes, heights, and colors. If you simply put them in here and there, taller roses may block shorter ones and bright pinks may clash with reds.

Since rose gardens highlight the roses, with few if any other plants to provide color or hide problem leggy stems, choose roses that are long-term or repeat bloomers and have an appealing form or growth habit.

For these reasons, floribundas, modern shrub roses, and miniature roses are excellent choices for the rose garden (though you can, of course, include just about any type of rose). They have continuous color throughout the season with plentiful clusters and sprays of flowers.

When planting roses in your rose garden, be sure to allow plenty of room for air circulation and access around the plants for deadheading, grooming, and cutting. Planting distance between hybrid teas, miniatures, and floribundas should be about 2 feet. The space between shrub or groundcover roses should be about 3 feet to allow for their greater sprawl.

You'll need to deadhead your rose garden regularly to encourage longer bloom. Also be sure to mulch to prevent disease and pests. An irrigation system is helpful because it will deliver water to the soil rather than the leaves, which encourages disease that can spread like wildfire in a concentrated planting of just roses.

Consider planting groundcovers or low-growing perennials in your rose garden to serve as a living mulch. Lavender, smaller catmint, and hardy geraniums are classics.

Great Roses for Rose Beds

Name	Zone
'Belle Story'	5-9
'Cotillion'	5-10
'Diana, Princess of Wales'	5-10
'Francois Rabelais'	5-10
'Johann Strauss'	5-10
'Margaret Merril'	5-11
'Miami Moon'	5-10
'Nicole'	5-10
'Pat Austin'	5-9
'Purple Heart'	5-10
'Rockin' Robin'	4-9
'Sexy Rexy'¶	5-11
'What a Peach'	5-10

Bright red 'Illusion', pale pink 'Lavender Lassie' and the small shrub 'Pillow Fight' combine well in a rose garden.

How to Use Roses *continued*

As a Hedge

Roses make beautiful, often fragrant, thicket-like hedges. They're not meant for tightly pruned hedges, but if you want an informal, lovely country-look hedge, a rose hedge can serve you well.

They are ideal for creating privacy, barriers, blocking out ugly views, or dividing a large garden into more intimate rooms.

Rose hedges can vary in height but tend to be between 3 to 6 feet and usually grow roughly as wide, though some, such as 'Simplicity' and its other-colored cousins, grow very upright.

In fact, 'Simplicity,' which is pink, started a craze for informal hedges because of its long bloom time and tidy, upright growth habit.

But just about any rose can be used in a hedge. Miniatures just several inches high can be used as a low hedge around flower beds, patios, or paths. Climbers and ramblers can be trained along a rough fence, such as a split rail fence, and form a living fence.

Height and shape also depends on how you prune the rose in early spring. Canes left higher in spring will grow taller; cutting back a rose hard in the spring will result in a shorter plant.

The Best Roses for Hedges

Name	Zone
'Betty Boop'	5-10
'Betty Prior'	4-9
'Bonica'	4-10
'Confetti'	5-10
'F.J. Grootendorst'	3-9
'Gizmo'	5-10
'Iceberg'	5-10
'Knock Out'	4-10
'Livin' Easy'	5-10
'Purple Simplicity'	5-10
'Red Simplicity'	5-10
'Simplicity'	5-11
'Sunsprite'	5-11
'White Simplicity'	5-10

'Red Fountain' roses make a splendid informal hedge when faced with perennials to hide their bare legs.

For Cutting

Not all roses are created equal for cutting.

The best roses for cutting naturally have long stems and smaller thorns. They have large flowers with petals that look good for a long time after cutting.

The pointed, oval shaped buds of hybrid teas are the gold standard for cut roses, but many clustered roses are great for cutting, too. Good clustered roses for cutting have most of the flowers in the cluster open at the same time, preventing you from having to trim out those that withered early. They have flowers that look good even as they fade (for example, they stay true pink rather than rapidly browning and their petals don't curl). Also, their petals are securely attached so they don't "shatter" (that is, fall off easily). Some roses, such as hybrid teas, have very tightly attached petals while others, such as some rugosas and some David Austin roses, shatter easily.

Roses such as hybrid teas and grandifloras naturally produce long straight stems with single flowers at the tip of each. Others can form clusters that are themselves pretty mini bouquets.

Some roses, especially hybrid teas, will last for up to three weeks in the vase if you do the following to assure longest life:

- Cut early in the morning. This assures that the roses will be their most hydrated (that is, stiff with water).
- Choose newer flowers, especially buds that are just starting to open. They'll finish opening in the vase and you'll have the pleasure of watching the process, besides.
- Condition your roses. Soak them in a tall narrow pitcher or vase up to their necks in tepid water for several hours before arranging. This allows them to soak up more water into the stems.
- Cut them a second time under water. When arranging the roses, right before putting the flowers in the vase or floral foam, make a final cut under water in a bowl of water; then immediately put the stem in water or foam again. This assures that the pores in the plant will stay open and the stems will take up water better than if you exposed them to air.
- Strip off any leaves that would be below the water line. Leaves foul the water, shortening the flowers' staying power.
- Use a floral preservative in the vase water. It can add days to the life of your arrangement.

WORK SMARTER

THORNS BE GONE

When cutting roses for arrangements, thorns can be a real problem so it's best to remove them either in the garden or once you bring them inside to work with them.

There are rose thorn strippers made especially for this, but if you have just a few stems to remove thorns from, an easy way to handle them is simply to take a nail clippers and clip off the thorns so you can go about your arrangement without pain.

Hybrid tea roses fresh from the garden are the royalty of cut flowers.

Long-Stemmed Roses for Cutting

Name	Zone
'Barbra Streisand'	5-10
'Bride's Dream'	5-10
'Crystalline'	5-10
'Elina'	5-10
'Jardins de Bagatelle'	5-9
'Kardinal'	5-10
'Love & Peace'	5-10
'Moonstone'	5-10
'New Zealand'	5-10
'Peter Mayle'	5-10
'Royal Highness'	5-10
'Toulouse Lautrec'	5-9
'Valencia'	5-10
'Veteran's Honor'	5-10

Clustered Roses for Cutting

Name	Zone
'Berries 'n' Cream'	5-10
'Blueberry Hill'	5-10
'Brass Band'	5-10
'Brilliant Pink Iceberg'	5-10
'Easy Going'	5-10
'Fabulous!'	5-10
'Fragrant Apricot'	5-10
'French Lace'	6-10
'Lavaglut'	5-10
'Love Potion'	5-10
'Marina'	5-10
'Sexy Rexy'	5-11
'Show Biz'	5-10
'Trumpeter'	5-10

How to Use Roses

continued

3

Design and Planning Basics

As a Climber or Rambler

Nothing makes a statement as dramatic and romantic as an explosion of roses on an arbor, wall, or large trellis.

Heights vary from a petite 6 feet to more than 20 feet; flowers range from 2 to 6 inches. Some bloom heavily in late spring or early summer with few, if any, flowers later; others have a heavy flush of bloom followed by intermittent blooms, then a final flush of bloom in early autumn. All climbers need full sun and moderate water, as well as a sturdy support that can accommodate their full height.

Availability of the roses listed here will vary by region and source. If you can't find a particular rose, ask the retailer about other roses with similar characteristics.

Climbing Roses

Also called large-flowered climbing roses, these are better behaved than ramblers, seldom reaching more than 15 to 20 feet in height. Climbers have long, flexible stems (canes) that need to be tied or gently intertwined with their support. They usually bloom heavily just once in late spring or early summer, then intermittently in fall once temperatures drop.

They need regular feeding and are prone to all the usual rose pests and diseases. Keeping them looking good requires some attention. (See pages 196–199 for pruning tips, and page 219 for pest and disease information.)

Name	Zones	Height
'Alberic Barbier'	6-9	20 feet
'Aloha'	6-10	10 feet
'Altissimo'	6-9	10 feet
'America'	6-10	12 feet
'Belle Portugaise'	8-9	20 feet
'Blaze Improved'	5-10	14 feet
'Climbing Cecile Brunner'	6-9	12 feet
'Climbing Etoile de Hollande'	6-9	18 feet
'Climbing Iceberg'	6-9	15 feet
'Climbing Peace'	6-9	20 feet
'Don Juan'	6-9	10 feet
'Dortmund'	6-9	10 feet
'Dublin Bay'	6-11	10 feet
'Fourth of July'	6-11	14 feet
'Golden Showers'	6-9	8 feet
'Henry Kelsey'	4-8	7 feet
'John Cabot'	4-8	6 feet
'Joseph's Coat'	5-10	12 feet
'Madame Alfred Carriere'	7-9	18 feet
'New Dawn'	4-9	20 feet
'Pink Pillar'	6-9	10 feet
'Rhonda'	6-9	8 feet
Rosa wichuraiana	6-10	10-20 feet
'Silver Moon'	7-9	18-20 feet
'White Dawn'	6-9	12 feet
'William Baffin'	4-8	8 feet

'Joseph's Coat' climbing rose

Rambler Roses

If you have space and a sturdy support, rambler roses will thrive, blanketing a large arbor, wall, fence—or even a whole tree—with breathtaking blooms. They flower for several weeks in early to midsummer.

They need a large, strong support because few grow less than 20 feet, and some can reach 50 feet. They can easily pull down any support that's not large enough to accommodate their sprawl and weight, including modest-size trees. Ramblers usually must be tied to their supports, though their large thorns sometimes help them scramble up trees. They bloom on wood grown the previous year, so prune immediately after blooming. (See pages 196–199.)

They're fairly pest-resistant but are particularly prone to mildew if air circulation is poor or humidity is high.

Name	Zones	Height
'Bobbie James'	4-9	30 feet
'Dorothy Perkins'	6-9	10-12 feet
'Dr. W. Van Fleet'	5-9	20 feet
'Etain'	4-9	15 feet
'Felicite Perpetue'	6-9	20 feet
'Lady Banks'	8-10	20 feet
'Leontine Gervais'	5-9	20 feet
'Paul's Himalayan Musk Rambler'	4-9	30 feet

As a Miniature

Sweet little undersized versions of the larger roses, miniature roses grow just 6 to 18 inches tall with small flowers to match. They're wonderful massed in flower beds, dotted along paths, or tucked into containers or window boxes. And they're generally fairly cold hardy. Miniflora roses are a new classification of roses with plant, leaf, and flower size intermediate between miniatures and shrub roses. Both miniature and miniflora roses are usually grown on their own roots (that is, without grafting), and therefore are generally hardier than many other roses (Usually Zones 5–10).

Miniature roses should be mulched to conserve moisture and minimize disease. Fertilize every 2 to 4 weeks, halting one month before your region's first average frost date in fall. Trim spent flowers to promote long blooming.

In Zones 7 to 10 no winter protection is needed. In Zones 5 and 6, mound the base with a few inches of soil or compost and cover the roses as shown on page 201. In late winter or early spring, prune by removing all but five to seven of the strongest stems, evenly spaced around the base. Then cut those back by half (see page 198 for tips on where to make cuts).

'Sun Sprinkles' miniature rose

Miniature Roses

'Angel Darling'	'Orange Sunblaze'
'Candy Mountain'	'Popcorn'
'Cupcake'	'Red Cascade'
'Fire Princess'	'Rise 'n' Shine'
'Gypsy Dancer'	'Rosy Dawn'
'Happy Trails'	'Sun Sprinkles'
'Lady of the Dawn'	'Sweet Dream'
'Little Bo Peep'	'Tear Drop'

As a Groundcover

A groundcover rose is any low-growing rose that can be planted in a grouping to cover an area. Many miniature roses can be used as groundcover roses, for example. However, most groundcover roses are low, spreading roses that grow perhaps 2 to 3 feet high and roughly twice to three times as wide. Some climbing or rambling roses are used as groundcovers on steep or large slopes. Many spreading groundcover roses as well as many climbing roses have the sprawling *Rosa wichuraiana* in their breeding.

Mulch groundcover roses to conserve moisture and to suppress weeds. Fertilize with a slow-release granular fertilizer as package directs. Avoid pruning, or prune lightly as needed for maximum coverage.

Groundcover Roses

'Alba Meidiland'	'Red Cascade'
'Bonica'	*Rosa wichuraiana*
'Carefree Beauty'	'Royal Bonica'
'China Doll'	'Scarlet Meidiland'
'Flower Carpet'	'The Fairy'
'Max Graf'	'White Meidiland'
'Paulii'	

As a Standard

Like something out of a fairy tale, standard roses, also called tree roses, seem too lovely to be real. But they're simply traditional roses (they often even have the same cultivar name) pruned and grafted as a shrub on top of a long, straight stem.

Standard roses vary in height, with 2 to 3 feet being the most common. However, some standards are 4 to 5 feet. Standard roses can be planted in the garden but do especially well in pots. Most need a stake the length of the trunk alongside for support.

Mulch standard roses; never allow to dry out. Fertilize every 2 to 4 weeks, halting 4 weeks before your region's first average frost date in fall. Trim spent flowers to prolong bloom time.

In Zones 8 and colder, where temperatures drop below 28°F (-2°C), protect plants in pots by storing in a garage or basement. For plants grown in the ground in Zone 7, wrap with burlap. In Zone 6 and colder, dig up the rose and bury it completely horizontal in soil. Remove the soil in spring after it thaws, and replant the rose upright.

In spring, when danger of frost has passed, prune out old, dead, and weak canes and remove any suckers at the base. Then prune selectively to maintain rounded shape.

Standard roses are highly prone to the usual rose diseases and pests (see page 219).

'Bonica' is a shrub rose that also makes an excellent groundcover when planted in masses.

A rose trained as a standard and planted in a pot.

Standard Roses

''Bill Warriner'
'Candelabra'
'Double Delight'
'Fame!'
'French Lace'
'Honor'
'Intrigue'
'Melody Parfumee'
'Mister Lincoln'
'Opening Night'
'Pat Austin'
'Peace'
'Rio Samba'
'Sun Flare'
'Ultimate Pink'

How to Choose and Design with Groundcovers

WORK SMARTER

GROUNDCOVER CARE

It's true that groundcovers are usually low-maintenance, but that doesn't mean they're no maintenance.

Like any plant, they need good soil, watering, and weeding. Groundcovers are usually planted densely enough that many weeds are crowded out, but some still manage to grow. Once a groundcover is badly infested with weeds, it can be difficult to get the weeds out.

Groundcovers are beautiful and they're easy. But they do require a bit of care.

A groundcover is any relatively low, somewhat spreading plant that is planted in groups for a massed effect.

Groundcovers are popular solutions for problem areas. When well-chosen for the region and the specific site, they're usually a low-maintenance way to landscape an area.

They seem so easy-care, in fact, that you need to be careful. Some gardeners plant vast areas in nothing but one type of vigorous groundcover, such as pachysandra or English ivy. But that can cause problems: The groundcover can become invasive, and it can be visually boring.

When faced with a large area that you're tempted to carpet with nothing but groundcover, mix in some other elements, such as shrubs and small trees. The result will be a better design and better gardening.

Groundcovers for Slopes

Groundcovers that grow quickly are an excellent solution for slopes, both shady and sunny. They're an ideal alternative to grass, which would need to be mowed at an angle and would require a lot of water. Just be sure when planting groundcovers to disturb the soil as little as possible to prevent erosion. A loose mulch such as wood chips at planting time can also reduce erosion if the slope isn't steep.

If the slope is steep, use biodegradable burlap, pinned into place with soil pins or stiff wire formed into long U-shapes, to prevent erosion until the plants fill in.

For a list of groundcovers that perform especially well on slopes, see the opposite page.

Groundcovers for Edging

Groundcovers can also look good along beds or borders planted with trees, shrubs, perennials, herbs, or annuals.

Whereas groundcovers planted on slopes need to spread quickly, groundcovers used as an edging need to behave themselves to avoid overtaking other plants in the bed.

Good groundcovers for edging include plumbago, goldenstar, liriope, small hostas, lady's mantle, and low-growing ferns.

Groundcovers as a Shade Solution

Many groundcovers thrive in the shade and make an ideal alternative to grass that may be struggling for survival under a large tree, along the north side of a house, or in another shady spot.

However, few groundcovers can withstand much foot traffic. A good landscaping solution for an area where grass won't grow but there's moderate foot traffic is to install a path or stepping-stones and plant a groundcover on either side of or among the pavers.

Rockcress grows only 6 to 8 inches high but forms a spreading mat up to 2 feet across covered with bright purple flowers in midspring.

Many groundcovers, such as creeping phlox, are smothered with flowers for a few weeks each year.

Good Groundcovers for Shade, Sun, and Slopes

Common Name	Botanical Name	Zones
Groundcovers for Shade		
Ajuga	*Ajuga reptans*	3-9
Archangel, yellow	*Lamiostrum galeobdolon* 'Variegatum'	3-9
Blue-eyed Mary	*Omphalodes verna*	5-9
Bog rosemary	*Andromeda polifolia*	2-6
Bunchberry	*Cornus canadensis*	2-7
Christmas rose; Lenten rose	*Helleborus niger; H. orientalis*	4-9
Coralberry, prostrate Chenault	*Symphoricarpos ×chenaultii* 'Hancock'	4-7
Cotoneaster, bearberry	*Cotoneaster dammeri*	5-9
Ferns	Various	Varies
Foam flower, Allegheny	*Tiarella cordifolia*	4-9
Forget-me-not	*Myosotis scorpioides*	3-8
Goldenstar	*Chrysogonum virginianum*	5-8
Hosta	*Hosta* spp.	3-8
Italian arum	*Arum italicum*	6-10
Ivy, English	*Hedera helix*	5-9
Lily-of-the-valley	*Convallaria majalis*	2-9
Pachysandra	*Pachysandra terminalis*	4-10
Phlox, creeping	*Phlox stolonifera*	2-8
Snow-on-the-mountain	*Aegopodium podagraria* 'Variegatum'	3-9
Strawberry, Alpine	*Fragaria vesca*	3-9
Sweet woodruff	*Galium odoratum*	4-8
Vinca	*Vinca minor, Vinca major*	4 (7)-8
Wintergreen	*Gaultheria procumbens*	3-8
Groundcovers for Hot, Sunny Areas		
Artemisia, Silver Brocade	*Artemisia stelleriana* 'Silver Brocade'	3-9
Basket-of-gold	*Aurinia saxatilis*	4-8
Bath's pink	*Dianthus gratianopolitanus* 'Bath's Pink'	4-9
Bearberry cotoneaster	*Cotoneaster dammeri*	5-9
Blue star	*Amsonia tabernaemontana*	3-9
Bog rosemary	*Andromeda polifolia*	2-6
Catmint	*Nepeta ×faassenii*	4-8
Dwarf blue fescue	*Festuca glauca*	4-9
Evergreen candytuft	*Iberis sempervirens*	4-8
Germander	*Teucrium prostratum*	4-9
Ice plant, hardy	*Delosperma nubigenum*	6-9
Hens and chicks	*Sempervivum tectorum*	4-10
Junipers, low types	*Juniperus* spp.	Varies
Lily turf	*Liriope muscari*	7-10
Mountain sandwort	*Arenaria montana*	3-6

Common Name	Botanical Name	Zones
Phlox, moss	*Phlox subulata*	2-9
Prostrate rosemary	*Rosmarinus officinalis* 'Irene'	7-10
Rock rose	*Helianthemum nummularium*	5-8
Spring cinquefoil	*Potentilla neumannii*	4-8
Sea thrift	*Armeria maritima*	3-8
Sedum, dragon's blood	*Sedum spurium* 'Dragon's Blood'	3-8
Sedum, goldmoss	*Sedum acre*	4-9
Stonecrop	*Sedum spectabile*	3-10
Thyme, creeping types	*Thymus* spp.	5-9
Veronica, low types	*Veronica* spp.	Varies
Wall rockcress	*Arabis caucasica*	3-7
Groundcovers for Slopes		
Basket-of-gold	*Aurinia saxatilis*	4-8
Blanket flower	*Gaillardia ×grandiflora*	2-9
Candytuft, evergreen	*Iberis sempervirens*	4-8
Coralberry, prostrate Chenault	*Symphoricarpos ×chenaultii* 'Hancock'	4-7
Cotoneaster, bearberry	*Cotoneaster dammeri*	5-9
Freeway daisy	*Osteospermum fruticosum*	8-10
Hens and chicks	*Sempervivum tectorum*	4-10
Ice plant, hardy	*Delosperma nubigenum*	6-9
Ivy, English	*Hedera helix*	5-9
Juniper, Andorra compact	*Juniperus horizontalis* 'Plumosa Compacta'	3-9
Jasmine, Asiatic	*Trachelospermum asiaticum*	7-10
Juniper, Bar Harbor	*Juniperus horizontalis* 'Bar Harbor'	3-9
Juniper, Blue Chip	*Juniperus horizontalis* 'Blue Chip'	3-9
Juniper, Blue Pacific shore	*Juniperus conferta* 'Blue Pacific'	5-9
Juniper, Blue Rug	*Juniperus horizontalis* 'Wiltonii'	3-9
Lilyturf	*Liriope muscari*	7-10
Mondo grass	*Ophiopogon japonicus*	7-9
Phlox, moss	*Phlox subulata*	2-9
Pink, Bath's	*Dianthus gratianopolitanus* 'Bath's Pink'	4-9
Rose, Alba Meidiland	*Rosa* 'Alba Meidiland'	4-8
Sedum, goldmoss	*Sedum acre*	4-9
Spurge, cypress	*Euphorbia cyparissias*	4-8
Strawberry, alpine	*Fragaria vesca*	3-9
Verbena, moss	*Verbena pulchella*	8-10
Vinca, little-leaf	*Vinca minor*	4-8

How to Choose and Design with Vines

A CLOSER LOOK

TOO MUCH OF A GOOD THING
Depending on where you live, some vines may be invasive. The classic example is wisteria. In warm climates, it can reach 100 feet. Many a homeowner has planted it right next to a house without proper support, then had the vine cut down only a few years later as it threatens to engulf the house. Wisteria and other vigorous vines often also send out shoots 6 feet or more away from their base, creating another problem.

Other problematically vigorous vines include Oriental bittersweet, trumpet creeper, and Japanese honeysuckle.

Then there's the issue of reseeding. Seeds of Oriental bittersweet and porcelain berry vine are spread by birds and become invasive in Northeast woodlands. Morning glories such as 'Heavenly Blue' are usually well-behaved in northern climates, but in mild-winter climates they reseed and spread so prolifically that they can become weeds.

Vines are immensely versatile plants. They can cover an ugly fence or grace a beautiful trellis. They can sprawl and be used as a groundcover, or can climb great heights and provide shade on a pergola or porch.

The key is to choose the right vine and use it wisely. Here's how:

Choosing the Right Vine

Consider the following when selecting a vine:

- How tall does it grow? Some vines will grow a modest 4 to 5 feet; others can reach 40 or even 60 feet.
- What kind of support does it need? A large-flowered clematis will politely climb a 6-foot wood trellis inserted into the ground. Big climbers such as wisteria and bittersweet form woody vines more akin to small trunks and can engulf even small trees. They need sturdy, well-constructed supports, pergolas, or porches to climb. Match the vine to the support.
- What is its climbing habit? A twining vine may be all right for a trellis attached to wood siding. But a climber that attaches with holdfasts can be difficult to remove when it comes time for painting.

Using Vines in the Landscape

- Camouflage an ugly fence. Plant annuals such as morning glories, black-eyed Susan vine, or scarlet runner bean at the base of the fence. Or plant perennials such as sweet autumn clematis, silver fleece vine, or cup-and-saucer vine.
- Camouflage an ugly building. For masonry, choose a self-clinging vine, such as climbing hydrangea or Boston ivy. For wood, erect a trellis using galvanized nails and wire and plant twining vines, such as morning glory, star jasmine, or akebia. The nails and wire allow you to pull down the trellis and cut back the vines, if needed, at painting time.
- Frame a window. Build a permanent lattice up the sides and over the top of a window. Plant a relatively tame 12-foot annual, such as black-eyed Susan vine, or a perennial such as a large-flowered clematis, on either side for living shutters.
- Interplant with tall, vertical plants. Large-flowered clematis are beautiful next to roses or tree peonies. They climb the larger plant and bloom on top of it.
- Avoid blocking the irrigation system. Plant vines away from areas where they might block sprinkler heads at maturity.

How Vines Climb

Clinging tendrils

Twining

Adhesive discs

Clinging rootlets

Started from seed, by early in the summer this annual black-eyed Susan vine has quickly covered an arbor and is just about ready to burst into yellow-orange bloom.

Mandevilla is an annual in colder regions and a perennial in warmer areas. It produces lovely 3-inch flowers.

Late summer into fall sweet autumn clematis fills the garden with its rich vanilla scent.

Fragrant Vines

Common Name	Botanical Name	Zone
Clematis, evergreen	*Clematis armandii*	7–9
Clematis, sweet autumn	*Clematis paniculata*	4–9
Honeysuckles, some types	*Lonicera* spp.	Varies
Hoya	*Hoya* spp.	11
Jasmine, Madagascar	*Stephanotis floribunda*	10–11
Jasmines, some types	*Jasminum* spp.	9–11
Jasmine, star	*Trachelospermum jasminoides*	8–10
Moonflower	*Ipomoea alba*	Annual
Roses, climbing, some types	*Rosa* spp.	Varies
Sweet pea	*Lathyrus latifolius*	Annual
Wisteria	*Wisteria floribunda*	5–9

Vines by Height

Height is influenced by the amount of sun and shade, water, and nutrients in the soil. With annual vines, it is also affected by the length of the growing season.

Common Name	Botanical Name	Zone
Small (10 feet and under)		
Black-eyed Susan vine	*Thunbergia alata*	Up to 10 feet
Clematis, large-flowered, some types	*Clematis* spp.	Up to 10 feet
Jasmine, star	*Trachelospermum jasminoides*	Up to 6 feet
Nasturtium	*Tropaeolum majus*	Up to 10 feet
Bean, scarlet runner	*Phaseolus coccineus*	Up to 10 feet
Sweet pea	*Lathyrus odoratus*	Up to 8 feet
Sweet potato vine	*Ipomoea batatas*	Up to 8 feet
Medium (10 to 20 feet)		
Cardinal climber	*Ipomoea ×sloteri*	Up to 20 feet
Hyacinth bean	*Lablab purpureus*	Up to 20 feet
Moonflower	*Ipomoea alba*	Up to 20 feet
Morning glory	*Ipomoea tricolor*	Up to 20 feet
Tall (20 feet or more)		
Bittersweet, American	*Celastrus scandens*	Up to 25 feet
Euonymus, wintercreeper	*Euonymus fortunei*	Up to 40 feet
Hydrangea, climbing	*Hydrangea anomala*	Up to 80 feet
Ivy, English	*Hedera helix*	Up to 50 feet
Firethorn	*Pyracantha coccinea*	Up to 15 feet
Honeysuckles	*Lonicera* spp.	Up to 30 feet
Silver lace vine	*Polygonum aubertii*	Up to 30 feet
Trumpet creeper	*Campsis radicans*	Up to 40 feet
Virginia creeper	*Parthenocissus quinquefolia*	Up to 50 feet

Understanding Annuals And Perennials

The brilliant red and orange poppies in this flower bed are cool-season annuals that add gorgeous color in early summer. By midsummer, they'll begin to fade and brown and should be replaced with a summer-blooming annual.

Choosing a pretty flower is easy. But successfully choosing and designing with annuals, perennials, and even biennials is more tricky.

Confused about the difference among annuals, perennials, and biennials? Remember that an annual sets seed and dies in only one year or less, and a perennial (think "permanent") comes back year after year. Biennials take two years to bloom, then die (remember that "bi" means two and rhymes with "die").

Using these three groups of flowers successfully is the key to having a constant supply of gorgeous flowers.

Choosing Annuals and Perennials

- Read the label. Is the plant the right plant for the right place? Check light, soil, and height information. Look for awards or prizes the plant has won—a good sign that it's reliable and has good growing characteristics.
- Is it healthy? What you see is what you get, no matter how much you're paying. Annuals and perennials should be healthy looking, not wilted, not leggy, and not showing signs of disease.
- What is its growth habit? A tumbling, vinelike annual is perfect for a window box, but in the back of the border it will get lost. An Oriental poppy is glorious until right after it blooms, when its foliage gets scraggly. (Plant it behind other, later-blooming perennials to camouflage the fading foliage.)

Choosing Annuals

- Alternate warm-season and cool-season annuals (see page 148). Get more color longer in prime spots, such as window boxes or planters, by planting cool-season annuals in winter or spring. Then, when the cool-season flowers fade in late spring, replace them with warm-season annuals.

- Experiment with reseeding annuals, such as California poppies, larkspur, and columbine. Plant seeds or established plants in spring and allow them to go to seed in late summer. The following spring, thin and transplant as desired.
- Buy healthy plants. Avoid purchasing plants that look diseased or wilted. They may spread the problem. Also, it's best to buy when the plants are not in bloom. Although they look gorgeous, blooming plants will take longer to become established, because they have to put their energy into flowering as well as root development.

Choosing Perennials

- Look for good value in comparison to size. Mail-order perennials may arrive small or bare-root and may take years to get to good blooming size. The large one-gallon perennials will bloom sooner but often cost far more. Perennials in 3- or 4-inch pots are often the best value.
- Check the roots. You may want to ask first, but don't be afraid to knock the plant out of its pot in the store. You want a plant that has a well-developed root system, not a small, weak cutting that is hardly established.
- Consider foliage. Perennials are short bloomers. Most of the time you'll be looking at the foliage. Choose plants with foliage that looks fresh all season (hosta, fringed bleeding heart, Siberian iris) and contrasts in color and texture with the other foliage in the garden. If you can steel yourself, pinch off any flowers to encourage good root development.

Annual lobelia, which is a cool-season annual, does well as long as temperatures stay in the 80s or below. The petunias in the urn are a warm-season annual.

A CLOSER LOOK

WHAT IS AN ANNUAL?

Technically, an annual is a plant that blooms, sets seed, and dies in only one year or less.

However, complicating matters slightly is the fact that a perennial in the South might be grown as an annual (that is, a temporary or one-season plant) in a more northern region.

Then some labels and books make further distinctions, such as hardy annuals, half-hardy annuals, half-hardy perennials, or tender perennials. Those labels simply mean that the plant is borderline.

To further blur matters, some flowers have both annual and perennial varieties. For example, some salvias are true annuals and others are hardy perennials. (Read the label carefully to figure it out.)

If you're confused, look at the Plant Encyclopedia starting on page 292, check the label, or ask garden center staff.

Then there's the issue of cool-season annuals and warm-season annuals. In the North gardeners are probably most familiar with warm-season annuals—marigolds, petunias, impatiens—that are planted after the last spring frost and which thrive as temperatures soar. Cool-season annuals, such as pansies, like things more chilly and are used in early spring or fall in cold climates or as winter color in warm climates.

What Is a Perennial?

A perennial is a plant that comes back year after year.

That said, there are finer points to it. Some plants that are perennials in warmer parts are grown as annuals in colder regions because the harsher winters kill them out.

Sometimes you'll see perennials, such as flax, referred to as short-lived perennials. These are perennials that naturally last for only a few years, then die out. Other perennials, such as peonies, last for decades.

Some perennials are herbaceous—that is, they die back to the ground in winter. Others (especially in warm climates) are evergreen or semi-evergreen, with foliage that may need simply a little trimming, if that, come spring.

What Is a Biennial?

A handful of our favorite flowers are biennials—plants that take two years to flower. The first year they grow foliage. The second year they bloom, then die at the end of the season.

To flower gardeners, a biennial may not sound like a very desirable plant (all that waiting, only for it to die!), but favorite biennials are so lovely that they're worth the wait. Spectacular Canterbury bells (page 315) is an excellent example.

Some biennials, such as foxgloves and hollyhocks, are a bit erratic—in a good way. They often bloom their first year from seed, then reseed so prolifically that they seem like perennials.

How to Choose And Design with Annuals And Perennials

One of the rewards of gardening is combining a striking variety of flowers in a large bed that is beautiful throughout the growing season. Here's how to create a beautiful flower bed or border:

- Make the bed amply sized—at least 3 feet across and, if possible, 12 to 16 feet or more long. This will allow you to have a rich variety of flowers so you'll always have something in bloom.
- Plant in large groups. Twenty marigolds in a group have a bigger impact and look more attractive than three in a group. Most plants grow in groups in nature and look best that way in the garden too.
- Leave pockets for annuals. A border of only perennials, unless perfectly planned, can lack color at certain times of the year. Leaving open spaces at the front of the bed for annuals lets you plug in color where it's needed.
- Fertilize regularly, especially if you have a lot of annuals. Because they grow and flower in one season, annuals need abundant food. Work in a slow-release fertilizer or compost at planting time. Supplement with a liquid fertilizer four or five times during the growing season.
- Know bloom times. Some perennials, such as Oriental poppies, are glorious for a week in May, then fade, looking tattered as they go.

Many of these flowers, including the dramatic, tall delphiniums, are perennials that will return every spring, saving time, work, and money.

This perennial flower bed is designed with a subtle blue and yellow color scheme. For contrast it has silver foliage, which looks striking no matter what is in bloom.

Must-Have Annuals

Looking for some of the easiest, most colorful flowers around? Then try some of these—flowers so easy that they're also ideal for a child's garden.

Common Name	Botanical Name
Ageratum, flossflower	*Ageratum houstonianum*
Cockscomb, celosia	*Celosia* spp.
Coleus	*Solenostemum scutellariodes*
Cosmos	*Cosmos* spp.
Dusty miller	*Senecio cineraria*
Geranium	*Pelargonium* spp.
Impatiens	*Impatiens* spp.
Marigold	*Tagetes* spp.
Pansies	*Viola* spp.
Petunia	*Petunia* spp.
Salvia	*Salvia* spp.
Sweet alyssum	*Lobularia maritima*
Vinca, annual	*Catharanthus roseus*
Wax begonia	*Begonia ×semperflorens-cultorum*
Zinnia	*Zinnia* spp.

Others, such as coreopsis, bloom from midspring until frost. Orchestrate your garden so that something is always in bloom.

Look at what's blooming in your neighborhood, parks, and public gardens. Make a list of a dozen or more perennials with a succession of bloom times, and be sure to include those in your garden.

- Deadhead! Trim off spent blooms regularly (see page 206); with most flowers, this promotes more bloom. By cutting off flowers, you're frustrating a plant's goal of setting seed, causing the plant to go into overdrive to produce more flowers.
- Cut back fearlessly. If disease has felled a perennial, even if it's early summer, cut it back to just a few inches. It often will send out a flush of new foliage or flowers. This practice also helps prevent the disease from spreading to other plants.

Plants with Fragrant Flowers

Here are some of the most intensely fragrant flowers around. Note that certain types and cultivars of one type of plant may be fragrant while others may not. When in doubt, read the label or ask.

Common Name	Botanical Name	Zones
Annuals, Perennials, and Vines		
Bee balm	*Monarda didyma*	4–8
Clematis, sweet autumn	*Clematis* spp.	4–9
Daylily, 'Hyperion'	*Hemerocallis* 'Hyperion'	3–10
Flowering tobacco	*Nicotiana* spp.	Annual
Geraniums, scented	*Pelargonium* spp.	8–11
Heliotrope	*Heliotropium arborescens*	10–11
Honeysuckle, some	*Lonicera* spp.	3–9
Hosta, August lily	*Hosta plantaginea*	3–9
Iris, bearded, some	*Iris ×germanica*	3–10
Jasmine, some	*Jasminum* spp.	9–11
Jasmine, star	*Trachelospermum jasminoides*	8–10
Lavender	*Lavandula* spp.	5–10
Lilies, some, but especially Oriental	*Lilium* spp.	3–9
Peony, some	*Paeonia* spp.	2–7
Phlox, garden	*Phlox paniculata*	5–7
Pinks, some	*Dianthus* spp.	4–8
Stock	*Matthiola incana*	Annual
Sweet alyssum	*Lobularia maritima*	Annual
Sweet pea	*Lathyrus odoratus*	Annual
Violets *(odorata* species)	*Viola odorata*	7–9

Long-Blooming Perennials

These plants will bloom 10 or more weeks in good conditions.

Common Name	Botanical Name	Zones
Aster	*Aster* spp., especially 'Moench', 'September Ruby', and 'Wonder of Staffa'	4–8
Black-eyed Susan, perennial	*Rudbeckia fulgida,* especially 'Goldsturm'	3–9
Blanket flower, perennial	*Gaillardia ×grandiflora,* especially 'Baby Cole'	2–10
Bleeding heart, fringed	*Dicentra eximia*	3–9
Catmint	*Nepeta ×faassenii,* especially 'Dropmore' and 'Six Hills Giant'	4–9
Coreopsis	*Coreopsis* spp. specially 'Sunray', 'Early Sunrise', 'Zagreb', and 'Moonbeam'	3–9
Daylily	*Hemerocallis* spp., especially 'Stella de Oro', 'Happy Returns', 'Lemon Lollipop', and 'Black-Eyed Stella'	3–10
Goldenstar	*Chrysogonum virginianum*	5–9
Joe-pye weed	*Eupatorium purpureum*	3–10
Lavender, English	*Lavandula angustifolia*	5–8
Phlox, garden	*Phlox paniculata,* especially 'Eva Cullum' and 'Franz Schubert'	4–8
Pinks, Bath's	*Dianthus gratianopolitanus* 'Bath's Pink'	4–9
Pinks, sweet William	*Dianthus* spp.	3–8
Russian sage	*Perovskia atriplicifolia*	5–7
Salvia, perennial blue	*Salvia ×superba,* especially 'May Night'	4–8
Scabiosa	*Scabiosa caucasica,* especially 'Butterfly Blue'	3–7
Sedum	*Sedum* 'Autumn Joy'	3–10
Shasta daisy	*Leucanthemum ×superbum* especially 'Becky'	4–9
Thrift, sea	*Armeria maritima*	4–8
Verbena	*Verbena* spp.	8–10
Veronica	*Veronica* spp., especially 'Sunny Border Blue'	3–8
White gaura	*Gaura lindheimeri*	5–9
Yarrow	*Achillea* spp., especially 'Fire King' or 'Apple Blossom'	3–9

How to Choose And Design With Annuals and Perennials *continued*

A beautifully designed flower bed can be the showiest part of your garden. Use a variety of colors, plant shapes, textures, and bloom times. Here's how to create a flower bed that delights you from spring through fall:

Use Color Effectively

- As a rule, mix pastels with pastels and brights with brights. Otherwise, the bed can look chaotic. If you're a beginner, work with a reliable, easy color scheme such as pink, blue, and white.
- Colors change with the seasons. Pinks and blues are easier to find in spring flowers. Maroons, russets, and oranges are easier to find in autumn flowers. Summer allows a wide range with nearly every color imaginable.
- Use white to add punch and freshness. Most color schemes can benefit from the addition of white. It makes the colors near it stand out and is striking at dusk.
- Use color to make a space feel bigger or smaller. Blues and dark reds blend into the background, creating the effect of being farther away. Yellows, clear reds, oranges, whites, and bright pinks seem closer.
- Use color to set mood. A garden with lots of red is vibrant and exciting. A garden with blues feels soothing and almost misty. A white garden is serene. A garden with pink and blue together is sweet and romantic.
- Coordinate. Consider the color of your home, fences, and nearby buildings when choosing a garden color scheme. Orange flowers against a red house can be jarring, and white flowers in front of a white house can get lost.

Think About Foliage

A flower's foliage is as important as its bloom. A pretty flower with good-looking foliage is a treasure. Some plants, such as Oriental poppies, have spectacular flowers; however, the foliage shrivels shortly after bloom, presenting the gardener with camouflage problems. Other plants, such as astilbe and peonies, have pretty, glossy foliage throughout

The Well-Designed Perennial Border

A spiky plant or two adds contrasting shape to this border, which is dominated by sprawling, "fluffy" plants. Ornamental grasses have been included for a strong vertical element and another contrasting shape.

White flowers freshen the look and add welcome contrast.

Plants are placed fairly close together for a lush look.

This border has a subtle color scheme: purple flowers are used with touches of yellow flowers and plants with gold foliage.

DESIGN TIP

MIX IT UP

There's a garden saying, "Put a roundy by a frilly by a spiky." And it works. A composition using these shapes will look good for months, long before and after the flowers have peaked.

the growing season. Some plants, such as hosta, lamb's-ears, and dusty miller, have such attractive foliage that they are planted primarily for their leaves. Many plants have variegated forms, with striking leaf markings.

Green is also a color. In the garden it ranges from the palest gray-green to deep burgundy-green to almost yellow spring green. Mix in a variety of foliage colors.

Mix Textures and Shapes

When combining plants in your flower garden, use a contrast in leaf shape, size, texture, and color. For example, put a hairy-leaved silvery plant next to a glossy, large-leaved plant. Tuck in a feathery plant next to one with strappy, grasslike leaves.

Experiment with plant combinations by plucking a leaf from each plant and holding them together in your hand. If you like the combination, it will probably look good in your flower bed too.

Plant According to Height

Arranging plants by height is easy. Put the tall ones (4 to 6 feet) in the back, the midsize ones (2 to 4 feet) in the middle, and the short ones (2 feet and less) in the front. Other height issues to keep in mind:

- How will your flower bed be viewed? If it will be viewed from all sides, put tall plants in the center, short ones along the edges, and midheight ones in between.
- How do you know how tall a plant will get? Checking the plant in the Plant Encyclopedia (page 292) or simply reading the label will guide you, but be aware that plant heights can vary according to growing conditions.

Plan for Seasonality

Plant color, height, texture, and shape change with the seasons. In spring, bulbs may fill your garden with color, then fade. For fall, plant ornamental grasses and other perennials that have good color or persist through the winter. Make note of a plant's characteristics from earliest spring through late fall and winter, and plant accordingly.

Work with Growing Conditions

To promote healthy plants and to make watering easier and more efficient, group plants with similar water requirements together as well as those with similar light and soil requirements.

This border has an attractive background—a wooded area. Other good backgrounds include tall fences or the side of a building.

Tall, unruly perennials are placed in back where they lend height while other plants disguise their leggy habit.

Midheight plants are placed in the middle.

Foliage is as important to this border as flowers. The border contains plants with a variety of leaf colors, including purple and yellow.

A purple-leaved plant breaks up what would otherwise be an expanse of green.

Lower, neater perennials are used as edging plants.

How to Choose And Design with Ornamental Grasses

Ornamental grasses can add four seasons of interest to the garden. In spring their emerging blades blend in well with other plantings; in summer their foliage adds movement and sometimes striking color; in fall they grace the landscape with intriguing seed heads; in winter, many remain standing as they dry, and the foliage and seed heads lend winter interest.

Many ornamental grasses have stunning color. Japanese blood grass is aptly named for its rich russet-red leaves.

Choosing Grasses

Many ornamental grasses are green, but others include blue oat grass, which is a striking steel blue-gray; to Japanese forest grass, a brilliant yellow-green; to black mondo grass, darkest green-black; to Japanese blood grass, a rich red.

Heights and shapes vary also. Low grasses such as blue fescue grow only several inches high and can be excellent groundcovers. Medium grasses such as fountain grass and blue oat grass have endless uses, including mixing into flower beds, borders, and foundation plantings in front of your home. Tall grasses, such as silver grass and pampas grass, work well in the back of borders or as specimen plantings all by themselves.

Seed heads are the glory of many grasses, and these, too, come in many different forms: open sheaves, foxtails, showy plumes, and bottlebrushes.

Depending on how tall and how stiff or soft the leaves are, ornamental grasses can add unforgettable movement to a garden when the wind blows, making it come alive. The rustling of the grasses, too, adds pleasant sound and yet another delightful element to the garden.

Grasses are an ideal companion to shorter, spreading plants with large leaves. Grasses' upward lines add something akin to exclamation points to the garden.

Plant grasses with flowers, or use them alone for a regal effect. Tall grasses such as Japanese silver grass, ravenna grass, and pampas grass work well as specimen plants.

Perennial grasses are less than attractive in late winter or early spring, when they should be cut back almost to the ground to make way for new growth. A way to brighten the resulting unattractive spot in the garden is to plant around the grasses with spring-blooming bulbs such as daffodils and crocuses. The bulbs add color to the barren spot, and the emerging new grass covers the dying bulb foliage.

Small, clump-forming grasses, such as dwarf blue fescue, make a striking edging for flower beds and other plantings.

Annual vs. Perennial Grasses

Most grasses are perennials, coming back year after year. But some are annuals lasting only one year—they will not come back in spring.

Complicating matters is the fact that some grasses are perennials in warm climates but in cold climates are grown as annuals. Read labels carefully to determine whether a grass is a perennial or an annual in your area. Purple fountain

GOOD IDEA

CONTROLLING INVASIVE GRASSES

If you have fallen in love with an ornamental grass but know that it can be invasive, slow it down by containing its roots in a pot in the ground.

Invasive grasses can include, depending on your climate, pampas grass, ribbon grass, Japanese blood grass, and blue lyme grass.

Plant the potentially problem grass in a several-gallon black plastic pot that gives the grass some room to grow, then sink the pot, plant and all, in the ground. Be sure to leave ½ to 1 inch of the pot's rim protruding above the soil to contain any roots that may run above ground.

If after two to three years there's no sign of the plant jumping its pot, leave it be. However, some grasses are so invasive that even a pot can't contain them. In this case, it's best to cut your losses and save yourself a weeding headache by digging up and disposing of the culprit.

How to Choose and Design with Ornamental Grasses *continued*

grass, for example, is a perennial only in Zones 8 to 10 but is often erroneously sold as a perennial in colder zones. Research how much cold the grass can tolerate, and use that to determine whether it will overwinter in your garden.

Clump-Forming Grasses vs. Running Grasses

Clumping grasses form tufts that grow larger each year while the plants stay put and don't spread.

In comparison, running grasses spread rapidly with stolons (aboveground stems) or rhizomes (underground stems)—so rapidly, in fact, that they can be invasive and create problems in planting beds and lawns.

Invasive types of ornamental grasses to use with caution include pampas grass, ribbon grass, blue lymegrass, and Japanese blood grass.

Cool-Season vs. Warm-Season Grasses

Cool-season grasses start to grow in late winter or early spring and begin producing seed heads in summer. They are usually evergreen in warm climates, though they may die back to the ground in cold climates. They may look tattered in late summer but will recover in the cooler temperatures of autumn. They include quaking grass, feather reed grass, tufted hair grass, blue lyme grass, blue fescue, Japanese wind grass, golden wood millet, and giant feather grass.

Warm-season perennial grasses start growing again only when the soil warms up later in spring. They thrive in summer's heat, and most are drought tolerant. They produce seed heads in fall, and their foliage often turns beautiful, rich colors. The seed heads then dry on the plant and remain through the winter. These grasses include sea oats, switch grass, silver grass, and fountain grass.

Ornamental Grasses for Shade, Meadows, and Dry Conditions

Common Name	Botanical Name	Zones
Shade-Tolerant Ornamental Grasses		
Blue oat grass	*Helictotrichon sempervirens*	4–9
Sedge, Golden	*Carex elata* 'Bowles Golden'	5–9
Sedge, Japanese	*Carex morrowii*	6–9
Japanese forest grass	*Hakonechloa macra* 'Aureola'	4–8
Northern sea oats	*Chasmanthium latifolium*	5–9
Ornamental Grasses for Meadow And Prairie Plantings		
Northern sea oats	*Chasmanthium latifolium*	5–9
Feather grass	*Stipa* spp.	8–11
Feather reed grass	*Calamagrostis ×acutiflora* 'Karl Foerster'	5–9
Purple moor grass	*Molinia caerulea*	4–8
Switch grass	*Panicum virgatum*	4–9
Drought-Tolerant Ornamental Grasses		
Dwarf pampas grass	*Cortaderia selloana* 'Pumila'	7–10
Blue fescue	*Festuca glauca*	4–9
Blue oat grass	*Helictotrichon sempervirens*	4–9
Feather grass	*Stipa* spp.	Varies
Silver grass; miscanthus	*Miscanthus sinensis*	5-10
Switch grass	*Panicum virgatum*	4–9

Japanese variegated sedge

How to Choose And Design with Ferns

Few plants add as much grace and elegance to a landscape as ferns. Most thrive in cool, moist, shady places, and make you feel rested just by looking at them.

There is a surprisingly wide variety of ferns available as more and more gardeners are smitten by their long, lovely fronds and are seeking interesting plants for shady areas.

Where to Plant

All ferns do best with some shade, though some, such as lady fern and hay-scented fern, will tolerate full sun if kept constantly moist. Though ferns tolerate varying amounts of light, the dappled light under clusters of trees is ideal.

As a rule, ferns do fine in full shade—that is, an area that receives less than four hours of full, direct light a day. They prefer gentle morning light over the more harsh, drying afternoon sun.

Ferns also need rich, moisture-retentive soil. They are natives of wooded areas where centuries of falling leaves have broken down to enrich the soil. If your soil is less than perfect, work 3 to 4 inches of compost into the soil where you'll be planting the ferns.

Ferns also prefer areas out of the wind, so planting along a building or fence (especially on the north side) is ideal.

Soil acidity also is important for ferns (see page 23). Most ferns do best in acidic soil (pH 5.5 to 6.5).

Cold Hardiness

Dozens of ferns are hardy to Zone 4 and above, but as a group there are far more ferns that do best in the southern half of the United States and in the temperate, moister regions of the Pacific Northwest.

Read the label carefully to make sure your fern is cold-hardy in your climate.

Ferns That Spread

Many ferns, such as marginal wood fern, remain single plants for years. Others, such as hay-scented fern, spread rapidly and can take over an area if not kept in bounds.

When choosing a fern, check into how quickly it spreads. Spreading can be a plus when you're trying to fill an area but a minus if you want to tuck a plant into a bed where space is limited.

In the right conditions, ferns spread beautifully, filling what would otherwise be a problem shady spot.

BUYER'S GUIDE

WILD FERNS

It's tempting to supplement your garden plantings with some of the beautiful ferns you may see growing wild. But it's not a good idea.

A number of ferns are rare and/or endangered and may be protected by law. In fact, in many states it's against the law to dig up any plant growing on public lands, including ditches along the roadside.

Evergreen Ferns

Most ferns in cold climates are perennials that die back to the ground each fall and send up fresh growth each spring. A few, however, are evergreen all year long in warmer climates. They include asparagus fern, holly fern, mother fern, and Western sword fern.

See the section on ferns starting on page 292 in the back of the book in the Plant Encyclopedia for details.

How to Choose And Design With Bulbs

Bulbs are a welcome part of the mix of plants in a garden. Spring-blooming bulbs such as tulips and daffodils provide color early in the season when few other plants are in flower. Summer-blooming bulbs such as lilies and dahlias are so spectacular that they stand out even when surrounded by other summer flowers.

Say "bulbs" and most people think of spring bloomers such as tulips and daffodils. However, the term *bulbs* can be loosely used to include lilies, cannas, gladiolus, irises, and others that are not strictly bulbs (see "What Is a Bulb?," below).

Spring-blooming bulbs are planted in fall, about the time they show up in garden centers for sale. They are hardy in even the coldest climates and in fact *need* a cold period to bloom. In warm climates where winters don't get cold enough, gardeners need to prechill spring bulbs (see page 162), such as tulips and hyacinths, or purchase prechilled bulbs and plant them in early spring. As a rule, bulbs must be prechilled in Zone 9 and warmer, with the exception of the Northwest.

Tender summer-blooming bulbs, on the other hand, can't take much cold. In most gardens in Zone 7 and colder, these bulbs are planted in spring and many need to be dug up in fall and stored indoors (see page 205). If in doubt, check individual bulb listings in the Plant Encyclopedia, starting on page 292.

For more on growing bulbs, see page 204 for planting information and page 205 on digging and storing tender summer-blooming bulbs.

Orchestrating a Bulb Display

Bulbs have a wide variety of bloom times, heights, and planting depths, making it fun to orchestrate their blooms in long successions that explode with color among your perennials and annuals.

For a year of color from bulbs, check the list on the next page. From autumn crocuses to snowdrops, you can have bulbs that bloom throughout the growing season.

Bulbs are magnificently space-efficient; you can plant them in the same spot as other flowers and even on top of one another. For instance, you can plant several daffodils 6 to 8 inches deep, then plant crocuses above the daffodils.

Bulbs have modest needs for food and water, so they are unlikely to interfere with other flowers planted nearby. Most bulb foliage begins to brown after bloom, and the unattractive foliage *must* be left to replenish the bulb for next year's bloom. Planting bulbs with other plants allows the emerging companion plants to screen the bulb foliage, or at least lets you push down the foliage so it's concealed by the emerging plant. The fresh, emerging foliage of daylilies, for example, will hide daffodils' dying foliage. See page 101 for specific combination ideas.

For information on planting bulbs, see pages 160–163.

A CLOSER LOOK

WHAT IS A BULB?

Some flowers we commonly think of as bulbs really aren't bulbs at all. True bulbs look a little like an onion, with many layers. Lilies, hyacinths, amaryllis, and daffodils, for example, are true bulbs. Others are actually corms, tubers, or rhizomes (see page 160 for planting information). Don't let the terminology throw you, though. They're not treated any differently. Just follow the label directions.

TYPES OF BULBS

Tulip bulb

Crocus corm

Iris rhizome

Anemone tuber

Dahlia tuber

Giant ranunculus tuberous root

Tulips are among the showiest of bulbs. Although they usually last only two or three years, their glowing beauty is worth the effort.

TOOL TIP

BULB PLANTERS

If you'll be planting more than a dozen or so bulbs, you'll want to check out the different kinds of bulb planters now available. These planters make quick work out of tucking dozens or even hundreds of bulbs into your garden, even in the hard, dry soil so common in fall, the time (in cold-winter regions) you plant tulips and daffodils and other spring-blooming bulbs.

Some are simply held in the hand, others you can push with your foot. Peruse the selection at your Home Depot store and always, if in doubt, ask your Home Depot garden associate for help in deciding.

DESIGN TIPS

BULB COMPANIONS

In late spring, the dying foliage of tulips, daffodils, and other bulbs can look tattered. It must be left in place to rejuvenate the bulbs, but it can be camouflaged. One way to do this is to tuck the bulbs among perennials and other plants that will hide the ripening foliage. Sun-loving bulbs can be interplanted with shade-loving plants as long as they're under a deciduous shrub or tree that allows ample sun in spring before the tree is in full leaf.

- Daffodils and hostas
- Daffodils and daylilies
- Daffodils and ferns
- Small bulbs, such as crocuses or grape hyacinths with vinca
- Tulips and forget-me-nots
- Early tulips and columbine
- Early tulips and creeping phlox
- Any small bulbs under a deciduous shrub or tree
- Tulips or hyacinths with lady's mantle
- Ornamental onion and artemisia
- Daffodils or tulips with hardy geraniums

DESIGN TIPS

MAKE A MAP

Spring, when many bulbs are in bloom, is an ideal time to note where the bulbs are so that in fall, when it's time to plant but no evidence of the bulbs remains, you can avoid digging up existing bulbs.

There are several ways to record where your bulbs are. A plant label works well but may become dislodged. Instead, take a photo or draw a rough map of your flower beds in spring so that, come fall, you'll know exactly where the bulbs are located.

A Year of Bulbs

Note: Exact bloom times will vary somewhat by region, especially in late winter and early spring. The sequence of bloom, however, is the same across the country.

Common Name	Botanical Name	Zones
Late-Winter/Early-Spring Flowering		
Crocus	*Crocus* spp.	3–8
Daffodil, early types	*Narcissus* spp.	3–9
Ranunculus	*Ranunculus asiaticus*	7–10
Snowdrops	*Galanthus nivalis*	3–7
Squill	*Scilla* spp.	2–8
Midspring Flowering		
Daffodil, mid and late	*Narcissus* spp.	3–9
Freesia	*Freesia* spp.	8–11
Fritillary; checkered lily	*Fritillaria meleagris*	3–8
Grape hyacinth	*Muscari* spp.	3–8
Tulip, midseason types	*Tulipa* spp.	3–7
Windflower	*Anemone* spp.	Varies
Late-Spring Flowering		
Fritillary; crown imperial	*Fritillaria imperialis*	5–8
Gladiolus	*Gladiolus* hybrids	8–11
Hyacinth	*Hyacinthus orientalis*	3–11
Iris	*Iris* spp.	Varies
Lily-of-the-valley	*Convallaria majalis*	3–7
Tulip, late	*Tulipa* spp.	3–7
Early-Summer Flowering		
Calla lily	*Zantedeschia aethiopica*	8–11
Cyclamen, hardy	*Cyclamen hederifolium*	7–9
Gladiolus	*Gladiolus* hybrids	8–11
Lily, Asiatic	*Lilium* spp.	3–9
Society garlic	*Tulbaghia violacea*	8–11
Mid- through Late-Summer Flowering		
Begonia, tuberous	*Begonia ×tuberhybrida*	9–11
Caladium	*Caladium bicolor*	8–11
Canna	*Canna* hybrids	7–11
Crocosmia	*Crocosmia ×crocosmiiflora*	5–10
Dahlia	*Dahlia* spp.	8–11
Gladiolus	*Gladiolus* hybrids	8–11
Gladiolus, Abyssinian	*Gladiolus callianthus*	7–11
Lilies, Oriental and Easter	*Lilium* spp.	3–9
Naked ladies	*Lycoris squamigera*	5–8
Autumn Flowering		
Begonia, tuberous	*Begonia ×tuberhybrida*	9–11
Caladium	*Caladium bicolor*	8–11
Canna	*Canna* hybrids	7–11
Crocus, Autumn	*Colchicum autumnale*	5–9
Dahlia	*Dahlia* spp.	8–11
Gladiolus	*Gladiolus* hybrids	8–11

Specialty Gardening

Gardens are as varied as the people who create them. Some are in dry areas, others in shade. Some require plantings that always look good for guests; others demand fun, safe plantings for children. In this chapter, you'll get

Chapter 4 Specialty Gardening

a wealth of ideas for creating the kind of garden that you, your site, and your lifestyle demand. It will help you start a garden that is as unique as you are.

Entry and Front Gardens

4

Specialty Gardening

GOOD IDEA!

ALWAYS BEAUTIFUL

Brighten entries in winter by inserting boughs of cut evergreens into the soil of window boxes and pots. The greenery adds a fresh, welcoming touch for months in cold climates.

Whether it's your front door or the side door you use when returning from work every day, you can create a cheerful, welcoming approach to your home with a few simple touches and a wealth of flowers.

Clean Up Your Act

Set the stage for new plantings with a little home improvement. Steady any wobbly railings, give the front door a fresh coat of paint, put out a welcoming doormat, and invest in an attractive mailbox. If there's room, set out a good-quality bench or chair. Even if you never use this furniture, it has a beckoning quality that makes the space more inviting. These small touches add to the beauty and sense of well-being in your home.

An interesting front walk, thoughtful plantings, several potted plants, and a comfortable seat make an entry irresistible.

Use Bright Colors

Because the entry is viewed first from far off, it's a smart strategy to use strong colors there. Brightly colored flowers are eye-catching and help announce, "This is the entrance." Red is an especially warm and welcoming color at a front entry—one of the reasons that so many front doors are painted red. Blue flowers can get lost visually when viewed from a distance. Use them as elements that are part of a closer look.

Use Containers Liberally

A big pot or planter filled with flowers on either side of the door is a classic. Line the steps with pots too. Use varying sizes for interest, making sure the pots work together as a group. Give them a unifying theme, such as the material (clay, concrete, wood) or the color.

Flank That Door

An easy way to add drama around the entry is to put something matched and striking on either side of the door—two columnar evergreens, two large pots filled with brightly flowering plants, or two distinctive shrubs. This further emphasizes the door and adds a pleasant symmetry.

Have Fun with Accessories

An entry is the ideal place for practical and pretty accessories. A bench beckons visitors to come closer, and it's a practical place to set down a parcel or a bag of groceries. Small sculptures, wreaths, swags, a decorative door knocker, and other touches all say that the people who live here care about their home and have put some thought into welcoming you to it.

Light Up Your Life

Low-voltage outdoor lighting is perfect for illuminating walks and plantings in your front yard. It lets you and your guests enjoy your flowers after dark, creates a dramatic effect, and softly lights up steps and paths to prevent falls. Look for uplighting to tuck under shrubs to light the sides of your home and footlights to line a path.

The classic yard light requires more elaborate wiring (you'll probably want to hire a professional), but it can make a walk safer and more secure. It's also an ideal support for a small flowering vine, such as clematis.

Break Out of the Mold

Flower gardens are often relegated to the backyard, and the front yard has only staid foundation shrubs, a tree or two,

A front patio equipped with table and chairs makes the perfect evening spot from which to say hello to neighbors and watch the world go by.

and lawn. Yet a front yard may get the most sun, which makes it a logical location for an herb garden or a flower garden. A good way to start is to line the front walk with flower beds, each at least 3 feet wide. With permission from the city, you can even turn the strip between the sidewalk and street into a delightful flower garden.

Enjoy Your Front Yard

Many homeowners neglect to take advantage of their front yard to relax and enjoy it. Instead, they spend time in the backyard.

The front yard has a charm all its own. If space permits, a porch swing is a comfortable place to relax with a cold drink and get acquainted with neighbors strolling by. Even in a limited space, a small outdoor table with one or two chairs can make a mini retreat, the perfect place to savor a cup of coffee with the morning paper or enjoy a glass of wine after a long day at work.

If there's no space on a front porch, consider creating an informal patio in the front yard with flagstones or pavers. It need be only 8 feet or so across to accommodate a table and chairs, expanding your outdoor living space considerably.

If privacy is a concern, plant fast-growing tall shrubs, such as lilacs, junipers, or spirea, or dense, small trees such as saucer magnolia or dogwoods for a living fence.

Gardening With Children

Children and gardens are a natural combination. Children love being outside and exploring nature, so your backyard is the perfect spot for them to play and learn.

Take It Easy

Many children have grown up disliking gardening because a parent forced them to weed, water, and do other garden chores. As much as is reasonable and fair, avoid forcing your hobby on your child. (Save their energy for washing dishes and cleaning their room.) They'll learn a lot simply by being outside with you and casually observing.

As the summer progresses, these pole bean vines will sprawl over this colorful children's tepee, creating a one-of-a-kind hideaway.

Toys for Gardening

Good children's garden tools encourage garden play. Look for appropriately sized buckets, hoes, rakes, spades, wheelbarrows, wagons, and other tools that encourage kids to have fun digging in the dirt, gathering leaves, or poking away at a weed patch.

Inexpensive plastic tools are fine, especially for very young children. Elementary-age children, however, can have even more fun with metal and wood tools that can get down to business. And the children might actually provide a little help.

Get 'Em Going

Playing outside among plants fosters a love of gardening. Here are some ideas to get your children started.

- Let them cut away. Give your child a blunt-end scissors and permission to go out and cut any, say, 10 flowers. Then let him or her arrange the flowers in a jar or vase.
- Create a personal garden. This tried-and-true favorite works. Give a child a space of his or her own to plant, even if it's just a large flower pot and some seeds.
- Make a fort/playhouse/hideout. Remember that empty space behind the lilacs? Pull the weeds and tote out a few weather-resistant child's chairs or boxes. You'll create a play space for them they'll remember all their lives.
- Grow a sunflower house. Plant giant sunflower seeds in a rectangle in a sunny spot, leaving a space for the door. Once the sunflowers have germinated, plant morning glories alongside. The sunflowers grow up for walls and the morning glories clamber overhead for a delightful living "house."
- Plant a bean tepee. Prop several 8-foot bamboo poles or slender limbs together tepee fashion and tie at the top. Plant at the base with pole beans, hyacinth beans, morning glories, or other fast-growing annual vines to grow an inviting play space.
- Plant a gourd tunnel. Bend a length of 6-foot hog or other livestock wire into a half circle and insert the cut ends into the ground. Plant along each cut end with gourd seeds. The foliage covers the tunnel, and the gourds, as they mature, hang down inside the tunnel.

Great Plants for Kids

Some plants are more intriguing to kids than others. Here are some of the best for pint-size gardeners:

- Big plants. Kids love things that grow fast. Giant sunflowers, morning glories, tall zinnias, and giant pumpkins wow 'em.
- Tasty treats. Just like adults, kids get excited about growing things they know they like. Good choices include strawberries, watermelons, sweet cherries, raspberries, blueberries, and just about anything else that's sweet.
- Interactive plants. Everything is more intriguing if you can play with it. Soft woolly lamb's ears feel good to stroke. Sensitive plant closes up when touched. Herbs release their scent when rubbed, as do scented geraniums, which have fascinating smells such as chocolate and lemon.
- Houseplants. Some kids become as attached to their houseplants as they are to a pet. Let them paint and decorate the pot. Keep the plant in the child's room and give him or her responsibility for watering it (with some reminding, perhaps).

This children's garden is inspired by a pizza, both in shape and plants. It's filled with basil, tomatoes, parsley, oregano, thyme, peppers, onions, and other key ingredients of a child's favorite treat.

A CLOSER LOOK

SAFETY CONSIDERATIONS

A landscape that is welcoming to children is also a safe landscape. Keep in mind the following:

- Design water gardens for safety. Opt for a fountain or a spray of water over stones. Even a water garden just a few inches deep poses a drowning hazard (think of a half-filled wading pool). Plus, liners become slick with mosses and algae, which can cause children to lose their footing. Even container water gardens that kids will be around should be filled with small stones, because a toddler who falls in a large container of water could drown.
- Avoid poisonous plants. Nearly any plant can be toxic if a certain part is ingested in enough quantity. (The leaves of rhubarb, for example, are toxic, whereas the stems are edible.) But some plants that are particularly alluring to children can be fatal even in small quantities. They include castor bean seeds, wisteria seeds, the berries produced by jasmine and lantana, and bittersweet, which has bright orange berries that look like candy. Keep an eye on children young enough to eat plant parts when they're in the garden.
- Avoid plants that scratch skin and tear clothes. Plant soft grasses in play areas so children are cushioned when playing on the ground. Avoid shrubs, especially rugosa roses, that have large thorns.
- Beware of bees. Bees are a valuable part of a garden's ecosystem. But some plants are bee magnets, posing a hazard for children, especially those going barefoot (many bee stings occur when the bee is stepped on). Until the kids get older, avoid these plants, and also plants touted as attracting butterflies. Many of them have nectar that is also irresistible to bees.

Shade Gardening

Even though you have lots of shade, you can still have a varied garden. True, the widest variety of plants—especially those that have colorful flowers—thrive in sunny conditions. But many plants do well in shade, and a shady garden is a relaxing spot on a warm day.

Types of Sun and Shade

Not all shade is the same. The lightly dappled shade underneath the loose, high canopy of a locust tree, for example, is different from the solid shade cast by a tall building or the deep shade underneath a stand of maples.

The basic types of sunlight and shade can be categorized as follows:

- Full sun. This is six or more hours of full, direct (not dappled) sun a day. If plants that need full sun fail to get it, they tend to be weaker and more spindly, have fewer flowers, and are more prone to disease than if they were planted in full sun. Most gardeners overestimate how much sun a spot gets, so keep that in mind.
- Part shade or part sun. These two terms mean the same thing—the area receives at least four hours of direct sun a day. Plants that need part shade or part sun also do well in areas with dappled shade for a large part of the day.

An area with part shade/part sun might receive full sun part of the day and full shade part of the day. Most plants, especially in the hot climates of the South and West, prefer morning sun. It dries the dew off foliage quickly to prevent fungal disease, and is in general kinder to plants than the often-beating afternoon sun.

- Full shade. This is less than four hours a day of sun. In these conditions, plant choice is relatively limited, but it still includes a number of attractive choices, such as lily-of-the-valley, caladium, and azaleas.

How Much Light Do You Get?

Here are other factors that influence how much sunlight an area gets:

- The ever-moving sun. The amount of light an area gets changes over the course of the year. An area might get less sun in spring, more in summer, and less again in fall. Observe patterns of sun and shade in your garden throughout the growing season.

Also be sure to check the area at different times of the day. It may be getting baked in the afternoon but be in full shade in the morning.

- Light levels can also vary as plants leaf out. Areas in full sun in early spring may be in deep shade when surrounding oak and maple trees leaf out. So you can grow sun-loving daffodils underneath your trees in early spring but will have to rule out sun-loving petunias in late spring.
- Large, well-lit areas such as gravel driveways or concrete sidewalks reflect light and increase the effects of the sun.
- The north side of a house is nearly always in part shade.
- Sunlight intensity varies in different parts of the country.

BUYER'S GUIDE

LABELS AND LIGHT LEVELS

When shopping for plants, check the label for light needs. Often you'll see a little sunlike symbol. A full white or yellow symbol means full sun. A symbol that is cut in half or is half black and half white means part sun/part shade. A blackened symbol means full shade.

One of the most beautiful shade-loving plants is the Japanese painted fern.

Even though this yard is shady, the homeowners have successfully created a beautiful garden with limited light. Hostas in a variety of shapes, colors, sizes, and textures predominate.

In the South and the Southwest, plants thrive with more shade than they do in other parts of the country, because the sun is more intense. So the wax begonias that need light shade in Maine do fine in deeper shade in Alabama.

- Intensity also varies with altitude. Plants at high elevations receive more intense sunlight.

Designing a Shade Garden

Often, gardeners with shade try to fight the site or the light. To make gardening easier, work with your climate and site by choosing plants that will thrive in existing conditions.

Here are some issues to keep in mind while designing a shade garden:

- If you're lucky, any trees you're planting underneath will be deep-rooted, and the falling leaves over the years will add valuable organic matter to the soil. If you're less lucky, you'll have to cope with the shallow roots of some trees, such as silver maple and pine, that rob surrounding plants of moisture. For these conditions, choose plants that thrive in dry shade (see chart on page 116).
- Plant around shallow roots. Depending on the size of the tree and the size of the roots, you may be able to cut off small roots. (Cutting off too many roots will damage the tree.) If in doubt, ask your Home Depot garden center associate.
- You may be tempted to build raised beds on top of problem roots, but mounding additional soil on tree roots can harm the tree.
- In areas with oak or walnut trees, the soil may be acidic. Choose plants that thrive in acid soils and shade, such as azaleas, hollies, hydrangeas, and rhododendrons.
- You can create a bit more sun by cutting off the lower limbs of trees, allowing in more light.

For more information on gardening in shade and sun, see page 24.

A CLOSER LOOK

LISTEN TO YOUR PLANTS

Plants will let you know when something is wrong. In the case of getting the right light, they'll tell you when they're getting too much or too little.

If a plant is getting too much sun, it will wilt (even shortly after being watered). It may have whitish burn marks or crispy brown marks, as though it had been fried.

If a plant is getting too much shade, its growth may be tall, weak, and spindly. Stems may lean toward the light. Foliage and flowers may be sparse.

Plants That Thrive in Shade

Deep shade, part shade, dappled shade, half shade—gardeners seem to recognize as many kinds of shade as Eskimos do snow. The plants on this list will all thrive in partial shade, and some even require it.

* Thrives even in deep shade with four hours or less of sun a day or several hours of dappled shade a day.

+ Will do well under deciduous trees because plants grow and bloom before the trees leaf out and cast much shade.

4

Specialty Gardening

Common Name	Botanical Name	Zones
Annuals and Perennials		
Agapanthus	*Agapanthus* spp.	8-10
Ajuga	*Ajuga* spp.	3-9
Amethyst flower	*Browallia speciosa*	Annual
*Arum, Italian	*Arum italicum*	6-10
*Astilbe	*Astilbe* spp.	3-8
Begonia, hardy	*Begonia grandis*	6-10
Begonia, wax	*Begonia ×semperflorens-cultorum*	Annual
*Bleeding heart	*Dicentra* spp.	3-9
Brunnera, heart-leaf	*Brunnera macrophylla*	3-8
*Bugbane	*Cimicifuga* spp.	3-8
Cardinal flower	*Lobelia* spp.	2-9
*Cast iron plant	*Aspidistra elatior*	8-10
*Christmas rose	*Helleborus niger*	3-9
*Coleus	*Solenostemum scuttellarioides*	Annual
Columbine	*Aquilegia* spp.	3-9
Coral bells	*Heuchera sanguinea*	3-9
Corydalis	*Corydalis* spp.	4-8
Cupflower	*Nierembergia* spp.	Annual
Cyclamen, hardy	*Cyclamen hederifolium*	7-9
Daylily	*Hemerocallis* spp.	3-10
Dead nettle, spotted	*Lamium maculatum*	3-9
*Epimedium	*Epimedium* spp.	4-9
Ferns (see pages 374-378 for descriptions of individual types)		Varies
Flowering tobacco	*Nicotiana* spp.	Annual
Foam Flower, Allegheny	*Tiarella cordifolia*	4-9
Forget-me-not, Chinese	*Cynoglossum amabile*	Annual
Forget-me-not, Woodland	*Myosotis sylvatica*	Annual
Foxglove	*Digitalis purpurea*	4-8
Fuchsia	*Fuchsia* spp.	8-10
Geranium, hardy	*Geranium* spp.	3-8
Goatsbeard	*Aruncus dioicus*	3-7
Goldenstar	*Chrysogonum virginianum*	5-9
Hellebore	*Helleborus* spp.	5-9
*Hosta	*Hosta cultivars*	3-8
*Impatiens	*Impatiens* spp.	Annual
Kafir lily; clivia	*Clivia miniata*	9-11
Lady's mantle	*Alchemilla mollis*	4-7
*Lenten rose	*Helleborus orientalis*	4-9
*Ligularia	*Ligularia* spp.	5-8
Lily-of-the-valley	*Convallaria majalis*	3-8
Lilyturf	*Liriope muscari*	7-10
Mimulus	*Mimulus × hybridus*	Annual
Mondo grass	*Ophiopogon japonicus*	7-9
Money plant; honesty	*Lunaria annua*	4-8
Monkshood	*Aconitum* spp.	3-7
Obedient plant	*Physostegia virginiana*	2-9
Pansy	*Viola ×wittrockiana*	Annual
Phlox, creeping	*Phlox stolonifera*	2-8
*Pigsqueak; Bergenia	*Bergenia* spp.	3-8
Primrose	*Primula* spp.	5-8
*Pulmonaria; Lungwort	*Pulmonaria saccharata*	3-8
Queen-of-the-prairie	*Filipendula rubra*	3-8
Salvia, annual red	*Salvia splendens*	Annual
Sweet alyssum	*Lobularia maritima*	Annual
*Sweet woodruff	*Galium odoratum*	4-8
Trillium	*Trillium* spp.	4-8
Turtlehead, pink	*Chelone lyonii*	3-8
Vinca; periwinkle	*Vinca* spp.	Varies
Violet	*Viola* spp.	Varies
*Virginia bluebells	*Mertensia virginica*	3-7
Wishbone flower	*Torenia fournieri*	Annual

Lily-of-the-valley

Goldenstar

Common Name	Botanical Name	Zones
Broad-Leaved Evergreens		
Aucuba, Japanese	*Aucuba japonica*	7–10
Boxwood	*Buxus* spp.	Varies
Daphne	*Daphne* spp.	Varies
Euonymus, Japanese	*Eunoymus japonica*	7–9
Gardenia	*Gardenia jasminoides*	8–10
Holly	*Ilex* spp.	Varies
Honeysuckle, Royal Carpet	*Lonicera pileata*	5–9
*Laurel, cherry	*Prunus laurocerasus*	6–9
Leucothoe, drooping	*Leucothoe fontanesiana*	5–8
Magnolia, southern	*Magnolia grandiflora*	6–10
Mahonia	*Mahonia* spp.	Varies
Mountain laurel	*Kalmia latifolia*	4–9
Pieris	*Pieris* spp.	Varies
Pittosporum, Japanese	*Pittosporum tobira*	8–10
*Rhododendrons and azaleas	*Rhododendron* spp. and hybrids	Varies
*Skimmia, Japanese	*Skimmia japonica*	6–9
Sweet olive	*Osmanthus* spp.	8–9
Viburnum, sweet	*Viburnum odoratissimum*	8–10

continued on next page

Goldflame honeysuckle

For a list of deciduous trees that do well in shade, see page 69.
For a list of shrubs that do well in shade, see page 76.
For a list of groundcovers that do well in shade, see page 87.

Plants That Thrive in Shade *continued*

Star jasmine

* Thrives even in deep shade with four hours or less of sun a day or several hours of dappled shade a day.

\+ Will do well under deciduous trees because plants grow and bloom before the trees leaf out and cast much shade.

Common Name	Botanical Name	Zones
Conifers		
Cryptomeria, Japanese	*Cryptomeria japonica*	6–8
False cypress	*Chamaecyparis* spp.	Varies
Incense cedar	*Calocedrus decurrens*	5–8
Hemlock, Canada	*Tsuga canadensis*	3–7
*Podocarpus; yew pine	*Podocarpus macrophyllus*	8–10
Spruce, white	*Picea glauca*	2–6
*Yew	*Taxus* spp.	4–7
*Yew, Japanese plum	*Cephalotaxus harringtonia*	6–9

Hardy cyclamen

Caladium

Common Name	Botanical Name	Zones
Vines		
Clematis, large-flowered	*Clematis ×hybrida*	3–9
Clematis, sweet autumn	*Clematis ternifolia*	4–9
*Cross vine	*Bignonia capreolata*	6–9
Honeysuckle, goldflame	*Lonicera ×heckrottii*	4–9
Hydrangea, climbing	*Hydrangea petiolaris*	4–7
*Ivy, English	*Hedera helix*	5–9
Jasmine, Madagascar	*Stephanotis floribunda*	10–11
Jasmine, star	*Trachelospermum jasminoides*	8–10
Silver lace vine	*Polygonum aubertii*	4–9
Trumpet creeper	*Campsis radicans*	4–9
*Virginia creeper	*Parthenocissus quinquefolia*	4–9

Columbine

Tuberous Begonia, 'Nonstop' hybrids

* Thrives even in deep shade with 4 hours or less of sun a day or several hours of dappled shade a day.

+ Will do well under deciduous trees because plants grow and bloom before the trees leaf out and cast much shade.

Common Name	Botanical Name	Zones
Bulbs		
Agapanthus	*Agapanthus* hybrids	8–10
*Begonia, tuberous	*Begonia ×tuberhybrida*	10–11
*Caladium	*Caladium bicolor*	8–11
+Crocus	*Crocus* spp.	3–8
Cyclamen, hardy	*Cyclamen hederifolium*	7–9
+Daffodil	*Narcissus* spp.	3–8
Naked ladies	*Lycoris squamigera*	5–9
+Squill	*Scilla* spp.	2–8

Common Name	Botanical Name	Zones
Plants That Compete Well With Shallow Tree Roots		
*Aucuba, Japanese	*Aucuba japonica*	7–10
Dead nettle, spotted	*Lamium maculatum*	3–9
Euonymus, Japanese	*Eunoymus japonica*	7–9
*Ivy, English	*Hedera helix*	5–9
Kerria, Japonica	*Kerria japonica*	5–9
*Pigsqueak, bergenia	*Bergenia*	3–8
*Sweet woodruff	*Galium odoratum*	4–8
Vinca, littleaf	*Vinca minor*	4–8

Virginia Bluebells

Double-flowered Japanese Kerria

Drought-Tolerant Gardens

4

Specialty Gardening

Like many drought-tolerant plants, artemisia sports silvery foliage.

BUYER'S GUIDE

A WALK ON THE DRY SIDE

You can conserve water by choosing drought-tolerant plants. Plants that use less water tend to have at least one of the following characteristics:

- **Silver leaves**
- **Hairy or furry leaves**
- **Thick, waxy, succulent leaves**
- **Thorns**
- **Small, fine-textured leaves**

No matter where you live, following basic water-smart gardening practices will save you money and time. Sometimes referred to as xeriscaping, water-conserving gardening doesn't mean your garden needs to look like a desert. Rather, it means making the most of your watering time and dollar. Here's how:

Reduce Lawn Space

Most lawns need water, and plenty of it. Minimize lawn area by installing patios and decks in high-use spots near the house. Farther out, create beds and borders filled with drought-tolerant small trees, shrubs, and perennials.

Turn grassy slopes into rock or terraced gardens. Avoid growing grass in shady areas under trees; instead plant those areas as woodland gardens full of low, drought-tolerant groundcovers such as periwinkle, forget-me-not, or hosta.

Prepare Good Soil

Create the richest, most moisture-retentive soil you can. Good, crumbly soil helps water trickle down deeper, so plants develop deep, strong root systems.

The key to improving soil is working in plenty of compost at the time you create a new bed, spreading 6 inches or more of compost on top of the bed, then digging or tilling it in. If you have an existing bed, spread 1 to 2 inches of compost on the ground each spring, then scratch it in among the plants. (See page 136 for more soil improvement tips.)

Mulch Well

Mulching in summer suppresses weeds and keeps the soil cool and moist, minimizing the need to water. Beds do best with 1 to 3 inches (any more and you'll suffocate them) of mulch (see page 184 for more information). Mulch around trees out to their dripline—that is, as far as their branches spread.

Group Plants

Save yourself work by grouping together plants that need more water, and put them close to the house—and the outdoor faucet. Moisture-lovers include hydrangeas, impatiens, lungwort, azaleas, astilbe, and hibiscus. Put plants that need less water together as well, and farther from the house, if desired.

Use the Shade

If you live in a hot region, especially Zone 7 or warmer (see page 26), plants will need more shade than they do in other parts of the country. They particularly like afternoon shade. Limiting afternoon sun is especially important for plants in pots, window boxes, and other containers.

Have the Right Tools

Sprinklers are not expensive, so keep two or three on hand. Have one that will cover a large area and one or two that will cover small or odd-shaped areas. A timer will allow you to set sprinklers to water before sunrise in order to minimize evaporation.

Stock up on garden hoses, too, so you have one for each outdoor faucet and can reach every corner of your landscape.

Water wands and watering cans are essential for potted plants and spot watering.

Check Into an Irrigation System

In arid Western states, an irrigation system is a must to keep plants alive during the months with no rain. In other parts of the country, it's less critical but still useful, saving money and time.

Check out the do-it-yourself irrigation supplies at your local Home Depot. It may be unnecessary to equip your whole yard, but you might find ways to minimize the most problematic areas. Also, there are irrigation systems specifically for container gardens. If you have a number of pots, one of them could be a huge timesaver.

Even annuals can be drought tolerant. This established planting of purple globe amaranth, annual blue salvia, annual geraniums, and marigolds needs minimal water.

Drought-Tolerant Plants

The following is a list of plants that do well in dry conditions. However, what gardeners in Maine might call dry is different than what gardeners in New Mexico might call dry. The plants below will do well for fairly dry conditions in the zones (see page 26) listed. In the warmer range of their zones, they will need more watering than they would in the cooler range of their zones.

Skyrocket Juniper

Common Name	Botanical Name	Zones
Drought-Tolerant Trees		
Acacia, Bailey	*Acacia baileyana*	8–10
Ash, green	*Fraxinus pennsylvanica*	3-9
Bald cypress	*Taxodium distichum*	4-10
Bay, sweet bay	*Laurus nobilis*	8-11
Birch, river	*Betula nigra*	4-9
Birch, Whitespire	*Betula mandschurica japonica* 'Whitespire'	4–7
Buckeye, California	*Aesculus californica*	6-10
Buckeye, Ohio	*Aesculus glabra*	3-7
Cedar, blue atlas	*Cedrus libani* 'Glauca'	6-9
Cedar, deodar	*Cedrus deodara*	6-9
Crape myrtle	*Lagerstroemia indica*	7-9
Cypress	*Cupressus* spp.	Varies
Desert willow	*Chilopsis linearis*	8-9
Elm, Chinese	*Ulmus parvifolia*	5-9
Fir, white	*Abies concolor*	3-7
Ginkgo	*Ginkgo biloba*	3-9
Hawthorn, Washington	*Crataegus phaenopyrum*	3-9
Honey locust, thornless	*Gleditsia triacanthos var. inermis*	3-8
Incense cedar	*Calocedrus decurrens*	5-8
Junipers	*Juniperus* spp.	Varies
Linden, silver	*Tilia tomentosa*	3-7
Magnolia, southern	*Magnolia grandiflora*	6-10
*Mahonia, leatherleaf	*Mahonia bealei*	6-9
Maple, Amur	*Acer tartaricum* ssp. *ginnala*	2-6
Maple, Norway	*Acer platanoides*	3-7
Maple, red	*Acer rubrum*	3-9
Maple, silver	*Acer saccharinum*	3-9
Mesquite	*Prosopis glandulosa*	10-11
Mountain ash, European	*Sorbus aucuparia*	3-6
Oak, bur	*Quercus macrocarpa*	2-8
Oak, pin	*Quercus palustris*	4-8
Oak, white	*Quercus alba*	4-9
Oak, willow	*Quercus phellos*	4-8
Olive	*Olea europaea*	8-10
Pagoda tree, Japanese	*Sophora japonica*	6-8
Palo verde	*Cercidium*	9-10
Pine, Austrian	*Pinus nigra*	4-7
Pine, Jack	*Pinus banksiana*	2-6
Pine, Japanese black	*Pinus thunbergii*	5-7
Pine, mugo	*Pinus mugo*	2-7
Pine, Scotch	*Pinus sylvestris*	3-7
Pine, white	*Pinus strobus*	3-8
Pistachio	*Pistacia chinensis*	6-9
Redbud	*Cercis canadensis*	3-9
Russian olive	*Elaeagnus angustifolia*	3-8
Serviceberry, shadblow	*Amelanchier* spp.	3-8
Sugarberry; hackberry	*Celtis* spp.	Varies
Yellowwood	*Cladrastis lutea*	6-8
Yuccas	*Yucca* spp.	4-10
Drought-Tolerant Annuals and Perennials		
Agapanthus	*Agapanthus* spp.	8-10
Agave	*Agave* spp.	8-11
Aloe	*Aloe* spp.	8-11
Artemisia	*Artemisia* spp.	Varies
Baby's breath	*Gypsophila paniculata*	3-9
Basket-of-gold	*Aurinia saxatilis*	4-8
Bear's breeches	*Acanthus mollis*	6-10
Black-eyed Susan	*Rudbeckia fulgida*	3-10
Blanket flower	*Gaillardia ×grandiflora*	2-10
Blazing star	*Liatris spicata*	3-9
Butter daisy	*Melampodium leucanthum*	Annual
Butterfly weed	*Asclepias tuberosa*	4-10
California poppy	*Eschscholzia californica*	Annual
Catmint	*Nepeta ×faasenii*	4-9
Coneflower, purple	*Echinacea purpurea*	3-9
Coreopsis	*Coreopsis* spp.	4-9
Cosmos	*Cosmos* spp.	Annual
Echeveria (most)	*Echeveria* spp.	8-11
Euphorbia (most)	*Euphorbia* spp.	Varies
Evening primrose, showy	*Oenothera speciosa*	3-9
False sunflower	*Heliopsis helianthoides*	4-9
Feather grass	*Stipa* spp.	Varies
Flax	*Linum perenne*	5-8
Flax, New Zealand	*Phormium tenax*	8-11
Fountain grass	*Pennisetum alopecuroides*	5-9
Gaura	*Gaura lindheimeri*	5-9
Geranium, hardy	*Geranium sanguineum*	3-8
Iris, bearded	*Iris ×germanica*	3-10
Lamb's ears	*Stachys byzantina*	4-8

4

Specialty Gardening

Drought-Tolerant Plants

Common Name	Botanical Name	Zones
Lavender, English	*Lavandula angustifolia*	5–8
Love-in-a-mist	*Nigella damascena*	Annual
Marigold	*Tagetes* spp.	Annual
Mexican sunflower	*Tithonia rotundifolia*	Annual
Moss rose	*Portulaca grandiflora*	Annual
Muhly grass	*Muhlenbergia* spp.	7–10
Naked ladies	*Amaryllis belladonna*	5–9
Penstemon	*Penstemon* spp. (many)	Varies
Poppy	*Papaver* spp.	Varies
Pot marigold	*Calendula officinalis*	Annual
Red-hot poker	*Kniphofia uvaria*	5–9
Red valerian	*Centranthus ruber*	4–8
Russian sage	*Perovskia atriplicifolia*	3–9
Santolina	*Santolina chamaecyparisus*	6–9
Sea lavender	*Limonium perezii*	8–11
Sea thrift	*Armeria maritima*	3–8
Sedums; stonecrop	*Sedum* spp.	4–9
Snow-in-summer	*Cerastium tomentosum*	3–7
Spider flower	*Cleome hasslerana*	Annual
Spurge, cushion	*Euphorbia polychroma*	4–8
Statice	*Limonium* spp.	Varies
Strawflower	*Helichrysum bracteatum*	Annual
Sunflower	*Helianthus annuus*	Annual
Swan river daisy	*Brachycome iberidifolia*	Annual
Verbena (most)	*Verbena* spp.	Varies
Yarrow	*Achillea* spp.	3–9
Yucca	*Yucca* spp.	4–10
Zinnia	*Zinnia elegans*	Annual
Zinnia, narrow-leaf	*Zinnia angustifolia*	Annual

Catmint

Common Name	Botanical Name	Zones
Drought-Tolerant Vines		
Bittersweet, American	*Celastrus scandens*	3-8
Black-Eyed Susan vine	*Thunbergia alata*	Annual
Boston ivy	*Parthenocissus tricuspidata*	4-8
Bougainvillea	*Bougainvillea*	9–10
Euonymus, wintercreeper	*Euonymus fortunei*	4-8
Firethorn	*Pyracantha coccinea*	6-9
Honeysuckle, trumpet	*Lonicera sempervirens*	4-9
Morning glory	*Ipomoea tricolor*	Annual
Porcelain berry vine	*Ampelopsis brevipedunculata*	4-8
Silver lace vine	*Polygonum aubertii*	4-9
Trumpet creeper	*Campsis radicans*	4-9
Virginia creeper	*Parthenocissus quinquefolia*	4-9
Wistera	*Wisteria* spp.	5-9

Weihenstephaner Gold Kamchatka sedum

Drought-Tolerant Bulbs

Allium; ornamental onion	*Allium* spp.	4–10
Amaryllis	*Hippeastrum* spp.	7–11
Crocosmia	Crocosmia ×*crocosmiiflora*	6–9
Crocus	*Crocus* spp.	3–8
Iris, German bearded	*Iris* hybrids	3–10
Iris, African	*Dietes iridioides*	8–10
Peruvian lily	*Alstroemeria* spp.	6–10
Society garlic	*Tulbaghia violacea*	8–11
Tulip	*Tulipa* spp.	3–7

For a list of drought-tolerant groundcovers, see page 87
For a list of drought-tolerant shrubs, see page 77

Rock Gardening

Hens and chicks are a low-growing, tough succulent that spreads well and is a beautiful, heat- and cold-tolerant addition to a rock garden.

A rock garden can be as elaborate as dozens of giant boulders embedded in a hillside or as simple as a small arrangement of modest-size rocks in a favored spot in your backyard.

A serious rock garden incorporates precise layers of gravel and grit with a careful selection of stones and a knowledgeable positioning of plants around those stones. But even beginners can get in on the fun with smaller, less complicated rock gardens. After all, rock gardens are simply an interesting way to incorporate beautiful stones into your yard, creating the ideal climate for plants that thrive with excellent drainage.

Planning a Rock Garden

Find a site in your garden where a rock garden would look natural. Slopes are an ideal location. But even if you have a flat site, you can create a raised bed of stone, or work in rock garden plants between flat pavers laid flush with the ground.

For inspiration, check out naturally occurring stone formations in your area. Notice how the rocks are positioned, what size they are, how they fit into the terrain, and how plants grow in the formations. Replicate that look on a smaller scale in your own rock garden.

Whenever possible, use local stone. It will look more natural in your part of the country, and it's likely to create better growing conditions for plants native to your area, making a lower-maintenance garden. Use the same stone throughout your garden for a uniform look.

Tufa is considered the stone of choice among rock-garden aficionados, but it's expensive and local only in a few tropical areas. Working with sandstone and limestone is good because they weather well and are porous enough to retain moisture. Irregularly shaped stones make the most interesting rock gardens. Rounded boulders and river rocks lack the character of craggier stones, making them less desirable in a rock garden.

Building and Planting a Rock Garden

If you will be including alpine plants, which demand perfect drainage and precise microclimates, or if you're creating a flat rock garden, put a drainage layer behind or beneath your rock garden. Dig out a 6-inch layer of soil (save it to backfill later), and fill the area with broken bricks, stones, sand, gravel, and similar loose material.

Top the fill with the stones you've chosen, arranging them carefully to achieve a natural look. Many stones look best if buried by one- to two-thirds. Wear heavy leather gloves and sturdy shoes or boots when working with stone.

Very large stones require the help of a friend or two. Extremely large stones are best left to the professionals. (Ask the home and garden center or landscaping company from which you purchased the stones if they will position some or all of them for you for a fee.)

Backfill with topsoil, working it around your arranged stones. For the top 6 inches or so of the rock garden, mix special soil, consisting of one part topsoil, one part compost, and one part grit or stone chips. This soil mixture ensures the perfect combination of fertile soil and excellent drainage.

When planting, consider the position of the plant in relation to the stones. Plants that sprawl or drape, such as creeping phlox or creeping thyme, look best if given stones to flow over. Plants that prefer shade or cooler conditions will do better on the north side of a large stone, whereas plants that like it warmer and sunnier will thrive on the south side. Stone absorbs heat during the day and releases it during the evening, a plus for heat-loving plants.

Add interest to rock gardens with an occasional vertical element, such as an upright evergreen. Most rock garden plants are low growers, so breaking up the overall profile creates a more dynamic garden.

Good Rock Garden Plants

Common Name	Botanical Name	Zones
Agapanthus	*Agapanthus* spp.	8–10
Allium; ornamental onion	*Allium* spp.	4–10
Basket-of-gold	*Aurinia saxatilis*	4–8
Bellflower	*Campanula* spp.	Varies
Bleeding heart	*Dicentra* spp.	2–9
Broom	*Cytisus* spp.; *Genista* spp.	Varies
Candytuft	*Iberis* spp.	4–8
Columbine	*Aquilegia* spp.	3–9
Conifers, dwarf	Various	Varies
Geranium, hardy	*Geranium sanguineum*	4–8
Crocus	*Crocus* spp.	3–8
Daffodil	*Narcissus* spp.	3–8
Grape hyacinth	*Muscari* spp.	3–8
Heather, Scotch	*Calluna vulgaris*	3–8
Heath	*Erica* spp.	4–8
Hens and chicks	*Sempervivum tectorum*	4–10
Junipers, various	*Juniperus* spp.	Varies
Moss rose	*Portulaca grandiflora*	Annual
Phlox, Creeping	*Phlox stolonifera*	2–8
Phlox, moss	*Phlox subulata*	2–9
Pinks, various	*Dianthus* spp.	Varies
Rock rose	*Cistus ×hybridus*	8–10
Rockcress, false	*Aubrieta deltoidea*	4–8
Rosemary	*Rosmarinus officinalis*	7–10
Sea thrift	*Armeria* spp.	3–8
Sedum, various	*Sedum* spp.	3–10
Squill	*Scilla* spp.	2–8
Thyme, Creeping	*Thymus* spp.	5–9
Tulip	*Tulipa* spp.	3–7
Yarrow	*Achillea* spp.	3–9

Cut Flowers From Your Garden

Even a small garden, if well designed, can provide lots of flowers to bring indoors. With some smart planning and a little know-how, you can bring in armloads of flowers and beautiful boughs all year long.

Choosing Good Plants for Arrangements

Nearly any flower, twig, berry, or leaf can be brought indoors and put in a vase. However, some flowers and branches are easier to arrange. Those flowers have the following characteristics:

- Last a long time in the vase, anywhere from a week to three weeks.
- Have sturdy, slender stems that make them easy to arrange.
- Have petals or leaves that are firmly attached and unlikely to fall off.
- Are free of sticky sap that makes them difficult to handle or that fouls the water (such as petunias).
- Stay open for several days. Flowers such as morning glories and daylilies last only a day but hybrid tea roses can last for up to two weeks.
- Have a pleasant or no fragrance. Some plants have a strong scent that is fine outdoors but unpleasant indoors, such as marigolds and catmint.

Growing Flowers for Cutting

If you have the space, you can indulge in a cutting garden just for flowers to bring indoors. When space is limited, you can still harvest lots of flowers from your regular beds and borders. In fact, cutting them makes your garden prettier, because it encourages flower production.

Another way to grow flowers for cutting is to plant them in rows in your vegetable garden. This is especially practical with fast-growing annuals planted from seed, such as zinnias and cosmos.

A special garden just for flowers is nice but not necessary. Even a small mixed display garden can provide many bouquets and still look good.

Top Flowers for Cutting

Common Name	Botanical Name	Zones
Aster	*Aster* spp.	4–8
Astilbe	*Astilbe* spp.	3–8
Baby's breath	*Gypsophila paniculata*	3–9
Black-eyed Susan	*Rudbeckia* spp.	3–10
Blazing star	*Liatris spicata*	3–9
Celosia	*Celosia* spp.	Annual
Chrysanthemum	*Chrysanthemum* spp.	4–9
Cosmos	*Cosmos* spp.	Annual
Daffodil	*Narcissus* spp.	3–8
Dahlia	*Dahlia*	8–11
Delphinium	*Delphinium elatum*	2–7
Freesia	*Freesia* spp.	8–11
Gerbera daisy	*Gerbera* spp.	7–10
Gladiolus	*Gladiolus* hybrids	8–11
Goldenrod	*Solidago* hybrids	3–9
Iris, all types	*Iris* spp.	3–10
Larkspur	*Consolida ambigua*	Annual
Lavender, English	*Lavandula angustifolia*	5–8
Lilac	*Syringa* spp.	Varies
Lily	*Lilium* spp.	Varies
Lily-of-the-valley	*Convallaria majalis*	3–7
Lisianthus	*Eustoma grandiflorum*	Annual
Peony	*Paeonia* spp.	2–8
Roses	*Rosa* spp.	Varies
Scabiosa	*Scabiosa caucasica*	3–7
Shasta daisy	*Leucanthemum ×superbum*	4–9
Snapdragon	*Antirrhinum majus*	Annual
Sunflower, annual	*Helianthus annuus*	Annual
Sweet pea	*Lathyrus odoratus*	Annual
Tulip	*Tulipa* spp.	3–7
Yarrow	*Achillea* spp.	3–9
Zinnia	*Zinnia* spp.	Annual

Gardening With Native Plants

Gardening with native plants is a great problem solver.

You no longer have to fight the conditions in your garden; you can celebrate them. Fatal pests and diseases are less likely to strike. Because native plants have naturally adapted to local growing conditions, including extremes of heat and cold, and drought and heavy rainfall, you have to do less to keep the plants healthy.

Many native plants also attract birds, butterflies, and helpful insects to your garden.

And gardening with native plants gives your garden a decided sense of regional style, whether your region is the Southwest, the Rockies, a Southern lowland, or a Great Plains prairie.

This bed of native wildflowers, including yarrow and coneflower, needs little maintenance other than weeding and an occasional watering.

Finding Native Plants

Native plants are specific to particular regions. A plant native to Northern California may not also be native to Southern California, and a plant native to the coast of Georgia may not also be native to the mountains of Georgia.

Because these plants are so specialized, it can be tricky to find them. Ask at your local Home Depot garden center which plants are natives or are their hybridized cousins (see "Talking Naturally" below). Or get online and search "native plants" followed by your state's name, or check with your local cooperative extension service for plant listings.

Remember that native plants are more than only flowers, bulbs, and grasses. They include shrubs, trees, and vines.

And tempting though it may be, avoid digging wild plants to bring into your garden. It's usually prohibited by law, because many wild plants are rare or endangered.

Designing with Native Plants

Native plants can be used in formal, meticulously tended gardens as well as in casual, naturalistic gardens.

In a garden where neatness is important, use the hybridized cousins of natives rather than the true natives to ensure longer bloom time and neater growth habit.

In a more wild-looking garden, true natives often fit in with the sprawling, blowsy look. However, this may look messy in a tight area, such as a small flower bed. True native plantings look more at home when, as in nature, they have room to sprawl, such as all of a sunny front yard or an entire slope.

A CLOSER LOOK

TALKING NATURALLY

There are subtle distinctions between the different types of plants that grow in nature—or are grown as though they were.

Native Plants: Plants indigenous to a region, growing there long before it was settled. These plants have adapted to the extremes of your particular climate, be that heat, humidity, drought, wet, or cold.

Hybrids of Native Plants: Plants that are cousins of the native plant, bred for better performance. Native goldenrod, for example, is prone to mildew, grows tall and rather floppy, and spreads to the point of invasiveness. Its hybridized cultivars grow shorter, are more resistant to mildew, and spread slowly, if at all. The flowers are usually larger and come in a wider variety of colors and forms.

Wildflowers: A loose term that encompasses native flowers as well as non-native flowers that are grown in a naturalistic setting. Wildflowers can include hybridized native plants as well (see page 122 for growing a wildflower meadow).

Naturalized Plants: Plants that are grown in a naturalistic way and often spread, as in lawns or other open areas. They may or may not be native plants. They often grow in untended areas, such as lots and ditches.

Native Plants

The following are plants that are native to a large portion of North America or grow easily in most parts of the country. Check the zone map (page 26) to be sure that the plant will survive in your region.

Common Name	Botanical Name	Zones
Flowers		
Aster	*Aster* spp.	4-8
Bee balm	*Monarda didyma*	4-8
Black-eyed Susan	*Rudbeckia* spp.	3-10
Blanket flower	*Gaillardia* spp.	2-10
Blazing star	*Liatris* spp.	3-9
Butterfly weed	*Asclepias tuberosa*	4-10
California poppy	*Eschscholzia californica*	Annual
Columbine	*Aquilegia* spp.	3-9
Coneflower, purple	*Echinacea purpurea*	3-9
Coreopsis	*Coreopsis* spp.	4-9
Evening primrose, showy	*Oenothera speciosa*	3-9
False indigo, blue	*Baptisia australis*	3-9
Goldenrod	*Solidago* spp.	4-8
Joe-Pye weed	*Eupatorium* spp.	3-10
Penstemon	*Penstemon* spp.	3-7
Queen-of-the-prairie	*Filipendula rubra*	3-8
Sneezeweed	*Helenium autumnale*	3-7
Turtlehead, pink	*Chelone lyonii*	3-8
Virginia bluebells	*Mertensia virginica*	3-7
Yarrow	*Achillea* spp.	3-9

Common Name	Botanical Name	Zones
Shrubs		
Plum, American	*Prunus americana*	4-10
Rhodendrons and azaleas, native types	*Rhododendron* spp.	4-10
Bayberry, northern	*Myrica pensylvanica*	2-6
Potentilla, shrubby	*Potentilla fruticosa*	2-11
Ceanothus	*Ceanothus* spp.	8-10
Dogwood, red-osier	*Cornus stolonifera*	2-8
Mahonia	*Mahonia* spp.	Varies
Mountain laurel	*Kalmia latifolia*	4-9
Holly, winterberry	*Ilex verticillata*	3-9
Trees		
Birch	*Betula* spp.	Varies
Dogwood	*Cornus* spp.	Varies
Maples	*Acer* spp.	Varies
Oaks	*Quercus* spp.	Varies
Redbud	*Cercis canadensis*	3-9
Serviceberry, downy	*Amelanchier arborea*	4-9
Staghorn sumac	*Rhus* spp.	3-8
Tulip tree	*Lirodendron tulipifera*	5-9
Yellowwood, American	*Cladrastis kentukea*	6-8

This type of columbine, a native wildflower that thrives in light shade, will reseed prolifically.

GOOD IDEA!

CHECK ORDINANCES FIRST

If you want to do a highly naturalistic planting, such as a prairie planting in your front yard or native grasses in the strip between the sidewalk and the street, first check local ordinances and laws regarding mowing, pruning, plant height, and overall yard care. As much as possible, comply with the regulations. If the regulations interfere with your plans for a naturalistic planting, talk to city officials. It's better to get clearance in advance than have to mow down—or, worse yet, remove—prized plants.

It also helps to explain your plans to your neighbors to generate goodwill and prevent surprises later.

A Wildflower Meadow Garden

Wildflower gardens are increasingly popular—and for good reason. Once established they require little work, and they tend to attract birds and butterflies. Gardeners are learning to appreciate their casual, easygoing look and are finding ways to incorporate them into their backyards—and sometimes even their front yards.

Some gardeners like to use strictly native plants in their wildflower garden. Others simply include whatever plant or flower lends itself to the casual jumble, especially if it reseeds.

Designing a Wildflower Garden

An open, sunny area is an ideal spot for a meadowlike wildflower garden—a happy mix of colorful, loosely arranged wildflowers. However, many wildflowers like shade, so a shady site is also a candidate for a wildflower garden.

The overall design of a garden with wildflowers can be as simple as many flowers growing together in no real pattern. You can also incorporate wildflowers into even the tidiest of flower beds, although you'll need to choose carefully for a neat growth habit that looks at home in a more cultivated setting. Remember that wildflowers include more than annuals or perennials. Many native flowers are shrubs—easy-to-incorporate natives for your garden.

Choosing Seeds

Wildflower mixes vary widely. Some are a mix of perennials and annuals; others are one or the other. (Perennials take time to establish but are long-lived. Annuals create fast color but are gone in a year unless they reseed.) Other mixes are tailored to certain regions or growing conditions. Read labels carefully and remember that you get what you pay for. The best, most regional wildflower mixes can be pricey.

Planting and Caring for Wildflowers

There's a myth that starting a wildflower garden requires only sprinkling some seeds on the ground, watering them, and watching them grow. Like any garden, wildflower gardens need preparation and care, especially the first year or two. It's in subsequent years that they become nearly maintenance-free.

To start a wildflower garden from seed, first remove existing vegetation and weeds, then work the soil to create a seedbed. Spread the seed and water well. Keep the area moist, and weed by hand. The second year, it's still important to keep the area weeded. That fall or the following spring, mow dead foliage.

After that, your wildflower garden should need little more than annual weeding, mowing, and perhaps reseeding to keep annual flowers going.

Wildflowers by Region

Common Name	Botanical Name
Arid West and Southwest	
Baby blue-eyes	*Nemophila menziesii*
California poppy	*Eschscholzia californica*
Larkspur	*Consolida ambigua*
Mexican hat	*Ratibida columnifera*
Shasta daisy	*Leucanthemum ×superbum*
Florida	
Common rose mallow	*Hibiscus moscheutos*
Coreopsis	*Coreopsis* spp.
Blanket flower	*Gaillardia* spp.
Sea lavender	*Limonium latifolium*
Summersweet	*Clethra alnifolia*
Mountainous West	
Blue flax	*Linum perenne*
Catchfly	*Lychnis alpina*
Columbine	*Aquilegia* spp.
Evening primrose	*Oenothera* spp.
Blanket flower	*Gaillardia* spp.
Larkspur	*Consolida ambigua*
Penstemon	*Penstemon* spp.
Wallflower	*Erysimum* spp.

Common Name	Botanical Name
Northeast/Midwest/Plains	
Aster	*Aster* spp.
Bee balm	*Monarda didyma*
Black-eyed Susan	*Rudbeckia* spp.
Blanket flower	*Gaillardia* spp.
Butterfly weed	*Asclepias tuberosa*
Coreopsis	*Coreopsis* spp.
Dames rocket	*Hesperis matronalis*
Lupine	*Lupinus* hybrids
Purple coneflower	*Echinacea purpurea*
Shirley poppy	*Papaver rhoeas*
Yarrow	*Achillea* spp.
Southeast	
Annual phlox	*Phlox drummondii*
Butterfly weed	*Asclepias tuberosa*
Cosmos	*Cosmos* spp.
Evening primrose	*Oenothera speciosa*
Blanket flower	*Gaillardia* spp.
Moss verbena	*Verbena tenuisecta*
Purple coneflower	*Echinacea purpurea*

Common Name	Botanical Name
Texas/Oklahoma	
Bachelor's button	*Centaurea cyanus*
Spike gayfeather	*Liatris spicata*
Ox-eye daisy	*Heliopsis helianthoides*
Texas bluebonnet	*Lupinus texensis*
Indian paintbrush	*Castilleja coccinea*
Toadflax	*Linaria* spp.
West/Pacific Northwest	
Birds' eyes	*Gilia tricolor*
California bluebell	*Phacelia campanularia*
California poppy	*Eschscholzia californica*
Five spot	*Nemophila maculata*
Blanket flower	*Gaillardia* spp.
Larkspur	*Consollida ambigua*
Shasta daisy	*Leucanthemum ×superbum*
Statice	*Limonium* spp.
Tidy tips	*Layia platyglossa*
Wallflower	*Erysimum* spp.

Landscaping Wooded Areas

Some homeowners think that trying to impose any order on a wooded area is hopeless. Certainly, the trees need to dominate the landscaping, but there are ways to lend color and order to even a heavily wooded lot.

Designing a Woodland Garden

To design a woodland garden, let mature trees be your guide. Dig out small, weedy trees less than 4 inches in diameter. Then step back and see where a path suggests itself. Lay fieldstones along the path as stepping-stones, or put down a 3-inch layer of wood-chip or pine-needle mulch. The path will be more weed-free and permanent if you lay down landscape fabric first.

Once the path is laid out, design and install the planting areas. These may be no more than clusters of colorful plants, such as azaleas or daffodils or columbine. Then create focal points with benches, a sundial, a birdbath, or gazing balls. Remember to keep the accessories simple.

Planting a Woodland Garden

The soil of many woodlands is riddled with tree roots. The best strategy for dealing with shallow roots is to plant between them. If you're doing extensive planting, you may need to remove some roots, but proceed carefully, because you can damage the tree. Avoid cutting roots closer than 1 to 2 yards from the base of a tree, and leave any roots thicker than an inch intact.

Good Plants for Woodland Gardens

Common Name	Botanical Name	Zones
Astilbe	*Astilbe* hybrids	3-8
Aucuba, Japanese	*Aucuba japonica*	7-10
Bleeding heart	*Dicentra* spp.	2-9
Brunnera, heart-leaf	*Brunnera macrophylla*	3-8
Christmas and lenten rose	*Helleborus* spp.	5-9
Columbine	*Aquilegia* spp. and hybrids	3-9
Crocus	*Crocus* spp.	3-8
Daffodil	*Narcissus* spp.	3-8
Fern	Various	Varies
Foamflower	*Tiarella cordifolia*	4-9
Hosta	*Hosta* spp.	3-8
Hydrangea	*Hydrangea* spp.	Varies
Mountain laurel	*Kalmia latifolia*	4-9
Phlox, woodland	*Phlox divaricata*	3-9
Pieris	*Pieris* spp.	Varies
Rhododendrons, azaleas	*Rhododendron* spp.	Varies
Squill	*Scilla* spp.	2-8
Virginia bluebell	*Mertensia virginica*	3-7

Less Is More

Creating a woodland garden primarily involves appreciating what you have. Years of leaf litter will have created rich soil, so there's no need for enriching or mulching.

Choose plants that can do without additional watering, so your woodland garden will be fairly self-sufficient. Water only for the first year to encourage plants to get established. The only real maintenance it may need is an annual pruning or two to remove branches that threaten to fall on anyone walking through. Fallen branches are less of a problem, because they host a variety of beneficial insects and animals.

It's helpful to rake away most of the leaves every other year or so to allow plants to reseed. Also, if problem colonies of plants occur, it's a good idea to dig or pull them a few times a year.

A CLOSER LOOK

COPING WITH DRY SHADE

Most woodland plants love moist, rich soil. However, some trees with shallow roots are water robbers, sucking the moisture out of the soil. In these conditions use plants that are both shade- and drought-tolerant.

A small clearing in a wooded area creates an ideal spot to plant a small-scale shade garden, complete with bench and flagstone path.

Designing a Water Garden

Siting a water garden below a high deck rewards viewers with sights from above and sounds from a small waterfall.

Installing a water garden in your landscape adds entirely new elements—the sound of splashing water, the visually and physically cooling effects of water, the introduction of new and interesting plantings, the fascination of fish, and the creation of a beautiful, restful focal point.

It's little wonder, then, that water gardens have exploded in popularity in recent years. And now, designing and installing your own water garden has never been easier.

Basically, creating a water garden involves digging a hole, putting in a liner, and connecting the garden to a water source. Many a homeowner has begun with a water garden no bigger than their kitchen sink. Building on that first experience, the gardener often installs a second water garden, either replacing the first one with a bigger and better one or creating an additional one.

A water garden should work with the landscape and its style. In a tiny urban garden with lots of potted plants, a container water garden in a large pot might be appropriate. In a wooded area, a small pool fed by a stream and waterfall would be a natural addition. In a small formal garden, a tiered fountain would fit in nicely.

When planning your water garden, ask yourself the following:

- What size? A small pond—about the size of a bathtub—will cost about \$500 to \$600 or so to install, including the liner, an electrical source for the pump, the pump/filter, and the plants, fish, and any edging materials. It will take about a half hour or so a week to maintain.

A medium-size pond—perhaps 10-foot by 12-foot—will cost about \$600 to \$800 or up. It will take about an hour or so a week to maintain.

Larger ponds can easily cost \$1,000 or more and take an hour or two a week to maintain.

- Flexible liner or preformed liner? Preformed liners take some of the pressure off designing a shape, but they limit you in the best shape and depth for your garden.
- Where to put it? Position the water garden in an area where you can sit and enjoy it, either alone or with friends and family. Avoid putting it under a deciduous tree or it can fill with leaves. Shaded gardens have fewer algae problems, however. Also, in warm climates, small water gardens with fish that like cooler water, such as goldfish, can overheat in full sun.
- How deep to make it? You can make your water garden just a few inches deep. If you want fish, it must be at least 18 inches deep.

In climates where winter temperatures reach from -10°F (-23°C) to -20°F (-29°C), at least part of the pond should be 24 inches deep to allow fish to overwinter. In climates where temperatures get to -30°F (-34°C) to -40°F (-40°C), part of the pond should be 30 to 36 inches deep. (An alternative is to use a water heater. See page 131.)

Some water gardens have ledges or shallow portions on which to set water plants that like shallow water. Make these ledges about 10 to 12 inches deep, just enough to let water cover your largest pot.

Some of the most satisfying water gardens are the smallest. With only a few plants and a tub, you can create a water garden in minutes.

A CLOSER LOOK

KIDS AND WATER GARDEN SAFETY

Water attracts children. They can't resist touching it, walking along the side of a pond, bending down and splashing in it.

Whether you have children, grandchildren, or a neighborhood with kids, when planning a water feature you'll want to keep child safety in mind. A toddler can drown in only a few inches of water, especially if that water is combined with an algae-slicked liner.

- Consider incorporating stone or rock into the water feature. In a small pool full of pebbles or river rock, it is nearly impossible for even a small child to come to harm.
- If the area around the water garden will be open, consider installing fencing. Check local planning and zoning regulations. Depending on the size and design of your water feature, you may be required by law to have a fence.
- Position your water garden where you can see it easily from the house so you can keep an eye on it.

BUYER'S GUIDE

WATER GARDEN KITS

An easy way to create your first water garden is to purchase a kit. Whether it uses a flexible or rigid liner, it will include an appropriately sized pump and other elements, making the sometimes complex process of design and installation simple. Be sure to follow package directions exactly and check out pages 128 and 129 for helpful installation tips.

Water Garden Depth

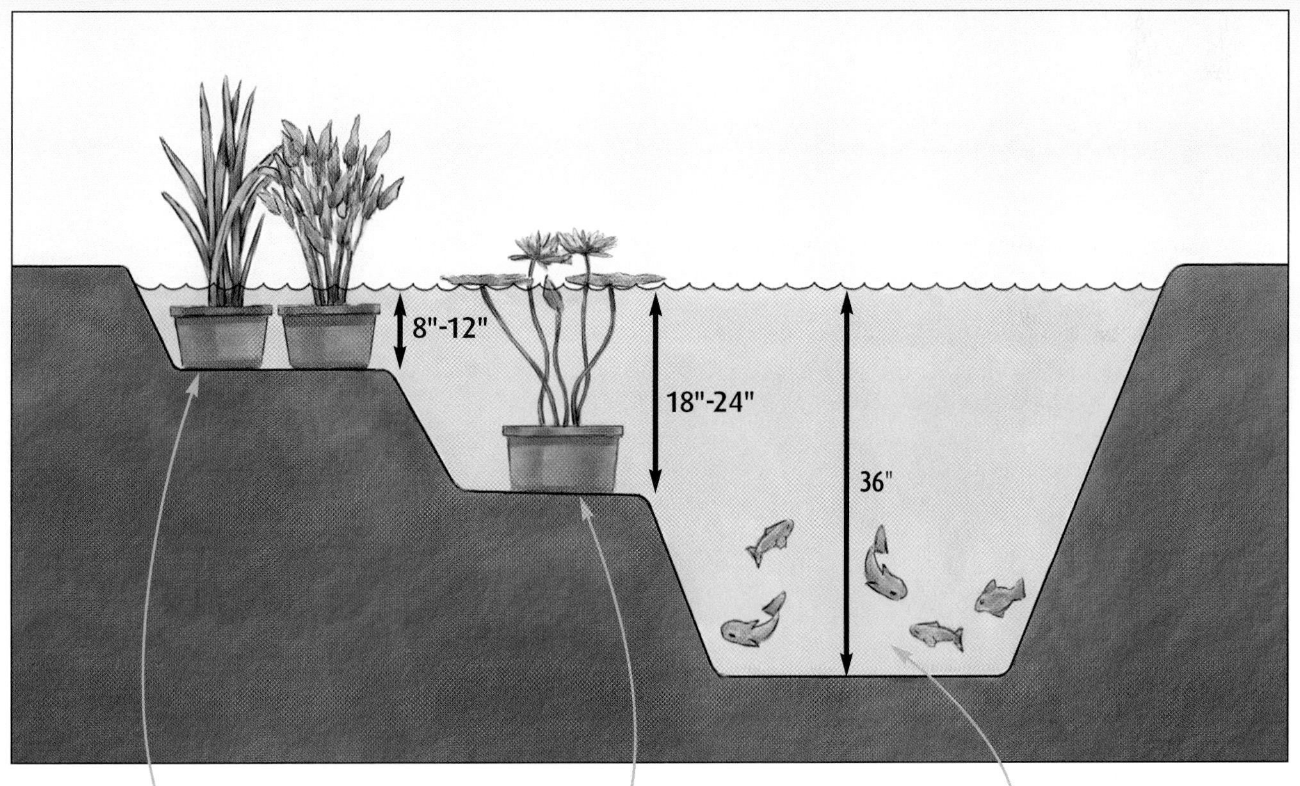

A marginal shelf is ideal for plants that like shallow water

A deeper area is needed for taller plants such as water lilies. In fact, you could make the whole pond this depth, if desired.

A very deep zone is excellent for overwintering fish.

The Mechanics of Water Gardening

A pump adds movement to the water garden. It recirculates the water, sucking it in and spurting it out again. This recirculation aerates the water, keeping it clear and healthy, especially for fish.

Most pumps also have a fountain head, which controls the way the water spurts out, whether in a naturalistic burble or nifty rotating jets.

Choosing a Pump

Choosing the right pump for your water garden is part art, part science.

Choose a pump too small and you won't have the spray or water movement you want. Choose one too large and it may look like a geyser and may create too much water movement for fish, stressing and even killing them. Look for a flow adjuster on the pumps you're considering; it can help keep the flow within a certain range.

You can roughly calculate an appropriate flow for your water garden if you know how much water your garden holds. (If it's a small garden, estimate how many 5-gallon buckets would fill the pond.) Then check the pump package for the number of gallons of water per hour the pump can move. Choose a pump that can move half the amount of water in your pond in an hour. So, if your pond holds 500 gallons of water, you'll need a pump that delivers at least 250 gallons an hour.

Filters

Unless you have a tiny container garden, any pump you choose will need a filter to prevent the motor from clogging with algae, leaves, and other debris. The larger the filter, the less often you'll have to rinse it. (A filter

Pumps, Filters, and More

The Fountain Head

This part usually slips on top of the extender. Different fountain heads produce different spray patterns (see the opposite page). Fountain heads can be sold either separately or with the rest of the pump.

The Filter

The filter on a pump keeps gunk and debris from the pond from clogging the motor and also helps keep the water clear. This box-style filter is designed so that the pump sits inside with sponges and a grid snapping on top. Many pumps are attached or built alongside the motor, as with the pump above and below. However, for extra filtration, even a pump with its own filter may be placed inside a box-type filter.

The Extender

This is the tube-like portion of the pump through which water rises. Extenders are usually sold with the pump. Select an extender that it is long enough to reach the water surface or you may have to set the pump on a riser of some sort. If the extender is too long, you can usually trim it with a hacksaw.

needs to be rinsed as often as daily; as seldom as once every few weeks or so.) You can seldom have too much filtration.

Most pumps with an attached filter (often called a prefilter) need to have the filter rinsed every day or two, depending on your garden. For more efficient filtration, consider a filter that looks like a box with a mesh top with a hole. The pump fits into the box and is topped with various spongelike foam layers. A mesh lid snaps on top, and the fountain head fits through the hole.

Even if your pump already has a prefilter built into it, it's often a good idea to set the pump inside a box-type filter to better protect the motor, since if too much algae or debris gets inside it can harm the motor. The additional filtration also keeps the water clearer.

A CLOSER LOOK

SUPPLYING ELECTRICITY

Most pumps need an electrical source to operate. (Solar-operated pumps are available but are harder to find.)

Because the pump will be in water, you need a GFCI (ground fault circuit interrupter) outlet, the kind you see in bathrooms that have a button you reset. They prevent electrocution.

If you already have one of these outlets outside your home, you may be able to run the cord to the outlet. If you want the electrical source to be more than a few yards from a building, however, you'll need to have one installed. Local codes may require a certified electrician to install the outlet. Costs for installation generally start at $100.

The outlet below has its reset button installed on the wall of a nearby garage. The cover on the outlet in the garden closes to protect the electrical connection from moisture and dirt.

Fountain Heads

When choosing a fountain head, choose a spray pattern that will complement your water garden. A naturalistic water garden, for example, looks good with a simple bubbler that percolates water upward and allows it to fall downward again, like a spring entering a pool. On the other hand, a more sleek, contemporary water garden or pool might look best with a dome-shaped spray.

Below are some of the most popular spray patterns.

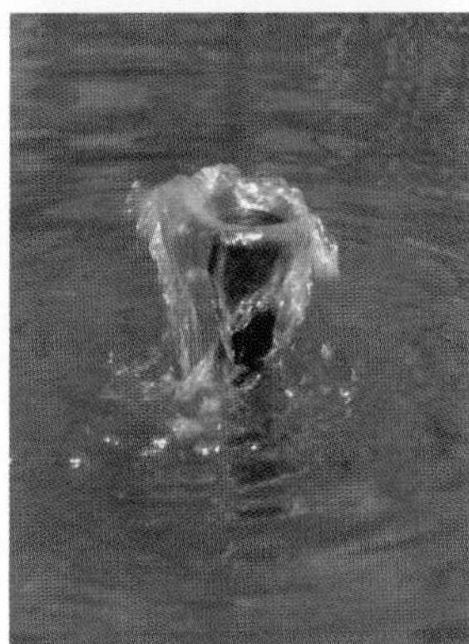

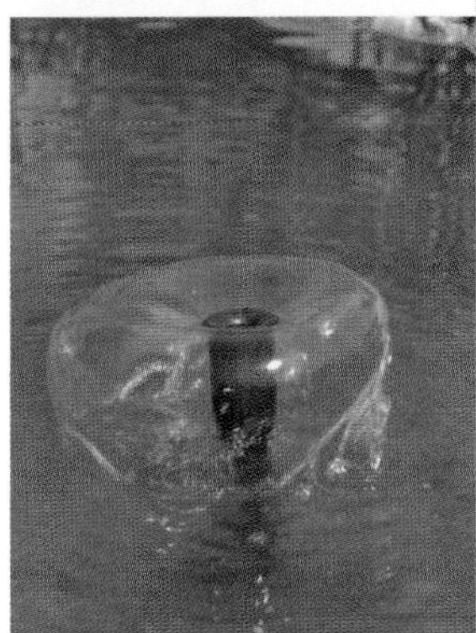

Installing a Water Garden

PROJECT DETAILS

SKILLS: Designing, digging
PROJECT: Installing a water garden

TIME TO COMPLETE

EXPERIENCED: A couple of days
HANDY: A few days
NOVICE: A week or two

STUFF YOU'LL NEED

TOOLS: Spade, level, length of lumber, ground rake, broad hoe, work gloves, sturdy shoes or boots
MATERIALS: Sand, water garden liner, edging materials, pump kit (optional), plants (optional), fish (optional)

Digging the Hole

When you install your water garden, give yourself plenty of time. Even if the pond is small, you may want to spread the project out over several days.

If your soil is very stony or hard, make digging easier by watering the area thoroughly, a few hours at a time, to soften the soil. Avoid making it muddy.

As you dig, toss the soil onto a tarp to protect your lawn. Dispose of the soil elsewhere on the property or, if you have too much, contact a landscaping service about removing it.

Dig carefully, lifting with your legs, not your back. Take frequent breaks to minimize strain.

How to Install a Water Garden with a Flexible Liner

A flexible liner allows you to create a water garden that is exactly the size and shape you want. It's also easier to hide the edges and make sure the water comes all the way up to the edging.

1 **Digging the Hole**
Mark the shape of the garden with a hose, string, or spray paint. Dig the hole, making shallow spots for setting out pots of plants and deeper spots to accommodate fish as needed. Make sure the edges are perfectly level or the water will slope within the pond, revealing the liner. Spread an inch or two of sand in the bottom to prevent liner tears.

2 **Positioning the Liner**
Allow the liner to warm in the sun for an hour or so to make it easier to arrange. Spread the liner, working out as many of the wrinkles as possible and making sure it conforms to the shape of the hole perfectly. As needed, use a brick or stone to hold it into place. Check the level once again, mounding or removing soil as needed.

3 **Installing Edging**
Once the liner is in place, put a few inches of water into the pond to settle it further and anchor it. Check the level once again. Add the edging and trim the liner with a scissors. The goal is to have little or no liner showing. It's best to wrap the liner up around the back and top of a first course of stone, which is then topped with a second course of stone. This way, the water can overlap the edging slightly without overflowing.

Fill the pond about two-thirds full and adjust the liner and edging further as needed.

4 **Filling the Water Garden**
Once you feel that the liner is installed correctly and it is perfectly level, completely fill the pond. Adjust the edging as needed to better conceal the liner. Plant around the pond as desired. You can add the pump and plants immediately. Wait three or more days before adding fish to allow water chemicals to dissipate.

How to Install a Water Garden with a Preformed Liner

A preformed, rigid liner takes some of the guesswork out of designing a water garden. It also has less chance of springing a leak. However, it's critical that it be installed in such a way that it's perfectly level and settles perfectly level.

1 Digging the Hole

Dig the hole, making it a few inches wider and a few inches deeper than the liner. Lay a base of about 2 inches of sand at the bottom to assist in positioning and settling.

2 Positioning the Liner

Position the liner, making sure it's level by stretching a level across the top. If the level isn't long enough, lay a board across the liner and set the level atop the board.

3 Filling and Edging

Partly fill the liner, positioning as you fill as needed. Check the level repeatedly as you work. Position stones or other edging.

4 Add Accessories

Position and plug in the fountain, adjusting the flow and extender as necessary. Add plants if desired. After three days, you may also add fish.

Final Touches

Adding Edging

Most water gardens look best with some type of edging, such as stone, pavers, or brick. With a preformed liner, position the stones so they protrude over the edge by a few inches and conceal the edge of the liner. With a flexible liner, wrap the liner up around the back and top of the edging.

Adding the Pump

Set the pump into the pond. You may want to position it on some bricks or flat stones to get it to the proper depth and to prevent bottom matter from clogging the pump.

Some pumps tend to float, especially when first added, so weight as needed with small stones. Avoid blocking the filter significantly.

As much as possible, hide the cord. Disguise it by running it down along the bottom and up the side, through gaps in the edging material. Bury the cord in the soil along the water garden to cover it up to the point where it connects with the electrical outlet.

Adding Fish and Plants

As long as any danger of frost is passed, you can add plants right away. (Frost damages most water plants.)

Before adding fish, however, allow the water to sit for three days so the chlorine and other chemicals dissipate. When adding fish purchased in a plastic bag, allow the sealed bag to rest in the pond water for 1 to 1½ hours so the fish gradually adapt to the temperature. Then open the bag and release the fish.

Water Garden Plants

Plants add yet another element to a water garden and are fun to watch and grow.

You don't need much space to grow water garden plants. Even in a dish or container water garden, you can easily grow water lettuces or fairy moss, for example. Most water garden plants prefer light shade to full sun.

There are four basic types of water garden plants:

Floaters

These plants float on the surface with visible or tiny roots dangling down in the water. Floaters play an important role in water gardens because they shade the water, keeping down algae growth. They're also a favorite of fish to nibble on.

Marginal Plants

These plants are grown in pots or special baskets made for water garden plants, and are set along the margins of the pond on a ledge. They usually need to be set just deep enough to cover the top of the pot or a few inches deeper.

If your pond lacks a ledge, you can set the plants on stacked bricks, stones, or even a dark plastic storage crate set upside down.

Submerged Plants

These plants are grown in pots on the bottom of the water garden, a foot or more deep. The foliage thrives underwater, rising upward and peeking out at the surface. Submerged plants are often tasty for fish and also provide them excellent hiding places from predators.

Water Lilies and Lotuses

Stars of any water garden, these beautiful blooming plants are grown in pots set a few inches to a foot or two below the surface of the water, depending on the plant's type and size. Some bloom during the day and some at night.

Favorite Water Garden Plants

Water Lettuce *(Pistia stratiotes)*
Also called shellflower, this floater has deeply creased lime green leaves that form lettucelike heads. It spreads by plantlets that break off the mother plant. Mature plants can stretch to 6 inches across and form a colony several feet wide by summer's end. Plant after your area's last frost date in spring. Prohibited in some states because it can be invasive, especially in warm climates.

Water Lily *(Nymphaea spp.)*
This beauty blooms in just about every color. Flowers have no scent, a slight scent, or a heavy scent depending on the type. Planted in baskets that should be set anywhere from a few inches to 2 feet below the water's surface, they first develop their classic round leaves, then send out flowers. Water lilies need fairly still water to thrive.

Some water lilies are cold-hardy and do poorly when the temperature is 95°F or above for prolonged periods. However, they will overwinter at the bottom of a deeper pond. Hardy in Zones 4 to 10. Other water lilies are tropicals and must be in water warmer than 70°F. Hardy only in Zones 10 and 11.

Water Hyacinth *(Eichhornia crassipes)*
This floater has shiny, whorled leaves and pretty blue midsummer flowers. It spreads rapidly and is invasive, and its sale is banned is some parts of the country. But it's still a good choice for small water gardens, especially in cooler regions where even a light frost will kill it completely. Its trailing roots provide good spawning spaces for fish. Winter-hardy in Zones 9 to 10.

Fairy Moss *(Azolla spp.)*
Also called water fern, this is one of the most commonly available floating plants. The 1/2-inch-across green leaves turn pale green or purplish green in summer and are a favorite food for goldfish. Plant after your region's last frost date in spring, though it is cold hardy through Zone 7. It is invasive, so plant it only in small water gardens where you can net or pull it out regularly to keep it under control.

Cattail *(Typha spp.)*
The brown flower heads of this familiar marginal plant peak in late summer to early fall. Many species are too invasive to grow in garden ponds, but the species sold at garden centers is better behaved. Cattails can reach up to 4 feet; dwarf varieties reach only 12 to 18 inches or so. Hardy in Zones 2 to 10, depending on the species.

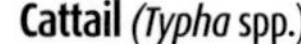

Lotus *(Nelumbo spp.)*
Water-lily like flowers but exceptionally large and fragrant with blooms up to 6 inches across and on stalks up to 5 feet high. Fascinating centers. Come in many colors. These tropical plants need several weeks of 80°F (26°C) or higher to bloom well. Hardy in Zones 4 to 11 if properly overwintered in deep water.

Water Garden Fish and Maintenance

Fish add sparkle, movement, and color to your water garden.

Before adding fish, check with your water supplier to see whether the water has chlorine or chloramines. Both can be removed by adding special chemicals, available where water garden supplies are sold or at pet stores.

When choosing fish or designing a pond, keep in mind that the smaller the pond, the more tolerant of temperature extremes your fish must be. Goldfish, for example, do well in cooler waters, whereas tropical fish must have warm water. The temperature of a small water garden changes dramatically depending on the sun and weather.

Different fish also need different depths. Koi, for example, need plenty of space in water at least 2 feet deep, whereas orfe, another kind of fish, spend most of their time in the upper levels of the pond.

The ideal time to add fish to a garden is in spring when water temperatures reach 50°F (10°C). As a rule, the number of fish you include depends on the size of a pond. Figure that each inch of fish should have 6 to 12 square inches of water. Further, koi need to swim up and down as well as horitzontally and so need at least 3 feet deep to accommodate their vertical swimming.

Nearly any fish will do well outside, but, as a rule, tougher, less finicky fish are best-suited to outdoor life. First-time water gardeners will want to start with inexpensive little goldfish before graduating to more expensive (and usually less tough) fish, some of which can cost upward of $200 each.

Add the fish by floating the plastic bag in which they were sold in the pond for 1 to 1½ hours to allow them to adapt to the water temperatures, or they might die of temperature shock.

Also be aware that predators such as raccoons, herons, and even cats might try to eat the fish. Protect expensive or beloved fish with netting made for ponds.

In fall, when temperatures outside drop to 60°F (17°C), bring tropical fish indoors (or all fish if there's danger that the pool could freeze solid). Or if the fish can tolerate cold, such as goldfish, and the pond is small, you can simply remove the pump and add a water heater.

Maintaining Your Water Garden

- Add water to your water garden whenever the level drops more than an inch or two, but avoid replacing more than one-third of the total water at one time. Doing so could kill the fish and throw off the balance of healthy bacterial growth.
- Skim off leaves and other debris that blow into the water garden.
- Feed fish every couple of days, if they need it. They may well have enough to eat with plant roots, algae, and mosquito larvae. They should appear ravenous each time you feed them.
- An easy way to overwinter fish and plants in a small water garden is to add a water heater. It will keep the water cold but not frozen all winter long.
- In winter, cut back any plants in pots and place them in the lowest portion of the garden. (Toss out floating plants, which will be killed by heavy frost.) Remove the pump and clean it thoroughly. Store it in a bucket of water until spring to keep critical parts from drying out.
- Garden pond water is seldom perfectly clear. A healthy-looking green tinge is fine. However, if your pond starts producing filamentous algae (algae that grows like fibers) remove it as soon and as thoroughly as possible. Use an algae killer that's safe for fish and plants as needed.
- With small ponds, you may want to clean them each spring. Bail out the water and remove the plants. Put the fish in a bucket of pond water while you clean the pond. Treat the new water with a dechlorinator, available in a bottle, before replacing the fish. Also, before placing the fish back in the pond, put them in plastic bags with water from the bucket, then set the bags in the pond for an hour or so to allow the fish to adjust to the temperature.

Water heaters can plug into the same power source as the fountain and float in the water all winter long, keeping water thawed.

If chosen well, water garden fish such as koi can live for decades.

Gardening For Wildlife

Attracting wildlife to your garden is easy. In fact, just by planting a garden filled with a variety of trees, shrubs, and flowers, you're likely to attract songbirds, butterflies, and hummingbirds that will be drawn by the shelter and food supply.

You can attract even more wildlife—or particular types of birds and butterflies—by doing the following:

- Provide shelter. Trees and shrubs are the best shelter there is. Plant only one or two, and the birds will start flocking. In limited spaces, plant large shrubs and vines. Both provide good spots for nesting and hiding from predators. Birdhouses are a nice touch, too, and they add a decorative element. (Clean them out in late winter or early spring to encourage returning birds and deter mold and diseases.)
- Provide water. Water attracts birds and other animals. Even a basic birdbath will do. The most attractive water setup, however, is a low basin or pool where water falls or bubbles up from a fountain. The splashing sound attracts many types of wildlife. Birds love to bathe in this, and butterflies will drink from water splashed along the edge.
- Provide food. Many flowers naturally provide food (such as berries) for wildlife, especially if you let the flowers go to seed—a real bird treat.

A bird feeder will attract even more birds. A flat-tray bird feeder filled with a general blend of seed will attract the widest variety of birds. To attract specific types of birds, check with your local seed and bird feeder supplier. Goldfinches, for example, love niger seed delivered from a tube feeder.

- Use bright colors. As a rule, birds, butterflies, and hummingbirds are most attracted to clear reds and brilliant pinks. Red zinnias, for example, will attract more butterflies than white ones. And magenta morning glories will attract more hummingbirds than blue ones.
- Use chemicals sparingly, especially insecticides. Many chemicals create conditions that discourage wildlife. And many insecticides—even organic ones—kill helpful insects as well as harmful ones.
- Be messy. When it comes to gardening for wildlife, you need to be more casual about maintenance. Birds love to feast on the seed heads of flowers left to mature on the stem. They favor tall grass, and thrive in unpruned shrubs where loose branches offer protection.

GOOD IDEA!

CARING FOR YOUR BIRDBATH

Birdbaths are a great way to attract birds to your garden, but if the water gets murky (which it can do in just a day or two in certain conditions), no birds will want to come.

Avoid this problem by positioning your birdbath in easy reach of your garden hose so you can flush out the water every day or two. Also, two or three times a year, be sure to give your birdbath a good scrubbing with a scrub brush and a little chlorine bleach (as long as the birdbath isn't colored) to kill algae.

A hummingbird moth is drawn to the tubular flowers with sweet nectar of bellflower.

Plants That Attract Butterflies

Common Name	Botanical Name	Zones
Ageratum	*Ageratum houstonianum*	Annual
Aster	*Aster* spp.	4-8
Azalea	*Rhododendron* spp.	4-10
Basket-of-gold	*Aurinia saxatilis*	4-8
Bee balm	*Monarda didyma*	4-8
Black-eyed Susan	*Rudbeckia* spp.	3-10
Blanket flower	*Gaillardia* spp.	2-10
Blazing star	*Liatris spicata*	3-9
Blue marguarite	*Felicia amelloides*	9-10
Butterfly bush	*Buddleia* spp.	5-10
Butterfly weed	*Asclepias tuberosa*	4-10
Candytuft	*Iberis* spp.	4-8
Coneflower, purple	*Echinacea purpurea*	3-9
Coreopsis	*Coreopsis* spp.	4-9
Cornflower, annual	*Centaurea cyanus*	Annual
Cosmos	*Cosmos* spp.	Annual
Dahlia	*Dahlia* spp.	8-11
False indigo, blue	*Baptisia australis*	3-9
Globe thistle	*Echinops* spp.	3-8
Goldenrod	*Solidago* hybrids	4-8
Heliotrope	*Heliotropium arborescens*	Annual
Hollyhock	*Alcea rosea*	3-11
Hyssop	*Agastache* spp.	5-10
Joe-Pye weed	*Eupatorium* spp.	3-10
Lantana	*Lantana camara*	8-10
Larkspur	*Consolida ambigua*	Annual
Lily	*Lilium* spp.	Varies
Marigold	*Tagetes* spp.	Annual
Mexican sunflower	*Tithonia rotundifolia*	Annual
Morning glory	*Ipomoea* spp.	Annual
Allium; ornamental onion	*Allium* spp.	4-8
Passionflower	*Passiflora* spp.	Varies
Petunia	*Petunia* spp.	Annual
Phlox, various	*Phlox* spp.	Varies
Scabiosa; pincushion flower	*Scabiosa caucasica*	3-7
Pinks, China	*Dianthus chinensis*	7-10
Primrose	*Primula* spp.	5-8
Rhododendron	*Rhododendron* spp.	Varies
Sedum	*Sedum* spp.	3-10
Snapdragon	*Antirrhinum majus*	Annual
Strawflower	*Helichrysum bracteatum*	Annual
Sunflower, perennial	*Helianthus* spp.	4-9
Sweet alyssum	*Lobularia maritima*	Annual
Sweet william	*Dianthus barbatus*	3-8
Thyme	*Thymus* spp.	5-8
Verbena	*Verbena* spp.	Varies
Viburnum	*Viburnum* spp.	Varies
Violet	*Viola* spp.	Varies
Wisteria	*Wisteria* spp.	5-9
Yarrow	*Achillea* spp.	3-9
Zinnia	*Zinnia* spp.	Annual

Plants That Attract Songbirds

Note: Nearly any tree or shrub over 8 feet tall will attract songbirds, because it provides excellent shelter. Trees that produce berries, such as serviceberry and dogwood, are especially favored, because they also provide food.

Common Name	Botanical Name	Zones
Aster	*Aster* spp.	4-8
Beautyberry, American	*Callicarpa americana*	7-10
Bittersweet, American	*Celastrus scandens*	3-8
Black-eyed Susan	*Rudbeckia* spp.	3-10
California poppy	*Eschscholzia californica*	Annual
Coneflower, purple	*Echinacea purpurea*	3-9
Coreopsis	*Coreopsis* spp.	4-9
Cosmos	*Cosmos* spp.	Annual
Goldenrod	*Solidago* hybrids	4-8
Honeysuckle	*Lonicera* spp.	3-9
Marigold	*Tagetes* spp.	Annual
Scabiosa; pincushion flower	*Scabiosa caucasica*	3-7
Staghorn sumac	*Rhus typhina*	3-8
Trumpet creeper	*Campsis radicans*	4-9
Zinnia	*Zinnia* spp.	Annual

Plants That Attract Hummingbirds

Common Name	Botanical Name	Zones
Bee balm	*Monarda didyma*	4-8
Butterfly bush	*Buddleia* spp.	5-10
Canna	*Canna* hybrids	2-11
Cardinal flower	*Lobelia* spp.	2-9
Cross-vine	*Bignonia capreolata*	6-9
Dahlia	*Dahlia*	2-11
Fuchsia	*Fuchsia* spp.	2-11
Geranium	*Pelargonium* spp.	2-11
Gladiolus	*Gladiolus* hybrids	2-11
Hollyhock	*Alcea rosea*	2-11
Honeysuckle, various	*Lonicera* spp.	3-9
Lantana	*Lantana camara*	2-11
Larkspur	*Consolida ambigua*	2-11
Morning glory	*Ipomoea* spp.	2-11
Penstemon	*Penstemon* spp.	3-7
Phlox, annual	*Phlox drummondii*	2-11
Petunia	*Petunia* spp.	2-11
Quince, flowering	*Chaenomeles speciosa*	4-9
Rose of Sharon	*Hibiscus syriacus*	5-9
Salvia, red annual	*Salvia splendens*	2-11
Snapdragon	*Antirrhinum majus*	2-11
Tobacco, flowering	*Nicotiana* spp.	2-11
Trumpet creeper	*Campsis radicans*	3-11
Weigela	*Weigela florida*	4-9

Preparation, Planting, and Propagation

Starting a garden is for some people the most exciting part—the smell of the earth, the pleasure of planting, the joy of beginning a new project with new possibilities.

So set yourself up for success by doing it right. On the following pages, you'll see the best way to create new beds, the best way to plant them, and the best way to start new plants to fill those beds. You'll also find nifty tricks for getting a wider variety of plants to grow in your garden, even when the weather doesn't cooperate. So dig in!

Chapter 5 Preparation, Planting, and Propagation

Building Good Soil

Even if your property is not blessed with naturally good soil, you can still have a beautiful garden. The key lies in investing time and resources in your soil.

Spending time on mere "dirt" may seem dull, but soil is the foundation of any garden. Take the time to improve it, and fewer plants will become sick or die, you'll spend less time and money watering, and you'll be able to grow a wider variety of plants. Your gardening experience overall will be infinitely more pleasurable because you took the time and effort to tend to the basics.

Before embarking on any soil improvement, however, it's important to understand what kind of soil you have (see page 22).

Improving Your Soil

Depending on the quality of your soil, you can take one of several approaches.

One of the most surefire is to build raised beds (see page 143). A raised bed can be anywhere from 3 to 4 inches high—just enough to somewhat improve the planting area—to 2 to 3 feet high, enough to create what are essentially planters that allow you to grow even where the soil had been terrible.

Another way to improve your soil is at the time you create a new bed. This involves adding several inches of organic matter and other amendments (see page 138), then tilling or double-digging them in (see page 142).

BUYER'S GUIDE

TIP-TOP TOPSOIL

Topsoil is the top layer of soil that, because it contains a high proportion of decomposing organic matter, is usually the most biologically active. It is often removed from one site and sold for delivery to another. It's less rich than compost, but it should still be high-quality soil. You can purchase it in bags or in bulk.

When you buy topsoil or compost in bulk for a garden project, look at it and feel it first. What is sold as topsoil (or even compost) is often poor-quality, clay-laden material or full of debris and other undesirable materials.

Anything sold as topsoil should be dark, rich, and heavy, crumbling easily with no debris, such as large strips of plastic bags or shards of glass. Compost should be coal-black, feel moist, and give off an earthy smell reminiscent of mushrooms. A little debris is acceptable, but you should find no large pieces.

If you can't look at the soil before it arrives at your house, be there at delivery time. If the soil or compost is less than top-notch, refuse the delivery.

The ideal soil is black and crumbly with a pleasant, earthy smell. This soil is dark from the addition of much compost.

Or build a berm (see page 145). Berms are a close relative of raised beds. Simply pile compost and topsoil on top of your existing soil to form a mound a few inches to a few feet above the existing soil.

If you want to improve the soil in an existing bed or border, you can do a total renovation, first digging out the perennials and working around small shrubs. Then you can spread several inches of soil amendments, and double-dig or till them in.

The easiest way to improve soil in an existing bed is to add organic matter—compost is ideal—as often as possible. Start by adding a 1- to 2-inch layer of compost on your beds and borders each spring. Add more compost each time you plant or are otherwise working the soil.

Which Soil Amendments to Add?

A soil amendment is anything you add to the soil to change its fertility and texture. It can range from sand to compost to a special soil conditioner purchased at the garden center.

Some soil amendments are organic—that is, they are plant-based and will break down with time. These include compost, sphagnum peat moss, sawdust, shredded newspaper, and leaf mold. Other amendments, such as sand or lime or gypsum, can improve the structure and chemical composition of the soil, but they lack organic matter (sometimes called humus), which results from decomposing plants.

One soil amendment stands out from the rest: compost. It does many things that no other single soil amendment can. It offers readily available nutrients to plants and improves microbial action in the soil. (Soil microbes break down organic matter so plants can use it.) It makes sandy soils more absorbent and clay soils more porous. It's hard to add too much compost to your soil. No wonder it's called "black gold" by gardeners.

Taking Care of Your Soil

It's important not only to improve your soil but also to keep from messing it up. If you work your soil when it's wet (as it often is in early spring) or dry (as it often is in late summer), it will form hard clumps that may take years to get broken up again.

Work the soil only when it's evenly moist. It will be easier to dig, and soil amendments will be better incorporated. Also, plants do best when planted in evenly moist—not soggy or hard—soils.

Mulches other than compost also help maintain soil. Grass clippings, pine needles, chopped leaves, bark mulches, and other organic mulches that break down slowly feed the soil over the years, adding to its fertility and texture.

One way to add more compost to your soil is to add mulch with it each spring. Add a layer 1 to 2 inches deep.

GOOD IDEA!

EVERY TIME YOU PLANT

A good way to improve your soil is to follow this rule: Always plant with a bag, bucket, or wheelbarrow of compost at your side. That way you can work a few spadefuls of compost into the bottom of large planting holes or work a little compost into the top several inches of soil when planting small things, such as annuals.

Soil Amendments

A soil amendment is anything you work into the soil to improve its fertility and texture. Some soil amendments also alter the pH. Check the following and decide which amendments you need:

BLOOD MEAL: Made of dried animal blood. A rich organic source of nitrogen. Slightly improves soil texture. Sprinkle lightly on the soil's surface or follow package directions, and rake in.

BONEMEAL: Source of phosphorus. Made of finely ground, steamed animal bones. Popular as a fertilizer for bulbs, although a synthetic fertilizer made specifically for bulbs is much more effective. Slightly improves soil texture. Work into planting holes, or sprinkle on the soil's surface and rake in. May attract dogs.

COMPOST: Nearly the perfect soil amendment. Improves soil fertility, breaks up clay, improves sand's ability to hold water, improves the texture of all soils, and encourages beneficial earthworms and microbes. It's nearly impossible to add too much. Add to planting holes, work into planting areas, mulch with 1 to 2 inches, or spread several inches on top of new beds and borders and work it into the soil.

GARDEN SULFUR: Lowers the pH of soil, making neutral and alkaline soils better for acid-loving plants. Add according to package directions only if you're certain of your soil's pH.

GYPSUM: Breaks up some clay soils, but its effectiveness is limited. Liquid gypsum is faster-acting than the powder form, which is spread on the soil's surface or dug in to a depth of several inches. Still, it takes 6 to 12 months to work. Gypsum also has the benefit of leaching out salt and can somewhat lower the pH of soils. Follow package directions exactly.

LIME: Made of ground limestone. Raises the pH of soil. Should be applied only on acidic soils to accommodate plants that need more alkaline conditions. Folk wisdom prescribes liming your soil each spring, but this creates pH problems unless your soil is very acidic. Processed lime takes effect in a few weeks; dolomitic limestone takes a few months.

MANURE: Usually sold as composted manure, not to be confused with regular compost. Fresh manure applied to the soil can burn plants. Allow fresh manure to compost or age for one year before applying. Composted (also referred to as aged or well-rotted) manure has a lower concentration of nutrients. Too much manure can adversely affect plants. Improves soil texture as well as fertility. Usually has a slight odor that disappears in a week or two. Work manure into the top inch or two of the soil.

PERLITE: Made of tiny, heat-popped volcanic rock. Keeps soil loose and improves its ability to hold water. Good for clay and sandy soils. Too expensive to use for projects much larger than containers. Work into the soil before planting containers or into the top several inches of soil. Very lightweight so sometimes floats to the top when soil is heavily watered.

SAND AND GRAVEL: Often worked in to break up clay soils. Sharp or builder's sand or sharp gravel is best. Sandbox sand is too fine to be effective. Beach sand has too much salt and can damage many plants. In some clay soils, especially those with a greenish cast, the addition of sand can create something akin to concrete. Experiment with a small area first before using on a large scale. Work to a depth of 18 to 24 inches.

SOIL CONDITIONER: A loose term for any material that improves the texture and/or fertility of the soil. Sometimes it's nothing more than compost, but materials can include anything from bark dust to crushed coral. Includes planter's mix, which is a blend of soil amendments. As with any product, read the package carefully. Work into the top 18 to 24 inches.

SPHAGNUM PEAT MOSS: Harvested from bogs, then dried. Acts like a sponge to help soils retain water. Also helps soil texture and slightly lowers pH. Good for sandy and clay soils alike, though it can worsen soil texture in some clay soils. Experiment in a small area first. Can be a problem if used extensively because it's difficult to rewet once it dries out.

Soil Troubleshooting

PROBLEM	SYMPTOMS	SOLUTION
Heavy clay	Difficult to work either wet or dry; water puddles rather than soaks in; soil usually has a red or orange cast; plants fail to thrive.	When soil is lightly moist (never when very wet or dry), spread with 4 to 6 inches of compost, sand, gravel, and/or sphagnum peat moss and work in to a depth of 18 inches. However, because sand and sphagnum peat moss can create soil texture problems in some clays, experiment on a small area first and wait at least 4 weeks before proceeding with the rest of the area. A power tiller is useful in some clay soils because it saves work and more thoroughly blends the soil amendments. Each year, add compost in planting holes, and mulch the entire bed with 1 to 2 inches of compost each spring. A raised bed or berm is often the best solution.
Sandy soil	Very loose whether wet or dry; water drains quickly; difficult to keep plants well-watered.	Spread 2 to 3 inches of compost and/or sphagnum peat moss over the top of the soil and work it in to a depth of 18 to 24 inches. Add compost to planting holes, and mulch with 1 to 2 inches of compost each spring.
Poor, light, dry soil	Most plants fail to thrive, but some, such as lavender and thyme, do well; soil is light in color.	Spread 2 to 3 inches of compost over the top of the soil and work in to a depth of 1 foot. Work compost into planting holes, and mulch with 1 to 2 inches of compost each spring.
Boggy, wet soil	Often damp even during dry spells, usually in low-lying areas; may give off a marshy smell; flowers planted there often have yellowing foliage.	Consider draining the soil by installing drainage tile in a bed of gravel (see page 56). Otherwise, build raised beds (page 143), and/or use moisture-loving plants.
Hardpan	Soil workable on top, but a few inches or a foot or so down is a hard, rocklike layer.	Experiment with the depth of the hardpan by removing topsoil from a small area and chipping away at it with a small pickax. If the hardpan breaks easily, proceed. If not, build a raised bed or berm.
Rocky soil	Difficult to dig; spade hits many rocks, large and small.	If the rocks are reasonably small and sparse, old-fashioned digging and removal are called for. If the rocks are more numerous, consider constructing a rock garden (page 118) or raised bed (page 143). Berms (page 145) with rocks incorporated on the surface of the soil are also an excellent option.
Soil filled with tree roots	Difficult to dig; spade hits tree roots.	As much as possible, plant between roots. With a small ax, cut out small (less than 1 inch in diameter) roots 3 to 6 feet out from the base of the tree. Extensive cutting of roots can damage trees, so proceed with caution. You can build raised beds in the root zone, but they should be lower than 2 inches high; more could harm the tree's roots.

Building New Beds, Borders, and Gardens

Digging Basics

There are a number of ways to dig a flower bed.

The "lazy bed" method involves minimal labor but can take weeks to months. Double-digging (page 142) is labor-intensive, but you can't beat it for thoroughly loosening and enriching the soil. It's most feasible in small areas.

Combining tilling and digging (page 142) falls between the two. A power tiller, which can go down no more than a foot, works the top layer of soil and saves labor. Then hand digging allows you to go down the 18 to 24 inches that are ideal for most flower gardens.

Whatever method you use, it's best to dig the flower bed on a day when the soil is slightly moist. If the soil is dry, turn on the sprinkler and soak it, then let the water trickle down for several hours. If the soil is wet, put off digging until it doesn't clump, to avoid ruining the texture.

A bed can be created about any time of year. Most gardeners like to do it in spring so they can plant immediately. But a fall bed has its advantages too. In all but the coldest parts of the country (Zone 3 and colder), you can still plant trees, shrubs, and perennials through October. Plus, you can plant spring-blooming bulbs.

DESIGN TIP

SCALE IS EVERYTHING

Scale the size of your beds and borders to fit the size of your yard. If flower beds are too small, they get lost in the landscape. In a medium-size yard, a bed at least 6 feet wide and at least 14 feet long would be appropriate. Before you dig, think big!

There are a number of ways to create a new bed. This one is being built first by stripping off the turf. Then soil amendments will be worked in with a spade.

You can put off planting the bed. In fact, in cold regions, soil that has been through a winter tends to be finer and better broken up, and organic material has had more time to break down. Also, fall is usually a less busy time for gardeners, so you enter the spring garden cleanup and planting frenzy ready to go.

Before digging or building your bed, mark the area to be dug with spray paint, flour, a garden hose, or lime. Do this several days before digging so you have time to consider the size and shape of the bed and can alter it as needed.

In most cases when building a new bed, you can leave the existing sod in place. It will break down and enrich the soil. Just pluck out or rake away any tufts or clods that remain on the surface when you're done. However, if you have bermudagrass or another vigorous grass, you should kill it first with a nonselective herbicide or remove it altogether.

Your digging tool is a matter of preference. Some gardeners swear by a round-point or a flat-edged spade, both of which slice through the soil and lift it up as well. Others prefer a spading fork, using it to loosen and sift through the soil without much lifting.

When you're done digging, smooth the soil with a broad hoe. Then follow with a ground rake to break up clumps and make a finer soil.

WORK SMARTER

DIGGING TIPS

- **Keep your shovel sharp. Have a file on hand to sharpen the shovel as necessary so it will slice through turf and soil easily.**
- **Lift soil with your legs, not your back, to prevent back strain or injury.**
- **Invest in good work gloves. They'll prevent many blisters.**
- **Wear sturdy work boots; they make digging easier.**

5

Preparation, Planting, and Propagation

The Lazy-Bed Method

1 If dealing with Bermudagrass, invasive weeds, or other problem plants, consider killing them with a non-selective herbicide first to prevent them from cropping up later.

Otherwise, smother grass or weeds by covering them with several layers of newspaper. Top with soil amendments (page 138), preferably a few inches of compost or high-quality topsoil. Allow everything to break down for at least 2 months or, better yet, over a season, such as winter.

2 When the newspaper has broken down, turn everything under to a depth of 12–18 inches. It's fine if a few chunks remain. Leave them in to further break down. Rake the surface smooth, removing larger bits of paper or sod as needed.

PROJECT DETAILS

SKILLS: Digging
PROJECT: Creating a flower bed with minimal effort and converting turf into valuable organic matter

TIME TO COMPLETE

EXPERIENCED: About 1 hour to prepare a medium-size bed
HANDY: About 1 hour
NOVICE: About 1 hour

STUFF YOU'LL NEED

TOOLS: Spade, wheelbarrow, garden gloves, sturdy shoes or boots, power tiller (optional)
MATERIALS: Soil amendments (page 138), newspapers (use black and white portions; glossy colored pages may contain heavy metals)

The Double-Digging Method

PROJECT DETAILS

SKILLS: Extensive digging
PROJECT: Digging a new bed very deep to prepare the soil exceptionally well

TIME TO COMPLETE

EXPERIENCED: A few hours, with frequent breaks, for a medium-size bed
HANDY: Several hours, with frequent breaks
NOVICE: Several hours, with frequent breaks

STUFF YOU'LL NEED

TOOLS: Spade, garden gloves, good work boots, wheelbarrow or tarp
MATERIALS: Soil amendments (see page 138)

1 Start by digging a trench 8 to 12 inches deep across the length of the bed. Set aside this better-quality topsoil in a wheelbarrow or on a tarp.

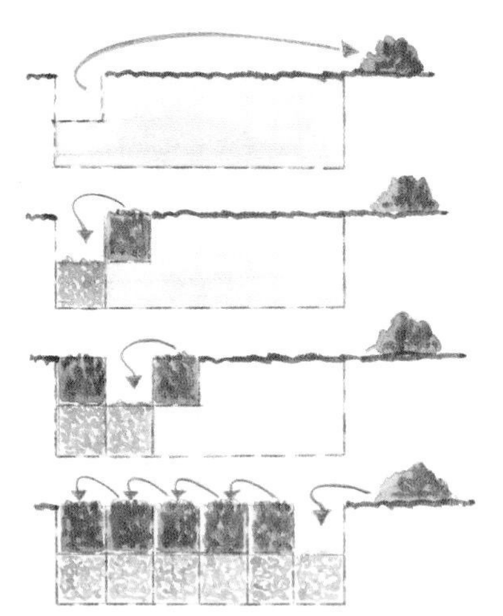

2 Work soil amendments (page 138) into the lesser-quality subsoil to a total depth of 16 to 24 inches. Then, in a sort of soil shell game, remove another row of topsoil alongside the first, and toss it on top of the newly improved subsoil. Repeat until the bed is complete, filling the last trench with the reserved topsoil from the first row.

The Tilling/Digging Method

PROJECT DETAILS

SKILLS: Running a power tiller, digging
PROJECT: Using man- and machine-power to dig a reasonably well-prepared bed

TIME TO COMPLETE

EXPERIENCED: A few hours, with frequent breaks, for a medium-size bed
HANDY: Several hours, with frequent breaks
NOVICE: Several hours, with frequent breaks

STUFF YOU'LL NEED

TOOLS: Power tiller, good work boots, heavy gloves, spading fork or spade
MATERIALS: Soil amendments (see page 138)

1 Spread soil amendments (page 138) on top of the soil and till in as deeply as possible, usually 8 to 12 inches depending on the design of the tiller. Be sure to wear sturdy shoes or boots to protect your feet. Pass the tiller over the soil several times.

2 Use a spading fork or a spade to loosen the soil further to a total depth of 16 to 24 inches. This well-loosened soil allows plant roots to reach down deep, making them more resistant to drought, cold, and other challenges.

Raised Bed Basics

Raised beds are the great cure-all for any type of soil problem. You can even build them right on top of concrete! They create a perfect garden environment of good soil and excellent drainage.

Designing Raised Beds

How high you make your raised beds and what you use to make them depends on several things:

• How bad is the soil? If your soil is fairly workable, you can get away with raised beds only 3 to 8 inches high. However, if the soil is completely unworkable—the kind of soil that can hardly be dented by a spade—make the raised beds 1 to 3 feet high.

• What will you grow in your raised beds? Annual flowers, herbs, and vegetables need about 1 foot of good soil to grow in; perennial flowers, fruits, herbs, and vegetables need about 18 inches. Shrubs have deep roots but can tolerate less-perfect soil, so give them about 18 inches of good topsoil.

You'll have to guesstimate how much good topsoil you'll have in your raised beds. If the underlying soil is adequate and you build a 6-inch raised bed on top, you'll have about a foot of good-quality soil—enough to grow annuals. If the underlying soil is terrible, you'll need to make beds raised at least 18 inches to grow perennials.

• What materials should you use to build the raised beds? Local materials are less expensive. Possibilities include fieldstone collected from local ditches and fields (get owner permission first, and stay away from public land) as well as river rock, small boulders, plain concrete blocks, concrete and retaining wall blocks, landscape timbers, wood boards, and scrap lumber. As long as lumber is rot-resistant and won't seep harmful chemicals (the way creosote-treated railroad ties might), you can use it in a raised bed that will not contain edibles. Any wood you use should be naturally rot-resistant (cedar, redwood, and others) or have been pressure-treated to prevent decay.

Preparing the Soil for Raised Beds

If the soil is at all workable, it should be loosened and improved (see page 136). Ideally, it should be turned over, and compost or other soil amendments worked in to a depth of a foot or more.

If mice or moles or other burrowing creatures are a problem, design the raised beds on top of a layer of hardware cloth (for smaller animals) or chicken wire (for larger animals). Make sure the wire is attached to or well-weighted by the base of the raised bed material so that animals can't wriggle in. Also, the wire openings must be large enough for the roots of plants to pass through. Hardware cloth buried several inches deep is fine for most annuals, but perennials and shrubs will need chicken wire buried at least 10 to 12 inches deep.

Filling the Raised Beds

If you're lucky, you may have the ideal source for filling the raised beds on your property—an overflowing compost heap or good-quality topsoil.

Otherwise, you'll need to purchase topsoil and compost to fill the beds. Purchase the best quality you can, making sure you see any topsoil before you buy it to avoid ending up with poor-quality "fill dirt" (see "Tip-Top Topsoil," on page 136). For all but the smallest projects, it's more economical to purchase topsoil and compost in bulk and have it dumped on your driveway. You can work in other soil amendments, such as sphagnum peat moss, but good topsoil and compost are the most economical and give the best results.

PROJECT DETAILS

SKILLS: Digging, stacking modular-type stone or block
PROJECT: Building a raised bed out of stone, concrete block, or solid concrete block made for such projects

TIME TO COMPLETE

EXPERIENCED: 3 hours for a small bed
HANDY: 4 hours for a small bed
NOVICE: 6 hours for a small bed

STUFF YOU'LL NEED

TOOLS: Ground rake, spade, stakes
MATERIALS: Concrete, stone, or landscaping concrete block, topsoil, soil amendments (optional)

How to Build a Stone or Concrete Block Raised Bed

1 Mark out the area for your raised bed with stakes. If the raised sides of the bed will be less than 1 foot, dig the soil to a depth of 1 foot, working in soil amendments as needed (see page 138).

2 Position the stones or blocks along the edges. In cold regions where frost heave can occur, bury the bottoms of the block or stone 1 to 3 inches below the soil's surface.

3 Add more courses to the raised bed as desired. However, keep simple raised beds like these to no more than 18 inches to prevent them from tumbling. Fill with good-quality topsoil and more soil amendments as needed.

Building New Beds, Borders, And Gardens

continued

PROJECT DETAILS

SKILLS: Basic woodworking, digging
PROJECT: Creating a raised bed with wood boards

TIME TO COMPLETE

EXPERIENCED: 1 hour for a medium bed
HANDY: A couple of hours for a medium bed
NOVICE: A few hours for a medium bed

STUFF YOU'LL NEED

TOOLS: Saw, screwdriver or hammer, spade, ground rake, work boots, work gloves, power drill (optional)
MATERIALS: Galvanized screws or nails; rot-resistant lumber, such as cedar or pressure-treated pine (Avoid pressure- or creosote-treated wood if you'll be growing edibles and use wood rated for ground contact); topsoil and soil amendments

How to Build a Wood Raised Bed

1 Screw or nail together pieces of rot-resistant lumber. Use galvanized nails or screws. Nails are easier and faster, but screws are stronger and longer-lasting.

2 Dig a trench 1 to 2 inches deep where you want the raised bed to rest. Position the frame on the trench and make it level by adding soil or digging out more.

3 Loosen the soil to a depth of 6 to 12 inches, working in soil amendments as needed (see page 138). There's no need to remove turf (except for bermudagrass) or most small weeds; they'll break down and feed the soil.

4 Fill with high-quality topsoil and rake smooth. The topsoil can be purchased or moved from elsewhere on the site.

Building A Berm

A berm is an excellent way to improve your soil easily as well as provide good drainage for the wide variety of plants that do best in rich, well-drained soil.

Whether your soil is rocky, heavy with clay, or very sandy, a berm is a fairly easy way to create a planting bed without the sides of a raised bed (though some gardeners like to place rounded boulders into the base of their berms as well as here and there around the surface of the berm to better stabilize the soil). You'll often see berms in the landscapes of newly built homes, where the good topsoil has been scraped away and what remains is lesser-quality subsoil. Berms allow you to put your topsoil investment exactly where you need it.

Berms can be any size. One of their advantages is that it's easier, less expensive, and more natural looking to have a large berm than a large raised bed. Many berms are 20 to 30 feet in length and 10 feet across. Few raised beds, especially raised beds of any significant height, are that large, whereas a berm of that size might be as high as 3 to 4 feet.

Therefore, the larger the berm, the bigger the benefit. You can get 3 to 4 feet of excellent-quality soil in which to grow small trees, shrubs, and about any annual and perennial that your climate and light conditions will allow.

Berms have other benefits too. They add privacy, especially in the fronts of homes where traffic and passersby may be an issue.

Berms can also be small—only several feet long and a few feet across. However, these berms can be only a foot or so high, because anything with steeper sides would quickly wash away.

Creating a berm is straightforward. You just pile up soil and sculpt it. Here are pointers that make berm-building even easier:

- Several days before you build the berm, mark the spot on the ground with a garden hose or spray paint. Think and rethink its position and shape. It's easier to change your plans before you start moving soil than after.
- In some cases you can use rubble in the center of large berms. Old bricks, broken concrete block, or stones dug up from around your property can be put in the center of the berm as long as they won't break down the way lumber or twigs would, making the berm sink as they decompose. Keep any rubble to the center of the berm so that plants have plenty of soil in which to grow—at least a foot or so for perennials and 2 feet for small shrubs. With anything else, avoid using rubble.
- Build a berm with top-quality soil. With the smallest of berms, purchasing topsoil and/or compost in bags is fairly inexpensive. For larger or multiple berms you'll want to purchase soil in bulk.

DESIGN TIP

DETERMINING THE SHAPE OF YOUR BERM

Berms lend themselves to curving, graceful sweeps, so design them with that in mind. Perfect circles and ovals can work in some situations but can look rigid if not designed and positioned exactly right.

Drainage Issues

When planning your berm, take into consideration how it will affect drainage around the base of your house. Some homeowners position the berm close to the house in such a way that it channels or traps water near the foundation, creating water problems in the basement.

Position a berm so that water will run away from, not toward the house. When in doubt, position the berm at least 10 feet away from the house to prevent basement water problems.

PROJECT DETAILS

SKILLS: Digging
PROJECT: Building a raised bed called a berm

TIME TO COMPLETE

EXPERIENCED: A couple of hours, depending on the size of the berm
HANDY: 3 hours
NOVICE: 4 hours

STUFF YOU'LL NEED

TOOLS: Hose, spade
MATERIALS: Newspaper (avoid glossy color inserts), good-quality topsoil and/or compost, mulch (optional)

How to Build a Berm

1 Kill existing grass or vegetation by smothering it with several layers of newspaper. Wet it to keep it in place.

2 Mound soil atop the newspaper. As you work, tamp it down by lightly walking atop the berm.

3 Allow the soil to settle for a day or two, then plant. Mulch will help prevent erosion until plants get settled.

Installing Edging

Edging on your beds and borders does many things: It prevents spreading plants inside the bed from invading the lawn, and it prevents turf from spreading into the bed. If well designed and installed, it makes mowing around the bed easier by clearly delineating between bed and lawn and by creating a smooth, flat surface against which to mow or trim. When designed so it's slightly higher than the original soil's surface, it can better hold the looser, fluffed-up soil of the bed in place, especially if you've raised the soil level a bit with amendments. Best of all, it adds a neat, groomed appearance to the landscape.

Edging Materials

Edging materials are limited only by your imagination and their ease of upkeep.

Brick, pavers, stone, plastic and metal strips, and wood edging are sold for this purpose. Depending on your region and garden style, small boulders, large sea shells, even upturned colored glass bottles can be used for edging.

Another popular way to edge beds is to trim the surrounding turf crisply. (See "How to Create a Turf Edge," at right.) Simply slice through the turf once or twice a year for cool-season grasses, two to four times a year for more aggressive warm-season grasses.

TOOL TIP

POWER EDGERS

If you have a large area to edge, or you'll be edging fairly frequently, consider renting or purchasing a power edger.

This nifty tool is ideal for creating crisp, fast, neat turf edges around beds and borders, edging around walks and drives, or digging quick, perfect mini trenches for installing plastic, metal, and other narrow edging.

See page 15 for more information on power edgers.

PROJECT DETAILS

SKILLS: Basic

PROJECT: Installing plastic edging, usually sold as a kit

TIME TO COMPLETE

EXPERIENCED: About 1 hour for 20 feet of edging

HANDY: About 2 hours

NOVICE: About 2½ hours

STUFF YOU'LL NEED

TOOLS: Mallet

MATERIALS: Plastic edging kit

How to Install Plastic Edging

1 Position the edging along the bed or border. (This is easier to do if you let the edging warm in the sun first.)

2 With a mallet, pound the stakes (which come with the edging) into the soil.

3 Backfill over the tabs with soil and/or mulch.

How to Install Brick Edging

1 Remove plants or weeds that are where the edging will be set. In Zone 6 and colder, dig a small trench and fill it with 1 to 2 inches of sand to ensure that the bricks stay in place even during freezing and thawing.

2 Position the bricks, filling in under them or digging out from under them as needed to get them to follow the curve of the bed and the land.

3 Pat sand and soil around the bricks to secure them in place. Spray with a hose to wash off the bricks and further settle the sand.

PROJECT DETAILS

SKILLS: Digging, positioning bricks
PROJECT: Laying brick to serve as an edging around planting beds

TIME TO COMPLETE

EXPERIENCED: About an hour for 10 feet of edging
HANDY: About 2 hours
NOVICE: About 3 hours

STUFF YOU'LL NEED

TOOLS: Trowel, flat-edged shovel
MATERIALS: Bricks or pavers, sand, garden hose

PROJECT DETAILS

SKILLS: Digging
PROJECT: Using an edger to slice through turf to make a neat edge around planting beds

TIME TO COMPLETE

EXPERIENCED: About 15 minutes for 10 feet of edging
HANDY: About 30 minutes
NOVICE: About 45 minutes

STUFF YOU'LL NEED

TOOLS: Half-moon edger (shown) or other edging tool, bucket or wheelbarrow to haul away turf, trowel or hand cultivator to lift turf

How to Create a Turf Edge

1 Use a half-moon edger to slice through the turf.

2 Tilt the edger upward to tear out the turf by the roots.

3 With your hands or a trowel, pull or dig up the bits of turf. Use a bucket or wheelbarrow to transport them to the compost heap.

Planting Basics

The fundamentals of planting are basic—dig a hole, put in a plant, fill in with soil, and water. Done!

But you'll have a better chance of getting your plant off to a faster start with better growth, health, and, in some cases, flowering, if you do it right.

Choosing the Right Time

Different plants do best depending on the time of year they're planted. Some thrive in cool conditions, whereas others like it hot. So it's important to know your region's last frost date in spring (if any), found on page 29. It's from this date that most planting is calculated.

- Cool-season annuals: Includes plants such as pansies, calendula, and snapdragons. These like to be planted in spring, several weeks before your region's last frost date. In warm-climate regions, plant cool-season annuals in fall for winter color.
- Warm-season annuals: Includes marigolds, celosia, petunias, and impatiens. These plants do not tolerate frost, so they should be planted anytime after your region's last frost date in spring.
- Perennials and shrubs: These survive through the winter, so they can tolerate some cold at planting time. Plant in spring, summer, or fall, as long as the weather won't be too cold (staying above freezing for a few days), too sunny and hot, or the temperature isn't above 85°F (29°C).
- Roses: Plant bare-root roses up to a month before your region's last frost date in spring, and container roses up to a week before. In Zone 6 and warmer, container roses may also be planted in fall.
- Bulbs: Plant spring-blooming bulbs such as tulips and daffodils in the fall. Plant summer-blooming bulbs such as lilies, cannas, and gladioli in the spring.

WORK SMARTER

WHEN TO PLANT

There's a myth that you can plant only in spring. Actually, you can plant almost anytime during the summer as long as high temperatures aren't above 80 degrees. (Any warmer and plants will wilt and possibly die.) The best days to plant are those that are cool and cloudy, with no strong sun to stress the plant. If rain threatens, new plants will benefit from the moisture.

In Zones 6 and warmer, fall is also a good time to plant. Cool temperatures and plentiful rainfall establish plants quickly and give them a jump start on spring.

Believe it or not, when planting, it's wise to pinch off flowers so plants can direct their energy into all-important root development, which will encourage better flowering and overall plant health later on.

If you have to plant on a sunny day, provide some shade. An overturned laundry basket is an easy, quick solution.

Preparing the Soil Well

Whether you're planting only one shrub or 50 annuals, it's important to prepare the soil. This is true even if you're planting in an existing flower bed. Prepare new flower beds well (see page 140). In existing flower beds, work a few spadefuls of a soil amendment, such as compost, into the area you'll be planting.

Especially if planting annuals, work a slow-release fertilizer into the ground. Annuals are hungry, fast-growing plants that thrive when given plenty of nutrients.

Putting the Plants in the Ground

Before planting, make sure your plants are well-watered and not wilting. If they are indeed looking droopy, water them in their existing pots and wait a day for them to recover. If a plant is bare-root, soak the roots in cool water for several hours before planting.

To plant, remove the plant gently from its pot. If the roots are wrapped in circles or are thickly knotted, loosen them with your fingers. If the roots are very large and tough, you may even need to slice through them slightly with a spade to loosen them.

Position the plant so the soil level is the same as it was in the pot. If the plant is bare-root, plant it at the depth specified on the package.

Difficult as it may seem, pinch or trim off any flowers. They're taking energy that would be better put into establishing the plant's root system for bigger, better, and more flowers later on. You'll lose a few pretty blooms, but you'll be rewarded with a healthier, longer-blooming plant.

Watering

Water the plant well. If it's a shrub or a rose, position a hose at the base just barely at a trickle and let it run for a half hour or more. For annuals and perennials, water so the soil is soaked a foot down.

Keep the plants well watered for the first two weeks, checking them daily for soil moisture and signs of wilting. Once they're established, they'll need less water.

For details on planting trees, see page 150; for details on planting shrubs, see page 152; for specifics on planting roses, see page 154; for annuals and perennials, see page 156; for details on planting vines, see page 158; for planting groundcovers, see page 159; and for planting bulbs, see page 160.

A CLOSER LOOK

GET THOSE ROOTS GOING!

When planting, it's a good idea to add something that will get the roots off to a fast start. Well-developed root systems make for healthier plants that are better at taking up water and critical nutrients.

A so-called starter fertilizer is heavy on phosphorus, which encourages root growth. (Avoid high-nitrogen fertilizer, which will encourage green leafy growth immediately. The poor plant has to get its bottom established first before it works on top growth!)

Another way to get roots going is to use a root stimulator. Root stimulators contain hormones that encourage rapid root growth.

Planting A Tree

Planting a tree is easy. There are some ways to ensure that the tree will take off faster with less stress and will have fewer problems in years to come.

Try these tips for planting trees:

- Position trees carefully so that even when they're fully grown they won't brush houses or power lines.
- Plant trees when the weather is mild—85° F (30°C) or below—and preferably calm and overcast. Bright sun and windy conditions dry out and stress transplants. Also, time planting for when there are months of temperate growing conditions ahead.
- In southern Canada and the northern third of the United States, that means planting in spring or during a cool spell during the summer. In the southern two-thirds of the United States, that means planting in early spring or in autumn.
- You don't have to dig a huge hole. Recent research shows that trees do just as well or better when a modest-size hole is dug. Dig a hole that's one-and-a-half to two times as wide as the tree's container or root ball and only slightly deeper than the container or root ball.
- Avoid extensive soil amending. Recent research indicates that tree roots do better when starting out in soil much like what they'll encounter beyond the planting hole. Add several spadefuls of compost to the planting hole, but nothing more.
- Every plant has its best side. Trees often have one side that looks better than the other sides. Before planting, examine the tree from all sides, and position its best "face" accordingly.
- Rough up the roots. If the roots are tangled or pot-bound, loosen them with your fingers or a cultivator claw, or even slice through them with the sharp edge of a spade to break them up and encourage them to grow outward.
- Avoid planting too high. Gardeners commonly plant trees so that the rim of the container soil or the rising mound of the roots is revealed. This dries out the plant. Measure the depth of the root ball and also the planting hole as you dig, then measure again before positioning the tree.
- Use a starter fertilizer. It will stimulate strong root growth. Especially if you've purchased a large or expensive tree, it's worth the investment.

How to Plant a Wrapped Tree

Some trees are sold wrapped in burlap, a plastic version of burlap, or sometimes a type of webbing. Remove as much of it as possible before planting to allow the roots to grow and spread easily. Even more critical is that you cut or at least pull away the twine or wire wrapped around the trunk to keep it from strangling the tree as the tree grows.

If the tree is small or the soil is compacted around the roots, you can cut away the burlap and twine, then carry or roll the tree into the planting hole. (Always move the tree by lifting or rolling the roots, never the trunk, or it may break off.)

If the tree is large, you or the landscaper may have to set it in the hole fully wrapped. In this case, after positioning the plant in the hole, cut away as much twine and burlap as possible, being certain to remove at least the twine around the trunk and loosen the burlap.

Proceed with filling around the root ball with soil, then watering and mulching.

WORK SMARTER

STAKES OUT

Unless a tree is in a very windy site, it's not necessary to stake it. Research has shown that trees are more likely to send out long, strengthening roots to stabilize themselves if they are not staked.

Furthermore, staking could cause more problems than it solves. Many gardeners use rough twine or, even worse, wire, both of which rub the bark or cut into the tree. Or they tie the tree to the stake in such a way that the twine girdles the trunk and over time starts growing into the tree.

A benefit of staking is that it helps protect the tree from string trimmers and mowers bumping against it. A better solution is to mulch the newly planted tree 2 to 3 inches deep at least 1 to 2 feet out from the trunk of the tree.

How to Plant a Bare-Root Tree

Bare-root trees are commonly sold by mail-order suppliers, who ship bare-root to cut costs. Planting a bare-root tree is much like planting a container-grown tree, except you need to do a little preparation first and position it a bit more carefully. First soak the roots in a bucket of water for 8 to 24 hours to hydrate them thoroughly. For best results, add root stimulator to the water to get the plant off to a faster start.

Prepare the planting hole as you would for a container tree. Then make a rough cone shape of dirt at the bottom of the hole, and spread the roots over the cone. Position the tree so that the point where the trunk meets the roots is only an inch or so below the soil level.

Fill in, tamp lightly, water well, and mulch—just as you would with a container-grown tree.

PROJECT DETAILS

SKILLS: Digging and basic planting skills
PROJECT: Planting a small tree sold in a container

TIME TO COMPLETE

EXPERIENCED: 20 minutes
HANDY: 30 minutes
NOVICE: 40 minutes

STUFF YOU'LL NEED

TOOLS: Shovel, hose, garden gloves
MATERIALS: Root stimulator (optional), compost (optional), mulch

How to Plant a Container-Grown Tree

1 Dig the hole for the tree making it only as deep as the container is tall to prevent the tree from settling below grade. There is no need to amend the soil, although you can add several spadefuls of compost if desired.

2 Remove the tree from the container. If the roots are tangled, loosen them with your fingers or by slicing through the outer roots with a trowel.

3 Position the root ball in the hole. Use the handle of the spade to make sure the soil level around the tree will be the same as the soil level in the container once you fill in.

4 Mound the soil around the tree to create a moat to hold water. Water well, and allow it to soak in. Repeat two, three, or even four times. Finish off with a 2- to 3-inch layer of mulch.

Planting Shrubs

Planting shrubs well ensures that they have a good chance of taking off better and faster and sets them up for better general health and vigor in years to come. It also keeps you from having to move them because they were positioned incorrectly in the first place.

Handling Shrubs

If your shrubs will be sitting around for a few days before you plant them, be sure to keep them well watered, especially in hot weather. Stressed, dehydrated shrubs transplant poorly.

When handling your shrubs, be sure to carry them by their container, not the branches, which could stress or even break the stems.

Positioning Shrubs

Shrubs should be spaced according to their full-grown width, listed on the label. Plant them as far apart as their ultimate width. If a shrub will get 4 feet wide, plant each one 4 feet apart on center—that is, plant them so that the base of each shrub is 4 feet from the base of adjacent ones.

If you're planting a hedge, be sure to plant the shrubs in a perfectly straight line. If you will have just a few plants, it's fairly easy to get the row straight. However, with long hedges, it's a good idea to stretch a string between two stakes along the row where the hedge will be, to make sure your planting holes are perfectly aligned.

PROJECT DETAILS

SKILLS: Digging, basic planting
PROJECT: Planting a hedge of shrubs or trees

TIME TO COMPLETE

EXPERIENCED: About 1 hour to plant a hedge of 8 or so plants
HANDY: About 2 hours
NOVICE: About 2 hours

STUFF YOU'LL NEED

TOOLS: Spade, garden hose, garden gloves (optional)
MATERIALS: Mulch, root stimulator or starter fertilizer (optional), used according to package directions

How To Plant a Hedge

1 Dig the holes for the shrubs. Position the plants as desired. If you want a perfectly straight line, run a string between two stakes where the hedge will be and plant.

2 Position the shrubs in the holes, making sure they are still perfectly in line with the others. Loosen their roots if they are badly entangled, as these are.

3 Water each shrub well, allowing a hose to just barely trickle at the base of each for a half hour or more to soak the soil. Finish off with a layer of mulch.

Planting Shrubs on Slopes

Shrubs should be planted upright, even if they're on sloping ground. Most upright stems will naturally reach vertically as they grow, even if they have to bend to do so. Dig holes for shrubs on a sloping site much the way you would on a level site. Make sure that the plants are positioned straight up and down once they are placed in the hole. Build the soil moat only on the downhill side of the plant (see below). The top of the moat should be level with the uphill soil. This prevents water from rushing down past the shrub before having a chance to soak in. If your soil is heavy clay, omit the moat, but build up the soil to form a level planting area before setting your new shrub in place.

Aftercare

New shrubs need daily watering for the first few weeks, especially during hot weather. In cool seasons, you can water every other day for the first week. After that, cut back to once a week for two to three months, then reduce to once a month, until the shrubs have weathered a full growing season. Water faithfully unless nature supplies at least ½ inch of water a week. Once established, properly sited plants will need supplemental water only during hot, dry spells.

If winters are harsh in your region or your plant is only marginally cold-hardy in your region, in fall you can wrap the shrub to prevent winter burn (see page 187). Also, if rabbits are a problem in your garden, you'll want to make a small round fence of chicken wire and bury it about an inch into the soil around the shrub to protect it while it's young and delicious to rabbits. Remove the fence after a year or so.

How To Plant a Container Shrub

1 Select a spot to plant your new shrub. Make sure that the growing conditions match the needs of your plant. There should be enough space for the shrub to grow undisturbed for many years to come.

Dig a hole twice as wide as the plant's container. This will give the roots room to grow into the loosened soil before venturing into the native soil. Dig the hole only as deep as the container is tall to prevent the shrub from settling below grade.

2 Remove the shrub from its plastic pot and lay it on the ground. (Avoid tugging on the plant to pull it from the pot.) If the roots are pot-bound, use the shovel blade to score the root ball. Scoring encourages feeder roots to grow beyond the root ball, establishing the plant faster. If your plant seems stuck in the pot, cut away the bottom and set the plant in the hole. Slice the sides of the pot and gently remove it. This will help prevent damage to young roots.

3 Set the shrub in the hole to check the depth. The top of the root ball—where stems emerge from the soil—should be level with the surface of the undisturbed ground around the hole. If your shrub sits too low, the hole is too deep. Planting your shrub at this level will cause stems to rot. Remove the plant and shovel additional soil into the hole. Press the loose soil firmly to prevent settling later. Put the plant into the hole to check the depth again. If the top of the root ball sits too high, remove the plant and dig the hole deeper.

4 Once the shrub is at the proper depth, fill in around the root ball, mixing a spadeful or two of compost or other organic matter, such as sphagnum peat moss, into the soil as you go. Avoid tamping the soil in place; loose soil helps the shrub get water and air. Water well to settle the soil, and allow the water to soak in. Then add more soil to create a moat of soil, to allow water to collect around the shrub. Mulch with a 2- to 3-inch layer of mulch (see page 184). Water again by putting a garden hose at the base and setting it at the slightest trickle. Let it run for an hour or two, or until the water puddles.

PROJECT DETAILS

SKILLS: Basic planting skills
PROJECT: Planting a shrub sold in a pot

TIME TO COMPLETE

EXPERIENCED: About 20 minutes per shrub
HANDY: About 30 minutes per shrub
NOVICE: About 30 minutes per shrub

STUFF YOU'LL NEED

TOOLS: Round-point shovel, tarp for collecting soil, wheelbarrow for mixing soil, sturdy garden gloves, garden hose
MATERIALS: Organic material for amending the soil, mulch

Planting Roses

WORK SMARTER

HOW DEEP TO PLANT?

The graft union (also called the bud union) is the knobby part of the plant where the top has been grafted onto the roots. In most climates, plant the bud union 1 to 2 inches above the soil level. In cold-winter regions (Zones 5 and colder), plant it at soil level or up to 2 inches below the soil. If in doubt, follow the instructions that come with the rose, or check with your Home Depot garden associate.

Roses are sold in one of two ways—in containers or as bare-root plants. Which type you buy determines how and when you'll plant the rose.

Bare-root roses can be planted in early spring a month or two before your region's last frost date (see page 29) and tend to be less expensive. Container roses can be planted later in the season (a month before and after the last frost date) and usually cost a little more. Either way, be sure to take the time to get them started right.

Bare-Root Roses

These are often sold in cardboard cartons or foil or plastic bags. (Be sure to remove the container before planting!) Look for bare-root roses with firm, sound-looking stems and no shriveling. It's all right if a few leaves are starting to sprout. If the rose is sending out new stems and leaves longer than 3 to 4 inches, it has probably been sitting around too long and may have problems getting established in your garden.

Choose a site for your roses in full sun—a spot receiving at least 6 full hours of direct sun a day. The site also should have excellent drainage, because roses dislike soggy roots.

Prepare the soil by digging a hole about a foot deeper and wider than the roots of the plant. Work in several spadefuls of compost to enrich the soil, improve drainage, and feed the roses. Plant to the right depth for your climate (see box at left). Use a broomstick or spade handle laid across the planting hole to judge the depth accurately.

If desired, also work in a slow-release granular fertilizer, following package directions. Some fertilizers are made specifically for roses and also contain a systemic pesticide.

After planting, mound soil around the rose to prevent the graft union from drying out at its base. Water well and keep moist for the next few weeks, then gently hose or push the mound away from the plant.

Container Roses

In Zone 5 and colder, plant container roses only in spring, so they have time to become well established before winter sets in. In Zone 6 and warmer, you can plant roses in spring or fall. Choose sturdy-looking plants with healthy green leaves and no wilted, spotted, yellow, or chewed leaves.

Aftercare

Keep the rose well-watered, making sure the soil is neither too dry nor soggy. In a week or two, the rose should start sending out new growth, a sign that it's taking off. This is a good time to apply a fertilizer to encourage new, strong growth. A slow-release rose fertilizer, available at most garden centers, is ideal. Just work it into the soil around the base of the rose. It's also a good idea to mulch around the base of the rose, 1 to 3 inches deep, to suppress weeds, prevent disease, and conserve moisture. Also keep the rose well fertilized into late summer (see page 181); in cold regions, provide winter protection (see page 201).

PROJECT DETAILS

SKILLS: Basic planting skills
PROJECT: Planting a rose sold in a pot

TIME TO COMPLETE

EXPERIENCED: 20 minutes
HANDY: 30 minutes
NOVICE: 40 minutes

STUFF YOU'LL NEED

TOOLS: Spade, hand pruners, bucket, hose or watering can
MATERIALS: Rose in container, compost or other soil amendments, root stimulator or starter fertilizer (optional), used according to package directions

How to Plant a Container-Grown Rose

1 Remove the rose from its pot. You may need to step on the side of the pot once or twice to loosen the root ball. Dig a hole about 6–10 inches deeper than the rose's roots, working in abundant compost.

2 Position the rose in the hole so the soil is level with the surrounding soil. Mound soil slightly to form a moat so water will puddle around the rose. Water well, and allow the water to soak in; then water two or three times more to make sure that the water reaches all the roots.

How to Plant a Bare-Root Rose

1 Prune the rose unless it has been prepruned by the seller (see box at right). Cut off any damaged branches and roots, and thin it (ideally) to three to six healthy branches at least as thick as a pencil.

2 Soak the roots in a bucket for about 12 hours. This helps hydrate the rose and keep it from drying out once you've planted it in the ground. Then prepare a hole, working in several spadefuls of compost to improve drainage and feed the rose.

3 Position the rose in the hole so the graft union is the correct height (see box on opposite page). Spread out the roots. Fill the hole with soil, and mound it in a small moat around the rose so water will collect at its base.

4 Water well, allowing the water to soak in; repeat two or three times. After watering, mound soil about 6 inches over the base of the plant to prevent the graft union from drying out. Push aside the soil after 2 to 3 weeks or gently wash it away.

PROJECT DETAILS

SKILLS: Digging, perhaps some pruning

PROJECT: Planting a rose sold bare-root, that is, without soil and without foliage

TIME TO COMPLETE

EXPERIENCED: About 20 minutes per rose, once it's soaked

HANDY: About 30 minutes per rose, once it's soaked

NOVICE: About 30 minutes per rose, once it's soaked

STUFF YOU'LL NEED

TOOLS: Spade, hand pruners, bucket, watering can or hose

MATERIALS: Bare-root rose, compost or other soil amendments, root stimulator or starter fertilizer (optional), applied according to package directions

BUYER'S GUIDE

PLANTING-TIME PRUNING

Most bare-root roses are sold "prepruned"—that is, they have no more than three to six stems, each only a foot or two long. Check the package to make sure. If still in doubt, use your good judgment on the general shape of the rose. Remove any damaged canes. Then evaluate it: It should have three to six stems cupping outward into an open vaselike shape, and the branches should each be about 8 to 12 inches long. If not, prune them (see page 198).

Planting Annuals And Perennials

For some gardeners, planting annuals and perennials is their favorite garden task. It's fun to mix and match flowers, and the payoff is often instant—just stand back and admire your handiwork.

Your flowers will take off faster and require less watering, weeding, and all-around work if you plant them properly. Choose the optimum time, prepare the soil, and plant smart. You'll be rewarded with lush plants and plentiful blooms for months to come.

Preparation

- Choose only full, healthy plants at the garden center. They should look large for their pots and look healthy with no wilting or yellowing. (Unhealthy plants will probably only go downhill.) Annuals, especially, may be flowering but have tiny, underdeveloped root systems. If you aren't sure, with the garden center's permission, knock or lift one of the plants out of its pot or cell pack to check.
- Plant as soon as possible after purchase. When plants sit around for days (and even weeks) in pots, they become stressed.
- Plant cool-season annuals, such as pansies and snapdragons, four to six weeks before your region's last frost date in spring. (Plant in late fall or early winter in warm-winter climates for winter color.) Plant warm-season annuals, such as marigolds and impatiens, after danger of frost has passed.
- Plant perennials just about anytime as long as it's not excessively hot—daytime highs of 85°F (29°C)—or cold (dipping regularly below freezing).

Planting

- Always work and amend the soil. Each time you plant annuals and perennials, be sure to dig down with your spade a foot or so to loosen the soil to encourage good drainage. Also be sure to work in plenty of compost, sphagnum peat moss, or another amendments (see page 138). In the short run, your immediate planting will be more likely to thrive. In the long run, you'll greatly improve your soil over the years.
- If you like to plant annuals each year, leave "pockets" for them in your mixed beds of perennials, bulbs, and annuals. Filling these pockets will add bursts of color, and the pockets will keep you from digging up any bulbs or late-emerging perennials.
- Mass annuals or perennials. Depending on the size, plant six or eight perennials or a dozen or more annuals in drifts for best effect and to avoid a patchwork look.

BUYER'S GUIDE

UNDERSTANDING BARE-ROOT PERENNIALS

Plants are sometimes sold bare-root, that is, they look as though they were just dug up and the soil shaken off, exposing the roots. They are usually packaged in bags or boxes, allowing growers to keep down packaging and handling costs and pass those savings on to you.

Because they're sold while dormant (not actively growing), they often look dead and not very promising. But with proper planting and care, they'll do just fine.

Choose bare-root perennials with care. The plant might be brown, but it should be healthy-looking and firm, not withered. Sometimes plants will start sending up new growth, which is fine as long as the growth is green and healthy, not pale and spindly or recently green and now brown and withered.

Plant bare-root perennials in the four weeks preceding and following your region's last average frost date in spring. In warm climates (Zone 7 and warmer), you can also plant bare-root perennials in fall.

Anyone can plant a flower, but if you plant them well they'll take off faster, be healthier, and bloom heavier.

• Water deeply. When you water, give the plants a good, deep soaking. Allow the water to seep in for 15 to 20 minutes, then water a second and even a third time to make sure the soil is thoroughly soaked several inches down.

• Protect your plants from wildlife and pets as needed. If rabbits are a problem in your area, you may want to create a temporary fence of chicken or other mesh wire around your succulent, tender new plantings for a week or so. Once plants get larger, they are less tasty to rabbits; and the soil settles, making it less tempting for pets to go digging. You can then remove the fencing with more confidence.

Aftercare

• For a few days after planting, check on your annuals and perennials each day and water if needed.

• Mulch. Add 1 to 2 inches of a mulch such as wood chips, pine needles, or grass clippings. Mulch does a superb job of retaining moisture, preventing weeds, and preventing mud from splashing on plants, which encourages disease.

• Avoid fertilizing right away. Instead, allow the plants to get established. Then, a couple of weeks after planting, fertilize with a slow-release fertilizer as desired. (See page 176 for more fertilizing tips.)

How to Plant Annuals and Perennials

1 Dig the hole. Use a shovel for large plants and a trowel for small plants in loose soil. In most cases, make the hole a few inches wider and deeper than the plant's pot. If the soil is heavy clay, make the hole twice as deep as the pot to improve drainage.

2 Amend the soil. Even if you've improved the soil in past years, work in the equivalent of a spadeful or two of compost or other soil amendment for large holes, or a trowelful or two for small holes. Then remove the plant from its pot.

PROJECT DETAILS

SKILLS: Digging, planting
PROJECT: Planting annuals and perennials

TIME TO COMPLETE

EXPERIENCED: 10 to 15 minutes for a few plants
HANDY: 15 to 20 minutes
NOVICE: 20 to 25 minutes

STUFF YOU'LL NEED

TOOLS: Shovel, trowel, hose, watering can
MATERIALS: Annuals and/or perennials, compost or other soil amendments, mulch

3 Loosen the roots as needed. If the roots are knotted or circling around the pot, loosen them with your fingers to stimulate them and encourage them to spread out in the soil.

4 Set the plant in the ground. The base of the plant should be level with the surrounding soil. Then make a small moat around the plant with your hands or a trowel to help water puddle around the plant.

5 Mulch, then water thoroughly. Soak the ground and not the plant; with small plants it's almost impossible to avoid dousing the whole plant. Keep the soil evenly moist for the next several weeks.

Planting Vines

The basics of planting a vine are the same as for any other plant.

If the vine is to be started from seed, see page 166 for tips on starting plants from seed indoors and out. If it's in a pot, see page 148 on planting basics. If it's bare-root in a bag or box, see page 156 for tips on planting bare-root perennials.

Providing the Right Support

Different vines do well on different types of supports.

Vigorous, borderline invasive twining vines, such as bittersweet, wisteria, honeysuckle, and morning glory, will twine up about any vertical support with ease, even a single wire.

More timid twining vines or those with delicate clinging tendrils, such as clematis, sweet peas, and black-eyed Susan vine, do best if given a gridded, closely spaced support, such as latticework or mesh.

Vines that attach themselves with stickfasts or aerial rootlets, such as trumpet vine, English ivy, Boston ivy, and climbing hydrangea, will do beautifully on walls and buildings. They also do well on latticework, attaching themselves to the flat surface of the wood. However, avoid planting them on wood or stucco that must be painted, because they're difficult to remove without leaving behind tiny bits of rootlets.

If the support starts several inches off the ground and the vine is small or will be started from seed, tuck a stick in next to the vine to give it something to climb on from the soil to the support.

See page 88 for illustrations of the ways that various vines climb.

Aftercare

Most vines benefit from a layer of mulch to help keep the surrounding soil moist. Also, a couple of weeks after they're planted, most vines, especially fast-growing annual vines, which need a lot of food to fuel their rapid growth, appreciate an application of fertilizer.

Mandevilla is a beautiful vine that will reward you with many flowers as long as you position and plant it well.

5

Preparation, Planting, and Propagation

PROJECT DETAILS

SKILLS: A bit of patience
PROJECT: Training a vine up a support

TIME TO COMPLETE

EXPERIENCED: 5 minutes
HANDY: 10 minutes
NOVICE: 10 minutes

STUFF YOU'LL NEED

TOOLS: Scissors
MATERIALS: Soft twine, strips of neutral-colored rag, or strips of pantyhose

How to Train a Vine

1 When the vine is small and as long as it is soft and pliable, twist it gently once or twice around the support. Some vines have a natural tendency to twine clockwise or counterclockwise, so work with their natural pattern, as much as you can determine it. Stiffer vines may need the help of stretch tape, strips of pantyhose or rag, or soft twine.

2 Keep tying. Every week or so, as the vine grows, check how well it's climbing. Depending on the support and the vine, it may simply scramble up by itself, but some may need tying all the way up.

Planting Groundcovers

The process of planting groundcovers is basically the same as that for any other plant (see "Planting Basics" on page 148): Prepare the soil, plant, water, and mulch.

The difference is in scale. With a groundcover, you're going to plant more than just one or two perennials or a small shrub or two; you're going to plant several or even dozens of plants.

Efficiency, then, is paramount to save time, money, and effort.

Start with measuring. It's important to space groundcovers the optimum distance apart. Plant them too closely and they'll choke one another out; plant them too far apart and the planting will look sparse.

To prevent this, measure and write down the square footage of the area you want to fill so that you purchase the right number of plants.

What is the right number? As a rule, plant groundcovers about 10 percent closer than their expected mature width. So if a label says that a plant grows 12 inches wide, plant individuals about 10 inches apart. If it says 18 to 24 inches wide, plant them 21 inches apart.

The exception is plants that spread indefinitely, such as bishop's weed, ajuga, periwinkle, English ivy, purple-leaf winter creeper, and creeping St. Johnswort. You could plant each several feet apart, and in several years they'd form a carpet of plants. If that is too long to wait, check with your Home Depot garden associate on the best spacing for your conditions and climate.

To plant groundcovers, first remove any grass or weeds from the area by digging and weeding. Then amend the soil as needed (see pages 136 to 139), working in plenty of organic matter. This is a permanent planting where you will be working the soil little in the future. It's good to take the opportunity now to loosen and enrich the soil several inches deep or more.

If the area is on a slope, however, work the soil as little as possible to prevent erosion. Then cover the area with landscape fabric or burlap. Cut through the fabric and enrich and loosen only the area within a few inches of where each plant will be positioned.

Mulch the groundcover after planting. Mulch deters weeds and conserves moisture. If you used landscape fabric, top it with wood chips or another loose mulch (see pages 184 to 185). Also, a week or two after planting, it's a good idea to sprinkle the planting with a granular preemergent herbicide/fertilizer combination or any other weed killer that destroys weeds before they germinate. Once a weed takes hold in a planting of groundcover, it can be difficult to get it all out without digging up the groundcover, weeds and all, and picking the weeds out of each plant. It's a laborious job, so stay on top of weeding from planting time onward.

GOOD IDEA

FENCE IT IN

If a groundcover is vigorous, it's a good idea to make sure its roots are blocked on all sides to keep it from creeping into other plantings or the lawn. Make sure that an edging separates any vigorous groundcover from the lawn and the rest of the flower bed. You may want to run edging right through the flower bed to hem in the groundcover, especially if you have perennials, annuals, or other small plants there that you want to protect from being overtaken.

PROJECT DETAILS

SKILLS: Basic planting skills
PROJECT: Planting a group of groundcovers

TIME TO COMPLETE

EXPERIENCED: An hour or so to plant several
HANDY: An hour or so
NOVICE: A couple of hours

STUFF YOU'LL NEED

TOOLS: Shovel, trowel, hose
MATERIALS: Groundcover plants, soil amendments

How to Plant Groundcovers

1 Prepare the soil for planting by working in soil amendments. Position the groundcovers while still in their pots and space them evenly. If the groundcovers are in cell packs, pull them out and lay them on the ground to position them.

2 Remove plants from the pots. Dig holes for each groundcover, then plant them, firming the soil around each one.

3 Mulch and water well. Keep well watered for the first two weeks or so, or until the plants are established.

Planting Bulbs

Bulbs come in two categories: spring-blooming and summer-blooming.

Each fall, garden centers fill up with enticing displays of spring-blooming bulbs. Spring may seem a long way off at that point, but spring-blooming bulbs, such as tulips, daffodils, crocuses, hyacinths, scilla, and grape hyacinths, are planted in fall to add a dash of color first thing in spring.

Summer-blooming bulbs, which include cannas, dahlias, gladioli, and lilies, are usually planted in spring, then bloom a few months later. They can be purchased loose as bulbs or already potted up and growing. Many (with the notable exception of lilies and irises) will not last the winter in Zone 7 and colder (see page 26 for a zone map) unless they are dug up and stored indoors for the winter (see page 205).

Because bulbs are seasonal, buy when you first see them available to ensure the best selection. Choose full, firm bulbs that appear unwithered and without any mold or brown discoloration. Whenever possible, buy "full-size" bulbs—that is, bulbs that are the top size for their type. This helps ensure that the bulb will thrive and produce generous numbers of full-size flowers.

Whatever type of bulbs you choose, always plant them in clusters of at least 10 or more so the planting will have a presence in the landscape.

When to Plant

- Plant spring-blooming bulbs in October or November, usually for up to four weeks after your region's first average frost date (see page 29).
- Plant summer-blooming bulbs in spring, anytime after your region's last average frost date (see page 29).
- Don't plant too early. Even if spring-blooming bulbs are available in,

GOOD IDEA!

PREVENT SQUIRREL DAMAGE

If squirrels tend to dig up and damage the bulbs you plant in fall, try this easy trick. Plant them in a cluster in a large hole. Top with a piece of chicken wire cut to fit the hole. Cover with soil. The squirrels will be thwarted and the bulbs will grow up easily through the wire.

Bulb planting depth

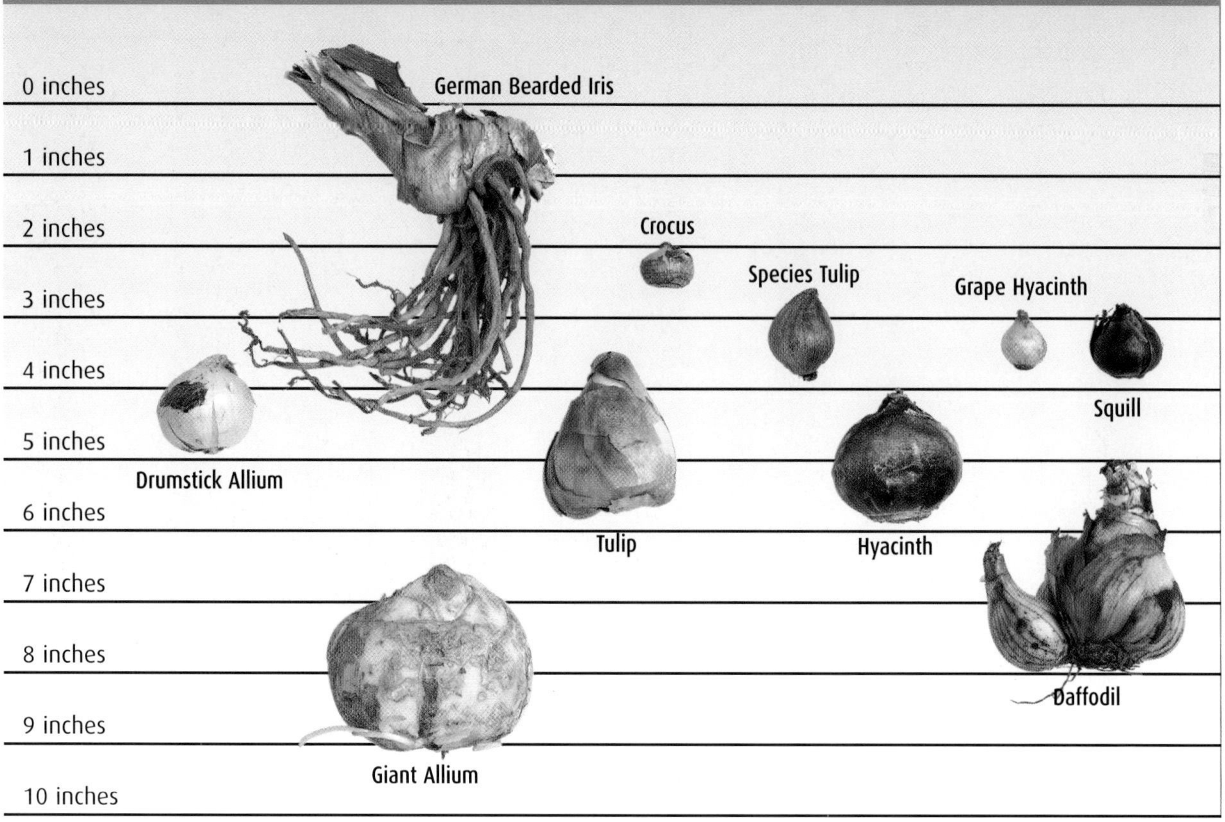

0 inches
1 inches
2 inches
3 inches
4 inches
5 inches
6 inches
7 inches
8 inches
9 inches
10 inches

German Bearded Iris
Crocus
Species Tulip
Grape Hyacinth
Squill
Drumstick Allium
Tulip
Hyacinth
Daffodil
Giant Allium

say, September and planting time in your region isn't until October, don't plant them early or they'll start growing prematurely and peter out. If in doubt, check with your Home Depot garden associate.

- In warm climates, those in Zones 8 and warmer, you can stagger plantings of many bulbs every 2 weeks to assure the longest period of bloom of your favorite bulbs.

How to Plant

- Purchase bulbs as close to planting time as possible and then plant them as soon as possible after purchasing, especially those that shrivel or spoil quickly, such as hyacinths and tulips. All other bulbs can be kept in a cool, dry place for a few weeks.
- Provide excellent drainage. Bulbs are prone to rot, so loosen the soil several inches deeper than the bulbs, and work in a little compost.
- Cluster bulbs in groups. The smaller the bulb, the larger the group. Group small bulbs, such as crocuses, in clumps of 30 or more. Group large bulbs, such as daffodils and tulips, in clumps of 15 to 20 or more. They look unnatural planted singly or in straight rows.
- Use a fertilizer made specifically for bulbs. Although bonemeal is a popular fertilizer for bulbs, it is missing some necessary nutrients, and it may attract rodents if used too close to the surface. Use compost or a commercial bulb fertilizer instead.
- Plant at the correct depth. The depth listed in the planting instructions is from the bottom of the bulb and includes any mulch you're applying (avoid applying more than 3 inches). In Zone 5 and colder, plant bulbs about an inch deeper than specified.

A CLOSER LOOK

WHICH SIDE IS UP?

Bulbs come in many different forms, and it can be confusing to figure out which way to plant each bulb. As a general rule, if there's a pointed side, it goes up. This is where the flower will emerge. The exceptions are ranunculus and dahlias. On these, any pointed parts are emerging roots; therefore, the pointed parts should be planted facing down.

In the long run, however, it really matters little. Bulbs will send up shoots and send out roots regardless; it may simply take them slightly longer to bloom if they start out pointed the wrong way.

How to Plant Bulbs

1 Dig the hole. Add compost or soil amendments to the bottom, loosening the soil a few inches below where the bulbs will be. Add bulb fertilizer, following package directions.

2 Position the bulbs at the recommended depth (check the label or bag). Put the base of the bulbs at the depth recommended by the supplier. Then fill the hole with soil, and water well. Label the area to avoid accidentally digging up the bulbs later.

PROJECT DETAILS

SKILLS: Digging, planting
PROJECT: Planting spring-blooming bulbs in the ground in autumn

TIME TO COMPLETE

EXPERIENCED: About 15 minutes for a grouping of a dozen or so bulbs
HANDY: About 20 minutes
NOVICE: About 20 minutes

STUFF YOU'LL NEED

TOOLS: Spade, plant labels and marker, watering can, hose
MATERIALS: Bulbs, commercial bulb fertilizer, compost or soil amendments

Chilling Bulbs for Outdoor Bloom in Warm Climates

A CLOSER LOOK

HOW LONG TO CHILL BULBS TO PLANT OUTDOORS?

Different bulbs require different chilling times to plant outdoors in warm climates

Tulip: Chill for 14 to 16 weeks
Crocus: Chill for 12 to 14 weeks
Hyacinth: Chill for 14 to 16 weeks
Daffodil, Paper-white, and Ranunculus:
No chilling needed.

Some of the most popular spring-blooming bulbs need to undergo a cold winter of some sort. In the hottest regions, nature needs a little help.

In the northern two-thirds of the United States and in Canada, nature supplies the chill. But in the southern portions of the United States and portions of California (Zones 9 to 11; see page 26), to successfully grow tulips, crocuses, and hyacinths, you first must chill the bulbs in the refrigerator before planting them outdoors. Some bulbs are sold prechilled, but even these will benefit from additional chilling. The easiest way to prechill bulbs is to store them in the refrigerator where temperatures stay between 40 and 45°F (4–7°C). Store them in breathable mesh bags, which many bulbs are sold in, or paper bags. Allow them to chill for 12 to 16 weeks. Keep the bulbs separate from fruits, because the ethylene gas given off by ripening fruit can kill the bulbs. Plant the bulbs outside in December or January in warm climates. They'll bloom just one year, but you'll love the show.

Even in warm climates, beautiful tulips such as these can be grown as long as you chill the bulbs in the refrigerator first to mimic winter's cold.

PROJECT DETAILS

SKILLS: Basic planting skills
PROJECT: In warm-winter climates, chilling bulbs to encourage bloom

TIME TO COMPLETE

EXPERIENCED: 10 minutes
HANDY: 10 minutes
NOVICE: 10 minutes

STUFF YOU'LL NEED

TOOLS: Shovel for planting
MATERIALS: Paper bag, bulbs

Chilling Bulbs for Outdoor Planting

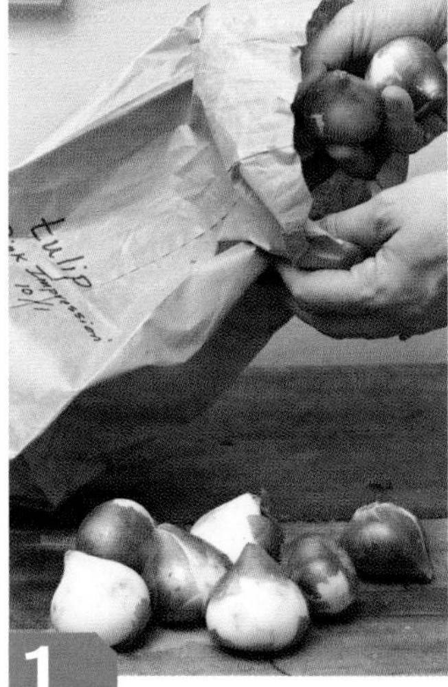

1 Slip the bulbs into the paper bag, labeling it to keep track. List the type of bulb as well as the date the bulbs were put in and when they should be removed.

2 Chill the bulbs in the crisper drawer for the appropriate period of time (see chart above).

3 Plant the bulbs outdoors immediately. They are unlikely to return year after year, but will give you a beautiful show for one spring.

Forcing Bulbs for Indoor Winter Bloom

Forcing bulbs is a harsh-sounding name for a delightful process. Pot up bulbs in fall, place them in the refrigerator for a few weeks to trick them into thinking it's winter, then pull them out again later in winter so they'll grow and bloom indoors, bringing cheer to even the gloomiest winter day.

Start by buying bulbs in fall when they go on display. You can force many types of bulbs, but tulips, daffodils, and hyacinths are among the easiest to force in pots. Paper-white narcissus and amaryllis need no prechilling and are easy to grow. They can be forced simply by planting them in a bowl of pebbles and water. They will bloom in just a few weeks.

Most other bulbs need to chill for several weeks at 50 to 55°F (10 to 13°C). It's easiest to chill the bulbs, potted up and slipped into a clear plastic bag, in the refrigerator, but an unheated garage, a cold frame, or an uninsulated crawlspace that is always cool but never freezing will work as well.

Forced 'Red Apeldoorn' tulips add color in late winter when you need it most.

A CLOSER LOOK

HOW LONG UNTIL BLOOM WHEN FORCING INDOORS FOR WINTER BLOOM?

Different bulbs need different treatments to bloom indoors in winter.

Amaryllis: No chilling; blooms 4 to 10 weeks after planting in pots.

Paper-white narcissus: No chilling; blooms 3 to 5 weeks after planting in pebbles and water.

Daffodil: Chill 14 to 17 weeks; blooms 2 to 3 weeks after planting in pots.

Hyacinth: Chill potted bulbs 10 to 12 weeks; unpotted 11 to 14. Blooms 2 to 3 weeks after.

Tulip: Chill planted in pots 14 to 20 weeks; blooms 2 to 3 weeks after.

Crocus: Chill planted in pots 14 weeks; blooms 2 to 3 weeks after.

Grape hyacinth: Chill 13 to 15 weeks; blooms 2 to 3 weeks after.

PROJECT DETAILS

SKILLS: Potting up

PROJECT: Planting spring-blooming bulbs indoors for winter bloom

TIME TO COMPLETE

EXPERIENCED: About 20 minutes

HANDY: About 25 minutes

NOVICE: About 30 minutes

STUFF YOU'LL NEED

TOOLS: None

MATERIALS: Tulips, daffodils, hyacinths, or other bulbs that force when potted up, pot or pots, potting soil

How to Force Bulbs for Indoor Bloom

1 Plant the bulbs in fall in a pot, placing them pointed side up as close together as possible. Barely cover their tops with soil. Water well. Put the pot in a plastic bag in the refrigerator or other cold spot. Keep moist.

2 Remove from the cold when shoots are an inch or so high. Put the pot in the sunniest spot available, such as a south-facing window. Keep watered.

Transplanting a Tree

WORK SMARTER

WHEN IS A TREE TOO BIG TO TRANSPLANT?

There are two rules to use when deciding if a tree can be successfully transplanted.

First is its size. The roots extend about as far as the branches do. To determine how deep to dig, figure on digging as deep as the spread of the branches.

The exception is a tree that has been planted in the past two years or so. In that case, the roots have probably grown only a foot or so beyond the original container size.

Transplanting a tree less than 6 feet tall is an easy enough job for the fairly fit, but transplanting larger trees takes strong arms and a good friend.

Do the transplanting on an calm, overcast day on which rain is predicted. Beating sun and wind wreak havoc with newly planted trees, drying them out quickly. Make sure the tree is well hydrated; water well two or three days before if necessary to make sure it's up for transplanting.

Evergreens can be transplanted anytime that the soil can easily be worked and when temperatures are not above 80°F (27°C).

With a deciduous tree, the ideal time of year to plant is when the tree is just starting to leaf out, so there's less water loss through mature leaves. However, in the southern half of the United States, another good time is autumn, when a tree is beginning to lose its leaves.

To transplant a tree that is less than 6 feet tall, start digging at the dripline, the circle that goes out as far as the branches do. Dig approximately the same distance down. If the dripline extends 2 feet from the trunk, dig down 2 feet. With a little luck, much of the soil will cling to the roots as you dig.

Position a tarp next to the tree. With the help of a friend, lift the root ball—avoid lifting by the stem or it may break—onto the tarp. Drag the tarp to the tree's new home.

Plant as you would a container-grown tree, as directed on page 151.

PROJECT DETAILS

SKILLS: Digging, good strength
PROJECT: Digging up a small tree to transplant it elsewhere

TIME TO COMPLETE

EXPERIENCED: 1 hour
HANDY: 2 hours
NOVICE: 2 hours

STUFF YOU'LL NEED

TOOLS: Root stimulator (optional; follow package directions), spade, tarp, a friend if the tree is large

How to Move a Tree

1 Move only those trees that you or you and a friend can dig up and handle. Move them in spring, or in fall in warm regions. Start by digging a circle around the dripline—the reach of the outermost branches.

2 Dig the hole as deep as you dug wide. Remove the tree with as much of the root ball intact as possible.

3 Roll or drag the root ball (handle the trunk as little as possible to keep it from snapping) onto a tarp. Drag the tarp to the tree's new location and plant it (see page 151 for details on how to plant a tree.) Keep it well watered for several weeks, or until it starts sending out new growth.

Dividing Perennials

Dividing perennials keeps them healthy and vigorous; it also gives you more plants to put around your garden or to share with friends and family.

What Time of Year to Divide?

- Divide spring-blooming plants immediately after flowering.
- Divide summer- and fall-blooming plants in early spring when they have 2 to 4 inches of top growth.
- In the South and Southwest, divide all but fall bloomers in fall. They love the cooler, wetter weather of autumn.
- Give your perennials at least four weeks to establish themselves before 90°F (32°C) temperatures or above, or freezing temperatures, arrive.
- Divide perennials on a cool, overcast day on which rain is forecast. Gentle, moist weather helps prevent heat stress on the tender new divisions.

Dividing Basics

Different plants require slightly different approaches, but basically, to divide a plant, you dig up the plant, break it into sections, and replant.

Depending on the size of the plant, you'll get from two or three new plants to a dozen. The new divisions can then be planted. Cut back the foliage by two-thirds, or to only a few inches high. Prepare the soil where any of the divisions will be planted, working in ample compost or other organic matter (see page 148 for planting basics).

Water the divisions well and keep them well watered for at least the next four weeks. Apply a 2-inch layer of mulch around the plants to protect them from extremes of heat and cold and to conserve moisture.

A CLOSER LOOK

SIGNS THAT A PERENNIAL NEEDS DIVIDING

Some plants need dividing more often than others. Most perennials need division every three to five years. Peonies are happy with no division for 10 years or more, whereas 'Autumn Joy' sedum needs dividing as often as every other year. As a rule, the faster the plant grows, the more often it needs dividing. These clues indicate it's time:

- The center of the crown at the base of the plant shows no new growth, and the plant may be forming a ring, as shown with the Siberian iris above.
- Flowering is reduced.
- The plant had been doing well for a year or two but is now floppy when it flowers.

How to Divide Perennials

Flowers with Fibrous Roots
Use a spade to dig up the shallow, sometimes loosely knotted roots. They often will break apart as they're dug, or you can easily break them apart with your hands. If not, a little prod with a trowel or a spade usually will do the trick.

Flowers with a Large Root Ball
Dig up the entire root. If the roots won't break apart with a spade, use a small hand ax to cut them apart. This works best if you lay the root ball on its side and cut from the sides inward rather than from the top downward.

Flowers with Tough Roots
If a plant's root ball is large but fairly easy to cut through, divide it by slicing off portions of the plant from its outside edges rather than digging up the entire plant.

Starting Plants From Seed

Nothing will save you more money—or make you swell up with a proud parent's satisfaction—like starting plants from seeds. And it's simple, once you get the knack and as long as you use easy-to-grow seeds.

How to Achieve Success with Seeds

Begin with flowers that are easy to start from seed (see the chart on page 167). One way to tell is to check how many days the seeds take to germinate—that is, sprout. If they germinate in a week or less, they're very easy. If it takes a week or two, they're somewhat easy. Plants that need more than two weeks to germinate or have special requirements, such as freezing, are difficult to start from seed.

For best success, follow package directions *exactly*. Follow the recommended date and temperature suggestions to the letter. It's especially important to avoid starting too early in the season, or seedlings will get leggy before you can plant them.

A temporary greenhouse is perfect for starting large amounts of seed each spring.

You can plant in about any container that can be punched with a drainage hole—an egg carton, a clear plastic produce container, or a paper cup, for example.

Choose the Right Soil

Choose a mix made specifically for seed (avoid regular potting mixes or soil from the garden). Otherwise, seeds may rot or become prone to diseases.

Some seeds should be left uncovered—they need light to germinate. Others need to be covered with soil because they germinate best in the dark. A few, such as morning glories and sweet peas, need to be soaked several hours in warm water. Check the seed packet to find out. Then sprinkle soil lightly over the seeds, if necessary, to the depth specified on the packet.

Water Carefully

Tiny seeds are easily washed out. To prevent this, set the container in a tray filled with water halfway up the sides of the container. Water will slowly seep up from the bottom. Remove the seed container after a half hour or so, when the soil's surface becomes moist. With very tiny seeds, fill the container with damp seed-starting medium, plant the seeds, and then water with a spray bottle. Slip into a clear plastic bag to retain moisture.

Keep Seeds at the Right Temperature

Allow the planted seeds to germinate at the temperature suggested on the seed packet. "Warm" usually means 70 to 80°F (21 to 26°C); "cool" means 55 to 65°F (13 to 18°C). Set a room thermometer next to the seeds to make sure they're at the right temperature. Move the seed containers to different spots in the house until you find one cool or warm enough (a bathroom with the door kept shut is often quite warm; the floor in the basement or garage is often quite cool). You can also purchase warming mats to set containers of seeds on if you're worried that they need more warmth.

Light the Seedlings

As soon as the seeds start to sprout, remove the plastic bag and put them in a south-facing window or directly under a grow-light. Better yet, combine the two. Too little light is a leading cause of sickly seedlings.

Unless the weather is extremely cold, you can also put them in a cold frame (see page 31) or one of the new small greenhouses now available. Be sure to bring in the plants on very cold nights and to open the cold frame or greenhouse on sunny days to prevent overheating.

How to Start Seeds Indoors

1 Fill an egg carton or a shallow container that will drain well with a mix made for starting seeds. Sprinkle with seeds. Cover with more mix as directed. Set the container in a tray of water to moisten, or sprinkle water on the mix gently with your hands, or use a spray bottle to water the seeds to keep them from being dislodged.

2 Slip the container into a plastic bag to keep it warm and moist. Position a room thermometer nearby to make sure the temperature is right for the type of seed (check the package). After a few days or weeks, once the seeds germinate, remove the bag.

3 Provide light as soon as the seeds germinate. Use a sunny south-facing window, a grow-light just a few inches above the plants, or both. Raise the grow-light as the seedlings grow.

PROJECT DETAILS

SKILLS: Basic planting skills
PROJECT: Starting seeds indoors in early spring to get a jump on the growing season

TIME TO COMPLETE

EXPERIENCED: 15 minutes
HANDY: 20 minutes
NOVICE: 30 minutes

STUFF YOU'LL NEED

TOOLS: Grow-light (or a sunny south-facing window), room thermometer
MATERIALS: Seeds, seed-starting mix, seed-starting container, plastic bag

Easiest Plants to Start From Seed

Common Name	Botanical Name	Zones
Annual and Perennial Flowers		
Black-eyed Susan	*Rudbeckia* spp.	3–10
Celosia	*Celosia* spp.	Annual
Coneflower, purple	*Echinacea purpurea*	3–9
Cornflower, annual	*Centaurea cyanus*	Annual
Cosmos	*Cosmos* spp.	Annual
Hollyhock	*Alcea rosea*	3–11
Marigold	*Tagetes* spp.	Annual
Morning glory	*Ipomoea tricolor*	Annual
Pansy	*Viola* spp.	Annual
Shasta daisy	*Leucanthemum* ×*superbum*	4–9
Snapdragon	*Antirrhinum majus*	Annual
Sunflower, annual	*Helianthus annuus*	Annual
Sweet pea	*Lathyrus odoratus*	Annual
Yarrow	*Achillea* spp.	3–9
Zinnia	*Zinnia* spp.	Annual

Common Name
Vegetables
Cucumber
Lettuce
Melon
Pepper
Radish
Squash
Tomato
Zucchini

A Timeline of Favorite Annuals For Starting Indoors from Seed

Some seeds should be started indoors because they need the special warmth and attention you can give them by carefully controlling soil, moisture, and temperature. Also, some, such as tomatoes, have a long growing season and need the extra time they get by being started early.

Common Name	Botanical Name
10 Weeks Before Last Frost Date in Spring	
Impatiens	*Impatiens walleriana*
Onion	
Parsley	*Petroselinum crispum*
Petunia	*Petunia* spp.
Sweet pea	*Lathrus odoratus*
6 to 8 Weeks Before Last Frost Date in Spring	
Basil	*Ocimum* spp.
Celosia	*Celosia* spp.
Marigold	*Tagetes* spp.
Pepper	
Salvia, annual types	*Salvia* spp.
Snapdragon	*Antirrhinum majus*
Tomato	
2 to 4 Weeks Before Last Frost Date in Spring	
Cosmos	*Cosmos* spp.
Hollyhock	*Alcea rosea*
Nasturium	*Tropaeolum majus*
Sunflower, annual types	*Helianthus annuus*

Annuals to Start Outdoors from Seed

Some seeds can be planted directly in the ground. They usually need to be thinned, however, once they germinate, because the seed gets scattered so thickly that the maturing plants are too crowded to grow.

Common Name	Botanical Name
Flowers	
Cornflower, annual	
Cosmos	*Cosmos* spp.
Larkspur	*Consolida ambigua*
Marigold	*Tagetes*
Moonflower	*Impomea alba*
Morning Glory	*Ipomoea tricolor*
Poppies, annual types	*Papaver* spp.
Sunflower	*Helianthus annuus*
Zinnia	*Zinnia elegans*
Vegetables	
Beet	
Cucumber	
Green bean	
Lettuce	
Melon	
Pea	
Spinach, collard, other greens	
Squash, pumpkin	
Zucchini	

Starting Seeds Outdoors

There are times when you'll want to start seeds outdoors directly in the soil.

Many vegetables are commonly started from seed outdoors, such as lettuces, green beans, beets, cucumbers, and squash. They grow quickly and may resist transplanting, so starting them outdoors makes sense.

Sow the seeds once the soil has warmed enough for your plant (check the package). Some plants, such as lettuce, annual poppies, and larkspur, like cool soil in early spring. But cucumbers and beans will fail to germinate unless the soil is warm enough, usually about two weeks after your region's last frost date.

Work the soil well, adding soil amendments (see page 138) as needed to make a high-quality area in which to start seeds. Plant at the depth specified on the packet. Keep well watered for the first two weeks, or until the plants are well-established.

5 Preparation, Planting, and Propagation

Taking Cuttings

Taking cuttings is a good way to multiply the plants in your garden or share favorite varieties with friends. Roses, especially, are worth the experimentation, because they're such valued plants.

But many plants besides roses can also be started readily from cuttings. Shrubs that lend themselves well to cutting include azaleas, rhododendrons, lilacs, boxwood, yew, willow, lavender, rosemary, hibiscus, holly, and hydrangeas. You can start a whole hedge, in fact, from cuttings.

Some perennials, too, are favorites for cuttings. Mum fanciers, for example, often take cuttings to increase their collection.

To take a cutting, trim off the tip of a perennial, shrub, or even a tree. The cutting can be a few to several inches long, depending on the size of the plant. Take smaller cuttings of smaller plants, larger cuttings of larger plants.

At the bottom of the cutting, include a few nodes—the swollen spots on a stem where a leaf or smaller stem grows. Strip off any leaves from the bottom third to half of the cutting. If the cutting has a number of large leaves, pinch off a few. A plant without roots should support as few large leaves as possible, yet have enough leaves to conduct photosynthesis and grow.

Moisten the end of the cutting, then dip it in rooting hormone, a white powder that comes in a little plastic jar, available at garden centers. Tap off any excess.

Insert the cutting into a pot filled with potting soil. (Tip: Use a pencil to poke a hole to slip the stem into to keep the powder from rubbing off. Then pat the soil in around the stem.)

Water well, and slip the pot into a clear plastic bag to retain moisture.

Keep it near a window or under a grow-light. Keep the soil moist. If the cutting roots, it will show signs of new growth in a few weeks. When it starts rooting, remove the bag and continue to grow as you would any seedling.

How to Take Cuttings

1 Take the cutting. Make sure it has a few stems and is a few inches long. Strip off the small stems to expose the nodes, where roots will start.

2 Dip the bottom 1 to 2 inches in rooting hormone powder. Insert into a mixture of half perlite, half potting soil.

3 Water and label the cuttings, and slip them into a clear plastic bag or a tray with a clear lid. The warm, humid environment encourages growth. Check for root growth every few days. Plant outdoors once roots are well-developed.

WORK SMARTER

STARTING CUTTINGS IN THE GROUND

During long, extended cool seasons, such as spring in the Pacific Northwest or winter in the South and Southwest, you can often start cuttings right in the ground. It's trickier than starting cuttings in pots, but in some cases you can get the cutting to grow to full size right where you started it.

Take the cutting as you would for one to be started in a pot. Dip it in rooting hormone, and insert it into well-amended, loose soil (see page 136). Water well. For protection, cover the cutting with a plastic milk jug with the bottom cut out and the cap left off for ventilation.

Keep the soil moist and check the cutting weekly for signs of new growth and/or root development by loosening the soil around it. With luck, the cutting will start growing actively in a few weeks.

PROJECT DETAILS

SKILLS: Basic planting skills
PROJECT: Cutting off part of a plant and rooting it

TIME TO COMPLETE

EXPERIENCED: 15 minutes for a few cuttings
HANDY: 20 minutes
NOVICE: 30 minutes

STUFF YOU'LL NEED

TOOLS: Hand shears, rooting hormone, pots, plastic bag or plastic tray with clear cover
MATERIALS: Perlite, potting soil

Maintenance

Any garden, no matter how modest, becomes even more beautiful when well-maintained. From watering to weeding, staking to pruning, fertilizing to deadheading—all tasks are critical to keeping plants attractive from earliest spring to the last chilly breath of winter.

In this chapter you'll learn what tasks are necessary to keep your garden attractive, and find out ways to make the chores a breeze. You may even discover what many gardeners already know—that caring for your plantings is a wonderfully relaxing part of gardening.

Chapter 6 Maintenance

The Rules Of Watering

Watering plants according to their specific needs is essential to a successful garden. And if you learn to water right, you'll spend less time at it. As a bonus, your plants will grow better and cost less to maintain. What a deal!

Don't Let 'Em Wilt

Many gardeners wait until their flowers are drooping to water them. Wilting stresses plants, causing dropped flowers and discolored leaves. Also, a wilted plant becomes more susceptible to insect and disease problems.

Instead, look for early warning signs that the plant needs water, such as leaves becoming less glossy or soil appearing hard and crusted. Also, do what experienced gardeners do. Keep an eye on the impatiens. These thirsty little annuals are usually the first flowers to wilt during dry conditions. If they're looking dry, turn on the hose.

Water Early in the Day

Start your sprinkler early in the day (four in the morning is not too soon). By watering early, you'll avoid the heat of the day and prevent evaporation. Early watering also allows plants to dry off well before nightfall, when fungal diseases take hold.

In some parts of the country, watering early also prevents leaf burn. Leaf burn occurs when droplets of water fall on leaves in the heat of the day, acting like tiny magnifying glasses and burning the leaf or flower tissue beneath them.

GOOD IDEA!

THE STICK TEST

What's the easiest way to see how dry soil is? Feel it! Wiggle your finger or poke a stick 2 to 3 inches into the ground. If it's bone dry at that depth, it's time to water.

Keeping plantings well watered is important to having a lush, healthy garden with plenty of flowers.

Water Deeply

Plants do best when they receive a deep soaking once in a while rather than a shallow watering often. Deep watering encourages plants to send their roots far into the soil. These deep roots help plants find moisture during dry spells, making them more resilient to drought.

Most plants do best with approximately 1 inch of water a week, though drought-tolerant plants can do with far less. But for general landscaping, if less than an inch of rain has fallen for a week, apply an inch of water from the hose. (When watering trees and large shrubs, water the dripline rather than just the base of the plant. The dripline is the imaginary circle defined by how far the branches stretch out. Everything below the tip of those branches is the dripline.)

If you're watering by hand, thoroughly soak the plants. If you're watering a shrub, for example, set the hose so it barely dribbles, and let it drip there for an hour or more. If you're watering with a spray attachment or watering wand, let the water soak in, then come back in a half hour or so and repeat the watering. It's much better to do a small area well than to just mist a large area.

Water the Soil Instead of the Plant

Many leaves and flowers resent getting wet; it makes them more prone to disease. Some flowers, such as petunias, rebel by closing. Of course, sometimes you'll need to use a sprinkler, and getting the leaves and flowers wet will be unavoidable. But when using a hose or watering can, water only the soil. Your flowers will be happier for it, and it saves water.

Better yet, consider investing in a drip-emitter system, microsprinklers, or soaker hoses (see page 175). These slowly apply water exactly where you want it. And because water is not dispersed through the air, these systems are highly efficient, using minimal water.

Although fancy metal pipe systems are available through professionals, there are many easy do-it-yourself water systems available at your garden center.

WORK SMARTER

WATER DEEPLY AND WELL

One of the best rules to remember when watering your plants is this: Water deeply and well, rather than shallowly and often.

That's because plants do best when the soil is moist several inches down, encouraging them to put down deep roots and making them more drought resistant. If you water shallowly, roots are not encouraged to go deep. Plus, wetting the foliage promotes fungal diseases.

WORK SMARTER

HOW MUCH IS ENOUGH?

As a rule, your garden needs 1 inch of water a week. How can you tell how much water you've applied?

Set out an old cake pan or other shallow, flat container where the sprinkler will hit it. For best accuracy, position the pan midway between the sprinkler and the farthest point that the water falls.

Measure the water in the pan to determine how much water is being added to the garden.

Irrigation Systems

In some climates, such as Southern California, an irrigation system is about a must. It's difficult to have a varied landscape or lawn without it. In other climates, such as moister parts of the Midwest and Northeast, gardeners can do quite well without an elaborate irrigation system.

As interest in gardening and water conservation has increased, so has interest in irrigation systems. Microsprinklers, bubblers, drip emitters, soaker hoses, and other devices can deliver the precise amount of water needed to the exact area at the optimum time with minimal work.

Costs for irrigation systems have been coming down in recent years. Elaborate irrigation systems are for the pros, but the more simple systems are easy for even beginners to set up. A do-it-yourself system can cost very little—you can even do just one flower bed, if you like. Professionally installed systems for an entire yard usually start at around $1,000 and can easily cost several thousand dollars depending on the system and the size of the property. However, depending on what part of the country you live in, a well-installed irrigation system may add to the value and salability of your home.

Do-It-Yourself or Hire a Pro?

In some parts of the country, homeowners install nearly 75 percent of all irrigation systems. Installing an irrigation system is well within the ability of a capable homeowner who plans thoroughly and works carefully. But digging trenches, installing piping, making connections, and carrying out verifications can be a lengthy process.

If you want to install an irrigation system, it's important to do your homework and plan well. If you're going to do more than just a small, basic irrigation project, invest in a book on irrigation systems—you'll save the price of the book many times over. Or attend one of the free clinics or workshops offered at many Home Depot garden centers. Also be sure to check with the municipal planning, zoning, and water departments about regulations concerning issues such as what you are allowed to install in the parking strip between your house and street, codes concerning underground irrigation, or getting underground cables marked before digging.

Consider hiring a professional if you have severe erosion problems,

Is an Irrigation System for Me?

If you answer yes to at least a few of the questions below, an irrigation system is probably a wise choice for you:

- Do I sometimes have to water garden areas as often as every one to three days?
- Does my lawn have problem spots from lack of water, especially around driveways and sidewalks?
- Am I unable or unwilling to water by hand in the early hours of the morning, the optimum time?
- Am I unable or unwilling to set up sprinklers manually and run them as long as I should (often a few hours) when lawn and plantings need it?
- When I run sprinklers, do they get a lot of water on pavement, patios, or the street?
- Would a well-installed and well-designed irrigation system add to my home's resale value?

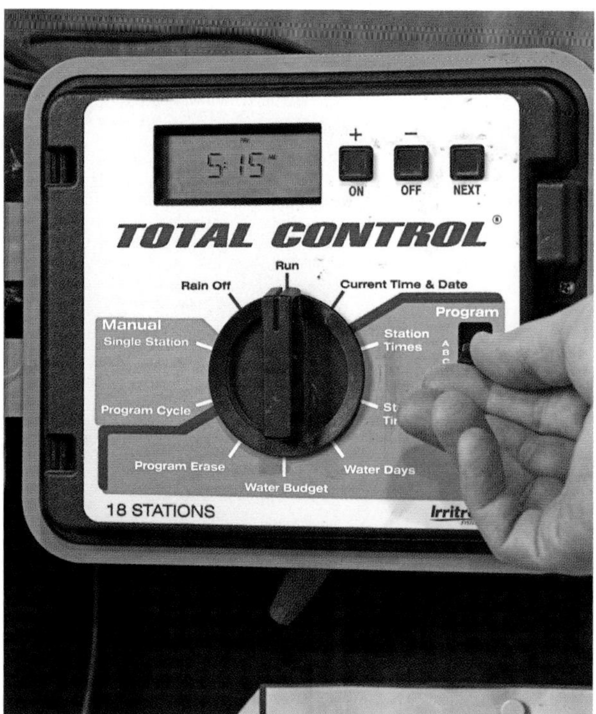

A timer mounted in the garage is the master control, allowing you to program watering for specific areas, changing weather conditions, and local rules governing water use.

Irrigation systems are vastly more efficient than traditional sprinklers. They deliver water in precise patterns low to the ground early in the day.

very rocky soil, steep slopes, or delicate or highly valuable plantings that need protection. Also, in some municipalities, you may have limited do-it-yourself options. Many cities require a licensed plumber to install the copper pipe from the city water main to the backflow preventer on your house, the beginning of an irrigation system.

If you're still uncertain, start small. Choose a section of your landscape that seems simple to get set up. The following year, add on to it, and the next year add on further. You'll learn as you go and will be able to pay for the system a little bit at a time.

Micro-Irrigation vs. Sprinkler Systems

Sprinkler systems, also called high-pressure irrigation, are by far the most common irrigation system used in North America. Sprinkler systems are the more traditional systems of piping underground, leading to pop-up sprinklers positioned around the landscape. These systems, which are nearly invisible, tend to be lower maintenance (all they really need is an annual flushing) but more expensive initially because trenching is needed.

Micro-irrigation, or low-pressure systems, are the newcomers. A micro-irrigation system uses a series of devices to apply water very slowly, usually right at soil level—the best way to prevent water loss through evaporation. Drip irrigation is a form of micro-irrigation.

Micro-irrigation systems tend to be more visible (but can be hidden under mulch) and easier to install than sprinkler systems. They are therefore less expensive. And because micro-irrigation systems are aboveground, they're easier to alter as your flower beds, vegetable gardens, and other plantings change. They usually work less well in lawns, because most are not buried, or at least not buried deeply. (However, even this is changing as manufacturers start to create do-it-yourself systems for lawns.) Also, micro-irrigation systems need a little more maintenance than sprinkler systems, because they can become clogged or damaged more easily.

Still, as the technology develops, the line between traditional sprinkler systems and micro-irrigation systems is blurring, and many homes now have a combination of the two.

Whatever system you choose, it's important to do a pressure test of your system. You can contact your water company or municipality to find out the water pressure of your system or you can use a purchased water gauge. You probably will then need to use a pressure reducer at your outdoor faucet, especially with a microirrigation system or you can blow out the ends of the system.

It's also important not to put a micro (low-pressure) system with a high-pressure traditional system since their pressure needs are different. Use separate outdoor faucets or an adapter that creates two faucets from one.

Micro-Irrigation System Elements

These are some of the elements you are likely to use when creating a micro-irrigation system:

Bubbler

Bubblers flood the immediate area a foot or so out. Ideal for shrubs and groundcover plantings.

Drip Emitter

Drip emitters literally drip water very, very slowly. They can be inserted directly into the main flexible tubing or into thin lines that run out from the main tubing.

Microsprinklers

Unlike their larger counterparts, these tiny sprinklers can be positioned all over the landscape to deliver water in the precise areas needed. They put out small amounts of water at a time, so the soil can absorb it easily, and because they're close to the ground, less water is lost to evaporation. Ideal for flower beds and shrub beds or in groundcovers.

Ring Drip Emitter

These emitters are designed to fit around small trees and shrubs as well as large perennials. Water slowly drips in a ring pattern around the plant.

Soaker Hose

These hoses have thousands of tiny pores all over them and slowly seep water. Best for rows of plantings, such as in vegetable gardens. The hoses are easy to set up and can be repositioned easily as plantings change.

Fertilizing Basics

GOOD IDEA!

NO-BRAINER FERTILIZING

If figuring out the best fertilizing for different plants and gardens in your landscape sounds too complicated, just do this:

Buy a big container (or two) of a slow-release, all-purpose fertilizer. On an early spring day when the foliage is dry and rain is forecast (rain will dissolve and release the fertilizer), sprinkle the fertilizer all over your landscape plantings according to package directions. This should be enough to provide the minimum nutrition for your plants for the season.

Avoid the lawn, however, because you or a lawn service are likely to fertilize it separately with a product specifically for lawns.

Ask 10 different gardeners once a year over 10 years how they're fertilizing that year and you'll probably hear a hundred different answers.

Fertilizing is part science, part art. Even experienced gardeners are constantly experimenting to come up with the perfect regimen for them and their gardens.

In some parts of the country, such as in the north-central United States, the soil naturally contains enough nutrients to grow healthy plants. However, that's not the case in most regions, where you'll need to fertilize your plants regularly for best results.

Fertilizers fall into one of two basic categories: synthetic and natural.

Synthetic vs. Natural

Synthetic fertilizers are man-made. Developed in the 1940s, they are inexpensive and, as long as they're used correctly, precise in their strength and in the mix of nutrients they deliver.

Synthetic fertilizers may be dry—in granular, powder, or pellet form—or liquid. Liquid types tend to be fast-acting and should be used with special caution, because it's easy to overfertilize with them. (Remember the rule: The faster-acting the fertilizer, the sooner it's likely to leave the soil. So a fast-acting fertilizer may last only two weeks, whereas a slow-release fertilizer may keep working for up to six months.)

Synthetic fertilizers have the advantage of coming in fast-acting formulations and of being more concentrated, but there are also drawbacks. Because synthetic fertilizers tend to be more potent than their natural counterparts, they can burn delicate roots and leaves. They are also highly soluble and, if over- or improperly used, can leach into groundwater. Overuse of synthetics also may inhibit the activity of beneficial soil microbes, decreasing their populations and interfering with their breakdown of organic matter.

All fertilizers come with instructions for proper use. Follow those instructions *exactly* to prevent problems.

Slow-release fertilizers have coated pellets that disintegrate, releasing fertilizer over a longer period of time. Hence, they are unlikely to burn plants. Liquid fertilizers, which are sprayed on leaves or mixed and poured onto the base of plants, allow quick nutrient uptake.

Natural fertilizers also come in dry or liquid form. Many provide only one nutrient and are not complete fertilizers. For example, blood meal supplies nitrogen, which will quickly green up failing plants. Bonemeal provides

Follow Directions

More is not better! When using a fertilizer, read the package carefully. Fertilizing too much or mixing the fertilizer incorrectly—at worst—can burn plants . Mixing incorrectly also can be a waste of time and money when you mix it too weak. As with all things, read the label.

An easy way to keep your plantings well fertilized is to work in compost or slow-release fertilizer at the base of each plant. It will feed them slowly and evenly for months.

A CLOSER LOOK

owering Plan
11-40-6
Great For Annuals, Perennials Roses & Other Flowering Plants
Promotes Maximum Blooms & Strong Roots
Granular Easy-To-Use Formula

UP, DOWN, ALL AROUND

The main plant nutrients in chemical fertilizers are N (nitrogen—for green, leafy growth), P (phosphorus—for root development, flowering, fruiting, and seed formation), and K (potassium—for disease resistance and general growth). Different proportions of these nutrients provide different results. The proportion of these nutrients is on fertilizer packages, always in the same order as their chemical symbols, N-P-K.

An easy way to remember their functions in order is: "Up (N), down (P), all around (K)."

phosphorus, for root growth and flower formation. You might need to use more than one product to provide complete fertilization. Fish emulsion is a liquid fertilizer that can be applied to damp soil or directly to leaves.

Natural fertilizers can also be used to alter soil pH. Cottonseed meal makes soil more acidic; limestone makes it more alkaline. Check the label of each natural fertilizer you're considering to find out its benefits.

Compost can also be considered a natural fertilizer and is probably the best all-around fertilizer because it does so many other things. First it provides an excellent balance of nutrients plus many micronutrients. Many gardeners use nothing but compost to feed their gardens. Compost also greatly improves soil texture and encourages helpful earthworm and microbial activity.

Natural fertilizers have no specific application rates. Because their nutrients are less concentrated than those in synthetic fertilizers, and they release their nutrients more slowly, they are less likely to harm your plants. With compost, work it into the soil freely. It's difficult to add too much compost.

Getting the Most from Your Fertilizers

No matter what type of fertilizer you use, there are some gardening practices that you should follow:

- Do a soil test. It's smart to start with the results of a soil test (see pages 540–541 for resources). That way, you'll know if there are any serious deficiencies and can correct them.
- Apply a fertilizer when the plant is most likely to be hungry, as in early spring when the plant is getting ready to do a lot of growth, or at the times it's producing flowers, fruit, or vegetables.
- Avoid applying a fertilizer right before a plant is going to stop growing. In hot regions, this is in late spring because summer's heat halts the growth of many plants. In cold regions, this is in fall, when winter is about to cause many plants to go dormant. Applying fertilizer right before a plant is going to shut down forces it to keep going and produces tender new growth that is susceptible to the stresses of heat and cold.
- Keep improving your soil texture. Even if you choose to use solely synthetic fertilizers, it's important that you have

continued on page 178

WORK SMARTER

FERTILIZER IS A FOOD

Often, gardeners confronted with a sick or ailing plant reach for the fertilizer in hopes that it might be the cure. But it's important to remember this rule: Fertilizer is a food, not a medicine.

Fertilizer is something you apply regularly to make sure your plant is receiving good nourishment. Applying fertilizer simply because a plant is doing poorly may actually do harm if the plant is overfertilized.

6

Maintenance

A Fertilizer Glossary

A bit confused about the different types of fertilizers and how to use them? Here's a glossary of terms found on fertilizer boxes and bags:

Balanced: Roughly equal proportions of the major three nutrients—nitrogen (N), phosphorus (P), and potassium (K)—and therefore a good general-purpose fertilizer. Package may read, for example, 10-10-10 or 5-10-5.

Complete: Contains all three primary plant nutrients (N, P, and K).

Foliar: To be sprayed on the plants, which quickly absorb the nutrients through their leaves. Usually used to supplement more conventional fertilizer.

Granular: Looks like tiny pellets or sand. Easy to apply; can use your hand, a measuring cup, or a spreader. Balance of N-P-K may vary, such as 11-40-6.

Liquid: May come as a liquid concentrate or as a water-soluble powder. Liquid fertilizers work well for heavy soils where a granular form may dissolve but be poorly absorbed. Fish emulsion is one of the few commercial organic liquid fertilizers available.

Slow-Release: A fertilizer that releases its nutrients slowly over a period of months. It can be organic (as with compost, bonemeal, and blood meal) or synthetic.

Soluble: Dissolves in water or after watering. Usually, a substance labeled soluble can be applied as a liquid fertilizer, but soluble can also mean that the fertilizer is activated when it comes in contact with water. Check the label to be sure.

Specialty Fertilizers: Some fertilizers are designed for the specific needs of a particular plant, such as an African violet or a rose. Others go beyond fertilizing, with added benefits of built-in insecticides or of changing the pH for acid-loving plants. Still others are designed for the specific needs of a plant at a particular time, such as a fertilizer rich in phosphorus (P) to help newly planted flowers establish their roots. Read the package carefully or ask garden center staff to make sure the fertilizer is right for your needs.

Spikes or Tablets: A super-easy way to fertilize over a period of weeks or even months. Just read the label carefully to choose the right fertilizer for the plant (they're made for everything from trees to houseplants) and follow directions exactly.

Timed-Release: Fine-tuned to release nutrients at various times in the growing cycle to match the plants' changing needs.

Fertilizing Basics *continued*

good, loose, well-drained soil so the fertilizers can percolate downward to deeper roots.

- Read the package. Fertilizer is a potent chemical, and applying it badly can harm your plants. Pause for a moment and really read the package, front and back. Is the fertilizer formulated for your type of plants? How do you use it or mix it up? Do you have the right equipment to apply the fertilizer, such as a spreader or sprayer? What time of year should you apply the fertilizer, and during what type of weather? How often should you apply the fertilizer?
- Apply natural fertilizers on warm days, because the warmth helps them begin to break down and release their nutrients.

Applying Fertilizers

When applying granular fertilizers, activate them and prevent them from burning leaves by scratching in the particles at the base of the plants or along rows. Water in quick-release fertilizers to prevent them from burning plants.

You can also fertilize plants with liquid and water-soluble fertilizers. Spray them directly onto the plants or mix them in a watering can and pour them onto the base of the plants. With larger plants, such as trees or large shrubs, apply fertilizer in a circle along the dripline, the imaginary circle beneath the outer tips of the branches.

Time the applications for early morning, early evening, or a cloudy day. Because water evaporates more slowly at these times, the plants have time to absorb more nutrients.

Forms of Fertilizer

Fertilizer comes in different forms. Choose the right form that's easiest for you and best for your plants.

Granular fertilizers are sprinkled on the ground and worked into the soil by lightly scratching the surface. (With containers, they are mixed into the soil when filling the pot at planting time, though you can later add more on the top of the soil.) Many formulations of granular fertilizer are available, but most are slow-release.

Liquid fertilizers are mixed with water and applied to the base or dripline of the plant. Liquid fertilizers are available in many formulations for many different plants, including houseplants, but are generally fast-acting.

Spray fertilizers are sprayed onto the leaves and are absorbed by the leaves for a foliar feeding. Foliar feeding is very fast-acting and, in the right situation, can green up plants stressed by iron chlorosis or other problems within hours. Many spray fertilizers are sold as shown with a special sprayer that simply screws onto the hose and is automatically mixed as you spray.

Fertilizer stakes are an easy way to fertilize a limited area. Stakes come in many sizes. Some are about as big as a matchstick and are used in houseplant and container plantings. Very large ones, such as this tree fertilizer spike, are hammered into the soil in several spots along the dripline of the plant, that is, the circular area underneath the outside perimeter of the branches.

For full, healthy plantings with plenty of bloom, most landscapes need to rely on fertilizers of one type or another.

Fertilizing Trees and Shrubs The First Year

To give prized plants a good start, use root stimulator at planting time. Root stimulators prompt the growth of feeder roots, helping new plants to settle into their new environment. Root stimulators are especially smart to use with higher-investment plants, such as trees and shrubs. Bare-root roses benefit from having their roots soaked in diluted liquid root stimulator before planting.

Follow package directions when using root-stimulating fertilizers. Add them to the planting holes prior to setting plants in them.

However, avoid high-nitrogen fertilizers during a tree's or shrub's first year. Nitrogen stimulates green leafy growth and during their first year, plants need to focus on growing good roots to assure healthier plants for years to come.

The exception is roses. Roses are hungry nitrogen-lovers. Two weeks after planting, you can start fertilizing with a high-nitrogen fertilizer. Again, be sure to follow package directions and underdo it rather than overdo it.

Overfertilizing and Underfertilizing

To be effective, fertilizer must be applied correctly. Too much and you harm plants; too little and you can starve them. If in doubt, however, use less rather than more. The dangers of overfertilizing are greater than those of underfertilizing.

Overfertilizing

Symptoms: Plants that are overfertilized often compensate by shutting down and slowing growth. Foliage turns yellow or brown but remains on branches. Plants take on a burned appearance.

If the plant is getting too much nitrogen, it will get tall and leggy with lots of fast, lush green growth, which is susceptible to disease. And because the plant is putting so much of its energy into green growth, it usually compensates by reducing flowering or fruit or vegetable production.

Solution: Check the soil. If the soil moisture is normal and you've been fertilizing frequently, stop fertilizing immediately. Supply the plant with plenty of water to leach excess chemicals from the soil.

Underfertilizing

Symptoms: Foliage becomes discolored, turning a yellowish hue. Growth is distorted or stunted.

Solution: Observe the plant carefully. Sometimes underwatering can masquerade as underfertilizing. If moisture is not the issue, find a fertilizer that describes or lists your plant on the label. Follow directions exactly and regularly.

How to Fertilize Different Types of Plants

How you fertilize depends in part on what type of plants you have and the time of year.

Perennial Flowers: Work in plenty of compost at planting time to improve soil fertility and texture. Each spring, work a slow-release fertilizer into the top inch or two of soil to feed plants gradually over the season. You may need to reapply later in the growing season; check the label. For existing beds, spread an inch of compost on top of the soil each spring, and work it around the plants.

In arid regions where foliage tends to yellow from lack of iron (chlorosis) or for top performance in other regions, give a foliar feeding in late summer to green up plants and promote growth and flowering.

Annual Flowers: Feed as for perennials. However, because annuals are fast growers, they benefit from periodic "snacks" throughout the season. Applying a liquid or foliar fertilizer to annuals several times during the growing season also helps assure more lush plants. Follow package directions. Avoid overapplying.

Container Flowers: At planting time, work in a slow release fertilizer, or use plant spikes. Apply a liquid fertilizer several times, as often as every two weeks, during the growing season, to replace the nutrients that are continually washed out with watering.

For more information on fertilizing containers, see page 280.

Roses: See opposite page.

Shrubs: Newly planted shrubs or those that completely regenerate foliage each year, such as butterfly bush or some hibiscus, benefit from an application of compost or low-release fertilizer. However, in most cases, established flowering shrubs do not need fertilizing. In arid regions where foliage tends to yellow from iron chlorosis, consider an occasional foliar feeding to green up plants.

Trees: The best way to keep trees well nourished is to keep grass from growing underneath them. Turf is a nitrogen gobbler. With newly planted trees, especially, it's important to mulch 2 to 3 feet out from the trunk to allow nutrients to trickle down to the roots. If desired, work in a slow-release fertilizer for the first couple of years of a newly planted tree's life around the dripline, the area beneath the outer perimeter of the branches. Established, mature trees usually do not need fertilizing.

Bulbs: When planting bulbs, add a bit of compost to the bottom of the planting hole. Also add a granular fertilizer made specifically for bulbs, following package directions. You may use bonemeal, but it attracts animals and needs to be combined with blood meal for a better balanced fertilizer.

Vegetables: The best way to fertilize overall is to spade or till in plenty of compost (a 2-inch layer or so) each spring. Or plant a cover crop of annual rye or a legume each fall and till that in each spring.

Otherwise, vegetables do well with a slow-release fertilizer. Some especially nitrogen-hungry vegetables, such as corn and lettuces, do well with a booster application of a liquid fertilizer. Be careful to avoid overfertilizing tomatoes with a nitrogen-rich fertilizer or you'll get very tall plants with lots of leafy growth and few tomatoes.

For more information on fertilizing vegetables, see page 260.

Houseplants: Although there are many different ways to fertilize houseplants, the easiest method is to choose a liquid houseplant fertilizer or houseplant fertilizer spikes and use as directed on the package.

Avoid fertilizing during the winter months, when houseplant growth slows because of shorter days and less light.

For more information on fertilizing houseplants, see page 290.

Fertilizing Roses

Fertilizing is as much art as science and varies according to region, overall gardening practices, and personal philosophy.

The only thing on which everyone agrees is that roses need nutrients.

Here are some ways to provide them:

The Organic Approach

Make sure your roses are well-fed by working in a spadeful or two of compost around the base of each rose each spring.

Once a month thereafter, fertilize your roses with a liquid organic fertilizer, such as manure tea or fish emulsion.

If you want to pamper your roses, each spring make a batch of "spring tonic" for them. Mix together in a 5-gallon bucket the following: 2 cups alfalfa meal, 2 cups Epsom salts, 2 cups fish meal, 2 cups greensand, 2 cups gypsum, and 1 cup bonemeal. Work approximately 1 cup of this spring tonic into the top inch or so of the soil for small rosebushes, using a trowel or hand cultivator. Large rosebushes (6 feet or taller) need 3 to 4 cups.

The No-Brainer Approach

At planting time and in early spring each year following, sprinkle a slow-release, granular combination fertilizer-insecticide at the base of each rose. It feeds and protects your roses for weeks and even months. Reapply as the package directs, usually every six weeks.

The Intense Approach

If you want the biggest and best roses, fertilize with a liquid fertilizer every two to three weeks. It will give them a quick, easily absorbed snack. Mix into a watering can, or attach a spray feeder to your garden hose.

Good Soil Makes for Good Roses

No matter which fertilizing approach you choose, roses love rich, moisture-retentive soil. Loose soil allows nutrients to percolate deeply, reaching the rose's roots and giving nutrition where it's needed.

Provide good soil by working in abundant compost at planting time. After a rose is planted, you can further improve the soil each spring by working a gallon or two of compost into the surface of the soil around the rose.

WORK SMARTER

WHEN TO STOP FEEDING ROSES

Stop feeding roses 2 months before your region's first frost date in fall (see page 29). Otherwise, you'll stimulate tender new growth that will be killed by winter's cold.

Also, if you live in a hot climate, as in the southern third of the United States, it's a good idea to stop feeding roses for about a month during the hottest weather, in August or so.

One of the fastest, easiest ways to feed roses—as well as prevent insect problems—is to apply a systemic rose fertilizer a few times during the growing season. Follow package directions exactly.

Composting Basics

There's an old saying that the three best things you can do for your plants are add compost, compost, and compost.

After all, the list of what compost can do for your garden goes on and on: It feeds plants, improves drainage, retains moisture, makes weeding easier, helps distribute fertilizer, attracts beneficial earthworms, promotes microbial activity in the soil (soil microbes break down organic matter so it can be used by plants), prevents disease in some cases, and provides micronutrients.

Composting is not only important, it's easy. Pile up materials and let them break down. In fact, composting makes daily work in the garden easier because it's a convenient way to dispose of leaves, grass clippings, and other yard wastes. You can forget bagging!

Although fancy compost bins are on the market and easy to install, they are unnecessary. Wire fencing works fine. It's nice to have three bins (one for finished compost, one for partly composted materials, and one for fresh materials). But that's also unnecessary, especially for the beginning composter. Once you have a bin, add materials as you gather them in the ordinary course of your yard work. You'll have compost in several months, usually at the bottom of the pile.

To use the compost, just pull off the rough material on top until you get down to the crumbly black compost at the bottom of the pile. (A pitchfork or spading fork makes this process easier.)

Cold Compost vs. Hot Compost

- Cold compost, the easiest method, is done by piling up materials and letting them break down for a year or two with an occasional turn if possible. Add cold compost to the bottom of a planting hole, but avoid mulching with it. When used on the soil's surface, incompletely composted weeds or plants you've added, such as tomatoes or hollyhocks, may sprout and create problems.
- Hot compost comes from a compost pile constructed with a balance of nitrogen-rich and carbon-rich materials that are turned regularly, at least once every week or two. It is also kept evenly moist with occasional watering. Hot compost becomes hot to the touch, and the heat kills weed seeds and many disease pathogens.

Tips for Faster, Better Compost

- Keep the pile a manageable size. Make it no more than 4 feet across and 3 feet high so you can turn it easily.
- Turn the compost regularly, as often as every few days, with a spading fork or pitchfork. Any turning is helpful, but more is better, because oxygen activates compost piles.
- Cut up or shred materials. The smaller the materials, the faster they'll break down.
- Layer nitrogen-rich materials (green materials) with carbon-rich

A CLOSER LOOK

DO COMPOST HEAPS STINK?

If you're adding significant amounts of manure, for several days to several weeks, yes, your compost heap will have a barnyard smell. But if you refrain from adding manure, your compost heap should give off minimal smell, if any.

And what about flies? Kitchen scraps will indeed attract flies. If you're adding those to the pile, sprinkle dry material from the existing heap over the scraps to take care of the problem. Some gardeners are afraid that compost piles will attract rodents and snakes. That is unlikely to happen as long as you turn the heap regularly, avoid adding too many kitchen scraps, and keep it from becoming an inviting-looking brush pile.

Composting is one of the best things you can do for your garden. Compost feeds plants and improves soil texture, making everything from watering to weeding easier. It also encourages earthworms and beneficial microbial activity in the soil.

6 Maintenance

materials (brown materials). If a pile has too much nitrogen, it will get slimy. If it has too much carbon, it will fail to break down quickly.

- Keep it moist. A damp environment speeds up decomposition. During dry spells, soak the compost heap with a hose. However, avoid keeping the compost heap wet all the time, because that also prevents good decomposition. In cool, rainy climates, such as the Pacific Northwest, you may want to cover the compost heap with a tarp or even build a shelter overhead to keep it from being too wet.
- If you have trouble producing enough compost for your garden, consider purchasing it. It's available in bags, sometimes labeled "humus," and in bulk for delivery via truck if you need a lot.

Building a Compost Heap

PROJECT DETAILS

SKILLS: Basic assembly, hauling
PROJECT: Setting up one or more compost heaps to collect yard waste

TIME TO COMPLETE

EXPERIENCED: An hour to a day, depending on the construction involved
HANDY: An hour to a couple of days
NOVICE: An hour to 2 to 3 days

STUFF YOU'LL NEED

TOOLS: Compost bin, spading fork or pitchfork
MATERIALS: Materials to compost, such as weeds, grass clippings, autumn leaves

1 Build a framework. A wire bin is shown, but concrete blocks or even straw bales stacked several feet high will also work. There are also a number of compost bin kits available, or you can build one from scratch. The ideal setup, especially for a large garden, has three bins to hold compost in various states of decomposition, but one bin is sufficient.

2 Alternate "brown" and "green" materials (see "Materials to Compost" below). You can simply dump materials onto the pile; but to heat up the pile for the fastest compost, layer one part nitrogen-rich materials to three parts carbon-rich materials. If the weather is dry, further speed the process by watering the pile.

3 Turn as often as possible. The more you turn the pile, the faster and hotter your compost will be. Turning once or twice a week is ideal. If you never turn your pile, you'll still get compost, but the decomposition takes much longer.

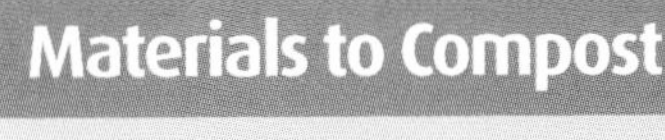

Materials to Compost

Nitrogen-Rich (Green) Materials to Compost

Alfalfa hay
Fruit and vegetable scraps
Grass clippings
Green leaves and weeds
Manure
Seaweed

Carbon-Rich (Brown) Materials to Compost

Dried leaves
Shredded newspaper
Straw
Woody stems and sticks

Other Materials to Add

Coffee grounds/tea leaves
Eggshells
Pine needles
Wood ashes

Do Not Compost

Black walnut leaves, nuts, and branches
Bones
Cat, dog, or other pet wastes
Diseased or invasive plants
Meat or meat products
Oils, fats, greases
Seed heads

6

Maintenance

Mulch Basics

WORK SMARTER

HOW MUCH MULCH TO BUY?

To figure out how much mulch you need, first figure the square footage of your area—the length times the width.

Then multiply the square footage times the depth of inches of mulch you want and divide by 324 square feet, which is one cubic yard, one inch deep. This will tell you how many cubic yards you will need.

So if, for example, you have 100 square feet and want to add three inches of mulch, multiply 100 by three, and then divide by 324 to convert to cubic yards. This equals .92 cubic yards that you need, so you can buy nine of the three-cubic-feet bags and you'll have a little leftover.

If in doubt, ask your Home Depot garden center associate.

Mulch does many things. It conserves moisture, prevents weeds, slows the spread of disease, adds organic material to the soil, protects plants from weather extremes, and encourages beneficial earthworms.

Mulch is used in two different ways. In warm weather, it's laid around the base of plants in a thin layer to cool them. In cold weather, it's mounded up around the base of plants to protect them.

Warm-Weather Mulch

Warm-weather mulch keeps the soil cool so it holds moisture better. The mulch suppresses weeds by shading them out before they can start. Warm-weather mulch serves as a barrier between the soil and the plant, so soilborne diseases are kept from splashing on the plant during rain or watering. The mulch absorbs water readily, preventing runoff and allowing the soil to better take in water. Organic mulches (those that break down) improve the soil's texture and feed plants.

Apply warm-weather mulch at about the time that tulips stop blooming. Spread it 1 to 3 inches thick—not thicker, or you'll risk rotting or suffocating the plants and invite diseases and pests, such as rodents. Keep the mulch about a half inch away from the base of plants.

When mulching trees or shrubs set in the lawn, mulch out as far as the branches reach. This prevents competition for food and water from hungry grass and also protects the trunks from string trimmers and mowers.

Apply warm-weather mulch in spring for best results, but you can apply it almost any time of year. Mulch needs to be reapplied from time to time, anywhere from annually to every few years, depending on the type of mulch and the climate. Fine, organic mulches break down fastest; large stone mulches last indefinitely.

Winter Mulch

In cold regions of the country, Zone 7 and colder, winter mulch is used to protect plants from winter's extremes. Even in warm parts of the country, plants that are less cold-hardy to that region should be protected with a winter mulch.

Mulch in winter prevents frost heaves—the eruption of the soil as it freezes and thaws in late winter, which damages the roots of many perennials.

Plants well-adapted to a region (with the exception of roses in most parts of the country, see pages 200–201) need little or no winter mulch. If you plan to winterize your roses, see page 201.

Apply winter mulch in fall after your region has had 48 hours of below-freezing temperatures. Remove and discard winter mulch in early spring, just as perennials are starting to send up fresh growth.

PROJECT DETAILS

SKILLS: Measuring, mulching
PROJECT: Surrounding trees, shrubs, and other permanent plantings with landscape fabric topped with loose mulch

TIME TO COMPLETE

EXPERIENCED: 1 hour for a large bed
HANDY: 2 hours
NOVICE: 3 hours

STUFF YOU'LL NEED

TOOLS: Scissors, sharp knife, buckets, shovel, wheelbarrow (optional)
MATERIALS: Landscape fabric/weed block, mulch to top it with

How to Lay Landscape Fabric

1 Spread the landscape fabric over the area to be covered. Get it as smooth as possible, but a few wrinkles are OK. Trim to fit with scissors.

2 If planting in the fabric, cut X-shaped slashes or holes and plant. Otherwise, top with mulch, gravel, or other materials.

Which Mulch is for You?

Cocoa Hulls: These add nutrients. Chocolate aroma for a short time. May mold or attract rodents or blow off. Can be expensive for large areas. Dark color is attractive.

Leaves: When chopped or shredded, leaves greatly improve soil texture and fertility. May blow. Thick, heavy layers of leaves that aren't shredded may mat, suffocating plants. Oak leaves make soil more acidic only if used for many, many years and even then only slightly so.

Compost: Greatly improves soil texture and fertility; dark color is attractive. If making your own compost, use only hot compost (see page 182) for mulching; cold compost contains weed seeds that can germinate.

Pine Needles: Available only in certain regions, but they are inexpensive and plentiful. They last two to four seasons. Can be a fire hazard where used extensively.

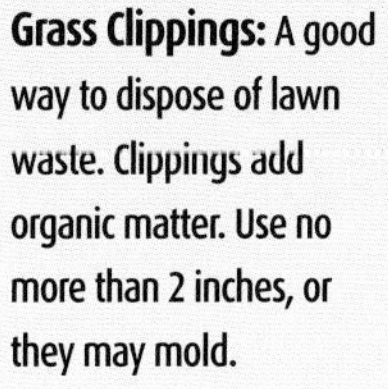

Grass Clippings: A good way to dispose of lawn waste. Clippings add organic matter. Use no more than 2 inches, or they may mold.

Straw/Hay: Fluffy and therefore good as a winter mulch. Neither very attractive nor compact enough for a warm-weather mulch. Hay often contains weed seeds.

Gravel and Stone: Best for arid and rock gardens. White or light-colored rock reflects sunlight and heat onto plants.

Wood Bark, Nuggets: Longer-lasting than wood chips. Large nuggets suppress weeds better than small chips, though chips look more attractive. Needs to be aged or will rob nutrients from the soil.

Landscape Fabric: Also called weed block. Made of a porous black material that allows water to trickle into the soil but deters weeds. Cover with at least 3 inches of a loose mulch, such as wood chips, to disguise it. Use only in permanent plantings where you will have little need to work the soil, such as around shrubs and trees. Works less well with annuals, where plants need to be moved around.

Wood Chips: Needs to be aged at least one year or will rob nutrients from the soil. Cedar, redwood, and cypress chips last the longest.

Caring For Trees

Trees are relatively self-sufficient, so caring for a tree once it's established is mostly a matter of protecting it from damage.

Mulch Away

Spreading a 2- to 3-inch layer of mulch around a tree is one of the best things you can do for it. Spread wood chips or other mulch as far as the branches extend—to the area called the dripline. Mulch suppresses weeds and conserves moisture. It also is far better than lawn, which steals critical water and nutrients from the tree. Mulch also keeps mowers and string trimmers from harming the bark of the tree, a common cause of tree disease and death.

Leave the Soil Level Alone

It's tempting to build raised beds around trees, but it's a poor idea. Raising the soil level around a tree by just 2 inches can cut off feeder roots, dry out others, cut off oxygen, and result in the death of the tree. It's fine to create a flower bed around a tree—just avoid changing the level of the soil.

Mulch trees out to to the dripline—that is, as far as the branches extend. This prevents competition from nitrogen-robbing grass.

Watering and Fertilizing

Watering an established tree (assuming that it's been well-chosen for your climate and site in the first place) is necessary only in cases of severe drought. If that occurs, it's essential to water deeply and seldom rather than shallowly and often. Water the entire area underneath the branches—many trees take up water better farther out from the trunk around the dripline—until the soil is soaked 6 inches down. Repeat once a week until you are out of the severe drought.

Fertilizing healthy trees is seldom necessary either. In fact, fertilizing otherwise fine trees can promote succulent new growth that's vulnerable to pests.

Salt Damage

Salt damage is characterized by tree leaves that are dried and brown along the edges. Salt damage occurs with the overuse of chemical fertilizers or when road salt continually runs off onto a tree's roots. If the soil is well-drained, you may be able to flush out the salts with large volumes of water each spring. Working gypsum into the top few inches also helps in saline Western soils. But the best method is to protect the tree from the salt by directing the runoff away from the tree with regrading or the use of other barriers.

WORK SMARTER

WRAPPING TREES

If you have a newly planted tree and live in a cold climate, wrap the tree for the first few winters. It will protect the tender bark from nibbling rabbits and rodents and from sunscald, a common and severe winter problem.

Wrap the tree in fall, sometime after the first frost but before the first snowfall. Many wraps are available; follow package directions. Wrap from the soil line up the trunk to the first significant branches.

Be sure to remove the wrap in spring about a month or so before your region's last frost date—about the time you do your first lawn mowing. Otherwise, fungal diseases and insects may start multiplying underneath the wrapping.

Prevent Construction Damage

Whether you're building a new home or simply doing some work around the house, it's important to protect your trees. Make sure that walks or driveways or the basement are kept from within 3 feet of the projected mature width of the tree. Adding pavement and digging too close to the roots can kill even a 100-year-old tree.

It's also critical to keep heavy equipment and trucks away from trees. The weight can compact soil and/or damage roots, resulting in tree death.

The best way to protect a tree during construction is to fence it off. Erect sturdy metal stakes about 3 feet farther than the branches extend (the dripline). Invest in some orange plastic tape, the kind used on construction sites, and wrap it around the stakes. It's also worth your while to have a discussion with workers about staying away from the trees with trucks, heavy equipment, and all other vehicles—even wheelbarrows.

Caring For Shrubs

Shrubs are wonderfully easy plants, so caring for them after they're established is quite simple.

Here's how to keep your shrubs happy and healthy:

- Mulch. Add 2 to 3 inches of mulch around shrubs to conserve moisture and suppress weeds.
- Water as needed. Many shrubs are drought-tolerant and do fine with no additional water. Others are quite thirsty and may need regular watering. Check the label or look up the shrub in the Plant Encyclopedia, starting on page 292. If the shrub wilts or the leaves lose their sheen, the shrub probably is getting too little water.
- Fertilize lightly, if at all. The best way to feed any shrub is to spread a ½-inch layer of compost around the base of the plant each spring. However, young shrubs can benefit from a once-a-year light fertilizing with a slow-release granular fertilizer.
- Deadhead flowers after blooming for a neat appearance.
- Cut out dead, diseased, or damaged plant parts.
- Act quickly when pests appear. Identify the problem using the disease and pest section starting on page 214. Otherwise, trim off a problem part of the plant and take it to your Home Depot garden center for identification of the problem and to get a remedy, if appropriate.
- Each spring, rake up leaves and dead branches around the shrub. These harbor pests and diseases, and it's best to remove them.

A CLOSER LOOK

SHRUBS THAT NEED ACIDIC SOIL

A number of shrubs, including azaleas, hollies, and hydrangeas, do best in the moist, acidic soils found in many woodlands.

If your soil is alkaline (has a soil pH of 7.5 or higher), it's best to avoid growing these acid lovers. However, if it's closer to neutral (a soil pH of 6.0–6.5), you can probably grow acid-loving shrubs successfully with some minor soil amending.

When planting, work in plenty of garden sulfur, available at garden centers, according to package directions. Work additional sulfur into the soil each spring, or fertilize with a product that also acidifies the soil.

For most acid-loving plants, this treatment helps them grow stronger and healthier. With hydrangeas that can flower in blue, such as 'Nikko Blue', however, the acid does something extra: It ensures a blue flower. In neutral soils, the flower color is pink.

How to Wrap a Shrub

1 Wrap the burlap around most or all of the small tree or shrub.

2 Secure the burlap in place with twine. Be sure to remove the wrap in spring, four to six weeks before your region's last frost date.

PROJECT DETAILS

SKILLS: Basic wrapping

PROJECT: Using burlap in cold climates to protect evergreens and other shrubs or trees for winter that were planted in the last year or two or are marginally hardy in your area

TIME TO COMPLETE

EXPERIENCED: 10 minutes

HANDY: 15 minutes

NOVICE: 20 minutes

STUFF YOU'LL NEED

TOOLS: Scissors

MATERIALS: Burlap, twine

Pruning Dos and Don'ts

Pruning is an important skill for a gardener to have. When plants are well pruned (or, in some cases, judiciously left alone), they grow healthier and are more productive and beautiful.

Pruning Dos

- Prune at the right time. For most plants, this is when the plant is least active. With most plants at most times in most parts of the country, this is late winter or very early spring. Check the plant's listing in the Plant Encyclopedia in the back of this book to be sure. Avoid pruning when a plant is in flower.
- Understand the concept of old wood and new wood. Some flowering plants bloom only on wood grown the previous year. Others bloom only on wood grown during the current season. Check a plant's listing in the Plant Encyclopedia in the back of the book for pruning guidance for each plant, but the general rule of thumb is to prune flowering shrubs within a month of when they stop flowering. This works for most flowering shrubs.
- Stock up on the right tools. It's just about impossible to do a proper pruning job without them. See "Tools for Pruning" (opposite page) for the right tools for the job.
- Take your time. Work slowly and walk around the plant as you work. Step back and observe frequently. Some gardeners even like to take a day or two to prune a tree or shrub so they can come back to it with a fresh eye for a second or even third pass. Pruning well is an art.
- Prune out dead or damaged wood at any time. It's dead—you don't have to worry about harming the plant by trimming it off.
- Be brave. Many people are afraid of pruning. But the only way you'll learn is to just do it.

Pruning Don'ts

- Avoid getting overly ambitious with trees. Cutting large, high branches is a job for the pros. They wear hard hats and safety gear for a reason. A large falling branch can seriously hurt people and property alike.
- Don't remove too much on trees. As a rule, don't remove more than 20 to 30 percent of the foliage.
- Leave tree wounds alone. The latest research says that tree and shrub wounds should be left alone to heal on their own without any special sprays or salves.
- Don't forget safety. Wear gloves to protect hands. When using power tools, use safety glasses, sturdy shoes, and earplugs.

Stumping Shrubs

There are times when drastic pruning measures are justified. Neglected shrubs become too large and develop poor shape. You could just start over with a new plant, but that old shrub may be far from hopeless. What may be hidden is the most valuable part of the plant. Overgrown shrubs have had time to establish big, healthy root systems. It will take years for a replacement plant to do as well.

You can still save the most valuable part of the shrub. But you have to be ruthless. Prune individual branches nearly to the ground. Stagger cutting heights to keep from having all branches the same level. This will make the new growth appear to fill out faster.

Late winter or early spring, before new growth emerges, is the ideal time for hard pruning. (You can do it any time of year except just before a freeze.) Pruning this severely might keep flowers from appearing for a season or two. In the meantime, you'll be pleased at how quickly your shrub will recover and how much better it looks despite your previous lack of care.

WORK SMARTER

THE THREE RULES OF PRUNING

These three rules of pruning will keep you on the path to success:

1. Cut out dead and dying wood. It's always OK to cut out dead or severely damaged wood any time of year.

2. Remove rubbing or crossed branches. If a branch is rubbing another, it will probably create a raw spot that would be an excellent entry point for disease. Also, plants should have an even, balanced shape that crossed branches interfere with. Remove these branches at the proper pruning time for your plant (when it's dormant or least actively growing).

3. Preserve the shape of the plant. With a few exceptions, such as formal hedges or topiary, pruning should preserve the natural shape of the plant. If possible, avoid cutting back so severely as to interfere with the natural shape.

WORK SMARTER

CLEAN UP YOUR ACT

Rubbing alcohol is a bargain shopper's dream for plant disease prevention. Fill a spray bottle with the alcohol, and make it a habit to spritz pruning tools to sterilize them between cuts, even when you're working on just a single plant. Tools that are not sterilized can transfer diseases from one branch to another and spread infections throughout your entire landscape.

Tools for Pruning

Correctly pruning trees and shrubs around your landscape is possible only if you have the right pruning tools. The right tool also turns a difficult job into an easy one that takes less time and effort, and causes less aching of arms, shoulders, and wrists. Every home gardener should have at least a pair of hand pruners, loppers, a pruning saw, and hedge clippers.

Hand Pruners

Hand pruners are operated with one hand, so they should be used only for cutting small branches. You can buy them in various sizes to match your needs. Trying to force pruners to cut through too-big stems can cause wood and stems to rip, leaving a jagged edge that becomes an entry point for insects or disease. Choose the bypass type of pruner for a clean cut.

Loppers

Operated with both hands, loppers have long handles that give you greater leverage to cut larger branches. Sharp bypass blades work like scissors for smooth, clean cuts. Use loppers whenever stems are too thick for hand pruners, usually more than an inch or so thick. If the loppers aren't big enough (for, say, a 2-inch-thick branch), use a pruning saw.

Pruning Saw

Unlike other saws, a pruning saw has a tapered end and a bowed shape that is designed specifically for making cuts through round limbs. The teeth are usually larger for faster cutting (as opposed to the fine cuts needed for woodworking). Look for a saw that cuts on both the push and the pull strokes for faster, easier cutting.

Power Hedge Trimmer

If you have to trim a large hedge, a power hedge trimmer will make quick work of the job with minimal strain. Gas-powered models are powerful and cordless, but they're heavier and require slightly more maintenance than electrical models. These are lighter (remember that you may be holding this tool at eye level) with slightly less maintenance, but you have a cord to deal with.

Hand Hedge Shears

These inexpensive shears are ideal for small shaping jobs around the home landscape. Look for comfortable handles and solid construction because they'll get a real workout. They're meant for trimming the tips of branches, so avoid cutting larger branches (more than ¼-inch or so). Use hand pruners for those instead.

Pole Saw

When you need to reach a branch high up, a pole saw may be the solution. It cuts with a pulling action of a cord. It's unsuitable for very large branches, but is a good way to reach high branches without a ladder.

6

Maintenance

Cutting a Large Branch

1 Cut off the branch several inches from the trunk. This will take the weight off the final cut and prevent tearing.

2 Make an undercut. Even with the shortened branch, tearing of the bark, resulting in a ragged final cut, can result without this important step. Allow for the final cut to protrude slightly more at the bottom, following the natural "collar" produced by the tree.

3 Make an overcut. This cut, too should allow for a final cut that slopes slightly outward.

4 The resulting final cut should be clean and smooth and follow the natural "collar" of the tree branch. The cut therefore is slightly closer to the trunk at the top of the cut and protrudes slightly at the bottom of the cut.

Pruning a Deciduous Tree

When it comes to pruning a deciduous tree, less is more. Most trees do fine with minimal pruning. After all, they grow in the wild without any pruning at all.

However, trees do benefit from judicious pruning. Here's how:

- Check the best time to prune. For most trees, this is in late winter and early spring while they're still dormant. Check the tree's listing in the Plant Encyclopedia in the back of this book to be sure.
- Cut out dead or severely diseased wood. If there are any stumps from previous bad cuts or broken wood, trim those off as well. Any time of year, it's fine to cut these off.
- Create scaffolding branches in spreading trees. If a tree is meant to have a spreading shape (see page 66 for shapes of trees), choose three or four lower branches, no lower than the top of your head, as scaffolding branches. These branches will create a strong, balanced tier of limbs at the bottom of the tree's greenery.
- Remove secondary leaders. Most spreading trees have a single central trunk that grows upward. Once in a while, a tree will send out a second large branch that is competing for the role of central trunk. This weakens the tree and can lead to the tree splitting down the middle during an ice storm or high winds. Cut off any secondary leaders that appear.
- Cut out suckers. Many trees, especially crabapples and other flowering trees, send up suckers from the roots. Trim these as closely as possible as often as once to several times a year.
- Remove water sprouts. On limbs, especially horizontal limbs, tiny water sprouts no thicker than a pencil will emerge. Remove these once to several times a year as needed or else they'll turn into large branches that will crowd one another out and ruin the overall shape of the tree. While they're still only a leaf or two on a tiny stem sprouting out of the trunk or branches of the tree, you can pull them off with your hand.
- Cut out small limbs that crowd the main limbs. Keep the overall shape of the tree, but remove the spindly growth.
- Cut off large branches in sections for safety's sake and to prevent the bark from tearing. If a branch is large, cut off the end, then cut off another section so you are left with a stump only a foot or so long. Then make an undercut an inch or so deep on the underside of the branch (this will prevent the bark from ripping). Then make the final cut from the top of the branch down, cutting as close as possible to the trunk. Remove as little bark as possible.

What to Prune from a Deciduous Tree

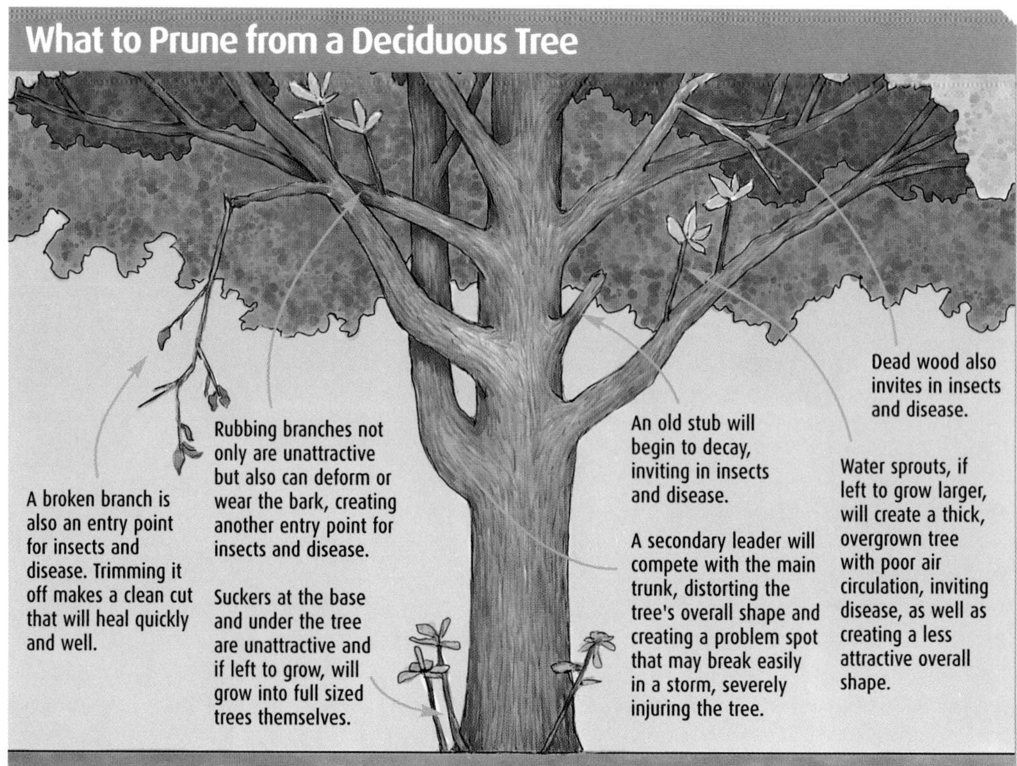

Even mature trees need ongoing pruning. Shown here are various problems that need to be removed.

Pruning Flowering Shrubs

With most flowering shrubs, the less pruning you do, the better. Most flowering shrubs have a naturally lovely shape that can be ruined by severe pruning. Besides, if pruned incorrectly, these shrubs will fail to produce flowers.

Prune a flowering shrub only if it has dead or dying wood or there are obviously problem branches that are rubbing or crossing. If you have a shrub that is too large, you can stump it (see page 188) to avoid fighting the shrub's size, although you will probably destroy flowers in the process. It may be best to transplant the shrub to where it has more space, or remove it from the garden altogether.

If you must prune a flowering shrub, prune it as soon as the flowers fade. Many spring-flowering shrubs, such as azaleas, bloom on old wood—that is, they develop flowers on wood grown the previous year. So if you wait too late in the season to prune, you will remove the next spring's show of blossoms. Summer-blooming shrubs can be pruned in early spring before new growth begins.

Unless a shrub is severely overgrown and warrants hard pruning, make selective pruning your goal. Selective pruning is simply cutting back a shrub here and there, one branch at a time, with hand pruners. Selective pruning reduces size and refines shape. Work to keep the cuts from being evident.

To prune selectively, locate an overgrown branch. Reach into the center of the plant so the cut is made deep within the shrub, hiding the cut. Make your cut right above a leaf or where the stem emerges from a main branch. New growth will begin at this point.

Pruning in this way achieves three things. First, the foliage hides ugly stubs from view. Second, removing individual branches preserves the plant's natural form. Finally, selective pruning encourages prolific flowering. Sunlight reaches the center of the plant, promoting the growth of new buds and leaves.

Give flowering shrubs a light pruning whenever you notice stray stems that give your plant a hairy look. Use selective pruning methods to remove such branches so the natural form of the plant is preserved. (Avoid getting carried away!)

Avoid shearing a flowering shrub—that is, giving it an all-over "haircut" and trimming off only the outer tips of the branches. This eventually damages the plant. Dense, twiggy growth emerges from the multiple cuts, shading the center of the shrub. In time, leaves and flowers only grow along the outside edges of the plant, giving it a thin, scalped look. Some flowering shrubs send up long, stray shoots in protest, making trimming necessary all over again to alter the odd appearance of the plant.

WORK SMARTER

WHEN TO PRUNE FLOWERING SHRUBS

The overall rule for pruning flowering shrubs is to do so in early spring unless the plant is a spring bloomer—you don't want to trim off the flowers.

That means:

- Prune **spring-flowering shrubs** in late spring, right after they've flowered.
- Prune **summer-flowering shrubs** in very early spring, giving them enough time to develop flowers later in the season.
- Prune **shrubs with late-summer or fall flowers or berries** in very early spring. They'll have plenty of time to develop flowers or fruits.

Some shrubs benefit from thinning, that is, cutting out entirely certain branches at the base of the plant. This shows a shrub before thinning.

Older wood on which flowers are less likely to form are removed. This shows the same shrub after thinning.

Pruning Evergreens

Evergreens, as a rule, are low-maintenance plants that seldom need serious pruning. Most evergreen trees and shrubs do beautifully with nary a nip nor tuck from a pruning tool.

However, some homeowners like to shear their evergreens to give them a tight, clipped shape, as with hedges or yews and boxwoods trimmed into balls and fanciful shapes.

GOOD IDEA!

HOLIDAY PRUNING

The best time of year in most parts of the country to prune most evergreens is in winter, when the plants have ceased to actively grow.

Time your pruning for the winter holidays to provide festive greens. Make cuts carefully (remember that they're pruning cuts), then gather the greenery and use it to decorate your home in style.

This bristlecone fir is so beautifully shaped, in part, because it underwent minimal pruning when young. With many evergreens, one of the best ways to assure a nice shape is to leave them alone.

Prune Carefully

Be aware that some evergreens take poorly to shearing or hard pruning. Some, such as junipers and arborvitae, grow only on the perimeter. If you cut them back hard to get out what appears to be dead wood, you'll be left only with trunk and branches and no needles, and it won't grow back.

Boxwood, yew, and holly are notable exceptions. They can be trimmed back hard and still do beautifully. They will regenerate even from the trunk.

As a rule, the larger the leaf, the less pruning an evergreen shrub requires and the less it can withstand without being ruined. Broad-leaved evergreens with big leaves, such as rhododendrons, are poorly suited for shearing. The result will be ragged brown-edged foliage and blunted stems producing few leaves. If you want shrubs that can be clipped neatly into smooth forms, choose evergreens with naturally compact shapes. These shrubs have either needled foliage or small leaves.

Keep the Shape

Know the mature form of a young plant before you prune. Save labels that have pictures; check the Plant Encyclopedia, starting on page 292; or ask a garden associate to describe the plant's natural mature form. Many beautiful plants have been ruined by improper pruning.

Many pyramid-shaped evergreens, for example, have a point at the top—a single branch that reaches upward, like the tip of a Christmas tree that you'd slip the star on. It's critical that, when you prune, you do avoid trimming off this point. It directs the tree's tapered upward climb. If you trim off the tip, the tree will fork at the top, distorting its graceful shape.

Pruning Flowering Evergreens

Trim flowering evergreens when their flowers fade. Use hand pruners to cut off the dead blooms and tips of small branches. This keeps plants from becoming shaggy and overgrown. Also, trimming prompts fresh growth and flower bud development for the next year.

Three Ways to Prune Evergreens

Selective Pruning

Selective pruning removes wayward branches while retaining a plant's natural form.

Why: To keep shrubs neat and control their size while maintaining their natural, informal shape.

When: Prune needled evergreen shrubs in late winter or early spring. Prune flowering, broad-leaved evergreens right after they bloom.

How: Reach inside shrubs and find where each long shoot emerges from stiff, older wood. Make pruning cuts here, inside the shrub, removing only the flexible shoot. (Cuts on stiff, older wood will not sprout again.) Avoid leaving any stubs. Make cuts toward the top of the plant where sunlight will prompt the most new growth. Avoid pruning evergreens severely at the bottom, which receives less sunlight.

Shearing

To give shrubs a tightly clipped, formal look, shear them on the surface, shaping them to the desired form. Plants suitable for shearing grow new twigs and leaves from each cut, making the foliage thick and dense.

Why: To create a formal, sculpted look in the landscape.

When: Shear in warm weather, which promotes fresh growth. Clip frequently to keep the shrubs neatly trimmed and to control their size.

How: Angle the blades of a sharpened hedge trimmer as needed to cut the plant's surface and to shape it. Stand back frequently to assess your work. An electric hedge trimmer makes shearing a large hedge easy. Use care to avoid whittling away your shrubs to bare branches.

Pinching

Bright green new growth on pines, spruce, and fir are called candles. Pinching of the candles by hand is the best way to control plant size and keep these evergreens neat without causing browned tips.

Why: To control size and shape quickly and neatly during the early part of the growing season.

When: Pinch soft, new growth on nonflowering evergreens in late spring or early summer before the shoots harden off (become stiff and woody).

How: Clasp the stem of the plant where the new growth emerges from the older wood. Pinch off the portion of new growth you want removed, even the entire shoot. Buds for next year's growth will form at this point.

Pruning A Hedge

Some hedges are informal and some are formal.

Informal hedges seldom need pruning. Some hedge plants may actually be harmed by pruning. If your hedge consists of bridalwreath spirea or azaleas, doing anything more than cutting out dead or damaged wood, or doing a little selective pruning on a branch here or there, will ruin the lovely natural shape of the plants.

Formal hedges, those trimmed into neat shapes, add a well-groomed appearance to the landscape. Hedges of privet, boxwood, yew, and holly all take well to tight pruning.

Neat Cuts

Unless you are a perfectionist, pruning a hedge using your eye as the measuring tool will work nicely. But for a precisely trimmed hedge, use a simple, wedge-shaped template (which you can build from three pieces of wood) to define your chosen form.

Alternatively, with the help of a second person, you can check how true your lines are by stretching a length of twine along the hedge.

WORK SMARTER

BATTERING A HEDGE

Formal hedges should be wider at the bottom than the top. Pruning this way, called battering, encourages light to reach even the lower branches, stimulating new leaf growth and preventing lower branches from dying out—a common problem with hedges. A hedge 5 feet tall, for example, could have a base 2 1/2 feet wide and a top only 1 foot wide.

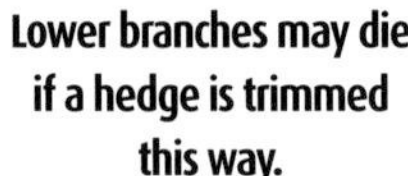

Lower branches may die if a hedge is trimmed this way.

A hedge trimmed to be wider on the bottom lets more sunlight in.

A yew hedge needs to be trimmed only once or twice a year. Faster-growing hedges may need to be pruned three or four times.

Pruning A Vine

Annual vines need no pruning or cutting back. In all but the warmest regions of the United States, they die when frost hits and can be pulled or cut down from their supports. Perennial vines require more management. They need an occasional bit of dead wood pruned out and often need to be cut back to prevent them from creeping into places you don't want them.

The best time to prune most vines is in late winter or early spring, just as the vine is leafing out. At this point you can tell dead wood from live yet can still see the vine's structure easily. Cut out any dead wood, using hand pruners or loppers, or a small saw for large stems.

As a general rule, follow each branch back to its origin at a main branch. Cut back side branches from a few inches to 2 feet from the main trunk. Then remove any suckers from the base.

This bittersweet is getting a hard pruning to the main branches in early spring, so it has plenty of time to develop berries in fall.

How to Prune Specific Vines

The first time to prune a vine is immediately after planting it. Although it may seem as though you're reducing your investment, you'll spur the vine into new and faster growth if you cut it back to about half the size it was when you bought it.

Most vines need little pruning for a season or two after that as they grow into their new home. But if, as the vines grow, the stems appear leggy with few leaves or flowers, trim them back to encourage new growth to develop more branches. Most vines will eventually require trimming to shape them and keep their size under control. Here's how to prune some popular vines:

American Bittersweet *(Celastrus scandens)*
Late winter or early spring is the time to cut back this vine to keep it in bounds, although trimming in fall produces attractive cuttings for arrangements. Trim stems as needed to keep vines the size and shape you desire. Overgrown vines require yearly pruning to keep them under control.

Chinese Wisteria (*Wisteria chinensis*)
When your wisteria has reached the desired height, thin three times a year to promote flowering. Prune first in winter when the vine is dormant. Locate the second bud from the tip on new growth and trim half the shoots on the plant back to this point. In spring, remove all young, leafless branches. Cut side branches, leaving two or three buds and allowing all nubby spurs to remain. Follow up with summer pruning to reduce by one-half the size of side branches.

Clematis (*Clematis* spp.)
Pruning varies according to bloom time. Clematis that bloom in spring should be pruned, if needed, right after flowering. Those that bloom in early summer, or those that bloom nearly year-round, should be pruned in early spring when new growth is apparent, back to perhaps 6–8 inches and a pair of well-formed leaf buds. Clematis that bloom in fall should be pruned in early spring to about 1 foot in height.

Climbing Hydrangea *(Hydrangea petiolaris)*
Trim these vines only as needed to keep them growing in the area you want and to keep their aerial rootlets off wood structures. Make cuts after flowering.

Hardy Kiwi *(Actinidia arguta)*
Regular pruning is needed only to maintain size. If you must prune, trim stems back immediately after flowering to avoid cutting off next year's blossoms.

Trumpet Honeysuckle *(Lonicera sempervirens)* and
Dropmore Scarlet Honeysuckle (*Lonicera* × *brownii* 'Dropmore Scarlet')
Prune these vines only if they've outgrown their allotted space. You can cut them anytime except right before a freeze, but the best time to prune honeysuckle is right after it finishes flowering.

Trumpet Vine *(Campsis radicans)*
Prune as needed in late winter or early spring to control this vigorous vine's size and reduce its weight. Cut back side shoots to develop a strong main framework of woody stems. Leave stubs with three or four buds when cutting off shoots.

Virginia Creeper *(Parthenocissus quinquefolia)* and
Boston Ivy *(Parthenocissus tricuspidata)*
Let these vines grow, but cut them back as needed to keep them off wood structures. If you must control their size, cut back the growing ends of stems in early winter. Repeat if necessary at the beginning of summer. Avoid cutting these vines at the base; if you do, you'll end up with the hard-to-remove dead stems clinging to the wall.

Pruning Roses

A CLOSER LOOK

NEW WOOD AND OLD WOOD

Some roses bloom on new wood— that is, wood produced during the current growing season. Others bloom on old wood—wood that grew the previous year. If you cut off that old wood when pruning this type of rose, you'll prevent flowers from forming.

Here's how to figure out if a rose blooms on new or old wood. As a rule, most bush roses bloom on new wood. Cut them back hard. Some old garden or antique roses as well as some climbing and rambler roses bloom on old wood.

Roses that bloom on new wood should be pruned hard in late winter or early spring. Roses that bloom on old wood should be pruned lightly after they bloom, giving them enough time to grow more wood for the next year.

If you're in doubt about what type of rose you have, prune back hard in spring. The worst result will be that flower buds will fail to form on the plant that year. And if there are none, you'll know that you probably have a rose that blooms on old wood. So from here on out, you should prune as soon as the rose is finished flowering.

Pruning roses is easy if you follow a few time-tested rules. The basic principle for all roses except climbers is to direct all growth outward in a regular and even fashion, keeping the center of the rose open so air can circulate to prevent disease.

When to Prune

You can cut out diseased or dead (black or dark gray) wood any time of year. But roses need a major pruning in late winter or early spring when they're first starting to send out new growth. The new growth is usually little red buds or shoots that will turn into new stems and leaves.

To get blooms as profuse as those on this 'Climbing Cécile Brúnner,' you have to prune properly early each spring.

What to Use

You need sharp bypass pruners for most jobs. Dull blades crush and damage wood, and damaged wood invites disease. You may need a pair of loppers (long-handled pruners for large branches) as well. Loppers can handle stems from a half inch to one inch thick. For heavy pruning jobs, you could use a small saw, but that's seldom necessary for roses.

A pair of heavy gloves is a must. Rose thorns can cause nasty gashes and cuts, and even small thorns have an unpleasant way of staying embedded in your skin. Long sleeves are also a good idea.

Keep rubbing alcohol or a weak bleach solution and paper towels on hand to sterilize the pruner blades after pruning each rosebush, to avoid spreading disease.

What to Prune

The first step in an early-spring pruning job is to cut out all completely dead wood, which is black or dark gray. When you cut into it, the dead center (called the pith) will also be black or dark gray. Wood is still alive, even if the outside is black, as long as the pith is white and firm. It's simply less vigorous than wood that's green on the outside.

Next, cut out any branches that are rubbing against others, crossing one another, or damaged or diseased.

Then choose three to six canes as your "keepers." These canes should be at least as thick as a pencil, but trim out stems that are too thick and old. The keepers should also spread outward from the center.

Remove other thin, spindly growth. Then cut the canes you are going to keep to a height of 1 to 3 feet, depending on how high you want your rosebush. As a rule, cut the rose canes about one-fifth as high as the desired mature height of the rose stalks, or longer in warm climates (Zone 7 and warmer). It may seem like drastic surgery, but the rose will survive. As long as you leave at least a few inches of cane, it will do fine.

Make the cut at the top of the cane so it's at a 45-degree angle ¼ inch above an outward-facing bud (see "Making a Cut Correctly," at right). This assures that new growth will be outward and upward, creating a healthy plant and an attractive shape. Avoid painting or dabbing any substance on the cuts. They'll heal nicely by themselves.

WORK SMARTER

MAKING A CUT CORRECTLY

When pruning roses, it's important that you make a 45-degree cut ¼ inch above an outward-facing bud. This ensures that the resulting stem will grow up and away from the center of the bush. This creates a more nicely shaped bush with an open center that allows better air circulation and is less susceptible to disease.

WORK SMARTER

THE FIVE-LEAFLET RULE

When you're deadheading roses or cutting a few to take indoors, you're pruning, affecting the ultimate shape and health of your rose. Therefore, it's important to cut carefully and correctly.

When cutting flowers or deadheading, make the cut just above a leaf with five little leaflets facing away from the center of the bush. This ensures strong new growth at the point of the cut.

Pruning Roses *continued*

How to Prune Climbers

Climbing roses get a different treatment from bush roses, and that treatment depends on whether they're ramblers or large-flowered climbers.

Ramblers usually have smaller flowers and grow rampantly, up to 20 feet in a season. If they are left unpruned, they'll grow into a thorny, overgrown thicket.

Ramblers bloom only once a year and do so on old wood grown the previous season. After they're done blooming, cut back the canes by a foot or so. This encourages fresh, rapid growth this year so they'll have lots of wood to bloom on next year. Tie this new growth to a fence or trellis.

Large-flowered climbers are less vigorous. In their first year, you must train them up the arbor or the trellis they're planted on. Tie them with soft twine or strips of cut pantyhose. Sometimes you can carefully weave the pliable stems in and out of the support.

Most large-flowered climbers bloom on new wood, so prune them every year in late winter or early spring while they're still dormant or just as they start sending out red buds of new growth. However, in their first two to four years, you need to prune them very little other than to remove dead or damaged wood. As the rose grows, prune as needed to shape it and control its height.

Pruning Roses in Mild Climates

Gardeners in warm parts of the country—the mid-South downward, the Southwest, and the Pacific coast—prune in a

PROJECT DETAILS

SKILLS: An eye for preserving the shape of the rose
PROJECT: Pruning

TIME TO COMPLETE

EXPERIENCED: 15 minutes
HANDY: 20 minutes
NOVICE: 30 minutes

STUFF YOU'LL NEED

TOOLS: Bypass hand pruners, loppers for large branches, protective gloves
MATERIALS: Rubbing alcohol, paper towels

How to Prune a Rose*

1 First remove dead wood—it's black or dark gray. Then remove rubbing, or damaged stems. Then step back to assess the plant. (The black bars above indicate where cuts would be made on this rose.)

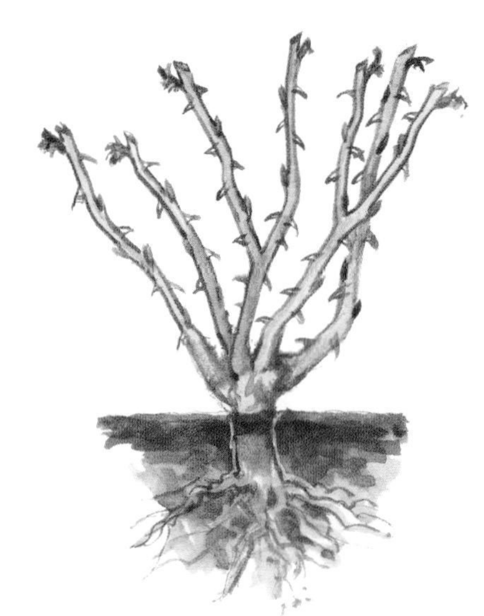

2 Prune the rest. Cut out any spindly growth that's thinner than a pencil. Leave only four or five thick, healthy canes 1 to 3 feet tall. After pruning each plant, sterilize the shears using rubbing alcohol and paper towels to prevent spreading disease.

* These steps apply to a bush rose, such as a shrub rose or hybrid tea, in a cold climate (Zone 6 or so and colder).

slightly different way. Because they lack harsh winters that kill back much of their rose growth, each late winter they need to decide how much of the roses to cut back.

As a rule, cut back shrub roses and hybrid teas to 2 to 4 feet. Give old garden roses, which bloom on old wood, a light overall selective pruning, cutting back some of the oldest stems to the base to keep the plants from becoming too lanky.

Climbers in warm climates do best if trained on a horizontal plane with each branch cut back to about the place where it's slightly thicker than a pencil. Then cut each side stem that has flowered to the lowest possible five-leaflet stem, about 1 to 2 inches from the main cane. This causes the cane to flower along its entire length for a spectacular display.

With any climbing or rambling rose, the more horizontally you can prune or train it the better. This encourages more vertical branches to grow up from the hortizontal branches, covering the plant more heavily with blooms.

How to Prune a Climbing Rose*

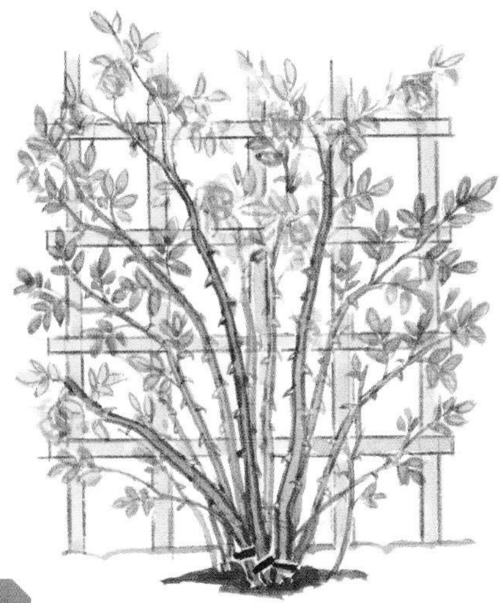

1 Prune in early spring. Cut out old branches (canes) that flowered the year before. The black marks indicate cuts.

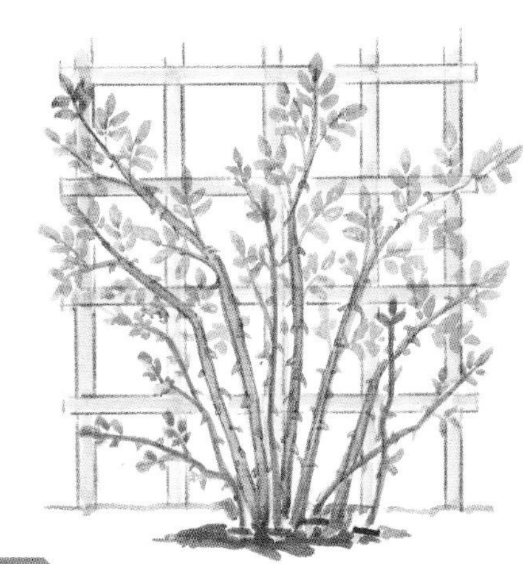

2 Cut out all dead, weak, or thin canes, leaving four or five strong new ones.

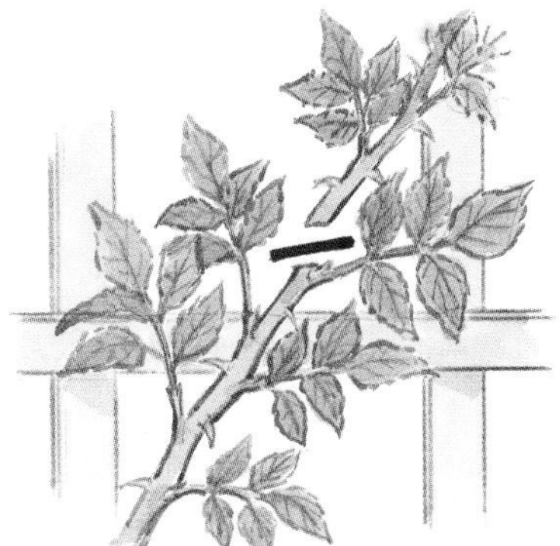

3 Cut back the selected canes. Cut to four or five sets of five-leaved leaflets. After pruning each plant, sterilize the shears using rubbing alcohol and paper towels to prevent spreading disease.

4 Now that you've done all that, tie the selected canes to the support with soft twine or strips of pantyhose.

* These steps are for a climbing rose that blooms on new wood in cold climates (Zone 6 or so and colder).

PROJECT DETAILS

SKILLS: An eye for preserving the shape of the rose
PROJECT: Pruning

TIME TO COMPLETE

EXPERIENCED: 20 minutes
HANDY: 25 minutes
NOVICE: 35 minutes

STUFF YOU'LL NEED

TOOLS: Bypass hand pruners, loppers for large branches, protective gloves
MATERIALS: Old pantyhose or soft twine for tying, rubbing alcohol, paper towels

Caring For Roses

Roses have an undeserved reputation for being high-maintenance. But as long as you choose a low-maintenance rose, it will take little more time than any other flowering shrub.

Yes, roses do best with regular pruning and fertilizing (see pages 196 and 181). Some rose fanciers, in order to grow show-perfect roses, set out on a strict regimen of heavy fertilizing and spraying, and often provide extensive winter protection.

But aside from contest-perfect, especially large flowers, your roses will do fine if grown in full sunlight—six hours or more of direct, unfiltered light a day—and given ample water and fertilizer (see page 181). In fact, a low-maintenance rose (see page 79) will take about the same amount of work as any other flowering plant.

More Rose Information

- For information on choosing low-maintenance roses, see page 79.
- For information on fertilizing roses, see page 181.
- For information on pruning roses, see pages 196–199.
- For information on rose pests and diseases, see page 219.

WORK SMARTER

KEEP THAT WATER COMING

Roses do best if they go into winter well watered. If the weather is dry in autumn, continue to water roses sparingly even after frost. Avoid watering once the ground freezes.

This 'Morden Blush' rose is very winter-hardy, requiring little winter protection except in Zone 4 or colder.

Winterizing Roses

How much winter protection you need to give your roses depends on your climate and the rose. It also varies depending on the severity of each winter. But in general, do the following, depending on which zone you live in (see page 26):

Zone 5 and Colder

In late fall, before the first snowfall, mound all roses with soil or compost to a height of 10 to 12 inches. In Zones 4 and 5, the hardiest roses, such as rugosas, Morden, Canadian Explorer, and most David Austins, will survive normal winters without additional protection. But hybrid teas and other borderline-hardy roses need their top growth protected as well (see illustrations below). And in Zone 3, all roses need their top growth protected.

Remove the top protection when daytime temperatures regularly are in the 50s, usually in March or so. Two or three weeks later, gently hose or push away the mounded soil.

Zones 6 to 8

In late fall, after the ground freezes, mound roses with 4 to 8 inches of soil, compost, or mulch. Remove in late February or early March.

Zone 9 and Warmer

No mounding or mulch is needed except for the least cold-hardy roses, such as hybrid teas, during the coldest winters. Even then, they'll need only 3 to 4 inches of mulch around their base.

A CLOSER LOOK

WHEN TO CUT BACK

Some gardeners cut back their roses to prepare them for winter. But roses are more likely to survive if the canes are left intact. Cut back only if you're concerned about severe wind damage; otherwise, tie in bundles. Prune roses in late winter or early spring.

6

Maintenance

Winter Protection for Roses

Mounding. In all but the warmest climates (Zone 9 and warmer), roses need to be protected in late fall with soil or compost mounded 6–12 inches high.

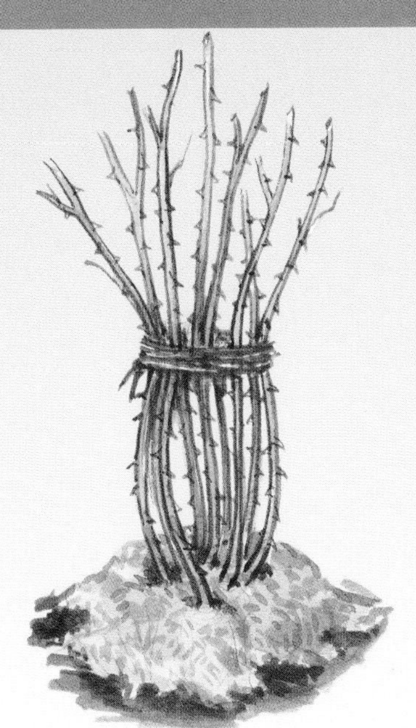

Tying canes. In high-wind areas, it's a good idea to tie together tall canes to prevent whipping wind from damaging them.

Wrapping. In Zone 5 and colder, less hardy roses should be wrapped with burlap and twine for further protection. Remove the covering in early spring, about the time the snow melts permanently.

Caring for Annuals and Perennials

WORK SMARTER

MANAGING RESEEDERS

Annuals that reseed themselves, properly tended, can be a gardener's great friend. Hollyhocks, cleome, sunflowers, bachelor's buttons, larkspur, California poppies, ox-eye daisies, and others sow themselves around the garden, multiplying rapidly each year. However, if they're too prolific, they can be a headache.

Keep them in check by thinning them as needed each spring or fall. Or dig up small (under 1 inch) reseeded plants and group or rearrange them for better effect.

If you want fewer reseeded plants, be sure to deadhead the parent plant as soon as it's finished flowering to keep it from setting seed. If you want more reseeded plants, leave the flowers on the parent plants and let them set seed.

Compost reseeders with caution. Avoid throwing spent flower heads on the compost pile unless you're making hot compost, which kills seeds. Cold compost will spread the reseeders with the compost, creating weed problems later.

A beautifully cared-for flower bed is a pleasure to work in and to behold. Here's how to care for your beds and borders in the most effective way:

- Improve the soil whenever you can. Each time you plant anything, take the opportunity to work some compost into the soil. You'll feed your plants and improve the soil texture, making watering and weeding much easier.
- Consider a preemergent herbicide. In spring when plants start new growth, sprinkle a granular fertilizer/preemergent herbicide on flower beds. It will send them off to a strong start and prevent weed seeds from germinating.
- Mulch. Each spring, apply 1 to 2 inches of mulch around annuals and perennials. It helps deter weeds and conserve moisture. It also prevents soilborne diseases from splashing on plants during watering or rain.
- Weed early. Get weeds while they're small and you'll save yourself hours. And avoid ever letting a weed flower set seed, or it will scatter hundreds if not thousands of seeds around your landscape.
- Keep up with basic chores. Every day go out and enjoy your flowers with hand pruners and a weeding tool in hand. You'll catch weeding and deadheading tasks early and be able to take care of them in just a few minutes. It's a relaxing way to start or end your day.

More Annuals and Perennials Information

- For information on fertilizing annuals and perennials, see page 180.
- For information on mulching, see page 184.
- For information on watering annuals and perennials, see page 172.
- For information on deadheading flowers, see page 206.
- For information on staking flowers, see page 207.

These richly colored coleus and yellow marigolds thrive in a partly sunny spot in the garden. These coleus are exceptionally large because of excellent soil and regular fertilizing.

Renovating a Flower Bed

Once in a while, a flower bed becomes a tangle of weeds and overenthusiastically spreading flowers. Or, as plants grow and mature, you realize that those tall plants should be in the back of the border, the lower plants in the front, and perhaps a plant or two shouldn't be there at all. When this happens, it's time to renovate the flower bed.

You can renovate just a small portion of a flower bed or, if you're ambitious, do an entire bed at a time.

Renovation consists of completely digging up the perennials, sprucing them up a bit, and replacing them in the bed. While they're out (set them on a tarp), you can divide the perennials as needed, remove weeds from the garden, and improve the soil. Then put the plants back in place. (Be careful not to dig up spring-blooming bulbs such as tulips and daffodils.)

It's best to renovate gardens in fall or spring. Do it on an overcast day right before rain is predicted to minimize stress on plants.

Tasks to do while renovating include:

- Breaking apart perennials in which weeds or grasses have become hopelessly entangled.
- Working compost or other soil amendments (see page 138) into the bottom of planting holes where it can feed plants and improve drainage. This is also a good opportunity to improve the soil generally throughout the renovation area by turning it over and working an inch or two of compost or other soil amendments into the top several inches of soil.
- Reposition flowers into a more pleasing arrangement, and relocate or discard problem plants.
- Divide plants that need dividing (see page 165).

A CLOSER LOOK

WINTERIZING YOUR FLOWER BEDS AND BORDERS

In Zone 6 and colder, you'll want to protect your flower beds and borders from winter's ravages.

In fall, after frost zaps most of the plants, pull up dead annuals. Cut back most perennials except those with attractive flower or seed heads, such as ornamental grasses and many sedums.

Then apply a layer of winter mulch. Like a winter coat, this insulates perennials from extremes of cold and damaging late-winter thaws. Winter mulch should be fluffy and light, but substantial enough to keep it from blowing away. Chopped leaves layered a few inches thick make an excellent winter mulch.

In spring, as soon as bulbs and perennials show signs of new growth, gently rake away the winter mulch.

Caring For Bulbs

Spring-Blooming Bulb Care

• Fertilize lightly in fall. Bulbs appreciate the nutrient boost. A fertilizer made especially for bulbs is ideal, but a general-purpose, slow-release granular fertilizer or a 1-inch layer of compost around the bulbs will also do nicely. Avoid feeding in spring at bloom time. The burst of nitrogen could encourage fungal problems.

• Deadhead spent flowers. This way the bulb's energy goes to strengthening the plant instead of producing seeds.

• Mulch. Bulbs do best after bloom and into the summer if the soil around them is cool and moist but not wet. Mulch helps keep the soil temperature lower and the moisture level higher.

• Keep them watered. Avoid letting bulbs bake and dry out. Keep the soil reasonably well watered, although keeping it a little on the dry side is ideal to prevent fungal problems. One way to achieve this is to plant annuals in a layer on top of the bulbs. You'll need to keep them watered, which in turn will keep the bulbs watered too.

• Label or mark bulbs after bloom. It's easy to slice through bulbs once their foliage dies back. Plant labels can help to prevent this, as can an attractive, flat stone, which blends in better. (If you wish, mark the bulbs with permanent labels.)

Summer-Blooming Bulb Care

• Use a general fertilizer on summer-blooming bulbs when their foliage appears in spring, then once a month while the plants are in bloom.

• Some bulbs, such as naked lady lilies or autumn crocus, bloom after the foliage has died. Fertilize them while their foliage is green and growing, then hold back while they're blooming later in the year. It's a good idea to mark these plants, too, so you can avoid digging them up or damaging the emerging flowers while weeding.

In a few weeks, the foliage of these bulbs will turn brown and unattractive, but the surrounding perennials will be large enough to camouflage it.

Hands Off That Foliage!

After spring-blooming bulbs, such as daffodils, tulips, and hyacinths, bloom, resist the temptation to remove the foliage as it browns and does what bulb experts call ripening.

Leaving the browning foliage in place helps bulbs store up energy for next year's bloom. If you remove it, as shown here, you weaken the bulb—a bad thing. Allow the foliage to fully brown and wither. Once it pulls away with little or no resistance, you can remove it.

Avoid covering the dying foliage with mulch. The foliage needs sunlight to help feed the bulb. And avoid braiding or tying up the foliage with rubber bands. The foliage also needs oxygen.

In warm climates where you must chill bulbs before planting (see page 162), the bulbs will not return the next year, so after they bloom you can simply pull them out and plant something else.

Digging and Storing Summer-Blooming Bulbs

In cold-winter regions, most summer-blooming bulbs must be dug up and stored indoors if you want to keep them year after year. (See the chart at right.) Of course, you could replant fresh bulbs each year, but it's far less expensive to save them.

Tender (that is, not winter-hardy) bulbs should be dug in fall after frost has nipped the leaves (see page 29 for average first frost dates). Dig before the leaves die back completely so you can find the bulbs.

Dig bulbs with a garden fork or spade, taking care to avoid damaging any bulbs. Brush off the soil and allow the bulbs to dry. Then store them indoors.

Storing bulbs requires care. Even experienced gardeners lose a few bulbs each year when they rot or shrivel. Minimize your losses by following these basic steps:

- Experiment with storage methods. Some gardeners prefer wooden boxes, cardboard boxes, or paper bags (the container needs to breathe, so avoid plastic). Others prefer to store bulbs in slightly damp sawdust or sphagnum peat moss.
- Store bulbs at the right temperature. Bulbs such as tuberous begonias, dahlias, cannas, and gladioli like cool temperatures, 35 to 55°F (2 to 13°C). Others, such as tuberoses and caladiums, like warmer conditions, 60 to 75°F (16 to 24°C). Cool spots include unheated garages, attics, and basements or crawlspaces. Warm spots include closets, underneath beds, or heated basements and attics. Place a thermometer in the spot so you can check the temperature throughout bulb storage to be sure.
- Check on bulbs at least once a month. Check the temperature and move the bulbs if it is too warm or too cool. Examine bulbs for rot or softness, and throw out bad bulbs. Moisten the packing material as needed to keep it slightly moist.

Summer-Blooming Bulbs to Dig

Common Name	Botanical Name	Dig and Store in These Zones
Abyssinian gladiolus	*Gladiolus callianthus*	Dig in 6 and colder
African lily	*Agapanthus*	Dig in 6 and colder
Caladium	*Caladium* hybrids	Dig in 9 and colder
Canna lily	*Canna* hybrids	Dig in 6 and colder
Crocosmia	*Crocosmia* ×*crocosmiifora*	Dig in 5 and colder
Dahlia	*Dahlia* hybrids	Dig in 7 and colder
Freesia	*Freesia* spp.	Dig in 8 and colder
Gladiolus	*Gladiolus* hybrids	Dig in 6 and colder
Persian buttercup	*Ranunculus asiaticus*	Dig in 7 and colder

PROJECT DETAILS

SKILLS: Digging
PROJECT: Digging up bulbs in fall that would die if left to winter outdoors

TIME TO COMPLETE

EXPERIENCED: 1 hour for a few dozen bulbs
HANDY: 1 to 2 hours
NOVICE: 2 to 3 hours

STUFF YOU'LL NEED

TOOLS: Spading fork or spade, soft brush (optional), hand pruners
MATERIALS: Storage box, newspaper, material such as sawdust in which to store bulbs

Digging and Storing Bulbs

1 After fall frost has blackened the bulb foliage, dig up bulbs carefully to avoid injuring them. A spading fork is less likely to do damage than a spade. Cut off the dead foliage for easier handling.

2 Shake or rub the soil from the bulbs, using a soft brush if necessary. Then spread the bulbs to dry for a few days on newspapers in a shady but dry and breezy spot, such as a porch or a garage with the door left open.

3 Store the dried bulbs in a cardboard box or paper bag. Avoid plastic because it promotes mold. Fill the box or bag with slightly damp sawdust or other packing material, and label it. Store in a cool to moderate—35 to 75°F (7 to 23°C)—room. Check every month or so, and remove any shriveled, moldy bulbs.

Deadheading

Deadheading—removing fading blooms—keeps your garden looking tidy, and it encourages many plants to continue flowering longer.

A plant's job is to set seed and reproduce. Seeds are produced from flowers. When you remove the flowers, the plant starts to produce more blooms in an effort to set seed. Without deadheading, the plant will likely stop or reduce its bloom production.

Which Flowers Need It

Annuals benefit the most from deadheading. With proper deadheading, many will produce more than double the flowers they would without. Perennials usually bloom for only a few weeks, but some perennials will continue to bloom for months with diligent deadheading. Others will respond with a second flush of bloom, sometimes as late as fall. Bulbs and shrubs tend to be the least responsive to deadheading, but some will bloom longer with diligent trimming of spent blooms. (Be sure to leave the foliage on bulbs to help them rejuvenate for the next year.)

How to Deadhead

The method of deadheading depends on the plant. Tall, tough stalks such as those on daylilies and irises need to be removed individually at the base of the plant with hand pruners. Flower stalks will fade and can then be pulled off easily by hand.

On some plants, such as marigolds, the flowers can be pinched off. If only a flower or two in a large cluster is fading, pinch or cut it off to allow the others to develop better.

Some plants look unattractive when first deadheaded but fill out again in a week or two. When deadheading individual flowers, reach into the plant as much as possible to minimize unattractive stubs.

You can deadhead with a variety of tools. Sometimes your fingers are all you need to pinch or snap off a fading flower. At other times, scissors are useful. Woody plants require hand pruners. Soft, bushy plants sometimes are easiest to deadhead with a sharp pair of grass clippers or hedge shears.

When deadheading a flowering shrub, reach into the plant and cut close to the center. That way, the stub resulting from the cut will be hidden by the foliage.

Cutting Back

Some annuals and perennials look tattered near the middle or end of the season and benefit from a hard cutting back rather than a mere deadheading. Cut back the plant by one-third to two-thirds with hand pruners. The plant will look ragged for a week or two but will soon regenerate with fresh foliage and a new burst of bloom.

Good candidates for cutting back include petunia, many bellflowers, coreopsis, perennial blue salvia, balloon flower, golden marguerite, lobelia, hardy geranium, gaura, and verbena.

WORK SMARTER

DEADHEAD EARLY AND OFTEN

Deadheading regularly is important for maximum flowering in your garden. Although it's best to deadhead daily, at least once a week should be sufficient.

How to Deadhead

Roses: If only a few flowers on a cluster have faded, pinch or trim them off. If the whole cluster is fading, cut it off at the first leaflet with five leaves (see page 197 for details).

Perennials with Tall Stalks: Cut off the stalk as near to the base as possible. In some cases, the stalk dries up enough that you can gently tug it off.

Perennials and Annuals with Partly Faded Flower Clusters: Cut or pinch off only the faded flower. When the entire cluster fades, remove the whole stem.

Bushy Annuals and Perennials with Many Small Flowers: It's difficult to get only the faded flowers, so when most flowers have faded, give the plant a haircut by shearing back by about one-third and removing all the blooms.

Staking Flowers

For the neatest, best-groomed garden, you'll probably need to do a little staking. Staking keeps your garden tidy looking even in late summer when mature plants tend to flop under their own weight.

Know When to Stake

The best staking is done when the plant is about a foot tall. That way the plant can grow tall and straight with the stake. But there are times when you may have to stake after the plant has begun to sprawl and spread. The effects are less graceful, but staking is still helpful because staking keeps plants off the ground, where moisture invites disease.

Keep Your Work From Showing

The best staking is nearly invisible. Choose staking materials in dark neutrals or deep greens rather than shiny metal or white. If shiny or white is all you have, give it a coat of dark green spray paint. Materials for tying should be soft and stretchy to prevent damaging stems. Good choices include cut strips of pantyhose, rags, or soft twine.

Stakes can be sticks or branches salvaged from your yard (keep a pile in the garage) or bits of scrap lumber. Bamboo rods are classic. Metal supports include rounded grids for plants to grow through; others create a fence to provide support.

Tall lilies, such as Asiatic and Oriental varieties, tend to lean. Cleverly designed stakes keep them attractive and upright.

How to Stake Flowers

Different types of flowers need different types of staking at different times of the year. Use one of these staking methods, or browse your local garden center for various staking materials and supports.

Staking Mature Bushy Flowers: Often the need for staking isn't apparent until the plant has begun to bend or lean. In that case, make a little fencelike structure with stakes and twine to keep the plant upright.

Staking Young, Tall, Slender Flowers: Tall individual flowers, such as delphiniums and many lilies, need sturdy stakes. Install natural-colored stakes when the plants are only a foot or so high. As the plants grow, tie them loosely to the stakes using soft twine, stretch tape, or strips of pantyhose.

Natural Support: Bushy plants that tend to sprawl, such as sweet peas and bush morning glory, will twine easily around a shrubby branch or two gently pushed into the ground at planting time. Branches make free, natural-looking supports.

Grid Support: Bushy flowers, such as peonies, yarrow, and asters, benefit from a gridlike plant support. Position the grid over the plant in spring when it's only several inches tall, and allow the growing plant to push through it.

Keeping Your Garden Healthy

GOOD IDEA!

MOVE IT

If a perennial fails to thrive, it may be in the wrong spot. The light may be too low or too harsh, or the plant might not like the soil or drainage in that particular location, or it may be getting too much competition from nearby plants.

So if after a year or two a plant is doing poorly, dig it up (early spring is best) and move it to a new place. Even experienced gardeners are amazed at how moving a plant from one spot to another in their gardens can make a difference.

That old saying about an ounce of prevention being worth a pound of cure is absolutely right.

In your garden, you will save unlimited amounts of time, energy, money, and frustration if you take some basic steps to prevent pest and disease problems before they strike.

Choose Disease-Resistant Cultivars

Some plants are more prone to diseases than others. If, for example, hollyhocks in your region tend to have rust spots on them, substitute another tall, slender plant instead, such as delphinium.

Read labels and plant descriptions carefully for mention of disease resistance. Look up the plant in the Plant Encyclopedia starting on page 292, to check for any mention of disease problems. And ask garden center staff when considering a purchase.

Even if a plant is vulnerable to a disease or pest, there may be a particular cultivar of that plant that is resistant to that disease or pest. For example, many tall garden phlox get powdery mildew. Some cultivars such as 'David' have been bred to resist diseases that normally would fell their less tough counterparts.

Avoid Monoculture

Monoculture—extensive plantings of the same thing—can be too much of a good thing. A garden planted only with roses is like a flashing sign welcoming Japanese beetles, aphids, and black spot pathogens. However, if you break up the rose plantings with perennials, annuals, and flowering shrubs, it's tougher for diseases and pests to move from plant to plant.

Rotate Plantings

With annuals—everything from marigolds to tomatoes—avoid repeating a planting year after year in the same spot. In fact, it's a good idea to wait three years before planting the same plant in the same spot. This allows any disease spores or overwintering insects that are particularly fond of that plant to disperse or die over time in the absence of their favored host.

Also, if that type of plant drains the soil of any one nutrient, plant rotation prevents the same plant from draining the same nutrient from the soil year after year.

Avoid planting the same plant within 20 to 30 feet of the old planting spot. With small properties, that may be difficult, but the farther away the better.

Use Good Gardening Practices

Be sure to follow practices for good gardening and your plants will respond beautifully.

Keep plants weeded. This prevents competition for water and nutrients and sometimes even light.

Keep them watered. Plants may spring back after a watering, but wilting plants send an SOS signal to insects and pathogens. They are less able to fight off problems. Avoid letting your plants wilt, and they'll stay healthier longer. Give them the water, soil, and sun they prefer.

Provide the right light. Most gardeners overestimate how much sunlight their gardens get. Fungal diseases take over when plants get too little light. On the other hand, if a shade-loving plant is placed in too much sun, it will wilt and may even suffer leaf burn.

Provide Good Air Circulation

Adequate air flow prevents fungal and other diseases from getting a foothold. Space plants according to label directions, and avoid placing plants against walls or fences.

Mulch

Mulch prevents soilborne disease pathogens from splashing onto stems and leaves, especially with annuals and perennials. Mulch 1 to 3 inches deep, and keep it ½ inch or so away from the plant to prevent excessive moisture on the stem and possibly rot.

Wood chip mulch is an excellent mulch for most trees, shrubs, perennials, and annuals. In vegetable gardens, you can use newspaper topped with grass clippings from your lawn, as long as the grass hasn't been treated with chemicals in the previous two weeks.

Water the Soil Rather than the Plants

Whenever possible, water the soil instead of the plant, keeping leaves and stems dry and preventing fungal disease.

Water in the Early Morning

If you have to water from overhead, do it early in the morning. The sun dries plants quickly. Otherwise, consider installing an irrigation system that will water plants right at soil level (see page 174).

Trim Off Problem Parts

If a tree or shrub has a dead or damaged branch, cut it off. It will only invite disease and insects.

If a perennial or annual has a diseased portion, pinch or cut it off. Doing so may slow or even stop the spread of the problem.

When pruning, be sure to wipe off your pruning tools with a rag dipped in rubbing alcohol between plants (especially roses and fruit trees). Pruning tools can spread diseases, even before disease symptoms are detected.

What to Do When Diseases and Pests Strike

When you notice that a plant is ailing, there are some quick, inexpensive, and earth-friendly things you can do:

- Look up the symptoms. Check the following sections on plant pests and diseases in this book (pages 214–219). Or ask your garden center staff to help figure out what the problem is. (Take a portion of the diseased plant with you to the garden center for staff to evaluate.) You may be able to take simple, specific measures to stop the problem.
- Spray the plant with water. A good, hard burst of water often will knock off even tiny insects, reducing their population and giving the plant a chance to recover. Keep an eye on the plant, and repeat the spray treatment every day for several days.
- Trim it or get rid of it. Trim off diseased plant parts to prevent spreading the disease. (Sterilize tools with rubbing alcohol between plants.) If the entire top of the plant is diseased and it's a perennial, cut it back to a few inches above the soil. If it's an annual, consider pulling it out to prevent the spread of the disease.
- Keep it out of the compost pile. Avoid putting diseased plants in the compost heap unless you make hot compost (see page 182), which will kill most disease pathogens. Otherwise, you'll spread the disease when you spread the compost.
- Tolerate it. To a degree, every garden will have some disease and pest problems. If you have some in your garden, just remember—it's all part of nature.

A hard spray of water can slow down many pest problems.

Trimming off diseased plant parts prevents further spreading of the problem.

6

Maintenance

Controlling Weeds

There's a reason why experienced gardeners have relatively few weeds in their landscapes. They've learned the best, most efficient ways to deal with them.

Using an Ounce of Prevention

Save hours of work by attacking weeds early. Weeds that have been allowed to get large are harder to pull or hoe out, and they can set seed, dispersing seeds into your garden. Here's how to prevent weeds from becoming a problem in the first place:

- Know your weeds. There's an old saying that a weed is just a plant in the wrong place. Be ruthless about pulling up those ox-eye daisies, those hollyhocks, those morning glories when they're reseeding too much.
- Attack weeds before they get more than an inch long or wide. If you get them early, they have less chance to compete with other plants, they are easier to remove, and you will prevent them from setting seed. Heed the old saying, "One year of seeds means seven years of weeds."
- Use a preemergent herbicide when needed. Sold under a variety of brand names, these granular herbicides are sprinkled onto the ground to prevent weed seeds from germinating. They ignore existing weeds but are useful in late winter or early spring, about the time the forsythia is blooming, when weeds get their start. (Be cautious, though. Preemergents can also kill the seeds you planted on purpose, such as lawn grasses, poppies, larkspur, and many others.)

  To minimize chemical use, apply a preemergent only where weeds were a severe problem the previous year. Hoeing, pulling, cultivating, and mulching are still the best ways to deal with weeds.
- Mulch. Mulch blocks light from weed seeds so they are prevented from germinating. Spread a 1- to 3-inch layer of mulch around plants in midspring, after the soil begins to warm up—about the time the daffodils stop blooming. In areas with permanent plantings, such as shrubs, use landscape fabric. Also called weed block, it looks like black plastic but has thousands of tiny holes to allow moisture and air to reach plant roots.

Dealing with Weeds After the Fact

Try these solutions for weeds that have gotten large or out of control:

- First remove the weeds that are flowering. Do everything you can to prevent them from setting seed, which would create a new generation of problems later on.
- Know when to pull and when to hoe. Hoeing is best for broad sweeps of small weeds in open areas; pulling is better when weeds are in tight areas or are large. Pulling is also the only method for getting weeds that spread and resprout if chopped up by a hoe (see chart starting on page 212).
- Renovate when things get out of hand. If weeds have badly infested a perennial planting, and have become hopelessly entwined with desirable plants, the best solution is to wait until fall or spring, then dig up the whole mass or clump. Break apart each perennial, and pick out the weeds. Add a spadeful or two of compost or other soil amendment to the area to enrich the soil. Cut back the top of the perennial by two-thirds, and replant it in the original spot.
- Know annual weeds from perennial weeds. This will help you figure out which ones are the most pressing to remove. If a frost is imminent and your annual weeds are a problem (but not flowering!), you can leave them alone. They'll die in a week or two anyway. Perennial weeds, however, will only get bigger, even after a frost. They need to be pulled immediately.
- Use chemicals as a last resort. Herbicides are somewhat effective on mature weeds. Some herbicides attack grasses only and are good choices for flower beds. Other herbicides are "nonselective"—that is, they kill everything they touch. Be careful! These herbicides are sprayed on, and sometimes they drift onto plants you want to keep. Repeat herbicide applications may be necessary to kill mature weeds.

A pre-emergent herbicide, sprinkled onto the soil in early spring, stops weed seeds before they start.

How to Control Weed Grasses

Some of the most common weeds in beds and borders are weedy grasses. Weed grasses can include crabgrass, Bermudagrass, goosegrass, quackgrass, and countless others.

The best way to control grasses of any sort is the way you'd control most weeds: Pull what you can and mulch to prevent new weedy grasses from getting started.

It's important to get the roots of weedy grasses (weed when the soil is moist) and to toss pulled weeds in the compost heap or they may reroot. Also never let them form those seductively attractive seedheads—each can produce hundreds of seeds.

When controlling weeds, it's important to figure out if they're annuals or perennials so you can treat them accordingly. This foxtail is an annual.

If the problem grass is an annual grass, such as crabgrass, sprinkling a preemergent herbicide over the bed in early spring will prevent any crabgrass seeds from germinating, as well as any other weed seeds in the bed.

With both annual and perennial weedy grasses, you can spot treat with a nonselective herbicide as long as you're sure not to get any on desirable plants.

WORK SMARTER

EASIER WEEDING

Follow these tips, and weeding may be a joy—almost.

- Weed when the soil is moist. Do it right after a rain or give the bed a thorough soaking with the sprinkler.
- Weed on a dry, sunny day. The weeds you behead with the hoe or drop onto the ground after pulling will shrivel and dry in the sun. On cool, overcast, moist days, weeds may reestablish themselves where they lie.
- Wear close-fitting gloves. Regular garden gloves can be too bulky for weeding, but your hands still need protection. Use tough, well-fitting latex gloves or cloth gloves with the tips and palms dipped in latex. Latex gloves are found in garden centers, and often in automotive or paint stores.
- Invest in a kneeling pad or knee pads. These pads make work more comfortable and keep your knees (and pants) cleaner.

A Weed Sprayer Makes Weed Control Easy

A weed sprayer doesn't cost much but can really speed along your weed control efforts. Simply unscrew or otherwise remove the top, mix the herbicide with water, put back on the top, give 'er a few pumps, and start to spray.

A small one-gallon sprayer is fine for smaller gardens. Larger sprayers, which are geared for large areas, have a strap so you can carry it on your shoulder or back.

An important tip: Don't mix different chemicals in the same sprayer. If there are residues of say, a nonselective herbicide in the sprayer and you fill it with a foliar fertilizer, when you spray your roses you might damage or even kill them with the weed killer residue. Mark the sprayer with a permanent marker and designate it for one type of mixture only. Use one for fertilizers; one for insecticides; and then separate sprayers for different sorts of weed control measures since they all work so differently.

Be sure to use a different sprayer for herbicides and for foliar fertilizing, shown here. Weed killer residues could harm desirable plants.

Common Weeds

Bindweed

Perennial. This relative of the morning glory has deep roots that are hard to eradicate. Roots or pieces of roots left from pulling or hand tilling resprout easily. Pull small (under 3 inches) bindweed as soon as you see it. Dig up at least the top 6 inches of the roots of larger plants. Repeated removal may be necessary. In severe infestations, repeat application of a nonselective herbicide may be necessary.

Black Medic

Annual. Has a small yellow flower and is a prolific seed producer, so pull or hoe as much as possible. The following spring, if the infestation has been severe, use a preemergent herbicide to prevent seeds from germinating. Black medic dislikes hot, dry summers and often dies out at that time.

Knotweed

Annual in all but the warmest regions. It has a long taproot, so it's best to pull this weed when the soil is moist. Be sure to sever the crown from its roots, or it will resprout. After weeding, work compacted soil lightly to prevent further invasion.

Chickweed

Annual in all but the warmest regions. Shallow roots make this weed easy to pull. Remove plants from the garden, because they can easily reroot.

Clover

Perennial. Pull clover as soon as you see it. Remove plants from the garden, because they can easily reroot. You can spot-treat with a nonselective herbicide, but be sure to avoid getting any on desirable plants.

Curly Dock

Perennial. Develops a large taproot, so be sure to dig at least the top inch or two. Pull or dig when the soil is moist for best results. Curly dock dislikes cultivated soil, so regular hoeing or cultivating can prevent a large infestation. You can spot-treat with a nonselective herbicide, but be sure not to get any on desirable plants.

Dandelion

Perennial. This weed must be dug up. Get at least the top 2 inches of its long, slender taproot, or it will return. Treat with a nonselective herbicide, but be sure not to get any on desirable plants.

Fennel

Perennial. Easy to identify because of leafy foliage, and when brushed, it releases a characteristic black licorice smell. Dig out by the root. There is no need to remove the entire taproot, but do remove the bulb at the top of the root. Cut the stalk to ground level; repeated cuttings over the season will kill the plant. Spray with a nonselective herbicide if needed.

Henbit

An annual or biennial. A member of the mint family, it likes cool, rich, moist soil and partial shade. Pull diligently, being sure to get as much of the root as possible.

Horsetail

Perennial. This weed loves wet conditions when small but can tolerate dry soil once established. Correcting drainage on a boggy or wet site will make it less vigorous. It has deep, spreading roots, so pull as best you can or simply cut as low as possible repeatedly. Treat with a nonselective herbicide, but be sure not to get any on desirable plants.

Ground Ivy

Perennial. It is also called creeping Charlie and cat's-foot. Shallow roots make it easy to pull. Weeds left lying on the ground can reroot. It's a good addition to the compost heap because of its high iron content. Treat with a nonselective herbicide, but be sure not to get any on desirable plants.

Lamb's Quarters

Annual in all but the warmest regions. A sturdy stalk and shallow roots make this easy to pull. Small plants are easy to hoe.

Lespedeza

Annual. This low-growing plant is commonly found in soils with low fertility. Fertilizing the area makes conditions less favorable for this weed while boosting desirable plants' growth, helping to crowd it out. Pull this weed, or apply a nonselective herbicide to extensive infestations.

Invasive Ornamental Grasses

Escapees from beds and borders, these grasses can sometimes spread rapidly to the point of being invasive. Many have underground runners that are nearly impossible to completely eliminate. Dig out the plants when the soil is moist so you can pull out as many of the runners as possible. Also, if the parent plant remains, consider digging it up and disposing of it to prevent further problems.

Plantain

Perennial. Remove at least the top inch of taproot to kill the plant. After weeding, work the compacted soil lightly to prevent further invasion. Treat with a nonselective herbicide, but be sure not to get any on desirable plants.

Purslane

Annual. Most common in the Northeast, least common in the Pacific Northwest, it is easy to pull. If you hoe it into pieces or allow stems to break off and lie on the ground, it can reroot and spread.

Red Sorrel

Perennial. Also called sheep sorrel or sour grass. Grows best in acidic soils and in soils with low fertility, so applying lime to raise the pH and using a fertilizer can reduce chronic infestations. Fertilizing also may help surrounding plants crowd it out. Red sorrel likes wet conditions, so improving drainage will make it less vigorous. Red sorrel spreads by rhizomes, and trying to hoe or pull it often results in additional plants. Use a nonselective herbicide to remove it, making sure to keep spray off neighboring desirable plants. Repeated applications may be needed.

Wild Onion and Wild Garlic

Perennial. Easy to identify because crushing one of the long, grasslike leaves releases the characteristic onion or garlic odor. Pull as much as possible; otherwise, use a nonselective herbicide. Will probably need repeated treatment.

Wild Violet

Perennial. Prefers cool, moist, partially shady sites. Control by digging, being sure to get the spreading roots. A thick layer of mulch (up to 3 inches) suppresses growth. Violets tend to become entwined in the base of perennials, especially those with an open growth habit, such as some irises. If this happens, dig and divide the perennial and pull out the violets. Spot treat with a nonselective herbicide, but be sure not to get any on desirable plants. May need repeated applications.

Pests and Diseases

A CLOSER LOOK

BEES AND EARTHWORMS

Some gardeners mistakenly think that bees and earthworms are pests. Quite the contrary. Bees play a critical role in pollinating blossoms. Without bees, there would be no fruits or flowers.

Earthworms also play a crucial role in a garden's ecosystem. They aerate the soil, and their castings greatly enrich the soil. The more earthworms in your soil, the more fertile it will be.

The best way to deal with pests and diseases is to prevent them in the first place (see page 208). However, when all else fails, identifying the problem, then taking measures to control it can also be effective.

Don't just dump whatever chemical you have handy on the problem—a tempting proposition when you're short on time. Instead, take a moment to identify the problem. Look carefully at the plant for clues, such as the pattern of the damage and on what part of the plant it occurs. Look for pests, although they're not always evident.

The most common pests and diseases are highlighted on the following pages. If you fail to find your problem here, cut off an affected portion of the plant and take it to your Home Depot garden center for identification and for a recommendation on how to treat the pest or disease.

WORK SMARTER

USING DISEASE AND PEST CONTROLS WISELY

Pest controls in the forms of sprays and powders are useful in your garden, but they're far from a cure-all. Even organic controls can kill some beneficial insects, including butterflies, ladybugs, bees, praying mantises, and lacewings. Remember, more is not better. Follow package directions carefully, and use all controls in moderation.

A Chemicals Glossary

When you are standing in the garden center aisle, trying to find a cure for a garden problem, it helps if you know some terms.

Weed Killers (also called herbicides)

Nonselective: Kills all parts of all plants it touches, including the roots. Good for large areas, but be sure to keep it from drifting onto neighboring plants.
Broadleaf: Kills plants with broad leaves. Usually a weed killer for lawns. The narrow-leaved plants (grass) are spared, but dandelions (among others) are killed.

Pesticides and Other Controls

Fungicide: Formulation that kills fungus-based diseases, including powdery mildew, damping off of seedlings, rust, gray mold, and some leaf spots.
Systemic: Formulation that gets into the system of the plant and kills insects that nibble on any part of the plant.
Pathogen: Organism, such as a fungus, bacterium, or virus, capable of causing a disease.

Common Pests

Ants

Symptoms: Leaves are curled, distorted, and yellowing. Ants are seen crawling on the plant.
How to control: Ants generally do little damage to plants. Instead, they may be feeding on the honeydew secreted by other damaging insects, such as aphids, scale insects, mealybugs, and whitefly. Treat these problems and the ants are likely to go away. On peonies, ants are feeding on a substance secreted by the plant and do no damage to the plant itself. Merely brush them off if you want to bring flowers indoors.

Aphids

Symptoms: Minute pale yellow, pink, or black insects appear on soft stems, new leaves, and flowers. Leaves curl, and new growth is stunted. Sometimes a sticky honeydew and a sooty mold are produced. Ants may be crawling on the honeydew.

How to control: Give plants a hard spray of water once a day for 10 days or more. Use insecticidal soap or pyrethrin. For roses and shrubs, if the problem is chronic from year to year, use dormant oil spray in early spring to control overwintering eggs.

Cabbage Worms

Symptoms: White moths fluttering about during the day are a sign that their larvae, cabbage worms, are present. They attack members of the cabbage family, including cauliflower, chewing round or irregular holes in leaves. The green worms are up to 1½ inches long with light stripes down their backs.
How to control: If damage is spotted, use an insecticide containing carbaryl, pyrethrin, insecticidal soap, or rotenone. Destroy plants immediately after harvest but keep them out of the compost heap.

Common Pests *continued*

Colorado Potato Beetles

Symptoms: Yellow-orange beetles with black stripes and spots. Larvae are dark red with black spots on sides. They feed on potatoes, tomatoes, and eggplant as well as petunias and other members of the nightshade family. Beetles and larvae eat leaves and stems to the extent of stunting or killing plants.
How to control: Plant resistant cultivars. Mulch deeply with straw in spring to prevent pests from emerging from soil. Spray with Bt *(Bacillus thuringiensis)* or pyrethrin.

Cutworms

Symptoms: Gray or brown caterpillars at night sever stems of just about any type of tender seedling near the soil level in early to midspring.
How to control: If cutworms have been a problem in the past, circle each seedling with a cardboard collar made from a length of paper towel tube, pushed slightly into the soil. Plant larger plants, which cutworms find far less attractive.

Flea Beetles

Symptoms: Leaves have numerous small round holes that are so extensive they can kill plants. Tiny dark beetles leap like fleas from leaf undersides. Favorite plants are eggplant, tomatoes, peppers, potatoes, spinach, cabbage-family vegetables, melons, lettuces, sweet potatoes, and petunias.
How to control: Till soil in fall or spring. Remove debris. Keep weeds down. Use white sticky traps, pyrethrin, or rotenone.

Grasshoppers

Symptoms: Large, chewed holes in leaves; many grasshoppers present. Worst in dry weather and arid regions.
How to control: Use acephate, spraying as soon as you see grasshoppers. Grasshoppers usually move into gardens from fields or weedy areas. The first few act as scouts and alert the rest about the available food in your garden.

Japanese Beetles/Grubs

Symptoms: Shiny blue-green beetles eat holes in leaves and flowers, especially roses.
How to control: Pick off beetles in early morning and drown in water. Use pheromone traps. Apply milky spore disease (available at some garden centers) or a product made specifically for grub control to kill lawn grubs, which are Japanese beetle larvae. Spray plants with rotenone.

Leaf Miners

Symptoms: Light-colored irregular trails twist and wind through leaves, with spots or blotches appearing on severely infested leaves, the result of leaf miner maggots feeding on inner leaf tissue. Common on columbine and dahlias.
How to control: Pick off and destroy infested leaves. Remove and destroy all plant parts in fall (keep out of compost heap). Spray infested plants with acephate.

Leaf Hoppers

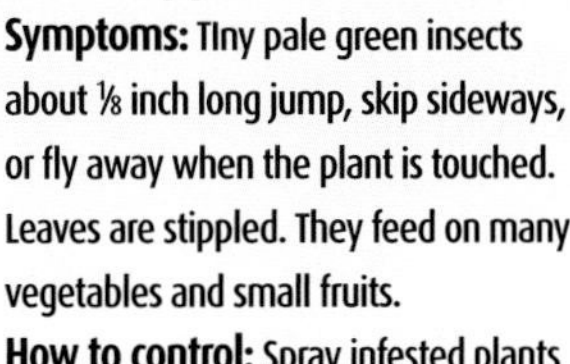

Symptoms: Tiny pale green insects about ⅛ inch long jump, skip sideways, or fly away when the plant is touched. Leaves are stippled. They feed on many vegetables and small fruits.
How to control: Spray infested plants with insecticide containing pyrethrin. Repeat applications as needed. Remove nearby weeds, which may harbor more leaf hoppers.

Mealybugs

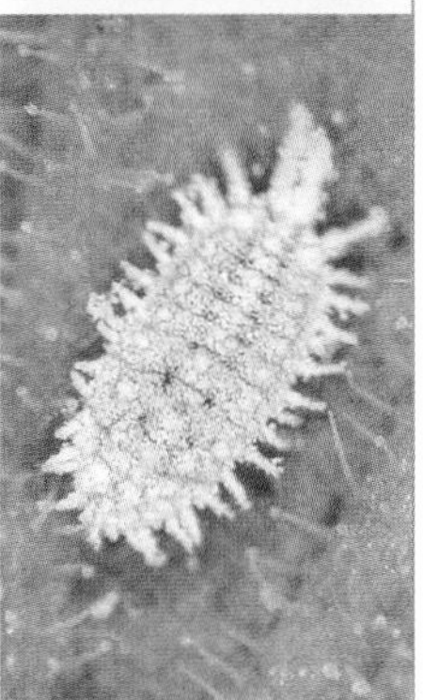

Symptoms: Clusters of insects create cottonlike white masses on stems and leaf axils. Can slow growth and kill plants. They secrete a honeydew substance that attracts mold.
How to control: Hose off mild infestations. For more serious problems, apply insecticidal soap or an insecticide containing acephate. Parasitic wasps provide some control. Horticultural oil can be used on some plants.

Common Pests *continued*

Nematodes

Symptoms: Invisible to the naked eye, these wormlike creatures live in the soil and attack plants, causing stunting of roots (as shown at right), swollen roots, yellowing, dead plant parts, reduced growth, and fewer flowers.
How to control: Test for nematodes if year after year you have chronic problems with plants that wilt, yellow, and slowly die, and you've eliminated other possible causes. Contact your county extension service, which can make recommendations about chemical control measures for nematodes.

Scale Insects

Symptoms: Hard, round- or oval-shaped insects adhere to stems and leaf undersides. Clustered together, they look like a pattern.
How to control: If the problem is chronic, spray with dormant oil in very early spring. Or, treat immediately with a systemic insecticide, following package directions.

Slugs and Snails

Symptoms: Chewed leaves, particularly those close to or touching the ground. Slime trails are visible. Damaged plants usually are in shady or cool, moist areas. Most prevalent in cool, moist climates.
How to control: Place short pieces of board or flat rocks around garden; slugs and snails will take refuge under them during the day. Each morning, collect the boards or rocks along with any clinging slugs or snails and dunk them in a pail of soapy water. Edge garden beds with copper flashing to disrupt slug paths. Sprinkle wood ashes heavily on soil of most bothered plants. If problem is severe, use slug bait, following package directions.

Spider Mites

Symptoms: Tiny spiders, often forming fine webs on plant and sucking its juices, cause speckled, pale foliage. Worst during hot, dry weather.
How to control: Keep plants well watered. Hose off undersides of infested leaves. If the problem is chronic on shrubs each year, spray in early spring with dormant oil. Choose a spray that specifies control of spider mites on the plant you want to spray.

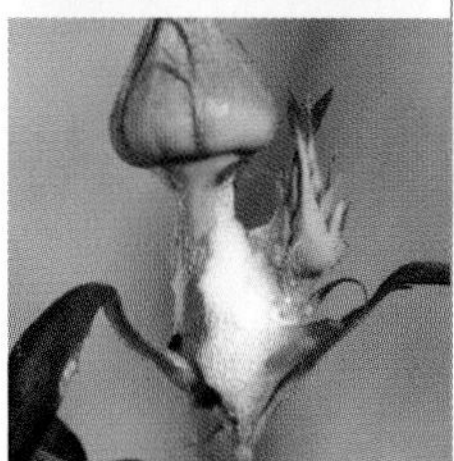

Spittlebugs

Symptoms: Distinctive frothy white foam collects between leaves and stems. Plant growth may be stunted if the infestation is heavy. Common on asters and pines.
How to control: Use a garden hose to blast away insects and froth. If plant is heavily infested, use an insecticide containing acephate or methoxychlor (make sure that the infested plant is listed on the product's label).

Squash Vine Borers

Symptoms: Leaves on squash, zucchini, and pumpkins wilt; may become black and crisp in advanced stages. Flat-backed green, gray, or brown bugs cluster on the plants when the infestation is advanced.
How to control: As soon as insects first appear, treat the plant with an insecticide containing carbaryl, insecticidal soap, or pyrethrin. Repeat treatment once a week. In the future, plant varieties that are resistant to squash vine borers. If infestations happen year after year, treat plants at planting time and once every one to two weeks thereafter.

Thrips

Symptoms: Tiny, darting black insects cause streaks and spots on flowers and young leaves. Common on roses, especially pale-colored ones.
How to control: Apply insecticidal soap or pyrethrin, or spray with a chemical specifying thrip control. If problem is chronic each year, use a systemic insecticide that specifies thrip control starting in spring.

Whiteflies

Symptoms: Tiny white insects fly around when plant is brushed or moved.
How to control: Apply horticultural oil, insecticidal soap, rotenone, or pyrethrin. Repeat applications as label directs.

Tomato Hornworm

Symptoms: Plump green or brown worms, up to 5 inches long with slender white stripes chew up leaves on tomatoes, peppers, eggplants, and others. Each worm has a tiny horn-like projection on its rear.
How to control: Treat plants with an insecticide containing carbaryl or *Bacillus thuringiensis*.

Common Diseases

Scab

Symptoms: On fruit trees, especially apples, crabapples, and pears, brown spots and patches form on fruits and leaves and may develop into corklike lesions. Fruit is often deformed and small and may drop prematurely.
How to control: If disease is less serious, fruit is still edible. Prevent scab next year by removing infected leaves and fruit this year. In the spring, spray with a fungicide containing captan.

Aster Yellows

Symptoms: Plants are generally stunted with flowers and leaves that have turned pale and lost most or all of their color as foliage turns yellow. Edges may be brown. Plant may have many thin stems with spindly leaves. Especially common on asters, mums, celosia, coneflower, dianthus, petunias, phlox, marigolds, broccoli, parsley, spinach, tomatoes, blanket flower, and snapdragons.
How to control: Control by removing and disposing of infected plants to prevent further spread. Often spread by leafhoppers, so if these are present, spray plants with malathion. Reapply whenever leafhoppers are seen.

Codling Moth

Symptoms: Found on fruit and nut trees. Fruit is marred by small holes surrounded by dead tissue. White worms up to 1 inch long may be found in the fruit.
How to control: There's little to be done for a season's fruits or nuts that are already infected. To prevent problems in the future, clean up leaf debris and fallen fruit each fall. If worms have been a problem, the following spring start spraying with an insecticide containing carbaryl or malathion every 10 days.

Bacterial Wilt

Symptoms: Plants repeatedly wilt and recover, but finally wilt permanently, and leaves turn yellow and brown. Can kill plants. Infected stems ooze slime if cut. Especially common in mums, delphiniums, nasturtiums, petunias, dahlias, and zinnias.
How to control: Remove and destroy infected plants to keep the bacteria from spreading. Dip all tools used on infected plants in rubbing alcohol. Wash hands well with soap and water after handling the plants to prevent spread to other plants.

Black Spot

Symptoms: A fungal disease that causes tiny black spots on leaves. Yellow and orange rings usually develop around the dark spots. Leaves yellow and drop. Common on roses. Unusual in arid West where dry conditions inhibit fungus growth.
How to control: Water in early morning and avoid overhead watering. Mulch to prevent water or mud from splashing onto plants. Give plants as much sun as practical. Spray with a fungicide, following timing and repeat spray directions.

Blight

Symptoms: Various fungal diseases of flowers, leaves, or stems. Results in sudden wilting and browning. Worst in humid, moist weather.
How to control: Water in early morning and avoid overhead watering. Mulch to prevent water or mud from splashing onto plants. Give plants as much sun as practical. Spray with a fungicide, following timing and repeat spray directions.

Blossom End Rot

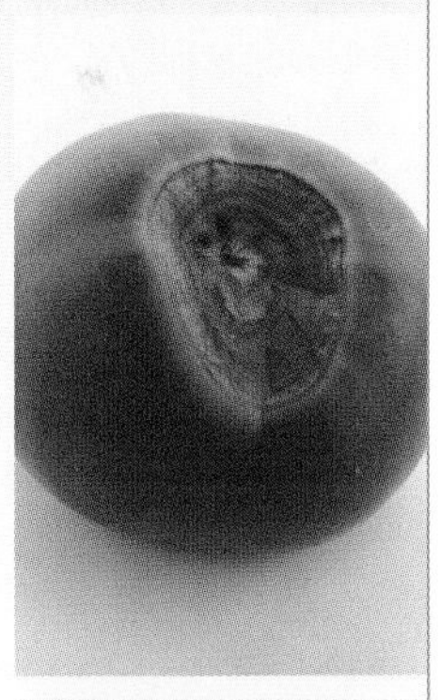

Symptoms: A problem found primarily on tomatoes but also peppers and melons. A large, sunken brownish-black spot develops on the end of the fruit.
How to control: Prevent by providing an even supply of moisture to plants. Avoid using high-nitrogen fertilizers or large quantities of fresh manure, which can encourage too-rapid growth.

Canker and Dieback

Symptoms: A problem on spruce and pine, especially those 15 years or older. Needles near the ground turn brown and dry and, over a year or two, drop. Eventually entire branch dies. Pitch may ooze from infected area. To test, slice off bark where dead area meets healthy area; you may see small black spore-producing bodies.
How to control: Prune off and dispose of dead or dying branches, sterilizing tools with rubbing alcohol between cuts and performing the task during dry weather.

Fusarium Wilt

Symptoms: Yellowing, stunted plants wilt and die. If cut open, infected stems have dark streaks.

How to control: Avoid planting the same plants in the same place each year. Mulch well to prevent water or mud from splashing onto plants. Give plants as much sun as practical.

Gall

Symptoms: Strange-looking bump or bumps, mainly on trees and shrubs. Can appear to be part of the plant or wrapped around it or almost like a fruit hanging from it.

How to control: Insects cause most gall formations by laying eggs, which the plant grows around. With the exception of crown gall, most do little damage to the plant. The best control is to trim off and dispose of the galls.

Gray Mold (Botrytis blight)

Symptoms: Yellow or orange spots turn into masses of fuzzy gray mold, which then turns into a slimy rot. Occurs during damp weather or in moist climates.

How to control: Avoid planting moldy plants or bulbs. Space plants as recommended on label to ensure good air circulation. Remove fading flowers (deadhead) promptly. Give plants as much sun as practical. In severe cases, apply an organic or chemical fungicide as package directs.

Leaf Spot

Symptoms: Spots on leaves look water-soaked or are brick red with yellow rings and black spots. Common during rainy or humid weather.

How to control: Rotate plantings yearly. Mulch well to keep water or mud from splashing on plants. Space plants to ensure good air circulation. Avoid handling wet plants, or disease may spread. Provide adequate sun. In severe cases, apply sprays specifying leaf spot control.

Powdery Mildew

Symptoms: Powdery white or gray areas show up on leaf surface. Leaves shrivel, dry, and drop. Common on lilacs, bee balm, roses, and tall garden phlox.

How to control: Mulch well to prevent water or mud from splashing onto plants. Space plants as recommended on label to ensure good air circulation. Give plants as much sun as practical. If using a commercial fungicide, apply it a few times in spring, which is before powdery mildew shows up. If a plant has chronic powdery mildew problems, make a practice of spraying a few times in early spring.

Rust

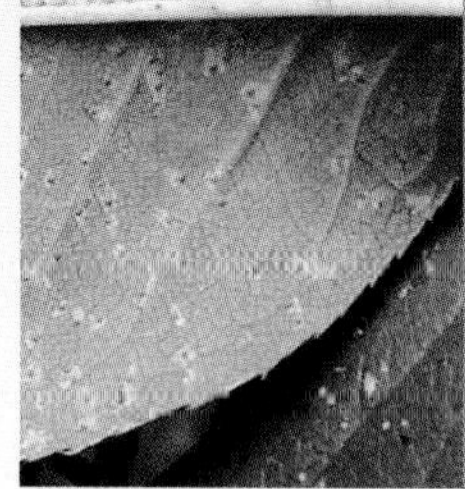

Symptoms: Bright red, orange, or yellow lesions occur on underside and tops of leaves and stems. Rust weakens and stunts plants in severe cases.

How to control: Avoid overhead watering. Mulch well to keep water or mud from splashing on plants. Space plants as recommended on label to ensure good air circulation. Give plants as much sun as practical. Avoid handling wet plants, or the disease may spread. In severe cases, spray with a product specifying rust control.

Verticillium Wilt

Symptoms: Lower leaves turn pale green, then yellow, then brown, and then drop. Branches wilt. In severe cases, plants die. Cut into an infected branch to check for dark streaks.

How to control: Destroy infected plants to prevent spread of disease. Trim off infected branches of shrubs or trees. No chemical control is available.

Common Rose Pests and Diseases

Aphids

Aphids are easy to spot as tiny white or pale green ovals that attach themselves to buds and tender new growth. If the problem is limited, just hose them off, then swab the area liberally with a half-and-half solution of liquid dish soap and water. For more serious problems, spray with an insecticide specifying control of aphids, or use a systemic insecticide early in the season the next year to prevent a recurrence.

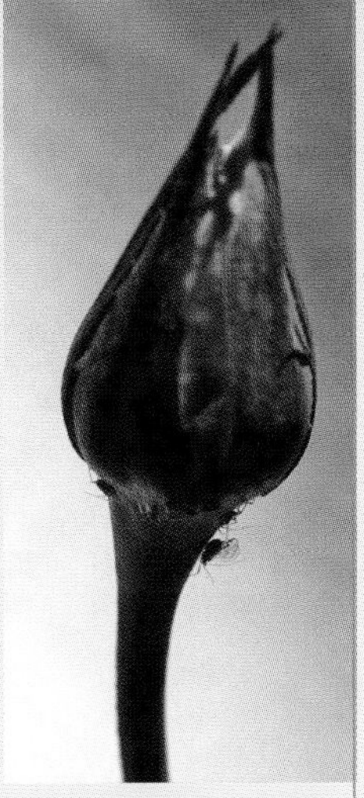

Black Spot

Black spot is one of the most common rose diseases. In fact, by summer's end, only the most disease-resistant roses have no black spot at all. Black spot starts with the appearance of tiny black dots on leaves. The leaves eventually turn yellow and brown and fall off. Black spot is a fungal disease that likes moist conditions and therefore is less common in arid regions or in a dry year. Planting roses in full sun will lessen the problem. Prevent spread of the disease by picking up fallen leaves and trimming off affected leaves. Water the roots of the plant only, not the leaves. If the problem has been severe, spray with a fungicide in early spring. This is a preventive measure. Once black spot shows up, it's untreatable until the following year.

Japanese Beetles

A common rose problem east of the Mississippi. Japanese beetles eat all parts of the plant (although the flowers are their favorite), leaving holes where they've chewed. Small infestations can be controlled by picking off the beetles and dropping them into a can of water with a thin film of oil on top. If the problem is severe, spray as soon as you notice them with a spray specifying control of Japanese beetles. Japanese beetle traps may also be effective.

Mildew

Mildew shows up in mid- to late-summer, primarily in regions with cool, humid evenings. Gray or white splotches appear on leaves and stems. Leaves eventually yellow, then brown, then fall. Planting in full sun will lessen this problem. Prevent spread of the disease by picking up fallen leaves and trimming off affected leaves. Water the roots of the plant only. Severe problems can be controlled by spraying with a fungicide in spring before the mildew becomes visible; follow package directions exactly. This usually means repeating the application until temperatures reach 75°F (24°C) or so.

Rust

Rust likes warm, damp conditions and becomes evident in early summer in the form of bright orange spots on the underside of leaves. Spots turn brown, then black. Planting in full sun will lessen this problem. Prevent spread of the disease by picking up fallen leaves and trimming off affected leaves. Water the roots of the plant only. Severe problems can be controlled by spraying in spring before the rust becomes visible, using a fungicide and following package directions. This usually means repeating the application until temperatures reach 75°F (24°C) or so.

Thrips

Tiny brown insects that love hot, dry weather. They nibble buds and flowers, discoloring and deforming them, especially light-colored roses. Repeated spraying with a chemical specifying thrip control is one option, but even this has limited effectiveness. If thrips are a problem year after year, use a systemic insecticide early in the season to stop this pest before its damage can be seen.

Protecting Your Garden from Wildlife

GOOD IDEA

NO MORE NIBBLING

The bark of young trees, especially fruit trees, is often susceptible to the nibblings of deer, rabbits, and rodents during the lean times of winter and very early spring.

Protecting the tree with a paper wrap (see page 186) will offer protection from wildlife and the elements. A solution that offers purely wildlife protection is to loosely wrap the trunk with ¼-inch hardware cloth or similar material. Be sure to extend the wrap from the ground up to the lower scaffolding branches of the tree (and into the soil for a few inches to thwart burrowing animals).

Gardening means working with nature. But nature also provides some critters that like to munch, knock down, or burrow in our gardens. The good news is that, to some degree, you can minimize the damage.

Deer

Often called rats with antlers, deer can wipe out hundreds of dollars' worth of plants in a single night.

Unfortunately, the only sure way to deter deer is to fence them out. Even the best repellents reduce deer feeding by only half, according to research. Deer fencing is expensive. Because deer are such high jumpers, the fencing needs to be at least 8 feet high, or as high as 12 feet in areas with large deer populations.

Electric fence is the most cost-effective option for large properties. It needs to be about 5 feet high with the first wire 10 inches off the ground and four spaced wires about 12 inches apart.

You can also deter deer with mesh fences. Although deer can jump very high, their jumps aren't long. Take advantage of this with two 4-foot-high wire mesh fences spaced about 4 feet apart. Deer avoid tight spaces, so they'll be wary of crossing the fence.

If you decide to use repellents, choose commercial formulations that repel deer with their putrid scent. Home remedies such as bars of soap, human hair, and hot pepper sprays are the least effective. All repellents need to be reapplied or replenished every 10 days or so.

Another strategy is to plant flowers that deer dislike. (See the chart on page 222). However, although deer may not be fond of these plants, they will eat almost anything if they become hungry enough. Of course, if you have a deer problem, avoid plants that deer love, which include azaleas, roses, tulips, lilies, daylilies, rhododendrons, and hostas.

Moles, Voles, Mice, and Other Burrowing Animals

It's nearly impossible to prevent moles, mice, voles (meadow mice), and other burrowing animals from pestering your garden. You can slow them down with a wire barrier.

For moles, voles, and mice, install hardware cloth 2 feet deep around garden beds and lawns. For gophers, the hardware cloth will have to extend aboveground by 2 feet for a total height of 4 feet.

Erect these barriers when there is no active burrowing in the bed, or you'll simply be sealing in the pests.

Also, remove piles of brush and debris where these animals might nest. And avoid mulching more than 2 to 3 inches thick.

A hungry deer will eat almost any kind of plant, even ones they normally avoid.

Fencing is the single most effective way to keep out unwanted wildlife. This vegetable garden is virtually deerproof.

Rabbits are small, but they can do amazing amounts of damage, especially during years when their populations are high.

To protect bulbs, add gravel or crushed stone to the planting hole. It provides drainage for the bulbs and is thought to discourage moles. You can also make wire cages from hardware cloth to bury underground and plant bulbs and other plants in. The cage should be topless and buried so the sides barely protrude from the ground.

Squirrels

Squirrels love burrowing and digging, especially around newly planted bulbs.

Protect bulbs by planting them in groups, then laying a piece of chicken wire over the top of the bulbs, and covering it with soil. The flowers will grow through the wire, and it will be difficult for the squirrels to get to them.

If squirrels are digging in other areas, especially around new plantings, lay a piece of chicken wire over the top of these, crimping the sides slightly to make a rough cage. Remove it when the plants become established and the loose soil has firmed, discouraging squirrels from digging.

Rabbits

The best way to keep out rabbits is to fence them out. Use wire mesh with openings of less than 1 inch. The fence must be 2 feet high and buried 3 inches beneath the soil to prevent burrowing. This works especially well for vegetable gardens where appearance isn't an issue.

Another option for individual plants, especially tender young annuals that rabbits love, is to make individual cages for susceptible plants or small plantings. Make the cages several inches high and tuck them over the young plants, burying the edges 3 inches into the soil. When the plants are several inches high and less tempting to rabbits, remove the cages.

Birds

As anyone who has grown fruits can tell you, birds can be persistent pests. One way to deter them is to cover fruit trees and berry patches with nylon netting as soon as the fruit starts to change color. (Mend any holes that develop in the netting; determined birds will find a way through.) Erect a frame over the fruit and stretch the net over the frame. Otherwise, if the netting rests on the fruit, the birds will peck through the net to the fruit on the other side.

Many gardeners swear by planting a mulberry tree on their property. The thought is that the birds will be so busy feasting on the mulberries that they will stay away from the strawberries or cherries. If you choose this option, plant the tree well away from walking and living areas. These trees drop huge numbers of juicy purple fruits that can stain. Flies are attracted to the overripe fruit as it decomposes on the ground, and the birds that devour the fruits have a habit of eliminating the purple remains all over the surrounding area. For these reasons, the planting of mulberry trees is prohibited in some cities and towns.

GOOD IDEA

WHEN IN DOUBT

There are a number of gadgets, gizmos, lotions, and potions that claim to deter deer, birds, rabbits, and other pests. When in doubt, check with your cooperative extension service wildlife specialist. That person is up on all the latest research on what works well to deter animal pests, what is less effective, and the best ways to use the products on the market.

Check the county government listings in your phone book for contact information.

Plants That Deer and Rabbits Don't Like

Although a deer or rabbit will eat about anything if it's hungry enough, there are plants that they will eat as a last resort. Here are some of the most deer- and rabbit-resistant plants:

Deer-Resistant Plants

Common Name	Botanical Name	Zones
Trees		
Birch, paper	*Betula papyrifera*	2-5
Boxwood	*Buxus* spp.	5-9
Flowering dogwood	*Cornus florida*	5-9
Honeylocust	*Gleditsia triacanthos*	3-8
Kousa dogwood	*Cornus kousa*	5-8
Magnolia	*Magnolia* spp.	5-9
Russian olive	*Elaeagnus angustifolia*	3-8
Serviceberry	*Amelanchier canadensis*	4-9
Smoke tree	*Cotinus coggygria*	5-8
Shrubs		
Butterfly bush	*Buddleia davidii*	5-10
Barberry, Japanese	*Berberis thunbergii*	4-8
Bayberry, Northern	*Myrica pensylvanica*	2-6
Mockorange	*Philadelphus* spp.	4-8
Oleander	*Oleander* spp.	8-10
Potentilla, shrubby	*Potentilla fruticosa*	2-11
Rose of Sharon	*Hibiscus syriacus*	5-9
Rosemary	*Rosmarinus officinalis*	7-11
Spirea	*Spiraea* spp.	2-9
Annuals, Perennials, and Bulbs		
Ageratum	*Ageratum houstonianum*	Annual
Astilbe	*Astilbe* spp.	3-8
Christmas rose	*Helleborus* spp.	3-9
Columbine	*Aquilegia* spp.	3-9
Coneflower, purple	*Echinacea purpurea*	3-9
Coreopsis	*Coreopsis* spp.	4-9
Daffodil	*Narcissus* spp.	3-8
Dahlias	*Dahlia* spp.	8-10
Forsythia	*Forsythia* spp.	5-9
Foxglove	*Digitalis purpurea*	4-8
Grape hyacinth	*Muscari* spp.	3-8
Irises, all types	*Iris* spp.	3-10
Lamb's ear	*Stachys byzantina*	4-8
Lavender	*Lavandula* spp.	5-8
Lilac	*Syringa* spp.	3-7
Monkshood	*Aconitum carmichaelii*	3-7
Peony	*Paeonia* spp.	2-8
Shasta daisy	*Leucanthemum × superbum*	4-9
Yarrow	*Achillea* spp.	3-9

Rabbit-Resistant Plants

Wrapping trees and shrubs (see page 186) not only provides winter protection, it also makes them unattractive to rabbits.

Common Name	Botanical Name	Zones
Ageratum	*Ageratum houstonianum*	Annual
Amethyst flower	*Browallia speciosa*	Annual
Astilbe	*Astilbe* spp.	3-8
Bear's breeches, spiny	*Acanthus spinosus*	6-10
Bee balm	*Monarda didyma*	4-8
Blanket flower	*Gaillardia* spp.	2-10
Bleeding heart	*Dicentra* spp.	2-9
Blue salvia, perennial	*Salvia × superba*	4-8
Butterfly bush	*Buddleia davidii*	5-10
Candytuft	*Iberis* spp.	3-10
Cardinal flower	*Lobelia cardinalis*	3-9
Chrysanthemum	*Chrysanthemum* spp.	4-9
Clematis	*Clematis* spp.	4-9
Columbine	*Aquilegia* spp.	3-10
Coreopsis	*Coreopsis* spp.	3-9
Corydalis	*Corydalis* spp.	4-9
Creeping phlox	*Phlox stolonifera*	2-8
Daffodil	*Narcissus* spp.	3-11
Daylily	*Hemerocallis* spp.	3-10
Four-o-clock	*Mirabilis jalapa*	9-11
Foxglove	*Digitalis purpurea*	4-9
Geranium	*Pelargonium* spp.	8-11
Globe thistle	*Echinops* spp.	3-8
Goatsbeard	*Aruncus dioicus*	3-7
Geranium, hardy	*Geranium* spp.	4-8
Hollyhock	*Alcea rosea*	3-11
Hyacinth	*Hyacinthus orientalis*	3-11
Hydrangea	*Hydrangea* spp.	3-9
Lady's mantle	*Alchemilla mollis*	4-7
Lavender	*Lavandula* spp.	5-8
Lily-of-the-valley	*Convallaria majalis*	3-8
Marigold	*Tagetes* spp.	Annual
Peony	*Paeonia* spp.	2-8
Potentilla, shrubby	*Potentilla* spp.	2-7
Queen-of-the-prairie	*Filipendula rubra*	3-8
Red-hot poker	*Kniphofia uvaria*	5-9
Russian sage	*Perovskia atriplicifolia*	3-9
Sedum	*Sedum* spp.	3-10
Shasta daisy	*Leucanthemum × superbum*	4-9
Iris, Siberian	*Iris sibirica*	3-10
Trumpet creeper	*Campsis radicans*	3-11
Veronica	*Veronica* spp.	3-8
Vinca, annual	*Catharanthus roseus*	Annual
Virginia bluebells	*Mertensia virginica*	3-7

Pests That Bother People

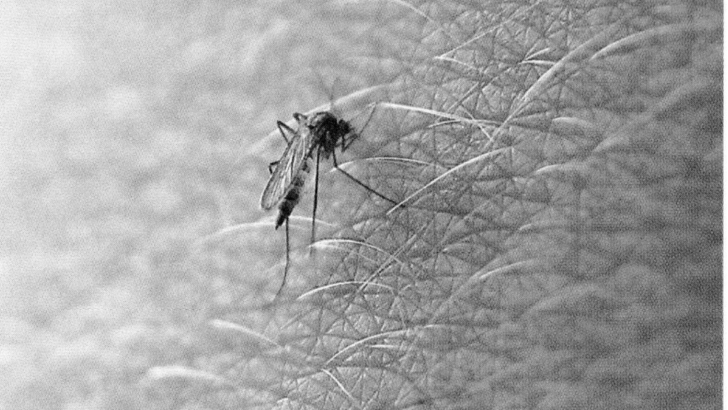

Mosquitoes can make gardening miserable but fortunately there are a number of measures you can take to prevent them from biting you.

Enjoying the great outdoors is less than great when you have to fight off biting and stinging insects. Here's how to enjoy your landscape more with fewer bugs bugging you:

Mosquitoes

The best way to protect yourself from mosquitoes is to have a good supply of insect repellent. Keep an array, including those combined with sunblock, lower concentrations made for children, water- and perspiration-resistant types, stick type for faces, and odorless formulations. Apply, getting every inch of exposed skin, before venturing outdoors in mosquito weather.

Other tips for avoiding mosquito bites:

- Avoid working in the garden at dawn or dusk. These times are when mosquitoes bite the most.
- Avoid tight or dark clothing. Mosquitoes can bite right through these. Loose, light-colored clothing is the best for avoiding bites.
- If you have a pond or other water feature, make sure that the water is moving, which disturbs mosquitoes, or stock it with fish, which eat mosquito larvae.
- Mosquitoes will avoid a breeze. If you have a porch or deck that's sheltered overhead, consider installing a ceiling fan, which will discourage mosquitoes and keep you cool and comfortable. In areas where it's tough to generate some moving air, consider a power mosquito eliminator, such as the Mosquito Magnet.

Bees and Wasps

Bees are wonderful pollinators in the landscape, and many gardeners welcome them. They will leave you alone and feed happily on flower nectar unless threatened. Wearing shoes and making sure that children wear shoes in the garden when bees are active is a good idea, because many bee stings occur when bees are stepped on.

Wasps, by comparison to gentle, helpful bees, pollinate far fewer plants, and some such as hornets and yellow jackets, are quite aggressive and will sting repeatedly with only slight provocation.

However, it's recommended to apply sprays that kill bees and wasps in your garden only if someone who gardens has a severe allergy. Bees are highly beneficial, and these sprays kill many other helpful insects as well. You can, however, avoid or remove plants that attract bees, including tall sedums, lavender, rosemary, broom, heath, honeysuckle, lantana, thyme, star jasmine, and salvias.

Avoid wasp stings by doing the following:

- Be aware that wasps are especially active and aggressive in late summer and early fall. Plan accordingly those activities where you're likely to have sodas and other sweet food they love. Swarming yellow jackets have ruined many a picnic.
- Remove food sources that attract wasps by sealing garbage cans, keeping uncovered food out of compost heaps, and picking up fallen fruits from trees. Wasps develop memory for food sources and will come back for some time even after the food is gone.
- Avoid wearing bright colors and florals, especially anything with bright yellow. If you look like a flower, wasps and bees will flock to you.
- Avoid wearing perfume outdoors. If you smell like a flower, you'll be treated like one.
- Go easy on swatting. Swatting and squashing wasps is counter-productive. When a wasp is squashed, a pheromone is released that attracts and incites other nearby wasps. It's best to simply walk away.

Fire Ants

Found throughout much of the South and the warmer West, fire ants deliver a painful sting that causes allergic reactions in some people. In a yard infested with fire ants, avoid playing in the grass, or even walking over it barefoot.

Pest control services will apply fire ant controls for you. Or you can control them yourself by spot-treating existing fire ant mounds, then, in the fall, applying fire ant bait to prevent future infestations.

First, spot-treat mounds. Apply fire ant dusts, liquid drenches, or granular products following package directions exactly. You can also pour 2 to 3 gallons of very hot or boiling water on the mound, which will kill ants much of the time, although in some cases the ants will merely move elsewhere.

Then, in late August through early October, when ants are still foraging and weather patterns are more predictable, apply bait when no rain is expected for several days. Fall is a good time to apply fire ant bait because it is slow-acting, taking weeks to months to reduce ant mound numbers. And it's easier to wait for the bait to take effect during the winter than it is in spring when there's more outdoor activity.

Because fire ants travel from yard to yard, team with your neighbors to implement simultaneous fire ant control programs. Decide what control method to use, and possibly plan to treat the entire neighborhood as a group effort.

Fire ant mound

Gnats, Midges, and Biting Flies

Gnats and midges may swarm and be annoying to watch or walk through, but they do not bite.

However, there are many species of biting flies, ranging in size from barely visible up to an inch, that deliver annoying bites. They include deerflies, blackflies, horseflies, and sand flies and can in some rare cases produce allergic reactions, though seldom as severe as those caused by bees, wasps, hornets, or yellow jackets.

Avoiding biting flies is much like avoiding mosquitoes. Use lots of insect repellent on your skin; avoid working at dawn or dusk; wear loose, light-colored clothing rather than dark and tight clothing; and make sure your landscape is free of standing water.

Lawns

A healthy lawn does many things. It sets off your home and your plantings. It gives a well-kept, restful look to your home and improves its value. It's an ideal place for children and adults alike to romp and relax. It keeps your property cleaner by holding soil in place, preventing mud from being tracked and the ground from eroding. A beautiful lawn is a point of pride for many homeowners, who work hard to have lush, green turf.

Chapter 7 Lawns

A beautiful lawn doesn't have to be difficult or expensive to maintain. In this chapter you'll find out ways to work smarter rather than harder and to spend wisely rather than extravagantly. You'll learn how to choose the right grass, water well, fertilize appropriately, and deal with problems effectively when they do crop up—setting you on the way to cultivating a lawn that will be the pride of the neighborhood.

Lawn Basics

A healthy, well-kept lawn is the goal of just about every homeowner.

We all know that such a lawn is beautiful and peaceful looking and is a good place to play and relax. But it also adds substantially to the value of your home. Real estate agents estimate that a beautiful lawn can add as much as 5 to 15 percent to a home's value, because it signals that the rest of the home is well-kept and is worth top dollar.

A beautiful lawn also keeps your home cooler and quieter. Streets, sidewalks, and driveways in hot, sunny weather can reach 100°F (38°C), whereas grass remains at a pleasant 75°F (24°C). This cool pocket around your home keeps the air cooler, significantly reducing air-conditioning costs.

Grass also absorbs and deflects sound. Especially when combined with trees and shrubs, it can substantially deaden neighborhood and traffic sounds.

Grass, like other plants, helps purify the air, and it produces oxygen. Just 625 square feet of grass supplies all the oxygen that one adult needs for a day. This means that an average home lawn of 5,000 square feet produces more than enough oxygen for a large family and produces as much oxygen as two 100-foot-tall trees.

Turf also fights pollution. Over the period of a year, the grass blades and roots in an acre of healthy lawn absorb hundreds of pounds of pollutants from air and rainwater, including nitrates, sulfur dioxide, nitrogen oxide, hydrogen fluoride, and other gases blamed for acid rain and the greenhouse effect.

Lawns and turf also play an important role in holding precious topsoil in place. Grass roots knit soil together, even on slopes, and a healthy lawn absorbs rainfall six times more effectively than a wheat field.

Grass also serves as a dust trap, rather like the filter on a vacuum cleaner. Grass slows the air that moves constantly across its surface, causing dust particles to settle onto the blades, where they are washed back into the soil by rain and dew. Every year, grass traps millions of tons of dust that would otherwise be

The Golden Rules for a Beautiful Lawn

Creating an attractive lawn can be a straightforward proposition. Follow these basic rules, and your lawn will look good:

1 Water regularly. Lawns need 1 inch of water a week, either from irrigation or rain. Make sure your lawn gets it in one form or the other.

2 Mow high and regularly. Tall grass shades the soil, keeping it cooler and moister and preventing weed seeds from germinating. Check the best grass height for your grass on page 235. Then mow at that height at least once a week. As a rule, you should remove less than one-third of a blade of grass, to avoid stressing it.

3 Fertilize. An optimum fertilizing schedule can be rather complex, but as a rough guide, if you fertilize in early spring and fall, you'll be doing enough to have a healthy lawn. See page 240 for more information.

4 Control weeds with two applications. In spring, apply a preemergent herbicide on your lawn when the bright yellow forsythia is blooming. This is the herbicide that prevents weed seeds from germinating in the first place and takes care of most annual weeds that spread by seed. Then, in fall, apply a broad-leaf herbicide. This takes care of perennial lawn weeds, which carry the herbicide along with nutrients down into their roots as they prepare for overwintering.

5 Grow grass only where grass should be grown. Avoid growing grass in deep shade or under a mature tree, especially one with shallow roots such as many maples and pines; grow an attractive groundcover instead (see page 159). Avoid growing grass in high-traffic areas; install a path or patio there instead. On steep slopes where turf is hard to maintain and erosion and/or baked conditions make grass unhealthy, plant flowers or a groundcover.

airborne, making for difficult breathing, irritated eyes, and reduced visibility.

Fortunately, a good lawn is less difficult to create and maintain than you might think. It just takes a little know-how and a commitment to regular watering, mowing, and basic care. With good basic care, a lawn grows lush and thick; naturally resists pests, disease, and drought; withstands traffic better; and is more likely to endure other problems.

Having a good lawn is easier than ever. Lawn care companies have come up with a wide range of products that you can tailor to your region and your needs.

Lawn breeders and researchers have created a number of new grass varieties with an eye toward reducing diseases and pests, resisting drought better, and producing lawns with a finer and softer texture that will stay greener with less fertilizer.

Perhaps best of all, researchers have worked on developing grasses that need less mowing.

WORK SMARTER

MADE IN THE SHADE

Lawn grasses grow less successfully in deep shade, but you may be able to grow grass in an area that gets at least four hours of direct light and six to eight hours of lightly dappled sun per day. Here's how:

- Choose a shade lawn mix, and plant or overseed with it.
- Mow grass 1/2–1 inch longer than normal. Because the grass blades are getting less light, they need more blade to take in the limited light and grow well.
- Apply half as much fertilizer as you would to lawns in sunny sites. Grasses in shade grow less and need less fertilizer, and too much nitrogen can be harmful.
- If growing under a mature tree in so-called dry shade, water more frequently.
- As much as is practical, trim up lower branches of trees to allow in more light.
- Be especially diligent about raking up fallen leaves and debris; grass grown in shade needs all the light it can get.

So-called cattle paths occur in high-traffic areas. Paths of stone or brick are an easy solution in these spots.

In areas with deep shade and shallow roots, shade-loving groundcovers are a wiser choice than turf.

Understanding Lawn Grasses

An element critical to having an attractive lawn with the least work, least expense, and fewest problems is planting the right grass for your region.

Always choose a premium seed blend. Buy top-of-the-line seed—it costs only a bit more and is well worth the small investment.

Read the Package

Spend a little time at the garden center reading the labels and comparing the different types of grasses. (This is a good point at which to consult with your Home Depot garden associate on your particular needs in order to find the right grass for you.) Look at the white stick-on label that lists the types of grass in the blend. Look for the blend that has the lowest percentage of weed seed (it should be less than 1 percent). Also look for varieties of grass that are named, such as perennial ryegrass or fine fescue, and avoid those that merely list VNS (variety not stated). Germination percentages should be at least 85 percent.

Also note whether it's a sun mix or a shade mix, whether it's good for high-traffic areas, and whether the seed is coated or treated or mixed with a special mulch to stay moister longer when sown on the ground.

Basic Characteristics

Lawn grasses can be annuals, perennials, or a blend of the two. Annual grasses germinate quickly, adding fast color. Perennial grasses get larger and lusher with the years.

Know if the grass you're planting is a bunching or a creeping type. Bunchgrasses, such as annual and perennial ryegrass, blue gramagrass, and tall fescue, spread by shooting out runners from their crown. Bunchgrass grows in low clumps and is rougher but more drought tolerant.

Grasses also can be divided into fine-textured and coarse-textured. Fine grasses, including creeping red bentgrass, Kentucky bluegrass, Bermudagrass, and zoysiagrass, create a smooth-looking, refined lawn. They're soft underfoot and comfortable for children to play on.

Wider-bladed grasses are tough and drought tolerant. They include tall fescue, buffalograss, and some varieties of perennial ryegrass.

A CLOSER LOOK

COOL-SEASON VS. WARM-SEASON GRASSES

Lawn grasses can be divided into two groups: cool season and warm season.

Cool-season grasses do best in the cool temperatures of spring and fall. They include fine fescues, tall fescues, Kentucky bluegrass, perennial ryegrass, rough bluegrass, and others. In warm climates, they look good year-round as long as they have ample water.

Warm-season grasses grow best when the weather is warm—in late spring through summer and into early fall and as a group tend to be more heat and drought tolerant. They include bahiagrass, blue gramagrass, buffalograss, carpetgrass, centipedegrass, Bermudagrass, St. Augustinegrass, and zoysiagrass. In winter, they go brown and dormant and tend to green up later than cool-season grasses.

Let the grasses' growth-spurt times help you decide when to tackle major lawn projects. Whenever tackling tasks that stress the grass, such as dethatching, aerating, or renovating the lawn, time them for early in the period of most active growth or just before growth starts.

This means that the best times to work on cool-season grasses are early spring, or late summer to early fall. Early to midsummer is best for warm-season grasses. When renovating cool-season lawns, be aware that competition from germinating weed seeds is lowest in late summer to early fall, so that may be the best time to schedule this task.

GOOD IDEA

FIND OUT WHAT KIND OF GRASS YOU HAVE

To figure out the best way to take care of your lawn, you need to know what kind of grass or different types of grass make it up.

To find out, dig up a small patch or two (about 1 inch by 1 inch each) from your lawn (fill in the space with a little soil) and take it to your Home Depot garden center for identification. Because front lawns are often planted in different grasses from back lawns, take a patch from each.

Or call a reputable lawn service and ask them to identify the grasses for you.

Cool-season grasses such as this fescue lawn provide a fine-textured yet tough surface for outdoor sports and games.

Warm-season grasses provide an even, dense activity surface that stays green all summer, even in southern cimates.

Lawn Grass Climate Map

This map shows the five major climate regions for turfgrass in the United States. Use the map to help you further narrow your choice of grasses for your lawn.

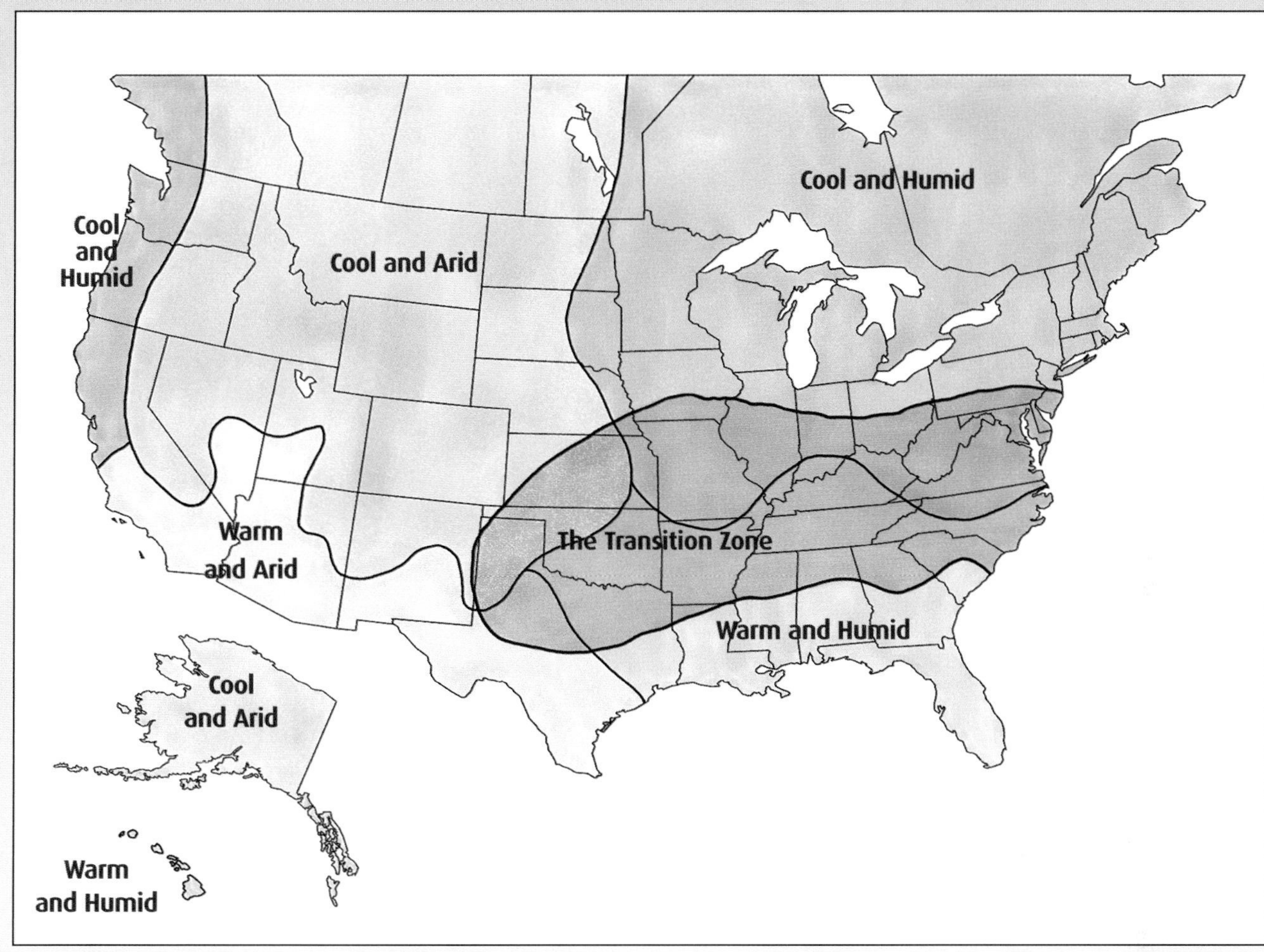

Cool and Humid

This region is highly diverse and includes areas with mild, wet winters and warm, dry summers, and areas with frigid winters and hot summers. Rainfall totals 30 inches or more per year. All of the cool-season grasses grow well here, although where little rain falls in summer they may go dormant for short periods unless watered. Zoysiagrass also grows in the southern portion of this region and along the Atlantic coast. It has a short growing season here and is brown much of the year. Buffalograss grows in western areas of the region.

Cool and Arid

This region has cold to mild, snowy to dry winters, and warm to hot, dry summers. Rainfall totals less than 20 inches per year. Cool-season grasses, especially Kentucky bluegrass and fine fescue, grow here but will stay green only if irrigated. To avoid having to irrigate, choose buffalograss, which does well on rainfall alone.

Warm and Arid

This region has hot summers, mild winters, and little to no rain at any time of year. Warm-season grasses do best here, with Bermudagrass being the most common. Buffalograss can be grown in northern parts of the region. The soil is alkaline and often saline, so check with your local Home Depot garden associate for more specialized grasses that are appropriate for some parts of this region.

Warm and Humid

In this region, winters are mild, rainfall is high, and summers are hot and humid. The area along the Gulf Coast is almost tropical, with rainfall totaling 60 inches or more per year. Warm-season grasses dominate in this region. Bermudagrass grows throughout; zoysiagrass is better adapted to the northern portions; and St. Augustinegrass, bahiagrass, and centipedegrass do better along the Gulf Coast. In the mountainous sections, cool-season grasses will grow.

The Transition Zone

The Transition Zone has characteristics of all four other regions. It has hot summers, cold winters, and wet and dry periods throughout the year. Most cool-season grasses and warm-season varieties fail to thrive here. However, a handful do well. These include tall fescue, a cool-season grass that is better suited to hot summers than most of the other cool-season grasses and can survive the winter in most of the Transition Zone. Of the warm-season grasses, cold-tolerant varieties of Bermudagrass do well in the southern part of the zone, and zoysiagrass grows farther north, although it is brown for much of the year. Kentucky bluegrass and perennial ryegrass, or a mix of these two with tall fescue, would be a successful combination for the cooler parts of this zone.

Planting A Lawn

There are three basic ways to start a lawn: from sod, from seed, or from sprigs.

Soil Preparation First

Regardless of the method you choose, you'll need to improve the soil, especially with a newly constructed home where the builder has probably scraped off and taken away the topsoil before building. Even if topsoil is put back on, it's often a thin layer less conducive to lush green grass.

Prepare the soil by first raking away debris and killing small weeds with hoeing or tilling. Take care of more extensive weed problems with a nonselective herbicide. (If using this, wait a week or two before planting. And if the infestation is really bad, water the area to stimulate new growth and then apply the nonselective herbicide again to zap it.)

Improve the soil by spreading at least an inch and preferably 2 to 3 inches of soil amendments (see page 138). Till in with a power tiller, which you can rent. Smooth the soil with a ground rake.

Laying Sod

Sod has a number of advantages over seed. You can sod a lawn almost anytime during the growing season. You can sod where seed may be hard to establish, such as in areas with heavy foot traffic or on sloping terrain. And sod is fast. A sod lawn can be walked on in as little as three weeks. However, it also costs considerably more than seed.

To lay a sod lawn, some preparation beyond tilling and amending the soil is necessary. A few days before the sod is delivered, water the area thoroughly; then allow the soil's surface to dry a little before laying the sod.

Plan to lay the sod on the day it arrives. Have the pallets stacked as close as possible to the planting area. If you must plant on a later day, have the sod stacked in a cool, shaded area and keep the outer rolls moist with a good watering. Lay the sod as soon as possible.

Starting a Lawn from Seed

Starting a lawn from seed is economical, and you have a wide variety of grass seed types to choose from, so you can use the one that's right for your conditions.

After preparing the soil, use a ground rake to make it as smooth as possible. Then roll it lightly with a lawn roller (these can be rented) about half full of water.

After planting, rope off the area with stakes and twine to keep foot traffic from compacting the soil. Keep the soil constantly moist; even a short dry period can kill the germinating seed. Lightly water with a sprinkler as often as three or four times daily until the grass is established—that is, until it's a half inch or so high. Use a fine spray or nozzle with a mist setting to avoid washing away soil and seed.

Allow the young grass to reach its maximum recommended height before mowing. At that point, it can receive some light foot traffic, but heavy play or traffic should be kept off it for another two to four weeks.

Starting with Sprigs or Plugs

Only warm-season grasses are started from sprigs or plugs. That's because some warm-season grasses fail to set viable seed and can be grown only from tiny divisions called sprigs and plugs.

Sprigs (also called stolons or runners) are pieces of the torn-up sod of creeping grasses. Plugs are small squares or circles of sod. Plant each type at intervals, several inches apart; eventually they will grow together.

PROJECT DETAILS

SKILLS: Tilling and planting
PROJECT: Planting a lawn from seed

TIME TO COMPLETE

EXPERIENCED: A couple of hours for a small area
HANDY: An hour
NOVICE: An hour

STUFF YOU'LL NEED

TOOLS: Tiller, rake, sprinkler
MATERIALS: Soil amendments (see page 138), seed

How to Start a Lawn from Seed

1 After removing weeds by hand or with a nonselective herbicide, till the soil, working in soil amendments as needed (see page 138). Smooth with a ground rake.

2 Sprinkle seed evenly, using a broadcast spreader. Consult the package directions for rate of coverage, but when in doubt, spread the seed more heavily rather than lightly.

3 Ensure good contact between seed and soil by lightly raking the entire area. Avoid raking roughly. Doing so could redistribute the seed. Water daily until established.

How to Plant Sprigs

Sprig planting is best done from late spring to the middle of summer. There are several ways to plant sprigs. Dig 2- to 3-inch-deep furrows 4 to 12 inches apart; place the sprigs in the furrows, and firm the soil around each stem. Or lay sprigs on the soil at desired intervals and lightly press them in with a notched stick. The fastest planting method is broadcast sprigging. Strew sprigs over the soil by hand, then cover them with soil and roll lightly with a water-filled roller. Whichever method you use, apply a special starter fertilizer after planting and water in well.

How to Plant Plugs

Plugs should be planted in early spring. Before they arrive, use a steel plugger (or a trowel or small spade) to dig holes the proper size in the soil, spacing them 6 to 12 inches apart, depending on the size of the plugs and type of grass. To help the lawn take hold evenly, offset the rows of plugs in a checkerboard pattern.

When the plugs arrive, lightly moisten the soil and place the plugs in the holes. Firm the soil around them so the crowns are level with the ground. After planting, roll as with sod and sprigs.

Water sprigs and plugs daily for the first two weeks after planting to keep them from drying out. They may take up to two years to fill in completely, so it is important to keep the soil around them free of weeds until they have filled in.

PROJECT DETAILS

SKILLS: Tilling, planting
PROJECT: Laying sod on bare soil

TIME TO COMPLETE

EXPERIENCED: A couple of hours for a small area
HANDY: 2 hours for a small area
NOVICE: 3 hours for a small area

STUFF YOU'LL NEED

TOOLS: Tiller, wheelbarrow, ground rake
MATERIALS: Soil amendments (see page 138), sod, sprinklers

How to Lay Sod

1 Remove problem weeds as needed with a nonselective herbicide. Till the soil, working in soil amendments as needed (see page 138).

2 Unroll the sod gently and position, being sure to butt ends and sides tightly so air doesn't get between them and dry them out. Stagger rolls, the way bricks are, so they start and stop in various areas.

3 Water well. Let water soak down a few inches through the sod and an inch or two into the soil. Water daily and deeply for a week or two until the sod establishes and starts to send out new growth of its own. Thereafter, make sure it receives rain or a watering weekly.

Fixing a Problem Lawn

It's thin. It's weedy. It has ugly brown patches and big bare spots. A problem lawn can ruin the appearance of your property.

If the problem is mild to moderate, you can take some steps to repair your lawn and improve it dramatically.

If the problem is severe, you will need to start over.

Patching a Lawn

Patching a lawn is simply repairing the occasional problem spot of a foot or two across or changing the way you care for your lawn to remedy chronic overall problems.

Repairing is called for if more than 70 percent of your lawn is in good shape, the grasses seem fairly well adapted to your climate and maintenance routine, and the only weeds are annual ones that are easy to remedy, such as crabgrass.

In these cases, you can repair by patching. Annual weeds such as crabgrass, which spreads by reseeding, can be controlled by applying a preemergent herbicide in spring.

Should I Repair or Replace?

When evaluating a problem lawn, it can be difficult to decide whether to repair it or dig it up and start over. Even if your lawn is troublesome, it may not require such a drastic step. Before you make the decision to replace or repair, decide whether the following statements are true:

- Most of the grass is fine bladed and deep green.
- The grass may be slightly thin but is generally healthy.
- The lawn is less than 50 percent weeds.
- The weeds that are there are mainly annual weeds, such as crabgrass.
- Diseases occur only occasionally, if at all.
- The grass turns brown only during the most severe drought.

If all of these statements are true, a lawn repair is likely all you need. If one or more statements is false, starting a new lawn is likely the best tactic. If you're still unsure, consult with a Home Depot garden associate (bring photographs), or have a reputable lawn service examine your lawn.

If the lawn is only a bit thin, overseed it (see page 246) in spring or fall. Otherwise, check the maintenance schedule (see page 240) to make sure you are watering and fertilizing as needed.

Renovating a Lawn

A lawn needs to be renovated when it's generally thin or is extensively infested with a variety of perennial broadleaf weeds, such as dandelions.

To renovate, you kill the existing lawn with a nonselective herbicide containing glysophate. This is the best solution when you don't need to work on the soil but the grass is in poor condition.

Reestablishing a Lawn

When the lawn stops thriving because of poor soil, poor drainage, or a steep slope, it's time to start from scratch by reestablishing the lawn.

Check the depth of the topsoil. There should be at least 6 inches of good-quality topsoil. If not, you'll need to truck some in before replanting.

If drainage is poor or a slope is the issue, you may want to consider regrading the site and installing drainage.

Reestablishing or renovating a lawn is a major step. Consult with a lawn care professional to get an idea of the scope of the project and the underlying reasons for the repair work. You must correct the underlying problems for your repairs to take. Otherwise, you'll have expended a lot of effort for little or no return.

Is Grass the Right Plant?

If your lawn is in such poor shape that you are considering renovating or reestablishing the lawn, it's wise to pause and ask yourself whether there is another solution besides growing lawn.

A low-lying spot might be better dealt with by turning it into a planting bed for flowers, shrubs, and trees that like wet conditions (see page 68, 76, and 130). A slope on which grass is difficult to grow is a prime candidate for planting with groundcovers and flowers that like good drainage and hot, dry conditions (see page 87 and 118).

Also ask yourself why the grass is so thin, allowing weeds to take over. If shade is the issue, it might be wiser to create a landscape of shade-loving planting beds and groundcovers, with mulch or flagstone paths, patios, or paving.

How to Patch a Problem Lawn

1 Rake the area to expose bare soil. Grass seed needs to make firm contact with the soil if it is to germinate well.

2 Sprinkle the grass seed onto the problem spot. The seed used here has a built-in mulch to keep it moister longer, encouraging better germination, and to protect it from birds that might eat exposed seed.

PROJECT DETAILS

SKILLS: Basic planting skills
PROJECT: Patching bare spots in lawns

TIME TO COMPLETE

EXPERIENCED: About 15 minutes
HANDY: 20 minutes
NOVICE: 20 minutes

STUFF YOU'LL NEED

TOOLS: Hand cultivator, hose with watering wand or spray nozzle
MATERIALS: Seed for patching (a product made especially for patching is best, especially if it has a mulch built in)

3 Water well, being careful not to wash away the seed. Water every day or twice a day to keep the soil moist for two weeks, until the grass is established.

GOOD IDEA

SMOOTHING A BUMPY LAWN

Most lawns, over the years, develop lumps and bumps from things being driven or wheeled over them when they were wet or from various animals burrowing under the surface.

The best way to fix a lawn that is uneven all over is to fix it bit by bit each year.

Each spring and each fall, top-dress the lawn by raking ¼ inch of topsoil or compost onto the lawn, adding more to low spots. If the low spots are large, overseed (see page 246) or use a lawn patch product on them. They will look sparse for a few days, but then the soil will wash downward.

If there are especially high large spots, remove the turf in horizontal slices. With a ground rake or broad hoe, scrape down the area and replace the sliced turf, filling in any gaps or bare spots with compost or topsoil. Reseed to fill in quickly and thickly.

Mowing Basics

Mowing your grass is fundamental to having a good lawn. Mowing properly is fundamental to having a *beautiful* lawn.

Mowing is essentially a form of pruning, encouraging grass to grow low and spread wide rather than grow tall and sparsely, thereby producing a thick lawn. And a thick lawn chokes out weeds.

To mow your lawn effectively, follow these tips:

Mow Regularly

When mowing, you should remove one-third of the grass blade or less. Otherwise, you'll stress the plant.

WORK SMARTER

EACH TIME YOU MOW, VARY YOUR MOWING PATTERN

Always mowing in the same direction or pattern can compact the soil. Also, grass leans or grows in the direction it's mowed, so changing the direction each time you mow encourages upright grass.

Mowing often and correctly is key to maintaining a thick, lush lawn that is free of problem weeds.

That means mowing anywhere from once every couple of weeks to twice a week, depending on your type of grass (some types grow faster than others) and the amount of moisture (more rain and more irrigation make grass grow faster) and fertilizer (more fertilizer makes grass grow faster).

Mow at the Right Height

Most mowers have mechanisms that allow you to adjust the mowing height. This is because different types of grasses do best at different heights. Also, in hot weather, grasses need to be longer to protect themselves and the soil.

Some grasses, such as zoysiagrass, can be cut as low as 1/2 inch in spring and fall. Others, such as bahiagrass, should be cut as high as 4 inches in summer and until they go dormant in late fall.

Check the chart at right for the correct mowing height for your grass, or at least check the range for cool-season or warm-season grasses. Cut your grass at the minimum height in spring and late fall; cut it at the maximum height in summer and early fall.

Most homeowners cut their grass too low in the hope that they'll have to cut less often. Plus, they think that a closely clipped lawn looks better.

But cutting extremely low can scalp the lawn, damaging the crown of the grass plants, stunting root growth, and encouraging thinner grass and more weeds. Also, if you scalp after letting the grass grow too long in the first place, you are greatly stressing the grass plants.

Cutting high in summer and early fall does a number of good things: It shades the soil, preventing weed seeds from germinating and keeping the soil cooler and moister. And because of the way grasses grow, when the plants are a little taller the roots grow a little deeper.

Mow Smart

Here's how you can mow better and more efficiently:

- Avoid cutting wet grass. It clogs the mower and cuts unevenly, and clumps of wet grass mat on the lawn, blocking light and air.
- Keep the blade sharp. Dull blades make for ragged lawns and ripped grass blades, which turn brown and give lawns a beige cast.
- For safety's sake, mow slopes on a diagonal. If a slope is very steep, it probably should be planted with something besides grass. See "Taming a Slope" on page 58.
- When using a power mower, it's a good idea to wear earplugs to minimize hearing loss. Thick garden gloves will help absorb vibrations from the machine. Of course, always wear sturdy shoes to prevent slipping and to prevent the mower blades and flying debris from hitting your feet.

Best Lawn Mowing Heights

Grass	Minimum Height	Maximum Height
Cool-Season Grasses		
Annual ryegrass	1 1/2"	2 1/2"
Bentgrass	1/2"	3/4"
Canada bluegrass	3"	4"
Chewings fescue	1 1/2"	2 1/2"
Hard fescue	1 1/2"	2 1/2"
Kentucky bluegrass	1 1/2"	2 1/2"
Perennial ryegrass	1 1/2"	2 1/2"
Red fescue	1 1/2"	2 1/2"
Rough bluegrass	2"	3"
Sheep fescue	2"	4"
Tall fescue	2 1/2"	3"
Wheatgrass	2"	2 1/2"
Warm-Season Grasses		
Bahiagrass	2"	4"
Hybrid Bermudagrass	1/2"	2"
Blue gramagrass	2"	3"
Buffalograss	2"	3"
Carpetgrass	1"	2"
Centipedegrass	1"	3"
Seashore paspalum	2"	4"
St. Augustinegrass	2"	4"
Zoysiagrass	3/4"	2"

Mowing Safety

When mowing, prevent serious injury with a few things:

- Wear sturdy shoes. It's easy for blades to slice a toe or toss a sharp object.
- Ear plugs are smart. Mowing every week for years can take its toll on your hearing. They're inexpensive and disposable, so use 'em!
- Thick gloves help absorb the vibrations on the machine so your wrists, elbows, and shoulders don't.
- Keep kids and friends away while mowing. Mowers can toss rocks and other debris with amazing force.

Mower Selection

BUYER'S GUIDE

LAWN TRACTOR, YARD TRACTOR, OR GARDEN TRACTOR?
They all sound similar, but they're each different.

A lawn tractor is made specifically for cutting grass, though it also can haul some light accessories, such as a small trailer.

Yard or garden tractors are more powerful and more general purpose. They can cut grass, but they also have the power to pull plows, rakes, and harrows and pull larger trailers carrying heavier loads.

Buying a mower is a little like buying a car. Some of us have the need and budget for a compact car; others are in the market for a luxury car or a powerful SUV. Know the basic features of each mower before you buy.

Reel Mower

Reel mowers have made a comeback. Standard before the advent of power mowers, they have gained favor with homeowners with small or steep lawns who don't mind a bit of a workout when they mow. Many also like the relatively low price and super-simple maintenance. Reel mowers are valued for their fine cut, which produces a manicured look. They're especially good for bentgrass and Bermudagrass, because they can be adjusted to cut quite low. Look for models that you can adjust the height without removing the wheels. Sharpen once or twice a year.

Rotary Power Mower

Power mowers are the most widely used type of mower. They are available in push or self-propelled models. Self-propelled models make mowing much easier and come with two basic types of drive systems: front-wheel drive and rear-wheel drive. Front-wheel drive has better maneuverability around trees and flower beds. It has good traction only on flat terrain and with thinner grasses. Rear-wheel drive offers the best traction for a variety of terrains as well as thicker grasses. Multispeed options are available for more flexible ground speed.

Make sure you get a bag with the machine. Otherwise, you'll have to rake clippings. Also, with a bag, you can mow over autumn leaves to chop them and collect them.

Mulching Mower

A mulching mower is a rotary power mower with a specially designed deck and blades that cut clippings into fine particles, which are thrown back onto the lawn. The "mulched" clippings act as a mulch among the grass blades, deterring weeds and conserving moisture. Eventually the clippings break down, feeding the soil. There are conversion blades on the market to turn a regular mower into a mulching mower. However, mulching mowers overall do a better job of finely chopping the grass. Look for a mower with at least a 5-hp engine for the best mulching.

Riding Mower/Lawn Tractor

If you have a relatively flat lawn of a half acre or more, a riding mower is probably for you. Features to consider include:

- Deck width. The wider the mower deck, the wider the cut and the faster the mowing job. However, the wider the deck, the less maneuverability you'll have around trees and flower beds, so you'll want to keep this in mind for your landscape. Before shopping, measure the width of any gates and other tight spots to make sure a mower can go through.
- Transmission type. Riding mowers have two types of transmissions: manual gear drive and automatic. A manual gear-drive transmission requires the use of a manual clutch to start, stop, or change ground speed. An automatic transmission (also called hydrostatic) requires no clutch, so it's easier to use and allows more control over speed.

- Foot or hand operation. A foot-operated riding mower allows you to control forward and reverse with your foot while having both hands on the wheel. A hand-operated riding mower controls forward and reverse with a lever on the fender, so you need to take one hand off the wheel to move the lever.
- Power. Lawn tractors are asked to do a lot, so the more power, the better, though of course you pay more for more power. The most powerful is a V-twin (2-cylinder) overhead valve. The next most powerful is an overhead-valve (OHV), single-cylinder type or a twin-opposed 2-cylinder. The least powerful is a standard single cylinder.

Mower Care

Once you've invested in a mower, it's important to keep it well maintained. Otherwise, it will cut poorly, operate inefficiently, and break down before its time.

Here's how to keep your mower operating smoothly for years to come:

- Keep it clean. After each use of the mower, give it a quick brushing off with a gloved hand or rag or whisk broom. It's a good idea, too, after the mower has stopped running completely, to reach under the deck with a gloved hand and do a quick brushing off of caked grass under the deck and on the blade.
- Once or twice a year, preferably right before you store the mower for the winter, give the mower a good cleaning. With the gas tank empty, disconnect the spark plug wire and turn the mower on its side. Spray it hard with a garden hose to loosen dirt and dried-on grass. Scrub with a soft brush and soapy water. Rinse.
- Clean or replace the air filter once or twice a year. Replace paper filters when they look dirty (keep a few on hand). Plastic foam filters should be removed and washed with warm, soapy water. Air-dry thoroughly. Then work about 2 tablespoons of clean mower oil evenly across the filter to lightly coat it.
- At the end of the mowing season, empty the gas tank by letting the mower run until the tank is dry. If the mower has a separate tank for oil, empty and refill it with fresh oil.
- Keep the blade sharp. A dull mower blade cuts unevenly and shreds the tip of grass blades, which then turn brown and give a lawn a beige cast that makes it look dry. The ragged ends are also good entry points for disease.

You can sharpen the blade yourself, as shown below. Or you can take it to a scissors sharpener or lawn mower repair place for sharpening. Keep a spare blade on hand so you'll have it while you're waiting for a convenient time to sharpen the other one or waiting for the sharpener to return a blade.

How to Sharpen a Mower Blade

1 Drain the gas and disconnect the spark plug wire in your power mower so the motor doesn't start while you're working.

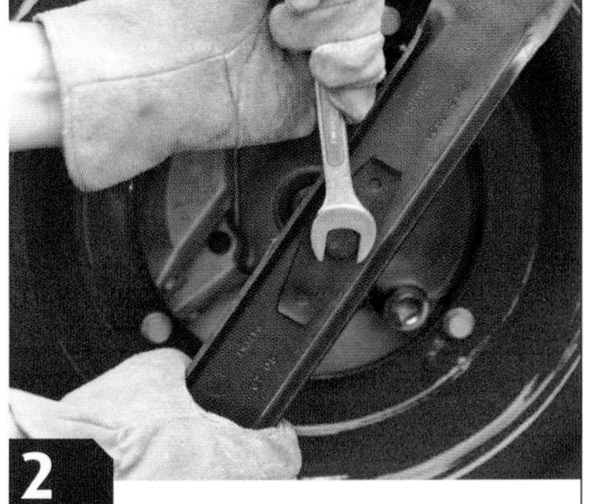

2 Wedge a block of wood between the blade and the mower deck to keep the blade from turning. Using an adjustable wrench, remove the bolt from the center of the blade.

3 Pull off the blade and clamp it in a bench vise. Sharpen it with a hand or power file with smooth, even strokes. Follow the original bevel of the blade as closely as you can. Make the same number of strokes on each edge to keep the blade perfectly in balance or else the blade may cut unevenly or make the mower vibrate, which can damage the engine.

4 Test the balance by resting the blade on the handle of a screwdriver or any other upright slender object. If one side points up, sharpen the other until the blade lies flat.

PROJECT DETAILS

SKILLS: Basic sharpening
PROJECT: Sharpening a mower blade

TIME TO COMPLETE

EXPERIENCED: 15 minutes
HANDY: 30 minutes
NOVICE: 60 minutes

STUFF YOU'LL NEED

TOOLS: wrench, C-clamp, power or hand file, object to balance blade

Watering Lawns

Lawns are thirsty plantings, and keeping them well watered is critical to their health.

As a rule, most lawns need 1 inch of water a week from rain, watering, or a combination of the two. Drought-tolerant grasses do well with less.

Water According to Soil Type

The soil under the lawn affects how often you need to water. Sandy soils drain quickly, so a lawn grown in those conditions may have to be watered two or three times a week if rain is inadequate. Clay retains water well, and a lawn on clay soil may require watering only once a week.

When you do water, water slowly and deeply, moistening soil to a depth of 6 to 12 inches. Running a sprinkler for a few minutes every evening is the worst way to water a lawn. Roots grow only where there is

Water in the early morning to prevent excessive evaporation. You can even set a timer to start the sprinkler before sunrise.

water, so if you consistently wet only the top few inches of soil, the roots stay near the surface. Eventually, the limited depth of the root system forces you to water more often. That means trouble, because frequent watering keeps the surface wet, which is ideal for disease development. If roots go deep into the soil, they can draw on a larger underground water supply, and the lawn can go much longer between waterings.

In heavy clay soils, it's smart to cycle your sprinklers off and on three or more times to allow the water to absorb deeply and to prevent puddling and runoff. You should still apply the water for the same amount of time, but break the time into sections. A timer can do much of the work for you.

When and How to Water

Lawns tell you when they need water. The grass blades roll up lengthwise to conserve moisture. At the same time, they lose their bright green color, and the entire lawn may take on a grayish cast. Thirsty grass plants also lose their resiliency, so if you walk across a lawn in need of water, the grass will spring back slowly, and your footprints may remain visible.

You can keep a lawn well watered with portable sprinklers, especially if you live in the eastern half of North America. But in the West, it's difficult to keep grass sufficiently watered, and wasting water through evaporation or watering pavement is expensive and irresponsible.

In the West, having a sprinkler system pays off in terms of saved labor, a better-looking lawn, and the more responsible use of a limited natural resource. Inground lawn sprinklers pop up before dawn and water close to the ground. The air right before dawn tends to be still with minimal wind, so little water blows in the wrong places, and the lack of sun greatly reduces evaporation because of heat.

Watering on a Slope

Watering on a slope can be tricky, because water can run down to the base of the slope before it can soak in.

One way to compensate is to use an oscillating sprinkler or a soaker hose that disperses water slowly. As with clay soils, you may want to cycle off and on to allow the water to trickle down.

Set a portable sprinkler at the top of the slope to allow for the downward flow of the water.

With inground irrigation systems, it is wise to design the system to apply the greatest amount of water at the top of the slope, less at the middle, and still less at the bottom, to compensate for the downward flow of the water.

Minimize watering problems by planting drought-tolerant grasses on the slope. If the problem is severe, plant drought-tolerant groundcovers (see page 117).

It's helpful to keep the slope aerated (see page 244), which allows water to trickle down into the ground more quickly. However, because power aerators may be difficult to use on slopes, use a manual aerator.

WORK SMARTER

DORMANT LAWNS

In late summer, without steady rain or watering, many cool-season lawns will go dormant—that is, they'll turn beige and dry looking.

Some homeowners figure this is part of nature's cycle. They know that dormant lawns green up again nicely when adequate rainfall returns. Other people are determined to have a green lawn throughout the growing season, and water it diligently.

The one thing to avoid doing is to cycle a lawn in and out of dormancy. That stresses the grass considerably. Keep the lawn steadily and thoroughly watered once a week, or stop watering at all.

If you choose to have a dormant lawn, avoid mowing it until it's green again. Leave the grass 3 to 4 inches tall to prevent the roots from burning. Stop fertilizing—and walking—on it.

WORK SMARTER

BETTER LAWN, LESS WATER

Keep your water bills down, use water responsibly—and have a great landscape. Here's how:

- Water early in the morning, ideally before sunrise. (Set an irrigation timer.) Watering later means more evaporation. Avoid watering in the evening; the foliage remains wetter longer, which encourages fungal diseases.
- Avoid watering on a windy day. It blows much of the water away and evaporates it.
- Water deeply and less often rather than shallowly and often. If water is allowed to sink deeply into the soil, it is less likely to evaporate quickly. Also, it encourages deep root growth, which makes grasses more drought tolerant.
- Water the grass rather than the driveway or the sidewalk. If you're using a sprinkler, have several on hand so you always have the right type for watering each particular space.
- Consider investing in an irrigation system, especially if you live in the western half of North America. These are designed and programmed to fine-tune watering for optimum times, perfect coverage, and little blowing or misting.
- Add water-smart plantings. These may replace a huge expanse of lawn. Plantings of trees, shrubs, groundcovers, and perennials, even if they're not labeled as drought tolerant, in general use far less water and take less maintenance than grass if they're planned and mulched well.

Fertilizing Lawns

Fertilizer comes in three basic types. Different types work for different needs and do slightly different things at different times of the year.

Water-Soluble Synthetic Fertilizers

Water-soluble synthetic fertilizers, as their name suggests, readily dissolve in water and are produced with a chemical reaction from organic and inorganic materials. These fertilizers are often also called quick release or fast acting. They act fast and can be applied during a wide range of times. Grass quickly greens up after application. And because soluble synthetics use mechanisms other than microbial action to release nutrients, they are effective even when the soil is cold.

Soluble synthetics have several disadvantages, however. Their effects are short-lived, so you must apply them multiple times in a growing season for best results. Grass grows rapidly after application, requiring frequent mowing, then goes through a slump as the fertilizer runs out. During rainy periods or in well-watered areas, the nitrogen can leach through the soil beyond the reach of the grass's roots.

Also, because these fertilizers are so intense, they can cause fertilizer burn in plants unless they are applied exactly according to package directions. To reduce the risk of fertilizer burn, many manufacturers combine soluble synthetics with the next category of fertilizers: slow release.

When to Fertilize Your Lawn

When you're trying to figure the best time to fertilize your lawn, it can seem like rocket science. There are many different approaches to fertilizing, from minimum to maximum.

Minimum fertilizing is fine for homeowners who don't care about a perfect lawn. Heavier fertilizing is good for homeowners who want a truly beautiful lawn or those lawns that have high traffic or other stresses. Lawns in sandy soil also benefit from more frequent feedings since the nutrients quickly wash out of the soil.

MINIMUM MAINTENANCE/ONE FEEDING

- Give your lawn an application of a slow-release fertilizer in spring when it first starts to green up. One feeding will make the lawn denser than if you didn't fertilize at all and will prevent weeds and make the lawn overall a little healthier.

MEDIUM MAINTENANCE/TWO FEEDINGS

- Give cool-season grasses (see page 228 for an explanation of cool- and warm-season grasses) a second feeding with a slow-release fertilizer in late spring to help thicken the lawn and to help them better withstand the stresses of summer.
- Give warm-season grasses a second feeding in early summer for the same reason.

MAXIMUM MAINTENANCE/THREE TO FOUR FEEDINGS

- Give cool-season grasses a third feeding in fall when they start growing faster again after summer's heat. It helps them better survive the winter and green up faster the following spring. If you want them to green up faster in the spring, give them a late fall feeding as well.
- Give warm-season grasses a third feeding in late spring and, if desired, a fourth feeding in mid-summer.

Lawn grasses are hungry plants and need plenty of nitrogen and other nutrients in order to thrive and achieve a rich, deep green.

Slow-Release Fertilizers

Also called controlled-release or timed-release, slow-release fertilizers provide nutrients at a predictable rate over a period of time. They ensure uniform turf growth throughout the season. You can apply them heavily without fear of burning the lawn. However, lawns green up more slowly than with granular or water-soluble fertilizers, and they may be expensive to use.

Some slow-release fertilizers are designed to act only after the soil warms to a certain temperature. Other slow-release fertilizers are coated. Individual particles of quick-release nitrogen are covered with a material that lets out only small amounts of nutrients at a time, usually only when the fertilizer is wet. Other coated fertilizers are a mix of pellets having coatings of varying thicknesses, which release the fertilizer at different rates.

Natural Organic Fertilizers

The term "natural organic" refers to any fertilizer that is made of dried or composted plant or animal waste.

A wide variety of natural organic fertilizers can be found on the market. Among the ones most suitable for use on turf are those made from sewage sludge and poultry waste.

Organic fertilizers have many advantages. While synthetic fertilizers add only nutrients, organic fertilizers also improve all-important soil structure and often contain valuable micronutrients. Also, organic fertilizers release nutrients slowly, an advantage or a disadvantage depending on your needs.

Because natural organics rely on soil microorganisms for the release of nutrients, they are weather-dependent. They will work only if the soil temperature is above 50°F (10°C).

TOOL TIP

THE RIGHT SPREADER FOR YOU

A good spreader is important for applying fertilizer and other lawn treatments quickly, easily, and accurately. If you have a spreader that works badly, it can burn grass or give it an uneven color.

There are three types of spreaders:

- A handheld crank spreader is good for small lawns. Simply put the correct amount of fertilizer in the little bin (check the package directions) and wind the crank as you walk to broadcast the granular product. Application is imprecise but adequate.
- A drop spreader (shown at right) looks like a small cart with a handle. It simply drops fertilizer from the bin. Application is precise but narrower than that of a broadcast spreader, so more passes have to be made to cover a lawn. Good for medium-size lawns.
- A broadcast spreader looks like a cart with a handle but throws granules or pellets over a wide area with a whirling wheel. Good for large lawns.

7

Lawns

Controlling Lawn Weeds, Pests, And Diseases

When you've been working hard on your lawn, it's frustrating to see problems with your beautiful green carpet.

Lawn problems happen for a reason: wet or dry weather, climate or site conditions that help a weed or pest or disease get a foothold, growing the wrong kind of grass for your region, or simply poor maintenance. Mowing infrequently or too low, watering too little or too shallowly, and fertilizing too much or too little can also contribute to lawn problems.

Lawn Diseases

The majority of lawn diseases are caused by soil-dwelling fungi. Lawn fungal problems are easier to prevent than cure. If you grow grass in full sun (rather than shade), plant the right grass for your climate and conditions, and water only in the early morning, you can avoid many fungal diseases.

If a fungal disease does strike, you can choose from a number of products for treating lawn fungal diseases. However, be sure to identify the problem first (see "Dealing with Lawn Pests and Diseases," right) and follow package directions exactly. Fungicides can be toxic if ingested and can irritate the skin upon contact.

Lawn Pests

As with lawn diseases, dealing with lawn pests requires you to identify the problem.

Pests are most often found in stressed areas of a lawn, such as the edge of the lawn or in wet, dry, or shady places. It's uncommon to find pests distributed evenly throughout the lawn. When you spot a problem, get down on your hands and knees and look at the area carefully. Insects tend to proceed outward from a central point, so look most carefully on the outside edges of the problem, where the culprits are most likely to be lurking.

Some insects, such as adult billbugs, chinch bugs, clover mites, greenbugs, and leafhoppers, feed on grass blades, so examine the blades carefully.

Others, such as cutworms, fiery skippers, sod webworms, armyworms, and billbug larvae, feed on the crowns of grass plants. Poke into the thatch area with a trowel or sharp stick and look carefully for signs of these insects.

Still other lawn pests feed on grass roots, including ground pearls, mole crickets, grubs, and wireworms.

If you do find a pest or signs of a pest, such as the pellet-shape green droppings left by sod webworms, put the evidence in a plastic bag along with a small portion of damaged turf and take it to your Home Depot garden center for help identifying the problem and determining the best way to remedy it.

Three Ways to Apply Lawn Products

Depending on when and what you're applying to your lawn to kill weeds, diseases, or pests, you will apply it with one of three devices:

Spreader: A drop or hand or broadcast spreader on wheels (see page 241) applies dry, granular products. Good for covering large areas.

Spray Container: Ideal for spot treatments. For small applications, you can often purchase the product premixed in a spray bottle. For large areas, you may want to mix the product in a 2-gallon or larger sprayer. With any type of spraying, be sure to spray only the plant you want to treat. Use a sprayer only on a still day, and use newspaper or a piece of cardboard to prevent drift onto other plants.

Hose-End Sprayer: Good for large lawns as long as the hose will reach. The product bottle has a portion to which you attach the hose. Then simply spray. For even application, use an even sweeping motion and follow a pattern as you move across the lawn. You may need to refill the bottle more than once before finishing.

Dealing with Lawn Pests and Diseases

Although some lawn pests and diseases are easy to identify, it can be difficult to identify many other problems because the symptoms are so similar—brown patches and yellowing dead spots.

Before trying to treat the problem, it's important to know what it is. Take a photo of your lawn with a digital camera, or dig up a small patch of problem turf and bring it to your Home Depot garden center. Or call a reputable lawn service and ask them to diagnose the problem for you. Another way to identify the problem is by calling your county extension office.

In some cases, the best solution may be to alter your fertilization or watering program (too much or too little causes problems) or apply a chemical control. In some cases the best solution may be to simply tolerate the problem and do nothing.

A Guide to Lawn Weed Killers

NAME	WHAT IT DOES	WHEN IT DOES IT
Broadleaf herbicide	Kills weeds with larger (not grassy) leaves, including dandelions.	Any time of year weeds are actively growing, but most effective in lawns in spring and early summer as first crop of broadleaf weeds are emerging and rapidly growing.
Grass herbicide	Kills grassy plants, such as Johnsongrass (and lawn grass). Doesn't affect broad-leaved plants. If used in lawns the area treated will have to be reseeded and patched. Good for flower beds and borders or groundcover plantings where grasses have invaded.	Any time of year weedy grasses are actively growing.
Non-selective herbicide	Kills all plants it touches. Need to be careful not to spray desirable plants. Best used in lawns to kill out patches off problem lawn	Any time of year plants to be destroyed are actively growing.
Pre-emergent herbicide	Kills annual weeds (such as crabgrass) as their seeds germinate. Do not use for several weeks where you've planted or will be planting seeds. Excellent in established lawns or in plantings of established perennials, annuals, shrubs, and groundcovers.	To control crabgrass and other cool-season annuals, apply in early spring about the time the bright yellow forsythia is blooming.

Reading Lawn Product and Other Chemical Labels

Get the most for your money—and get better results besides—by reading the label of any type of weed control (an herbicide) as well as any insect control (an insecticide) carefully. A minute or two spent reading the label can prevent many problems later on.

Problems occur when a label isn't read and followed *exactly*. For example, applying at the wrong time for the wrong problem or applying too much or too little or during the wrong kinds of weather can result in major problems, and sometimes even dead plants.

The main front label tells what exactly the product does and which plants it works on. (This one kills all major broadleaf weeds in the lawn. It also fertilizes.) It also often offers a listing of active ingredients as well as a caution in storing and using. Increasingly, label information is being offered in both English and Spanish.

The back label often has more detail of the overview offered on the front.

Look for phone and computer icons. A quick call or checking of a website can be very helpful.

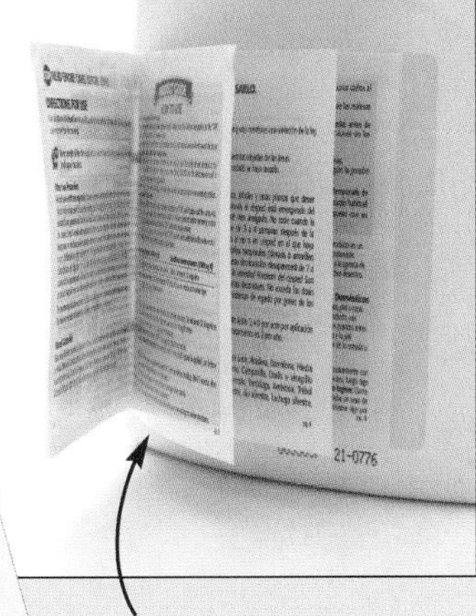

Increasingly, garden chemicals have peel-back booklets attached. This one holds the all-important Directions for Use, a must for every chemical label. It will include how to mix the chemical, if necessary, and how and when to apply.

Storage and disposal information is also included. You can't just dump leftover lawn chemicals on the ground or down a sink because they may contaminate drinking or groundwater supplies. So it's critical to dispose of chemicals properly.

This peel-back booklet also has a complete list of exactly which broadleaf weeds are controlled by the product. It reseals, so you can open it in the store and close it back up.

Aerating A Lawn

GOOD IDEA

TESTING FOR COMPACTION

If you are unsure whether your lawn is compacted, you can conduct this simple test:

When the soil is relatively moist and soft, plunge a 3/4- to 1-inch metal pipe into the soil to remove a plug of turf. (You may need a mallet to help you do this.) Remove the pipe and tap it until the plug is released, then examine the plug closely. If the grass roots are only an inch or so deep, your soil is compacted. If they extend 4–6 inches, the roots are growing nicely into the lawn and the plants are healthy.

Aerating a lawn does a number of good things for your turf. This process of punching holes every few inches across your lawn loosens soil and breaks up thatch, allowing water, air, and fertilizer to get to grass roots. Aerating enables the roots to grow deeply and produces a more vigorous, healthy, and disease- and drought-resistant lawn.

How Often to Aerate?

Many lawns, particularly heavily used ones, have compacted soil, which restricts the movement of air and water to roots. The soil under lawns tends to compact readily, because—unlike garden soil—it is virtually never worked or turned. So for a lawn, aerating is the alternative to tilling.

Intensively maintained lawns should be aerated once a year; those that receive moderate maintenance, every two years. Lawns with heavily compacted soil or severe thatch problems may need twice-yearly aeration.

How to Aerate

Several types of tools are available for aerating lawns. If your lawn is small, there's a foot-press aerator that you push into the soil like a spade. It's large and flat with a big U-shape handle. For large lawns, you can buy or rent an engine-powered aerator or have a lawn service use such a machine on your lawn. A core aerator resembles a lawn mower. You steer it across the lawn, aerating as you go. Whatever tool you use, make sure that the soil is moist—but not too wet—during aeration so the aerator can penetrate easily.

Aerating tools remove thin, cigar-shape plugs of soil and deposit them on the surface of the lawn. You can leave them indefinitely, if you wish. If their appearance bothers you, leave them there to dry for a day or so, then break them up with energetic raking to create a thin, beneficial topdressing.

When to Aerate

With cool-season grasses, such as Kentucky bluegrass, aerate in fall, ideally about four to six weeks before your region's first frost date. With warm-season grasses, such as Bermudagrass, aerate in midsummer.

A power aerator, which can be rented, takes out plugs of soil every few inches. The resulting holes allow water and air to penetrate deeply and also to break up thatch.

Dethatching A Lawn

Thatch is dead organic matter—grass stems, dead roots, and debris—that builds up in a lawn faster than it decomposes. Lawn clippings are often erroneously thought to add to thatch, but most clippings break down and nurture the soil.

Examining Thatch

Thatch is the dry beige stuff that accumulates on top of the soil at the base of the grass blades. A layer of ½ inch or less is normal and harmless. In fact, it protects the crown of the grass and reduces soil compaction. However, a layer thicker than ½ inch is a problem because it prevents water from reaching the roots. A layer of thatch thicker than 2 inches is a severe problem.

An easy test for thatch is this: Walk around on your lawn with firm-soled shoes. If your lawn feels spongy underfoot, it has excessive thatch.

Many things can cause thatch: poorly aerated soil, overabundance of nitrogen, and watering shallow and often rather than deep and less frequently, which encourages shallow roots. Infrequent mowing also is a culprit. (You should mow often enough that you remove one-third of the blade or less.) Mowing too low also encourages thatch (see page 235 for correct mowing heights).

You can dethatch in a variety of ways:

- For lawns with moderate thatch, simply aerating the lawn will alleviate thatch problems.
- For small lawns—if you have strong arms—use a thatching or cavex rake to take up the thatch. The long, knifelike blades of these specialized rakes cut through the sod and pull up thatch. A simple ground rake will help, too, if you rake vigorously.
- For large lawns or those with serious thatch problems, the most effective tool is a vertical mower. Resembling a heavy-duty power mower, this machine has a series of revolving vertical knives that cut and pull through the thatch, bringing it to the surface. You can purchase or rent this machine, or ask a lawn service to perform the task. Use a leaf rake to rake up the material afterward.

After dethatching, water the lawn well to keep the grass hydrated. About a week after dethatching, fertilize the lawn to stimulate new growth.

Regardless of the method you use to remove thatch, it's seldom a problem that is solved in one year. Repeat an annual thatch removal for two or more years until the thatch is less than 1 inch.

When to Dethatch

Dethatching is rather traumatic for turfgrasses, so they need some time to recover after the process. For cool-season lawns, that means dethatching in late summer or early fall when they're less actively growing. For warm-season grasses, that means dethatching in late summer or early fall.

7

Lawns

A Cross-Section of Thatch

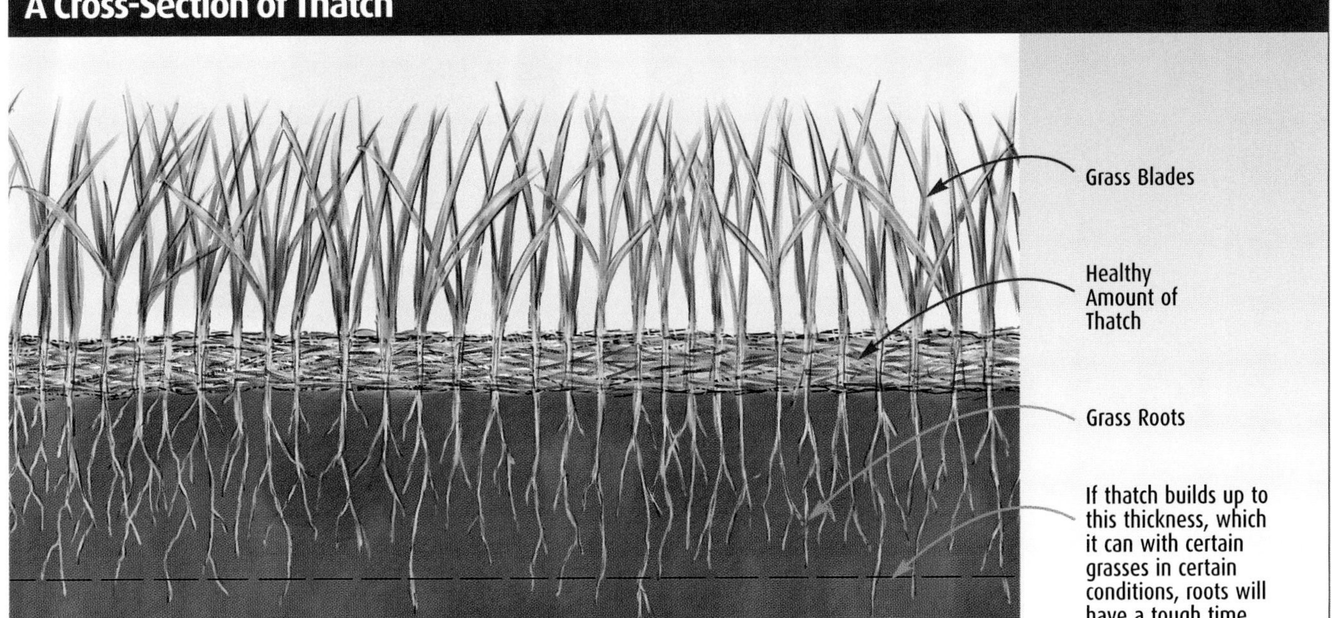

Every lawn should have a certain amount of thatch for optimum health, as shown above. However, if thatch gets too deep roots will have problem reaching the soil for nutrients and water.

Overseeding a Lawn

Overseeding is an excellent way to boost a browning or ailing lawn.

In warm regions, homeowners overseed their permanent warm-season grasses with a quick-growing cool-season grass that will thrive during the winter months while their warm-season grasses go dormant.

All across North America, homeowners with problem or thin lawns overseed to make their lawn lusher and more full. It's a good way, too, to introduce improved new grass varieties to an older lawn planted with a type of grass that is less than ideal.

Overseeding for a Thicker Lawn

Before overseeding, analyze the condition of your current lawn. If it has less than 50 percent good grass, overseeding may be less effective. Instead, your best choice would be to remove the existing turf and start over. However, if more than 50 percent of the lawn is strong, vigorous grass, overseeding is a good option.

Scattering seed over an existing lawn, called overseeding, can make sparse lawns thicker. It is also used to green up lawns in warmer climates.

Next, determine what caused the deterioration of your existing turf. Was it shade? Drought? Insects or disease? Starvation? Only after you've determined the cause can you choose an appropriate new grass for overseeding. For example, select a shade-tolerant seed blend for shady lawns or a blend containing insect-resistant perennial ryegrass if insect infestations have ruined your cool-season lawn. If in doubt, talk to your Home Depot garden center associate, or call a reputable lawn service.

When it's time to overseed, choose the optimum season: fall for cool-season turfgrasses and spring for warm-season grasses.

Then prepare the soil so seeds can make contact with it. If they simply rest on old turf, they may fail to germinate well. Prepare the old lawn by mowing it as short as possible. Rake up the clippings, then mow and rake again. This helps expose the soil.

Next, scratch the soil vigorously with a metal garden rake or garden claw to rough it up and create a good seedbed.

You'll need to sow seed at two to three times the amount recommended on the package. Then cover the seed with a ¼- to ½-inch layer of topsoil. Keep the soil constantly moist, which means watering daily or even two or three times a day, until the seed sprouts and is ½ inch high.

Allow the new seedlings to grow to the maximum cutting height, then mow. This helps thicken the lawn. You should take off one-third or less of their height.

Once the grasses are established, continue with your normal feeding, watering, and mowing regime; in time, the new grasses will take over the lawn.

Overseeding for Winter Color

In the South and West, warm-season grasses go dormant early in winter, leaving a brown lawn the rest of the season. Because cool-season grasses thrive in the temperatures of a mild winter, you can sow them over warm-season grasses to add some temporary color.

Choose a vigorous grass that germinates quickly in fall and dies back as the warm-season grass greens up in spring. If the cool-season grass grows too late in spring, it could compete with the warm-season species. Annual ryegrass and red fescue are two popular species fitting these criteria.

Sow seed when temperatures begin to drop, usually in October or November. If you start too early, still-active warm-season grasses crowd out the cool-season grass. Start too late and cold weather may inhibit germination.

The next spring, encourage the regrowth of the warm-season grass by closely mowing the cool-season cover. The latter will die out as the temperatures rise.

Lawn Moss And Grub Control

Moss Control

Moss is beautiful, and lawns of nothing but moss are slowly gaining favor in the United States (they're a long-held tradition in Japan).

Still, when moss is invading your turfgrass, it's a problem.

Hundreds of species of moss grow in North America. In lawns, they're hardly aggressive; the fact is they gradually fill in spots where grass already isn't growing.

When moss appears, it's usually in areas where drainage is poor or air circulation is restricted or there's too much shade or the soil lacks fertility.

First test the soil to check the pH. Mosses thrive in acidic soils with a pH of 5.0 or less. If your soil is acidic, dust it with lime each year to raise the pH.

To further control moss, first remove as much as is practical with a hand or power rake. If grass is scant in the area, improve drainage by spreading ½ inch of sand or 1 inch of compost onto the soil and tilling it in. Smooth with a rake, and roll or tamp flat. Reseed with a grass seed mix made specifically for shady areas.

Improve air circulation as much as possible by pruning nearby trees and shrubs.

When grubs attack you can often lift the dead grass like a carpet. If skunks, raccoons or birds have been tearing up the lawn it's often for grubs.

Moss is beautiful but prevents grass from growing thick and healthy. Minimize it with moss control products.

Also use a lawn product for eliminating moss. Apply shortly after the grass has been mowed and while the grass is wet from heavy dew or rain.

Grub Control

There are two types of grubs. One is the black turfgrass ataenius grub, which is the larva of the adult black shiny beetle. The other is the white grub, a catchall term for the larvae of Japanese beetles, June bugs, crane fly, rose chafers, Asiatic beetles, and others. Both types look similar, do similar damage, and are controlled the same way.

Grub damage is apparent in late spring or early fall as the larvae start to feed and patches of lawn start to turn brown. Test for grubs by lifting a 1-foot square of sod in late spring or early fall. If you see more than six of the plump, C-shape white creatures, which range in size from ¼- to ¾-inch long, it's time to use control methods.

Use a lawn grub control product as soon as damage is apparent. Water well after applying. The following spring, check for grubs again. A second application at that time may be needed.

Vegetables, Herbs, Fruits, and Other Garden Edibles

Chapter 8 Vegetables, Herbs, Fruits, And Other Garden Edibles

Food tastes better when you grow it yourself. Somehow you can taste in every bite the effort you put into planting, caring for, and harvesting.

In this chapter, you'll learn all about edibles and how, even in small yards, there's room for them. Grow some herbs in pots by the back door, a little cherry tree in the front yard, and a couple of rows of strawberries as edging plants in a flower bed.

Growing it yourself takes less time if you choose the lowest-maintenance plants. And edible gardening is an excellent activity to do with kids. It teaches them how food is grown and shows how wonderful a perfectly ripe strawberry, still warm from the sun, can taste. In fact, that's a pleasure we can all enjoy!

Edible Gardening

There's an old tradition of planting things you're going to eat back where they are out of sight—behind the garage, in the farthest reaches of the backyard, off to the side of the house.

But vegetables, herbs, fruits, and other edibles can be an attractive part of the landscape, be that in the back, the front, or the side. Especially when space in a garden is limited, it's useful to think outside the box and get creative in the way you plant your edibles.

Front-Yard Edibles

Vegetable gardens can move beyond the backyard. In many landscapes, the front yard is the only place with the full sun needed to grow tomatoes, strawberries, squashes, peppers, and other favorite edibles.

Concerns about what the neighbors might think prevents some homeowners from planting in the front. Consider telling your neighbors in advance what you're doing, with a pledge to keep the garden neat and attractive.

Another concern in planting front-yard edibles is that passersby might take the produce. You may lose the odd apple or handful of raspberries, but, all in all, you may well be pleased with how respectful of your plantings people are.

Many areas of a front yard lend themselves to a vegetable garden, herb bed, or planting of small fruit trees.

BUYER'S GUIDE

DOWNSIZED FRUIT

These days, many favorite fruits are available as miniature plants. Miniature fruit trees are different from the more commonly found dwarf fruit trees. Dwarf trees can reach 10 to 15 feet (standard fruit trees can reach 20 to 30 feet), but miniature trees seldom grow taller than 6 to 8 feet. And some miniature fruit trees, such as apples, pears, cherries, and peaches, are more like bushes, growing only 3 to 4 feet, yet producing full-size fruit.

Raised beds are a great idea for vegetable gardens. In areas with poor soil, they create an ideal planting bed. In cold regions, they thaw and drain the soil earlier, assuring more successful spring planting.

How about a vegetable garden or strawberry patch in the strip between the sidewalk and street? Or a vegetable garden running the length of the driveway? Or you could create a large bed or series of beds and plant your favorite vegetables laid out in interesting patterns.

Beautiful Vegetable Gardens

When well-designed and well-tended, a vegetable garden can be attractive enough to serve as the focal point of the landscape.

The key is providing good structure for the layout. Design your vegetable garden with a pleasing shape in mind. Some vegetable gardens consist of a series of raised beds, laid out in regular geometric shapes. Others are distinguished with brick paths. You might choose circles, a series of rectangles or squares, or a formal pattern much like those found on old European estates.

However, even a simple vegetable garden with straw paths can be a thing of beauty as long as it's planted with an eye for overall design.

Attractive Plants

Some cultivars are more attractive than others. Look for more unusual cultivars of your favorite vegetables that will add interest to your vegetable garden.

Some herbs, for example, have interesting variegation on the leaves or are bred to produce larger flowers than traditional types. With vegetables, look for interesting leaf color, such as red lettuces, purple cabbages, or chile peppers in a wild variety of colors.

Edibles in the Landscape

Edible plantings are often tucked behind buildings or in the back of the yard. But many edibles are so attractive that it's a shame to hide them.

Here are some of the most attractive edible plants, with suggestions on how to use them in beds, borders, and other places in your landscape:

Blueberries: These bushes have lovely green leaves and nice fall color. Highbush blueberries make a handsome hedge.

Corn: Need a quick screen? Plant corn, which reaches 7 feet by late summer. Be sure to plant at least eight to ten rows for best pollination and production.

Grapes: Plant grapes along a lattice fence or over an arbor or pergola. The leaves are large and lovely and turn a rich red in fall.

Herbs: Nearly any herb lends itself to planting among perennials and annuals. Try sage, especially the multicolored type, or one of the variegated thymes or deep purple basil. A number of other herbs, such as lavender, thyme, and oregano, like hot, dry conditions with excellent drainage—perfect for planting among stones and pavers.

Lettuces and Kales: Lettuces and other greens can be dark green, spring green, or deep red and purple; many have touches of cream or pink as well. Many have ruffled edges. Plant along paths or use as edging in the front of beds and borders.

Peppers and Eggplants: Pepper and eggplant foliage is green and attractive all growing season. The fruits are shiny and eye-catching, especially those of chile peppers.

Pole Beans: Plant pole beans up trellises, arbors, or even bamboo tepees in the middle or back of beds and borders. The vines have small, attractive flowers. The more unusual cultivars with purple or multicolored beans are a knockout.

Rhubarb: This plant features big, beautiful leaves and tall, attractive flower stalks. Use in the back of large flower beds and borders.

Strawberries: Leaves stay green all season, then turn deep russet in fall. Strawberries appeal as edging along paths or in the front of beds and borders.

Choosing Vegetables And Other Edibles

When shopping for seedlings of vegetables and other edibles, it's tempting to grab what looks good and interesting at the moment. But the result may be food that your family dislikes and little of what they do like.

Here's how to decide what to plant:

Is It Worth the Work?

For many vegetables, the answer is yes. Homegrown tomatoes, for example, are easy to grow, taste much better than the supermarket equivalent, and are cheaper to grow than to purchase in the store. On the other hand, growing cabbage when your family dislikes it, and when the result tastes much like what you'd buy at the grocery, may be a wasted effort.

When deciding which edibles to grow, consider the following:

- Do my family and I like it enough to care for and harvest it?
- Can I grow it more cheaply than what I can buy?
- Is the quality at the supermarket close to that from the garden? Or would I prefer to purchase it at a farmer's market?
- Do I have the space for it?
- Do I have enough sun for it?
- Is it prone to disease in my garden?

Lettuces are some of the most beautiful, productive vegetables around. Considering supermarket prices, it pays to grow a variety each year.

Cool-Season vs. Warm-Season Edibles

Some edibles grow and produce well in cooler weather, whereas others need hot weather. By planting both types, you'll ensure a steady supply of edibles throughout the growing season.

Cool-season annual vegetables include lettuce, spinach, kale, peas, onions, beets, radishes, Brussels sprouts, cabbage, broccoli, and cauliflower. All these need to be planted in early spring in cold-winter climates and in winter in warm-season climates. That's because if they are exposed too long to temperatures over 80 to 85°F (27 to 30°C), they will get bitter or stop producing. Plant seedlings of these cool-weather lovers about one month before your region's last frost date in spring. Plant seeds directly in the garden about six weeks before your last frost date in spring.

Warm-season annual vegetables need adequately warm soil temperatures to thrive. They include tomatoes, eggplant, peppers, melons, squash, pumpkins, and cucumbers. Start seeds for these indoors four to six weeks before your region's last frost date in spring, or plant seedlings outdoors after all danger of frost has passed. A handful of other seeds need very warm soil: Plant green beans and corn seeds directly in the soil two weeks after your region's last frost date in spring.

In late summer or early autumn, you can plant seeds or seedlings of cool-season annuals for fall harvest. Be sure to keep them well watered, and consider covering them with shade cloth to prevent them from getting too warm.

See "A Vegetable Garden Planting Timeline," on page 255, for a chronological listing of when to plant what.

A Starter Vegetable Garden

Many a beginning gardener in spring has tucked in a few plants here, a few seeds there, only to be overwhelmed by produce come September. Here's a list of what to plant in a 10- by 15-foot vegetable garden to provide enough for a family of four, depending on your preferences:

1 beefsteak-type tomato plant
1 cherry tomato plant
2 sauce-type tomato plants
1 eggplant plant
1 zucchini plant
1 hot pepper plant
2 green bell pepper plants
1 5-foot row mixed lettuces
1 5-foot row spinach
1 5-foot row carrots interplanted with radishes
1 melon plant
1 acorn or butternut squash plant
1 5-foot row bush green beans
1 10-foot row sweet or snap peas
1 parsley plant
1 basil plant

Big-Space and Small-Space Edibles

Some fruits and vegetables take up more space than others. They're delicious, to be sure. Make sure you have enough room to grow them. Conversely, some edibles lend themselves to growing in a planter or very large pot.

Big-Space Edibles

Artichokes: Plants grow 6 to 8 feet tall and can shade other plants unless positioned well. Position with care, away from other plantings.

Asparagus: A large patch, approximately 6 by 8 feet, is needed to provide enough asparagus at one time for a meal for four people.

Corn: You need several rows of corn for it to pollinate well, about enough to fill a 6- by 8-foot area.

Pumpkins: Plan on a 5-foot-square area for large pumpkins; 4-foot-square for smaller types.

Raspberries and Blackberries: A 5-foot-square patch will produce enough for a modest bowlful of berries every day or so during the fruiting period.

Strawberries: Plants are only a few inches tall and wide, but dozens of plants are needed to produce a significant amount of fruit. About 40 plants would produce enough fruit at once to serve a meal for four.

Watermelon: Plant a 4-foot-square for most types.

Small-Space Edibles

Carrots: A 2-foot row can produce enough for a few meals.

Dwarf or Bush-Type Cucumbers: One plant will be enough to keep you in salads for the summer.

Dwarf or Bush-Type Squash: One plant will be adequate to produce enough squash for several meals.

Eggplant: One plant will be enough to produce perhaps five to nine eggplants in late summer.

Herbs: Depending on the plant, you should have enough from one plant for dozens of dishes.

Lettuce and Spinach: Plant leaf-type lettuces and spinach in rows 6 to 8 inches wide and use the "cut and come again method" (see page 261) to make a 2-foot row produce enough lettuces for several meals.

Miniature Fruit Trees or Bushes: Depending on the type and size, you'll get dozens of fruits.

Patio-Type and Cherry Tomatoes: Depending on the type and size, you'll get dozens of large tomatoes; several dozen of the cherry types.

Pole Beans: Plant three to four vines at the base of a tepee or trellis for enough for several meals.

Radishes: Just a 1-foot row will produce dozens of radishes.

Sweet Bell Peppers: One plant will produce a dozen or so peppers.

Hot Chile Peppers: One plant will produce a couple of dozen peppers.

Planting Vegetables

Planting a vegetable garden is a great pleasure. It's a good feeling to fill a plot with tiny seedlings and seeds, all holding the promise of bounteous harvests within only a few weeks.

Selecting the Site

Nearly all vegetables and most other edibles need full sun—six hours of direct, unfiltered light a day.

Vegetables also need good drainage. A slope or raised beds is the ideal, especially in cold northern climates where poorly drained soil stays colder in spring, subtracting weeks of valuable growing season. Also, whenever possible, orient vegetable rows from north to south to assure the most even distribution of light and best production.

Improving the Soil

Fall is the ideal time to take measures to improve the soil for spring planting. Cover crops are excellent sources of nutrients. Sow seed of an annual legume or nitrogen-rich grass, one designated specifically as a cover crop, over the bare vegetable garden. The legume or grass grows for a few weeks before being killed by early winter weather. In spring, you can till the dead but nutrient-rich plants back into the soil.

GOOD IDEA!

SUCCESSION PLANTING

You can ensure a long supply of your favorite vegetables with succession planting—that is, planting another crop every two weeks or so.

Lettuces, spinach, and radishes are fast-maturing vegetables ideal for succession planting. You can get in two or three plantings before temperatures get too warm for these cool-season plants.

Corn is also popular for succession planting. Plant a crop every two weeks for a total of three or so crops to give yourself harvests of succulent sweet corn for several weeks.

Raised beds are excellent for vegetable gardens, assuring the rich soil they need and making weeding a snap.

Another way to improve vegetable-garden soil is to spread a 1- to 3-inch layer of finely chopped autumn leaves into the bare garden in fall. Dig or till into the soil. By spring, most of the leaves will have broken down, adding valuable organic matter and nutrients.

Preparing the Soil

Vegetables have a lot of growing and producing to do, often in only a few weeks, so it's important that they have top-quality rich, well-drained soil. Raised beds are often the easiest way to provide this. Raised beds also have the advantage of warming up earlier in spring in cool climates, allowing you to plant earlier and therefore harvest earlier.

Whether or not you have raised beds, working 3 to 4 inches of compost into the soil is a great substitute, as long as you can work it in a foot or so deep to ensure good drainage.

Seedlings vs. Seeds

Vegetables and herbs can be planted as seeds or seedlings, depending on the type and availability in your area. Some garden centers might have lettuce seedlings whereas others have only seeds, and still others might have both. You can plant the seedlings rather than the seeds for earlier harvests.

Keep in mind that the seeds of warm-season crops, such as tomatoes and peppers, must be started indoors, where

continued on page 256

A Vegetable Garden Planting Timeline

See page 252 for details on cool- and warm-season edibles. The suggestions below are for planting in cold-winter climates (Zone 7 and colder). In Zones 8 and warmer, follow the guidelines here in winter through early spring.

6–8 weeks before the last frost date in spring

- Plant seeds indoors of warm-season vegetables, such as tomatoes, peppers, and eggplant. (Otherwise, purchase established seedlings later.)
- Start fast-growing, cool-season veggies directly from seed in the soil as soon as it is well thawed and can easily be worked. These include radishes, carrots, lettuces, spinach, kale, beets, and peas.

4 weeks before the last frost date in spring

- Start fast-growing warm-season edibles indoors. (Otherwise, purchase as established seedlings later.) These include melons, squashes, pumpkins, and cucumbers.
- Plant seedlings of cool-season veggies outdoors. These include broccoli, cabbage, onion sets, and cauliflower.
- Plant herbs that like cool weather, including parsley and cilantro.
- Do another sowing of radishes, lettuces, spinach, and peas to ensure a longer supply.

After the last frost date in spring

- Plant seedlings outdoors of warm-season annuals (either purchased or started indoors), including tomatoes, peppers, and eggplant.
- Do a sowing of heat-tolerant lettuces and spinach to ensure an uninterrupted supply.
- Plant seedlings of fast-growing, warm-season veggies, including melons, squashes, pumpkins, and cucumber. However, they may do better if you wait another week or two for the soil to warm up more.

2 weeks after the last frost date in spring

- Plant seedlings of fast-growing, warm-season veggies, including melons, squashes, pumpkins, and cucumber.
- Plant seeds of green and pole beans directly in the soil.

6–8 weeks before your region's first frost date in fall:*

- Start fast-growing, cool-season veggies directly from seed. These include radishes, carrots, peas, lettuces, spinach, kale, beets, and peas. Keep well watered, and shade soil if necessary. You'll be able to harvest these in fall.

* Not applicable for mild-winter climates.

growing conditions are warm enough. The seeds of other crops, such as radishes and green beans, do better when planted directly in the garden. (See "A Vegetable Garden Planting Timeline," on page 255, for specifics.)

Starting plants indoors from seeds saves money. There are also more seeds to choose from in garden centers than there are established seedlings. Most garden centers carry only two or three types of melon seedlings, for example, whereas the seed rack might have a half dozen or more types.

Purchased seedlings are more convenient than seeds. Also, if you want only a plant or two, the cost difference between seeds and seedlings is nominal.

Some vegetables are sold in forms particular to them. In early spring, you'll see onion sets sold in stores. These are tiny starter onions that are planted stem side up in the soil. You'll also see what are called seed potatoes. These are small potatoes that, unlike supermarket potatoes, are untreated with any chemical to inhibit growth from the eyes, the parts of the potato from which stems start to grow.

Crop Rotation

Avoid planting the same kind of vegetable in the same spot year after year. That practice makes it more likely that diseases and pests will strike.

Many diseases occur when a certain type of plant, such as a tomato, picks up disease pathogens or insects living in the soil. If you grow a plant in the same place year after year, you create an ideal environment for those same tomato

WORK SMARTER

THINNING VEGETABLES

When you plant tiny seeds in a row, such as lettuce, carrots, and radishes, you'll end up with a too-thick stand of the plant. The tiny seedlings will crowd one another out.

To encourage healthy, full-size plants, pull or snip out the extra seedlings, a process called thinning. You can discard the extras or eat them. Tiny lettuce seedlings and radish tops are quite tasty.

Even a small container can be the host for a few heads of lettuce. Container plantings of vegetables are often as attractive as they are productive.

diseases and pests to build up, because they have their favorite host plant handy on which they can multiply. Lettuce planted there probably would have less of a problem, because it is susceptible to a different set of pests and diseases.

So it's a good idea to move plants around from year to year. Ideally, you should plant at least 50 feet from last year's planting spot and should avoid planting in the same spot more often than every three years. With small spaces, do the best you can to keep from planting in the same spot, and wait a year or two before replanting in the original spot.

Square-Foot Gardening

In recent years, the technique of planting in blocks rather than rows has become popular.

Instead of long rows in the garden, a plot is divided up into 3- by 3- or 4- by 4-foot or so squares. You might have one tomato plant per square or 16 bush bean plants or four pepper plants and so on. The blocks can be raised beds with narrow straw paths in between, or they can be separated by paths made of pieces of lumber, which suppress weeds and give you firm footing in all weather.

Proponents of this method think that the blocks make it easier to amend the soil and rotate plantings. Also, the plants in block plantings shade the soil more efficiently than row planting, keeping it cooler and moister as well—in effect serving as a living mulch.

A CLOSER LOOK

WHAT'S A HILL?

Sometimes on seed packets you'll see mention of planting on a hill. The reference is to a small mound perhaps two to three feet across and a few to several inches high.

These hills work as small-scale raised beds. They ensure that the soil is well-drained and well-warmed, critical for good germination of seeds such as cucumbers, squash, zucchini, beans, and melon.

Some vegetables, such as this purple cabbage, need to be planted in late winter or early spring while temperatures are cool. Others, such as tomatoes and peppers, should be planted after all danger of frost has passed.

Space-Saving Techniques

Few gardeners have as much space as they'd like for vegetables. So it's important for them to plant edibles as efficiently as possible.

Blocks Rather Than Rows

Traditional vegetable gardens have long rows, but the paths between all those rows take up a lot of space. In the past 25 years, more gardeners have experimented with planting in blocks perhaps 3 by 3 feet across, minimizing path space. This method is often called square-foot gardening. Paths between the blocks are usually a wood plank or some pavers.

Blocks also allow for efficient equidistant positioning of plants such as peppers and eggplants and blanket plantings of crops such as lettuces and greens.

See page 257 for more information on square-foot gardening.

Seek Out Smaller Cultivars

As more gardeners look for small-space solutions, plant breeders are responding with plants that are more compact. Traditional zucchini and cucumbers, for example, are sprawlers, taking up several square feet per plant. New varieties are now available that have a more compact mounding habit, producing abundant vegetables in an area perhaps only 2 feet by 2 feet.

Grow Vertically

Training vegetables to grow upward uses less ground space and keeps most vegetables healthier, because it improves air circulation around the plants.

Pole beans, tomatoes, and peas are naturals for training up trellises, but even many melons, zucchini, and summer squash do well when trained upward. Smaller melons and squash also do well when trained upward. Tie them as they grow with strips of soft, stretchy rag or cut pantyhose.

You can use a variety of supports for vertical gardening. If growing plants against a building, experiment with wire and string trellises stretched between large galvanized nails or eye hooks screwed into the siding. You can also make tepees with bamboo, strips of lumber, or long limbs saved from pruning projects.

Pole beans and peas, which twine naturally up supports, are ideal. But tomatoes also can be grown vertically, trained up a single 8-foot 2 × 2 pole, one end buried a couple of feet in the ground. (Be sure to pinch off all suckers and side shoots to keep the tomato from branching too much.)

Pole beans are a great space saver. In just a foot or two of square space, you can grow enough green beans for several meals.

Raised Beds

Tall raised beds, those 2 feet or higher, save space, because you can make use of the sides, allowing plants to trail downward.

The benefits of allowing plants to trail is the same as training them upward—air circulates around them better and prevents disease.

Also, with raised beds, you can fill the beds with top-quality soil and compost, allowing you to plant closer together than you might in a regular vegetable garden with less ideal soil. Another space- and labor-saving aspect of raised beds is that the rows between these permanent beds can stay weed free. In traditional beds, you need to hoe between the rows. But if you lay down newspaper topped with straw or grass clippings between raised beds, weeds will be kept from growing on the paths. Another advantage is that sprawling fruit such as melons and squash can grow on top of the material, staying high and dry and ripening better.

Paths between raised beds can also be made of crushed stone on top of landscape fabric. If you want to get fancy and permanent, you can also use brick or pavers.

Containers

Containers are good space utilizers, because you can use them wherever you have a little bit of sun—even if it's on a patio or the front step or a strip of pavement.

The larger the container, the better most vegetables will do and the more varieties you'll be able to grow (see Chapter 9 for more details on container gardening). Consider building a large planter 2 to 3 feet deep and as wide and perhaps 6 to 10 feet long. You'll be able to grow a surprising variety and quantity of patio-type tomatoes, peppers, cucumbers, lettuces, green beans, herbs, and other edibles.

GOOD IDEA!

WINDOW BOX EDIBLES

Even a tiny window box in a sunny location can be a productive source of food. In early spring, about six weeks before your last frost date, sow a mesclun or leaf lettuce mix in the window box. About the time you've harvested all the lettuces (use the cut-and-come-again method on page 261), dig up the plants and replant the window box with chile peppers, sweet peppers, or eggplant. Or plant a box with herbs such as basil, parsley, sage, rosemary, oregano, or tarragon. Thyme makes an attractive plant. You'll be able to harvest from the window box even after a light frost.

The window box can be positioned in the traditional spot under a window, or a few can be lined up like planters on a patio, along a driveway, or in any other sunny spot.

Interplanting Vegetables

Interplanting is planting together two or more complementary plants. One classic combination is radishes and carrots. Mix the seeds of the two together and sow in a row directly in the garden soil in early spring. The radishes send up foliage in only a few days, marking the spot where you planted the much slower-growing carrots, which take about two weeks to send up foliage. The radishes grow only a few inches deep and mature in about two weeks. As you harvest the radishes, you can thin the planting of the still-maturing carrots.

After the radish harvest, the carrots continue to grow and mature and are ready to harvest in about two more months, depending on the type.

Other good interplanting combinations include:

- Squash and corn. Plant the squash on the perimeter of the corn patch. It will weave in and out along the base of the corn, acting as a living mulch to suppress weeds, and its nutrient needs complement those of corn.
- Beans and corn. Plant a row of bush beans or other beans along the base of a row of corn or between patches of corn. Beans are a nitrogen fixer, adding that essential nutrient to the soil. Corn is a nitrogen-hungry plant and thrives on the nitrogen the beans add to the soil.
- Tomatoes, basil, and garlic. Plant sweet basil and garlic in between tomato plants. It's thought that the basil and garlic have properties that keep the tomatoes healthier. As a bonus, all three taste delicious together.
- Tomatoes and lettuces. When you plant tomatoes, plant small (1 foot by 1 foot or so) patches of lettuce in between. The lettuce makes good use of the space between the tomatoes until they get larger. And as the tomatoes get larger as the weather gets hotter, the tomatoes shade the cool-loving lettuces. Remove the lettuces after the first harvest or two to make room for the expanding tomatoes.

Caring for Vegetables

If you've chosen a good site for your vegetables and taken the time and money to improve the soil, tending your vegetables will be easy.

Watering Vegetables

Most vegetables need 1 inch of water a week, from rain or irrigation. Follow the basic rules for watering (page 172), watering only early in the morning and being sure to water the soil rather than the plants. Many vegetables are highly susceptible to the fungal diseases that can result from foliage that stays wet too long.

Mulch

Mulch is critical in a vegetable garden. Without it, weeds can take over, watering is less effective, and soilborne diseases plague plants. Newspaper topped with grass clippings or straw is an excellent mulch, especially under melons and cucumbers, where the mulch keeps the developing fruit off the ground and away from disease pathogens and insects.

Fertilizing

Most vegetables are hungry plants and need lots of nutrients. After all, they must grow and produce in only one season. Feed in moderation, however, especially with nitrogen, which fuels leafy green growth. Otherwise, your veggies may have lots of foliage but bear little produce.

The best vegetable fertilizer is compost. Work a 1- to 2-inch layer of it into the garden at planting time.

Alternatively, you can use a slow-release synthetic fertilizer at planting time for the all-around general feeding of plants. Additionally, a few nitrogen-hungry plants, such as tomatoes, corn, and lettuces, appreciate a snack of a fast-acting liquid fertilizer. Tomatoes should get this fertilizing about two weeks after planting. Corn should get this additional fertilizing when it's 1 foot high. Lettuce should get it right after the plants are thinned, about one to two weeks after sowing lettuce seed in the garden.

Caring for Tomatoes

Tomatoes are the most popular plant for vegetable gardens, but they're also one of the most prone to pests and diseases and problems associated with irregular watering. Here's how to keep them healthy:

- Plant tomatoes in full sun, where they will get at least six full hours of straight, unfiltered light.
- At planting time, mulch with several layers of wet newspaper, topped with about an inch of grass clippings or 3 inches of straw. This conserves moisture, suppresses weeds, and does an excellent job of preventing soilborne diseases from getting on the leaves and stems.
- Give plants ample support. Indeterminate tomatoes are the taller types and include most beefsteak tomatoes. Indeterminate tomatoes will grow to 6 feet-plus in a season compared to smaller determinate tomatoes, which are most sauce-type and cherry tomatoes.
- Provide 5- to 6-foot tomato cages made from fencing wire, or other ample support. These promote good air circulation.
- Pinch suckers. Many tomatoes send out little sprouts at the crotch where a smaller stem attaches to the main stem. Once a week, pinch off these suckers or each will grow into a whole new stem, creating a tangled mass with poor air circulation.

Harvesting Vegetables

The most rewarding part of vegetable gardening is harvesting, gathering the fruits—and vegetables—of your labor.

Here's how to harvest better and more easily:

- Harvest often. If you leave produce on some plants, it's a signal to the plants that they can stop producing. Harvest daily to encourage plants to produce more.
- Harvest when plants are dry. Handling vegetable foliage when it's wet can encourage the spread of disease. Green beans are especially vulnerable. Harvesting them when wet can spread rust.
- Harvest early. When in doubt, it's generally better to harvest slightly underripe vegetables, before they get tough or bitter.
- Harvest early in the day. Produce tends to be better hydrated and at the peak of its flavor in the early morning. Keep in a cool place (but not necessarily refrigerated, because overchilling most produce reduces flavor) until you're ready to eat it. For maximum flavor and freshness, eat it within a day or two.

It's important to harvest vegetables as soon as they're ripe. Leaving them on the plant causes the plant to slow or even cease production.

GOOD IDEA!

THE CUT AND COME AGAIN METHOD

Lettuces come in two types—leaf and head lettuce. Head lettuces, when allowed to get large, form heads, such as Iceberg, Romaine, and Bibb.

Leaf lettuces are sown in rows and not thinned as much as head lettuces. They are harvested when their leaves are 3–6 inches high. (Many head lettuces can also be grown as leaf lettuces by growing them closely together and harvesting when small.)

Some gardeners harvest leaf lettuces by pulling up the whole plant and trimming off the tiny roots. But you can get more harvests from the same planting by using a scissors or sharp knife to cut off the lettuces just an inch or so high. You'll get a tasty salad, and the plants will grow back two or three more times, giving you more lettuce faster with less work.

Is It Ready to Be Harvested?

Here's how to tell if your favorite vegetables are ready to be harvested:

Corn: Harvest after silk starts to turn brown. Most of the kernels should be nicely filled out. When a kernel is pierced with your fingernail, it should run milky, rather than clear, to show that the sugars have developed. Eat the same day.

Green beans: Should be smooth and still have their sheen with few bumps from developing seeds inside. Pick as soon as possible—smaller green beans are more tender. Eat within two to three days.

Green peas: Pods should be nicely filled out but still barely have their sheen. When a pod is opened, the peas should taste fresh, green, sweet, and not at all starchy. Eat the same day.

Lettuce: As soon as you can see it, you can eat it. Lettuce foliage is delicious even when tiny. However, when lettuce starts to get leggy, it's starting to bolt—that is, send up flower stalks. It is bitter at this point and should be pulled up and discarded.

Melons: Fruit is ripe when the stem pulls away from the fruit with only a slight tug. The blossom end—the end opposite the stem—may soften. The fruit develops a pleasant aroma.

Tomatoes: Tomatoes feel heavy for their size. They will be fully colored, though there may be green or other uneven coloration on the shoulders, at the top of the fruit. Fruits should pull away easily from the plant. They often taste even better if allowed to sit on a windowsill for another day. Refrigeration diminishes flavor.

Zucchini: As soon as the bright golden flower drops off the blossom end, harvest. Some gardeners, to ensure tenderness and flavor, even harvest with the flower on. Allowing the zucchini to get large makes them tough and bitter.

Choosing and Growing Herbs

Herbs give so much pleasure for so little work. They look good, often smell good, usually taste good—and they thrive with little fuss.

Choosing Herbs

Some herbs you'll want to plant simply for the pleasure of looking at them. Enjoy the pretty blue flowers of catmint, the low carpet of thyme, the splotches of gray, burgundy, and cream on a variegated sage.

Other herbs you'll grow to brush them with your hand and take in their intense fragrance: lemon balm, lemon verbena, lavender, and any of the many scented geraniums (some of which smell like chocolate, mint, pineapple, and rose).

Then there are all the herbs for cooking (see "Starter Herbs and How to Use Them" on page 263). Fresh herbs are less pungent than their dried counterparts but have a greener, fresher flavor. Add them during the last minute or two of cooking, or use them fresh, chopped, and scattered on top of dishes at the last minute before serving.

Designing with Herbs

Herb plants can be scattered around the garden, tucked in here and there wherever they'll be happy. Nearly all are attractive enough to be at home in flower beds. Plant only one if you want, but many herbs look good when massed.

Or grow herbs in a bed of their own. There's something satisfying about walking out to your herb garden while cooking and cutting whatever looks freshest and best.

An herb garden can be formal or informal. An informal bed might be a small patch near the kitchen, just big enough to grow your favorite herbs within easy reach.

In just a few feet of space, you can grow dozens of different types of herbs to enliven your cooking and beautify your garden.

Or your herb garden could be reminiscent of the formal gardens of European estates, with symmetrical, geometric designs and brick or crushed stone paths. Many have the pattern of the garden further outlined with rows of low or pruned plants as edging, such as boxwood or herbs that grow only 6 inches or so high and wide. These formal herb gardens are a thing of beauty and delightful to walk through.

Growing Herbs

However you choose to use herbs, your site will dictate what exactly you can grow.

Nearly all herbs prefer full sun, although some will do well in partial shade. Many favorite herbs hail from sunny spots around the Mediterranean: thyme, lavender, rosemary, oregano, and tarragon. Others thrive in more cool, moist conditions: chives, mint, lemon balm. Check the listings for each herb at right to make sure you put each in the correct spot.

Nearly all herbs need good drainage. That makes them excellent candidates for raised beds or planting on slopes. Many, such as chamomile and dill, love to reseed in nooks in pavement and stone as well as along crushed stone paths.

Starter Herbs and How to Use Them

With hundreds of herbs to choose from, it can be tough to decide which ones to grow. Here are some that are the most useful in the kitchen—a good reason to grow herbs.

Basil: The ultimate herb to use with tomatoes—good in tomato sauces, soups containing tomatoes, or snipped over fresh tomatoes with a drizzle of olive oil and vinegar. Perk up a green salad with a few chopped leaves added to the other greens.

Cilantro: Excellent in Mexican and Indian dishes. Also good with about anything containing lime, except desserts.

Mint: Good with fruit but also tasty in many Indian dishes. Add a few leaves to iced tea or brew a whole pot of mint tea. Essential for mint juleps.

Oregano: Good with roast or grilled chicken and red meats. Excellent in red sauces and other tomato-based dishes.

Parsley: More than just a garnish, it's good in pasta dishes or on top of casseroles or a bowl of soup to add a fresh green taste. Toss a handful into a green salad.

Rosemary: A classic with anything containing lamb. Also good with chicken. Stuff a chicken's cavity with rosemary before roasting.

Thyme: Use in about any dish, but it's especially good in tomato sauces, with roast or grilled chicken or red meats, and in most any soup.

Growing Herbs in Containers

Herbs are ideal for growing in pots. Many thrive in hot, dry conditions with excellent drainage—the kind of conditions often found in a clay pot. Also, many herbs tend to be vigorous to the point of being invasive, so it's good to have them contained.

Herbs that do best in pots in hot, dry conditions include thyme, oregano, rosemary, tarragon, and lavender. Herbs that do well in pots but prefer cooler, moister conditions include parsley, cilantro, and mint.

Choosing and Growing Fruits

Many fruits are as beautiful as they are productive. They flower, usually in spring, and those flowers turn into the fruits. As a bonus, many fruit trees also have an attractive shape and richly colored fall foliage.

For trees such as apple, plum, cherry, and almond, the flowers are so stunning that you could grow the trees for those alone. It's almost a bonus that the tree also produces fruit.

Other fruit-bearing plants are also quite attractive. Blueberry bushes are easy to grow and look good enough in the landscape that whole hedges of highbush blueberries are often grown. Strawberries (see "Growing Strawberries," page 265) are small, compact, attractive plants. Grapes are lovely vines with fresh green foliage in spring and summer and excellent autumn color as well.

Where to Grow Fruits

Most fruits need full sun, but a handful, such as gooseberries, elderberries, alpine strawberries, and raspberries, will grow and produce well in light shade.

Most fruits need rich soil with ample moisture. Most prefer neutral soil. Blueberries are the exception; they need acid soil, with a pH of about 4.5.

Put fruit trees and small fruits anywhere in your garden. Some homeowners think fruit trees need to be off by themselves, but they work well in both front yards and backyards as decorative trees. Their smaller size and beautiful flowers lend themselves nicely to ornamental gardening. However, be sure to consider where fruit will fall, such as on a driveway or walk, when siting them.

Choosing a Type of Fruit

When choosing a fruit tree or other fruit-bearing plant, it pays to do a little research and find the best cultivars for your region and your garden. Seek out the most disease-resistant cultivars. Fruit-producing plants are susceptible to a host of fruit-mangling and -damaging diseases, so it's important to choose those that need the least spraying and care.

Also make sure that whatever fruit you choose is self-pollinating or that you can plant more than one tree. Many apple trees, for example, need a second tree so the two can cross-pollinate in order to produce fruit. Grow only one and it may be healthy and flower, but it will fail to produce fruit.

Check the cold-hardiness of the fruit tree. Many can be damaged by a late frost or cold temperatures.

If you live in a warm-winter region, check the fruit's chilling requirement—the number of hours of temperatures below 45°F (8°C) that a plant needs for a period of dormancy.

If late frosts are a concern, avoid planting trees in low-lying areas where cold air may settle. Instead, plant them in higher spots where cold air will flow freely past them.

Dwarf and Miniature Fruit Trees

Gone are the days when every household had a 30-foot fruit tree in the backyard to supply the kitchen with mountains of produce for pies and jams.

These days, gardeners usually choose semidwarf, dwarf, or even miniature trees to avoid the onslaught of fruit that a large tree can produce. Smaller trees have other advantages too. They start producing fruit earlier, in only three to four years rather than the six to eight years it takes a standard tree. And because the tree is smaller, it's easier to spot and control disease problems earlier.

A dwarf tree is created by grafting the species with the desired fruit onto a rootstock that will control size. It results in a tree that's as much as one-quarter the parent tree's height. A standard apple tree may be 30 to 35 feet. A dwarf may be only 8 to 10. A semidwarf, also created through grafting, reaches perhaps half the parent tree's height. So a semidwarf of that apple tree would reach only 10 to 15 feet.

Miniature trees are quite small, about the size of a medium shrub, and can be grown in large containers or whiskey barrel halves. The fruit is full-size.

Even in a pot, this orange tree will produce fruit. In cold climates, it should be brought indoors when temperatures threaten to dip below freezing.

Controlling Fruit Pests and Diseases

Pests and diseases can be a real problem with fruits, ruining what would otherwise be a delicious harvest. Here's how to avoid pest and disease problems:

- Choose disease- and pest-resistant cultivars. Apple cultivars such as 'Liberty' and 'Freedom' are resistant to many common apple problems and seldom need spraying.
- Keep up with pruning. Good pruning lets in air and light, assuring healthier plants and better fruiting.
- In early spring, before the plants break dormancy, spray fruit trees with horticultural oil. It's an organic measure and prevents a host of pest problems.
- If birds stealing fruit are a problem, toss a bird net over the fruit right before it ripens.
- At harvest time, remove any excess fruits that fall to the ground. Allowing them to rot where they fall attracts problem pests and encourages diseases that might infect the rest of the tree.

How Easy Is It to Grow?

The following is a list of commonly grown fruits according to how easy or difficult they are to grow, assuming they are well-suited to your climate:

Easy

Apricots
Avocados
Blueberries
Cherries
Citrus
Fall-bearing raspberries
Figs
Oranges
Peaches
Plums

Moderately Easy

Apples
Pears
Summer-bearing raspberries

High Care

Almond
Everbearing strawberries
Grapes

Growing Strawberries

Strawberries are immensely rewarding and easy plants to grow in your garden. They require little space and are pretty enough to plant along paths, among flowers, or in any other sunny spot with good drainage and moderately rich soil. Strawberries bloom with tiny white flowers in early spring; their leaves turn rich russet and gold in fall.

Choose from two main types: June-bearing (a heavy harvest in June) or everbearing (a light harvest from June through September). Also consider the less-common alpine strawberry, which produces tiny, intensely flavored fruits in spring and fall.

Strawberries need at least six hours of full sun, though alpine types will tolerate light shade. Strawberries thrive in rich, well-drained soil, so consider raised beds filled with compost. In winter in cold regions, protect the plants with a thick layer of straw. These cool-weather lovers also like a thick mulch of straw (hence the name) in summer.

Supermarket strawberries with their pithy white centers can't beat homegrown strawberries, which are immensely flavorful all the way through.

Pruning Fruit Trees

If you've ever seen a fruit tree growing untended on an old lot or near an abandoned house, you'll know what happens if pruning is left undone.

The tree grows thick and unruly, almost a bramble of thin, weedy-looking sucker branches and water sprouts growing from the main branches and base of the tree. Damaged or broken branches, left on the tree, have invited pest and disease problems. Fruits are small and may be sparse. They usually ripen poorly.

Good pruning, on the other hand, creates a tree that has a selected number of strong branches, free of weedy suckers, that are open to sunlight, promoting good fruit production and ripening as well as easy picking. Trees are healthier, too, and are attractive enough to hold their own visually in the landscape.

The age of a tree will affect the scope and importance of your pruning. When planting a new tree, decide on your pruning style. Remove the leader, if necessary. Then remove all but three or four well-spaced branches that spread horizontally around the central leader. These will be the main framework of the tree for years to come.

During the tree's first growing season in your garden, cut off little branches that begin to grow along the trunk, a process you'll need to continue throughout the first years of the tree's life and perhaps permanently.

When the tree is three to four years old, you'll need to continue to prune it with considerable thought, because the cuts you make now will dictate its growth pattern for decades to come. The pruning may take only 10 minutes, but it will be critical.

At the other end of the spectrum is a mature (say 20 years old) tree for which the growth pattern is determined. How you prune is less critical. However, because the tree is large, pruning is more time-consuming and could easily take a couple of hours each spring.

How to Prune a Fruit Tree

Different fruit trees require different pruning methods.

Central Leader Method

Best for apple and pear trees. A tall, central branch dominates, so following the natural growing pattern is easy. This method can also be used for cherry and plum trees.

Open Center Method

Apricot, peach, and nectarine trees do well with this method; it helps them produce well and makes the fruit easier to pick. The branches go out and up as though following the sides of a bowl, allowing sunlight into the center and encouraging maximum production and ripening. Also good with almond, hazelnut, cherry, and plum trees.

Modified Leader Method

A cross between the other two methods. Fairly easy to achieve because it accommodates a tree's natural tendency to grow straight up, but also trains branches out and up with an open center to keep picking easier and allowing in sunlight.

Fruit trees produce best in the parts of the tree that receive good light. This cherry tree is pruned in such a way that sunlight reaches even the center, making for easier picking and better production.

WORK SMARTER

FRUIT TREE PRUNING BASICS

As you work, keep the ultimate overall shape of the tree in mind. Step back after each major cut to consider your work. Some gardeners like to prune a large tree in two or three separate sessions over a couple of days, so they have time to look at the tree and think about where they are going to make their next cuts.

1. Cut out any dead, damaged, crossed, or rubbing branches before making other cuts.

2. Cut out any suckers or water sprouts (see page 190 for an illustration of these).

3. Cut out any limbs that are growing too low or are heavily shaded by other limbs.

4. Finally, cut branches that will help you achieve the final shape and growth pattern you desire.

Pruning Pointers

- Have the right tools. Good loppers and a good pruning saw (see page 189) will make the job easy with cleaner cuts and less strain on you. If you have large, mature trees, consider investing in a small chain saw to speed the work.
- Prune in late winter or very early spring, before growth starts for the season.
- Keep up with suckers and water sprouts. On some trees, especially older varieties of apples and plums, these are so vigorous that you'll have to trim them out three or four times a growing season. Do it often, however, and the job will take only a few minutes each time, unless the tree is very large.
- Sterilize tools between trees by rubbing cutting parts with a rag dipped in rubbing alcohol or one part bleach to four parts water.
- It's tempting to hire out the pruning of fruit trees. However, do so with caution. Few lawn or landscape services have anyone knowledgeable about various fruit trees and the best way to prune them. Ask what training or background the person has in pruning fruit trees, or your trees may be mangled by an overconfident, overzealous worker.

Container Gardening

Gardening in containers is an exercise in instant gratification. Get a pot, buy some plants and a little potting soil, and there you have it—a pretty container garden. For that reason, most gardens have at least a few containers, usually filled with long-blooming annuals. In this chapter, you'll learn how to design stunning

Chapter 9 Container Gardening

container gardens, large and small, in a variety of containers with a variety of plants.

You'll also learn insider tips on how to plant your containers for minimal maintenance but good looks. And you'll get valuable tips for designing and growing containers in your climate, be it arid, sunny Southern California or chilly northern Maine.

Designing With Containers

What could be easier than container gardening? Choose a pot, select some plants, and position the result wherever you want greenery, color, and fragrance. Here's how to get the best effect for your investment of time and money:

Choosing a Container

There are nearly as many types of containers as there are plants to put in them. If it will hold soil and has drainage, it can successfully grow plants.

Innovative gardeners plant in everything from grand urns to old sneakers. Other unusual containers include watering cans, metal buckets, bushel baskets, wicker baskets (line them with sphagnum peat moss first), wheelbarrows, horse troughs, old ceramic bowls and pitchers, cereal bowls, and teacups.

The container's material affects its function. Clay pots are beautiful but are porous and tend to dry out. Plastic, resin, and fiberglass pots are inexpensive, hold moisture well, and are lightweight, but they may not be as attractive as other containers. Wooden containers, including whiskey barrels and window boxes, hold moisture well but are prone to rotting. Metal containers have few drawbacks other than weight and price.

Container Size and Shape

The size of the container also plays a role. Large containers can be heavy and expensive but retain moisture well and make a strong impact. Small containers are less expensive but dry out quickly. Also, left on a front step, they could be snatched by unethical admirers.

When in doubt, use large containers. Many gardeners scatter a number of smaller containers around instead of using only a few large ones to create a more dramatic effect.

The shape of the container also influences what plants will go into it and how it will be used. Low, shallow containers are best for low, trailing plants. Tall containers look good with tall plants that capitalize on the container's generous size.

Where to Put a Container

You need to be sure that the container is placed so the plants get the amount of sun or shade they need. If you put it on a porch or under an eave or other shelter, you'll need to

DESIGN TIP

POTS AS FILLERS

Each spring, plant a large pot or two with colorful annuals such as impatiens, marigolds, periwinkle, begonias, and other long, intense bloomers. If a bare or problem spot appears in one of your flower beds, camouflage the problem by setting the pot right in the bed for instant color and an instant solution.

Containers can go about anywhere, including the middle of a planting bed, to add color and structure.

provide more watering than might be needed if the pot was in the open.

Otherwise, there are seemingly endless ways to position containers around your yard. Here are ideas to get you started:

- Make a garden of just containers. Group three or more containers that have like characteristics (such as all clay or all wood). Or fill different containers with plants that fit together into a theme, such as all herbs or all red blooms.
- Flank a door or a path. Position two large containers on either side of a front or back door—or even a garage door. Or set them on either side of an entry or a path.
- Line steps. Set pots alongside a railing, or flanking outdoor steps.
- Hang or mount containers. Baskets of plants look good hanging from a porch or flanking a doorway. Mount them along a tall, bare fence to break up the expanse. (Mount them securely; they'll be heavy when wet.) Also check out your garden center for rings and other devices that allow regular flower pots to hang on walls and fences.
- Create a focal point in a border. If you have a flower bed that lacks interest, position a large (18 inches or wider) pot in it and plant it with colorful annuals or a striking shrub.

High, low, and all around—with containers you can have color and greenery at all levels.

TOOL TIP

MASONRY BITS

A simple masonry bit can turn ceramic, clay, or pottery containers without holes into pots with good drainage. Simply drill a hole or two with the bit. (Wear safety glasses.) Some containers may crack even with a masonry bit, so this technique is best saved for a pot or container you're willing to risk losing.

Choosing Plants For Containers

Nearly any plant can be grown in a container, but some plants perform better than others.

Annual flowers are favorites because they bloom quickly and for months at a time. However, long-blooming perennials also make good choices for containers, as do small shrubs and even trees.

Many gardeners think they have to mix plants in containers, but some of the most striking plantings are of just one type.

A good container plant should have the following characteristics:

- Foliage that is attractive for months at a time
- Blooms that last a long time, at least several weeks
- Roots that are OK with being crowded
- Form that makes it suitable for a container, such as a graceful trailing habit or handsome upright habit that's good for the back or center of a planting.
- Moderate drought tolerance. It can be tough to keep container plantings moist all the time. Plants that die or are permanently damaged by a little dryness can be risky propositions for containers.

Solo Plants in Pots

A single type of plant in a pot can be striking, making a strong impact as long as the plant is full and healthy. Fill containers with enough plants for a lush look. With annuals, that means planting about 50 percent closer than what the plant label recommends.

So if you're planting a 14-inch-diameter pot with marigolds, for example, first choose marigolds that grow 12 inches or taller, so they'll be in scale with the pot. If the label recommends planting them 8 to 10 inches apart, plant them 4 or 5 inches apart.

Underplanting

When planting a slender tree or shrub or a standard (lollipop-shape) plant in a large pot, add even more color by underplanting. Proceed with planting the larger plant as you normally would. But instead of leaving bare soil, underplant with a small, low-growing or trailing plant, such as ivy, sweet alyssum, lobelia, or impatiens.

DESIGN TIP

A SUMMER VACATION FOR YOUR HOUSEPLANTS

As with their owners, houseplants enjoy a break from their routine during the summer. Letting them spend a few months outdoors rejuvenates them.

Except in arid climates, an easy way to give your houseplants a summer vacation is to use them outside in containers—in the pot they were in indoors or in a new one just for the summer. (Set the original pot inside a new one and fill in with potting soil to camouflage.) If the houseplant is small, tuck it—pot and all—into a larger container planting with annuals or perennials. Either way, place it in light to full shade, because outdoor sun is too intense for most houseplants. In fall, remove the houseplant, with its pot still intact, clean it up, and bring it back indoors.

A cracked birdbath, no longer suitable for filling with water, can make a great container for annual flowers.

Small trees are great choices for pots. Keep them year-round in warm climates; treat them like annuals in cold climates.

A CLOSER LOOK

SPRING BULBS IN POTS

Spring bulbs, such as daffodils and tulips, make a gorgeous show in pots, planters, window boxes, and other containers.

In temperate regions with moderately cold winters (most of Zone 7, including the Pacific Northwest and parts of the South), plant bulbs directly in large pots in fall.

In warm climates (warmer parts of Zones 8 to 11), plant prechilled bulbs (or chill your own; see page 162) in late autumn or early winter.

In very cold climates (Zones 4 and 5), potted bulbs will freeze solid over the winter. If you want potted spring bulbs in these climates, plant preforced bulbs in containers in early spring.

GOOD IDEA!

HANGING BASKET PLANTS USED CREATIVELY

Hard to wait for little plants to grow and fill a large pot?

For instant color, get a hanging basket with a fully mature plant with lots of flowers. Remove the hangers and gently knock the plant out of the basket. Loosen the matted roots, if any, with your fingers. Then plant in a large pot filled partially with potting soil.

Tuck in more potting soil around the edges, carefully lifting the cascading stems of the plant and using your fingers to push the soil around the roots. Water well once, then check the soil level again. Add more potting soil as needed to fill any gaps.

Combining Plants in Pots

If you choose to combine plants in pots, follow this formula: Plant at least three different plants—one tall and spiky, one low and trailing, and one of medium height as a filler.

Follow a color scheme with your pots, just as you would when decorating a room in your home or when planting an entire bed of flowers. Consider how the flowers will look together when everything is in bloom. You may wish to avoid hot pink blooming alongside bright red.

Keep in mind the plant's foliage too. Foliage comes in different shades of green and has different textures and leaf sizes and shapes. For greatest interest, mix silvery greens with deep greens, fuzzy-leaved plants with shiny-leaved plants, and large leaves with tiny, feathery leaves.

It's also important to combine plants with like growing needs. Grow full-sun plants in one container and shade-tolerant plants in another.

Good Plants for Containers

Common Name	Botanical Name
Tall, Spiky Plants	
Bells of Ireland	*Moluccella laevis*
Canna	*Canna* hybrids
Celosia	*Celosia* spp.
Flax, New Zealand	*Phormium* spp.
Salvia, annual blue	*Salvia farinacea*
Snapdragon	*Antirrhinum majus*
Spider flower	*Cleome hassleriana*
Tobacco, flowering	*Nicotiana* spp.
Midheight Filler Plants	
Ageratum	*Ageratum houstonianum*
Begonia, various	*Begonia* spp.
Dusty miller	*Senecio cineraria*
Flowering cabbage, kale	*Brassica oleracea*
Geranium, upright types	*Pelargonium* spp.
Globe amaranth	*Gomphrena globosa*
Grasses	Various
Heliotrope	*Heliotropium arborescens*
Impatiens	*Impatiens* spp.
Marigold	*Tagetes* spp.
Pansy	*Viola* spp.
Tuberous begonia	*Begonia* ×*tuberhybrida*
Vinca, annual	*Catharanthus roseus*
Wishbone flower	*Torenia fournieri*
Zinnia	*Zinnia* spp.
Low, Trailing Plants	
Dahlberg daisy	*Thymophylla tenuiloba*
Lobelia, edging	*Lobelia erinus*
Fan flower	*Scaevola aemula*
Fuchsia	*Fuchsia* spp.
Geranium, ivy type	*Pelargonium* spp.
Ivy	Various
Lantana	*Lantana camara*
Licorice plant	*Helichrysum petiolare*
Nasturtium	*Tropaeolum majus*
Petunia	*Petunia* spp.
Swan River daisy	*Brachycome iberidifolia*
Sweet alyssum	*Lobularia maritima*
Sweet pea	*Lathyrus odoratus*
Sweet potato vine	*Ipomoea batatas*
Verbena, trailing forms	*Verbena* spp.

Common Name	Botanical Name
Drought-Tolerant Container Plants	
Agapanthus	*Agapanthus* spp.
Artemisia	*Artemisia* spp.
Cactus	Various
Dusty miller	*Senecio cineraria*
Geranium, annual	*Pelargonium* spp.
Flax, New Zealand	*Phormium* spp.
Hens and chicks	*Sempervivum* spp.
Kalanchoe	*Kalanchoe*
Lantana	*Lantana* spp.
Licorice plant	*Helichrysum petiolare*
Moss rose	*Portulaca* spp.
Salvia, annual blue	*Salvia farinacea*
Sedum, various	*Sedum* spp.
Thyme	*Thymus* spp.
Verbena	especially *Verbena* 'Imagination'
Yucca	*Yucca filamentos*

When combining plants in a container, include those with varied growth habits. Here, filler plants bridge the spaces between trailing plants and upright plants.

Container Planting Basics

Planting a container is easy. You'll have good results if you follow these tips:

- Start with high-quality potting soil—purchased or made by you. Avoid regular garden soil. It's too heavy and lacks the necessary combination of richness and good drainage.
- Making your own potting soil is economical. And if you're an experienced gardener, you can create the blend that's perfect for your plants and your climate. A good starter mix is six parts compost, sifted through a wire screen, to one part perlite and one part sphagnum peat moss.
- Make sure your pots are clean. It's best to wash them with warm, soapy water and rinse them thoroughly before planting. If small pots have held diseased plants, disinfect them by soaking in 1 gallon hot water with about ¼ cup chlorine bleach added.
- When using a clay pot for the first time, soak it in a bucket of water for about 15 minutes. Otherwise, the dry clay will wick moisture from the potting soil.
- If the container is very large, put in an inverted plastic pot to minimize the amount of soil you need to fill it and to keep the pot lighter so you can move it around. (See "How to Repot Container Plants," below.)
- If you want to make a large pot heavier to deter thieves, put a few bricks or large stones at the bottom.
- Allow at least ½ to 1 inch below the top of a container for water to puddle when watering.
- When you're done planting, water the container thoroughly and put it in a shady or sheltered place for a day or two to avoid stressing the plants.
- Keep the plants especially well watered for the next 10 days or so until they're thoroughly established.

A CLOSER LOOK

PERFECT POTTING SOIL

For the healthiest, most vigorous container plantings, choose your potting soil carefully. Avoid using soil straight out of the yard—it can be too heavy or too light for pots, or drain poorly. Instead, use purchased potting soil. Commercial mixes vary greatly, so read the label carefully. Some are billed as soilless and are a combination of soil amendments (see page 138). Others have fertilizers and moisture-retaining polymer crystals worked in. Or make your own potting soil (see directions at left).

Avoid selecting potting soils based on weight only; some contain a lot of heavy sand, and some lightweight potting mixes have excellent ingredients. If in doubt, ask your garden center associate about which mix is best.

WORK SMARTER

DOUBLE POTTING

Keep plants moister longer with double potting—that is, setting the pot inside a larger one. Fill around the smaller pot with soil, moss, or mulch, insulating the smaller pot from heat and cold, and keeping it cooler and moister longer. Double potting is especially useful when you want to use a porous clay outer pot or if you plan to eventually remove the plant from the larger container. It can also increase humidity around the plant.

PROJECT DETAILS

SKILLS: Potting plants
PROJECT: Repotting root-bound permanent plantings from a smaller pot to a larger one

TIME TO COMPLETE

EXPERIENCED: 30 minutes
HANDY: 1 hour
NOVICE: 1 hour

STUFF YOU'LL NEED

TOOLS: Trowel, hose or watering can
MATERIALS: New pot, potting soil

How to Repot Container Plants

In warm climates where containers can be left outside year-round, plants grow large enough to require repotting into a larger pot, or division and repotting into the original pot. They also often need to have the soil replenished with fresh potting soil.

1 Plants are rootbound when the lower roots curl around the bottom of the pot or the roots start coming out of the top of the pot. Knock the plant out of the pot to check as needed.

2 Loosen the roots and repot in a pot 1 to 2 inches wider than the original pot. Use top-quality potting soil.

3 Fill with soil, being sure to leave ½ to 1 inch of space at the top for water to collect. Water well.

Container Planting Basics *continued*

PROJECT DETAILS

SKILLS: Potting
PROJECT: Planting a large container to use outdoors

TIME TO COMPLETE

EXPERIENCED: ½ hour
HANDY: 1 hour
NOVICE: 1 hour

STUFF YOU'LL NEED

TOOLS: Watering can/hose
MATERIALS: Pot, material to cover drainage hole, plastic pot (optional), top-quality potting soil, assorted plants, slow-release fertilizer

How to Pot Container Plants

1 Cover the hole at the bottom of the pot to prevent soil from washing out of it. If the container will stay outdoors permanently, as in mild-winter climates, use a clay shard or piece of screen. In climates where the pot will be out only for a few mild-weather months, a folded piece of newspaper will do.

2 Knock plants from their original pots and loosen the roots. Position the plants in the new pot and fill it with soil made specifically for potting. Be sure to leave ½ to 1 inch of room at the top for water to pool.

GOOD IDEA!

SAVING SOIL

Here's a tip: If the pot is large, save soil and lighten the load by inverting a plastic pot at the bottom.

PROJECT DETAILS

SKILLS: Basic planting skills
PROJECT: Lining a wire basket with sphagnum peat moss, and planting it

TIME TO COMPLETE

EXPERIENCED: ½ hour
HANDY: 1 hour
NOVICE: 1 hour

STUFF YOU'LL NEED

TOOLS: Shears, trowel, watering can
MATERIALS: A wire basket, sphagnum peat moss or preformed liner for lining basket, potting, soil, plants

How to Plant a Wire Basket

1 Line the basket with the moss. Some mosses come preshaped into a liner. Others require you to pat the moss into shape. Use shears to cut planting holes along the side of the basket.

2 Partly fill the basket with potting soil, using an empty flower pot to balance the basket. Gently insert the plants through the holes, adding more potting soil on top of them.

3 Fill with the remaining plants, water well, and hang.

How to Rotate Container Plantings

Containers are invaluable for their ability to add color and greenery to important spots, such as window boxes on the front of the house, near the front door, or near other frequently used entries.

In cold-winter climates, many gardeners fill their containers only during the late spring and summer months, when warm-season annuals such as marigolds and impatiens abound.

Even in warm-winter climates, where plantings can thrive in containers all season long, some gardeners leave their containers empty—a waste of space and opportunity.

Instead, get more pleasure from your containers and brighten key areas of your landscape by filling containers with plants all year-round.

The key is changing the plantings throughout the year. Plant and replant your window boxes, planters, and pots in winter, spring, summer, and fall for a look that reflects the season.

DESIGN TIP

CONTAINER ACCENTS FROM THE GARDEN

Not all the elements in your containers and window boxes need to be live and growing.

In cold regions of the country, where winter makes growing anything outdoors impossible, consider cutting boughs of evergreens such as pine, holly, and spruce and tucking them into the soil of various containers.

In early spring, take cuttings of blossoming branches of forsythia, pussy willow, and other flowering plants and add them into containers for color and interest.

In fall, after frost fells annuals, cut branches of colorful autumn trees and shrubs and poke them into the container's soil. Or cut the dried seed heads and dried flower heads of favorite perennials, such as tall sedums, ornamental grasses, false indigo, rose hips, and others. You can even include pumpkins, gourds, pinecones, and other accents in your containers.

How to Change Plantings with the Season

1 In spring, about a month before your region's last frost date, plant the container with cool-season annuals that can withstand frost, such as pansies and violas, lobelia, and snapdragons. You can even sink whole pots of forced spring-blooming bulbs into the soil. Fertilize with a slow-release fertilizer.

2 In late spring or early summer, after all danger of frost has passed, remove the spring flowers, which by now will probably be leggy and tired looking. Replace with heat-loving annuals such as marigolds, impatiens, petunias, vinca, and ageratum. Add more potting soil as needed. Fertilize with a slow-release fertilizer.

3 In fall, when the warm-season flowers have been nipped by frost, remove them and replace with cold-loving flowering cabbages or kale, mums, or a new planting of pansies. Add more potting soil as needed. Pumpkins or gourds make a handsome accent.

PROJECT DETAILS

SKILLS: Planting

PROJECT: Removing and adding plants every few months to keep container plantings looking great

TIME TO COMPLETE

EXPERIENCED: ½ hour

HANDY: 1 hour

NOVICE: 1 hour

STUFF YOU'LL NEED

TOOLS: Trowel, bucket to collect dead plants, extra soil

MATERIALS: Potting soil, new plants , granular slow-release fertilizer

Watering Container Plantings

WORK SMARTER

VACATION CARE FOR CONTAINERS

Going away for a long weekend or on a business trip? Avoid the problem of finding someone to water your plants by setting the plants in a pan with a few inches of water in it. The water will wick up through the drainage hole (and, if you're using clay pots, through the walls of the pot). Set large pots in a plastic storage box filled with several inches of water.

This foot soak will keep most plants moist for up to four days. It even works with hanging pots. Just take down the pot and set it in the water. The water will be drawn up through the drainage holes.

Keeping containers well watered is essential. Many gardeners lose plants because they fail to keep up with a container's watering needs.

Pots dry out quickly, often in a matter of hours if they're small. Check a container's soil daily, poking your finger down into the soil a half inch or so to see how dry it is. In hot, windy weather, you may need to water twice a day. Completely soak the pot every time you water.

Container plants also need plenty of nutrients, because each watering flushes them out. Even if you worked in a fertilizer at planting time, most container plants benefit from snacks throughout the growing season. Consider adding a water-soluble fertilizer to your watering can every two to four weeks (for more information on fertilizing container plantings, see page 280).

If you're having problems keeping a container well watered, you can try a few things. If it's on the west or south side of a house or other building, try moving it to the east side where the sun is less direct. You can even move it to the north side of the house. If it's a plant that needs partial to full sun, position it at least a few feet away from the house to keep it from being in too much shade.

Another strategy is to repot the plant. Put it in a larger pot, which will stay moister longer. Or double-pot it (see page 275), putting its existing pot inside a larger one.

If you constantly have problems keeping plants watered in one particular spot or container, such as a window box on the west side of your house or a clay strawberry pot, next time be sure to plant with drought-tolerant plants suited to containers (see page 274).

Consistent, ample watering is a must for large, lush plantings in containers. In hot weather, this pot needs thorough watering once and sometimes even twice a day.

Setting Up Drip Irrigation for Containers

If you live in an arid climate or have extensive container plantings, you'll want to consider installing a drip irrigation system designed specifically for containers. It's surprisingly easy even for beginners. Start by visiting your garden center and checking out the supplies for ideas. Or set up a system like the one shown here. (See page 174 for more information on drip irrigation systems for the larger landscape.)

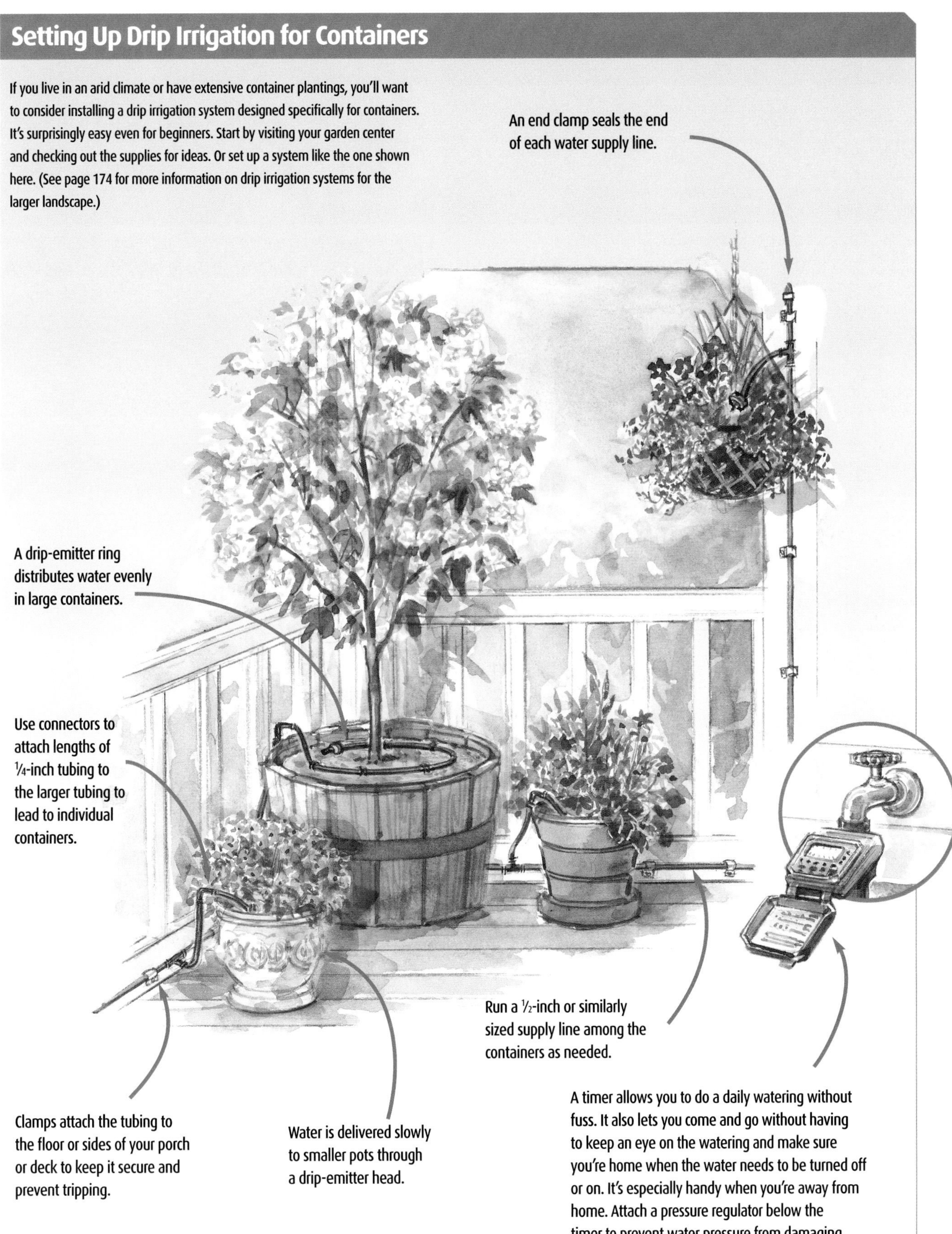

Fertilizing Containers

Container plantings are hungry. Watering constantly flushes nutrients out of the soil, so to keep container plantings lush and full and, in some cases, flowering well, you need to make sure they are well-fertilized.

Good fertilizing starts with good soil. When planting containers, make sure you use top-quality potting soil, not ordinary garden soil. Loose, rich, freely draining potting soil allows water, air—and fertilizer—to percolate down to all levels of the roots.

Check your potting mix to see what fertilizers are already worked in. If so, it's probably a slow-release fertilizer that will last several weeks or even a few months. You will probably need to replenish the slow-release fertilizer after that time.

Containers, especially flowering containers, also appreciate a snack of liquid fertilizer every two to three weeks. But be careful to avoid overfertilizing. If a flowering plant gets too much nitrogen, it will grow tall and leggy and have lots of lush green foliage but few flowers.

BUYER'S GUIDE

STOCK UP

Because the most full, lush containers are fertilized regularly, it's easy to run out of fertilizer. And having to make a special trip to the garden center may delay your applying the fertilizer by days or weeks.

So it's a good idea to buy enough fertilizer to easily last the season. That way, you'll always have some when you need it. You can always use up any leftovers next year.

Fertilizers for Containers

Containers can be fed in a variety of ways:

Compost: In large pots and planters, filling the bottom of the pot with compost before topping it with regular potting soil is a good way to make sure plants get plenty of the major nutrients and important micronutrients and activity from helpful microbes. In plantings that will be around for a few years, you can also add an inch or two of compost to the soil's surface of the container each spring to keep plants happy and healthy.

Slow-Release Fertilizers: Slow-release fertilizers, which are usually granular, release their nutrients slowly over a period of weeks and even months. They're a great fertilizing foundation for your containers, making sure plants have a slow, steady source of nutrients. Work slow-release fertilizers into the soil at planting time, then scratch some more into the top of the soil periodically according to package directions. Do this in addition to or instead of liquid fertilizing (see below).

Fertilizer Spikes and Tablets: Be sure to use those labeled for containers. An easy way to apply a slow-release fertilizer.

Liquid Fertilizers: Think of these as quick snacks for your plants. Every two to three weeks, most container plantings (especially hard-working flowering ones) benefit from an application of liquid fertilizer, usually as a solution that's applied from a watering can or perhaps with the use of a special applicator at the end of a hose. This quick burst of nutrients is helpful but short-lived, which is why it needs to be repeated frequently throughout the growing season.

Cold-Climate Container Care

Lucky gardeners in mild-winter climates (Zones 7 and 8 and warmer) can have container plantings outdoors all year long. Gardeners in colder climates need to replant their containers each spring.

Take In Those Pots

Clay and plastic pots can stay outside in Zone 6, but in Zone 5 and colder, they may freeze and shatter (even most plastic and fiberglass ones) if you leave them out.

In fall, after frost fells the plantings in your containers, remove the plants and soil and do a little basic container care so they'll be ready to go in spring. Hose off excess dirt, then scrub them with hot, soapy water. Mix about ¼ cup bleach into 1 gallon water and swab it onto the container to sterilize it. Let it sit 10 minutes, then rinse again. (Avoid doing this on grass or other plantings; the bleach could harm them.) Let air-dry, then store the containers in a garage, shed, or other sheltered place.

The exception is concrete pots, which are exceptionally sturdy. If they're in a place sheltered from rain and other moisture, such as a porch, they can be left outside in Zone 5. The plants in the pot will almost certainly die, but at least you will be spared having to move the heavy pot.

In Zones 6 and colder, empty and clean containers each fall. Leaving them outside will cause cracking, even in plastic and concrete containers.

Burying Pots in Cold Climates

Planting trees and shrubs in pots provides a classic look during the growing season, but in Zone 6 and colder, the pots will likely freeze solid in winter and kill the plants unless you take extra measures.

Protect each pot from the extremes of winter by burying it, plant and all, in a hole or trench. The soil and surrounding material act as insulators to prevent freezing.

Dig a hole or trench deep enough for the pot or pots in a protected area, such as the side of the house or behind a garage. After your area's first fall frost, set the pot, plant and all, in the hole. Top with alternating layers of dry leaves and soil. (If the autumn is dry, you may want to water the pots first.) In spring, about the time the bulbs start pushing up out of the soil, dig out the pots. Scrub them off and put them back in place.

Houseplants

Since ancient times, people have brought plants inside from the outdoors to enliven their rooms. In fact, some traditions hold that every room must have at least one plant to produce feelings of peace and comfort. Indeed, houseplants do just that.

Chapter 10 Houseplants

In this chapter, you'll learn how to incorporate houseplants into your home with skill and style. You'll also learn which houseplants are right for different spots in your home and simple tricks for giving houseplants the appropriate light, water, and food.

One of the best things about the most common houseplants is that they're easy to grow—so easy, in fact, that they're excellent projects for children.

So, fill your home with houseplants, then sit back and enjoy the serenity that they bring to every room.

Using Houseplants In Your Home

Houseplants add texture, color, and fragrance, and can even purify the air. Here's how to use houseplants well in your home:

- Choose the right size and shape plant for the space. A foyer with a cathedral ceiling would show off a 6- to 8-foot tree, such as a palm or fig. A coffee table would look elegant with a low, spreading ivy or pothos. The tops of bookcases and kitchen cabinets can be softened with cascading ivy.
- Group houseplants together. If you have an ideal spot in your home for houseplants, such as a sunroom, it's fun to create an indoor garden with clusters of pots. Mix a variety of heights, shapes, leaf textures, colors, and sizes. Use similar pots for a unified look.
- Take advantage of windows. Most plants do best in front of a window. Create ideal spaces for houseplants by putting them on a plant stand or a small, narrow, inexpensive wicker or rattan table in front of a window. Or get out a hammer and nails and build a special shelf for houseplants in front of the window, or an indoor window box into which you can set pots.
- Kitchen and bathroom windows are natural spots for houseplants because they offer light, humidity, and a ready water source. Install narrow shelves of wood or glass, supported with brackets attached to the cabinets or window frame.

The Golden Rules of Growing Houseplants

Follow these fundamentals and you'll seldom go wrong when growing houseplants in your home:

1 Provide enough water. Usually, watering a plant once a week is enough. Be sure to water thoroughly, enough that water comes out the bottom drainage hole.

2 Provide enough light. Many houseplants suffer from lack of light. Few houseplants do well if they aren't in front of a window. See page 287, however, for a list of plants that do well in a dark corner.

3 Discard when necessary. Many homeowners expect their plants to grow indoors for decades. Truth is, houseplants are really just plants from outdoors that we hope will look gorgeous in a highly artificial environment. It's hard to keep a houseplant alive and thriving for more than a few years. When a plant gets sick or leggy and isn't attractive anymore, don't chastise yourself for having a black thumb. Just toss the tired-out plant and replace it with a fresh one.

Houseplants such as this orchid lend vital color and interest to a home. Without the orchid, this space, tucked away in a corner, would be lost. The orchid transforms it into a charming vignette.

- Utilize the area in front of the stationary half of a sliding glass door. It is an ideal place to grow houseplants because of the abundant light. Find an attractive plant stand or bookshelf with no back that can hold a variety of pots.
- Use saucers. Protect furniture and floors with waterproof saucers. Plain clay saucers can wick moisture, so look for glazed types or plastic look-alikes. Further protect surfaces by setting the saucers on top of coasters or cork mats to allow for air circulation underneath.
- Keep colors in mind. Houseplant foliage comes in a surprising variety of colors; choose those that will harmonize or contrast with the colors in the room. Also consider flower color, and choose colors that will look good with your home's decor.

African violets thrive when placed in the ideal spot—the soft, diffused light found in a north window. The humidity from the kitchen also benefits these rather particular plants.

Growing Orchids

Interest in orchids has undergone a renaissance in the past several years. New breeding techniques have brought down costs, making many orchids as inexpensive as other houseplants.

Homeowners, too, are finding that growing orchids is easier than they thought. True, some orchids are demanding about having the right light, humidity, and temperature, but many are easy to grow in average conditions, including Brassavola, Brassia, Cattleya, Cymbidium, Dendrobium, Encyclia, Epidendrum, Oncidium, some Paphiopedilum, Phalaenopsis and Vanda.

Given good light, proper potting in bark or fiber, and appropriate humidity, an orchid can thrive and flower for years in the average home. Read the plant label carefully for more exact growing requirements.

For more information, see the orchid entries in the Plant Encyclopedia starting on page 292.

This Cattleya hybrid is an intergeneric cross as gorgeous as its name is long: *Brassolaeliocattleya* 'Helen Brown'.

How to Choose Houseplants

Houseplants are usually selected in one of two ways. You have a spot in your home that you want to fill with a little greenery, or you see a houseplant, fall in love with it, and take it home, determined to find a place for it.

Regardless how you decide to purchase a houseplant, it's important to be a smart buyer:

- Buy only healthy plants. If a plant is sickly, has drooping or yellowing foliage, is dry, or otherwise looks unappealing, leave it at the store. It's almost certainly going to continue to fail and may transfer pests or diseases to other houseplants in your home.
- Buy often. Houseplants are a great picker-upper, especially in the middle of winter when many homeowners are starved for living plants and color. Experiment with houseplants throughout the house. If you're willing to enjoy them for a limited time only, you can keep them even in very low-light areas, including the basement, before they start to fail. In the meantime, for a modest cost, you'll brighten your home.
- Invest in an attractive pot. Why spend money on a beautiful plant if you're going to keep it in green plastic? A beautiful pot or pretty basket sets off a houseplant and enhances your enjoyment of it.

Flowering Plants

It's easy to fall in love with flowering plants, sometimes called florist's plants or gift plants. They're the beauties we spot at garden centers, flower shops, even the supermarket, in full, glorious bloom, often in the dead of winter.

Florist's plants include azaleas, tulips, daffodils, hydrangeas, miniature roses, nonhardy mums, cyclamen, poinsettias, and cineraria.

Many homeowners buy these plants in the hope that they'll keep blooming for months and keep growing for years. The truth is, these plants are meant to add a burst of color to our homes for perhaps two to four weeks. Think of them as a longer-lived alternative to cut flowers. After a few weeks, the flowers fade and the foliage loses it freshness. That means it's time to dispose of the plant and purchase a new one.

Easy-to-Grow Houseplants

Aloe	Dracaena	Peperomia
Arrowhead vine	English ivy	Philodendron
Artillery plant	Ficus	Ponytail palm
Asparagus fern	Fishtail palm	Snake plant
Bamboo palm	Hoya; wax plant	Spider plant
Cape primrose	Japanese aralia	Swedish ivy
Cast-iron plant	Lady palm	Sweet olive
Chinese evergreen	Living-vase plant	Umbrella plant
Devil's ivy	Old-man cactus	Wandering Jew

Wandering Jew

Plants Harmful to Kids and Pets

These plants may result in vomiting or more severe reactions if ingested, or in rashes and other problems if sap gets on skin.

Caladium	English ivy	Philodendron
Clivia	Ficus	Pothos
Croton	Fishtail palm	Swiss-cheese plant
Crown-of-thorns	Flamingo flower	
Dumb cane	Peace lily	

Dumb Cane

Plants for Every Room

Steamy bathroom

Cape primrose
Coleus
Croton
Ferns
Flamingo flower
Hibiscus

Low Light

Cast-iron plant
Chinese evergreen
Dracaenas
Fishtail palm
Lady palm
Philodendron
Snake plant

Cool Sunroom

(For areas that seldom get over 60°F (16°C) in winter. Do well outdoors in summer.)

Artillery plant
Asparagus fern
Cactus
Christmas cactus
Clivia
English ivy
Swedish ivy

Cool Hallway With Drafts

Cactus
Citrus
Japanese fatsia
Spider plant
Umbrella plant

Warm Sunroom

(Areas with full sun and temperatures of 90°F (32°C) or more. In winter, if the room will be significantly cooler, you'll need to move the plant to another space.)

Bromeliads
Cactus
Crown-of-thorns
Grape ivy
Hoya; wax plant
Jade
Kalanchoe
Nerve plant
Ponytail palm

Kalanchoe

Best Plants for Absorbing Indoor Air Pollutants

Bamboo palm	Peace lily	Snake plant
Dracaena	Philodendron	Spider plant
English ivy	Pothos	

Snake Plant

The Right Houseplant In the Right Spot

Finding just the right spot for just the right houseplant could mean the difference between a plant that struggles and fails and a plant that grows and thrives year after year.

Light is key and varies to a surprising degree in different parts of your home, depending on which direction your windows face. Daytime and nighttime room temperatures and humidity levels also are important.

Light

Generally, plants are categorized as low-, medium-, or high-light plants. Plants may do fine with slightly more or less light than their category. However, drastically different light will often cause problems. Plants may be damaged from too much light or direct sun, or they may stretch and become spindly with too little light.

A plant may be able to barely survive with certain levels of light. Lower light, for example, may be sufficient to maintain a plant and keep it looking good, but be insufficient to promote bloom.

Heat and Humidity

The best temperature range for most plants is 60 to 75°F (16 to 24°C). Even more critical is a 5 to 10°F (3 to 6°C) drop at night.

Additionally, note the different microclimates in your house relative to light intensity and humidity. Plants that like cooler temperatures may do well on a sunny, unheated porch or a spot close to a window during the winter. Foyers and entryways can also provide cool temperatures, but not consistently—an opening door tends to deliver cold blasts of air. In summer, this same entryway or foyer will be filled with bursts of hot air, fine for a cactus but deadly to a sensitive, thin-leaved tropical plant.

So an area with rapid temperature changes demands a fairly tough plant. It must be tolerant of summer breezes and drying drafts. Less tolerant plants may do less well.

Which Window for Which Plant?

Many plants prefer one type of exposure over another. A plant that might do beautifully in a north window, for example, would burn in a south window.

As a rule, plants that need high light usually do best in a southern or western exposure. Plants that do well in medium light usually thrive in a western or eastern exposure. In a west- or east-facing window, plants receive a few hours of sun each day—morning sun in an east window and late afternoon sun in a west window. Low-light plants usually do best with light from an east- or north-facing window. It's OK to place them farther away from the window than you would other plants.

Other guidelines for deciding where to position plants:

- A sheer curtain lessens the light intensity and heat in a south- or west-facing window, making the situation appropriate for a medium-light plant.
- Trees outside the windows greatly affect the light. Evergreen trees filter light all year long; deciduous trees filter it only when the trees are in leaf.
- The intensity of direct light varies according to the season. When the sun is high in the sky in summer in the Northern Hemisphere, it is more intense and hotter. In winter the sun is lower in the sky and less intense. Also, of course, days are longer in the summer and shorter in the winter, further affecting plant growth.
- A west-facing window is usually hotter than a south-facing window because of the concentrated sunlight in the late afternoon.

10 Houseplants

Because hot air rises, the top shelf of a bookcase or the top of a kitchen cabinet can provide extra warmth for a plant that dislikes cold. These locations are also out of the way of air movement. However, because they are remote you will need to remember to feed and water them.

The tendency for hot air to rise means that the floor will be cooler, so that is a good place for plants that do poorly in natural summer heat or home heating in winter.

Turning on the heat in the house for the winter naturally dries the air, so be ready with your pebble trays or humidifier to make up for lost moisture. If you are growing only arid plants or plants that can tolerate low humidity levels (see "Easy-to-Grow Houseplants" on page 287), this is not an issue. But tropical plants suddenly deprived of moisture can suffer, sometimes dramatically.

Summer brings other changes for plants. Keep them away from vents when the air-conditioning is running—the blowing cold air is the equivalent of a draft. Also remember that if you close the shades to keep the house cool in summer, you may need to give high-light plants some additional illumination.

WORK SMARTER

PROVIDING HUMIDITY

Many houseplants need high humidity. Misting is a popular way to try increase humidity, although only for a few minutes.

A more effective way to provide humidity is a pebble tray. Take any tray—even a plain rectangular cake pan, though there are attractive trays made just for this purpose—and fill it with crushed stone or pebbles ½ to 1 inch deep. Add water until it's level with the pebbles. Set plants in pots on top of the pebbles.

Another solution is to equip the room with a humidifier. It adds moisture to the air fairly effectively.

Whatever method you use, be sure to put a thermometer that also measures humidity in rooms with houseplants. That way you can see how the temperature and humidity can vary widely throughout your house. These devices cost only a few dollars.

GOOD IDEA!

LIGHT WHERE YOU NEED IT

A grow-light can take other forms besides an elaborate setup in a basement. Experiment with grow lights used in attractive ways around your home. An architect's clamp-on lamp is perfect for outfitting with a grow bulb and positioning over a plant in a dark corner. Try floor lamps over taller plants set on the floor. Even regular lamps, equipped with a grow bulb, are helpful to plants on end tables and nightstands. If it can hold a bulb, it can probably be equipped with a grow bulb and used to keep your houseplants healthy.

Houseplant Care Basics

If your houseplants are in the right spot, they will need minimal attention, but here's how to keep them happy and healthy for a long time.

Water Regularly

Most houseplants do fine with a regular weekly watering. Make sure the soil is soaked enough that water runs out the drainage hole at the bottom; then empty the saucer. Every couple of months or so, it's a good idea to put the plant in the kitchen sink or bathtub where you can spray the leaves with water to remove dust, and thoroughly soak the soil. In area with high salts, if possible, water with rain water.

Fertilize As Needed

Plant fertilizer spikes make feeding plants easy. If you'd rather use another type of fertilizer, choose one that specifies houseplants, and follow package directions.

Most houseplants have less need for fertilizer in the winter months when reduced light slows their growth. Restart feeding in spring.

Groom Weekly

When you're doing your weekly watering, pinch off yellowing or problem leaves, trim back dying stems, and generally give the plant a quick spruce-up. If the soil looks hard and compacted, even after watering, cultivate the soil lightly with a kitchen fork to help it better absorb water in the future. Every several months, as soil slowly washes out of the pot, add a handful or two of potting soil to replenish nutrients.

GOOD IDEA!

BOTTOM WATERING

Once in a while your houseplants may get so dry that the soil hardens and pulls away from the sides of the pot. When this happens, water tends to run over the hard surface of the soil, down the inside of the pot, and out the drainage hole, doing little good. You can remedy this problem in pots with a drainage hole by watering from the bottom up. Put the pot in a deep dish or saucer and fill the dish as full as possible. Let it sit for one to two hours. If all the water is absorbed, repeat. The soil will slowly get soaked through and swell back to its previous state, thoroughly watering the plant in the process.

PROJECT DETAILS

SKILLS: Basic planting
PROJECT: Planting a newly purchased houseplant in a permanent pot

TIME TO COMPLETE

EXPERIENCED: 10 minutes
HANDY: 15 minutes
NOVICE: 20 minutes

STUFF YOU'LL NEED

MATERIALS: Flower pot, potting soil

How to Plant a Houseplant

1 Pull out or knock the plant from its plastic pot. If the roots are tangled, loosen them with your fingers or a kitchen fork.

2 Put a single small stone or handful of crushed stone in the bottom of the pot to promote drainage. Position the plant, then fill around it with potting soil, firming it with your fingers.

3 Make sure there's at least ½ inch of space at the top for water to pool. Water well. If the soil settles, top with more soil.

Houseplant Pests and Diseases

To be happy when growing houseplants you'll need to be able to tolerate imperfections. Yellowing or dropping leaves are part of a plant's life cycle. If a plant is healthy, the yellowed or fallen leaves will be replaced by new green ones.

Giving a houseplant the best care possible can take a little experimentation. It's often necessary to shift the light to see what works best, or hold back water or water a little extra, or move the plant to a cooler or warmer room to find just the right spot.

When a problem does occur, try to figure out what's causing it and how to remedy it. Sometimes the best approach is to trim off the problem part and give the plant a good all-over rinse in the shower or kitchen sink. After that, make sure you give the plant regular watering, fertilizing, and correct light, and in a few weeks the problem may disappear.

Houseplant Problems

Brown Leaf Tips

Brown leaf tips and edges can be caused by many things: overwatering, underwatering, too little light, too much light, too much heat, overfeeding, dry air, or cold drafts. Read up on the plant in the Plant Encyclopedia, starting on page 292, to better understand its needs, and make sure to provide for them. Also look for other symptoms for further clues.

Dropped Leaves

A few dropped leaves, especially a few bottom leaves that yellow and drop off occasionally, are normal. Also, a plant that is repotted or moved from one location to another may go into slight shock and drop a few leaves. (Weeping figs are notorious for this.) However, if a tree suddenly loses many leaves, it's a sign of severe shock in the form of too much dryness, blasts of cold air, or a large drop or rise in temperature. Remedy the stresses, and the plant may recover in several weeks. If it fails to rally, and it has lost most of its leaves, discard it.

Dying Foliage

Some dying foliage is fine, a normal part of the renewal process. Simply trim it off as it occurs. Under- or erratic watering can cause dying foliage; water at regular intervals. If the foliage is yellowing first before dying and most of the dying leaves are at the bottom of the plant, the plant may be getting too little light.

Frequent Wilting Between Waterings

Wilting between regular waterings is probably a symptom of a plant's being potbound—that is, the roots are outgrowing the pot. Repot the plant. Also, if the plant likes shade, make sure it isn't getting too much sun, especially in the late afternoon.

Mealybugs

These tiny pests look almost like cottony fluff. Take care of a modest infestation (a few clusters) by wiping the plant's leaves liberally with a cotton swab dipped in rubbing alcohol. Treat more severe infestations with a houseplant insecticide that specifies mealybug control.

Scale

Scale insects are present when tiny, roundish, crusty plates attach to the underside of leaves and stems. Wipe leaves with a cotton swab dipped in rubbing alcohol. Wait a week or two to see if the scales reappear. If they do, apply a houseplant insecticide that specifies scale control.

Whitefly

These tiny white insects fly up in the air when the plant is brushed. Control small infestations with an insecticidal soap or an insecticide formulated for houseplants that specifies whitefly control.

Yellowing

If the upper leaves are firm and yellow, the problem may be the result of using hard water for acid-loving plants such as hydrangeas and azaleas. Yellowing and falling of a few lower leaves is normal. If the leaves are pale yellow-green and spindly or underdeveloped, the cause may be underfeeding or too little light.

Plant Encyclopedia

One of the smartest things a gardener can do is to read up on the plants already growing in the garden as well as scout out potential new additions. Doing this background work will help you better provide ideal growing conditions for the plants you already have and also seek out the most beautiful, best-performing plants for future planting.

That's why in the second half of this book, you'll find a comprehensive Plant Encyclopedia. This is a listing of the most commonly grown and widely available plants in North America.

In it, you'll find a color photograph for each plant, as well as detailed growing and selection information. The alphabetical listings are by the name most commonly used for that plant. Listings are then also cross-referenced by other common names and botanical names.

So dive in. Whether you're looking for a specific plant or just wanting to get some ideas for new plants, you're sure to learn plenty about the best plants for your garden.

How to Use This Plant Encyclopedia

This plant encyclopedia was designed with beginning to intermediate gardeners in mind—gardeners who tend to call a daylily a daylily rather than by its fancy, botanical name: *Hemerocallis*.

That means plants in this encyclopedia are listed alphabetically by their common rather than their botanical name. In the cases where a plant has more than one common name (the same plant might be called African lily or Lily-of-the-Nile but is most commonly referred to by its botanical name: *Agapanthus)* the plant is listed under the most commonly used name. Elsewhere in the encyclopedia, then, there are cross-references by its other various names.

Space limits this book from listing all the plants grown in North American gardens, so only the most readily available and widely grown plants are highlighted here.
For each, you'll find complete growing information and maybe even a tip or two, setting you on your way to creating a beautiful garden filled with a wide variety of plants.

Since some readers know the botanical name only for a plant, we've also cross-referenced plants by botanical name. In this case, *Baptisia australis* is the botanical name for blue false indigo.

The encyclopedia is alphabetical with each section labeled by letter.

Each plant has a color photo for easy indentification.

The range of hardiness—that is, the parts of the country that are warm enough to grow each plant—is also listed. For a map showing the hardiness zones, see page 26. Some annuals, however, may not have any hardiness listing; because they die out each winter, their cold-hardiness is irrelevant.

The range of the plant's mature height and width is listed for each plant.

Banana - *Bauhinia* spp.

rich, moist soil that is fertile and well-amended with organic matter. Plant in a protected area where wind won't damage its broad leaves. Fertilize regularly and keep soil moist. In areas at the northern edge of its hardiness range, plants will die back in winter but resprout from the roots. Even in mild areas, bananas are short-lived and will die back after a few years (usually after they have flowered and fruited), at which time they produce offsets that can be replanted to create new plants. Indoors, keep in a warm location with medium to bright light. High humidity is preferred.
▶ ***Choices:*** A number of cultivars of this banana are available, some with reddish or red-splotched and striped leaves. 'Zebrina' is particularly attractive, with deep green leaves striped in maroon. Japanese banana *(Musa basjoo)* is one of the hardiest bananas and reaches 15' high with gigantic 8' leaves. It is hardy in Zones 8-10, and will usually resprout after winter dieback in Zone 7. *M. ×paradisiaca* is a popular ornamental banana in Southern California and Florida. It forms huge clumps 20' high and 20' wide with multiple trunks. The leaves are up to 10' long. Zones 9-11.

Baptisia australis
see False Indigo, Blue

Barberry, Japanese
Berberis thunbergii
Deciduous shrub

Berberis thunbergii 'Atropurpurea'

▶ ***Hardiness:*** Zones 4-8
▶ ***Size:*** 3' tall, 4'-7' wide
▶ ***Features:*** Leaves appear early in the spring. Fantastic foliage color in summer and fall.
Thorny plants create dense barriers. This spiny shrub will grow anywhere. It can tolerate tight root quarters, urban pollution, and neglect. Green summer foliage turns shades of orange, scarlet, or reddish purple in the fall. Spines are sharp and make effective barrier plantings, but avoid siting plants where children play, or use thornless varieties. Plants tend to collect blowing debris and require cleaning out in the spring. Growth in Zone 8 is limited.
▶ ***Uses:*** Hedges, barriers, foundation plantings, or border shrubs
▶ ***Needs:*** Plant anywhere except in standing water. Japanese barberry performs best in full sun in well-drained, fertile soil. Prune to shape after flowering. Plants tolerate urban conditions well.
▶ ***Choices:*** 'Atropurpurea' has reddish or purple leaves, turning red in fall. 'Crimson Pygmy' has deep red leaves that turn orange-scarlet in fall and grows 2'-3' tall and wide. 'Rose Glow' leaves turn rose-red in fall. The variety 'Thornless' is a better selection for areas where children play. Turning orange-red in the fall, it grows 3'-5' tall and 4'-6' wide.

Barrenwort
see Epimedium

Basil
Ocimum basilicum
Warm-season annual herb

Sweet basil

▶ ***Hardiness:*** Not applicable
▶ ***Size:*** Grows 9"-18" tall, 6"-12" wide, depending on the cultivar
▶ ***Features:*** Leaves have distinctive flavor; the perfect complement to nearly any dish containing tomatoes.
▶ ***Uses:*** Excellent chopped and sprinkled over fresh tomatoes, salads, or pasta dishes.
▶ ***Needs:*** Full sun. Rich, well-drained soil with ample moisture. Start from seed indoors 6 weeks before your region's last frost date or buy established plants. Plant outdoors after all danger of frost is past. Can harvest as soon as leaves appear. Trim off flowers to focus plant on producing maximum foliage. Slugs can sometimes be a problem.
▶ ***Choices:*** Sweet basil has traditional basil flavor. Spicy globe basil is smaller, globe-shaped, and has a spicier flavor. Purple-leaved types are available,

B

Plant encyclopedia

310 Gardening 1-2-3

Plant encyclopedia

Plants are listed first by their common, rather than botanical name. This is the name most people know.

The botanical name is also listed. A plant may have several common names but most have just one botanical name. (The exception is when botanists reclassify plants and change botanical names. In most cases, then, the other less current or less used botanical name is listed later on in the plant description.)

The "feature" section describes the chief characteristics of the plant, why you might want to grow it, and, where appropriate, the liabilities you should watch out for.

Here's where you can get an idea of the best way to use a plant.

The growing needs of each plant are described in detail, complete with sun, soil, and water needs as well as growing tips.

In this section, some of the most popular or best species or cultivars of the plant are listed. This section may also steer you to similar plants that are better-suited for your growing conditions or your garden.

Bringing it Home

Whether you fall in love with a plant on the pages of this Plant Encyclopedia or in a glossy magazine or in your Aunt Nellie's garden in Pasadena, it can be a challenge to get the plant you want. Here's how:

- First, find out (and jot down on paper) as much about the plant's name and the plant itself as possible. Asking a garden center if they have "this pretty blue plant that blooms in summer" won't be very helpful. And even if you have only an old-fashioned regional common name ("Kiss-me-by-the-garden-gate" is a perfect example), that might not be helpful, either.

  As much as possible, find out and write down the full botanical name of the plant. Note exactly when it was in flower, if it was, and what the flower was like. Take note of other plant characteristics, such as height, spread, leaf shape and texture, etc. Better yet, take a picture, if you can.
- Read up on the plant. If possible, find the plant in the Plant Encyclopedia and read up on its needs. Do you have enough sun or shade? Can you supply enough water? Are you in the right growing zone (see page 26)? Do you have the right soil? Even if you can get your hands on the plant, it won't do well unless you have the right growing conditions for it.
- At the garden center, if you can't find the plant, ask. Since different plants should be planted at different times, shipments come in constantly during the growing season. If a garden center doesn't have a plant in March, they might in May. Or maybe even October, depending on the plant.
- Plant it in the right spot. If you decided you just love those beautiful regal astilbes, which need part to full shade and plenty of rich, moisture-retentive soil, but your new flower bed is a rock-garden filled otherwise with drought-tolerant plants, find a different, shadier location and enrich the soil amply, or better yet, build a raised bed.

There are some tricks to finding just the right plants for your garden. Reading up on the plant's description in the Plant Encyclopedia is a good first step.

Aaron's Beard
see St. Johnswort

Abelia, Glossy
Abelia ×grandiflora

Semievergreen shrub

Abelia ×grandiflora

▶**Hardiness:** Zones 6-9
▶**Size:** Grows 4'-6' tall, 3'-5' wide
▶**Features:** A low-maintenance shrub, abelia produces pink, white, or lavender flowers summer through fall. Fine-textured, glossy foliage has bronze cast when new. Heat tolerant, excellent for the South and West in sun or part shade. Hot weather promotes flowering.
▶**Uses:** Informal settings suit abelia best—an informal hedge, mass planting, or bank cover. Combine it in the shrub border with large-leaved evergreens for textural contrast.
▶**Needs:** Plant in sun or part shade in rich, well-drained, acidic soil (although alkaline soil is tolerated well). Pinch new growth to maintain compact plants. Blooms appear on new growth each year, so prune in late winter or early spring. Although abelia makes a good hedge, it's prettiest when left unsheared. Instead, to preserve this shrub's graceful form, cut out selected branches at the plant's base. It is prone to leaf spot, though usually pest and disease free.
▶**Choices:** 'Edward Goucher'—4' high, lavender flowers; 'Francis Mason'—pinkish-white flowers and variegated leaves; 'Prostrata'—2' high, white flowers; 'Sherwood'—2'-3' high cascading form, white flowers.

Abeliophyllum distichum
see Forsythia, White

Abies spp.
see Firs

Abutilon ×hybridum
see Flowering Maple

Acacia, Bailey
Acacia baileyana

Evergreen flowering tree

Acacia baileyana

▶**Hardiness:** Zones 8-10
▶**Size:** 20'-30' tall, 20'-40' wide
▶**Features:** Bailey acacia is a fast-growing tree that provides a spectacular display of fragrant, brilliant yellow flower clusters in midwinter (January and February in California). Fine-textured fernlike foliage. Grows quickly, but short-lived, lasting only 20 to 30 years. Pest resistant. Tolerates dry soil and neglect.
▶**Uses:** Attractive as single-stemmed specimen or multistemmed hedge. Good for massing on banks and hillsides. Often planted along freeways in California.
▶**Needs:** Plant in well-drained soil and full sun. Water when new; established plants need little watering. Prune back the main stem to encourage a shrublike shape or remove lower branches to train as a small tree. Needs little attention after establishment to thrive.
▶**Choices:** 'Purpurea' has foliage with purplish new growth.

Acanthus spinosus
see Bear's Breeches, Spiny

Acer spp.
see Maples

Achillea spp.
see Yarrow

Aconitum carmichaelii
see Monkshood, Azure

Actinidia arguta
see Kiwi, Hardy

Actinidia chinensis
see Kiwi, Chinese Gooseberry

Adiantum pedatum
see Ferns, Maidenhair Fern

Aechmea fasciata
see Bromeliads: Silver Vase Plant

Aegopodium podagraria 'Variegatum'
see Bishop's Weed

Aeschynanthus spp.
see Lipstick Plant

Aesculus spp.
see Buckeye

African Daisy (*Osteospermum fruticosum*)
see Freeway Daisy

African Daisy (*Dimorphotheca* spp.)
see Cape Marigold

African Daisy
Arctotis hybrids

Short-lived perennial usually grown as an annual

Arctotis hybrid

▶**Hardiness:** All zones when grown as an annual; perennial in Zones 8-10.
▶**Size:** 1' tall, 1½' wide
▶**Features:** Masses of brilliant 3-inch daisies in purple, pink, red, orange, yellow, cream, and white, often with a contrasting dark "bullseye." Plants form clumps of woolly, dark green lobed leaves with silvery undersides. In favorable climates (coastal

A

Plant encyclopedia

West with dry, cool summers) they often reseed, but tend to revert to orange.

▶ **Uses:** Bedding annual, also excellent in containers

▶ **Needs:** Plant in full sun and extremely well-drained, loose, and preferably gravelly soil. Provide moderate, even watering. In Zones 2–6 plant established seedlings in early spring. In Zones 7–11 (especially in the Southwest) plant in late fall or early winter for blooms winter through spring. Mulch to conserve moisture. Fertilize lightly, if at all. Thrives in areas with extended cool weather and moderate moisture. Does less well in excessive heat or humidity.

▶ **Choices:** Retail and mail-order nurseries sell hybrids in many colors, usually as a mix. *Dimorphotheca* spp. (see Cape Marigold) and *Osteospermum* spp. (see Freeway Daisy) are also sometimes sold as African daisy.

African Milk Tree

see Cactus and Succulents

African Violet

Saintpaulia spp.

Tropical herbaceous perennial grown as a houseplant

Saintpaulia spp.

▶ **Size:** Grows from 2"–5" tall and 3"–10" wide, depending on the type

▶ **Features:** Tiny flowers in pink, reds, corals, purple, lavender, and white on top of fuzzy leaves. Resemble violets. Most types bloom several times a year.

▶ **Uses:** As a houseplant

▶ **Needs:** Bright light, such as that from an east window or a south window in winter. Always protect from strong light, however. To induce winter bloom, provide artificial light at night. Does well long-term under grow lights. Minimum 60°F/16°C in winter. Avoid drafts. Plant in top-quality potting soil or a special mix for African violets. Needs high humidity; set on a tray filled with pebbles and water. Keep water off leaves; water by setting the pot in a small bowl of water and letting the water soak upward. Fertilize with a half-strength 10-30-10 liquid fertilizer every time you water; fertilizers especially for African violets are ideal.

▶ **Choices:** Hundreds of types are available. Choose from standard varieties that come in many sizes, from microminiatures that grow 2" to large types that grow up to 18" wide. Leaves can be plain or variegated or have interesting rolled, crinkled, or serrated edges. Flowers come in a variety of forms, from single to semidouble, frilled, star, bicolors, and multicolors. Trailing types of African violets are also available.

Agapanthus; African Lily; Lily-of-the-Nile

Agapanthus spp.

Evergreen perennial

Agapanthus africanus

▶ **Hardiness:** Zones 8–10

▶ **Size:** 1'–1½' tall and wide with flower stems 2'–4' tall

▶ **Features:** Hot weather brings clusters of blue blossoms on stalks rising above straplike leaves. Plants establish easily and require minimal care. Foliage is normally yellow-green in color; if leaves turn too yellow, feed with balanced liquid fertilizer. Big clusters of blue flowers on erect stalks. Clumps of flat, coarse-textured foliage. Easy-care and trouble-free plantings.

▶ **Uses:** Groundcover, containers, accent planting, flowerbeds, edging for walks or shrub beds

▶ **Needs:** Plant in any well-drained soil in full sun or partial shade. Water regularly during the summer months for best bloom. Established plants can get by with little or no extra water.

▶ **Choices:** 'Queen Anne'—2' tall, blue flowers; 'Peter Pan'—1' tall, deep blue flowers.

Agastache spp.

see Hyssop

Agave americana

see Cactus and Succulents: Century Plant

Agave victoriae-reginae

see Cactus and Succulents: Queen Victoria Century Plant

Ageratum; Flossflower

Ageratum houstonianum

Annual

Ageratum houstonianum

▶ **Size:** 6" tall and wide to 30" tall and 20" wide, depending on cultivar

▶ **Features:** Blooms early summer to frost.

▶ **Uses:** Lower-growing cultivars are excellent as bedding or edging plants in the front of the border. Taller types are best in the mixed border or in the cutting garden.

▶ **Needs:** Full sun in cooler parts of the country; partial shade where summers are hot. Needs rich, well-drained soil with plenty of water. Plant seedlings in spring after all danger of frost has passed. Mulch to conserve moisture. Fertilize regularly, every 4 weeks, or work in a slow-release fertilizer at planting time. Trim spent blooms regularly. In Zones 8–11 replant if desired in late summer for fall bloom. This plant often reseeds in warm, moist climates.

▶ **Choices:** Choose from pinks, whites, purples, and blues. Dwarf varieties, such as 'Hawaii', grow 6" tall, while 'Blue Mink' grows 12". 'Blue Horizon' grows 30" and is excellent as a cut flower.

Aglaonema commutatum
see Chinese Evergreen

Ajuga; Bugleweed
Ajuga reptans

Spreading semievergreen perennial (evergreen in mild-winter climates)

Ajuga reptans

▶***Hardiness:*** Zones 3-9
▶***Size:*** 4"-6" tall, spreading 24"-36" wide
▶***Features:*** Fast-growing groundcover for shaded locations. Blue, white, or pink flowers combine well with spring-blooming bulbs and azaleas. Wide availability of foliage variations. Spring brings spikes of sky blue flowers. Ajuga will grow where grass fails. Dry or dense shade is not a problem for this adaptable, low-growing groundcover. Ajuga will spread easily into lawns. Avoid locating it where it will take advantage of this situation.
▶***Uses:*** Groundcover good for rock gardens, edging patios, stepping-stone paths, formal or informal gardens, front layer of planting beds
▶***Needs:*** Plant in any soil that's moist but well drained. Plants won't thrive in soggy soil or in drought conditions. Grow in partial shade.
▶***Choices:*** 'Alba'—white flowers; 'Burgundy Lace'—dark pink flowers; 'Atropurpurea'—blue flowers, bronze-purple leaves; 'Tricolor'—pink, cream, green leaves.

Akebia quinata
see Chocolate Vine

Alcea rosea
see Hollyhock

Alchemilla mollis
see Lady's Mantle

Algerian Ivy
see Ivy, Algerian

Allegheny Foam Flower
see Foam Flower, Allegheny

Allamanda
Allamanda cathartica

Tropical evergreen vine

Allamanda cathartica

▶***Hardiness:*** Zone 10
▶***Size:*** Where hardy and when grown in the ground, allamanda can grow 50' or more as a vine. It is often maintained as a shrub 4'-6' high and wide. In large containers as a vine it can reach 8' or more in a season.
▶***Features:*** Covered with large yellow trumpet-shaped blossoms for much of the year, allamanda's colorful impact, fast growth, and low maintenance make it a popular pick to grow either as a vine or trained as a shrub. It tolerates hot, sunny locations.
▶***Uses:*** Good for covering walls, fences, gates, and arbors, or as a freestanding shrub and colorful accent. North of Zone 10 where winters reach freezing temperatures, allamanda is excellent grown in containers as a patio plant for color all summer, or as an annual in the ground.
▶***Needs:*** Plant in any well-drained soil in full sun. Water regularly. Feed several times during the growing season with a balanced fertilizer. Provide support to encourage climbing. To grow allamanda as a shrub, pinch or prune back new growth frequently to keep it bushy. Allamanda does not tolerate frost, so protect from freezing temperatures. To overwinter container patio plants, bring indoors and place in bright, direct sunlight.

Allium; Ornamental Onion
Allium spp.

Flowering bulb

Allium giganteum

▶***Hardiness:*** Most species are hardy in Zones 4-8
▶***Size:*** 8" to 4' tall, depending on species
▶***Features:*** Flowers come in blue, purple, pink, yellow, and white; most species bloom in late spring or early summer. There are many species, all with long grassy or straplike leaves and spherical clusters of small flowers forming a ball on top of tall, sturdy stems.
▶***Uses:*** Best used in the mixed-flower border where the taller-blooming stems lift the beautiful flowers above surrounding plants.
▶***Needs:*** Full sun or light shade, especially in Zones 7-10. Sandy, well-drained soil. Ample water. Plant bulbs in fall. Depth will vary with type; check label. Plant in masses of a dozen or more for best effect. Fertilize rarely. Keep up on weeding with those that have dense, hard-to-weed, grasslike foliage. Trim spent blooms. Divide every few years when crowded and blooming diminishes. Rodents may eat this plant.
▶***Choices:*** Popular species and varieties include, from small to large: Golden garlic *(Allium moly,* 6"-8" tall, yellow flowers) and rosy garlic *(A. roseum,* 6"-8" tall, pink flowers); star-of-Persia *(A. christophii,* 1'-2' tall, huge 10" spheres of silvery purple); drumstick allium *(A. sphaerocephalum,* 2' tall, 2" egg-shaped flower clusters in pinkish purple); blue globe onion *(A. caeruleum,* 2' tall, 1" sky blue flower clusters); Persian onion *(A. aflatunense,* 3' tall, 3" purple spheres); and giant allium *(A. giganteum,* 4' tall, huge

10" globes of purple flowers.) *A. g.* 'Globemaster' has even larger flower heads (12" across).

Allium schoenoprasum
see Chives

Almond
Prunus dulcis

Deciduous nut-bearing tree

Almond

►***Hardiness:*** Zones 6–9
►***Size:*** Dwarf types grow 8'–12' tall, 8'–12' wide; others grow 20'–30' tall, 20' wide
►***Features:*** Beautiful flowers in spring followed by delicious nuts in summer. Likes hot summers and low humidity; does well in the Southwest. Drought-tolerant once established. Trees produce for 50 years or more.
►***Uses:*** Almond trees are pretty enough to use as a decorative tree anywhere in the landscape.
►***Needs:*** Full sun. Likes rich, well-drained soil but tolerates a range of soil types. Harvest by picking or shaking the tree after the leathery hulls begin to split. Spread nuts in a layer on newspaper in a cool, breezy, shady spot to dry for 2–3 days. Remove hulls. Dry nuts in their shells for another 7–10 days. Prune as an open-center tree (see page 266).
►***Choices:*** Some almonds need a second almond tree for cross-pollination; others do not.

Almond, Flowering
see Plum, Ornamental

Aloe vera
see Cactus and Succulents: Aloe

Alstroemeria spp.
see Peruvian Lily

Alyssum
see Basket-of-Gold or Sweet Alyssum

Amaranth; Love-Lies-Bleeding
Amaranthus caudatus

Annual

Amaranthus caudatus

►***Size:*** 2'–3' tall
►***Features:*** Long dark flower tassels are an old-fashioned favorite. Blooms early summer through frost. Though usually grown for its dripping red flowers, upright as well as green and golden flower variations of this plant are available, as are variations in foliage color, including deep purple-red.
►***Uses:*** In the mixed flower border; excellent as a featured upright plant in the middle of a mixed container.
►***Needs:*** Full sun in Zones 6–7 and the Pacific Northwest; partial shade Zones 8–11. This plant likes rich, well-drained soil and ample moisture but will rot if kept too moist. Plant established seedlings outdoors in spring after all danger of frost has passed. Mulch to help keep soil moist. This plant benefits from an application of compost or slow-release fertilizer when flowering starts. Stake taller varieties. Amaranth is susceptible to aphids, spider mites, and aster yellows virus.
►***Choices:*** Joseph's coat *(Amaranthus tricolor)* is a related species grown for its imposing form and dramatic, boldly colored foliage that lends a tropical feeling to the flower border. 'Illumination' grows 4'–5' tall with crimson and gold leaves. 'Aurora Yellow' is 3' tall with bright yellow foliage on top, green below. 'Early Splendor' is similar with bright scarlet foliage above, green below.

Amaryllis belladonna
see Naked Ladies

Amaryllis
Hippeastrum spp.

Subtropical perennial bulb

Hippeastrum spp.

►***Hardiness:*** Zones 7–10
►***Size:*** Grows 1'–3' tall
►***Features:*** Spectacular large 6"–10" flowers in white, pink, salmon, or red rise above thick, strappy leaves emerging from a bulb as large as a baseball.
►***Uses:*** As a houseplant for seasonal color; or outdoors as a flowering garden plant in Zones 7 and warmer.
►***Needs:*** You can buy amaryllis already in bloom, as a planted bulb in a pot ready to start sending out growth, or as a dormant bulb to plant yourself. To bring amaryllis into bloom indoors starting with a dormant loose bulb, plant between October and May for flowering between December and June. Plant one bulb per 6" pot with a third of the bulb showing above the pot's rim. Place the pot in a 70°F/21°C room in direct to bright light. In the first few weeks, water sparingly. After the leaves and bud develop—or if you have purchased a bulb that is beginning to send out foliage—water more frequently. Direct sunlight and warm temperatures encourage best growth. Amaryllis generally blooms 6 to 8 weeks after planting; the flowers last about 2 weeks.
After the flower has started to bloom, keeping it in indirect bright light will prolong flowering. Cut the stem close to the bulb after the flower fades. The long, thin leaves will continue to grow. In mid- to late summer, stop watering and allow the leaves to die back. In September or October, place the bulb in

a cool dark place for 8–12 weeks to simulate dormancy. Bring the bulb back to room temperature, begin watering, and its flowering cycle will begin again.
▶**Choices:** Many cultivars are available, including striped and double flowers.

Amelanchier spp.
see Serviceberries

Amethyst Flower; Sapphire Flower
Browallia spp.
Annual

Browallia spp.

▶**Size:** 8"–18" tall, depending on variety
▶**Features:** Deep blue, mid-blue, purple, and white blooms from late spring through fall on compact, mounding plants.
▶**Uses:** Lovely in the front of the border or in beds. Excellent in containers. In cooler climates (Zones 2–5) it mixes well with impatiens and lobelia.
▶**Needs:** Best in full sun in Zones 2–5; light shade in Zones 6–11. Rich, well-drained soil. Ample water. Plant established seedlings in spring, working in compost. Mulch to retain moisture. For best health and flowering, fertilize regularly, every 4 weeks, or work in a 9-month slow-release fertilizer at planting time. Amethyst flower may not bloom where summers are cool or short. In mild-winter areas, it may survive the winter. If this happens, cut back plants to a few inches in spring and fertilize to spur new growth. In warm climates this plant may also reseed. It is prone to aphids and whiteflies.
▶**Choices:** Bells hybrids produce deep blue, mid-blue, and white flowers on 12" plants. Trolls hybrids have white or blue flowers on more compact 10" plants. Starlight hybrids bear dark blue, sky blue, and white flowers earlier than other selections.

Ampelopsis brevipedunculata
see Porcelain Berry

Amsonia tabernaemontana
see Blue Star

Andromeda
see Pieris

Andromeda polifolia
see Bog Rosemary

Anemone spp.
see Windflower

Anethum graveolens
see Dill

Angel's Trumpet
see Datura

Antirrhinum majus
see Snapdragon

Aphelandra squarrosa
see Zebra Plant

Aporocactus flagelliformis
see Cactus and Succulents: Rattail Cactus

Apple
Malus sylvestris var. *domestica*
Deciduous fruit tree

Apple 'Grayburn'

▶**Hardiness:** Zones 3–9
▶**Size:** Miniatures grow a mere 6' tall; standards can hit 30'; 2'–20' wide
▶**Features:** Delicious fruits from summer through fall
▶**Uses:** Apple trees are pretty enough to use as a decorative tree anywhere in the landscape.
▶**Needs:** Full sun. Prefers deep, rich, moist soil with a neutral pH. Choose cultivars suited to your region's heat or cold. Depending on the type, may need a second apple or crabapple tree with which to cross-pollinate.

For best fruit, spray with horticultural oil in very early spring. Prune in very early spring (see page 266). Best trained with a central leader. Harvest when apples turn color and have fully developed flavor and sweetness.
▶**Choices:** Hundreds of cultivars available, including heritage varieties. 'Liberty' and 'Freedom' are the most disease resistant. Choose low-chill types for warm climates. Early-, mid-, and late-season cultivars available. Also sometimes divided into eating apples, which are crisp and fully flavored, and baking apples, which are softer fleshed and tarter for more contrast when turned into applesauce, apple butter, cobblers, or pie.

Apricot
Prunus armeniaca
Deciduous fruit tree

Apricot 'Goldbar'

▶**Hardiness:** Zones 6–9
▶**Size:** Dwarf types grow 6'–12' tall; others can reach 25' high and 6'–25' wide
▶**Features:** Juicy fruits for a two-week period in summer
▶**Uses:** Pretty enough to use as a decorative tree anywhere in the landscape.
▶**Needs:** Full sun. Plant on north or east side of slopes and buildings to prevent frost damage to early blossoms. Likes moist, rich, neutral soil but will tolerate drier conditions. Train as an open-center tree. Spray in early spring or late winter with horticultural oil to prevent pests. Prune annually after blooming. Bears on spurs that are productive for up to 4 years. Thin fruits as they develop to just 2"–3"

A

Plant encyclopedia

apart. Usually doesn't need a second tree for cross-pollination, but it will produce more heavily with a second tree.

▶ **Choices:** In the North, plant late-blooming cultivars. Early- and mid-season cultivars also are available.

Apricot, Flowering
see Plum, Ornamental

Aquilegia spp.
see Columbine

Arabis spp.
see Rockcress, Wall

Aralia
Polyscias spp.

Subtropical shrub or small tree

Polyscias fruticosa

▶ **Hardiness:** Zones 10–11

▶ **Size:** 3'–15' tall, depending on the type

▶ **Features**: Treelike houseplant with twisted stems and interesting, Asian-looking foliage

▶ **Uses:** As a houseplant; in tropical areas of southern Florida and Hawaii it is sometimes grown as a hedge, or as a small patio tree or shrub in a large container.

▶ **Needs:** Very particular about humidity; must have ample humidity or it will drop its leaves. A humidifier running nearby or a conservatory setting is a must. Keep in bright light away from direct sun. Needs to be kept warm; doesn't like cool; a minimum of 65°F/18°C in winter. Keep soil moist most of the year and on the dry side in winter when growth is less active. Fertilize with a half-strength 10-10-10 fertilizer with each watering—this delicate plant is shocked by a heavier influx of fertilizer. Drops its leaves when conditions are less than ideal or when conditions change

▶ **Choices:** Most aralia leaves are fernlike, but the most popular aralia is dinner-plate aralia *(P. scutellaria). P. scutellaria* var. *pennockii* is yellow-veined. *P. scutellaria* 'Marginata' has white-edged foliage. Ming aralia *(P. fruticosa)* has almost bamboolike leaves.

Araucaria araucana
See Monkey Puzzle Tree

Araucaria heterophylla
see Norfolk Island Pine

ARBORVITAE

While the native species are tall forest trees, most of the varieties of arborvitae you'll find in nurseries are low-care evergreens that come in an assortment of shapes and sizes. There's easily one to fit every landscape setting. The foliage of some varieties turns a purplish mahogany in the cold months, but many retain good foliage color throughout winter.

ARBORVITAE

American Arborvitae; Eastern White Cedar
Thuja occidentalis

Evergreen tree

Thuja occidentalis 'Emerald'

Thuja occidentalis 'Hetz Midget'

Thuja occidentalis 'Little Giant'

▶ **Hardiness:** Zones 3–7

▶ **Size:** 30'–60' tall with a spread of 10'–15'. There are many dwarf cultivars.

▶ **Features:** This low-maintenance evergreen tree comes in shapes and sizes from globe-shaped dwarfs to narrow, vertical pillars. Because of its slow-to-medium growth rate, it is easy to maintain in a desired shape. Native to northeastern North America.

▶ **Uses:** Good for specimen shrub, screen, foundation planting, or anchoring the corner of planting beds. Because of a tendency toward winter burn in exposed areas, it is a poor choice for a windbreak.

▶ **Needs:** Easy to establish. Plant in full sun. Moist, well-drained soils are best, but performance is good in any soil that isn't extremely wet. Rocky, poor, dry, or highly alkaline soils are fine. Protect from winter winds, snow, and ice. Heavy snow or ice can break branches; knock snow away with a broom after it falls. Plants can be susceptible to spider mites. At the first sign of fading foliage or silky webbing, spray with an insecticide that lists spider mites on the label. Prune to shape during the warm growing season.

▶Choices: 'Emerald'—Narrow, pyramidal shrub or small tree 10'-15' high, 3'-4' wide; leaves stay bright green through winter; Zones 3-8. May also be sold as 'Smaragd.'

'Pyramidalis'—Narrow pyramidal shape; new leaves bright green; 12'-15' high, 3'-4' wide; Zones 3-8.

'Techny'—Slow-growing, pyramidal form, 15' high, green all year.

'Globosa'—Rounded shape, 4'-6' high and wide, gray-green foliage.

'Golden Globe'—bright golden foliage, 3' high and wide.

'Hetz Midget'—Dwarf, rounded, evergreen shrub stays short and tidy for years, eventually reaching 3' tall and wide. Good for specimen use, lining a walkway, small entry plantings, rock gardens, containers. Foliage retains rich green color all winter.

'Little Giant'—Rounded slow-growing dwarf that reaches 4'-6' high after 10-15 years. Deep green foliage maintains rich color all winter.

ARBORVITAE

Giant Arborvitae; Western Red Cedar

Thuja plicata

Evergreen tree

Thuja plicata 'Zebrina'

▶Hardiness: Zones 6-7; some cultivars are hardy to Zone 4.

▶Size: 60'-100' tall over time

▶Features: A forest giant where it grows wild in the Pacific Northwest, this slow-growing upright, cone-shaped evergreen makes an effective screen or vertical accent in the home landscape for many years. Because it is less susceptible to winter damage than American arborvitae, and is distasteful to deer, it is considered more trouble-free in many parts of the country.

▶Uses: Grouped as a screen or planted alone as a tall accent—a punctuation mark in the landscape.

▶Needs: Plant in full sun and any well-drained soil as long as it is not wet, although moist, well-drained woodland soils are best. Foliage tends to bronze in winter in full sun. Selections developed from inland plants are considerably hardier than ones developed from coastal plants. Needs little pruning.

▶Choices: 'Elegantissima'—an especially hardy cultivar (Zones 4-7) with yellow new foliage in early summer.

'Atrovirens'—another very hardy form (Zones 4-7) with deep green, almost black foliage that holds its color well into winter.

ARBORVITAE

Oriental Arborvitae

Platycladus orientalis, previously *Thuja orientalis, Biota orientalis*

Evergreen tree

Platycladus orientalis 'Conspicua'

▶Hardiness: Zones 6 (southern)-9

▶Size: The many cultivars range from 2' to 15' tall

▶Features: Best known for its popular golden or bright yellow forms, this arborvitae is unique in its flat, vertical branches covered with tiny scalelike leaves. Cultivars are available in many shapes, sizes, and foliage colors. Many are reliably dwarf, slow-growing, and easy to maintain.

▶Uses: The brighter-colored forms are useful wherever you need year-round accents and tidy growth. A matched pair or a single plant will catch the eye without overdoing. Foliage may clash with house colors, so use carefully near your home.

▶Needs: Plant in sun to part shade in any soil that isn't extremely wet. Poor, dry soil is fine. Very tolerant of heat. Grow colored-foliaged forms in full sun for best color development. Protect from winter winds, especially when grown in full sun, and avoid growing this plant where it is not hardy (it is often sold as far north as Zone 5).

▶Choices: 'Aurea Nana'—A long-time favorite for its low cost, bright—almost neon—golden-chartreuse color and tight, gumdrop shape. It rarely exceeds 1½'-2' in height.

'Conspicua'—Golden arborvitae. This popular plant has more aliases than any criminal. It may also be sold as Berckman's Golden Arborvitae, Berckman's Golden Biota, or Golden American Arborvitae. It is even frequently mislabeled 'Aurea Nana.' By whatever name, it's also a popular choice for its brilliant, yellow-green foliage and tight, upright conical form that eventually reaches 6½' tall and 2½' wide.

'Blue Cone'—Bluish-green foliage on a pyramidal, egg-shaped cone, it slowly reaches 6' tall.

Archangel, Yellow

Lamiastrum galeobdolon

Perennial groundcover

Lamiastrum galeobdolon 'Variegatum'

▶Hardiness: Zones 3-9

▶Size: 12"-18" tall with indefinite spread

▶Features: This rapidly spreading groundcover is an excellent choice for difficult deep shade and dry soil under trees where few other plants can grow. Silver and green leaves all summer, and hooded yellow flowers in late spring and early summer, help to brighten dark spots. Use with care where you can let it romp, since this plant can become an aggressive weed. Keep it out of flower beds unless it's the only flower you want there.

▶Uses: Groundcover beneath trees; rapid cover and erosion control on shady slopes and banks; containers.

▶Needs: While the most vigorous growth is in moist, well-drained soil in dense or partial shade, with this plant vigorous growth may not be a benefit. It performs beautifully in dry soil too. Cut plants back after summer flowers fade to promote thick foliage growth.

▶Choices: 'Herman's Pride' has more silver in the leaves than the species and is somewhat less invasive.

Archontophoenix cunninghamiana (Seaforthia cunninghamiana)
see Palms: King Palm

Arctostaphylos spp.
see Manzanitas

Arctotis spp.
see African Daisy

Arecastrum romanzoffianum
see Palms: Queen Palm

Arenaria montana
see Sandwort, Mountain

Arenaria verna caespitosa
see Irish Moss

Arizona Cypress
see Cypresses

Armeria maritima
see Sea Thrift

Aronia melanocarpa
see Chokeberry, Black

Arrowhead Vine
Syngonium podophyllum

Tropical trailing or upright evergreen perennial

Syngonium podophyllum

▶***Hardiness:*** Tropical
▶***Size:*** Grows 1'-3' tall and up to 5' wide
▶***Features:*** Distinctive arrow-shaped leaves are borne on tall, slender, somewhat vining stems. Easy to grow.
▶***Uses:*** As a houseplant; good for hanging baskets
▶***Needs:*** Bright, indirect light. Average house temperatures are fine but at least 60°F/16°C in winter. Keep soil moist at all times, less moist in the winter when growth is less. Appreciates a tray of pebbles filled with water for more humidity. Fertilize 2-3 times in summer when growth is most active. Mealybugs and spider mites can be problems. Rinse off plant in the sink every month or so to avoid infestations. Otherwise, treat with a houseplant insecticide.
▶***Choices:*** Look for a variety of markings on leaves. Some are solid green, while others have pale yellow or creamy veins, and still others have white or gold speckles.

Artemisia
Artemisia spp.

Perennials grown for their attractive foliage

Artemisia stellerana 'Silver Brocade'

▶***Hardiness:*** Zones 3-10, but differs according to species
▶***Size:*** 3'-4' tall and 24" wide; can easily be kept to 18" mounds
▶***Features:*** Mounds of striking silvery foliage are effective foils next to perennials that bear brightly colored flowers. Somewhat sprawling, floppy habit can be controlled into neat mounds by cutting back in midsummer after blooming. Flowers are inconspicuous.
▶***Uses:*** Combine with perennials in the mixed border, or use as an accent. Excellent filler between roses in the rose garden. Good in containers.
▶***Needs:*** Sandy, quick-draining soil in full sun. This plant is drought tolerant. Plant established plants in spring, summer, or fall; in Zones 9-10 plant also in winter. Mulch to prevent disease. Avoid fertilizing and overwatering. Plants get floppy in certain conditions and will look more attractive when cut back by about half in midsummer after blooming. Divide every year or two to keep in bounds if invasiveness is a problem. Also pull out unwanted sprouts and runners. Root rot or fungal diseases are problems in wet or humid areas.
▶***Choices:*** Silver mound artemisia *(Artemisia schmidtiana* 'Silver Mound') forms mounds, flops less, and is less aggressive. It has feathery, fine-textured silvery foliage, delightful for touching. Shear after blooming to maintain neat mounded shape. Hardy in Zones 4-10. Silver Brocade artemisia (*A. stellerana* 'Silver Brocade'), sometimes sold as *A.s.* 'Boughton Silver') is a bushy perennial with feathery, deeply lobed silvery-white leaves. It grows about 1' tall and 2' wide, and is hardy in Zones 3-9. Silver Queen and Silver King artemisia (*A. ludoviciana* 'Silver Queen', *A.l.* 'Silver King') have almost white, very silvery lance-shaped leaves. They form bushy plants 2-4' tall and 2' wide, and can be invasive. They are both often used in wreaths. They are hardy in Zones 4-7.

Artemisia dracunculus
see Tarragon

Artichoke
Cynara scolymus

Perennial vegetable

Artichoke

▶***Hardiness:*** Zones 7-11
▶***Size:*** 3'-6' tall, 2'-3' wide
▶***Features:*** Thistlelike plant produces an edible flower bud.
▶***Uses:*** In the vegetable garden. Sometimes grown in the flower border to show off its bold-textured foliage.
▶***Needs:*** Full sun. Artichoke prefers rich, well-drained soil with ample moisture but will tolerate poorer soils and less moisture. May die out in winters with freezing temperatures. Plants lose productivity after 4 years. Plant established plants in late winter after all danger of frost has passed. Plant 2'-3' apart in rows 3' apart. Cut off the artichoke with 1"-1½" stem before it begins to open. In winter, cut back plants to 10" and cover with loose winter mulch. In colder regions, grow as an annual. Few pests or diseases.
▶***Choices:*** Look for cultivars that are thornless, mature quickly, and produce many artichokes per plant. 'Green Globe Improved' matures in 90 days. 'Imperial Star' matures in 90 days, is thornless, and

has high yields. It's a good choice for growing as an annual. 'Violetto' is a lovely purple color and more cold hardy than other types.

Artillery Fern

Pilea microphylla (formerly *Pilea serpyllacea* 'Rotundifolia')

Tropical perennial

Pilea microphylla

► ***Hardiness:*** Zones 9–10
► ***Size:*** 6"–8" tall, 18"–24" wide
► ***Features:*** This plant, which is not a fern, produces inconspicuous flowers and is grown chiefly for its foliage. Its chartreuse, fine-textured foliage and low, dense form with horizontal branching make for a refined appearance tucked into tight spaces. It's named for its ability to shoot its seeds several feet away when they ripen.
► ***Uses:*** Plant artillery fern in narrow, confined spaces, beneath eaves, as edging along walkways or beds, near entries, beside steps. It makes an excellent container plant and is a favorite grown indoors as a houseplant.
► ***Needs:*** Plant in moist but well drained soil; fertile is best. Plants tolerate sandy soil but will need extra fertilization. Grow in full sun or partial shade—it makes a beautiful substitute for ferns in places that are too sunny. Tolerates reflected heat from paving and walls. It may be short-lived.

Arugula

Eruca sativa

Cool-season annual vegetable

Arugula

► ***Hardiness:*** Not applicable
► ***Size:*** Grows several inches tall, a few inches wide
► ***Features:*** Also called rocket or roquette, this salad green has a distinctive, piquant bite that adds zest to salads. Can also be steamed.
► ***Uses:*** In the vegetable garden
► ***Needs:*** Full sun to light shade, especially in regions where spring is early and hot. Prefers rich, well-drained soil with moderate moisture but will tolerate poorer, drier conditions as well. Does well in windowboxes, planters, and other containers. Plant in fall, winter, or spring as soon as you can work the thawed soil or as long as you can expect a few weeks of temperatures hovering above freezing and below 80°F/27°C. Arugula tolerates light frosts well but gets bitter in hot weather. Plant seeds ¼" deep. Harvest when leaves are 4"–6" tall. Few pests or diseases.
► ***Choices:*** 'Sylvetta' is smaller and more bolt-resistant than other types. Or try selvatica arugula *(Diplotaxis erucoides),* not a true arugula but similar and more heat-tolerant.

Arum, Italian

Arum italicum

Perennial

Arum italicum

► ***Hardiness:*** Zones 6–10
► ***Size:*** Forms clumps 12"–18" tall and wide
► ***Features:*** Arum is a bulblike plant with an unusual growth cycle: Its beautiful arrow-shaped leaves emerge in the fall, last through the winter, and wither in spring, to be followed by exotic hooded flowers in summer that transform into spikes of brilliant reddish-orange berries in late summer and early fall.
► ***Uses:*** Plant among lower-growing groundcovers such as vinca or pachysandra beside patios and shady pathways, beneath covered porticos and in courtyards, and in woodland areas.
► ***Needs:*** Plant in well-drained soil that's rich in organic matter. Grow in shade or sun.
► ***Choices:*** 'Marmoratum' has large leaves with silvery veins; 'Pictum' has leaves veined with gray and cream.

Aruncus dioicus

see Goatsbeard

Asclepias tuberosa

see Butterfly Weed

Ash, Green; Red Ash

Fraxinus pennsylvanica

Deciduous shade tree

Fraxinus pennsylvanica

► ***Hardiness:*** Zones 3–9
► ***Size:*** Grows 50' tall and 30' wide
► ***Features:*** Sometimes called red ash, this tree grows fast, lives a long life, and tolerates whatever growing conditions are thrown its way. Roots are well-behaved and will not buckle paving, although they will clog drains if given the opportunity. In good years fall color can be yellow. Trees are widely planted because of their ease of growth. Choose seedless varieties for less mess in the landscape.
► ***Uses:*** Good shade tree, street tree. Plant along walks or drives, next to patios, in open lawns and parking areas.

▶ Needs: Plant in soils ranging from acidic to alkaline, wet to dry, compacted or loose. Green ash tolerates drought, reflected heat from paving, and car exhaust.
▶ Choices: 'Marshall's Seedless' has especially rapid growth, is seedless and insect resistant. 'Summit' has a narrow, egg-shaped crown. Autumn Purple white ash *(Fraxinus americana* 'Autumn Purple') is a slower-growing shade tree with excellent purple to chocolate-brown fall color.

Ash, Mountain
see Mountain Ash, European

Asparagus
Asparagus officinalis

Perennial vegetable

Asparagus

▶ Hardiness: Zones 4–8
▶ Size: Grows 4' tall
▶ Features: Once established, an asparagus bed will produce early spring harvests for 10–30 years. The large plants are attractive in summer with sprays of feathery, fine-textured foliage.
▶ Uses: In the vegetable garden or a patch of its own
▶ Needs: Full sun to light shade. Deep, loose, rich soil that is well drained. Work soil well, digging 12"–18" deep and adding plenty of compost. Plant crowns (dormant plants) in spring 4–6 weeks before average last frost date, spacing 15"–18" apart and covering with 2" of soil. Keep well weeded and watered in first year. Mulch is helpful. Allow to grow to full height and to develop feathery foliage. Wait 2 years to harvest. Each spring, apply 1" compost to soil. Harvest in spring by cutting or snapping off plumper spears at base when 6"–8" tall.
▶ Choices: Choose all-male hybrids for best production. 'Jersey Knight' is one of the most popular. In California, the South, and the Pacific Northwest, plant 'UC157', which needs less chilling in winter.

Asparagus Fern; Sprengeri Fern
Asparagus densiflorus

Subtropical perennial

Asparagus densiflorus

Asparagus densiflorus 'Meyersii'

▶ Hardiness: Zones 9–11
▶ Size: Cascading branches that arch up to 1' tall and can be 2' or more long
▶ Features: This is not a fern, but a heat-tolerant, easy-to-grow plant with beautiful feathery leaves.
▶ Uses: As a houseplant; or outdoors as a perennial in mild-winter areas.
▶ Needs: Bright to minimal light; dislikes direct light. Keep soil moist; may need watering 2–3 times a week. Plants tend to become easily rootbound, so about once a month set the pot in a bowl partly filled with water to allow the soil to become thoroughly soaked. Divide and repot every spring; does beautifully outdoors in containers or hanging baskets in bright shade. Protect from constant high temperatures; provide a minimum of 50°F/10°C in winter. Fertilize each time you water with a half-strength 10-10-10 fertilizer. Sheds its tiny leaves as they yellow and die regularly. Keeping the plant cool and moist slows the process; shake out the leaves gently once a week.
▶ Choices: *Asparagus densiflorus* is by far the most popular asparagus fern. Plume asparagus fern *(A. d.* 'Myersii') is upright and distinctive, with compact, narrow "fronds." Plumose asparagus fern—also called emerald feather fern or lace fern *(A. setaceus,* formerly *A. plumosus)*—has gracefully arching, almost layered, feathery leaves that are mistaken for ferns more often than any other asparagus fern.

Aspen, Quaking
see Quaking Aspen

Asperula odorata (Galium odoratum)
see Sweet Woodruff

Aspidistra elatior
see Cast-Iron Plant

Asplenium nidus
see Ferns: Bird's Nest Fern

Aster
Aster spp.

Herbaceous perennial

Aster spp.

▶ Hardiness: Zones 4–8, but varies according to species
▶ Size: Ranges from 15" to 5' tall, depending on species
▶ Features: Valuable for its showy, late-season daisies that bloom late summer through fall. Colors range from blue through purple, pink, and deep rose, as well as white.
▶ Uses: In the mixed flower border; taller varieties are best in the back of the border where staking is less noticable. Excellent as a cut flower.
▶ Needs: Best in full sun but will tolerate light shade. This plant needs rich, well-drained but moist soil and does best where fall is cool and moist. Plant established plants in spring or fall. Pinch taller varieties back by half in early summer to prevent flopping, though they may still need staking. Fertilize lightly, if at all. Mulch well after cutting back in fall to prevent dying out during the winter. Mildew and fungal diseases are a chronic problem, so avoid watering overhead and choose disease-resistant cultivars. Protect from browsing deer, as this plant is a favorite of theirs.
▶ Choices: Many cultivars in numerous species and hybrids are available. New England aster *(Aster novae-angliae)* is hardy in Zones 4–8; it grows 5' tall and 2' wide. Michaelmas daisy, also called New York aster *(A. novi-belgii)*, is hardy in Zones 4–8. It reaches 4' tall and grows 3' wide. Frikart's aster *(A. ×frikartii)* is hardy in Zones 5–8 and grows 30" tall and 15" wide. *A. ×frikartii* 'Monch' is a popular selection of Frikart's aster with deeper, almost blue flowers.

Aster, China

see China Aster

Astilbe; False Spirea

Astilbe ×arendsii

Herbaceous perennial

Astilbe ×arendsii

▶ ***Hardiness:*** Zones 3-8

▶ ***Size:*** From 1'-4' tall, and 10"-3' wide, depending on species

▶ ***Features:*** Plumey spikes in mid- to late summer are an important source of color in the shade garden. Left on the plants after blooming, the spikes ripen into rich russet seedheads that remain attractive well into winter. Lush, dark green foliage is much-divided and fine-textured.

▶ ***Uses:*** Plant in large areas as a perennial groundcover for dramatic summer color.

▶ ***Needs:*** Needs shade, more in the South and less in the North. Astilbe requires rich, constantly moist but well-drained, deep soil. Plant established plants in spring or fall, working in compost. Fertilize regularly, every 4 weeks, for best health and flowering. Mulch to conserve moisture. After plant blooms, cut off fading flower stalks. Keep well watered. Leaves will scorch and shrivel if soil dries. Divide every 3-4 years in spring or fall. This plant is susceptible to crown rot in wet soil in winter. Japanese beetles and spider mites can also be problems.

▶ ***Choices:*** Numerous cultivars are available in rich reds, pinks, lilacs, salmons, creams, and whites. Choose for flower color, height, and early-, mid-, and late-season blooming. Chinese astilbe (*Astilbe chinensis* 'Pumila') is a low-growing variety with spiky pink flowers that blooms later in the summer than any other astilbe, making it excellent for extending the season.

Athyrium spp.

see Ferns: Japanese Painted Fern

Aubrieta deltoidea

see Rockcress, False

Aucuba, Japanese

Aucuba japonica

Subtropical broadleaf evergreen shrub

Aucuba japonica

▶ ***Hardiness:*** Zones 7-10

▶ ***Size:*** 5'-8' tall, 3'-4' wide

▶ ***Features:*** Japanese aucuba is a broadleaved evergreen that thrives in poor soil, partial sun, or deep shade. Attractive large, lustrous leaves range from solid deep green to speckled, to mostly yellow depending on variety, lending a tropical appearance to the garden. The foliage is neat in appearance, little troubled by insects or disease, and dense even in heavy shade.

▶ ***Uses:*** Good for shady corners, foundation planting, as understory shrub beneath shady trees where soil is dry, as background or accent (depending on foliage color). Performs well in large containers.

▶ ***Needs:*** Plant in partial sun or shade in rich to poor soil. The hotter the climate, the shadier your planting spot should be. Prune in spring. Variegated forms brighten dark, shady spots, but use them sparingly—it is easy to overdo.

▶ ***Choices:*** 'Crassifolia' has dark green leaves. 'Crotonifolia' has brightly colored leaves in gold and white. 'Longfolia' has bright green leaves with an unusual long and narrow shape. 'Nana' is a dwarf variety that grows 2' tall. Many other cultivars are available; choose for leaf color and form.

Aurinia saxatilis

see Basket-of-Gold

Autumn Crocus

Colchicum autumnale

Perennial fall-blooming bulb

Colchicum autumnale

▶ ***Hardiness:*** Zones 5-9

▶ ***Size:*** 4"-6" tall, 4" wide

▶ ***Features:*** This important source of late-season color bears large crocuslike blossoms in pink, white, and lavender hues in early fall, followed by foliage that remains green all winter then disappears in spring. Each bulb produces up to 6 flowers. All parts of the plants are toxic.

▶ ***Uses:*** Most effective in clumps planted among trees and shrubs and in the front of the border. Excellent in containers.

▶ ***Needs:*** Full sun to light shade. Average, well-drained soil. Provide ample water while plants are blooming; otherwise water moderately. Plant corms in mid- to late summer, 3-4" deep, in average, well-drained soil. Plant in groups of a dozen or more for best effect. This plant is usually pest free, and little bothered by deer and rabbits.

▶ ***Choices:*** Flowers come in pink, lavender, or white.

Avocado
Persea americana

Subtropical evergreen fruit-bearing tree

Avocado 'Haas'

▶***Hardiness:*** Zones 8–11, depending on the cultivar
▶***Size:*** Grows up to 40' tall and wide, depending on the type
▶***Features:*** Large trees produce delicious fruit.
▶***Uses:*** In the landscape, provides dense shade; otherwise use as edible landscaping.
▶***Needs:*** Full sun. Well-drained soil is essential; drought tolerant once established. Plant where this tree's shallow roots will be undisturbed; avoid digging around the tree. Mulch lightly. Plants bloom in late winter; production is heavier if two or more selections are planted. Fruit ripens from summer into winter, depending on type.
▶***Choices:*** Avocados are one of three types. Mexican types are hardy to 18°F/-8°C. Guatemalan are hardy to 21°-25°F/-6°- -5°C, and West Indian are hardy to 25°F/-5°C. Although the plants will survive these temperatures, the fruit-producing flowers are damaged by subfreezing temperatures. In years with a frost, the trees will not produce avocados.

Azalea
see Rhododendron

Baby's Breath
Gypsophila paniculata

Perennial

Gypsophila paniculata

▶***Hardiness:*** Zones 3–9
▶***Size:*** 18"–30" tall, 2'–4' wide
▶***Features:*** Lovely cloudlike sprays of tiny white or pink blossoms create a soft, ethereal effect in the mixed border. Drought tolerant. Blooms early to midsummer. An outstanding cut flower.
▶***Uses:*** Filler in the mixed border and in rock gardens; a mainstay for the cutting garden.
▶***Needs:*** Average to poor, well-drained soil. Thrives in alkaline soil; perishes if soil is too acidic. Does best if kept evenly moist, but will tolerate drought once mature. Dislikes extreme humidity. Plant seedlings in spring. Staking is usually needed to support top-heavy stems. Fertilize sparingly if at all. Cut back immediately after first bloom to encourage a second, late-summer bloom. This plant is usually pest free.
▶***Choices:*** Flowers come in whites or pinks. 'Bristol Fairy' is a popular white type. 'Compacta Plena' grows 18" tall.

Baby's Tears
Soleirolia soleirolii

Subtropical groundcover

Soleirolia soleirolii

▶***Hardiness:*** Zones 9–10
▶***Size:*** Grows 2"–3" tall and spreads indefinitely
▶***Features:*** Tiny round leaves grow along pink, succulent stems to form dense, mounding mats. Easy to grow. Used as a groundcover for shady areas in mild climates; good in containers and baskets. Does well in terrariums, though it tends to crowd out other plants.
▶***Uses:*** Easy to grow in containers indoors and out; useful as a perennial groundcover for moist, shady spots in mild-winter areas without hard frosts.
▶***Needs:*** Keep soil evenly moist. Baby's tears grows in about any light, but it prefers bright, indirect light. Does well in average home conditions with a minimum of 45°F/7°C in winter. Fertilizing is usually not necessary.
▶***Choices:*** Most baby's tears have solid gray-green leaves. *Soleirolia soleirolii* 'Argentea' has silvery leaves.

Bachelor's Button
see Cornflower

Bacopa; Water Hyssop
Sutera cordata

Subtropical perennial grown as an annual

Sutera cordata

▶***Hardiness:*** Zones 9–10
▶***Size:*** 6"–8" tall, 10"–14" wide
▶***Features:*** Hundreds of tiny, delicate white flowers sparkle among bright green, fine-textured leaves. Cascading habit is perfect for hanging baskets. Blooms summer to frost.
▶***Uses:*** Containers such as hanging baskets where its spilling, cascading form is effective. Or plant in the ground in the front of beds where it can flow out over the walk or along walls where it can drape.
▶***Needs:*** Full sun or light shade, especially Zones 7–11. Rich, well-drained, moist soil. Ample moisture; never allow to dry out. Dislikes heat, so keep out of hot situations, such as near a driveway or on a sunny patio. Plant established plants outdoors in spring after all danger of frost has passed. Because this is a thirsty plant that dies quickly if dried out, work water-retaining crystals into the soil under the plant. Mulch to conserve moisture. Fertilize occasionally, every 4–5 weeks, or work in a slow-release fertilizer at planting time. Bacopa will grow as a perennial in Zones 9–11, but it is best grown as an annual.
▶***Choices:*** Pink- and lavender-flowered selections are becoming available.

Bald Cypress

Taxodium distichum

Deciduous coniferous tree

Taxodium distichum

▶***Hardiness:*** Zones 4-10
▶***Size:*** Grows 50'-70' tall with a 20'-30' spread
▶***Features:*** This swamp native can tolerate the extremes, from soggy soils to hot areas surrounded with paving. Trees form towering cones of feathery foliage. Bright green spring foliage matures to a soft sage green in summer; fall color is a rusty brown before dropping. Trunks become massive and buttressed with age. When grown in water or in damp, marshy spots, trees develop knobby, protruding roots known as knees. Cones are green to purple in color and mature to brown in a single growing season. Growth is moderate to fast.
▶***Uses:*** Wet areas, compacted soils of newly constructed homes, natural areas, beside ponds or streams, swampy sites, specimen use
▶***Needs:*** Bald cypress grows in soil that's poor and dry, rich and moist, or just plain wet. Acidic soils are preferred; chlorosis develops on alkaline sites. Grow in full sun. Plants are very wind tolerant.

Balloon Flower

Platycodon grandiflorus

Herbaceous perennial

Platycodon grandiflorus

▶***Hardiness:*** Zones 3-8
▶***Size:*** 2'-3' tall, 1'-2' wide
▶***Features:*** Balloon flower is popular for its big, bell-shaped flowers in blue as well as pink and white. Buds swell into puffy "balloons" before opening into rounded bells. Blooms midsummer to fall for a long season of color. Foliage often turns a clear yellow in fall.
▶***Uses:*** In the mixed flower garden, beds and border. Excellent for a casual cottage-garden look.
▶***Needs:*** Full sun in Zones 3-6; light shade in Zones 7-8. Rich, deep, well-drained soil. Ample moisture. Plant established plants in spring. Mulch. Fertilize occasionally or work in a slow-release fertilizer each spring. Tall types may need staking. Trim individual flowers to promote longest bloom. After the first flush of bloom in spring, cut back by one-third to one-half for more blooms. In fall mark plants with stakes. Plants emerge late in spring and may be accidentally dug up during weeding. This plant needs no division but may be divided in spring for more plants. It is usually pest free.
▶***Choices:*** Flowers come in purples and whites, more rarely pink.

Bamboo Muhly

see Grasses, Ornamental: Muhly

BAMBOO

Indispensable for an Asian or tropical effect, this large group of tropical and subtropical grasses possesses an amazing variety of sizes, colors, growth habits, and textures, from low-spreading groundcovers 8" high to giant timber bamboos with trunks (called *culms*) 6" or more in diameter that grow 40' or more tall. Forms range from narrow, vertical columns to fine-textured, fountainlike sprays that arch to the ground; and from light and dark green culms to ones that are bright yellow and even pure black, shiny as lacquer, and sometimes dramatically striped. Bamboos are some of the fastest-growing plants in the world, and are famous for aggressively spreading, but there are clump-forming species that are refined and restrained in their growth habit. Most bamboos have a running habit, however, and are best grown where their growth can be confined, such as in a large container or a firmly confined planting bed, or where you can let them spread indefinitely into thickets and groves without worry. For running bamboo, remember that the underground rhizomes reach as far, and grow as quickly, as the aboveground culms—and instead of leaves sprouting from each node, a new culm shoots into the air. Underground barriers intended to prevent bamboos from spreading must be very strong and go 4 to 5 feet deep into the ground—bamboo rhizomes can penetrate the smallest crack in an underground barrier, and descend as far as 4 feet to go under a barrier and escape to the other side. Most bamboos are tropical or subtropical and intolerant of the slightest frost, but a few species are hardy as far north as Zone 5. All bamboos need a constant supply of moisture; drought causes the evergreen leaves to quickly turn an unsightly brown, and you'll have to wait until next year's culms arise to hide them.

BAMBOO

Hedge Bamboo

Bambusa multiplex

Tropical evergreen grass

Bambusa vulgaris 'Vittata'

▶***Hardiness:*** Zones 8 (southern)-11
▶***Size:*** 8'-35' tall, depending on variety
▶***Features:*** In mild-winter, subtropical climates where winter temperatures never go lower than 15°F, this species of bamboo is popular for several varieties that are outstanding for their restrained, clump-forming habit, arching gracefully with a fountainlike effect. All have narrow (¼"-1½") but interesting, shiny culms that you will want to expose by pruning away the lower leaves.
▶***Uses:*** Indispensable for Asian-themed gardens. Plant as a specimen in the lawn or incorporate into the shrub border at a woodland's edge—wherever you would use a large arching shrub with a tropical effect. Good for privacy screening, informal hedges. Smaller varieties make good container plants, although they may be short-lived. Leaf litter can be a nuisance around pools.
▶***Needs:*** Best in evenly moist, well-drained soil well-amended with organic matter and full sun to part shade. It's prone to winterburn at the northern edge of its climate tolerance, as well as scorch in hot-summer areas, so plant it where it is protected from drying winds.

▶Choices: 'Alphonse Karr' is a tall variety that reaches 35' in frost-free areas, 20' high farther north. It has 1" culms, striking for their horizontal green and yellow stripes. Chinese goddess bamboo ('Riviereorum') is a small variety that grows 6'-10' tall with narrow ¼" culms and lacy, fine-textured foliage. It is beautiful in containers for its graceful fountain shape. Golden goddess bamboo ('Golden Goddess') is similar but with bright golden yellow culms. 'Stripestem Fernleaf' is another small selection 6'-10' tall with white-and-green-striped leaves and stems. It is also good for containers. Clumping giant timber bamboo *(Bambusa oldhamii)* is a related species that can grow 50'-60' tall with massive 4" culms—very dramatic in large sites.

BAMBOO

Dwarf Bamboo

Pleiblastus spp.

Evergreen subtropical grass

Pleioblastus auricoma 'Dwarf Golden'

▶Hardiness: Zones 5-10

▶Size: 1'-3' tall, with indefinite spread

▶Features: If you have a well-contained area where you can let this baby romp, it makes a fast-growing, tropical-looking groundcover. In winter the deep green leaves turn tan along the edges for an attractive striped effect.

▶Uses: Excellent in Japanese gardens if well-contained. Good for erosion control on slopes. Performs well in containers.

▶Needs: Plant in sun or shade in virtually any soil. Be sure to contain this rampant spreader in beds with a deep concrete barrier or paving. In areas where the ground freezes in winter, mow every year in the spring before new growth emerges. In mild-winter areas, mow every few years to keep plants looking neat.

▶Choices: There are a number of dwarf running bamboos, and all are aggressive spreaders that need to be well-contained. *Pleioblastus argenteostriatus* grows 2'-3' tall with dark green leaves striped with white along the edge. It is a good choice for shade. Zones 8-11. Dwarf fernleaf bamboo *(P. distichus)* makes a lacy, fine-textured groundcover 2'-3' high. Zones 7-10. Pygmy bamboo *(P. pygmaeus)* is a very low-growing, aggressively spreading species (6"-12" tall) with narrow, fine-textured leaves. Zones 6-10.

BAMBOO

Fountain Bamboo

Fargesia nitida
(formerly *Sinarundinaria nitida)*

Evergreen hardy clump-forming bamboo

Fargesia nitida

▶Hardiness: Zones 5-10

▶Size: 6'-8' tall, arching as wide

▶Features: Restrained and graceful in size and form, this arching fountain of fine-textured foliage is becoming increasingly popular as the only hardy, clump-forming, nonrunning bamboo.

▶Uses: In Asian-themed gardens, in the mixed shrub border, as a screen, in the lawn as a specimen

▶Needs: Plant in rich, moist but well-drained soil well-amended with organic matter. Tolerates full sun if protected from drying winds, but partial shade is best. Tolerates shady areas well. In northern areas if foliage suffers winterburn, cut the clump to the ground in early spring before new growth emerges.

BAMBOO

Hardy Bamboo

Phyllostachys spp.

Evergreen subtropical grass

Phyllostachys aurea

▶Hardiness: Zones 5-10, but varies according to species

▶Size: 6'-25' tall with indefinite spread; varies according to species and region

▶Features: This group of running bamboos includes some of the hardiest bamboo varieties. Culms range from bright green to rich golden yellow, deep shiny black, and striped. All species in this genus spread aggressively and should be well-contained with concrete barriers at least 4' deep or wide expanses of pavement. In northern areas where the foliage suffers winterburn, cut to the ground in early spring before new culms emerge.

▶Uses: As groves and thickets in Asian-themed gardens, in beds and containers. Makes a good screen or hedge.

▶Choices: Yellowgroove bamboo *(Phyllostachys aureosulcata)* is one of the hardiest of all bamboos. It grows 12'-15' tall in northern areas, and up to 25' tall where winters are mild without freezing. Its culms are 1½" wide and deep green with a striking yellow groove running the entire length. Golden bamboo *(P. aurea)* grows 6'-10' tall with bright golden 1" culms. It's a good choice for a large container. Giant timber bamboo *(P. bambusoides)* is a more tender species with massive culms 6" in diameter that reach a height of 45'. It is spectacular in groves. Zones 8-10.

Banana

Musa acuminata

Tropical perennial

Musa ×paradisiaca

▶Hardiness: Zones 8-11

▶Size: 5'-10' tall, depending on variety

▶Features: The enormous, paddle-shaped leaves of banana bring the essence of the tropics into any garden. Even in areas out of its hardiness range, it's easy to grow in containers and bring indoors over the winter. And since it's fast-growing where summers are warm and long, it can even be grown as an annual, from seed that's easy to start indoors in winter. This banana may produce inedible fruit, but only in areas where it doesn't freeze.

▶Uses: For a tropical effect around swimming pools, water features, and patios, for dramatic tropical texture and form in the shrub or perennial border, as a patio plant, as a houseplant indoors.

▶Needs: Good in full sun to deep shade in deep,

rich, moist soil that is fertile and well-amended with organic matter. Plant in a protected area where wind won't damage its broad leaves. Fertilize regularly and keep soil moist. In areas at the northern edge of its hardiness range, plants will die back in winter but resprout from the roots. Even in mild areas, bananas are short-lived and will die back after a few years (usually after they have flowered and fruited), at which time they produce offsets that can be replanted to create new plants. Indoors, keep in a warm location with medium to bright light. High humidity is preferred.

▶***Choices:*** A number of cultivars of this banana are available, some with reddish or red-splotched and striped leaves. 'Zebrina' is particularly attractive, with deep green leaves striped in maroon. Japanese banana *(Musa basjoo)* is one of the hardiest bananas and reaches 15' high with gigantic 8' leaves. It is hardy in Zones 8–10, and will usually resprout after winter dieback in Zone 7. *M. ×paradisiaca* is a popular ornamental banana in Southern California and Florida. It forms huge clumps 20' high and 20' wide with multiple trunks. The leaves are up to 10' long. Zones 9–11.

Baptisia australis

see False Indigo, Blue

Barberry, Japanese

Berberis thunbergii

Deciduous shrub

Berberis thunbergii 'Atropurpurea'

▶***Hardiness:*** Zones 4–8

▶***Size:*** 3' tall, 4'–7' wide

▶***Features:*** Leaves appear early in the spring. Fantastic foliage color in summer and fall. Thorny plants create dense barriers. This spiny shrub will grow anywhere. It can tolerate tight root quarters, urban pollution, and neglect. Green summer foliage turns shades of orange, scarlet, or reddish purple in the fall. Spines are sharp and make effective barrier plantings, but avoid siting plants where children play, or use thornless varieties. Plants tend to collect blowing debris and require cleaning out in the spring. Growth in Zone 8 is limited.

▶***Uses:*** Hedges, barriers, foundation plantings, or border shrubs

▶***Needs:*** Plant anywhere except in standing water. Japanese barberry performs best in full sun in well-drained, fertile soil. Prune to shape after flowering. Plants tolerate urban conditions well.

▶***Choices:*** 'Atropurpurea' has reddish or purple leaves, turning red in fall. 'Crimson Pygmy' has deep red leaves that turn orange-scarlet in fall and grows 2'–3' tall and wide. 'Rose Glow' leaves turn rose-red in fall. The variety 'Thornless' is a better selection for areas where children play. Turning orange-red in the fall, it grows 3'–5' tall and 4'–6' wide.

Barrenwort

see Epimedium

Basil

Ocimum basilicum

Warm-season annual herb

Sweet basil

▶***Hardiness:*** Not applicable

▶***Size:*** Grows 9"–18" tall, 6"–12" wide, depending on the cultivar

▶***Features:*** Leaves have distinctive flavor; the perfect complement to nearly any dish containing tomatoes.

▶***Uses:*** Excellent chopped and sprinkled over fresh tomatoes, salads, or pasta dishes.

▶***Needs:*** Full sun. Rich, well-drained soil with ample moisture. Start from seed indoors 6 weeks before your region's last frost date or buy established plants. Plant outdoors after all danger of frost is past. Can harvest as soon as leaves appear. Trim off flowers to focus plant on producing maximum foliage. Slugs can sometimes be a problem.

▶***Choices:*** Sweet basil has traditional basil flavor. Spicy globe basil is smaller, globe-shaped, and has a spicier flavor. Purple-leaved types are available, including 'Purple Ruffles' and 'Purple Opal.' Thai basil has a distinctive flavor for Southeast Asian dishes.

Basket-of-Gold; Gold Dust Alyssum

Aurinia saxatilis

Herbaceous evergreen perennial

Aurinia saxatilis

▶***Hardiness:*** Zones 4–8

▶***Size:*** 8"–12" tall, 12"–18" wide

▶***Features:*** Rapid growth. Bright yellow flowers in late spring. Tolerates drought and rocky soil. Low clumps of gray-green foliage. Plant this evergreen cover in dry, rocky spots. You'll enjoy attractive clusters of bright yellow flowers from spring into summer. Not for areas that are hot and humid. May also be sold as cloth-of-gold or gold dust. Sometimes listed as *Alyssum saxatile.*

▶***Uses:*** Rock gardens, slopes, raised planters, planting beds, edging walkways or patios, entries, parking areas, arid landscapes, Xeriscaping, cascading over retaining walls

▶***Needs:*** Plant in any soil that's dry, including rocky soil. Grow in full sun. Trim after flowering to keep plants neat and compact. Water only during periods of extreme drought. Plant in spring or fall in loose, well-drained soil, adding sand or grit if the soil has much clay. Fertilize lightly if at all; plants will become floppy if the soil is too rich. Mulch to conserve moisture. After blooming cut back by one- to two-thirds to keep the plant neat and to encourage reblooming. Basket-of-gold dislikes transplanting but can usually be transplanted with success in the fall. This plant is prone to aphids.

▶***Choices:*** 'Variegata' has leaves edged with pale green; 10" high. 'Tom Thumb' is 3"–6" high. 'Citrina' bears pale lemon yellow flowers. 'Sunny Border Apricot' has apricot flowers.

Bauhinia spp.

see Orchid Tree

Bay; Sweet Bay; Grecian Laurel

Laurus nobilis

Shrub or tree with leaves used as an herb

Sweet bay

▶ ***Hardiness:*** Zones 8–11
▶ ***Size:*** Grows to 50' tall
▶ ***Features:*** Large evergreen broadleaf shrub providing pungent leaves used for cooking.
▶ ***Uses:*** A landscape shrub or at the edge of a vegetable or herb garden. Or prune into a standard small tree. Where not hardy, it is often grown in a large container as a patio plant and kept in a sunny spot indoors for the winter.
▶ ***Needs:*** Full sun to light shade. Bay prefers rich, well-drained neutral soil but will tolerate variations. Moderate moisture. Plant outdoors in spring. Can be grown as a container plant. Susceptible to scale. Spray in summer with a horticultural oil if scale occurs. Harvest by picking leaves. Preserve leaves by placing between layers of paper toweling and pressing for a few weeks between heavy books as you would pressed flowers.
▶ ***Choices:*** 'Angustifolia' has green wavy-edged leaves; 'Aurea' has green leaves tinged with gold.

Bayberry; Northern Bayberry

Myrica pensylvanica

Semievergreen to deciduous shrub

Myrica pensylvanica

▶ ***Hardiness:*** Zones 2–6
▶ ***Size:*** 5½' tall and wide
▶ ***Features:*** Northern bayberry is a tough shrub, surviving in any kind of soil and withstanding harsh salt spray and soil salts. Its bright green leaves release a familiar scent when rustled or crushed. Aromatic silvery berries ripen in late summer and fall, linger on branches through winter into spring, and are attractive to many birds. Cuttings make a lovely addition to fall or holiday flower arrangements. Plants are evergreen in warmer areas and deciduous in colder climates.
▶ ***Needs:*** Plant in full sun or partial shade. This shrub is easy to grow and adapts to a variety of soils, thriving in heavy clay, sandy, fertile, or poor soil. Prune in late winter to remove dead wood and to shape shrubs. To produce fruit, both female and male plants are needed (check plant tags).
▶ ***Uses:*** Hedges, screens, fencerows, foundation plantings mixed with broadleaf evergreens. Use along streets where salt from winter snow removal is a problem. Popular for dried flower arrangements. Excellent for seaside gardens and harsh exposures.

Bean

Phaseolus spp.

Warm-season annual vegetable

Pole bean 'Spanish Emeralds'

▶ ***Hardiness:*** Not applicable
▶ ***Size:*** Bush types grow 1'–2' tall and as wide; pole types grow 6'–8' tall and 1' wide
▶ ***Features***: Tender green beans grow on bushes or vinelike plants.
▶ ***Uses:*** In the vegetable garden
▶ ***Needs:*** Full sun. Good, well-drained soil with consistent moisture. Plant from seed 1" deep and 12"–18" apart two weeks after your region's last frost date. Provide teepees or other supports for pole beans. Beans start to produce in 40–100 days. Harvest daily for best production, picking beans while small and tender. If growing beans for drying, allow to dry on plants, then remove from pods and store. For longest harvest, plant a new crop every two weeks. Avoid high-nitrogen fertilizers, which decrease yields. Working with plants when wet can spread rust. Mexican bean beetle is this plant's worst pest; control with pyrethrin.
▶ ***Choices:*** Many types of interesting beans, including green, yellow, purple, and variegated beans. Bush types: Try disease-resistant 'Kentucky Blue', purple-streaked 'Marbel', or purple 'Royal Burgundy', or delightfully tender tiny French filet beans. Pole types: 'Kentucky Blue Pole', a disease-resistant vine; 'Kentucky Wonder', can be used fresh and green or dried. Choose a vegetable type of scarlet runner bean, such as 'Scarlet Emperor', for pretty flowers as well as foliage. Also try shelling beans for drying.

Bearberry

see Manzanitas

Beard-Tongue

see Penstemon

Bear's Breeches, Spiny

Acanthus spinosus

Perennial

Acanthus spinosus

▶ ***Hardiness:*** Zones 6–10
▶ ***Size:*** 3'–4' tall, 2'–3' wide
▶ ***Features:*** Dramatic, tropical-looking large leaves with oodles of sharp spines. Spikes of mauve-purple flowers that can reach 4' tall add to the drama in early summer. Plants can be invasive.
▶ ***Uses:*** Large sunny beds and hillsides, or shady ravines and wooded areas where a tropical look is wanted and plants can spread without worry.
▶ ***Needs:*** Plant in sun to part shade or even full shade; in hot climates provide more shade. Does best in average to sandy soil. Drought tolerant, it needs to be planted where roots won't be overly wet in winter. During extended periods of summer drought, it may go dormant and lose leaves if not watered. Choose a site where this vigorous spreader will have room to expand. Plant seedlings in spring or fall, keeping well watered for the first few months. Fertilize lightly if at all. Divide in spring. Handle mature plants with leather gloves to cushion sharp plant parts. Slugs and snails are sometimes a problem.

▶ ***Choices:*** *Acanthus mollis* is a more tender bear's breeches (Zones 8-11) with much larger, broader, even more tropical-appearing leaves than *A. spinosus*—and without the nasty spines. *A. mollis* 'Latifolius' is a variety with even larger leaves. It is the most popular acanthus for California and the Deep South.

Beautyberry, American

Callicarpa americana

Deciduous shrub

Callicarpa americana

▶ ***Hardiness:*** Zones 7–10
▶ ***Size:*** 4'-8' tall and wide
▶ ***Features:*** Upright stems bear coarse-textured leaves. Clusters of magenta berries circle stems like thick wreaths in autumn. Cut berried stems for use in indoor arrangements. Sprawling, arching form makes this shrub a poor choice for formal gardens. Tolerates a range of growing conditions.
▶ ***Uses:*** Good as specimen plants or seasonal accents or in seaside landscapes, natural areas, woodlands, shrub borders, and mass plantings. Attracts birds.
▶ ***Needs:*** Tolerant of shade or sun; plant in full sun for best-formed berries, but light shade helps berries last longer. Nearly any type of soil from wet to dry is OK, but moist, slightly acidic soil is best. Provide moderate to ample moisture. Beautyberry is salt tolerant and tolerates smog and seaside conditions well. Plant established plants in spring or fall. No need to fertilize. Mulch to conserve moisture. This plant produces small flowers in late summer that turn into berries in fall. Birds may eat berries. Throw a net over the shrub to protect and save it for cutting. In late winter or early spring, when it shows signs of new growth, trim back hard to 6"–12" from the ground. It blooms on new growth, so hard pruning ensures good berry production and tames its sprawling habit. Protect from rabbits, since they like this plant's new growth.
▶ ***Choices:*** 'Lactea' has blazing white fruit and is very effective. *C. bodinieri* 'Profusion' is a beautyberry from China with effective pink flowers in late summer, outstanding fruit display, and pink, rose, and purple fall foliage. It is hardy in Zones 6–9.

Beautyberry, Chinese

Callicarpa dichotoma

Deciduous shrub

Callicarpa dichotoma

▶ ***Hardiness:*** Zones 5–8
▶ ***Size:*** 3'-4' tall and wide
▶ ***Features:*** This easy-to-grow shrub has lovely lavender-pink flowers on arching stems in summer, but autumn is when it puts on its best show. Bright clusters of purple berries combine with yellow foliage to provide a colorful contrast. Berries linger after the leaves fall, covering stems.
▶ ***Uses:*** Specimen use, mass planting, shrub borders; use along driveways, walkways, and areas of high visibility
▶ ***Needs:*** Plant in full sun or light shade in well-drained, fertile soil. Cut plants back in spring, leaving only 4"–6" of stem. Let them resprout each year for vigorous growth and abundant flowering and fruiting.
▶ ***Choices:*** *C. dichotoma* var. *albifructus* has white berries and grows 3'-4' tall and wide; Zones 5–8. *C. japonica* (Japanese beautyberry) bears deeper purple berries and brilliant yellow fall foliage; 4'-6' tall; Zones 5–8.

Bedding Begonia

see Begonias: Wax Begonia

Bee Balm; Bergamot

Monarda didyma

Perennial

Monarda didyma

▶ ***Hardiness:*** Zones 4–8
▶ ***Size:*** 2'-4' tall, 1' 3' wide. Dwarf varieties are 12"–18" tall.
▶ ***Features:*** It's hard to find a better hummingbird-and-butterfly magnet than bee balm. Bees like it, too, of course. This prairie native produces scads of bright pink, lavender, magenta, or red flowers over a long season in midsummer. Flowers and leaves have a spicy fragrance. Blooms mid- to late summer.
▶ ***Uses:*** In mixed border, cottage garden, and wilder native meadow and prairie plantings
▶ ***Needs:*** Full sun in cooler regions (Zones 4–6) to part shade in warmer areas (Zones 7–8). Rich, well-drained soil. Moderate to ample moisture. Plant established plants in spring or fall. Feed occasionally, every 6 weeks, or work in a slow-release fertilizer at planting time. Trim spent blossoms to prolong flowering. Mulch to retain soil moisture. This plant spreads easily and can be invasive Divide every 2–4 years as needed. It is prone to mildew, so plant openly to allow for good air circulation, and cut plants back to the ground after flowering to promote growth of fresh, disease-free foliage.
▶ ***Choices:*** Choose mildew-resistant varieties such as 'Marshall's Delight' (pink), 'Gardenview Scarlet', 'Stone's Throw Pink', and 'Violet Queen'. Also look for new dwarf varieties from the Morden Research Station in Canada. They are reliably dwarf, growing 12"–18" tall, but don't spread aggressively, and are mildew resistant too.

Beech, American

Fagus grandiflora

Deciduous tree

Fagus grandiflora

▶Hardiness: Zones 3–9
▶Size: 50'–70' tall and wide
▶Features: Smooth, gray trunks; golden fall foliage; and dried brown leaves that linger through the long winter months make American beech an attractive landscape addition. Low, wide branches make a beautiful specimen in large open areas. The root system is shallow and the canopy dense; growing grass beneath it can be a challenge. Mulch instead for improved tree health and less work for you, or allow moss to grow by keeping the area clear of fallen leaves. If lower branches are left unpruned they will eventually cover the ground, eliminating the need to grow anything underneath. Nuts are edible and enjoyed by birds and squirrels.
▶Uses: Specimen use, woodland and naturalized areas, attracting birds and wildlife, providing winter interest. Because of low branches and surface roots, it does not make a good street tree.
▶Needs: Trees thrive in moist, well-drained, acidic soil. Avoid heavy clay or areas where construction equipment has compacted the planting site. Trees grow best in full sun or partial shade. This tree is intolerant of drought; in Zones 8 and 9 especially provide adequate moisture through hot summer dry spells.

Fagus sylvatica 'Rohan Obelisk'

▶Choices: European beech *(Fagus sylvatica)* is a similar tree that is somewhat more tolerant of dry spells than American beech. It is hardy in Zones 5–9. Fall foliage color is more muted than American beech, usually bronze to brown. In Zones 5–7, grow it in full sun; farther south, give it partial shade. Numerous cultivars come in a wide range of forms and foliage color. Weeping European beech, *F. sylvatica pendula*, has dramatically weeping branches that drape the ground. Tricolored European beech, *F. s.* 'Purpurea Tricolor', has fantastic purple leaves edged with pink and pinkish white.

Beet

Beta vulgaris

Cool-season annual vegetable

Beet 'Detroit Dark Red'

▶Hardiness: Not applicable
▶Size: Greens grow 10" or so tall, roots go several inches deep
▶Features: Brightly colored roots for salads, soups, and side dishes; tasty greens for cooking
▶Uses: In the vegetable garden
▶Needs: Full sun to light shade. Loose, deep soil with lots of organic matter (work in compost at planting time) with poor to moderate fertility. Likes slightly alkaline soil and consistent moisture. Well adapted to cool, moist climates. Plant seeds as soon as soil is thawed and can be worked well, up to 2–3 weeks before your region's last frost date. Plant seeds ½"–1" deep in rows 16" apart. When plants are a few inches tall, thin to 3"–4". Keep soil moist; do not allow to dry out. Mulch helps prevent drying. As the shoulders of the beets start to emerge, hill them by hoeing loose soil up and over them. Harvest baby beets when roots start to get round. Flavor is best when beets are 1½"–3" wide.
▶Choices: Many interesting colors are available. Red types are classics, but also try yellow, white, carrot-shaped, and varieties that when cut have colorful rings in the interior.

BEGONIAS

Begonia spp.

Begonias are a varied group of plants with a vast array of leaf shapes, colors, and textures as well as some spectacular flowers. Houseplants in colder climates, some types are also grown as annuals outdoors. Still others are grown as perennials in mild-winter climates in the South and Southwest.

BEGONIAS

Rex Begonia

Begonia ×Rex Cultorum hybrids

Tropical perennial

Begonia ×Rex Cultorum hybrid

▶Hardiness: Zones 10–11
▶Size: 10"–18" tall
▶Features: Gorgeous, roughly heart-shaped large leaves up to several inches across with stunning veined markings in burgundy, red, green, cream, silver, and brown. Grown for the beautiful foliage.
▶Uses: As a houseplant
▶Needs: Medium light; no direct light. Keep soil evenly moist; allow soil to dry slightly in winter. Overwatering may cause the crowns of the plant to rot. Average warmth. Good humidity; set on a tray of pebbles with water or double pot (see page 275)

with damp peat packed in between the two pots. Good air circulation is a plus as long as there are no cold drafts. Fertilize with a half-strength 10-30-10 solution at every watering during the growing season; stop fertilizing during the winter. Repot every spring. Pot-bound plants tend to lose color in their leaves.

▶ ***Choices:*** 'Merry Christmas' has beautiful green and red markings. 'Silver Queen' has elegant green and silver markings. 'Yuletide' has red, burgundy, and brown markings. 'Her Majesty' is cream, tan, and brown.

BEGONIAS

Angel-Wing Begonia

Begonia coccinea

Tropical perennial

Begonia coccinea

▶ ***Hardiness:*** Zones 10–11

▶ ***Size:*** Grows up to 6' if left unpruned

▶ ***Features:*** The largest of the begonias, these grow on bamboolike stems, called canes, and can grow as tall as a person. They produce lovely dangling waxy flowers in salmon, pink, red, and white. The leaves are glossy and up to 5" long.

▶ ***Uses:*** As a houseplant

▶ ***Needs:*** Medium light. When plants start to form buds, brighter light is needed. Keep soil evenly moist; allow soil to dry out slightly in winter. Overwatering may cause the crowns of the plant to rot. Average warmth. Good humidity; set on a tray of pebbles with water or double pot (see page 275) with damp peat packed in between the two pots. Good air circulation is a plus as long as there are no cold drafts. Fertilize with a half-strength 10-30-10 solution at every watering during the growing season; stop fertilizing during the winter. Pinch back branches each spring to encourage bushiness and fullness.

▶ ***Choices:*** *Begonia* 'Lucerna' is another cane-type begonia that looks very like the true angel-wing begonia and is grown the same way. The leaves, however, are splotched with white.

BEGONIAS

Tuberous Begonia

Begonia ×tuberhybrida hybrids

Tuberous perennial grown as an annual

Begonia ×tuberhybrida 'Nonstop Hybrids'

▶ ***Hardiness:*** Annual in all zones; can be perennial in Zones 10–11

▶ ***Size:*** 12"–18" tall, 8"–18" wide

▶ ***Features:*** Huge tropical flowers in rich, glowing colors brighten up any shady spot.

▶ ***Uses:*** Bedding, color accent, containers, hanging baskets

▶ ***Needs:*** Light shade to almost full sun in Zones 2–5; light shade in Zones 6–11. Tolerates even deeper shade in all zones. Rich, moist, but extremely well-drained soil (most successful in containers). Water well during bloom. Plant tubers indoors in spring in pots just deep enough to cover, 2–4 weeks before the last frost date. Transplant outdoors after all danger of frost has passed. Or plant in a permanent place outdoors when nights are above 50°F/10°C. Work a slow-release fertilizer or compost into planting spot. Fertilize every 4–6 weeks. Keep evenly moist. Trim spent blooms. Lift and store tubers in fall (page 204).

BEGONIAS

Wax Begonia; Bedding Begonia

Begonia ×semperflorens-cultorum hybrids

Short-lived perennial grown as an annual

Begonia ×semperflorens-cultorum 'Cocktail Brandy'

▶ ***Hardiness:*** Annual in all zones

▶ ***Size:*** 6"–12" tall and wide

▶ ***Features:*** A staple of Victorian beds, wax begonias are easy-to-grow, hard-working bedding annuals that provide bright color over a long season of bloom, spring to frost. Bronze-leaved forms have the added attraction of colorful foliage.

▶ ***Uses:*** Annual bedding plant. Peforms well in containers.

▶ ***Needs:*** Best in full sun to light shade in Zones 2–5; light to deep shade in Zones 6–11. Bronze-leaved types tolerate more sun, even in the South. Rich, well-drained soil and moderate moisture. Plant established seedlings in spring or anytime after danger of frost has passed. Mulch to conserve moisture and prevent disease. Fertilize regularly for best bloom and health. Water moderately, but overwatering will cause roots to rot. Pinch or brush off spent blooms. Usually pest and disease free; spider mites, leaf rot, and whiteflies can be problems.

▶ ***Choices:*** Wax begonia has flowers in pinks, whites, reds, and peaches. Leaves are bright green, bronze, or mottled.

Belgian Endive; Chicory

Cichorium endiva

Cool-season annual

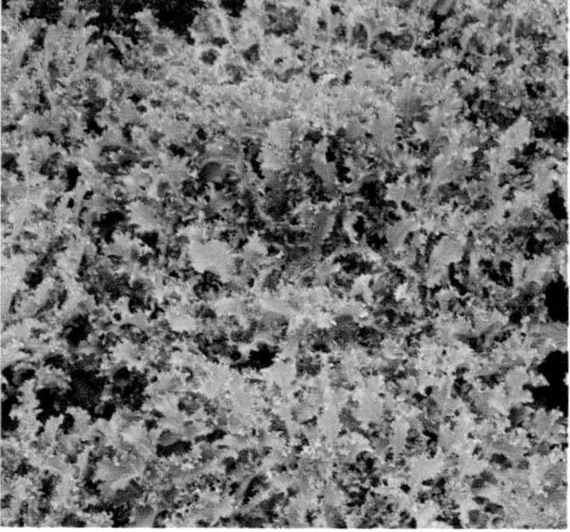

Belgian endive 'Salad King'

B

Plant encyclopedia

▶ **Hardiness:** Not applicable
▶ **Size:** Grows 8"-10" tall, a few inches wide
▶ **Features:** Tender heads resemble lettuce but are usually served braised. The taproot is used for a coffeelike drink.
▶ **Uses:** Indoor edible plant
▶ **Needs:** Belgian endive is usually grown indoors away from strong sunlight, which can make it bitter. Purchase roots to grow or dig up roots from chicory (the name for Belgian endive when it's grown outdoors for its tasty root) from the garden, if you already have some. Use roots 8"-10" long. Cut off foliage to 1". Closely pack roots upright in a 12" tall container with a drainage hole. Cover with sand 4" above roots. Cover with plastic bag to keep moist. Put in a dark place 50°-60°F/10°-16°C. When plants start to emerge from sand in about 3 weeks, harvest them by digging down to the crown and cutting off the long, pale, pointed head where it meets the root. Return potted roots to the sand; you should be able to get a few more harvests. Newer cultivars can be forced without soil in a cool, dark area. Simply put roots in the container without soil.
▶ **Choices:** 'Witloof Zoom' and 'Witloof Robin' need no soil.

Bell Peppers

see Peppers

Bellflower

Campanula spp.

Perennial or biennial

Campanula poscharskyana

▶ **Hardiness:** Zones 4-9
▶ **Size:** 8"-12" tall and wide
▶ **Features:** Lavender-blue star-shaped flowers appear over a long season from midsummer to fall on spreading stems covered all year long—even in winter—with bright green, heart-shaped leaves. Bellflower is a durable, easy plant that tolerates harsh winters and drought.
▶ **Uses:** Filling planting beds, in rock gardens, covering bare spots, as a groundcover on slopes, and in raised planters where it can sprawl over retaining walls. It's a good spiller for hanging baskets and other containers.
▶ **Needs:** Full sun or partial shade in Zones 4-5, although flowering is best in full sun; prefers part shade in Zones 6-9. Best in rich, moisture-retentive but well-drained soil, although any average garden soil is fine. It's tolerant of some drought, but performs best with moderate to ample moisture. Plant in spring or fall. Mulch to keep soil cool and moist. Fertilize lightly.

Campanula persicifolia

▶ **Choices:** There are many perennial bellflowers. Carpathian bellflower *(C. carpatica)* is a hardy perennial forming mounds of blue, violet, and white flowers all summer. It's best in northern cool-summer climates and rich, moist soil. 'Blue Clips', 'White Clips', 'Bressingham White', and 'Jewel' are some of the best cultivars. Zones 2-7. Italian bellflower *(C. isophylla)* is a more tender, mat-forming, trailing bellflower, useful as a groundcover in mild-winter climates, especially in cool coastal climates such as coastal California and Oregon. Its blue or white flowers are very effective in hanging baskets. Where summers are hot give it shade and plenty of moisture. Zones 6-10. Peach-leaf bellflower *(C. persicifolia)* produces a showy display of blue or white bells on erect stalks 2'-3' tall in early to midsummer. It is more tolerant of heat than most bellflowers, and the best choice for the South. Zones 3-8. Canterbury bells *(C. medium)* is a popular old-fashioned biennial producing tall erect stalks 1½'-4' tall with big bell-shaped flowers in blue, pink, and white. Planted in spring or fall the first year, it blooms the second year. Zones 3-8.

Bellis perennis

see English Daisy

Bells of Ireland

Moluccella laevis

Annual

Moluccella laevis

▶ **Hardiness:** Not applicable
▶ **Size:** 2'-3' tall, 6"-8" wide
▶ **Features:** Tall vertical stems cloaked in luminous green bell-shaped flowers are a favorite for flower arrangements, either fresh or dried. Blooms in summer. Reseeds prolifically; excellent for wild meadow areas where it can be allowed to multiply.
▶ **Uses:** Excellent in the vase. Best confined to the cutting garden or to wild, rough areas where its ungainly vertical form and ability to reseed are less of a problem.
▶ **Needs:** Full sun. Rich, loose, well-drained soil. Moderate moisture. In Zones 2-6 sow seeds directly on soil's surface in early spring, a few weeks before last frost date. In Zones 8-11 sow seeds in late autumn. Fertilize occasionally, every 4-6 weeks, or work in a slow-release fertilizer at planting time. Mulch if desired. Cut flowers at their peak for arrangements or drying. Few pests or diseases bother this plant.

Berberis thunbergii

see Barberry, Japanese

Bergamot

see Bee Balm

Bergenia cordifolia

see Pigsqueak

Betula spp.

see Birches

Bignonia capreolata

see Cross Vine

BIRCHES

Betula spp.

In nature, most birches play the role of pioneer trees, being among the first woody plants to repopulate an old field or burned area that's on its way back to becoming a forest. They reproduce prolifically and grow quickly, and are often susceptible to diseases and pests. They are thus relatively short-lived—especially compared with the taller forest trees that eventually overtake and shade them out, such as the maples and beeches of the Northeast or the oaks and hickories of the Midwest. In the home landscape, birches can serve a similar role. Enjoy their beautiful bark and trunk in new landscapes for rapid effect while you wait for slower-growing trees to take over. Single-trunk or multitrunk specimens planted in groves of five to seven provide more immediate impact when individual trees are young and small.

BIRCHES

Canoe Birch; Paper Birch

Betula papyrifera

Deciduous tree

Betula papyrifera

▶ ***Hardiness:*** Zones 2–5
▶ ***Size:*** 50'–70' tall, 25'–40' wide.
▶ ***Features:*** When you plant a canoe birch, you're planting a piece of history. Native Americans used the bark for making utensils, wigwam covers, and, of course, canoes. Its chalky white bark peels away in papery layers. Canoe birch is especially striking when planted against a backdrop of evergreens. The trees grow quickly to as much as 70' tall and add to fall's color show with leaves that turn shades of yellow and orange. Will not thrive in polluted areas.
▶ ***Uses:*** Specimen tree, planting in groves or natural areas, adding interest to winter landscapes, large yards
▶ ***Needs:*** Plant in full sun in acidic soil that's moist but well drained. This birch thrives in cool northern climates and transplants easily. In hot-summer climates stressed trees often succumb to insects and diseases, especially the bronze birch borer. Plant where low branches will not pose a problem. Or, remove obstructing branches in summer or fall when sap flow is less and bleeding from cuts is reduced.

BIRCHES

European White Birch

Betula pendula

Deciduous tree

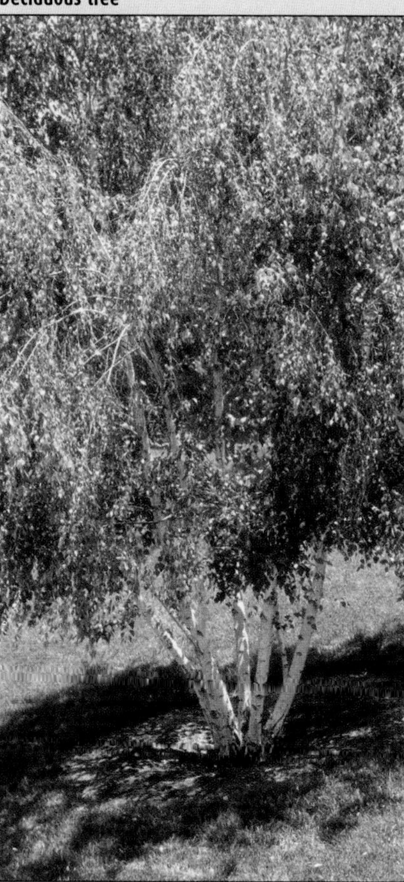

Betula pendula

▶ ***Hardiness:*** Zones 2–7
▶ ***Size:*** 40'–80' tall, 25'–50' wide
▶ ***Features:*** Striking black-and-white bark and graceful, almost weeping form are the hallmarks of this birch species. Trees grow best where summers are cool and moist. Glossy green summer leaves turn yellow in the fall. Very attractive planted against evergreens. This is not a tree for heat and drought. Stressful growing conditions like these invite birch borer insects and a wide variety of diseases. Look for multitrunked specimens for maximum effect. Rapid growth rate.
▶ ***Uses:*** Specimen tree, winter interest, groves, deciduous screen, corners of yards, cold growing regions
▶ ***Needs:*** Plant in moist, well-drained soil. Keep roots cool with mulch or groundcover. Adaptable to alkaline soil. Grow in full sun to partial shade. To prevent excessive bleeding of sap, prune in summer or fall.

BIRCHES

River Birch

Betula nigra

Deciduous tree

Betula nigra

▶ ***Hardiness:*** Zones 4–9
▶ ***Size:*** 40'–80' tall, 40'–70' wide
▶ ***Features:*** A great way to make a brand new or flat landscape look better is to add a fast-growing tree, especially a multitrunk specimen. An even better way is to plant a grove of them. River birch adds height, shade, and texture quickly. Cinnamon-colored peeling bark adds to its ornamental value throughout the year. River birch tolerates a variety of growing conditions; it will even tolerate standing in water. Heat tolerant, too, this is the best birch tree for the South. Other birches become stressed when temperatures rise, making them more susceptible to pests. River birch is resistant to borers. It's the largest of the birches and possibly the longest-lived. Where it grows in nature along rivers and in flood plains, an older specimen can reach 90' with a massive trunk and branches that spread almost as wide.
▶ ***Uses:*** Boggy areas, watersides, natural areas, beside patios and decks, along walkways. In open areas plant river birch in groves for rapid effect. Makes a good shade tree or deciduous screen. Provides winter interest.
▶ ***Needs:*** Plant in almost any soil from dry to soggy, poor or fertile. Acidic soil suits it best. Grow in full sun or partial shade. Prune only to remove obstructing low-hanging branches. Avoid planting near sewer lines and septic tanks; its roots will seek them out.
▶ ***Choices:*** 'Heritage' has outstanding peeling bark.

BIRCHES

Whitespire Birch

Betula platyphylla var. *japonica* 'Whitespire'

Deciduous tree

Betula platyphylla var. *japonica* 'Whitespire'

▶ ***Hardiness:*** Zones 4-7
▶ ***Size:*** 30'-50' tall, 20'-25' wide
▶ ***Features:*** The glossy green leaves of this tree shimmer in summer breezes, turn bright yellow in autumn, and fall to reveal showy chalk-white branches in winter. Bark turns white when branches are about 3 to 4 years old. Bark does not peel like other species of birch. Very resistant to bronze birch borers. Rapid growth rate.
▶ ***Uses:*** As a specimen tree, planting in groves in lawns and natural areas, adding winter interest, planting beside patios
▶ ***Needs:*** Plant in acidic soil that's either moist or dry. Grow in full sun. To prevent bleeding of sap, prune in summer or fall.

Bird-of-Paradise, Mexican

Caesalpinia mexicana

Tropical evergreen flowering tree

Caesalpinia mexicana

▶ ***Hardiness:*** Zones 10–11
▶ ***Size:*** 12'-15' tall and wide
▶ ***Features:*** Producing bright lemon-yellow flowers with long red "streamers" (stamens) during all but the coolest months, Mexican bird-of-paradise is a colorful addition to the landscape. Foliage adds interesting texture. Not frost tolerant. Needs little water once established.
▶ ***Uses:*** Small accent tree near patios or beside entries; adds shade and texture as well as color.
▶ ***Needs:*** Grow in well-drained soil and full sun. Water new plants frequently to establish; after that, water only during drought.
▶ ***Choices:*** Red bird-of-paradise *(C. pulcherrima)* is a red-and-yellow flowered shrub to 10' tall. Zones 9–10. Red bird-of-paradise is more hardy and may sprout again if damaged by frost.

BIRD-OF-PARADISE

Bird-of-paradise plants seem to embody the very meaning of "tropical" in the landscape. Huge, dramatic, bananalike leaves appear on top of long stalks; exotic, other-worldly flowers bloom nearly all year long. Described as a shrub and a tree, both species listed here are large evergreen perennials.

BIRD-OF-PARADISE

Bird-of-Paradise

Strelitzia reginae

Evergreen shrub

Strelitzia reginae

▶ ***Hardiness:*** Zones 10–11
▶ ***Size:*** 5'-6' tall, 3'-6' wide
▶ ***Features:*** Brilliant, exotic flowers are orange and blue. Clumps of big, coarse foliage. Excellent, long-lasting cut flowers. Plants are neat and virtually litter-free.
▶ ***Uses:*** Accent plants, single specimen use, entries, courtyards, shrub beds, containers, patio plantings; excellent beside the pool and near paving
▶ ***Needs:*** Plant in fertile soil that's moist but well drained. Grow in full sun or provide some afternoon shade. For the most spectacular blooms, feed once a month with a balanced fertilizer during the hot season and water regularly. Bright birdlike blooms are showiest during cool months, but you'll enjoy the clumps of foliage year-round. Protect plants if frost is a possibility. Remove dead foliage after new leaves emerge.

BIRD-OF-PARADISE

White Bird-of-Paradise; Giant Bird-of-Paradise

Strelitzia nicolai

Evergreen tree

Strelitzia nicolai

▶ ***Hardiness:*** Zones 9–10
▶ ***Size:*** 25'-30' tall, 12'-15' wide
▶ ***Features:*** Slow-growing. Big, dramatic leaves provide accent. Upright shape and form. White blooms resemble perching birds. Tall sprays of leaves make a dramatic accent in the landscape.
▶ ***Uses:*** Large, coarse-textured accent, tropical appearance, single specimen, entry areas, around swimming pools, hiding blank walls
▶ ***Needs:*** Plant in full sun or partial shade. Soil must be well drained. Water regularly for best appearance. Feed frequently when first planted to help plants gain in size. Once established, taper off feeding to twice a year. Leaf damage occurs during even short freezes. Prolonged freezes will kill plants. Provide shelter in Zone 9.

Bishop's Hat

see Epimedium

Bishop's Weed; Silver-Edge Goutweed; Snow-on-the-Mountain

Aegopodium podagraria 'Variegatum'

Perennial groundcover

Aegopodium podagraria 'Variegatum'

► ***Hardiness:*** Zones 3-9
► ***Size:*** 1' tall with indefinite spread; flower stalks can reach 2'
► ***Features:*** Groundcover performs well in sun or shade. Lustrous green-and-white foliage spreads quickly; vigorous growth is a hallmark of this plant. Isolate from other types of groundcovers and perennials; its vigorous growth will choke other plants out. Small white flowers clustered on 2' stems appear in early summer.
► ***Uses:*** Filling in where grass won't grow, massing, erosion control, hillsides, dry shade around tree roots, naturalized areas, large planting beds, brightening dim, shaded areas
► ***Needs:*** Plant in any kind of soil. Bishop's weed will grow in full sun, partial or dense shade; protect from afternoon sun in hotter climates. Tolerates full sun where summers are cool. Remove any solid green foliage that appears, or patches may revert to all-green foliage. Prune away flower stalks after blooming.

Bittersweet, American

Celastrus scandens

Deciduous vine

Celastrus scandens

► ***Hardiness:*** Zones 3-8
► ***Size:*** Can grow 20' in a season
► ***Features:*** Maturing in autumn, bright red berries are nestled inside yellow capsules. The fruit is widely used in dried arrangements in fall and winter. Plants are easy to grow and vigorous. Vines can girdle the trunks of young trees, killing them.
► ***Uses:*** Autumn accent; growing on fences, trellises, or arbors; natural areas; hiding scars in the landscape
► ***Needs:*** Plant in any kind of soil, damp or dry, average to poor fertility. This vine grows in sun or shade, but full sun yields the most fruit. Plant established plants in spring or fall. Both a male and female plant are necessary for berry production. This vine climbs by twining and needs a large, heavy arbor, large tree, sturdy fence, or pergola that will accommodate its full 15'-25' size. Fertilizing is unnecessary. Prune heavily each spring to control size. The colorful berries are poisonous.
► ***Choices:*** Insignificant flowers are produced; grown primarily for orange and scarlet berries. Avoid planting Oriental bittersweet *(Celastrus orbiculatus)*, which is spread by birds in Northeast woodlands and is invasive. It is often mislabeled as American bittersweet.

Blackberry

Rubus hybrids

Shrublike bramble with berries

Blackberry

► ***Hardiness:*** Zones 4-9
► ***Size:*** Grows 8'-15' tall, depending on the type
► ***Features:*** Succulent tiny dark fruits in summer
► ***Uses:*** In a berry patch
► ***Needs:*** Full sun. Likes sandy, moist, acidic loam but does well in drier and poorer soils. Tolerates heat better than raspberries. Blackberries, especially trailing types, are easiest to harvest and most manageable to prune when trained on a trellis. Plant dormant woody suckers in spring, planting 1" deeper than the container and 30" apart. Prune trailing types back hard. Prune erect types lightly. Harvest when fruit is shiny, soft, deeply colored, and pulls off easily.
► ***Choices:*** Trailing types can have canes up to 15' long. Erect or upright types have canes that grow only 8' or so. Thornless cultivars are available but are usually less cold-hardy than other types.

Black Chokeberry

see Chokeberry, Black

Black-Eyed Susan; Gloriosa Daisy

Rudbeckia spp.

Perennial; some grown as annual

Rudbeckia fulgida 'Goldsturm'

▶Hardiness: Zones 3–10
▶Size: 8"–4' tall, 2'–4' wide, depending on variety
▶Features: Goldsturm black-eyed Susan is a popular perennial for its golden, almost neon blooms with striking black centers. It blooms over a long season from mid- to late summer; the flowers are followed by black seed heads that are effective all winter, especially against snow. Gloriosa daisies are short-lived perennials usually grown as annuals, with broad daisy flowers in yellow to orange and chocolate brown, often bicolored and striped with contrasting colors. Both are beautiful grown among ornamental grasses, the larger sedums, blazing star, Joe-pye weed, asters, and other late-season perennials.
▶Uses: In the mixed border (use the dominant, intense yellow of Goldsturm with care) and cottage garden. Large beds have an almost overpowering effect. All types are excellent as cut flowers.
▶Needs: Full sun. Rich to average soil; tolerates clay. Abundant moisture is best but will tolerate heat and drought once established. Plant perennial types in spring or fall. Plant annual types in spring after all danger of frost has passed. Mulch to conserve moisture. Fertilize rarely. Tall types may need staking. Trim spent blooms to promote longer flowering. Powdery mildew may be a problem.
▶Choices: Perennial black-eyed Susan or orange coneflower *(R. fulgida)* is a popular flower, especially 'Goldsturm'. It's hardy in Zones 3–9. Gloriosa daisy *(R. hirta)* is a short-lived perennial usually grown as an annual. It may come back for a second year in Zones 3–10. Shining coneflower *(R. nitida)* is a 4' tall perennial in Zones 4–10. It performs well in the South.

Black-Eyed Susan Vine

Thunbergia alata

Tropical perennial vine grown as an annual

Thunbergia alata

▶Hardiness: Zones 10–11
▶Size: 6'–10' tall and wide
▶Features: Restrained and small in size as vines go, this annual nevertheless grows quickly from seedling to flowering size in early summer to provide a long season of bloom. The funnel-shaped flowers are yellow, orange, or creamy white with dark centers and make a good show.
▶Uses: Covering trellises, lattice, small fences, and mailboxes
▶Needs: Rich, well-drained soil. Ample moisture. Grow as an annual in Zones 2–9, a perennial in Zones 10–11. Plant established seedlings or sow seeds directly in soil in late winter or spring, after all danger of frost. Work a few spadefuls of compost into soil or add a slow-release fertilizer. Once they are about 1" high, thin plants to at least 12" apart. This vine climbs by twining; support can include trellises, string trellises, teepees, lattice, chain link fencing, or mailboxes. In Zones 2–9 tear or cut down after frost or when it gets ragged in early winter. In Zones 10–11, frost will kill to the ground but plants will reemerge.
▶Choices: 'Susie' series is the most popular, with flowers that are yellow, orange, and cream with dark brown centers.

Black Mondo Grass

see Mondo Grass, Black

Blanket Flower

Gaillardia spp.

Annuals and perennials

Gaillardia ×grandiflora

▶Hardiness: Zones 2–10
▶Size: 10"–3' tall, 10"–2' wide, depending on variety
▶Features: You can grow this bright bloomer anywhere soil stays dry. It thrives in hot, warm, or cold climates—even in harsh seashore areas. Fiery yellow, maroon, and reddish flowers appear nonstop summer through frost, even through hot spells. It flowers well without regular deadheading.
▶Uses: Seaside gardens, hillsides, ditches, raised beds, berms, parking areas, seasonal accent, along sunny walkways or patios, containers, covering bare, dry hot spots
▶Needs: Plant in well-drained soil. Poor, dry, sandy soil is fine. Grow in full sun. This plant tolerates heat and drought. It is salt tolerant. Plant in spring; perennial types can also be planted in fall. Divide perennials every few years in the spring. Allow to dry between waterings. Fertilize lightly, if at all; trim spent blooms to keep plant blooming until early autumn or even frost. This plant is prone to powdery mildew and leaf hoppers. It is also susceptible to crown rot in wet conditions.
▶Choices: Flowers are usually bicolored in autumn colors—reds, golds, yellow, burgundy, and cream. *Gaillardia pulchella* is the annual blanket flower and can be grown in Zones 2–11; *G. ×grandiflora* is the perennial type and can be grown in Zones 2–10.

Blazing Star; Gayfeather

Liatris spp.

Perennial

Liatris spicata

▶Hardiness: Zones 3–9
▶Size: 18"–3' tall, 8"–2' wide, depending on variety
▶Features: This beloved native of prairies and meadows produces tall spikes of bright pink, purple, or white flowers. Plant it in generous masses and drifts for a truly spectacular effect in midsummer. Flowers attract butterflies.
▶Uses: A must for the natural meadow garden and for butterfly gardens, blazing star is also a refined plant for the mixed border and cottage garden.
▶Needs: Full sun. Average to sandy, rich soil. Moderate moisture. Plant established plants in spring. Mulch to conserve moisture. Fertilize occasionally, every 6 weeks or so, or work in a slow-release fertilizer each spring. Stake as needed; plants withstand crowding well and seem to appreciate a close neighbor they can lean against for support. Trim spent blooms promptly to encourage a second bloom. Divide about every 4 years or so if needed. This plant is generally trouble free, though root knot nematodes can be a problem in the South.
▶Choices: Blooms come in pinks, purples, and whites. 'Kobold' is an especially refined cultivar that grows 18" to 2' feet tall and produces thick clumps

of flowering stems over time. Unlike those of other varieties, its blooms open starting from the top of the spike and work their way down, which provides a neater and more colorful appearance over a longer time. Kansas gayfeather *(Liatris pycnostachya)* grows to 5' tall.

Bleeding Heart; Fringed Bleeding Heart

Dicentra spp.

Perennial

Dicentra spectabilis

▶***Hardiness:*** Zones 2–9
▶***Size:*** 9"–4' tall and wide, depending on variety
▶***Features:*** Old-fashioned bleeding heart is a favorite shady-garden plant valued for its romantic strings of pink or white heart-shaped flowers that appear for a couple of weeks in early spring with the tulips. Fringed bleeding hearts are more delicate in size, with soft, ferny foliage, and produce flowers in woodland gardens over a longer season, sometimes as long as spring to fall.
▶***Uses:*** In the shade garden or natural woodland areas
▶***Needs:*** Full sun to light shade in Zones 2–5; light to full shade in Zones 5–9. Rich, well-drained soil with plenty of compost. Keep constantly moist, especially in full sun. Plant established plants in fall or spring. Mulch. Trim spent blooms.
▶***Choices:*** *Dicentra eximia*, everblooming or fringed bleeding heart, blooms with the daffodils and, in Zones 2–5, continues lightly until frost. Its ferny foliage stays pretty all season long in Zones 3–9. 'Luxurient' is a hybrid between fringed bleeding heart and western bleeding heart that puts on a continuous, outstanding show of deep rose flowers all summer. *D. spectabilis*, common or old-fashioned bleeding heart, makes a spectacular show in early spring, but the whole plant goes dormant by midsummer. Hostas planted nearby can cover bare spots in Zones 2–9.

Bloody Cranesbill

see Geranium, Hardy

Blue-Eyed Mary

Omphalodes verna

Semievergreen perennial groundcover

Omphalodes verna

▶***Hardiness:*** Zones 5–9
▶***Size:*** 2"–8" tall, 8"–12" wide
▶***Features:*** Try this groundcover for bright blue, white-eyed blossoms in shady places. Plants bloom in spring with daffodils and early tulips. The heart-shape leaves are semievergreen and effective well into winter. Plants quickly fill bare areas and return every year without fail.
▶***Uses:*** Planting beneath trees and shrubs, pairing with spring flowering bulbs, woodland gardens
▶***Needs:*** Grow in partial shade. Plant in moist, fertile soil that's well drained and somewhat acidic. Plants will tolerate poor soil or dry shady spots but will spread less quickly. Dig and divide plants in fall or spring to increase plantings or to control spread. Plants reseed prolifically, but seedlings are easy to pull. Apply slug repellent in early spring.
▶***Choices:*** 'Alba' has white flowers.

Blue False Indigo

see False Indigo

Blue Flax

see Flax, Blue

Blue Lilyturf

see Lilyturf, Blue

Blue Marguerite

Felicia amelloides

Subtropical perennial grown as an annual

Felicia amelloides

▶***Hardiness:*** Perennial in Zones 9–10
▶***Size:*** 1'–3' tall, 2'–5' wide
▶***Features:*** Blooms very early spring to midspring, or nearly all year in cool coastal climates.
▶***Uses:*** Containers, seasonal bedding
▶***Needs:*** Rich, well-drained soil. Tolerates drought, but flowers better with moderate water. Plant in early spring in Zones 7–8; in fall in Zones 9–11. Pinch, deadhead, and cut back by about one-quarter frequently to keep plant looking neat and flowering abundantly. This will also prevent it from spreading too much. Fertilize every 4–6 weeks or work in a 9-month slow-release fertilizer in spring. Plants will usually overwinter in Zones 9–11 but get shabby after a year or two. Better grown as an annual. It is usually pest free.
▶***Choices:*** Flowers come in shades of blue. 'Astrid Thomas' is a dwarf type and stays open at night. 'Midnight' is a lovely dark blue.

Blue Star

Amsonia tabernaemontana

Perennial

Amsonia tabernaemontana

▶***Hardiness:*** Zones 3–9
▶***Size:*** 1½'–2' tall and wide
▶***Features:*** Starry cool blue flowers cover this perennial from late spring and continue through the middle of summer for a quiet, restrained effect that sets off other, brighter-colored flowers. Its neat, upright form makes a nice addition to areas where shorter groundcovers may be hidden from view. In fall, however, this plant takes center stage when its narrow green leaves turn a blazing yellow. Best of all, it's easy to grow—plants adapt well to poor soil.
▶***Uses:*** Good for wildflower gardens, perennial beds, entries, along fences, around decks, or at the foot of rock walls
▶***Needs:*** Plant in well-drained soil. Avoid excessively fertile soil or extra fertilization. Growth will be floppy and open if plants are overfertilized. Trim plants back after flowering to increase density. In cool areas plant in full sun, but pick a spot that's partially shaded if your summer temperatures are warm.
▶***Choices:*** Arkansas amsonia *(Amsonia hubrechtii)* has narrow, willowlike leaves that present a fountain of feathery, fine texture. Its fall color is especially impressive, even in the South, and it's more tolerant of heat than *A. tabernaemontana*.

Blue Star Creeper

Pratia pedunculata (formerly *Isotoma fluviatilis* and *Laurentia fluviatilis*)

Evergreen groundcover

Pratia pedunculata

▶**Hardiness:** Zones 5–10
▶**Size:** 1"–5" tall, 18"–24" wide
▶**Features:** Fine-textured, mosslike leaves are sprinkled with tiny light-blue flowers in late spring and summer. Plants spread to form a refined, mossy groundcover that blankets the soil, seeming to flow around rocks and pavers.
▶**Uses:** Effective as a groundcover around rocks and between paving stones or stepping-stones.
▶**Needs:** Full sun to part shade in cool-summer climates; part shade to shade in hot-summer climates. Average garden soil. Space plants 6"–12" apart. Water regularly and generously in summer. Fertilize monthly from spring to fall.

Bluebeard

Caryopteris ×*clandonensis*

Deciduous flowering shrub

Caryopteris ×*clandonensis* 'Longwood Blue'

▶**Hardiness:** Zones 5–8
▶**Size:** 2'–3' tall and wide; grows quickly
▶**Features:** Airy sprays of light blue flowers and grayish leaves give this shrub a charming, hazy effect in the landscape. Valuable for its late-season flowers in late summer and early fall, when most other shrubs are not blooming. Foliage is aromatic when bruised.
▶**Uses:** In the mixed shrub or perennial border. Most effective massed in groups. Makes a beautiful contrast with Moonbeam coreopsis.
▶**Needs:** Full sun. Appreciates good, well-drained garden soil amended with organic matter. Cut to the ground each spring for a neater habit and more flowers.
▶**Choices:** 'Azure' and 'Heavenly Blue' have bright blue blooms; 'Longwood Blue' has light blue flowers and gray-green leaves.

Blueberry

Vaccinium spp.

Berry-producing deciduous shrub

Blueberry 'Blueband'

▶**Hardiness:** Zones: 4–9
▶**Size:** Grows 18"–15' tall and 18"–10' wide, depending on the type
▶**Features:** Easy, attractive bushes that produce tasty fruits in summer. It's one of the best bird-attracting plants around, so be sure to plant one for the birds and one for you, and plan on draping plants with nets if you want all the berries. Makes an outstanding ornamental shrub with lustrous green leaves and attractive white bell-shaped flowers in spring. Some varieties have good fall color.
▶**Uses:** In the berry patch or as a hedge
▶**Needs:** Full sun. Moist, acidic soil (see page 136) is a must. Grow in 1' raised beds with acidified soil in regions with neutral or alkaline soils. Prune each spring. If soil is not naturally acid, fertilize with ammonium sulfate or another acidifying agent.
▶**Choices:** Highbush types grow 8'–15' producing much fruit; berries are especially tasty. Lowbush types grow up to 3' tall, short enough for snow to protect them, and are good choices for the North. Choose low-chill types for the South. Early-, mid-, and late-season cultivars are available.

Blushing Bromeliad

see Bromeliads

Bog Rosemary

Andromeda polifolia, formerly *A. rosmarinifolia*

Evergreen shrub

Andromeda polifolia

▶**Hardiness:** Zones 2–6
▶**Size:** 16"–18" tall, 18"–24" wide
▶**Features:** As long as soil is acidic, bog rosemary tolerates dampness. Tiny white-to-pink, balloon-shaped flowers open in spring and continue through early summer. Leaves stay lustrous dark green in all seasons. Small size and slow growth make this an excellent plant for tight corners and small spaces.
▶**Uses:** Shady beds, rock gardens, woodland areas, moist locations
▶**Needs:** Plant in well-drained, fertile, moist, acidic soil. Increase soil acidity by adding peat moss or composted oak leaves at planting time. Mulch well to conserve moisture. Plant in full sun or partial shade for best growth.
▶**Choices:** 'Alba'—abundant white blooms; 6" tall, 8" wide; 'Compacta'—pink blooms, glaucous leaves; 12" tall, 8" wide.

Bok Choy; Pak Choi

Brassica rapa

Cool-season annual vegetable

Bok Choy 'Mei Quing Choi'

▶**Hardiness:** Not applicable
▶**Size:** Grows 4"–8" tall, 4"–8" wide
▶**Features:** Dark green leaves with thick, crunchy midribs; excellent for stir-fry.
▶**Uses:** In the vegetable garden
▶**Needs:** Full sun to light shade. Rich soil, tolerates sand and clay. Plentiful moisture.

Most cultivars need short days or they'll bolt (send up flower stalks), going bitter. Others will tolerate any day length. Check package for planting directions. Those types that can be grown no matter how long the days are can be planted in spring on the average last frost date for spring harvests or in mid- to late summer for fall harvests. Those that need short days should be planted only in mid- to late summer for fall harvests. Plant seeds ½" apart in rows 2'–2½' apart. Thin emerging plants to 10" apart. Thinnings can be used in stir-fries and salads. Keep soil evenly moist. Fertilize every 2–4 weeks to encourage rapid growth. Harvest by picking outer leaves as needed. Cut whole head when large and weighing up to 3 pounds.

▶ ***Choices:*** 'Shanghai' tolerates warm weather and can be planted in spring or fall.

Boltonia

Boltonia asteroides

Perennial

Boltonia asteroides

▶ ***Hardiness:*** Zones 4–9

▶ ***Size:*** 3'–7' tall, 3'–4' wide

▶ ***Features:*** Good late-season perennial flowers can be hard to come by, but boltonia blooms late in spades. Its bushy, strongly upright plants are covered with an explosion of small white, pink, or blue daisies in early to late fall. They look great in the mixed border with ornamental grasses, Joe-Pye weed, Autumn Joy sedum , and other plants with attractive fall seed heads, as well as with asters, chrysanthemums, black-eyed Susans, and other fall-blooming flowers.

▶ ***Uses:*** Toward the rear of the mixed border or in natural meadow or prairie plantings.

▶ ***Needs:*** Prefers full sun but will tolerate very light shade. It needs rich, moist, but well-drained soil and moderate water the first year. It is drought tolerant when mature. Plant established plants in spring. Mulch to prevent disease. Fertilize lightly. Stake in rich soil or in shade. Divide plants every 3–4 years. Boltonia is fairly pest and disease free.

▶ ***Choices:*** Boltonia flowers come in pink, blue, and white. 'Snowbank' is a popular white-flowered variety with a neat, tightly upright form 4' tall. 'Pink Beauty' has pale lilac-pink flowers and grows 3–4' tall.

Boston Ivy

Parthenocissus tricuspidata

Deciduous vine

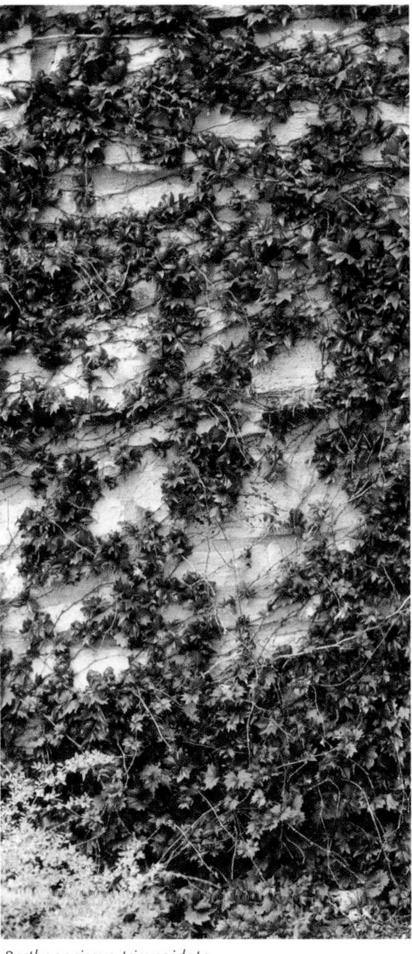

Parthenocissus tricuspidata

▶ ***Hardiness:*** Zones 4–8

▶ ***Size:*** Indefinite; can climb at least 20'–40' in all directions

▶ ***Features:*** Grow this vine to enjoy foliage that changes with the seasons. Large leaves are glossy green in summer, turning russet to rich wine red in fall. Bare winter stems lend pattern to hard surfaces for vertical interest. It climbs by attaching adhesive disks to solid surfaces; disks can damage wood.

▶ ***Uses:*** Growing on masonry walls, fences, or buildings; hiding blank walls; adding coarse texture; backgrounds; seasonal accents; giving new homes an aged look

▶ ***Needs:*** Grow in any soil, from alkaline to acidic, dry to moist. Plant in full sun or partial shade. Full sun brings out intense fall color. Plants may require more water in hotter climates. It spreads aggressively by underground runners and must be controlled to keep it from overwhelming nearby plants such as foundation shrubs.

Bottlebrush Buckeye

see Buckeye

Bottlebrush, Crimson

see Crimson Bottlebrush

Bougainvillea

Bougainvillea spp.

Subtropical evergreen flowering shrub often grown as a vine

Bougainvillea spp.

▶ ***Hardiness:*** Zones 9–10

▶ ***Size:*** 20'–40' tall and wide

▶ ***Features:*** Bougainvillea is a flamboyant addition to the landscape. The brilliantly colored crepe-paperlike blooms are impossible to miss. Its arching, sprawling, thorny stems can grow 10' to 15' in a season, so it's stunning when trained and tied as a climbing vine, forming a thick canopy of foliage and blazing flowers. Bougainvillea is also effective when allowed to billow and sprawl as a groundcover, especially on slopes. And it's excellent in containers, where it's easy to control into smaller sizes on a teepee, or arching and cascading from a hanging basket.

▶ ***Uses:*** Covering walls, sturdy trellises and pergolas, and fences; growing as a low shrub or allowed to sprawl across the ground as a groundcover; in containers. Long, sharp thorns make bougainvillea a good barrier plant, but keep it away from places where passersby or cars might brush against it.

▶ ***Needs:*** Plant in well-drained soil in full sun—provide light afternoon shade in hottest regions. Plant in spring after all danger of frost has passed. Plant carefully because the roots are fragile. Will climb by leaning and "grabbing" with its long thorns if tied to a supporting structure, which should be sturdy, since mature plants can be massive. Tie securely to prevent wind from shredding leaves against plant thorns. Fertilize in spring and summer. Water regularly until established, then moderately, in spring only. Keep soil from getting soggy; drought tolerant once established. Use balanced fertilizer throughout the growing season. Prune in spring after flowering to encourage new growth. Bougainvillea blooms on new growth and takes hard pruning well. This vine does well outdoors all year in Zones 9–11 but can be planted in a protected site in hot summer areas of Zone 8. Low-shrubbery types will also grow all year in Zone 8 as container plants, if they are moved to a protected area over the winter.

▶ ***Choices:*** Flowers are available in white, pink, salmon, orange, red, magenta, purple, and lavender hues, often of neon intensity.

Bouvardia

Bouvardia longiflora 'Albatross'

Evergreen shrub

Bouvardia longiflora 'Albatross'

▶ ***Hardiness:*** Zones 9–10
▶ ***Size:*** 2'–3' tall and wide
▶ ***Features:*** Grow bouvardia—a Mexican native—for its dangling clusters of delicious-smelling flowers on refined, fine-textured, evergreen foliage. It's perfect in pots placed around a terrace or patio. Does not tolerate cold; plants are damaged or killed when temperatures approach freezing.
▶ ***Uses:*** Good for accent plantings, entries, patios, and containers. Place it near windows, doorways, benches, and walkways where its fragrance can be enjoyed.
▶ ***Needs:*** Plant bouvardia in partial shade—a spot that gets morning sun followed by afternoon shade is ideal. Grow in moist, well-drained soil, and water frequently. Cut flowering stems back to encourage new growth and more blooms. Make cuts a little above a leaf or remove stems completely, cutting to the base.

Bower Vine

Pandorea pandorana

Subtropical evergreen vine

Pandorea jasminoides 'Rosea Superba'

▶ ***Hardiness:*** Zones 9–11
▶ ***Size:*** Can reach 40'–50' in all directions
▶ ***Features:*** Big, white funnel-shaped flowers with purple throats cover this big beauty in spring and early summer, and its large, glossy leaves are lovely all year long. This is a large vine for southern climates, especially California and Florida. Plant it where you need a lot of coverage fast, and give it plenty of room and a sturdy structure to climb on.
▶ ***Uses:*** Covering large, unsightly structures; climbing on large pergolas; draping over tall masonry walls
▶ ***Needs:*** This Australian native is best in rich soil well-conditioned with organic matter. Plant it in full sun to light shade; in hot-summer climates give it more shade. Water moderately; it can tolerate some drought but is best with even moisture. It blooms on old wood, so if you need to prune it do so right after flowering.
▶ ***Choices:*** 'Golden Showers' has deep yellow flowers. *Pandorea jasminoides* grows about half the size of *P. pandorana*, and produces white flowers with pink throats. It is less tolerant of drying winds and frost. 'Rosea Superba' is a pink-flowered cultivar that is fragrant. Zones 10–11.

Box, Sweet

see Sweet Box

BOXWOODS

Buxus spp.

Boxwood is a shrub that is equally at home tucked into formal planters flanking a front porch or in a more informal perennial border. The evergreen, bright green leaves of boxwood make it a shrub that establishes the "bones" of a landscape in all seasons. While its natural billowing shape is attractive, boxwood tolerates shearing into various shapes and can be used to create a lovely formal hedge or topiary.

BOXWOODS

Edging Boxwood

Buxus sempervirens 'Suffruticosa'

Evergreen shrub

Buxus sempervirens 'Suffruticosa'

▶ ***Hardiness:*** Zones 6–8
▶ ***Size:*** In many years, without pruning, boxwood can grow 4' tall, 6'–9' wide
▶ ***Features:*** This tiny boxwood grows slowly and, with regular pruning, will form a neat and tidy hedge around other plantings, seating areas, or walkways. One of the best plants for a low-growing edging hedge, boxwood can be maintained at any height from a few inches to several feet. Glossy green foliage is fragrant. Plants are resistant to leaf miner infestations.
▶ ***Uses:*** Good for low, formal hedges; specimens; mass plantings; topiaries; edging gardens
▶ ***Needs:*** Plant in full sun or light shade in well-drained, fertile soil. Boxwoods have shallow roots that prefer cool conditions. Mulch the root area with peat or compost. Protect shrubs from strong, drying winds. Prune boxwood in early to midsummer, after flowering.

BOXWOODS

Green Beauty Boxwood

Buxus microphylla 'Green Beauty'

Evergreen shrub

Buxus microphylla 'Green Beauty'

▶ ***Hardiness:*** Zones 5–9
▶ ***Size:*** 3'–4' tall and wide
▶ ***Features:*** This cultivar is hardier than the species and has bright green leaves, a more rounded form, and smaller mature size.
▶ ***Uses:*** Hedges, specimen use, topiaries, accenting entrances, formal gardens, planting beds
▶ ***Needs:*** Plant in full sun or light shade in well-drained, fertile soil. Boxwoods prefer cool conditions. Mulch the root area with peat or compost. Protect shrubs from strong, drying winds, especially in winter. Prune boxwood after flowering.
▶ ***Choices:*** 'Winter Gem'—compact form; 'Compacta'—12" high and wide.

BOXWOODS

Japanese Boxwood

Buxus microphylla var. *japonica*

Evergreen shrub

Buxus microphylla var. *japonica*

▶ ***Hardiness:*** Zones 6–9
▶ ***Size:*** 3'–6' tall and wide
▶ ***Features:*** Japanese boxwood is a dense, upright shrub with lustrous evergreen leaves. Shape it to meet your yard's needs—or just let it grow. Protect plants from drying winds, especially in colder areas.
▶ ***Uses:*** Good for specimen shrub or hedge, foundations, edging, formal gardens
▶ ***Needs:*** Plant in full sun or light shade in well-drained, fertile soil. Shallow roots prefer cool growing conditions. Mulch the root area with peat or compost. Protect shrubs from strong, drying winds. Prune boxwood after flowering.

BOXWOODS

Korean Boxwood

Buxus microphylla var. *koreana*

Evergreen shrub

Buxus microphylla var. *koreana*

▶ ***Hardiness:*** Zones 5–9
▶ ***Size:*** 1'–2' tall, 2'–3' wide
▶ ***Features:*** The toughest of all boxwoods, this one withstands hot, cold, and humid climates. Shrubs grow slowly, stay low, and take pruning well. Plants are easily trimmed into a variety of shapes for formal landscapes. Also sold as Korean littleleaf boxwood. Fine-textured foliage remains bright green all year.
▶ ***Uses:*** Low hedges; massing; surrounding vegetable, rose, or herb gardens; formal landscapes; courtyards; entries; winter interest; edging planting beds
▶ ***Needs:*** Plant in fertile soil that's moist but well drained. Slightly acidic soil is best. Mulch well to keep shallow roots cool; peat or compost is good for mulching. Protect shrubs from strong, drying winds. Prune to shape in early or midsummer.
▶ ***Choices:*** 'Tide Hill' is an even hardier cultivar that stays low and spreads wide over many years—15" high, 5' wide, Zones 4–9.

BOXWOODS

Wintergreen Boxwood

Buxus microphylla 'Wintergreen'

Evergreen shrub

Buxus microphylla 'Wintergreen'

▶ ***Hardiness:*** Zones 4–6
▶ ***Size:*** 3'–4' tall and wide
▶ ***Features:*** This shrub earns its place in the landscape for year-round beauty—it's a particularly hardy selection that keeps its color during the winter. Its tidy form stays neat summer through winter and looks great under snow. Plants make beautiful low hedges or edges.
▶ ***Needs:*** Plant in fertile soil that's moist but well drained. Avoid soggy soil and mulch to keep roots cool. Plants are shallow-rooted, and deep cultivation should be avoided. Although winter hardy, plants are less tolerant of hot weather. Grow in full sun or partial shade.
▶ ***Uses:*** Edging flowerbeds, formal gardens, foundation planting, low hedges, planting beside patios, along walkways, in courtyards or entries, for winter interest
▶ ***Choices:*** 'Green Pillow' is another hardy selection that forms a small, rounded green cushion 18" tall by 3' wide.

Brachycome iberidifolia

see Swan River Daisy

Bradford Pear

see Callery Pear

Brassaia spp.

see Schefflera

Brassica oleracea

see Cabbage, Brussels Sprouts, and Flowering Cabbage

Brassica rapa

see Bok Choi, Pak Choi

Broccoli

Brassica oleracea

Cool-season annual vegetable

Broccoli 'Packman'

▶ ***Hardiness:*** Not applicable
▶ ***Size:*** Grows up to 1' tall, 1' wide
▶ ***Features:*** This classic vegetable has crunchy green heads
▶ ***Uses:*** In the vegetable garden
▶ ***Needs:*** Full sun to light shade. Rich, neutral soil with plentiful moisture. Dislikes weather above 80°F/27°C. Plant established seedlings 12"–14" apart outdoors 4–6 weeks before your region's last frost date for a late spring harvest. For fall harvest, plant established plants in midsummer in the North or in the fall in mild-winter climates in the South and Southwest. Avoid high-nitrogen fertilizers, which can make stems hollow. Keep soil moist. Harvest when central head is full with plump flower buds but before flower buds open.
▶ ***Choices:*** Broccoli matures in 40–120 days. Look for fast-maturing types (50–55 days) for spring plantings to avoid hot weather.

BROMELIADS

Some bromeliads are grown for their beautiful foliage, which grows in a rosette pattern with leathery, strappy foliage. Others are grown for their exotic, pineapple-like flowers—and a few bromeliads are grown for both. Some are easy to grow, while others are more demanding.

Unlike most plants, bromeliads are epiphytic—so-called air plants that do not need soil to grow. In nature, they use trees, rocks, and other plants to support their tiny root systems. Some grow in loose, fast-draining soil and are called terrestrial (growing in the earth) bromeliads. In the home, bromeliads as a rule need an extremely well-drained medium in which to grow. They are grown on slabs or on bark or in mixes of loose bark. If you can find them, potting mixes for epiphytes are ideal.

With all bromeliads, avoid overwatering and make sure the mix or bark in which they're planted has excellent drainage but remains constantly moist.

Most bromeliads have a natural vase formed by the tightly packed rosette of leaves. In the wild, since the plants' roots are minimal, rainwater collects in this vase to slowly deliver water to the plant. Water this type by pouring water into the center of the plant, into the empty vase. Refill the vase every month or so. Occasionally add a half-strength fertilizer to the vase water.

Humidity for all bromeliads is essential. Keeping the potting mix damp helps, but plants should also be set on trays of pebbles with water. Alternatively, run a humidifier nearby.

BROMELIADS

Blushing Bromeliad

Neoregelia carolinae

Tropical epiphytic perennial

Neoregelia carolinae

▶ ***Size:*** Leaves grow about 1' long
▶ ***Features:*** Glossy, strappy leaves with sometimes subtle color variations
▶ ***Uses:*** As a houseplant
▶ ***Needs:*** Bright but not direct light; average household warmth
▶ ***Choices:*** *Neoregelia carolinae* f. *tricolor* is the most popular variety with leaves that are red near the vase and then change to green and white. *N. spectabilis,* called fingernail plant, has green leaves with a distinctive red pointed tip that looks like a sharp red fingernail.

BROMELIADS

Earth Star

Cryptanthus bivittatus

Tropical epiphytic perennial

Cryptanthus bivittatus

▶ ***Size:*** Grows 4" tall and wide, depending on the type
▶ ***Features:*** Outstanding leaf colors of pink, green, and silver. The plant is small for a bromeliad and the leaves are flat. Plants do well in dish gardens. The humidity need for this plant is especially high, so it's an excellent choice for a large terrarium or miniature conservatory.
▶ ***Uses:*** As a houseplant
▶ ***Needs:*** Direct, brightest light. Average home warmth is fine.
▶ ***Choices:*** Other earth stars include *Cryptanthus fosterianus,* which grows 15" long. The rainbow star is *C. bromelioides* var. *tricolor,* with beautiful stripes on its leaves in red, green, and cream.

BROMELIADS

Flaming Sword

Vriesea splendens

Tropical epiphytic perennial

Vriesea splendens 'Splenriet'

▶ ***Size:*** Grows leaves 12"–18" long with a flower head up to 2' tall
▶ ***Features:*** Most have especially showy large, narrow flower heads
▶ ***Uses:*** As a houseplant
▶ ***Needs:*** Bright but not direct light. Average household warmth, but more warmth (75°F/24°C) to induce flowering.
▶ ***Choices:*** *Vriesea splendens* is the most commonly found. Other types usually have broader flower heads. *V. vulcana* has an all-red flower head. *V. carinata* has a yellow, red, and green flower head. A few, including *V. hieroglyphica* and *V. fenestralis,* are grown only for their mottled foliage.

BROMELIADS

Guzmania

Guzmania lingulata

Tropical epiphytic perennial

Guzmania lingulata 'Ultra'

▶ ***Size:*** Grows leaves 4"–2' long and flower heads 6"–2' tall, depending on the species
▶ ***Features:*** A broad, spreading flower head in brilliant colors
▶ ***Uses:*** As a houseplant
▶ ***Needs:*** Bright but not direct light. Average household warmth, but more warmth (75°F/24°C) to induce flowering.
▶ ***Choices:*** *Guzmania lingulata* has orange and red bracts; *G. l.* var. *minor* grows leaves 4" long with a proportional flower head. *G. zahnii* is the largest, with leaves 2' long.

BROMELIADS

Pineapple Dyckia

Dyckia brevifolia

Tropical epiphytic perennial

Dyckia brevifolia

▶ ***Size:*** 1' high, 2' wide
▶ ***Features:*** This bromeliad acts more like a cactus or an agave, preferring a bright, sunny spot

and low humidity—and it's armed with sharp spines at the edges of each leaf. The neat rosettes of leaves would be at home in any cactus and succulent garden.

▶**Uses:** As a houseplant

▶**Needs:** Provide bright, direct sun, preferably in a south- or west-facing window. Unlike most bromeliads, pineapple dyckia prefers low humidity. Nighttime temperatures of 50°–55°F and daytime temperatures above 68°F are ideal, but this plant is less fussy. Grow it in a heavy terra-cotta pot in cactus soil and allow it to dry fairly well between waterings. Root rot can be a problem if the plant is grown in low light and kept too moist. Apply fertilizer only once a year. Remove any yellow leaves that appear. Move it outside to a sunny spot in the summer.

BROMELIADS

Pink Quill

Tillandsia cyanea

Tropical epiphytic perennial

Tillandsia cyanea

▶**Size:** Grows 12" tall; 16" wide

▶**Features:** Pretty dark green leaves up to 14" long. Sends out flattened, paddle-shaped deep pink and purple flowers a little over an inch long in late spring or autumn.

▶**Uses:** As a houseplant

▶**Needs:** Grow as for most bromeliads. Pink quill does not form a vase, however, so keep potting medium very moist during the growing season, barely moist during winter. Fertilize monthly with a solution of half-strength fertilizer.

BROMELIADS

Silver Vase Plant

Aechmea fasciata

Tropical epiphytic perennial

Aechmea fasciata 'Variegata'

▶**Size:** Leaves grow about 1'; flower head 1' tall

▶**Features:** Beautiful thick, spined bluish to gray leaves are sometimes streaked with silver and white. Sends up large heads in pink to purple, which then send out bracts of tiny flowers.

▶**Uses:** As a houseplant

▶**Needs:** Bright but not direct light. Average warmth, but quite a lot of warmth (75°F/24°C) is needed to induce flowering. When the main flower has faded, the plant develops side shoots. When the shoots are about 6", prune out the main vase to keep the plant growing.

▶**Choices:** *Aechmea chantinii*, also called zebra plant, has a deep orange bract that droops to show yellow flowers. *A. fulgens* var. *discolor*, also called coral berry, has purple flowers with red berries, and the undersides of the green-topped leaves are purple.

Brooms

Cytisus spp. and *Genista* spp.

Flowering shrubs with evergreen stems

Genista pilosa

▶**Hardiness:** Zones 6–8, some species Zones 4–8

▶**Size:** 1'–6' tall and wide, depending on species

▶**Features:** Brooms are spectacular in bloom, literally covered in small, fragrant, pea-shaped blossoms for 2 weeks in spring. Most are in yellow hues, but some are pink, deep rose, or cream. All year long they're attractive shrubs with dense bright green vertical or arching stems that are reminiscent of grasses. Most brooms have small, inconspicuous leaves and conduct most of their photosynthesis in their green stems. The texture of these stems is beautiful combined with ornamental grasses, low-growing junipers, and yucca.

▶**Uses:** Mass in beds or mix in among other shrubs in the border, especially where soil is sandy and infertile. The low, spreading types, mostly in the genus *Genista*, are good groundcovers for rock gardens and slopes. All brooms perform well in harsh seashore conditions.

▶**Needs:** Average to poor, sandy, rocky soil. Moderate moisture at first; then highly drought tolerant. Does well in windy and seashore conditions; good for erosion control.

Plant established plants in spring. Do not fertilize. Pruning is unnecessary, especially in naturalistic settings, but cut stems back by one-third immediately after blooming. Shrubs can be invasive. Brooms are bothered by few diseases or pests.

▶**Choices:** Warminster broom *(Cytisus ×praecox)* is widely grown and is hardy in Zones 6–9. It grows 4'–6' tall with upright to arching branches. Cultivars are available with yellow, pale yellow, cream, pink, rose, and maroon blossoms, and are less invasive than other brooms. Silky-leaf broom *(Genista pilosa)* grows 18" tall and can spread 4' or more wide. Hardy in Zones 4–8, it makes an outstanding groundcover in rock gardens and for erosion control on slopes. Avoid Canary Island broom *(G. canariensis)* or Scotch broom *(C. scoparius)* in the West, where they've taken over in some areas.

Browallia spp.

see Amethyst Flower, Sapphire Flower

Brugmansia

see Datura, Angel's Trumpet

Brunnera, Heart-Leaf

Brunnera macrophylla

Perennial

Brunnera macrophylla

B

Plant encyclopedia

►**Hardiness:** Zones 3–8
►**Size:** 18" tall, 24" wide in bloom
►**Features**: Airy haze of bright blue forget-me-not flowers hovers above attractive heart-shaped leaves in early to mid-spring. Foliage looks good all summer.
►**Uses:** Massed as groundcover in woodland gardens, shady beds, other shady spots in the landcape. It's a good partner for fringed bleeding heart, meadow rue, astilbe, and ferns.
►**Needs:** Plant in shade to dense shade and moist, well-drained soil—the more sun, the more moisture is required. Avoid hot, sunny sites where foliage will scorch. Plants self-sow prolifically. Cut spent blooms back to the leaves before seeds form and dig out excess plants and seedlings annually. This is especially important for the variegated cultivars, since seedlings will revert to green and crowd out the parents. This plant is basically pest free and slug resistant.
►**Choices:** 'Langtrees' is variegated with splashes of silver. 'Jack Frost' is silver with darker veins.

Brussels Sprouts

Brassica oleracea

Cool-season annual vegetable

Brussels sprouts

►**Hardiness:** Not applicable
►**Size:** Grows 2'–3' tall, 6" wide
►**Features:** Small, round, cabbagelike sprouts grow on the sides of trunklike stem
►**Uses:** In the vegetable garden
►**Needs:** Full sun to light shade. Likes moist, neutral soil and 80 days of cool weather below 80°F/27°C to mature. Plant established plants in early spring 4–6 weeks before your region's last frost date. In mild-winter areas, plant in fall. Space plants 20" apart. Keep soil moist. To assure sprouts mature at the same time, pinch off top 6" of plants when lower sprouts are ½"–¾" in diameter. Frost improves the flavor.
►**Choices:** Dwarf and regular types available. 'Green Jade', a dwarf, is one of the most popular; matures in just 80 days. 'Rubine', a regular type, matures in 125 days with ruby-red sprouts.

BUCKEYE AND HORSECHESTNUT

Aesculus spp.

Buckeyes are generally small trees or large, suckering shrubs, while horsechestnuts are large shade trees. Both are useful for making a big statement in the landscape, especially when they bloom with their large, erect clusters of flowers in white, pink, or red—usually in mid- to late summer, when few other trees and shrubs are blooming. Some have a good yellow fall color. All produce shiny, polished fruits encased in a spiny, leathery covering. The fruits are poisonous, and their spiny outer covering can make them a nuisance when they drop. Site these plants away from patios, driveways, and other paved surfaces, or where people are likely to walk barefooted.

BUCKEYE AND HORSECHESTNUT

Bottlebrush Buckeye

Aesculus parviflora

Deciduous shrub

Aesculus parviflora

►**Hardiness:** Zones 5–8
►**Size:** 10' tall, 15' wide
►**Features:** A big, bodacious shrub, bottlebrush buckeye can cover a large shady area under maples or oaks. Plants grow at a moderate to slow rate into rounded shrubs. In midsummer they produce loads of spectacular 1' spikes of white, fragrant flowers with protuberant red anthers. The foliage turns a good yellow in fall and is seldom bothered by leaf scorch, unlike most other buckeyes.
►**Uses:** Makes a massive statement for a large area under mature trees. Good in combination with other late-blooming shrubs such as summersweet and oakleaf hydrangea.
►**Needs:** Plant in moist, well-drained soil high in organic matter. Best in light to deep shade, but performs well in full sun if soil is kept moist. Suckering habit can be troublesome if it has inadequate room to grow. Leaf and fruit litter are less of a problem since this shrub is cloaked with foliage clear to the ground.
►**Choices:** The variety *serotina* blooms about 3 weeks later than the species, in late summer. 'Rogers' produces enormous flower clusters 18"–2' long about 2 weeks later than the species. Red buckeye *(A. pavia)* is a shrubby small tree that produces a good show of dark red flowers in midsummer. It grows 20'–25' tall and wide, and is hardy in Zones 5–9.

BUCKEYE AND HORSECHESTNUT

Common Horsechestnut

Aesculus hippocastanum

Deciduous tree

Aesculus hippocastanum

►**Hardiness:** Zones 3–7
►**Size:** 50'–75' tall, 40'–70' wide
►**Features:** This attractive tree gets big and is best planted in large open spaces. Spikes of white flowers rise above coarse-textured leaves in late spring. Individual flowers have hints of yellow and pink on each petal. The buckeye fruits ripen in September.
►**Uses:** In large open areas, as a shade tree, contributing seasonal color and coarse texture, large properties
►**Needs:** Plant in deep, fertile soil that's moist but well drained. Tolerates acidic or alkaline soils. Grow in full sun or partial shade. Mulch to keep roots moist and cool; avoid dry conditions, which can bring on leaf scorch. These large trees are unsuitable for small yards.

Aesculus ×carnea 'Rosea'

►**Choices:** Red horsechestnut *(Aesculus ×carnea)* is a hybrid between common horsechestnut and red buckeye. It's a large, stately tree that slowly grows to 50' tall and 40' wide, and produces a beautiful display of pink to red flowers in 8"–10" erect clusters in late spring. It is hardy in Zones 5–8. Ruby horsechestnut *(A. ×carnea* 'Briotii') bears bright rose-red flowers, and 'O'Neill Red' produces showy double red flowers.

BUCKEYE AND HORSECHESTNUT

Ohio Buckeye

Aesculus glabra

Deciduous tree

Aesculus glabra

▶ ***Hardiness:*** Zones 3–7
▶ ***Size:*** 20'–50' tall, 20'–50' wide
▶ ***Features:*** Medium growth rate. Large, yellow-green flowers in summer. Low, branched, broad, rounded form. Dense canopy of coarse-textured foliage. Give this tree room to grow and you'll enjoy cool, leafy shade for many years. Scented flowers in summer are an added bonus. Flowers are followed by inedible fruit. The seed is poisonous.
▶ ***Uses:*** Shade tree or specimen use, natural areas, riverbanks, woodlands, large open areas, parks
▶ ***Needs:*** Plant in deep, fertile soil that's moist but well drained. Trees prefer moist locations and will not tolerate drought. Grow in full sun or partial shade. Mulch to keep roots moist and cool.

Buddhist Pine

see Podocarpus

Buddleia davidii

see Butterfly Bush

Bugbane

Cimicifuga spp.

Perennial

Cimicifuga racemosa

▶ ***Hardiness:*** Zones 3–8
▶ ***Size:*** 3'–6' tall, 2'–3' wide
▶ ***Features:*** A valuable addition to the shade garden for its elegant, tall spikes of white flowers when few other shade plants are blooming. Adapts well to wet soils. Blooms late summer to late fall.
▶ ***Uses:*** In woodland gardens and shady natural areas. Good for problem wet spots even in full sun if soil is constantly moist.
▶ ***Needs:*** Part shade is best; will tolerate full sun if constantly moist. Rich, deep, moist, preferably acidic soil. Plant established plants in spring. Mulch to retain moisture. Keep well watered, or leaves will brown and plants will be stunted. Fertilize occasionally. Plants seldom need division, perhaps every several years. Diseases and pests are seldom a problem as long as conditions are good.
▶ ***Choices:*** Flowers are white. 'The Pearl' is a popular cultivar. *Cimicifuga racemosa* may grow to 6' tall and may need staking. 'Atropurpurea' has dark purple foliage.

Bugleweed

see Ajuga

Bugloss

see Brunnera, Heart-Leaf

Bunchberry

Cornus canadensis

Deciduous flowering shrub grown as groundcover

Cornus canadensis

▶ ***Hardiness:*** Zones 2–7
▶ ***Size:*** 3"–6" tall with indefinite spread
▶ ***Features:*** This low-growing relative of dogwood blooms in late spring or early summer. White or pinkish flowers are followed by showy red berries that are attractive to birds. The ground-hugging green leaves turn red in fall. Bunchberry is a little more challenging to get started than other groundcovers, but it's worth the extra effort. Slow to medium growth rate.
▶ ***Uses:*** In shady beds, woodland gardens, under acid-loving shrubs and trees, cool locations
▶ ***Needs:*** Plant in well-drained, fertile, acidic soil. Choose a spot in partial to full shade and where moisture is available. Plants can be slow to get started; improve soil acidity with peat, composted oak leaves, or pine straw mulch at planting time. Regions with cool summers are best.

Bunny Ears Cactus

see Cactus and Succulents

Burning Bush, Dwarf; Dwarf Winged Euonymus

Euonymus alatus 'Compacta'

Deciduous shrub

Euonymus alatus

▶ ***Hardiness:*** Zones 3–8
▶ ***Size:*** 5'–10' tall and as wide
▶ ***Features:*** Leaves turn brilliant red in autumn. Also sold as dwarf winged euonymus, named for corky ridges present on stems. Leaves grow in horizontal layers. Naturally dense, rounded outline.
▶ ***Uses:*** Specimen shrubs, seasonal accents, deciduous screens, massing, parking areas, beside patios, along walkways or paths, hedges
▶ ***Needs:*** Plant in any well-drained soil, acidic or alkaline. Grow in full sun or partial shade. Pruning s seldom needed or desired; maintain plants in their natural rounded form.
▶ ***Choices:*** Burning bush (not dwarf) grows 12'–15' tall and wide.

B

Plant encyclopedia

Burro's Tail
see Cactus and Succulents

Bush Cinquefoil
see Potentilla

Butia capitata
see Palms: Pindo Palm

Butter Bean
see Lima Bean

Butter Daisy
Melampodium paludosum

Annual

Melampodium paludosum

▶ ***Size:*** 10"-14" tall and wide

▶ ***Features:*** Butter daisy is one tough customer, withstanding heat, humidity, and drought while remaining covered with brilliant gold-medallion daisies all summer. It's a good annual for the South. Blooms early summer to frost.

▶ ***Uses:*** Bedding, containers

▶ ***Needs:*** Full sun but will tolerate light shade, especially in hot summer areas. Average to poor soil. Drought tolerant, but does far better with even moisture. Plant established plants in spring after all danger of frost has passed. Avoid fertilizing, which will reduce blooms. There is no need to deadhead. Slugs can be a problem in moist conditions. Otherwise, aphids and red spider mites are sometimes present.

Butterfly Bush
Buddleia davidii

Perennial or semievergreen shrub

Buddleia davidii

▶ ***Hardiness:*** Zones 5–10

▶ ***Size:*** 4'-8" tall, 3'-6' wide

▶ ***Features:*** Butterfly bush is easy to grow; hot sun and limited water do little to discourage abundant flowers in shades of pink, white, purple, or red. Blooms attract butterflies. Excellent vase life for cut flower use.

▶ ***Uses:*** At the rear of sunny flowerbeds or natural areas, beside patios or decks to show off butterflies and blossoms, cut flowers

▶ ***Needs:*** Give plants a good start by mixing organic matter such as compost into the planting hole. Full sun yields the most flowers. Prune in either spring or fall to encourage blooming. Full sun in Zones 5–6; full sun to light shade in Zones 7–10. Average to sandy, fertile to poor, well-drained soil. Ample moisture is best; will tolerate drought. Plant established plants in spring or fall. Mulch. Do not fertilize. This plant dies back to the ground each winter in northern climates. *Buddleia davidii*, the most commonly available buddleia, blooms on new wood produced each spring. In Zones 5–6, cut back to the ground in late winter or early spring. In Zones 7–11 cut back less severely, to a foot or 2. Some species bloom only on the wood they grew the previous year. In these cases prune the shrubs back by one-fifth to one-third immediately after they flower in summer.

▶ ***Choices:*** 'Empire Blue'—large dark blue flowers; 'Fascination'—salmon-pink blossoms; 'Harlequin'—variegated leaves, maroon flowers; 'Royal Red'—dark purple-red flowers; 'Black Knight'—deep purple flowers; 'White Bouquet'—white blossoms; 'Wilsonii'—drooping, light pink-purple flower spikes.

Butterfly Milkweed
see Butterfly Weed

Butterfly Vine
Mascagnia macroptera

Deciduous flowering vine

Mascagnia macroptera

▶ ***Hardiness:*** Zones 9–10

▶ ***Size:*** Grows 12'-15' a season in all directions

▶ ***Features:*** This Mexican desert native sports colorful yellow, orchidlike flowers all summer. Once established it requires little in the way of care and grows quickly, even in dry, sunny locations. Butterfly vine can tolerate cold weather and survives temperatures down to 25°F. Also known as yellow orchid vine.

▶ ***Uses:*** Arid landscapes; xeriscaping; covering fences, gates, arbors, and other outdoor structures; colorful accent

▶ ***Needs:*** Grow in any well-drained soil in full sun. Water regularly until established. Plants can tolerate drought, but weekly watering during the growing season will yield best results. Provide support for these twining vines to climb on.

▶ ***Choices:*** Lavender butterfly vine, *Mascagnia lilacina*, produces lilac-colored flowers.

Butterfly Weed

Asclepias tuberosa

Perennial

Asclepias tuberosa

► ***Hardiness:*** Zones 4-10
► ***Size:*** 2'-4' tall, 10"-2' wide
► ***Features:*** You may see butterflies tussling over these flowers or a caterpillar munching on the leaves—it's the favorite food of the monarch butterfly. In fact, this drought-tolerant native's cheerful orange flower heads are attractive to many butterflies and bees. Blooms midsummer.
► ***Uses:*** A must for meadows and naturalized prairie gardens, and a valuable addition to the cottage garden. Very effective massed in large numbers with spring bulbs planted underneath; butterfly weed emerges late to cover the browning bulb foliage.
► ***Needs:*** Average to poor soil with good drainage. This plant likes sandy soil and is fairly drought tolerant. Plant established plants in spring. Mulch to prevent disease. Avoid fertilizing. Cut flowers freely for arrangements; deadheading often sparks a second bloom. This plant has a long, brittle taproot, and it's tough to divide or transplant. It's slow to emerge each spring, so mark it in fall to avoid damaging or hoeing it out while doing early weeding. It is susceptible to aphids and powdery mildew.

Buxus spp.

see Boxwoods

Cabbage

Brassica oleracea

Cool-season annual vegetable

Cabbage 'Atlantis'

► ***Hardiness:*** Not applicable
► ***Size:*** Grows 1'-3' tall and as wide depending on growing conditions and type
► ***Features:*** Large, beautiful, tasty heads surrounded by larger leaves
► ***Uses:*** In the vegetable garden
► ***Needs:*** Full sun to light shade. Rich, neutral soil; tolerates sandy to clay soils. Plentiful, consistent soil moisture helps prevent heads from splitting. Needs 60-90 days of temperatures between 25°-80°F/ 9°-27°C. Plant established plants in spring 4-6 weeks before your region's last average frost date or in fall in Zones 8 and warmer. Space 18"-24" depending on mature size; check package label. Keep soil moist. Treat cabbage worms, root maggots, and cabbage loopers with *Bt*. Harvest as soon as heads are firm and solid; waiting beyond that risks splitting.
► ***Choices:*** Red cabbages are less disease prone than green. Choose from early-, mid-, and late-season maturing types. Also try deeply crinkled savoy cabbages.

Cabbage, Flowering

see Flowering Cabbage

Cabbage Palm

see Palms

CACTUS AND SUCCULENTS

This huge group of plants encompasses a wide variety of interesting plants with waxy, often spined foliage. These arid-climate natives are mostly low-maintenance as long as they have plenty of sun and are not overwatered. For all, unless otherwise specified, plant in a special fast-draining mix formulated for succulents and cactus that mimics the sandy soil they often grow in. Water with tepid, never cold, water. Allow the soil to dry out thoroughly between waterings and withhold water in winter. High humidity can cause problems such as leaf scarring and rotting. A mulch of gravel, especially around cactus, is helpful because it helps keep the bases of plants drier. Direct sun is ideal, and nearly all can be summered outdoors as long as you transition them by giving them just an hour or two a day of sun at first. Average to hot home temperatures are fine. However, for a cactus to flower, a cool period is necessary to trigger bloom. Fertilize cactus and succulents only in spring and summer when their growth is active; once or twice during that period with a 10-10-10 liquid fertilizer is plenty. Some cactus will flower, but most need to be at least a few years old before they do so. They will then bloom annually, usually in the spring. To encourage flowering, withhold water and food in winter, followed by more water and a fertilizer in spring.

CACTUS AND SUCCULENTS

African Milk Tree

Euphorbia trigona

Succulent evergreen perennial

Euphorbia trigona

► ***Hardiness:*** Zones 10-11
► ***Size:*** 4'-6' tall, 2' wide
► ***Features:*** This plant may look and behave like a cactus, but it comes from an unrelated genus of plants—*Euphorbia*—that are the African equivalents of the cacti of the Western Hemisphere.
► ***Uses:*** As a houseplant. In arid mild-winter climates it is sometimes grown as a landscape plant in the cactus garden.
► ***Needs:*** Grow as for most cacti, but keep it out of direct sun. Water stress can cause the leaves to drop, but plants soon recover without injury and grow new leaves.

CACTUS AND SUCCULENTS

Aloe

Aloe spp.

Subtropical succulent perennials

Aloe striata

►***Hardiness:*** Zones 8–11

►***Size:*** Depending on variety, can be a tiny 6" rosette or a 30' tree

►***Features:*** These are the South African versions of the Mexican agaves. Their thick, pointed, succulent leaves form attractive stemless rosettes. Unlike agaves, these plants don't die after they produce flowers, but multiply to form large clumps. Mature plants usually bloom every year with long-lasting, brightly colored flowers in yellow, orange, pink, or red on tall spikes. The sap from nearly all species can be a skin irritant.

►***Uses:*** As a houseplant in all zones. In arid, mild-winter climates, aloes are used in outdoor containers, as specimen plants in the ground, and as groundcover or edging plants

►***Needs:*** Indoors provide bright light, preferably a south-facing window. Plants do fine in average home temperatures, but the ideal is at least a 10°F/5°C degree difference between day and night with temperatures as low as 40°F/10°C in winter. Average humidity. Water when dry; keep soil on the dry side in winter. Fertilize 2–3 times in summer.

►***Choices:*** There are hundreds of species of aloes, in many shapes and sizes. *Aloe vera* is a popular species—the sap from the fleshy leaves is thought to soothe burns, hence its nickname medicine plant. It is often kept on a sunny kitchen windowsill. *A. variegata* has upright 6" leaves with distinctive white bands. *A. aristata* is smaller, with 4" leaves and a more globelike shape. *A. jucunda* is a dwarf and forms several small 3" rosettes. *A. humilis* is another dwarf with blue-green leaves. *A mitriformis* has interesting thorns along the edges of its leaves.

CACTUS AND SUCCULENTS

Bunny Ears Cactus

Opuntia microdasys

Succulent evergreen perennial

Opuntia microdasys

►***Hardiness:*** Zones 10–11

►***Size:*** 1'–2' tall, 3'–5' wide

►***Features:*** If you hate to water or watering restrictions make it difficult, try bunny ears cactus. Once it's planted, no further care is required. Flat, oval pads give this plant its name. Interesting shape and polka-dot bristles. Thrives in drought and heat. Coarse texture.

►***Uses:*** Outdoors in arid landscapes, Xeriscaping, seaside and desert areas, containers, raised beds or berms, rock gardens, dry slopes, areas that receive little water. It is also a popular houseplant.

►***Needs:*** Grow in full sun. Plant in well-drained, sandy, or gritty soil. Improve soil drainage with gravel or sand. Grow where water will drain from the roots. Overwatering will kill this plant.

►***Choices***: *Opuntia* is a large genus of cacti with species native mostly to the arid, mild-winter areas of Southwestern United States and Mexico to Brazil and Argentina, but with a few hardier species native to the Great Plains and even as far north as Canada. It includes two main types: prickly pears, with flat, paddle-shape stem segments, and those known as cholla, with cylindrical, spiny stem segments. Popular prickly-pear species include beavertail cactus *(O. basilaris),* a low-growing, wide-spreading plant 1' tall and 4' wide; tree prickly pear *(O. ficus-indica),* a shrubby or treelike plant that forms great masses of paddle-shape stem segments up to 15' tall and 12' wide; and hardy prickly pear *(O. humifusa),* a usually low, spreading plant 1'–2' tall and 4' or more wide that is native across many of the drier parts of North America to the Canadian border. *O. phaeacantha* is another hardy prickly pear that can be grown outdoors as far north as Kansas and Colorado. One of the more attractive cholla types sometimes used in desert landscaping in the Southwest is desert Christmas cactus *(O. leptocaulis),* also called pencil cactus for its narrow, pencil-thin stem segments that can each grow as long as 12"; it forms 2'–4' shrubby clumps. It is called desert Christmas cactus for the many bright red and yellow prickly-pear fruits that it produces, usually around Christmastime. It can be grown as far north as Oklahoma.

CACTUS AND SUCCULENTS

Burro's Tail

Sedum morganianum

Succulent evergreen perennial

Sedum morganianum

►***Hardiness:*** Zones 10–11

►***Size:*** Stems trail up to 3' long

►***Features:*** Also called donkey's tail. Stems with tiny pointed succulent leaves trail beautifully from hanging baskets or out of pots positioned on pedestals or shelves.

►***Uses:*** As a houseplant. In mild-winter areas, sometimes grown as an outdoor container plant year-round, or in a raised cactus-and-succulent bed spilling over a wall.

►***Needs:*** Grow as you would any other cactus or succulent, except avoid fertilizing. Also, the leaves fall off easily if bumped; put the plant where it will be undisturbed. Best in a terra-cotta pot with a rounded edge; sharp-edged pots could damage leaves and stems.

CACTUS AND SUCCULENTS

Century Plant

Agave americana

Succulent evergreen perennial

Agave americana 'Mediopicta'

▶***Hardiness:*** Zones 8-11
▶***Size:*** Outdoors in the ground, this desert native grows into a huge plant as wide as 8'-10' with individual leaves as long as 4'. In large containers it grows 3'-4' across when fully mature; most houseplants are younger and much smaller, no more than 1'
▶***Features:*** Thick, long, pointed, sharp leaves edged with dangerous spines fan out from this plant's base to form a gigantic rosette. It's called century plant because, mistakenly, it is thought to bloom once every 100 years. When it does bloom (often after 15 or 20 years when grown outdoors in Southwestern desert gardens), the effect is awe-inspiring, with a towering stalk reaching 10' to as much as 40' into the air topped with a magnificent 3'-6' "candelabra" of hundreds of creamy white blossoms. After it blooms the plant dies. The good news is that it sends out young pups, called offsets, that you can plant to start the cycle over again.
▶***Uses:*** As a houseplant with a cactus collection, or outdoors in the ground from as far north as Sacramento, California, to southern Mexico
▶***Needs:*** Grow as you would any other cactus or succulent: in stony or sandy, sharply drained soil and in full sun. When growing this plant outdoors in regions moister than its native desert, protect these plants from rain, especially in winter. In the relatively moist areas of central and northern California it can grow so rapidly that it blooms in 5 years—and removing this huge plant from the back of a border can take a crane (individual leaves can weigh 40 pounds or more). In containers use a cactus potting mix and give the plant lots of sun. Agaves prefer a shallow pot to a deep one.
▶***Choices:*** There are many species of this Mexican native that range in size from 1' across to the huge century plant. Other varieties suited for growing indoors include 'Marginata', with green, yellow-edged leaves, and 'Mediopicta', with cream leaves edged in green.

CACTUS AND SUCCULENTS

Crown-of-Thorns

Euphorbia milii

Succulent evergreen perennial

Euphorbia milii

▶***Hardiness:*** Zones 9-11
▶***Size:*** Grows 3' tall
▶***Features:*** Aptly named, this interesting plant has rounded leaves on leggy, thorny stalks. As long as it has plenty of direct light, it produces tiny flowers nearly year-round in red, yellow, or salmon.
▶***Uses:*** As a houseplant; in mild-winter climates it grows to a woody shrub
▶***Needs:*** When plant is in bloom, allow the top inch or so of soil to dry out. When not in bloom, let about half the soil ball dry out (test it by poking it with a pencil) but do not let the entire soil ball dry out or the plant will drop its leaves. Otherwise, grow as you would any other cactus or succulent.

CACTUS AND SUCCULENTS

Echeveria

Echeveria spp.

Succulent evergreen perennial

Echeveria elegans

▶***Hardiness:*** Zones 8-11
▶***Size:*** Grows 4"-2' tall, depending on species
▶***Features:*** Like the hardier but otherwise similar genus *Sempervivum,* this group of succulents is sometimes called hen and chicks because of its ability to spread into clumps by forming small offsets clustered around a mother plant every year. The plants have pointed leaves that form tight rosettes of green, blue-green, whitish, or bronze, sometimes tipped in red. Pink, red, or yellow flowers on tall stems emerge from the center of the plant in summer.
▶***Uses:*** As a houseplant. In mild climates echeveria are popular as evergreen perennials in the border, in beds as groundcover, as specimens, and in outdoor containers
▶***Needs:*** Very susceptible to overwatering. In containers, plant in a well-drained soil such as a cactus mix. Fertilize once or twice in summer with a 10-10-10 fertilizer. Outdoors plant in well-drained sandy or gravelly soil. Best in cooler coastal climates, where plants should be grown in full sun. In hot-summer areas, provide some shade.
▶***Choices:*** *Echeveria harmsii* forms a rosette above branching stems with obvious red tips. *Echeveria glauca* has blue-green leaves.

CACTUS AND SUCCULENTS

Golden Barrel Cactus

Echinocactus grusonii

Succulent evergreen perennial

Echinocactus grusonii

C

Plant encyclopedia

▶**Hardiness:** Zones 8–11
▶**Size**: Grows 9" tall
▶**Features:** Slow-growing globe-shape plant, prominent ribs covered with golden woolly hairs
▶**Uses:** As a houseplant. In mild-winter desert climates it is popular as a landscape specimen in cactus gardens and in containers outdoors
▶**Needs:** Easy to grow if given a warm, bright spot indoors and low humidity. Grow in well-drained cactus mix and allow to dry out completely between waterings. In winter give it a cooler spot and longer periods of rest between waterings. Under the right conditions it may produce a flower. Repot only when the barrel begins to extend beyond the edge of the pot.

CACTUS AND SUCCULENTS

Hen and Chicks

Sempervivum spp.

Succulent evergreen perennial

Sempervivum tectorum

▶**Hardiness:** Zones 4–10
▶**Size:** 3"–6" tall, indefinite spread over time
▶**Features:** This succulent plant produces plump rosettes (the "hens"), which rapidly grow young offsets (the "chicks"). Plants tolerate heat, drought, and neglect. Tall reddish flower stems occur on mature plants and reach about 2' tall. Fleshy rosettes are gray tinged with purple. Spreads easily with little care.
▶**Uses:** Rock gardens, arid landscapes, xeriscaping, slopes, areas that lack regular watering, as edging and in beds. Adaptable as to culture, hen and chicks mixes well with other perennials in the front of the mixed border. Excellent in containers.
▶**Needs:** Best in gritty, sandy, well-drained soil, but faster growth occurs in more average garden loam. Grow in full sun most places, but plant in partial to dense shade in hot desert climates.
Like sedums, sempervivums tolerate more water than many succulents. Water moderately during dry periods to prevent shriveling. Pinch and replant offsets to multiply.
▶**Choices:** A seemingly infinite variety of foliage colors are available, from reddish to maroon to cobwebby white. If you live in a mild-winter climate (Zones 8-11), for an even wider selection of hens and chicks to grow outdoors, see the similar group of plants called echeveria.

CACTUS AND SUCCULENTS

Jade Plant

Crassula ovata

Succulent evergreen perennial

Crassula ovata

▶**Hardiness:** Zones 8–11
▶**Size:** Grows from a few inches to 5' tall, depending on the plant's age
▶**Features:** Thick, succulent leaves that are jade green, tinged on the edges with red. Very slow growing; large plants are unusual and costly. Thrives easily.
▶**Uses:** As a houseplant. In mild, arid climates jade plant is often grown outdoors as a hedge, specimen, or patio container plant.
▶**Needs:** Bright, direct light is best, but plants will tolerate medium light. Average household temperatures. Allow soil to dry thoroughly between waterings; avoid overwatering. When repotting, use a mix for cactus and succulents. As the plants grow, you can either allow the new plants around the base of the main plant to grow for a shrubby look or cut them off. Also pinch off any leaves growing along main stems for a more treelike appearance.
▶**Choices:** *Crassula argentea* 'Hummel's Sunset' has golden leaves.

CACTUS AND SUCCULENTS

Kalanchoe

Kalanchoe blossfeldiana

Succulent evergreen perennial

Kalanchoe blossfeldiana

▶**Hardiness:** Zones 9–11
▶**Size:** Grows 12"–18" tall
▶**Features:** One of the most popular flowering houseplants, this succulent produces pretty flowers in large heads in red, pink, lilac, orange, yellow, or white on a neat mound of waxy, rounded leaves.
▶**Uses:** As a houseplant. It's sometimes grown as a perennial in arid mild-winter regions.
▶**Needs:** Many gardeners purchase these plants and simply discard them when they stop blooming after a few weeks. But they can be kept and tended like any other cactus or succulent. Will bloom annually, usually in spring, but greenhouse-grown plants are difficult to bring back into bloom in the home. Blooms heaviest when it has direct sun, which turns the leaves reddish. Also will do well in an east or west window as long as it has a south window in winter.
▶**Choices:** Many cultivars are available, but usually are not specified on the plant label. Miniatures include 'Tom Thumb' and 'Compact Lilliput.'

CACTUS AND SUCCULENTS

Living Stones

Lithops spp.

Succulent evergreen perennial

Lithops spp.

▶ ***Hardiness:*** Zones 10–11
▶ ***Size:*** Grows 1"–2" tall and wide
▶ ***Features:*** Tiny rounded columns with mosaic markings of browns, pinks, and golds. In late summer, a daisylike bloom may appear on two leaves. A plant may remain as one plant or develop into clumps.
▶ ***Uses:*** As a houseplant
▶ ***Needs:*** Grow like any other cactus or succulent, except stop watering completely after bloom until two new leaves appear.

CACTUS AND SUCCULENTS

Mother-of-Thousands

Kalanchoe daigremontiana

Succulent evergreen perennial

Kalanchoe daigremontiana

▶ ***Hardiness:*** Zones 10–11
▶ ***Size:*** Grows 18"–36" tall
▶ ***Features:*** Also called maternity plant and Daigremont kalanchoe. Grows on a slender stem with 1"–2"-long blue-green leaves splotched in reddish purple. The edges of the leaves have shallow teeth, and between each pair of teeth is a tiny replica of the whole plant. These drop off readily and, in the right conditions, root and grow, forming a clump around the mother plant.
▶ ***Uses:*** As a houseplant
▶ ***Needs:*** Same as other cactus and succulents. Hold off fertilizing for the first 6 months after you purchase the plant.
▶ ***Choices:*** Sometimes sold as *Bryophyllum daigremontianum.*

CACTUS AND SUCCULENTS

Old Man Cactus

Cephalocereus senilis

Succulent evergreen perennial

Cephalocereus senilis

▶ ***Hardiness:*** Zones 8–11
▶ ***Size:*** Grows 1' tall
▶ ***Features:*** 5" long soft white "hairs," hence its name. Small sharp spines are under the hairs.
▶ ***Uses:*** As a houseplant; outdoors in Southwestern cactus gardens as a specimen
▶ ***Needs:*** Needs more winter warmth than other cactus. Keep temperatures above 60°F/16°C.

CACTUS AND SUCCULENTS

Panda Plant

Kalanchoe tomentosa

Succulent evergreen perennial

Kalanchoe tomentosa

▶ ***Hardiness:*** Zones 10–11
▶ ***Size:*** Grows to 18" tall and wide
▶ ***Features:*** Attractive thick leaves covered with soft silver hairs. Edges are tipped with chocolate-brown or rust hairs. Leaves are borne in a rosette pattern on slightly elongated stems.
▶ ***Uses:*** As a houseplant
▶ ***Needs:*** Same as other cactus and succulents. Hold off fertilizing for the first 6 months after you purchase the plant. Repot infrequently.

CACTUS AND SUCCULENTS

Queen Victoria Century Plant

Agave victoriae-reginae

Succulent evergreen perennial

Agave victoriae-reginae 'Compacta'

▶ ***Hardiness:*** Zones 8–11
▶ ***Size:*** Grows 6"–1' across
▶ ***Features:*** This is one of the smallest agaves,

forming a rosette of triangular leaves in dark green edged in white.
▶ **Uses:** As a specimen outdoors in arid regions, or indoors as a houseplant
▶ **Needs**: Grow as any cactus or succulent. Agaves prefer a shallow pot to a deep one.

CACTUS AND SUCCULENTS

Rattail Cactus

Aporocactus flagelliformis

Succulent evergreen perennial

Aporocactus flagelliformis

▶ **Hardiness:** Zones 10–11
▶ **Size:** Grows up to 6' long in natural conditions; anywhere from a few inches to a few feet as a houseplant, depending on growing conditions and pot size
▶ **Features:** Interesting long, trailing rounded stems covered with delicate spines. Spectacular magenta flowers last up to two months along the stems.
▶ **Uses:** As a houseplant
▶ **Needs**: Does best in a hanging basket or on a pedestal to show off the trailing stems.

CACTUS AND SUCCULENTS

Snowball Cactus

Mammillaria bocasana

Succulent evergreen perennial

Mammillaria bocasana

▶ **Hardiness:** Zones 8–11
▶ **Size:** Grows 4"–6" tall and 6"–12" wide
▶ **Features:** Also called pincushion cactus, this is probably the most commonly grown cactus for the house. It comes in a wide variety of colors and textures. It stays small but may form a single ball or many balls in clumps. It is among the easiest cactus to get to flower.
▶ **Uses:** As a houseplant
▶ **Needs:** Same as for other cactus.
▶ **Choices:** *Mammillaria bocasana* forms a cluster of balls with silvery hairs. *M. wildii* is oval-shape. *M. rhodantha* and *M. hahniana* have pink flowers.

CACTUS AND SUCCULENTS

Zebra Haworthia

Haworthia fasciata

Succulent evergreen perennial

Haworthia fasciata

▶ **Hardiness:** Zones 10–11
▶ **Size:** Grows 3"–8" tall and wide, depending on the type
▶ **Features:** Sometimes simply called zebra plant. Forms rosettes of sharply pointed, fleshy brownish to green leaves with a network of white veins.
▶ **Uses:** As a houseplant
▶ **Needs:** Give zebra haworthia a warm spot on the windowsill in bright to medium light, but no direct light. During active growth (September through May), water whenever soil's surface feels dry to the touch, and fertilize once or twice with a general houseplant fertilizer. During the plant's rest phase (June through September), water only when soil feels dry 1" below the surface.
▶ **Choices:** *Haworthia cymbiformis,* also called window plant, has semitransparent "windows" instead of bumps on the tops of leaves.

Caesalpinia mexicana

see Bird-of-Paradise, Mexican

Caladium

Caladium hybrids

Subtropical bulb

Caladium hybrid

▶ **Hardiness:** Annual in Zones 2–9; perennial in Zones 8–11
▶ **Size:** 1'–3' tall and wide
▶ **Features:** The large, bold-colored leaves available with caladium bring welcome drama to shady spots where, outside of impatiens, there are few choices for season-long color. Brilliant reds, delicate pinks, cool whites, and silvery streaks are all part of the caladium show.
▶ **Uses:** Color in shady areas
▶ **Needs:** Light shade in Zones 2–6; deeper shade in Zones 7–11. Some cultivars are more tolerant of sun than others. Rich, well-drained but moist soil, neutral to acidic. Ample moisture. Plant tubers 2" deep in spring when ground is thoroughly warm and nights are above 60°F (16°C). Work in a few spadefuls of compost and a slow-release fertilizer. Many gardeners like to start plants 6–8 weeks ahead indoors in pots for later transplanting. After plant emerges, mulch to conserve moisture. Protect from snails and slugs. In fall, after first frost, lift and store tubers if desired (see page 205) or simply buy more tubers the next spring. Store at 40°F (4°C). Bring small pots indoors as winter houseplants or allow plants to go dormant in the pots.
▶ **Choices:** Leaves are marked in reds, greens, pinks, and whites. Dozens of cultivars are available in many sizes, markings, and color combinations.

Calamagrostis ×acutiflora 'Karl Foerster'

see Grasses, Ornamental: Feather Reed Grass

Calendula

see Pot Marigold

California Incense Cedar

see Incense Cedar, California

California Lilac

see Ceanothus

California Poppy

Eschscholzia californica

Annual

Eschscholzia californica

▶ Hardiness: Not applicable
▶ Size: 6"-12" tall and wide
▶ Features: Blooms spring or summer
▶ Uses: Excellent for mixed flower border and beds, meadow gardens, rock gardens, and wherever a loose, natural look is desired. Performs well in containers.
▶ Needs: Sandy, poor, neutral soil; dislikes acidic soil. Moderate moisture at first; becomes drought tolerant once established. Plant seeds directly in soil in early spring for early summer bloom; in Zones 7-11 also sow in fall for spring bloom. Hold off on fertilizing; rich soil may prevent bloom. To prevent seedlings from sprouting, tear out plants after bloom has passed; this plant often self-seeds. It is usually pest free.
▶ Choices: Flowers are oranges, yellows, creams, and whites. Reds, pinks, and violets are also becoming available. Most cultivars are single flowers, but 'Ballerina' is semidouble and 'Mission Bells' is double.

Calla Lily

Zantedeschia spp.

Subtropical perennial bulb

Zantedeschia aethiopica

▶ Hardiness: Zones 8-11
▶ Size: 18"-4' tall, 10"-2' wide
▶ Features: These elegant flowers impart an exotic, tropical look to any planting. Many varieties have attractive mottled leaves.
▶ Uses: Excellent to plant in shady and wet sites outdoors as an annual in Zones 7-11 or a perennial farther south. In mild coastal climates it performs well in full sun. This is a superb container plant—probably its most popular use.
▶ Needs: Grow as an annual in Zones 2-7; as a perennial in Zones 8-11. Full sun to light shade, especially in hot-summer areas of Zones 8-11. Average to rich, always moist soil. Provide ample moisture. In Zones 2-7 plant in containers in spring after all danger of frost has passed. In Zones 8-11 plant outdoors in containers or in the ground. Plant 4" deep. Mulch to conserve moisture. Fertilize once or twice during bloom. This plant will often naturalize. It is prone to leaf spots, slugs, and snails. In fall in Zones 2-7, store plant, pot and all, in garage or cool basement over the winter.
▶ Choices: Flowers are usually white, but yellow, orange, purple, red, and nearly black species and cultivars are available.

Callery Pear

Pyrus calleryana

Deciduous tree

Pyrus calleryana 'Bradford'

▶ Hardiness: Zones 4-8
▶ Size: 30'-50' tall, 20'-35' wide
▶ Features: No wonder this tree is so popular—callery pear combines all the features desired in an ornamental tree: rapid growth, attractive, uniform shape (like big lollipops); white spring flowers before leaves; summer shade; no fruit—and its foliage turns shiny scarlet to purple in fall. It does tend to be weak-wooded (the commonly offered cultivar 'Bradford' is more prone than most to developing weak crotches that often split the trunk under heavy snowfall). Some people find the flowers to have an unpleasant odor.
▶ Uses: Parking areas, lawns, street trees, specimens, patios, courtyards, entries, lining driveways, growing in large planting beds, providing seasonal accent
▶ Needs: Plant in any soil that's well drained and receives full sun. Trees tolerate city conditions including polluted air and reflected heat from paving. Roots are well behaved and won't buckle paving. Prune in late winter or early spring.
▶ Choices: 'Aristocrat'—less prone to trunk-splitting than the more commonly offered 'Bradford', 30'-35' tall, 20'-25' wide; 'Capital'—coppery fall leaves, 40' tall, 15' wide; 'Chanticleer'—less susceptible to freeze damage than 'Bradford', 30' tall, 20' wide; 'Cleveland Select'—blooms very young, 30'-35' tall, 20' wide.

Callibrachoa

see Million Bells

Callicarpa spp.

see Beautyberry

Callistemon citrinus

see Crimson Bottlebrush

Callistephus chinensis

see China Aster

Calluna vulgaris

see Heather, Scotch

Calycanthus floridus

see Sweet Shrub

Calocendrus decurrens

see Incense Cedar, California

Camellia

Camellia spp.

Broadleaf evergreen shrub

Camellia japonica 'Admiral Nimitz'

Camellia japonica hybrid

Camellia japonica 'Art Howard'

Camellia sasanqua

▶ ***Hardiness:*** Zones 7–11
▶ ***Size:*** 1'–15' tall, 3'–12' wide, depending on variety
▶ ***Features:*** This dark-green shrub adds elegant flowers to the landscape at an unexpected time of year. Large roselike blooms, in an array of colors, open in late fall and early winter *(Camellia sasanqua)* or late winter and early spring *(C. japonica)*. The lush, glossy evergreen leaves are beautiful in all seasons. Some varieties are low-growing, spreading in form; in mild climates larger varieties are sometimes pruned with a single trunk as a small tree. Most develop a full rounded form that is covered in beautiful blossoms once a year. Camellia blossoms are lovely in flower arrangements, holding their color and shape well.
▶ ***Uses:*** Good for corners of houses and porches, accents, background. Group plants together to grow hedges or set alone for a specimen plant. Excellent in woodland gardens with a high tree canopy and dappled shade, combined with evergreen azaleas and rhododendrons and spring-blooming bulbs. Performs well in large containers.
▶ ***Needs:*** Best in part shade, but will tolerate full shade and full sun. Does best in rich, moist, acidic soil. Ample moisture. Plant established plants in spring or fall. Mulch 2" deep. Keep moist first three years; after that most in-ground plants survive on natural rainfall. Fertilize plants shorter than 8' every 6–8 weeks or so with an acidic plant food. Read label carefully; do not overfertilize. Prune immediately after flowering. Cut out any dead or weak wood, shape shrub, and thin growth as desired. This plant is prone to disease if soil is poorly drained or if there are excessive salts in the soil. It is also prone to camellia petal blight, a bacterial disease. Pick up fallen leaves and petals immediately to help control this problem.
▶ ***Choices:*** Common camellia *(Camellia japonica)* and its many hybrids are hardy in Zones 8–11. There are hundreds, if not thousands, of cultivars to choose from, including those with double and single flowers in various shades and markings of pink, red, and white. They appear in late winter and early spring. Sasanqua camellia *(C. sasanqua)* is the hardier species, useful in Zones 7–11. It also has many hybrids to choose from.

Campanula spp.
see Bellflower

Campsis radicans
see Trumpet Creeper

Canada Hemlock
see Hemlock, Canada

Canary Island Date Palm
see Palms

Candytuft
Iberis spp.

Evergreen perennial or cool-season annual

Iberis sempervirens

▶ ***Hardiness:*** Zones 4–8 (perennial species)
▶ ***Size:*** 6"–12" tall, 12"–36" wide
▶ ***Features:*** White is valuable for adding sparkle to landscapes; plant candytuft to brighten areas or line walkways with snowy blooms in early spring. Plants will thrive poorly in soggy soil. Perennial species is covered in blazing white blossoms in early spring and has attractive fine-textured foliage that looks good the rest of the year. It forms low, spreading mats. The annual species has white or pink blossoms that are effective from spring to early summer.
▶ ***Uses:*** Rock gardens, edging walkways, patios, courtyards, narrow confined spaces, raised planters, retaining walls, slopes, perennial beds, stone pathways, entries, moonlight gardens
▶ ***Needs:*** Average, well-drained, neutral to alkaline soil. Moderate moisture. Plant established plants in spring or fall. They look best in groups of eight or more. Mulch. Fertilize lightly in spring with a slow-release fertilizer. After flowering is over, cut back by one-third to one-half. Perennial types seldom need division, but divide if desired. Every few years, after flowering, cut back perennial candytuft especially hard—by one-half to two-thirds—to ensure compact growth.
▶ ***Choices:*** In Zones 4–8 grow evergreen candytuft *(Iberis sempervirens)* as a perennial. In Zones 9–10 grow either evergreen candytuft or globe candytuft *(I. umbellata)* as a cool-season annual, planting in fall or late winter.

Canna; Canna Lily
Canna hybrids

Perennial often grown as an annual

Canna 'Wyoming'

▶ ***Hardiness:*** Zones 8–11 (perennial)
▶ ***Size:*** 18"–7' tall, 10"–3' wide
▶ ***Features:*** While canna's exotic-looking flowers in bright, hot colors can be outstanding, the foliage creates the real drama in the garden. Huge leaves, often tinted with red to varying degrees or striped or blotched in yellow or red, lend an unmistakably tropical effect. And this plant is easy to grow just about anywhere in full sun. Flowers attract hummingbirds.

▶Uses: Good for a strong vertical accent wherever a bold stroke is needed. Excellent in containers.
▶Needs: Annual in Zones 2-7; perennial in Zones 8-11. Full sun. Tolerates a variety of soils, but does best in rich, well-drained soil. Provide abundant moisture. Plant in spring after soil has warmed, a week or two after last frost date. Work in ample compost or a slow-release fertilizer at planting time. Protect from snails and slugs. In fall, in Zones 2-7, after first frost, lift and store tubers (see page 205). Store at 40-50°F (4-10°C).
▶Choices: Flowers come in pinks, reds, oranges, yellows, and whites. Foliage has markings of greens, yellows, whites, and purples. 'Pretoria' has lime-green and lemon-yellow tigerlike stripes. 'Wyoming' has deep purple foliage. 'Pfitzer's' dwarf hybrids grow only 30" tall.

Cantaloupe
see Melons

Cape Honeysuckle
Tecomaria capensis
Evergreen shrub, vine, or groundcover

Tecomaria capensis

▶Hardiness: Zones 10-11
▶Size: 8' tall, 4' wide
▶Features: Any way you grow it, cape honeysuckle will fill your landscaping needs—and fast. Train this evergreen plant as an upright shrub, climbing vine, or trailing groundcover, and enjoy bright red-orange blossoms all winter long.
▶Uses: Informal hedges or screens, accent shrub, groundcover, climbing vine, adding color and fine texture to the landscape
▶Needs: Plant in any soil, as long as it's well drained. Water new plants frequently until well-established, then water moderately when soil is dry. Severe pruning will keep plants in shrub form. For climbing vine or groundcover use, pruning is unnecessary.

Cape Marigold; African Daisy
Dimorphotheca spp.
Annual

Dimorphotheca spp.

▶Hardiness: Not applicable
▶Size: 4"-16" tall, 6"-14" wide
▶Features: Blooms late winter through spring in mild-winter climates, all summer in cold-winter climates. Blooms close up at night and during overcast weather.
▶Uses: Annual bedding color massed as groundcover, excellent in containers
▶Needs: Average to poor, loose, well-drained soil. Light to moderate moisture. Plant seeds directly in soil in early spring for summer bloom. In Zones 9-11 plant seeds this way in late fall or early winter for blooms in late winter and early spring. Avoid fertilizing. Trim spent blooms regularly to promote longest flowering time. Discard plants after blooming has ceased.
▶Choices: Flowers are white, oranges, yellows, creams, or apricot, and are often sold as mixes. 'Glistening White' is purest white.

Cape Jasmine
see Gardenia

Cape Leadwort
Plumbago auriculata (formerly *P. capensis*)
Subtropical evergreen or semievergreen shrub or vine

Plumbago auriculata

▶Hardiness: Zones 8-11
▶Size: 6' tall, 8' wide when grown as a shrub
▶Features: White, pale blue, or intense robin's-egg blue flower clusters on long, arching branches appear over a long season from spring through summer, or even all year long in mild frost-free climates. If tied to a support and trained as a vine, this shrub can climb up to 12' tall.
▶Uses: Excellent massed on slopes and banks, grown as a loose, natural hedge; between perennials and other blooming shrubs in the mixed border; or against fences and walls as a vine
▶Needs: Plant in any soil that is well drained, in full sun. To keep shape dense or to speed recovery after winter frosts in colder areas, prune back hard annually in late winter.
▶Choices: To ensure good color select plants when in bloom. 'Royal Cape' and 'Imperial Blue' are good selections for intense blue color.

Cardinal Climber
Ipomoea ×sloteri
Annual vine

Ipomoea ×sloteri

▶Hardiness: Not applicable
▶Size: 10' in all directions
▶Features: Bright red blossoms; deeply lobed, ferny leaves; and a more restrained growth habit make this vine a winner. The flowers appear from midsummer into fall and are attractive to hummingbirds. Like the flowers of cardinal climber's relative, morning glory, they open in the morning and close later in the day.
▶Uses: A good choice for training onto mailboxes and lampposts, or growing on a small lattice in a container
▶Needs: Best in full sun with moderately moist, well-drained soil. Plant seeds directly where you want the plants; as with morning glory, for fastest germination nick the hard seed coat with a file and soak the seed overnight before sowing. Fertilize sparingly; too much nitrogen will encourage foliage rather than flowers. The vine climbs by twining; proper supports include netting, small lattice, bamboo poles and teepees, and chain-link fence.
▶Choices: Cypress vine *(Ipomoea quamoclit)* is a similar annual vine with finer-textured, feathery foliage. Its flowers come in red and white; sometimes both red and white flowers appear on the same plant.

Cardinal Flower

Lobelia cardinalis

Perennial

Lobelia cardinalis

▶ ***Hardiness:*** Zones 2–9
▶ ***Size:*** 2'–4' tall, 1'–2' wide
▶ ***Features:*** Native wildflower has tall spikes of brilliant red flowers in late season that are attractive to hummingbirds. Thrives in any low spots in the garden that stay wet or even boggy. Blooms in late summer or early autumn.
▶ ***Uses:*** At the edge of water gardens and streamsides where soil is constantly moist, bog gardens, rain gardens in low wet spots
▶ ***Needs:*** Full sun in Zones 2–5; shade, especially afternoon shade, in Zones 5 and warmer. Rich, moist, preferably boggy soil; ample moisture. Plant established plants in spring or fall. Fertilize at planting time and each following spring with a slow-release fertilizer. Mulch. Trim spent blooms. Cardinal flower is a short-lived perennial, lasting only a few years. Plants may self-sow. Otherwise, divide every other year to assure an ongoing supply. It is pest free.
▶ ***Choices:*** Great blue lobelia *(Lobelia siphilitica)* tolerates dryer conditions in Zones 4–8. It produces blue or purple spikes instead of red.

Carex morrowii

see Sedge, Variegated Japanese

Carnation

see Pinks

Carolina Allspice

see Sweet Shrub

Carolina Laurelcherry

see Laurels

Carpinus spp.

see Hornbeams

Carrot

Daucus carota var. *sativus*

Cool-season annual vegetable

Carrot

▶ ***Hardiness:*** Not applicable
▶ ***Size:*** Tops grow 4"–8" tall and roots grow about the same
▶ ***Features:*** Vitamin-rich roots that taste great cooked or raw
▶ ***Uses:*** In the vegetable garden
▶ ***Needs:*** Full sun to light shade. Rich, deep, loose soil with plentiful, consistent moisture to keep carrots from splitting. Needs 65–80 days of temperatures between 40°–85°F/5°–30°C.

Before planting, work soil to a depth of 1', adding plenty of compost. Plant in the north 2–3 weeks before average date of last frost. In Zones 8 and warmer, plant from midwinter to early spring. Plant seeds ½" deep in rows 1' apart. Thin seedlings to 2"–3". Keep soil moist; mulch to assist in this. Add mulch later in season to cover up shoulders of carrots as they emerge from the soil; sunlight turns them green and bitter. Harvest anytime after full color develops but while roots are still tender and sweet.
▶ ***Choices:*** Choose from hybrids as well as Imperator (8"–10" long and slender), Chantenay (4"–5" long, does well in heavy soil), Danvers (6"–7" long and wider than other types), and Nantes (5"–7" long and cylindrical rather than tapering). 'Caroline' is a popular Chantenay type with excellent flavor.

Carya illinoiensis

see Pecan

Caryopteris ×*clandonensis*

see Bluebeard

Caryota mitis

see Palms: Clustered Fishtail Palm

Cast-Iron Plant

Aspidistra elatior

Subtropical evergreen perennial

Aspidistra elatior

▶ ***Hardiness:*** Zones 8–11
▶ ***Size:*** 2'–3' tall, 1'–2' wide
▶ ***Features:*** Cast-iron plant is a good choice for shady places. It requires little attention and adapts easily to poor soil and other tough conditions. Too much sun and lack of moisture turn leaves crispy brown on the edges. Plants spread slowly into thick clumps of large, attractive dark green leaves. It's exceptionally easy to both grow in the landscape in the South and in containers indoors—hence its name.
▶ ***Uses:*** As a houseplant in most regions; in Zones 8–11 outdoors it is good for covering bare, shady areas; planting beneath eaves, decks, and overhangs; as a coarse-textured accent; in containers; as a groundcover beneath trees.
▶ ***Needs:*** Indoors, give it low to bright light; grows best in medium light and dislikes direct sun. Does well in average household temperatures and average household humidity. Allow soil to dry slightly between waterings; dislikes constantly wet soil. Rinse or wipe off the plant's broad leaves once a month or so with water. Outdoors, plant in any soil except one that is soggy and wet. Sandy soil enriched with organic matter is ideal for helping hold moisture. Grow in filtered or dense shade. Water when dry and temperatures are high. Feed with a balanced fertilizer in spring and again in summer.
▶ ***Choices:*** A lovely variegated type *(Aspidistra elatior* 'Variegata') is also available.

Catharanthus roseus

see Vinca (*Catharanthus* spp.)

Catmint

Nepeta ×faassenii

Perennial

Nepeta ×faassenii 'Walker's Low'

▶Hardiness: Zones 4–9
▶Size: 1'–3' high, 1'–4' wide
▶Features: Plant catmint where you need a low-growing bloomer to tumble over the edges of patios, walkways, and rock walls. Purple-blue flowers bloom steadily in summer sun, forming a ribbon of blue where they are used. They are very attractive in combination with yellow and pink flowers. The cascading blue-green foliage is aromatic. Blooms early summer and continues to frost.
▶Uses: Xeriscaping, rock gardens, filling in hot spots, edging planting beds, walkways, entries, or patios
▶Needs: Full sun preferred but will tolerate light shade. Average to sandy, well-drained soil; it tends to die out in clay or wet soils. Moderate to light moisture. Plant established plants in spring or fall. Avoid fertilizing. Mulch. After blooming occurs, shear back by about one-third to one-half to promote fresh growth and more bloom. Divide in spring every 3–4 years as needed. It is usually pest and disease free, though cats may roll on it.
▶Choices: Technically, *Nepeta ×faassenii* is catmint and *N. cataria* is catnip, but the two are now used interchangeably to describe nearly any *Nepeta. N. ×faassenii* is the showiest catmint. *N.* 'Six Hills Giant' is the largest, spreading to 4'. It has violet-blue flowers on 24"–36" spikes. 'Walker's Low' is a low-growing variety about 12"–18" tall that looks lovely cascading over the edge of a walkway.

Catnip

see Catmint

Cattleya

see Orchids

Cauliflower

Brassica oleracea

Cool-season annual vegetable

Cauliflower

▶Size: Grows 1'–2' tall and as wide
▶Features: Crunchy white heads are tasty raw or cooked
▶Uses: In the vegetable garden
▶Needs: Full sun to light shade. Well-drained soil high in organic matter. Dislikes hot or dry conditions, which make heads loose and "ricey." Grow only in regions where it can have 2 months of temperatures between 55°F and 80°F (13°C and 27°C). Plentiful moisture. Add compost to soil at planting time. Plant established plants in spring or fall, 18"–24" apart, working in ample compost. Mulch to keep soil cool and moist. When small heads are visible, blanch them to prevent brown spots and ensure sweetness by pulling leaves over the head and fastening them with a rubber band or spring-type clothespin. Cut off heads when full and compact, usually 1–2 weeks after heads first appear.
▶Choices: Self-blanching types are available. Cauliflowers mature in as little as 55 days; quick-maturing types work best in regions where high heat may be a problem.

Ceanothus, California Lilac

Ceanothus spp.

Evergreen shrub

Ceanothus 'Dark Star'

▶Hardiness: Zones 8–10; some species hardier
▶Size: 6" to 15' tall, 3' to 30' wide, depending on variety
▶Features: Mostly native to California and Oregon from the coastal fog belt to higher elevations of the Sierra Nevada, these evergreen shrubs are valuable landscape plants in western gardens for their early spring bloom and carefree nature. There are hundreds of species and hybrids available. Some are low, prostrate groundcovers that spread rapidly. Others are tall, almost treelike in form. And many fall somewhere in between—small to large shrubs of varying sizes. All are fairly short-lived under the best conditions: 10–12 years at most. The most popular selections bear pleasantly scented flowers in the blue range, from sparkling pale blue to vibrant, deep blue. Some varieties are white, pink, or lavender.
▶Uses: A must for natural-looking California native plant landscapes. Excellent for xeriscaping and erosion control on banks and slopes with stony, dry soil. Low-growing, spreading forms make a good groundcover; medium-size shrubs are good screens and hedges.
▶Needs: All species native to the West should be planted in soil with perfect, sharp drainage—stony, sandy soil is best ("Plant 'em on a pile of rocks," says one noted California horticulturist). Full sun. Most should be watered only during establishment, and rarely fertilized. Some of the low-growing species native to the coastal fog belt, however, appreciate occasional water during the summer dry spell. Prune lightly if at all, and leave branches larger than 1" in diameter. If you live in the East and want to try your luck with this Western native, choose a variety native to moister coastal areas, give it perfect drainage, try to protect it from summer rain, and hope for the best.
▶Choices: Carmel creeper *(Ceanothus griseus* var. *horizontalis)* and its many cultivars are popular selections for the cool, mild climates in the California coastal fog belt from San Francisco south. Most grow 1'–2' tall and spread quite wide; 'Hurricane Point' can quickly spread as wide as 30'. Flowers range from pale to medium to deep, intense blue, depending on cultivar. *C. thyrsiflorus* is one of the hardiest California lilac species (Zones 7–10); it grows up to 20' tall, 30' wide with light to deep blue flowers, but has many cultivars of varying heights and flower colors (including white)—some as low as 3' tall and 5' wide. *Ceanothus* 'Dark Star' and 'Julia Phelps' are medium-size shrubs popular for their dark, intense, midnight-blue flowers. They both can grow 8' tall and wide, and make good hedges.

Cedar, California Incense

see Incense Cedar

Cedar, Eastern Red

see Junipers

Cedar, Japanese

see Cryptomeria, Japanese

Cedar, Western Red

see Arborvitae

CEDARS

Cedrus spp.

Many plants go by the common name of cedar, including juniper and arborvitae. The genus *Cedrus*, however, includes the true cedars, native to the Middle East. Israel, Palestine, Lebanon, and Syria are thought to have been covered long ago in great forests of these majestic trees, and they were the trees from which the original Temple of Solomon was built. In the landscape, both species described here form grand specimens of picturesque form.

CEDARS

Blue Atlas Cedar

Cedrus libani 'Glauca'

Evergreen coniferous tree

Cedrus libani 'Glauca'

▶***Hardiness:*** Zones 6-9
▶***Size:*** 40'-60' tall, 30'-40' wide
▶***Features:*** Known for its sweeping branches and silvery blue needles, blue atlas cedar grows slowly to a majestic size and requires plenty of room to develop fully. Pruning ruins the form of this picturesque tree. Allow a minimum of 30 feet of open space per tree. May grow 120' tall and 100' wide after many years.
▶***Uses:*** Single specimen, matched pairs, large estates, background, screening, winter interest
▶***Needs:*** Plant in a sunny site with well-drained, fertile soil. Plants will tolerate sandy and clay soils too. Best growth occurs in acidic soil, although they will tolerate alkaline. Protect from strong winds. If two shoots emerge from tree's top, remove the weaker shoot to allow the other to form a central leader.
▶***Choices:*** Also try: 'Pendula'—weeping form.

CEDARS

Deodar Cedar

Cedrus deodara

Evergreen coniferous tree

Cedrus deodara

▶***Hardiness:*** Zones 6-9
▶***Size:*** 40'-70' tall, 25'-30' wide
▶***Features:*** Even if you live where it's too hot to grow most wintery-looking evergreen trees, you can grow this one. Deodar cedar tolerates heat and poor, dry soils, growing slowly to make excellent specimen plantings with graceful, pendulous branching. As trees mature, they widen out and become flat-topped. Older trees also produce green cones that turn reddish brown at maturity. Cones take two years to mature. Green foliage is silvery with hints of blue.
▶***Uses:*** Specimen use, screening to block poor views and add year-round privacy, background for deciduous trees and shrubs, winter interest, and large, open areas
▶***Needs:*** Plant in any well-drained or dry soil, from acidic to alkaline. Grow in full sun; protect from sweeping winds that can deform the tree.
▶***Choices:*** 'Aurea' has golden foliage.

Cedrus spp.

see Cedars

Celastrus scandens

see Bittersweet, American

Celery

Apium graveolens var. *dulce*

Cool-season annual vegetable

Celery

▶***Hardiness:*** Not applicable
▶***Size:*** Grows about 1' tall, 3"-4" wide
▶***Features:*** Crisp green vegetable for snacking and salads
▶***Uses:*** In the vegetable garden
▶***Needs:*** Must have evenly cool temperatures with ample moisture. Plants must not be exposed to temperatures below 55°-85°F/13°C-30°C. May bolt, turning bitter and tough. Full sun to part shade. Moist to wet, rich soil. Work soil to a depth of several inches, adding plenty of compost. In Zones 7

C

Plant encyclopedia

and colder, start seeds indoors 10 weeks before planting outside. Plant outdoors 4-6 weeks before your region's last frost date in spring. In warm-winter regions, Zones 8 and warmer, sow directly in the garden. Space or thin to 12"-18" apart. Keep soil moist. Fertilize with liquid fertilizer every 3 weeks. Blanch when plants are 8" or so for milder, sweeter flavor by covering with heavy paper or an inverted cardboard milk carton with the top cut off. Harvest when base is 2"-3" wide. Prolong harvest in mild-winter climates by cutting off only outer ribs, leaving smaller interior ribs to continue growing.
▶ ***Choices:*** Look for cultivars that are self-blanching.

Celtis laevigata
see Sugarberry

Celosia spp.
see Cockscomb

Centaurea spp.
see Dusty Miller; Cornflower

Centranthus ruber
see Red Valerian

Century Plant
see Cactus and Succulents

Cephalocereus senilis
see Cactus and Succulents: Old Man Cactus

Cerastium tomentosum
see Snow-in-Summer

Ceratostigma plumbaginoides
see Plumbago

Cercidiphyllum japonicum
see Katsura Tree

Cercidium texanum
see Palo Verde, Texas

Cercis canadensis
see Redbud

Cestrum nocturnum
See Jessamine, Night-Blooming

Chaenomeles speciosa
see Quince, Flowering

Chamaecyparis spp.
see False Cypresses

Chamaedorea elegans
see Palms: Parlor Palm

Chamaerops humilis
see Palms: Mediterranean Fan Palm

Chameleon Plant
see Houttuynia

Chard; Swiss Chard
Beta vulgaris

Cool-season annual vegetable

Chard 'Rhubarb'

▶ ***Hardiness:*** Not applicable
▶ ***Size:*** Grows 1'-2' tall, a few inches wide
▶ ***Features:*** Beautifully veined leaves grow on richly colored stalks; excellent for stir-fry
▶ ***Uses:*** In the vegetable garden
▶ ***Needs:*** Full sun to light shade. Rich, loose soil high in organic matter that is neutral to alkaline. Plentiful, consistent moisture. Needs at least 60 days of temperatures below 80°F/27°C. In Zones 6 and colder, plant seeds directly in soil in spring 2-3 weeks before your region's last average frost date. In Zones 7 and warmer, plant anytime from fall to early spring. Plant seeds 1" deep and thin to 9"-12". Keep soil moist. Harvest by cutting off at soil level. Prolong the harvest by cutting off outer leaves first. Leave smaller interior leaves to mature for harvest a week or two later.
▶ ***Choices:*** 'Bright Lights' stems grow in many brilliant colors. 'Fordhook Giant' is more tolerant of cold and heat than other types.

Chasmanthium latifolium
see Grasses, Ornamental: Northern Sea Oats

Chaste Tree; Lilac Chaste Tree
Vitex agnus-castus

Deciduous small tree or large shrub

Vitex agnus-castus

▶ ***Hardiness:*** Zones 6-10
▶ ***Size:*** 6'-25' tall and wide
▶ ***Features:*** Grows well and blooms profusely in hot, dry areas with alkaline soils. Fragrant summertime flowers are usually lilac, but also come in blue, pink, or white. They attract butterflies. Faster growth occurs in hotter areas. Can also be grown as a shrub. Plants are low maintenance and adaptable.
▶ ***Uses:*** Accents (single specimen or in groups); growing near patios, decks, porches, and entries; informal hedges
▶ ***Needs:*** Plant in full sun or light, dappled shade. Any type of soil will do as long as it is well drained. Water new plants regularly. Once established, water only in times of severe drought. To encourage treelike shape, remove lower limbs as the plant grows.

Checkered Lily
see Fritillary

Chelone lyonii
see Turtlehead, Pink

Cherry
Prunus spp.

Deciduous fruit tree

Cherry 'Early Richmond'

▶ ***Hardiness:*** Sweet cherries Zones 5-9; tart types Zones 4-8
▶ ***Size:*** Grows 10'-50' tall and 10'-30' wide, depending on variety
▶ ***Features:*** Delicious sweet or tart red fruits on a beautiful tree
▶ ***Uses:*** In the home orchard; pretty enough to plant anywhere in the landscape
▶ ***Needs:*** Full sun. Fares poorly in the warmest parts of the country because of summer heat. Rich, well-drained soil with average moisture; will tolerate some variation. Sour cherries do not need a second tree for cross-pollination. Most sweet cherries except 'Stella' do. Prune very early each spring as an

open-center or central-leader tree (see page 266). Fertilize sweet cherries for higher yields. May need to throw a net over trees to protect from birds eating the cherries.

▶ ***Choices:*** Sweet cherries are excellent for eating fresh and include 'Bing.' Sour cherries are preferred for baking. 'Montmorency' is considered the most flavorful; 'Northstar' is cold hardy and disease resistant. Nanking cherries are the smallest trees; also look for bush types 'Jan' and 'Joy'.

Cherry Laurel
see Laurel

Cherry, Ornamental
see Plum

Cherry-Pie Plant
see Heliotrope

Chicory
see Belgian Endive

Chilopsis linearis
see Desert Willow

China Aster
Callistephus chinensis

Annual

Callistephus chinensis

▶ ***Hardiness:*** Not applicable

▶ ***Size:*** 6"–36" tall, 6"–12" wide

▶ ***Features:*** Cheerful daisies in nearly every color, especially pink, red, and blue. Blooms in late summer to early fall

▶ ***Uses:*** Annual bedding plant for late-season color. Good cut flower. Nice in combination with pot marigold

▶ ***Needs:*** Rich, well-drained soil. Moderate water. Plant established seedlings in spring after all danger of frost has passed. Feed regularly, every 4 weeks, or work in a 9-month, slow-release fertilizer. Mulch to conserve moisture. If continuous bloom is desired, replant every few weeks. Stake tall varieties. This plant is prone to a number of diseases and pests, including aster yellows virus, septoria leaf spot, aphids, mealybugs, rust, wilt diseases, and gray mold. Avoid replanting in the same area to minimize these problems.

▶ ***Choices:*** 'Ostrich Plume' is wilt resistant; 'Florette Champagne' has unusual pink quilled petals.

Chinese Beautyberry
see Beautyberry

Chinese Cabbage
see Cabbage

Chinese Elm
see Elm, Chinese

Chinese Evergreen
Aglaonema commutatum

Tropical evergreen perennial

Aglaonema commutatum

▶ ***Hardiness:*** Zones 10–11

▶ ***Size:*** Grows 1'–2'

▶ ***Features:*** An easy plant that looks good with minimal fuss. When grown in good conditions, it will send up an elegant white flower that looks like an open pod

▶ ***Uses:*** As a houseplant

▶ ***Needs:*** Low to medium light for all-green types; somewhat brighter light for variegated types. Average household temperatures and humidity are fine, but appreciates a tray of pebbles and water in winter. Allow the soil to dry slightly between watering; roots can rot if left standing in water. Fertilize once a year with a 10-10-10 fertilizer.

▶ ***Choices:*** *Aglaonema pictum* grows only 6" and has speckled, silvery leaves. *A. nitidum* is the largest at 18" with plain green leaves. *A.* 'Silver King' and *A.* 'Silver Queen' are choices with foliage that is almost entirely silver-gray with green markings.

Chinese Forget-Me-Not
see Forget-Me-Not, Chinese

Chinese Fountain Palm
see Palms

Chinese Fringe Flower
see Fringe Flower, Chinese

Chinese Fringe Tree
see Fringe Tree

Chinese Gooseberry
see Kiwi; Chinese Gooseberry

Chinese Hibiscus
see Hibiscus, Chinese

Chinese Pistachio
see Pistachio

Chionanthus retusus
see Fringe Tree, Chinese

Chives
Allium schoenoprasum

Perennial herb

Chives

▶ ***Hardiness:*** Zones 3–9

▶ ***Size:*** Grows 12" tall, 8" wide

▶ ***Features:*** This member of the onion family also produces striking pink globe-shape flowers in spring

▶ ***Uses:*** Can be used as an edging plant. Snip the

fresh soft, hollow, grasslike leaves of chives over potatoes, soups, and salads. Flowers are edible and can be used in salads.

▶ ***Needs:*** Full sun but tolerates light shade. Prefers rich, well-drained soil with average moisture, but will tolerate some variety in soils and moisture. Start from seed 10 weeks before last frost date or buy established plants. Plant outdoors as long as weather is only moderately hot or nighttime temperatures are above 20°F/-7°C. Reseeds prolifically; deadhead to prevent reseeding. Usually pest free.

▶ ***Choices:*** Garlic chives *(Allium tuberosum)* have white flowers and a distinctive onion flavor.

Chlorophytum spp.

see Spider Plant

Chocolate Vine

Akebia quinata

Semievergreen flowering vine

Akebia quinata

▶ ***Hardiness:*** Zones 5–9

▶ ***Size:*** Grows 20'–40' in all directions

▶ ***Features:*** This vine earns its name with purplish-brown blooms in spring that smell hauntingly of chocolate. Delicious and calorie free! Delicate leaves make a fine-textured screen. Long purple seedpods in fall. Also sold as five-leaved akebia. Vines climb by twining and will not damage sturdy wooden structures, but can become weedy with bird-distributed seedlings as well as horizontal shoots sent out from the mother plant.

▶ ***Uses:*** Screening for privacy or blocking poor views, covering fences, trellises, or arbors, twining up posts and rails

▶ ***Needs:*** Plant in full sun or partial shade in fertile soil that's moist but well drained. Prune chocolate vine hard every year after flowering to control growth and limit seed production. You'll need two vines for cross-pollination, however, if you want it to produce the long purple pods.

▶ ***Choices:*** 'Variegata'—leaves display patches of cream on vines that are less vigorous than the species.

Chokecherry

see Plum, Ornamental

Chokeberry, Black

Aronia melanocarpa

Deciduous flowering shrub

Aronia melanocarpa

▶ ***Hardiness:*** Zones 4–9

▶ ***Size:*** 3'–6' tall and 6'–10' wide

▶ ***Features:*** You'll enjoy this easy-to-grow shrub throughout the seasons. White spring flowers are followed by black berries and wine-colored fall foliage. Fruit persists through much of fall and early winter. This plant rarely requires pruning, but you'll need to give it room to grow. Forming thickets of leggy stems, plants are perfect for naturalizing, especially in low, poorly-drained spots with problem wet soil, but are unsuitable for formal gardens.

▶ ***Uses:*** Natural areas, edges of woodlands, wet areas, planting beside sunny ponds, shrub beds, massing, attracting birds

▶ ***Needs:*** Plant in any moist soil except shallow, alkaline sites. These swamp natives tolerate wet areas with heavy soil; they'll also endure dry, sandy conditions. Grow in full sun or partial shade. Fruiting is heavier in full sun.

▶ ***Choices:*** For a shrub with glossy foliage that turns a flashy red in fall, choose 'Elata'. Red chokeberry, *A. arbutifolia*, produces red berries and red to purple fall color. 'Brilliant' is the most popular cultivar for its blazing red berries and excellent red fall foliage.

Christmas Cactus; Thanksgiving Cactus

Schlumbergera spp.

Tropical evergreen succulent perennials

Schlumbergera ×buckleyi

▶ ***Hardiness:*** Zones 10–11

▶ ***Size:*** Grows 12"–18"

▶ ***Features:*** Interesting segmented, trailing succulent stems that produce bright red, salmon, purple, or white flowers in winter, often around the holidays they're named after.

▶ ***Uses:*** As a houseplant in hanging baskets

▶ ***Needs:*** Medium to bright light. Pot in a soil mix that is well drained but not as coarse as cactus mix; in nature this plant grows in moist, jungle conditions. Allow the top 2" of soil to dry between waterings, and keep drier still in winter. However, when plants are forming buds, keep the soil evenly and lightly moist or the buds may fall off. Average household temperatures and humidity are fine most times of the year, but cooler temperatures of below 55°F/13°C are needed in fall for the plant to start bud formation. In June, July, and August, place it outdoors in a shady spot protected from pests. Fertilize three times with a 10-10-10 fertilizer. Around mid-September, or after outdoor temperatures have fallen to 45°F/7°C, bring it indoors to a cool room or the garage where temperatures remain around 55°F/13°C. Reduce watering, keeping the soil only slightly moist. Continue to keep the plant somewhat dry and cool as it forms flower buds; it may drop its buds if the growing conditions are changed. Around the beginning of November, bring plants into warmth and begin watering more frequently. After blooming, allow them to rest for a couple of months by keeping again at 55°F/13°C and keeping soil on the dry side.

▶ ***Choices:*** Look for a variety of colors as well as flower forms.

Christmas Rose; Lenten Rose

Helleborus species and hybrids

Evergreen perennials

Helleborus orientalis

▶ ***Hardiness:*** Zones 3–9
▶ ***Size:*** 14"–18" tall, 18"–2' wide
▶ ***Features:*** Because of its hardiness, lush evergreen foliage, showy winter blossoms that last for 2 months or more, and easy, accommodating nature in the garden, hellebores are challenging hostas as America's favorite perennial for shade. The bell-shape blossoms and lush leaves may look delicate, but they're actually thick and leathery, with a substance that makes them persist through harsh winters and low temperatures; a glorious sight against snow. Many hybrids are available in a wide range of blossom colors and forms. Blooms mid- or late winter.
▶ ***Uses:*** Winter interest, pathways, shady patios, natural areas, beneath trees, in raised beds or on woodsy slopes. Best in large masses as a woodland groundcover in naturalistic shade gardens, although it makes a showy specimen too.
▶ ***Needs:*** Very rich, well-drained soil with ample moisture is best. Plant established plants in spring, working in compost. Give them partial shade and protect from hot afternoon sun in hotter climates. Plant will fail in extreme heat or drought. Water regularly when conditions are dry. Mulch each spring to help conserve moisture. Once plants are blooming, trim any winter-worn foliage to better show off flowers. Plants spread rapidly in good conditions, so there is usually little need to divide. This plant is usually pest and disease free in suitable climates.
▶ ***Choices:*** Flowers are white or soft pinks. Lenten rose *(Helleborus orientalis)* is hardy in Zones 4–9 and blooms in late winter. Christmas rose *(H. niger)* blooms mid- to late winter, depending on the climate, and is hardy in Zones 3–8. 'Royal Heritage' is a popular, highly variable seed strain for Zones 5–9 with single and double flowers that range from cream to pastel pink, electric chartreuse, magenta, and deep maroon, some with attractive, contrasting streaks and splotches. For best colors choose individual plants when in bloom, or purchase named selections.

Chrysanthemum; Perennial Mum

Chrysanthemum ×*grandiflorum*

Perennial

Chrysanthemum ×grandiflorum

▶ ***Hardiness:*** Zones 4–9
▶ ***Size:*** 1'–3' tall, 8"–3' wide
▶ ***Features:*** Available in nearly every color except blue and a wide variety of flower forms, perennial mums provide welcome color late in the season—perhaps the last of all perennials to bloom in crisp fall weather.
▶ ***Uses:*** Late-season color in the mixed border or in the cut flower garden. Very effective massed in groups and in combination with flowering cabbage and kale, late-blooming asters, and perennials with bright fall foliage such as blue star and blue plumbago.
▶ ***Needs:*** Rich, well-drained soil, preferably slightly acidic. Ample moisture. Plant established plants in spring. Fertilize regularly. Mulch to keep roots cool and moist. Pinch tips every 2 weeks to promote bushiness and better flowering, stopping mid-July in Zones 4–6 and mid- to late August in Zones 7–9. The shallow roots of mums die out easily in winter, so mulch well in fall, especially in Zones 4–6. Wait to cut back foliage until early spring. This plant is usually problem free unless soil is too wet.
▶ ***Choices:*** Perennial mums may also be labeled with the botanical name *Dendranthema*. There are hundreds of varieties available; choose for color and flower form.

Chrysogonum virginianum

see Goldenstar

Cigar Plant

see Mexican Heather

Cilantro

see Coriander

Cimicifuga spp.

see Bugbane

Cinquefoil

see Potentilla

Cissus antarctica

see Grape Ivy; Kangaroo Vine

Cissus rhombifolia

see Grape Ivy

Cistus ×hybridus

see Rock Rose

Citrus

Citrus spp.

Fruit-producing evergreen tree or shrub

Lemon 'Eureka'

Lime 'Rangpur'

Orange 'Valencia'

▶ ***Hardiness:*** Zones 8-11, depending on the type
▶ ***Size:*** Dwarf types grow 4'-12' tall and almost as wide; standard types usually grow 20'-30' tall and almost as wide
▶ ***Features:*** Nicely shaped trees or shrubs with glossy evergreen leaves produce fragrant blossoms in spring and attractive, delicious fruit in season. Good for containers.
▶ ***Uses:*** In the orchard; these are also beautiful plants in their own right for landscaping and containers; edible landscaping
▶ ***Needs:*** Full sun. Excellent drainage a must. Prefers soil moist but will not tolerate wet soil. Raised beds or planting on berms or mounded soil recommended. Cold hardiness is critical. Most types of citrus can be grown where temperatures do not fall below 20°F/-7°C. However, some, such as Mexican lime, cannot tolerate temperatures below 28°F/-2°C. Sufficient heat is also important. Lemons and limes need the least heat. Valencia oranges need more heat and navel oranges more heat yet. Citrus is somewhat drought tolerant once established, but do not let tree wilt. Irrigation often required. Mulch to protect shallow roots and to conserve moisture. Fertilize mature trees, once in later winter, once in June, and once in August. If iron chlorosis develops, you may be overwatering. Prune as needed, preserving lower branches as much as possible since heaviest production is on those. In Zones 7 and colder, many citrus trees are grown as container plants. Bring indoors before frost and overwinter in a sunny, south-facing window. Let summer outdoors, being sure to acclimate the plant to sun and variations in temperature first by leaving it out for one hour on the first day, two hours on the second, and so on.
▶ ***Choices:*** Citrus plants can survive at below-freezing temperatures, but freezing temperatures destroy flowers and therefore the year's fruit. In colder regions, choose early-ripening types to beat the frost. Orange trees usually form dense globes up to 25' tall. Grapefruit trees reach up to 30' tall. Lemon trees reach up to 20'; they have low heat requirements and therefore are the most likely to produce indoors. Limes reach 15'-20' and are the most adaptable; there's a lime for nearly every landscape in Zones 8 and warmer.

Cladrastis kentukea

see Yellowwood

Clarkia amoena

see Godetia

CLEMATIS

The genus *Clematis* contains some of the showiest of the flowering vines. The large-flowered hybrids are perhaps the best known—and there are hundreds, if not thousands, of cultivars that have been developed over the years in almost every conceivable color from white, pink, and red to purple, violet, and blue. There are even some recent cultivars in the yellow range. Perhaps not as well-known but equally as useful are the species clematis, of which there are dozens in commerce. Besides the two most popular ones described in this section, others to look for include pink anemone clematis *(Clematis montana* var. *rubens,* Zones 5-8), a large vine to 15' high with huge mounds of 3" pink, vanilla-scented flowers in spring; golden clematis *(Clematis tangutica,* Zones 3-8), a 10' vine with small yellow bell-shape flowers in early summer; scarlet clematis *(Clematis texensis,* Zones 4-8), a 7' vine with red or deep pink bottle-shape flowers from midsummer to autumn; and alpine clematis *(Clematis alpina,* Zones 5-8), a small 5'-7' vine with violet blue bell-shape blooms in spring.

Clematis

Clematis spp.

Deciduous and evergreen perennial vines

Clematis 'Mrs. P.B. Truax'

CLEMATIS

Evergreen Clematis

Clematis armandii

Evergreen flowering vine

Clematis armandii

▶ ***Hardiness:*** Zones 7-9
▶ ***Size:*** 20' in all directions
▶ ***Features:*** Choose this fast-growing vine when you desire white, deliciously fragrant flowers in spring as well as year-round foliage. Take the time to make new plants happy and you'll be rewarded with vigorous growth. May require support to get started. Initial growth may be slow. Plants can grow to great lengths and heights.
▶ ***Uses:*** Screening for privacy or to block poor views, trellises, arbors, rails, fence tops, climbing through trees, seasonal accents
▶ ***Needs:*** Plant in well-drained acidic to slightly alkaline soil that's rich in organic matter. Vines prefer to grow in the sun but roots need to be kept shaded and cool. Prune after flowering to remove tangled or dead trailers. Vines climb by twisting leaf petioles that resemble tendrils, and by multiple branches weaving in and around a support and one another (not quite twining). Provide a sturdy, large support.

C

CLEMATIS

Large-Flowered Hybrid Clematis

Clematis hybrids

Deciduous flowering vine

Clematis ×jackmanii

Clematis 'Ville de Lyon'

Clematis 'Hagley Hybrid'

Clematis ×jackmanii

▶***Hardiness:*** Zones 3–9
▶***Size:*** 10' tall and wide; some varieties can reach 20'
▶***Features:*** When you think of flowering vines, hybrid clematis is probably a plant that comes to mind. Large, showy blossoms 3"–6" across appear as a big flush each spring, with some varieties producing repeat blooms into late summer. Numerous colors and flower forms are available. Best of all, most varieties are restrained in growth habit, with a smaller size than most vines, and seldom require pruning to control growth. Fuzzy fall seed heads add seasonal interest.
▶***Uses:*** Colorful accent, coarse texture, entries, growing up arbors, trellises, fences, posts, and poles. Excellent in containers. Makes a good companion for early-blooming species and once-blooming old garden roses; allow the vine to grow up and over the rose to provide blooms after the roses are through (it won't damage the rose). For the same reason, makes a good companion growing up into flowering dogwood.
▶***Needs:*** Plant in fertile, well-drained soil that's rich in organic matter (add compost or composted manure). Set new plants about 2" deeper in the soil than they were in nursery pots. Keep roots cool and shaded but position vines to spread into sunny areas. In nature these vines emerge from the cool, humus-rich soil beneath deciduous shrubs, and grow up and over the shrubs into the warm sunlight. After planting, cut back all stems to right above a pair of strong, healthy buds about a foot higher than soil level. Tie young plants to supports. Prune to control growth and remove dead stems. Prune after blooming. It the plant blooms in the spring, prune by midsummer; winter pruning will remove flower buds. Plants that bloom in the summer produce flowers on the current season's growth; prune these anytime during the winter (pruning after new growth starts will delay or prevent flowering).
▶***Choices:*** *C. ×jackmanii* is highly popular for its massive display of intense deep purple blossoms. It repeats well for at least one more showy display later in the summer; 'Ville de Lyon' has red flowers; 'Nelly Moser' is an old-fashioned favorite with two-toned flowers of light and dark pink. 'Ramona' has large 6" flowers of lavender-blue; 'Niobe' has deep ruby flowers with yellow centers and blooms in late spring and into the summer on new wood; 'H.F. Young' has large Wedgewood blue flowers; 'Duchess of Edinburgh' has white double flowers; 'Sugar Candy' is pink with a darker pink stripe down the center of each petal. 'Moonlight' produces a good show of unusual pale yellow blossoms. There are many more hybrid cultivars.

CLEMATIS

Sweet Autumn Clematis

Clematis paniculata

Deciduous flowering vine

Clematis paniculata

▶***Hardiness:*** Zones 4–9
▶***Size:*** 20' tall, 20' or more wide
▶***Features:*** In late summer, when most other summer flowers fade, this easy-to-grow vine bursts into bloom. Tiny pinwheel flowers cover green leaves with mounds of frothy cream. Delicate tendrils will not damage wood. The flowers are deliciously and powerfully fragrant from as much as a block away. Vigorous growth covers large, sturdy structures quickly, but can outgrow small spaces and supports. It tends to spread by reseeding, too, so plant with care.
▶***Uses:*** Growing on sturdy fences, trellises, arbors, natural areas, rails, posts, growing as a groundcover in ditches and along banks, seasonal accents.
▶***Needs:*** This native vine will grow in any kind of soil that isn't soggy, although slightly acidic soil is best. Grow in full sun or partial shade. This vigorous vine thrives on neglect.

Cleome hassleriana
see Spider Flower

Clethra alnifolia
see Summersweet

Cleyera
Cleyera japonica

Evergreen shrub

Cleyera japonica

▶ ***Hardiness:*** Zones 7–10
▶ ***Size:*** 8–10' tall, 5'–6' wide
▶ ***Features:*** If you live in the South, as long as your soil isn't alkaline or boggy you can grow cleyera. This upright shrub keeps its dark glossy leaves year-round; as new foliage emerges it is glossy bronze with dark red tips. The main reasons for growing this shrub are its gorgeous foliage and neat form that never needs pruning to maintain its rounded shape. But in early fall, on older plants, you can expect the bonus of small, intensely fragrant white flowers borne in clusters. They turn into dark red berries that hang on to the plant all winter. This camellia relative may also be sold as *Ternstroemia gymnanthera*.
▶ ***Uses:*** Formal or informal landscapes, tight spots and city conditions, backgrounds, near corners of houses
▶ ***Needs:*** Plant in sun or shade in acidic, moist soil. Prune to shape any time of year. On the coast, plants must be protected from salt spray to prevent desiccation.

Clivia miniata
see Kafir Lily

Clustered Fishtail Palm
see Palms

Coccoloba uvifera
see Sea Grape

Cockscomb; Celosia
Celosia spp.

Annuals

Celosia plumosa 'Apricot Beauty'

▶ ***Hardiness:*** Not applicable
▶ ***Size:*** 4"–3' tall and 4"–18" wide, depending on variety
▶ ***Features:*** There are many varieties of celosia, and nearly all of them are known for their brilliant hot colors from neon magenta and red through orange and yellow. Plume celosia *(Celosia plumosa)* has vertical, feathery flowers that look like flames. Cockscomb *(C. argentea* var. *cristata)* has tight, convoluted, somewhat bizarre flowers that have been described by some as roosters' combs (and by others as brightly colored brains). Wheat celosia *(C. spicata)* is a more refined species, producing tall stalks with wheatlike flowers at the top in delicate shades of ivory or pink. These plants are lovely in combination with ornamental grasses such as fountain grass. Depending on how soon you set out plants in spring, all celosias bloom contantly from late spring or early summer through fall.
▶ ***Uses:*** Annual bedding plant, in the mixed flower border, in the cutting garden. Excellent for cutting or drying. Good performer in containers.
▶ ***Needs:*** Rich, well-drained soil. Moderate moisture. Plant established seedlings in spring after all danger of frost has passed. Mulch to conserve water and prevent disease. Fertilize regularly, every 4 weeks, or work in a 9-month slow-release fertilizer at planting time. Trim fading blooms to encourage further flowering. Celosia is generally trouble free, but spider mites can be a problem as can root rot.
▶ ***Choices:*** Flowers come in oranges, peach, gold, pink, red, magenta, and maroon. Dwarf cultivars 4" high are available. 'Century' is a popular plumed type; 'Apricot Beauty' is an especially lovely plumed type. 'Toreador' and 'Fireglow' are two well-known crested types.

Codiaeum spp.
see Croton

Colchicum autumnale
see Autumn Crocus

Coleus
Solenostemum scutellarioides hybrids

Tropical evergreen perennial grown as an annual

Solenostemum ×hybridus 'Alabama Sunrise'

▶ ***Hardiness:*** Not applicable
▶ ***Size:*** 6"–36" tall and 12"–36" wide
▶ ***Features:*** Whether indoors as a houseplant or outdoors as a bedding or container annual, coleus is grown for its spectacular foliage rather than its lavender flowers (which most people remove as they form). Plants grown from seed are highly variable in leaf color and size, as well as ultimate plant height, but in the past few years vegetatively propagated cultivars have become popular for their consistently dependable appearance, making them more useful as a bedding plant.
▶ ***Uses:*** Annual bedding plant and container plant for sun or part shade. Sometimes overwintered indoors as a houseplant.
▶ ***Needs:*** Best in partial shade, but quite tolerant of full sun to deep shade. Newer varieties tolerate more sun. Plant 12"–24" apart in late spring after last frosts and when ground has warmed. Fertilize with a slow-release fertilizer. Apply 3" of vegetative mulch in summer. When soil feels dry 2" below surface, water deeply. Remove flowers as they form to help keep plants compact. Cuttings root easily and grow quickly in water or in soil. Grow indoors in a bright location, keep soil evenly moist, and protect from whiteflies and mealybugs. If plants become leggy, take cuttings and begin again.
▶ ***Choices:*** Many varieties are available; choose plants after they have leafed out. Bellevue Hybrid Blend is a seed mix with leaves variously splashed with pink, red, ivory, and green. Dragon Series leaves are dark, with combinations of purple, black, and red, and rimmed in gold.

Colewort
see Crambe

Collard Greens
see Greens

Columbine

Aquilegia spp.

Perennial

Aquilegia hybrid

▶ ***Hardiness:*** Zones 3-9
▶ ***Size:*** 30" tall and 24" wide
▶ ***Features:*** Striking spurred flowers—some varieties have double flowers—in a wide range of colors and bicolors, on refined, gray-green foliage reminiscent of maidenhair ferns. Flowers attract hummingbirds. Blooms late spring to early summer.
▶ ***Uses:*** Naturalize in shaded or semishaded woodlands; lovely in cottage gardens and in the mixed border
▶ ***Needs:*** Full sun to part shade in areas where temperatures seldom hit 100°F/38°C; in warmer climates plant in shade to part shade. Rich, loose, well-drained soil. This plant will rot in soil that is too wet, especially during the winter. Prefers moderate moisture, but will survive some dryness. Plant established seedlings in spring or fall. Fertilize occasionally, every 6 weeks, or apply a 9-month slow-release fertilizer in spring. If plants get shabby in late summer, cut back by half or more. Mulch well over winter. Plants usually live only 3 or 4 years and therefore need no division. They often reseed, but seedlings usually revert to the red-and-yellow flowers of the species. Space different-colored varieties at least 50 feet apart to prevent new plants from crossbreeding.
▶ ***Choices:*** McKana Hybrids Improved is a hybrid seed strain with bicolored blossoms in a mix of colors. Canadian columbine *(Aquilegia canadensis)* is a native wildflower with red spurs and yellow sepals; it makes a dependable naturalizer. *A. flabellata* 'Ministar' has bright blue and white flowers on dwarf 6" plants.

Coneflower, Purple

Echinacea purpurea

Perennials

Echinacea purpurea 'Kim's Kneehigh'

Echinacea purpurea 'Big Sky Sunrise'

▶ ***Hardiness***: Zones 3-9
▶ ***Size:*** 2'-4' tall, 2'-3' wide
▶ ***Features:*** Bold, colorful daisies grace this stately prairie native from mid- to late summer, when they turn into bronze seed heads that remain attractive well into winter—especially against snow. The flowers attract butterflies; the seeds attract goldfinches.
▶ ***Uses:*** Showy in the mixed border; combines well with ornamental grasses. Often naturalizes and is effective in meadow and prairie wildflower gardens.
▶ ***Needs:*** Average to poor, well-drained soil. Moderate moisture, but tolerates drought well. Plant established plants in spring or autumn. Avoid fertilizing. If soil is rich or moist, may need staking. Deadhead for longer bloom or leave flower heads standing to attract birds and butterflies. This plant spreads easily in most conditions. Divide every 3-4 years. It usually is pest and disease free, but caterpillars and Japanese beetle are sometimes a problem.
▶ ***Choices:*** Flowers are pinks, whites, and reds with reflexed, drooping petals. 'White Swan' is an unusual white cultivar; 'Crimson Star' is a red type. 'Magnus' is a particularly choice pink cultivar with huge 7" deep purple flowers; the petals are held straight out, and not reflexed. Recent breeding has resulted in the introduction of green-petaled and double-flowered forms. 'Razzmatazz' is an unusual double-flowered cultivar with fluffy, pompomlike flowers in brilliant raspberry red. 'Kim's Knee High' is a dwarf variety only 2' tall.

Consolida ambigua

see Larkspur

Convallaria majalis

see Lily-of-the-Valley

Convolvus tricolor

see Morning Glory, Dwarf

Coral Bells

Heuchera sanguinea

Perennial

Heuchera sanguinea

▶ ***Hardiness:*** Zones 3-9
▶ ***Size:*** 12"-24" tall, 12" wide
▶ ***Features:*** Forming tidy mounds of heart-shape leaves, this plant is grown as much for the evergreen foliage as the tall, wispy spikes of tiny bell-shape flowers that are showy in early to late spring. Many hybrids have been introduced recently with spectacular foliage in red, maroon, nearly black, bronze, yellow, and green, sometimes with contrasting markings in gold and silver.
▶ ***Uses:*** Effective massed as a groundcover in sun to part shade. Performs well in containers. Pretty in combination with late-blooming tulips.
▶ ***Needs:*** Full sun to light shade in Zones 3-5; partial shade in Zones 6-8. Rich, well-drained soil; likes slightly alkaline conditions. Moderate moisture; will tolerate slight drought. Plant established plants in spring or fall. Mulch. Fertilize occasionally, perhaps every 6 weeks, or work in a 9-month slow-release fertilizer each spring. Trim off spent flower stalks to encourage longer blooming. Divide plants every 3-4 years as needed. They are usually pest and disease free.
▶ ***Choices:*** Flowers come in pinks, reds, and whites. Most coral bells *(Heuchera sanguinea)* have green leaves. Hybrids are now available with yellow, pink, bronze, and silvery foliage colors. Purple-leaf coral bells *(H. micrantha × H. americana)* is grown primarily for its larger, more colorful leaves. 'Palace Purple' has dark purple foliage. 'Pewter Veil' has silvery foliage.

Coralberry

Symphoricarpos species

Deciduous flowering shrub

Symphoricarpos ×*chenaultii* 'Hancock'

▶*Hardiness:* Zones 4-7
▶*Size:* 1'-5' tall, 3'-10' wide, depending on variety
▶*Features:* Grow this plant to quickly cover ground that's moist or dry, in full sun or shade. Its self-layering habit forms a broad mound of foliage, and low-growing forms are available. White or pink flowers that look like tiny roses and pink, purple, or white berries add seasonal appeal and attract birds—be sure to plant it where you can see the show in winter. This plant tolerates air pollution and heavy shade, so it's a great choice for city gardens.
▶*Uses:* Stabilizing hillsides and slopes, woodland gardens, shrub borders, informal hedges, screens, planting beds, attracting birds, shady urban gardens, winter interest
▶*Needs:* Plant in soil that's moist or dry, fertile or poor. Tolerates alkaline soil and will thrive in sun or shade. Prune in early spring to stimulate abundant bloom.
▶*Choices:* Prostrate Chenault coralberry *(Symphoricarpos* ×*chenaultii* 'Hancock'*)* is a low-growing, wide-spreading coralberry that grows 1'-2' tall and 6'-10' wide, with pink and white flowers and berries. It makes an easy-to-grow and hardworking groundcover for slopes. Indian currant coralberry *(S. orbiculatus)* has dark rose to purplish-red berries and grows 2'-4' tall and 4'-8' wide. 'Amethyst' is a new, hardier hybrid introduction with vivid deep purple-pink berries in late summer. It reaches 3'-5' tall and wide. Zones 3-7. Snowberry *(S. albus)* bears an abundance of white berries in fall. It grows 3' tall, 3'-6' wide. Zones 3-7.

Cordyline spp.

see Dracaena; Ti Plant; Spike Plant

Coreopsis; Tickseed

Coreopsis spp.

Perennial

Coreopsis grandiflora

▶*Hardiness:* Zones 4-9
▶*Size:* 2'-3' tall, 1'-2' wide
▶*Features:* Cheerful yellow, golden, or pink 1" summer flowers on upright plants. Easy to grow. Blooms summer through fall.
▶*Uses:* In the mixed flower border. Looks best massed in groups. Threadleaf coreopsis is good at the front of beds and borders and is effective spilling over the edge onto walks.
▶*Needs:* Average to sandy, well-drained soil; doesn't need to be particularly fertile. Moderate water for pink coreopsis *(Coreopsis rosea),* but others are fairly drought tolerant. Plant seedlings in spring or fall. It is important to shear off spent blooms to keep plant blooming for long periods. Fertilize occasionally. Taller types may sprawl; in spring push a ring-type support into the soil when plants are several inches high. Plants may last only a few years, so divide every 3 or so years to assure an ongoing supply. Few pests, with the exception of rabbits, bother coreopsis.
▶*Choices:* *Coreopsis grandiflora* produces bright golden yellow summer daisies on 3' upright plants. Some cultivars have flowers with red centers.

Threadleaf coreopsis *(C. verticillata)* has fine-textured, feathery foliage and a relaxed, draping form about 18" tall and wide. It is best known for the cultivar 'Moonbeam', which has beautiful pale yellow flowers. 'Zagreb' has golden yellow flowers. Pink coreopsis *(C. rosea)* also has threadleaf foliage but with a more upright form and pink flowers.

Coriander; Cilantro

Coriandrum sativum

Grow as a cool-season annual herb

Coriander

▶*Hardiness:* Not applicable
▶*Size:* Grows 2'-3' tall, 1' wide
▶*Features:* Coriander is the English name and cilantro is the Spanish name for the same plant. Leaves have a distinctive, tangy flavor and seeds are pungent and smell almost like lime. A staple of Southeast Asian, Indian, and Hispanic dishes.
▶*Uses:* Snip leaves over ethnic dishes for an exotic, fresh flavor. Let seeds dry and use them ground in many other dishes.
▶*Needs:* Full sun in the North; light shade in hotter areas. Average soil, good drainage. Ample water. Bolts and goes to seed in hot weather, so plant in fall or late winter/early spring. Can tolerate light frost. Sow seed directly in garden in fall or late winter/early spring. Or plant established plants; dislikes transplanting so smaller plants do best. Usually pest-free.
▶*Choices:* 'Slo-bolt' is more heat tolerant than other types.

Corn
Zea mays

Warm-season annual vegetable

Corn

▶ ***Size:*** Grows 4'-8' tall, 1' wide
▶ ***Features:*** Sweet, tender ears that are a staple of summertime dining
▶ ***Uses:*** In the vegetable garden
▶ ***Needs:*** Full sun. Deep, rich soil with ample moisture. Does best in climates with warm summers, especially warm humid summers. Plant after all danger of frost has passed and soil is therefore adequately warmed. Plant seeds 1" deep. Plant at least 8 rows (can be planted in very short rows) to assure good cross-pollination. Thin to 2' for short types, 3' for tall types. Keep soil moist. Fertilize with a slow-release fertilizer at planting time, again when corn is 8" tall, and then a third time when 18". Harvest when silks turn brown and a kernel, when pierced with your thumbnail, oozes milky rather than clear sap. Eat within the day to ensure maximum tenderness and sweetness. For longest harvest, plant quicker- and longer-maturing types at 2-week intervals. If planting the newer Super Sweet hybrids, isolate them from other varieties by at least 200' or 14 days' planting time.
▶ ***Choices:*** In cool-summer areas, such as the Pacific Northwest and Zone 3, plant short cultivars that mature early (65–70 days) such as 'Sugar Buns' or 'Earlivee'. Favorite tall types include 'Silver Queen', 'Silver King', and 'Peaches and Cream'.

Corn Plant
see Dracaena

Cornflower, Annual; Bachelor's Button
Centaurea cyanus

Annual

Centaurea cyanus

▶ ***Hardiness:*** Not applicable
▶ ***Size:*** 12"–18" tall, 10"–12" wide
▶ ***Features:*** These cheerful cottage-garden favorites are best known for their blue flowers, but they also bloom in shades of pink, purple, and white. Blooms early to midsummer, then on and off again until frost.
▶ ***Uses:*** In beds, borders, and cottage gardens (it is often included in wildflower seed mixes, even though it is a native of Europe). Use shorter varieties in mixed containers. Excellent as a cut flower; the taller types are a favorite for the cutting garden.
▶ ***Needs:*** Average, well-drained soil. If soil is acidic, add lime. Moderate to light moisture. Plant from seed directly in soil for best results. In Zones 5–8 sow seeds outdoors 2 weeks before spring's last frost date. In Zones 9–10 plant seeds outdoors in fall for spring bloom. Plant just deep enough to cover and keep soil moist. When plants are about 1" tall, thin to 8" apart. If planting established seedlings, do so outdoors after last frost date. Keep seeds and young plants evenly moist; they are somewhat drought tolerant once established. Trim spent blooms to prevent excessive reseeding, but plant will still reseed freely. Fertilize lightly, if at all.
▶ ***Choices:*** 'Blue Diadem' has 2" intense blue flowers on 30" plants. 'Blue Midget' has sky blue flowers on 10" plants. 'Florence Mix' has blue, pink, white, red, and blue flowers.

Cornflower, Perennial; Mountain Bluet
Centaurea montana

Perennial

Centaurea montana

▶ ***Hardiness:*** Zones 3–8
▶ ***Size:*** 18"–24" tall and wide
▶ ***Features:*** Renowned for their startlingly deep blue color, the large flowers have an unusual starburst form. Blooms late spring through midsummer.
▶ ***Uses:*** Effective when allowed to spread into large colonies in beds, cottage gardens, and meadow gardens.
▶ ***Needs:*** Average to sandy, poor soil; must have excellent drainage. Moderate moisture. Plant established plants in spring. Mulch to conserve moisture. Fertilize lightly if at all. Trim spent blooms to prevent excessive reseeding. In late summer cut plant back to a few inches to promote fall bloom. Stake to prevent floppiness. This plant may spread aggressively where well suited to conditions and often will spread and form a large colony. Divide every 3–4 years as desired. It is susceptible to slugs and snails.
▶ ***Choices:*** White and pink varieties are sometimes offered.

Cornus spp.
see Dogwoods

Cortaderia selloana
see Grasses, Ornamental: Pampas Grass, Dwarf

Corydalis; Fumewort
Corydalis spp.

Perennial

Corydalis ochroleuca

▶Hardiness: Zones 4-8
▶Size: 10"-16" tall, 8"-14" wide
▶Features: The fernlike leaves of this mounding, shade-tolerant plant are so beautiful that its showy flowers seem almost like a bonus. Blooms late spring to midsummer; in cool-summer climates it may bloom until frost.
▶Uses: A choice plant for the woodland garden in dappled shade—lovely in combination with maidenhair fern and columbine.
▶Needs: Average to fertile, well-drained soil. Especially likes gravelly soil. It will tolerate alkaline soil and light drought but does best with ample moisture. Plant tubers 3" deep in fall or plant established seedlings in spring. It needs no deadheading. Fertilize occasionally; divide in fall every 2-3 years as needed. Plants may die back after blooming, especially where summers are hot. Mark the spot to prevent digging up; plants should come back next year. The yellow species may spread vigorously in ideal conditions. Fumewort is usually pest free and is not attractive to deer and rabbits.
▶Choices: Best known for the yellow species, *Corydalis lutea*, which bears mounds of cheerful lemon yellow flowers in late spring and early summer. *C. flexuosa* is a new introduction that has made quite a sensation with its neon blue flowers on 12" mounds. 'Blue Panda' has equally brilliant blue flowers on 8" mounds. Both prefer a cool spot in partial shade. Zones 6-8.

Corylus avellana 'Contorta'
See Harry Lauder's Walking Stick

Cosmos
Cosmos spp.

Annual

Cosmos bipinnatus

▶Hardiness: Not applicable
▶Size: 1'-6' tall, 10"-36" wide, depending on variety
▶Features: Cosmos are old-fashioned favorites bearing clouds of blossoms in summer. The pink type, *Cosmos bipinnatus,* grows 3'-4' tall with 3"-4" saucer-shape single flowers in pink, rose, and white. Yellow cosmos *(C. sulphureus)* is a smaller plant growing 18"-36" tall with 1"-2" semidouble blossoms in vibrant yellow, orange, and scarlet. All cosmos bloom midsummer to frost.
▶Uses: Most effective when massed in beds. Bright blue larkspur is beautiful combined with pink cosmos—and truly electric with orange and scarlet cosmos. Makes a good cut flower.
▶Needs: Poor to average, well-drained soil. Moderate moisture, but tolerates some drought. Plant seedlings outdoors after all danger of frost has passed. You can also plant seed directly in soil at that time, but it will take longer to bloom. Pinch plants' tops when they're a few inches tall to encourage bushier growth. Avoid fertilizing. Water regularly as needed. Stake as needed. Trim spent blooms or regularly cut for bouquets to promote longer bloom time. It is usually pest and disease free.
▶Choices: *Cosmos bipinnatus* 'Sensation' is the classic seed strain with white and pink flowers, some with picotee edges. 'Seashells Mix' has flowers with curiously rolled, tubular petals, starlike in effect. The 'Sonata' Series is a more compact 2' tall with flowers in pink, deep rose, and white. Among the *C. sulphureus* varieties are 'Bright Lights,' a tall-growing mix (3') of yellow, orange, and scarlet flowers and the 'Ladybird' series, with yellow, orange, and scarlet flowers that grow only 10"-14" tall.

Cotinus spp.
see Smoke Trees

COTONEASTERS
Cotoneaster spp.

Cotoneasters are the workhorse shrubs of the landscape. Covered with small white or pink flowers in spring, or brilliant red berries in fall and winter, or fine-textured, semievergreen foliage nearly year-round, these shrubs are always handsome. Some are low, spreading groundcovers; others are rounded or arching masses from medium to large size. All are dependable, adaptable, and easy to care for in any landscape.

COTONEASTERS

Bearberry Cotoneaster
Cotoneaster dammeri

Semievergreen shrub

Cotoneaster dammeri 'Coral Beauty'

▶Hardiness: Zones 6-9
▶Size: 6"-18" tall, 4'-8' wide
▶Features: Choose as a quick-growing groundcover for its glossy, semievergreen leaves (evergreen in Zones 8 and 9), white flowers in late spring, and colorful bright red fruits in autumn.
▶Uses: Groundcover, good on slopes, around rocks, and next to retaining walls over which it can cascade
▶Needs: Best in full sun and well-drained soil; tolerant of hot, dry spots and stony soil. Protect from insects, especially Japanese beetles in the East. Fireblight can be a problem.
▶Choices: *C. dammeri* 'Coral Beauty' and 'Lowfast' have excellent displays of bright red fruits and are both a bit hardier than the species, to southern Zone 5. 'Lowfast' is prostrate, forming a mat that seldom exceeds 4" tall.

COTONEASTERS

Cranberry Cotoneaster

Cotoneaster apiculatus

Semievergreen shrub

Cotoneaster apiculatus

▶ **Hardiness:** Zones 5–8
▶ **Size:** 18"–24" tall, 4'–6' wide
▶ **Features:** This low, mounding shrub bears rosy pink flowers in spring, lustrous dark green leaves that turn deep red in the fall, and scads of bright red berries in autumn and winter. It's among the most tolerant of the cotoneasters to adverse conditions of drought and heat, and more resistant to insects too.
▶ **Uses:** Attractive in the shrub border, on slopes and banks, in rock gardens
▶ **Needs:** Plant in full sun and well-drained soil. Avoid crowding plants too much; as with all cotoneasters, good air circulation is beneficial.

COTONEASTERS

Spreading Cotoneaster

Cotoneaster divaricatus

Semievergreen shrub

Cotoneaster divaricatus

▶ **Hardiness**: Zones 4–7
▶ **Size:** 5'–6' tall, 6'–8' wide
▶ **Features:** One of the most beautiful cotoneasters for its graceful form, flower and fruit display, and summer and fall foliage. Rose-colored flowers appear in late spring and are followed by heavy crops of brilliant red fruit from fall into winter. Fall leaf color turns neon shades of yellow, orange, and scarlet.
▶ **Uses:** In the shrub border, as informal hedges and screens. A good choice for harsh seaside locations.
▶ **Needs:** Best in full sun and moist, well-drained soil, but tolerates dry, rocky soils. Less bothered by pests than most cotoneasters, but occasional treatment for scale, spider mites, and fireblight may be necessary.
▶ **Choices:** Hedge cotoneaster *(Cotoneaster lucidus)* has a similar rounded form and is excellent as an informal hedge. Its glossy dark green foliage turns dark red in the fall. It produces inconspicuous black fruits. It is one of the hardiest of all the cotoneasters, hardy in Zones 2–6. Many-flowered cotoneaster, *C. multiflorus,* is covered with huge numbers of tiny white flowers in late spring, followed by a good display of fruits in fall. In summer the dull, medium-green foliage makes a good background. Zones 4–7.

COTONEASTERS

Rockspray Cotoneaster

Cotoneaster horizontalis

Evergreen or semievergreen shrub

Cotoneaster horizontalis

▶ **Hardiness:** Zones 5–8
▶ **Size:** 2'–3' tall and 5'–8' wide.
▶ **Features:** Rockspray cotoneaster offers effortless seasonal interest. Showy spring flowers are followed by loads of red berries in fall; leaves stay green year-round. Branches form an interesting fish-bone pattern and create a horizontal layered effect. Plants are deciduous in cooler regions.
▶ **Uses:** Slopes; planters; behind and cascading over retaining walls; in sunny, dry beds; and as groundcover
▶ **Needs:** Plant in full sun and well-drained soil. Susceptible to fireblight. Remove and destroy affected branches. Use spray containing streptomycin.
▶ **Choices:** 'Little Gem'—12" high; 'Robusta'—vigorous, upright growth, heavy fruiting; 'Saxatilis'—compact, few berries; 'Tom Thumb'—broad spreading, dense.

COTONEASTERS

Willowleaf Cotoneaster

Cotoneaster salicifolius

Semievergreen shrub

Cotoneaster salicifolius

▶ **Hardiness:** Zones 6–8
▶ **Size:** 10' tall, 12' wide.
▶ **Features:** Popular in California and the South, this large shrub has a graceful, arching form, attractive gray-green, elongated leaves, and an effective fruit display that lasts all fall and winter. The small white flowers appear in summer and are less showy.
▶ **Uses:** This is a popular large shrub for screening, large-scale massing, and informal hedges. It needs a large area.
▶ **Needs:** Best in moist, well-drained soil but tolerant of drier situations when established. Full sun to partial shade; best fruit display is in full sun. Will need occasional treatment for fireblight.

Crabapple
Malus spp.

Deciduous flowering tree

Malus floribunda

▶ ***Hardiness:*** Zones 4–8
▶ ***Size:*** 15' tall and wide, but varies according to variety
▶ ***Features:*** Showy flowers in late spring; attractive small, bright red or yellow fruits in fall; handsome small stature, excellent for urban gardens—it's little wonder that crabapples are among America's most popular flowering trees. Numerous hybrids and cultivars are available with single and double flowers in red, pink, and white; with a variety of forms from wide-spreading to columnar to weeping; and with fruit that is yellow, orange, and red. Best of all are the cultivars that have been bred for disease resistance. Especially in the South it's important to select varieties resistant to fireblight, apple scab, and powdery mildew.
▶ ***Uses:*** Specimen tree; suitable for small yards; seasonal accent; lining driveways; framing patios, low decks, or shrub beds; lawn tree; planting along fences; adding winter interest; attracting birds. Avoid planting near pavement since fruit can be messy.
▶ ***Needs:*** Grow in full sun. A heavy loam soil that's well drained, moist, and acidic is ideal, but trees will grow in sites less than ideal. Best in open areas with good air circulation. Remove water sprouts—nonblooming, thin twigs growing straight up from main branches—in mid- to late winter. Rake away fallen leaves and fruit to help control apple scab disease. Watch out for fireblight; if it occurs, treat it right away.
▶ ***Choices:*** Japanese flowering crabapple *(Malus floribunda)* is one of the best species, with excellent resistance to Japanese beetles. Plumleaf crabapple *(M. prunifolia)* produces clouds of white flowers in spring and bright, dangling red fruit in fall. Sargent's flowering crabapple *(M. sargentii)* is a horizontal, spreading tree that rarely exceeds 9' high but can reach 15' wide. Some of the more popular hybrid cultivars include: 'Indian Magic'—pink flowers, red-orange fruits and orange fall foliage color; 'Mary Potter'—white flowers, red fruit, attractive spreading form; 'Prairiefire'—coral red flowers, purple-red fruit, reddish foliage that turns orange in the fall; 'Red Jade'—white to pink flowers, red fruit, weeping form; 'Sugar Tyme'—white flowers, red fruit, bred for southern regions. Selections known for disease-resistance, dark reddish foliage and and persistent fruit include 'Pink Spires'—rose-pink flowers, deep red fruit, and red-purple to bronze foliage; 'Red Splendor'—deep pink blossoms, bright red fruit, dark reddish-green foliage; 'Royalty'—dark red-purple foliage; 'Profusion'—rose-red, scented flowers that open before leaves appear, maroon fruit, purplish to bronze-green foliage. There are hundreds of crabapple cultivars; ask your garden associate for recommendations for your area.

Crambe; Colewort
Crambe cordifolia

Perennial

Crambe cordifolia

▶ ***Hardiness:*** Zones 5–9
▶ ***Size:*** 4'–6' tall, 2'–4' wide
▶ ***Features:*** Clouds of white flowers like baby's breath in early summer, and bold, interesting foliage
▶ ***Uses:*** In the mixed flower border
▶ ***Needs:*** Average to rich, well-drained soil; neutral to alkaline. Ample moisture; never allow to dry out. Plant established plants in spring or fall. Fertilize occasionally, every 4 weeks, or work in a 9-month slow-release fertilizer each spring. Stake the tall, flowering stalk to prevent flopping. Trim off fading stalk to prevent reseeding. Dividing is unnecessary. This plant is susceptible to caterpillars and aphids. It may need a regular pesticide program if problems are chronic.
▶ ***Choices:*** Blooms are white. *Crambe maritima* (sea kale) grows 2' tall and tolerates the sand and salt found in seaside conditions.

Cranberrybush, European
see Viburnums: European Cranberrybush Viburnum

Cranesbill, Bloody
see Geranium, Hardy

Crape Myrtle
Lagerstroemia indica

Deciduous flowering tree

Lagerstroemia indica

Lagerstroemia indica

▶ ***Hardiness:*** Zones 7–9; some varieties are hardy to Zone 6. Dwarf shrub varieties can be grown as a perennial in Zone 5.
▶ ***Size:*** 15'–25' tall and 12'–20' wide
▶ ***Features:*** This tree has fabulous summer flowers, blazing autumn foliage color, attractive multicolored peeling bark, and sculptural form—not to mention its fast growth and heat tolerance. Flowers bloom from mid- to late summer in white, lavender, pink, and red. Glossy green foliage turns orange, red, and yellow before dropping in the fall. Smooth gray bark peels off to reveal an underbark of various colors. Many superior selections are named after Native American tribes. Dwarf, shrubby varieties are available that are hardy aboveground in Zone 6 and as a die-back perennial in Zone 5.

C

Plant encyclopedia

▶**Uses:** Specimen, patio tree, poolside, parking areas, entries, courtyards, providing privacy, seasonal accent, winter interest, massed plantings, or hedge rows

▶**Needs:** Plant in full sun in any moist, well-drained soil. Add peat moss or organic matter to soil at planting time. Remove dead wood when it occurs. To encourage larger blooms, remove suckers from the base. Otherwise little pruning is necessary or advised; it is best to avoid severe pruning and allow plants to achieve natural form.

Crassula spp.

see Cactus and Succulents: Jade Plant

Crataegus spp.

see Hawthorns

Creeping Jenny

see Moneywort

Creeping Myrtle

see Vinca; Littleleaf Periwinkle

Creeping Thyme

see Thyme, Creeping

Crimson Bottlebrush

Callistemon citrinus

Evergreen flowering tree

Callistemon citrinus

▶**Hardiness:** Zones 8-11

▶**Size:** 10'-15' tall and wide

▶**Features:** This is one of the longest-blooming of all flowering trees; its arching to pendulous branches bear loads of brilliant red, bristle-shape blooms over what seems like an impossibly long bloom season—from late winter through spring and summer and well into fall. The flowers attract hummingbirds. Foliage smells of lemons when crushed. Best of all, it's the closest thing to carefree that there is in the garden.

▶**Uses:** Best in warm climates of California and Florida. Small accent tree, either a single specimen or in groups; patio plantings; and around decks.

▶**Needs:** Plant in full sun and well-drained soil. Water young plants frequently to speed growth. Mature trees rarely need watering—or attention of any kind. Can be pruned to obtain a shrublike form.

▶**Choices:** 'Compacta'—4'-5' tall; 'Mauve Mist'—bright pink-purple flowers, 6'-12' tall. Weeping bottlebrush *(C. viminalis)*—weeping branches.

Crocosmia; Montbretia

Crocosmia ×crocosmiiflora

Perennial corm

Crocosmia ×crocosmiiflora

▶**Hardiness:** Zones 6-9

▶**Size:** 2'-3' tall, 1' wide

▶**Features:** Bright, hot colors in reds, oranges, and yellows float above swordlike leaves, powerfully effective when massed into clouds of blooms. Blooms appear midsummer to late summer.

▶**Uses:** Flower beds and borders, massed in large groups or in smaller groups in the mixed border. Beautiful combined with ornamental grasses.

▶**Needs:** Full sun or light shade. Average to rich, well-drained soil. Drought tolerant but best with moderate water. Plant corms in spring 3"-5" deep after all danger of frost has passed. Work in a slow-release fertilizer at planting time and every spring or every other spring thereafter. In fall in Zone 6, provide a thick layer of winter-protecting mulch. Can be grown successfully in Zone 5 if corms are lifted in the fall, stored in a cool place over winter, and replanted the following spring.

▶**Choices:** Flowers are red, orange, gold, or yellow. 'Lucifer' (red-orange) is one of the few crocosmias hardy to Zone 5, as well as the most popular variety in California.

Crocus, Autumn

see Autumn Crocus

Crocus

Crocus spp.

Spring-blooming perennial bulb

Crocus hybrids

▶**Hardiness:** Zones 3-8

▶**Size:** 4"-6" tall, 6" wide

▶**Features:** For many gardeners the flowers of crocus popping out above the melting snow are the first sign of spring. Flower colors are yellow, white, purple, and pink.

▶**Uses:** Under deciduous shrubs and trees, in flower beds and borders, naturalized in the lawn, in containers. Most effective when planted in groups of 2 or 3 dozen.

▶**Needs:** Full sun or light shade, especially the shade found under deciduous trees and shrubs. Rich, well-drained soil. Moderate water. Plant in October in Zones 3-6 or in November in Zones 7-8, positioning 2-5" deep. An inch or two of mulch is good winter protection in Zones 3-6. Rodents may eat corms.

▶**Choices:** Flowers come in yellow, white, purple, and pink. Snow or bunch crocus *(Crocus chrysanthus)* grows 2-3" tall and blooms especially early; each bulb will form a little clump. Dutch or giant crocus *(C. vernus* var. *vernus)* grows 3-4" tall and blooms as soon as the snow crocuses finish.

Cross Vine

Bignonia capreolata

Evergreen or semievergreen flowering vine

Bignonia capreolata

▶ ***Hardiness:*** Zones 6-9
▶ ***Size:*** 30'-50' in all directions
▶ ***Features:*** This fast-growing vine features bright orange-red, funnel-shape blooms in mid- to late spring with a delicious fragrance reminiscent of mocha. Thick foliage hides whatever the plant grows over. Climbing by tendrils, plants will not damage wood, but they do need a sturdy support.
▶ ***Uses:*** Screening, trellises, arbors, fences, walls, posts, rails, natural areas, seasonal accents, erosion control on slopes, covering chain-link fences.
▶ ***Needs:*** Plant in acidic soil that's moist but well drained. Can tolerate standing water for short periods of time. Prune in winter. Grow in sun for best flowering.
▶ ***Choices:*** 'Madame Galen' has deep scarlet flowers.

Croton

Codiaeum spp.

Tropical shrub

Codiaeum variegatum var. *pictum* 'Miss Peters'

▶ ***Hardiness:*** Zones 10-11
▶ ***Size:*** Grows 6"-3' tall
▶ ***Features:*** Spice up an all-green area of your yard, patio, or bright spot indoors with variegated croton. Its large leaves are mottled with eye-catching patterns of red, yellow, or pink. Croton is damaged or killed by freezing temperatures.
▶ ***Uses:*** As a houseplant, though it is a landscape plant in shrub beds outdoors in the warmest regions of the United States. It is also effective planted in the ground as annual bedding or accent in all zones where summers are warm. Excellent in containers on the patio or deck.
▶ ***Needs:*** Bright light for best color in leaves. Keep soil evenly moist with tepid, never cold, water and on a tray of pebbles and water for higher humidity. Does well enough in medium to warm household temperatures, but prefers warmth and falters in temperatures below 60°F/16°C. Keep away from cold drafts. Fertilize three times in the summer when growth is heaviest with a 10-10-10 fertilizer. Immediately remove any tiny flowers that might form, as they attract pests. Loves a summer outside in a bright location with heat and humidity. In the ground, plant in full sun and in rich, moist soil high in organic matter.
▶ ***Choices:*** *Codiaeum variegatum* var. *pictum*, sometimes called 'Joseph's Coat', is the most commonly available. Most crotons have pointed, somewhat oval leaves, so look for unusual leaf shapes, such as corkscrew shape, or slender, elongated and deeply lobed leaves. 'Norma' has mostly red veins with some pink, orange, and yellow veins.

Crown-of-Thorns

see Cactus and Succulents

Crown Imperial

see Fritillary

Cryptanthus bivittatus

see Bromeliads: Earth Star

Cryptomeria, Japanese; Japanese Cedar

Cryptomeria japonica

Evergreen coniferous tree

Cryptomeria japonica 'Jindai-Sugi'

▶ ***Hardiness:*** Zones 6-8
▶ ***Size:*** 50'-60' tall, 20'-25' wide
▶ ***Features:*** A neat, pyramidal, upright habit makes this conifer a good choice for southern and western formal gardens. Foliage is dark green; trees are densely clothed to the ground.
▶ ***Uses:*** Screening, specimen in larger landscapes. Makes a good backdrop for perennial flower gardens.
▶ ***Needs:*** Plant in full sun but where it is protected from drying winds, especially in winter. It will tolerate light shade. Best in rich, deep, light and well-drained soil with abundant moisture. Trees do not tolerate drought well. Keep soil evenly moist during growing season.
▶ ***Choices:*** 'Yoshino' is relatively fast-growing, and its bright green summer foliage bronzes slightly in winter. 'Ben Franklin' grows 30' tall and is salt tolerant. There are many shrubby dwarf varieties available, some reaching no higher than 3' tall.

Cucumber

Cucumis sativus

Warm-season annual vegetable

Cucumber 'County Fair'

▶ ***Hardiness:*** Not applicable
▶ ***Size:*** Grows 10" tall, 1'-4' wide, depending on the cultivar
▶ ***Features:*** Produces crisp vegetables excellent for salads and pickles
▶ ***Uses:*** In the vegetable garden
▶ ***Needs:*** Full sun to light shade. Will do well in a variety of soils, but does best in rich, well-drained alkaline soil with ample organic matter and moisture. Will grow in a wide range of climates but does need temperatures above 70°F/21°C for three months. Plant seeds 1½" deep or established seedlings two weeks after your region's last frost date. Plant in raised beds or hills (2' wide; 4" high mounds) to assure faster-warming soil. Space plants 3'-4' apart, depending on the type. Check the package or label. Mulch to conserve moisture and keep developing cucumbers clean. Pick as soon as they hit full size. Otherwise, they become filled with large seeds, and the plant stops producing.

▶ Choices: Choose between slicing-type cucumbers and smaller, denser pickling cucumbers. Compact bush-type cucumbers conserve space. Also look for cucumbers that are nonbitter or burpless, They have thin, tender skin that makes for pleasant eating, and they lack a compound that makes them hard for some to digest.

Cupflower

Nierembergia hippomanica

Perennial grown as an annual

Nierembergia hippomanica 'Violet Robe'

▶ Hardiness: Short-lived perennial in Zones 7–10
▶ Size: 10" high and wide
▶ Features: Mounds of white or light blue cup-shape flowers bloom all summer and well into fall.
▶ Uses: Plant in groups in the front of the mixed border or as edging. Mass as a bedding plant, or grow in mixed containers.
▶ Needs: Full sun in cool summer areas in Zones 3–6; part shade in hot summer areas in Zones 7–11. Rich, well-drained soil. Ample moisture. Grow as a cool-season annual everywhere except the wetter parts of Zones 8–9, where it can be grown as a perennial. Plant established plants in late winter or in spring a week or two before the last frost date. Group in clusters of 10 or more for best effect. Fertilize occasionally. Mulch. After first bloom cut back by one-third to one-half to prompt further bloom.
▶ Choices: Flowers are purple or white. 'Mont Blanc' and 'Violet Robe' are two favorites.

Cuphea spp.
see Mexican Heather

×Cupressocyparis leylandii
see Cypresses, Leyland Cypress

Cupressus arizonica
see Cypresses, Arizona Cypress

Cupressus sempervirens
see Cypresses, Italian Cypress

Currant, Green Mound Alpine

Ribes alpinum

Deciduous flowering shrub

Ribes alpinum 'Green Mound'

▶ Hardiness: Zones 2–7
▶ Size: 2'–3' tall and wide
▶ Features: Grow this plant for its neat, compact form and maintenance-free care. Shrubs thrive in cold weather, all types of soil, sun or shade, and everything in between. 'Green Mound' is a male form and has better disease resistance than most female varieties. Fruiting is rare.
▶ Uses: Deciduous hedges, lower layers in front of evergreens, foundation plantings, shrub beds, filling in bare areas, seasonal accents
▶ Needs: Plant in any kind of soil, including acidic to alkaline, fertile to poor, wet to dry. Grow in sun or shade. Trim hedges anytime; removal of flowers isn't a concern. Easy to transplant and grow.
▶ Choices: Clove currant, *R. odoratum*—6' to 8' high, scented flowers, Zones 4 to 6

Cushion Spurge
see Spurge, Cushion

Cut-Leaf Staghorn Sumac
see Staghorn Sumac

Cycas revoluta
see Palms: Sago Palm; King Sago

Cyclamen, Hardy

Cyclamen hederifolium

Perennial

Cyclamen hederifolium

▶ Hardiness: Zones 7–9
▶ Size: 3"–6" tall, 4"–8" wide
▶ Features: Beloved for its rosy pink blooms in late summer and early fall, this is one of the easiest cyclamens to grow in the garden.
▶ Uses: In the woodland garden, in beds under deciduous trees and shrubs. Group in masses of a dozen or more for best effect.
▶ Needs: Light shade, preferably shade under tall deciduous trees or shrubs. Rich, well-drained but moist soil. Ample moisture during growth; otherwise moderate. Best in climates where summers are relatively dry with cool nights. Plant established plants or tubers in spring or fall, working in ample compost. Position tubers just below the soil's surface. Mark clearly to avoid disturbing. This plant is unlikely to bloom much for the first year or two but, once established, will take off and even self-sow if not disturbed. Each fall, mulch with 2"–3" of chopped autumn leaves for winter protection as well as nutrients. In spring, spread 1"–2" of compost on the planting.

Cynoglossum amabile
see Forget-Me-Not, Chinese

Cypress, Bald
see Bald Cypress

CYPRESSES

Many trees and shrubs go by the name of cypress—in this section you'll find trees described in three different genera. All are evergreen conifers with impressive and distinctive forms.

CYPRESSES

Arizona Cypress

Cupressus arizonica

Evergreen coniferous tree

Cupressus arizonica var. *glabra* 'Blue Ice'

▶***Hardiness:*** Zones 7–9
▶***Size:*** 30'–40' tall, 15'–20' wide
▶***Features:*** Arizona cypress has a tall, pyramidal shape and grows quickly. In great age it can spread majestically into picturesque shapes. It is less successful in humid areas with plentiful rainfall.
▶***Uses:*** Screening to block views or add privacy, windbreaks or tall hedges, single specimen for year-round greenery, xeriscaping in dry areas
▶***Needs:*** Plant in well-drained soil—dry, rocky, alkaline sites are ideal. Plant in full sun. Once established, plants can do without supplemental watering.
▶***Choices:*** 'Blue Pyramid' has blue-gray foliage.

CYPRESSES

Italian Cypress

Cupressus sempervirens 'Stricta'

Evergreen tree

Cupressus sempervirens 'Stricta'

▶***Hardiness:*** Zones 7–10
▶***Size:*** 60' tall, 5'–10' wide
▶***Features:*** This is arguably the narrowest tall tree in existence—a mature specimen is like an exclamation point in the landscape. It's a familiar sight in the hillside towns and countrysides of Italy, often lining drives and marking the location of a villa. And it's common in California.
▶***Uses:*** Focal point, screen, colonnade, allée
▶***Needs:*** Most at home in the mediterranean climate of California with its dry summers and moist winters. In the Southeast it often succumbs to disease resulting from the high summer humidity. Plant in well-drained soil in full sun.

CYPRESSES

Leyland Cypress

×*Cupressocyparis leylandii*

Evergreen tree

×*Cupressocyparis leylandii*

▶***Hardiness:*** Zones 6–9
▶***Size:*** 60'–70' tall, 10'–15' wide
▶***Features:*** Dense, fluffy foliage stays green year-round. Fast-growing; more than 3' a year. Low maintenance. Tolerant of soil extremes. Feathery evergreen foliage and columnar form make a graceful, airy addition to the landscape. Bluish green color provides interesting contrast. Tolerant of salt spray.
▶***Uses:*** Quick screening of unwanted views, provides privacy, evergreen background for deciduous trees and shrubs
▶***Needs:*** Grow in any soil that's well drained. Plant in full sun and water regularly for fastest growth. Supply extra water during dry spells. Be sure to plant this tree with an eye to its ultimate size; it can quickly outgrow a small space. While this is a low-maintenance tree tolerant of poor soils, trees may decline in hot climates without regular watering. Design tip: When planting a screen, stagger trees so they form a zigzag pattern. This will provide a thicker planting and add depth to the area.
▶***Choices:*** If you can't water regularly, substitute Eastern red cedar, *Juniperus virginiana,* or Southern red cedar, *J. silicicola,* in areas with long, hot summers and sandy soils.

CYPRESSES

Russian Cypress

Microbiota decussata

Evergreen shrub

Microbiota decussata

▶***Hardiness:*** Zones 3–7
▶***Size:*** 6"–36" high, 8'–12' wide
▶***Features:*** This mat-forming Siberian native shrugs off cold weather, diseases, and insects. Scaly green foliage blushes with a reddish or purplish brown tinge in winter. Plants return to midgreen color when warm weather returns. Russian cypress grows low and wide and is useful in a variety of landscaping situations. If you have a spot in partial shade that's too shady for a creeping juniper, this is a better choice.
▶***Uses:*** Including in the front layer of shrub beds; filling blank spots on hillsides; planting beneath low windows; parking areas; cold, dry, or windswept areas; winter interest
▶***Needs:*** Plant in moist, well-drained soil. Grow in full sun or partial shade. Pruning is rarely needed; cut to remove stray growth as it occurs. Plants are disease and pest free.

Cypress Spurge
see Spurge, Cypress

Cypress Vine
see Cardinal Climber

Cyrtomium falcatum
see Ferns: Japanese Holly Fern

Cytisus spp.
see Brooms

Dancing Ladies
see Orchids

Daffodils
Narcissus spp.

Perennial bulb

Narcissus 'King Alfred'

▶ ***Hardiness:*** Zones 3-8
▶ ***Size:*** 5"-24" tall, 6"-12" wide, depending on variety
▶ ***Features:*** Nothing says spring like daffodils. Planted in generous groups and drifts, their cheerful yellow blossoms are a spectacular welcome to the season. By early summer their foliage dies off and disappears without a trace. Plant them among later-emerging perennials such as daylilies and hosta that will grow to hide the dying foliage.
▶ ***Uses:*** Most effective planted in groups of 6 or more or in large, generous drifts of 30 or more bulbs. Use in flower beds and planted between perennials in the mixed border, under shrubs and trees, naturalized in meadow gardens. Excellent in containers, although container bulbs rarely rebloom, even when planted outdoors.
▶ ***Needs:*** Full sun, although light shade from deciduous trees later in season is ideal. Rich, well-drained soil, neutral to slightly acidic. Ample water during growth and bloom; moderate water after. Plant 5-8 inches deep in October in Zones 3-7 and in November to early December in Zones 8-11. Work in compost and bulb fertilizer.
▶ ***Choices:*** Thousands of cultivars offer a variety of sizes, flower forms, and colorings in yellow, orange, pink, and white. Flower forms range from tiny and flat to trumpet and cupped, and from single to double flowers. Choose for early, mid- and late-season bloom for the longest effect. Trumpet and large-cup hybrids, the most commonly available, are hardy in Zones 3-9. Jonquils *(Narcissus jonquilla)*, pheasant's-eye *(N. poeticus)*, and angel's tears *(N. triandrus)* are hardy in Zones 4-9 in the East; in Zones 4-11 in the West. Paperwhite narcissus are tender (Zones 7-9) and most often grown indoors as a winter-blooming annual.

Dahlberg Daisy; Golden Fleece
Thymophylla tenuiloba, (formerly *Dyssodia tenuiloba)*

Annual

Thymophylla tenuiloba

▶ ***Size:*** 4"-8" tall, 6"-12" wide
▶ ***Features:*** This low-growing delight bears tiny, bright yellow daisies above soft, ferny, fine-textured foliage. The flowers are effective against the bright green leaves all summer long.
▶ ***Uses:*** Ideal for edging, bedding, spilling out of walls or the edge of containers, and in between paving stones. While it's adapted to nearly all climates if the soil is well drained, it's especially useful in desert and rock gardens. Performs well in containers and hanging baskets.
▶ ***Needs:*** Poor, well-drained soil is this plant's preferred home. Drought tolerant. Plant established seedlings in spring as soon as danger of frost has passed. Avoid fertilizing. Discard after frost. This plant may overwinter in warm climates but usually looks too shabby to keep growing. Pests and diseases are uncommon.

Dahlia
Dahlia hybrids

Perennial tuber often grown as an annual

Dahlia hybrid

▶ ***Hardiness:*** Zones 8-11
▶ ***Size:*** From 12"-24" tall (bedding types) to 1'-7' tall (exhibition types)
▶ ***Features:*** Colorful daisylike flowers from delicate 3" single-petaled blossoms to huge pompoms the size of a dinner plate bloom in late season, some as early as midsummer, and some as late as fall. Bedding dahlias are short and bushy in stature and profuse in their 2"-3" blooms from midsummer to fall. Exhibition dahlias can be huge, as tall as sunflowers, and are often pruned to develop one huge blossom.
▶ ***Uses:*** Bedding dahlias are most effective massed in beds and borders. They also perform well in containers. Exhibition dahlias are usually grown in the cutting garden. Both types are superb for cutting.
▶ ***Needs:*** Perennial in Zones 8-11; annual in colder regions. Full sun is essential; light shade at midday is appreciated in Zones 8-11. Rich, well-drained soil. Ample moisture. Feed regularly and protect from insects and disease. In spring after all danger of frost has passed, plant 6" deep, 12"-15" apart for bedding dahlias, 3" deep and 12"-36" apart for exhibition dahlias. Place stakes at planting time to avoid damaging roots later. After the first three sets of leaves have developed, pinch the tip of the shoots. A few weeks later, pinch the shoots a second time. Fertilize with a low-nitrogen formula every 6 weeks. Trim spent blooms. In Zones 2-7, in fall, after the first frost, lift and store tubers in a dry spot that stays about 40°F/4°C (see page 205). In spring, divide clumps and then replant, including part of the old stem in the division.
▶ ***Choices:*** Hundreds, if not thousands, of cultivars are available from specialty suppliers. Flowers come in every color except blue, and in a wide range of forms from single and double to round pompoms and balls.

Daisy, Butter
see Butter Daisy

Daisy, Freeway
see Freeway Daisy

Daisy, Shasta

see Shasta Daisy

Daphne

Daphne spp.

Evergreen shrub

Daphne ×burkwoodii 'Carol Mackie'

Daphne odora 'Marginata'

▶***Hardiness:*** Zones 5–9, but varies according to species.

▶***Size:*** 1'–4'

▶***Features:*** Few plants are as memorable for fragrance as daphne, and there's a variety to suit nearly every climate. Flowers are white, sometimes rosy pink or delicate lavender. Most varieties bloom for a few weeks in spring with the later tulips. All have attractive, fine-textured foliage, and some varieties have variegated leaves. For most gardens daphne is a short-lived shrub—it can thrive for several years and then suddenly die. But its fabulous fragrance makes it worth the trouble.

▶***Uses:*** Plant near walks, decks and patios, garden benches, and windows where its fragrance can be enjoyed. Good in rock gardens, the mixed border or as a specimen.

▶***Needs:*** Full sun to light shade, depending on the species. Rich to average, well-drained but moist soil. Moderate to ample water during bloom; otherwise moderate to dry. Plant in spring or fall. Mulch well. Pruning is unnecessary. It dies out easily if soil is too soggy.

▶***Choices:*** Flowers are white or pink. Burkwood daphne *(Daphne ×burkwoodii)* is semievergreen and has a number of lovely variegated cultivars. Grows 3'–4' tall and wide. It blooms late spring and sometimes again in late summer, and is hardy in Zones 5–7. 'Carol Mackie' is popular for its variegated foliage. Garland and rose daphne *(D. cneorum)* grows 1' tall by 3' wide. Good for rock gardens, with deep rosy-pink flowers in early spring and dark green, persistent leaves. Zones 5–7. February daphne *(D. mezereum)* has pale lavender flowers very early, before the leaves. Zones 6–9. Winter daphne *(D. odora)* is the most fragrant of the daphnes, and also the most tender. It can grow as large as 4' tall and spread 8'–10' wide, covered in evergreen foliage. 'Variegata' is the most popular cultivar for its creamy variegated leaves. Zones 7–9.

Date Palm

see Palms

Datura; Angel's Trumpet

Brugmansia spp. and *Datura* spp.

Tropical perennial or shrub, and annual

Brugmansia spp.

▶***Hardiness:*** Zones 9–11

▶***Size:*** 3'–10' tall, 3'–7' wide

▶***Features:*** The huge, dangling trumpets and large leaves of this plant create a drama reminiscent of the tropics. The flowers come in a range of colors from yellow, peach, and pink to white and cream, some with blushes and picotee edges. Many cultivars are intensely fragrant. Grow as a patio plant that you bring indoors to rest for the winter; in mild-winter climates it can be grown in the ground as a large evergreen shrub. Datura is most often grown as an annual from seed. All parts of these plants are poisonous.

▶***Uses:*** Excellent in containers as a patio plant in the summer. Datura performs well in beds and the mixed border as an annual, growing quickly to a 3' blooming size from seed.

▶***Needs:*** Grow as a perennial or shrub where temperatures don't go below 45°F/7°C. Elsewhere grow as an annual or indoor/outdoor patio plant. Full sun in most areas, part shade in hot summer regions, Zones 7–11. Site should also be protected from wind, which damages the oversized flowers. Water often; never allow plant to dry out. Plant established plants in spring in rich, well-drained soil. If growing as an annual, fertilize frequently, every 2–4 weeks, with liquid fertilizer to fuel this plant's rapid growth. In Zones 4–8 if the plant is in a pot, bring it indoors in fall before the first frost and place in a sunny spot to overwinter, if desired. It is susceptible to aphids and whiteflies.

▶***Choices:*** Brugmansias are quite variable from seed, and there are many cultivars in a range of colors and potency of fragrance, with single or double flowers. Try to choose plants while in bloom. *Datura innoxia* is the most commonly offered datura for use as an annual. Its flowers are white blushed with pale lavender, and are only lightly fragrant.

Davallia fejeensis

see Ferns: Rabbit's Foot Fern

Dawn Redwood

Metasequoia glyptostroboides

Deciduous coniferous tree

Metasequoia glyptostroboides

▶***Hardiness:*** Zones 4–8

▶***Size:*** 70'–100' tall, 25'–30' wide

▶***Features:*** If you have room for a big tree, dawn redwood can top 100' in as many years. Feathery bright green foliage turns bronze in autumn before dropping. Growth is rapid at first, slowing with age. The size of this tree will dwarf most single-story houses. Plant away from smaller buildings to avoid comparison or place near larger structures. Trunks of older trees develop buttressed, fluted bases with beautiful reddish exfoliating bark.

▶***Uses:*** Large, open lawns or natural areas; groves; lining streets or long driveways; large estates

▶***Needs:*** Plant in moist—but not soggy—soil. Acidic soils are preferred over alkaline. Grow in full sun. Seldom requires pruning.

Daylily

Hemerocallis spp.

Perennial

Hemerocallis 'Black-Eyed Stella'

Hemerocallis 'Stella de Oro'

Hemerocallis 'Pushmataha'

Hemerocallis 'Elmo Jackson'

Hemerocallis 'Queen's Castle'

Hemerocallis 'Joyful Occasion'

▶***Hardiness:*** Zones 3–10
▶***Size:*** 10"–4' tall in bloom; 6"–10' wide, depending on variety
▶***Features:*** This is the classic low-maintenance perennial, famous for its profuse flowers in every color except blue, and its fountains of narrow leaves that emerge in time to cover the dying foliage of spring-blooming bulbs. Multiple flower stems each have many buds; the flowers last only a day, but many open every day over a long season in early summer, midsummer, or late summer, according to variety—and some even bloom a second time in fall. Most varieties are deciduous, but some that are adapted to southern climates are virtually evergreen.
▶***Uses:*** Highly effective massed in large beds that combine early-, mid- and late-seaon varieties. Also looks good as a specimen. They are favorite subjects to combine with other plants in the mixed flower border.
▶***Needs:*** Full sun. Tolerates shade but flowers less. Rich, well-drained soil, but thrives in many different soils. Best with moderate to ample moisture but will also tolerate drought. Plant established plants in spring or fall. Group in clusters of 6 or more for best effect. Fertilize occasionally, about every 6 weeks, or work in a 9-month, slow-release fertilizer. Pinch off any spent flowers daily and trim off spent flower stalks to promote further bloom. Divide every 3–4 years as needed. Some types spread easily. This plant is usually pest free, although rust is becoming a serious problem with some varieties, and the succulent flower buds are a favorite food of deer.
▶***Choices:*** There are a huge number of cultivars available—some 6,000 new ones are introduced each year. If possible, choose plants when they're in bloom, and if you want an award-winning new introduction expect to pay $100 or more. The color range available is astonishing, from the more common oranges and yellows to pinks, bright reds, and deep maroons, many of them bicolored. Creams and near-whites are also available, and even lavenders that begin to approach blue. Flower forms vary from simple singles to doubles, some with ruffled edges—and some varieties have a delicious fragrance. Plant size ranges from miniatures only 10" tall to large plants with blooming stems more than 4' tall. Choose early-, mid-, and late-season varieties for blooms all summer. Recent introductions include more and more varieties that exhibit dependable rebloom, producing flowers at least twice each year. Some of the better-known rebloomers include the famous golden 'Stella de Oro', its progeny 'Black-Eyed Stella', and the clear lemon-yellow 'Happy Returns'.

Dead Nettle, Spotted

Lamium maculatum

Perennial groundcover

Lamium maculatum 'Pink Pewter'

▶ **Hardiness:** Zones 3-9
▶ **Size:** 8"-12" tall, 12"-24" wide
▶ **Features:** Even shady spots kept dry by thirsty tree roots are no problem for this plant. Choose spotted dead nettle for its silvery mottled leaves and durability. Pink or purple blooms appear in spring through summer. Trailing stems cover ground quickly; plants can be very vigorous and may outgrow some garden situations.
▶ **Uses:** As groundcover beneath trees and covering bare, shady spots—even places with dry soil.
▶ **Needs:** Can handle full sun, especially in Zones 3-5, but prefers light shade. Average to rich, moist soil. Ample moisture best, especially in full sun, but will tolerate drought once established. Plant established plants in spring or fall. Plant several together for best effect. This plant benefits from occasional fertilizing but seldom needs it because it tends to be invasive, especially in moist conditions. However, bare spots may occur if a planting is too dry. Cut back by one-third or so after bloom time if plants become straggly. Divide in spring or fall as desired. Slugs, leaf spot, and root rot are sometimes a problem.
▶ **Choices:** 'Beacon Silver' is one of the most popular varieties. It has pale pink blooms. 'White Nancy' has white flowers. 'Pink Pewter' has pink flowers.

Delosperma spp.

see Ice Plant, Hardy

Delphinium

Delphinium elatum

Perennial

Delphinium elatum, Pacific hybrid

▶ **Hardiness:** Zones 2-7
▶ **Size:** 3'-7' tall, 1'-3' wide
▶ **Features:** Famous for its intensely blue flower spikes on tall, stately plants, delphiniums also come in shades of light blue, lavender, pink, purple, red, and white. The flowers appear in early summer, about the same time as Shasta daisies. Although short-lived and prone to disease, especially where summers are warm, this majestic perennial is well worth the effort.
▶ **Uses:** A classic plant for the rear of the mixed border in combination with Shasta daisy and veronica, delphiniums combine well with many other plants. This is perhaps the signature plant of English gardens; where climates in North America have similar cool summers, such as the northeastern United States, the Pacific Northwest, high-altitude gardens, and around the Great Lakes into Canada, delphiniums thrive.
▶ **Needs:** Demands very rich, fertile, deep, moist soil and moderate conditions away from extreme heat. Keep evenly moist; never allow to dry out. Grow as an annual in Zones 2-7; can grow as a perennial in Zones 6-7 where summers are cool. Plant established plants in spring and fertilize regularly. Mulch to keep soil cool and moist. Staking is a must; stake when plants are about 18" high. Trim spent blooms to promote longer flowering. This plant is prone to mildew, slugs, and snails. A regular pesticide program should be considered.
▶ **Choices:** Pacific hybrids grow to 7'; white 'Connecticut Yankee' grows 2'-3' and is more heat resistant.

Dendranthema

see Chrysanthemum

Dendrobium

see Orchids

Dennstaedtia punctilobula

see Ferns: Hay-Scented Fern

Deodar Cedar

see Cedars

Deschampsia caespitosa

see Grasses, Ornamental: Tufted Hair Grass

Desert Candle

see Foxtail Lily

Desert Willow

Chilopsis linearis

Deciduous flowering tree

Chilopsis linearis

▶ **Hardiness:** Zones 8-9
▶ **Size:** 20'-25' tall, 20'-30' wide
▶ **Features:** Add this airy, attractive tree to your yard for spring and summer flowers that come in a wide range of colors. Not a willow, this is a relative of trumpet vine and cross vine. Desert willow needs very little water and, as its name implies, is best grown in arid climates. It is a poor choice if you live in a wet, humid area. Its dangling clusters of bright lavender-pink blooms attract hummingbirds, which makes it popular in southern Arizona, where as many as 9 species of hummingbirds might visit a garden.
▶ **Uses:** Arid landscapes, single specimens or groups of accent trees, Xeriscaping, attracting hummingbirds, very nice around patios
▶ **Needs:** Plant in full sun and alkaline, dry soil. You won't need to give this Southwestern desert native much water. Cut out extra branches to emphasize the tree's airy, arching shape.
▶ **Choices:** The unimproved species is the most attractive to hummingbirds, but 'Barranco' has prettier deep lavender flowers that are almost as attractive. 'Hope' is a white-flowered cultivar; it may take hummingbirds a while to notice its flowers.

Deutzia, Slender

Deutzia gracilis

Deciduous flowering shrub

Deutzia gracilis

▶ **Hardiness:** Zones 5-8
▶ **Size:** 5'-7' high; 6'-8' wide
▶ **Features:** Expect a lavish display of sparkling white flowers for a week or two every spring from this dependable old-fashioned favorite. Blooms in May. Its shrubby form is graceful and arching, wider than it is tall.
▶ **Uses:** In the mixed-shrub border
▶ **Needs:** Easy to grow and adaptable. Plant in any good garden soil in full sun to light shade. Prune immediately after flowering. Early spring growth is sometimes damaged by late-spring frosts.
▶ **Choices:** *Deutzia ×lemoinei* is a similar shrub with white flowers that appear a week or two later than those of slender deutzia. *D. crenata* 'Nikko' grows only 18" tall and 2' wide. *D. ×rosea* 'Carminea' is also dwarf, but with rosy pink flowers.

D

Plant encyclopedia

Dianthus spp.

see Pinks

Diascia spp.

see Twinspur

Dicentra spp.

see Bleeding Heart

Dieffenbachia spp.

see Dumb Cane

Digitalis purpurea

see Foxglove

Dill

Anethum graveolens

Cool-season annual herb

Dill

▶***Size:*** 3'-4' tall, 1'-2' wide
▶***Features:*** Lovely feathery leaves and Queen-Anne's-lacelike flowers grace this herb, a favorite for pickles, salads, and salmon
▶***Uses***: Snip leaves over potato and cucumber salads, salmon dishes, or nearly any dish with an oil and vinegar dressing. A key ingredient in dill pickles.
▶***Needs:*** Full sun. Prefers rich, well-drained soil with ample moisture, but will tolerate some variety in soils and moisture. In hot climates, sow seeds in fall and early spring. In colder climates, sow in spring. Or buy small established plants, although dill is hard to transplant. Will reseed prolifically, ensuring an ongoing supply of new plants for years to come.
▶***Choices:*** 'Smokey' is a beautiful deep gray-green. 'Dukat' is one of the most commonly grown. 'Fernleaf' is 18" and is slow to bolt.

Dimorphotheca spp.

see Cape Marigold

Dionaea muscipula

see Venus Flytrap

Diospyros spp.

see Persimmon

Distictis spp.

see Trumpet Vine

Dizygotheca

see False Aralia

DOGWOODS

Cornus spp.

There seems to be a dogwood for nearly every landscape purpose, from low groundcovering mats (see Bunchberry, page 328), to rounded shrubs that provide winter color in even the coldest regions (red-stemmed and yellow-stemmed dogwoods) to elegant small trees that provide spectacular effects in all seasons (flowering and kousa dogwoods). A planting of flowering and kousa dogwoods and the hybrids between the two, in fact, will provide continuous flowers for six weeks from May to mid-June, colorful red berries in August and September, blazing fall foliage color in October, and attractive bark all winter long.

DOGWOODS

Cornelian Cherry Dogwood

Cornus mas

Deciduous flowering shrub or small tree

Cornus mas

▶***Hardiness:*** Zones 4-8
▶***Size:*** 10'-20' tall and 10'-15' wide
▶***Features:*** Cornelian cherry dogwood steals the show in early spring with golden blooms that burst open even before forsythia. Edible cherry-red fruit ripens in midsummer and can be made into flavorful preserves. Or let the birds enjoy the fruit. These shrubs require little care after plants become established. Plants are attractive planted against a dark green or red background.
▶***Uses:*** Specimen use, shrub borders, hedges, screens, foundation plantings
▶***Needs:*** Plant in full sun in moist, well-drained soil. While neutral pH is best, it tolerates acidic and alkaline soils well. Prune any dead or damaged stems in late winter or early spring; prune to shape after flowering. Pest free.
▶***Choices:*** 'Aureo-elegantissima'—leaves are yellow or brushed with pink. 'Variegata'—leaf margins are creamy white.

DOGWOODS

Flowering Dogwood

Cornus florida

Deciduous flowering tree

Cornus florida

▶***Hardiness:*** Zones 5-9
▶***Size:*** 20'-25' tall, 20'-25' wide
▶***Features:*** Slow to medium growth. Plant a single dogwood or several together to welcome middle or late spring with drifts of white. Flowers appear before the foliage for maximum effect. The leaves of these graceful, horizontally tiered trees turn varying shades of red to purple in autumn. Bare trees form interesting irregular silhouettes in winter. The lovely pink-flowering selections are less heat tolerant than white-flowering cultivars.
▶***Uses:*** Specimen trees; seasonal accents; understory plantings; natural areas; edges of woodlands; filling empty corners of yards; near patios, decks, or benches; corners of houses; attracting birds in fall and winter
▶***Needs:*** Plant in rich, acidic soil that's moist but well drained. Grow in partial to dense shade. Trees bloom best in sun but require afternoon shade in hotter climates unless watered regularly. Supply all dogwoods with extra water during droughts. Avoid nicking or damaging trunks in any way (lawnmowers are common culprits) since this allows entry to dogwood borer, which is a serious problem.
▶***Choices:*** 'Cherokee Chief'—dark pink flowers and reddish-colored new foliage; 'Plena'—white, double flowers. In areas of Zone 4 and northern Zone 5 where flowering dogwood is not reliably hardy, pagoda dogwood *(Cornus alternifolia)* is a popular substitute. Its umbels of white flowers lack

the conspicuous bracts of flowering dogwood, but the form of this graceful small tree is similar, with beautiful horizontal layered branching, good red fall color, and blue-black winter fruits that are attractive to birds. 'Variegata' is a popular selection for its white and green variegated leaves. It is resistant to anthracnose and dogwood borer. Zones 4–8.

DOGWOODS

Gray Dogwood

Cornus racemosa

Deciduous flowering shrub

Cornus racemosa

▶***Hardiness:*** Zones 4–7
▶***Size:*** 10'–15' tall, 10'–15' wide
▶***Features:*** Umbels of white spring flowers turn into white, berrylike fruits that are savored by numerous species of birds. After the fruits are gone and leaves have fallen, the stems that held the fruits become visible. Three-year-old and older stems develop the gray bark color; younger wood is reddish brown. The pinkish stems contrast with the gray stems of the shrub, and the result is picture perfect—all winter long.
▶***Uses:*** Shrub borders, hedges, poor soils, naturalized areas, winter interest, massed plantings
▶***Needs:*** Plant in full sun in moist, well-drained soil. Prune any dead or damaged stems in late winter or early spring; prune to shape after flowering. It has suckers and can be difficult to maintain in small settings. In colder climates, shield from northwest winds by planting in a protected area, rather than out in the open.
▶***Choices:*** 'Slavinii'—dwarf with twisted leaves; 2'–3' high, suckering spread.

DOGWOODS

Kousa Dogwood

Cornus kousa

Deciduous flowering tree

Cornus kousa

▶***Hardiness:*** Zones 5–8
▶***Size:*** 20'–30' tall, 20'–30' wide
▶***Features:*** This picturesque Chinese tree extends the dogwood season by blooming about a month later than the flowering dogwoods. Unlike flowering dogwood, the horizontal layers of leaves are in place before the flowers appear. White in color, they remain attractive for more than 6 weeks. Edible, pinkish-colored fruit develops in late summer through fall. Fall foliage is eye-catching in shades of red and purple. The plant's form and beautiful peeling, multicolored bark provide winter interest for the landscape. Named selections are more pest resistant than many cultivars of *C. florida.*
▶***Uses:*** Specimen tree, seasonal accents, courtyards and patios, edges of woodlands, natural areas, shrub and groundcover beds
▶***Needs:*** Plant in well-drained, acidic soil with some organic matter. Grow in partial shade or full sun with regular watering. Roots are shallow; all dogwoods need extra water during dry spells.
▶***Choices:*** 'Gold Star' has yellow and green variegated leaves and white flowers. If you really want to extend the flowering dogwood season, plant some of the Rutgers Hybrids *(C. rutgersensis)* too. These hybrids between flowering and kousa dogwoods bloom midway between the two, about 2 weeks after flowering dogwood and 2 weeks before kousa dogwood. They are also resistant to anthracnose and dogwood borer. There are pink and white selections, all with star-shape blooms. Aurora, Galaxy, Constellation, and Ruth Ellen are white; Stellar Pink is rosy pink.

DOGWOODS

Red-osier Dogwood, Redtwig Dogwood

Cornus stolonifera

Deciduous flowering shrub

Cornus stolonifera

▶***Hardiness:*** Zones 2–8
▶***Size:*** 8'–10' tall, 5'–10' wide
▶***Features:*** Rapid growth. Winter interest against evergreen background. Fast growth and soil adaptability. Useful in large planting areas. Brighten your yard's winter appeal with red-osier dogwood. The new stems have a greenish color with a hint of red. With the onset of cool weather, stems turn bright red to linger and glow against winter snows after the leaves blow away in the fall. The more sun plants receive, the brighter the twig color will be.
▶***Uses:*** Shrub borders, along fences or driveways, around ponds, large displays
▶***Needs:*** Plant in full sun in moist, well-drained soil. Will tolerate partial shade. The red stem color is brightest on young wood. Prune all stems to within 4"–6" of the ground in early spring, before new growth begins.
▶***Choices:*** 'Cardinal'—showy red twigs, 6' tall, 12' wide; 'Elegantissima'—gray-green leaves with irregular, twisted white margins; 'Aurea'—leaves are soft yellow.

DOGWOODS

Yellow-twig Dogwood

Cornus stolonifera 'Flaviramea'

Deciduous shrub

Cornus stolonifera 'Flaviramea'

▶ ***Hardiness:*** Zones 3–8
▶ ***Size:*** 6'–8' tall, 8'–10' wide.
▶ ***Features:*** Plant yellow-twig dogwood to brighten winter scenes around your home. This plant requires only well-drained soil and well-timed pruning in early spring to encourage growth of new yellow stems. Use with caution in the landscape; the color effect can be overwhelming.
▶ ***Uses:*** Shrub borders, mass plantings, along drives or fences
▶ ***Needs:*** Plant in full sun or part shade in moist or wet soil. The yellow stem color is brightest on young wood. Prune all stems to within 4"–6" of the ground in early spring, before new growth begins.
▶ ***Choices:*** 'Isanti'—bright red stems; 5'–6' high, 8'–10' wide; Zones 3–8.

Douglas Fir

see Fir, Douglas

DRACAENAS

Dracaena spp.

These extremely popular houseplants are sometimes called false palms for their often thick, trunklike stems and flourish of long, tapering leaves along, and sometimes only at the top of, the trunk. They have a modern, architectural look. It's easy to confuse dracaenas with cordylines, and you'll sometimes find one mislabeled as the other. The main difference is the roots. Dracaena has smooth roots that are deep yellow and orange; cordylines have white knobby roots. However, they are grown in a similar manner. Dracaenas need light shade to medium light—near an east or west window is ideal. In less light, the interesting variegation on leaves may fade. Does fine in average household warmth. Keep soil evenly moist; reduce watering in winter but avoid drying out. Fertilize once a year. Humidity is important to these natives of African jungles. With too little humidity, their tips brown and edges yellow. Double-pot them surrounded by wet peat (see page 275), run a humidifier, or set them on a tray filled with pebbles and water.

DRACAENAS

Green Dracaena

Dracaena deremensis

Tropical evergreen perennial

Dracaena deremensis

▶ ***Hardiness:*** Zones 10–11
▶ ***Size:*** Grows up to 4' tall with 1'-long leaves
▶ ***Features:*** Some cultivars sport beautiful stripes in white, green, yellow, or red.
▶ ***Uses:*** As a houseplant, but sometimes grown as a landscape specimen plant in a sheltered spot in the warmest regions of the United States.
▶ ***Needs:*** Grow as for any dracaena.
▶ ***Choices:*** All-green 'Janet Craig' is the most popular type of this dracaena. The Stripe series offers leaves with distinct stripes with white, yellow, and green. 'Compacta' is much smaller than the others.

DRACAENAS

Corn Plant

Dracaena fragrans

Tropical evergreen perennial

Dracaena fragrans

▶ ***Hardiness:*** Zones 10–11
▶ ***Size:*** Grows up to 20' tall outdoors, but is a slow grower that seldom tops 4' in pots indoors
▶ ***Features:*** The most commonly available dracaena is nicknamed corn plant because of the similarity in foliage. Also called mass cane because the leaves mass at the base of the plant. Older plants tend to lose their lower leaves, giving the plants a palmlike look.
▶ ***Uses:*** As a houseplant, but sometimes grown as a landscape specimen plant in a sheltered spot in the warmest regions of the United States.
▶ ***Needs:*** Can do with less light than other dracaenas. Tolerates very low light. Otherwise, grow as for any dracaena.
▶ ***Choices:*** Several types available. 'Massangeana', which has a yellow central stripe, is the most popular. 'Lindenii' has yellow leaves with multiple green stripes.

DRACAENAS

Madagascar Dragon Tree

Dracaena marginata

Tropical evergreen perennial

Dracaena marginata

▶ ***Hardiness:*** Zones 10–11
▶ ***Size:*** Grows up to 8' tall
▶ ***Features:*** Long, narrow leaves make a spiky flourish on top of the thick stems of this popular plant. As the plants grow, they lose their bottom leaves, making them look even more architectural and like a palm. Especially easy to grow, these are often planted as an annual in mixed containers and beds for a vertical, spiky effect.
▶ ***Uses:*** As a houseplant, but sometimes grown as a landscape specimen plant in a sheltered spot in the warmest regions of the United States.
▶ ***Needs:*** Can do with less light than other dracaenas. Tolerates very low light. Otherwise, grow as for any dracaena.
▶ ***Choices:*** Most Madagascar dragon trees sold are green edged with deep reddish purple, giving them an overall deep purple appearance. 'Tricolor' has even bands of green, cream, and red. 'Colorama' looks mainly red with narrow cream and green stripes. These dracaenas also are sometimes available as trees. These are simply 1' or longer lengths of the thick, loglike main stems cut into a section and planted in potting soil. Leaves sprout out the top.

DRACAENAS

Song of India

Dracaena reflexa

Tropical evergreen perennial

Dracaena reflexa

▶ ***Hardiness:*** Zones 10–11
▶ ***Size:*** Grows 4' or more tall with 6" leaves
▶ ***Features:*** Classic dracaena, corn plant shape with attractive striping
▶ ***Uses:*** As a houseplant
▶ ***Needs:*** Grow as any dracaena, but is especially demanding of high humidity.
▶ ***Choices:*** Sometimes sold as *Dracaena pleomele* or *Pleomele reflexa*. 'Variegata' is by far the most commonly sold. It has yellow-edged leaves and must have at least medium light to maintain the yellow. Sometimes plain green types are available.

DRACAENAS

Lucky Bamboo

Dracaena sanderiana

Tropical evergreen perennial

Dracaena sanderiana

▶ ***Hardiness:*** Zones 10–11
▶ ***Size:*** Grows up to 2'–3' tall, 1'–2' wide
▶ ***Features:*** Sometimes sold as a smaller version of the classic corn plant dracaena. Recently, small cuttings of this plant have been sold to grow in small vases or trays of water. It is easy to train the stems into fantastic curls, twists, and other shapes by manipulating the light source or wiring the stems.
▶ ***Uses:*** As a houseplant, but sometimes grown as a landscape specimen plant in a sheltered spot in the warmest regions of the United States.
▶ ***Needs:*** When potted in soil, grow as for any dracaena, but keep the soil constantly wet. When sold growing in water, change the water every 3–5 days and never allow the water to evaporate completely. Use bottled water to prevent the minerals found in most tap water from turning the tips brown (fluoride is especially destructive). Add a half-strength foliage plant food to the water every 2 weeks. If you want to train the stems into unusual shapes, put a young plant in a darkened spot with a single light source directed to the stem. The plant will respond by growing toward the light.
▶ ***Choices:*** 'Borinquensis' has dark green-edged leaves.

DRACAENAS

Gold Dust Dracaena

Dracaena surculosa

Tropical evergreen perennial

Dracaena surculosa

▶ ***Hardiness:*** Zones 10–11
▶ ***Size:*** Grows 30" tall
▶ ***Features:*** Looks unlike many dracaenas. Dark green leaves heavily speckled with creamy yellow to white. Thin stems and thin, flat, pointed oval leaves.
▶ ***Uses:*** As a houseplant
▶ ***Needs:*** Grow as any dracaena.
▶ ***Choices:*** 'Florida Beauty' is nearly all yellow and white. Gold dust dracaena is sometimes sold as *Dracaena godseffiana*.

Dragon Tree, Madagascar
see Dracaena

Drummond Phlox
see Phlox: Annual Phlox

Dryopteris erythrosora
see Ferns: Autumn Fern

Dumb Cane; Dieffenbachia
Dieffenbachia seguine

Tropical evergreen perennial

Dieffenbachia seguine

▶***Hardiness:*** Zone 11
▶***Size:*** Grows 1'–6' depending on the type, age, and growing conditions
▶***Features:*** An extremely easy houseplant with variegated leaves in green, cream, and gold.
▶***Uses:*** As a houseplant
▶***Needs:*** Medium light; too little causes lower leaves to drop. Allow the top inch of soil to dry out between waterings. Does best on a tray of pebbles and water for higher humidity, but will tolerate drier situations. Average household temperatures are fine as long as there are no cold drafts. Fertilize three times in summer with a 10-10-10 fertilizer. Rinse or wipe off the large, broad leaves with a damp cloth about once a month or so.

Sap from this plant can irritate skin, stain clothes, and is slightly toxic, so keep away from children and animals.
▶***Choices:*** 'Exotica' has gold-speckled leaves, 'Rudolph Roehrs' is nearly all cream with green veins, 'Camilla' has primarily cream leaves that deepen to green at the margins.

Dusty Miller
Senecio cineraria
(formerly *Centaurea cineraria*)

Perennial often grown as an annual

Senecio cineraria

▶***Hardiness:*** Zones 6–11
▶***Size:*** 6"–24" high, 6"–18" wide
▶***Features:*** This plant is grown for its beautiful silver, lacy, feltlike foliage; in some varieties the leaves appear practically white. It's particularly complementary to purple and pink flowers. The small yellow flowers appear in its second year of growth, but since it's almost always grown as an annual they are rarely seen.
▶***Uses:*** Mix with pink or purple flowers in sunny flower beds. Effective massed into groups where the garden is viewed at night, especially by moonlight, such as near a dining patio or front entrance. Makes a good contrast with dark-foliaged plants, such as dark-leaved perilla.
▶***Needs:*** Average, well-drained soil. If soil is acidic, add lime. Moderate to light moisture; most types are heat and drought tolerant once established. Plant established seedlings in spring after danger of frost has passed. Fertilize rarely, if at all. When watering avoid getting leaves wet. Dusty miller produces small white or yellow flowers; trim them off to preserve foliage effect. Annual in Zones 2–5; perennial in Zones 6–11. It is most attractive if pulled out at the end of the growing season. Aphids are sometimes a problem.
▶***Choices:*** 'Silver Dust' and 'Silver Lace' are both beautifully lacy. 'Cirrus' has more solid, rounded foliage.

Dutch Iris
see Iris

Dutchman's Breeches
see Bleeding Heart

Dyckia brevifolia
see Bromeliads: Pineapple Dyckia

Dyssodia tenuiloba
see Dahlberg Daisy

Earth Star
see Bromeliads

Easter Cactus
Hatiora gaertneri

Tropical forest cactus

Hatiora gaertneri

▶***Size:*** Grows 12"–18" tall and wide
▶***Features:*** Similar to Christmas cactus but with differently formed flowers and a bloom time in April or May, often around Easter. Sometimes will bloom again in fall if the conditions are right.
▶***Uses:*** As a houseplant, especially appropriate for hanging baskets
▶***Needs:*** Medium to bright light. Allow the top 2" of soil to dry between waterings and keep drier still in winter. However, when the plant is forming buds, keep the soil evenly and lightly moist or the buds may fall off. Average household temperatures and humidity are fine most times of the year, but cooler temperatures of below 55°F/13°C are needed in fall to cause the plant to start bud formation. Fertilize three times in summer with a 10-10-10 fertilizer. To encourage bloom, in the fall from about October to January let the plant rest by keeping it cool, about 55°F/13°C. From February to March, keep dry and cool. In April, water normally and keep at a minimum of 60°F/16°C.
▶***Choices:*** Look for a variety of colors as well as flower forms.

Eastern Red Cedar
see Junipers

Eastern White Cedar
see Arborvitae

Echeveria spp.
see Cactus and Succulents: Echeveria

Echinacea purpurea
see Coneflower, Purple

Echinocactus grusonii
see Cactus and Succulents: Golden Barrel Cactus

Echinops spp.
see Globe Thistle

Edging Lobelia
see Lobelia, Edging

Eggplant
Solanum melongena var. *esculentum*

Warm-season annual vegetable

Eggplant 'Ichiban'

▶***Size:*** Grows 1'-2' tall and about as wide
▶***Features:*** Lovely purple or white shiny vegetables that are used in many Mediterranean dishes
▶***Uses:*** In the vegetable garden. It is attractive in the mixed border, too, with its purple flowers and shiny fruits.
▶***Needs:*** Full sun. Prefers rich, well-drained soil but will tolerate a variety. Moderate moisture. Needs warm days with highs up to 80°-90°F/27°-32°C and cooler nights for about 75 days. Plant established seedlings outdoors 2 weeks after your region's last frost date in spring. In the South, also plant in midsummer for a fall harvest. Space 18"-24". Harvest by cutting off the eggplants as soon as they are plump and firm. Frequent harvesting encourages more production.
▶***Choices:*** Choose from deep purple, nearly black, white, and pinkish ('Lavender Touch'). Baby types are especially tender and nonbitter. Also try Asian-type eggplants, which are long and slender like cucumbers and stand up well in stir-fries.

Egyptian Star Cluster
see Pentas

Elaeagnus angustifolia
see Russian Olive

Eleagnus pungens
see Eleagnus, Thorny

Eleagnus, Thorny
Eleagnus pungens

Broadleaf evergreen shrub

Eleagnus pungens

▶***Hardiness:*** Zones 7-9
▶***Size:*** 8'-11' tall, 6'-10' wide
▶***Features:*** If you give it room to grow, thorny eleagnus is an easy shrub. Arching branches bearing silvery foliage stay green year-round; tiny fall flowers are fragrant with a scent similar to that of gardenia. It grows rapidly, and tolerates pollution and salt spray.
▶***Uses:*** Hillsides, large informal hedges, screening, background planting, natural areas
▶***Needs:*** Plant in full sun in any kind of soil, including sand, clay, acidic, alkaline, or poor and dry. Choose a spot where plants will have room to grow. Size is not easy to control. Pruning promotes long, unattractive shoots. This shrub is unsuitable for a formal garden.
▶***Choices:*** 'Aurea'—leaves have yellow coloration around their edges.

Elm, American
Ulmus americana 'Princeton'

Deciduous tree

Ulmus americana

▶***Hardiness:*** Zones 3-9
▶***Size:*** 90' high, 50' wide
▶***Features:*** The unique, vase-shape habit of the American elm has made this one of the most beloved shade and street trees in North America. Unfortunately many thousands of stately older trees have been killed by Dutch Elm Disease since that pathogen was introduced many years ago. Princeton is a cultivar introduced in the 1920s that has recently been found to have good resistance to Dutch Elm Disease.
▶***Uses:*** Unparalleled as a street tree, in time arching high overhead. Excellent shade tree. Give it plenty of room to grow.
▶***Needs:*** Best in full sun and average well-drained but moist soil. Tolerates occasional flooding

and drought (its natural habitat is along rivers and streams). Susceptible to a range of debilitating diseases besides Dutch Elm Disease; keep trees healthy through judicious pruning and debris removal.

Elm, Chinese

Ulmus parvifolia

Deciduous tree, evergreen in frost-free areas

Ulmus parvifolia

Ulmus parvifolia

▶ ***Hardiness:*** Zones 5-9
▶ ***Size:*** 35'-45' tall, 20'-25' wide
▶ ***Features:*** Chinese elm may be the ultimate patio shade tree. Its small size, neat habit, fast growth, and leafy shade make it ideal for sitting areas. Dark green summer foliage changes to yellow and finally to reddish purple in the fall. And the bark is quite ornamental—especially when viewed at close range—a mottled combination of gray, green, orange, and brown. Its ample, shallow root system makes growing grass beneath this tree difficult.
▶ ***Uses:*** Shading small areas such as decks, patios, courtyards, and entries; streetside use; parking areas; side yards; narrow spaces; urban landscapes
▶ ***Needs:*** Plant in moist, loamy soil for best results, though trees will also grow in dry, sandy, or alkaline soils. Grow in full sun. Roots will not buckle paving. Trees are rapid growing and endure heat, drought, and pollution.
▶ ***Choices:*** 'Sempervirens' has a pendulous canopy. 'Drake' has exceptional heat tolerance.

Endive

see Belgian Endive

English Daisy

Bellis perennis

Perennial often grown as an annual

Bellis perennis

▶ ***Hardiness:*** Zones 4-7
▶ ***Size:*** 4"-8" tall, 5"-9" wide
▶ ***Features:*** If you live where summers are cool, such as northern, coastal, and high-altitude areas, you can grow this delightful daisy with little trouble. It's a well-known and beloved flower planted with spring bulbs in Europe, where summers are generally milder than in most of North America. In southern climates (Zones 8-10) it makes a good winter annual. Its bright, cheerful daisies come in red, pink, and white with yellow centers above compact mounds. Blooms early to late spring, or through winter with fall planting in southern climates.
▶ ***Uses:*** Annual or perennial bedding plant for midspring bloom in cool-summer climates of Zones 4-7; or annual winter bloom in southern climates (Zones 8-10). Performs well in containers.
▶ ***Needs:*** Full sun in cool, moist climates but more shade in drier, warmer climates. This plant needs ample moisture and rich soil that never dries out, especially in full sun. Grow as a perennial by planting established seedlings in spring or fall in Zones 4-7. In warm, humid Zones 8-10, plant in fall as an annual for spring bloom and then tear out when summer heat hits. Cut back after flowering stops in late spring or early summer. Apply a winter mulch in Zones 6 and colder. English daisy is prone to powdery mildew.
▶ ***Choices:*** Flowers come in pinks, reds, or whites. Some varieties bear single flowers, while others look more like tiny pompons.

English Ivy

see Ivy, English

English Laurel

see Laurels

Epimedium; Bishop's Hat; Barrenwort

Epimedium spp.

Evergreen groundcover

Epimedium ×youngianum 'Niveum'

▶ ***Hardiness:*** Zones 4-9
▶ ***Size:*** 6"-15" tall, 12"-18" wide
▶ ***Features:*** Delicate white, pink, red or yellow flowers (depending on the species or hybrid) are subtly attractive in early spring, but it's the neat, clean, heart-shape foliage of this perennial groundcover that steals the show. The new leaves emerge all bronzy and glowing in early spring, turn bright green in summer, then bronze again in fall and winter. Best of all this is one of the few plants that grow well in dry shade.
▶ ***Uses:*** Excellent for shady beds under trees where greedy tree roots make life difficult for plants. Makes a neat, clean groundcover. Excellent in combination with other shade perennials that have foliage that persists over winter, such as coral bells and foam flower.
▶ ***Needs:*** Plant in shade to part shade. Although most rapid growth is in rich, moist, woodland soils well-amended with organic matter, this plant is highly tolerant of dry, difficult, root-filled soils under trees and shrubs. It is largely pest free.

Epipremnum spp.

see Pothos

Eremurus spp.

see Foxtail Lily

Erica spp.

see Heath

Erigeron hybrid

see Fleabane

Eriobotrya japonica

see Loquat

Eryngium spp.

see Sea Holly

Escallonia, Frades

Escallonia ×exoniensis 'Frades'

Evergreen flowering shrub

Escallonia ×exoniensis 'Frades'

▶ ***Hardiness:*** Zones 9–10
▶ ***Size:*** 5'–6' tall and wide
▶ ***Features:*** Rapid growth. Pink flowers in summer and fall. Small, glossy green leaves on a dense plant. Tolerant of salty and windy conditions. Small glossy leaves have a fine texture; pink flowers bloom nearly all year. Plants damaged by hard freezes will often recover. Prune dead branches after new growth emerges. Will grow in coastal areas of Zone 8.
▶ ***Uses:*** Coastal areas, massing, shrub borders, entries, patio planting or around semishaded decks, screening, low windbreaks, espalier
▶ ***Needs:*** Plant in any soil except highly alkaline ones. Water regularly. Grow in partial shade. After flowers fade, prune lightly to keep plants compact. Tolerates salt and wind.
▶ ***Choices:*** 'Newport Dwarf'—less than 3' tall, about 4' wide; dark pink to red flowers.

Eschscholzia californica

see California Poppy

Eulalia Grass

see Grasses, Ornamental: Silver Grass

EUONYMUS

Euonymus spp.

The evergreen euonymus are an amazing group of plants. Some of them are both shrubs and vines; similar to English ivy—as juvenile plants they behave like vines, climbing with holdfasts (tiny rootlike structures) that adhere to surfaces. But when it reaches the top of the structure it's climbing, the plant undergoes a metamorphosis into an adult, changing its leaf shape, growth structure, and overall form into a bushy shrub, losing its power to develop holdfasts and climb, and—something else it could not do as a juvenile—developing flowers and fruits. Cuttings can be taken from this adult portion of the plant, and when they are grown they retain all the characteristics of the adult. Some of the evergreen euonymus you find at nurseries are shrubs, and some are vines. Like English ivy, the vining types make good groundcovers (although they are generally much hardier), but as soon as they reach a vertical structure such as a tree trunk or wall, they will climb up it. There are deciduous euonymus species, too, but they are very different in appearance and behavior. For a description of a popular one, see Burning Bush on page 328.

EUONYMUS

Golden Euonymus

Euonymus japonicus 'Aureus'

Broadleaf evergreen shrub

Euonymus japonicus 'Aureus'

▶ ***Hardiness:*** Zones 7–9
▶ ***Size:*** 8'–10' tall, 6' wide
▶ ***Features:*** With gold and green variegated leaves brighter than many flowers, golden euonymus is a real head-turner. This evergreen shrub is easy to grow—it's rapid-growing and tough, tolerant of salt spray and harsh coastal conditions, and works as well in a container as it does in the ground. A little of this plant goes a long way in the landscape. Avoid placing it where the bright foliage will clash with house colors or other plants.
▶ ***Uses:*** Accents, coastal gardens, and specimen plants
▶ ***Needs:*** Golden euonymus thrives in sunny or shady spots with good air circulation. Heat, poor soil, and coastal conditions are no problem. Plants can withstand heavy pruning. To help prevent powdery mildew, space plants growing in shade far enough apart to keep air circulating. Remove branches that revert to solid green.

EUONYMUS

Manhattan Spreading Euonymus

Euonymus kiautschovicus 'Manhattan'

Broadleaf evergreen shrub

Euonymus kiautschovicus 'Manhattan'

▶ ***Hardiness:*** Zones 4–8
▶ ***Size:*** 6'–8' tall, 8'–12' wide
▶ ***Features:*** This is one of the hardiest broadleaf evergreens in gardening—and one of the fastest growing. The dark green leaves of this shrub appear on spreading branches, making it a natural choice to create a screen or to form a loose, informal hedge. Pretty pink capsules surround orange-red fruits in fall. Manhattan spreading euonymus is easy to grow. Late summer flowers can attract flies. Locate plants away from patios and outdoor seating areas. Leaves can winter-burn in colder climates; plant where you won't view daily from inside your home.
▶ ***Uses:*** Informal hedges, screens, or mass plantings
▶ ***Needs:*** Plant in full sun, part shade, or shade. Soil can be fertile or poor, but should be well drained. Plants may die back during hard winters. Prune to remove dead branches when buds swell in spring. Shrubs will quickly regrow.

EUONYMUS

Purple-leaf Wintercreeper

Euonymus fortunei 'Coloratus'

Broadleaf evergreen shrub or vine often used as groundcover

Euonymus fortunei 'Coloratus'

▶ ***Hardiness:*** Zones 4–8
▶ ***Size:*** 6"–24" high as a groundcover, with indefinite spread
▶ ***Features:*** One of the hardiest broadleaf vines, this sprawling groundcover isn't picky about soil. Plant it in full sun so green foliage will turn wine-red in fall and winter. Control scale with an insecticide spray labeled for euonymus. This plant spreads fast, so be sure you want it.
▶ ***Uses:*** Filling in bare spots beneath trees, on hills, or dry areas surrounded with paving
▶ ***Needs:*** Plant in full sun in any soil that is well drained. Tolerant of high and low soil pH. Trim midspring to keep it in bounds and to remove dead or damaged stems. Underplant with spring bulbs. Mulch for winter in colder growing zones.

Euonymus alatus

see Burning Bush

Eupatorium purpureum

see Joe-Pye Weed

Euphorbia cyparissias

see Spurge, Cypress

Euphorbia milii

see Cactus and Succulents: Crown-of-Thorns

Euphorbia polychroma

(E. epithymoides)

see Spurge, Cushion

Euphorbia pulcherrima

see Poinsettia

Euphorbia trigona

see Cactus and Succulents: African Milk Tree

European Mountain Ash

see Mountain Ash, European

Eustoma grandiflorum

see Lisianthus

Evening Primrose, Showy

Oenothera speciosa

Perennial

Oenothera speciosa

▶ ***Hardiness:*** Zones 3–9
▶ ***Size:*** 12"–18" tall and wide, but can spread indefinitely
▶ ***Features:*** Often included with bluebonnets in wildflower mixes for Texas, the showy evening primrose is not a primrose, and it blooms during the day—but it is immensely showy, blanketed with flowers from late spring to early summer that open early in the day as a creamy white that quickly darkens to a lovely shell pink. The silvery gray foliage makes a beautiful contrast to the pink, and is attractive in its own right for quite awhile after blooming is over. This plant spreads rapidly into large colonies—which can be a boon in large, rough areas or where it's well contained, but a bane in more controlled gardens where it can overwhelm its neighbors.
▶ ***Uses:*** Naturalized in meadow gardens and cottage gardens, especially where soil is dry and stony. Effective as a solid cover in a self-contained raised bed.
▶ ***Needs:*** Full sun. Average to poor, well-drained soil. Moderate moisture but will tolerate drought. Plant established plants in spring. No need to deadhead, mulch, or fertilize. This plant spreads rapidly by underground runners and can become a nuisance, especially in rich soil. Each fall and spring, dig up unwanted plants to keep in bounds. It is usually pest and disease free, though spittlebugs can sometimes be a problem.
▶ ***Choices:*** For yellow-flowered *Oenothera* species, see Sundrops on page 516.

Fagus spp.

see Beech

False Aralia

Schefflera veitchii
(Dizygotheca elegantissima)

Tropical broadleaf evergreen shrub

Schefflera veitchii

▶ ***Hardiness:*** Zones 10–11
▶ ***Size:*** Grows up to 6' tall
▶ ***Features:*** Tall, multiple stems with flourishes of elegant narrow, serrated leaves in deep, glossy, almost black green. Leaves are coppery when young.
▶ ***Uses:*** As a houseplant
▶ ***Needs:*** Medium to bright, filtered light. Keep soil evenly moist; allowing the soil to dry out at all will cause leaves to drop. Use a tray with pebbles and water to raise humidity. Does fine in the average to warm temperatures of a house. Fertilize three times in summer with a 10-10-10 fertilizer. The plant naturally loses lower leaves as it ages.

FALSE CYPRESSES

Chamaecyparis spp.

Although better known for many smaller, shrublike cultivars, the false cypress species are large coniferous trees that in their natural habitat grow 100' tall or more. Prized for their elegant soft foliage, they are excellent specimen trees for large spaces, and make good screens. Because they take pruning well, they are sometimes used as hedges. They all prefer a cool, humid climate and moist, acidic, well-drained soil rich in organic matter, although some cultivars of Hinoki false cypress and Japanese false cypress tolerate heat well.

FALSE CYPRESSES

Hinoki False cypress

Chamaecyparis obtusa

Evergreen coniferous tree or shrub

Chamaecyparis obtusa 'Nana Gracilis'

► ***Hardiness:*** Zones 5–8
► ***Size:*** 40–50' high, 10–20' wide
► ***Features:*** This slow-growing tree's graceful, soft-textured foliage on frondlike, semipendulous branches retains its color well all year long. The species has a broad, sweeping form cloaked in a rich, dark, velvety green, but cultivars are available that are smaller trees and shrublike mounds, some with yellowish leaves. The bark of the tree is an attractive shredding reddish brown.
► ***Uses:*** The species, if you can find it, makes a beautiful landscape specimen, but this plant is better known for its many cultivars. Some are smaller trees and many are low-growing dwarf types that are used more like shrubs. Even slower-growing than the species, they are useful in foundation plantings, in the shrub border, and in rock gardens. All of the smaller cultivars perform well in containers, and are popular subjects for bonsai.
► ***Needs:*** Best in cool, humid climates such as the Pacific Northwest, and moist, well-drained, acidic soil high in organic matter. Plant in full sun, but in a spot that is protected from wind. Many cultivars are more heat tolerant than the species as well as other false cypresses. Keep soil evenly moist; a 2"–4" layer of shredded bark mulch is helpful to retain soil moisture. In dry summers, spider mites can be a problem.
► ***Choices:*** Dwarf Hinoki false cypress *(Chamaecyparis obtusa* 'Nana'*)* is popular for its slow growth habit and small ultimate size (2'–3' tall, 3'–4' wide). Its tufted foliage is a velvety dark green, its form like a tiny Christmas tree. 'Nana Gracilis' has similar dark green foliage, but grows 6'–10' tall into a more pyramidal shape. 'Nana Lutea' is an extremely dwarf type with bright golden yellow leaves; it grows only 10" tall, 12" wide, and is a popular subject for rock gardens. 'Crippsii' forms a broad pyramid, very slow-growing to 10'–15' tall, with golden yellow new foliage where it is exposed to sun. The yellow foliage eventually fades to a darker green, creating the effect of a bright yellow glow with velvety dark green depths. 'Filicoides' has pendulous fernlike foliage and is slow-growing to about 10' tall.

FALSE CYPRESSES

Japanese False cypress; Sawara False cypress

Chamaecyparis pisifera

Evergreen coniferous tree or shrub

Chamaecyparis pisifera 'Snow'

► ***Hardiness:*** Zones 5–8
► ***Size:*** 50–70' high; 10–20' wide
► ***Features:*** The species is a large, imposing dark to bright green forest tree in its native Japan, but is seldom planted in North American gardens. The smaller, usually dwarf, cultivars are of three types: threadleaf, with long, pendulous, narrow branchlets that create a stringy effect; plumed, with soft sprays of foliage that have a feathery effect; and moss, with foliage tufted for a lush, velvety, mosslike effect.
► ***Uses:*** The slow-growing dwarf cultivars are useful in foundation plantings, the shrub border, and as specimens in rock gardens and collections of dwarf conifers. The species, which is rarely available, needs space as a landscape specimen.
► ***Needs:*** Most of the cultivars are better adapted to harsh Midwest conditions than other false cypresses, although best growth is in cool, humid climates such as the Pacific Northwest and parts of the Northeast. Deep, moist soil that is well drained and high in organic matter is best, although this plant is reasonably tolerant of more average soils. Keep soil evenly moist during dry spells. In hot, dry weather watch out for spider mites.
► ***Choices:*** Threadleaf cultivars: 'Filifera' is slow-growing to about 10' in as many years, although in time it may reach 25' tall. 'Filifera Aurea' is similar but with bright yellow new foliage. 'Golden Mop' is a rounded dwarf to 3' tall with bright yellow threadlike foliage. Plumed cultivars: 'Plumosa' has an open habit and soft, feathery sprays of foliage. It grows at a medium rate to become a large tree nearly as tall as the species. 'Plumosa Aurea' is similar, but with golden yellow foliage where it is exposed to direct sun. 'Plumosa Compacta' is a slow-growing rounded dwarf that reaches 3' tall and wide. 'Plumosa Nana' is even smaller and more flattened in shape, rarely growing taller than 18". Moss cultivars: 'Squarrosa' is a wide cone of velvety bluish foliage that reaches 15'–25' tall. 'Boulevard' is a slow-growing cone to 15' tall with blue-green mossy foliage, needlelike but soft to the touch. 'Squarrosa Pygmaea' is a tight mound 3' tall with bluish foliage.

FALSE CYPRESSES

Lawson False cypress

Chamaecyparis lawsoniana

Evergreen coniferous tree

Chamaecyparis lawsoniana 'Aurea Densa'

► ***Hardiness:*** Zones 6–8
► ***Size:*** 40'–60' high, 10'–20' wide; many cultivars are smaller
► ***Features:*** Mainly grown in the Pacific Northwest, this species and its cultivars have soft, needlelike foliage borne in flattened sprays held in somewhat vertical planes. The species is a large tree with gray-green to dark green foliage. Cultivars range in foliage color from yellow and blue to deep,

F

Plant encyclopedia

dark green, and in form from large conical trees to tiny pillows.

▶ ***Uses:*** The tree is useful as a landscape specimen or screen. The smaller cultivars work well in foundation planting, in the shrub border, and in formal gardens. The smallest cultivars are good in the rock garden and in dwarf conifer collections. All make good subjects for bonsai.

▶ ***Needs:*** Best in cool, humid climates with relatively high annual rainfall. Needs deep, moist soil that is well drained and high in organic matter. Subject to serious mite infestations in hot summers.

▶ ***Choices:*** 'Alumnii' is a narrow column of rich blue foliage held in rigidly vertical fans. It grows 6'-13' tall and is a good choice for formal gardens. 'Nana' has a rounded shrubby form to 6' tall with deep green foliage. 'Golden Showers' has pendulous, bright yellow branch tips on yellow-green foliage. 'Oregon Blue' grows into a 25' conical tree at a rapid rate, unusual for false cypresses. It has rich blue foliage.

False Dragonhead

see Obedient Plant

False Indigo, Blue

Baptisia australis

Perennial

Baptisia australis

▶ ***Hardiness:*** Zones 3-9

▶ ***Size:*** 3'-5' tall, 3'-5' wide

▶ ***Features:*** Showy indigo-blue flower spikes in late spring and early summer; a shrubby habit with attractive summer foliage; handsome blue-black seedpods and grassy stems in fall and winter—false indigo is a perennial for all seasons. This prairie native is easy to grow and well-adapted to many climates and soils. Blooms in early summer.

▶ ***Uses:*** The rear of the mixed flower border, as a screen. Nice in the wildflower meadow. The decorative seedpods are attractive in dried arrangements.

▶ ***Needs:*** Full sun in Zones 3-6 and Pacific Northwest; light shade in hot summer in Zones 7-9. Prefers rich, well-drained soil but tolerates many different soils. It needs moderate to light moisture and is fairly drought tolerant once mature. Plant established plants in spring or fall and avoid moving because it has a deep taproot that resists transplanting. Mulch to conserve moisture in all but the wettest climates. This plant benefits from light fertilizing, especially an application of an inch or two of compost in spring. It is usually pest and disease free. Stake lightly to prevent flopping.

▶ ***Choices:*** 'Prairie Smoke' has pale lilac flowers and smoky gray-green stems in winter. A white variety, *Baptisia alba*, is also available.

False Rockcress

see Rockcress, False

False Spirea

see Astilbe

False Sunflower

Heliopsis helianthoides

Perennial

Heliopsis helianthoides

▶ ***Hardiness:*** Zones 4-9

▶ ***Size:*** 3'-6' tall, 1'-2' wide

▶ ***Features:*** This easy-to-grow native of the North American prairies bears cheerful daisies in clouds of yellow and gold over a long season. There are many refined cultivars with double and single flowers in yellow and gold, some with green centers. Blooms late summer.

▶ ***Uses:*** Plant in groups for best effect. In the mixed border, this plant is a "leaner" and good to plant with others it can lean against for support. It's excellent planted in groups in and among ornamental grasses.

▶ ***Needs:*** Rich, moist to well-drained soil. Adequate to ample moisture. Plant established plants in spring. Fertilize occasionally, every 6 weeks, or work in a 9-month slow-release fertilizer each spring. Trim spent flowers for longest bloom. Divide every 2-4 years to maintain vigorous, healthy plants. This plant is prone to powdery mildew and rust.

Fan Flower

Scaevola aemula

Perennial grown as an annual

Scaevola aemula

▶ ***Hardiness:*** Zones 9-11 in the West

▶ ***Size:*** 6"-18' tall, 18" wide

▶ ***Features:*** Trailing, spreading form and rich blue or purple flowers make this Australian native a favorite annual groundcover and hanging basket plant. Blooms spring to frost.

▶ ***Uses:*** As a spiller cascading out of hanging baskets and other mixed containers. Also pretty as a bedding plant and annual groundcover, especially where it can spill out over the edge of a bed or cascade down a wall or raised planter.

▶ ***Needs:*** Full sun in Zones 2-6; full sun to light shade in Zones 7-11. Usually grown as an annual but can be grown as a perennial in Zones 9-11. Plant in rich to average, moist but well-drained soil. It needs moderate moisture and excellent drainage. This plant works best in containers or rock gardens. Fertilize regularly, every 4-6 weeks, or work in a slow-release fertilizer in spring. It is usually pest and disease free.

▶ ***Choices:*** Flowers are a lovely intense blue, though light blue, sky blue, blue-violet, lavender, pink, and white are also available. 'Blue Wonder' is the most readily available, but other selections, such as 'New Wonder' and 'Purple Fanfare', are also good.

Fatshedera; Aralia Ivy

×Fatshedera lizei

Subtropical broadleaf evergreen shrub

×Fatshedera lizei

▶ ***Hardiness:*** Zones 8–10
▶ ***Size:*** 6"–10' tall and wide
▶ ***Features:*** Rapid growth. Rich green leaves resemble large ivy; sprawling form allows plants to climb. Thrives in both dense and partial shade. This unusual intergeneric cross between the hardy vine English ivy and the tropical shrub fatsia *(Fatsia japonica)* is not quite a vine and not quite a shrub. Its rich green leaves resemble a large English ivy or a small tropical fatsia—you decide. While it is not a natural climber, its long stems can be trained (by tying) to grow against a wall or up a post, or they can be allowed to clamber on the ground where they will mound up into a shrublike form. It thrives in partial shade as well as in difficult, fully shady spots. Use it to add bold, tropical-looking texture to shady areas. It's especially useful in protected, walled entry gardens or courtyards.
▶ ***Uses:*** Trained on walls in courtyards, around shaded entries, adding coarse texture, providing background, beside shaded ponds or swimming pools
▶ ***Needs:*** Plant in any soil that's moist but not soggy. Grow in partial shade or dense shade. Protect from hot, drying winds and late frosts. Pinch tips for bushier growth. Tie to a support if you want it to grow upward.

Fatsia, Japanese; Japanese Aralia

Fatsia japonica

Evergreen shrub

Fatsia japonica

▶ ***Hardiness:*** Zones 8–10
▶ ***Size:*** 3'–4' tall, 6'–8' wide
▶ ***Features:*** Grow this shade-loving shrub for its leaves and its ability to grow well in difficult shady spots. Large glossy foliage is lobed and adds a noticeably bold, tropical texture to landscape compositions. White flowers appear in October and November. Protect plants from extreme wind.
▶ ***Uses:*** Courtyards, against walls, poolside, shaded entries or patios, contrasting with fine-textured plants
▶ ***Needs:*** Plant in moist, acidic soil that's rich with organic matter for ideal growing conditions. Shrubs also tolerate soils from sandy to heavy clay, but not soggy soils. Grow in partial to dense shade; protect from afternoon or winter sun. Water regularly for optimal growth.

Felicia amelloides

see Blue Marguerite

Fennel

Foeniculum vulgare

Perennial herb

Fennel 'Purpurascens'

▶ ***Hardiness:*** Zones 6–9 but usually grown as an annual in all zones
▶ ***Size:*** 3'–7' tall, 2'–3' wide, depending on the cultivar
▶ ***Features:*** Lovely, feathery foliage and height make this a favorite for edible landscaping. Delightful aniselike taste.
▶ ***Uses:*** Leaves are tasty chopped fresh over dishes; bulbs are served raw or cooked in many other dishes. Seeds are used in many Southern Italian and German dishes.
▶ ***Needs:*** Full sun. Prefers rich, well-drained soil with average moisture, but will tolerate some variety in soils and moisture. Drought tolerant once established. In hot climates, sow seeds in fall and early spring. In colder climates, sow in spring. Or buy small established plants, although plants usually transplant poorly. Will reseed prolifically, assuring an ongoing supply of new plants for years to come.
▶ ***Choices:*** 'Rubrum' is also known as bronze fennel and is prized for its dark reddish-bronze foliage. Florence fennel *(Foeniculum vulgare* var. *dulce)* can be grown as an annual vegetable with its edible bulbous base.

Fern, Artillery

see Artillery Fern

FERNS

There is a staggering variety of ferns and some gardeners have collections of nothing but. Shapes, sizes, and hardiness vary tremendously, but all have the same graceful, cooling, peaceful effect. There are ferns native to tropical rainforests, to hot sunny deserts, to temperate forests, and to harsh mountaintops. There are species that climb like a vine, that spread into thick colonies and groundcovering mats, that tower as 15' trees, and that float in ponds. Some are evergreen, some are deciduous. Some are grown in containers indoors, some as patio plants that are brought indoors for the winter, and still others outdoors in the woodland garden.

For all their differences, most of the ferns grown in gardens and indoors as houseplants have the same basic needs. They dislike intense, bright light and their leaves can burn when exposed to too much. Give them medium to bright, filtered light. Placing them in a dark spot may cause them to become thin and disease prone. Ferns are moisture lovers and need always moist (but never waterlogged) soil and ample humidity. Outdoors they grow best in rich, moist, well-drained woodland soil high in organic matter, and under the boughs of a high tree canopy where the air is cool and moist. Indoors, bathrooms are ideal. Otherwise run a humidifier or set them on trays of pebbles and water. Most ferns grown as houseplants thrive when put outside for the summer in regions with humid summers as long as they're in a shady protected spot, such as a porch. They like average to warm household temperatures between 60°–75°F/16°–24°C. Fertilize three times in summer with a 10-10-10 fertilizer or fertilize every time you water with a one-quarter strength solution. Many ferns, even the evergreen ones, have fronds that turn yellow and die back, especially on the underside of the plant. Lift the healthy green leaves and trim off the dead fronds; this stimulates vigorous new growth on the plant.

FERNS

Autumn Fern

Dryopteris erythrosora

Perennial

Dryopteris erythrosora

▶***Hardiness:*** Zones 5–9
▶***Size:*** 1'–2' tall, 1'–2' wide
▶***Features:*** Seasonal color. Fronds are reddish, pink, or yellow as they emerge in spring, green in summer, and russet in fall and winter. Red spores are visible in winter. Plants tolerate some drought but perform best where soil never dries out. Great for covering moist, shady areas.
▶***Uses:*** Filling shady areas where grass won't grow, edging walkways, planting beds or patios, courtyards, entries, beside benches, massing, woodlands, winter interest
▶***Needs:*** Moist soil, rich with organic matter; mix compost into planting holes. Grow in partial or dense shade. Mulch for winter. Protect from wind in winter.

FERNS

Bird's Nest Fern

Asplenium nidus

Tropical evergreen epiphyte

Asplenium nidus

▶***Hardiness:*** Zones 10–11
▶***Size:*** Grows 10"–15" tall
▶***Features:*** This unusual houseplant is unfernlike for a variety of reasons. Its fronds are simple and undivided and straplike in shape, unlike the highly divided, lacy leaves normally associated with ferns. Like many orchids and bromeliads, it is an epiphyte, or "air plant"—it grows without any soil to speak of, up in the air on tree trunks. It's named for the way its wide, long, wavy-edged leaves surround the fibrous "nest" at its center.
▶***Uses:*** As a houseplant. Excellent in terrariums.
▶***Needs:*** Grow as you would any fern, except that the potting medium must be very coarse to allow plenty of air. It's important to provide a humid environment (65% or more); in especially humid environments this plant can be grown on a slab without any potting medium at all. Keep potting medium evenly moist or tips will turn brown. Avoid getting water in the cup that is formed by the fronds. And avoid handling new fronds; they're very delicate.

FERNS

Boston Fern

Nephrolepis exaltata

Tropical evergreen perennial

Nephrolepis exaltata

▶***Hardiness:*** Zones 9–11
▶***Size:*** Fronds grow as long as 3'
▶***Features:*** Classic, trailing, graceful deep green fern fronds that are usually 1'–2' long but can reach 3' in ideal conditions.
▶***Uses:*** As a houseplant
▶***Needs:*** Grow as you would any houseplant fern (see section introduction, page 374).
▶***Choices:*** Interesting variations available, including those with more wavy leaflets and more compact types.

FERNS

Christmas Fern

Polystichum acrostichoides

Evergreen perennial

Polystichum acrostichoides

▶***Hardiness:*** Zones 4–8
▶***Size:*** 18"–24" tall and wide
▶***Features:*** Lustrous, glossy fronds; one of the few hardy evergreen ferns for woodland gardens in the North.
▶***Uses:*** Singly as a specimen or grouped as a groundcover in the woodland garden. The cut fronds are popular for holiday decorations.
▶***Needs:*** Plant in spring; if planting in groups space 2' apart. Plant in moist, well-drained soil high in organic matter, and keep continuously moist. Dense to partial shade.

FERNS

Cinnamon Fern

Osmunda cinnamomea

Deciduous perennial

Osmunda cinnamomea

▶ **Hardiness:** Zones 3–7
▶ **Size:** 36" tall, 18" wide
▶ **Features:** Stately tall, erect fronds are finely divided. In spring, beautiful fertile fronds emerge covered with rusty spores, which is where this plant gets its name. It tends to colonize into large stands.
▶ **Uses:** Ideal at the edges of ponds and streams, or where water stands. A good choice for sunny, low-lying spots with wet soil.
▶ **Needs:** Best in acidic soil that is continuously moist to soggy, in full sun. In cool climates it will tolerate somewhat drier soil in partial shade. Plant 2' apart.

FERNS

Hay-Scented Fern

Dennstaedtia punctilobula

Perennial

Dennstaedtia punctilobula

▶ **Hardiness:** Zones 3–8
▶ **Size:** 6"–18" tall, indefinite spread
▶ **Features:** Fill in bare, shady spots with this fast-growing fern that tolerates a variety of soils. You'll enjoy arching, feathery fronds that are green in summer and yellow in autumn. Allow plenty of room for this fern to spread.
▶ **Uses:** Shade gardens, massing, contrasting with coarse-textured plants, large planting beds, natural areas, shaded woodlands
▶ **Needs:** Plant in acidic soil; adapts to poor, dry soil. Grow in partial to dense shade. Established plants require little watering.

FERNS

Japanese Holly Fern

Cyrtomium falcatum

Evergreen perennial

Cyrtomium falcatum

▶ **Hardiness:** Zones 8–10
▶ **Size:** 18"–24" high; 24"–30" wide
▶ **Features:** Medium growth rate. Fills moist, shady beds. Glossy dark green leaves seem to shine in dim light; their coarse texture contrasts well with smaller-leaved plants. Avoid poor, dry soils.
▶ **Uses:** Shady areas where grass won't grow; edging shady walkways, planting beds, or patios; courtyards; entries; beside benches
▶ **Needs:** Plant in soil that's moist but well drained and rich in organic matter. Set plants high in planting holes; plants are intolerant of water around roots. Grow in partial or dense shade. Mulch for winter.

FERNS

Japanese Painted Fern

Athyrium nipponicum 'Pictum'

Perennial

Athyrium nipponicum 'Pictum'

▶ **Hardiness:** Zones 4–9
▶ **Size:** 12"–18" tall and wide
▶ **Features:** This slow grower is one of the most colorful ferns, with dark purplish foliage that has pink and silvery highlights. Use it to brighten moist, shaded spots. Because this fern grows slowly, plant it in clusters for faster impact. Plants may disappear during droughts. Leaves emerge again when soil is moistened. In Zones 4 and 5 protect it over winter with a loose covering of evergreen boughs.
▶ **Uses:** Shady areas, front layer of planting beds, growing beneath trees or tall shrubs, beside shady creeks, ponds, or downspouts, at the foot of a shaded bench, woodlands
▶ **Needs:** Plant in moist soil that's rich in organic matter. Grow in partial or dense shade. Mulch for winter. Don't remove freeze-damaged foliage until new leaves begin to emerge.

FERNS

Maidenhair Fern

Adiantum pedatum

Perennial

Adiantum pedatum

▶ **Hardiness:** Zones 3–8
▶ **Size:** 12"–16" tall, 12"–16" wide
▶ **Features:** Medium growth rate. Bright green, fine-textured foliage thrives in damp, shady locations. Returns every year in the spring. Lightens shady, damp spots with bright green, delicate fronds. Leaflets seem to hover above dark, purplish stems. The fine texture combines nicely with hostas. May be sold as northern maidenhair fern.
▶ **Uses:** Natural areas, damp sites, woodland paths, shady courtyards and entries, textural contrast among plants or stones, narrow confined spaces, shady ponds or creeks, near downspouts
▶ **Needs:** In its natural habitat this fern is often found around moist seepages and springs. Plant in moist soil that's rich in organic matter, and keep the soil contantly moist. Soil should be neutral or slightly acidic. Grow in partial to dense shade; protect from afternoon sun in hotter climates. This fern has delicate foliage that burns easily. Mulch for winter protection.

FERNS

Ostrich Fern

Matteuccia struthiopteris
(formerly *M. pensylvanica)*

Perennial

Matteuccia struthiopteris

▶ ***Hardiness:*** Zones 3–8
▶ ***Size:*** 5' tall, 3' wide
▶ ***Features:*** This is one of the largest hardy ferns for the garden, yet in spite of its hardiness it creates an imposing impression of tropical drama. In good conditions it tends to colonize into large masses, so it may be too aggressive for the smaller garden.
▶ ***Uses:*** Naturalizing in large areas of partial shade
▶ ***Needs:*** Grows in about any garden soil from those with average moisture to the continuously moist. Most vigorous in dappled shade, but tolerates full sun to dense shade; the sunnier the spot, the more moisture is required. Prone to leaf scorch in dry soils, especially with a lot of sun. This is a less satisfactory choice for hot southern gardens.

FERNS

Rabbit's Foot Fern

Davallia fejeensis

Tropical perennial

Davallia fejeensis

▶ ***Size:*** Grows 2' tall
▶ ***Features:*** Fronds grown on top of thick hairy stems that push out of the soil at the plant's base, hence this fern's name.
▶ ***Uses:*** As a houseplant
▶ ***Needs:*** Grow as you would any fern (see section introduction, page 374).

FERNS

Royal Fern

Osmunda regalis

Perennial

Osmunda regalis

▶ ***Hardiness:*** Zones 3–9
▶ ***Size:*** 6' tall, 6' wide
▶ ***Features:*** This is the largest hardy fern in North America, with imposing broad, bold-textured fronds that impart a tropical appearance even though this fern is native into Alaska. The form is upright and arching. Fertile fronds covered with rust-colored spores appear in spring. In fall the fronds turn an appealing yellow before dying back to the ground.
▶ ***Uses:*** Dramatic when planted in groups. Use in the shady garden where a big statement with large size and bold texture is desired.
▶ ***Needs:*** Best in moist, rich, woodland soil that is well drained and high in organic matter. Plants tolerate wet soil as well. This fern prefers dense to partial shade and protection from midday sun. Plant 3'-6' apart in spring or fall. Apply 3" of mulch around, but not touching, the plants in summer and winter. Keep soil moist. Remove fronds after they wither and fall to the ground in late fall.

FERNS

Staghorn Fern

Platycerium bifurcatum

Tropical evergreen epiphyte

Platycerium bifurcatum

▶ ***Hardiness:*** Zones 10–11
▶ ***Size:*** Grows 2' or more across
▶ ***Features:*** Like bird's nest fern and some orchids and bromeliads, this native of tropical rain forests is an epiphyte, or air plant, that grows on trees with virtually no soil. It has distinctively shaped, unfernlike fronds that look like antlers. It's usually grown on a log, plank, or other flat surface outfitted with a ball of sphagnum moss. The whole thing can be hung on a wall, especially outside on a porch or other sheltered, shady spot.
▶ ***Uses:*** As a houseplant. In southern Florida and southern California where winter temperatures never go lower than 45°F, it is sometimes grown on tree trunks outdoors.
▶ ***Needs:*** Same light and humidity needs as other ferns. If grown in a pot, use a very coarse medium to make sure air gets to the roots. Keep the medium evenly moist, watering frequently as needed.
If grown on a log or plank, keep the moss ball moist, which usually means a daily watering. Outdoors in subtropical climates with low humidity—such as southern California in the summer—it will grow best with frequent misting or near a pool or fountain where air is humid.

FERNS

Western Sword Fern

Polystichum munitum

Evergreen perennial

Polystichum munitum

▶**Hardiness:** Zones 7–9
▶**Size:** Can reach 4' tall and 7' wide
▶**Features:** With its glossy bright green leathery fronds, western sword fern is similar in appearance to Christmas fern but is larger. It is a native of the redwood forests of coastal California and the milder coastal regions of southern Oregon. It is a useful landscape plant not only in natural wild gardens but also, with its neat form and clean evergreen foliage, in more formal landscapes.
▶**Uses:** As a specimen or in large groups as a tall groundcover in wooded areas along the California and Oregon coasts.
▶**Needs:** Plant any time of the year in western gardens, spacing plants 3' apart in dense to partial shade. It will take more sun in cool fog-belt areas of the coast. Best in moist, well-drained soil high in organic matter. Mulch plants well to help retain moisture, but avoid overwatering in summer.

Festuca spp.

see Grasses, Ornamental: Fescue

Ficus spp.

see Figs

Fig, Edible

Ficus carica

Deciduous fruit tree

Fig 'Brown Turkey'

▶**Hardiness:** Zone 7 with winter protection; otherwise Zones 8–11
▶**Size:** Grows 6'–30' tall; 4'–25' wide, depending on type and climate
▶**Features:** Plump, rich fruits on a tree with interesting deeply lobed leaves
▶**Uses:** Attractive enough to use anywhere in the landscape. Makes a good espalier.
▶**Needs:** Full sun for best production; light shade tolerated. Average, well drained soil. Plant trees in spring before they leaf out. Space 8'–25' apart, following label directions. Prune to grow as a central leader (see page 266). In Zone 7, can be grown if planted in a protected spot, especially one against a warm wall, and wrapped in burlap each winter. Prune hard each spring before the tree leafs out and keep under 8' tall to accommodate wrapping. Or plant a dwarf type.
▶**Choices:** Dwarf types seldom top 10'. Standards can reach 30'. In Southern California, 'Black Mission', and 'Violette de Bordeaux', are good choices. In Northern California, try 'White Genoa' or 'Desert King'. In the Southeast, try 'Celeste' and along the Gulf Coast 'Tena'.

FIGS

Ficus spp.

Ornamental figs vary widely from stately spreading weeping figs that can grow up to 6' tall to low, creeping types. Leaves can be small and papery or large and rubbery, as with the classic rubber plant. Most are grown as houseplants or in the mild climates of southern Florida, California, and Hawaii.

FIGS

Weeping Fig

Ficus benjamina

Tropical broadleaf evergreen tree

Ficus benjamina

▶**Hardiness:** Zones 10–11
▶**Size:** As a houseplant can grow 6'–12' tall
▶**Features:** Dramatic treelike form with branches that spread and tend to form a weeping pattern. Glossy, pointed oval leaves.
▶**Uses:** As a houseplant, though sometimes grown as a landscape plant in the warmest regions of the United States.
▶**Needs:** Bright light. Allow soil to dry out slightly between waterings, especially in winter. Average home humidity and air temperatures fine. Fertilize three times in summer with a 10-10-10 fertilizer. Drops leaves very easily with any changes in care or site. Will drop leaves heavily when first purchased and moved to its new home. Will drop leaves also if over- or underwatered. With proper care, will regrow new leaves.
▶**Choices:** Interesting variegated-leaf types available, including 'Starlight'.

FIGS

Mistletoe Fig

Ficus deltoidea var. *diversifolia*

Tropical broadleaf evergreen shrub

Ficus deltoidea var. *diversifolia*

▶**Hardiness:** Zones 10–11
▶**Size:** Grows up to 3' tall
▶**Features:** Slow-growing bush has teardrop-shape leaves. Leaves have small brown spots and the plant produces pea-size inedible fruits year-round.
▶**Uses:** As a houseplant, though sometimes grown as an evergreen shrub in the warmest regions of the United States.
▶**Needs:** Bright light. Allow soil to dry out slightly between waterings, especially in winter. Average home humidity and air temperatures fine. Fertilize three times in summer with a 10-10-10 fertilizer.

FIGS

Rubber Tree

Ficus elastica

Tropical broadleaf evergreen tree

Ficus elastica

▶**Hardiness:** Zones 10–11
▶**Size:** Grows up to 4'–5' tall indoors
▶**Features:** Easy to grow. Nearly oval, thick, shiny dark green, broad leaves are 8"–12" long.
▶**Uses:** As a houseplant, though sometimes grown as an evergreen tree or shrub in the warmest regions of the United States.

►**Needs:** Bright light. Allow soil to dry out slightly between waterings, especially in winter. Average home humidity and air temperatures fine. Fertilize three times in summer with a 10-10-10 fertilizer. Wipe off the broad leaves every month or so with a damp cloth to remove dust.
►**Choices:** *Ficus elastica* 'Robusta' has especially broad leaves. 'Black Prince' has almost black leaves.

FIGS

Fiddle-leaf Fig

Ficus lyrata

Tropical broadleaf evergreen tree

Ficus lyrata

►**Hardiness:** Zone 11
►**Size:** Grows to 20' tall outdoors, seldom more than 6'-10' tall indoors depending on the growing conditions and size of pot
►**Features:** Large violin-shape leaves can get as long as 18"
►**Uses:** As a houseplant, though sometimes grown as an evergreen tree or shrub in the warmest regions of the United States.
►**Needs:** Average home humidity and air temperatures fine
►**Choices:** Sometimes sold as *Ficus pandurata.*

FIGS

Indian Laurel Fig

Ficus microcarpa

Tropical broadleaf evergreen tree

Ficus microcarpa 'Variegata'

►**Hardiness:** Zones 10–11
►**Size:** Grows 4'-12' tall
►**Features:** Similar to weeping fig but with upright branches and dark oval waxy green leaves 3"–4" long. It can handle lower light levels than weeping fig.
►**Uses:** As a houseplant, though sometimes grown as an evergreen tree in the warmest regions of the United States.
►**Needs:** Bright, indirect light is best. Keep soil barely moist; never soggy. Allow soil to get slightly drier in winter. Avoid feeding for the first several months after purchasing. After that, feed every three or four months. Average household humidity. Prefers warm nights of 65°–70°F/18°–21°C and very warm days of 75°–85°F/24°–29°C.

FIGS

Fig, Creeping

Ficus pumila

Tropical evergreen vine

Ficus pumila

►**Hardiness:** Zones 8–10
►**Size:** Indefinite; can spread 30' or more in all directions
►**Features:** Choose creeping fig when you want a vigorous, fast-growing vine to quickly cloak walls with greenery. Stems cling tightly to hard surfaces, covering them completely with a close mat of fine-textured foliage. Avoid planting on wood structures—it traps moisture, causing rot and damage. Tolerates drought in both sun and shade.
►**Uses:** Covering walls and fences made of masonry, stucco, or metal; making new landscapes look older and established; providing green backgrounds for accent. Sometimes used like English ivy for temporary topiary indoors.
►**Needs:** Plant in well-drained soil in sun or shade. In hottest areas, provide some afternoon shade. Water regularly until established, then moderately or not at all. Prune or shear mature plants to keep foliage flat and neat. Like some evergreen euonymus and ivy, this plant will change into an adult form with larger leaves and a bushy habit when it reaches the top of its climbing structure.

Filipendula rubra

see Queen-of-the-Prairie

FIRS

Abies spp.

Firs bring a wide range of climatic tolerance, shapes, and sizes to the landscape. Many are available in silvery forms, their stiff blue-green needles good for a contrast in the garden. Because their upright, pyramidal form is attractive in itself, they make good specimens.

FIRS

Balsam Fir

Abies balsamea

Evergreen coniferous tree

Abies balsamea

►**Hardiness:** Zones 3–6
►**Size:** 45'-75' tall, 15'-25' wide
►**Features:** Tolerates cold weather, wind, and shade. Dark green foliage all year-round. Narrow, upright form is ideal for specimen use. Although it grows more than 50' high, a balsam fir may fit in a small yard. This pretty tree only gets about 15'-20' wide. This tree is a good choice for higher elevations and temperature extremes, and it tolerates wind and shade well. Trees are widely used for Christmas trees and wreaths. Slow to medium growth rate.
►**Uses:** Screening for privacy or blocking poor views, vertical accent, providing background for deciduous trees and shrubs
►**Needs:** Plant in moist, acidic soils; trees will also grow in boggy areas and on windswept summits. Plants look their best when grown in well-drained soil. Grow in partial shade. Prune only diseased or broken branches. Won't tolerate pollution.

FIRS

Dwarf Balsam Fir

Abies balsamea 'Nana'

Evergreen coniferous shrub

Abies balsamea 'Nana'

▶ ***Hardiness:*** Zones 3–6
▶ ***Size:*** 2'–3' tall and wide
▶ ***Features:*** Sometimes a green plant is just what's needed in the landscape. Dwarf balsam fir fits the bill, staying tidy and rounded at only 3' tall with little or no pruning. This shrub thrives where summers are cool and moist. Water regularly in the warmer areas of its growing range, especially during dry periods. Slow growth rate.
▶ ***Uses:*** Foundation planting, low background for perennials, shrub beds, beside patios, along walkways, narrow areas, rock gardens, specimen planting
▶ ***Needs:*** Plant in fertile soil that's moist but well drained. Slightly acidic soil is best. Grow in partial shade. Plants adapt well to cold locations. Provide supplemental water when conditions are dry or when growing in warmer areas.

FIRS

Bristlecone Fir

Abies bracteata

Evergreen coniferous tree

Abies bracteata

▶ ***Hardiness:*** Zones 3–9
▶ ***Size:*** 50'–70' tall and 15'–20' wide
▶ ***Features:*** Try bristlecone fir for a fluffy evergreen if your area is warm and dry. Its symmetrical shape, especially in youth, adds a formal look to the landscape. Leave lowest branches all the way to the ground for best appearance. This tree is also sold as Santa Lucia fir and may be listed as *A. venusta*. Cones are rounded.
▶ ***Uses:*** Northern California landscapes, mountainsides, rock gardens, specimen trees, screening, providing a background for deciduous plants
▶ ***Needs:*** Grow in well-drained soil that's neutral to acidic. Rocky soils are fine. Plant in partial to deep shade. Humidity and wet soil are not good for this tree.

FIRS

Frasier Fir

Abies fraseri

Evergreen coniferous tree

Abies fraseri

▶ ***Hardiness:*** Zones 4–7
▶ ***Size:*** 30'–40' tall, 20'–25' high
▶ ***Features:*** These easy-care evergreens offer a sweet fragrance in a classic Christmas tree-shape package. Frasier firs are not picky about where they sink their roots; they will thrive in most ordinary, well-drained soils. Their only demand is that they be kept away from hot, dry locations. For a family activity that will bring joy for years to come, plant Frasier firs in your yard and decorate them for the holiday season. The dark green foliage will also provide a backdrop to more colorful plants throughout the year. Slow growth rate. May be sold as southern balsam fir.
▶ ***Uses:*** Specimen use, winter interest, screening to add privacy or to block poor views, providing background for shrubs and other trees
▶ ***Needs:*** Grow in full sun or partial shade. Plant in moist, well-drained soil. Trees tolerate dry soil, but young trees will require watering during the first few years until well established. Not tolerant of heat or excessive drought.

FIRS

Veitch Fir

Abies veitchii

Evergreen coniferous tree

Abies veitchii

▶ ***Hardiness:*** 3–6
▶ ***Size:*** 50'–75' tall, 12'–25' wide
▶ ***Features:*** Evergreens are traditionally slow growing. Choose this species of fir when you need an evergreen tree that grows relatively quickly. Veitch fir will provide a neat, pyramidal form and clean dark green foliage with silvery undersides even in urban areas. Young cones are especially attractive, a bright blue-gray color.
▶ ***Uses:*** Screening for privacy or blocking poor views, winter interest, providing background for deciduous trees and shrubs, cold regions of the country
▶ ***Needs:*** Plant in acidic soils that are moist but well drained. Grow in sun or partial shade. Prune only diseased or broken branches. Somewhat tolerant of urban growing conditions.

FIRS

White Fir

Abies concolor

Evergreen coniferous tree

Abies concolor

▶ ***Hardiness:*** Zones 3–7
▶ ***Size:*** 30'–50' tall, 15'–30' wide
▶ ***Features:*** Grow white fir where its blue-tinted needles can show off against the sky or dark green plants. This easy-care tree keeps fresh foliage year-round and a conical Christmas tree shape throughout its life. This is the best fir for the Midwest and Eastern seaboard. More tolerant of city conditions than other firs. Also known as concolor fir. Foliage is fragrant.
▶ ***Uses:*** Specimen tree use; windbreaks; screening; background; adding fine texture, winter interest, and blue color to landscape compositions
▶ ***Needs:*** Plant in rich, moist, well-drained, sandy loam soil. Trees will tolerate rocky or dry soil, but growth is slower. Tolerates heat and cold equally well. Grow in full sun. Plant in a location where you won't need to prune.

Fir, Douglas

Pseudotsuga menziesii

Evergreen coniferous tree

Pseudotsuga menziesii

▶ ***Hardiness:*** Zones 4–6
▶ ***Size:*** 40'–80' high, 12'–20' wide
▶ ***Features:*** Plant this stately tree where it will have room to grow. Slightly curving branches grow in pyramidal fashion. A traditional forest tree, it makes the transition to the landscape beautifully. Trees are not suitable for use in windbreaks. May be sold as *P. douglasii.*
▶ ***Uses:*** Specimen use, large groves, corners of yards, large estates, screening views, mass plantings
▶ ***Needs:*** Plant in well-drained, moist, acidic soil. Dry, poor soils or windy conditions are unsuitable. Grow in full sun.
▶ ***Choices:*** 'Fastigiata'—upright, conical shape; 40'–80' tall, spread to 20'. *P. menziesii glauca*—needles are blue-green; 40'–80' tall, spread 12'–20'. 'Oudemansii'—15'–30' tall, spread 12'–20'.

Firethorn; Pyracantha

Pyracantha coccinea

Evergreen shrub

Pyracantha coccinea

▶ ***Hardiness:*** Zones 6–8
▶ ***Size:*** 6'–18' tall and wide
▶ ***Features:*** In spring the stiff, sprawling branches of firethorn are covered with foamy white flowers; in late summer, fall, and winter they boast heavy loads of orange-red berries. The evergreen foliage is attractive throughout the year. Plants adapt to any kind of dry soil. Stems are thorny. Berries are produced on 2-year-old wood; overpruning will reduce fruiting. Berries attract birds; over the course of winter the berries that persist ferment, and robins returning in spring often become inebriated on them.
▶ ***Uses:*** Hedges, barriers, espalier, slopes, massing, specimen plants, seasonal accents, attracting birds, filling in hot, dry areas in yards
▶ ***Needs:*** Plant in any well-drained soil; dry soil is fine, as is alkaline or acidic soil. Grow in full sun or partial shade.

Firethorn, Yukon Belle

Pyracantha angustifolia 'Yukon Belle'

Semievergreen to evergreen shrub

Pyracantha angustifolia 'Yukon Belle'

▶ ***Hardiness:*** Zones 5–9
▶ ***Size:*** 5'–8' tall, 4'–6' wide
▶ ***Features:*** This thorny shrub spills out fountains of white flowers in early summer. Bright orange berries follow in autumn and linger through winter, long after the leaves are gone. Birds love this shrub because of its berries and protection for nests. This shrub is thorny; avoid placing it in areas where children play or near walkways.
▶ ***Uses:*** Hedges, barriers, espalier on a wall or chimney
▶ ***Needs:*** Plant in fertile, moist, well-drained soil. Full sun yields best flowering and fruiting, but this shrub will grow in partial shade. Prune as needed in any season. Once this shrub is established, it doesn't take well to transplanting.
▶ ***Choices:*** 'Gnome'—orange berries; to 6' tall and wide; Zones 4–9.

Fittonia spp.
see Nerve Plant

Flaming Sword
see Bromeliads

Flax, Blue
Linum perenne

Perennial

Linum perenne

▶***Hardiness:*** Zones 5-8
▶***Size:*** 18"-24" tall, 12" wide
▶***Features:*** Violet, blue-violet, or white flowers appear late spring to early summer on arching stems.
▶***Uses:*** In the mixed flower bed and border, as a filler between earlier- and later-blooming plants. Good for naturalizing in meadow and informal cottage gardens.
▶***Needs:*** Full sun to part shade. Average to sandy, well-drained soil. Moderate moisture. Drought-tolerant. Plant established plants in spring. Avoid fertilizing. Mulch, if desired, to conserve moisture. However, mulch will retard this plant's light self-sowing. Cut back by one-half to two-thirds after flowering to prevent floppiness. This plant tends to die out after a few years but often will reseed, ensuring an ongoing supply. Seedlings are easy to pull or move to another location. Prone to damage by grasshoppers.
▶***Choices:*** 'Saphyr' is a popular cultivar with sapphire blue flowers on 8"-10" plants. 'Diamond' has white flowers and grows to about the same height.

Flax, New Zealand
Phormium tenax

Subtropical evergreen perennial

Phormium colensoi 'Sunset'

▶***Hardiness:*** Zones 8-11
▶***Size:*** 7'-9' tall, 7'-10' wide. Flower stalks can rise 15' tall
▶***Features:*** Few plants exceed the drama of this New Zealand native. Huge pointed, sword-shape leaves arch stiffly 7' or more out of clumps that can grow 10' wide. Numerous cultivars are available with multicolored, striped, and solid leaves in a variety of hues from bronze and gray-green to yellow, pink, and red. Established plants send up towering flower stalks topped with red or red-orange flowers. Best in western climates of California, where summers are dry and winters are moist. Plants are tough and low maintenance.
▶***Uses:*** As a big, dramatic accent in the landscape
▶***Needs:*** Well-drained soil, full sun to light shade. Be sure to give this plant plenty of room to grow. It is natural for the outer leaves of plants to fade and die as the clump grows; remove these by cutting them at the base for a neater appearance. Remove flower stalks after flowers wither.
▶***Choices:*** Many cultivars are available for a wide range of leaf color and pattern. Recently, many hybrids between New Zealand flax and mountain flax *(Phormium colensoi)* have been introduced. Most are smaller plants well-adapted to growing in containers as patio plants, and are increasingly sold as annuals to grow for a single summer in a mixed container. In mixed containers they make beautiful fountain-shape anchors in the center.

Fleabane
Erigeron hybrids

Perennial

Erigeron hybrid

▶***Hardiness:*** Zones 2-10
▶***Size:*** 9"-30" tall, 24" wide
▶***Features:*** Daisylike flowers with bright yellow centers grow in neat clumps of mounded foliage. Suitable for moist growing areas. Locate fleabane where you'll be able to water regularly, since plants like moist soils and are not drought tolerant. Group them together in odd numbers of at least three plants for the best effect. Flowers are good for cutting. This plant often self-sows and can become a nuisance.
▶***Uses:*** Entries, beside patios, along walkways, in front of taller shrubs, in mixed flower beds
▶***Needs:*** Plant in full sun in well-drained, fertile soil. Soil should not dry out between waterings. Put plants in midday shade in warmer climates. Remove spent blooms to increase flowering. Shape plants by cutting stems back to just above a leaf.

Flossflower
see *Ageratum*

Flowering Cabbage, Flowering Kale

Brassica oleracea

Cool-season annual

Brassica oleracea

▶ ***Size:*** 12"–24" tall and 12"–18" wide
▶ ***Features:*** These plants are grown for their marvelous, brilliantly colored foliage that is showy from late summer long into winter when everything else has gone to bed. In mild climates they are sometimes grown for effect from winter through the spring bulb season, and even interplanted with tulips. Flowering kale differs from flowering cabbage in having crinkled and ruffled leaves. The two are varieties of the same species.
▶ ***Uses:*** Cool-season annual bedding color. Performs well in containers. Good in combination with spring bulbs in mild climates where it can be started early outdoors.
▶ ***Needs:*** Average, well-drained soil. Moderate water. Plant established plants in fall. Fertilize at planting time. Mulch to conserve moisture. This plant looks good well past first frost in all zones and will hold its color through winter in Zones 8–11. Tear out in spring or as soon as plants become unattractive. It is prone to cabbageworms, slugs, cutworms, and clubroot.
▶ ***Choices:*** Deep green outer leaves set off showy inner leaves of red, cream, and pink. 'Peacock' is colorful and feathery.

Flowering Maple

Abutilon ×hybridum

Subtropical shrub

Abutilon ×hybridum 'Souvenir de Bonn'

▶ ***Hardiness:*** Zones 8–11
▶ ***Size:*** Grows up to 5' tall and wide depending on growing conditions and pot size
▶ ***Features:*** Also called Chinese lantern or parlor maple. Has large, 3" maplelike leaves in varying shades of green or variegated with white or yellow. The 2" pink, red, or yellow flowers that bloom in spring through summer hang down like earrings and look like small hibiscus flowers. Easy to grow.
▶ ***Uses:*** As a houseplant, though in mild-winter climates it can be grown as a shrub.
▶ ***Needs:*** Blooms best in direct light, but bright to medium light is fine. Plant will bloom less and get leggy in lower light. Likes plenty of moisture; keep soil evenly moist. Average temperatures and humidity. In late fall, cut back by about half to ensure a bushier plant in spring. Also during this time, allow soil to dry out somewhat between waterings and keep in a cool place between 50°–60°F/10°–16°C until late winter.
▶ ***Choices:*** Look for variegated leaves and different flower colors. 'Canary Bird' has yellow flowers, 'Boule de Neige' has white, 'Fireball' is red, and 'Souvenir de Bonn' is pink.

Flowering Tobacco

Nicotiana hybrids

Warm-season annual

Nicotiana 'Domino'

▶ ***Size:*** 6"–18" tall, 6"–10" wide, depending on cultivar
▶ ***Features:*** The many hybrid cultivars of flowering tobacco come in shades of pink, white, red, and chartreuse, and a range of sizes from 6" to 14" tall. They are outstanding for summer-long color when massed. Some varieties are lightly fragrant.
▶ ***Uses:*** Summer-long annual bedding color. Excellent in containers.
▶ ***Needs:*** Usually light shade, but full sun if humid or in Zones 2–3. Rich, well-drained soil. Moderate moisture. Likes heat. Plant established plants in spring after all danger of frost has passed. Mulch. Fertilize occasionally. This plant is usually killed by frost; in Zones 10–11 it may last the winter and act as a perennial.
▶ ***Choices:*** 'Nicki' and 'Domino' are two long-popular hybrids that grow about 18" tall. *Nicotiana sylvestris* grows up to 6' tall, blooms in white, stays open all day, is richly fragrant at night, and attracts hummingbird moths. It will reseed profusely but is easy to control. *N. langsdorffii* has chartreuse tubular flowers that attract hummingbirds. It grows 3'–5' tall.

Foam Flower, Allegheny

Tiarella cordifolia

Perennial

Tiarella cordifolia

▶ ***Hardiness:*** Zones 4–9
▶ ***Size:*** 6"–12" tall, 12"–24" wide
▶ ***Features:*** Feathery white flowers appear in spring above light-green foliage. In fall the foliage turns a lovely bronze-red. When grown with the proper conditions, plants spread quickly to make large, lush patches. Plants spread by underground stems and can quickly take over in moist, shady areas.
▶ ***Uses:*** Moist shaded areas, planting beneath acid-loving shrubs and trees, woodland gardens, rock gardens, perennial flower borders
▶ ***Needs:*** Grow in deep or partial shade. Plant in well-drained, moist, fertile, slightly acidic soil. Mix in peat moss or composted leaves at planting and apply a 3-inch-thick layer to the soil's surface each spring. Avoid sunny, dry, alkaline conditions. Plants prefer cool locations.
▶ ***Choices:*** 'Dark Eyes' has leaves marked with burgundy; 'Tiger Stripe' has light-green leaves with red centers. Wherry's oakleaf foam flower *(Tiarella wherryi* 'Oakleaf'*)* has deeply lobed leaves and showy pink-tinged flowers.

Forget-Me-Not, Chinese

Cynoglossum amabile

Annual

Cynoglossum amabile

►**Size:** 18"–30" tall, 10"–20" wide
►**Features:** Dense clusters of blue flowers in late spring or early summer, showier than *Myosotis*.
►**Uses:** In the flower border
►**Needs:** Sun or light shade. Average to rich, well-drained soil. Plenty of moisture. Sow seed directly onto soil, or plant as seedlings. Plant in early spring as soon as soil can be worked in Zones 2–7; in fall in Zones 8–9. Avoid fertilizing. Trim spent blooms to promote flowering. Pull out plants when they have finished blooming in summer. This plant usually reseeds freely, coming back year after year. It is prone to mildew, especially if not well watered.
►**Choices:** Plants are renowned for electric blue color, but white and pink cultivars are available. 'Firmament' is especially stocky and less prone to flopping.

Forget-Me-Not, Woodland

Myosotis sylvatica

Annual or biennial

Myosotis sylvatica

►**Size:** 6"–18" tall and wide
►**Features:** Delicate, open and airy sprays of tiny, intensely blue flowers in early to late spring. Some cultivars are smaller and more compact, producing dense mounds of blue or pink blossoms.
►**Uses:** Let it naturalize freely in the woodland garden. Gorgeous planted between spring bulbs.
►**Needs:** Full sun to part shade in Zones 4–6; part shade in Zones 7–9. Rich to poor, well-drained soil that stays moist. Ample to moderate moisture. In Zones 4–6 plant by scattering seed on prepared soil 2–3 weeks in early spring before last frost date. In Zones 7–9 plant seeds in late autumn. In all zones plant established plants outdoors in late winter or early spring, a few weeks before last frost. Avoid fertilizing. Deadhead to prevent reseeding. Mulch if desired, but this will reduce reseeding.
►**Choices:** Blue, but sometimes pink varieties are available. It is sometimes sold incorrectly as *Myosotis alpestris*. 'Victoria' is a popular intense blue. 'Victoria Rosea' is pink.

Forget-Me-Not, Hybrid

Myosotis hybrids

Perennial

Myosotis 'Ball Pink'

►**Hardiness:** Zones 3–8
►**Size:** 6"–12" tall, 8"–12" wide
►**Features:** Dainty blue or pink flowers with yellow eyes cover low-growing plants in midspring. They require abundant moisture to perform their best; the perfect locations are damp, shady spots near water or naturalized in moist woodlands. Prostrate plants spread by stolons. Rapid growth.
►**Uses:** Moist areas, planting beside water features, edges of woodlands, near downspouts, banks of streams
►**Needs:** Plant in fertile, moist soil. Partial shade is best, but plants can handle full sun in cooler areas where moisture is consistent. Cutting back after flowering promotes compact growth.

Forsythia, Border

Forsythia ×intermedia

Deciduous flowering shrub

Forsythia ×intermedia

►**Hardiness:** Zones 5–9
►**Size:** 8'–10' tall, 7'–10' wide
►**Features:** This big, arching shrub welcomes spring in daffodil season with sunshine yellow blooms. It's easy to grow, but give this rapid grower plenty of room. Prune after flowering by removing oldest wood to the ground. Tolerant of city conditions.
►**Uses:** Informal hedge or screen, massed plantings, and banks
►**Needs:** Full sun for best flowering; will tolerate light shade. Average to rich, well-drained soil is best, but tolerates a wide variety of soils, from moist to dry and acidic to alkaline. Ample to moderate moisture is best. Plant established plants in spring or fall. No need to fertilize or trim spent blooms. Mulch to conserve moisture. Flowers bloom on old wood grown the previous year. Little pruning is needed, but do any necessary pruning immediately after flowering. Large, arching form is inappropriate for formal gardens or shaping. Shearing destroys the plant's natural shape. If pruning is desired, selectively cut out the oldest and weakest stems to right above the ground. Every few years, cut the entire shrub back to about a foot to renew and control size. This shrub is prone to few serious pests or diseases.
►**Choices:** 'Lynwood' and 'Spring Gold' are the most popular varieties. 'Northern Sun', 'Northern Gold', and 'Meadowlark' are good choices for colder areas; they are hardy to Zone 4. *Forsythia suspensa* has a gracefully pendulous form good for spilling down banks.

Forsythia, Vermont Sun
Forsythia mandshurica 'Vermont Sun'

Deciduous flowering shrub

Forsythia mandshurica 'Vermont Sun'

▶ ***Hardiness:*** Zones 4-8
▶ ***Size:*** 6'-8' tall, 4'-6' wide
▶ ***Features:*** Vermont sun forsythia is the ideal forsythia for colder regions. Its yellow flowers in early spring make an attractive shrub border or screen. Flower buds will withstand temperatures as low as -30°F/-34°C and open about 1 week before other types of forsythia. Foliage turns beautiful shades of yellow, pink, and red in the fall.
▶ ***Uses:*** Seasonal accent, informal screens or hedges, hillsides, natural areas, massing, shrub beds
▶ ***Choices:*** *Forsythia ovata* 'Northern Gold' is hardy to -25°F/-32°C.

Forsythia, White
Abeliophyllum distichum

Deciduous flowering shrub

Abeliophyllum distichum

▶ ***Hardiness:*** Zones 4-8
▶ ***Size:*** 3'-5' tall, 3'-4' wide
▶ ***Features:*** This ugly duckling becomes a swan when covered with fragrant white flowers. Blooms have a blush of pale pink. One of the first shrubs to bloom; flowers appear in March and early April. Plant in front of a dark background for contrast. Prune annually immediately after flowering to encourage vigorous new growth and abundant blooms next year.
▶ ***Uses:*** Specimen shrub, seasonal accent, late winter interest, informal deciduous screen, natural areas, hillsides, sunny areas
▶ ***Needs:*** Plant in fertile, well-drained soil that's acidic or alkaline. Grow in full sun. Prune heavily immediately after flowering to control size. Cutting late will remove flower buds for the following spring. Easy to transplant.

Fothergilla, Large
Fothergilla major (formerly *F. monticola*)

Deciduous shrub

Fothergilla major

▶ ***Hardiness:*** 4-8
▶ ***Size:*** 6'-10' tall; 5'-9' wide
▶ ***Features:*** Position large fothergilla prominently where you can enjoy the show. The curtain rises in spring with the appearance of white bottlebrushlike blooms that smell sweetly of honey. Summer leaves are dark, leathery, and free of holes and disease. In fall, the foliage explodes into a display of red-orange-scarlet-yellow fireworks. All colors are possible on the same plant and at the same time.
▶ ***Uses:*** Shrub borders, foundations, mass plantings, near patios and outdoor seating areas, planting near other acid-loving shrubs and perennials
▶ ***Needs:*** Plant in well-drained, fertile, acidic soil. Does not tolerate alkaline soil. Full sun is best for the most flowers and best fall color; in southern locales, some shade is required. Moderate moisture. Plant in spring or fall, working ample compost into the planting hole. Avoid pruning or removing lower stems, which help fill out the plant. This shrub produces suckers; trim these regularly. Few diseases or pests bother this plant.
▶ ***Choices:*** 'Mt. Airy'—larger flowers, more reliable fall color; *F. gardenii* (dwarf fothergilla)—Only 2'-3' tall and wide, with a blue cast to the summer foliage. The fragrant white flowers are smaller too. Fall color is spectacularly neon and multicolored.

Four-o-Clock; Marvel-of-Peru
Mirabilis jalapa

Warm-season annual; tuberous-rooted perennial in mild climates

Mirabilis jalapa

▶ ***Hardiness:*** Zones 8-11
▶ ***Size:*** 2'-3' tall and wide
▶ ***Features:*** Cheerful bushy plants are loaded with multicolored, fragrant flowers that open in late afternoon and into the evening. The flowers come in white, red, yellow, pink, orange, and bicolors, sometimes with many different colors on the same plant. Blooms midsummer to frost.
▶ ***Uses:*** Lovely in the mixed flower border with other hot colors, or used as a low, temporary hedge or shrub. Plant it around pools, patios, entrances and windows where you can enjoy the evening fragrance.
▶ ***Needs:*** Annual in Zones 2-6; perennial in Zones 7-11. Prefers full sun; tolerates light shade. Average to rich, well-drained soil. Best with ample moisture but will tolerate heat, drought, and neglect. Plant established plants in spring after all danger of frost has passed. This plant looks best in groups of a dozen or more. It often self-sows freely. Mulch to keep soil moist and control weeds and reseeding. Fertilize occasionally, every 4-6 weeks, or work in a slow-release fertilizer in spring. Deadheading not

needed. In Zones 6-7, provide winter mulch to help plants survive the winter. In colder zones tuberous roots can be dug and stored. Plants are usually pest and disease free.
▶ **Choices:** Flowers come in brilliant pinks, reds, yellows, and whites; often mottled.

Foxglove

Digitalis purpurea

Biennial or perennial

Digitalis purpurea

▶ **Hardiness:** Zones 4-8
▶ **Size:** 2'-5' tall, 1'-2' wide
▶ **Features:** Tall, stately spikes of charming bell-shape flowers are as essential as hollyhocks for the informal cottage garden. Flowers are in shades of rose, pink, white, and yellow. This is a biennial that forms a rosette of evergreen leaves in the first year and blooms the second. After blooming the plants die, but they reseed freely in good locations. Blooms appear in late spring or early summer.
▶ **Uses:** Gorgeous in cottage gardens planted with old garden roses (they bloom in the same season). Lovely against a picket fence. Makes a good vertical accent in any garden.
▶ **Needs:** Full sun in Zones 4-7; partial shade in Zones 8-9. Rich, well-drained soil. Some types tolerate less water, but moderate to ample moisture is ideal. Plant established seedlings of any type of common foxglove in spring. For biennial types you can plant seeds directly in soil in midsummer and keep moist. In warm Zones 7-9, you can plant established seedlings in fall for bloom the following spring. Plant in groups of 10 or more for best effect and easiest care. Stake as needed. Mulch. This plant reseeds. It has naturalized in the open woodlands of the Pacific Northwest.
▶ **Choices:** Depending on climate and the type, foxglove can be grown as an annual, biennial or perennial. 'Excelsior' hybrids bloom the first year from seed with a mix of pastel pink, rose, white, and yellow flowers. *Digitalis grandiflora* is a true perennial; it has pale yellow tubular flowers and grows 3' tall. Strawberry foxglove (*D.* ×*mertonensis*) had 5'-7' spires of coppery rose flowers; it is a short-lived perennial that often blooms for two or three successive years.

Foxtail Lily

Eremurus spp.

Perennial grown from a rhizome

Eremurus spp.

▶ **Hardiness:** Zones 5-8
▶ **Size:** 2'-7' tall, 2'-3' wide
▶ **Features:** Plant foxtail lily for a dramatic vertical accent in late spring and early summer. Hundreds of small white or pastel blooms cover the upper half of each dense, bottlebrush-shape spike that rises 3'-7' above fountains of strappy foliage. As many as 7 or 8 spikes may arise from a single established plant. It makes a superb cut flower that may last for several weeks in the vase. After bloom is over the foliage dies back to the ground.
▶ **Uses:** The mixed flower border, meadows, cottage gardens, the cut flower garden. Like *Allium gigantium,* foxtail lily is gorgeous interplanted with ornamental grasses that expand later in the summer to cover the bulbs' dying foliage.
▶ **Needs:** This plant must have full sun. Rich, very well-drained (sandy is good) soil. Moderate moisture while growing; tolerates drought once dormant in late summer and fall. Plant rhizomes in fall; plant established plants in spring. Fertilize during bloom time. Handle roots carefully; they're brittle and tend to rot if damaged. Stake taller types. Foliage dies down after blooming; mark spot to avoid injuring the roots. It is susceptible to slugs and snails.
▶ **Choices:** Plants come in whites, pinks, yellows, and oranges. Read label carefully to choose desired height. *Eremurus stenophyllus* grows 2'-3'. *E. robustus* may reach 10'.

Fragaria 'Pink Panda'

see Strawberry, Pink Panda

Fragaria vesca

see Strawberry, Alpine

Fraxinus spp.

see Ash

Freesia

Freesia spp.

Perennial bulb

Freesia spp.

▶ **Hardiness:** Zones 8-11 in the West
▶ **Size:** 12"-18" tall, 6"-12" wide
▶ **Features:** Clusters of luminous flowers in yellow, gold, orange, pink, purple, violet, or white appear in spring.
▶ **Uses:** Except where it acts as a perennial—in the dry-summer, wet-winter, mild climates of southern California—freesia is most often grown as a houseplant or purchased in bloom in containers. It makes an interesting annual in nearly all climates.
▶ **Needs:** Perennial in Zones 9-11 where summers are dry and winters are cool and moist; grow as an annual elsewhere. Full sun or very light shade, especially in Zones 8-11. Average, well-drained, preferably sandy soil. Ample moisture during growth; less during summer dormancy. In Zones 2-8 plant corms in spring after all danger of frost has passed. In Zones 9-11 plant corms in fall. Plant 2" deep. Cluster in groups of a dozen or more for support; stake as needed. Temperatures of 60°-70°F/16°-21°C in the day and 50°-60°F/10°-16°C at night are best; it will go dormant in summer in hot regions. In wet-summer regions, corms should be dug and stored or treated as annuals. In Zones 2-8 dig corms in fall.

Freeway Daisy

Osteospermum fruticosum

Perennial or annual groundcover

Osteospermum fruticosum

▶Hardiness: Zones 9–11
▶Size: 1'-2' tall, 10'-15' wide
▶Features: Named for its ability to grow along Southern California freeways, this tough plant likes it hot. White daisylike blooms with purple centers appear throughout the year, though flowering is most profuse in spring. Hybrid varieties are compact and bloom heavily; they are often vegetatively propagated and sold as annual bedding plants. This tough plant is tolerant of heat, drought, wind, and salt air.
▶Uses: Groundcover, seaside landscapes, Xeriscaping, arid landscapes, slopes, parking areas, accent, massing in shrub beds
▶Needs: Plant in well-drained soil, including sand. Full sun provides best bloom. Thrives with regular watering. Pinch tips to encourage bushy growth. Cut back long branches on older plants.

Freeway Ice Plant

see Ice Plant, Freeway

Fringed Bleeding Heart

see Bleeding Heart

Fringe Flower, Chinese

Loropetalum chinense

Semievergreen flowering shrub

Loropetalum chinense ssp. *rubrum* 'Razzleberri'

▶Hardiness: Zones 7–9
▶Size: 6'-10' tall and wide
▶Features: Showy pink, red, or white flowers in late winter and early spring, good fall and winter foliage color, horizontally layered shape, and attractive red-leaved cultivars have made this recent introduction from China a winner among Southern gardeners. The flowers have drooping, straplike petals that create a feathery effect; they are borne in profusion and are especially attractive against the burgundy or bronze leaves of some cultivars.
Its graceful form makes it the perfect foundation plant, especially near entrances.
▶Uses: Foundation plant, in the shrub border, as a specimen. There are lower-growing cultivars useful as a large-scale groundcover.
▶Needs: Best in acidic, moist, well-drained soils high in organic matter. Will not survive in alkaline soils or dry, stony soils. Partial shade is best, although it tolerates full sun.

Fringe Tree, Chinese

Chionanthus retusus

Deciduous flowering tree

Chionanthus retusus

▶Hardiness: Zones 6–8
▶Size: 10'-25' tall, 8'-10' wide
▶Features: Pretty little round tree is covered with unusual-looking blooms in late spring. Fleecy panicles are snow white and fragrant. Male trees produce larger, showier blooms and no fruit. Females produce attractive flowers as well as ornamental fruit. Older plants develop ornamental bark that is gray to brown and peeling. Trees are not picky about growing conditions; they will tolerate almost anything. May be sold as grancy graybeard.
▶Uses: Specimen use, small yards, seasonal accent, empty corners, attracting birds, natural areas, planting beds
▶Needs: Plant in full sun or deep shade in fertile soil that's wet or dry. Acidic soils are ideal, but alkaline conditions are tolerable. Grow as a small tree or large shrub. To grow as a small tree, prune away undesired stems in late winter or early spring.

Fritillary; Crown Imperial; Checkered Lily

Fritillaria spp.

Spring-blooming bulb

Fritillaria imperialis

▶Hardiness: Zones 3–7
▶Size: 6"-4' tall, depending on variety
▶Features: Charming clusters of bell-shape blooms, usually mottled or streaked in contrasting colors, dangle from relaxed stems in spring.
▶Uses: In borders, meadows, woodland gardens. Performs well in containers.
▶Needs: Full sun or part shade. Rich, well-drained soil. Moderate water, though less once dormant in summer. Plant bulbs as soon as available in fall, usually September, to keep them from drying out. Plant 4"-6" deep. Crown imperial is spaced 8"-12"; checkered lily 3"-4". Place in ground at a 45-degree angle to prevent tops from collecting water. Best in groups of 2 to 3. After blooming, leave browning foliage. It's needed to rejuvenate the plant. Remove brown foliage when it pulls off without resistance.
▶Choices: Crown imperial *(Fritillaria imperialis,* Zones 5–8) is a tall, dramatic species, lovely in beds and borders. It produces 2'-4' stems that at the top bear a ring of orange, red, or yellow flowers capped by a dense tuft of small leaves. Mulch for winter protection. Checkered lily *(F. meleagris,* Zones 3–8) does less well in hot, dry climates. It bears 1 to 3 checked and veined flowers from deep brown to rosy lilac, wine, or white.

Fuchsia

Fuchsia hybrids

Evergreen and deciduous shrubs

Fuchsia hybrid

▶***Hardiness:*** Zones 8–10, but varies
▶***Size:*** 18"–3' or more tall, depending on variety
▶***Features:*** Blooms spring through frost
▶***Uses:*** Outdoors in the shrub border or in patio containers and hanging baskets in Zones 8–10. In more northern zones grow as an annual in containers and hanging baskets.
▶***Needs:*** Grown as an annual in Zones 2–7; as a woody perennial or small to large shrub in Zones 8–11. Average, neutral to acidic, well-drained soil. Needs moderate to ample moisture. Never allow to dry out. Plant established plants in spring. Use potting soil if plants are grown in a container. Pinch tips of small plants at planting time for better bushiness. Mulch to conserve moisture. Fertilize with a liquid fertilizer every 2–3 weeks. Pinch off spent blooms to promote more flowering. This plant is prone to mites, spider mites, whiteflies, and aphids.
▶***Choices:*** The elaborate flowers come in pinks, purples, reds, and white. Often the same flower may have two colors. There are hundreds of cultivars.

Fumewort

see Corydalis

Gaillardia spp.

see Blanket Flower

Galium odoratum

see Sweet Woodruff

Gardener's Garters

see Grasses, Ornamental: Ribbon Grass

Gardenia; Cape Jasmine

Gardenia jasminoides, (formerly *Gardenia augusta*)

Evergreen shrub

Gardenia jasminoides

▶***Hardiness:*** Zones 8–10
▶***Size:*** 2'–4' tall, 3'–6' wide
▶***Features:*** Gardenia will reward you with irresistible fragrant white blossoms and attractive glossy evergreen foliage in many sizes and varieties. Problem insects are common. Control with insecticide at the first sign of infestation.
▶***Uses:*** Low hedges or screens, containers, accents in planting beds
▶***Needs:*** Full sun to light shade. Extremely well-drained, humus-rich, moist, acidic soil. Improve soil by working shredded leaves, sphagnum peat moss, ground bark, bagged humus, or compost into the planting hole. Where soil is poor-draining, grow in large pots. Needs ample moisture; water frequently. Specific climate requirements. Survives to 0°F/-18°C, but dies back to ground. Hardy to about 10°F/-12°C without damage. When forming flower buds, it needs nighttime temperatures of 50°–55°F/10°–13°C and sufficient summer heat to bloom. Mulch with 2"–3" of mulch to prevent cultivating around shallow roots. Feed monthly with an acidic fertilizer. Prune only to remove straggly branches or trim spent blooms.

Garlic

Allium sativum

Annual vegetable

Garlic

▶***Hardiness:*** Zones 2–11
▶***Size:*** 1' tall, 2"–3" wide
▶***Features:*** Versatile vegetable adds flavor to many foods
▶***Uses:*** In the vegetable garden
▶***Needs:*** Full sun. Rich, well-drained soil with moderate moisture; tolerates dry soil. Will rot in wet soils. Adapted to many climates. Plant in October in Zones 7 and colder with a few inches of lightweight mulch on top; in November–January in Zones 8 and warmer. Break apart heads into cloves and insert into worked soil 1½"–2" deep, spaced 4"–6". Plant elephant garlic 4"–6" deep and space 6"–8". Near harvest, allow soil to become dry. Harvest in summer when half the leaves have yellowed and the necks of the leaves become soft. Gently dig up entire plant. Cure for a few weeks by laying on newspapers in a cool, airy place, such as a porch. Trim off tops or braid the foliage. Store indoors for several months.
▶***Choices:*** Large elephant garlic has recently become popular, partly for its more mild flavor. If you like intense garlic, plant more pungent cultivars, such as 'Spanish Roja'.

Gaultheria procumbens

see Wintergreen

Gaura, White

Gaura lindheimeri

Perennial

Gaura lindheimeri 'Pink Cloud'

▶***Hardiness:*** Zones 5–9
▶***Size:*** 3'–5' tall, 2'–3' wide
▶***Features:*** Dancing on wiry stems like clouds of butterflies, gaura's dainty flowers are pink in bud, open to white, then fade to pink again. This plant is a "leaner," ideal for growing among other perennials in the border that it can lean on for support. Blooms appear midsummer into fall and need no deadheading. Plants form clumps and are fast growing.
▶***Uses:*** In the mixed flower border; gorgeous planted among ornamental grasses
▶***Needs:*** Full sun; tolerates light shade in Zones 7–9. Sandy, well-drained soil; will tolerate some clay. Drought tolerant, but moderate moisture is best. Plant established plants in spring. Trim spent blooms to prolong flowering. Cut back in midsummer to control size and to encourage further flowering. If soil is too moist and rich, plants may sprawl; stake as needed. This plant has a deep taproot; division is seldom needed. Where well suited to existing conditions, it self-seeds to the point of being invasive. It is prone to leaf spot, rust, and mildews.
▶***Choices:*** 'Pink Cloud' has pale pink flowers. 'Whirling Butterfly' grows just 18"–24" tall and seldom reseeds. 'Siskiyou Pink' is deep pink and only 18"–24" tall. 'Crimson Butterfly' has reddish foliage and stems, and it grows only 18"–24" tall.

Gayfeather

see Blazing Star

Gazania

Gazania spp.

Annual or perennial

Gazania spp.

▶***Hardiness:*** Annual in Zones 2–7; perennial in Zones 8–11
▶***Size:*** 6"–12" tall, 6"–10" wide
▶***Features:*** Bears bright daisies in yellow, orange, red, or muted pink—often dazzlingly striped and banded in darker color. The flowers close at night. Blooms appear summer through frost or even all year in warmer climates. Thrives in heat.
▶***Uses:*** In borders, beds, and containers, as edgers and groundcovers. Gazania is often used as a groundcover in the mild climates of California, planted 12" apart.
▶***Needs:*** Grow as an annual in Zones 2–7; as a perennial in Zones 8–11. Full sun in Zones 2–8; will tolerate some shade in Zones 9–11. Average to poor, sandy, well-drained soil. Tolerates drought and heat well. Plant established plants in spring after all danger of frost has passed. Fertilize lightly if at all. Keep spent blooms trimmed to promote longest blooming; gazania will bloom year-round in warm-winter climates. In wet climates this plant is prone to crown rot.
▶***Choices:*** Flowers come in yellows, reds, and bronzes. 'Chansonette' is a compact early flowering variety.

Gelsemium sempervirens

see Jasmines; Jessamines

Genista spp.

see Brooms

Geranium, Hardy; Bloody Cranesbill

Geranium sanguineum

Perennial

Geranium sanguineum

▶***Hardiness:*** Zones 3–8
▶***Size:*** 9"–12" tall; 18"–24" wide
▶***Features:*** Summer flowers in shades of pink bloom abundantly in partial shade or sun. Tolerates heat, drought, and harsh winters. This long-lived perennial—available in magenta, pink, and lavender—is perfect for small gardens or for covering ground beneath shrubs. Foliage grown in full sun turns red in autumn. Moist soil aids plants in spreading.
▶***Uses:*** Planting beds, growing beneath shrubs or roses, beside patios, along walkways, in small spaces, formal or informal gardens, seasonal accents
▶***Needs:*** Plant in any soil that's well-drained; fertile soil is best. Full sun in Zones 4–6; part shade in Zones 7–8. Protect from afternoon sun in hotter climates. Mulch. Fertilize occasionally, every 4–6 weeks, or work in a 9-month slow-release fertilizer each spring. After the first flowering, shear back by as much as half once or twice during the growing season to keep growth compact and to encourage better blooming. This plant spreads rapidly; divide every 2–4 years as needed. This plant is pest and disease resistant.
▶***Choices:*** There are many species and hybrid cultivars of hardy geraniums, and all are lovely. They come in pinks, blues, whites, and purples. 'Johnson's Blue' is an especially lovely clear blue; 'Wargrave Pink' blooms all summer and fall.

Geranium; Bedding Geranium; Pelargonium

Pelargonium spp.

Annual; perennial in mild climates

Pelargonium ×*hortorum*

▶***Hardiness:*** Zones 8–11
▶***Size:*** Usually 18"–24" tall and wide, but can grow into a large shrub outdoors in frost-free climates.
▶***Features:*** Easy and vigorous, geraniums are a familiar sight in beds and containers throughout North America. One of the most highly bred of annuals, they are available in every warm hue imaginable, from white and pink to salmon, orange, and red. They bloom spring through frost or all year in mild climates. In the West they go by the common name of pelargonium.
▶***Uses:*** Often grown by themselves in pots or in bedding schemes, they are also useful in mixed borders and containers, hanging baskets, and window boxes, and are sometimes grown as houseplants.
▶***Needs:*** Full sun in Zones 2–8; light shade in Zones 9–11. Rich, well-drained soil. Moderate water, but ivy geranium (sold as *Pelargonium peltatum)* is drought tolerant. Grow as annuals in Zones 2–9 and as perennials in Zones 10–11. Plant established plants in spring after all danger of frost has passed. Mulch. Fertilize frequently. Trim spent blooms to encourage long flowering. Overwinter by digging up and potting. Keep in a sunny area indoors.
▶***Choices:*** Zonal geraniums (sold as *P. ×hortorum)* are the most common and are available in hundreds of varieties and seed strains. Scented geraniums (various species) are a large group, with scents including apple, coconut, lemon, peppermint, rose, and many others (citronella, reported to repel mosquitoes, is a scented geranium). They are popular subjects for collections. Ivy geraniums have small, starry flowers and a cascading habit that particularly suits them to hanging baskets and window boxes.

Gerbera

Gerbera spp.

Annual or perennial

Gerbera spp.

▶***Hardiness:*** Zones 7–10
▶***Size:*** 8"–24" tall, 6"–20" wide
▶***Features:*** Famous as a cut flower for the pure, intense colors of its sculptural daisies, gerbera is every bit as eye-catching in the garden. Flowers come in striking reds, yellows, peaches, pinks, and creams. Blooms midsummer through fall.
▶***Uses:*** In the front of the mixed flower or shrub border, in beds, in containers, in the cutting garden
▶***Needs:*** Grow as a cool-season annual in Zones 3–6; as a perennial in Zones 7–10. Full sun in Zones 3–6; part shade in hot summer in Zones 7–10. Rich, well-drained, preferably sandy soil. Moderate, even moisture. Plant established plants in early spring in Zones 3–6; in spring or fall in Zones 8–10. Fertilize occasionally, every 6 weeks, or work in a 9-month slow-release fertilizer in spring. Trim spent blooms regularly to promote flowering. It is prone to gray mold, aphids, whiteflies, thrips, and leaf miners.
▶***Choices:*** 'Rainbow' is especially easy to grow. 'California Giants' hits 2', while 'Skipper' is a compact 8" tall.

German Bearded Iris

see Iris

Germander, Wall

Teucrium chamaedrys

Evergreen shrub

Teucrium chamaedrys

▶***Hardiness:*** Zones 4–9
▶***Size:*** 12"–20" tall, 12"–24" wide
▶***Features:*** Medium to rapid growth. Carmine rose blooms in mid- to late summer. Grow germander where you want a little row of green. Plants adapt to both formal and informal gardens. Trim into desired forms or allow them to remain in their natural mounded form.
▶***Uses:*** Formal knot gardens; edging rose, herb, or flower beds; rock gardens; entries; edging patios or walkways
▶***Needs:*** Grow in full sun. Plant in well-drained, alkaline to neutral soil. Work lime into soil to increase alkalinity. Tolerates pruning to form a low hedge. For formal hedges, cut plants in early spring to within a few inches of the ground.

Geum

Geum spp.

Perennial

Geum chiloense 'Mrs. Bradshaw'

▶***Hardiness:*** Zones 4–7
▶***Size:*** 12"–24" tall, 12"–24" wide
▶***Features:*** The combination of hot, bright colors and an open, airy form make geum a good plant for the mixed border, especially planted among flowers with cooler hues such as larkspurs and *Verbena bonariensis,* or whites such as baby's breath. The flowers bloom over a long season from late spring through summer.
▶***Uses:*** The front of the mixed border; meadow gardens; cottage gardens. It makes a good cut flower.
▶***Needs:*** Best in full sun in cool regions, but in areas with hot summers afternoon shade is a must. Give it well-drained soil rich in organic matter. Space plants 12"–18" apart for shoulder-to-shoulder coverage. Water abundantly during the growing season. Deadhead to prolong bloom. This plant has few serious pests or diseases.
▶***Choices:*** 'Mrs. Bradshaw' is a popular old-time favorite with deep orange-red semi-double flowers. 'Mrs. Bradshaw Improved' is a newer version with larger flowers. 'Lady Stratheden' has hot-yellow flowers.

Ginkgo; Maidenhair Tree

Ginkgo biloba

Deciduous tree

Ginkgo biloba

▶ ***Hardiness:*** Zones 3-9
▶ ***Size:*** 50'-80' tall, 30'-50' wide
▶ ***Features:*** When Ginkgo's fan-shape leaves turn golden in autumn, they hold their color even after dropping to the ground. With its angular limbs and pyramidal to spreading form, this tree is considered one of the most attractive deciduous trees. Female trees produce messy fruit with an objectionable odor.
▶ ***Uses:*** Specimen use, seasonal accent, street trees, lining walkways or drives, parking areas, open lawns, large estates
▶ ***Needs:*** Plant in a range of soils including acidic, alkaline, sandy, or clay. Ginkgo grows best in full sun. Trees are drought resistant but grow faster with regular watering and a spring feeding of balanced fertilizer. Pruning is unnecessary except to remove lower limbs for clearance beneath the tree. Tolerates urban conditions, confined root spaces, heat, and cold. Easy to grow and pest free.
▶ ***Choices:*** Male clones without fruit include 'Autumn Gold' and the narrow, columnar-formed 'Fastigiata'.

Gladiolus

Gladiolus hybrids

Perennial corm often grown as an annual

Gladiolus hybrid

▶ ***Hardiness:*** Zones 8-11
▶ ***Size:*** 3'-5' tall, 8"-18" wide
▶ ***Features:*** This is one of the most beloved of cut flowers. Its tall, narrow form and heavy, magnificent flowers—which must be staked—are best kept in the cut-flower garden, although plants can be beautiful in the back of the border. Blooms in midsummer.
▶ ***Uses:*** In the cut flower garden or the rear of the mixed border where a vertical accent is desired
▶ ***Needs:*** Perennial in Zones 8-11 but best if grown as an annual. Full sun. Average to rich, well-drained soil. Ample water while growing and blooming, then moderate water.

Plant corms as soon as danger of frost has passed. In hot-summer areas (Zones 8-11) plant in late winter. Plant 4"-6" deep and work in compost or slow-release low-nitrogen fertilizer. For a succession of blooms, plant more every 2 or 3 weeks (they bloom 60 to 100 days after planting). Support by staking, especially in windy sites, or mound soil 6" around stems. Remove faded flower stalks immediately. When cutting flowers, leave at least 3 to 4 leaves so corms will have energy to mature next year. In late fall, lift and store corms to replant next year.

Gladiolus, Abyssinian

Gladiolus callianthus

Perennial

Gladiolus callianthus

▶ ***Hardiness:*** Zones 7-11
▶ ***Size:*** 30"-4' tall, 4"-6" wide
▶ ***Features:*** This smaller, more delicate- and wild-appearing cousin of the florist gladiolus is considerably hardier too. It's lovely in meadow gardens, cottage gardens, and the mixed border growing among ornamental grasses and other perennials and annuals that it can lean on for support. Like its more highly bred cousins, it makes an outstanding cut flower—and best of all, it's richly fragrant.
▶ ***Uses:*** The mixed border, cottage gardens, meadow gardens, the cut-flower garden
▶ ***Needs:*** Grown as an annual in Zones 3-6; as a perennial in Zones 7-11. Full sun. Rich, well-drained soil in a site protected from wind. Ample water. In Zones 3-6 start indoors in peat pots 4 weeks before last frost date, then transplant after all danger of frost. In Zones 7-11 plant in spring after all danger of frost. Plant 4"-6" deep. After plant emerges mulch to conserve moisture. Work in compost or a slow-release fertilizer each spring. Stake as needed. Trim spent blooms to prolong flowering for up to 2 months. In fall in Zones 3-6, if desired, lift and store the bulbs for the winter (see page 205). This plant is prone to thrips and mosaic virus.

Gleditsia triacanthos inermis

see Honeylocust, Thornless

Globe Amaranth

Gomphrena globosa

Annual

Gomphrena globosa 'Lavender Lady'

▶ ***Size:*** 8"-2' tall, 10"-20" wide
▶ ***Features:*** While most of the taller-growing varieties of globe amaranth are best in the cutting garden, the newer lower-growing forms make outstanding bedding plants for hot, dry places. This is an excellent cut flower and a favorite for drying. Blooms midsummer through fall.
▶ ***Uses:*** The cutting garden, bedding, the mixed flower border. Performs well in containers.
▶ ***Needs:*** Average to poor or sandy, well-drained soil. Does best with moderate water, but tolerates drought. Plant seedlings in spring after all danger of frost has passed. Fertilize regularly, every 4 weeks, or work in a 9-month slow-release fertilizer at planting time. Taller varieties may flop; stake as needed. Aphids and spider mites are sometimes a problem.
▶ ***Choices:*** Flowers are pinks, whites, purples, reds, and oranges. 'Strawberry Fields' is a popular red type; 'Lavender Lady' is an elegant lavender. 'Buddy' grows only 8" tall.

Globe Thistle

Echinops ritro

Perennial

Echinops ritro

▶ ***Hardiness:*** Zones 3–8
▶ ***Size:*** 2'–4' tall, 2'–3' wide
▶ ***Features:*** Spiky spheres of lavender or steely blue bloom in mid- or late summer on plants that are tall, prickly columns. Interesting foliage texture combines well with ornamental grasses, false sunflowers.
▶ ***Uses:*** The mixed border; this is not a stand-alone plant.
▶ ***Needs:*** Average to poor, well-drained soil. Best with moderate water but will tolerate drought when mature. Plant established seedlings in spring or autumn. Avoid fertilizing; if soil is too rich, staking will be needed. Deadhead after bloom is finished. Divide plants in spring or fall every 3–4 years as needed. This plant is usually pest free.
▶ ***Choices:*** 'Taplow Blue' is a popular cultivar.

Gloriosa Daisy

see Black-Eyed Susan

Gloxinia

Sinningia speciosa

Tropical perennial

Sinningia speciosa

▶ ***Size:*** 8" tall and wide
▶ ***Features:*** Stunning, bell-shape velvety flowers in red, white, violet, and pink with plain or ruffled edges bloom for 2 months or more. Often bought as a potted plant and then discarded after flowering stops. However, if provided with the right conditions, it can be coaxed into flowering again.
▶ ***Uses:*** Flowering houseplant
▶ ***Needs:*** Bright, indirect light. Water with tepid, not cold, water and keep the water off leaves and flowers. Average household warmth. Ample humidity is a must; set on a tray of pebbles and water—but a humidifier in the area is much better—or grow in a miniature conservatory. Fertilize with a half-strength fertilizer every time you water. To encourage repeat bloom, reduce watering after flowering and do not feed. Allow soil to dry out once leaves turn yellow. Store the pot in a cool area, about 50°F/10°C. In spring, repot the roots in fresh potting soil. Keep warm and rather dry until leaves appear. Then resume regular care.
▶ ***Choices:*** Some plants have double flowers. The Maxima group has nodding flowers; the Fyfiana group has large, upright flowers.

Goatsbeard

Aruncus dioicus

Perennial

Aruncus dioicus

▶ ***Hardiness:*** Zones 3–7
▶ ***Size:*** 4'–6' tall, 6' wide
▶ ***Features:*** Like a giant astilbe, goatsbeard produces huge white panicles of blooms that look like feathers. They are followed by shiny black berries that if left on the plant provide winter interest. This is a big perennial that should be used as a shrub in the landscape. It blooms in late spring to early summer.
▶ ***Uses:*** For mass in the woodland garden. Beautiful as a large-scale echo when planted as a backdrop for a bed of astilbe. In a sunnier spot, goatsbeard is a good support for a late-blooming clematis that can be cut back hard each spring; the clematis will give the goatsbeard needed shade during the height of summer, while extending the bloom effect.
▶ ***Needs:*** Will tolerate full sun in Zones 3–4 but needs shade in Zones 5–7. It needs rich, moist, deep soil high in organic matter. Always keep soil moist. Plant established plants in spring or fall, working compost into the soil. Mulch to conserve moisture. Fertilize occasionally, every 6 weeks, or work in a 9-month slow-release fertilizer each spring. Division is usually not necessary but can be done in spring with difficulty. The roots are large and hard to cut. Plants are troubled by few pests or diseases, but leaf edges will turn brown with insufficient water.
▶ ***Choices:*** Flowers are creamy white. 'Kneiffii' is a popular dwarf cultivar that is only 3' high when in bloom. It has finely divided, lacy foliage. Dwarf goatsbeard *(A. aethusifolius)* is just 12" tall in bloom, which occurs 2 weeks earlier than for other goatsbeards.

Godetia

Clarkia amoena

Annual

Clarkia amoena

▶ ***Size:*** 18"–24" tall, 9"–12" wide
▶ ***Features:*** Godetia is a lovely addition to the spring garden, especially in the West. Cup-shape blooms with contrasting margins and centers come in shades of white, pink, and red. Blooms appear for a few weeks in late spring and early summer. They quit when the summer heats up.
▶ ***Uses:*** Seasonal color in beds and borders.
▶ ***Needs:*** Full sun in Zones 2–5; partial shade in Zones 6–11. Poor, well-drained soil. Moderate moisture. In Zones 2–7 plant seeds directly in soil in early spring, as early as 2 weeks before last frost

date and no later than the last frost date itself. In Zones 9–11 plant seeds in fall for early spring color. When plants are about 1" high, thin to 4" to 1' apart, depending on how bushy the plants will get (check the seed packet). Godetia looks and blooms best when thickly planted. When plants are 2" high, pinch by half to promote bushier, less floppy plants. Push a few twiggy branches into the ground among the planting to help support the flowers. Avoid fertilizing.

▶ **Choices:** *Clarkia unguiculata* has narrow, strap-shape petals for a fluffy effect to its single or double flowers. It is often called farewell-to-spring and has the same height, culture, and bloom season as *C. amoena*. Both species are native to the West Coast.

Gold Dust Alyssum
see Basket-of-Gold

Golden Fleece
see Dahlberg Daisy

Gold Flower
see St. Johnswort

Golden Barrel Cactus
see Cactus and Succulents

Goldenrod
Solidago hybrids

Perennial

Solidago hybrid

▶ **Hardiness:** Zones 4–8

▶ **Size:** 12"–36" tall, 12"–20" wide, depending on variety

▶ **Features:** Contrary to popular belief, goldenrod does not aggravate allergies. Its pollen is waxy and heavy, not airborne (the culprit is usually the less conspicuous ragweed, which blooms at the same time). Europeans have seen the value of the American native wildflower and have bred it into some fantastic plants for the garden. They range from tall fountains of gold when in bloom to low, tidy cushions for the front of the border. The species is valuable for late-season bloom in late summer or fall; many of the hybrids bloom earlier, in mid- to late summer.

▶ **Uses:** In the mixed border, the meadow garden, the cottage garden, and the cutting garden

▶ **Needs:** Full sun. Average to poor, well-drained soil. Does best with moderate moisture but is drought tolerant. Plant established plants in spring. Mulch to conserve moisture. Avoid fertilizing; tall types may need staking if soil is too rich. Trim spent blooms or cut frequently for bouquets. This plant is usually pest and disease free.

▶ **Choices:** Wild goldenrod that seeds itself in your garden should be removed—it's invasive. Choose a hybrid that will spread less and is more compact and disease resistant. 'Golden Baby' is 18"–24" tall with dark yellow blooms. 'Fireworks' creates a fountain of pure yellow flowers and red-tinged foliage; it grows 2'–4' tall. 'Peter Pan' is bright yellow and grows 2'–3' tall.

Goldenstar; Green-and-Gold
Chrysogonum virginianum

Perennial groundcover

Chrysogonum virginianum

▶ **Hardiness:** Zones 5–8

▶ **Size:** 8"–10" tall, 12"–24" wide

▶ **Features:** Growing less than 1' tall, plants are covered with star-shape golden flowers in spring, sporadically in summer, and then heavily again in fall. Plants are evergreen in mild winters and may survive in cooler locations with winter mulch. They thrive in shaded, moist locations. Plants spread quickly by runners.

▶ **Uses:** Groundcover for bare, shady spots, woodland gardens, planting beneath shade trees, moist areas beside downspouts, wildflower gardens, near ponds

▶ **Needs:** Plant in spring or fall in rich, moist soil that's somewhat acidic. Full sun to part shade in Zones 5–6; part to full shade in Zones 7–9. The cooler the climate, the sunnier the planting area can be. Provide ample moisture, especially if grown in full sun. Plant in groups of 10 or more for best effect. Fertilize occasionally. Divide in spring or fall every 3 or so years as needed. This plant often reseeds, but not problematically. It is prone to mildew if it gets too little sun.

Choices: Flowers are bright yellow. 'Allen Bush' is especially long-blooming.

Goldmoss
see Sedums

Gomphrena globosa
see Globe Amaranth

Gooseneck Loosestrife
see Loosestrife, Gooseneck

Goutweed
see Bishop's Weed

Grape
Vitus spp.

Fruit-producing vine

Vitis vinifera 'Cabernet Franc'

▶ **Hardiness:** Zones 4–10

▶ **Size:** Up to 30'–40' in all directions, but plants are generally pruned hard to control size and for best production

▶ **Features:** Delicious purple, red, or green fruits on an attractive vine that turns russet in autumn.

▶ ***Uses:*** Along a tall fence, arbor, or on a special trellis; vine is attractive enough to use in edible landscaping.
▶ ***Needs:*** Full sun. Prefers well-drained sandy loam but tolerates less drainage. Drought tolerant once established. Plant vines in early spring 8' apart along a trellis or arbor. Train and prune heavily each spring. From the second year onward, fertilize each spring with a balanced fertilizer. Vines start producing in the third year. Harvest in fall once grapes are fully ripe and sweet-tasting. In North, try harvesting after a frost, which can sweeten many grapes.
▶ ***Choices:*** Check label descriptions to see if grapes are seeded or seedless and good for juicing or as table grapes, that is, they are good eaten fresh. American grapes are hardy in Zones 4–10 and include 'Concord' and 'Catawba'. European grapes are usually used in wine-making and are suited to Zones 6–10; hybrids Zones 5–10. Muscadine grapes are a native with a distinctive musky flavor.

Grapeholly
see Mahonias

Grape Hyacinth
Muscari botryoides
Spring-blooming bulb

Muscari botryoides

▶ ***Hardiness:*** Zones 3–8
▶ ***Size:*** 6"–8" tall
▶ ***Features:*** This diminutive flowering bulb is an essential companion to daffodils in spring, most effective when planted in generous drifts. Tiny, intense deep blue, purple, or white blossoms are held tightly in clusters on low spikes above narrow, grasslike foliage.
▶ ***Uses:*** Beds for spring bloom. Grape hyacinth is an excellent subject for containers.
▶ ***Needs:*** Full sun or light shade. Average to poor, well-drained, preferably sandy soil. Abundant to moderate water. Plant in October 2"–3" deep. Fertilizing is unnecessary. For best effect plant in groups of 3–4 dozen. Where well situated, this plant may spread. Foliage after bloom will gradually fade and "ripen." This is needed to feed the plant for next year. Remove foliage only when it pulls away with no resistance. This plant is usually pest free.
▶ ***Choices:*** Flowers are usually purple but sometimes are white. The most commonly grown species *(M. botryoides* and *M. armeniacum)* have little round flowers. 'Blue Spike' has double flowers. Tassel grape hyacinth *(M. comosum)* has unusual feathery flowers.

Grape Ivy; Kangaroo Vine
Cissus spp.
Tropical evergreen vine

Cissus rhombifolia

▶ ***Size:*** Grows a few to several feet long in ideal conditions
▶ ***Features:*** Easy to grow. A lush tropical vine that does beautifully in hanging containers or those on shelves or pedestals. Can also be trained into a topiary form.
▶ ***Uses:*** As a houseplant in most regions but used as a vine or groundcover in the warmest regions of the United States.
▶ ***Needs:*** Medium light. Will tolerate low light if kept dry. Likes average to hot temperatures. Allow soil to dry out between soakings. Needs at least medium humidity. Fertilize 3 times in summer with a 10-10-10 fertilizer. Pinch regularly to keep full and bushy. Also can be planted at the base of a large upright plant in a pot.
▶ ***Choices:*** *Cissus rhombifolia* is known as grape ivy (but it is sometimes sold as *C. rhomboidea*), and its leaves are usually made up of 3 leaflets. *C. antarctica*, kangaroo vine, can have larger single leaves or can have leaves made up of 5 leaflets. Usually sold in plain deep green, but both are available with interesting leaf variegations that include red and cream.

Grapefruit
see Citrus

Grass, Mondo
see Mondo Grass

GRASSES, ORNAMENTAL

Tough and easy to grow, yet spectacular in their effect, ornamental grasses offer more reward for the effort than almost any other group of plants. And the variety to choose from is enormous, from low tufts of colorful foliage to huge tropical-looking fountains of feathery blooms taller than a horse. Most ornamental grasses are late to emerge in spring and come into their own only in mid- or late summer, when their astonishing textural effects are mature. But they become real garden stars in fall and winter when most other plants are asleep—many varieties have colorful fall and winter leaves, and nearly all have showy seed heads that are effective until the whole plant is cut back in late winter or early spring. Consider planting ornamental grasses with more ephemeral spring-blooming plants that have foliage that could stand covering up after their flowers are over, such as spring bulbs and the taller early summer-blooming bulbs such as *Allium giganteum*.

GRASSES

Blood Grass, Japanese
Imperata cylindrica 'Red Baron'
Perennial grass

Imperata cylindrica 'Red Baron'

G

Plant encyclopedia

▶**Hardiness:** Zones 5–9
▶**Size:** 18"–24" tall and wide
▶**Features:** Though it dislikes hot, dry areas, Japanese blood grass will quickly fill an area with bright red foliage if conditions are right. Leaves are green at the bottom and red above. Texture contrasts with other plants. Most effective when planted in groups. Avoid poorly drained sites with this plant.
▶**Uses:** Accents and planting beds in front of walls, fences, and evergreen shrubs, massed plantings
▶**Needs:** Plant in well-drained, fertile soil that's moist. Foliage color is best in full sun, but plants need afternoon shade in hotter climates. Mulch well. Cut plants back to the ground in spring before new growth emerges.

GRASSES

Blue Fescue

Festuca glauca

Perennial grass

Festuca glauca

▶**Hardiness:** Zones 4–9
▶**Size:** 6"–10" tall and wide
▶**Features:** Blue, grassy foliage in fine-textured tufts is tough, durable, and drought tolerant. Foliage color contrasts with other plants. Position plants close together to form a dense groundcover.
▶**Uses:** Rock gardens, parking areas, entries, edging walkways, perennial beds, planting in front of shrubs
▶**Needs:** Plant in full sun in well-drained soil. Dig and divide plants every 2 or 3 years. Trim plants to the ground in early spring to allow emergence of new growth and to clean up plants.
▶**Choices:** 'Elijah Blue' is 6" to 10" high and wide and has powdery blue foliage.

GRASSES

Blue Oat Grass

Helictotrichon sempervirens

Perennial grass

Helictotrichon sempervirens

▶**Hardiness:** Zones 4–9
▶**Size:** 12"–18" tall and wide; flower stalks can arch 6'–8'
▶**Features:** With gray-blue foliage that looks like a large blue fescue, this plant bears remarkably delicate flower stalks that arch and wave in the breeze. The flowers appear earlier in the summer than most grasses, and create a gauzy effect that makes a lovely light screen, especially when planted in front of windows. Foliage is evergreen in mild climates.
▶**Uses:** In the mixed border it combines well with lavender, *Verbena bonariensis,* and the pink forms of gaura. Looks good with the smaller echoes of blue fescue in front. Makes a good groundcover massed in large beds. Performs well in rock gardens and in containers.
▶**Needs:** Best in moist, well-drained soil, but tolerant of drier ones. Plant in early spring and allow room between plants for them to grow. Water abundantly until established. Best in full sun but tolerant of partial shade.

GRASSES

Feather Reed Grass

Calamagrostis ×acutiflora 'Karl Foerster'

Perennial grass

Calamagrostis ×acutiflora 'Karl Foerster'

▶**Hardiness:** Zones 3–9
▶**Size:** 4'–6' tall, 18"–24" wide
▶**Features:** Extremely upright, erect, wheatlike flower stalks in summer and winter are effective earlier than those of most other ornamental grasses. They make an outstanding light screen around patios and pools that lends the sense of enclosure without being claustrophobic.
▶**Uses:** Most effective planted in groups and masses in large beds. Performs well in containers.
▶**Needs:** Best in moist, slightly acidic soils, but tolerates drier ones. Tolerates clay soil. Full sun. Cut back to 3"–4" in late winter or early spring. Expect no pest or disease problems.

GRASSES

Feather Grass, Giant

Stipa gigantea

Perennial grass

Stipa gigantea

▶**Hardiness:** Zones 5–9
▶**Size:** 18"–24" tall, 2'–3' wide, with flower stems 6'–8' tall
▶**Features:** Huge, airy clouds of flowers followed by seed heads hover above these plants from late summer long into winter. The foliage is fine-textured and often evergreen in mild climates. The tall flowers and seed heads angle out from the plant, so give it plenty of room in the landscape. It's quite impressive rising out of a bed of low-growing junipers.
▶**Uses:** Specimen planted as accent in large beds of lower-growing plants such as lavender or juniper.
▶**Needs:** Best in the cool climates of the Pacific Northwest south to coastal central California. Must have full sun and well-drained soil. Water until established, then infrequently.

GRASSES

Feather Grass, Mexican

Stipa tenuissima

Perennial grass sometimes grown as an annual

Stipa tenuissima

►***Hardiness:*** Zones 8–11
►***Size:*** 12"–18" tall and wide
►***Features:*** There is no plant more fine-textured than this delicate beauty. Its clumps of hairlike leaves arch and drape gracefully, and when it blooms the flowers and seed heads that follow are soft and feathery, often with a pink cast. Plants grow quickly from seed, making this plant a good annual north of its hardiness range.
►***Uses:*** Stunning massed in beds, as edging, in the front of the flower border, in rock gardens, in containers. Lovely at the edge of pools and streams.
►***Needs:*** Any well-drained soil and full sun.

GRASSES

Fountain Grass

Pennisetum alopecuroides

Perennial grass

Pennisetum alopecuroides

►***Hardiness:*** Zones 5–9
►***Size:*** 18"–48" tall, 24"–36" wide
►***Features:*** Fountain grass adds movement to the landscape with arching foliage that sways in the slightest breeze. Fine-textured leaves turn red in fall; maroon seed heads are showy through winter. This plant is easy to grow in sunny spots. Also try the annual purple fountain grass, *P. alopecuroides* 'Rubrum', with its reddish-purple foliage.
►***Uses:*** Growing in masses to fill bare, sunny spots, adding winter color to landscapes, growing as accent plants, edging patios, and containers
►***Needs:*** Plant in average soil (dry is better than wet) and full sun. Allow leaves and seed heads to remain on plants through the winter. Cut them off in spring just as new growth is emerging.

GRASSES

Japanese Forest Grass

Hakonechloa macra 'Aureola'

Perennial grass

Hakonechloa macra 'Aureola'

►***Hardiness:*** Zones 4–8
►***Size:*** 1'–3' tall, 2'–4' wide
►***Features:*** Few ornamental grasses tolerate shade, so for that alone this grass is valuable. It is also one of the most beautiful ornamental grasses, with long leaves that arch and drape gracefully all in the same direction for a highly elegant effect reminiscent of falling water. Its variegated forms are the most often grown and offered in nurseries. All turn bright yellow in autumn.
►***Uses:*** Outstanding in the front of the shady border, especially when massed in groups. Use it in the front of beds and borders where its graceful foliage can spill out, or plant it at the base of rhododendrons and witch hazels. Lovely in containers.
►***Needs:*** Best in rich, well-drained soil high in organic matter. Needs a cool spot in the garden. Partial shade is best, but will tolerate both denser shade and full sun in cool climates. Plant in early spring. Mulch to conserve moisture, and keep moist until established.
►***Choices:*** 'Aureola' has bright chartreuse to creamy yellow leaves, and 'Albovariegata' has white-striped leaves.

GRASSES

Muhly Grass

Muhlenbergia spp.

Perennial grass

Muhlenbergia capillaris

►***Hardiness:*** Generally Zones 7–10, but varies by species
►***Size:*** Most are 3' high, 3' wide, but varies by species
►***Features:*** These mostly evergreen or semievergreen perennial grasses are becoming increasingly popular in mild-climate southern and western gardens. In foliage they have attractive pincushion form. Some have airy, foamy clouds of flowers and seed heads, others fountainlike sprays .
►***Uses:*** Excellent in rock gardens, containers, and difficult, dry sites as a specimen or accent. Lower-growing species are attractive massed as groundcovers.
►***Needs:*** All muhly grasses need full sun and well-drained soil, and are good choices for hot, dry sites.
►***Choices:*** Gulf muhly *(Muhlenbergia capillaris)* is a somewhat hardier (Zones 6–9), deciduous perennial species that produces elegant, misty clouds of bright magenta blooms that float above a stiff 3' mound of foliage. It is the best choice for the Southeast. Bamboo muhly *(M. dumosa)* produces large, arching clumps of feathery foliage that can reach 6' tall and wide. Resembling bamboo, this is an excellent, well-behaved, evergreen substitute for bamboo in hot, dry sites. Largest size, however, is attained with adequate soil moisture. Zones 7–10.

Lindheimer muhly *(M. lindheimeri)* is a good choice for Texas and southwestern gardens (Zones 7–9). It produces 3' pincushion mounds of blue-green foliage and erect, feathery rose-tan flower spikes that reach 5' high. Deer grass *(M. rigens)* is similar in appearance to Lindheimer muhly but better adapted to gardens in California (Zones 7–9).

GRASSES

Pampas Grass, Dwarf

Cortaderia selloana

Perennial grass

Cortaderia selloana 'Pumila'

▶***Hardiness:*** Zones 7–10
▶***Size:*** 6'–10' tall and wide, with plumes up to 12' tall
▶***Features:*** This Argentinian native is one of the largest ornamental grasses, and one of the most dramatic—its clumps of arching foliage grow 6' or more tall and as big across, and the tall plumes reach higher than a gaucho on a horse. The species can be invasive in California, so choose from the better-behaved cultivars. Avoid pampas grass where people may brush against the foliage. The grass blades are sharply serrated and can cause injury. It's best used in large areas where it is viewed from a distance.
▶***Uses:*** Large areas, summer screening, accents, or solving background problems; poor fit for small spaces
▶***Needs:*** Plant in full sun to partial shade in any kind of soil as long as it's well drained. Cut clumps to the ground in early spring. Pampas grass is insect and disease resistant.
▶***Choices:*** 'Argenteum' grows to 12' high with silvery plumes; 'Gold Band' has yellow-striped foliage; 'Pumila' reaches just 4'–6' tall in bloom; 'Rendatleri' matures at 8'–10' tall with large, pink feathery flowers.

GRASSES

Ribbon Grass

Phalaris arundinacea 'Picta'

Perennial grass

Phalaris arundinacea 'Tricolor'

▶***Hardiness:*** Zones 4–9
▶***Size:*** 2'–3' tall, spreads indefinitely
▶***Features:*** Be careful with this grass—it spreads aggressively, especially in moist soils, and is difficult to root out. But in areas where it is contained it is beautiful for its creamy green and white leaves.
▶***Uses:*** Well-contained beds where it cannot escape. Gorgeous in containers.
▶***Needs:*** Most vigorous (not necessarily a good thing) with abundant moisture, even soggy soils. If growing in a container, water frequently and abundantly, or stand container in a saucer of water.

GRASSES

Northern Sea Oats

Chasmanthium latifolium

Perennial grass

Chasmanthium latifolium

▶***Hardiness:*** Zones 5–9
▶***Size:*** 3'–4' tall, 2' wide
▶***Features:*** Dangling spikelets of flattened seed heads are attractive from midsummer on. Clumps of fine-textured, bamboolike foliage turn golden wheat colors in fall. Plants are tolerant of difficult sites that are flooded during wet spells.
▶***Uses:*** Difficult low, wet spots in the garden. Most attractive when massed, especially among shrubs that have red fall foliage.
▶***Needs:*** Moist, even wet, soil is best, but this grass tolerates a wide variety of soils. Full sun is best, but considerable shade is well tolerated. Plants will self-sow; mulch to help control this. Cut back in late winter or early spring before new growth emerges.

GRASSES

Silver Grass; Miscanthus; Zebra Grass; Eulalia Grass

Miscanthus sinensis

Perennial grass

Miscanthus sinensis 'Morning Light'

▶***Hardiness:*** Zones 5–9
▶***Size:*** 4'–6' tall, 3'–4' wide
▶***Features:*** Perhaps the most popular of the ornamental grasses, it has fine-textured foliage and graceful fountains of feathery flowers and seed heads in late summer and winter. There are many cultivars available that range in foliage from silvery gray to variegated, and are of different sizes. Sometimes mistakenly called fountain grass (which is *Pennisetum* spp.).
▶***Uses:*** Specimen, screening, winter effect
▶***Needs:*** Full sun in nearly any soil, but rich soils and too much fertilizer may cause floppy growth. Mulch and water well until established. Cut back in late winter or early spring before new growth starts.
▶***Choices:*** Many cultivars available. 'Gracillimus', the most common, has graceful, arching, fine-textured leaves and the latest-appearing flowers. 'Morning Light' is upright with lighter silvery foliage. 'Zebrinus' is tall and upright with green and cream-striped foliage. 'Purpurascens' is a smaller plant about 3' high with red-tinted foliage that turns to outstanding reds and purples in autumn. *M. ×giganteus* is a huge, dramatic upright species that can reach 14' high and 4'–6' wide. Unlike *M. floridulus*—a more tender (Zones 7–11) large species that runs aggressively—*M. ×giganteus* is clump-forming and hardy in Zones 4–9.

GRASSES

Switch Grass

Panicum virgatum

Perennial grass

Panicum virgatum 'Warrior'

►**Hardiness:** Zones 4–9
►**Size:** 3'–10' tall, 1'–3' wide, depending on variety
►**Features:** This North American native is one of the easiest grasses to grow in the garden, tolerant of a wide range of soils and environments. It forms erect to arching clumps of blue-green foliage that are topped in late summer with airy clouds of tiny flowers followed by seed heads. The seed heads often have a pink or reddish glow to them, and in autumn the foliage of most varieties turns to lovely shades of red and gold.
►**Uses:** Massed as a large-scale groundcover in beds or on banks and slopes; as an accent in the mixed flower border.
►**Needs:** Best in sun and dry to moderately moist soil, but tolerant of a wide variety of soils from dry and stony to heavy clay. The moister the soil, the taller it grows. Cut back in late winter after new growth emerges.
►**Choices:** 'Heavy Metal' is strongly upright to 4'–6' tall with blue-gray foliage. Autumn foliage is a dull tan. 'Shenandoah' gradually turns reddish through the summer to an excellent bright ruby red in fall. 'Cloud Nine' is a larger plant, to 8' tall, with excellent fall color and reddish seed panicles.

GRASSES

Tufted Hair Grass

Deschampsia caespitosa

Perennial grass

Deschampsia caespitosa

►**Hardiness:** Zones 4–9
►**Size:** 1'–3' tall, 2' wide
►**Features:** Mounds of fine-textured foliage produce puffy clouds of tan to golden yellow seed heads in late summer. Clumping foliage is evergreen.
►**Uses:** Best when massed in large groups as a groundcover, although also effective as a specimen among lower-growing groundcovers
►**Needs:** Best in cool, damp, heavy clay and full sun to fairly dense shade—it's more tolerant of shade than most ornamental grasses. Foliage will discolor in hot, dry conditions.
►**Choices:** Any of the many named cultivars (most are from Germany) are far superior to the species, which has dull tan seed heads. 'Bronzeshleier' produces clouds of bronze seed heads. 'Goldstaub' has yellow flowers and seed heads.

Green-and-Gold

see Goldenstar

Greens, Salad

(other than lettuces)

Cool-season annual vegetables

Mustard green 'Red Giant'

►**Size:** Most grow up to 8" tall, a few inches wide by harvest
►**Features:** Add variety to salads with a range of shapes, colors, and flavors
►**Uses:** In containers, in edible landscaping, in the vegetable garden
►**Needs:** Grow like lettuces (see Lettuce, page 423). Full sun to light shade, especially in areas with hot summers. Rich, loose soil with plenty of compost worked in. Ample moisture. Plant seeds directly in soil just deep enough for soil to cover in spring as soon as soil can be worked or 4–6 weeks before your region's last frost date. Can also be planted in fall in Zones 8 and warmer. Thin small clusters of plants to about 1" apart; use the thinnings in early salads. Keep soil moist. Mulch to conserve moisture. Fertilize every two weeks with a liquid fertilizer. Harvest by cutting all but 1" of the plants. They will regrow for 2–3 more harvests.
►**Choices:** Includes cress (tangy, often curly leaves), purslane (succulent and mildly acerbic), miner's lettuce or claytonia (tender leaves that form a rosette), corn salad or mâche (mild, nutty flavor), cutting or annual chicory (adds bite), and tangy mustard greens such as mizuna or tatsoi.

Grecian Laurel

see Bay

Guzmania lingulata

see Bromeliads: Guzmania

Gypsophila paniculata

see Baby's Breath

Hakonechloa macra 'Aureola'

see Grasses, Ornamental: Hakone Grass

Hamamelis spp.

see Witch Hazels

Hardy Ice Plant

see Ice Plant, Hardy

Harry Lauder's Walking Stick

Corylus avellana 'Contorta'

Deciduous shrub

Corylus avellana 'Contorta'

G

Plant encyclopedia

▶ Hardiness: Zones 5–7
▶ Size: 4'–7' high and wide.
▶ Features: The dramatically twisted and gnarled stems of this round shrub never fail to elicit comments and, especially when the leaves that have fallen, present a striking sight against snow or a light-colored wall. In late winter and early spring before the leaves appear, the branches are covered with long, pendulous yellow catkins that are very showy.
▶ Uses: As a specimen, accent, or focal point for its striking form and texture. Effective next to a light-colored masonry or stucco wall.
▶ Needs: Very adaptable and easy to grow in sun or shade and in nearly any soil. Excellent in poor, dry soil. For grafted plants, remove root suckers as they arise or the plant will eventually overgrow and revert to the straight-stemmed species.

Hatiora gaertneri

see Easter Cactus

Hawaiian Ti Plant

see Ti Plant

Haworthia fasciata

see Cactus and Succulents: Zebra Haworthia

Hawthorn, Indian

see Indian Hawthorn

HAWTHORNS

Crataegus spp.

The list of trees that provide a showy effect in several seasons is pretty short. And the hawthorns have to rank near the top. Outstanding in flower and fruit, some have the added advantage of beautiful fall foliage color. All are favorite havens for birds, which seek out both the fruits and the dense, twiggy, and often thorny growth that makes a good home for a nest. Best of all, hawthorns are undemanding and easy to grow.

HAWTHORNS

Thornless Cockspur Hawthorn

Crataegus crus-galli var. *inermis*

Deciduous flowering tree

Crataegus crus-galli var. *inermis*

▶ Hardiness: Zones 4–7
▶ Size: 20'–30' tall, 20'–35' wide
▶ Features: Medium growth rate. White flowers appear in early spring. Orange fall color; red berries last into winter. Thornless stems. Drought resistant. This tough little tree provides flowers in spring, bright leaves in fall, and showy red fruit in winter. Look for the variety *inermis;* other kinds have thorns that can be dangerous to children and adults walking by. Plants grow vigorously in the landscape.
▶ Uses: Specimen trees, seasonal accents, entries and courtyards, patio areas, coastal or urban landscapes, tall hedges, planting at corners of houses
▶ Needs: Plant in any soil that's well-drained, including acidic, alkaline, sandy, or clay. Grow in full sun to partial shade. Tolerates wind, coastal conditions, cold weather, and urban pollution. Little pruning is required.

HAWTHORNS

Washington Hawthorn

Crataegus phaenopyrum

Deciduous flowering tree

Crataegus phaenopyrum

▶ Hardiness: Zones 3–9
▶ Size: 25'–30' tall, 20'–25' wide
▶ Features: Medium growth rate. Clusters of white flowers in spring. Leaves turn orange or red in autumn; red berries provide winter interest. Small tree tolerates a variety of growing conditions. Plant anywhere you want to add year-round color in the yard. White flowers tinged with pink start off the spring followed by glossy green summer foliage. Colorful fall foliage raises the curtain for red fruits that persist throughout the winter. Thorny twigs add texture during the winter as well.
▶ Uses: Specimen trees, seasonal accents, natural areas, growing in clusters, attracting birds, winter interest, narrow spaces, and hedges
▶ Needs: Plant in any soil, from acidic to alkaline, dry to moist, poor to fertile. Grow in full sun or partial shade. Tolerates urban pollution and paving. Remove low-hanging branches for clearance, if desired. Avoid planting in high-traffic areas because of the thorns.

Heather, Mexican

see Mexican Heather

Heather, Scotch

Calluna vulgaris

Evergreen shrub

Calluna vulgaris

▶ Hardiness: Zones 3–8
▶ Size: 4"–24" tall, 24"–30" wide
▶ Features: Medium to fast growth rate. Late summer blooms attract bees. Numerous varieties to choose from. Scotch heather's bright foliage is as eye-catching as the blooms, and its leaves last year-round. Flowers occur from midsummer to fall in shades of gold, white, rose, lilac, and crimson. Scotch heather is low maintenance.

▶ ***Uses:*** Massing, edging walkways, flower beds, groundcover for bare areas, planting in front of shrubs
▶ ***Needs:*** Full sun best, especially on the east side of a building or hedge for protection from winter sun and wind. Well-drained or sandy soil, rich in organic matter but low in nutrients, is ideal. Acidic soil and moderate moisture are preferable. Plant established plants in spring. Keep moderately moist. Too much water will cause root rot. Avoid fertilizing. In winters with sparse snow cover protect with boughs of pine or other cut evergreens until spring. This plant is usually pest free.
▶ ***Choices:*** 'Allegro'—dark red flowers; 'Beoley Gold'—yellow foliage; 'County Wicklow'—pink flowers.

Heath; Winter Heath

Erica carnea

Evergreen shrub

Erica carnea

▶ ***Hardiness:*** Zones 4-8
▶ ***Size:*** 8"-10" tall, 18"-22" wide
▶ ***Features:*** Medium growth rate. Flowers appear from late winter into spring. Needlelike foliage retains color year-round. Many cultivars are available. This groundcover puts on its flower show when winter is winding down, but plants are attractive all year long. Flower colors range from white to shades of pink and purple. Foliage is available in various hues as well.
▶ ***Uses:*** Entries, parking areas, walkways, positioning in front of larger shrubs
▶ ***Needs:*** Full sun best, especially the east side of a building or hedge for protection from winter sun and wind. Well-drained or sandy soil, rich in organic matter but low in nutrients, is ideal. Prefers acidic soil. Plant established plants in spring. Keep moderately moist, but too much water causes root rot. Keep from fertilizing. In winters with sparse snow cover, protect smaller heathers with boughs of pine or other cut evergreens until spring. Plants are usually pest free.
▶ ***Choices:*** Colors are pinks, lavenders, whites, and creams. Many cultivars have striking golden foliage.

Heavenly Bamboo

see Nandina

Hedera spp.

see Ivy

Helenium autumnale

see Sneezeweed

Helen's Flower

see Sneezeweed

Helianthemum nummularium

see Rock Rose

Helianthus spp.

see Sunflower

Helichrysum bracteatum

see Strawflower

Helichrysum petiolare

see Licorice Plant

Helictotrichon sempervirens

see Grasses, Ornamental: Blue Oat Grass

Heliopsis helianthoides

see False Sunflower

Heliotrope

Heliotropium arborescens

Annual or perennial

Heliotropium arborescens 'Mini Marine'

▶ ***Hardiness:*** Zones 10-11
▶ ***Size:*** 1'-2' tall and as wide
▶ ***Features:*** Delicious, fruity vanilla fragrance (some think it smells like cherry pie) and beautiful tight clusters of deep purple flowers are this plant's claims to fame. Blooms summer through frost.
▶ ***Uses:*** Excellent in containers (try combining with sweet alyssum and ivy geraniums). Also good for edging or in mixed plantings with other summer-blooming annuals. Place where the fragrance can be enjoyed. Can be brought indoors for the winter as a houseplant.
▶ ***Needs:*** Annual in Zones 2-10; perennial in Zones 10-11. Full sun, though appreciates some afternoon shade in hot summer areas in Zones 7-11. Rich to average, well-drained soil. Keep evenly moist, though plants thrive with occasional slightly dry periods. Plant seedlings in spring after all danger of frost has passed. Apply a 1"-2" layer of mulch to prevent disease. Fertilize regularly, every 4 weeks. Trim spent blooms to encourage more flowering. In Zone 10 mulch in fall to protect from winter cold and ensure regrowth in spring. Or dig up right before the first autumn frost and bring indoors. It will last several months as a fragrant houseplant.
▶ ***Choices:*** Most varieties are bred for compactness: 'Blue Wonder' grows 12" tall, 'Mini Marine' grows only 10" tall. Other varieties, such as 'Fragrant Delight', have been bred for fragrance.

Helleborus spp.

see Christmas Rose; Lenten Rose

Hemerocallis spp.

see Daylily

Hemlock, Canadian

Tsuga canadensis

Evergreen tree

Tsuga canadensis

▶ ***Hardiness:*** Zones 3-7
▶ ***Size:*** 40'-70' tall, 25'-35' wide
▶ ***Features:*** Give your garden a look reminiscent of a cool, green mountainside by planting Canadian hemlock. Fine-textured foliage will form a screen concealing undesirable views or provide a backdrop for other shrubs in the planting bed. Plants can tolerate heavy pruning and are often planted in hedges. Trees look best when lower branches can remain in place all the way to the ground. Low maintenance once established.
▶ ***Uses:*** Screening, background, hedging along property lines, natural areas, woodlands, mountainsides, large estates
▶ ***Needs:*** Plant in acidic soil that's moist but well drained. Grow in sun or partial shade in areas protected from the wind. Water new trees for 2 growing seasons to ensure good establishment. Afterward, water during severe droughts. Trees are intolerant of pollution.
▶ ***Choices:*** 'Pendula' is slow-growing with gracefully drooping branches and a pyramidal form in youth and old age.

Hen and Chicks

see Cactus and Succulents

Heuchera spp.

see Coral Bells

HIBISCUS

Hibiscus spp.

Hibiscus cover the gamut from tropical evergreen shrubs to hardy perennials, shrubs, and small trees. All are grown for their showy, colorful flowers—broad and round with a prominent column of stamens in the center—made famous by the dancing ballerina flowers in the Disney film *Fantasia.*

HIBISCUS

Chinese Hibiscus

Hibiscus rosa-sinensis

Evergreen shrub

Hibiscus rosa-sinensis

▶ ***Hardiness:*** Zones 9–10
▶ ***Size:*** 8'-15' tall, 3'-10' wide
▶ ***Features:*** If you have hot sun and sandy soil, you have a spot for Chinese hibiscus, a quick-growing shrub or small tree. Big flowers last only a day but are opening nearly nonstop when grown in full sun. Glossy, evergreen foliage; coarse texture. Many colors, sizes, and forms are available.
▶ ***Uses:*** Foundation planting, hedges and screens, patios and entries, accent shrubs, single specimen, containers
▶ ***Needs:*** Grow in full sun or dappled shade for best flowering. Plant in well-drained, sandy, acidic soil. Water regularly to prevent wilting and stress. Water often and feed monthly during growing season with balanced fertilizer. Prune regularly to control size and shape. In early spring, prune out one-third of the mature wood to keep plants vigorous. Chinese hibiscus is hardy only to about 30°F/-1°C.

HIBISCUS

Hardy Hibiscus; Rose Mallow

Hibiscus moscheutos

Perennial

Hibiscus moscheutos

▶ ***Hardiness:*** Zones 5-9
▶ ***Size:*** 3'-5' tall, 3' wide
▶ ***Features:*** Remember that catalog picture with the girl standing next to a flower bigger than her head? With hardy hibiscus, even northern gardens can look tropical with large, lobed leaves and flowers the size of hubcaps. These are tall, relatively narrow moisture-loving plants that look best massed in large, powerful groups—the perfect treatment for that problem low area in your yard that always stays wet.
▶ ***Uses:*** Mass in large groupings in beds or as a hedge, or work into the mixed border as a bold-textured accent. Good choice for the edge of ponds and streams. The smaller cultivars perform well in containers.
▶ ***Needs:*** Full sun in Zones 2-5; partial shade in hot summer areas in Zones 6-11. Rich, well-drained but moist soil. Needs ample water; thrives in wet, hot conditions. Plant established plants in spring after all danger of frost has passed. Mulch. Fertilize occasionally, every 6 weeks, or work in a 9-month, slow-release fertilizer each spring. Stake tallest types. Perennial types are slow to emerge from the soil in spring; be careful to avoid hoeing or pulling out.
▶ ***Choices:*** Disco Belle series is a seed strain with 9-inch pink, red, or white flowers on 20"-30" plants. The Southern Belle group is another seed strain with huge 10"-12" red, pink, or white blooms. Plants reach 3'-4' tall.

HIBISCUS

Rose of Sharon

Hibiscus syriacus

Deciduous shrub

Hibiscus syriacus

▶ ***Hardiness:*** Zones 5-9
▶ ***Size:*** 8'-12' tall, 6'-8' wide
▶ ***Features***: Large flowers in pinks, reds, whites, and blues dress up this old-fashioned shrub. Rose of Sharon is a fast-growing plant that withstands poor soil, heat, and drought. May also be sold as althea.
▶ ***Uses:*** Informal shrub bed or screen, narrow areas or beside paving and swimming pools, single specimen in beds and containers
▶ ***Needs:*** Plant in full sun to partial shade in any soil that's well drained, from acidic to alkaline. Trim only as needed to shape plants; make cuts in winter to avoid removing flower buds. Underplant with shorter shrubs.
▶ ***Choices:*** 'Aphrodite'—dark pink petals with dark red centers; 'Blue Bird'—large lavender flowers with red centers; 'Diana'—large, pure white flowers; 'Oiseau Bleu'—azure blue flower with purple veining; 'Paeoniflorus'—double light pink flowers from June to September.

Hippeastrum spp.

see Amaryllis

HOLLIES

Ilex spp.

The hollies include a wide variety of valuable and popular evergreen and deciduous shrubs and small trees. Some produce ornamental bright red or orange berries that are attractive all winter long.

HOLLIES

American Holly

Ilex opaca

Broadleaf evergreen tree

Ilex opaca and *Ilex opaca* fruit (inset)

▶ ***Hardiness:*** Zones 6–9
▶ ***Size:*** 40' tall, 20' wide
▶ ***Features:*** Glossy evergreen leaves edged in short, sharp spines make this small native tree a good choice for background and massing. The bright red berries and evergreen leaves are favorites for winter decorations. Although mature trees can reach 40' tall in great age, they grow slowly, around 5"–7" per year. Only female trees produce berries; plant one male for every three female trees to ensure good fruit set.
▶ ***Uses:*** Background, massing in groups, thorny barrier, winter effect. Berries and leaves last long when cut and brought indoors in winter. Slow growth makes this tree suitable for small gardens. Avoid planting where people may walk barefoot.
▶ ***Needs:*** Plant in moist, well-drained soil high in organic matter. Best in full sun but protect from dry winter winds. Tolerates part shade well.
▶ ***Choices:*** 'Merry Christmas' is faster-growing with rich, dark leaves. 'Groonenberg' remains compact and bears heavy crops of fruit.

HOLLIES

Blue Holly

Ilex ×meserveae

Evergreen tree

Ilex ×meserveae 'Blue Girl'

▶ ***Hardiness:*** Zones 5–8
▶ ***Size:*** 10'–15' tall, 8'–10' wide
▶ ***Features:*** Glossy blue-green leaves earn this holly its name. Plant one male for every dozen female plants if you want the attractive red berries. Protect plants from desiccating winter winds, especially in colder climates. This is one of the most cold hardy of the hollies. Neat, small size fits in with many landscapes.
▶ ***Uses:*** Specimen use, screening poor views, privacy, winter interest, hedges, attracting birds
▶ ***Needs:*** Grow in fertile, moist, acidic soil. Use a fertilizer formulated for acid-loving plants in the spring. Grows well in full sun and partial shade. Prune to shape in late winter or early spring.
▶ ***Choices:*** 'Blue Girl'—female, glossy blue-green foliage; abundant, bright red berries; 'Blue Boy'—male pollinator, glossy leaves.

HOLLIES

Burford Holly, Dwarf

Ilex cornuta 'Burfordii Nana'

Evergreen shrub

Ilex cornuta 'Burfordii Nana'

▶ ***Hardiness:*** Zones 6–9
▶ ***Size:*** 12'–18' tall, 10'–15' wide
▶ ***Features:*** This tough shrub gets much larger than its name implies. You can keep hedges trimmed between 4' and 6' tall. Or, let single specimen plants grow tall enough to form small trees (remove lower branches to reveal trunks), as shown here. Foliage stays a glossy dark green year-round. Heavy crops of red berries appear in winter.
▶ ***Uses:*** Foundation planting, parking areas, hedges, barriers, or as a background plant
▶ ***Needs:*** Plant in full sun to partial shade in acidic soil that's either rich or poor but not too wet. Prune as needed to control size. Allow plants to form a dense mass instead of individual shapes.

HOLLIES

Foster's Holly

Ilex xattenuata 'Fosteri'

Broadleaf evergreen tree or shrub

Ilex ×attenuata 'Sunny Foster' and 'Foster 2' (inset)

▶ ***Hardiness:*** Zones 6–9
▶ ***Size:*** 20' tall, 8' wide

H

Plant encyclopedia

▶ ***Features:*** This narrow, conical small tree is cloaked to the ground in lustrous, narrow evergreen leaves. Because of its dense evergreen foliage, narrow habit, and relatively fast rate of growth, it has become a favorite holly in the southeastern United States for screens and hedges. The spiny leaves are a rich, dark green. In fall and early winter, female plants produce heavy crops of bright red berries. Plant one male plant for every three female plants for best fruit production.
▶ ***Uses:*** Excellent for screening or as a tall hedge. Spiny leaves are good for barrier. Makes a good vertical accent.
▶ ***Needs:*** Plant in deep, moist, well-drained soil high in organic matter. Tolerates acidic soils well. Best in full sun, but tolerant of light shade. Protect from dry winter winds. Quite trouble-free and easy to grow.

HOLLIES

Inkberry, Compact

Ilex glabra 'Compacta'

Evergreen shrub

Ilex glabra 'Compacta'

▶ ***Hardiness:*** Zones 3–9
▶ ***Size:*** 4'–6' tall and wide
▶ ***Features:*** Few shrubs are as adaptable as glossy-leaved inkberry. You can grow it at the beach, in snow, in alkaline or acidic soils, in sunny or shady spots. Also sold as gallberry. Thrives in the eastern United States.
▶ ***Uses:*** Foundation planting, screening, massing, winter interest, providing background, seaside landscapes, formal or informal gardens, parking areas, poolside, planting beside patios and walkways
▶ ***Needs:*** Plant in acidic soil that's moist but well drained. Grow in full sun or partial shade. Pest and disease-resistant. Shear or prune heavily as needed to maintain compact size.
▶ ***Choices:*** Compact varieties are more desired for home landscape use. Choose 'Compacta' unless you want a 10'-tall shrub. Also try: 'Nigra'—3'-4' tall; 'Shamrock'—5'-6' tall.

HOLLIES

Japanese Holly, Compact

Ilex crenata 'Compacta'

Evergreen shrub

Ilex crenata 'Compacta'

▶ ***Hardiness:*** Zones 5–8
▶ ***Size:*** 3'–5' tall, 3'–4' wide
▶ ***Features:*** Consider this shrub a substitute for boxwood. Although inexpensive and fast-growing in comparison, the dense form of this disease-resistant shrub has similar classic appeal. Plants are easily trimmed into formal shapes.
▶ ***Uses:*** Entries, specimen use, formal gardens, foundation or background planting in shrub beds
▶ ***Needs:*** Plant in sun or shade in well-drained soil. Prune if desired to maintain compact form. This disease-resistant shrub is easy to transplant.

HOLLIES

Japanese Holly, Green Lustre

Ilex crenata 'Green Lustre'

Evergreen shrub

Ilex crenata 'Green Lustre'

▶ ***Hardiness:*** Zones 4–6
▶ ***Size:*** 3'–6' tall, 5'–10' wide
▶ ***Features:*** This holly is hardy and sturdy. Its dense branching habit and thick leaf cover make it an excellent choice for creating a privacy screen or barrier hedge. Japanese holly adapts well to urban growing conditions and to small yards. Though it prefers acidic soil, it will tolerate neutral soil pH. This holly is easy to grow or maintain. Grow in the warmer areas of Zone 4 by planting in a location shielded from harsh winter winds.
▶ ***Uses:*** Specimen use, hedges, screening, massing in planting beds
▶ ***Needs:*** Plant in either full sun or partial shade in fertile, moist soil that's high in organic matter. Prefers acidic soils. Alkaline soil will cause leaves to turn yellow; add peat at planting to lower pH. Prune to shape shrubs in summer, after the new growth is mature. Tolerates city conditions and confined growing spaces.

HOLLIES

Japanese Holly, Heller

Ilex crenata 'Helleri'

Evergreen shrub

Ilex crenata 'Helleri'

▶ ***Hardiness:*** Zones 5–8
▶ ***Size:*** 2'–3' tall, 3'–5' wide
▶ ***Features:*** If you hate pruning, Heller Japanese holly stays low and tidy all by itself. This evergreen shrub grows slowly. Start with larger plants if you want instant impact. Transplants easily into the landscape. Tolerant of city conditions.
▶ ***Uses:*** In front of low windows or taller plants, filling large shrub beds, edging around patios and decks
▶ ***Needs:*** Plant in sun or shade in soil of medium fertility and moisture. Requires acidic soil. Pick a shadier spot if your soil is poor. Water regularly during hot, dry spells. Space new plants 2' apart and let them grow together to form a dense mass.

HOLLIES

Lusterleaf Holly

Ilex latifolia

Evergreen tree

Ilex latifolia

▶***Hardiness:*** Zones 7–9
▶***Size:*** 20'–25' tall, 10'–12' wide
▶***Features:*** Lusterleaf holly trees form dense pyramids of shiny green leaves highlighted by bright red berries in fall that persist through the winter. Female plants produce the showy red berries if properly pollinated; male plants are necessary for pollination.
▶***Uses:*** Screening to provide privacy or block poor views, an evergreen background for deciduous plants, winter interest, specimen use, windbreaks, woodland gardens
▶***Needs:*** Grow in moist, well-drained acidic soil; established plants will tolerate drought. Grow in sun or shade. Little if any pruning is required. Leave lower limbs to maintain attractive pyramidal form.

HOLLIES

Nellie R. Stevens Holly

Ilex × 'Nellie R. Stevens'

Evergreen shrub

Ilex ×'Nellie R. Stevens'

▶***Hardiness:*** Zones 6–9
▶***Size:*** 15'–20' tall, 10'–15' wide
▶***Features:*** With its naturally broad, pyramidal form and dark, glossy green leaves, Nellie R. Stevens holly is a longtime favorite in the landscape. Plants grow big, so give them plenty of room. They resemble fat Christmas trees growing in the yard. Female plants fruit heavily.
▶***Uses:*** Corners of tall houses, screening poor views, privacy, windbreaks, specimen plants
▶***Needs:*** Plant in full sun or partial shade in well-drained, acidic soil. Give new plants plenty of room to grow. Mature plants can withstand drought.

HOLLIES

Possumhaw

Ilex decidua

Deciduous tree

Ilex decidua

▶***Hardiness:*** Zones 3–9
▶***Size:*** 15'–25' tall, 8'–20' wide
▶***Features:*** This tough holly is different from most; it loses its leaves in the winter and grows well in swampy, alkaline soils. Irregular in form, the branches are horizontal and ascending. Red and red-orange berries show off against dark green foliage in late summer and fall, and against bare winter branches. Plant female trees in showy locations, but be sure to include a male tree nearby for pollination.
▶***Uses:*** Small specimen use, winter interest, natural areas, understory use, parking areas, soggy locations, courtyards and entries
▶***Needs:*** Plant in soil that's well drained or swampy, acidic or alkaline. Provide a location with full sun or partial shade. Trees require little if any pruning; they look best when maintained in their naturally irregular form.
▶***Choices:*** 'Warren's Red'—upright form, profuse berries.

HOLLIES

Savannah American Holly

Ilex opaca 'Savannah'

Deciduous tree

Ilex opaca 'Savannah'

▶***Hardiness:*** Zones 5–9
▶***Size:*** 20'–25' tall, 10'–15' wide
▶***Features:*** This versatile holly produces bumper crops of berries that last from late fall through the winter. Trees have naturally pyramidal forms. Leave lower branches all the way to the ground or prune them to expose a portion of the trunk. Foliage is normally a yellow-green color; if leaves turn noticeably yellow, fertilize with acid-loving plant food.
▶***Uses:*** Specimen use, low-growing street tree, providing winter interest, patio plantings, parking areas, screening, background plantings in shrub beds
▶***Needs:*** Plant in full sun or partial shade. Soil conditions should be fertile, acidic, moist, yet well drained. Prune trees in the winter if they need shaping. Female plants produce showy red berries. Males are necessary for pollination. Plant one male for every two to three females.

HOLLIES

Winterberry

Ilex verticillata

Deciduous flowering shrub

Ilex verticillata 'Winter Red'

▶***Hardiness:*** Zones 3–9
▶***Size:*** 6'–10' tall and wide

H

Plant encyclopedia

▶**Features:** Grow this holly to add color to the winter landscape. Twigs covered with bright red berries attract hungry birds in cold weather. Plants require acidic soils; alkaline soil will cause leaves to turn yellow and plants will not thrive. You must plant both male and female plants to get berries. Plant one male for every 10 to 12 females.
▶**Uses:** Wet, boggy areas, winter interest, screens or hedges, attracting birds, training as a small tree, massing
▶**Needs:** Plant in full sun or partial shade in fertile, moist soil that's high in organic matter. Plants prefer acidic soil. They will adapt to wet soils.
▶**Choices:** 'Sparkleberry'—quarter-inch berries, 15' tall, 12' wide, Zones 5-9; 'Winter Red'—dark green leaves turn bronze in fall, berries last until spring, 8' tall, 10' wide, Zones 3-9.

HOLLIES

Yaupon Holly

Ilex vomitoria

Evergreen tree

Ilex vomitoria

▶**Hardiness:** Zones 7-10
▶**Size:** 15'-20' tall, 6'-8' wide
▶**Feature:** Yaupon holly will live anywhere you put it. Glossy gray-green leaves provide a change in texture that lasts year-round. Stems are whitish to gray in color; young stems are covered with down. Scarlet-red berries cover trees fall through winter and are great for attracting flocks of birds into the landscape. Plants can be grown as small trees or large shrubs. Dwarf cultivars are a better choice for shrub use.
▶**Uses:** Seaside landscapes including dune plantings, screening, specimen trees, planting beside patios, in natural areas or woodland gardens, attracting birds, foundation plantings, espalier
▶**Needs:** Plant in any soil from dry to wet, acidic to alkaline. Very adaptable. Grows in sun or shade. Tolerates salt spray, wind, heat, and pruning.
▶**Choices:** Weeping yaupon ('Pendula')—narrow shape, attractive drooping branches.

HOLLIES

Yaupon Holly, Dwarf

Ilex vomitoria 'Nana'

Evergreen shrub

Ilex vomitoria 'Nana'

▶**Hardiness:** Zones 7-10
▶**Size:** 3'-4' tall, 3'-5' wide
▶**Features:** Sun or shade, wet or dry—this plant is happy anywhere. Dwarf yaupon holly is slow-growing and compact, although plants eventually get big with age. Fruit is hidden by the foliage.
▶**Uses:** Foundation planting, low hedges, formal gardens, coastal areas, Xeriscaping, massed plantings
▶**Needs:** Plant in sun or shade and in about any soil, including acidic, alkaline, poor, or sandy. Established plants are drought tolerant. Pruning is unnecessary unless old plants outgrow their space. Then, cut back severely.
▶**Choices:** 'Schilling's Dwarf'—good for hotter climates (Zones 9 and 10).

Hollyhock

Alcea rosea

Biennial or short-lived perennial

Alcea rosea

▶**Hardiness:** Zones 3-7
▶**Size:** 4'-8' tall, 2' wide
▶**Features:** Hollyhocks are the very essence of the cottage garden. Their pleasantly rough foliage has an informal attitude, and their tall, vertical presence complements a host of lower-growing, bushier flowers. Like the earlier blooms of foxglove, the spikes of hollyhocks are naturals to grow against a picket fence or the warm, rough tones of wood or shingle siding. Blooms appear over a long season, peaking in midsummer.
▶**Uses:** The cottage garden or at the rear of more informal mixed borders with flowers such as purple coneflower, black-eyed Susan, and sunflower. Effective massed against large stone, brick, or natural wood walls and fences.
▶**Needs:** Rich, well-drained soil with moderate water. Depending on the region and the hollyhock type, this plant may behave as an annual, biennial, or perennial. Read package directions carefully. In Zones 3-8 start seeds of any hollyhock indoors 2-4 weeks before last average frost date or sow directly outdoors after frost. In Zones 9-11 plant seedlings in fall or late winter for spring bloom. If planting established plants, plant outdoors after all danger of frost has passed. Mulch to prevent disease. Work a 9-month slow-release fertilizer into the soil each spring. Stake for best appearance. Prone to rust disease; use a fungicide labeled for hollyhock control.
▶**Choices:** 'Chater's Double' is a seed strain with double flowers in maroon, red, rose, white, or yellow. 'Nigra' is a single-flowered cultivar with the darkest flower of all hollyhocks, a deep maroon.

Hollyhock Mallow

Malva alcea 'Fastigiata'

Perennial

Malva alcea 'Fastigiata'

▶**Hardiness:** Zones 3-8
▶**Size:** 24"-36" tall, 18"-24" wide
▶**Features:** A profusion of deep, clear pink flowers like miniature 2" hollyhocks blooms midsummer to fall on neat, bushy 3' mounds of foliage. Lovely in combination with obedient plant and balloon flower.
▶**Uses:** In the mixed border or planted in masses as a summer hedge
▶**Needs:** Full sun, but prefers light shade in hot summer areas in Zone 6 and warmer. Rich to average, well-drained soil. Drought tolerant in cool-summer areas in Zones 4-5; moderate moisture in hot summer areas in Zones 6-8. Plant established plants in spring. Fertilize occasionally or work in a slow-release fertilizer. It self-sows excessively; mulch and cut back in fall to control reseeding. Stake as needed. Each plant lasts only a few years but reseeds to ensure an ongoing supply.
▶**Choices:** High mallow *(Malva sylvestris* 'Zebrina') has eye-catching pale pink flowers veined with deep purple.

Holly, Sea
see Sea Holly

Honesty
see Money Plant

Honeylocust, Thornless
Gleditsia triacanthos var. *inermis*

Deciduous tree

Gleditsia triacanthos var. *inermis*

▶***Hardiness:*** Zones 3–8
▶***Size:*** 70'–100' tall, 50'–70' wide
▶***Features:*** You can grow grass beneath this broad shade tree. Fine-textured leaves are yellow-green in spring, bright green in summer, and golden yellow in fall. The true honeylocust tree has dangerous thorns on the trunk. Named selections are all thornless and most are seedless as well. Select one with the growth habit you desire for your yard.
▶***Uses:*** Shade, lawn, street, or specimen use; coastal areas; city conditions; areas prone to salting by winter road crews
▶***Needs:*** Plant in fertile, well-drained soil in full sun. Trees tolerate salt, drought, polluted air, and alkaline soils. Prune as needed to shape or remove dead wood.
▶***Choices:*** 'Shademaster'—seedless, 30'–45' tall and wide; 'Skyline'—pyramidal shape, to 50' tall; 'Sunburst'—conical shape, new leaves yellow, 40' tall by 30' wide.

Honeysuckle, Cape
see Cape Honeysuckle

HONEYSUCKLES
Lonicera spp.

While not all honeysuckles have scent, the ones that are fragrant are the stuff of legend. These mostly deciduous plants are either shrubs or vines. Some are invasive, with berries that are spread by birds. One of these vines—Japanese honeysuckle *(Lonicera japonica)*—is a rampant weed species that is banned from commerce in many states in the East. Encounters in woods and meadows with this extremely fragrant honeysuckle may be what imbues the entire genus with a reputation for delicious, almost overpowering scent.

HONEYSUCKLES

Dropmore Scarlet Honeysuckle
Lonicera ×brownii 'Dropmore Scarlet'

Semievergreen flowering vine

Lonicera ×brownii 'Dropmore Scarlet'

▶***Hardiness:*** Zones 3–7
▶***Size:*** 7'–10' tall and wide
▶***Features:*** Enjoy the trumpet-shape flowers as well as the hummingbirds they attract from June all the way through September. Flowers are scentless. Twining stems climb and clamber on vertical structures, but this vine won't damage wood. Control major aphid infestations if they occur with insecticide or insecticidal soap. May also be sold as scarlet trumpet honeysuckle.
▶***Uses:*** Climbing chain-link fences, trellises, scaling picket or privacy fences, arbors, posts, seasonal accents
▶***Needs:*** Plant in any type of soil that's well drained. Grow in full sun. Water during dry periods. Fertilize using a balanced liquid fertilizer at half-strength every 2 months. New plants may require strings to help them start scaling posts.
▶***Choices:*** Goldflame honeysuckle *(Lonicera ×heckrottii)* grows a modest 10' tall; its maroon flowers with yellow centers bloom over a long season and are highly fragrant. Zones 4–9.

HONEYSUCKLES

Royal Carpet Honeysuckle
Lonicera pileata

Evergreen to semievergreen shrub

Lonicera pileata

▶***Hardiness:*** Zones 5–9
▶***Size:*** 12"–24" tall, 3'–8' wide
▶***Features:*** This groundcovering shrub is easy to grow. You'll enjoy creamy spring blossoms, purple berries in summer, and shiny green leaves year-round. Royal carpet honeysuckle is not invasive.
▶***Uses:*** Planting beds, foundation planting, attracting birds, covering banks and slopes
▶***Needs:*** Plant in well-drained, fertile soil in full sun or partial shade. Prune after flowering to shape the plant. Tame wayward stems and control size anytime.

HONEYSUCKLES

Tatarian Honeysuckle, Arnold's Red
Lonicera tatarica 'Arnold's Red'

Deciduous flowering shrub

Lonicera tatarica 'Arnold's Red'

▶***Hardiness:*** Zones 3–9
▶***Size:*** 10'–12' tall, 8'–10' wide
▶***Features:*** When 'Arnold's Red' bursts into

H

Plant encyclopedia

bloom, the effect is that of a red waterfall. Blossoms give way to bright red berries that are a favorite among birds. This shrub is easy to establish and easy to maintain. Fallen fruit can stain paving. Use near outside living areas but keep a bit of distance. Dense masses of branches can catch all kinds of wind-borne trash; spring cleanup will be needed, especially if planted in open areas or near roadsides.
▶ ***Uses:*** Hedges, dense screens, fence-row planting
▶ ***Needs:*** Plant in full sun or partial shade in well-drained, fertile soil. Prune annually after flowering to shape and maintain size. Prune anytime to tame wayward stems.
▶ ***Choices:*** 'Alba' or 'Parvifolia'—fragrant white flowers; 'Hack's Red'—deep purplish-red flowers; 'Virginalis'—rose-pink buds and the largest flowers of any *L. tatarica* form.

HONEYSUCKLES

Trumpet Honeysuckle

Lonicera sempervirens

Deciduous flowering vine (evergreen in frost-free zones)

Lonicera sempervirens

▶ ***Hardiness:*** Zones 4-9
▶ ***Size:*** 10'-20' tall and wide
▶ ***Features:*** Grow this gently twisting climber to cover fences, posts, arbors, or rails with blue-green foliage and scarlet summer flowers. Bright red berries ripen in fall. Easy to grow and nondamaging to garden structures.
▶ ***Uses:*** Entries, courtyards, sitting areas; covering fences, trellises, arbors, rails, and posts; attracting hummingbirds to the garden
▶ ***Needs:*** Plant in well-drained, moist soil that's rich in organic matter. Water regularly, especially during dry spells. Grow in full sun. Prune in late winter or early spring to control growth as needed.

HORNBEAMS

Carpinus spp.

Hornbeams are handsome, well-behaved deciduous trees for the landscape. The native American hornbeam is an elegant smallish tree with trunks and large limbs covered in smooth gray bark and shaped distinctively like well-developed muscles. Use it in informal naturalistic landscapes for its picturesque structure and bright fall colors. Its cousin from across the seas is a little more aristocratic and formal in its regular shape and clean foliage. It takes pruning well and is often shaped into formal hedges and pollarded into tight, formal canopies.

HORNBEAMS

American Hornbeam

Carpinus caroliniana

Deciduous tree

Carpinus caroliniana

▶ ***Hardiness:*** Zones 3-9
▶ ***Size:*** 20'-30' tall and wide
▶ ***Features:*** Slow growth rate. Thrives in soggy, acidic soils. Leaves turn yellow, orange, and red in fall. Long-lived tree when sited properly.
Plant an American hornbeam now and you'll enjoy it for many years to come. Brightly colored fall foliage is one good reason; tolerance of boggy soils is another. Smooth gray bark earns this tree its nickname of musclewood. Trees are best used in naturalized areas as an understory tree.
▶ ***Uses:*** Small street trees, lawn trees, wet, boggy areas, waterside locations, natural areas, woodlands, beside patios
▶ ***Needs:*** Plant in deep, rich soil that's slightly acidic. Trees thrive in moist soil but will tolerate drier ground. Wet, boggy soil is fine. Will grow in partial to full shade. Plant in spring.

HORNBEAMS

European Hornbeam

Carpinus betulus

Deciduous tree

Carpinus betulus

▶ ***Hardiness:*** Zones 4-7
▶ ***Size:*** 40'-60' tall, 30'-40' wide
▶ ***Features:*** This small, adaptable tree is easy to grow. Branches are arranged around trunks like a spiral staircase to form dense, tidy canopies. Trees are pest and disease free. Foliage turns yellow in fall.
▶ ***Uses:*** Parking areas; entries; street trees, including in small yards; lawns; near patios; in paving cut-outs; lining driveways; high hedges
▶ ***Needs:*** Grow in full sun or partial shade and provide well-drained soil. Roots won't tolerate standing water. Plants tolerate either acidic or alkaline soil.
▶ ***Choices***: 'Asplenifolia'—leaves are deeply lobed; 'Columnaris'—slow-growing columnar form, 30' tall by 20' wide; 'Fastigiata' (also sold as 'Pyramidalis')—vase-shape tree, 30'-50' tall by 20'-40' wide.

Horsechestnut

see Buckeye

Hosta

Hosta spp.

Perennial

Hosta 'Frances Williams'

H

Plant encyclopedia

Hosta plantaginea

►***Hardiness:*** Zones 3–8
►***Size:*** 3"–48" tall, 3"–48" wide, depending on variety
►***Features:*** If you find composing with textures to be an elusive concept, plant beds filled with hostas. These large-leaved plants add coarse texture, a variety of hues, and erect stems of often fragrant flowers. Use variegation with care to avoid clashing foliage colors. Blooms mid- or late summer.
►***Uses:*** Shade gardens, front layer of beds, natural areas, massing, specimen plants, coarse-textured accent, shady courtyards, entries, patio areas
►***Needs:*** Rich, well-drained soil; moderate to plentiful moisture, though some tolerate dry soil. Mix compost at planting and mulch with humus each spring. Plant established plants in spring or fall. Fertilize occasionally, every 6 weeks, or work in a slow-release fertilizer in spring. Supply extra water during dry periods. Trim spent flower stalks for a neater appearance. These plants are susceptible to slugs and snails, although those with thicker, more leathery leaves are less susceptible. See page 216 for tips on controlling. Grow in partial or dense shade. Sun tolerance varies with the cultivar grown; in general, the more yellow in the foliage, the more sun the variety will tolerate. In fact, yellow-foliaged varieties need more sun for good color.
►***Choices:*** There are hundreds of varieties. *Hosta plantaginea* is fragrant. 'Sum and Substance' grows 3' wide with yellow-green leaves, is fairly slug resistant, and tolerates light sun. 'Blue Angel'—oval, bluish-green leaves; 36" tall by 48" wide; white flowers. 'Blue Moon'—blue-green leaves; 4" tall by 12" wide; pale mauve flowers. 'Diamond Tiara'—thin, wavy, olive-green leaves splashed with gray-green and edged with creamy white; 14" tall by 26" wide; violet flowers. 'Frances Williams'—heart-shape, puckered blue-green foliage with yellowish margins; 24" tall by 36" wide; white flowers. 'Golden Prayers'—deep yellow, slightly puckered leaves; 14" tall by 24" wide; pale lavender flowers. 'Kabitan'—lance-shape, bright yellow leaves edged with green; 8" tall by 10" wide; violet flowers. 'Love Pat'—heart-shape, thick puckered foliage; 18" tall by 36" wide, off-white flowers. 'Ryan's Big One'—heart-shape, grayish blue leaves are thick and deeply puckered; 34" tall by 60" wide; white flowers. 'Sugar and Cream'—wavy, heart-shape green leaves are edged with cream; 30" tall and wide; white flowers. 'Zounds'—puckered, thick yellow heart-shape foliage, 22" tall by 36" wide; pale lavender-blue flowers.

Hot Pepper

see Peppers

Houttuynia; Chameleon Plant

Houttuynia cordata 'Chameleon'

Perennial

Houttuynia cordata

►***Hardiness:*** Zones 5–9
►***Size:*** 6"–18" tall, indefinite spread
►***Features:*** Rapid growth rate. Colorfully variegated heart-shape leaves. Thrives in sunny areas with abundant water. For a moist, sunny spot, plant houttuynia. You'll enjoy care-free, colorful leaves throughout warm summer months. Houttuynia spreads quickly by underground roots and can be difficult to remove. This plant is a vigorous grower.
►***Uses:*** Filling in bare, moist areas, planting near downspouts, growing in or along ponds, portable water gardens
►***Needs:*** Plant in well-drained soil that's rich in humus. Add peat moss or composted leaves at planting time and mulch beds heavily each spring. Keep moist at all times. Plants will tolerate partial shade, but full sun produces the most colorful leaves. In colder climates, apply a winter mulch when the ground freezes.
►***Choices:*** 'Flore Pleno'—leaves tinged purple, double white flowers.

Howea forsteriana

see Palms: Kentia Palm

Hoya; Wax Plant

Hoya spp.

Tropical evergreen succulent vine

Hoya carnosa 'Picta'

►***Hardiness:*** Zone 11
►***Size:*** Grows as long as 15'
►***Features:*** Long trailing stems with waxy succulent leaves. Produces clusters of flowers that resemble milkweed flowers; the white flowers with their reddish-purple centers have a delicious, honeylike scent.
►***Uses:*** As a houseplant in most regions; however, can be grown as a permanent outdoor container plant in the warmest regions of the United States in a protected spot as long as temperatures always stay above freezing. Can be trained on trellises. Excellent in hanging baskets. Sometimes trained onto topiary structures.
►***Needs:*** Medium to bright light. Direct morning light encourages flowering. Allow the soil's surface to get dry between waterings. In the winter, water slightly less. Not fussy about humidity, but higher humidity encourages flowering. Does best in average to warm conditions; avoid cold drafts. Fertilize three times in summer with a 10-30-10 fertilizer.
►***Choices:*** *Hoya carnosa* is the most commonly grown. 'Variegata' has cream-edged leaves. 'Exotica' has leaves with yellow centers. 'Krimson Princess' has reddish young leaves. *H. australis* has round leaves. *H. multiflora* has pale yellow flowers.

Hyacinth

Hyacinthus orientalis

Spring-blooming bulb

Hyacinthus orientalis

▶ ***Hardiness:*** Zones 3-11
▶ ***Size:*** 6"-12" tall, 4"-8" wide
▶ ***Features:*** Heavenly fragrance that perfumes the entire garden—or the entire house—in spring exudes from these showy spikes of flowers.
▶ ***Uses:*** Effective massed in beds for midspring blooms. Excellent in containers, either outdoors or forced indoors for early spring bloom.
▶ ***Needs:*** Perennial in Zones 3-7; annual in Zones 7-11. Full sun, though light shade from deciduous trees later in season is ideal. Rich, very well-drained soil, acidic to neutral. Ample water during growth and bloom; moderate water after. Plant in October in Zones 3-7, working compost and bulb fertilizer into the soil. In Zones 8-11, purchase bulbs and chill in refrigerator for 6-8 weeks (or purchase prechilled) and then plant outdoors. Plant 8" deep. Mulch for winter protection in Zones 3-4. After blooming, allow foliage to brown and "ripen." Leave it alone until foliage pulls away easily This plant may come back for several years. Hyacinth are good for forcing (see page 163).
▶ ***Choices:*** Many named varieties available in blue, purple, red, pink and white.

HYDRANGEAS

Hydrangea spp.

Well-known for their big showy clusters of late-season flowers, hydrangeas are valuable shrubs for their easy culture and shade tolerance, and are often considered the workhorses of the shade garden. Most are big shrubs, 5' or more tall and wide, although some of the more popular large species have new dwarf cultivars that grow only 3' tall and wide.

HYDRANGEA

Smooth Hydrangea

Hydrangea arborescens 'Annabelle'

Deciduous shrub

Hydrangea arborescens 'Annabelle'

▶ ***Hardiness:*** Zones 3-9
▶ ***Size:*** 3'-5' tall, 4'-6' wide
▶ ***Features:*** Big blossoms are showy from spring into fall and change colors with the seasons. They start off apple green in late spring, then become white, then back to green, and finally fade to pink-blushed beige in cool weather. Position these shrubs where you can enjoy them throughout the growing season. Flowers may reach nearly 1' in diameter. Cut blossoms dry well.
▶ ***Uses:*** Specimen shrubs, seasonal accent, massing, entries, courtyards, beside patios, include in flower or shrub beds, narrow spaces between walkways and walls
▶ ***Needs:*** Plant in fertile, slightly acidic soil that's well drained but moist. Water regularly. Grow in full sun or partial shade—blooms best in sun but may require afternoon shade in hotter regions. Prune in late winter or early spring, cutting stems right above a bud to remove one-quarter of stem's length.

HYDRANGEA

Climbing Hydrangea

Hydrangea anomela petiolaris

Deciduous flowering vine

Hydrangea anomela petiolaris

▶ ***Hardiness:*** Zones 4-7
▶ ***Size:*** Climbs slowly to 40' tall or more
▶ ***Features:*** This hydrangea is an easy-growing and beautiful vine. It will cover buildings or tree trunks with yards of foliage and elegant, lacy caps of creamy white flowers in late spring and early summer. Older stems develop exfoliating bark. The combination of flowers, foliage, and bark gives this plant appeal in all seasons.
▶ ***Uses:*** Adding texture to brick or stone walls, chimneys, courtyard walls, and tree trunks; seasonal accent; providing coarse-textured background
▶ ***Needs:*** Plant in fertile, well-drained, moist soil in either full sun or shade. Prune as needed in late winter or early spring to control growth. This vine tolerates alkaline soil. Climbs by rootlets that cling to surfaces; large trunks of older trees are ideal supports. Because the vine doesn't twine, it's safe around larger trees. The rootlets will also cling to masonry walls.
▶ ***Choices:*** False climbing hydrangea *(Schizophragma hydrangeoides)* looks and behaves almost exactly like climbing hydrangea even though it's unrelated—only botanists can easily tell the difference. It's less hardy, to Zones 6-8, blooms about 2 weeks later than climbing hydrangea, and, also unlike climbing hydrangea, its leaves turn a bright, clear yellow in the fall before dropping. 'Moonlight' has attractive gray-green foliage. 'Rosea' is an exciting new cultivar with deep, bright rosy pink flowers. It is reportedly hardier too—to Zones 5-9.

HYDRANGEA

Bigleaf Hydrangea

Hydrangea macrophylla

Deciduous flowering shrub

Hydrangea macrophylla 'Nikko Blue' (above) and pink lacecap form (inset)

▶ ***Hardiness:*** Zones 6-9
▶ ***Size:*** 3'-6' tall, 3'-6' wide
▶ ***Features:*** Big, bodacious globes of flowers in late summer; large, coarse-textured green leaves; fast growth with salt tolerance—bigleaf hydrangeas will make you look like a gardening genius. The huge blue or pink flowers appear in warm weather set against rich green leaves. Acidic soil yields blue flowers, while plants grown in alkaline soil bloom pink. Add aluminum sulfate to soil for blue, lime for pink. Treat plants individually within a bed for a medley of blue and pink flowers.
▶ ***Uses:*** Specimen shrubs, massing, brightening shady beds, entries, courtyards, coastal landscapes, planting in shrub beds, perennial beds
▶ ***Needs:*** Plant in fertile soil that's moist but well drained. Grow in full sun in cooler regions, afternoon shade in hotter areas. Water regularly; plants wilt when roots are dry. Tolerates salt. Remove flower heads after color fades. The plants are hardy in Zone 5, but they die to the ground, and because they bloom on the previous year's wood will never produce flowers.
▶ ***Choices:*** Bigleaf hydrangea has many cultivars, some of which have been bred for the florist trade and are less successful performers in the garden. All bigleaf hydrangea cultivars come in two flower forms: mophead, with those big round globes of pink or blue; and lacecap, with big elegant flowerheads in which an outer ring of large florets

surrounds a central, tight cluster of tiny ones. Among the garden-worthy mopheads: 'Nikko Blue' has been bred to remain blue, but it will develop pink tints in alkaline soil. 'Pia' is a 3' dwarf that has been bred to remain pink even in acidic soil, and it does so remarkably well. 'Forever Pink' is a larger shrub that also has flowers that remain pink in acidic soils. 'Glowing Embers' is a large shrub with bright red flowers. Among the garden-worthy lacecaps are 'Blue Billow', with violet-and-white lacecap flowers, and 'Mariesii', a blue lacecap with ivory-variegated leaves. Recently bigleaf hydrangeas have been bred to bloom on new wood—which means that even if they die back to the ground like a perennial, they will bloom the next year, both earlier than the older cultivars and over a longer season. This makes these marvelous plants accessible to gardeners in Zone 5. 'Endless Summer' is the first of these new cultivars, and has blue mophead flowers in acidic soils. More are being introduced every year.

HYDRANGEA

Oakleaf Hydrangea

Hydrangea quercifolia

Deciduous flowering shrub

Hydrangea quercifolia

►***Hardiness:*** Zones 3-8
►***Size:*** 4'-8' tall, 3'-10' wide
►***Features:*** Slow to medium growth rate. Big, drooping cones of creamy flowers. Large, coarse leaves turn scarlet in autumn. Mounded, irregular plant form. These shrubs are big, their flowers are big, and so are their leaves. Prune after flowering if necessary, but plants look best when grown into their naturally irregular form. Less suited for formal landscapes.
►***Uses:*** Specimen shrubs, planting beneath trees, massing, coarse-textured backgrounds, shrub borders, edges of woodlands, natural areas
►***Needs:*** Plant in moist, acidic or alkaline soil that's rich in organic matter. Grow in full sun in cooler regions, partial shade in hotter areas. Shrubs grow best with regular watering but will tolerate drought.

►***Choices:*** 'Snow Queen' is a selection with showier, larger flowers that are held nicely erect, instead of drooping down like the species. 'Pee Wee' is a dwarf that remains 30"-40" tall and a bit wider, which is a valuable trait for an otherwise large species.

HYDRANGEA

Peegee Hydrangea

Hydrangea paniculata 'Grandiflora'

Deciduous flowering shrub

Hydrangea paniculata 'Grandiflora'

►***Hardiness:*** Zones 3-8
►***Size:*** 10'-20' tall and wide
►***Features:*** Plant this tough, fast-growing shrub where it has room to get big. Plants fade into the background until midsummer flowers put them in the spotlight. Large, cone-shape white flowers, fade to pink, beige, and then to rust. Flowers are produced on new wood. Flower heads can reach 12"-18" in length. Plants should be pruned to 5 or 10 main shoots to produce the largest heads. Ultimate plant size is variable.
►***Uses:*** Specimen shrub, seasonal accent, informal deciduous screen, coarse-textured background, beside blank walls or fences
►***Needs:*** Plant in rich soil that's moist but well drained. Slightly acidic soils are best. Shrubs will adapt to any soil condition except soggy. Grow in full sun or partial shade. Avoid pruning by giving plants plenty of room; shrubs grow vigorously and get large enough to be trained into small trees.

Hypericum calycinum

see St. Johnswort

Hypoestes phyllostachya

see Polka-Dot Plant

Hyssop

Agastache spp.

Perennial

Agastache spp.

►***Hardiness:*** Zones 5-10
►***Size:*** 20"-36" tall, 15"-30" wide
►***Features:*** Hyssop is an erect perennial with fragrant foliage that produces mauve and light pink or purplish spikes from midsummer to fall. The flowers are attractive to bees.
►***Uses:*** Best used in the mixed border or informal cottage garden, hyssop is a good, sturdy companion to purple coneflower, bee balm, and spike speedwell. It also performs well in containers.
►***Needs:*** Thrives in average, well-drained soil with only moderate water. This plant dislikes wet conditions; most types are drought tolerant. Most species last through the winter only in Zones 6 and warmer. In other areas, grow as an annual. Plant in spring in Zones 2-5; in spring or fall in Zones 6-11. Fertilize lightly. Divide in spring as needed. Hyssop is prone to mildew, rust, downy mildew, and some other fungal leaf diseases.
►***Choices:*** Hyssop comes in orange, apricot, red, purple, pink, blue, and white. 'Firebird' has copper-orange flowers; 'Tutti Fruitti' is a good substitute for the beautiful but invasive purple loosestrife. Anise hyssop *(A. foeniculum)* has bluish-purple or white flowers and foliage that smells like anise. Mexican hyssop *(A. cana)* bears dark pink or purple flowers in late summer and fall.

H
Plant encyclopedia

Iberis spp.
see Candytuft

Ice Plant, Hardy
Delosperma spp.

Perennial

Delosperma cooperi

▶ ***Hardiness:*** Zones 6–9
▶ ***Size:*** 1"–2" tall, 2'–3' spread
▶ ***Features:*** This ground-hugging creeper needs very little water to survive and prefers poor, dry soil. Plant it to cover bare spots and enjoy orange-red flowers in summer. Numerous daisylike flowers cover plants. Small, succulent leaves add texture.
▶ ***Uses:*** Rock gardens, hillsides, bare spots where there's little topsoil, beside paving
▶ ***Needs:*** Plant in any soil, no matter how poor, as long as it's well drained. Grow in full sun.
▶ ***Choices:*** *D. cooperi*—magenta flowers; *D. velutinum*—white flowers.

Ice Plant
Malephora crocea

Evergreen perennial groundcover

Malephora crocea

▶ ***Hardiness:*** Zones 9–11
▶ ***Size:*** 4"–9" tall and 4'–6' wide
▶ ***Features:*** Scattered with bright yellow flowers, this succulent from South Africa is a familiar sight along the highways and roadsides of southern California. It spreads quickly to hold down sandy soil and is a good choice to cover moderately steep slopes in a jiffy. Also makes a good fire retardant when planted around structures. Good for windy, hot, dry areas.
▶ ***Uses:*** Groundcover for large areas. Good for erosion control on moderately steep slopes, but not for steeper slopes where mud slides are possible. Plant this as a firebreak around homes in areas prone to wildfires.
▶ ***Needs:*** Carefree in well-drained soil and full sun. Needs little or no supplemental water even through drought. Little bothered by pests and disease. Plant it and forget about it.
▶ ***Choices:*** *Carpobrotus edulis* is the common freeway ice plant used in coastal areas from Oregon to Southern California. It bears scattered magenta flowers all year above thick, succulent leaves. It's also as carefree as you can get for covering large areas. Zones 8–11.

Ilex spp.
see Hollies

Imperata cylindrica 'Red Baron'
see Grasses, Ornamental: Blood Grass, Japanese

Impatiens
Impatiens walleriana and hybrids

Annual

Impatiens walleriana hybrid

▶ ***Size:*** Usually 12"–18" tall and wide
▶ ***Features:*** This is America's favorite annual for shade, blooming spring through frost with loads of brightly colored blossoms. Its continuous bloom, luminous flower colors, and ability to flourish in shady conditions make it a garden treasure. There are hundreds of varieties to choose from. Select for compact, dense habit; size of bloom; and color ranging from magenta and violet through pink, salmon, white, and even yellow. Double flowers reminiscent of roses have recently become available.
▶ ***Uses:*** Bedding plant in shady areas. Tolerates sun well with adequate, constant supply of moisture. Excellent in containers.
▶ ***Needs:*** Light shade in Zones 2–5; deep shade in hot-summer areas in Zones 6–11; lots of moisture. Plant in spring after all danger of frost has passed. Best in groups of a dozen or more. Fertilize occasionally, every 6 weeks, or work a slow-release fertilizer into the soil once or twice during the growing season. Mulch. In Zones 10–11 grow as a perennial but cut back hard—by two-thirds or more—in spring to promote fresh growth. It is usually pest and disease free.
▶ ***Choices:*** Choose plants by the flat when in bloom to select colors, flower shape, and size. Look for the recently introduced varieties with delicate small flowers and trailing habit, bred for hanging baskets, as well as new yellow and fully double-flowered selections. New Guinea impatiens are more tropical-appearing, with larger foliage that is often brightly colored with yellow or bronze. The flowers are larger, too, usually in hot shades of orange, red, and salmon. In fact, the whole plant is larger, reaching 24" high and wide in a season. It tolerates more sun heat than other kinds of impatiens, too, and is often grown in containers on the patio as well as indoors as a pot plant.

Inca Lily
see Peruvian Lily

Incense Cedar, California
Calocedrus decurrens

Evergreen tree

Calocedrus decurrens

▶ **Hardiness:** Zones 5-8
▶ **Size:** 30'-60' tall, 8'-10' wide
▶ **Features:** These trees stand like soldiers at attention, lending an air of formality to the large landscape. Their height complements larger landscapes but may prove overpowering for small lots or single-story homes. Though it prefers moist sites, California incense cedar is adaptable to the heat and drought found in southern growing areas. Makes a beautiful large specimen tree.
▶ **Uses:** Specimen use, windbreaks, planting in groves beside large lawns and formal estates
▶ **Needs:** This cedar thrives in fertile soil that's moist or wet. Grow in full sun or partial shade. Trees dislike windswept or smoggy conditions, but they can survive the heat and humidity of the Southeast.

Indian Hawthorn

Raphiolepis indica

Evergreen shrub

Raphiolepis indica

▶ **Hardiness:** Zones 8-10
▶ **Size:** 3'-6' tall and wide
▶ **Features:** You can't go wrong choosing Indian hawthorn for your landscape. It's tough and easy to maintain, and features glossy green leaves, fragrant spring flowers, and purple-black berries that ripen in the fall and persist through winter.
▶ **Uses:** Foundation planting, parking areas, seaside landscapes, low hedges, massing in planting beds, entries
▶ **Needs:** Grow in full sun or partial shade. Plant in moist, fertile, well-drained soil that's acidic or alkaline. Water regularly until established, moderately thereafter. Fertilize two to three times a year. Pinch back branch tips after spring flowering to keep plants bushy. Allow shrubs to grow together to form a mass.

Inkberry

see Hollies

Ipomoea spp.

see Morning Glory; Moonflower; Sweet Potato; and Cardinal Climber

Iris, African

Dietes iridioides (formerly *Moraea iridioides)*

Evergreen perennial

Dietes iridioides

▶ **Hardiness:** Zones 8-10
▶ **Size:** 2'-3' tall, 3'-4' wide
▶ **Features:** Irislike blooms of white and purple resemble butterflies. Spiky foliage stays green year-round. Tolerates heat and drought. Plants are grown for foliage as well as flowers. Clumps of spiky, upright leaves contrast with rounded shrubs in the landscape. Blossoms appear during the hottest summer months. Also known as *Dietes vegeta.*
▶ **Uses:** Accents, single-specimen clumps, containers, entries, patios, near pools, low decks, parking areas
▶ **Needs:** Plant in well-drained soil in full sun or partial shade. Add organic matter to sandy soils for water retention. Plants will thrive with very little water, but blooms increase with regular watering and abundant light. Plant in protected, frost-free spots. Mulch in areas with occasional cold weather.

Iris: German Bearded Iris; Siberian Iris; Dutch Iris

Iris spp.

Perennials

German Bearded Iris

▶ **Hardiness:** Zones 3-10
▶ **Size:** 12"-36" tall
▶ **Features:** Blooms early to midsummer
▶ **Uses:** Beds, borders, containers
▶ **Needs:** Growing conditions vary depending on the type of iris. Read label carefully. German bearded iris *(Iris germanica)* does best in full sun and average, well-drained soil. It needs moderate moisture but is drought tolerant once established in Zones 3-10. Siberian iris *(I. sibirica)* prefers rich to average, well-drained soil with moderate moisture, but will tolerate both very wet and moderately dry conditions in Zones 3-9. It does less well in the Southwest. This plant is very pest and disease resistant. Dutch iris *(I. xiphium)* is grown as an annual in Zones 3-7 but is perennial in Zones 8-10. It requires rich, well-drained soil and moderate water during growth. It is drought tolerant when dormant in summer.
▶ **Choices:** Thousands of cultivars are introduced every year. Choose when in bloom.

Irish Moss

see Scotch Moss

Isotoma fluviatilis

see Blue Star Creeper

Italian Arum

see Arum, Italian

Italian Cypress

see Cypresses

Ivy, Algerian

Hedera canariensis

Evergreen vine

Hedera canariensis 'Variegata'

▶ **Hardiness:** Zones 7-10
▶ **Size:** 10'-15' or more in all directions
▶ **Features:** This ivy makes a neat, dependable

groundcover in shady areas. Variegated heart-shape leaves help lighten dark nooks and crannies. Can also be grown on buildings or in trees. Vigorous growth even in dense shade. Tolerates heat better than English Ivy.
▶ ***Uses:*** Groundcover in shady areas, growing beneath trees, erosion control on shady slopes, framing lawns with coarse texture
▶ ***Needs:*** Plant in fertile soil that's moist but well drained. Grow in dense shade and water regularly. Feed in spring and fall with high-nitrogen fertilizer to encourage lush growth. Trim two or three times a year to keep beds neat.

Ivy, English

Hedera helix

Evergreen vine

Hedera helix

▶ ***Hardiness:*** Zones 5–9
▶ ***Size:*** 10'–20' in all directions
▶ ***Features:*** Grow English ivy to blanket shady beds or slopes with layers of dark, glossy foliage. Frame a lawn with an ivy-filled bed for a classic look. In areas with high rainfall, English Ivy is a nuisance plant that may climb high in trees where it can build up heavy masses that break limbs.
▶ ***Uses:*** Hillsides, shady areas, planting beds, natural areas, formal gardens, aging new structures, clinging to and covering solid walls, topiary. Makes a good houseplant.
▶ ***Needs:*** Grow in any soil that's moist or damp. Plant in full sun or partial shade where summers are cool; plant in partial or dense shade where summers are hot (protect from afternoon sun). Vines will adapt to poor, dry soil in shade.
▶ ***Choices:*** There are dozens of cultivars available; some people enjoy collecting them. They vary by foliage size from tiny-leaved needlepoint ivies to big, broad leaves, and by leaf coloration from deep and light greens to yellow, white, and silver markings.

Ixora; Jungle Geranium

Ixora coccinea

Evergreen shrub

Ixora coccinea

▶ ***Hardiness:*** Zones 10–11
▶ ***Size:*** 4'–6' tall, 4'–6' wide
▶ ***Features:*** Grow ixora for an accent or colorful hedge in frost-free areas. Plants are covered with clusters of red, pink, yellow, or orange blooms for several months. Good hedge plant; withstands pruning. Tolerates salt air and reflected heat. Regular fertilization ensures repeated blooms.
▶ ***Uses:*** Foundation planting, hedges, accent, parking areas, entries, coastal locations, poolside, adding fine texture and color to landscapes
▶ ***Needs:*** Plant in moist, fertile soil that's acidic and well drained. Provide full sun or partial shade and water regularly. Feed several times a year with a balanced fertilizer. For hedges, prune as needed to keep plants neat.

Jade Plant

see Cactus and Succulents

Japanese Aralia

see Fatsia, Japanese

Japanese Aucuba

see Aucuba, Japanese

Japanese Barberry

see Barberry, Japanese

Japanese Cedar

see Cryptomeria, Japanese

Japanese Painted Fern

see Ferns

JASMINES; JESSAMINES

Jasminum spp.; *Trachelospermum* spp.; *Stephanotis* spp.; *Cestrum* spp.; *Gelsemium* spp.

The true jasmine genus with the legendary fragrance is *Jasminum,* but several other intensely fragrant plants commonly go by the name. Star jasmine and its close relative Asiatic jasmine (both *Trachelospermum* species) are important landscape plants in California and the Southeast. And the flowering vine called Madagascar jasmine—well known as both a houseplant and as a flower for bridal bouquets—is a *Stephanotis* species.

JASMINES; JESSAMINES

Asiatic Jasmine; Yellow Star Jasmine

Trachelospermum asiaticum

Evergreen flowering vine

Trachelospermum asiaticum

▶ ***Hardiness:*** Zones 8–10
▶ ***Size:*** 10'–15' in all directions; as groundcover reachs 12"–24" tall, indefinite spread
▶ ***Features:*** Asiatic jasmine sprawls, spreads, and stays green year-round. Pale yellow flowers are intensely fragrant. Glossy foliage forms a thick mat that easily covers bare ground and hillsides. Leaves are a blush wine-red in cool winters. May be sold as Asian jasmine.
▶ ***Uses:*** Groundcover on hillsides, parking areas, large spaces, covering bare spots, cascading over retaining walls, trained on a tripod in containers
▶ ***Needs:*** Plant in acidic or alkaline soil that's well drained. Moist, rich soil gives best results, although plants can adapt to poor soils. Grow in full sun or partial shade. Trim regularly to keep edges and top layers neat.

JASMINES; JESSAMINES

Downy Jasmine

Jasminum multiflorum

Evergreen shrub

Jasminum multiflorum

►***Hardiness:*** Zones 9–10
►***Size:*** 3'–5' tall, 5' wide. Or can be trained as a vine to 15' in all directions.
►***Features:*** Here's a plant you can use as a shrub, climbing vine, or groundcover, whatever your landscape needs. Tiny white flowers cover the plants from late winter through spring and exude a delicious, powerful fragrance. Rapid grower.
►***Uses:*** Informal hedges, groundcover, parking areas, poolside, shrub beds, or growing up trellises, arbors, and fence posts
►***Needs:*** Plant in well-drained soil in full sun or light shade. Water regularly. Feed two to three times during the growing season with a balanced fertilizer. Downy jasmine is a sprawling shrub with long stems that, without training, will pile onto one another. Prune as a neat shrub or hedge; train the long stems to grow up a support by tying them; or allow the stems to sprawl across the ground as a groundcover.

JASMINES; JESSAMINES

Madagascar Jasmine

Stephanotis floribunda

Evergreen flowering vine

Stephanotis floribunda

►***Hardiness:*** Zones 10–11
►***Size:*** 10'–15' in all directions
►***Features:*** Although many flowering vines need sun to bloom, this one flowers happily in a semishaded spot. White blossoms are extremely fragrant.
►***Uses:*** Planting near sitting areas, covering fences and arbors, training on posts, screening for privacy, containers; flowering houseplant indoors
►***Needs:*** Plant in moist, well-drained soil enriched with humus or compost. Water regularly and feed with balanced fertilizer throughout the growing season. Place the roots in shade and the vine in filtered sun if possible. Climbs by twining; provide support. Indoors, give it the brightest location in your house, keep consistently moist, and feed heavily and regularly. In winter allow for a rest period by letting the soil dry before watering. In summer move it gradually to the patio, placing it in a spot with filtered sun.

JASMINES; JESSAMINES

Poet's Jasmine

Jasminum officinale

Semievergreen or deciduous vine

Jasminum officinale 'Grandiflorum'

►***Hardiness***: Zones 9–11
►***Size:*** Up to 25' in all directions
►***Features:*** This is the most commonly grown jasmine in southern California, Florida, and Hawaii; a large twining vine with dark, lustrous foliage and white, intensely fragrant flowers that bloom all summer and into fall.
►***Uses:*** Trellises, arbors, over pergolas
►***Needs:*** Full sun or light shade in rich, moist soil high in organic matter. Water abundantly. Pinch and prune to control size and shape.

JASMINES; JESSAMINES

Pink Chinese Jasmine

Jasminum polyanthum

Evergreen vine

Jasminum polyanthum 'Variegata'

►***Hardiness:*** Zones 8–11
►***Size:*** 15'–20' in all directions
►***Features:*** This is a favorite vine for coastal California, the Southern Atlantic and Gulf coasts from Charleston to New Orleans, and Hawaii. Fast-growing and vigorous, it bears large, showy clusters of funnel-shape flowers that are rosy pink on the outside with white interiors. They are immensely, almost overpoweringly fragrant with a scent that can fill a neighborhood. They appear in late winter and early spring, which makes this an ideal plant to combine with poet's jasmine for fragrance that lasts nearly the entire year.
►***Uses:*** Trellises, arbors, pergolas. Also used as a groundcover. Performs well in containers and hanging baskets.
►***Needs:*** Best in full sun to partial shade, and a rich, moist soil high in organic matter. Water and fertilize regularly. Prune as needed to control growth and shape; it recovers quickly from pruning.
►***Choices:*** 'Variegata' has leaves edged in light yellow.

JASMINES; JESSAMINES

Showy Jasmine

Jasminum floridum

Semievergreen flowering shrub

Jasminum floridum

▶ **Hardiness:** Zones 7–9
▶ **Size:** 4'–6' tall, 4'–6' wide
▶ **Features:** This vigorous shrub is just right for hillsides. The stems arch gracefully downhill, and the roots can handle the dry conditions. The tiny yellow scentless flowers produced over several months from spring into fall are a bonus. It's evergreen in the southern parts of its range. This plant may be sold as Florida jasmine.
▶ **Uses:** Xeriscaping, slopes and banks, massing, trailing over walls
▶ **Needs:** Plant in any soil—including acidic or alkaline—unless it stays wet. Grow in full sun or partial shade. Prune to control plant size.

JASMINES; JESSAMINES

Star Jasmine; Confederate Jasmine

Trachelospermum jasminoides

Evergreen flowering vine

Trachelospermum jasminoides

▶ **Hardiness:** Zones 8–10
▶ **Size:** 6'–8' in all directions
▶ **Features:** Clusters of white star-shape flowers show off against a background of glossy leaves. Flowers are very fragrant; some people find the scent overpowering.
▶ **Uses:** Covering chain link and other fences, arbors, posts, screening for privacy or to block poor views, covering bare soil. Makes a good container plant tied to a tripod for support
▶ **Needs:** Average, evenly moist, well-drained soil. Moderate to ample moisture. Plant established plants in spring or fall. As needed, tie to support to get vine started, or plant in beds as groundcover. Growth may be slow at first, but will speed up when plants become established. Prune for shrub form. Avoid fertilizing; if soil is too rich, blooms are diminished. Seldom needs pruning, but if desired, do so in late winter or early spring. This vine is sometimes bothered by whiteflies, scale, and mites.

JASMINES; JESSAMINES

Carolina Jessamine; Yellow Jessamine

Gelsemium sempervirens

Evergreen flowering vine

Gelsemium sempervirens

▶ **Hardiness:** Zones 7–9
▶ **Size:** Climbs 10'–20' in all directions
▶ **Features:** Easy-to-grow shrub tolerates a range of conditions. Bright yellow flowers in late winter and early spring. Stems form thick tangles of glossy foliage covered with dark green leaves that turn purple-green in fall. Vines are naturally thin at the bottom and thick and woolly at the top. A poor choice for formal gardens. Twining stems will not damage wood. Flowers are scentless.
▶ **Uses:** Fences, arbors, downspouts, trellises, blank walls, screening, poolside, seasonal accents, parking areas
▶ **Needs:** Plant in any soil, including alkaline or acidic, clay or sand, wet or dry. Grow in sun or partial shade. Dense shade reduces bloom. Prune overgrown vines after flowering to regain control; stray trailers can be removed at any time. Full sun to light shade. Average to rich soil. Moderate moisture; plants are drought tolerant after 2–3 years. Plant established plants in spring or fall. Mulch to conserve moisture. Tie to supports; plant will twine upward. Fertilize with slow-release fertilizer each spring. Every few years, prune severely right after flowering—by half to two-thirds—to control growth. This vine is usually pest and disease free.
▶ **Choices:** The species has single yellow flowers. 'Pride of Augusta' is a popular cultivar with double yellow flowers.

JASMINES; JESSAMINES

Night-Blooming Jessamine

Cestrum nocturnum

Tropical broadleaf evergreen shrub

Cestrum nocturnum

▶ **Hardiness:** Zones 9–11
▶ **Size:** 10'–12' tall, 8'–12' wide
▶ **Features:** Unbelievably delicious fragrance at night is the hallmark of this beloved shrub. The leaves are large and long and quite tropical-looking. The flowers are white and especially showy in the moonlight. Although poisonous to people, the white berries that follow are attractive to birds.
▶ **Uses:** Plant near bedroom windows, entranceways, and outdoor entertaining areas where evening fragrance is best appreciated.
▶ **Needs:** Plant in a warm spot protected from wind. Flowers are most profuse in full sun, although partial shade is well tolerated. Best in a fertile, deep, moist soil high in organic matter. Plants grow quickly and can get rangy if not pruned regularly; but the rapid growth is a plus for quick recovery after occasional frost damage. Feed and water regularly.

Joe-Pye Weed

Eupatorium purpureum

Perennial

Eupatorium purpureum

▶ **Hardiness:** Zones 3–10
▶ **Size:** 4'–7' tall, 3' or more wide

▶Features: Lovely big clusters of mauve flowers top tall, stately plants. Blooms appear late summer or early fall and attract butterflies. The seed heads remain effective well into winter.
▶Uses: Joe-Pye weed is most effective massed in large groups where it can occupy a sizable space. It combines beautifully with ornamental grasses and Autumn Joy sedum. It can be used in the rear of the mixed border, but clumps spread and can enlarge to hard-to-manage proportions.
▶Needs: Average to rich, moist soil. Tolerates wet soil; needs ample moisture. Best in full to half sun; with too much shade the stems will flop and need staking. Plant established plants in spring. Fertilize occasionally. Mulch to conserve moisture. Pinch back in midsummer, if desired, to control height, but flowers will be smaller. This plant seldom needs division. It is usually pest free.
▶Choices: Flowers are reddish-purple or white. 'Atropurpureum' has striking deep-purple stems. 'Gateway' has bronze stems that bear huge, light-colored blooms.

Jonquil
see Daffodils

Juneberry
see Serviceberries

JUNIPERS
Juniperus spp.

Junipers are the hardest-working plants in the landscape. There's one for nearly every purpose, from flat, spreading groundcovers to shrubs of every shape and size, to trees as broad as an oak or as narrow as a telephone pole. The evergreen foliage can be a deep green that's almost black, bright green, chartreuse, yellow, or nearly sky blue—or more muted in grays and cool steely blue. The textures of junipers combine well with many ornamental grasses and other plants with narrow, grasslike foliage and easy culture in poor dry soils and harsh climates, such as brooms.

JUNIPERS

Andorra Compact Juniper
Juniperus horizontalis 'Plumosa Compacta'
Evergreen shrub

Juniperus horizontalis 'Plumosa Compacta'

▶Hardiness: Zones 3-9
▶Size: 12"-18" tall, 6'-10' wide
▶Features: Low plumes of foliage are blue-green to gray-green. Forms a dense mat of evergreen foliage. Drought and salt tolerant. If you're looking for a groundcover for a bed surrounded by paving, this juniper can handle the reflected heat as long as the soil drains well. Plants stay full at the center. They are susceptible to Kabatina twig blight.
▶Uses: Groundcover in parking areas, coastal gardens, raised planters, hillsides, beside patios, filling in hot, dry beds and bare spots, foundations
▶Needs: Plant in full sun in any well-drained soil, including alkaline. Little pruning required—remove dead or damaged branches as needed. Needs little extra water.

JUNIPERS

Bar Harbor Creeping Juniper
Juniperus horizontalis 'Bar Harbor'
Evergreen shrub

Juniperus horizontalis 'Bar Harbor'

▶Hardiness: Zones 3-9
▶Size: 10"-12" tall, 4'-6' wide
▶Features: This spreading shrub tolerates heat, salt, and drought, and it turns shades of plum in winter. Makes a handsome groundcover. Twig blight can be a problem. Remove affected branches and destroy. Rinse pruners in alcohol between cuts.
▶Uses: Groundcover in parking areas, coastal gardens, raised planters, hillsides, beside patios; filling in hot, dry beds, bare spots, and foundations
▶Needs: Plant in full sun in well-drained soil. Slightly alkaline soil is preferred. Little pruning required—remove dead or damaged branches as needed. Extra watering is not required.

JUNIPERS

Blue Chip Creeping Juniper
Juniperus horizontalis 'Blue Chip'
Evergreen shrub

Juniperus horizontalis 'Blue Chip'

▶Hardiness: Zones 3-9
▶Size: 8"-10" tall, 8'-10' wide
▶Features: Grow blue chip juniper for its blue needlelike summer foliage that becomes tipped with purple during winter months. This plant loves sunny, dry locations and tolerates salt.
▶Uses: Groundcover in parking areas, coastal gardens, raised planters, hillsides, beside patios; filling in hot, dry beds, bare spots, and foundations
▶Needs: Plant in full sun in any well-drained soil, including alkaline. Little pruning or watering required.
▶Choices: 'Prince of Wales'—bright green leaves turn purplish in winter.

JUNIPERS

Blue Pacific Juniper
Juniperus conferta 'Blue Pacific'
Evergreen shrub

Juniperus conferta 'Blue Pacific'

▶Hardiness: Zones 5-9
▶Size: 10"-12" tall, 3'-6' wide
▶Features: Keep extra watering to a minimum, and this sun-loving groundcover will thrive. Blue-green foliage stays fresh-looking year-round and provides great contrast with other foliage and flowers.

J

Plant encyclopedia

▶**Uses:** Parking areas, entries, planting beds, hillsides, planter boxes, as a low layer in front of taller shrubs
▶**Needs:** Plant in full sun and any well-drained soil, from acidic to alkaline. Little pruning required—remove dead or damaged branches as needed.
▶**Choices:** 'Emerald Sea'—emerald-green leaves; 'Silver Mist'—silvery foliage.

JUNIPERS

Blue Rug Creeping Juniper

Juniperus horizontalis 'Wiltonii'

Evergreen shrub

Juniperus horizontalis 'Wiltonii'

▶**Hardiness:** Zones 3-9
▶**Size:** 3"-6" tall, 6'-8' wide
▶**Features:** This plant is aptly named: Its intense blue foliage is flat like a rug. Grow this juniper in hot, dry soil to carpet difficult spots or drape over retaining walls. This plant is susceptible to Kabatina twig blight.
▶**Uses:** Groundcover in parking areas, coastal gardens, dry planting beds, beside walkways and patios, behind retaining walls
▶**Needs:** Plant in full sun in any well-drained soil, including alkaline. Little pruning required—remove dead or damaged branches as needed. Extra water is seldom needed.

JUNIPERS

Dwarf Japanese Garden Juniper

Juniperus procumbens 'Nana'

Evergreen shrub

Juniperus procumbens 'Nana'

▶**Hardiness:** Zones 4-9
▶**Size:** 4"-12" tall, 8'-10' wide
▶**Features:** This ground-hugging juniper has branches that are densely packed with blue-green foliage. Plants thrive in heat and dry soil; they'll even tolerate pollution. The brighter the sunlight, the better for this sun-loving plant.
▶**Uses:** Groundcover in parking areas, planting beds, growing beside walkways and patios
▶**Needs:** Plant in full sun in any well-drained soil, including acidic or alkaline. Little pruning required—remove dead or damaged branches as needed. Extra water is seldom required.
▶**Choices:** 'Nana Greenmound'—resembles bright green cushions, 4" to 6" tall, 6' to 8' wide.

JUNIPERS

Eastern Red Cedar

Juniperus virginiana

Evergreen tree

Juniperus virginiana

▶**Hardiness:** Zones 3-9
▶**Size:** 40'-50' tall, 8'-20' wide
▶**Features:** Grow this durable native to block winds and screen poor views, provide a background for your garden, or to add needed privacy in the landscape. Trees are tough enough to plant at the beach and anywhere else you need their wide adaptability. Conical form becomes pendulous with age. Numerous cultivars are available with varying sizes, forms, and foliage color.
▶**Uses:** Screening, privacy, windbreaks, shelter belts, seaside landscapes, hillsides, natural areas, providing background for deciduous trees and shrubs, attracting birds, hedges, topiaries
▶**Needs:** Grow in any soil from acidic to alkaline, sandy to clay, wet to dry. Plant in full sun for densest growth. Trees grown in partial shade will be more open. Tolerates wind, salt, and drought. Water new trees regularly the first year to help them establish.

JUNIPERS

Hollywood Juniper

Juniperus chinensis 'Torulosa' or 'Kaizuka'

Evergreen tree

Juniperus chinensis 'Torulosa'

▶**Hardiness:** Zones 6-9
▶**Size:** 15'-20' tall, 8'-12' wide
▶**Features:** Rich green foliage year-round; interesting, slightly twisting branches. Tough and carefree, Hollywood juniper thrives in dry conditions and tolerates salt spray. Plants have an irregular form; pruning is unnecessary.
▶**Uses:** Xeriscaping, single-specimen plant, entry areas, at the corner of a tall house, seaside landscapes, or along a property line for privacy
▶**Needs:** Grow in full sun or partial shade. Plant in almost any kind of soil—acidic, alkaline, clay, or sand—as long as it's well drained. Will die in soil that stays wet. Needs water during periods of prolonged drought or when plants are new.

JUNIPERS

Old Gold Chinese Juniper

Juniperus chinensis 'Old Gold'

Evergreen shrub

Juniperus chinensis 'Old Gold'

▶ ***Hardiness:*** Zones 4–10
▶ ***Size:*** 2'–3' tall, 3'–4' wide
▶ ***Features:*** Old gold juniper features foliage as bright as its name implies. With its strong color, a little of this plant goes a long way. Locate near dark or neutral backgrounds. Foliage may clash with house color or the foliage of other variegated plants.
▶ ***Uses:*** Specimen plants, dry areas, hillsides, winter interest, Xeriscaping, arid landscapes
▶ ***Needs:*** Plant in any soil that's well drained, including acidic or alkaline. Hot, dry, and poor soil is fine; avoid wet soil. Does poorly in extreme heat or desert conditions. Grow in full sun.
▶ ***Choices:*** 'Spartan'—20' tall pyramidal shrub, green foliage, fast-growing.

JUNIPERS

Parson's Chinese Juniper

Juniperus chinensis 'Parsonii'

Evergreen shrub

Juniperus chinensis 'Parsonii'

▶ ***Hardiness:*** Zones 3–9
▶ ***Size:*** 2'–3' tall, 3'–4' wide
▶ ***Features:*** Forms a low-growing mound of grey-green foliage and maintains leaf color through the seasons. Once established, plants are carefree. Occasional pruning to remove any dead or damaged growth is all that is needed. Avoid overwatering.
▶ ***Uses:*** Low-growing hedge, low plantings along a walkway, or surrounding a patio or deck
▶ ***Needs:*** Plant in full sun in moist, well-drained soil. Will also grow in chalky, sandy soils that are dry. Little pruning is needed.

JUNIPERS

Pfitzer Juniper

Juniperus ×media 'Pfitzeriana'

Evergreen shrub

Juniperus ×media 'Pfitzeriana'

▶ ***Hardiness:*** Zones 4–9
▶ ***Size:*** 6'–8' tall, 15'–18' wide
▶ ***Features:*** This is a big, wide-spreading shrub too large for foundation planting but useful in large beds and open areas. It has gray-green foliage.
▶ ***Uses:*** For massing in large open areas.
▶ ***Needs:*** Easy to grow in full sun and in about any well-drained soil; it's quite tolerant of dry soil and substantial periods of drought. Bagworms, mites and Phomopsis twig blight are sometimes a problem. Pruning is seldom advised, but if necessary do so by cutting back individual branches. Shearing will ruin the natural, graceful form of this shrub.
▶ ***Choices:*** 'Pfitzeriana Compacta' has a similar horizontally-spreading form but is smaller, growing 3'–4' tall and 6'–8' wide. 'Pfitzeriana Aurea' is similar to 'Pfitzeriana' but with bright yellow foliage. 'Old Gold' and Gold Coast have yellow foliage but are smaller than 'Pfitzeriana Aurea', growing 3' high and 5' wide. 'Pfitzeriana Glauca' is a blue-green version of 'Pfitzeriana'.

JUNIPERS

Sea Green Chinese Juniper

Juniperus chinensis 'Sea Green'

Evergreen shrub

Juniperus chinensis 'Sea Green'

▶ ***Hardiness:*** Zones 4–8
▶ ***Size:*** 4'–6' tall, 3'–4' wide
▶ ***Features:*** Graceful and elegant, with a fountainlike form, sea green juniper has foliage that darkens with cooler temperatures. Grow it for year-round frothy foliage in moist or poor soils in full sun.
▶ ***Uses:*** Foundation plantings around homes, decks, porches
▶ ***Needs:*** Plant in full sun in moist to dry, well-drained soil. Will also grow in chalky, sandy soils that are dry. Little pruning is needed.

JUNIPERS

Skyrocket Rocky Mountain Juniper

Juniperus scopulorum 'Skyrocket'

Evergreen tree

Juniperus scopulorum 'Skyrocket'

▶ ***Hardiness:*** Zones 4–8
▶ ***Size:*** 15'–20' tall, 1'–2' wide
▶ ***Features:*** Sometimes sold as Rocky Mountain juniper, 'Skyrocket' is a preferred selection chosen especially for its narrow, upright form and silvery blue coloration. Plants tolerate the harsh growing conditions of the Midwest. Growth may be limited in clay soils.
▶ ***Uses:*** Vertical accent, arid landscapes, hedges, screens, growing in groups as windbreaks, urban landscapes, Xeriscaping
▶ ***Needs:*** Plant in full sun. This tree thrives in moist, well-drained soil but will grow in poor, dry soil, too. Tolerant of city conditions. Avoid planting in soggy soil.

JUNIPERS

Tam Savin Juniper

Juniperus sabina 'Tamariscifolia'

Evergreen shrub

Juniperus sabina 'Tamariscifolia'

► ***Hardiness:*** Zones 3–7
► ***Size:*** 3'–6' tall, 5'–6' wide
► ***Features:*** This easy-to-grow evergreen requires little effort to grow or to maintain. Simply plant it, water it in, and let it grow. Tam juniper grows in a mounded shape of blue-green branches, making it the perfect choice for including as part of a foundation planting or for rounding the corner of a house or deck.
► ***Uses:*** Low-growing hedges, planting along walkways, surrounding patios or decks, mass plantings
► ***Needs:*** Plant in full sun in well-drained soil. Grows well in chalky, sandy soils that are dry. It also can take urban growing conditions. Little pruning is needed. Remove dead or damaged branches or shape anytime from early summer to fall.
► ***Choices:*** 'Arcadia'—leaves are grass green; 1' tall, 4' wide; Zones 3–7.

Jupiter's Beard

see Red Valerian

Kafir-Lily; Clivia

Clivia miniata

Tropical evergreen perennial

Clivia miniata

► ***Hardiness:*** Zones 9–11
► ***Size:*** Grows 1'–2' tall
► ***Features:*** Gorgeous orange, yellow, or red flower balls 3" across are followed by berries on thick, strappy green foliage.
► ***Uses:*** As a houseplant. In southern areas it is used outdoors as a tall groundcover in deep shade.
► ***Needs:*** Morning or afternoon direct sun; otherwise simply bright light. Direct noon sun can scorch the leaves. Average humidity. Keep soil evenly moist. Reduce watering slightly in fall; reduce even more in winter to encourage a resting period. Resume regular watering when flower stalks appear in early spring. Average household temperatures are fine most of the time, but plants must have temperatures below 50°F/10°C during the winter rest period to encourage good flower formation. Fertilize with a half-strength fertilizer of 10-30-10 every 2 or 3 weeks, but hold off fertilizing during the winter rest period. After blooming, trim off stalk to divert energy into other parts of the plant. Keep the offsets that develop attached to the mother plant to encourage an attractive cluster of blooming plants. Blooms best when slightly potbound. Use a heavy pot with a broad base, because the large flower heads tend to make this plant tip over.

Kalanchoe

see Cactus and Succulents: Kalanchoe; Mother-of-Thousands; and Panda Plant

Kale

Brassica oleracea

Cool-season annual vegetable

Kale

► ***Hardiness:*** Zones 2–11
► ***Size:*** 1'–2' tall, 6"–12" wide
► ***Features:*** Beautiful pink, purple, green, and white leaves
► ***Uses:*** In edible landscaping, in containers, in the vegetable garden
► ***Needs:*** Full sun to light shade, especially in hot-summer regions. Rich, well-drained soil with ample moisture and neutral to slight alkalinity. Cool temperatures below 80°F/27°C for about 2 months. Extremely cold hardy; it can be harvested even in deepest winter. Plant seeds ½" deep or established plants in spring 4–6 weeks before your region's last frost date or as soon as you can work the soil. For fall or winter harvest, do the same in fall. Thin to 6"–12" apart, depending on the leaves' mature size. Keep soil moist. Harvest by cutting off near soil level.
► ***Choices:*** 'Lacinato' or dinosaur kale is tall, blue-green, with unusual shape and crinkling. 'Dwarf Blue Curled Vates' is heat resistant and cold tolerant. 'Verdura' has curled dark blue-green leaves on compact plants.

Kale, Flowering

see Flowering Cabbage

Kalmia latifolia

see Mountain Laurel

Kangaroo Vine

see Grape Ivy

Katsura Tree

Cercidiphyllum japonicum

Deciduous tree

Cercidiphyllum japonicum

▶Hardiness: Zones 4-8
▶Size: 40'-60' tall, 20'-30' wide
▶Features: This is a tree anyone can grow. Its size fits well with small home landscapes. Foliage emerges a reddish color in the spring, matures to a blue-green hue, and turns red and gold in the fall, providing three-season interest. Fall color is best when grown in acidic soil. Fallen leaves smell of cinnamon or burnt sugar. Avoid planting in areas with northwestern exposure in the winter or where winds are extremely harsh.
▶Uses: Specimen use, patio areas, small yards, street trees, entries, courtyards, and parking areas
▶Needs: Plant in full sun in soil that's well drained and fertile. Grow in alkaline or acidic soils. Water young trees during periods of heat and drought. If several main stems emerge, prune the tree to a single trunk in late winter or early spring.

Kentia Palm
see Palms

Kerria, Japanese
Kerria japonica
Deciduous flowering shrub

Kerria japonica 'Pleniflora'

▶Hardiness: Zones 5-9
▶Size: 5'-7' tall, 6'-10' wide. Growth rate is slow to get going, fast once established.
▶Features: Kerria's bright yellow spring flowers are as showy and as welcome as those of forsythia—only kerria is the better of the two for shade. Its bright green stems make this plant attractive even in winter after the leaves have dropped. This rough, carefree plant works best in more natural spots such as the woodland garden.
▶Uses: Use wherever the landscape is shady—in the woodlands, in the shrub border, massed in large groups for stunning effect
▶Needs: Moderate sun; flowers will fade in strong sun. Well-drained, humus-rich, moist soil. Ample water. Plant in spring, summer, or fall. Mulch. This shrub blooms on previous year's growth. Immediately after flowering, cut out flowering shoots to ground or cut back severely. If plant becomes overgrown, renew by cutting entire shrub down to a few inches. Add an application of compost around the base of the plant each spring. This plant is usually pest free.
▶Choices: This bush covers itself with golden flowers in midspring. 'Pleniflora' has double, pomponlike flowers. Variegated forms are also available.

King Palm
see Palms

King Sago
see Palms: Sago Palm

Kinnikinnick
see Manzanitas: Bearberry

Kiwi; Chinese Gooseberry
Actinidia chinensis (Actinidia deliciosa)
Fruiting vine

Kiwi 'Hayward'

▶Hardiness: Zones 7-9
▶Size: Grows up to 40' tall but can be managed with hard pruning
▶Features: Edible fruits on an attractive large vine
▶Uses: Edible landscaping
▶Needs: Full sun. Prefers moist, well-drained, acidic soil. Plant a male plant with a female plant for vines to produce fruit. One male can pollinate as many as 9 female vines. Plant on the north side of buildings and slopes; this plant breaks bud early and can be damaged by late frosts. Work compost into soil and plant 10' apart. Prune back to one or two buds. As the vine grows, select one strong shoot to train upward as a trunk (which can get quite thick) and remove all others. Prune heavily each early spring; it produces fruits only on those shoots that grow from canes grown the previous year.

Kiwi, Hardy
Actinidia arguta
Deciduous vine

Actinidia arguta

▶Hardiness: Zones 4-8
▶Size: 25'-30' in all directions
▶Features: This deciduous, twining vine is easygoing about its growing conditions. Poor or fertile soil, wet or dry, this vine will take off wherever it is planted. Attractive foliage adds coarse textural background in the landscape. White flowers open in early summer. They are fragrant but not showy. Fruits ripen from September to October; they are small (about the size of a large grape), hairless, thin-skinned, and delicious. For added protection in colder climates, plant on southern walls.
▶Uses: Screening; privacy; covering a fence, trellis, or arbor; edible landscaping

▶ **Needs:** Plant in full sun or partial shade in any kind of soil. Growth rate is fastest in rich soil. To slow it down, plant in poor soil. Prune anytime during the growing season to keep it in bounds. Grow both male and female plants for fruit production.
▶ **Choices:** 'Issai'—bears purple fruits. *A. kolomikta* (variegated kiwi vine) is an ornamental plant with multicolored leaves, green with pink and white blotches. It grows to 15' tall, does not produce fruit, Zones 5-8.

Kniphofia uvaria
see Red Hot Poker; Torch Lily

Kumquat
see Citrus

Lady's Eardrops
see Fuchsia

Lady's Mantle
Alchemilla mollis

Perennial

Alchemilla mollis

▶ **Hardiness:** Zones 4-7
▶ **Size:** 12"-18" tall, 20"-24" wide
▶ **Features:** Lady's mantle is a good low plant for in-between areas that are both shady and sunny. Chartreuse blooms are set off by silky gray-green leaves. Morning dew or rain caught by the leaves is a beautiful sight.
▶ **Uses:** Edging a planting bed, planting beneath shrubs, lining a walkway
▶ **Needs:** Full sun in Zones 3-6 and Pacific Northwest; otherwise partial shade. This plant likes rich, well-drained soil that remains moist but will tolerate drier soil with more shade. It needs moderate moisture. Plant established plants in spring or fall. Work a 9-month slow-release fertilizer into the soil's surface each spring. Mulch to conserve moisture. Trim spent blooms to promote second bloom and prevent reseeding (it will readily resow in most climates). Cut back plant by half if foliage gets ratty, to promote fresh growth. This plant is prone to fungal diseases, especially in the South.

Lagerstroemia indica
see Crape Myrtle

Lamb's Ears
Stachys byzantina

Perennial

Stachys byzantina

Stachys byzantina—flowers

▶ **Hardiness:** Zones 4-8
▶ **Size:** 12"-15" tall; 12"-18" wide
▶ **Features:** Lamb's ears are as soft and fuzzy as their name suggests. Grow these summer bloomers in patches to fill in flower beds or to edge planting areas. Velvety leaves are silvery and touchable; flowers are pink, white, or purplish. Water plants early in the day so leaves will dry before nightfall.
▶ **Uses:** Entries, children's gardens, moonlight gardens, edging planting beds, patios, walkways
▶ **Needs:** Plant in fertile soil that's moist but well drained. Tolerates poor soil as long as it is well drained. Grow in full sun (with afternoon shade in hotter climates). Trim heat-damaged plants to encourage growth in fall. Dig and divide plants every 3 to 4 years. Moderate moisture but also drought tolerant. Plant established plants in spring or fall. Fertilizing is unnecessary. Avoid getting leaves wet when watering. If desired, cut off flowers to keep focus on foliage. Each spring, gently rake or pull out tattered leaves to make way for new growth. This plant is prone to crown and root rot in moist or humid conditions.
▶ **Choices:** Flowers are pink, but plant is grown mainly for its silver-gray foliage. 'Silver Carpet' has no blooms and is a good choice for edging.

Lamium galeobdolon
see Archangel, Yellow

Lamium maculatum
see Dead Nettle, Spotted

Lantana
Lantana camara

Evergreen shrub

Lantana camara

▶ **Hardiness:** Zones 8-10
▶ **Size:** 18"-24" tall, 6' or more wide
▶ **Features:** Lantana makes a rewarding groundcover and container plant. This tough plant produces bright yellow blooms almost nonstop during hot weather. Leaves are evergreen. Tolerates heat, drought, salt, wind.
▶ **Uses:** Groundcover on bare, sunny spots; xeriscaping, seaside areas, arid landscapes, entries, parking areas, seasonal accent, containers
▶ **Needs:** Warm-season annual in Zones 2-9; perennial in Zones 10-11. Average to rich, well-drained soil. Moderate water; will tolerate slightly

dry conditions, but does far better with adequate moisture. Plant established plants in spring. Fertilize in spring with a 9-month slow-release fertilizer. Mulch to conserve moisture. If plant gets shabby, shape lightly to retain attractive shape. It is prone to whiteflies, aphids, caterpillars, mealybugs, and mites.
►***Choices:*** Flowers come in white, orange, yellow, red, and lavender. 'Camara Mixed Hybrids' is a dwarf, growing just 18" tall. 'Gold Mound' has golden yellow flowers.

Larkspur

Consolida ambigua

Annual

Consolida ambigua

►***Size:*** 1'-3' tall, 8"-12" wide, depending on variety
►***Features:*** This charming annual relative of delphiniums provides a good source of intense blue flowers from spring to midsummer in most areas, and clear into fall in cool-summer regions. The flowers and foliage are delicate and refined. Also available in whites and pinks, it reseeds freely; the seedlings are a boon for informal gardens, and easy to remove where unwanted. The taller cultivars are "leaner" plants that are perfect to grow up through other plants in the mixed border that they can lean on for support, or in large, closely packed groups.
►***Uses:*** A must for informal cottage gardens and meadow gardens, especially in cool-summer areas where the bloom season is spectacularly long. Also a welcome addition to the more formal mixed border, growing up among other plants. The lower-growing varieties are good for massing in beds.
►***Needs:*** Full sun in Zones 2-7; light shade in Zones 8-11. Plenty of moisture. In Zones 2-8 plant seeds directly in soil outdoors in early to midspring. In Zones 9-11 plant in fall for winter or very early spring bloom. Thin seeds according to package directions. This plant looks best in large stands of 20 or more plants. Stake tall varieties. Fertilize occasionally. Keep well watered but avoid wetting leaves. When plants are done blooming, tear them out and shake them upside down to scatter seeds, assuring reseeders next spring. Weed carefully the following spring to avoid disturbing tiny larkspur seedlings.
►***Choices:*** There are many varieties to choose from. 'Dwarf Hyacinth Mixed' (blue, white, and pink mix) and 'Frosted Skies' (white flowers with blue edges) are only 12"-18" tall. 'Early Bird Hybrids' are 20" tall, 'Sublime Mix' are 3'-4' tall, and 'Giant Imperials' are 4'-5' tall.

Lathyrus odoratus

see Sweet Pea

LAURELS

Laurels are large evergreen shrubs or small trees popular in the South as backbones of the garden. . They are grown mostly for their lustrous, dark green foliage that is attractive all year long. Relatives of cherries and plums, they produce spikes of small white or ivory flowers in spring that are followed by small black fruits that attract birds.

LAURELS

Cherry Laurel; Carolina Laurelcherry

Prunus caroliniana

Evergreen shrub

Prunus caroliniana

►***Hardiness:*** Zones 6-9
►***Size:*** 6'-8' tall, 4'-6' wide
►***Features:*** Grow this tough shrub when you need an easy, fast-growing hedge or green background. Rapid growth rate. Bronze new growth turns glossy green. Tolerates heat, salt, and drought. Plants can be left natural or pruned into shapes. Falling berries and leaves are messy near paving.
►***Uses:*** Hedges, screening, informal or formal gardens, coastal areas, quick background, attracting birds, xeriscaping, natural areas
►***Needs:*** Plant in average soil. After the first summer, watering unnecessary. Grow in full sun or partial shade. Prune anytime. Shears well. Shrubs can be trained as small trees. Plants grown in alkaline soil may require iron sulfate to keep foliage from yellowing.

LAURELS

Otto Luyken English Laurel

Prunus laurocerasus 'Otto Luyken'

Evergreen shrub

Prunus laurocerasus 'Otto Luyken'

►***Hardiness:*** Zones 6-8
►***Size:*** 5'-6' tall, 6'-8' wide
►***Features:*** White spring flowers will bloom in shade. Compact form with upright branches; glossy, dark green foliage. The large leaves add coarse texture as neat, spreading plants fill in shady spots. Allow shrubs to grow together to form a mass of dark green.
►***Uses:*** Foundation planting, massing beneath trees, shrub beds, background to shade gardens and perennial borders, entries, low hedges
►***Needs:*** Plant in moist, well-drained soil in partial or dense shade. Mulch roots well and water regularly. Protect from afternoon sun in hot climates. Pruning unnecessary.
►***Choices:*** Schip laurel, 'Schipkaensis' is a bit more hardy; 10'-15' tall, good for screening; Zones 5-8.

Laurel, Bay
see Bay

Laurentia fluviatilis
see Blue Star Creeper

Lauristinus
see Viburnums

Laurus nobilis
see Bay

Lavandula spp.
see Lavender

Lavender Cotton
see Santolina

Lavender, English
Lavandula angustifolia

Shrub or perennial, sometimes evergreen

Lavandula angustifolia

▶***Hardiness:*** Zones 5–8
▶***Size:*** 1'–2' tall, 2–3' wide.
▶***Features:*** Cultivated for hundreds of years as an herb for its fragrance, English lavender is also a lovely garden plant. Its low mounds of silvery or blue-green fine-textured leaves and lavender-purple flower spikes are famously fragrant, and especially beautiful when in bloom from early to late summer.
▶***Uses:*** In mixed flower borders and the front of the shrub border. Makes a good low hedge in a formal parterre or herb garden. It performs well in containers.
▶***Needs:*** Full sun. Poor, well-drained, neutral to alkaline soil; dislikes rich or wet clay soils. Very drought tolerant; dislikes too much water or humidity. Fungal diseases may occur where too wet or humid. Plant in spring. If needed, work sand or grit into the soil to loosen and improve drainage. Do not fertilize. Water with care in areas with ample moisture. A gravel mulch is useful. Cut back foliage by half or more after first blooming to prompt fresh growth and more blooms. Mulch for winter protection in Zones 5–6.
▶***Choices:*** 'Munstead' is the most hardy. 'Lavender Lady' blooms the first year from seed and can be treated as an annual. Useful in cold climates where it may die out. 'Hidcote' flowers are a very deep purple.

Leek
Allium porrum

Cool-season annual vegetable

Leek 'Amor'

▶***Hardiness:*** Zones 2–11
▶***Size:*** Grows 2' tall, 1"–2" wide
▶***Features:*** Subtle onionlike flavor for French and many other dishes, especially soups
▶***Uses:*** In the vegetable garden
▶***Needs:*** Full sun to light shade. Rich, deep, well-drained soil with plentiful moisture. Grows in a wide variety of climates but grows best in temperatures of 60°–70°F/16°–24°C. For extra-early plants and to prevent having to blanch, start seeds indoors 10 weeks before your region's average last frost date. When several inches high, plant outdoors in trenches 6" apart. Allow rain and wind to wash the soil into the trench to keep from having to blanch the leeks later. Otherwise, sow seeds directly in the garden in spring 4–6 weeks before the average last frost date. Thin emerging seedlings to ½" and then to 1" when a few inches tall. As plants grow, mound soil around the bases to make sure the tasty white portion is as long, white, and tender as possible. Harvest when base is about 1" thick. Overwinter by covering bases with several inches of straw and harvesting in spring.
▶***Choices:*** Choose from tender summer leeks or long-season, winter-hardy leeks. Summer leeks mature in one season, 70–80 days, and include 'King Richard', 'Varna', and 'Otina'. Winter-hardy leeks mature in 100–140 days and include 'Giant Musselburgh' and 'Blue Solaise'. Also look for leeks billed as self-blanching to minimize work.

Lemon
see Citrus

Lenten Rose
see Christmas Rose

Leopard Plant
see *Ligularia*

Leptospermum scoparium
see Tea Tree, New Zealand

Lettuce
Lactuca sativa

Cool-season annual vegetable

Lettuce 'Black-Seeded Simpson'

Lettuce 'Buttercrunch'

L

Plant encyclopedia

Romaine lettuce 'Devil's Tongue'

Romaine lettuce 'Freckles'

▶ ***Hardiness:*** Zones 2–11
▶ ***Size:*** Grows up to 8" tall, a few inches wide
▶ ***Features:*** Add variety to salads with a range of shapes, colors, and flavors
▶ ***Uses:*** In containers, in the vegetable garden
▶ ***Needs:*** Full sun to light shade, especially in areas with hot summers. Rich, loose soil with plenty of compost worked in. Ample moisture. Plant seeds directly in soil just deep enough for soil to cover in spring as soon as soil can be worked or 4–6 weeks before your region's last frost date. Can also be planted in fall in Zones 8 and warmer. Dislikes warm weather, will bolt (that is, send up a seed stalk and grow bitter) when temperatures are regularly above 80°F/27°C. Thin small clusters of plants to about 1" apart; use the thinnings in early salads. Keep soil moist. Mulch to conserve moisture. Fertilize every 2 weeks with a liquid fertilizer. Harvest by cutting all but 1" of the plants. They will regrow for 2–3 more harvests. Replant every 2 weeks to ensure an ongoing supply.
▶ ***Choices:*** Hundreds of cultivars and several types available. The most popular are informally called leaf lettuces and include old-time favorites such as 'Black-Seeded Simpson', 'Red Sails', and 'Oakleaf'. Butterhead types ('Summer Bibb', 'Buttercrunch', 'Little Gem') can be grown as leaf lettuces or thinned to several inches apart and allowed to mature as heads. You can do the same with Romaine lettuces, such as 'Sierra'. Crisphead or iceberg lettuces form attractive heads and are crisp and crunchy, including 'Green Ice' and 'Nevada'. Mesclun lettuce mixes of a variety of greens are planted like leaf lettuces. Allow them to grow 2"–4" high and cut off to about 1". Choose from blends for spring, summer, and fall planting.

Leucanthemum ×superbum
see Shasta Daisy

Leucophyllum frutescens
see Texas Ranger

Leucothoe, Drooping
Leucothoe fontanesiana

Evergreen shrub

Leucothoe fontanesiana. Inset: *Leucothoe axillaris*

▶ ***Hardiness:*** Zones 5–8
▶ ***Size:*** 3'–6' high, 3'–6' wide
▶ ***Features:*** Drooping leucothoe opens its fragrant white flowers in spring. They dangle and droop among the bright, bronzy-colored leaves. Leucothoe maintains its lustrous evergreen foliage through winter. Use this shrub to accompany azaleas or rhododendrons for a lovely spring show.
▶ ***Uses:*** Shrub borders, beneath shade trees, with acid-loving plants, fences, hiding leggy plants, massing, covering shady banks. Plant on retaining walls for cascading effect
▶ ***Needs:*** Plant in partial to full shade in acidic, moist, well-drained soil. Rich, fertile soil is best. Protect plants from drying winds and drought. Rejuvenate plants by pruning them to the ground after flowering.
▶ ***Choices:*** 'Rainbow'—new leaves are mottled with rosy pink and creamy yellow; 5' tall, 6' wide. Dwarf leucothoe *(Leucothoe axillaris)*—graceful compact form, 2'–4' tall, 3'–6' wide, not as susceptible to leaf spot diseases as drooping leucothoe. Sometime sold as coastal leucothoe. Zones 5–9.

Leyland Cypress
see Cypresses

Liatris spicata
see Blazing Star

Licorice Plant
Helichrysum petiolare

Perennial grown as an annual

Helichrysum petiolare 'Silver'

Helichrysum petiolare 'Limelight'

▶ ***Hardiness:*** Zones 10–11
▶ ***Size:*** 2' high, 5' wide
▶ ***Features:*** Popular in containers and as a bedding annual for its spreading, cascading form and beautiful woolly leaves in shades of silver, gray-green, white, and chartreuse. The leaves of this plant have a pleasant licorice scent when bruised.
▶ ***Uses:*** Licorice plant is beautiful arching through other plants in the mixed container; try the silver-leaf forms with pink petunias. Hanging baskets and pots, window boxes, or in the ground at the top of a retaining wall that it can spill over.

▶ ***Needs:*** Most are best in full sun, but the yellow and chartreuse forms prefer partial shade. Plant in spring in well-drained soil high in organic matter. Withstands dry soil when established but tolerates regular watering. Prune to shape if needed.
▶ ***Choices:*** The species has beautiful silvery-green leaves. 'Variegatum' has two-toned leaves of gray-green and light green. 'Limelight' has pale, glowing chartreuse leaves.

Ligularia; Leopard Plant

Ligularia spp.

Perennial

Ligularia dentata 'Desdemona'

▶ ***Hardiness:*** Zones 5-8
▶ ***Size:*** 3'-4' tall, 3'-5' wide
▶ ***Features:*** Bright yellow flowers and large, bold, tropical-looking leaves have made ligularia a favorite for shady beds. One variety produces its flowers on tall spikes; another bears big yellow daisies in clusters like a bouquet. Both are effective accents as a specimen, and provide spectacular drama when massed in large groups. Plants bloom in mid- to late summer.
▶ ***Uses:*** Excellent for shady beds, in the woodland garden, near water, such as on the edges of pools and streams. Dramatic massed in groups of 5 or more spaced 2'-3' apart.
▶ ***Needs:*** Rather picky about light; afternoon shade preferred in Zone 5 and a must in hot-summer regions of Zones 6-8. Rich, moist to wet soil. Ample moisture; never let dry out. Plant established plants in spring, working in ample compost. Mulch to help conserve moisture. Feed occasionally, every 6 weeks, or apply a slow-release fertilizer each spring. Trim off spent flower spikes after blooming. During periods of warm, humid weather the leaves may droop, but they will recover when the humidity drops. Protect plants from slugs and snails.
▶ ***Choices:*** Flower spikes are bright yellow or orange. 'The Rocket' is the most popular cultivar, with pointed, serrated leaves and yellow flower spikes rising to 5' tall; 'Desdemona' has huge, round, deep-red spring leaves that turn green on top. It produces large yellow daisies in clusters on stems about 1'-2' above the foliage. Leopard plant *(Farfugium japonicum* 'Aureo-maculatum') used to be grouped with ligularias as *L. tussilaginea,* and is still sold under that name in most garden centers and nurseries. It is a tender plant (Zones 8-10) popular in the South and coastal California for its unusual deep-green round leaves with bright yellow polka dots. Most often grown as a container plant, it thrives in moist soil and dense shade.

Ligustrum spp.

see Privets

Lilac Chaste Tree

see Chaste Tree

LILACS

Syringa spp.

Ah, lilacs—one marvelous sniff and you're transported to your grandmother's garden. Most lilacs are every bit as fragrant as the legends and stories that surround them promise. But fragrance is a subjective thing, and very personal—so to make sure the lilacs you plant have the fragrance you want, purchase them in bloom and give them the sniff test. Because most lilacs are hardy and like cool summers, they are excellent plants for the North and the Northeast. Prone to mildew in all climates, they are especially so in hot, humid ones. Most lilacs also need a period of winter chill to set the next year's flower buds. For both reasons they are less successful choices for the mild-winter climates of the South and the West, including California.

LILACS

Common Lilac

Syringa vulgaris

Deciduous flowering shrub

Syringa vulgaris var. *alba*

▶ ***Hardiness:*** Zones 3-7
▶ ***Size:*** 8'-15' tall, 6'-12' wide
▶ ***Features:*** Mid- to late-spring flowers are extremely fragrant. Numerous colors from which to choose. Dense hedges for privacy and screening.
▶ ***Uses:*** Shrub borders, informal hedges, screening, specimen use, planting beside entries or patios
▶ ***Needs:*** Plant in full sun to partial shade in well-drained, fertile soil. Best flowering occurs in full sun. Add composted leaves or peat moss to soil at planting time to boost fertility. Remove faded blooms to keep plants looking neat. Prune after flowering to shape the shrub and encourage vigorous new growth.
▶ ***Choices:*** French hybrids offer big double flowers in a variety of colors including burgundy, pink, white, and deep purple. Powdery mildew is common on lilacs, but plants will survive. Look for these varieties: *S. vulgaris* var. *alba*—white flowers; 'Arch McKean'—reddish-purple flowers, produces few suckers; 'Charm'—pink flowers; 'Miss Ellen Willmott'—double white flowers; 'Little Boy Blue'—single sky blue flowers, 4'-5' high, 5'-6' wide; 'Primrose'—yellow flowers; 'Wedgwood Blue'—lilac pink buds open to true blue flowers, 6' tall, 6'-8' wide.

LILACS

Cutleaf Lilac

Syringa ×laciniata

Deciduous flowering shrub

Syringa ×laciniata

▶ ***Hardiness:*** Zones 4-8
▶ ***Size:*** 6'-8' tall, 6'-10' wide
▶ ***Features:*** Cutleaf lilac is the best lilac to grow in the warmer parts of the country, even Zone 8. Use it to frame a porch or other outdoor seating area so you can enjoy the flowers' perfume to the fullest. Lacy foliage looks like it has been cut with scissors.
▶ ***Uses:*** Shrub borders, hedges, screens, specimen use, entries
▶ ***Needs:*** Plant in full sun or partial shade in well-drained, fertile soil. Best flowering occurs in full sun. Add composted leaves or peat moss to soil at planting time to boost fertility. Remove faded blooms to keep plants looking neat. Prune after flowering to shape the shrub and encourage new, vigorous growth.

LILACS

Japanese Tree Lilac

Syringa reticulata

Deciduous tree

Syringa reticulata

▶ ***Hardiness:*** Zones 3–7
▶ ***Size:*** 20'–30' tall, 15'–25' wide
▶ ***Features:*** A Japanese tree lilac in bloom is a sight to see. Covered with warm white flowers, the dark leaves provide the ideal backdrop. Trees thrive in areas with cold winters and cool summers. The flower show may be stronger on alternate years. Bark is a glossy reddish-brown.
▶ ***Uses:*** Small specimen trees, seasonal accents, entries, patios, planting beside the corners of houses, planted in groups for screening and as backgrounds to deciduous shrubs and perennials
▶ ***Needs:*** Plant in well-drained, slightly acidic soil. Grow in full sun for best bloom. Remove spent flowers to keep plants looking neat. Prune unwanted branches in late winter or early spring. This tree thrives where summers are cool.
▶ ***Choices:*** 'Summer Snow'—compact, rounded crown; profuse flowers; 'Ivory Silk'—flowers appear on younger plants; 'Regent'—abundant flower production, uniform shape.

LILACS

Miss Kim Lilac

Syringa patula 'Miss Kim'

Deciduous flowering shrub

Syringa patula 'Miss Kim'

▶ ***Hardiness:*** Zones 3–7
▶ ***Size:*** 6'–8' tall, 4'–5' high
▶ ***Features:*** This late-blooming lilac features single, pale lavender flowers that are rich with perfume. Leaves are glossy green in summer, then turn a burgundy red in fall. Miss Kim Lilac can survive winter temperatures of -40°F/-40C.
▶ ***Uses:*** Shrub border, informal hedge, screen, specimen shrub, near outdoor seating areas to enjoy the fragrance
▶ ***Needs:*** Plant in full sun to partial shade in well-drained, fertile soil. Clip blooms as they fade. Prune only if needed, after flowering, to shape the shrub.

LILACS

Persian Lilac

Syringa ×persica

Deciduous flowering shrub

Syringa ×persica

▶ ***Hardiness:*** Zones 3–7
▶ ***Size:*** 4'–8' tall, 5'–10' wide
▶ ***Features:*** This shrub has the same sweet, fragrant blooms as its larger lilac cousins but with more grace. Pale purple flowers grow in clusters at the tips of branches.
▶ ***Uses:*** Shrub borders, informal hedges, specimen use, perennial beds
▶ ***Needs:*** Plant in full sun to partial shade in well-drained, fertile soil. Best flowering occurs in full sun. Add composted leaves or peat moss to soil at planting time to boost fertility. Remove faded blooms to keep plants looking neat. Prune after flowering to shape plants and encourage vigorous new growth.

Lily

Lilium spp.

Perennial bulb

Lilium hybrid (Asiatic)

Lilium 'Stargazer'

Lilium longiflorum

▶Hardiness: Zones 3–9
▶Size: 18"–8' tall, depending on variety
▶Features: Large, showy flowers (some varieties intensely fragrant) clustered at the tops of tall, leafy stems bloom in early summer, midsummer, and late summer, depending on variety. These are "leaners," best grown among sturdier perennials and shrubs or massed together in large groups. Lilies have leaves along the flowering stem, while daylilies *(Hemerocallis* spp.) produce long, leafless flower stalks arising from low mounds of long, strap-shape leaves.
▶Uses: Excellent for the mixed border, grown among sturdier perennials and shrubs for support and to help mask the lily foliage after blooming. Spectacular massed in large groups. The shorter varieties are good in containers and in beds. All varieties make excellent cut flowers; trim off the stamens to prevent the rust-colored pollen from dropping and causing stains.
▶Needs: Full sun in Zones 3–5; full sun to light shade Zones 6–9. Rich, well-drained soil. Regular water during growth; then less. Plant bulbs in fall 8" deep, no later than a week or so after first frost date. Or plant established container plants in spring. Work in compost and bulb fertilizer at planting time. In spring, stake plants growing more than a few feet tall. Trim spent blooms. Allow foliage to brown on plant to rejuvenate for next year. When leaves die completely in late summer, cut off a few inches above soil level to mark spot.
▶Choices: Asiatic lilies grow 2'–5' tall and bloom early to midsummer. The flowers have no fragrance, but they come in many warm colors from cream to orange and salmon to scarlet, red and deep red, and are mostly open, flat, and star-shape. Oriental lily hybrids grow 2'–8' tall and are richly fragrant with more trumpet-shape or strongly recurved flowers. They bloom in midsummer or later, depending on cultivar. The color range is not as wide as for the Asiatic hybrids, limited to whites, pinks, and maroons, but many are richly striped, mottled, and variegated. One widely sold, long-favorite cultivar is 'Strawberry Shortcake', sometimes sold as 'Stargazer', which grows 18"–24" tall with intensely fragrant blooms that are creamy white, strikingly mottled and striped in deep pink and maroon. It is excellent in containers and massed in beds. Recently, hybrids have been developed that combine the intense, warm colors of the Asiatics with the rich fragrance of the orientals. They bloom later than the Asiatics and earlier than the orientals, and are all sturdy, large plants, with long-lasting, trumpet-shape flowers of thick substance. Easter lilies *(Lilium longiflorum),* well-known in the florist trade, are hardy in Zones 7–11 and are intensely fragrant.

Lily-of-the-Nile
see Agapanthus

Lily-of-the-Valley
Convallaria majalis

Perennial

Convallaria majalis

▶Hardiness: Zones 3–8
▶Size: 6"–8" tall, 6" wide
▶Features: Delicate-appearing stalks of deliciously fragrant white bell-shape blooms with scalloped edges emerge from among attractive leaves in midspring. Spreads nicely in moist, shady areas to make a dense groundcover that looks good all summer.
▶Uses: As groundcover in partial to dense shade in woodland gardens, in beds under trees and shrubs and at the north side of the house, walls, and fences. Makes a good cut flower for small vases.
▶Needs: Will take full sun in Zones 3–5 and the Pacific Northwest but needs at least part shade in Zones 6–7. Tolerates dense shade well. Average to poor, well-drained, acidic to neutral soil with plenty of moisture. It withstands drought well, but leaves will brown prematurely around the edges if conditions are too dry. In moist soil plants spread well into a large stand. Plant in fall or spring, working plenty of compost into the soil. Prone to leaf rot and stem rot if conditions are too wet.
▶Choices: Flowers are almost always white, but 'Rosea' is light pink; 'Plena' is a double-flowered white form.

Lilyturf; Monkey Grass
Liriope muscari

Evergreen perennial groundcover

Liriope muscari

▶Hardiness: Zones 7–10
▶Size: 12"–18" tall, 12"–18" wide
▶Features: This clumping cover will grow like crazy about anywhere you plant it. Blooms late summer on thick clumps of green, grassy foliage. Plant solid beds or neat rows. Divide clumps in spring or fall to make new plants.
▶Uses: Filling empty areas, massing, edging beds, walkways, or patios, entries, courtyards, slopes, narrow, confined spaces, parking areas, rock gardens, coastal areas
▶Needs: Best in partial shade, although tolerant of full sun to dense shade. Best in rich to average, well-drained soil. Moderate moisture, but will tolerate drought. Plant established plants in spring. Work in a slow-release fertilizer at planting time and again each spring. Mulch to conserve moisture. No need to divide, although clumps may be divided in spring for more plants. Every few years mow or cut back plants to a few inches in late winter (before new growth emerges) to remove tattered leaves and prompt new growth. These plants are susceptible to slugs and snails.
▶Choices: Flowers come in blues, purples, and whites. Variegated forms have leaves edged in white or yellow. 'Majestic' grows 8"–10" with dark blue flowers; 'Variegata' has green leaves with pretty white margins.

Lima Bean

Phaselous lunatus

Warm-season annual vegetable

Lima Bean

▶ ***Hardiness:*** Zones 4–11
▶ ***Size:*** Bush types grow 1'–2' tall and as wide, pole types grow 6'–8' tall and 1' wide
▶ ***Features:*** Tasty beans growing on a bush- or vine-like plant can be eaten fresh or dried.
▶ ***Uses:*** In the vegetable garden
▶ ***Needs:*** Full sun. Good, well-drained soil with consistent moisture. Plant from seeds 1" deep and 18"–24" apart two weeks after your region's last frost date. Provide teepees or other supports for pole beans. Beans start to produce in 70–90 days. Harvest when beans are plump in the pod. If growing beans for drying, allow to dry on plants, then remove from pods and store. For longest harvest, replant a new crop every 2 weeks.
▶ ***Choices:*** Lima beans do best in warm climates. 'Fordhook', however, is adapted to the North and 'Geneva' can be planted a week or two earlier than other types.

Lime

see Citrus

Limonium spp.

see Statice

Linaria spp.

see Toadflax

LINDENS

Tilia spp.

Lindens are excellent shade trees that have the delightful bonus of producing richly fragrant flowers in early summer. The flowers are not very showy, but are probably more responsible for people looking around and asking "What's that heavenly scent?" than any other plant. In Europe they are often called lime trees because of their citrusy fragrance. Lindens can drop a lot of litter—spent flowers and seeds—so plant them away from gutters and paving where that might be an issue.

LINDENS

American Linden

Tilia americana

Deciduous tree

Tilia americana

▶ ***Hardiness:*** Zones 2–8
▶ ***Size:*** 60'–80' tall, 30'–50' wide
▶ ***Features:*** Growing wild from Canada to Alabama, this tree is easy to transplant and grows very large. Coarse-textured leaves provide dense shade. Well suited for large areas. Selected varieties are more appropriate for home landscapes. May be sold as basswood. Trees often reach 100' tall with age. Dark green foliage has lighter underside; fragrant, pale-yellow flowers appear in summer.
▶ ***Uses:*** Specimen use, shade trees, large estates, natural areas, wooded sites
▶ ***Needs:*** Plant in moist soil that's well drained. Trees grow best in alkaline soil but will tolerate some acidity. Will grow in shallow, rocky soil but mature size may be reduced. Grow in full sun or partial shade. Dislikes polluted air but withstands cold winters. Easy to transplant.
▶ ***Choices:*** 'Redmond'—dense, pyramidal canopy; 45' tall by 25' wide; 'Fastigiata'—conical, upright form.

LINDENS

Littleleaf Linden

Tilia cordata

Deciduous tree

Tilia cordata

▶ ***Hardiness:*** Zones 3–7
▶ ***Size:*** 60'–70' tall, 30'–50' wide
▶ ***Features:*** This tree's uniform shape makes it a good choice for planting in neat rows or squares and to add symmetry to the landscape. Glossy green foliage turns yellow-green in fall. Small summer flowers are more fragrant than showy. Several cultivars are available that differ in form and growth rate. Trees can be grown in the warmer parts of Zone 3.
▶ ***Uses:*** Lawn, specimen, shade, and streetside use, parking areas, lining driveways, formal landscapes, patio trees
▶ ***Needs:*** Plant in any soil that's moist, including acidic or alkaline, fertile or poor. Trees can withstand the compacted soils of new construction as well as pollution and paving. Grow in full sun.

Linum perenne

see Flax, Blue

Lipstick Plant

Aeschynanthus spp.

Tropical perennial

Aeschynanthus spp.

▶ ***Size:*** Trailing stems 18"–36" long, depending on the type
▶ ***Features:*** Stunning-throated 2"–3" flowers in cream, yellow, orange, pink, and red that look like little lipsticks emerging from their cases grow on top of a trailing plant. Excellent in hanging pots and baskets.
▶ ***Uses:*** As a houseplant
▶ ***Needs:*** Bright but indirect light. Keep soil moist but cut back on water in winter. Fertilize once a month during the blooming season with a 10-30-10 fertilizer; hold off on fertilizing at other times, especially winter. Make sure the drainage is good or rot may occur. When repotting, use a mix that is half African violet mix and half epiphyte (air plant) mix. Needs high humidity; put on a tray filled with pebbles and water or run a humidifier. Cut back stems hard (as much as by half or two-thirds) after flowering to keep plants from becoming leggy.
▶ ***Choices:*** *Aeschynanthus lobbianus* is the most commonly sold, but *A. pulcher, A. javanicus,* and *A. radicans* are also sold and are similar with 18" stems. *A. speciosus* has stems up to 3' and larger flowers.

Liquidambar styraciflua
see Sweet Gum

Liriodendron tulipifera
see Tulip Tree

Liriope muscari
see Lilyturf

Lisianthus
Lisianthus grandifolia
(Eustoma grandiflorum)

Annual

Lisianthus grandifolia

▶***Size:*** 15"–20" tall, 12" wide
▶***Features:*** Ivory, pink, and purple cup-shape blooms on long, sturdy stems have made lisianthus popular in the cut-flower trade, and it's perfect for home cutting gardens as well. Some varieties have double, roselike blossoms. Blooms mid- to late summer.
▶***Uses:*** While often grown in the cutting garden, lisianthus is attractive in beds and borders too. In the mixed border it looks especially good with roses, snapdragons, and delphiniums.
▶***Needs:*** Average, well-drained soil; ample moisture. Plant established seedlings in spring after all danger of frost has passed. Pinch off tops at planting time to encourage bushier growth and more flowers. Mulch to conserve moisture. Fertilize regularly, every 4 weeks, or work in a 9-month slow-release fertilizer at planting time. Trim spent blooms to encourage further flowering. This plant is usually pest free.
▶***Choices:*** Flowers are pinks, whites, and blues. Dwarf types grow 6" tall; taller types are excellent for cutting. 'Flamenco' is especially heat tolerant.

Lithodora
Lithodora diffusa (formerly *Lithospermum prostratum)*

Evergreen shrub

Lithodora diffusa

▶***Hardiness:*** Zones 6–8
▶***Size:*** 6"–12" high, 12"–15" wide
▶***Features:*** This small evergreen shrub is covered with brilliant deep blue flowers in early summer. It has a somewhat trailing habit, with small, fuzzy, dark green leaves that remain attractive all year.
▶***Uses:*** Excellent in the rock garden or in the front of raised beds where its beautiful blue flowers can be appreciated up close. Most effective when massed in groups as a groundcover.
▶***Needs:*** Full sun. Best in acidic, moist but well-drained soil high in organic matter. Avoid alkaline soils. Prune flowers after blooming. Do not cultivate around roots and avoid transplanting after established.

Lithops spp.
see Cactus and Succulents: Living Stones

Lithospermum prostratum
see Lithodora

Living Stones
see Cactus and Succulents

Livistona chinensis
see Palms: Chinese Fan Palm

Lobelia cardinalis
see Cardinal Flower

Lobelia, Edging; Trailing Lobelia
Lobelia erinus

Annual

Lobelia erinus 'Riviera'

▶***Hardiness:*** Zones 4–11
▶***Size:*** 4"–8" tall, 6"–15" wide
▶***Features:*** These low, trailing plants produce masses of delicate tiny flowers in vivid shades of deep blue, sky blue, purple, lavender, pink, and white. They bloom best during cool weather, languish in hot summers.
▶***Uses:*** Excellent in hanging baskets, as edging, and massed in beds as a groundcover. Looks good in rock gardens, especially tucked into pockets to spill out of rock walls.
▶***Needs:*** Full sun in cooler regions in Zones 4–6, part shade in hot summer in Zones 7–11. Light, rich, well-drained soil. Moderate to ample moisture. Plant established plants outdoors after all danger of frost has passed. Feed occasionally, every 4–6 weeks, or work in a slow-release fertilizer at planting time. Mulch to conserve moisture and keep soil cool. When temperatures regularly get higher than 85°–89°F/29°–32°C, plants will stop blooming. Cut back by half to two-thirds when this happens; plants will rebloom in fall and continue until the first frost.
▶***Choices:*** 'Riviera' and 'Blue Moon' form compact mounds. The 'Fountain' and 'Cascade' series have cascading habits.

Lobularia maritima
see Sweet Alyssum

London Plane Tree
see Sycamores

Lonicera spp.
see Honeysuckles

Loosestrife, Gooseneck
Lysimachia clethroides

Perennial

Lysimachia clethroides

▶ ***Hardiness:*** Zones 3–8
▶ ***Size:*** 3' tall, 3' wide, spread is indefinite
▶ ***Features:*** In the right place where it can be allowed to spread into a dense, large colony, gooseneck loosestrife produces a spectacular effect in late summer, when its sea of white flower spikes crook their necks all in the same direction for a most charming picture.
▶ ***Uses:*** Large areas, planted in groups and allowed to spread into a large mass. Most vigorous in moist soils, at the edges of ponds and streams, and in low wet spots with poor drainage.
▶ ***Needs:*** Average to rich soil. Likes ample moisture but will tolerate somewhat dry conditions. Plant established plants in spring or fall. Mulch to conserve moisture. No need to fertilize. Contain plants with an underground barrier to prevent spread.
▶ ***Choices:*** Yellow loosestrife *(Lysimachia punctata)* has brilliant yellow flowers blooming along 3' stems. This plant needs even moisture but will also tolerate somewhat dry conditions. It can be invasive in Zones 4–8, but somewhat less so than gooseneck loosestrife. For a description of the groundcover *L. nummularia,* see Moneywort (also called Creeping Jenny) on page 440.

Loquat
Eriobotrya japonica

Subtropical evergreen tree

Eriobotrya japonica

▶ ***Hardiness:*** Zones 8–10
▶ ***Size:***20'–30' tall, 15'–25' wide
▶ ***Features:*** Large, dark green leaves are evergreen. Loquat works well as a background tree in hot regions, providing interesting texture. Can be trained as an espalier against walls. White fragrant flowers develop into pear-shape fruits that ripen April through June.
▶ ***Uses:*** Screening for privacy or to block views, coarse-textured background or accent tree, adding shade as a small ornamental tree
▶ ***Needs:*** Full sun or partial shade. Plant in any well-drained moist soil, from acidic to alkaline. Water regularly after planting, then only when conditions are extremely dry. Mulch area around trunk. Feed with a balanced fertilizer if soil is sandy.

Loropetalum chinense
see Fringe Flower, Chinese

Love-in-a-Mist
Nigella damascena

Annual

Nigella damascena

▶ ***Size:*** 15"–24" tall, 6"–8" wide
▶ ***Features:*** Pink, white, or blue flowers surrounded by feathery bracts, and fine threadlike foliage give love-in-a-mist an airy, misty quality in the garden. The flowers are followed by puffy seedpods that are beloved by flower arrangers. Plants self-sow prolifically, so plants will return year after year. Blooms late winter or spring.
▶ ***Uses:*** Lovely in the cottage garden or meadow garden with other self-sowing annuals. In the mixed border it combines beautifully with forget-me-nots and spring-blooming bulbs.
▶ ***Needs:*** Full sun. Sandy or gravelly soil with excellent drainage. Moderate moisture. In Zones 2–7 sow seeds outdoors in early spring a couple of weeks before last frost date. In Zones 8–11 do so in late autumn. Sow seed directly onto prepared soil and plant in generous clusters of 10 or more plants for best effect. Do not cover. Keep moist. Thin seedlings to 8"–12" apart. Avoid fertilizing. May need support; insert a shrubby branch or two into the ground. Trim spent blooms to prolong blooming. However, deadheading may reduce reseeding, which this plant will do nicely in ideal conditions.
▶ ***Choices:*** 'Persian Jewels' is the most commonly offered variety. It is an excellent mix of intense blue, deep pink, and white.

Love-Lies-Bleeding
see Amaranth

Lucky Bamboo
see Dracaenas

Lunaria annua
see Money Plant

Lungwort
see Pulmonaria

Lupine, Russell
Lupinus 'Russell Hybrids'

Perennials

Lupinus 'Russell Hybrids'

L

Plant encyclopedia

Lupinus texensis

▶ ***Hardiness:*** Zones 4–6
▶ ***Size:*** 24"–36" tall, 18"–24" wide
▶ ***Features:*** Lupines are a large group of wildflowers native to western North America. The Russell Hybrids are the result of sending many lupine species off to England for finishing school. They have become popular subjects for gardening in the cool-summer climates of England and similar humid, cool-summer climates in North America—the Northeast, around the Great Lakes, and the Pacific Northwest. Blooms early summer with poppies, peonies, hardy geraniums, bearded iris, and the first flush of roses.
▶ ***Uses:*** Excellent massed in beds, or planted in smaller groups of 3 or 5 in the mixed border.
▶ ***Needs:*** Full sun; tolerates light shade. Rich, acidic, well-drained soil. Ample moisture. In Zones 4–5 plant established plants in spring and grow as a short-lived perennial. In Zones 6–9 plant in fall as a cool-season annual. Plant in groups of 6 or more for best effect. Fertilize occasionally, every 4–6 weeks, or work in a slow-release fertilizer at planting time. Mulch to keep soil cool and moist. Trim spent flower stalks to encourage a second bloom. This plant is susceptible to aphids, powdery mildew, slugs, and crown rot.
▶ ***Choices:*** Nearly all colors are available. Texas bluebonnet *(Lupinus texensis)* is a wildflower native to Texas. It is a small plant, 6"–12" tall, with spikes of bright blue flowers with clear white eyes in early spring (about April 15 in the Texas hill country). It is often sold in Texas wildflower seed mixes with showy evening primrose and Indian paintbrush.

Lycoris squamigera
see Naked Ladies

Lysimachia clethroides
see Loosestrife, Gooseneck

Lysimachia nummularia
see Moneywort

Madagascar Dragon Tree
see Dracaenas

Madagascar Jasmine
see Jasmines

MAGNOLIAS
Magnolia spp.

This classic Southern plant comes in an amazing variety of colors, flower and leaf shapes, and plant forms. Magnolias also can be more cold hardy than commonly thought, with several types doing well as far north as Zone 5. Magnolias can be either evergreen or deciduous and range in size from 6' to as tall as 80', depending on the type and growing conditions. All have showy, lovely flowers characterized either as star type or larger cup type. Some magnolias are also fragrant.

MAGNOLIAS

Saucer Magnolia
Magnolia ×soulangiana

Deciduous flowering tree

Magnolia ×soulangiana

▶ ***Hardiness:*** Zones 5–9
▶ ***Size:*** 20'–30' tall, 20'–30' wide
▶ ***Features:*** Big, beautiful blooms in shades of white to pink and purple accent this ornamental tree. Often jumping the gun on spring, it blooms during the slightest warm spell, often resulting in flower loss because of frost. Flowering occurs before leaves emerge. Planting on a northern exposure may help delay flowering and reduce flower loss. Hybrids with girls' names bloom a bit later as well. Branches emerge low on the trunk and spread widely to form a crown with an attractive rounded outline.
▶ ***Uses:*** Specimen use, seasonal accents, open lawn areas, large planting beds, groupings, near buildings
▶ ***Needs:*** Plant in rich soil high in organic matter. Slightly acidic soil is best, but trees tolerate some alkalinity. Mulch well and water regularly in summer to keep soil moist. Prune after flowering and only as needed because cuts heal slowly.
▶ ***Choices:*** Northern Japanese magnolia, *M. kobus,* blooms in midspring.

MAGNOLIAS

Southern Magnolia
Magnolia grandiflora

Broadleaf evergreen flowering tree

Magnolia grandiflora

▶ ***Hardiness:*** Zones 6–10
▶ ***Size:*** 50'–80' tall, 30'–50' wide
▶ ***Features:*** Everything about this magnolia is big—its size, its foliage, its flowers, and its fruit. Blooms up to 12" across appear in late spring, emitting a perfumelike scent. Rose-red fruit ripens in late fall. Trees need plenty of room to grow and develop their stately form. Avoid planting this tree in small areas. Look for trees that are named; they are generally superior in strength and quality to unnamed varieties.
▶ ***Uses:*** Specimen tree, open lawn areas, large estates, screening, soggy soil, espalier blank walls
▶ ***Needs:*** Grows best in well-drained rich soil, but trees tolerate poor soils and wet locations. Soil should be acidic. Plant in full sun or partial shade. Protect from winter winds in northern areas.
▶ ***Choices:*** 'Bracken's Brown Beauty'—cold-tolerant, brown-backed leaves; 'Little Gem'—shrubby form, small sizes; 'DD Blanchard'—tree with upright form.

MAGNOLIAS

Star Magnolia

Magnolia stellata

Deciduous flowering tree

Magnolia stellata

► ***Hardiness:*** Zones 5–9
► ***Size:*** 15'–20' tall, 10'–15' wide
► ***Features:*** Fragrant, white starry blooms brighten shady spots during the gray days between winter and spring. This tree stays small and tidy. This is the earliest-blooming magnolia. Planting on a northern exposure may delay flowering and reduce flower loss due to freezing temperatures. Trees look great planted against red brick walls and buildings.
► ***Uses:*** Small specimen trees, seasonal accent, foundation planting, narrow spaces, beside walkways or steps, natural areas, understory trees, woodlands, shaded courtyards
► ***Needs:*** Plant in moist, well-drained soil that's rich in organic matter and acidic. Mulch trees well and water regularly to keep soil moist during summer months. Grows best in partial shade. May survive in warmer parts of Zone 4.

MAGNOLIAS

Sweet Bay Magnolia

Magnolia virginiana

Semievergreen tree

Magnolia virginiana

► ***Hardiness:*** Zones 5–9
► ***Size:*** 10'–30'+ tall, 15'–20' wide
► ***Features:*** This magnolia is a good choice if you're looking for a tidy tree with foliage, flowers, and form. White lemon-scented flowers begin blooming in late spring and continue sporadically through the summer months. Foliage is glossy green above with a silvery underside. Tree sizes and form vary, depending on the climate. Trees in Zone 9 may reach up to 50' tall and be completely evergreen. A tree in Zone 5 may reach 10' tall and lose all its foliage in the fall.
► ***Uses:*** Specimen tree use, patios, courtyards, damp locations, naturalized areas, narrow spaces, shrub beds, coastal areas, screening where winters are mild, confined spaces
► ***Needs:*** Plant in highly organic, acidic soil that's moist or even wet and boggy. Trees will not tolerate drought. Grow in sun or partial shade. Protect from winds where winters are cold. Roots will not buckle paving.

MAHONIA; GRAPEHOLLY

Mahonia spp.

The striking large spiny, often glossy leaves alone would warrant growing grapeholly, but as a bonus, this plant also has pretty yellow flowers in early spring that develop by late summer into clusters of purple-blue fruits that resemble grapes. Also attracts birds.

MAHONIA

Leatherleaf Mahonia

Mahonia japonica 'Bealei'

Evergreen shrub or small tree

Mahonia japonica 'Bealei'

► ***Hardiness:*** Zones 6–9
► ***Size:*** Grows up to 12' tall and 6' wide
► ***Features:*** Stems are vertical while leaves are horizontal. Leaves are 12" or more long and divided into 7–15 thick, broad leaflets 5" or more long. Flower clusters are 3"–6" long.
► ***Uses:*** As a specimen plant or in a hedge. Beautiful when planted against stone, brick, or wood so that striking shape and leaves stand out.
► ***Needs:*** Full sun in the North and the foggy Pacific Northwest. Rich, moist acidic soil with plentiful moisture. Disease resistant, although small looper caterpillars can be a problem. If so, treat with an insecticide containing Bt *(Bacillus thuringiensis)*.

MAHONIA

Oregon Grapeholly

Mahonia aquifolium

Evergreen shrub

Mahonia aquifolium

M

Plant encyclopedia

▶**Hardiness:** Zones 5-9
▶**Size:** Grows up to 6' tall and 4' wide
▶**Features:** Leaves are 4"-10" long with 5-9 oval leaflets that are glossy green in some cultivars, dull green in others. Young growth is bronze-colored.
▶**Uses:** As a specimen plant or in a hedge. Beautiful when planted against stone, brick, or wood so that its striking shape and leaves stand out.
▶**Needs:** Full sun in the North and the foggy Pacific Northwest. Rich, moist acidic soil with plentiful moisture. Disease resistant.
▶**Choices:** 'Compacta' is only 2' tall and spreads readily. 'Orange Flame' grows 5' tall with bronze-orange new growth that turns green in summer and burgundy in fall.

Maidenhair Fern
see Ferns, Maidenhair Fern

Maidenhair Tree
see Ginkgo

Malus spp.
see Apple and Crabapple

Malva spp.
see Hollyhock Mallow

Mammillaria bocasana
see Cactus and Succulents: Snowball Cactus

Mandevilla
Mandevilla spp.

Tropical evergreen flowering vine

Mandevilla splendens 'Red Riding Hood'

▶**Hardiness:** Zones 8-10; grow elsewhere as an annual
▶**Size:** 4'-12' tall, 1'-5' wide
▶**Features:** Mandevilla produces lots of big, irresistible pink blooms in hot weather. This tropical vine is not tolerant of cold temperatures but will grow about anywhere during the summer. May also be sold as *Dipladenia*.
▶**Uses:** This twining vine is ideal for small trellises and other supports. It performs well in containers.
▶**Needs:** Grow as an annual in Zones 2-7; as a perennial in Zones 8-10. Rich to average, well-drained soil. Moderate moisture. Plant established plant in spring, working some compost into the soil as well as some slow-release fertilizer. Pinch stems to encourage bushiness. Provide light support if growing as an annual; sturdy support where grown as a perennial. Mulch since roots like it cool (but foliage likes it sunny). Fertilize container plants every 2-3 weeks with a liquid fertilizer. In Zones 2-6, container plantings can be overwintered in a sunny spot indoors. In Zones 7 can be overwintered in a garage or other protected spot. Blooms on new wood, so where perennial, cut back by about one-third in late winter or early spring. Plants are prone to spider mites.
▶**Choices:** Pink 'Alice du Pont' is the most commonly sold. Red Riding Hood mandevilla (*M. splendens* 'Red Riding Hood') is also sometimes available.

MANZANITAS; BEARBERRY
Arctostaphylos spp.

This shrubby evergreen is a native of the West and can be a groundcover, a shrub, or even a small tree depending on the type and where it's grown. The most popular types, however, are used as groundcovers because they can thrive even in poor, sandy soils and seaside conditions with little moisture. They are ideal for controlling erosion or planting on slopes. Lustrous, dense leaves and tiny, waxy bell-shape flowers in spring top interesting crooked branches with smooth red to burgundy bark. Produces small, attractive ornamental fruits as well.

MANZANITAS

Common Manzanita
Arctostaphylos densiflora

Broadleaf evergreen shrub

Arctostaphylos densiflora 'Howard McMinn'

Arctostaphylos stanfordiana 'Palisades'

▶**Hardiness**: Zones 6-11
▶**Size:** Grows 6'-20' tall, 4-10' wide
▶**Features:** Delightfully crooked growth habit and smooth, polished, burgundy-colored bark. Leaves can be shiny or dull, depending on the type. Flowers are white to pink. White fruit ripens to rich red.
▶**Uses:** As a specimen, on a large slope for erosion control, as a hedge
▶**Needs:** Water weekly after planting. After a few months, however, plant needs water only once a month or so. Control growth by pinching every few weeks during the growing season.

MANZANITAS

Emerald Carpet Manzanita
Arctostaphylos 'Emerald Carpet'

Evergreen broadleaf shrub used as a groundcover

Arctostaphylos 'Emerald Carpet'

►**Hardiness:** Zones 6-9
►**Size:** Grows 9"-14" tall, up to 5' wide
►**Features:** This dense, uniform groundcover is green even in the hottest, driest weather. An excellent substitute for lawn on steep slopes where mowing is difficult. Flowers are small and not particularly showy.
►**Uses:** As a groundcover
►**Needs:** Plant 2'-3' apart. Water weekly after planting for the first several months. After a few months, however, plant needs water only once a month or so. In the hottest parts of the United States, however, watering every 2-3 weeks may be necessary. Control growth by pinching back every several weeks during the growing season.

MANZANITAS

Bearberry; Kinnikinnick

Arctostaphylos uva-ursi

Evergreen shrub groundcover

Arctostaphylos uva-ursi

►**Hardiness:** Zones 2-7
►**Size:** 4"-6" high, 18"-20" wide
►**Features:** This low evergreen can take sun, cold, poor soil, and heat without any help. It blooms mid- to late spring and produces red berries in the fall. Low-maintenance plants are ideal for sites you don't have time for yet want to look good. White flowers are tinged with pink. Bright red berries attract birds to the area.
►**Uses:** Planting near paving, seaside gardens, foundation plantings, perennial beds, poor soils, attracting birds
►**Needs:** Plant in poor, sandy, infertile soil in full sun or partial shade. Plants rarely require pruning or fertilizer.
►**Choices:** 'Massachusetts'—pale pink flowers.

Maple, Flowering

see Flowering Maple

MAPLES

Acer spp.

Maples in all their forms offer unbeatable fall color. They come in a wide range of heights, from small Japanese maples that may hit only 5' to stately tall maples that soar to 80'. Leaf shapes can also vary tremendously, as can overall shape. There's a maple for about every region of the country except the arid Southwest. Maples do best with constant, steady, deep moisture that even diligent watering can't provide. It's also important to choose maples with care. Some, such as silver maple, have shallow root systems that can compete with grass. Norway maple reseeds prolifically in some areas.

MAPLES

Amur Maple

Acer tataricum ginnala

Deciduous tree

Acer tataricum ginnala

►**Hardiness** Zones 2-6
►**Size:** 15'-18' tall, 18'-20' wide
►**Features:** You can grow this hardy little maple as a traditional single-stemmed tree or in a multitrunk form. Trees grown in full sun develop the best fall color. Leaves turn bright red or yellow in fall. Ornamental seeds turn from green to red to brown in late summer and fall. Trees are pest free and adaptable. They adapt well to life in aboveground containers. Known as a hard maple.
►**Uses:** Planting beside patios or decks, entries, or in front of blank walls, multistemmed specimen tree, containers
►**Needs:** Amur maple grows best in moist, well-drained soil, but will thrive in drier soils as well. Plant in full sun or partial shade. Prune in summer or fall to minimize bleeding sap. Can withstand heavy pruning. Easy to transplant.
►**Choices:** 'Red Fruit' boasts large quantities of bright red-winged seeds. 'Flame' has outstanding fall color.

MAPLES

Japanese Maple

Acer palmatum

Deciduous tree

Acer palmatum 'Atropurpureum'

►**Hardiness**: Zones 5-8
►**Size:** 15'-20' tall, 10'-15' wide
►**Features:** This tree is so graceful that it's an accent even in winter when it's as bare as a bone. It is small and neat with well-behaved roots. Delicate leaves vary among named selections in shape, color, size, and texture; all are shaped somewhat like a hand. Green-leaved selections tend to have the best fall color, turning brilliant shades of orange, gold, or crimson. Trees are often multitrunked. Picturesque form shows best against solid backgrounds, such as walls or tall evergreen shrubs.
►**Uses:** Specimen planting, accents and focal points, winter interest, patios, decks, entries, courtyards, understory trees, adding human scale, small gardens
►**Needs:** Plant in fertile soil that's moist but well drained. Add compost at planting; mulch roots well to keep them cool. Grow in full sun or partial shade; protect selections with fine-textured leaves from afternoon sun in hotter climates. Grow green-leaved varieties in sun for brilliant fall color. Trees tolerate confined spaces if watered regularly.
►**Choices:** 'Atropurpureum'—red-purple summer foliage turns brighter red in autumn, medium-textured leaves. 'Bloodgood'—red-purple summer foliage turns brighter red in autumn, fine-textured leaves. 'Linearilobum'—bright green, fine-textured leaves turn yellow in fall. 'Burgundy Lace'—red-purple leaves, deeply cut for a lacy look. 'Shishio'—new leaves and autumn foliage are red; summer leaves are green. Var. *heptalobum*—broader leaves

have coarser texture; green foliage turns bright orange to red in fall. 'Sango-kaku'—green leaves with coral bark; good winter interest. 'Oshio-beni'—bright red foliage during the growing season.

Weeping form, smaller size: 'Dissectum' (threadleaf)—very fine-textured foliage; mounding form. 'Crimson Queen'—reddish purple leaves; fine-textured foliage. 'Ever Red'—very fine-textured foliage, dark red-purple in color, mounding form. 'Inaba-shidore'—red leaves. 'Viridis'—green leaves.

MAPLES

Norway Maple

Acer platanoides

Deciduous tree

Acer platanoides 'Crimson King'

▶***Hardiness:*** Zones 3-7
▶***Size:*** 40'-50' tall, 30'-40' wide
▶***Features:*** Plant this tough tree for its large leaves that cast cooling shade in summer. Varieties are available with varying foliage colors and mature tree size. Roots can buckle nearby concrete. Grass grows sparsely under its dense shade and among its shallow roots. Known as a hard maple.
▶***Uses:*** Lawn, street, and shade tree use in large areas
▶***Needs:*** This maple grows in well-drained soil ranging from sandy to clay, acidic to alkaline. Can handle hot, dry conditions and polluted air.
▶***Choices:*** 'Crimson King'—slow growing, rich maroon-colored foliage; 'Deborah'—new foliage emerges red and matures dark green; golden yellow in fall; 'Royal Red'—maroon leaves turn bronze-red in autumn; 'Schwedleri'—new leaves are purple, turning dark green in summer and changing to gold in fall.

MAPLES

Paperbark Maple

Acer griseum

Deciduous tree

Acer griseum, with bark detail

▶***Hardiness:*** Zones 4-8
▶***Size:*** 20'-30' tall, 15'-30' wide
▶***Features:*** The cinnamon-colored bark on this maple peels away as the tree ages—the trunk looks as though it's covered with curly wood shavings. Snow cover provides an excellent foil for the winter interest this plant provides. Because it is slow-growing, plant this tree as soon as you begin your landscaping project. Three-lobed leaves are bluish green during the summer and develop a bronze or red color in the fall. Known as a hard maple.
▶***Uses:*** Planting near patios and decks, lawn and specimen use, near flower beds, adding interest to winter scenes
▶***Needs:*** Plant in full sun in moist soil. Clay or well-drained soil is fine as long as moisture is available; these maples are not drought tolerant. Adapts to a wide range of soil. Transplant balled-and-burlapped or container-grown trees in spring. Exfoliating bark characteristic develops with age.

MAPLES

Red Maple

Acer rubrum

Deciduous tree

Acer rubrum

▶***Hardiness:*** Zones 3-9
▶***Size:*** 40'-50' tall, 30'-40' wide
▶***Features:*** Grow this tough native tree for a delicate blush of red in spring, leafy shade in summer, and brightly colored foliage in fall. Red maples adapt to a variety of growing conditions. These trees grow naturally in swamps but are equally at home in a hot, dry parking area. Known as a hard maple.
▶***Uses:*** Shade trees, parking areas, street trees, lining long driveways, woodlands, patios, decks, fast-growing deciduous screens, beside ponds or creeks, boggy areas, hot and dry spots, natural areas
▶***Needs:*** Grow in any kind of soil, from alkaline to acidic, rich to poor, or wet to dry. Grow in full sun or partial shade. Water new trees regularly for the first growing season; after that, trees rarely need water. Tolerates heat and car exhaust.
▶***Choices***: 'Autumn Flame'—leaves turn vivid red in early fall; 'October Glory'—brilliant orange or red fall foliage; 'Red Sunset'—foliage turns red in early fall; 'Bowhall'—symmetrical, narrow canopy, yellow to red fall leaves; 'Columnare'—narrow canopy about 10' wide, red fall foliage; 'Indian Summer'—vigorous, cold-hardy; leaves turn red-orange in fall.

MAPLES

Silver Maple

Acer saccharinum

Deciduous tree

Acer saccharinum

▶***Hardiness:*** Zones 3–9

▶***Size:*** 50'–70' tall, 35'–50' wide

▶***Features:*** Plant a silver maple to provide quick shade in broad, open areas. Silvery-backed leaves turn lemon yellow in autumn. Because of its rapid growth, wood is weak and trees may break apart during storms; keep trees away from power lines or houses. Roots can invade septic or drainage systems. Keep roots away from paving. Short-lived compared with other maples. Known as a soft maple.

▶***Uses***: Shading, screening, adding quick shade and height to new yards while longer-lived trees mature, large open spaces

▶***Needs:*** Plant in full sun or partial shade. This tree tolerates a variety of soils, from acidic to alkaline and sandy loam to clay. Plant away from buildings, paving, and pipes.

▶***Choices:*** 'Silver Queen'—oval form, bears fewer seeds; 'Skinneri'—stronger wood, deeply cut leaves.

MAPLES

Sugar Maple

Acer saccharum

Deciduous tree

Acer saccharum

▶***Hardiness:*** Zones 4–8

▶***Size:*** 60'–75' tall, 40'–50' wide

▶***Features:*** Leafy summer shade followed by traffic-stopping fall color makes sugar maple an excellent choice for growing in large lawns or in rows along streets or driveways. Roots require large open spaces; avoid restricted growing areas. Plants will grow well in the cooler areas of Zone 8. Known as a hard maple.

▶***Uses:*** Shade trees, lawn trees, lining driveways and streets, large open spaces, seasonal accent, natural areas, large estates, formal landscapes, mountainsides

▶***Needs:*** Plant in acidic soil that's moist but well drained; avoid compacted clay, wet soil, or city conditions. Grow in full sun or partial shade. Fall color is best in sun.

▶***Choices:*** 'Green Mountain'—thick, deep green foliage; 'Bonfire'—grows slightly faster; 'Green Column'—leaves turn yellow-orange; 'Legacy'—drought resistant; 'Flax Mill Majesty'—faster growing, red-orange leaves.

MAPLES

Trident Maple

Acer buergerianum

Deciduous tree

Acer buergerianum

▶***Hardiness:*** Zones 4–8

▶***Size:*** 20'–30' tall and wide

▶***Features:*** Plant this small, graceful tree to add summer shade and head-turning fall color to your yard or outdoor sitting area. Three-lobed foliage is glossy green during the summer months and turns on the color show later in the fall than other maples. Old trunks exfoliate to reveal shades of gray, brown, and orange.

▶***Uses:*** Shade tree use, lawns, planting along streets, near patios and decks, in small yards, containers, bonsai

▶***Needs:*** Plant in spring in well-drained, acidic soil. Provide full sun for best growth. Can grow in partial shade. Trees are drought tolerant. Position where low branches can spread naturally, or remove limbs to allow room for walking or parking beneath trees. Make cuts in summer or autumn when sap flow is reduced.

Maranta leuconeura

see Prayer Plant

Marigold, Pot

see Pot Marigold

M

Plant encyclopedia

Marigold
Tagetes spp.

Annual

Tagetes patula

▶***Hardiness:*** Zones 9–11, or as annual
▶***Size:*** 6"–4' tall and 4"–2' wide, depending on the type and growing conditions
▶***Features:*** These workhorses of the flower garden are tough heavy bloomers that look great all growing season as long as they have plenty of heat. Flowers come in yellow, gold, orange, russet, deep red, or cream and are abundant as long as the soil is good and moisture is ample. Flowers may be single to fully double and range from 1" to 4" across.
▶***Uses:*** Outstanding in beds, borders, and containers
▶***Needs:*** Full sun in Zones 2–6; light shade appreciated in Zones 7–11. Rich to average, well-drained, preferably sandy soil. Moderate water. Plant established plants in spring after all danger of frost has passed, or start from seed indoors. Planting outdoors too early in cold soil will cause plants to sulk and make them more prone to disease. At planting time pinch off flowers and tips of seedlings to promote branching. Mulch to conserve moisture. Fertilize occasionally. Pluck, pinch, or trim off spent blooms to ensure the longest bloom time. Blooming tends to slow when temperatures top 90°F (32°C). Prone to botrytis, root rot, fusarium wilt, slugs, rust, leaf spot, and Japanese beetles.
▶***Choices:*** African marigold *(Tagetes erecta)* is the showstopper of the group, with plants up to 4' tall and flowers up to 4". 'Inca' and 'Perfection' are two widely available cultivars. French marigolds *(T. patula)* as small, very easy low plants with 2" flowers that are sometimes bicolored. Sizes range from the 6" dwarf French marigolds to full-size types reaching 18". 'Disco', 'Queen Sophia', and 'Boy' marigolds are included in this group. Signet marigolds *(T. tenuifolia)* form mounds of feathery foliage and have many small, single 1" flowers. They grow 6"–12" tall and as wide. 'Gem' is the most commonly sold cultivar of this type. *T. lemmonii* is grown almost exclusively in arid desert regions where it grows as a shrubby perennial up to 6' tall and wide. It covers itself with small golden flowers throughout the year and handles arid conditions well.

Marguerite, Blue
see Blue Daisy

Marjoram; Sweet Marjoram
Origanum majorana

Perennial or annual herb, depending on the climate

Origanum majorana

▶***Hardiness:*** Zones 6–9
▶***Size:*** 1' tall, 1' wide
▶***Features:*** Pretty green leaves with small white flowers in late summer; good for use in French, Italian, and Mediterranean dishes
▶***Uses:*** Excellent in cream-based soups or in pasta sauces. In early summer, dry by cutting 8" or so stems, bundling the ends together with a rubber band, and hanging in a cool dry place for a few weeks. Rub dried leaves to crumble; store in a jar.
▶***Needs:*** Full sun. Does best and has best flavor in light, stony, neutral to alkaline soil but will thrive in other conditions as well. Moderate moisture. Plant seedlings in late winter to early spring; can take some frost. Usually pest free.
▶***Choices:*** 'Aureum' has golden leaves.

Marvel-of-Peru
see Four-o-Clock

Mascagnia macroptera
see Butterfly Vine

Matteuccia spp.
see Ferns, Ostrich Fern

Matthiola incana
see Stock

Mayday Tree
see Plums

Maypop
see Passionflower

Melampodium paludosum
see Butter Daisy

Melons
Cucumis melo

Warm-season annual fruit

Hybrid Melon 'Flavor Bouquet'

▶***Size:*** Grows a few inches tall, 2'–4' wide
▶***Features:*** Juicy fruits growing on sprawling vines in mid- to late summer
▶***Uses:*** In the vegetable garden
▶***Needs:*** Full sun. Well-drained, well-warmed soil high in organic matter with a pH above 6.0. Ample moisture until fruit begins to ripen, then less. Does best in areas with long, warm summers. Plant seeds 1" deep or established seedlings 2 weeks after your region's last frost date. Plant in raised beds or hills (2' wide; 4" high mounds) to ensure faster-warming soil. Space plants 3'–4' apart, depending on the type. Check the package or label. Mulch to conserve moisture and keep developing fruit clean. Once the fruit are baseball size, put a board underneath each to prevent insect damage. Determining exactly when a melon is ripe is a fine art. Clues are that the fruit pulls away easily from the vine, the melon smells sweet and ripe, and the blossom end is slightly soft.
▶***Choices:*** Choose from cantaloupe, muskmelon, honeydew, crenshaw, and Charentais melons. Specific cultivars fall under each of these categories.

Mentha requienii
see Mint, Corsican

Mertensia virginica
see Virginia Bluebells

Mesquite

Prosopis glandulosa

Deciduous flowering tree

Prosopis glandulosa

►**Hardiness:** Zones 10–11 in the West
►**Size:** 20'-30' tall, 12'-15' wide
►**Features:** Mesquite thrives even in the driest conditions of the Southwest. Adds interest to arid landscapes with its irregular sculptural shape and spring bloom. Gnarled trunk is topped with airy foliage. Yellow-green flowers in spring. Long tap roots make moving difficult.
►**Uses:** Xeriscaping, arid landscapes, planting in lawns to cast light shade, controlling erosion on hills and slopes, screening, windbreaks
►**Needs:** Plant in dry, sandy, alkaline soil with full sun. This small tree is highly drought tolerant. Water very little or not at all. Extra watering—even lawn irrigation or poor drainage—can cause mesquite to sicken and die.

Metasequoia glyptostroboides

see Dawn Redwood

Mexican Bird-of-Paradise

see Bird-of-Paradise, Mexican

Mexican Fan Palm

see Palms

Mexican False Heather; Cigar Plant

Cuphea spp.

Sometimes evergreen perennial often grown as an annual

Cuphea hyssopifolia

►**Hardiness:** Zones 10–11; elsewhere grown as an annual
►**Size:** Up to 2' tall and wide, depending on growing conditions
►**Features:** Neatly shaped plants produce interesting tubular flowers in a variety of colors. Blooms summer through fall.
►**Uses:** As a shrubby perennial where cold hardy; otherwise in beds and borders and containers. Neat habit also makes it a good edging plant.
►**Needs:** Grow as an annual in Zones 2–9; as a perennial in Zones 10–11. Full sun in Zones 2–7; part shade in Zones 8–11. Needs very rich, moist, well-drained soil; never allow to dry out. Plant seedlings in spring after all danger of frost has passed. Pinch tips at planting time for bushier growth. Fertilize regularly, especially if growing as an annual. If growing as a perennial, cut back heavily each spring to prompt fresh growth. This plant is prone to whiteflies, aphids, and powdery mildew.
►**Choices:** Flower colors are pinks, purples, whites, oranges, and reds. *C. hyssopifolia* is evergreen and known as Mexican, Florida, or false heather. *C. ignea* is known as cigar plant.

Mexican Sunflower

Tithonia rotundifolia

Annual

Tithonia rotundifolia

►**Size:** 2'-5' tall, depending on the type
►**Features:** This often dramatically tall annual thrives in the heat, producing 2"-3" flowers in deep orange or yellow in late summer through fall. Leaves are large and velvety. Attracts butterflies. Flowers are good for cutting.
►**Uses:** Excellent back-of-border plant
►**Needs:** Full sun. Average to poor, well-drained soil. Moderate to light moisture; thrives in heat and humidity. Plant established plants in spring after all danger of frost has passed. Mulch to conserve moisture. Avoid fertilizing. Stake taller types. Snails and slugs may be problems.
►**Choices:** Flowers are deep orange or yellow. 'Fiesta del Sol' is a dwarf, growing just 30" tall but producing many flowers. Yellow 'Aztec Sun' is especially attractive to butterflies.

Michaelmas Daisy

see Aster

Microbiota decussata

see Cypresses, Russian Cypress

Millettia reticulata

see Wisteria, Evergreen

Million Bells; Callibrachoa

Callibrachoa spp.

Annual

Callibrachoa spp.

►**Size:** Grows 5"-8" tall; 6"-20" wide, depending on growing conditions
►**Features:** This petunia look-alike covers itself with tiny flowers all growing season long. Unlike petunias, however, the flowers are self-cleaning, that is, they simply dry up and fall off after they're done flowering—no pinching or deadheading needed. A new introduction but rapidly increasing in popularity.

M

Plant encyclopedia

▶**Uses:** Excellent in baskets, windowboxes, and containers where the long stems can trail. Will do fairly well in the ground as well as in flower beds and borders.
▶**Needs:** Grow much like its cousin, the petunia. Full sun in rich, well-drained soil. Moderate water; too much water encourages root rot and too little will stunt growth. Water the soil around the plant rather than the foliage and the flowers to keep both healthier and more attractive. In late summer, may need to trim back stems by one-third to encourage lusher, fuller growth. Space 8"–12" at planting time, and work in a slow-release fertilizer. Follow up with a dilute fertilizer every 2–4 weeks thereafter, especially in containers.
▶**Choices:** Cultivars come in colors including pink, cherry pink, white, yellow, purple, and terra-cotta.

Mimulus ×hybridus
see Monkey Flower

Mint
Mentha spp.
Perennial herb

Mentha ×piperita 'Black Peppermint'

▶**Hardiness:** Zones 4–10, depending on the type
▶**Size:** Grows 2' tall, spreads widely
▶**Features:** Characteristic mint flavor; scent releases when crushed.
▶**Uses:** Plant low-growing Corsican mint where you can step on it and release its fragrance. Use other mints to make mint tea, snip over fruit salads, or add to iced tea or Indian dishes.
▶**Needs:** Full sun to part shade. Prefers rich well-drained soil with average moisture, but will tolerate variety in soils and moisture. Plant established plants in spring or fall. Mint spreads aggressively by underground runners, so prevent problems by planting it in a contained area, such as a small spot between the house and driveway and sidewalk. Or plant it in a large pot sunk in the ground with about 1" of the rim of the pot protruding.
▶**Choices:** Spearmint *(M. spicata)* is one of the most intensely flavored mints. Also try apple mint, pineapple mint, and peppermint, including chocolate peppermint *(M. ×peperita* 'Chocolate'). Some mints have variegated leaves.

Mint, Corsican
Mentha requienii
Perennial groundcover

Mentha requienii

▶**Hardiness**: Zones 6–9
▶**Size:** 1"–2" tall, indefinite spread
▶**Features:** Plant this mosslike mint where you'll be sure to see and smell it up close. Bright green leaves grow together to form low, creeping, fuzzy mats. Tiny purple flowers appear in summer. Foliage is peppermint-scented.
▶**Uses:** Growing between stepping stones, covering soil beneath roses and leggy perennials, planting beds, growing under benches
▶**Needs:** Plant in moist, fertile soil; like most mints, will adapt to any soil other than soggy or bone dry. Grow in partial shade to shade. Water regularly in sunny locations.

Mirabilis jalapa
see Four-o-Clock

Miscanthus sinensis
see Grasses, Ornamental: Silver Grass

Mockorange
Philadelphus spp.
Deciduous flowering shrub

Philadelphus spp.

▶**Hardiness:** Zones 4–8
▶**Size:** 3'–12' tall and wide
▶**Features:** Grown for the lovely sweet scent of its spring flowers, reminiscent of orange blossoms. The shrub itself is rather ordinary, with medium green leaves and a ragged growth habit.
▶**Uses:** A background hedge or screen
▶**Needs:** Rich to poor, moist soil. Ample moisture best, but tolerates drought. Plant established plants in spring or fall. Mulch to conserve moisture. Do not fertilize mature plants or trim spent blooms. Prune regularly to avoid legginess. Immediately after flowering, remove branches at base. Also cut back individual branches to shape. This shrub is usually pest and disease free.
▶**Choices:** Flowers are white or yellow. Sweet mockorange *(P. coronarius)* is the most commonly grown and reaches 10'–12' tall, Zones 4–7. Lemoine mockorange *(P. ×lemoinei)* is hardy in Zones 4–8. 'Avalanche' grows 3' tall. *P. ×virginalis* is hardy in Zones 5–8.

Moluccella laevis
see Bells of Ireland

Monarda didyma
see Bee Balm

Mondo Grass
Ophiopogon japonicus
Evergreen groundcover

Ophiopogon japonicus

▶**Hardiness:** Zones 7–9
▶**Size:** 6"–10" tall, indefinite spreading clumps
▶**Features:** Turn barren, shady spots into lush carpets of dark green by planting mondo grass. Soft, thick clumps choke out most weeds. Known for its fine-textured, arching foliage. Separate from lawns with sturdy barriers.

▶ ***Uses:*** Filling in shady areas, hillsides, planting beneath trees and shrubs, narrow confined areas, forming the front layer of planting beds
▶ ***Needs:*** Plant in any soil except soggy. Tolerates varying levels of soil pH. Mow every few years in late winter before new growth emerges. Grow in full sun, partial shade, or dense shade.

Mondo Grass, Black

Ophiopogon planiscapus 'Nigrescens'

Evergreen groundcover

Ophiopogon planiscapus 'Nigrescens'

▶ ***Hardiness:*** Zones 6–9
▶ ***Size:*** 6" tall, 9" wide
▶ ***Features:*** Gorgeous strappy greenish-black foliage is a standout in the garden. Slowly forms clumps. Pinkish-white flowers on short spikes in summer are followed by black berries.
▶ ***Uses:*** As an edging plant, groupings in mixed beds and borders
▶ ***Needs:*** Full sun to light shade. Rich, well-drained soil. Ample moisture. Plant new plants 12" apart. Usually disease and pest free.

Money Plant; Honesty

Lunaria annua

Biennial

Lunaria annua

▶ ***Hardiness:*** Zones 4–8
▶ ***Size:*** 18"–36" tall, 1'–2' wide
▶ ***Features:*** Grown for the lovely translucent silvery disks about 1" across that are produced as part of the seedpods in late summer. The rest of the plant is undistinguished, with heart-shape leaves and small purple flowers in spring.
▶ ***Uses:*** In the flower bed or border
▶ ***Needs:*** This biennial prefers light shade but will tolerate full sun. Average to poor soil. Moderate water. In Zones 4–7 plant seeds directly in soil ⅛-inch deep in spring a week or two before the last frost date. In Zone 8 sow seeds in autumn. Thin to 12". Avoid fertilizing. If sowing in autumn, mulch to help plants survive winter. Flowers come in spring. Leave spent blooms on plants. This plant produces seedpods in late summer. It often reseeds and can become invasive in some areas. Usually free of diseases and pests.
▶ ***Choices:*** Colors are white, purples, and pinks.

Moneywort; Creeping Jenny

Lysimachia nummularia

Perennial groundcover

Lysimachia nummularia 'Aurea'

▶ ***Hardiness:*** Zones 3–8
▶ ***Size:*** 4"–8" tall, 12"–24" wide
▶ ***Features:*** Moneywort thrives in wet shade. Plants spread quickly and can take over small areas in no time. Plants are adaptable to sun or shade as long as moisture is available. Yellow flowers in early summer.
▶ ***Uses:*** Shady, damp areas where grass won't grow, beside ponds and water features, near downspouts
▶ ***Needs:*** Plant in well-drained, fertile, moist soil. Choose a spot in dense or partial shade. Cut plants back after flowering to promote compact growth. For low maintenance, let plants grow.
▶ ***Choices:*** 'Aurea'—lime green to yellow leaves.

Monkey Flower

Mimulus ×hybridus

Annual

Mimulus ×hybridus

▶ ***Size:*** 1'–2' tall and wide
▶ ***Features:*** Striking lipped flowers in a variety of colors on a mounded plant with large, glossy leaves. Blooms late spring to frost.
▶ ***Uses:*** In flower beds and borders, baskets and other containers
▶ ***Needs:*** Full sun tolerated in Zones 2–5; otherwise part to full shade. Rich, well-drained soil. Ample moisture. Plant established plants in spring after all danger of frost has passed. Mulch to keep soil cool and moist. Never allow plant to dry out. Fertilize regularly, every 2–4 weeks, or work in a slow-release fertilizer at planting time. Cut back after first bloom to promote further flowering. Dry spells can halt flowering. Water generously to restore bloom. This plant can be grown as a perennial in

M

Plant encyclopedia

Zones 9–11. It is prone to aphids and whiteflies.
▶**Choices:** The Magic series offers 14 colors, including yellows, roses, reds, oranges, and bicolors. 'Magic Yellow Flame' has striking orange and yellow flowers.

Monkey Grass
see Lilyturf

Monkey Puzzle Tree
Araucaria araucana
Evergreen tree

Araucaria araucana

▶**Hardiness:** Zones 8–11
▶**Size:** 65'–90' tall, 25'–35' wide
▶**Features:** This large forest tree from Chile has a strange, exotic form with widely-spaced, horizontal branches clothed in sharp, spiny, dark green leaves. It is dramatic against the sky. Cones are huge, heavy, and covered in sharp spines.
▶**Uses:** Best in large, parklike spaces where people do not walk or sit underneath. This is a tree that needs space.
▶**Needs:** Easy to grow in about any well-drained soil and either sun or shade.

Monkshood, Azure
Aconitum carmichaelii
Perennial

Aconitum carmichaelii

▶**Hardiness:** Zones 3–7
▶**Size:** Up to 3' tall, 2' wide
▶**Features:** Lovely hooded flowers in purple or deep purple grow on tall, slender stems with deeply lobed leaves. Plants resemble delphinium. Blooms late summer to early fall. All parts of the plant are poisonous.
▶**Uses:** In the flower bed or border
▶**Needs:** Likes well-drained, humus-rich, moist soil; add compost. Water moderately, more often if plant is in full sun. Plant established plants in spring or fall. Mulch to conserve moisture. Fertilize occasionally, every 6 weeks, or work in a slow-release fertilizer in spring. This plant dislikes dividing or transplanting. Stake if plant becomes floppy. It is prone to crown rot and mildew.
▶**Choices:** Monkshood is available with blue to violet flowers; some varieties, such as 'Bicolor', are available with blue and white flowers.

Monstera deliciosa
see Swiss Cheese Plant

Moonflower
Ipomoea alba
Annual vine

Ipomoea alba

▶**Size:** Grows 20'–30' tall
▶**Features:** Beautiful 6" lightly fragrant white flowers in the classic morning glory shape bloom in early evening or on overcast days.
▶**Uses:** Fast-growing vine for large fences, arbors, or trellises. Beautiful when planted alongside morning glory, which opens in the morning and closes in the late afternoon as moonflower opens.
▶**Needs:** Soak seed for 1 day in water. Plant directly in the soil at the base of a large and sturdy support after all danger of frost has passed. Work in a slow-release fertilizer. Keep soil moist. Once seed germinates, usually after a few days, check plants daily to gently guide them onto the support. After the first frost or at the end of the growing season, tear out the vine. May reseed in some conditions, becoming invasive.

Morning Glory
Ipomoea tricolor and hybrids
Annual vine

Ipomoea tricolor

▶**Size:** 6'–20' long, depending on growing conditions
▶**Features:** Beautiful trumpet-shape flowers bloom on vigorous, twining stems with heart-shape green leaves. The flowers open in the morning and on overcast days, hence the name. Flowers come in blues, reds, pinks, lavenders, and white as well as some bicolors.
▶**Uses:** On larger trellises
▶**Needs:** Average to poor, well-drained soil. Ample moisture. Plant seeds in late winter or spring directly in soil after all danger of frost, soaking first in water 24 hours to soften tough coat. Work a few spadefuls of compost into soil or add a slow-release fertilizer. When vines reaches 1" tall, thin to at least 18" apart. Limit fertilizer to keep size in check.
▶**Choices:** Most popular is the common morning glory *(I. tricolor),* which blooms morning to afternoon. 'Heavenly Blue' is a favorite, 10'–15'.

Morning Glory, Dwarf
Convolvulus tricolor
Annual

Convolvulus tricolor 'Royal Ensign'

▶ **Size:** 1' tall, 2' wide
▶ **Features:** A low-growing, somewhat spreading plant that much resembles morning glory with trumpetlike flowers. Blooms mid- through late summer.
▶ **Uses:** Edging plant; along a planter or wall
▶ **Needs:** Average, well-drained soil. Moderate moisture. After all danger of frost has passed in spring, soak seeds overnight and then plant directly in the soil outdoors. Avoid transplanting. Fertilize lightly. Plants thrive with little attention. Keep evenly moist. Deadhead regularly for most bloom. Although it's a perennial in Zones 9–11 and sometimes even as far north as Zone 7, it's best to pull in the fall and replant in the spring for fresh, attractive flowers.
▶ **Choices:** 'Royal Ensign', a beautiful blue, is popular, but now there are red and rose-colored varieties as well. Do not plant *C. arvensis* (bindweed), which is highly invasive.

Montbretia
see Crocosmia

Mosaic Plant
see Nerve Plant

Moses-in-the-Boat
Tradescantia spathacea

Tropical evergreen perennial

Tradescantia spathacea

▶ **Hardiness:** Zones 9–11; otherwise grown as a houseplant
▶ **Size:** 6"–1' tall
▶ **Features:** Forms clusters of long sword-shape leaves along a thick stem up to 8" tall. Leaves are dark teal-tinged deep green on top and rich violet below. The small white three-petaled flowers are hidden in boat-shape purple bracts, hence the name. Blooms all year outdoors.
▶ **Uses:** As a houseplant; as a groundcover in mildest areas of Southern California and Florida
▶ **Needs:** As a landscape plant: Bright sun to deep shade. Prefers rich soil high in organic matter but will make do in sandy soils or even rocky crevices. Will tolerate drought. As a houseplant: Bright light or filtered light through a sheer curtain. Likes cool nights of 50°–55°F/10°–13°C and daytime temperatures of 65°–70°F/18°–21°C. Keep soil barely moist. Hold off on feeding new plants for the first few months; after that, feed every few months. Average humidity.
▶ **Choices:** Sometimes sold as *Rhoeo spathacea* or *R. discolor.* Other common names include Moses-in-the-cradle, Moses-in-the-bulrushes, man-in-a-boat, boat-lily, and oyster plant.

Moss, Irish
see Scotch Moss

Moss, Scotch
see Scotch Moss

Moss Pink
see Phlox: Moss Phlox

Moss Rose
Portulaca grandiflora

Annual

Portulaca grandiflora

▶ **Size:** 4"–8" tall, up to 2' wide
▶ **Features:** This annual can take the hot and drought and can be found in all the toughest, baked situations. It produces red, orange, yellow, purple, or pink flowers on trailing stems lined with narrow, succulent leaves. Old types opened around noon and closed in the afternoon; new types, some of which have variegated flower petals, stay open all day. Blooms spring to frost.
▶ **Uses:** In beds and corners; excellent in containers in baked conditions
▶ **Needs:** Full sun. Average, well-drained soil, preferably sandy. Very drought tolerant. Plant established plants in spring after all danger of frost has passed. Water sparingly, allowing soil to dry well between waterings. Aphids, thrips, and white rust may cause problems.
▶ **Choices:** Flowers come in reds, oranges, yellows, purples, whites, and pinks. New types that remain open all day include 'Sundial' and 'Sundance'.

Moth Orchids
see Orchids

Mother-in-Law's Tongue
see Snake Plant

Mother-of-Thousands
see Cactus and Succulents

Mountain Ash, European
Sorbus aucuparia

Deciduous flowering tree

Sorbus aucuparia

▶ **Hardiness:** Zones 3–6
▶ **Size:** 30'–50' tall, 15'–25' wide
▶ **Features:** Three seasons of color make this tree a good choice for cooler climates. White spring flowers are followed by orange-red summer fruit and finally by yellow-red fall foliage. The scent of the flowers is unpleasant to some. Birds love the fruit and consume it as quickly as it ripens. Available as single or multitrunked trees.
▶ **Uses:** Specimen use, seasonal accent, patio trees, courtyards, entries, attracting birds to the landscape

▶**Needs:** Plant in fertile soil that's moist but well drained. Neutral to acidic soil is best. Grow in full sun or partial shade. This tree thrives where summers are cool. Plants do not tolerate summer heat or drought.
▶**Choices:** Showy mountain ash *(S. decora)*—white flowers, red berries, orange-red fall foliage; Zones 3-8.

Mountain Bluet
see Cornflower

Mountain Laurel
Kalmia latifolia

Broadleaf evergreen shrub

Kalmia latifolia 'Alba'

▶**Hardiness:** Zones 4-9
▶**Size:** 7'-15' tall and wide
▶**Features:** If you have the right soil condition for mountain laurel, you may wish to try this large-leaved evergreen shrub. You'll enjoy clusters of blossoms from May to June in white and shades of pink and red.
▶**Uses:** Natural areas, large planting beds and foundations, good background for summer perennials
▶**Needs:** Plant in acidic, moist soil in sun or shade. Fewer flowers are produced in dense shade. Pruning is unnecessary. Mulch plants well and provide water during hot, dry spells. Plants thrive poorly in alkaline or dry soil.
▶**Choices:** 'Alba'—white flowers; 'Myrtifolia'—stays under 6' tall; 'Ostbo Red'—deep red flower buds; 'Pink Charm'—pink flowers; 'Polypetala'—double feathery pink flowers; 'Sharon Rose'—deep red buds and light pink flowers, compact growth habit.

Muhlenbergia spp.
see Grasses, Ornamental: Muhly Grass

Mum
see Chrysanthemum

Musa acuminata
see Banana, Dwarf

Muscari spp.
see Grape Hyacinth

Mustard Greens
see Greens

Myosotis spp.
see Forget-Me-Not

Myrica cerifera
see Wax Myrtle

Myrica pensylvanica
see Bayberry

Naked Ladies; Surprise Lily
Lycoris squamigera

Flowering bulb

Lycoris squamigera

▶**Hardiness:** Zones 5-9
▶**Size:** 18"-24" tall, 12" wide
▶**Features:** This unusual plant first sends up a burst of fragrant pink 3" trumpet-shape flowers in late summer. After the flowers fade, the leaves appear and remain green until spring.
▶**Uses:** In the flower bed or border
▶**Needs:** Full sun. Rich, well-drained soil. Abundant moisture while growing; moderate while dormant. Plant bulbs in mid- to late summer, 5"-6" deep. This plant dislikes too much water in summer. Plant in clusters, crowding to promote better blooming. Plants are prone to root and bulb rot if overwatered.
▶**Choices:** In arid Western regions, grow *Amaryllis belladonna.* It's similar but is about a foot taller with slightly larger flowers.

Nandina; Heavenly Bamboo
Nandina domestica

Evergreen shrub

Nandina domestica

▶**Hardiness:** Zones 6-9
▶**Size:** 6'-8' tall, 4'-6' wide
▶**Features:** Grow this old-fashioned favorite for its lacy leaves and red winter berries, which make great decorations for holiday tables. Plants sucker, forming thickets. Tiny creamy flower clusters occur in late spring. Plants look best planted in drifts or massed.
▶**Uses:** Massing, growing in narrow spaces, adding fine texture, seasonal accents, screening, entries, beside driveways, walkways, or patios, screening the area beneath low decks
▶**Needs:** Plant in moist, fertile soil, but plants can adapt to any soil. Grow in full sun for best color; partial shade is OK. If leaves of plants grown in alkaline soil turn sickly yellow, remedy with iron sulfate. Keep nandina bushy by pruning in late winter. Cut two-thirds of randomly selected stalks at staggered heights. Allow the remaining third to remain at full height.
▶**Choices:** 'Harbor Dwarf'—compact 2'-3' tall, reddish purple in winter. 'Moon Bay'—smaller leaves, 18"-30" tall, bright red in winter.

Napa Cabbage
see Cabbage

Narcissus spp.
see Daffodils

Nasturtium
Tropaeolum majus
Annual

Tropaeolum majus

▶**Size:** 6"-18" tall; up to 6' wide depending on the type
▶**Features:** The pretty, rounded, shiny leaves and attractive bright red, orange, yellow, or peach flowers make nasturtium an easy-to-grow favorite. Simply plant seeds in early spring for weeks or even months of colorful bloom. Trailing types are great as a groundcover for a small area.
▶**Uses:** Flower beds and borders; containers, baskets. Climbing types will cover a small trellis.
▶**Needs:** Full sun in Zones 2-6; part shade in hot-summer areas in Zones 7-11. Average to poor, well-drained, preferably sandy soil. Drought tolerant. Plant seed directly in the garden. In Zones 2-7 plant in spring 1 week after last frost date. In Zones 8-11 sow in late autumn for winter or spring bloom. Fertilizing will cause leaves to grow higher than flowers. Blooms until temperatures regularly top 85°F (29°C).
▶**Choices:** Choose climbing types to cover trellises. Dwarf or trailing types are good for beds, borders, and containers. 'Alaska' sports variegated foliage.

Neanthe bella
see Palms: Parlor Palm

Nectarines
see Peaches

Neoregelia carolinae
see Bromeliads: Blushing Bromeliad

Nepeta spp.
see Catmint

Nephrolepis exaltata
see Ferns: Boston Fern

Nerium oleander
see Oleander

Nerve Plant, Mosaic Plant
Fittonia verschaffeltii
Tropical evergreen perennial

Fittonia verschaffeltii

Fittonia verschaffeltii var. *argyroneura*

▶**Size:** 8" tall and wide
▶**Features:** Also goes by net plant and snakeskin plant because of its beautifully veined leaves in red, pink, silver, and green. This low grower is good for shallow, wide containers; dish gardens, and terrariums. Also good as groundcover planted in the same container as a large, upright plant. Will trail somewhat in a larger pot.
▶**Uses:** As a houseplant
▶**Needs:** Medium to low light; direct sun can damage its leaves. Average to warm household temperatures, but tolerates slightly cooler temperatures. Keep evenly moist but not soggy. High, constant humidity a must to keep plant from dying. A miniature conservatory, terrarium, area with a humidifier or a steamy bathroom are about the only ways to accomplish this. Pinch regularly to keep plant full.
▶**Choices:** *Fittonia verschaffeltii* var. *argyroneura* (formerly *F. argyroneura*) 'Nana' is the easiest to grow because it's the least fussy about humidity.

New Guinea Impatiens
see Impatiens

New Zealand Flax
see Flax, New Zealand

New Zealand Tea Tree
see Tea Tree

Nicotiana hybrids
see Flowering Tobacco

Nierembergia hippomanica
see Cupflower

Nigella damascena
see Love-in-a-Mist

Norfolk Island Pine
Araucaria heterophylla
Tropical evergreen coniferous tree

Araucaria heterophylla

▶**Hardiness:** Zones 10-11
▶**Size:** Grows up to 5' tall indoors and in containers; up to 100' outdoors
▶**Features:** Indoors Norfolk Island pine is a charming little evergreen needled tree, like a miniature Christmas tree. Outdoors, its tiered leaves are striking.
▶**Uses:** As a houseplant; also grown as an outdoor container or specimen plant in mild-winter climates
▶**Needs:** Outdoors: cool, moist frost-free conditions. Indoors: medium light; bright light fine

N

Plant encyclopedia

as long as temperatures are cool—this plant prefers cool conditions. Keep soil evenly moist. Fertilize once or twice a year. Plant will naturally lose lower branches, so trim them out as they begin to die.

Northern Bayberry

see Bayberry

OAKS

Quercus spp.

The common names of oaks hint at their adaptability to various climates—swamp oak, canyon live oak, coast live oak, interior live oak, Rocky Mountain white oak. The most commonly grown oaks are described here, but check with your garden center to find the right oak for your region, ensuring minimal pest, disease, and cold-hardiness problems. When planting an oak, position it wisely. Give it plenty of room for its height and spread. Also take into consideration fallen acorns, which can be a problem on walks, drives, or grassy slopes.

OAKS

Bur Oak

Quercus macrocarpa

Deciduous tree

Quercus macrocarpa

▶ ***Hardiness:*** Zones 2–8
▶ ***Size:*** 70'–80' tall, 70'–80' wide
▶ ***Features:*** This shady oak will grow in difficult conditions that defeat many other oak trees. The only requirement: Make sure you have the room for a long-lived, massive tree sometimes reaching over 100' tall. Glossy green leaves turn yellow in the fall. Large acorns with distinctly fringy cups provide the other common name, mossycup oak.
▶ ***Uses:*** Large specimen or shade tree, open prairie and natural areas, parks
▶ ***Needs:*** Plant in about any soil, including alkaline, dry clay, or sand. Grow in full sun. Tolerates polluted air and a wide range of temperatures. One of the oaks most tolerant of life in the city.

OAKS

Coast Live Oak

Quercus agrifolia

Broadleaf evergreen tree

Quercus agrifolia

▶ ***Hardiness:*** Zones 7–10 in the West
▶ ***Size:*** 40'–50' tall, 40'–50' wide
▶ ***Features:*** If you have dry soil and low humidity, this is the oak for you. Small leaves make a thick crown for branches that twist with age. Sheds leaves in spring.
▶ ***Uses:*** Shade tree (not in lawn), natural areas, arid landscapes, xeriscaping, hillsides
▶ ***Needs:*** Plant in well-drained soil; trees will thrive poorly in wet soil. Grow in full sun or partial shade. Cover root zones beneath canopies with mulch; grass or flowers require too much additional water. Overly wet roots may develop oak root fungus.

OAKS

Laurel Oak

Quercus laurifolia

Deciduous tree

Quercus laurifolia

▶ ***Hardiness:*** Zones 7–10
▶ ***Size:*** 40'–60' tall; 50'–60' wide
▶ ***Features:*** Laurel oak grows quickly to form a pyramidal to rounded crown. Because they grow fast, trees may live only 50 years. Dark green leaves persist much of the winter.
▶ ***Uses:*** Xeriscaping, shade trees, parking areas, street trees, residential landscapes
▶ ***Needs:*** Plant laurel oak in full sun to partial shade. You can grow this tree in most soil types, including dry, sandy soil, but moist, acidic soil is optimal. Water new trees frequently to help them become established. Watering is rarely needed after that.

OAKS

Northern Red Oak

Quercus rubra

Deciduous tree

Quercus rubra

▶ ***Hardiness:*** Zones 4–7
▶ ***Size:*** 60'–80' tall, 50'–70' wide
▶ ***Features:*** Although it's native to many parts of the United States, Northern red oak grows particularly well in the Midwest. Trees produce large, rounded canopies upon maturity. New foliage has a pinkish or reddish color when unfolding, turning dark green in summer. Foliage is coarse-textured and lobed. Fall color varies from dark to bright red depending on environmental conditions. Trees produce dense shade; it may be difficult to grow grass beneath the leafy canopies.
▶ ***Uses:*** Shade and street tree use (in sites not confined by paving), specimen trees, large estates, open areas
▶ ***Needs:*** Plant in acidic soil that's moist but well drained. Trees lack taproots, so are easy to transplant. Trees tolerate polluted city air. Plant in full sun.

OAKS

Pin Oak

Quercus palustris

Deciduous tree

Quercus palustris

▶ ***Hardiness:*** Zones 4–8
▶ ***Size:*** 60'–70' tall, 25'–40' wide
▶ ***Features:*** Pin oak excels as a big, fast-growing shade tree. Roots won't buckle paving. Foliage turns scarlet in fall; brown leaves remain until spring. Surround with shade-tolerant groundcover, mulch, or paving; shade is too dense for a nice lawn. Avoid placing tree where you want to walk (or drive) under it; lower branches lean down to the ground. If you prune them off, the next higher branches will slowly drop just as low. Iron chlorosis is a common ailment of trees grown in alkaline soils. It may be nearly impossible to remedy on a long-term basis. Select another tree species more suited to alkaline locations.
▶ ***Uses:*** Shade tree, urban conditions, parks, golf courses
▶ ***Needs:*** Plant in moist, acidic soil—dry soil is OK. Grow in full sun or partial shade. Endures confined roots, reflected heat from paving, and air pollution.

OAKS

Scarlet Oak

Quercus coccinea

Deciduous tree

Quercus coccinea

▶ ***Hardiness:*** Zones 4–9
▶ ***Size:*** 70'–75' tall, 40'–50' wide
▶ ***Features:*** For dense summer shade and bright fall color, add scarlet oak to your yard—if you have room. Trees grow to an impressive size that works well with multistory homes and buildings. Young trees have a pyramidal form with a strong central leader and pendulous lower branches that drop off as the tree matures.
▶ ***Uses:*** Shade tree, large specimen tree, lawn tree, natural areas, woodland landscapes
▶ ***Needs:*** Plant in acidic soil that's moist and well drained. It will tolerate dry, sandy soils. Grow in full sun. Prune in late winter or early spring to prevent spread of disease.

OAKS

Shumard Oak

Quercus shumardii

Deciduous tree

Quercus shumardii

▶ ***Hardiness:*** Zones 5–9
▶ ***Size:*** 80'–100' tall, 50'–60' wide
▶ ***Features:*** Shumard oak is tough; it'll grow about anywhere. Fast-growing trees feature big canopies and red fall color.
▶ ***Uses:*** Shade, lawn, or street tree use; lining long driveways; parking areas; large patios; natural areas; damp locations
▶ ***Needs:*** Plant in soil that's acidic or alkaline, well drained or damp. Grow in full sun. Roots won't buckle paving. Tolerates reflected heat and air pollution. Easy to grow.

OAKS

Southern Live Oak

Quercus virginiana

Evergreen tree

Quercus virginiana

▶***Hardiness:*** Zones 8–10
▶***Size:*** 40'–80' tall, 60'–100' wide
▶***Features:*** If you want to grow a legacy, plant a southern live oak in your landscape. These broad, spreading trees become massive and live for generations. Horizontal, arching branches grow more picturesque with age. Trees are unsuitable for the small landscape, though; they're best used where they can spread out to their fullest.
▶***Uses:*** Shade, street, and large specimen use; large estates, coastal locations, open areas, new yards
▶***Needs:*** Grow in almost any soil, including poor, dry, sandy, and alkaline. Slightly acidic, moist soil is optimum. Tolerates wind, heat, salt spray, and compacted soil. Prune to develop a suitable leader if necessary.

OAKS

White Oak

Quercus alba

Deciduous tree

Quercus alba

▶***Hardiness:*** Zones 4–9
▶***Size:*** 80'–100'or more tall, 50'–80' wide
▶***Features:*** White oaks provide generations of leafy shade in a large landscape. Dark green summer foliage turns in the fall to a reddish wine and finally to brown. Leaves are large, coarse, and may remain on the tree throughout the winter. Wood is sturdy.
▶***Uses:*** Shade tree, large specimen tree, natural areas, woodlands
▶***Needs:*** Plant in acidic soil that's moist and well drained. Grow in full sun. Avoid planting in areas where construction has compacted soils. Make any pruning cuts in late winter or early spring.

OAKS

Willow Oak

Quercus phellos

Deciduous tree

Quercus phellos

▶***Hardiness:*** Zones 4–8
▶***Size:*** 40'–60' or more tall, 30'–40' wide
▶***Features:*** Majestic in size, this oak is big enough to shade your house and your landscape. Long, narrow leaves provide a more fine-textured appearance than other oaks. Leaves turn varying shades of yellow in the fall. Remove lower limbs to park or walk beneath your tree safely. Iron chlorosis may develop in alkaline soils. Check your soil's pH before planting. Acorns produce numerous seedlings for transplanting.
▶***Uses:*** Large specimen, shade tree, street tree, lining long driveways, large patio tree
▶***Needs:*** Grow in fertile, moist acidic soil. Wet clays and loams are OK. Trees will tolerate dry, slightly alkaline soil. Tolerates city conditions. Transplants easily.

Obedient Plant
Physostegia virginiana
Perennial

Physostegia virginiana

▶ ***Hardiness:*** Zones 2–9
▶ ***Size:*** 3'–4' tall, 3' wide although tends to spread indefinitely by runners
▶ ***Features:*** Spires of flowers bloom in pink or white on tall slender stems with dark green narrow leaves. The plant gets its name from the way long, slender flowerheads will bend and then "obediently" retain the bent shape. Also called false dragonhead because each individual flower looks like the head of a Chinese dragon. Blooms late summer through early fall.
▶ ***Uses:*** In flower beds and borders; does well in moist naturalistic plantings
▶ ***Needs:*** Full sun or part shade. Average, well-drained soil, preferably acidic. Moderate to abundant moisture. Plant established plants in spring or fall. Mulch to conserve moisture. Avoid fertilizing, which encourages the plant to become invasive. Cut back after blooming to encourage a second flush. Dig up spreading plants in spring and fall to keep in check. This plant is usually pest and disease free.
▶ ***Choices:*** Flowers are pink or white. 'Vivid' is one of the most popular. 'Summer Snow' is earlier-blooming and considerably less invasive.

Ocimum basilicum
see Basil

Oenothera spp.
see Evening Primrose

Ohio Buckeye
see Buckeye

Old Man Cactus
see Cactus and Succulents

Olea europaea
see Olive

Oleander
Nerium oleander
Broadleaf evergreen shrub

Nerium oleander

▶ ***Hardiness:*** Zones 8–10
▶ ***Size:*** 10'–15' tall and wide
▶ ***Features:*** This tough, low-maintenance shrub is just the thing for seaside and desert plantings. Featuring big, coarse evergreen leaves and colorful flowers, it blooms throughout summer and fall.
▶ ***Uses:*** Parking areas, seaside and desert landscapes, xeriscaping, hedges and screens, large containers
▶ ***Needs:*** Nearly any type of soil. Little or no additional watering once established. Plant in spring or fall from established plants. No need to fertilize, although those growing only 4'–5' may need slow-release fertilizer or compost worked into the soil in spring. Prune in winter. This bush flowers on new growth, so cut some stems of smaller types back to the ground and remove selected branches of larger types. It is prone to scale. Plant in well-drained soil and full sun—sandy soil is ideal. Water new plants regularly until established; rarely thereafter. Prune in early spring to keep plants neat and control size. Can plant in coastal areas of Zone 7.
▶ ***Choices:*** Flowers bloom in white, yellow, pink, and red. Mature size varies radically, from 3'–20' tall. Read label carefully. A few, such as 'Double Sister Agnes', are fragrant. Also check hardiness; some are more sensitive to frost than others.

Olive
Olea europaea
Evergreen tree

Olea europaea

▶ ***Hardiness:*** Zones 8–10
▶ ***Size:*** 25'–30' tall, 25'–30' wide
▶ ***Features:*** Southern California is perfect for growing olives. These elegant, gray-leaved trees thrive in the area's hot, arid climate, which is much like their native Mediterranean setting. Olives are poor choices for humid areas with lots of rainfall.
▶ ***Uses:*** Xeriscaping, single specimen use, adding shade, planting near parking areas or patios (choose fruitless varieties for cleanliness)
▶ ***Needs:*** Grow olives in full sun. When planting, prepare the soil by digging deeply; add gypsum if needed to improve drainage. Olives thrive in rich soil but will also grow in stony, alkaline sites. Water new plants; older plants rarely need watering.

Olive, Sweet
see Sweet Olive

Omphalodes verna
see Blue-Eyed Mary

Oncidium
see Orchids: Dancing Ladies Orchid

Onions
Allium cepa

Cool-season annual

Onion 'Simcoe'

▶ ***Hardiness:*** Zones 2–11

▶ ***Size:*** Foliage grows 1'–2' tall; roots grow a few inches deep

▶ ***Features:*** Pungent roots are a kitchen staple

▶ ***Uses:*** In the vegetable garden

▶ ***Needs:*** Full sun. Rich, well-drained soil with plenty of organic matter, such as compost. More acidic soil results in a more pungent flavor. Plant in early spring in the northern two-thirds of the United States and in Canada. Elsewhere, fall planting is best. To plant from seed, sow seed directly in the garden 4 weeks before your region's average last frost date, planting ¼" deep and 4"–6" apart. For earlier onions, you can start seeds indoors 10 weeks before your region's average last frost date. Plant outdoors 4"–6" apart. You can also plant from sets, small dormant bulbs. Plant 4 weeks before the average last frost date, 2"–3" deep and 4"–6" apart. Harvest after 4–8 weeks for scallions. Or harvest when onions are fully mature, when they are 2"–4" wide and the tops are starting to fall over. Gently dig up entire plant. Cure for a few weeks by laying on newspapers in a cool, airy place, such as a porch. Trim off tops or braid the foliage together. Store indoors for several months.

▶ ***Choices:*** The length of summer days determines how well certain types of onions develop bulbs. In the southern third of the United States, where summer days are only 14 hours long, choose short-day varieties such as 'Yellow Granex' or 'Red Creole'. In the central third of the United States plant intermediate types such as 'Super Star' or 'Candy.' In the northern third and Canada, where days are longer, try 'Walla Walla' and other sweet Spanish types.

Onion, Ornamental
see Allium

Ophiopogon japonicus
see Mondo Grass

Ophiopogon planiscapus 'Nigrescens'
see Mondo Grass, Black

Opuntia microdasys
see Cactus and Succulents: Bunny Ears Cactus

Orange
see Citrus

ORCHIDS
Tropical epiphytes

Few can resist orchids, with their intricate, beautifully colored flowers and elegant leathery, long foliage. In the past, orchids were regarded as difficult, fussy plants, but with breeding advances that have brought down their cost, an increasing number of people are trying their hand at growing the easiest orchids, listed below, and have been delighted with the results.

Each type of orchid has its own special needs, but as a rule, good light is important. An east or west window is ideal if sheer curtains or another filtering device is used. Orchids dislike direct sun, but they need 10–15 hours of sunlight a day. In winter you will need to supplement with artificial light. Turn the pot occasionally to promote even, straight growth, and on cold nights, move the orchids away from the window to avoid cold drafts, which can be fatal. Most orchids prefer daytime temperatures of about 70°F/21°C in summer and about 60°F/16°C in winter. It's also important to provide about a 10°F/5°C drop in temperature at night to encourage good growth and flowering.

Water regularly with soft, room-temperature water; orchids should be kept evenly moist but not soggy. Orchids also benefit from weak fertilizing along with their watering. Dilute a 10-10-10 fertilizer to one-fourth the rate recommended on the package and follow the adage of "weekly, weakly."

Humidity for orchids is critical. Set pots on a tray filled with pebbles and water or run a humidifier nearby. Most orchids do best with humidity of at least 60 to 70 percent.

Excellent ventilation is also a must. Avoid placing orchids in hot, stuffy rooms. They'll also enjoy being placed in a shady spot outdoors on warm days or even spending an entire summer outdoors. Most orchids like being pot-bound (some even send roots out from the pot into the air with no problem). However, if the potting medium starts to break down, which it usually does in 2–3 years, repot immediately, because decomposed medium can contribute to rot. Use a special orchid mix.

ORCHIDS

Cattleya Orchid
Cattleya hybrids

Tropical epiphyte

Cattleya 'Vandelleta'

▶ ***Size:*** Grows 1'–5' tall, depending on the type and growing conditions

▶ ***Features:*** Sometimes called the corsage orchid, this orchid is an excellent choice for novices. Comes in an astounding array of colors, patterns, and fragrances. The flowers last about 2 weeks on the plant, but if you touch them, they'll age prematurely.

▶ ***Uses:*** As a houseplant

▶ ***Needs:*** Grow as for most orchids. However, the humidity needs of cattleyas are especially high. Grow in a terrarium or miniature conservatory, if possible. Also less tolerant of temperature changes.

▶ ***Choices:*** Thousands of cattleya hybrids have been produced.

ORCHIDS

Cymbidium Orchid
Cymbidium spp.

Tropical epiphyte

Cymbidium spp.

▶ Size: Grows up to 3' tall, depending on the type
▶ Features: One of the easiest of all orchids to grow. Produces waxy, long-lasting flowers that make excellent cut flowers. Wide range of colors in everything but blue, often with lovely patterns. Flowers last 8–10 weeks on the plant.
▶ Uses: As a houseplant
▶ Needs: Grow as for other orchids. Cymbidiums especially love light. Leaves should be slightly yellowish green. If they are dark green, it's a sign plants are receiving too little light.
▶ Choices: Standard hybrids grow up to 3' tall with flowers 3"–5" across. Miniatures grow 1'–2' tall with flowers 1"–3" across.

ORCHIDS

Dancing Ladies Orchid

Oncidium spp.

Tropical epiphyte

Oncidium 'Sweet Sugar'

▶ Size: Grows from 4" to 4', depending on the type. With flower stalk, some of these types of orchids can top 5'.
▶ Features: A good orchid for beginners, this plant derives its name from the way the flowers, usually in yellow and brown, delicately dangle from the branched, arching flower stalks.
▶ Uses: As a houseplant
▶ Needs: Grow as for other orchids. Because of its size, it's a good idea to use a large, broader pot. Double potting (see page 275) is an excellent option that allows you to use peat moss kept wet to increase humidity.
▶ Choices: A number of species are available. *Oncidium cheirophorum* is one of the smallest, with leaves growing only 4" and flower stalks only 6".

ORCHIDS

Dendrobium Orchids

Dendrobium spp.

Tropical epiphyte

Dendrobium Jaq-Candy 'Udom Stripe'

▶ Size: Grows a few inches to several feet tall, depending on the type and growing conditions
▶ Features: This huge group of orchids encompasses more than 1,000 species and includes both evergreen and deciduous orchids. Some are excellent for beginners while others are more demanding.
▶ Uses: As a houseplant
▶ Needs: Grow as for other orchids. However, *Dendrobium nobile* needs to be cool and dry in the fall in order to set flower buds.
▶ Choices: *D. phalaenopsis* is by far the most commonly sold of the dendrobiums and for good reason—it may remain in bloom for up to 4 months.

ORCHIDS

Moth Orchids

Phalaenopsis spp.

Tropical epiphyte

Phalaenopsis Reve Rose

▶ Size: Grows 1' leaves with 2'–3' flower stalks
▶ Features: An especially rewarding orchid to grow because it doesn't need a period of rest as most other orchids do in order to flower. It also has a long bloom time, flowering for months, usually in summer. Some moth orchids are such heavy bloomers they're practically everblooming.
▶ Uses: As a houseplant
▶ Needs: Grow as for other orchids
▶ Choices: There are several species of *Phalaenopsis*. The hybrids, however, are especially easy to grow and are bred for longer bloom and bigger flowers, as well as a wider variety of colors and markings.

ORCHIDS

Slipper Orchids

Paphiopedilum spp.

Tropical terrestrial perennial

Paphiopedilum spp.

▶ Size: Foliage grows a few to several inches tall and wide
▶ Features: Slipper orchids look different from other orchids. Their foliage grows most distinctively; their flowers have a striking pouch, like the lady's slipper that grows in the wild. An especially easy orchid to grow because it doesn't need a period of rest as most other orchids do. Plants bloom for 1–3 months and are less fussy about moisture and humidity than some other orchids.
▶ Uses: As a houseplant
▶ Needs: Grow as for other orchids. However, these orchids appreciate a more marked difference between daytime and nighttime temperatures, preferring nights of 55°–60°F/13°–16°C and days of 70°–85°F/21°–27°C.
▶ Choices: Several species and many hybrids available. Divided into mottled-leaved species and green-leaved species. A hybrid, *Paphiopedilum maudiae,* is considered by some to be the best orchid for a beginner.

ORCHIDS

Vanda Orchids

Vanda spp.

Tropical epiphyte

Vanda spp.

▶ ***Size:*** Grows up to 6', depending on the species, but most are shorter
▶ ***Features:*** Vandas have distinctive foliage with a number of narrow leaves branching out in a flattened from a central stalk, like a brushy palm front.
▶ ***Uses:*** As a houseplant
▶ ***Needs:*** Grow as for most orchids. Does best when grown in a special orchid basket filled with orchid mix. Dislikes being pot-bound but is stressed by repotting, so choose generous-sized baskets. Top leaves to keep plants more compact.
▶ ***Choices:*** The species *V. coerulea* and *V. sanderiana* are available, but the hybrids usually have superior flowers.

Orchid Tree

Bauhinia spp.

Evergreen or deciduous trees and shrubs

Bauhinia ×blakeana

▶ ***Hardiness:*** Zones 9-11
▶ ***Size:*** 10'-35' tall, depending on species
▶ ***Features:*** Spectacular, exotic, orchidlike blooms covering these trees and shrubs for nearly half the year have made some species popular in the mild-winter climates of southern Arizona and California, and in Hawaii. Flower color ranges from white to pink and purple; one species has orange-red flowers.
▶ ***Uses:*** Tree species have a spreading, umbrellalike form good for casting shade over a patio. Larger species make glorious street trees. Smaller shrubby ones are beautiful trained as an espalier. All are excellent wherever a massive, long-season color display is wanted.
▶ ***Needs:*** Plant in a warm spot in full sun to part shade. Pruning to train growth habit should be accomplished right after blooming is over.
▶ ***Choices:*** Purple orchid tree *(Bauhinia purpurea)* is the largest and most widely grown, reaching to 30' tall and 40' wide, covered with pink or purple flowers from midwinter into spring. Red bauhinia *(B. galpinii)* is a large shrub that grows about 10' tall. Its orange-red flowers appear from early spring into fall. Chinese orchid tree *(B. xblakeana)* is a wide-spreading tree reaching 20' tall and 30' wide, excellent for shade as a patio tree. It blooms all winter long from late fall into spring with flowers that are white suffused with rose and purple.

Oregano, Greek

Origanum vulgare hirtum

Perennial herb

Origanum vulgare hirtum

▶ ***Hardiness:*** Zones 5-9
▶ ***Size:*** Grows 1'-2' tall, 2'-3' wide
▶ ***Features:*** Low-spreading plant is versatile in a variety of dishes. Pretty white flowers in spring.
▶ ***Uses:*** Does well in rock gardens, raised beds, or among flagstones or pavers. Excellent fresh or dried. Use in Italian, Greek, and other ethnic dishes. Ideal in tomato sauces as well as lamb, bean, egg, and cheese dishes. Good fresh in salads or snipped into salad dressings. In early summer, can dry by cutting 8" or so stems, bundling the ends together with a rubber band, and hanging in a cool, dry place for a few weeks. Rub dried leaves to crumble and store in a jar.
▶ ***Needs:*** Full sun. Well-drained, average to poor, rocky soil. Flavor is best with poor soil and excellent drainage. Plant established plants outdoors in spring or fall. Moderate water; somewhat drought tolerant once established.
▶ ***Choices:*** Greek oregano has the best flavor; other types are less fully flavored. Crush a leaf between your fingers to check for intense oregano scent. Variegated types are also available.

Oregon Grape; Oregon Grapeholly

see Mahonia

Oriental Arborvitae

see Arborvitae, Oriental

Oriental Poppy

see Poppy

Origanum majorana

see Marjoram

Origanum vulgare

see Oregano

Ornamental Onion

see Allium

Osmanthus fragrans

see Sweet Olive

Osmunda cinnamomea

see Ferns: Cinnamon Fern

Osmunda regalis

see Ferns: Royal Fern

Osteospermum fruticosum

see Freeway Daisy

Pachysandra

Pachysandra terminalis

Perennial groundcover

Pachysandra terminalis

▶ ***Hardiness:*** Zones 4-9
▶ ***Size:*** 9"-12" high, 24"-36" wide
▶ ***Features:*** This groundcover fills in bare shady spots where grass won't grow—but only if the soil is moist. It makes a good companion to hostas. Both are coarse-textured, grow in shade, and like the same type of soil.

▶**Uses:** Filling in shady spots where grass won't grow, planting beneath trees, raised beds, growing in shade gardens
▶**Needs:** Plant in dense to partial shade—protect from afternoon sun in hotter climates. Moist, fertile soil is essential. Mix in peat moss or composted leaves at planting and tuck around plants each spring. Mulch new plantings for their first and second winters in colder areas.

Paeonia spp.

see Peony

Pagoda Tree, Japanese

Sophora japonica

Deciduous tree

Sophora japonica

▶**Hardiness:** Zones 6–8
▶**Size:** 50'–75' tall, 50'–75' wide
▶**Features:** When most trees are plain green, Japanese pagoda tree puts on a summer spectacular with its show of scented, creamy flowers. Trees get big; give them room to grow and develop their broad, rounded crown. Can be messy when petals, leaves, and pods drop throughout the year, but summer flowers and leafy shade make it worth planting, even beside patios.
▶**Uses:** Large specimen, shade, and lawn tree; urban landscapes, open areas, large estates, golf courses, parks
▶**Needs:** Plant in loamy, well-drained soil. Tolerates polluted conditions of the city and poor soil. Once established, can tolerate heat and drought. Prune young trees to encourage the development of a main, central trunk.
▶**Choices:** 'Pendula'—weeping form for accent use.

Pak Choi

see Bok Choi

PALMS

Nothing lends a tropical feel to a landscape like palms. Their waving, graceful fronds and interesting trunks make them a staple in warm-climate landscapes. Although most palms are tropical or subtropical natives, some are amazingly hardy and can be grown as far north as Seattle. They also have a variety of heights and forms, with some working well as shrubs and others soaring to 80' or more. Unlike many other plants, palms don't drop leaves or other litter, making them desirable for poolside plantings. In cold climates, palms have been a favorite houseplant since Victorian times. They thrive in containers and even in limited light can reach several feet indoors, depending on the type and growing conditions.

PALMS

Areca Palm

Chrysalidocarpus lutescens
(formerly *Dypsis lutescens)*

Palm tree

Chrysalidocarpus lutescens

▶**Hardiness:** Zones 10–11
▶**Size:** Outdoors up to 10' tall; 6' wide; indoors almost as large if container is big enough
▶**Features:** Light, graceful green fronds and smooth, slender multiple trunks. Sometimes called butterfly palm. Be sure to give this plant plenty of room when using indoors.
▶**Uses:** As an accent or small specimen plant in the landscape; as a houseplant
▶**Needs:** Outdoors, plant areca palm in spring or early summer in a frost-free, shady, sheltered spot, working a few spadefuls of compost into the soil. Palms are drought tolerant but benefit from an occasional spray from the hose to rinse off dust.

Indoors, give palms medium to filtered bright light. Allow soil to dry slightly between waterings; palms do poorly in wet soil. Average household temperatures and humidity. Fertilize three times in summer with a 10-10-10 formulation. Palms are easily damaged, so keep out of high traffic areas. Trim off fronds as they die naturally.

PALMS

Cabbage Palm; Sabal Palm

Sabal palmetto

Palm tree

Sabal palmetto

▶**Hardiness:** Zones 8–10
▶**Size:** 40'–80' tall, 15'–25' wide
▶**Features:** Sabal palm is easy to grow, eventually reaching heights of about 80'. Tolerates drought, salt, and confined spaces, heat and light frosts. For uniform appearance, you can plant mature trees with some of the trunk buried so that all are even in height. Or, plant them in stair-step fashion for added interest.

▶ ***Uses:*** Parking areas, patios, street trees, xeriscaping, seaside planting, entry areas, single specimens or groups

▶ ***Needs:*** Plant in full sun to partial shade in spring or early summer, working a few spadesful of compost into the soil. Extremely adaptable—grows in most kinds of soil. Water frequently after planting until new growth appears. Once established, no extra water is needed. Prune only dead or damaged fronds to avoid ruining the rounded crown.

PALMS

Chinese Fan Palm

Livistona chinensis

Palm tree

Livistona chinensis

▶ ***Hardiness:*** Zones 10–11

▶ ***Size:*** 15' tall

▶ ***Features:*** The tall, slender trunk has interesting scarring and is topped with dark, shiny fan-shape leaves. A huge advantage over some other palms is that this plant is self-cleaning—old leaves simply drop off rather than needing to be pruned.

▶ ***Uses:*** As a specimen plant or shade tree; attractive when planted in groups

▶ ***Needs:*** Plant full sun in late spring or early summer, working a few spadesful of organic soil amendment, such as compost, into the soil. Keep well watered the first year; palms are drought tolerant after that. Will survive temperatures as low as 22°F/-6°C.

PALMS

Clustered Fishtail Palm

Caryota spp.

Palm tree

Caryota spp.

▶ ***Hardiness:*** Zones 10–11

▶ ***Size:*** As a landscape plant, 25'–100'. As a houseplant, 6'–10' tall, 4'–6' wide

▶ ***Features:*** Delightful ragged-edged leaves are shaped like tropical fish. Produces suckers at the base, making the plant nicely full and shrubby. Arching fronds have leaflets for their entire length.

▶ ***Uses:*** Parking areas, patios, street trees, xeriscaping, entry areas, single specimens or groups, outdoor containers. Also as a houseplant.

▶ ***Needs:*** Outdoors: Plant in spring or early summer in a frost-free, shady, sheltered spot, working a few spadesful of compost into the soil. Drought tolerant but benefits from an occasional spray from the hose to rinse off dust.

Indoors: Direct to bright light. Allow soil to dry slightly between waterings; palms do badly in wet soil. Average household temperatures and humidity. Fertilize three times in summer with a 10-10-10 formulation. Easily damaged; keep out of high-traffic areas. Trim off fronds as they die naturally.

▶ ***Choices:*** Clustered fishtail palm *(Caryota mitus)* is a slow grower that hits 25' and is badly damaged or killed by frost. Canton fishtail palm *(C. ochlandra)* reaches up to 25' and can survive some subfreezing temperatures. Wine fishtail palm *(C. urens)* has fewer leaves that are closer to a triangle shape. It can hit 100' but will die if exposed to frost.

PALMS

Date Palm

Phoenix dactylifera

Palm tree

Phoenix dactylifera

▶ ***Hardiness:*** Zones 9–10

▶ ***Size:*** 65'–80' tall, 40'–50' wide

▶ ***Features:*** Date palms are a dramatic and impressive sight, topping out at 70'–80' feet tall. Avoid planting trees too close to homes. May die during extended freezes.

▶ ***Uses:*** Xeriscaping, street trees, large lots, arid landscapes, seaside

▶ ***Needs:*** Plant in full sun with well-drained soil. Date palms are very drought tolerant. Discontinue supplemental watering when new plants show signs of fresh growth.

PALMS

Date Palm, Canary Island

Phoenix canariensis

Palm tree

Phoenix canariensis

▶ ***Hardiness:*** Zones 9–10
▶ ***Size:*** 50'–60' tall, 30'–50' wide
▶ ***Features:*** Thick trunks grow to impressive heights, crowned with stiff, wide fronds. Drought tolerant and easy care. Its trunk grows more slowly than its fronds. Start off with trees that have fronds above head height. Trees may die during extended freezes.
▶ ***Uses:*** Tropical effect, single-specimen accent plant, entries, parking areas, along streets
▶ ***Needs:*** Plant in full sun. Soil must be well drained; wet sites promote fungal problems. Select a planting location that will accommodate wide, stiff fronds without chance of human injury.

PALMS

Date Palm, Pygmy

Phoenix roebelenii

Palm tree

Phoenix roebelenii

▶ ***Hardiness:*** Zones 9–10
▶ ***Size:*** 8'–10' tall, spread to 8' wide
▶ ***Features:*** Rapid growth rate. Fine-textured fronds add contrast. Smaller, more manageable size; choose single, double, or triple specimens. Use in prominent places in your landscape for accenting with a tropical touch. Containers on patio, porch, or deck are stunning. Although it grows quickly, this palm is worth spending money on for a good-sized specimen from the start.
▶ ***Uses:*** Accent plants, single specimen, entries, courtyard, poolside, shrub beds, large containers
▶ ***Needs:*** Plant in fertile, well-drained soil. Grow in full sun or partial shade. Water new plants regularly; later, water only when dry. Feed three times a year with palm fertilizer. Protect from freezing temperatures.

PALMS

Kentia Palm, Paradise Palm

Howea forsteriana

Palm tree

Howea forsteriana

▶ ***Hardiness:*** Zones 9–10
▶ ***Size:*** Up to 10' tall and wide
▶ ***Features:*** Graceful, feathery palm leaves have made these slow-growing trees a favorite for hotel lobbies and malls. Easy to grow indoors or out in mild climates; tolerant of a wide variety of conditions.
▶ ***Uses:*** Outdoor containers, groupings, small specimen plant, planting under other larger trees outdoors, widely used as a houseplant
▶ ***Needs:*** Outdoors: Plant in spring or early summer in a frost-free, shady, sheltered spot, working a few spadefuls of compost into the soil. Drought tolerant but benefits from an occasional spray from the hose to rinse off dust.

Indoors: Medium to filtered bright light. Allow soil to dry slightly between waterings; palms do poorly in wet soil. Average household temperatures and humidity. Fertilize three times in summer with a 10-10-10 formulation. Easily damaged; keep out of high-traffic areas. Trim off fronds as they die naturally.
▶ ***Choices:*** Sentry or curly palm *(Howea belmoreana)* grows more upright to 6'–7'.

PALMS

King Palm

Archontophoenix cunninghamiana
(formerly *Seaforthia cunninghamiona)*

Palm tree

Archontophoenix cunninghamiana

P

Plant encyclopedia

▶ **Hardiness:** Zones 10–11
▶ **Size:** Grows 50' tall, 10'–15' wide
▶ **Features:** This tall, elegant palm grows 50' or more with feathering leaves that grow up to 10' long and produce a pleasing effect with gray-green under the leaves and deep green above. The old leaves are shed neatly.
▶ **Uses:** As a specimen plant or part of a grouping
▶ **Needs:** Plant in late spring or early summer in full sun to light shade; this palm can take more shade than most, especially when young. Work a few spadesful of organic soil amendment, such as compost, into the planting hole. Keep well watered the first year; palms become drought tolerant after that. When young, this plant can be killed by frost. Mature trees, however, can survive temperatures as low as 28°F/-3°C

PALMS

Lady Palm

Rhapis excelsa

Palm tree or shrub

Rhapis excelsa

▶ **Hardiness:** Zones 10–11, warmer parts of 9
▶ **Size:** Up to 12' outdoors; up to 8' indoors
▶ **Features:** This is one of the smallest palms, with a beautiful, elegant shape and short-stalked bluish-green fan leaves on multiple trunks. Plants are more tolerant of lower light and have a finer texture than other palms.
▶ **Uses:** As a garden plant in smaller-scale plantings; used as a houseplant as well
▶ **Needs:** Full sun to light shade. Plant in late spring or early summer. Work a few spadesful of organic soil amendment, such as compost, into the planting hole. Keep well watered the first year; palms become drought tolerant after that. Prone to iron chlorosis in soils with a high pH.

PALMS

Lady Palm, Slender

Rhapis humilis

Palm tree or shrub

Rhapis humilis

▶ **Hardiness:** Zones 9–11
▶ **Size:** 5'–15' tall and wide
▶ **Features:** Deep green fan palms form attractive bamboolike clumps. As a houseplant, one of the few fan-type palms sold because it's more upright than the others and fits better into home spaces. Also called rattan palm.
▶ **Uses:** As an accent plant or understory plant, excellent in outdoor containers, as a houseplant
▶ **Needs:** Outdoors: Plant in spring or early summer in a frost-free, shady, sheltered spot, working a few spadesful of compost into the soil. Drought tolerant but benefits from an occasional spray from the hose to rinse off dust. Hardy to 22°F/-6°C. Indoors: Medium to filtered bright light. Allow soil to dry slightly between waterings; palms do poorly in wet soil. Average household temperatures and humidity. Fertilize three times in summer with a 10-10-10 formulation. Easily damaged; keep away from high-traffic areas. Trim off fronds as they die naturally.

PALMS

Mediterranean Fan Palm

Chamaerops humilis

Palm tree

Chamaerops humilis

▶ **Hardiness:** Zones 8–10
▶ **Size:** 10'–20' high; 15'–20' wide
▶ **Features**: Handsome plants, available in multi- or single-stemmed forms, flourish in hot landscapes as well as cooler borderline areas. One of the hardiest palms, Mediterranean fan palm will tolerate temperatures as low as 6°F/-15°C. Adds tropical-looking accent to planters, patios, and decks.
▶ **Uses:** Accent, either as a single specimen or in groups; screening; forming an impenetrable hedge
▶ **Needs:** Place this palm in full sun to light shade; you can grow it in just about any soil that's well drained. Water frequently for the first year or two after planting, then only when dry. Keep the area around trunks free of grass and weeds.

PALMS

Mexican Fan Palm

Washingtonia robusta

Palm tree

Washingtonia robusta

▶ **Hardiness:** Zones 9–10
▶ **Size:** 60'–100' tall, 12'–15' wide
▶ **Features:** Growing between 60' and 100' tall, this palm is best used in large, open spaces. Very tall mature size makes it incorrectly proportioned for use beside most homes. Think big when using the Mexican fan palm.
▶ **Uses:** Single specimen, groups, parking areas, large landscapes

▶ Needs: Plant in just about any soil that's well drained and in full sun. This desert palm tolerates dry conditions but grows fastest when watered regularly. In humid semitropical regions, water less frequently. Overwatering can damage or kill these plants. Remove dead fronds periodically.

PALMS

Parlor Palm

Chamaedorea elegans (formerly *Neanthe bella*)

Palm tree or shrub

Chamaedorea elegans

▶ Hardiness: Zones 10–11
▶ Size: Up to 4' tall and wide outdoors; up to 2'–3' tall and wide indoors
▶ Features: Slow-growing palm has a single trunk. Its compact size is good for smaller spaces outdoors, especially containers and large planters. Leaves vary with type. The parlor palm often is sold as a 6" houseplant.
▶ Uses: As a garden plant in smaller-scale plantings; as a houseplant
▶ Needs: Outdoors: Plant in spring or early summer in a frost-free, shady, sheltered spot, working a few spadesful of compost into the soil. Drought tolerant but benefits from an occasional spray from the hose to rinse off dust.

Indoors: Medium to filtered bright light. Allow soil to dry slightly between waterings; palms do poorly in wet soil. Average household temperatures and humidity. Fertilize three times in summer with a 10-10-10 formulation. Easily damaged; keep out of high-traffic areas. Trim off fronds as they die naturally.
▶ Choices: Sometimes also sold as *Collinia elegans*

PALMS

Pindo Palm

Butia capitata

Palm tree

Butia capitata

▶ Hardiness: Zones 8–10
▶ Size: 12'–20' tall, 12'–15' wide
▶ Features: This tough palm features arching, blue-green fronds and a thick trunk. Good choice for hot, semitropical locations or areas that receive short bursts of freezing temperatures. Edible fruit gives this plant its nickname of jelly palm.
▶ Uses: Single specimen or coarse-textured accent, massed in groups or planted in rows: xeriscaping: parking areas and streetside
▶ Needs: Plant in full sun and well-drained soil. Allow plenty of room for this plant's mature spread of 15'. Pindo palm is fairly drought tolerant; water only when soil is dry. Fertilize yearly with palm food.

PALMS

Queen Palm

Syagrus romanzoffiana, formerly *Arecastrum romanzoffianum*

Palm tree

Syagrus romanzoffiana

▶ Hardiness: Zones 10–11
▶ Size: 40'–50' tall, 30' wide
▶ Features: The queen palm is a regal presence with its gracefully arching fine-textured fronds and tall, straight, smooth gray trunk that give it the quintessential palm tree appearance. Trunks grow to 40'–50' tall. Tolerates heat and confined conditions; but temperatures of 25°F/-4°C and below damage or kill this palm. Roots adapt well to confined conditions.
▶ Uses: Fine-textured accent, single specimen or in rows, cutouts in patios or decks, entry, parking, street tree
▶ Needs: Plant in moist, well-drained soil and full sun. Palms will grow in neutral to alkaline soils. Water and fertilize regularly with palm food. Grow where plants are protected from high winds. Remove dead fronds before they fall.

PALMS

Royal Palm

Roystonea elata

Palm tree

Roystonea elata

▶ Hardiness: Zones 10–11
▶ Size: 75'–80' tall, 25'–30' wide
▶ Features: Tall and stately, this Florida native gives landscapes a tropical touch. It features smooth gray and green trunks topped with graceful fronds. Trunks have a tendency to lean. Prolonged frost will kill this tree.
▶ Uses: Street trees, parking areas, beside multistory homes and buildings, large lawns
▶ Needs: Plant in full sun. Rich, moist to wet soil is ideal for this swamp native. Sandy, fast-draining soils will need regular watering for best results. Fertilize once or twice a year with palm food.

PALMS

Sago Palm; King Sago

Cycas revoluta

Palm tree or shrub

Cycas revoluta

► ***Hardiness:*** Zones 8-10
► ***Size:*** 6'-10' tall, 6'-8' wide
► ***Features:*** Add this slow-growing plant to your landscape for an exotic accent. Feathery-looking fronds are stiff and grow in a circle. Glossy green foliage color. Cold tolerant, hardy to 15°F/-9°C. Grows in poor, sandy soils, sun or shade.
► ***Uses:*** Accent plant, entry areas, including in a bed of groundcover, growing in large containers
► ***Needs:*** Plant king sago in any well-drained soil that receives full sun or shade. If you live in an area with occasional winter freezes, choose a spot that offers some protection, such as near a wall of your home away from the northern exposure.

PALMS

Senegal Date Palm

Phoenix reclinata

Palm tree

Phoenix reclinata

► ***Hardiness:*** Zones 9-10
► ***Size:*** 25'-35' tall, 20'-35' wide
► ***Features:*** This palm has arching, evergreen fronds and an attractive multitrunked form that grows in a big clump, giving a tropical look to the landscape. This palm is damaged when temperatures fall below 28°F/-3°C. Avoid planting where freezes are likely. Leaf stalks are thorny. Drought and salt tolerant.
► ***Uses:*** A multitrunked accent, hiding tall walls, tropical effect, xeriscaping, coastal areas (but not right on the beach)
► ***Needs:*** Plant in any soil that's well drained and stays sunny all day long. Senegal date palm is drought tolerant after plants are established. Avoid overwatering to prevent disease.

PALMS

Windmill Palm

Trachycarpus fortunei

Palm tree

Trachycarpus fortunei

► ***Hardiness:*** Zones 8-10
► ***Size:*** 20'-30' tall, 5'-10' wide
► ***Features:*** Windmill palm is an unusually adaptable palm that can be used in many different landscaping situations. Trees have neat fronds that are fanlike in appearance and hairy trunks that provide added texture. Grows well in the ground as well as large containers.
► ***Uses:*** Courtyards, entries, confined spaces, containers, beside swimming pools, accent plant
► ***Needs:*** Plant in full sun or light, dappled shade. These palms adapt to a range of soil conditions. Place the root ball a little below soil level at planting. Water regularly. Fertilize two to three times a year with palm food. Can tolerate temperatures down to 10°F/-12°C.

Palo verde, Texas

Cercidium texanum

Deciduous flowering tree

Cercidium texanum

► ***Hardiness:*** Zones 9-10
► ***Size:*** 15'-25' tall, 15'-20' wide
► ***Features:*** Palo verde is Spanish for "green tree," and this Texas native indeed sports unusual, smooth green bark. It also features clusters of yellow spring flowers. You may also find palo verde sold as *Parkinsonia texana var. texanum.*
► ***Uses:*** Adding color and shade to hot, arid landscapes and hillsides; Xeriscaping
► ***Needs:*** Give Texas palo verde a place in full sun. Plant in alkaline, well-drained soil. Water frequently to get new plants started, infrequently after that.

Panda Plant

see Cactus and Succulents

Pandorea spp.

see Bower Vine

Panicum virgatum

see Grasses, Ornamental: Switch Grass

Pansy; Viola; Violet

Viola spp.

Perennials and cool-season annuals

Viola spp.

► ***Hardiness:*** Zones 6-9 for perennial types; others are annuals
► ***Size:*** 2"-12" tall and wide, depending on type

▶Features: Violas and pansies, both perennial and annual types, are invaluable for bright, cheerful early spring color, and some are sweetly fragrant. The flat five-petaled flowers come in a wide array of colors and often have interesting splotches that form the so-called faces on the plants. In ideal conditions, some will spread considerably.
▶Needs: Full sun in Zones 2–7; full sun or preferably light shade in hot-summer areas in Zones 8–9. Humus-rich, well-drained but moist soil. Abundant moisture. Blooms only during cool weather. To grow pansies and violas, both of which are annuals, plant outdoors in spring in Zones 2–7 a few weeks before last frost date. In Zones 8–11 plant in late autumn for spring bloom. Work ample compost into the soil. Mulch to cool soil and conserve moisture. To grow perennial types of violets (Zones 6–9) plant established plants outdoors in spring. Keep spent blooms trimmed. Each spring, work more compost into the soil around the plants.
▶Choices: Perennial types include horned violet *(V. cornuta),* which grows 5"–12" tall with 1" flowers. Sweet violets *(V. odorata)* have highly fragrant flowers on plants 8"–15" tall.

Annual types include the pansy *(V. ×wittrockiana)* which has large flowers 2"–7" across on plants 4"–8" tall. Johnny-jump-up *(V. tricolor)* is a delicate-looking plant just 2"–6" tall, usually with purple and yellow flowers. It reseeds generously, hence its name.

Papaver orientale
see Poppy, Oriental Poppy

Papaver spp.
see Poppy

Paper birch
see Birches

Paphiopedilum
see Orchids: Slipper orchids

Paradise Palm
see Palms, Kentia Palm

Parlor Ivy
see Philodendrons: Heart-Leaf Philodendron

Parlor Palm
see Palms

Parsley
Petroselinum crispum

Grow as a cool-season annual

Italian parsley

▶Hardiness: Zones 2–11
▶Grows: 6"–12" tall, 6"–12" wide
▶Features: Emerald leaves on plants are attractive enough to grow in flower beds. Butterfly larvae love parsley as a host plant.
▶Uses: Snip fresh parsley over just about any soup, pasta, salad, and cheese or egg dish. Tuck a plant or two into the vegetable or herb garden but also consider including in a flower bed, especially as an edging plant.
▶Needs: Full sun to light shade. Prefers rich, well-drained soil with plenty of moisture, but will tolerate some variety in soils and moisture. Dislikes heat; bolts in hot weather. Plant established plants in early spring in cold-winter climates Zones 7 and colder; plant in fall in Zones 8 and warmer.
▶Choices: Flat-leaved parsley, sometimes called Italian parsley, is a bit taller (18") and preferred by gourmets over curly-leaved types.

Parsnip
Pastinaca sativa

Cool-season annual vegetable

Parsnip 'Cobham Improved Marrow'

▶Hardiness: Zones 2–11
▶Size: Leaves grow several inches tall, roots 6"–12" deep without taproot
▶Features: Roots excellent in soups, stews, and side dishes
▶Uses: In the vegetable garden
▶Needs: Full sun to part shade. Best in rich, well-drained soil deeply worked to at least a foot. Average moisture. Plant in spring 2–3 weeks before your region's last average frost date. Plant seeds ½"–1" deep. Thin to 6"–8". Keep soil moist. Mulch lightly to keep soil cool; mulch heavily if you want to harvest into winter; thicker mulch will delay soil from freezing. Harvest after the first frost, which sweetens parsnips.
Choices: 'Harris Model' is 2" wide and 12" long.

Parthenocissus spp.
see Virginia Creeper and Boston Ivy

Pasque Flower
Pulsatilla vulgaris, formerly *Anemone pulsatilla*

Perennial

Pulsatilla vulgaris

▶Hardiness: Zones 4–8
▶Size: 4"–6" tall and wide
▶Features: In earliest spring, the silvery, silky foliage of this fascinating native plant unfurls followed by deep purple, blue, white, or reddish 1"–3" flowers.
▶Uses: In beds and borders, prairie and other naturalistic plantings, among spring-blooming bulbs
▶Needs: Full sun in Zones 4–6; light shade in hot-summer regions in Zones 7–8. Average, well-drained soil. Moderate water; more drought tolerant in cool, shady sites. Plant in spring. Mulch to conserve moisture. Foliage dies back in summer. Avoid fertilizing. No need to divide or deadhead. May reseed modestly. Plants are prone to root rot in wet winter soil.
▶Choices: *Pulsatilla vulgaris* 'Alba' is white. Most pasque flowers are single, but 'Azure' is a semidouble violet and 'Polka' is semidouble white.

Passionflower; Maypop
Passiflora spp.

Evergreen or deciduous flowering vine

Passiflora coccinea

P Plant encyclopedia

▶ ***Hardiness:*** Zones 7–10
▶ ***Size:*** 15'–20' tall, 15'–20' wide
▶ ***Features:*** Grown for its exotic blooms, passionflower quickly covers garden structures with plenty of lush, glossy foliage. It dies to the ground during winter in the cooler parts of its range, but returns in spring. Try *P. edulis* as a woody climber.
▶ ***Uses:*** Covering fences and arbors, screening, erosion control, covering sunny bare spots, accent
▶ ***Needs:*** Plant in any well-drained soil in full sun or partial shade. Water regularly. Provide support—trellis, fencing, or string—for vines to climb, or let plants spread as groundcover. Prune as needed to keep this vigorous vine within bounds.
▶ ***Choices:*** Blue passionflower *(P. caerulea)* has 4" blue, hot pink and white flowers and grows to 30' tall. Scarlet passionflower *(P. coccinea)* has 3" red flowers and grows 30' in all directions.

Peace Lily

Spathiphyllum wallisii

Evergreen perennial

Spathyphyllum wallisii

▶ ***Hardiness:*** Zones 10–11
▶ ***Size:*** Up to 6' tall and wide as a landscape plant; usually 1'–2' tall and wide as a houseplant.
▶ ***Features:*** Peace lily displays large, glossy leaves—6" or more long—growing from a common base. Outdoors or in good conditions indoors, it will send up a fascinating 3" white flower that looks like half a pod with a pretty golden yellow center.
▶ ***Uses:*** As an accent plant in smaller areas or along walkways as a larger edging plant. Also as a houseplant
▶ ***Needs:*** Outdoors: Shade and loose, rich, well-drained soil with ample moisture. Frost kills plants. Indoors: Bright, indirect light. Direct sun can burn the leaves. Average home warmth fine as long as temperatures stay above 55°F/13°C and there are no cold drafts. Does best on a tray of pebbles with water for higher humidity but will tolerate average home humidity. Keep soil evenly moist. Avoid letting soil become either soggy or dry. Fertilize 2–3 times in the summer. Wipe leaves once a month with a damp cloth to keep glossy and healthy.
▶ ***Choices:*** *Spathiphyllum wallisii* grows about 1' tall and wide. *S.* 'Mauna Loa' grows about 3' tall.

Peaches and Nectarines

Prunus persica

Deciduous fruit tree

Peach 'Frost'

▶ ***Hardiness:*** Zones 5 (southern) to 9
▶ ***Size:*** Miniatures grow 3'–4' tall and as wide; standards up to 20' tall and as wide
▶ ***Features:*** Juicy fruits on a small to large tree in summer. Peaches have fuzz; nectarines, a variation of peaches, are smooth-skinned. Trees tend to be short-lived, lasting 10–15 years.
▶ ***Uses:*** In orchards and edible plantings, as an ornamental small tree
▶ ***Needs:*** Full sun. Likes rich, moist, well-drained soil with a pH of 6.2 to 6.5, but will tolerate other soils. Plant on north and east sides of buildings and slopes to prevent too-early blossoms that get zapped by late frost. Prune in early spring. Train to an open-center shape (see page 266).
▶ ***Choices:*** Peaches and nectarines dislike cold winters or late frosts. In the southern half of Zone 5, the only portion of 5 where you can grow these tender plants, plant 'Reliance', the most cold-hardy. Nectarines, which are less cold hardy, can be grown in Zones 6–9.

Peacock Orchid

see Gladiolus, Abyssinian

Pears and Asian Pears

Pyrus spp.

Deciduous fruit tree

Pear 'Doyenne De Cornice'

Asian Pear 'Chojura'

▶ ***Hardiness:*** Zones 4–9 (traditional pears); Zones 5–9 (Asian pears)
▶ ***Size:*** Grows from 5'–20' tall and 4'–15' wide, depending on the type
▶ ***Features:*** Crisp to soft fruits growing on a tree in late summer to early fall
▶ ***Uses:*** In orchards and edible plantings, as an ornamental small tree
▶ ***Needs:*** Full sun. Best in rich, well-drained soil but will tolerate wet soils. Prune in late winter or early spring to a single leader to accommodate pear's tendency to grow vertically. Spray with horticultural oil in late winter or early spring. Pick when fruit just begins to soften. Allow to finish ripening indoors for up to a month. Water trees during drought.
▶ ***Choices***: Traditional pears are *P. communis*. Asian pears are *P. serotina* and look like apples but are crunchy with pear flavor. Choose a cultivar suited to your region and one that is disease resistant.

Peas

Pisum sativum

Cool-season annual

Pea 'Green Arrow

▶ ***Hardiness:*** Zones 2-11
▶ ***Size:*** Grows 1'-3' tall, a few inches wide
▶ ***Features:*** Shelling peas are the traditional dinner table favorite. Snap peas fill out but have edible pods; snow peas are flat with edible pods.
▶ ***Uses:*** In the vegetable garden
▶ ***Needs:*** Full sun to light shade. Rich, well-drained soil with plentiful moisture. Prefers cool, damp weather. In cooler-summer regions (roughly Zones 6-7 and the Pacific Northwest) plant in early spring as soon as the soil can be worked and again in late summer for a fall harvest. Can be fussy about germinating; avoid soaking seed before planting. May need to replant after 2 weeks if peas fail to germinate. Plant seeds 2"-3" deep and 3" apart. As a rule, plant about 4' of shelling peas and 2' of snap or snow peas for each person to assure enough. Provide low (3') string trellis or other support. Folding fencing made especially for peas is convenient. Keep soil moist. Avoid high-nitrogen fertilizers. Cover with netting or erect a chicken-wire fence around the planting to protect from rabbits and deer. Pick shelling peas when pods have a sheen and are filled out. Open one or two to taste raw; peas should be sweet and tender, not starchy. If they have started to dent, they are past their prime. Harvest snap peas when the pods start to plump and they taste crisp, sweet, and tender when sampled raw. Harvest snow peas when the pods appear fully developed and they are sweet and tender when sampled raw.
▶ ***Choices:*** Many cultivars available. Try the award-winning 'Super Sugar Snap', which is very sweet and has a heavy crop. 'Mr. Big' is a shelling pea that has large pods and is very sweet. Leafless and semileafless peas are also good to look for because they put more of their energy into producing peas rather than foliage. 'Sugar Ann' is short and needs no support.

Pecan

Carya illinoinensis

Deciduous nut tree

Carya illinoinensis

▶ ***Hardiness:*** Zones 5-9
▶ ***Size:*** Grows 70'-100' tall, 40'-75' wide
▶ ***Features:*** A native tree that makes a pretty landscape tree but also produces delicious nuts. Where hot, dry conditions limit shade tree choices, pecans make the switch from farm to landscape. Low-branching and wide-spreading pecan trees drop catkins, leaves, limbs, and nuts at various times throughout the year. Seedlings often appear in planting beds where squirrels have buried nuts. Trees grow easily from seed but are difficult to transplant.
▶ ***Uses:*** Shade tree, edible landscaping
▶ ***Needs:*** Full sun. Deep, well-drained neutral rich soil is best but will tolerate considerable variation. Needs long, hot summers with warm nights seldom below 70°F/21°C. Need to plant two different cultivars to produce nuts. Plant in spring or fall. Little pruning needed other than to remove dead or damaged wood. Harvest in autumn after leaves and nuts begin to drop. Shake branches to speed harvest.
▶ ***Choices:*** Look for a cultivar well suited to your region. Ask a garden center associate or local cooperative extension service for recommendations.

Pelargonium spp.

see Geranium

Pennisetum spp.

see Grasses, Ornamental: Fountain Grass

Penstemon; Beard-tongue

Penstemon spp.

Perennials and annuals

Penstemon spp.

▶ ***Hardiness:*** Zones 3-7
▶ ***Size:*** 4"-30" tall, 6"-18" wide
▶ ***Features:*** This group of spectacular Western wildflowers can be finicky to grow, even in Western native plant gardens. But it has a number of species and hybrid cultivars that are suitable for gardens throughout the more northern zones of North America. All form spikes of colorful flowers in late spring or early summer.
▶ ***Needs:*** Full sun in most areas; part shade where summers are hot. Average to poor, loose, fast-draining soil. Water needs range from moderate to drought tolerant, depending on the type. Plant established plants in spring. Hold off on fertilizer and avoid overwatering. Trim spent blooms for second flush. This plant is prone to root rot and black spot. A short-lived perennial, beard-tongue usually dies out after 3-4 years.
▶ ***Choices:*** Flowers are red, pink, yellow, purple, lavender, white, and salmon. Many wild species are available, especially in the West. 'Husker Red', a bushy 3' plant that has white flowers and purple foliage that fades to bronze in summer heat, is one of the most commonly available. The Prairie series of hybrids are evergreen in warm regions. 'Prairie Dusk' has clear purple blooms; 'Prairie Fire' is red; 'Elfin Pink' has pink blooms. Heights vary dramatically; check the label. Hybrids that are perennial in Zones 7-10 and sometimes grown as annuals farther north include 'Garnet', with deep red flowers, and 'Sour Grape', with blue-violet flowers.

Pentas

Pentas lanceolata

Tropical shrub grown as an annual or houseplant

Pentas lanceolata

▶ ***Hardiness:*** Zones 10-11
▶ ***Size:*** A 6'-8' shrub in Hawaii and southern California and Florida, it can reach 2'-3' tall in a pot indoors and 6"-18" tall in a season as an annual bedding plant.
▶ ***Features:*** Pentas puts on a show with big, tight, round clusters of star-shape flowers in brilliant shades of pink, salmon, red, and white. The long leaves are dark green and fuzzy. Blooms summer through frost as an annual bedding plant, all year outdoors where hardy, and as a houseplant.
▶ ***Uses:*** Annual bedding plant and container plant, houseplant, in Zones 10-11 in the shrub border or as a specimen shrub or screen.
▶ ***Needs:*** Full sun, but part shade is appreciated when used as a bedding plant in Zones 7-11. Indoors, give it the brightest spot in the house,

preferably an unobstructed south-facing window. Rich, well-drained soil. Ample moisture. Plant started plants from the garden center in spring after all danger of frost has passed. Mulch to conserve moisture. Feed every 4–6 weeks, or work in a slow-release fertilizer at planting time. Trim spent blooms to encourage further flowering. In fall, a few weeks before the first frost date, bring inside and place in a sunny spot as a houseplant. It is prone to whiteflies.
▶ **Choices:** Flowers come in pink, lavender, white, and red. Some types grow as tall as 3', but the dwarf types generally sold for outdoor gardens grow just 6"–12" tall. 'New Look' is a dwarf cultivar.

Peony

Paeonia hybrids

Perennial

Paeonia hybrid

▶ **Hardiness:** Zones 2–8
▶ **Size:** 24"–36" tall and 30"–40" wide
▶ **Features:** Peonies are famous for their big, luscious, mostly fluffy double blossoms in late spring and early summer, about the same time as bearded iris, oriental poppies, and the early old garden roses. The flowers are often deliciously fragrant, although this varies widely among cultivars. They are wonderful cut for the vase, and come in a wide range of pinks, peaches, reds, lilacs, and whites. Some are single or semidouble with a prominent central mass of golden stamens. Plants form mounding shrubby masses of dark, lustrous foliage that can be an asset in the garden all summer. Some varieties produce colorful red seed heads in fall. Once established, peonies thrive for more than a human lifetime in the garden with little attention.
▶ **Uses:** In the mixed border with oriental poppies and bearded iris; as a specimen, massed in beds, or as a summer hedge. Superb for the cutting garden, lovely in informal cottage gardens.
▶ **Needs:** Full sun in Zones 2–6; partial shade beneficial in hot areas in Zones 7–8. Rich, well-drained soil; moderate to plentiful moisture. Plant in spring in Zones 2–6; spring or fall in Zones 7–8. Work in ample compost at planting. Mulch. Fertilize each spring. It may take 3–4 years to bloom after planting. Trim spent flowers after flowering. Provide support to herbaceous types with a tomato cage or other support once plants reach 1' tall each spring. Dividing is unnecessary unless more plants are wanted. Ants do not hurt peonies.
▶ **Choices:** Herbaceous peonies grow about 3' tall; tree peonies grow to 5' tall. Fern-leaf peony is an old-time favorite.

Peperomia

Peperomia spp.

Tropical evergreen perennial

Peperomia argyreia

▶ **Hardiness:** Zone 11
▶ **Size:** Grows 4" to 4' tall, depending on the type
▶ **Features:** There are a number of peperomias available. Most have roughly heart-shape, thick leaves, some waxy and some crinkled and many with beautiful variegations. Bushy types, the most commonly sold, grow 4"–6" tall and wide. Upright types are more elongated and grow as tall as 1'. The more unusual trailing types can grow as little as 6" or as much as 4', depending on the type.
▶ **Uses:** As a houseplant
▶ **Needs:** Bright, indirect light. Average household warmth and humidity are fine but plants will drop leaves if too cold or exposed to cold drafts. Allow soil to dry slightly between waterings to prevent root rot, but if soil gets too dry leaves will wilt or the plant may drop leaves.
▶ **Choices:** *P. caperata,* with its familiar, attractive crinkled leaves, is a popular plant. The metallic-looking green and silver striped leaves found on watermelon peperomia *(P. argyreia)* and ivy peperomia *(P. griseoargentea)* are also popular.

Peppers

Capsicum annuum

Warm-season annual vegetable

Bell Pepper

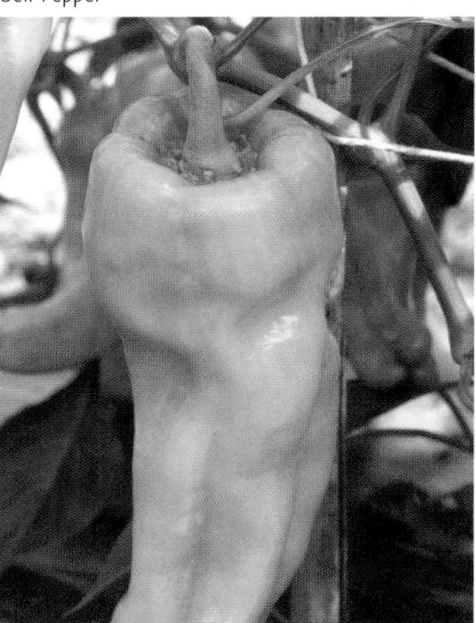

Pepper 'Aconcagua-Andes'

Pepper 'Hot Portugal'

▶Hardiness: Zones 2-11
▶Size: Grows 1'-2' tall and as wide
▶Features: Sweet and crisp or tender and spicy hot peppers grow on attractive deep green plants
▶Uses: In the vegetable garden
▶Needs: Full sun. Rich, well-drained soil high in organic matter for sweet (also called bell) peppers; sandy soil for hot peppers. Moderate moisture. Prefers warm climates, but tolerates a wide variety in soils and climates. If desired, start seeds indoors 6-8 weeks before your region's last frost date. Otherwise, plant established plants outdoors after all danger of frost has passed. Space 12"-24", depending on the mature size of the pepper plant (check the packet or label). Work a spadeful or two of compost into the soil at planting time. In cooler climates (Zones 6 and colder) it's helpful to cover new plants with a plastic gallon milk jug with the bottom cut off and the lid removed. Remove jug when flowering begins. Mulch with newspapers topped with straw or grass clippings to prevent soil-borne diseases. Provide steady rather than sporadic moisture to prevent blossom end rot. Fertilize every 2-3 weeks with a liquid fertilizer. Harvest when peppers appear to be fully sized and to have achieved their expected mature color. If left on the plant too long, production will decrease and peppers will start to deteriorate. Dry harvested hot peppers by using a needle to run a heavy thread through the bases. Hang in a cool, dry, airy place, such as a breezy porch or protected patio or in a cooler part of the summer kitchen. Peppers dry in a few weeks.
▶Choices: In cool-summer regions, choose peppers better adapted to shorter, cooler growing seasons, such as 'California Wonder' or 'Jingle Bells'. Sweet or bell peppers usually start out green and are perfectly tasty at that time but will mature into a different color, depending on the cultivar. At the end of the summer, many peppers ripen into orange, yellow, or red and become very sweet. Other more unusual types ripen into deep green-brown or deep purple. Sweet banana peppers are thin-walled, long, and yellow.
There are many types of hot peppers, with varying degrees of hotness. Jalapeño peppers are one of the milder types with serrano and any with the word 'Thai' in the name being quite hot. Habañero peppers are among the hottest. Poblano peppers are mild. As they mature, they turn red and wrinkle. When dried, they are called anchos.

Perennial Hibiscus
see Hibiscus

Perennial Lobelia
see Cardinal Flower

Perennial Mum
see Chrysanthemum

Periwinkle
see Vinca

Persian Buttercup
see Ranunculus

Persimmon
Diospyros spp.
Deciduous trees

Diospyros virginiana

▶Hardiness: Zones 5-9 (American persimmon) or Zones 8-10 (Japanese persimmon)
▶Size: 30'-50' tall, 20'-30' wide
▶Features: Both American and Japanese species are attractive landscape trees known for their edible fruits that are extremely bitter and astringent when unripe. Both species have good yellow-to-orange fall foliage color and interesting winter bark texture. The Japanese persimmon is best known in California and parts of the Southeast; it produces the large persimmons that are sold commercially.
▶Uses: Specimen and shade trees; American persimmon is attractive planted in groves. Plant where messy fruit drop is not a problem.
▶Needs: Plant in any well-drained soil and in full sun. The unimproved species of American persimmon needs both male and female trees for good fruit set.
▶Choices: American persimmon *(Diospyros virginiana)* has several cultivars bred for larger fruits. 'Early Golden', 'John Rick', and 'Meader' are three that will produce fruits without cross-pollination. Some of the popular varieties of Japanese persimmon *(D. kaki)* are 'Izu', 'Hachiya', and 'Fuyu'.

Peruvian Lily, Inca Lily
Alstroemeria spp.
Perennial bulb

Alstroemeria spp.

▶Hardiness: Zones 6-10
▶Size: 2'-4' tall, 4"-12" wide
▶Features: Best known as a cut flower, Peruvian lily produces large clusters of azalea-like flowers on tall, leafy stems. Colors range from hot red, salmon, pink, gold, orange, and yellow to cool mauve, lavender, purple, cream, and white. Some types—notably the salmon-orange *A. aurea*—spread aggressively where they're well-adapted (western Mediterranean climates from Oregon to southern California). Blooms late spring to midsummer.
▶Uses: Meadows, flower beds, in the cutting garden. Good massed in groups or in the mixed border growing among other perennials it can lean on for support.
▶Needs: Full sun Zones 6-7 and Pacific Northwest; otherwise part shade. Needs well-drained, acidic to neutral soil with plentiful water. Plant rhizomes 6"-8" deep in early spring in all zones or in fall in Zones 8-10. Plants benefit from an annual spring application of compost or a slow-release fertilizer. In Zone 7 Peruvian lily may survive winter with a 3" layer of mulch. In Zone 6 you can dig and store the bulbs for winter (see page 205), but the plants often don't survive. Attractive to deer and rodents.
▶Choices: The flowers come in bicolors and beautifully mottled patterns of yellows, oranges, apricots, creams, reds, purples, and whites.

Perovskia atriplicifolia
see Russian Sage

Persea Americana
see Avocado

Petroselinum crispum
see Parsley

Petunia
Petunia spp.
Annual

Petunia hybrid

P

Plant encyclopedia

▶Size: 6"-24" tall, 2'-6' wide
▶Features: Hundreds of varieties in every imaginable color and flower form have made petunias one of the top bedding annuals in North America. In recent years the plant has become even more exciting with a wide range of plant sizes and forms, from trailing, sprawling beauties lovely in hanging baskets to tiny, compact "roundie moundies" covered in miniature blooms. Flowers are available in red, pink, lavender, purple, white, and even pale yellow; many are striped in contrasting colors. Purple and white varieties are often richly fragrant, especially in the evening. Flowers range from the size of a penny to the size of a saucer. The typical plant form is of stems radiating horizontally out from the center of the plant and arching upward to a vertical position. New trailing varieties, such as the Wave and Surfinia series, have low, flat, trailing stems that can grow as long as 6'-10'. Blooms spring through frost.
▶Uses: Massed in beds and grown in every kind of container; trailing types are fantastic in hanging pots and window boxes
▶Needs: Full sun. Rich to poor, well-drained soil; tolerates alkaline soil. Moderate water. In Zones 2-7 plant established plants in spring after all danger of frost has passed. In hot-summer regions of Zone 8, plant in early fall. In Zones 9-11 plant in late fall for winter color. Pinch tips by ½"-1" to encourage bushiness. Mulch to conserve moisture and to keep sticky leaves clean. Fertilize every 2-4 weeks, or work a slow-release fertilizer into the soil at planting time and supplement with monthly fertilizing after that. Deadhead as time permits. In late summer when plants get leggy, cut back by one-third to one-half to tidy and rejuvenate.
▶Choices: Nearly infinite. Buy in bloom at the garden center.

Phalaenopsis
see Orchids: Moth Orchids

Phalaris arundinacea 'Picta'
see Grasses, Ornamental: Ribbon Grass

Philadelphus spp.
see Mockorange

PHILODENDRONS
Philodendron spp.

Among the easiest of houseplants to grow, philodendrons are tropical vines that come in a surprisingly large array of leaf shapes, colors, and sizes. Most have large, glossy, leathery leaves that give any home a tropical feel, reflecting the plant's tropical rain forest origins. Philodendrons are strong, sturdy plants that can tolerate a variety of conditions and have unfinicky light needs. All, however, do best in bright (not direct) light to fairly low light. The exceptions are those with variegated leaves—they need bright light to maintain the variegation. Keep soil evenly moist and slightly on the dry side in winter. Fertilize once to three times in summer. Average household warmth is fine, as is average household humidity. However, philodendrons will do best when their pots are set in a tray with pebbles and water or when double-potted (see page 275) surrounded with peat moss kept wet.

PHILODENDRONS

Heart-Leaf Philodendron
Philodendron scandens

Tropical evergreen vine

Philodendron scandens

▶Size: Grows several inches to several feet, depending on growing conditions and whether or not you pinch the ends
▶Features: Sometimes also called parlor ivy, this is one of the most familiar of all houseplants; 3"-5" heart-shape leaves grow thickly along several stems. Pinch the ends regularly to promote thicker, bushier growth. Or train up a moss pole or up a small string trellis or allow to trail from a hanging basket or shelf. Wipe off or rinse off the glossy leaves regularly to keep attractive and healthy.
▶Uses: As a houseplant
▶Needs: Easy to grow; provide even moisture, medium light, and average household temperatures. Tolerant of lower light and dryer soils. If plants get long and leggy, prune back to encourage bushiness.

PHILODENDRONS

Red-Leaf Philodendron
Philodendron erubescens

Tropical evergreen vine

Philodendron erubescens

▶Size: Grows several inches to several feet, depending on growing conditions and whether you pinch the ends
▶Features: Also called blushing philodendron, this plant has dark green leaves with a purplish sheen and red edges.
▶Uses: As a houseplant
▶Needs: Best in medium light. Too much sun will bleach the leaves and they will lose their beautiful color; too little light will cause them to revert to green. Allow soil to dry between waterings. Repot when the thick roots begin to fill the pot. Watch out for mealybugs and spider mites; wash leaves regularly.
▶Choices: 'Red Emerald' is a popular cultivar with red stems and leaves that are red as they begin to unfurl and then turn green as they mature.

PHILODENDRONS

Tree Philodendron; Cut-Leaf Philodendron
Philodendron bipinnatifidum, formerly *Philodendron selloum*

Tropical evergreen vine

Philodendron bipinnatifidum

▶Size: Grows up to 8' tall and wide
▶Features: Deeply cut, glossy leaves up to 2' long on long, arching stalks give these oversized plants an almost palmlike effect. Dramatic in a large hall or room with a high ceiling.
▶Uses: As a houseplant, although in the warmest regions of the United States also used as an outdoor plant
▶Needs: Medium to low light is best; too much sun will fade the leaves. Allow soil to dry out between waterings. Wash leaves regularly to control spider mites. If mealybugs become a problem control with horticultural oil.

Philodendron, Split-Leaf
See Swiss Cheese Plant

PHLOX

Phlox spp.

There are a number of phlox species and hybrids that are wonderful in the garden, and new ones seem to be entering the market every year. Annual phlox and garden phlox are both old-fashioned favorites for their fragrant, colorful, long-season flowers, and both are being improved every year. Annual phlox gets sturdier, more compact, and more floriferous with each new variety introduced, and the newer mildew-resistant hybrids of garden phlox are making it more popular than ever. Moss phlox is unbeatable for its neon electric colors in midspring and evergreen feathery foliage reminiscent of asparagus fern. But exciting new hybrids between moss phlox and garden phlox are achieving the best of both kinds. Creeping phlox and woodland phlox are shade-tolerant species lovely in the spring woodland garden for their bright blue color.

PHLOX

Annual Phlox

Phlox drummondii

Annual

Phlox drummondii

►***Hardiness:*** Not applicable
►***Size:*** 4"–12" tall, 6"–8" wide
►***Features:*** Tight clusters of brightly colored flowers are like tiny bouquets in shades of pink, red, salmon, purple, mauve, and white—with many of the flowers bicolored. Blooms all summer to frost.
►***Uses:*** Bedding, edging, rock gardens, informal cottage gardens; excellent in containers.
►***Needs:*** Full sun. Average to rich, well-drained soil. Moderate moisture. In Zones 2–6 sow directly from seed in prepared soil outdoors in very early spring a few weeks before last frost date. In Zones 7–11 sow in late autumn for late winter or early spring bloom, 2–4 weeks before first frost date. Thin to the distance recommended on seed packet. Cluster in groups of a dozen or more for best effect. Trim spent blooms. Heat stops bloom, but plants will revive in fall.
►***Choices:*** Blooms come in whites, pinks, reds, blues, purples, salmon, and yellow. 'Dwarf Beauty' is just 6" tall, while 'Brilliant' is 2' tall.

PHLOX

Creeping Phlox; Woodland Phlox

Phlox stolonifera

Perennial

Phlox stolonifera

►***Hardiness:*** Zones 2–8
►***Size:*** 6"–12" tall, 8"–12" wide
►***Features:*** Creeping phlox is the most shade tolerant of all phlox, thriving in either partial or deep shade. With abundant moisture, plants form a dense groundcover that combines beautifully with bulbs and shrubs. Plants will not prosper in dry shade.
►***Uses:*** Combining with spring flowering bulbs, shady areas, woodland plantings, growing at the base of shrubs and trees, moist locations
►***Needs:*** Light shade in Zones 2–6; full shade in Zones 7–8, preferably dappled. Plants in cooler climates can tolerate more sun. Needs rich, well-drained soil and ample moisture. Plant established plants in spring. Work in ample compost at planting time. Mulch to conserve moisture, but do so lightly—just 1" or so—to prevent smothering the evergreen leaves. Each following spring, top soil with 1" of compost. Plants will probably reseed if you let the flowers ripen on the plant; plants also spread by underground runners. Mildew and slugs are occasional problems.
►***Choices:*** 'Blue Ridge'—sky blue flowers; 12" tall stems. Flowers come in pinks, blues, purples, and white. The most fragrant is 'Sherwood Purple'.

PHLOX

Garden Phlox, Summer Phlox

Phlox paniculata

Perennial

Phlox paniculata

►***Hardiness:*** Zones 4–8
►***Size:*** 24"–40" tall, 18"–24" wide
►***Features:*** Wild forms are magenta; hybrids offered in the garden center are in spectacular shades of pink, red, lilac, or white, some of them bicolored. All are fragrant, some varieties more than others. Blooms early, mid-, or late summer, depending on variety.
►***Uses:*** A classic plant for the mixed border, spectacular massed in large groups
►***Needs:*** Full sun in Zones 3–6; light shade in hot-summer climates in Zones 7–9. Rich, well-drained soil; ample moisture. Plant established plants in spring or fall. Place far enough apart to prevent mildew diseases. Mulch. Work a long-term slow-release fertilizer into the soil each spring. Cut back by about one-third after blooming to encourage rebloom. If mildew becomes severe, cut plant back to just a few inches.
►***Choices:*** Especially resistant to mildew are 'Miss Lingard', 'Mt. Fuji', 'David', 'Franz Schubert', and 'Eva Cullum'. *P. maculata* (wild sweet William or spotted phlox, Zones 5–8), is slightly more resistant to mildew than *P. paniculata* (garden phlox, Zones 4–8).

PHLOX

Moss Phlox, Moss Pink

Phlox subulata

Evergreen perennial

Phlox subulata

▶ ***Hardiness:*** Zones 2-9
▶ ***Size:*** 6"-9" tall, 18"-24" wide
▶ ***Features:*** This matlike groundcover is the answer to dry hillsides and ditches. Plants are carpeted with white, pink, or lavender blooms in spring. Lush green foliage is present the remainder of the year.
▶ ***Uses:*** Xeriscaping, slopes, ditches, erosion control, beside steps, edging planting beds, rock gardens, entries, creeping over walls
▶ ***Needs:*** Plant in full sun in average or poor, rocky soil that's dry. Alkaline soil is preferred. Dig and divide plants in fall or let them spread naturally. Shear plants after bloom to encourage dense growth and later rebloom. Plants are sometimes prone to spider mites if grown in hot, dry conditions and to root rot in wet winter conditions.
▶ ***Choices:*** Flowers come in blues, purples, pinks, and white. Most moss phloxes dislike heat or drought, but *P. nana (P. mesoleuca)* does well in the arid Southwest.

PHLOX

Woodland Phlox, Wild Blue Phlox

Phlox divaricata

Perennial

Phlox divaricata

▶ ***Hardiness:*** Zones 3-9
▶ ***Size:*** 12"-18" tall, 1'-2' wide
▶ ***Features:*** These pale blue, pink, or white flowers brighten the woods of the Northeast in mid- to late spring. The bushy plants grow up to 18" tall.
▶ ***Uses:*** Best in light, open shade under the canopy of tall deciduous trees. Use in the woodland wildflower garden or in more open meadow gardens.
▶ ***Needs:*** Light shade, dappled if possible. Rich, well-drained soil that retains moisture. Plant established plants in spring. Work in ample compost at planting time. Mulch to conserve moisture. Each following spring, top soil with 1" of compost. Shear back by about half after flowers fade to tidy and to promote fresh foliage growth. This plant spreads slowly from the roots. For more plants, divide immediately after blooming or in fall. This plant is slightly more resistant to mildew than garden phlox. Slugs may be bothersome.
▶ ***Choices***: Flowers come in pink, blue, lavender, and white.

Phoenix canariensis
see Palms: Canary Island Date Palm

Phoenix dactylifera
see Palms: Date Palm

Phoenix reclinata
see Palms: Senegal Date Palm

Phoenix roebelenii
see Palms: Pygmy Date Palm

Phormium spp.
see Flax, New Zealand

Photinia, Oriental

Photinia villosa

Deciduous flowering shrub

Photinia villosa

▶ ***Hardiness:*** Zones 4-7
▶ ***Size:*** 10'-15' tall, 10'-12' wide
▶ ***Features:*** This shrub gets large; give it plenty of room to grow. You'll enjoy white spring flowers, reddish fall foliage, and bright red berries. Plants can be pruned to form an attractive small tree for use around patios and in foundation plantings.
▶ ***Uses:*** Specimen use, background plantings, deciduous screens, attracting birds, winter interest, seasonal accent, pruning into a small trees, shrub borders
▶ ***Needs:*** Plant in well-drained, acidic soil. Grow in full sun to partial shade. Plants can be susceptible to fire blight. Prune and destroy dying branches; sterilize tools between cuts. Apply a spray containing streptomycin or basic copper sulfate in spring before buds open if this disease is a problem in your area. Reapply throughout bloom.

Photinia, Redtip

Photinia ×fraseri

Evergreen shrub

Photinia ×fraseri

▶ ***Hardiness:*** Zones 6-9
▶ ***Size:*** 10'-15' tall, 5'-7' wide

▶Features: Redtip photinia grows quickly. New growth unfolds bright red at the tops of shrubs. If left unpruned, this shrub will grow very large; give it plenty of room or plan to prune. Flowers have an unpleasant smell. Fire blight can kill an entire hedge quickly. Remove diseased branches as soon as disease appears, rinsing loppers between cuts to avoid spreading the problem. Redtip photinia suffers in areas with high humidity.
▶Uses: Hedging or screening; specimen trained into a single-stemmed tree
▶Needs: Plant in full sun or partial shade in well-drained soil. Fertilize regularly with nitrogen to prevent deficiency. Prune heavily in late winter or early spring by cutting woody stems at their bases.

Physostegia virginiana
see Obedient Plant

Picea spp.
see Spruces

Pieris, Chinese
Pieris formosa var. *forrestii*

Evergreen flowering shrub

Pieris formosa var. *forrestii*

▶Hardiness: Zones 8-9
▶Size: 8'-10' tall, 4'-6' wide
▶Features: Larger and more tender than Japanese pieris, this plant bears even more spectacular floral displays. But it is known chiefly for its bright reddish-tinted new leaves. In some varieties the red foliage color persists long into summer. This is the best pieris for southern gardens and is a popular plant in California.
▶Uses: Either for massing or as a specimen in the shrub border or at the foundation. Beautiful combined with azaleas, to which it is related.
▶Needs: Best in well-drained, acidic soil high in organic matter. Plant in partial shade in a location protected from wind and hot afternoon sun. Keep soil evenly moist.
▶Choices: 'Wakehurst' has large leaves that are bright red when young. 'Forest Flame' is a hybrid with Japanese pieris that has especially brilliant red new foliage. It is hardy in Zones 7-9.

Pieris, Mountain; Andromeda
Pieris floribunda

Evergreen flowering shrub

Pieris floribunda

▶Hardiness: Zones 4-8
▶Size: 4'-6' tall, 3'-10' wide
▶Features: This low, mounded shrub is smothered with sweet-smelling white flowers in early to midspring. Individual blooms dangle like tiny floral earrings from stems. Dark green leaves emerge bronzy red, deepen to green, and stay green year-round. This undemanding shrub is easy to grow if provided the proper growing conditions. It is the hardiest of the pieris.
▶Uses: Specimen shrub, informal hedges: near walkways, doors, and outdoor seating areas where people can enjoy the fragrance.
▶Needs: Plant in full sun or partial shade in moist, well-drained, acidic soil. Boost soil acidity by mulching with composted oak leaves or by working peat moss into the soil at planting time. Very little pruning is required.

Pieris, Japanese; Andromeda
Pieris japonica

Evergreen flowering shrub

Pieris japonica

▶Hardiness: Zones 6-9
▶Size: 9'-12' tall, 6'-8' wide
▶Features: Each spring, andromeda is blanketed with blossoms of pure white that smell as lovely as they look. The individual blooms look like tiny bells. Rich bronze leaves deepen to glossy green. This plant is easy to grow in acidic, moist locations. In warm locations provide shade during the hottest part of the day. Plants are also sold as lily-of-the-valley bush. Slow growth rate.
▶Uses: Specimen use, informal hedges, shrub borders, mass plantings, plantings with evergreens, woodland areas
▶Needs: Plant in full sun or partial shade in moist, well-drained, acidic soil. Boost acidity by mulching with composted oak leaves or by working peat moss into the soil at planting time. Prune lightly after flowering to retain form. Shelter from strong wind.
▶Choices: Attractive cultivars are widely available. 'Purity'—white flowers on upright stems; 3' tall and wide. 'Valley Rose'—pastel pink flowers, to 8' tall and wide. 'Valley Valentine'—dusky red flowers, to 8' tall and wide. 'Brovwer's Beauty' and 'Karenoma' are hybrids between mountain pieris *(P. floribunda)* and Japanese pieris that are hardy in Zones 5-8.

Pigsqueak; Heart-Leaf Bergenia
Bergenia cordifolia

Perennial

Bergenia cordifolia

▶Hardiness: Zones 3-8
▶Size: 8"-12" tall, 12"-18" wide
▶Features: Pigsqueak offers something for every season—bell-shape flowers in spring, bright green leathery foliage in summer, and bronzy-red leaves in fall and winter. Add organic matter to the soil at planting time to help retain moisture.
▶Uses: Mass planting, edging perennial beds and borders, along walkways
▶Needs: Plant in moist but well-drained soil, in full sun or partial shade. The cooler the climate, the more sun plants can tolerate. Before new growth emerges, remove leaves burned by winter cold.
▶Choices: 'Bressingham Ruby'—ruby red flowers, purplish leaves in winter

Pilea microphylla 'Rotundifolia'

see Artillery Fern

Pindo Palm

see Palms

Pineapple Dyckia

see Bromeliads

PINES

Pinus spp.

Fast-growing pines are one of the workhorses of the landscape, growing quickly to provide greenery and color almost anywhere you need it. The pine family is amazingly diverse and there is a pine—or two—that works well in just about every North American climate. The attractive pine cones that most pines produce are beautiful on the tree and can serve as autumn and summer decorations in the home.

PINES

Austrian Pine

Pinus nigra

Evergreen coniferous tree

Pinus nigra

▶***Hardiness:*** Zones 4–7
▶***Size:*** 60'–100' tall, 30'–40' wide
▶***Features:*** Dense, dark green foliage forms the classic pyramidal shape. Interesting, rugged bark. Tolerates heat, salt, and drought. Grows as much as 1' a year. Loses lower branches as it ages.
▶***Uses:*** As a windbreak or large hedge; as a specimen planting
▶***Needs:*** Full sun. Prefers well-drained soil with moderate moisture, but highly tolerant of different soils and conditions. Prone to a number of diseases, including tip blight, needle blight, and pine moths. Check the plant frequently for signs of disease. Rake up and destroy dropped needles regularly, if possible, to prevent disease from being harbored in the dead needles.
▶***Choices:*** 'Arnold Sentinel' is columnar and grows 25' tall.

PINES

Himalayan White Pine

Pinus wallichiana

Evergreen coniferous tree

Pinus wallichiana

▶***Hardiness:*** Zones 5–8
▶***Size:*** Grows 30'–50' tall, 20'–30' wide
▶***Features:*** Long 6"–8" needles hang in somewhat pendulous cascades from the branches, creating a loose, fluffy effect. Needles are gray-green with white stripes, giving the tree a silvery effect. The tree has the classic pyramidal shape and bears 6"–12" long cones.
▶***Uses:*** As a specimen tree or in a hedge or windbreak
▶***Needs:*** Full sun. Himalayan white pine prefers well-drained, moist soil but tolerates a variety of conditions.
▶***Choices:*** 'Zebrina' is a cultivar whose needles cascade in an especially pronounced, beautiful manner.

PINES

Italian Stone Pine

Pinus pinea

Evergreen coniferous tree

Pinus pinea

▶***Hardiness:*** Zones 8–10
▶***Size:*** Grows 40'–60' tall and wide
▶***Features:*** An open, spreading umbrella shape and short needles give this pine a decidedly Mediterranean look. Produces cones that are the source of delicious pine nuts. Also called umbrella pine.
▶***Uses:*** As a specimen tree. Often planted along streets because it can take the heat generated from pavement.
▶***Needs:*** Plant in full sun. Tolerates a variety of soils, but highly heat and drought tolerant once established. A good choice for sandy soils and coastal gardens. Tolerates temperatures as low as 15°F/-9°C.

PINES

Jack Pine

Pinus banksiana

Evergreen coniferous tree

Pinus banksiana

▶***Hardiness:*** Zones 2–6
▶***Size:*** 35'–50' tall, 10'–15' wide
▶***Features:*** If winters in your area are known for blasting wind and frigid temperatures, and your site has impoverished soil, jack pine is the right plant for the place. Young trees are pyramidal while older trees may appear flat-topped. Jack pine holds its needles year-round.
▶***Uses:*** Arctic areas, windbreaks, mass plantings, screening, providing background in the landscape
▶***Needs:*** Plant in acidic soil; trees do poorly in areas with alkaline soils. However, very poor, sandy soil or clay soil is fine. Grow in full sun. Tolerates extreme cold and wind.

PINES

Japanese Black Pine

Pinus thunbergii

Evergreen coniferous tree

Pinus thunbergii

▶ ***Hardiness:*** Zones 5–7
▶ ***Size:*** 20'–80' tall, 20'–25' wide
▶ ***Features:*** The sculptural, irregular form of Japanese black pine suggests a dainty garden, but this tree is tough enough for growing at the beach. This pine will tolerate salt and sand. Prune to emphasize bonsailike form, if desired in the landscape. Knock heavy snow off branches to prevent them from breaking. Needles stay dark green year-round. Tolerates salt spray and sandy soil.
▶ ***Uses:*** Seaside landscapes, stabilizing sand dunes, specimen use, windbreaks and screening, Japanese gardens and bonsai.
▶ ***Needs:*** Plant in fertile soil that's moist but well drained. Will grow on sandy soils. Grow in full sun.
▶ ***Choices:*** Dragon's-eye pine ('Oculus-draconis') has yellow-banded needles.

PINES

Japanese Red Pine

Pinus densiflora

Evergreen coniferous tree

Pinus densiflora 'Umbraculifera'

▶ ***Hardiness:*** Zones 6–7
▶ ***Size:*** Grows 40'–60' tall and wide
▶ ***Features:*** With a twisted trunk that displays attractive orange-red flaking bark, and its somewhat horizontal orientation, Japanese red pine brings an interesting look to the landscape.
▶ ***Uses:*** As a specimen tree, as a large hedge
▶ ***Needs:*** Full sun. Well-drained soil. Does best with protection from wind. Allowing needles to accumulate around the base of the tree provides a natural mulch.
▶ ***Choices:*** 'Pendula' is a weeping form. Tanyosho pine ('Umbraculifera') is multitrunked and umbrella shape; it is popular for use as a large shrub.

PINES

Japanese White Pine

Pinus parviflora

Evergreen coniferous tree

Pinus parviflora

▶ ***Hardiness:*** Zones 4–7
▶ ***Size:*** Grows 20'–50' tall and wide
▶ ***Features:*** Nicely tiered wide, spreading branches with narrow, 2½" twisted blue-green needles. 4" oval upright cones. Bark on older trees becomes interestingly scaly and dark gray.
▶ ***Uses:*** As a specimen tree or planted in clusters
▶ ***Needs:*** Full sun to very light shade. Does best in cool, moist soil, which mulch helps maintain.
▶ ***Choices:*** 'Glauca' has silvery blue-green, tufted needles; it is slow growing and medium size. 'Brevifolia' is a slow-growing dwarf.

PINES

Lacebark Pine

Pinus bungeana

Evergreen coniferous tree

Pinus bungeana

▶ ***Hardiness:*** Zones 4–7
▶ ***Size:*** 30'–50' tall, 20'–35' wide
▶ ***Feature:*** Fat, fluffy, and always green—this slow-growing pine is worth the wait. Young trees form rounded pyramids often with multiple trunks. With maturity they become open, broad-spreading and flat-topped. Very picturesque. Flaking, light-colored mottled bark adds interest to drab winter scenes. Established trees tolerate drought.
▶ ***Uses:*** Specimen use; windbreaks; fine-textured background; dense, year-round screening for privacy or to block poor views; winter interest
▶ ***Needs:*** Plant in any well-drained soil; acidic or alkaline pH is fine. Grow in full sun. Prune as desired to form multi- or single-stemmed trees. Trees grow best in cool climates.

PINES

Mugo Pine; Dwarf Mountain Pine

Pinus mugo var. *mugo*

Evergreen coniferous shrub

Pinus mugo var. *mugo*

▶ ***Hardiness:*** Zones 2–7
▶ ***Size:*** 18"–20' tall, 18"–30' wide
▶ ***Features:*** Mugo pine grows slowly and makes a good filler for planting beds. There are many different varieties and forms of mugo pine available that range in height from just over 1' tall to small tree size. Be sure to read plant labels so you can select the growth habit you desire. If you want one that stays tiny, select a variety that grows less than a few feet tall. If you are looking for a larger plant or even a small tree, there are selections to fill your needs as well. Slow growth makes maintenance easy.
▶ ***Uses:*** Specimen use, mass planting, combining with perennials and alpines in rock gardens, year-round texture
▶ ***Needs:*** Plant in full sun or partial shade in deep, moist, well-drained soil. Pinch growing tips in late spring, removing 3" to 6" of new growth. This encourages thick, dense, bushy plants.
▶ ***Choices:*** 'Compacta'—4' tall by 5' wide; 'Gnome'—15" tall by 3' wide; 'Mops'—7'–10' tall, 8' wide.

PINES

Scotch Pine

Pinus sylvestris

Evergreen coniferous tree

Pinus sylvestris 'Edwin Hillier'

▶ ***Hardiness:*** Zones 3–7
▶ ***Size:*** 30'–60' tall, 30'–40' wide
▶ ***Features:*** You'll love Scotch pine for the tidy cones of blue-green or yellow-green they form. Older trees develop into a twisted, open shape like a living sculpture that reveals peeling, textured reddish brown bark. Young trees are conical and take shearing well—they're the classic Christmas tree. Medium growth rate.
▶ ***Uses:*** Screening for privacy or to block poor views, specimen use, winter interest, natural areas, planting in masses
▶ ***Needs:*** Plant in full sun. Adapts to a wide range of soil types, but prefers acidic pH. Requires well-drained sites. Tolerates poor, dry soils. Trees are easy to transplant.
▶ ***Choices:*** 'Aurea' has bright golden yellow foliage in winter. 'Edwin Hillier' shows silvery blue needles. 'Fastigiata' is narrow and upright with ascending branches; 25' tall, 3'–10' wide.

PINES

Swiss Stone Pine

Pinus cembra

Evergreen coniferous tree

Pinus cembra

▶ ***Hardiness:*** Zones 4–7
▶ ***Size:*** Grows 30'–40' tall, 15'–25' wide
▶ ***Features:*** This pine grows in a roughly columnar shape, slightly wider at the bottom than the top. It has 2"–3" soft, stiff needles with densely packed branches. It produces 2"–3" cones in purplish brown that never open.
▶ ***Uses:*** As specimen or accent, as a hedge
▶ ***Needs:*** Full sun. Moist, well-drained soil.
▶ ***Choices:*** 'Compacta' and 'Chalet' are cultivars.

PINES

White Pine

Pinus strobus

Evergreen coniferous tree

Pinus strobus

▶ ***Hardiness:*** Zones 3–8
▶ ***Size:*** 50'–80' tall, 20'–40' wide
▶ ***Features:*** It's difficult to find a screening tree that grows as quickly or is as pretty as white pine. This tree develops a full-skirted, graceful pyramidal form. Fluffy bluish-green needles are 3"–5" long, soft, and touchable. Given room to grow, trees may reach 150' tall. They can also be sheared for hedging use. Allow fallen needles to accumulate as water-conserving, weed-controlling mulch. Water during dry spells. In colder areas, protect from sweeping winds and road salt.
▶ ***Uses:*** Screening for privacy and blocking poor views, filling large empty areas, background plantings, clustering together or planting in rows or groves
▶ ***Needs:*** Plant in any well-drained soil; trees thrive in many extremes except heavy clay soil. Grow in full sun. Trees transplant easily into the landscape. Trees are not tolerant of high pollution levels.
▶ ***Choices:*** 'Nana'—dwarf globe white pine, a rounded shrub.

Pink Quill

see Bromeliads

PINKS; SWEET WILLIAM; CARNATION

Dianthus spp.

Delightful for their late spring, early summer flowers (some kinds bloom all summer), pinks are distinguished by the serrated edges of their flower petals, as though they were cut with pinking shears—hence their common name. Many are deliciously fragrant. Cheddar pinks, maiden pinks, cottage pinks, and the hybrids among them are mostly low, mounding plants that produce pink, red, or white blooms on relatively short stems. Carnations *(D. caryophyllus)* are familiar cut flowers with larger, more double blooms that often grow on taller stems. They are tender perennials hardy only to Zones 8–10, and are usually grown in greenhouses for the cut flower trade. China pinks and sweet William are tender or short-lived perennials usually grown as annuals. Both have wonderfully fragrant blooms nearly all summer long.

PINKS; SWEET WILLIAM; CARNATION

China pink

Dianthus chinensis

Perennial usually grown as an annual

Dianthus chinensis 'Baby Doll'

▶ ***Hardiness:*** Zones 7–10
▶ ***Size:*** 6"–24" tall, 6"–12" wide
▶ ***Features:*** This is an exceptional bedding plant with many cultivars that remain a compact 6"–12" mound covered in flowers all summer. The flowers come in multihued patterns of pink, red, and white. The grassy leaves are 3" long, gray-green, and attractive all season.
▶ ***Uses:*** Bedding plant, edging, excellent in containers
▶ ***Needs:*** Plant 6"–12" apart in late spring. Plants prefer sun in Zone 5 and north; light afternoon shade Zones 6 and south. Soil should be fertile, well drained, and alkaline (pH 7.0–7.5). Allow soil to dry between waterings, then water deeply. Deadheading hastens reblooming. Plants may self-sow.
▶ ***Choices:*** 'Baby Doll' series has red and white patterned flowers. 'Fire Carpet' has red flowers.

PINKS; SWEET WILLIAM; CARNATION

Sweet William

Dianthus barbatus

Biennial often grown as an annual

Dianthus barbatus

▶ ***Hardiness:*** Zones 3–8
▶ ***Size:*** 18"–24" tall, 8"–12" wide.
▶ ***Features:*** This old-fashioned flower is a favorite for early-season color in the mixed border, and an excellent cut flower. Its fragrant, cheerful red, pink, and white blooms (many strikingly bicolored) are produced in dense clusters at the ends of tall stems like nosegays. Blooms in late spring and early summer.
▶ ***Uses:*** A must for the cottage garden as well as the cutting garden for its early summer bloom, sweet William is also attractive in more formal mixed flower borders. It performs well in containers.
▶ ***Needs:*** Plant 12" apart in spring or fall, in full sun and rich, well-drained soil. Allow soil to dry between waterings, then water deeply. Plants reseed, which is a welcome trait. In the South they may overwinter and bloom a second year if the flower heads are cut before they develop seed.

PINKS; SWEET WILLIAM; CARNATION

Maiden pink

Dianthus deltoides

Perennial

Dianthus deltoides 'Arctic Fire'

▶ ***Hardiness:*** Zones 4–8
▶ ***Size:*** 4" tall, 12"–15" wide
▶ ***Features:*** Maiden pink is an evergreen, mat-forming perennial more tolerant of heat and humidity than many other pinks. It produces great quantities of red, pink, or white blooms over a long period, peaking in late spring or early summer, then reblooming quickly after shearing nearly until frost.
▶ ***Uses:*** An outstanding groundcover for its excellent dark gray-green grasslike foliage and long, showy bloom season; performs well in containers
▶ ***Needs:*** Best in full sun north of Zone 5, but in Zone 6 and south give it some protection from hot afternoon sun. Space plants 6"–12" apart in rich, well-drained soil. Allow soil to dry before watering, then water deeply. Shear spent blooms after each flush for optimum flower production.
▶ ***Choices:*** 'Tiny Rubies' has small deep raspberry-red flowers.

PINKS; SWEET WILLIAM; CARNATION

Cottage pink

Dianthus plumarius

Perennial

Dianthus plumarius

P

Plant encyclopedia

►**Hardiness:** Zones 3-8
►**Size:** 8"-20" tall, 15"-24" wide
►**Features:** Mounds of gray-green, grassy foliage are attractive enough just for the foliage, but the flowers make them spectacular. Hardier than most other pinks, these perennials bloom in late spring and early summer in shades of pink, deep rose, and white.
►**Uses:** Flower bed edging, borders, especially in cottage gardens, performs well in containers.
►**Choices:** 'Mountain Mist' is more mat-forming than other types, and also more tolerant of heat and humidity. It bears rosy-pink flowers. Allwood pinks *(D. allwoodii)* are taller-growing (12"-18" tall) with steely gray-green foliage. Many of its cultivars are double-flowered, resembling tiny carnations. Hardy to Zone 5.
►**Needs:** Full sun to light shade in Zones 3-6; light shade appreciated in Zones 7-9. Average to rich, well-drained, slightly alkaline soil. Moderate moisture.

PINKS; SWEET WILLIAM; CARNATION

Cheddar pink

Dianthus gratianopolitanus

Perennial

Dianthus gratianopolitanus 'Firewitch'

►**Hardiness:** Zones 3-8
►**Size:** 8"-12" tall, 18"-24" wide
►**Features:** Tufted mounds of silvery, grasslike foliage that is nearly evergreen spread to form mats. Attractive all year for their foliage, they are covered in fragrant white or pink blossoms in late spring.
►**Uses:** A good groundcover in beds, or at the front of the mixed border between taller perennials and low shrubs. Good edging plant.
►**Needs:** Best in full sun and well-drained soil of high fertility. Tolerates more heat and humidity than other *Dianthus*. Allow soil to dry between waterings, then water deeply. Bloom can be prolonged into summer with deadheading.

PINKS; SWEET WILLIAM; CARNATION

Bath's Pink

Dianthus gratianopolitanus 'Bath's Pink'

Perennial groundcover

Dianthus gratianopolitanus 'Bath's Pink'

►**Hardiness:** Zones 4-9
►**Size:** 9"-12" tall, 18"-24" wide
►**Features:** Fragrant fringed pink flowers adorn blue-green mats of fine-textured foliage each spring. If deadheaded, flowering will continue for more than six weeks. Bath's pink is nearly indestructible, tolerating heat, humidity, and drought.
►**Uses:** Hillsides, growing over retaining walls, raised beds, berms, rock gardens, bordering planting beds, patios, walkways, courtyards, Xeriscaping
►**Needs:** Plant on sloping soil where water can drain quickly; plants won't thrive in soggy soil. Grow in full sun or partial shade; too much shade discourages flowering. Pluck or shear wilted blooms to extend flowering and maintain tidy plants.

Pistachio; Chinese Pistachio

Pistacia chinensis

Deciduous tree

Pistacia chinensis

►**Hardiness:** Zones 6-9
►**Size:** 30'-35' tall, 25'-35' wide
►**Features:** Ungainly young plants, with a little training and care, mature into neatly rounded shade trees known for brilliant fall colors of orange to red. These are the closest trees providing the colors of sugar maple for the South. Summer foliage is dark green. Trees are disease and pest free. Medium growth rate. Roots won't buckle paving;
►**Uses:** Street, lawn, and patio use; entries; parking areas; city conditions; anchoring the corner of a yard
►**Needs:** Plant in full sun. Trees grow best in moist, well-drained soils, but they adapt to less than ideal conditions. Chinese pistachio is drought resistant and tolerant of moderately alkaline conditions. Prune and stake young trees to encourage the growth of a strong, central trunk.

Pittosporum, Japanese; Tobira

Pittosporum tobira

Evergreen shrub or small tree

Pittosporum tobira 'Variegata'

►**Hardiness:** Zones 8-10
►**Size:** 5'-10' tall, spread to 10'
►**Features:** These plants, with their rounded shape and dense sea green foliage with cream-colored edges, make a nice change of pace from the all-green shrubs often chosen for landscaping. Japanese pittosprum also features fragrant white spring flowers; the scent is similar to orange blossoms. Easily transplanted and adaptable. Medium growth rate. Tolerates heat, salt, and wind.
►**Needs:** Grow in full sun or partial shade. Plant in any fertile, well-drained soil. Slightly acidic soil is ideal but not necessary. Water regularly for best results. Feed in spring or summer with a balanced fertilizer. Clip stray stalks to maintain a natural form or shear into smooth, formal shapes.
►**Uses:** Foundations, hedges, seaside landscapes, parking areas, massed in shrub beds, barriers, background
►**Choices:** Variegated Japanese Pittosporum *(Pittosporum tobira* 'Variegata').

Plane Tree
see Sycamores

Platanus spp.
see Sycamores

Platycerium bifurcatum
see Ferns: Staghorn Fern

Platycodon grandiflorus
see Balloon Flower

Plum, Edible
Prunus spp.

Deciduous fruit tree

Prunus 'Blufire Plum'

▶ ***Hardiness:*** Zones 4-9
▶ ***Size:*** Grows 8'-20' tall and slightly wider, depending on the type
▶ ***Features:*** It's hard to find good plums in the store, so a plum tree in your backyard is a treat. Trees can be small or large, depending on the type, and produce beautiful white flowers in spring and fruits in summer.
▶ ***Uses:*** As an ornamental tree, for fruit production
▶ ***Needs:*** Full sun. Prefers rich, deep, moist, well-drained soil with a pH between 6.0 and 7.0. Plant a tree in a site protected from late spring frosts so blossoms aren't damaged as they develop. Mulch. Begins to bear in the third or fourth year.
▶ ***Choices:*** European plums *(P. domestica)* may or may not have pits. Japanese plums *(P. salicina)* are larger and juicer and have a slightly bitter taste around the pit. They also, as a group, tend to ripen earlier than European plums. In colder regions, choose a cultivar that is late-producing to avoid frost damage of developing flowers. May need to plant a second tree for cross-pollination, depending on the cultivar.

PLUMS, ORNAMENTAL
Prunus spp.

A wide variety of beautiful flowering trees and shrubs are found in the plum tribe, including flowering cherry, flowering almond, flowering apricot, flowering peach, and chokecherry. All are in the genus *Prunus,* and produce gorgeous flowers in pink, rose, and white in early to late spring. Other members of *Prunus* include the edible plum (above) and the evergreen laurels (see Laurels, page 422).

PLUMS, ORNAMENTAL

Amur Chokecherry
Prunus maackii

Deciduous flowering tree

Prunus maackii

▶ ***Hardiness:*** Zones 2-6
▶ ***Size:*** 35'-45' tall, 20'-25' wide
▶ ***Features:*** It seems the colder the better for this spring-flowering tree. White flowers are followed by small fruits ripening to black in August. Birds love them. Fruit can stain paving; avoid planting near walkways or patios. Yellow fall color completes the growing season display. The ornamental features of this tree don't end with leaf drop; shiny, cinnamon-colored bark brightens drab winter scenes. As trees mature, the bark exfoliates, providing additional winter interest. Medium to rapid growth rate.
▶ ***Uses:*** Specimen use, seasonal accent, adding winter interest, attracting birds, fall color
▶ ***Needs:*** Plant in well-drained soil in full sun or partial shade. Naturally rounded canopy needs little or no pruning.

PLUMS, ORNAMENTAL

Dwarf Flowering Almond
Prunus glandulosa 'Rosea Plena'

Deciduous flowering shrub

Prunus glandulosa 'Rosea Plena'

▶ ***Hardiness:*** Zones 4-8
▶ ***Size:*** 4'-5' tall, 3'-5' wide
▶ ***Features:*** In midspring, dull twigs transform into wands of bloom, turning dwarf flowering almond into a cloud of double pink blossoms. Blossoms appear before leaves unfurl. Plants look scraggly when not in bloom; skirt them with low-growing bloomers such as catmint, alpine strawberries, or flower carpet roses. Medium growth rate. Easily transplanted and grown.
▶ ***Uses:*** Specimen use, shrub or perennial border, seasonal interest

▶Needs: Plant in full sun in fertile, moist, well-drained soil. Full sun yields best flowering, but this shrub will grow in partial shade. Prune annually after flowering to shape the shrub. Remove any dead wood in early spring.

PLUMS, ORNAMENTAL

Kwanzan Cherry

Prunus serrulata 'Kwanzan'

Deciduous flowering tree

Prunus serrulata 'Kwanzan'

▶Hardiness: Zones 5–8
▶Size: 30'–40' tall, 30'–40' wide
▶Features: Welcome spring to your yard with the pink double blooms of kwanzan cherry. This tree boasts glossy, coppery-colored bark and bright fall foliage too. This tree may also be sold as Japanese flowering cherry. Kwanzan cherry is a particular selection. Selected varieties are often grafted onto *P. avium* rootstock. Trees grow quickly and are often short-lived in the landscape. Medium to rapid growth rate. Puffy double pink flowers open in spring; bronzy leaves turn orange-bronze in fall; shiny, smooth bark provides winter appeal.
▶Uses: Specimen use, lawn trees, street trees, patio trees, seasonal accents, courtyards, groves
▶Needs: Plant in moist, well-drained soil. Grow in full sun. Protect from harsh wind. Trees are naturally vase-shape (spreading upward like a "V") and require little or no pruning to keep them that way.
▶Choices: 'Mt. Fuji'—pink buds, white flowers; 20' tall by 25' wide; spreading. 'Shirofugen'—pink buds, white flowers that fade back to pink, leaves deep bronze at emergence; 25' tall by 30' wide.

PLUMS, ORNAMENTAL

Mayday Tree; European Birdcherry

Prunus padus var. *commutata*

Deciduous flowering tree

Prunus padus var. *commutata*

▶Hardiness: Zones 3–6
▶Size: 30'–50' tall, 20'–30' tall
▶Features: If you're prone to early bouts of spring fever, plant a mayday tree. Leaves emerge while most trees are still bare; it is one of the earliest trees to unfurl its leaves in the Midwest. Fragrant white flowers open in midspring, earlier than other kinds of birdcherry trees. Small black fruits attract birds. May also be sold as European birdcherry—mayday is a particular selection. Leaves turn shades of bronze and yellow in fall. Medium growth rate.
▶Uses: Specimen use, seasonal accents, attracting birds, including in shrub beds
▶Needs: Plant in moist, well-drained soil that's somewhat fertile. Grows best in full sun. Little pruning is needed if mature size was taken into account prior to planting. Trees are low-branching. Thrives where summers are cool.

PLUMS, ORNAMENTAL

Newport Plum

Prunus cerasifera 'Newport'

Deciduous flowering tree

Prunus cerasifera 'Newport'

▶Hardiness: Zones 4–8
▶Size: 15'–20' tall, 15'–20' wide
▶Features: Newport plum has all the assets needed for small landscape situations. Because of its compact size and rapid growth rate, it is perfect for areas such as patios, courtyards, and entries. As an added plus, plants provide color contrast in the landscape, showing pale pink to white flowers in spring and reddish-purple summer foliage.
▶Uses: Specimen use, seasonal accents, patio trees, courtyards, entries, planting in clusters at corners of lots or in shrub beds, small areas
▶Needs: Plant in any average, well-drained soil. Trees aren't particular about soil pH. Grow in full sun. Prune after flowering to shape and maintain size.
▶Choices: 'Newport' is a hardier variety than 'Atropurpurea'.

PLUMS, ORNAMENTAL

Purple-leaf Plum

Prunus cerasifera 'Atropurpurea'

Deciduous flowering tree

Prunus cerasifera 'Atropurpurea'

▶Hardiness: Zones 4–8
▶Size: 15'–30' tall, 15'–25' wide
▶Features: Fast growth and colorful foliage makes purple-leaf plum a popular plant for landscapes. Pink flowers appear in early spring

before the foliage; spring foliage emerges ruby red, changing to the summer color of dark purple. Trees are usually short-lived, surviving about 20 years under good growing conditions. Trees spread by suckering. Plant them where you can easily control sucker growth through mowing or pruning. Purple foliage may clash with some house colors.

▶ ***Uses:*** Specimen trees, seasonal accent, lining driveways, patio trees, planting in clusters at entries to property, groves

▶ ***Needs:*** Plant in any soil that is well drained. They will not tolerate wet feet. Trees aren't particular about soil pH. Grow in full sun for best color development. Prune after flowering. Keep plants growing vigorously for best pest resistance.

▶ ***Choices:*** 'Thundercloud'—dark pink, fragrant flowers; deep purple foliage; 20' tall and wide; Zones 5–8. 'Vesuvius'—double light pink flowers, purple foliage; *P. ×blireana*—ruffled pink flowers, greenish-red foliage.

PLUMS, ORNAMENTAL

Purple-leaf Sand Cherry

Prunus ×cistena

Deciduous flowering shrub

Prunus ×cistena

▶ ***Hardiness:*** Zones 2–8

▶ ***Size:*** 7'–10' tall, 5'–8' wide

▶ ***Features:*** Plant a few of these shrubs and you'll have a hedge—and a purple one at that. Broad plants take shaping well and bloom with pinkish-white flowers in midspring. Shrubs sometimes produce purple cherrylike fruit in summer. Place shrubs where purple foliage creates a desired color contrast and won't clash with the color of the your house. Slow growth rate. Tolerates cold winters and various soil types.

▶ ***Uses:*** Hedges, screens, specimen shrub, background planting in perennial beds

▶ ***Needs:*** Plant in any soil that's moist but well drained. Grow in full sun. Trim in spring after flowering to shape plants and maintain desired size.

PLUMS, ORNAMENTAL

Sargent Cherry

Prunus sargentii

Deciduous flowering tree

Prunus sargentii

▶ ***Hardiness:*** Zones 4–7

▶ ***Size:*** 40'–70' tall, 40'–50' wide

▶ ***Features:*** These trees combine beauty with usefulness for a tree suitable for almost any landscape. Clusters of light pink flowers appear in mid- to late spring followed by glossy crimson-colored fruit. The foliage emerges with a red tinge and turns a dark, glossy green during the summer. Orange-red fall foliage and polished, mahogany brown bark complete the fall wardrobe. Trees possess shiny reddish-brown bark that's pretty during winter months. Avoid planting near areas where fruit may stain paving. Medium to rapid growth rate.

▶ ***Uses:*** Specimen tree, seasonal accent, shade or lawn tree use, planting near corners of large houses, attracting birds

▶ ***Needs:*** Plant in well drained soil in full sun or partial shade. Prune to shape trees only as needed in late winter or early spring.

▶ ***Choices:*** 'Columnaris'—narrow, columnar form; 40' tall by 10' wide

PLUM, ORNAMENTAL

Weeping Higan Cherry

Prunus subhirtella 'Pendula'

Deciduous flowering tree

Prunus subhirtella 'Pendula'

▶ ***Hardiness:*** Zones 4–8

▶ ***Size:*** 20'–40' tall, 15'–30' wide

▶ ***Features:*** Each cascading branch of this tree is covered with pink flowers in spring and golden leaves in fall. Cherrylike red fruit ripens to nearly black. Bare weeping stems are attractive in winter. Plants make excellent specimen plantings in the landscape. Avoid planting near areas where fruits might drop and stain paving. Varieties are usually grafted about 4'–6' tall on *P. avium* rootstock. Medium to rapid growth rate.

▶ ***Uses:*** Specimen tree, accent, courtyards, entries, near patios and decks, Japanese gardens

▶ ***Needs:*** Plant in well-drained soil. Grow in full sun or partial shade. Prune to shape trees as needed after bloom.

▶ ***Choices:*** 'Yae-shidare-higan'—pink, double flowers are long-lasting, 'Autumnalis'—semidouble pink blooms appear in fall as well as in early spring.

PLUMS, ORNAMENTAL

Yoshino Cherry

Prunus ×yedoensis

Deciduous flowering tree

Prunus ×yedoensis

▶ ***Hardiness:*** Zones 5–8

▶ ***Size:*** 20'–40' tall, 20'–40' wide

▶ ***Features:*** The famous cherry tree of Washington, D.C., Yoshino cherry's light pink buds open into clouds of white blooms in early spring before the foliage appears; falling petals resemble snowflakes. Blooms possess a slight fragrance and are not overpowering. Rounded crowns form trees of spectacular spring beauty. Occasionally grow to 50' tall. Medium growth rate.

▶ ***Uses:*** Specimen trees, seasonal accent, planting near patios, entries, courtyards, street trees, city conditions

▶ ***Needs:*** Plant in moist, well-drained soil that's moderately fertile. Grow in full sun and provide protection from harsh winds. Keep trees growing vigorously by watering during drought and fertilizing annually.

▶ ***Choices:*** 'Shidare Yoshino'—weeping dwarf tree.

Plumbago, Cape
see Cape Plumbago

Plumbago auriculata
see Cape Plumbago

Plumbago; Blue Plumbago
Ceratostigma plumbaginoides

Perennial

Ceratostigma plumbaginoides

▶ ***Hardiness:*** Zones 5–9
▶ ***Size:*** 8"–18" tall, 12"–18" wide
▶ ***Features:*** Plumbago is a snap to grow as a fast-growing groundcover. Late summer blooms are brilliant blue; bright green leaves turn reddish in fall. Full sun, well-drained soil, and light pruning each spring will keep this blue-flowered grower looking great for years to come. Plants will survive in Zone 5 with winter mulch. Blooms late summer through fall.
▶ ***Uses:*** Rock gardens, large planting beds, growing in front of shrubs, underplanting with spring bulbs, rambling over rocks
▶ ***Needs:*** Full sun in Zones 5–6; light shade in Zones 7–9. Average, well-drained soil, moderate moisture. Plumbago will not tolerate soggy soil conditions. Plant seedlings in spring. Fertilize lightly. Mulch in winter in Zone 5. In late winter or very early spring, cut back woody stems to stimulate new growth. Plants are slow to emerge in the spring. This plant is prone to root rot in wet conditions, and powdery mildew.

Podocarpus; Yew Pine; Buddhist Pine
Podocarpus macrophyllus

Subtropical evergreen tree or shrub

Podocarpus macrophyllus

▶ ***Hardiness:*** Zones 8–10
▶ ***Size:*** 10'–30' tall, 5'–15' wide
▶ ***Features:*** Because its large, dark green, needlelike leaves resemble those of true yews (*Taxus* spp.), this small tree is often used as a substitute in warmer, mild-winter climates where yews are difficult to grow.
▶ ***Uses:*** As a specimen, background, street tree, screen, or hedge. Trains well as an espalier, and shears well into topiary or hedge.
▶ ***Needs***: Plant in full sun or part shade and in average, neutral to acidic, well-drained soil. Tolerates heat well. Tolerates shade but grows more slowly.
▶ ***Choices:*** 'Maki' is a popular compact, slow-growing cultivar 6'–10' tall often used in foundation plantings.

Poinsettia
Euphorbia pulcherrima

Tropical evergreen or deciduous shrub

Euphorbia pulcherrima 'Red Sails'

▶ ***Hardiness:*** Zones 9–11
▶ ***Size:*** 6'–12' high, 10'–12' wide
▶ ***Features:*** While poinsettia is grown as a colorful landscape shrub in southern Florida, California, and Mexico, most North Americans know it as the familiar pot plant sold during the holiday season. Some gardeners pride themselves on their ability to grow poinsettia as a houseplant and produce its colorful bracts year after year.
▶ ***Uses:*** Best known as indoor holiday decoration. Used as a large, somewhat rangy landscape shrub in warm climates without winter frost.
▶ ***Needs:*** Indoors place in a sunny spot and protect from sudden temperature changes both cold and hot. Water when soil is slightly dry to the touch. Be sure the container (and foil wrapping) that the plant comes in from the nursery has holes for drainage. To encourage poinsettia to rebloom, begin feeding in February once a month with houseplant fertilizer. In March cut stems back to 4"–6". In April repot into a slightly larger container. Move outdoors to a sunny spot after nighttime temperatures are above 60°F. Pinch out growing shoots once or twice to keep plant compact. Water regularly and feed every 2 weeks while outdoors. Before nighttime temperatures fall to 55°F, bring indoors to a sunny window. Starting in September, encourage the plant to initiate flower buds by moving it to a closet or other darkened room each night to give the plant more than 12 hours of darkness.

Polka-Dot Plant
Hypoestes phyllostachya

Tropical perennial

Hypoestes phyllostachya 'White Splash'

Hypoestes phyllostachya 'Ruby'

▶ ***Hardiness:*** Zones 10–11
▶ ***Size:*** Grows 1'–2' tall in ideal conditions with ample space; most plants sold when just a few inches tall and wide.
▶ ***Features:*** Also known as freckle face, this plant has distinctive spots in pale pink on smooth, green, roughly heart-shape leaves.
▶ ***Uses:*** As a houseplant, though sometimes used as a bedding plant in warmer parts of the United States
▶ ***Needs:*** Bright light; direct sun will bring out the color of the spots most. If the plant gets too little light, the spots will fade. Keep soil quite moist but not soggy; in winter keep soil slightly drier. Average household warmth and humidity are fine, but benefits from being grown on a tray with pebbles and water. Keep the plant bushy by pinching off the tiny lavender flowers when they appear.
▶ ***Choices:*** Sometimes sold as *H. sanguinolenta*. 'Splash' is a commonly available cultivar.

Polygonum aubertii
see Silver Lace Vine

Polypodium aureum
see Ferns: Rabbit's Foot Fern

Polyscias spp.
see Aralia

Polystichum acrostichoides
see Ferns: Christmas Fern

Polystichum munitum
see Ferns: Western Sword Fern

Poor Man's Orchid
See *Schizanthus*

Poppy, California
see California Poppy

Poppy, Annual
Papaver spp.

Annuals

Papaver rhoeas

▶***Size:*** 12"–24" tall, 6"–18" wide

▶***Features:*** Valuable for their early-season bloom (as early as midwinter in California), the delightful single, semidouble, and fully double flowers of annual poppies have a delicate crepe-papery texture. They are available in many warm colors, from yellow and gold to orange, salmon, pink, and red. Blooms appear in winter, spring, or early summer, depending on species and the region.

▶***Uses:*** Seasonal bedding color, meadow gardens, cottage gardens, excellent in containers

▶***Needs:*** Full sun in Zones 2–6; partial shade preferred in Zones 7–11. Average to poor, well-drained soil. Moderate moisture. Does best started from seed. In Zones 3–7 sow seeds directly onto prepared soil in early spring, 2–3 weeks before last frost date. In Zones 8–10 sow in late autumn. Barely cover seeds. Thin but leave in groups of at least a dozen or so. Mulch. Avoid fertilizing or transplanting.

▶***Choices:*** In cool-summer, low-humidity areas, Iceland poppy *(P. croceum* or *P. nudicaule)* may last as a perennial. Annual poppies include *P. rhoeas* (corn, Shirley, and Flanders poppy) and *P. somniferum* (opium poppy). See also California poppy.

Poppy, Oriental
Papaver orientale

Perennial

Papaver orientale

▶***Hardiness:*** Zones 3–7 (8 on the West Coast)

▶***Size:*** 24"–36" tall, 2'–3' wide

▶***Features:*** It's a thrilling show to watch a poppy bloom in late spring and early summer. Exotic prickly buds swell and unfurl like a snake's head to pop open into huge, magnificent crepe-papery blooms of rich hues (orange, red, pink, and white) with dramatic black centers. These are somewhat ephemeral perennials; their foliage quickly gets tatty and withers, and needs hiding by later-maturing plants. The blooms appear about the same time as peonies and bearded iris.

▶***Uses:*** This is a classic mixed-flower-border plant and a staple of the cottage garden, beautiful with peonies, iris, and the first flush of roses.

▶***Needs:*** Full sun in cool-summer areas and in Zones 2–6; part shade in warm areas in Zones 7–8. Rich to average, deep, well-drained soil. Does best with moderate moisture; somewhat drought tolerant. Plant established plants in spring or fall. Mulch. Fertilize occasionally or work in a slow-release fertilizer. Remove faded flowers unless seedpods will be harvested. Foliage dies back after blooming and is unattractive for a few weeks. After bloom time, interplant with African marigolds, cosmos, sunflowers, or other fast-growing annuals to fill the open spots. Or interplant with perennial baby's breath and other later-appearing plants, such as butterfly weed or Joe-pye weed. This plant spreads rapidly in good conditions. Keep in check by digging up new plants each spring.

▶***Choices:*** Cultivars are available in many shades of orange, salmon, pink, rose, and ivory.

Populus tremuloides
see Quaking Aspen

Porcelain Berry
Ampelopsis brevipedunculata

Deciduous vine

Ampelopsis brevipedunculata

▶***Hardiness:*** Zones 4–8

▶***Size:*** 10'–25' in all directions

▶***Features:*** The flowers on this vine aren't noticeable; but the colorful fruit appearing in fall certainly is, forming in shades of yellow, lavender, and bright blue, all on the same vine. Round, colored fruit is showiest when vines are spread out, as on a trellis. Porcelain berry is a fast-growing cover for all types of structures.

▶***Uses:*** Trellises, lattice, fences, arbors, entries, near patios, covering eyesores such as stumps or rock piles

▶***Needs:*** Vines will adapt to just about any soil except soggy. They grow best in full sun. Plant where root growth is restricted and climbing support is provided. Prune in winter to shape plants and encourage vigorous growth.

Portulaca grandiflora
see Moss Rose

Possumhaw
see Hollies

P

Plant encyclopedia

Potato Vine

Solanum jasminoides

Annual or perennial ornamental vine

Solanum jasminoides 'Album'

▶**Hardiness:** Zones 8-11
▶**Size:** 30' tall when grown as a perennial
▶**Features:** This inedible relative of the edible potato is a fast grower and is used as an annual to brighten baskets and window boxes in cold-winter climates and as a perennial to cover an arbor in warmer climates. Leaves are medium to purplish green and the plant produces 1" flowers in white or palest blue nearly all growing season. Can be poisonous if eaten.
▶**Uses:** As a flowering ornamental in baskets, large pots, and window boxes; as a shade-producing vine for arbors and pergolas
▶**Needs:** Plant established plants in spring in full sun to light shade. Keep soil evenly moist at first, but plant becomes drought tolerant once established. Feed at planting time in spring with a slow-release fertilizer. Will need to be tied to any support so it can climb. If grown as a perennial, reapply a fertilizer each spring. If the vine gets too rampant or leggy, cut back at any time to promote new growth. Cut or dig out runners that grow along the ground.
▶**Choices:** 'Album' has white flowers. 'Album Variegated' has variegated leaves.

Potatoes

Solanum tuberosum

Annual vegetable

Potato 'Desiree'

Potato 'Butterfinger'

Potato 'Red Thumb'

▶**Size:** Foliage grows a few inches tall; the roots—the potatoes—grow several inches deep
▶**Features:** Home-grown potatoes allow you to try a wide variety as well as harvest prized new potatoes early in the season.
▶**Uses:** In the vegetable garden
▶**Needs:** Full sun; light shade tolerated well in hot-summer regions. Does best in light to sandy, deeply loosened, well-drained soil with plenty of organic matter worked in. Does best in slightly acidic soils with a pH of 4.8-5.8 and particularly well in raised beds. Prefers cool summers. Plant certified seed potatoes only—not cut-up supermarket potatoes. If desired, for more reliable sprouting, a few weeks before planting, chit the potatoes by exposing them to light for a few weeks. Planting times vary. In cooler summer regions, plant in early spring as soon as soil can easily be worked (in Zones 5 and 6, this is often around St. Patrick's Day). In the South and Southwest, plant in the fall or winter to assure a longer, cooler growing season. Plant seed potatoes with at least one eye, that is, an area that's about to sprout or already has sprouted. You can cut seed potatoes into a few pieces as long as each piece has at least one eye.

Every gardener has a favorite method of growing potatoes. The key is to make sure that the potato tubers are not exposed to sunlight, which greens them and makes them bitter. Some of the most popular growing methods include:

Hilling: Plant in furrows or holes 1' deep and 10" apart. Cover with an inch or so of soil. As the foliage grows, cover with another inch or two of soil. This assures a long stem, which will produce more potatoes. When the trench or hole is filled, proceed to mound soil an inch or two at a time over the base of the foliage, continuing until the mounds are 6"-12" tall. Some gardeners stack old tires, one at a time, around each potato hill to assist in mounding.

Straw: In clay or very wet or stony soils, lay the seed potatoes on the ground. (Covering with 1"-2" of compost is helpful.) Top with 6" of straw.

Harvest: Take new potatoes from the sides of the main plant 7-8 weeks after planting. Do not disturb the whole plant because it will continue to produce. Potatoes have matured fully when the foliage starts to die. Dig gently. Rub loose soil off potatoes; do not wash. Let dry on newspapers in the sun for several hours.

Pests: Colorado potato beetle is often a problem. Handpick larva and adults if there are just a few. Otherwise, treat with Bt *(Bacillus thuringiensis)* or a neem-based insecticide.

▶**Choices:** Many interesting types available, including delightful, firm fingerling types that are excellent for roasting, boiling, and salads. Yellow-fleshed types such as 'Yukon Gold' are recently popular and tend to have a wonderful buttery flavor. For a traditional small red, firm potato ideal for salads, try 'Dark Red Norland'. For a fluffy potato for baking or mashing, try 'Kennebec'. Blue and pink potatoes also available.

Potentilla neumanniana

see Spring Cinquefoil

Potentilla, Shrubby; Bush Cinquefoil

Potentilla fruticosa

Deciduous flowering shrub

Potentilla fruticosa 'Primrose Beauty'

▶**Hardiness:** Zones 2-7
▶**Size:** 1'-4' tall, 2'-4' wide

P

Plant encyclopedia

►*Features:* This bloomer keeps going and going, from early summer until frost. The flowers of shrubby potentilla come in all shades, from white to yellow to pink and orange. The shrub stays a neat size—under 4' tall—and grows in all types of soil from poor to rich. Amazing cold tolerance allows this plant to grow where winter temperatures dip to a frigid -50°F/-45°C. Slow growth rate. Extended flowering from summer to frost; bright green foliage, yellow-brown in fall.
►*Uses:* Low hedges, shrub borders, foundation use, mass planting
►*Needs:* Plant in any kind of soil that is well drained. Though full sun yields best flowering, this shrub also will grow in partial shade. Remove one-third of the stems in late winter or early spring for best flowering.
►*Choices:* 'Abbotswood'—white flowers; bluish-green leaves; 30" tall, 4' wide. 'Goldfinger'—bright yellow flowers; dark green leaves. 'Yellow Gem'—grows just 2'-3' wide and flowers well. 'Jackman's Variety'—bright yellow flowers, 3'-4' tall. 'Primrose Beauty'—primrose flowers; 3' tall. 'Tangerine'—yellow-flushed-red flowers, 2' tall and 4' wide.

Pot Marigold
Calendula spp.
Annual

Calendula spp.

►*Features:* Blooms spring through summer.
►*Uses:* Beds, borders, containers, as a pest-deterring edging plant in vegetable beds
►*Needs:* Poor to rich, well-drained soil. Moderate water. In Zones 2-7 plant established seedlings in garden in early spring, no earlier than 2-3 weeks before last frost date. In Zones 8-11 plant in fall for winter and spring bloom. Fertilize regularly, every 4 weeks, or work a 9-month, slow-release fertilizer into the soil at planting time. Trim spent blooms for best flowering. This plant is prone to powdery mildew, leaf spot, cabbage loopers, and aphids.
►*Choices:* Flowers are mainly brilliant oranges and yellows, but apricots and creams are also available.

Pothos
Epipremnum aureum
Tropical perennial vine

Epipremnum aureum

►*Size:* Grows several feet long, depending on growing conditions and whether you pinch the ends
►*Features:* Related to the philodendron and often mistaken for one, this plant is equally easy to grow. Also called devil's ivy. The main difference from philodendrons is the creamy or yellow variegation of the shiny, heart-shape leaves that grow along pothos' long, vining stems.
►*Uses:* As a houseplant
►*Needs:* Not fussy about conditions, but does best in bright light to bring out the variegation. Allow soil to dry slightly between waterings. Fertilize once to three times in summer. Average household warmth is fine, as is average household humidity. Rinse plant or wipe off leaves with a damp cloth once a month or so to keep them shiny and healthy. Pothos is easy to propagate by rooting cuttings in a glass of water set on a sunny windowsill.

Pratia pedunculata
See Blue Star Creeper

Prayer Plant
Maranta leuconeura
Tropical evergreen perennial

Maranta leuconeura var. *erythroneura*

►*Size:* Grows 8" tall and several inches across on slightly vining stems
►*Features:* Lovely striped and variegated 6" leaves in greens, burgundy, reds, and silvers fold up at night, like hands in prayer, hence the name.
►*Uses:* As a houseplant
►*Needs:* Medium light; bright light tends to fade the colors. Keep soil evenly moist with tepid water; slightly drier in winter. Average household warmth fine but avoid cold drafts. Good humidity is important. Set pots on a tray with pebbles and water (see page 289) or double pot (see page 275) surrounded with peat moss kept wet.
►*Choices:* *M. leuconeura* var. *kerchoviana* is called rabbit's tracks for the interesting brown patches on its green leaves. *M. l.* var. *erythroneura,* the most commonly sold prayer plant, is also called herringbone plant for the way the red veins branch out from the center of the leaf. Also look for *M. l. massangeana,* which has blackish green leaves with silvery veins.

P

Plant encyclopedia

PRIMROSES

Primula spp.

Primroses are the aristocrats of the shade garden, a delight for their showy spring blooms and attractive, crinkly foliage. Some connoisseurs, especially in the cool-summer climates of the Northeast and Pacific Northwest, like to collect the many species and hybrids available from specialty growers. All are perennials with somewhat ephemeral foliage that declines and gets ratty as the summer progresses, especially during hot spells. The familiar polyantha hybrids are such ephemerals; because they bloom the first year from seed, they are usually grown as annual bedding plants.

PRIMROSES

English Primrose

Primula vulgaris

Perennial

Primula vulgaris

▶ ***Hardiness:*** Zones 4–8
▶ ***Size:*** 8"–10" tall, 10"–15" wide
▶ ***Features:*** The species is a beloved native of the English woodlands, with sweet-smelling small, pale yellow flowers in late spring and early summer. The modern cultivars are in nearly every color except true blue, with larger flowers, but they have lost most of their fragrance. The foliage is evergreen in the southern part of its range where summers are cool (high altitudes and coastal areas). This is a charming plant for the shade garden.
▶ ***Uses:*** Specimen accent or massed as edging, in beds, or underneath shrubs in shady woodland gardens. This old-fashioned favorite is a must for the cottage garden. It performs well in containers.
▶ ***Needs:*** Easy in rich, constantly moist, well-drained woodland soil that is high in organic matter. Neutral to acidic soil is best (pH 5.5–7.0) It's best in partial shade but tolerates full sun and heat, even in the South, if the soil is constantly moist. Plant 12"–15" apart in spring or fall. Mulch in summer and winter.
▶ ***Choices:*** Cultivars come in white, yellow, pink, purple, and red. Some are double-flowered and some are bicolored.

PRIMROSES

Japanese Primrose

Primula japonica

Perennial

Primula japonica

▶ ***Hardiness:*** Zones 5–8
▶ ***Size:*** 12"–24" tall, 12"–24" wide
▶ ***Features:*** Soggy, shaded spots cease to be problem areas when you plant Japanese primrose in them. Colorful flowers from spring through midsummer in shades of pink, crimson, and white won't grow anywhere else. Medium growth rate.
▶ ***Uses:*** Wet, boggy areas; beside water features; adding color to shaded spots
▶ ***Needs:*** Plant in fertile soil that doesn't dry out. Soil should be acidic to neutral. Mix in composted oak leaves or peat moss at planting and add a 3" layer of mulch around plants each spring to keep soil rich in humus. Grow in a shady spot. Provide plants with extra water during dry periods.

PRIMROSES

Polyantha Primrose

Primula ×*polyantha*

Perennial usually grown as an annual

Primula ×*polyantha*

▶ ***Hardiness:*** Zones 5–8
▶ ***Size:*** 6'–12" tall, 8"–12" wide
▶ ***Features:*** If you like bright colors, polyantha primroses are your ticket; where other primroses are ballerinas, these are straight from the circus. These old-fashioned bedding plants have brilliant large flowers that are produced in clusters so big they nearly cover the foliage. Most that you'll find in the garden centers are seed strains in a mix of neon colors—yellow, red, and blue. In mild climates, such as Coastal California, they can be bedded out for winter and early spring color. Everywhere else they are planted in early spring, provide lots of color for about 6 weeks, then are pulled up to make room for the next round of colorful annuals.
▶ ***Uses:*** Seasonal bedding plant, edging. Attractive with spring bulbs. Performs beautifully in containers.
▶ ***Needs:*** Full sun in Zones 3–6; light shade in Zones 7–10. Rich, moisture-retentive but well-drained soil. Ample moisture. Grow as an annual or a perennial, depending on the the climate. It will not last year after year in Zones 5 and colder, or in very hot, dry conditions, such as the arid Southwest. To grow as an annual, in Zones 3–7, plant in early spring, 2–3 weeks before last frost date. In Zones 8–10 plant in late autumn for winter and early spring color. Discard when hot weather hits. To grow as a perennial, plant in early spring. Water well during dry spells. In late fall cover with pine boughs or other lightweight mulch for winter protection.

***Primula* spp.**
see Primroses

PRIVETS

Ligustrum spp.

Privets are hard to beat as hedges and screens at the property's edge. Their clean foliage takes shearing well and rebounds quickly. These are tough plants that are easy to grow nearly anywhere; there's one for practically every climate in North America.

PRIVETS

Amur Privet

Ligustrum amurense

Deciduous shrub

Ligustrum amurense

▶ ***Hardiness:*** Zones 3–7
▶ ***Size:*** 12'–15' tall, 8'–10' wide
▶ ***Features:*** Some plants are common with good reason. Amur privet is easy to grow, tolerates a range of conditions, and can be sheared into neat hedges. Thrives even under tough Midwest growing conditions. Odor from small flowers in summer can

be objectionable. Although the neat, dense foliage takes shearing well, shearing or pruning in formal shapes often removes flowers. Rapid growth rate.
▶**Uses:** Hedging, screening, foundation planting, formal or informal landscapes, background plantings
▶**Needs:** Plant in any soil except those that are very wet. Grow in full sun or partial shade. Shrubs tolerate poor, dry, or compacted soils; polluted air; salt; and reflected heat from paving. Prune in summer.

PRIVETS

Border Privet

Ligustrum obtusifolium

Deciduous shrub

Ligustrum obtusifolium

▶**Hardiness:** Zones 4-8
▶**Size:** 6'-8' tall and wide
▶**Features:** This is the classic privet used for hedges throughout the North and the East. While it takes shearing well, its natural form is beautiful for its graceful horizontal branching. The foliage is a glossy medium to light green, small and fine-textured. The small white flowers emit an unpleasant smell.
▶**Uses:** Shears well as a formal hedge, although this plant's fast growth will require frequent attention to keep it neat. Better use is as an informal hedge with its naturally graceful growth habit allowed to shine.
▶**Needs:** Trouble free in just about any soil, wet to dry, acidic to alkaline, although most vigorous in rich, moist, well-drained soils. Best in full sun but tolerates partial shade.

PRIVETS

California Privet

Ligustrum ovalifolium

Deciduous or semievergreen shrub

Ligustrum ovalifolium 'Aureum'

▶**Hardiness:** Zones 6-9
▶**Size:** 10'-15' tall, 12' to 15' wide
▶**Features:** A popular hedge plant throughout its range (including the Southeast), California privet has glossy, dark green leaves that are relatively small and fine-textured. It takes shearing well.
▶**Uses:** Hedge, screen
▶**Needs:** Grow in any soil from acidic to alkaline, wet to dry. Best in full sun but quite tolerant of shade. Avoid fertilizing late in the season; succulent new growth that results could be severely injured by winter cold. Protect from aphids and scale insects.

PRIVETS

Chinese Variegated Privet

Ligustrum sinense 'Variegatum'

Evergreen shrub (semievergreen in cool climates)

Ligustrum sinense 'Variegatum'

▶**Hardiness:** Zones 7-10
▶**Size:** 6'-12' tall, 6'-12' wide
▶**Features:** This fast-growing shrub forms thickets of arching stems and displays clusters of white flowers with a fragrance described as both pleasant and unpleasant. Most widely used for hedges. Can be clipped into shapes for large containers. Remove any branches bearing solid green leaves. Seedlings will bear green leaves. This plant is difficult to kill; make sure you want it where you plant it.
▶**Uses:** Informal hedges, screening for privacy or to block poor views, specimen shrubs, accents
▶**Needs:** Plant in any kind of soil. Grow in any level of light. Mow over seedlings or pull them by hand. Prune to shape into desired forms.

PRIVETS

Golden Vicary Privet

Ligustrum ×vicaryi

Evergreen shrub

Ligustrum ×vicaryi

▶**Hardiness:** Zones 5-8
▶**Size:** 8'-10' tall, 8'-10' wide
▶**Features:** Let the sun shine and this shrub will too. Full sun brings out the bright, golden-colored foliage. Plants show off best when placed against a backdrop of dark-leafed evergreens. White flowers appear in midsummer and are followed by bluish-black fruit that birds relish. Slow to medium growth.
▶**Uses:** Specimen, foundation plantings, screens, planting against dark-colored backgrounds, hedging
▶**Needs:** Plant in full sun in well-drained soil. Full sun keeps the leaves bright gold instead of yellow-green. Prune shrubs to shape after flowering.

PRIVETS

Japanese Ptomrivet

Ligustrum japonicum

Broadleaf evergreen shrub

Ligustrum japonicum 'Rotundifolium'

P

Plant encyclopedia

▶ ***Hardiness:*** Zones 7–10
▶ ***Size:*** Grows 6'–12' tall and about half as wide
▶ ***Features:*** A classic hedge shrub, Japanese privet has large, lustrous leaves. It grows at a moderate rate—not too fast—so a good pruning once to twice a year in colder regions and 2–3 times a year in mild winter climates keeps it in shape. It also responds well to pruning, quickly recovering from a hard cut. It has a tidy growth habit, so you can also leave it unpruned for a softer effect.
▶ ***Uses:*** Excellent for hedges
▶ ***Needs:*** Full sun to light shade, especially in the southern half of the United States. Average soil, moderate moisture its first year or two. Tolerates some dryness after established.

PRIVETS

Wax-Leaf Privet

Ligustrum lucidum

Evergreen shrub

Ligustrum lucidum

▶ ***Hardiness:*** Zones 7–10
▶ ***Size:*** 8'–12' tall, 5'–10' wide
▶ ***Features:*** Easy-to-grow wax-leaf privet isn't known for showy flowers or brightly colored fruit. But it is invaluable for year-round thick, glossy greenery that thrives just about anywhere, shaped as a shrub or a small tree. Privet's flower fragrance is offensive to some. Rapid growth rate.
▶ ***Uses:*** Tree-form specimen, confined areas beside parking, near swimming pools, or in large planters. Shrubs make thick, dense hedges.
▶ ***Needs:*** Plant in medium-fertility soil in sun or shade. Prune stems as needed to shape; remove lower limbs to train into a small tree. Leaves are too large to clip plants into formal shapes.

Prosopis glandulosa

see Mesquite

Prunus armeniaca

see Apricot

Prunus caroliniana

see Laurels: Cherry Laurel

Prunus dulcis

see Almond

Prunus spp.

see Plum

Pseudotsuga menziesii

see Fir, Douglas

Pulmonaria, Lungwort

Pulmonaria spp.

Perennial

Pulmonaria saccharata 'Roy Davidson'

▶ ***Hardiness:*** Zones 3–8
▶ ***Size:*** Grows 12"–18" tall and to 2' wide, depending on the type
▶ ***Features:*** Funnel-shape blue to purple flowers in drooping clusters in late spring. Excellent for moist shade gardens. Evergreen in all but the harshest winters.
▶ ***Uses:*** In woodland gardens; in shady flower beds and borders. Can plant in large groups as a groundcover.
▶ ***Needs:*** Light to full shade. Rich, well-drained, moist soil with ample moisture. Work in plenty of compost at planting time. Space 1' apart. Divide after flowering when needed; remove faded flower stalks. Remove fading leaves in early summer to make way for fresh new growth. Powdery mildew can be a problem; keep soil moist to prevent problems.
▶ ***Choices:*** *P. angustifolia* grows 12"–18" tall and has dark blue flowers with dark green leaves. *P. saccharata* grows 18" tall or more and is 2' wide. Leaves are silvery-white spotted and flowers are violet-pink or white.

Pulsatilla vulgaris

see Pasque Flower

Pumpkins

see Squash

Purple Coneflower

see Coneflower, Purple

Purple Heart

Tradescantia pallida

Tropical evergreen perennial

Tradescantia pallida

▶ ***Hardiness:*** Zones 9–11
▶ ***Size:*** Grows trailing stems several feet long unless tips are pinched.
▶ ***Features:*** Sometimes also called purple wandering Jew, this trailing plant has lovely burgundy leaves. The leaves are slightly hairy and tiny pink flowers may appear in summer.
▶ ***Uses:*** As a houseplant; excellent in a hanging basket. In Southern California and Florida, it is sometimes grown as a groundcover in shade.
▶ ***Needs:*** Bright light and even some direct light are important to keep the rich color of the leaves and to prevent plants from getting leggy. Keep soil very moist during most of the year; keep slightly drier in winter. Average household warmth and humidity are fine, though a tray with pebbles and water is beneficial. Fertilize three times in summer. Pinch ends of stems to control size and encourage a bushier, lusher plant.
▶ ***Choices:*** May be sold under a variety of botanical names, including *T. zebrina*.

Pussy Willow

see Willows

Pygmy Date Palm

see Palms

Pyracantha

see Firethorn

Pyrus calleryana

see Callery Pear

Quaking Aspen
Populus tremuloides

Deciduous tree

Populus tremuloides

▶***Hardiness:*** Zones 2–6
▶***Size:*** 40'-50' tall, 20'-30' wide
▶***Features:*** When breezes blow, the leaves of quaking aspen shake, shimmer, and whisper in the wind. Yellow autumn leaves are showy against silvery trunks. Trees are very adaptable to a range of growing conditions and are fast-growing but short-lived. The usual life span is less than 35 years.
▶***Uses:*** Accent use, groves, natural areas, hillsides, new construction areas
▶***Needs:*** Transplants easily and grows quickly. Grow in full sun or part shade. Trees grow best in well-drained, fertile soil but will grow in any soil that isn't waterlogged.

Queen-of-the-Prairie
Filipendula rubra

Perennial

Filipendula rubra

▶***Hardiness:*** Zones 3–8
▶***Size:*** 6'-8' tall, 3'-4' wide
▶***Features:*** This is a large perennial that presents a striking vertical accent at the rear of the early summer border, with tall stems topped with fluffy cotton candy pink panicles of flowers for a few weeks in early to midsummer. It is quite happy in wet or even boggy soils. The large leaves reach 8" across and provide a dramatic bold texture when the plant is not in bloom.
▶***Uses:*** Excellent for difficult low, wet spots and swales where water drains poorly, as well as drier sites. Use it at the edge of ponds and streams. It's dramatic massed in large groups in large gardens.
▶***Needs:*** Best in full sun with plenty of moisture; keep soil moist to wet. Tolerates wet, even boggy, soil that's preferably slightly acidic (pH 5.5–7.0). Plant established plants in spring. Mulch to keep soil moist. Fertilize occasionally, every 4–6 weeks, or work in a 9-month, slow-release fertilizer each spring. Cease fertilizing 6–8 weeks prior to the first frost date. Trim off spent flowers after blooms are over. This plant rarely needs staking. Divide tough roots in spring as needed. Spider mites and mildew are a problem if plant isn't adequately watered.
▶***Choices:*** Flowers come in shades of pink. 'Venusta' has deep pink flowers that fade to lighter colors as they age. Queen-of-the-Meadow *(F. ulmaria)* has creamy white flowers and is a much smaller plant, about 24"–36" tall and 24" wide. It prefers afternoon shade. 'Aurea' is a cultivar with intensely yellow leaves in spring that become even lighter as they mature through the summer.

Queen Palm
see Palms

Quercus spp.
see Oaks

Quince, Flowering
Chaenomeles speciosa

Deciduous flowering shrub

Chaenomeles speciosa

▶***Hardiness:*** Zones 4–9
▶***Size:*** 5'-10' tall, 5'-8' wide
▶***Features:*** What this shrub lacks in graceful form it makes up for it with its spectacular early spring bloom. Besides white, the flowers come in hot shades of red, scarlet, peach, salmon, and pink, and they cover the plant. The form of this shrub is a bit rangy and sprawling. It's thorny, and makes a good barrier plant at the property boundary. In addition, the branches are excellent for cutting and forcing indoors for a welcome breath of spring in late winter. The flowering quince produces richly aromatic fruits that make excellent jams and jellies. Bring them indoors in the fall and let them ripen on the kitchen table for a few weeks before cooking them, and the whole house will be permeated with a delicious apple scent.
▶***Uses:*** This is an excellent barrier shrub because of its thorniness, but for the same reason don't plant it next to driveways, entryways, or walkways where it might scratch the passerby. It is also good in the shrub border.
▶***Needs:*** Quince prefers full sun and a heavy soil—average to heavy clay. Moderate water best, but drought tolerant. Plant established plants in spring or fall. Mulch to conserve moisture. No need to fertilize in most conditions. No need to trim spent blooms. This plant blooms on old wood. Best to leave unpruned except for removal of dead or damaged wood. Apple scab, fire blight, and aphids may be problems. Just as buds begin to swell in early spring, cut branches and bring indoors to bloom in a vase.
▶***Choices:*** Many cultivars are available in white, red, salmon or pink.

Rabbit's Foot Fern
see Ferns

Radicchio
Cichorium intybus

Annual vegetable

Radicchio

▶***Size:*** Grows a few to several inches tall, depending on the type
▶***Features:*** The purplish-red heads of this bitter salad green add bite, color, and crunch to salads
▶***Uses:*** Vegetable garden
▶***Needs:*** Full sun to light shade. Rich, well-drained soil with plentiful moisture. In Zones 6 or 7 and colder, plant in spring directly in the garden ½" deep, thinning to 1'. In hot-summer regions of Zones 7 or 8 and warmer, plant in late summer for winter harvest. If growing traditional types of radicchio, allow the plant to grow tall until the frost, then cut off the green tops. In warm climates, red heads will then sprout and be ready for harvest in

Q

Plant encyclopedia

4–6 weeks. Alternatively, you can plant newer types of radicchio that form new heads right away with no cutting back. The heads turn purple-red when cool fall or winter weather arrives, signaling time for their harvest. Harvest when heads feel firm. If heads fail to form, the loose leaves are still tasty.
▶ ***Choices:*** 'Red Treviso' and 'Red Verona' are traditional types. 'Giulio' and 'Rossana' are newer types that don't need cutting back to form heads.

Radishes

Raphanus sativus

Cool-season annual vegetable

Radish

▶ ***Size:*** Foliage grows a few to several inches tall; radishes grow a few to several inches deep
▶ ***Features:*** Fast, easy-to-grow vegetable for early spring
▶ ***Uses:*** Vegetable garden
▶ ***Needs:*** Full sun to light shade. Loose, rich, deeply worked soil without shallow roots or many stones. Plentiful moisture. Plant seeds in early spring directly in the garden 3–4 weeks before your region's last frost date or as soon as soil can easily be worked. In hot-summer regions of Zones 8 and warmer, plant in fall and winter for cool-season harvests. Plant seeds about ½" deep. Keep moist throughout growing or radishes will become pithy and bitter-hot. Thin to 1"–1½" apart. Radishes will be ready for harvest in 3–4 weeks. Pull up one or two to taste in the garden; they should be tender and not hot or bitter. If desired, sow another two or three plantings every 2 weeks to ensure an on-going supply.
▶ ***Choices:*** Choose from the more commonly found red, round radishes, the large, white daikon types used in Asian cooking, or the long French types. 'Easter Egg' is a round type that is an assortment of red, purple, and pink radishes. 'White Icicle' is a popular French type. 'April Cross' and 'Spring Leader' are popular daikon types.

Ranunculus; Persian Buttercup

Ranunculus asiaticus

Annual or perennial spring-blooming bulb.

Ranunculus asiaticus

▶ ***Hardiness:*** Zones 7–10 in the West
▶ ***Size:*** 12"–15" tall, 6"–12" wide
▶ ***Features:*** Large double flowers 3"–5" wide may be white or a range of hot colors from red, pink, and orange to gold and bronze. They appear in early to late spring, about the same time as annual poppies and the poppy anemone, so the three combine well in beds.
▶ ***Uses:*** Wonderful massed in beds with other spring-blooming bulbs, poppy-flowered anemones, and annual poppies. Excellent in containers.
▶ ***Needs:*** Actually not a bulb but a claw-shape tuberous root. Each tuberous root produces many flowers. Where winters do not drop below 0°F/-18°C (Zones 7–10), plant in fall. In colder areas, plant in spring. If the roots are dry and shriveled, soak in water for a few hours before planting. Best in full sun, tolerates light shade. Rich to average, very well-drained, preferably sandy soil. Ample moisture. In California, where winter temperatures don't drop below 0°F/18°C—roughly Zones 7–10—and where summers are dry, grow as a perennial. Plant in late fall to very early winter, 4" deep, and select a spot that won't get much summer water. In the South, where summers are wet, most gardeners lift and store after blooming is through and the foliage yellows (see page 205). Over the winter store the roots in slightly damp sand at 50°–55°F. In colder zones it can be grown as an annual planted in spring, and is especially successful in containers.
▶ ***Choices:*** Flowers come in yellows, oranges, reds, pinks, and whites.

Raphiolepis indica

see Indian hawthorn

Raspberry, Edible

Rubus spp.

Deciduous shrublike bramble with berries

Raspberry

▶ ***Hardiness:*** Zones 3–9: red raspberries; 5–9: black raspberries
▶ ***Size:*** Grows 4'–8', depending on the type
Features: Succulent tiny fruits in late summer and fall
▶ ***Needs:*** Full sun to light shade. Does best in slightly acidic, rich soil with good drainage, but will tolerate some variety in soils. Better in regions with cooler summers and moderate winters. Raspberries come in two types: those that bear on canes grown the first year (includes both everbearing and fall-bearing types) and those that grow on canes that have been growing for two years (includes the summer-bearing types). Prune right after producing by cutting fruit-bearing canes to the ground after harvesting. Thin canes each spring. Fertilize lightly in spring and mulch with 2" or so of wood chips, pine needles, grass clippings, or other biodegradable mulch. Can be grown in sprawling thickets, but easiest to harvest with fewest disease problems when grown on a trellis.
▶ ***Choices:*** 'Heritage' is an everbearing red raspberry that is widely adapted. Yellow and purple raspberries also are available. Black raspberries are more heat tolerant than red types.

Raspberry, Creeping

Rubus pentalobus

Evergreen groundcover

Rubus pentalobus

▶***Hardiness:*** Zones 7-10
▶***Size:*** 6"-1' tall, 2'-4' wide
▶***Features:*** This groundcover for southern gardens is gaining popularity for its dense habit and moderate rate of growth. Evergreen, reddish-tinted leaves have an interesting rough, puckered texture.
▶***Uses:*** Groundcover
▶***Needs:*** Plant in any well-drained soil in full sun or light shade.

Rattail Cactus

see Cactus and Succulents

Rattlesnake Grass

see Grasses, Ornamental: Quaking Grass

Redbud

Cercis canadensis

Deciduous flowering tree

Cercis canadensis 'Alba'

▶***Hardiness:*** Zones 3-9
▶***Size:*** 20'-30' tall, 25'-35' wide
▶***Features:*** Spring arrives early if you have a redbud in your yard. Purplish-pink flowers appear in April, before leaves, on trees just a few years old. Older trees actually form flower buds on tree trunks and provide a conversation topic through the entire neighborhood. Attractive, heart-shape leaves turn yellow in fall; color quality varies with genetics and light. Tree trunks divide close to the ground and then develop graceful, ascending branches. Medium growth rate. Native tree proves tough and adaptable.
▶***Uses:*** Specimen, patio, understory, small lawn tree use, seasonal accent, in groundcover, shrub beds, woodland areas
▶***Needs:*** Plant in any soil type from sandy to clay and soil pH from acidic to alkaline. Prefers dry over soggy soil. Grow in full sun to partial shade. Prune to remove dead wood and open the canopy for light penetration.
▶***Choices:*** 'Alba'—white flowers; 'Forest Pansy'—purple leaves in spring and fall.

Red Cedar, Eastern

see Junipers

Red Cedar, Western

see Arborvitae

Red Hot Poker; Torch Lily

Kniphofia uvaria

Perennial

Kniphofia uvaria

▶***Hardiness:*** Zones 5-9
▶***Size:*** 3'-4' tall, 3'-4' wide
▶***Features:*** These hot-colored, exotic-looking spikes of tubular flowers will put a blaze in your summer garden. The foliage is a grasslike mound of gray-green leaves. Bloom times vary from spring to fall according to species and variety.
▶***Uses:*** In the mixed border with other perennials, singly or in groups of three. Combines well with ornamental grasses and 'Moonbeam' coreopsis and, in Zones 8-10 in the West, aloes. Performs well in containers.
▶***Needs:*** Full sun in Zones 5-6; part shade in hot summer areas in Zones 7-9. Rich to average, well-drained soil; moderate moisture. Fertilize rarely, if at all. Cut off spent flower spikes. Plant in spring or fall. Cut back plant by half after flowering if leaves become unsightly. In Zones 5-7 tie leaves over crown with twine in winter to help the plant shed water; the crown rots if it's wet too long. There is no need to divide, though small plants that form around the base of the plant can be transplanted for more plants.
Choices: Flowers come in reds, yellows, oranges, and creams. 'Little Maid', 'Citrina', and 'Royal Castle' are especially long bloomers.

Red Valerian; Jupiter's Beard

Centranthus ruber

Perennial

Centranthus ruber

▶***Hardiness:*** Zones 4-8 (9 in the West)
▶***Size:*** 2'-3' tall, 1'-2' wide
▶***Features:*** This is one of the longest-blooming perennials, with clusters of glowing rosy red, creamy white, or coral pink blooms throughout the summer on bushy plants. The attractive silvery-green foliage contrasts nicely with the warm colors of the flowers. Individual plants are short-lived but reseed prolifically, so if conditions are good (especially if soil is well drained and not too rich) they can last for years in the garden.
▶***Uses:*** Most effective planted in large groups in beds where plants can reseed without worry. Beautiful with lamb's-ears planted in front.

▶Needs: Poor, average to alkaline soil, with excellent drainage; it will not thrive if soil is too rich. This plant needs even moisture at first, but then is drought tolerant. Plant established plants in spring. Do not fertilize. Keep spent blooms trimmed to minimize reseeding; this plant can become a slightly problematic (but beautiful) weed if left alone, especially in the West where it has naturalized. However, it is a short-lived plant, lasting only 3-5 years, so allow at least a few to reseed. It is trouble free if well suited to the site.
▶Choices: Flowers come in coral pink, white, and deep rose-red.

Redwood, Dawn
see Dawn Redwood

Rhapis excelsa
see Palms: Lady Palm

Rhapis humilis
see Palms: Slender Lady Palm

RHODODENDRONS AND AZALEAS
Rhododendron spp.

Beloved for their fabulous show of flowers—some deliciously fragrant—for a few weeks in spring or early summer, many azaleas and rhododendrons have other seasons of beauty, too, although perhaps not as loud and and eyecatching. Some have beautiful evergreen foliage that adds a welcome warmth to winter. And some of the deciduous azaleas have showy fall color in orange, yellow, red, and burgundy. There are hundreds, if not thousands, of azalea and rhododendron cultivars available. Besides the ones described below, ask your garden center associate for recommendations for your area.

RHODODENDRONS

Carolina Rhododendron
Rhododendron carolinianum

Evergreen flowering shrub

Rhododendron carolinianum

▶Hardiness: Zones 5-8
▶Size: 3'-6' tall, 3'-4' wide
▶Features: Celebrate late spring in your yard with Carolina rhododendrons. These shrubs feature flowers in a selection of springtime shades of pink and white. The medium-size leaves stay dark, shiny green throughout the year. Can grow in Zone 4 with winter protection. Avoid planting rhododendrons where exposed to harsh winds or strong winter sun. Native to the Blue Ridge Mountains of the Carolinas and Tennessee.
▶Uses: Seasonal accents, background planting, foundation planting, along fences, entries, along walkways, beside patios, massing in planting beds
▶Needs: Grow in full sun. Plant in fertile, acidic, moist, well-drained soil. Set new shrubs slightly higher to prevent water from collecting around roots. Mulch to keep roots moist. Provide extra water in autumn. Prune as soon as flowering finishes; reach into plants to remove woody stems—do not shear.
▶Choices: var. *album*—white flowers. *Rhododendron minus* is a similar native species that is somewhat more heat tolerant and open in form.

RHODODENDRONS

Catawba Rhododendron
Rhododendron catawbiense

Evergreen flowering shrub

Rhododendron catawbiense

▶Hardiness: Zones 4-8
▶Size: 6'-10' tall, 5'-8' wide
▶Features: The bright lilac-purple blossoms of catawba rhododendron are breathtaking against the dark green leaves. Dense plants form a broad, rounded outline. Catawba rhododendron can take cold weather without sacrificing flower buds, but protect from drying winter winds. Slow growth rate.
▶Uses: Specimen shrub, screen, massed, or foundation planting
▶Needs: Plant in moist, well-drained, acidic, fertile soil. Rhododendrons can take full sun in colder areas; in warmer climates, partial shade is best. Water plants in fall. Mulch beneath shrubs to help soil stay moist. Prune to remove dead branches after new growth has emerged. Snap off flowers after they fade.
▶Choices: 'P.J.M.'—lavender-pink flowers, shade and drought tolerant, 6' tall to 4' wide, Zones 4-8; 'P.J.M. White'—white flowers, leaves turn burgundy in winter, 3' to 4' high and wide, Zones 4-8; Mollis hybrids—large, waxy blooms; many flower colors, deciduous, 4'-5' tall and wide, Zones 4-8.

RHODODENDRONS

Cornell Pink Korean Azalea
Rhododendron mucronulatum 'Cornell Pink'

Deciduous flowering shrub

Rhododendron mucronulatum 'Cornell Pink'

▶Hardiness: Zones 5 (4 with protection)-8
▶Size: 4'-8' tall, 3'-5' wide
▶Features: Include these shrubs for early spring color. Flowers open before leaves unfurl, blanketing the plant in bright pink. One of the earliest azaleas to bloom. Leaves turn yellow to crimson in fall. Plant these shrubs in a protected location away from winter sun. This is especially important in colder climates where warming rays may coax buds into opening too early. Freezing temperatures damage or kill the blooms before you can enjoy them.
▶Uses: Specimen use, seasonal accents, foundation plantings (with evergreen shrubs), massing, filling in planting beds, natural areas
▶Needs: Plant in fertile, acidic soil that's moist but well drained. Set new shrubs slightly higher than existing ground to prevent water from collecting around roots. Mulch well to keep roots moist. Supply extra water during dry periods and in autumn. Grow in full sun. Remove woody stems after flowering; do not shear.

RHODODENDRONS

Exbury Azalea
Rhododendron Exbury hybrids

Deciduous flowering shrub

Rhododendron 'Gibraltar'

▶ ***Hardiness:*** Zones 4–8
▶ ***Size:*** 4'–8' tall, 4'–8' wide
▶ ***Features:*** Midspring flowers in a range of colors; leaves turn yellow, orange, or red in fall. Colorful accent in front of evergreens. These azaleas will add color to your yard in the spring when blossoms open and again in autumn when the leaves put on their fall show. Choose rose-pink, red, orange, white, or yellow flower colors. Plants are also known as Knap Hill or Rothschild hybrids.
▶ ***Uses:*** Seasonal accents, hedges, foundation plantings, massing, planting along fences, driveways, and beneath trees
▶ ***Needs:*** Plant in fertile, acidic soil that's moist but well drained. Set new shrubs slightly higher than existing ground to prevent water from collecting around roots. Mulch to keep roots moist. Supply extra water during dry periods and in autumn. Grow in full sun. Remove selected woody stems after flowering; do not shear.
▶ ***Choices:*** 'Berry Rose'—rose-pink blossoms; 'Firefly'—red flowers; 'Gibraltar'—bright orange flowers; 'White Swan'—white blooms.

RHODODENDRONS

Glenn Dale Azaleas

Rhododendron Glenn Dale hybrids

Evergreen flowering shrub

Rhododendron 'Pink Ice'

▶ ***Hardiness:*** Zones 6–9
▶ ***Size:*** 3'–8' tall, 3'–6' wide
▶ ***Features:*** These evergreen azaleas were bred with cold hardiness in mind. Choose from a range of flower colors and bloom times, from mid-April to mid-June. Flowers may be white, pink, purple, red, or orange-red. If you chose a speckled or striped selection, remove branches that bear solid-colored flowers. Plants have an upright, rounded habit and a medium growth rate.
▶ ***Uses:*** Shrub borders, woodland edges, foundation plantings, massing, beside patios, surrounding lawns, accents
▶ ***Needs:*** Plant in acidic soil that's moist but well drained. These plants won't tolerate wet soils. Grow in partial or dense shade. Hand-prune after flowering; do not shear. Cold hardy.

RHODODENDRONS

Gumpo Azalea

Rhododendron 'Gumpo'

Evergreen flowering shrub

Rhododendron 'Gumpo White'

▶ ***Hardiness:*** Zones 6–9
▶ ***Size:*** 6"–30" tall, 6"–30" wide
▶ ***Features:*** This little azalea blooms when it's hot. Although it requires acidic soil to grow optimally, very little care is needed beyond that. Plants come in the colors of white, red, pink, lavender, salmon, and rose. Flowers in late spring or summer. Slow to medium growth rate.
▶ ***Uses:*** Entries, planters, parking areas, beneath low windows or planted as the front layer of shrub beds, tidy growing for use in smaller landscapes
▶ ***Needs:*** Gumpo azaleas need partial shade and well-drained soil. Mix organic matter such as compost into the hole. If planting near concrete—which raises soil pH—mulch with pine bark or pine straw to increase acidity. Low growing—no pruning necessary.
▶ ***Choices:*** 'Gumpo Pink'—pink flowers; 'Gumpo White'—white flowers; 'Gumpo Rose'—reddish flowers.

RHODODENDRONS

Kurume Azaleas

Rhododendron Kurume hybrids

Evergreen flowering shrub (semievergreen in cool climates)

Rhododendron 'Blaauw's Pink'

▶ ***Hardiness:*** Zones 6–9
▶ ***Size:*** 2'–6' tall, 2'–6' wide
▶ ***Features:*** Grow these compact azaleas where you want dense shrubs covered with green leaves year-round and blankets of blossoms in spring. Kurumes are slow-growing, so they stay small longer than southern Indian azaleas.
▶ ***Uses:*** Massing in planting beds, bordering taller shrubs, entries, courtyards, beside patios and walkways, accents
▶ ***Needs:*** Plant in acidic soil that's moist but well drained. Shrubs grow faster with regular watering but can't tolerate soggy soil. Grow in full sun to partial shade. With proper watering, tolerates heat and sun. Feed with acid-loving plant food after blooming ceases.
▶ ***Choices:*** 'Hinode Giri'—purplish red, very hardy; 'Appleblossom'—white to pink flowers with darker blotches, occasional red stripes; 'Christmas Cheer'—red blooms; 'Coral Bells'—strong pink flowers.

RHODODENDRONS

Northern Lights Azaleas

Rhododendron Northern Lights series

Deciduous flowering shrub

Rhododendron 'Northern Lights'

▶ ***Hardiness:*** Zones 4–7
▶ ***Size:*** 4'–6' tall, 4'–6' wide
▶ ***Features:*** Developed at the University of Minnesota, these azaleas can take the cold. Buds will withstand temperatures down to -45°F/-42°C and still produce abundant blooms when spring arrives. Flowers possess a clovelike fragrance. Spring flowers are available in a range of colors including bronze and burgundy. Plants may have purple foliage in fall.
▶ ***Uses:*** Cold-tolerant accent for the spring garden, informal deciduous hedges, foundation plantings (with evergreen shrubs), massing, natural areas, filling in planting beds
▶ ***Needs:*** Grow in full sun. Plant in fertile, moist, well-drained, acidic soil. Set new shrubs slightly higher than existing ground to prevent water from collecting around roots. Mulch. Supply extra water during dry weather and again in autumn. Prune when flowers have finished to remove woody stems; do not shear.
▶ ***Choices:*** 'Golden Lights'—golden flowers in late spring, bronzy-red fall foliage; 'Northern Hi-Lights'—creamy white and yellow flowers in late spring, burgundy to purple fall foliage; 'Orchid Lights'—lilac

R

Plant encyclopedia

flowers in early spring, insignificant fall color; 'Rosy Lights'—rosy flowers in late spring, insignificant fall color; 'White Lights'—pink buds open to white blossoms in late spring, bronzy-purple fall foliage.

RHODODENDRONS

Rutherford Azaleas

Rhododendron Rutherford hybrids

Evergreen flowering shrub (semievergreen in cool climates)

Rhododendron 'Southern Belle'

▶ ***Hardiness:*** Zones 9–10
▶ ***Size:*** 2'-3' tall and wide
▶ ***Features:*** These slow-growing, wide plants are easy to keep neat and low. They thrive in hotter climates, tolerating heat, sun, and humidity, often blooming in early to late winter and repeating bloom in the fall. Leaves stay green year-round.
▶ ***Uses:*** Massing in planting beds, bordering tall shrubs, entries, courtyards, beside patios and walkways, seasonal accents, beneath low windows
▶ ***Needs:*** Plant in acidic soil that's moist but well drained. Shrubs grow rapidly with regular watering but can't tolerate soggy soil. Grow in partial sun to dense shade. Feed with acid-loving plant food after blooming ceases.
▶ ***Choices:*** 'Red Ruffles'—strong red; 'Alaska'—white blooms.

RHODODENDRONS

Southern Indica Hybrid Azaleas

Rhododendron Southern Indica hybrids

Evergreen flowering shrub

Rhododendron 'Formosa'

▶ ***Hardiness:*** Zones 8–10
▶ ***Size:*** 8'-10' tall, 4'-6' wide
▶ ***Features:*** Spring isn't official throughout much of the warmer climates until these evergreen shrubs are covered with blossoms. Flowers come in white, and shades of salmon, pink, red to purple. Southern Indica azaleas aren't hard to grow if your soil is acidic. Also sold as southern Indian hybrid azaleas. Though fall is the best time to plant woody shrubs in mild climates, it's worth waiting until spring for azaleas. Doing so will allow you to buy azaleas while they're in bloom so you can be sure of the color you're getting and match all the plants. Unintended colors could clash in an otherwise well-planned landscape.
▶ ***Uses:*** Shrub borders, entries, woodland edges, foundation plantings, massing, seasonal accents, planting beside patios and driveways, growing beneath tall trees
▶ ***Needs:*** Plant in acidic soil that's moist but well drained. Shrubs grow rapidly with regular watering but can't tolerate soggy soil. Morning sun with afternoon shade is ideal. Hand-prune after flowering; do not shear. Feed with acid-loving plant food after bloom. Mulch to conserve moisture and increase acidity.
▶ ***Choices:*** 'Duke de Rohan'—bright pink flowers with purplish blotches; 'Formosa'—vivid purplish red flowers; 'George Lindley Tabor'—white to soft pink blooms; 'Mrs. G.G. Gerbing'—white flowers; 'President Clay'—red flowers; 'Pride of Mobile'—strong pink blossoms with darker blotches.

Rhubarb

Rheum ×*cultorum*

Edible perennial

Rhubarb

▶ ***Hardiness:*** Perennial in Zones 2–7; grow as a cool-season annual in Zones 8 and warmer
▶ ***Size:*** Grows 1'-2' tall and wide
▶ ***Features:*** Large attractive leaves and ruby-red edible stalks. Sends up pretty flower stalks in early summer. One or two plants provide plenty of stalks for pies, rhubarb sauce, and other sweets.
▶ ***Uses:*** In the vegetable garden or flower bed
▶ ***Needs:*** Full sun to light shade. Prefers rich, well-drained soil. Plentiful moisture. Does best in areas with cool, moist summers and winters with regular sub-freezing temperatures. Plant crowns or divisions from another rhubarb plant in early spring or autumn. Keep moist; mulch is helpful. In cold-winter climates, usually Zones 6 and colder, rhubarb is a long-lived perennial and needs little care from year to year. In areas roughly Zones 7–8, it is usually a short-lived perennial and will die out after a few years. In hot-summer regions of Zones 8 and warmer, it must be grown as a winter annual. Plant several plants to assure enough stalks. Harvest in spring through summer by cutting off the stalks; both red and green portions are tasty. (However, the leaves are toxic.) Very large stalks or stalks that are no longer firm can be stringy or tough, so avoid harvesting those. Do not remove more than half the stalks in a season. The flower stalks are attractive; cut them off once they're done flowering for a neater appearance.
▶ ***Choices:*** Some cultivars available, but often sold merely as rhubarb.

Rhus typhina 'Laciniata'

see Staghorn Sumac, Cut-Leaf

Ribes spp.

see Currant

River Birch

see Birches

Rockcress, False

Aubrieta deltoidea

Perennial

Aubrieta deltoidea

▶ ***Hardiness:*** Zones 4–8
▶ ***Size:*** 6"-8" tall, 18"-24" wide
▶ ***Features:*** This mat-forming plant is a beautiful trailing groundcover for well-drained rocky, stony soils, and spills elegantly over and through rock walls. In midspring, at the height of the spring bulb season, it becomes a blanket of tiny, bright purple to pink flowers.
▶ ***Uses:*** A must for the rock garden; combines wonderfully with spring-blooming bulbs; performs well in containers
▶ ***Needs:*** Must have excellent drainage; plant only in rock gardens, slopes, along walls, or in other places where it will never have wet feet. False rockcress needs only moderate moisture. Plant established plants in spring. Work plenty of sand or

R

Plant encyclopedia

grit into the soil in all but the sandiest areas. Mulch to conserve moisture. Fertilize lightly if at all. Cut back by one-third to two-thirds after blooming to keep it neat and compact. False rockcress is a short-lived perennial, usually dying out after a few years. Be prepared to replace it as needed or to take cuttings every other year or so. This plant is prone to root rot if not well drained and is also susceptible to aphids, nematodes, and flea beetles.

Rockcress, Wall

Arabis caucasica (formerly *Arabis albida)*

Perennial

Arabis caucasica

▶***Hardiness:*** Zones 4–7

▶***Size:*** 10"–18" tall, 12"–18" wide

▶***Features:*** Spreading mounds of beautiful gray foliage are covered in white blossoms in early to midspring, a stunning sight when planted around daffodils and other spring-blooming bulbs. Excellent in combination with false rockcress, blooming somewhat earlier. Flowers also come in pink.

▶***Uses:*** Rock gardens, at the base of or tucked into planting pockets in rock walls. Good in containers. Excellent in association with false rockcress and spring-blooming bulbs.

▶***Needs:*** Poor, loose, very well-drained soil; moderate moisture. Full sun. Plant established plants in spring or fall. Mulch is helpful to keep soil cool. Avoid fertilizing. Cut back stems after flowering to keep plants tidy. Divide every 2–3 years. In the right climate, diseases are seldom a problem. Hot, humid, or wet climates encourage root or crown rot.

▶***Choices:*** Flowers come in whites and pinks, and some cultivars are double-flowered. *A. caucasica* 'Variegata' has white flowers with silvery leaves edged in white. 'Pink Charm' has pink flowers. *A. procurrens* tolerates light shade.

Rock Rose

Helianthemum nummularium

Evergreen shrub

Helianthemum nummularium

▶***Hardiness:*** Zones 5–8

▶***Size:*** 6"–12" tall, 2'–3' wide

▶***Features:*** Rock rose is a heavy bloomer in spring and early summer. Gray-green leaves last year-round. Medium growth rate.

▶***Uses:*** Rock gardens, raised beds, planters, hillsides, rock walls, front layer of shrub beds

▶***Needs:*** Plants perform best in poor soils. Little care is required if good drainage is present. Water around roots can freeze, killing rock rose in colder climates. Plant in full sun in well-drained, alkaline to neutral soil. Work lime into soil to increase alkalinity. Shear plants after the flowers fade to keep plants neat and promote new growth.

▶***Choices:*** 'Buttercup'—golden yellow flowers.

Rock Rose, White

Cistus ×hybridus

Evergreen shrub

Cistus ×hybridus

▶***Hardiness:*** Zones 8–10

▶***Size:*** 3'–5' tall, 3'–5' wide

▶***Features:*** This Mediterranean native doesn't mind dry heat, wind, or drought. Sprawling stems are covered with white flowers from spring to summer. Fine-textured foliage stays green year-round. Rapid growth rate.

▶***Uses:*** Low-maintenance areas, banks and slopes, along roadsides and driveways, beach plantings, informal hedges

▶***Needs:*** Plant in full sun. Grows successfully in poor or dry but well-drained soil. Tolerates drought, salt, and wind. Water regularly until the plant is established, then water little or not at all. Cut stems back occasionally to encourage thick, full growth.

ROSES

Unquestionably America's favorite flower. When hearing the word "rose" most people think of the long-stemmed red hybrid tea roses you find at the florist. And the hybrid tea—with a fully double, high-centered, sculptural blossom on a long, strong stem—is the most popular kind of rose for gardening too. Yet there are many other kinds of roses to grow in the rose garden and in the larger landscape. In fact, there is probably more diversity and landscape usefulness in this single genus of plants than in any other group of shrubs in horticulture. There are ramblers that will climb 40' or more and leap from tall tree to tall tree. There are miniatures that remain a tidy neat mound 12" tall and 20" wide with perfectly proportioned tiny flowers and leaves.
And there is everything in between—sprawling groundcovers that stay low and spread wide; arching shrubs, low rounded shrubs, tall upright shrubs, weeping shrubs, shrubs grafted onto standard trunks that resemble small trees; low climbers for spreading out over a fence or climbing a lamp post, larger climbers for covering an arbor or pergola, huge climbers for covering a house, if you wish. Some roses—especially the old garden roses, ramblers, and wild, or species, roses—save all their energy for one spectacular show of flowers, usually in spring or early summer. Many of these have showy fruits called hips that are red, orange, or yellow in late summer and fall. But an increasing number of landscape roses, capturing the most important trait of the hybrid tea, rebloom again and again throughout the summer in successive flushes.
Also from the hybrid tea comes an astonishingly wide range of "modern" colors, including yellows, salmons, lavenders, mauves, and purples, to add to the usual range of reds, pinks, and whites of this genus. Many of the flowers are deliciously fragrant. Add to this profusion of fragrance, summer-long color, and diversity of form the new breeding for carefree disease resistance, hardiness, and vigor, and you end up with nearly the perfect landscape plant. Simply put, there's a rose for just about every purpose in the landscape.

ROSES

Hybrid tea and grandiflora

▶***Hardiness:*** Zones 6 (5 with protection)–9.

▶***Size:*** 4"–7" tall, 2"–4" wide (larger in mild climates)

▶ Features: Upright and somewhat leggy, this group of modern roses has been bred for perfection of blooms for cutting. The typical flower form is full, double, and sculptural, with a high, pointed center, usually produced as one blossom on each long, strong stem. Grandifloras are similar but produce their long blooming stems in clusters. These are not especially good roses for the landscape and are most often grown in special rose gardens. Prone to disease and pests if neglected, they generally demand too much care and attention to be useful in the landscape. But unquestionably they are the ultimate cut flower, available in an astonishing array of colors, and many varieties are fragrant.
▶ Uses: Best in the rose garden, excellent for cutting. This is the most popular kind of rose in North America.
▶ Needs: Plant bare-root plants in spring before their buds swell, in well-drained, slightly acidic soil high in organic matter. Plant container-grown plants anytime during the growing season. Best in full sun; needs at least 6 hours of unobstructed direct sun per day during the growing season in order to bloom well. Fertilize and water abundantly, protect from disease and pests with a regular program of pest controls, and protect from winter damage in Zone 5. Remove spent flowers to promote faster reblooming. Prune back to induce dormant rest period in November in mild climates (Zones 8–10); farther north prune in late winter to remove all dead stems.
▶ Choices:

Peace—pink blend with gold highlights in the center blushing to pink at the petal edges. Very fragrant. Easy to grow.

Crystalline—pure white with spicy fragrance.

Crimson Bouquet—grandiflora with brilliant red blooms, good fragrance.

Gift of Life—yellow blend with soft yellow blooms fading to ivory at the edges.

Gold Medal—grandiflora with deep yellow blossoms that have burnt orange to red on the edges of the petals. Plants are upright and tall, to 7" high.

Peter Mayle—deep pink, almost red blooms are one of the most fragrant of all roses.

Love & Peace—a progeny of the famous Peace rose, a yellow blend with more deep pink in the petals, deepening to red at the petal edges. Mild fragrance.

ROSES

Floribunda and polyantha

▶ Hardiness: Zones 5 (4 with protection)
▶ Size: 3"–4" tall, 3"–4" wide
▶ Features: Floribundas and polyanthas are cluster roses, producing several flowers on short stems at the end of each blooming stem. Many of the floribundas have a high center similar to the hybrid tea, albeit individually smaller blossoms, but there is more variety in bloom form and more coverage of color on the bush than hybrid teas, with every bit as wide a color selection and good reblooming all summer long. The rounded form of these shrubs, usually cloaked to the ground in foliage, makes them more amenable to landscape use. However, floribundas are generally just as high-maintenance as hybrid teas and for best appearance need a regular program of feeding and pest and disease control. The polyanthas, on the other hand, offer some of the most low-maintenance shrubs there are for the landscape (most notably The Fairy).

►***Uses:*** Floribundas are generally best grown in the rose garden where they can receive a regular program of feeding, pest control, and deadheading. Polyanthas and some of the newer more disease-resistant floribundas are excellent subjects for the mixed perennial border and the shrub border.

►***Needs:*** Plant bare-root plants in spring before their buds swell, in well-drained, slightly acidic soil high in organic matter. Plant container-grown plants anytime during the growing season. Best in full sun; needs at least 6 hours of unobstructed direct sun per day during the growing season in order to bloom well. Fertilize and water abundantly, protect from disease and pests with a regular program of pest controls, and protect from winter damage in Zone 5. Remove spent flowers to promote faster reblooming. Prune back floribundas to induce dormant rest period in November in mild climates (Zones 8–10); farther north prune in late winter to remove all dead stems.

►***Choices:***

Betty Prior—huge clusters of medium pink blooms with white centers. Good disease resistance.

Gruss an Aachen—light pink blooms that fade to creamy white. Good disease resistance; takes a bit more shade than most roses.

Iceberg—one of the most popular roses in the world, and for good reason: pure white blossoms appear in open clusters all summer. Glossy foliage is always healthy.

Mlle. Cécile Brünner—a beloved old polyantha with small silvery-pink flowers in large airy clusters. Spicy, sweet fragrance. More tender, Zones 6–10.

Nearly Wild—single-petaled pink flowers with white eyes and an apple fragrance cover this small, 2"–3" bush in the first spring flush, sporadically thereafter. Don't crowd this plant or it will suffer from blackspot. Very hardy, Zones 4–9.

Sun Flare—lemon-yellow blooms hold their color well even in summer heat. Prolific bloom production all summer. Light fragrance.

The Fairy—this polyantha is hard to beat for lots of color all summer with easy care. Huge clusters of soft pink flowers all summer. No fragrance.

ROSES

Miniature and miniflora

▶ ***Hardiness:*** Zones 5 (4 with winter protection)–10
▶ ***Size:*** 12"–18" tall and as wide. Miniature climbers can grow 4'–8' tall.
▶ ***Features:*** Miniature roses combine small size and summer-long blooms with hardiness and a range for flower colors and forms every bit as wide as that of their larger cousins, the hybrid teas and floribundas. Many of them have the same high-pointed flower form as hybrid teas, but in miniature. Minifloras are a new class of small roses that are intermediate in size of both shrub and flower, between miniatures and floribundas. Most miniature roses are grown on their own roots and not grafted, which means they are generally hardier than hybrid teas and floribundas.
▶ ***Uses:*** Ideal for edging and massing in beds as a groundcover, and perfect for planting in front of hybrid teas to hide their "bare legs." They are unexcelled as a subject for containers.
▶ ***Needs:*** Although they are hardier, miniature roses generally require the same attention as the larger hybrid teas and floribundas to look their best—regular feeding and watering, attentive protection from pests and disease, and regular deadheading to encourage fast rebloom.
▶ ***Choices:***

Autumn Splendor—this miniflora is a yellow blend with generous sprays of high-centered flowers in brilliant yellow, gold, and orange. Grows 30" tall and wide.

Margo Koster—a tiny 12" plant with deep salmon flowers all summer long, disease resistant and easy to grow. Stems are nearly thornless.

Santa Claus—a popular red red rose; bushes can reach 3' tall in mild climates.

Scentsational—beautiful tiny lavender-mauve blossoms are deliciously fragrant. In cool climates the petal color deepens on the outer edges.

Sun Sprinkles—an award-winning new miniature with clear, deep yellow blossoms that hold their color a long time, even in hot sun.

ROSES

Classic and modern shrub

▶ ***Hardiness:*** Many hardy in Zones 4–9, but differs according to variety
▶ ***Size:*** Ranges from small rounded shrubs 2' high and 3' wide to large arching shrubs 7'–8' high and wide, to huge shrubs that, in mild climates, approach the size of a small tree.
▶ ***Features:*** All roses, from huge ramblers to hybrid teas to miniatures, are shrubs of one form or another. This classification is a rather arbitrary catch-all that botanists use for roses that don't fit well into any other category. Nevertheless, it includes many of the most useful rose varieties for the landscape, including some of the hardiest and most disease-resistant roses. Among them are the so-called English roses with their delightful old-fashioned antique flower forms and fragrance and modern colors; and the newer low-growing ones marketed by garden centers as groundcover roses.
▶ ***Uses:*** Depending on size and form, these are wonderful plants to integrate into the shrub border, or use as groundcover, or, in the case of some of the larger ones, train to climb a wall or fence. Most are bred to rebloom quickly throughout the summer.
▶ ***Needs:*** Generally less care is needed with this rose category, although all roses benefit from generous feeding, watering, and pest protection. Many, especially groundcover roses, are self-cleaning and rebloom well without deadheading.

▶ ***Choices:***

Adelaide Hoodless—this hardy rose, bred in Canada, has bright red blooms in early summer and sporadically thereafter. Protect from blackspot. Zones 3–9.

Bonica—a famous shrub rose that produces pink flowers all summer. Quite hardy, Zones 4–9, and easy to grow.

Country Dancer—this small, hardy shrub grows 3' tall and wide and produces large quantities of double deep rose blossoms all summer. Zones 4–9.

Alba Meidiland—this groundcover rose with blazing white blossoms can spread 5' or more while remaining 1'–2' high. First summer flush is the biggest; blooms appear sporadically thereafter. Zones 5–10.

F.J. Grootendorst—a rugosa rose with the typical dark, crinkly foliage, good disease resistance, and great hardiness, Zones 4–9. The flowers are deep pink and, after the first big early-summer flush, appear only sporadically the rest of the summer.

Flower Carpet—marketed as a groundcover, this is actually an arching shrub that grows 3' high and 4'–5' wide. The self-cleaning bright pink flowers rebloom all summer. Quite hardy, Zones 5–9.

Ballerina—like all the hybrid musk roses this one blooms well even in partial shade. The light pink flowers appear in one big spectacular flush in late spring or early summer. Zones 5–10.

Carefree Beauty—a very hardy upright shrub 4'–5' tall with large, fragrant, rich pink flowers all summer. Orange-red hips are showy in fall and winter. Zones 4–10.

Frau Dagmar Hartopp—a hybrid rugosa with the typical dark, wrinkled foliage and hardiness to Zones 4–9. The single pink flowers with golden centers are fragrant and repeat well all summer. Plants grow 4' tall. Large crimson hips are attractive in winter.

Graham Thomas—an English rose with beautiful yellow fragrant double flowers all summer on large, arching plants. The deeply cupped flowers have an old-fashioned look.

Hunter—red double blooms in a big flush in early summer and again in early fall. This hardy hybrid rugosa has wrinkled foliage and good disease resistance. Zones 4–9.

Morden Centennial—a very hardy Canadian shrub with rich deep pink double flowers that keep on coming all summer long.

Hansa—one of the older hybrid rugosas with wrinkled dark green foliage and large red double blooms that exude a clove fragrance. Red hips are striking in winter. Very hardy, Zones 3–9.

Knock Out—a new breakthrough shrub rose bred for complete immunity to blackspot. Deep cherry-red flowers are single and reblooming all summer. Hardy, Zones 4–10.

Pink Meidiland—deep pink single flowers with a bright white eye provide intense color. Zones 5–10.

Henry Kelsey—this hybrid kordesii is one of the hardiest of all climbers, with bright, dark rosy red semidouble flowers with yellow centers all summer. Spicy fragrance. Can be trained to climb 6'–8' high, and needs little winter protection even in the North. Zones 4–9.

Morden Blush—an extra-hardy rose from Canada, with elegant, light pink blossoms that last for weeks on the bush. Grows 2'–5' tall. Zones 3–10.

Sir Thomas Lipton—cupped, fragrant white double flowers bloom in successive flushes all summer. Plants are upright, 3'–5' tall, and hardy. A hybrid rugosa excellent for hedges. Zones 4–9.

Therese Bugnet—this hybrid rugosa is one of the hardiest, with ruffled, double blooms that have an old-fashioned appearance. Disease resistant. Zones 4–9.

William Baffin—this hybrid kordessii is one of the hardiest climbing roses, actually a big, upright shrub that can be trained as a climber to 10'-12' tall. The deep pink semidouble blooms have cheerful yellow centers, and repeat well all summer long. Disease resistant. Zones 3–9.

ROSES

Old garden roses and species

▶***Hardiness:*** Varies, from tender hybrid noisette, tea, and hybrid china roses (Zones 7–10) to the hardy alba, hybrid foetida, and hybrid spinosissima (hardy to Zone 3).

▶***Size:*** Range from 2'-15' tall, depending on variety, with some climbers reaching 40' or more. Most old garden roses, however, are arching-to-rounded shrubs 3'-6' tall and 4'-7' wide.

▶***Features:*** By definition the classification of old garden roses is made up of those varieties in existence before 1867, when the first modern hybrid tea was developed. Many of the most popular old garden roses have extremely double, even quartered blooms that are very romantic, and a wonderful fragrance. The colors are mostly in the white or light pink to dark pink range, although a few of the bourbons have deep burgundy flowers. Species roses nearly all have single-petaled flowers in white or various shades of pink. The hybrid foetida group is the source of yellow color in modern roses, and also the source of susceptibility to black spot—which is why most modern yellow (and salmon and peach) roses have problems with that disease. Old garden roses and species have a fairly undeserved reputation for pest resistance and low care, perhaps because most varieties bloom only once in late spring (and thus need no deadheading, and are often ignored the rest of the season). Unlike the other old-garden roses, the more tender hybrid China, hybrid perpetual, Portland, and tea roses are reblooming. Their genetics form the background for the modern hybrid teas and floribundas. This is also why many of the modern hybrid teas and floribundas are hardy only to Zone 6.

▶***Uses:*** Excellent in cottage gardens with other late-spring blooming flowers, such as peonies, poppies, and bearded iris, as well as foxgloves and hardy geraniums.

▶***Needs:*** Like any rose, these perform best in full sun and moist, rich, well-drained soil that is high in organic matter and slightly acidic (pH 6.0–6.5). Old garden roses, especially the hardy ones, need less pruning than other kinds, mostly to shape or to remove dead wood. The once-blooming roses need less protection from pests and disease since they are through blooming before many of the flower-eating insects arrive. Here's a trick to encourage more blooms on old roses that have an arching form: In early spring as the long new canes emerge, bend them over and peg them close to the ground with wire. The more horizontal the cane, the more flowers will be produced along its length.

▶***Choices:***

Baron Girod de l'Ain—1897. This hybrid perpetual has deep pink fragrant double blossoms with a ragged white deckle edge. Unlike many old roses it blooms repeatedly through the summer. Zones 6–10.

Celsiana—1750. This is a damask rose with light pink, semidouble blossoms with a strong musk fragrance. Blooms once in early summer. Zones 5–10.

Charles de Mills—1746. A hybrid gallica with deep pink, very full and huge blossoms that exude a rich fragrance. Blooms once in late spring. Zones 5–10.

Fantin-Latour—date unknown. This centifolia rose produces fantastically fragrant, elegantly light pink blossoms so full of petals they have what is called a cabbage form. Blooms once in late spring.

Memorial *(Rosa wichuriana)*—a species rose with small white single flowers in spring on long, sprawling canes; it is the parent of many modern groundcover and climbing roses. Excellent dark green, glossy foliage and hardiness. Zones 5–10.

Queen of Denmark—date unknown. This hardy, ancient alba produces bright pink double flowers with extraordinary fragrance. Blooms once in late spring. Beautiful red hips appear in fall and winter. 4'–6' tall. Zones 3–9.

Rosa rubrifolia—This species rose produces a flush of small pink single flowers for a week or so in late spring, but it isn't grown for the flowers as much as for the beautiful gray foliage and attractive small but numerous red hips in fall and winter.

Sombreuil—1850. This climbing tea rose produces immense numbers of very double, quartered white blossoms in repeating flushes all summer. Strong tea-rose fragrance. It can be trained to climb to 12', a good size for arbors. Unfortunately it is hardy only in Zones 7–10.

White Rugosa *(Rosa rugosa* 'Alba')—the white form of the species has large, single white flowers with yellow centers and a raspberry fragrance, one big flush in spring and sporadic blooms thereafter. Very hardy, vigorous, and disease resistant. Pretty red hips in winter. Zones 3–10.

Zephirine Drouhin—1868. This Bourbon from France is a well-behaved, thornless climber that produces masses of fragrant double cerise pink blooms all season. Can be trained to climb 8'–12' tall. It's disease resistant and tolerates more shade than most roses, although blooming will decrease. Zones 5–9.

ROSES

Climbers and ramblers

▶ ***Hardiness:*** Varies depending on variety. Most are hardy aboveground only in Zones 6 or 7, and need winter protection for the canes to survive further north.

▶ ***Size:*** Ranges from climbing miniatures only 4' tall to huge ramblers that grow up in trees or over houses 40' or more.

▶ ***Features:*** No rose actually climbs as a vine climbs. So-called climbing roses are actually shrubs that lean against a support with long, arching canes that grab on with their thorns. So all climbing roses need training by tying to get them to climb up. Ramblers are the biggest of the climbing roses; some develop trunks as thick as trees, and need very strong supports to climb on. All ramblers bloom only once each year, in late spring. Large-flowered climbers are generally climbing hybrid teas or floribundas, and a large number of some of the most popular roses in those groups have been developed into large-flowered climbing roses, for example, Climbing Peace and Climbing Iceberg.

▶ ***Uses:*** Train ramblers up into large, mature trees and on strong metal supports fixed to tall masonry walls. Train the taller climbers over arbors and pergolas and along fences, the shorter ones as pillar roses to climb trellises and lampposts, and on columns. Miniatures are beautiful trained up walls in small spaces, on fences and trellises, and on tripods in containers.

▶ ***Needs:*** Grow as for any rose, in full sun and rich, moist, well-drained soil high in organic matter. Feed and water regularly and protect from pests as needed. Deadheading will hasten reblooming in varieties that rebloom. In winters in Zone 6 and farther north, grow hardy varieties or protect canes from cold (see page 201).

Blaze Improved Climbing Rose—large brilliant red double flowers are produced in great quantities all along the canes of this climber, and all summer. Grows 12'–14' long, a classic growing on a white wooden fence. Roots are hardy Zones 5–10; protect canes in Zones 5 and 6.

Eden Climber—lots of old-fashioned blossoms packed with petals in a blend of light pink, cream, and yellow. Grows 12' high, ideal for pillars. Zones 6–10.

Fourth of July—blazing red and white striped blossoms are striking in big sprays all summer. Delicious apple and rose fragrance. Zones 6–11.

Iceberg Climbing Rose—all the great qualities of its famous floribunda parent, but unfortunately not as hardy. Grows 6'–12' tall. Zones 6–10.

Joseph's Coat Climbing Rose—flower colors include red, pink, orange, and yellow, and every combination in between. Grows 8'–12' tall, good on pillars and fences. Zones 7–10.

Mlle. Cécile Brünner Climbing Rose—the same summer-long silvery-pink sprays of small blossoms as its polyantha parent, but on a climber that can reach 20' high. Zones 7–10.

New Dawn—voted the most popular climber in the world by the World Rose Society. Fragrant double light pink blossoms are produced in great quantities all summer long with no deadheading required. Very vigorous and hardy, canes can reach 12'–20' long. Reportedly hardy aboveground in Zones 4–10.

Peace Climbing Rose—the climbing version of the revered hybrid tea, it blooms only on old wood and is not for cold climates. Zones 8–10.

Rainbow's End Climbing Rose—a climbing miniature with tiny multihued blossoms that open deep yellow with red edges and mature to deeper reds. Plants are covered in flowers all summer, but the flowers are not fragrant. Grows 8' tall. Zones 5–11.

Summer Wine—big single coral pink flowers with a light yellow eye appear all summer. Extremely fragrant. Canes grow 12' tall, good for growing on a pillar or arbor. Zones 6–10.

Rose Mallow
see Hibiscus, Perennial Hibiscus

Rose of Sharon
see Hibiscus

Rosemary
Rosmarinus officinalis

Evergreen shrub

Rosmarinus officinalis 'Arp'

▶ ***Hardiness:*** Zones 7–11
▶ ***Size:*** 5'–6' tall and wide as a perennial, 1'–2' as an annual
▶ ***Features:*** Lovely deep green, needled leaves with delicious pinelike flavor and aroma. Dainty white flowers in summer.
▶ ***Uses:*** In the herb bed, as a landscape plant, or as a container plant indoors and out. Often trained into topiary. Outstanding with lamb and chicken.
▶ ***Needs:*** Full sun. Poor to average well-drained soil. Drought tolerant. In Zones 7 and colder, does well as a container plant brought indoors each winter to a cool room with ample humidity in a sunny spot. Otherwise, plant established plants outdoors in spring (or also fall in Zones 8 and warmer). Root rot may be a problem if drainage is not good.
Choices: 'Benden Blue' has blue flowers.

Royal Palm
see Palms

Roystonea elata
see Palms: Royal Palm

Rubus spp.
see Raspberry

Rudbeckia spp.
see Black-Eyed Susan

Russian Cypress
see Cypresses

Russian Olive
Elaeagnus angustifolia

Deciduous tree

Elaeagnus angustifolia

▶ ***Hardiness:*** Zones 3–8
▶ ***Size:*** 12'–20' tall, 12'–20' wide
▶ ***Features:*** This tough tree takes cold, salt, wind, and dry soil. Foliage has silvery undersides and can't be beat for providing foliage contrast in the landscape. Trees add interest to areas enjoyed in the evening and tolerate troublesome areas. Tiny yellowish flowers are fragrant. Keep plants growing vigorously for best performance.
▶ ***Uses:*** Coastal areas, Xeriscaping, patio trees, street trees (withstands road salt), specimen use, natural areas, entries
▶ ***Needs:*** Plant in area with coastal winds, salty, poor soil, and drought. This tough tree can actually be planted in any kind of soil except soggy. Grow in full sun. Prune after flowering for a rounded shape. Or let trees grow naturally into irregular forms. Roots will not disturb paving.

Russian Sage
Perovskia atriplicifolia

Perennial

Perovskia atriplicifolia

▶**Hardiness:** Zones 3-9
▶**Size:** 3'-5' tall, 2'-4' wide
▶**Features:** Big, airy sprays of tiny blue-lavender blossoms are beautiful over one of the longest bloom seasons of any perennial—midsummer through fall. The foliage is silvery gray and delightfully aromatic (not edible).
▶**Uses:** In the mixed border with other late-summer and fall-blooming perennials. Especially beautiful with pale yellow and dusky pink colors, such as 'Moonbeam' coreopsis, purple coneflower, fountain grass, and Autumn Joy sedum.
▶**Needs:** Full sun. Average to sandy, loose, well-drained soil. Moderate moisture to drought tolerant. Plant established plants in spring. Fertilize lightly, if at all. Stake if needed. Doesn't need division. This plant is usually pest free.
▶**Choices:** Blue is the only color available.

Rutabaga
see Turnip

Sabal palmetto
see Palms: Cabbage Palm

Sage, Culinary
Salvia officinalis

Perennial herb

Salvia officinalis

▶**Hardiness:** Zones 4-8
▶**Size:** Grows 1'-2' tall and wide
▶**Features:** Lovely gray-green leaves with tall blue flower spikes.
▶**Uses:** In the herb bed or vegetable garden or as part of an edible landscape. Delicious with chicken, turkey, and in bread dressing and gravies, making it a prominent herb at Thanksgiving.
▶**Needs:** Full sun. Very well drained, average soil with moderate water. Plant established plants outdoors in spring or fall. Root rot may be a problem if drainage is not good.
▶**Choices:** Beautiful variegated types available, including 'Tricolor' with gray, white, and purple flowers and 'Aurea', gray with golden green.

Sage, Russian
see Russian Sage

SAGE; SALVIA
Salvia spp.

The ornamental sages are some of the showiest and most useful plants in the garden. Many are hardy evergreen perennials and shrubs used primarily in the mild climates of the West. Here we discuss some annuals and hardy perennials that are grown all over North America.

SAGE

Annual Red Salvia; Scarlet Sage
Salvia splendens

Annual

Salvia splendens 'Hotline'

▶**Size:** 6"-3' tall, 4"-2' wide
▶**Features:** Fire engine red; brilliant purple; neon rose; hot, glimmering salmon—the electric spikes of annual red salvia have come a long way in the past few years. This is one of the easiest annuals to grow for blooms summer to frost.
▶**Uses:** A classic bedding annual; excellent in containers.
▶**Needs:** Average, well-drained soil. Moisture varies depending on type. Plant in spring after any danger of frost has passed. Pinch off any flowers and top ½" of foliage section to promote branching. Mulch. Fertilize regularly, every 4 weeks, or work in a slow-release fertilizer. Trim spent flowers to promote longer bloom. Annual red salvia is prone to leaf spot, rust, aphids, and leafhoppers.
▶**Choices:** Usually red but also cream, purple, or salmon. Red sage *(S. splendens)* does well in full sun or light shade and needs ample water. 'Hotline' is especially heat and drought tolerant, Zones 2-9.

SAGE

Mealycup Sage; Annual Blue Salvia
Salvia farinacea

Annual

Salvia farinacea 'Victoria Blue'

▶**Size:** 1'-3' high, 4'-8' wide
▶**Features:** Bright blue spikes above gray-green leaves. More open and delicate in appearance than annual red salvia, but as tough and easy to grow. Blooms all summer.
▶**Uses:** A good bedding and container plant, this annual sage works better in the mixed flower border than do the brilliant tones of annual red salvia.
▶**Needs:** Full sun in Zones 2-6; light shade in hot summer areas in Zones 7-11. Average, well-drained soil. Moderate moisture. Likes warm weather and moderate to high humidity. Grow as an annual in Zones 2-7; as a perennial in Zones 8-11. Plant established plants in spring after all danger of frost has passed. Pinch off any flowers and top ½"-1" of foliage to promote much-needed branching. Mulch to conserve moisture. Fertilize occasionally, every 4-6 weeks, or work in a slow-release fertilizer in spring. It is prone to rust, aphids, and leafhoppers.
▶**Choices:** Flowers come in deep rich blues and silvery whites. 'Victoria Blue' is one of the best. 'Strata' has bicolored flowers.

SAGE

Perennial Blue Salvia
Salvia ×superba

Perennial

Salvia ×superba

▶ **Hardiness:** Zones 4–8
▶ **Size:** 1'–3' tall, 1'–2' wide
▶ **Features:** Blue or purple flowers on spikes appear over a long season from early to midsummer. Best known for its true blue cultivars that range from deep midnight blue to bright light blue. Gray-green foliage is attractive the rest of the season.
▶ **Uses:** Most effective planted in large groups in beds and borders. The dark blue 'Maynight' is spectacular in combination with shasta daisies and 'Moonshine' yarrow.
▶ **Needs:** Full sun to light shade, especially in Zones 7–8. Average to rich, well-drained soil. Needs moderate moisture until established, then drought tolerant. Plant established plants in spring or fall. Mulch. Fertilize every 6 weeks or so, or work in a slow-release fertilizer each spring. Keep spent flowers trimmed for several weeks of bloom. After first flush of bloom, cut plants back by one-third to one-half to promote yet further bloom. Tall types may need staking. It is usually pest and disease free. It seldom needs division but can be divided in spring for more plants.
▶ **Choices:** Color is usually deep blue or purple. 'May Night' is especially long-blooming. 'Blue Hill' has true blue flowers.

SAGE

Texas Sage
Salvia coccinea
Annual or perennial

Salvia coccinea 'Lady in Red'

▶ **Hardiness:** Zones 9–11
▶ **Size:** Grows up 3' tall and wide
▶ **Features:** This Texas native produces plenty of 1" scarlet-lipped flowers on top of pretty spires. It's very attractive to birds and butterflies. Loves heat.
▶ **Uses:** Flower beds and borders
▶ **Needs:** Fun sun in Zones 6 and colder; will also do well in light shade in warmer regions. Does best in poorer, drier soils but will thrive in a variety of conditions. Fertilize lightly; overfertilizing encourages legginess in an already naturally leggy plant. Cut back by one-third in late summer to encourage bushier, fuller growth. Drought tolerant and tolerates salt spray. Not attractive to deer. Will survive temperatures to 30°F/-1°C.

Sagina subulata 'Aurea'
see Scotch Moss

Sago Palm
see Palms

Saintpaulia spp.
see African Violet

Salix spp.
see Willows

Salvia spp.
see Sage

Sandwort, Mountain
Arenaria montana
Evergreen perennial

Arenaria montana

▶ **Hardiness:** Zones 3–6
▶ **Size:** 2"–6" tall, 10"–12" wide
▶ **Features:** Sandwort will grow in sunny spots and poor soil. Mounds of tiny, gray-green leaves last throughout the year. White flowers appear in mid- to late spring. Provide extra water during dry spells or plants will not survive. Slow to medium growth rate.
▶ **Uses:** Rock gardens, sunny niches, tucking into crevices of stone walls
▶ **Needs:** Plant in full sun in well-drained, yet moist soil. Prefers soils with low fertility. Plants are not drought tolerant and will need supplemental water during dry periods.
▶ **Choices:** Pink sandwort *(A. purpurascens)*—pink flowers; 2" tall by 8" wide; Zones 4–7.

Sansevieria trifasciata
see Snake Plant

Santolina; Lavender Cotton
Santolina chamaecyparissus
Perennial

Santolina chamaecyparissus

▶ **Hardiness:** Zones 6–9
▶ **Size:** 1'–2' tall, 2'–6' wide
▶ **Features:** Santolina is grown more for its beautiful silvery foliage than its small yellow flowers, but the two are lovely in combination. Low, spreading forms are valued for their use as miniature perennial hedges. Blooms all summer.
▶ **Uses:** As a textural accent in the front of the border, in rock gardens, as a low hedge or edging. A good choice for Xeriscaping.
▶ **Needs:** Full sun. Average to poor, sandy or gritty, well-drained soil. Very drought tolerant. Plant established plants in spring. Avoid fertilizing. Periodically shear off spent flowers with hedge clippers. Each year, in early spring, cut back to a few inches tall. After a few years, replace if plant becomes too woody. It is prone to root rot if site is too wet in winter.
▶ **Choices:** It has only yellow flowers. 'Compacta' is a useful dwarf form that needs less shearing to stay neat. 'Lemon Queen' has pale yellow flowers.

Sapphire Flower
see Amethyst Flower

Sarcococca
see Sweet Box

Savory
Satureja spp.
Annual herb

Satureja montana

▶Hardiness: Zones 4–9
▶Size: Grows 18" tall, 10" wide
▶Features: Pretty gray-green plant with pleasant peppery, thymelike flavor
▶Uses: In the herb or vegetable garden. Nice for edible landscaping. Good in containers. Snip fresh over bean, egg, chicken, and fish dishes. Also good in many soups as well as butters or vinegars.
▶Needs: Full sun. Average well-drained soil; neutral to slightly alkaline. Plant established plants in spring after danger of frost has passed.
▶Choices: Summer savory *(S. hortensis)* is the annual. Winter savory *(S. montana)* is a semievergreen perennial that is stronger and more reminiscent of pine than the annual type.

Scabiosa; Pincushion Flower

Scabiosa caucasica

Perennial

Scabiosa 'Butterfly Blue'

▶Hardiness: Zones 3–7
▶Size: 1'–2' tall, 6" 1' wide
▶Features: Pretty pink, blue, or white flowers on tall, wiry stems resemble pincushions. Taller forms make good cut flowers; the lower spreading forms are excellent perennial groundcovers for their extended bloom season from midsummer through fall. Attracts butterflies.
▶Uses: In the cutting garden or the mixed flower border; low-growing cultivars are beautiful massed as a groundcover in beds
▶Needs: Full sun in Zones 3–5; light shade in Zones 6–7. Rich, moist but well-drained soil. Abundant moisture. Plant established plants in spring. Mulch to conserve moisture. Fertilize occasionally, every 4–6 weeks, or work in a slow-release fertilizer at planting time. Trim spent flowers to promote several weeks of bloom. Slugs are sometimes a problem.
▶Choices: Flowers are lovely blues and lavenders; pinks and whites are also available. 'Butterfly Blue' is a 6"–12" dwarf and one of the most heat tolerant.

Scaevola aemula

see Fan Flower

Scallions

see Onions

Schefflera, Umbrella Tree

Schefflera spp. (formerly *Brassaia)*

Evergreen large shrub or small tree

Schefflera arboricola 'Green Gold'

▶Hardiness: Zones 10–11
▶Size: Grows up to 40' tall and 30' wide, depending on the type
▶Features: Attractive tropical-looking plants with deep green or variegated leaves divided into dramatic leaflets. Where ideally suited to the climate, it may produce dramatic 1' flower heads in yellowish-green aging to bronze, and purple-black fruits. In colder climates, used as a houseplant.
▶Uses: In frost-free zones, as a large shrub or small tree or specimen plant. Can also be worked into planting beds and borders, especially with other foliage plants such as ferns and shade-loving groundcovers. Excellent container plants.
▶Needs: Full sun near the coast and other moister conditions; light shade best in drier conditions. Rich, somewhat moist soil. Feed lightly throughout the year; a slow-release fertilizer is ideal. Thrives in high humidity. Mulch.
▶Choices: *S. actinophylla,* sometimes sold as *Brassaia actinophylla,* is commonly known as umbrella plant because of the way it holds its giant leaves. Grows 20'–40' tall. Invasive when well suited to the climate, as it is in Florida. *S. arboricola,* sometimes sold as *Heptapleurum arboricolum,* is commonly known as Hawaiian elf schefflera. It's easy to prune into a smaller plant. More shrublike than some other scheffleras. Grows 10'–20' tall.

Schizanthus; Poor Man's Orchid

Schizanthus pinnatus

Annual

Schizanthus pinnatus 'Royal Pierrot'

▶Size: 1'–2' tall, 12"–18" wide
▶Features: Small pink, rose, lavender, purple, or white flowers that resemble orchids have streaks and centers of various contrasting colors. Foliage is bright green and ferny, an attractive foil for the flowers. Best in cool weather of spring and fall, or through winter in frost-free areas. Mostly grown in mild-climate coastal areas.
▶Uses: Annual seasonal bedding or container plant in spring, or in fall and winter in frost-free zones.
▶Needs: Does not tolerate frost. Best in full sun but will melt out in heat of summer. Plant in moist, well-drained soil high in organic matter, and protect from wind. Start seeds 4 weeks ahead of planting out in early spring, or fall in mild-winter zones.

Schlumbergera spp.

see Christmas Cactus

Scilla spp.

see Squill

Scotch Heather

see Heather: Scotch

Scotch Moss, Irish Moss; Pearlwort

Sagina subulata

Perennial groundcover

Sagina subulata

► ***Hardiness:*** Zones 3-9
► ***Size:*** Grows 1" tall and spreads indefinitely over time
► ***Features:*** Although not a true moss, this plant looks like one with its velvety green carpet of tiny leaves that form low mats. It covers itself in tiny white flowers in spring. Perfect as a low-traffic groundcover or in between paving stones.
► ***Uses:*** As a groundcover
► ***Needs:*** Full sun in Zones 5 and cooler; light shade in warmer regions. Prefers rich, moist, fertile soil. Work in plenty of compost at planting time. Plant in spring or fall 6" apart. Be diligent in keeping weeded; once weeds take hold they can be very difficult to pry out of the tightly matted leaves. Can self-sow and become slightly invasive. Tends to start "hummocking" in the center over time. If this happens, cut out the overly tall portion in the center and smooth it flat. Replant with portions of the shorter moss off to the side.
► ***Choices:*** Garden centers list Irish and Scotch moss almost interchangeably. The golden-green versions of either are more tolerant of sun and heat. 'Aurea', with bright yellow-green foliage, is one of the most widely available.

Sea Grape

Coccoloba uvifera

Evergreen shrub

Coccoloba uvifera

► ***Hardiness:*** Zones 10-11
► ***Size:*** 20'-30' in all directions
► ***Features:*** Sea grape is the perfect choice for coastal landscapes. Picturesque twisting stems and large rounded leaves thrive in tough conditions. White, fragrant flowers develop into purple grapelike fruit that is both ornamental and edible. Medium growth rate. Withstands wind and salt spray. Needs little water once established.
► ***Uses:*** Seaside landscapes, hedges, windbreaks, adding shade, coarse-textured accents, Xeriscaping
► ***Needs:*** Plant in well-drained, sandy soil and full sun. Sea grape is an ideal seaside tree, standing up easily to salt spray and wind. Water new plants regularly to help establish. Plants rarely need extra water after that.

Sea Holly

Eryngium spp.

Perennial

Eryngium ×oliverianum

► ***Hardiness:*** Zones 2-8, depending on type
► ***Size:*** 2'-7' tall, depending on type
► ***Features:*** Blooms midsummer to frost.
► ***Uses:*** Middle of border, textural effect, dried for arrangements
► ***Needs:*** Poor, dry, sandy soil; thrives on drought and seashore conditions. Plant established plants in spring. Once mature, sea holly dislikes transplanting. Avoid fertilizing; plants may flop in soil that is too rich. If necessary, stake. Sea holly is prone to root rot in wet sites, especially if wet over the winter. Sooty mold is a problem in humid conditions.
► ***Choices:*** Amethyst sea holly, *E. amethystinum,* is the most cold hardy, thriving in Zones 2-8. Giant sea holly, *E. pandanifolium,* grows 6'-7' tall and 4' wide (Zones 8-10).

Sea Lavender

see Statice

Sea Thrift; Thrift

Armeria maritima

Evergreen perennial

Armeria maritima 'Dusseldorf Pride'

► ***Hardiness:*** Zones 3-8
► ***Size:*** 3"-8" tall, 10"-12" wide
► ***Features:*** Sea thrift thrives by the sea as well as in any garden that has plenty of sunshine and sandy soil. This grasslike evergreen features bright pink flowers during hot months. Flowering stems rise above the foliage. Foliage grows in grasslike tufts. Lollipoplike flowers appear in late spring. Tolerates poor, dry, sandy soil conditions. Slow to medium growth rate.
► ***Uses:*** Coastal areas, rock gardens, edging, planting beds
► ***Needs:*** Full sun in Zones 4-5; light shade in Zones 6-8. Well-drained, sandy soil and moderate moisture. Plant established plants in spring or fall. Mulch to keep soil moist. Fertilize infrequently, if at all. Keep spent flowers trimmed for longest bloom time. Plant in full sun and well-drained soil, including sand. Afternoon shade in hot regions. Divide every few years in spring or autumn when centers begin to die out and flowering is reduced.
► ***Choices:*** 'Alba'—white flowers, 6" tall; 'Dusseldorf Pride'—rose-pink blooms; 'Laucheana'—rose-pink blooms, 4"-6".

Sedge, Variegated Japanese

Carex morrowii 'Variegata'

Evergreen perennial

Carex morrowii 'Variegata'

▶ ***Hardiness:*** Zones 6–9
▶ ***Size:*** 18"–20" tall, 12" wide
▶ ***Features:*** Cream and green weeping foliage sways in the slightest breeze, bringing movement to the garden. The fine texture and bright color of variegated Japanese sedge contrasts nicely with the larger, dark green leaves of many shrubs. Flower spikes emerge in late spring. Rapid growth rate.
▶ ***Uses:*** Planting along walkways, on hillsides, or in front of bigger, dark green shrubs. Plant in groups of three or more for best effect.
▶ ***Needs:*** Plant in well-drained, fertile, moist soil in full sun or partial shade. Remove dead leaves during the growing season.
▶ ***Choices:*** 'Fisher'—cream-striped, cream-edged leaves.

Sedum morganianum

see Cactus and Succulents: Burro's Tail

SEDUMS; STONECROPS

Sedum spp.

Sedum kamtschaticum 'Weihenstephaner Gold'

There are hundreds of different sedums, ranging from low evergreen mat-forming plants with tiny succulent leaves to tall perennials with showy flowers in late summer. Each has its own needs, but generally they do well in full sun, appreciating light shade in hot summer climates (Zones 8–11). They do especially well in rock gardens, needing average to poor, sandy, well-drained soil, doing best with moderate moisture but tolerating drought well. Plant established plants in spring or fall. Avoid fertilizing. Trim spent flowers. Usually pest and disease free.

SEDUMS

Dragon's Blood Sedum

Sedum spurium 'Dragon's Blood'

Perennial

Sedum spurium 'Dragon's Blood'

▶ ***Hardiness:*** Zones 3–8
▶ ***Size:*** 2"–6" tall, 12"–18" wide
▶ ***Features:*** Red blooms appear in the heat of summer on this sedum and last into autumn. Foliage has reddish-bronze color. Plants grow quickly in poor, dry soil and in blazing sun. Spreads well, especially in northern gardens. It can be invasive in formal plantings. Divide anytime during the growing season.
▶ ***Uses:*** Filling in hot, dry spots where nothing else will grow; rock gardens; arid landscapes; sunny slopes; xeriscaping; edging beds; patios or walkways; containers; stone walls and crevices
▶ ***Needs:*** Plant in poor, dry soils that drain well; plants won't tolerate damp conditions. Grow in full sun. Plants are drought tolerant and pest resistant.

SEDUMS

Goldmoss

Sedum acre

Evergreen perennial

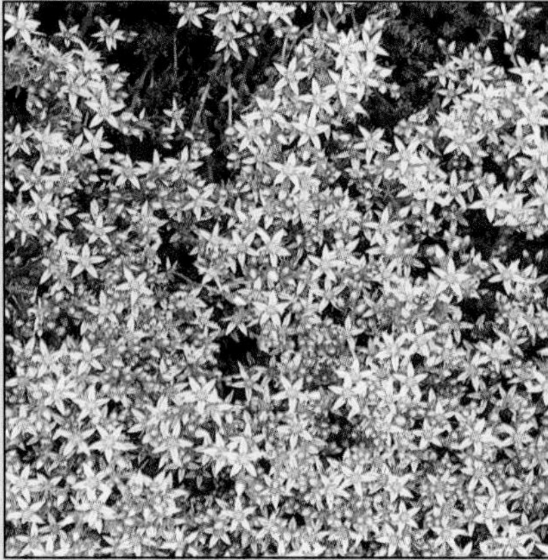

Sedum acre

▶ ***Hardiness:*** Zones 4–9
▶ ***Size:*** 2"–4" tall, 24"–36" wide
▶ ***Features:*** Here's a fast-growing groundcover that grows well in hot pockets or on barren slopes to form a low creeping mat of tiny starlike yellow-green flowers all summer. It may be sold as stonecrop sedum.
▶ ***Uses:*** Ditches, rock gardens, crevices in paving or walls, parking areas, growing beside steps, cascading over retaining walls, filling in hot, dry areas, confined spaces, perennial gardens, containers
▶ ***Needs:*** Grow in full sun in soil that's well drained; slightly alkaline soil is best. Adapts to poor, dry locations. Tolerates drought and reflected heat.

SEDUMS

Showy Stonecrop

Sedum spectabile, syn. *Hylotelephium*

Perennial

Sedum (Hylotelephium) 'Autumn Joy'

▶ **Hardiness:** Zones 3-10
▶ **Size:** 12"-18" tall, 18"-24" wide
▶ **Features:** Here's a plant that loves poor, dry soil—even rocky or sandy soil. Grow stonecrop in hot spots to enjoy thick foliage and clusters of late flowers. Butterflies are an added bonus. Support elongated stems of plants growing in partial shade. Medium to rapid growth rate. Blooms in late summer and fall. Grows with little water; drought tolerant. Thick, fleshy leaves add coarse texture.
▶ **Uses:** Rock gardens, arid landscapes, xeriscaping, slopes, entries, adding to the front of planting beds
▶ **Needs:** Plant in poor, dry soils that drain well; plants won't tolerate damp conditions. Grow in full sun. Divide plants in fall when clumps grow from outer edges instead of the center. Cut plants back in June for smaller plants with additional bloom and stems that don't flop over.

Sempervivum tectorum
see Cactus and Succulents: Hen and Chicks

Senecio cineraria
see Dusty Miller

Senegal Date Palm
see Palms

SERVICEBERRIES; JUNEBERRY; SHADBUSH
Amelanchier spp.

Serviceberries include a range of small understory trees and shrubs as valuable for their hardiness and adaptibility as for their multiple-season beauty. The tree forms, especially downy serviceberry *Amelanchier arborea),* shadblow serviceberry *(Amelanchier canadensis),* and the hybrid serviceberry *Amelanchier ×grandiflora,* are elegant, refined plants with snowy white early spring flowers (before the foliage), red or black berries in midsummer that are beloved by birds (and tasty in jams and jellies), and outstanding fall color.

SERVICEBERRIES

Allegheny Serviceberry
Amelanchier laevis

Deciduous tree

Amelanchier laevis

▶ **Hardiness:** Zones 4-8
▶ **Size:** 15'-25' tall, 15'-25' wide
▶ **Features:** This small, shrubby tree boasts white flowers followed by bronze leaves in spring. Foliage is green in summer and changes to a brilliant orange-red in fall. Sweet, blue-black berries attract birds. You can grow Allegheny serviceberry in damp soil. Medium growth rate.
▶ **Uses:** Small specimen tree, woodland gardens, naturalized areas, fall color, waterside locations, areas with wet soils
▶ **Needs:** Grow this tree in moist soil that's fertile and acidic. Wet, boggy soils are ideal. Provide a location with full sun or partial shade.

SERVICEBERRIES

Downy Serviceberry
Amelanchier arborea

Deciduous tree

Amelanchier arborea

▶ **Hardiness:** Zones 4-9
▶ **Size:** 15'-25' tall, 20'-30' wide
▶ **Features:** This easy-care tree goes on display three out of four seasons. Spring brings saucer-shape white flowers, summer brings purple-black berries, and fall brings golden yellow to dusky red foliage. Berries can stain paving but the birds usually take care of the fruit before that becomes a problem. Best used at the edges of woodlands or in naturalized settings. May be sold as juneberry. Medium growth rate.
▶ **Uses:** Planting along edges of woods, natural areas, small yards, side yards, perennial beds or near evergreens, accent, specimen use, use as a single or multistemmed small tree, attracting birds
▶ **Needs:** Plant in fertile, acidic soil that's moist but well drained. Tolerates a variety of soil conditions. Grow in full sun or partial shade. Little or no pruning is required.

SERVICEBERRIES

Serviceberry
Amelanchier alnifolia

Deciduous flowering shrub

Amelanchier alnifolia

▶ **Hardiness:** Zones 3-8
▶ **Size:** 8'-12' tall and wide
▶ **Features:** Choose serviceberry for beautiful spring flowers that blanket the bush with white stars in early spring. Plants in flower are especially showy when planted against an evergreen hedge. Bluish-purple fruit ripens in midsummer and is attractive to birds as well as humans. Rounded green leaves turn brilliant red and yellow in autumn. Once serviceberry is planted, it's basically carefree. Fallen fruit can stain paving surfaces, so it is best to keep this shrub away from patios, driveways, and walkways. Medium growth rate.
▶ **Uses:** Specimen, hedges, woodland areas, planting near ponds and streams, shrub borders, attracting birds
▶ **Needs:** Plant in full sun or partial shade in moist, well-drained, fertile soil. Will tolerate drier locations as well. Shrubs will grow in either acidic or alkaline soil. This shrub rarely requires pruning.
▶ **Choices:** 'Regent'—compact shrub with sweet fruit and attractive foliage. Grows 4' to 6' tall, spreads 12' wide.

SERVICEBERRIES

Shadblow Serviceberry

Amelanchier canadensis

Deciduous tree or shrub

Amelanchier canadensis

►***Hardiness:*** Zones 3–8
►***Size:*** 15'–20' tall, 8'–10' wide
►***Features:*** The wet, boggy soils found beside ponds and streams are ideal for growing this pretty little tree. Spring brings a cloud of white flowers that appear before the leaves; blue-black fruit attracts birds in summer; autumn brings beautifully colored yellow to orange to red foliage. Can be grown as a large shrub or multistemmed tree.
►***Uses:*** Specimen use, edges of woodlands, waterside areas, wet, boggy soils, seasonal accent, naturalized areas
►***Needs:*** Plant in acidic, fertile soil. Trees thrive in moist or boggy soil; they're native to swamps. Grow in full sun to partial shade. For an upright, multistemmed form, remove suckers from the base of plants to encourage several main trunks.
►***Choices:*** *A. ×grandiflora* (apple serviceberry)—young leaves purplish-red in fall; 25' tall; 30' wide.

Shadbush

see Serviceberries

Shallots

see Onions

Shasta Daisy

Leucanthemum ×superbum

Perennial

Leucanthemum ×superbum

►***Hardiness:*** Zones 4–9
►***Size:*** 6"–3' tall, 6"–2' wide, depending on variety
►***Features:*** These crisp white daisies on long, sturdy stems are as wonderful and long-lasting in the flower garden as they are in the vase. They bloom early summer to late summer.
►***Uses:*** A classic for the cottage garden and the mixed border, beautiful in combination with delphiniums and the blue forms of veronica. One of the best cut flowers, very long-lasting in the vase.
►***Needs:*** Full sun in most regions; part shade in hot, dry regions of Zones 8–9. Rich, well-drained, neutral to alkaline soil. Moderate moisture. Plant established plants in spring or fall. Mulch. Feed occasionally, every 6 weeks, or work a 9-month, slow-release fertilizer into the soil each spring. May need to stake. Keep spent flowers trimmed to ensure longer bloom. In Zones 4–5 protect in fall with more mulch. Plant dies if winter soil is too wet.
►***Choices:*** Flowers come in whites or creamy yellow. 'Becky' is one of the best cultivars with sturdy, heat-tolerant 3' plants that have a longer bloom season than any other Shasta daisy—starting earlier and finishing later. It is the best Shasta daisy for the South. 'Alaska' has large white flowers and grows to 20" tall. 'Lady' grows only 6"–8" inches and blooms early. 'Polaris' grows to 36". Some double and frilled types are also available.

Shrubby Cinquefoil

see Potentilla

Siberian Iris

see Iris

Silver-Edge Goutweed

see Bishop's Weed

Silver Lace Vine

Polygonum aubertii

Deciduous flowering vine

Polygonum aubertii

►***Hardiness:*** Zones 4–9
►***Size:*** 25'–35' in all directions
►***Features:*** Grow this quick climber in any kind of soil to cover almost anything. Blankets of foamy white blooms appear mid- to late summer. This vine can be hard to remove—be sure to plant it where you want it to be. Dense foliage provides quick screening. Grows in sun or shade.
►***Uses:*** Coastal areas, xeriscaping, dry shade, screening, privacy, growing on fences or arbors
►***Needs:*** Plant in any kind of soil, including poor and dry. Grow in sun or shade. Plant vines near well-anchored supports. Prune in late winter or early spring to control growth.

Silver Vase Plant

see Bromeliads: Silver Vase Plant

Silverleaf; Silverado Sage

see Texas Ranger

Sinningia speciosa

see Gloxinia

Skimmia, Japanese

Skimmia japonica

Evergreen shrub

Skimmia japonica

►***Hardiness:*** Zones 6–9
►***Size:*** 3'–4' tall, 3'–4' wide

S

Plant encyclopedia

▶ Features: Attractive flower buds open to showy, fragrant white blooms. Skimmia is a small evergreen shrub that thrives in shaded areas. Whether in full spring flower or covered with red berries in fall and winter, plants are a picturesque addition to the landscape. Plants will withstand air pollution. Provide a protected location, and plants can be grown in Zone 6. Slow growth rate.
▶ Uses: Fronts of planting beds, combining with shade-loving perennials, specimen, foundations, containers
▶ Needs: Plant in fertile, acidic soil that is both moist and well drained. Mix in peat moss or composted oak leaves at planting to improve acidity. Provide a shaded or partially shaded space. Separate male and female plants are needed for fruit production. Plant one male for every six females.
▶ Choices: 'Bronze Knight'—male plant with dark red flower buds. 'Fructo Albo'—green flower buds and white berries, 2' tall by 3' wide. 'Rubella'—a male plant with red flowers buds and fragrant white blooms.

Slender Lady Palm
see Palms

Slipper Orchid
see Orchids

Smoke Tree
Cotinus coggygria

Deciduous shrub or small tree

Cotinus coggygria 'Royal Purple'

▶ Hardiness: Zones 5–8
▶ Size: Grows 15' or more tall, 15' wide
▶ Features: This tree gets its name from the dramatic summer flower parts that resemble puffs of smoke. Leaves are bluish green to purple during summer. In the fall, leaves turn dramatic yellow, orange, or purplish red.
▶ Uses: As a specimen plant, in a mixed hedge, as a large back of border plant in beds and borders
▶ Needs: Full sun. Does well in a variety of soils, especially dry, rocky ones; best leaf color when slightly stressed. Drought tolerant once established. Although this plant is naturally multitrunked, it can be pruned as a small tree by selecting one trunk and removing others. Does not do well in wet soil.
▶ Choices: 'Royal Purple' has the deepest purple leaves, but 'Velvet Cloak' also has good color. 'Purpureus' starts out purple in spring and fades to green in summer.

Snake Plant
Sansevieria trifasciata

Tropical evergreen perennial

Sansevieria trifasciata 'Laurentii'

▶ Hardiness: Zones 10–11
▶ Size: Grows to 5' tall depending on the type and age of plant
▶ Features: Also called mother-in-law's tongue, this is one of the easiest houseplants to grow, withstanding a variety of conditions. It has tall, succulent, pointed foliage with white, yellow, or silver crossbanding and white or yellow edges.
▶ Uses: As a houseplant
▶ Needs: Bright light with some direct sun preferred but will grow in low light as well. Average household warmth and humidity is fine. Water lightly, allowing the soil to dry out somewhat between waterings. In winter, water only once a month or so. Overwatering is one of the few ways to kill snake plant. If the tall leaves start to flop, tie them together with soft, thick string or twine that won't rub the leaves.
▶ Choices: *S. cylindrica* can reach 5' feet tall but *S. trifasciata* 'Laurentii', the most commonly grown type, can top out at 3' in ideal conditions but usually grows to 1'–2' tall. 'Hahnii' grows only several inches tall with a more spreading habit.

Snapdragon
Antirrhinum majus

Annual

Antirrhinum majus 'Rocket Hybrid Pink'

▶ Size: 7"–3' tall, 6"–3' wide, depending on variety
▶ Features: Best known for their tall spikes of red, pink, yellow, and white in late spring to early summer and fall, snapdragons are increasingly available in many different forms, including low mounding dwarfs useful for bedding, and cascading forms for growing in hanging baskets. Some have bicolored blossoms, and some even have a delicious fruity fragrance. Blooms in winter (in mild climates), spring, or fall.
▶ Uses: Low-growing types make good winter bedding in mild-winter climates, otherwise annual seasonal bedding in spring, early summer, and fall. Good in the cutting garden; the taller types are outstanding cut flowers. Performs well in containers.
▶ Needs: Grow as an annual in Zones 2–8; as an annual or perennial in Zones 9–11. Full sun in Zones 2–9 and Pacific Northwest; light shade in Zones 9–11. Rich to average well-drained soil; moderate water. In Zones 2–8 plant established seedlings in spring for summer and fall color. In Zones 9–11, plant in fall or late winter for color winter through spring. Fertilize regularly, every 4 weeks, during flowering or work in a 9-month, slow-release fertilizer at planting time. Stake taller types. Deadhead for best production, but flowering usually slows or stops altogether when temperatures hit the high 80s°F/over 30°C. Cut back by two-thirds if plants get leggy.

Sneezeweed; Helen's Flower

Helenium autumnale

Perennial

Helenium autumnale

▶ ***Hardiness:*** Zones 3-7
▶ ***Size:*** 3'-5' tall
▶ ***Features:*** Blooms late summer through early autumn
▶ ***Uses:*** Borders, combined with asters or ornamental grasses
▶ ***Needs:*** Average, not fertile, moist to wet soil. Does best if kept evenly moist, but will tolerate drought once mature. Plant seedlings in spring. Fertilize rarely, if ever; overfertilizing makes these plants flop. Pinch back by about one-third in late spring to assure bushier, more sturdy plants. Stake as needed with taller types. Trim spent blooms for longest flowering. Divide every 2-3 years as needed. This plant is susceptible to rust, powdery mildew, and leaf spot.
▶ ***Choices:*** Flowers come in yellows, golds, reds, and burgundy.

Snowball Cactus

see Cactus and Succulents

Snowbell, Japanese

Styrax japonicus

Deciduous flowering tree

Styrax japonicus

▶ ***Hardiness:*** Zones 5-8
▶ ***Size:*** 20'-30' tall, 15'-25' wide
▶ ***Features:*** If you can find it, buy it. This sculptural tree features clusters of bell-like white flowers in May and June followed by red or yellow fall leaves. Leaves perch on the stems like butterflies and do not hide the pendulous blooms. Slender, smooth trunks have sculptural form. These trees should be planted more frequently, especially when soil conditions are appropriate. Also sold as Japanese snowdrop tree. Medium growth rate.
▶ ***Uses:*** Specimen tree, seasonal accents, hillsides, entries, beside patios or outdoor seating areas, planting beds, mixed borders
▶ ***Needs:*** Plant in fertile, acidic, well-drained soil; water regularly to keep soil moist. Add organic matter to the soil before planting. These will not tolerate extreme heat or drought. Grow in full sun or partial shade. Position plants in protected areas in cold climates. Prune to shape into small trees by removing shrubby branches from the base of plants.

Snowberry

Symphoricarpos albus

Deciduous flowering shrub

Symphoricarpos albus

▶ ***Hardiness:*** Zones 3-7
▶ ***Size:*** 3'-6' tall, 3'-6' wide
▶ ***Features:*** Snowberry earns its name from the abundance of white berries that cover its stems in fall. This rapid-growing shrub is tolerant of difficult growing conditions; use it in shady locations. Good for stabilizing steep banks and slopes, and in areas where air pollution is high.
▶ ***Uses:*** Informal landscapes, woodland areas, hillsides to stabilize soil, wildlife habitat plantings
▶ ***Needs:*** Snowberry grows in sun or shade, in any type of soil, and in areas where air pollution is high. Prune in early spring to stimulate flowering on new growth. Plants will sucker and spread.

Snow-in-Summer

Cerastium tomentosum

Evergreen perennial

Cerastium tomentosum

▶ ***Hardiness:*** Zones 3-7
▶ ***Size:*** 3"-6" tall, 8"-12" tall
▶ ***Features:*** Just as the name suggests, snowy white blossoms cover these plants from late spring through early summer. Silvery white leaves form mats of foliage. This groundcover thrives in dry soil. Plants may be short-lived in hot, humid areas. Divide plants to fill in thin patches and bare areas. Rapid growth rate.
▶ ***Uses:*** Dry soils, hillsides, banks, berms, raised planters, planting beds, xeriscaping, arid areas, entries, growing beside walkways or patios, sprawling over and out of walls
▶ ***Needs:*** Average to poor, sandy, well-drained soil. Moderate water. It is drought tolerant and dies out in hot, humid areas. Plant seedlings in spring in Zones 3-5; spring or fall in Zones 6-7. Cut back to foliage after flowering to keep plants neat and full. Fertilize little if at all. It can become invasive in sites where it's well suited and where soil is fertile. Usually pest and disease free, this plant may develop root rot in damper sites.
▶ ***Choices:*** It has white flowers only. 'Yo Yo' is less invasive than other cultivars.

Snow-on-the-Mountain

see Bishop's Weed

Society Garlic
Tulbaghia violacea

Perennial

Tulbaghia violacea

▶ ***Hardiness:*** Zones 8–11
▶ ***Size:*** 18"–2' tall, 6"–10" wide
▶ ***Features:*** Clusters of lavender tubular blooms on top of long, slender, wiry stems appear early summer and often keep blooming until fall. Silver-gray grassy foliage is attractive.
▶ ***Uses:*** Good in the rock garden or the front of the mixed border. Performs well in containers.
▶ ***Needs:*** Full sun to light shade. Average, moist, but well-drained soil. Best with moderate moisture but will tolerate some drought. Plant container-grown plants in spring or fall. Plant bulbs in spring 1"–2" deep. Trim spent blooms; otherwise this plant is low maintenance. It is bothered by few pests or diseases. In Zone 8, mulch for winter protection.
▶ ***Choices:*** Flowers are lavender. 'Silver Lace' has white-striped leaves.

Solanum jasminoides
see Potato Vine

Soleirolia soleirolii
see Baby's Tears

Solenostemum scutellarioides hybrids
see Coleus

Solidago hybrids
see Goldenrod

Song of India
see Dracaenas

Sophora japonica
see Pagoda Tree

Sorbus aucuparia
see Mountain Ash, European

Spathiphyllum wallisii
see Peace Lily

Speedwell
see Veronica

Spider Flower
Cleome hassleriana

Annual

Cleome hassleriana

▶ ***Size:*** 3'–5' tall, 3"–12" wide
▶ ***Features:*** Tall stems with circlets of spidery pink and white blooms appear midsummer and continue to frost. Plants self-sow into large stands, which is how this flower looks its best.
▶ ***Uses:*** Massed in large beds or as a temporary annual hedge. Good in loose, more natural-appearing cottage gardens, meadow gardens, and open areas where its self-sowing nature can be allowed free rein. Small thorns make it unpleasant to weed out.
▶ ***Needs:*** Full sun in Zones 2–5; full sun to part shade in Zones 6–11. Rich, moist soil. Ample water. Plant seedlings in spring after all danger of frost has passed. Fertilize sparingly to prevent from getting too tall. Stake when 1' tall, being careful around the small thorns. This plant often reseeds, sometimes problematically so. It is usually pest and disease free but is susceptible to rust, aphids, and leaf spot.
▶ ***Choices:*** Flowers are pinks, whites, roses, or lavender. 'Queen' is a popular variety.

Spider Plant
Chlorophytum comosum

Tropical perennial

Chlorophytum comosum 'Variegatum'

▶ ***Size:*** Grows several inches tall and wide with cascading stems that can extend up 3' long
▶ ***Features:*** Also called airplane plant, this plant's habit of throwing out cascading wiry stems that produce "babies," or plantlets, that will reroot readily if set atop soil. One of the most popular of houseplants, it has long, strappy, striped leaves.
▶ ***Uses:*** As a houseplant
▶ ***Needs:*** Bright to medium light. Allow soil to dry out slightly between waterings. However, if the plant is underwatered or watered irregularly, the tips of the leaves turn brown. Fertilize three times in summer. Average household temperatures and humidity fine, although it prefers temperatures on the cooler side, between 60°F/16°C to 70°F/21°C or so. This fast-growing plant quickly outgrows pots, so repot once or twice a year when the plant has tightly filled the pot.
▶ ***Choices:*** 'Vittatum' is the most commonly available spider plant variety with green leaves with white stripes down the center. 'Variegatum' has green leaves edged in white. 'Mandaianum' is more compact and has yellow-striped leaves.

Spiderwort
Tradescantia virginiana

Perennial

Tradescantia virginiana

▶ ***Hardiness:*** Zones 4–9
▶ ***Size:*** Grows up to 3' tall, 1' wide
▶ ***Features:*** This beautiful tiny three-petaled native flower comes in pink and red, but it's the strikingly deep or pale blue flowers in late spring that are the most distinctive. Has randomly arching, grasslike foliage. Sometimes sold as *T. andersoniana*. Some spiderworts reseed freely to the point of being a weed.
▶ ***Uses:*** Flower beds and borders, wildflower plantings
▶ ***Needs:*** Full sun to full shade. Prefers moist, even boglike conditions. Divide in early spring or fall. If desired, cut back after spring bloom. Foliage will recover well; plant may bloom a second time.

Spinach

Spinacia oleracea

Cool-season annual vegetable

Spinach 'Tyee'

► ***Hardiness:*** Zones 2–11
► ***Size:*** Grows several inches tall
► ***Features:*** Deep green leaves that are excellent to eat raw in salads or cooked
► ***Uses:*** In containers, in the vegetable garden
► ***Needs:*** Full sun to light shade, especially in hot-summer climates. Rich well-drained soil. Ample water. Does well in cold but not heat. Plant seeds directly in soil ½" deep in spring as soon as soil can be worked or 4–6 weeks before your region's last frost date. Can also be planted in fall in Zones 8 and warmer. Dislikes warm weather, will bolt (that is, send up a seed stalk and grow bitter) when temperatures are regularly above 80°F/27°C. Thin small clusters of plants to about 1" apart; use the thinnings in early salads. Keep soil moist. Mulch to conserve moisture. Fertilize every 2 weeks with a liquid fertilizer. Harvest by cutting all but 1" of the plants. They will regrow for 2–3 more harvests. Can also replant every 2 weeks to assure an ongoing supply. Withstands cold well; can be harvested even after covered in snow.
► ***Choices:*** 'Whale' and 'Indian Summer' are bolt resistant, making them good choices for spring planting. 'Bloomsdale Longstanding' is excellent to plant in early autumn for winter harvest.

Spiny Bear's Breeches

see Bear's Breeches, Spiny

SPIREAS

Spiraea spp.

This is a wide-ranging group of shrubs, perhaps best known for big, old-fashioned white-flowered forms such as bridalwreath, Vanhoutte, and baby's breath spireas that bloom for a couple of weeks in late spring or early summer. Increasingly, however, as more and more cultivars of the pink-flowering forms hit the market, they are commanding all the attention. Many are small in size, bloom over a long season, have outstanding foliage colors during the summer and turn to a riot of color in autumn.

SPIREAS

Anthony Waterer Spirea

Spiraea japonica 'Anthony Waterer'

Deciduous flowering shrub

Spiraea japonica 'Anthony Waterer'

► ***Hardiness:*** Zones 3–9
► ***Size:*** 3'–5' tall, 3'–5' wide
► ***Features:*** Not all spireas have white flowers in early spring. This one boasts dark pink blooms when spring is fading into summer. For durability nothing can take the place of spirea in home landscapes. May be sold as *S. ×bumalda* 'Anthony Waterer'. Medium to rapid growth rate. New foliage is reddish-purple. Durable and adaptable in any setting.
► ***Uses:*** Parking areas, entries, specimen plants, beside patios, background to summer flowerbeds, facing for taller shrubs, massed plantings, low hedges
► ***Needs:*** Plant in full sun to partial shade in any well-drained soil. Prune back in spring before new growth begins.
► ***Choices:*** 'Little Princess'—rounded shape, about 30" tall, pink flowers. 'Alpina'—12"–30" tall.

SPIREAS

Baby's Breath Spirea

Spiraea thunbergii

Deciduous flowering shrub

Spiraea thunbergii

► ***Hardiness:*** Zones 2–8
► ***Size:*** 3'–5' tall, 3'–5' wide
► ***Features:*** Bid goodbye to winter and usher in spring. This is the first spirea to bloom, and it shows delicate white flowers covering loosely spreading arching branches. Yellowish-green leaves turn orange-red in fall. Rapid growth rate.
► ***Uses:*** Entries, accent plants, informal hedges, beside patios, as a background to beds of spring-blooming bulbs
► ***Needs:*** Plant in full sun to partial shade in soil that's moderately fertile and doesn't stay very wet. Give plants room to grow. Prune as needed, but maintain naturally arching form.
► ***Choices:*** 'Compacta'—grows 2'–4' tall.

SPIREAS

Bridalwreath Spirea

Spiraea prunifolia

Deciduous flowering shrub

Spiraea prunifolia

▶ ***Hardiness:*** Zones 5-8
▶ ***Size:*** 5'-7' tall, 4'-6' wide
▶ ***Features:*** Little buttonlike white flowers cover the arching branches early each spring. This is a perfect backdrop for spring flowering bulbs. Shiny dark green foliage turns orange-red in fall. Best used in informal areas. Rapid growth rate.
▶ ***Uses:*** Arching branches form informal hedges, entries, specimen plants, background to spring flowerbeds
▶ ***Needs:*** Plant in full sun to partial shade in soil that's moderately fertile and doesn't stay wet. Prune with a light hand; over-pruning spoils the naturally arching form. Give plants room to grow.

SPIREAS

Limemound Spirea

Spiraea japonica 'Limemound'

Deciduous flowering shrub

Spiraea japonica 'Limemound'

▶ ***Hardiness:*** Zones 4-9
▶ ***Size:*** 2'-3' tall, 2'-3' wide
▶ ***Features:*** True to its name, limemound spirea is a little lump of bright, lime-green foliage. Tiny pink blooms cover plants in late spring and leaves turn bright orange in fall. Plants provide interest year-round. If desired, prune plants back in the spring before new growth begins. Rapid growth rate. Low-growing, low-maintenance shrub.
▶ ***Uses:*** Entries, parking areas, accents, or the front layer of shrub beds
▶ ***Needs:*** Plant in full sun and well-drained soil. No pruning is required, but plants can be pruned off near the ground in late winter or spring to encourage dense, compact plants.
▶ ***Choices:*** 'Golden Princess'—golden yellow leaves; 'Gold Mound'—heat tolerant, 30"-40" tall, pink flowers.

SPIREAS

Shibori Spirea

Spiraea japonica 'Shibori'

Deciduous flowering shrub

Spiraea japonica 'Shibori'

▶ ***Hardiness:*** Zones 4-8
▶ ***Size:*** 3'-4' tall, 3'-4' wide
▶ ***Features:*** Can't decide between pink or white flowers? This spirea blooms in both colors at the same time. Like all spireas, shibori is adaptable for a variety of uses in the home landscape. Medium growth rate.
▶ ***Uses:*** Entries, groups behind flowerbeds, specimen plants, beside patios and low decks, as low hedges
▶ ***Needs:*** Blooms best in sun but also does well in partial shade. Requires well-drained soil; it will not tolerate wet sites. Prune spirea in spring before new growth begins.

SPIREAS

Vanhoutte Spirea

Spiraea ×vanhouttei

Deciduous flowering shrub

Spiraea ×vanhouttei

▶ ***Hardiness:*** Zones 3-8
▶ ***Size:*** 6'-8' tall, 10'-12' wide
▶ ***Features:*** The flowers of Vanhoutte spirea look like tiny white bouquets in late spring and early summer. This shrub is easy to grow no matter where you put it. Not for small areas. Rapid growth rate.
▶ ***Uses:*** Entry areas, informal hedges, specimen plants, as a background to spring flowerbeds
▶ ***Needs:*** Plant in full sun to partial shade in soil that's moderately fertile and doesn't stay wet. Blooms best in sun. Set it where you have room for a big, arching shrub. Plants are not a choice for formal areas.

Spotted Dead Nettle

see Dead Nettle, Spotted

Sprengeri Fern

see Asparagus Fern

Spring Cinquefoil

Potentilla neumanniana

Perennial

Potentilla neumanniana

►***Hardiness:*** Zones 4–8
►***Size:*** 2"–4" tall, 8"–12" wide
►***Features:*** Spring cinquefoil thrives in dry, neglected areas. Vigorous growth forms a dense cover that reduces weed growth. Yellow flowers bloom nearly nonstop during warm summer months. Divide and plant where you want its yellow blooms. Medium to rapid growth rate.
►***Uses:*** Xeriscaping, rock gardens, slopes, edging planting beds, dry banks, rock walls
►***Needs:*** Spring cinquefoil will grow in soil that's rich or poor, even rocky, as long as it's dry. Full sun yields best flowering. Prune after blooms fade to reduce invasive tendencies. Divide in spring or fall.

Spring Heath
see Heath

SPRUCES
Picea spp.

Spruces are among the hardiest conifers around, excellent for northern gardens. They grow slowly and last a long time in the landscape. Some have a narrow conical form; others are known for their intense blue foliage.

SPRUCES

Alberta Spruce, Dwarf
Picea glauca 'Conica'

Evergreen shrub

Picea glauca 'Conica'

►***Hardiness:*** Zones 3–8
►***Size:*** 5'–8' tall, 6'–12' wide
►***Features:*** If you want a topiary but don't have time to train one, this is the plant for you. Slow-growing dwarf shrubs resemble tidy, miniature trees. These little shrubs often stay as small as 2'–3' tall for many years.
►***Uses:*** Single specimens or matched pairs; anchoring corners of flowerbeds; formal gardens; entries; courtyards; beside walkways, gates, and patios; growing in containers or confined spaces
►***Needs:*** Plant in neutral to acidic soil that's moist but well drained. Grow in full sun or partial shade. Provide regular watering in hot areas. If growing in containers, make sure pots drain well. Rarely needs pruning; cut stray branches on occasion to maintain shape.

SPRUCES

Bird's Nest Spruce
Picea abies 'Nidiformis'

Evergreen shrub

Picea abies 'Nidiformis'

►***Hardiness:*** Zones 2–7
►***Size:*** 2'–3' tall, 2'–3' wide
►***Features:*** Bird's nest spruce is an excellent plant for small gardens. Its slow growth rate and short stature (spreading more out than up) make it a natural choice for planting in areas where you do not want to block views. Plant this low-growing shrub and then forget about it. It's really that easy. Interesting plant form creates a living "nest." Tolerates cool climates and moist soils.
►***Uses:*** Specimen use, mass plantings, growing along walkways and drives, rock gardens, perennial borders
►***Needs:*** Plant in full sun in moist, well-drained soil. Spruces do poorly in polluted, dry conditions. Prune to remove damaged wood or to shape the shrub.

SPRUCES

Colorado Blue Spruce
Picea pungens glauca

Evergreen tree

Picea pungens 'Glauca'

►***Hardiness:*** Zones 2–7
►***Size:*** 30'–60' tall, 10'–20' wide
►***Features:*** The blue foliage color of a Colorado blue spruce is attractive year-round. The degree of blueness can vary from tree to tree. Compare the colors and select the trees that fit your needs. Blue tree color can conflict with house colors. Select the color appropriately or plant trees away from the house. Colorado blue spruce has dense branches that extend to the ground and produces 2"–4" long cones. Slow growth rate.
►***Uses:*** Large specimen, winter interest, windbreaks, grouping beside long driveways or in the corners of large yards, screening, sheltering birds
►***Needs:*** Grow in full sun. Trees grow best in rich, moist soil. They will tolerate dry soil conditions, and accept a wide range of soil conditions.
►***Choices:*** 'Koster'—silvery foliage. 'Hoopsii'—blue-white needles; dense, pyramidal form.

SPRUCES

Norway Spruce
Picea abies

Evergreen tree

Picea abies

►***Hardiness:*** Zones 2–7
►***Size:*** 40'–60' tall, 25'–30' wide
►***Features:*** Spruces have the toughness and durability necessary to survive in colder climates. Harsh winds and below-zero temperatures are no problem for Norway spruce. Trees grow to be quite large, so give them plenty of room from the start. Big cones, 4"–6" long, persist on pendulous branches through winter. Its pyramidal shape adds formality to landscapes. Medium to rapid growth rate.
►***Uses:*** Windbreaks, background planting, large specimen, defining property lines, screening, large estates, sheltering birds
►***Needs:*** Plant in acidic soil that's moist but well drained. Water diligently during the early years of growth. After establishment, spruces can tolerate drier conditions. Clean air is necessary. Plants require little pruning. Grows best in cool climates.
►***Choices:*** 'Aurea'—yellow-green needles; 'Pendula'—weeping shrub.

SPRUCES

Dwarf Norway Spruce

Picea abies 'Pumila'

Evergreen shrub

Picea abies 'Pumila'

▶ ***Hardiness:*** Zones 3-8
▶ ***Size:*** 3'-4' tall, 4'-6' wide
▶ ***Features:*** Dwarf Norway spruce is a cold-hardy shrub that tolerates severe winters and has a broad, rounded form that looks great even under snow. Grow this evergreen where you need a plant with year-round presence. Medium to rapid growth rate. Its broad, compact form rarely needs pruning.
▶ ***Uses:*** Foundation planting, hedges, background use, planting in shrub beds, winter interest, entries, corners of porches, patios, or low decks
▶ ***Needs:*** Plant in sandy, acidic soil that's moist but well drained. Grow in full sun. This plant is cold tolerant and thrives where summers are cool.

SPRUCES

Red Spruce

Picea rubens

Evergreen tree

Picea rubens

▶ ***Hardiness:*** Zones 2-5
▶ ***Size:*** 60'-70' tall, 30'-40' wide
▶ ***Features:*** Choose red spruce when you want a tall, evergreen tree that is well adapted to the cold. The conical form, reddish-brown bark, and evergreen needlelike foliage on upturned branches are attractive year-round, especially in snow. Cones add ornamental interest. Medium growth rate.
▶ ***Uses:*** Adapted to high mountain areas, vertical accent, specimen, winter interest, sheltering birds, screening, providing evergreen background for deciduous shrubs and trees
▶ ***Needs:*** Plant in deep, well-drained, neutral to acidic soil. Grow in full sun to partial shade. Prune only as needed to shape. Allow lower branches to remain on the tree and maintain conical form. Does not tolerate air pollution well.

SPRUCES

Serbian Spruce

Picea omorika

Evergreen tree

Picea omorika

▶ ***Hardiness:*** Zones 4-7
▶ ***Size:*** 50'-70' tall, 10'-20' wide
▶ ***Features:*** Growing much taller than it does wide, this graceful spruce with a pyramidal shape and graceful outline stands like a spire in the landscape. Serbian spruce withstands a variety of soil types, pH levels, and air pollution. Branches droop down near the trunk and turn up slightly at the ends. Cones are about 2" long, bluish-black when young, ripening to a cinnamon brown color. Trees can reach heights of 100' or more with time. Slow growth rate.
▶ ***Uses:*** Tall, narrow specimen tree; mass plantings in large yards; winter interest
▶ ***Needs:*** Grow in full sun or partial shade. Plant in soil that is deep, rich, and moist but well drained. Acidic or alkaline soil conditions are fine. Protect from strong winds, especially in cold winter climates. Very adaptable; tolerates city air.

SPRUCES

White Spruce

Picea glauca

Evergreen tree

Picea glauca

▶ ***Hardiness:*** Zones 2-6
▶ ***Size:*** 40'-60' tall, 10'-20' wide
▶ ***Features:*** This tree withstands wind, heat, cold, shade, and drought—all the growing conditions found in the Plains states, where it thrives. Trees can tolerate overcrowding and transplant easily. The dense foliage of the white spruce stays green year-round, and its conical form adds formality in the yard. Cones are less than 2" long, green at first, then turning brown upon maturity.
▶ ***Uses:*** Windbreaks, large specimen trees, screening to add privacy or block poor views, tall hedges
▶ ***Needs:*** Plant in acidic soil that's moist but well drained. Water diligently during the early years of growth. After establishment, spruces can tolerate drier conditions. Clean air is necessary. Little pruning is needed. Grow in full sun or shade.

Spurge, Cushion

Euphorbia polychroma
(formerly *E. epithymoides)*

Perennial

Euphorbia polychroma

▶ **Hardiness:** Zones 4–8
▶ **Size:** 12"–18" tall, 12"–18" wide
▶ **Features:** Bright yellow flowers surround charteuse bracts in midspring on neat, mounded plants. The foliage turns beautiful shades of purple, red, yellow, and orange in the fall.
▶ **Uses:** Good at the front of the border or as an edging plant. Performs well in containers. Combine with spring-blooming bulbs, hardy geraniums, and blue plumbago for a brilliant spring, summer, and fall show.
▶ **Needs:** Full sun in Zones 4–6 and Pacific Northwest; part shade in Zones 7–8. Average to sandy, well-drained soil; moderate moisture but will tolerate drought; can be invasive in moist soils. Plant established plants in spring or fall. Mulch to conserve moisture. Fertilize occasionally. Usually there is no need to trim spent blooms. Divide only when plants become floppy after a few years. Plants are usually pest free.

Spurge, Cypress
Euphorbia cyparissias
Perennial

Euphorbia cyparissias

▶ **Hardiness:** Zones 4–8
▶ **Size:** 8"–16" tall and wide
▶ **Features:** This fast-growing groundcover can withstand anything but dense shade and wet, boggy soil. Sprucelike needles fill in gaps in the landscape quickly. Plants are bare in winter. Neat mounds of sea-green foliage are covered with yellow spring flowers. Avoid planting cypress spurge near flowerbeds. Underground roots enable this plant to spread into areas where you may not want it.
▶ **Uses:** Groundcover on hillsides, dry areas, raised planters, banks, large planting beds
▶ **Needs:** Plant in full sun or partial shade in well-drained soil. Tolerates dry, infertile growing conditions.
▶ **Choices:** 'Orange Man'—flowers and fall leaves both tinted orange.

Squash, Winter; Pumpkin
Cucurbita spp.
Warm-season annual

Winter Squash 'Festival'

▶ **Size:** Grows 1'–2' tall, 3'–10' wide, depending on the type
▶ **Features:** Hard-rind squashes that will store for months indoors, including pumpkin, butternut, acorn, hubbard, and turban. Need to be cooked before eating; rinds not edible.
▶ **Uses:** In the vegetable garden
▶ **Needs:** Full sun. Light shade tolerated well in hot-summer areas Zones 7 and warmer. Rich, well-drained soil with plenty of organic matter. If desired, for earliest harvests, you can start seeds indoors in spring 3–4 weeks before your region's last frost date. Otherwise, plant established plants or seeds (1" deep) in the garden 2 weeks after the frost date. Work in a spadeful or two of compost at planting time. Squashes and pumpkins need warm soil, so plant in raised beds or create hills about 4"–6" tall and 12"–18" round. Space most squash 3'–4' apart. Depending on the size of the pumpkin, space 4'–10' apart (check the packet or label). Mulch with newspapers topped with grass clippings or straw to keep soil moist and developing squash clean and dry. Keep soil evenly moist. Harvest before the first frost when skins are hard and stems are brown and dry. For longest storage, rinse with a solution of 1 part chlorine bleach and 10 parts water. Then lay on newspapers in the sun for 10 days (bring in if frost or rain threatens). Will store indoors for several months. Squash beetles are often a problem. Pick off by hand as soon as they are spotted. Can also use pyrethrum or another pesticide labeled for squash beetles.
▶ **Choices:** Hundreds of winter squash cultivars are available, but they are often sold merely by type. Look for compact or bush types to save space. Pumpkins have a long growing season, up to 120 days for giant pumpkins such as 'Big Max' or 'Atlantic Giant.' In Zones 6 and colder with shorter growing seasons, choose smaller, faster maturing types such as 'Jack Be Little' (95 days).

Squash, Summer; Zucchini
Cucurbita spp.
Warm-season annual

Summer Squash 'Summer Crookneck'

▶ **Size:** Grows 1' tall, 3'–4' wide
▶ **Features:** Tender-rind squashes that can be eaten raw or cooked; rinds are edible. Includes pattypan, straightneck, crookneck, zucchini.
▶ **Uses:** In the vegetable garden
▶ **Needs:** Full sun. Light shade tolerated well in hot-summer areas Zones 7 and warmer. Rich, well-drained soil with plenty of organic matter. If desired, for earliest harvests, you can start seeds indoors in spring 3–4 weeks before your region's last frost date. Otherwise, plant established plants or seeds (1" deep) in the garden 2 weeks after the frost date. Work in a spadeful or two of compost at planting time. Squashes need warm soil, so plant in raised beds or create hills about 4"–6" tall and 12"–18" round. Space most summer squash 3'–4' apart. Mulch with newspapers topped with grass clippings or straw to keep soil moist and developing squash clean and dry. Keep soil evenly moist.
Harvest while small, even baby sized, when summer squash are still at their most tender and not bitter. Avoid letting them get more than several inches long. Can pick with blossom still attached. Squash beetles often a problem. Pick off by hand as soon as they are spotted. Can also use pyrethrum or another pesticide labeled for squash beetles.
▶ **Choices:** Dozens of summer squash cultivars available, but they are often sold merely by type. Look for bush cultivars, which grow only a 1'–2' tall and wide.

Squill
Scilla spp.

Spring-blooming bulb

Scilla sibirica

▶ ***Hardiness:*** Zones 2-8
▶ ***Size:*** 6"-12" tall
▶ ***Features:*** Such pretty little flowers on elegantly arching stalks might deserve a prettier name. This is an early spring flowering bulb that displays many small blooms per plant. Flowers are typically blue, but some types bloom in white or pink.
▶ ***Uses:*** Plant in groups of 3-4 dozen
▶ ***Needs:*** Full sun or light shade. Rich, well-drained soil. Ample water while blooming; moderate water when it goes dormant in late spring. Plant in October in Zones 2-6 and November in Zones 7-8. Position 2"-3" deep. Avoid watering in summer. No fertilizer needed. Where well-situated, it usually spreads. It is pest free.
▶ ***Choices:*** Siberian squill *(S. sibirica)* is the most commonly grown and hardy in Zones 2-7. Two-leaved squill *(S. bifolia)* grows 6" tall and has been grown in gardens since the 16th century. Cuban lily *(S. peruviana)* is hardy in Zones 4-8 and grows 10"-12" tall, blooming in late spring. It's good for warm climates.

St. Johnswort
Hypericum calycinum

Deciduous shrub used as groundcover

Hypericum calycinum

▶ ***Hardiness:*** Zones 5-9
▶ ***Size:*** 12"-18" tall and wide
▶ ***Features:*** St. Johnswort, also called Aaron's beard, produces bright yellow puffs of bloom in areas of the garden that get little sunlight, filling in bare spaces with layers of leaves. Plants spread quickly through stolons and can take over a planting bed.
▶ ***Uses:*** Filling in dry, shady areas; growing beneath trees; as a low layer in front of shrubs
▶ ***Needs:*** Plant in partial to dense shade in moist, rich, well-drained soil; tolerates drier conditions. Plant in spring or fall. Mulch to conserve moisture. Technically a shrub, this evergreen plant spreads low enough to serve as a groundcover. It spreads rapidly. In small gardens, divide plants every two to three years to keep in bounds. Each spring, cut back to ground to encourage good flowering. Plants are drought tolerant.

Stachys byzantina
see Lamb's Ears

Staghorn Sumac, Cut-leaf
Rhus typhina 'Laciniata'

Deciduous shrub

Rhus typhina 'Laciniata'

▶ ***Hardiness:*** Zones 3-8
▶ ***Size:*** 15'-25' tall, 15'-25' wide
▶ ***Features:*** For a surprisingly tropical look in cold climates, grow cut-leaf staghorn sumac. The fine-textured, deeply cut lacy leaves resemble fronds. This shrub will grow in any soil that isn't soggy, making this plant an excellent selection for problem areas. Use with care in landscape settings; its interesting texture can easily be overused. May be sold as 'Red Autumn Lace' because its dark green foliage turns orange-red in fall. Rusty-red fruit adds winter interest. Rapid growth rate.
▶ ***Uses:*** Seasonal accents, urban conditions, areas with poor soils, hillsides and banks, massing, naturalizing, waste areas, specimen use
▶ ***Needs:*** Plant in any soil that's well drained, from acidic to alkaline, poor to fertile. Plants decline in excessively wet soils. Grow in full sun. Tolerates pollution, reflected heat from paving, and seasonal heat and cold. Rejuvenate old plants by cutting to the ground in winter.

Statice; Sea Lavender
Limonium spp.

Perennial

Limonium latifolium

▶ ***Hardiness:*** Zones 2-11, depending on type
▶ ***Size:*** 2' tall and wide
▶ ***Features:*** Statice brings an airy mass of pale lavender blooms into the garden in mid- to late summer. This is a slow-growing, clump-forming plant with dark green leaves that turn red in autumn.
▶ ***Uses:*** Seaside plantings, bare patches, visual texture, pair with ornamental grasses, fall color, cut or dried flower arrangements
▶ ***Needs:*** Annual statice needs full sun; perennial will take some shade in Zones 8 and warmer. Sandy, well-drained soil. Somewhat drought tolerant but does best with even, moderate moisture. Plant established plants in spring after danger of frost has passed. Fertilize occasionally, every 6 weeks, or work in a slow-release fertilizer each spring. Stake tall types. Needs no division; propagate by digging up the small side rosettes that form at the plant's base.
▶ ***Choices:*** Annual statice (Zones 2-11) is ideal for drying. Perennials are sea lavender *L. latifolium* (Zones 3-9) and *L. perezii* (Zones 8-11).

Stephanotis floribunda
see Jasmines: Madagascar Jasmine

Stewartia, Japanese

Stewartia pseudocamellia

Deciduous flowering tree

Stewartia pseudocamellia

▶ ***Hardiness:*** Zones 5–7
▶ ***Size:*** 30'–40' tall, 20'–25' wide
▶ ***Features:*** This tree provides year-round interest in the landscape. Green spring and summer foliage; white camellialike blossoms in summer; excellent fall color in yellows, reds, and purples; and peeling bark for winter appeal make its slow growth worth the wait. Trees form an oval to pyramidal crown. Grows in the milder areas of Zone 5.
▶ ***Uses:*** Specimen use, seasonal accents, patio trees, entries, courtyards, small areas, planting in shrub or perennial beds, providing winter interest
▶ ***Needs:*** Plant in acidic soil that's moist but well drained. Add composted leaves or peat to the soil at planting time; fertilize with acid-loving plant food in spring. Grow in full sun or partial shade. Provide shade during the hottest part of the day in warm climates.

Stipa spp.

see Grasses, Ornamental: Feather Grass

Stock

Matthiola incana

Cool-season annual

Matthiola incana

▶ ***Size:*** Grows to 3' tall and 1' wide, depending on the type
▶ ***Features:*** The spicy-sweet scent of stock is the best reason to grow it. A large planting of these spired flowers, which come in nearly every color except blue and yellow, will perfume a corner of the garden on a sunny day, while a few added to a spring bouquet will fill a warm room with fragrance. Easy to grow as long as temperatures are cool.
▶ ***Uses:*** In flower beds or borders. Does especially well in pots.
▶ ***Needs:*** Full sun to light shade. Poor to average soil and moderate water. Plants will fail to bloom if temperatures are higher than 65°F/18°C. Plant established plants outdoors about one month before your region's last frost date; in the winter in Zones 9–11.
▶ ***Choices:*** Dwarf types grow 1' tall and wide. Good to use as bedding plants. Columnar types can grow 3' tall and 1' wide and are outstanding for cutting but often need staking and extended cool temperatures—5 months or more of temperatures at 65°F/18°C.

Stonecrop

see Sedums

Strawberry

Fragaria spp.

Berry-producing perennial

Strawberry 'Siskit'

▶ ***Hardiness:*** Zones 3–10: June-bearing; Zones 3–8: everbearing
▶ ***Size:*** Grows 6"–8" tall, 4"–6" wide
▶ ***Features:*** Delicious red berries in June and later, depending on the type
▶ ***Needs:*** Full sun to very light shade. All types thrive in rich, well-drained soil; consider raised beds filled with compost. Plants like moisture; water during dry spells. Choose from two main types: June-bearing (a heavy harvest in June) or everbearing (also called day-neutral, they provide a light harvest from June through September). In winter in cold regions, protect them with a thick layer of straw that covers tops. Remove in early spring. Mulch soil in summer. Grow by planting established plants in spring. Pinch off flowers for the first year to encourage strong roots. Keep well-watered and fertilize annually with a slow-release fertilizer in midspring. Renovate June-bearing patches annually by thinning or keeping paths between rows cleared with a tiller to keep at maximum production. Pull out everbearing types every third year and replant.

Strawberry, Pink Panda

Fragaria 'Pink Panda'

Perennial

Fragaria 'Pink Panda'

▶ ***Hardiness:*** Zones 3–9
▶ ***Size:*** 6"–8" tall, 8"–10" wide
▶ ***Features:*** If you have fertile, well-drained soil in partial shade, consider pink panda strawberry. Enjoy pink flowers, miniature berries, and spreading foliage. Plants spread by runners that root wherever they touch soil; plants need room to spread. Small, edible berries are sweet and tasty. Glossy green foliage forms a quick groundcover.
▶ ***Uses:*** Entries, planting beside patios and along walkways, containers
▶ ***Needs:*** Plant in full sun or partial shade in fertile, well-drained soil. Divide by digging up tiny rooted plants and clipping connecting stems. In spring, remove dead or winter-damaged leaves before new growth emerges. Mulch plants in cold winters to help keep them evergreen.

Strawberry, Alpine
Fragaria vesca
Perennial

Fragaria vesca

▶***Hardiness:*** Zones 3-9
▶***Size:*** 8"-12" tall, indefinite spread
▶***Features:*** Alpine strawberry, usually grown for its flavorful fruit, also makes a fine groundcover. Add it to herb gardens or window boxes for white flowers that appear in late spring and small, flavorful red fruit in late spring and summer. Plant where it has plenty of room to spread; this plant's rosettes of foliage spread quickly. When purchasing strawberry plants for their fruit, keep in mind that June-bearing plants produce a single crop of larger berries in the spring while everbearing plants produce two crops of smaller berries, one in the spring and another in late summer and fall.
▶***Uses:*** Filling in empty areas, shrub beds, planting beneath roses, confined spaces, natural areas, slopes, raised planters, berms, planting beside patios
▶***Needs:*** Plant in well-drained, fertile soil. Strawberries tolerate acidic soil but thrive in alkaline soil. Grow in full sun where summers are cool. Cover with mulch in late fall to prevent winter injury.

Strawflower
Helichrysum bracteatum
Annual

Helichrysum bracteatum 'Bikini Mix'

▶***Size:*** 1'-4' tall, 6"-10" wide
▶***Features:*** Orange, pink, red, white, bronze, and purple blooms have a dry, strawlike texture. Most often grown in the cutting garden for cutting and drying; some of the lower-growing varieties make good bedding plants for late-summer color. Blooms mid- through late summer.
▶***Uses:*** Excellent for drying to use in winter bouquets, the long-stemmed types need staking or they will flop, and are best grown in the cutting garden.
▶***Needs:*** Average to sandy, well-drained, alkaline soil. Light moisture; drought tolerant. Plant seedlings in spring after all danger of frost has passed. Fertilize little, if at all. This plant self-sows where conditions are favorable. It is prone to aster yellows virus and aphids.
▶***Choices:*** Flowers come in yellows, oranges, pinks, reds, white, bronzes, and purples. 'Bright Bikini Mix' is one of the most popular varieties, as are some of the pastel mixes.

Strelitzia spp.
see Bird-of-Paradise

Styrax japonicus
see Snowbell, Japanese

Succulents
see Cactus and Succulents

Sugarberry; Hackberry
Celtis laevigata
Deciduous tree

Celtis sinensis 'Green Cascade'

▶***Hardiness:*** Zones 5-9
▶***Size:*** 40'-60' tall, 40'-60' wide
▶***Features:*** This tree is tolerant of adverse conditions. It forms a broad canopy, and features smooth gray bark on massive limbs. It grows quickly even in compacted soil in urban landscapes. Proper pruning when trees are young prevents problems in old age. Avoid planting trees near sidewalks and drives since roots may buckle paving. Medium to rapid growth rate.
▶***Uses:*** Street and shade tree, urban landscapes, floodplains, compacted soils, large, open areas, damp or boggy locations
▶***Needs:*** Plant in full sun to partial shade. Thrives in soils that are wet, dry, sandy, or heavy clay. Tolerates compacted and alkaline soils, as well as urban conditions. Easily transplanted and grown.
▶***Choices:*** *C. occidentalis*—70' tall by 50' wide; Zones 2-9. *C. sinensis*—smooth bark, glossy leaves, orange fruit; Zones 6-9.

Sumac
see Staghorn Sumac

Summer Phlox
see Garden Phlox

Summersweet; Sweet Pepperbush
Clethra alnifolia
Deciduous flowering shrub

Clethra alnifolia 'Rosea'

▶***Hardiness:*** Zones 4-9
▶***Size:*** 4'-9' tall, 4'-6' wide
▶***Features:*** Lovely white flower spikes late in the summer when few other shrubs are blooming exude a warm, sweet fragrance redolent of honey, and they attract butterflies. And the fall foliage color is outstanding—a clear, brilliant yellow. This is a good choice for problem wet soils and partial shade, and some of the smaller dwarf cultivars are manageable even for the smaller garden.
▶***Uses:*** Shrub border, massed in larger beds
▶***Needs:*** Full sun to medium shade, especially in hot summer areas in Zones 7-9. Rich, moist to wet, acidic soil. Ample moisture. Plant established plants in spring or fall. Mulch 3"-4" deep to conserve moisture and keep soil cool. No need to fertilize in

most conditions. Slow to establish, but once it does, may need to dig up suckers to control spread. Blooms on new growth, so prune annually in mid- to late winter (before new growth begins or the plant will bleed sap). Cut out old or weak growth to base of plant. It is usually pest and disease free, but spider mites are a problem in dry conditions.
▶ ***Choices:*** Flowers are white or pink. 'Hummingbird' is a dwarf that grows 3' tall and 4' wide. 'Rosea' has pink flowers.

Sundrops; Sundrop Primrose
Oenothera spp.
Perennial

Oenothera macrocarpa

▶ ***Hardiness:*** 4-8
▶ ***Size:*** 12"-24" tall, 18"-24" wide
▶ ***Features:*** Big, bright yellow flowers like drops of sunshine on red-tinted foliage earn this plant its name. The blooms last a long time and appear over a long season from late spring to late summer. At the onset of cold weather, the basal rosette turns a nice maroon and remains attractive all winter. This is a good choice for difficult, hot, dry spots. This rapid grower spreads quickly to cover large areas.
▶ ***Uses:*** In the mixed border at entry areas, parking areas, in planting beds, rock gardens
▶ ***Needs:*** Plant in well-drained soil or poor, rocky sites. Full sun for flowering. Tolerates heat. Mulch in late fall in areas with cold winters. It can reseed prolifically; remove faded flowers for additional blooms and to control reseeding. Dig out excess plants annually. When blooming stops in late summer, shear plants back by one-half or cut plants back to their rosettes to encourage vegetative growth. Dig and divide in spring or fall every four or five years.
▶ ***Choices:*** 'Fireworks' is a popular new introduction of sundrops with bright red stems and red buds that open into yellow flowers. Flowering is profuse and effective all summer. Ozark sundrops (*O. macrocarpa*, formerly *O. missouriensis*) bears large, solitary lemon yellow flowers that individually last a long time. It prefers a moist (but well-drained) soil, but seems to languish in the heat and humidity of southern gardens. Zones 4-8. For a description of the pink and white *O. speciosa*, see Evening Primrose on page 371.

Sunflower, Annual
Helianthus annuus
Annual

Helianthus annuus

▶ ***Size:*** 2'-12' tall, 1'-3' wide, depending on variety
▶ ***Features:*** Most famous for those huge blooms on immensely tall stems, sunflowers come in a wide variety. Some are bushy dwarfs only 2' tall with lots of small blooms; others are lanky medium-size plants. The flowers can be single, double, or very double like a big pompom. And they can be golden yellow, lemon yellow, bronze, orange, and reddish brown. All are excellent for cutting and long-lasting in the vase. All are so easy to grow that they are excellent starter plants to introduce children to gardening. And all, alas, have relatively short bloom seasons over the height of summer. Blooms midsummer, late summer, or early autumn, depending on planting time.
▶ ***Uses:*** Mass small cultivars in flower beds or borders, tall types add appeal to vegetable and flower beds, along fences or as screens
▶ ***Needs:*** Average to poor, well-drained soil; moderate moisture. Plant seeds in spring directly in soil, or plant seedlings after all danger of frost has passed. Thin or transplant newly emerged seedlings to recommended spacing. Mulch. Fertilize lightly, if at all. Stake taller types. For a continuing supply of sunflowers, plant every 2 weeks until midsummer. This plant is prone to verticillium wilt, powdery mildew, and wilt.
▶ ***Choices:*** Flowers come in yellows, golds, oranges, burgundy, and creams. 'Italian White' is an elegant cream; 'Valentine' is long blooming; 'Sunspot' grows only 2'-3' tall; 'Soraya' needs no staking.

Sunflower, Perennial
Helianthus spp.
Perennial

Helianthus ×multiflorus

▶ ***Hardiness:*** Zones 4-9
▶ ***Size:*** 4'-8' tall, 3'-4' wide
▶ ***Features:*** Tall and lanky, this sunflower comes back every year to produce huge masses of golden yellow flowers with dark centers, late in the season when few other flowers are still blooming. Blooms late summer or early to late fall.
▶ ***Uses:*** At the rear of the border. Perhaps best in wildflower and native plant gardens since it has a tendency to spread.
▶ ***Needs:*** Rich, moist to well-drained soil. Adequate to ample moisture. Plant established plants in spring. Mulch to conserve moisture and prevent weeds. Fertilize occasionally, every 6 weeks, or work a 9-month slow-release fertilizer into the soil each spring. Trim spent flowers for longest bloom. Divide every 2-4 years as needed. This plant is prone to mildew, rust, and leaf spot.
▶ ***Choices:*** Flowers come in yellows and golds. *H. ×multiflorus* thrives in Zones 4-8. 'Lodden Gold' is especially nice variety. In the South choose swamp sunflower—*H. angustifolius*.

Sunflower, Mexican
see Mexican Sunflower

Surprise Lily
see Naked Ladies

Sutera cordata
see Bacopa

S

Plant encyclopedia

Swan River Daisy

Brachycome iberidifolia

Annual

Brachycome iberidifolia

▶ ***Size:*** 8"–18" tall, 8"–18" wide
▶ ***Features:*** Pale blue or lavender flowers with yellow centers are borne among feathery bright green leaves. The fine-textured foliage is attractive. Blooms late winter or early spring.
▶ ***Uses:*** Containers, hanging baskets, and windowboxes for early-season color
▶ ***Needs:*** Rich, well-drained soil. It needs moderate water but is somewhat drought tolerant once established. In Zones 2–8 plant established seedlings 3–4 weeks before last frost date. In Zones 9–11 plant in late fall or early winter for winter or early spring color. Mulch to conserve moisture and prevent weeds. Fertilize lightly, if at all. Shear by a few inches occasionally (every few weeks or so) to deadhead and promote further blooms. It will reseed in favorable climates. Plants fade when weather gets hot. In cooler regions cut back to a few inches for more blooms. This plant is sometimes prone to botrytis, aphids, and slugs.

Sweet Alyssum

Lobularia maritima

Annual

Lobularia maritima

▶ ***Size:*** 3'–1' tall, 8"–2' wide
▶ ***Features:*** Give this plant plenty of sun and well-drained soil and it's hard to beat for lots of reward for little effort. Puffy clouds of small white, pink, or lavender flowers smother these mounding, trailing plants with color so thick you can't see the foliage. Blooms during cool weather, although newer varieties tolerate more heat and continue blooming all summer.
▶ ***Uses:*** Excellent for edging, lovely growing between the cracks of flagstones set in sand or allowed to reseed in the front of the border. It's a good container plant too.
▶ ***Needs:*** Full sun in Zones 2–5; tolerates light shade in Zones 6–11. Average to poor, well-drained soil. Moderate moisture. Grow as an annual in Zones 2–9; as a perennial in Zones 10–11. Plant established seedlings in spring after all danger of frost has passed. Mulch. Fertilize lightly, every 4–6 weeks, or work in a slow-release fertilizer. This plant gets tall with sparse blooms when temperatures regularly hit the high 80s°F/29–32°C; cut back by about half to rejuvenate and promote further bloom. It reseeds readily in good conditions, but colors of new plants will be muddy. Downy mildew and caterpillars are sometimes a problem.
▶ ***Choices:*** Blooms come in white, purples, and roses.

Sweet Bay

see Bay

Sweet Box

Sarcococca humilis

Evergreen shrub

Sarcococca humilis

▶ ***Hardiness:*** Zones 6–9
▶ ***Size:*** Grows 18" tall, can spread to 6'–8'
▶ ***Features:*** This glossy broad-leaved evergreen grows only 18" tall but spreads readily. It appreciates a little shade and does well in lightly wooded areas under rhododendrons, azaleas, and other taller shrubs. In spring, it produces tiny white flowers that are intensely and sweetly fragrant.
▶ ***Uses:*** As a groundcover
▶ ***Needs:*** Full sun to light shade. Rich, moist soil. (Work in plenty of compost at planting time.) Space 2'–3' apart. Can burn in intense winter sun, so best to plant under other evergreens or on the north side of a building.

Sweet Olive; Tea Olive

Osmanthus fragrans

Broadleaf evergreen shrub or tree

Osmanthus fragrans

▶ ***Hardiness:*** Zones 8–9
▶ ***Size:*** Can reach 25' high and wide with age in warmer zones. Often maintained at 6'–10' tall.
▶ ***Features:*** The leathery lustrous dark green leaves of this shrub are beautiful all year and reason enough to grow it, but the real attraction is the heavenly fragrance exuded by its small white flowers nearly all year long (most abundant in spring and fall).
▶ ***Uses:*** In the shrub border or as a small specimen tree. Plant it near windows and patios where its fragrance can be appreciated.
▶ ***Needs:*** Easy to grow and tolerant of most garden soils from acidic to alkaline, moist to dry. Best in full sun. Best when left unpruned and allowed to develop its natural form.

Sweet Pea

Lathyrus odoratus

Annual

Lathyrus odoratus

► ***Size:*** 1'-8' tall, 1'-2' wide

► ***Features:*** This small climber is excellent in the cool weather of spring, sporting showy pink, white, red, and lavender blossoms from midspring until the summer heats up. Some varieties are delightfully fragrant. In mild climates it is often grown with stocks for winter color and bouquets. Blooms in winter, spring, or summer in cool climates.

► ***Uses:*** Good cut flower, effective on small trellises and fences that are fine-textured enough for its small tendrils to grasp. Lovely draping out of hanging baskets.

► ***Needs:*** Full sun. Rich, well-drained soil. Ample moisture; plant must never dry out during growth. First soak seeds in warm water for 24 hours and then plant ½" deep. Plant directly in the soil when the weather is cool and a light frost is still possible, perhaps 2-3 weeks before the last frost in late winter or early spring. In Zones 8-11 plant in late autumn or early winter. Provide support. Once plants have emerged, mulch to conserve moisture and keep soil cool. Fertilize regularly, every 2-4 weeks. Trim spent blooms or cut often for bouquets to encourage longer flowering. Plants die when temperatures get hot; discard.

Sweet Pepperbush

see Summersweet

Sweet Peppers

see Peppers

Sweet Potato

Ipomoea batatas

Warm-season annual vine/vegetable

Ipomoea batatus 'Beauregard'

Ipomoea batatus 'Margarita'

Ipomoea batatus 'Blackie'

► ***Hardiness:*** Zones 5-11

► ***Size:*** Grows 20' or more in a season, depending on growing conditions

► ***Features:*** Underground tubers are delicious boiled, mashed, or even in pies. Yams have a similar look and taste, but are a different plant.

► ***Uses:*** In the vegetable garden; decorative types make excellent groundcovers and container plants.

► ***Needs:*** Full sun. Ample water; needs at least 1" a week. For edible tubers, best in sandy soil that is deeply dug and free of roots or many stones. However, will tolerate a variety of soils. Best in the South and Southwest but can be grown in Zones 5 and colder if you choose early maturing types. Sweet potatoes need very warm soil, so plant in raised beds or create hills about 6" tall and 12" round. Or prewarm the soil by laying down black plastic mulch a week in advance and planting through an "X" in the mulch. Then plant slips, prestarted sweet potatoes, about 2 weeks after your region's last frost date. Space 2' or so apart. Mulch to conserve moisture and water regularly if rains are not sufficient to keep soil evenly moist. Avoid high-nitrogen fertilizers, which cause much leafy growth but smaller tubers. Harvest after the first frost or when the soil temperature drops below 50°F/10°C. Dig carefully to not bruise or scrape tubers. Brush off soil. Dry on newspapers in the sun for two hours. Store in a paper bag for 10 days; then in a cool dry place for up to 6 months.

► ***Choices:*** 'Georgia Jet' produces in only 90 days, useful in areas with shorter growing seasons.

Sweet William

see Pinks

Sweet Woodruff

Galium odoratum (formerly *Asperula odorata)*

Perennial

Galium odoratum

S

Plant encyclopedia

▶Hardiness: Zones 4-8
▶Size: 4"-1' tall, 1' wide
▶Features: This groundcover grows quickly in rich soil, making it a good choice to fill in bare areas. In spring, little white blossoms spread like snowflakes across a blanket of bright green hand-shape leaves.
▶Uses: Planting in groups beneath shade trees, along walkways, in the front of flower beds
▶Needs: Plant in well-drained, humus-rich, acidic soil; increase soil acidity by adding peat moss, composted oak leaves, or pine straw mulch. Sweet woodruff grows in full sun or partial shade. The hotter the climate, the more shade is required.

Sweet Gum, Fruitless

Liquidambar styraciflua 'Rotundiloba'

Deciduous tree

Liquidambar styraciflua 'Rotundiloba'

▶Hardiness: Zones 5-9
▶Size: 60'-75' tall, 40'-50' wide
▶Features: Young trees have a distinctly pyramidal outline that becomes more rounded as they mature. Neat in appearance and, because this variety is fruitless, it is neat all the way around. Give roots room to spread—avoid planting areas surrounded by paving. Large lobed leaves turn various hues in fall, from yellow to red to dark purple. In milder climates, fall color may not be as showy on fruitless sweet gums as on those that bear fruit. Medium growth rate.
▶Uses: Shading lawns, parking areas, or decks; street tree
▶Needs: Plant in full sun. Moist, slightly acidic soil is required for growth. Trees do not tolerate pollution, city life, or areas where their fleshy roots are limited. Remove lower branches in late winter if needed to walk or park beneath trees.
▶Choices: *L. styraciflua*—produces spiny gumballs, bright fall foliage. *L. formosana*—leaves are five-lobed; tree shape is conical; bright fall foliage.

Sweet Shrub; Carolina Allspice

Calycanthus floridus

Deciduous flowering shrub

Calycanthus floridus

▶Hardiness: Zones 4-9
▶Size: 6'-9' tall, 6'-12' wide
▶Features: Let this old-fashioned shrub welcome you home with its spicy perfume. Small, reddish-brown flowers unleash their fruity fragrance during warm, summer months. Bright green leaves turn yellow in fall. Shrubs grown from seed may have an unreliable scent; some are unpleasant. Purchase plants while in bloom to ensure a pleasing fragrance. Plants are easy to grow and form a rounded outline. Slow growth rate.
▶Uses: Massing; specimen; fragrance planting beside entries, windows, porches, patios, or benches; at gates, parking areas, courtyards, edges of woodlands, shrub beds
▶Needs: Plant in any soil type; shrubs grow best in deep, moist, loamy soil. Grow in sun or shade. Flowering is best and plants grow largest in full sun. Prune after flowering in the spring to remove older wood. Pest resistant.
▶Choices: 'Athens'—yellow-green flowers.

Swiss Chard

see Chard

Swiss Cheese Plant; Split-Leaf Philodendron

Monstera deliciosa

Tropical evergreen vine

Monstera deliciosa

▶Hardiness: Zones 10-11
▶Size: 10' high, 10' wide
▶Features: Attractive lustrous, dark green leaves are large and divided. This is a large vine that needs plenty of space to grow. Normally somewhat floppy, it can be trained to grow upright.
▶Uses: As a houseplant in a room with plenty of overhead space, such as a foyer with a vaulted ceiling.
▶Needs: Best in bright filtered light although quite tolerant of low light conditions. Average home temperatures of 65°-75°F are fine. Allow to dry between waterings during active growth. Repot infrequently. Small leaves or leaves with no splits result when light is too low. Rather than cutting off aerial roots, direct them back into the potting soil or onto a moss pole to give the plant more vertical support.

Switch Grass

see Grasses, Ornamental

Syagrus romanzoffiana

see Palms: Queen Palm

SYCAMORE; PLANE TREE

Platanus spp.

American sycamores are large forest trees not as frequently planted in the garden as their European cousin, the London plane tree, or the hybrids between the two. Nevertheless they are stately trees native to riverbanks and floodplains in North America, and are sometimes planted as a street tree, although not as frequently as London plane tree.

SYCAMORES

American Sycamore

Platanus occidentalis

Deciduous tree

Platanus occidentalis

▶ ***Hardiness:*** Zones 5-9
▶ ***Size:*** Grows up to 150' tall, 100' wide
▶ ***Features:*** Classic shade tree with a long, elegant trunk sheathed in gorgeous gray and white mottled bark. Very large, maplelike leaves. Grows well in nearly all parts of the United States. A rather fast grower, growing 1'-2' a year. Also known as buttonwood.
▶ ***Uses:*** Best in native or naturalized plantings
▶ ***Needs:*** Full sun. Does best in moist to wet soil. However, highly susceptible to anthracnose and mildew. Also tends to shed twig and branch litter.

SYCAMORES

London Plane Tree

Platanus ×acerifolia

Deciduous tree

Platanus ×acerifolia

▶ ***Hardiness:*** Zones 6-8
▶ ***Size:*** Grows to 100' tall and wide, depending on the type. Some may reach only 60' tall
▶ ***Features:*** The London plane tree is much like American sycamore in that it's a classic shade tree with a long, elegant trunk sheathed in gorgeous gray and white mottled bark. Very large, maplelike leaves. Grows well in nearly all parts of the United States. A rather fast grower, the London plane tree attains growth of 1'-2' a year. However, unlike the above native sycamore, this sycamore is far more disease resistant and more drought tolerant.
▶ ***Uses:*** As a specimen. Does well in urban plantings and is often used as a street tree or is pruned for formal effect. Many urban trees and walkways are lined beautifully with plane trees.
▶ ***Needs:*** Full sun. Prefers moist soils but thrives in a variety of soils and situations.
▶ ***Choices:*** 'Bloodgood' is rapid growing and resistant to anthracnose. 'Liberty' is also disease resistant. 'Metroshade' is a fast grower with new growth appearing as an attractive cinnamon color.

Symphoricarpos spp.

see Snowberry and Coralberry

Syngonium podophyllum

see Arrowhead Vine

Syringa spp.

see Lilacs

Tabebuia spp.

see Trumpet Tree, Golden and Trumpet Tree, Pink

Tagetes spp.

see Marigold

Tarragon, French

Artemisia dracunculus 'Sativa'

Perennial herb

Artemisia dracunculus 'Sativa'

▶ ***Hardiness:*** Zones 4-6
▶ ***Size:*** Grows 2'-3' tall, 1'-2' wide
▶ ***Features:*** Small shrublike herb has aniselike flavor that is a staple of many classic dishes
▶ ***Uses:*** To the side of the vegetable garden or in an herb garden. Snip fresh leaves into soups, stews, and salads. Excellent with chicken or fish. Also a classic in herb vinegar.
▶ ***Needs:*** Full sun to light shade. Prefers rich well-drained sandy soil with average moisture, but will tolerate some variety in soils and moisture. Dislikes wet soils; somewhat drought tolerant. Plant established plants in spring or fall. Divide every 2-3 years for manageable size and for better flavor.
▶ ***Choices:*** French tarragon *(A. dracunculus* 'Sativa') has far superior, more intense flavor. However, Russian tarragon *(A. dracunculus)* is commonly sold, and the two are not always labeled as anything more specific than tarragon. So if your tarragon isn't very flavorful, replant.

Taxodium distichum

see Bald Cypress

Taxus spp.

see Yews

Tea Olive

See Sweet Olive

Tea Tree, New Zealand

Leptospermum scoparium

Evergreen flowering shrub or small tree

Leptospermum scoparium 'Nana'

▶ ***Hardiness:*** 9-10
▶ ***Size:*** 6'-10' tall, 6'-10' wide
▶ ***Features:*** This big shrub has a soft look. Grow it to enjoy early summer flowers with white, pink, or red petals and dense foliage that stays green year-round. May be grown as a small tree. Tolerates heat and salty air. Thrives in southern California. Medium growth rate.

S

Plant encyclopedia

▶ ***Uses:*** Coastal areas, specimen shrubs, seasonal accent, background planting, screening, shrub beds
▶ ***Needs:*** Plant in fertile, acidic soil. Alkaline soil can lead to chlorosis; offset with supplemental iron. Requires soil that is moist but well drained; root rot may develop in wet soil. Grow in full sun or partial shade. Protect from harsh winds.
▶ ***Choices:*** 'Pink Pearl'—pink to white double flowers, 6'-10' tall; 'Snow White'—white double flowers, 2'-4' tall.

Tecomaria capensis
see Cape Honeysuckle

Teucrium chamaedrys
see Germander

Texas Bluebonnet
see Lupines

Texas Ranger
Leucophyllum frutescens 'Silverado'

Evergreen shrub

Leucophyllum frutescens 'Silverado'

▶ ***Hardiness:*** Zones 8-10
▶ ***Size:*** 6'-8' tall, 4'-6' wide
▶ ***Features:*** Grow this silvery shrub where sun is plentiful but water isn't. Poor, alkaline soils aren't a problem either. Rose-purple flowers will be enjoyed for several months. Avoid planting in humid regions with high rainfall. Slow growth rate.
▶ ***Uses:*** Arid areas, Xeriscaping, hedges, containers, flower beds, seaside plantings, rock gardens, slopes, areas that aren't often watered
▶ ***Needs:*** Plant in dry, well-drained soil—including sandy or chalky soil—in full sun. Water regularly until established; afterward, you'll rarely need to water this Southwestern desert native.
▶ ***Choices:*** 'Compactum'—3'-4' tall.

Thanksgiving Cactus
see Christmas Cactus

Thrift
see Sea Thrift

Thorny Eleagnus
see Eleagnus, Thorny

Thuja spp.
see Arborvitae

Thunbergia alata
see Black-Eyed Susan Vine

Thyme, Culinary
Thymus vulgaris

Perennial herb

Thymus vulgaris 'Argenteus'

▶ ***Hardiness:*** Zones 4-6
▶ ***Size:*** Grows 2' tall, 1' wide; low-growing varieties available
▶ ***Features:*** Delightful pungent thyme is as pretty as it is practical. Can be used in nearly any dish. Neatly growing plant has attractive, shiny gray-green leaves; also produces tiny white or lavender flowers. A favorite of beneficial bees.
▶ ***Uses:*** So pretty, thyme can be used anywhere in the landscape that provides good drainage. Outstanding on baked slopes, in rock gardens, or tucked among flagstones and pavers. Easy to dry. Cut a number of stems a few inches long, bundling the ends together with a rubber band and hanging in a cool dry place for a few weeks. Rub dried leaves to crumble and store in a jar.
▶ ***Needs:*** Full sun, though appreciates light shade in hot summer areas. Does best in light, dry, well-drained soil and moderate moisture, but also is drought tolerant.
▶ ***Choices:*** There are more than 40 types of thyme, including lemon, caraway, and oregano flavored types and variegated types.

Thyme, Creeping
Thymus praecox

Evergreen herb

Thymus leucotrichus

▶ ***Hardiness:*** Zones 5-9
▶ ***Size:*** 6"-8" tall, 8"-12" wide
▶ ***Features:*** Choose creeping thyme when you need a low-growing plant to tuck into hot, dry crevices or between stepping stones. Aromatic leaves stay gray-green year-round and can tolerate light foot traffic. Purplish pink flowers cover plants in spring. Medium to rapid growth rate.
▶ ***Uses:*** Tucking between stepping-stones, beneath benches, edging planting beds or walkways, entries, filling in between roses, growing over tops of retaining walls, tucking into rock walls
▶ ***Needs:*** Thrives in hot, dry soil with alkaline pH. Plant in full sun. Work lime into soil to increase alkalinity. Plants fail to thrive in damp soil; select a location that's well drained.

Thymophylla tenuiloba
see Dahlberg Daisy

Ti Plant
Cordyline fruticosa

Tropical shrub

Cordyline terminalis 'Lilliput'

▶ ***Hardiness:*** Zone 11
▶ ***Size:*** Grows up to 6' tall depending on type and age, though most sold are 1'-3' tall
▶ ***Features:*** Also goes by a variety of other names, including ti tree, good luck plant, red dracaena, Polynesian ti, and Hawaiian ti. The long, strappy leaves grow on top of a trunklike stem and the green types have traditionally been used as the so-called grass in Hawaiian grass skirts.
▶ ***Uses:*** As a houseplant, but also used as a landscape plant in subtropical and tropical regions.
▶ ***Needs:*** Bright, indirect light. Keep soil moist at all times; keep slightly drier in winter. Average home warmth fine. Needs higher humidity; grow on a tray with pebbles and water or double-pot surrounded with peat moss kept wet. Fertilize three times in summer.
▶ ***Choices:*** Sold under a variety of botanical names, including *C. terminalis* and *Dracaena terminalis*. 'Baby Doll' has small burgundy leaves with pink edges. 'Firebrand' has larger dark burgundy leaves. 'Kiwi' has small leaves with traces of red and yellow-green, yellow, and cream patterns.

Tiarella cordifolia
see Foam Flower, Allegheny

Tickseed
see Coreopsis

Tilia spp.
see Lindens

Tillandsia cyanea
see Bromeliads: Pink Quill

Tithonia rotundifolia
see Mexican Sunflower

Toadflax
Linaria spp.
Annual

Linaria spp.

▶ ***Size:*** 1'-3' tall, 9"-12" wide
▶ ***Features:*** Toadflax is best known for its colorful annual varieties often used for winter and early spring bedding in the mild-winter climates of the West. The flowers resemble miniature snapdragons (it is sometimes called baby snapdragon), and come in similar colors. Bloom times vary from late winter to late summer.
▶ ***Uses:*** Lower-growing annual types are good cool-season bedding plants. The taller perennial forms are best in informal to wild cottage and meadow gardens where they can reseed without worry to you.
▶ ***Needs:*** Full sun. Light, well-drained, preferably sandy soil. Moderate moisture; perennial type is drought tolerant once established. For annual types, in Zones 4-7, sow seeds directly in garden in early spring as soon as snow thaws. In Zones 8-9, sow seeds for annual types in fall for late-winter bloom. Thin to 6"-12" between plants. For perennial types, plant established plants in spring. Mulch both types. Shear plants after first bloom to encourage a second bloom.
▶ ***Choices:*** An annual, *L. maroccana* dies out when midsummer heat hits. A perennial, *L. purpurea* blooms all summer in many climates and reseeds prolifically throughout the garden.

Tobacco
see Flowering Tobacco

Tobira
see Pittosporum

Tomatillo
Physalis ixocarpa
Warm-season annual

Tomatillo 'Verde Puebla', flowers

Tomatillo fruit

▶ ***Hardiness:*** Zones 3-11
▶ ***Size:*** Grows 3' tall, 5' wide
▶ ***Features:*** Tiny green tomatolike fruits in papery husks that are key to many green Mexican sauces
▶ ***Uses:*** In the vegetable garden
▶ ***Needs:*** Full sun. Tolerates a variety of soils but does best in rich, well-drained soil. Needs plentiful moisture. If desired, start seeds indoors 6-8 weeks before your region's last frost date. Otherwise, plant established plants outdoors after all danger of frost has passed. Work a spadeful or two of compost into the soil at planting time. Mulch with newspapers topped with straw or grass clippings to prevent soil-borne diseases. Grow in 3' cages for support. Provide consistent moisture, about 1" of water a week. Using too much nitrogen-rich fertilizer on plants will produce much foliage and fewer tomatillos. Unlike their distant cousins, tomatoes, tomatillos are bothered by few pests or diseases. Harvest at any size, but best for cooking when the paper skin begins to split.
▶ ***Choices:*** Some cultivars are lower growing than others. Yellow tomatillos are also available and generally are sweeter.

Tomato
Lycopersicon esculentum
Warm-season annual vegetable

Tomato 'Tom Siletz'

▶ ***Hardiness:*** Zones 2-11
▶ ***Size:*** Determinate types, which include paste, cherry, and patio tomatoes, grow 2'-4' tall and 1'-2' wide; indeterminate types, which include most beefsteak and slicing types, grow 4' tall and taller as sprawling vines, easily topping 6'
▶ ***Features:*** One of the most popular plants for the vegetable garden, this juicy red vegetable is a summertime staple.
▶ ***Uses:*** In the vegetable garden
▶ ***Needs:*** Full sun. Well-drained soil high in organic matter. Prefers neutral soil. Easiest to grow in areas with hot summers. Gardeners in Zones 3 and colder should choose early-maturing varieties that produce in 70 days or less to accommodate the shorter growing season. Southern and Southwestern gardeners should seek out heat- and drought-tolerant cultivars. If desired, start seeds indoors 6-8 weeks before your region's last frost date. Otherwise, plant established plants outdoors after all danger of frost has passed. (In the South and Southwest, you can also plant in late summer for better fall harvests.)

Work a spadeful or two of compost into the soil at planting time. Mulch with newspapers topped with straw or grass clippings to prevent soil-borne diseases. Gardeners use a variety of staking techniques, but the simplest is to use premade tomato cages. Use 3' cages for smaller determinate-type tomatoes; use 6' cages for taller indeterminate types. Provide consistent moisture, about 1" of water a week, to prevent blossom end rot and to assure strong growth. Too much nitrogen-rich fertilizer on tomatoes produces much foliage and fewer tomatoes. As the plants grow, pinch off suckers, the small stems that start at the crotch of secondary stems from the main stems. These can grow very large, making the plant a tangled mess, encouraging disease and making harvest difficult. As practical, pinch off diseased leaves, especially lower leaves, to prevent the problem from spreading to other parts of the plant. Each year, if possible, plant in a spot 15' or more away from a spot where you planted tomatoes in the last 2 years to minimize disease problems.

▶***Choices:*** Hundreds of types available. Main categories include paste-type tomatoes, which are good for making into sauces and processing; cherry-type tomatoes, which are small and ideal for snacking and salads; and slicing tomatoes, which are large and juicy, ideal for slicing into platters for salads, sandwiches, and other fresh eating. ('Brandywine' is the beefsteak tomato that wins many taste testings for best flavor.) Tomatoes also come in a rainbow of colors. Most are red, of course, and many are yellow or orange. But others are green, whitish, striped, streaked, or deep purple-red. When shopping for tomatoes, look for the most disease-resistant types available since these plants are highly susceptible to an array of problems. As a rule, the more letters on a label, the more diseases a plant resists. A tomato that has VFFTNASt, such as 'Big Beef' or 'Celebrity', would be one of the most disease-resistant around. One that lists a VF or a VFT would be less disease resistant.

Torch Lily
see Red Hot Poker

Torenia fournieri
see Wishbone Flower

Trachelospermum jasminoides
see Jasmines: Asiatic Jasmine; Yellow Star Jasmine

Trachycarpus fortunei
see Palms: Windmill Palm

Tradescantia spp.
see Spiderwort; Wandering Jew; Moses-in-the-Boat; Purple Heart

Trailing Lobelia
see Lobelia, Edging

Transvaal Daisy
see Gerbera

Treasure Flower
see Gazania

Tree Ivy
see Fatshedera

Tree Lilac
see Lilacs: Japanese Tree Lilac

Trillium; Wake-Robin
Trillium spp.

Perennial

Trillium grandiflorum

▶***Hardiness:*** Zones 4-8
▶***Size:*** 1'-2' tall and wide
▶***Features:*** Stunning three-petaled flowers in pinks and whites above a whorl of three leaves have made this one of the most beloved spring wildflowers in North America. Plants will slowly multipy into dense clusters and stands in optimum conditions. Unfortunately, trilliums are difficult to propagate, and most offered at nurseries have been collected in the wild—a practice that is decimating the wild populations. Carefully check to make sure the ones you purchase are not collected from the wild, and be prepared to pay some money for ones that have been vegetatively propagated.
▶***Uses:*** The woodland shade garden under trees and shrubs.
▶***Needs:*** Light to medium shade. Rich, moist, neutral to acidic soil. Does well under deciduous trees and large shrubs. Abundant moisture. Plant rhizomes 4" deep in spring or plant container-grown plants. Work in ample compost. Mulch to conserve moisture. Plant will gradually spread to 1'-2' clumps. When plant is dormant, divide clumps if new plants are desired. It is pest and disease free.
▶***Choices:*** Flowers are usually white but also come in pinks, burgundy, and mahogany. *T. grandiflorum* has the showiest flowers, growing 2"-3" across. Others are *T. erectum, T. sessile,* and *T. chloropetalum,* which is large at 2' tall.

Tropaeolum majus
see Nasturtium

Trumpet Creeper
Campsis radicans

Deciduous flowering vine

Campsis radicans 'Minnesota Red'

▶***Hardiness:*** Zones 4-9
▶***Size:*** 40' or more in all directions
▶***Features:*** This blooming beauty of a vine is as easy to grow as a weed. Shiny green leaves and orange flowers are attractive from spring until frost. Rampant growth can destroy arbors and fences or choke trees. Keep this vine away from rooftops. Blossoms attract hummingbirds.
▶***Uses:*** Camouflaging eyesores; attracting hummingbirds; growing on tall, very sturdy supports; covering large, blank masonry walls
▶***Needs:*** Plant in any conditions; trumpet vine grows in sun, shade, rich soil or poor. It will even thrive in sidewalk cracks. Prune as needed to control. It blooms on new wood, so prune heavily each spring to achieve best flowering and to control size. Mow over stems in lawn. Do not fertilize. Trumpet vine climbs by twining as well as by rootlets that attach to surfaces, and will strangle any tree it grows on. Plant established plants in spring or fall. Aerial rootlets cling tightly to walls or supports and need no help attaching. Can reach 20'-40' tall, so site carefully, providing a heavy, large arbor or pergola. Rootlets and vigorous vines can damage stucco and wood shingles. This plant is bothered by few pests or diseases.
▶***Choices:*** 'Flava'—yellow flowers; 'Praecox'—red flowers.

Trumpet Tree, Golden

Tabebuia chrysotricha

Briefly deciduous, sometimes evergreen tropical tree

Tabebuia chrysotricha

▶ ***Hardiness:*** Zones 10-11
▶ ***Size:*** Grows 25'-30' tall and wide
▶ ***Features:*** Beautiful 3"-4" long trumpet-shape flowers in golden yellow often with deep purple stripes in throat. Blooms heaviest in April to May when trees temporarily lose leaves. Dark green leaves with three to seven leaflets.
▶ ***Uses:*** Excellent in a large container or as a specimen plant.
▶ ***Needs:*** Full sun. Tolerates a variety of soils, but needs good drainage and does best with regular watering along with fertilizing at least once or twice a year. Starts blooming as a young tree. Hardy to 24°F/-5°C.
Choices: Sometimes sold as *T. pulcherrima.*

Trumpet Tree, Pink

Tabebuia heterophylla

Tropical evergreen tree

Tabebuia heterophylla

▶ ***Hardiness:*** Zones 10-11
▶ ***Size:*** Grows 30' tall and wide
▶ ***Features:*** Lovely 2"-3" long trumpet-shape flowers in pink with a white throat and a touch of yellow. Blooms late winter and sometimes a second time in late summer or fall. Dark green leaves with three to seven leaflets. Takes several years to bloom.
▶ ***Uses:*** Excellent in a large container or as a specimen plant.
▶ ***Needs:*** Full sun. Tolerates a variety of soils, but needs good drainage and does best with regular watering. Fertilize at least once or twice a year. Hardy to 24°F/-5°C.
▶ ***Choices:*** Sometimes sold as *T. ipe.*

Trumpet Vine

Distictis spp.

Evergreen vine

Distictis buccinatoria

▶ ***Hardiness:*** Zones 10-11
▶ ***Size:*** Grows 20'-30' tall
▶ ***Features:*** This striking vine produces big, beautiful orange, red and yellow, or violet and white trumpetlike flowers for months at a time. Some are beautifully scented. Climbs by tendrils. Not to be confused with the trumpet vine that does well in colder climates, *Campsis radicans* (see Trumpet Creeper).
▶ ***Uses:*** Arbors, pergolas, fences
▶ ***Needs***: Full sun to light shade, especially in hot, dry areas. Keep newly planted plants well watered and fertilize lightly about once a month.
▶ ***Choices:*** The blood-red trumpet vine *(D. buccinatoria)* bears 3" flowers that are orange fading to softer red with a yellow throat. Flowers bloom lightly throughout the year. This is a rather rangy vine, so cut it back as needed to keep neat. Vanilla trumpet vine *(D. laxiflora)* is a neater-growing vine with 4" violet flowers with touches of white. Royal trumpet vine *(D.* 'Rivers') has larger leaves and flowers than the other types and because the leaves are glossy, they look better during the winter. Flowers can be up to 5" long in purple with orange inside.

Tsuga spp.

see Hemlock

Tuberous Begonia

see Begonia, Tuberous

Tulbaghia spp.

see Society Garlic

Tulip Tree; Tulip Poplar

Liriodendron tulipifera

Deciduous tree

Liriodendron tulipifera

▶ ***Hardiness:*** Zones 5-9
▶ ***Size:*** Grows 70'-100' tall, 35'-50' wide
▶ ***Features:*** This amazingly large native tree is also quite beautiful. A fast grower, spurting as much as 18" a year, it also produces beautiful yellow tuliplike flowers high up in the tree, where they are rather difficult to see.
▶ ***Uses:*** An excellent shade tree for large areas or in a planting of other large trees
▶ ***Needs:*** Full sun to light shade. Rich, well-drained, moist soil. Needs plenty of room for roots.
▶ ***Choices:*** Arnold ('Fastigiatum') has a more columnar habit. Majestic Beauty ('Aureo-marginatum') has leaves with a pretty golden-green margin.

Tulip

Tulipa spp.

Spring-blooming bulb

Tulipa 'Red Emperor'

▶ **Hardiness:** Perennial in Zones 3-7; annual in Zones 7-11
▶ **Size:** 4"-30" tall, 4"-10" wide
▶ **Features:** These small bulbs pack a lot of punch when it comes to spring display. It comes in nearly every color of the rainbow, in single and double flowers, and in fantastic flower forms from the familiar tulip-shape to star-shape, lily-shape, and frilly parrot tulips. The tiny species tulips are reliably perennial even in the South for years of enjoyment. Others need winter chill to bloom well year after year, and are most often planted as annuals in the South and the mild climates of the West. Even in the North where tulips are in their element, they don't last long in the garden if planted in wet, heavy soil.
▶ **Uses:** The ultimate spring bedding plant, often combined with pansies and wallflowers for spectacular effect. Tulips are best planted in tight groups of a dozen bulbs or more. Large beds are stunning.
▶ **Needs:** Full sun, though light shade from deciduous trees later in season is ideal. Rich, very well-drained soil. Ample water during growth and bloom; moderate water after. Plant in October in Zones 3-7, working compost and bulb fertilizer into the soil. In Zones 8-11 purchase bulbs and chill in the refrigerator for 6-10 weeks (or purchase prechilled) and then plant outdoors. Mulch for winter protection in Zones 3-4. In spring, after blooming, allow foliage to brown and "ripen." Where well-situated, plants will come back for several years, but often die out after 2 or 3 years. Tulips are also good for forcing indoors (see page 163).

Turnip

Brassica rapa

Cool-season annual vegetable

Turnip 'Market Express'

▶ **Hardiness:** Zones 2-11
▶ **Size:** Leaves grow several inches tall; roots 2"-6" deep without taproot
▶ **Features:** Roots are excellent in soups and side dishes. Greens are good cooked.
▶ **Uses:** In the vegetable garden
▶ **Needs:** Full sun to part shade. Best in rich, well-drained soil deeply worked with plenty of compost and a pH that is neutral to alkaline. Heat and too little water make turnips bitter. Plant in spring when soil is at least 60°F/16°C up to 6 weeks before your region's last average frost date. Plant seeds ¼"-½" deep. Thin to 4"-6"; thinnings are an excellent addition to salads. Keep soil moist. Mulch. Avoid nitrogen fertilizers, which force the plants' energy into foliage rather than the roots. Harvest when roots are 1½"-2½" and before heavy frosts. Pull up the entire plant. Can also sow a crop for fall harvest in late summer.
Choices: Choose fast-maturing cultivars to ensure rapid growing in cool weather, such as 'De Milan', which is ready in 35 days. Harvest while small.

Turtlehead, Pink

Chelone lyonii

Perennial

Chelone lyonii

▶ **Hardiness:** Zones 3-8
▶ **Size:** 2'-4' tall, 1'-2' wide
▶ **Features:** These are bushy, vertical plants best grown in groups for their rosy pink blossoms that resemble the heads of snapping turtles. Plants slowly spread to form large colonies. Blooms late summer to fall.
▶ **Uses:** Low wet spots in the garden, boggy areas, or the sides of ponds and streams where soil is heavy and wet
▶ **Needs:** Full sun if conditions are wet; partial shade in drier conditions. Rich, preferably acidic soil. Ample moisture; never allow soil to dry out. This plant loves boggy conditions. Plant established plants in spring. Pinch tips of plants in early summer for bushier plants with more flowers. Fertilize for best flowering. Stake if site is too shady. Pink turtlehead is pest and disease free as long as conditions are right.
▶ **Choices:** Flowers come in pink or white. *C. glabra* has pinkish-white flowers, grows 4' tall. Hardy in Zones 5-9. *C. obliqua* has deep pink or white flowers, grows 3' tall. Hardy in Zones 3-9.

Twinspur

Diascia spp.

Perennial or annual

Diascia spp.

▶ **Hardiness:** Zones 8-10
▶ **Size:** 10"-12" tall, 1'-2' wide
▶ **Features:** Low clumps of foliage are smothered in tiny pink or salmon blossoms all summer. Where hardy over winter, it grows into trailing plants that are lovely spilling over walls. Blooms in late winter or early spring and into fall.
▶ **Uses:** This is a superb container plant in all parts of North America. Where it is hardy, it is lovely tucked in at the feet of other perennials in the mixed border or allowed to spill over walls.
▶ **Needs:** Full sun in Zones 2-6; part shade in Zones 7-11. Average, well-drained soil. Somewhat drought tolerant, it will die out if soil is heavy and wet. In Zones 2-7 treat as an annual that thrives in the cool conditions of early spring. In Zones 8-10 grow as a perennial. Either way, plant seedlings in early spring after danger of frost has passed. When blooms begin to fade, shear back the plant by about one-quarter to rejuvenate. In Zones 2-7 tear out the plant when all blooming stops. This plant may spread vigorously. Divide every 2-3 years in autumn.
▶ **Choices:** *D. barberae* is an annual. Perennial types include *D.* 'Ruby Field', and *D. vigilis*. Flowers come in coral pink, salmon, rose, lilac, and apricot.

Umbrella Tree

see Schefflera

Ulmus parvifolia

see Elm, Chinese

Ulmus spp.

see Elm

Vaccinium spp.

see Blueberry

Valerian

see Red Valerian

Vanda

see Orchids

Venus Flytrap

Dionaea muscipula

Tropical evergreen perennial

Dionaea muscipula

▶ ***Size:*** Grows a few inches tall and wide, depending on the type and age of the plant
▶ ***Features:*** This fascinating plant produces leaves fringed with teeth that will clamp down on flies and bits of meat. A great plant for kids.
▶ ***Uses:*** As a houseplant, excellent in terrariums
▶ ***Needs:*** High humidity is critical; keep plant in a terrarium or cover the plant and pot with a large glass jar turned upside down. (Keep leaves from touching the glass or they may rot.) Medium light. Keep the soil constantly moist by watering with room-temperature rainwater. Feed once every other week or so with a bit of meat held out on the tip of a pencil or stick. Difficult to keep alive for more than a few months.

Verbena, Moss

Verbena tenuisecta

Perennial

Verbena tenuisecta

▶ ***Hardiness:*** Zones 8–10
▶ ***Size:*** 8"–12" tall, 18"–24" wide
▶ ***Features:*** Grow this heat-loving groundcover for its bright pink, violet, or white flowers. Fine, fernlike foliage adds textural contrast to planting beds. Sometimes sold as *V. tenera*. Rapid growth rate.
▶ ***Uses:*** Groundcover in hot, dry sites; filling in the front layer of shrub beds, slopes, courtyards, entries, edging walkways, patios, or containers
▶ ***Needs:*** Plant in well-drained soil and full sun. Avoid soggy soil. Water regularly until established. Afterward, water moderately.

Veronica; Speedwell

Veronica spp.

Perennial

Veronica 'Sunny Border Blue'

▶ ***Hardiness:*** Zones 3–8
▶ ***Size:*** 6'–3' tall, 6"–3' wide
▶ ***Features:*** Pretty blue spires rise from round, mounded clumps of foliage. Blooms late spring to midsummer, sometimes longer.
▶ ***Uses:*** Specimen plant, borders
▶ ***Needs:*** Full sun best but tolerates light shade, especially in Zones 7–8. Rich to average, moist but well-drained soil. Moderate to abundant moisture. Plant established plants in spring or fall. Mulch to conserve moisture. Fertilize occasionally, every 4–6 weeks, or work in a slow-release fertilizer in spring. Trim spent blooms to keep plant tidy and encourage flowering, which can last several weeks. Mildew and leaf spot are sometimes a problem.
▶ ***Choices:*** Flowers come in blues, purples, pinks, and white. 'Sunny Border Blue' is one of the most popular, growing 18" tall and blooming for an extraordinarily long season, early summer through fall. Groundcover types are also available.

VIBURNUMS

Viburnum spp.

Viburnums are a useful group of semievergreen or deciduous shrubs valuable for white flowers in spring or early summer. Many have spectacular late-summer and fall fruits and good fall foliage color, and some have flowers with a rich, powerful fragrance. Their culture varies somewhat, but most grow best in full sun to light shade and rich, well-drained soil. Moderate moisture is best for most, but some like wet soil, others drier conditions. Plant established plants in spring or fall, working a few spadefuls of compost into the planting hole. Mulch to conserve moisture. No further feeding needed in most conditions. Needs minimal or no pruning. Pest and disease problems vary by species, but most are fairly problem-free.

VIBURNUMS

Arrowwood Viburnum

Viburnum dentatum

Deciduous flowering shrub

Viburnum dentatum

▶ ***Hardiness:*** Zones 3–8
▶ ***Size:*** 6'–15' tall, 6'–15' wide
▶ ***Features:*** This flowering shrub is tough and durable. Clusters of tiny, white flowers appear in late spring. Dark green leaves turn yellow or red in fall. Arrowwood viburnum is cold hardy, adaptable, and gets big quickly. Plant it to create a living wall in your landscape or for other utilitarian uses. Birds enjoy the bluish-black fruits that ripen in late summer and fall. Plants sucker freely and may need restriction from growing out of their given area.
▶ ***Uses:*** Deciduous hedge, screening, coastal areas, attracting birds, background for garden rooms, shrub beds and flowerbeds
▶ ***Needs:*** Plant in moist but well-drained soil. Shrubs will adapt to a variety of other soils. Grow in full sun or partial shade. Give this plant plenty of room to grow since it suckers readily. Salt tolerant.

VIBURNUMS

Blackhaw Viburnum

Viburnum prunifolium

Deciduous flowering shrub

Viburnum prunifolium

V

Plant encyclopedia

▶**Hardiness:** Zones 3-9
▶**Size:** 12'-15' tall, 8'-12' wide
▶**Features:** Whether you live where winters are cold or summers are hot, this shrub will adapt to your climate. It offers creamy colored flowers in the spring, edible berries in the fall, and colorful autumn foliage. Fall foliage varies from purplish to shining red to deep red or bronze. This large-growing shrub can be pruned in the form of a small tree.
▶**Uses:** Specimen use, seasonal accents, shrub beds, courtyards, entries, areas beside patios, gates, fences, or walls, natural areas, massing, attracting birds to the landscape
▶**Needs:** Plant in slightly acidic soil that's moist but well drained; however, shrubs will adapt to other soil types. Will tolerate dry soils. Grow in full sun or partial shade. Resists mildew.

VIBURNUMS

Compact American Cranberrybush Viburnum

Viburnum trilobum 'Alfredo'

Deciduous flowering shrub

Viburnum trilobum 'Alfredo'

▶**Hardiness:** Zones 2-7
▶**Size:** 5'-6' tall, 5'-6' wide
▶**Features:** This hardworking, fast-growing shrub for all seasons is easy to grow. It offers white flower clusters in spring, bright red fall foliage, and decorative red fruit in fall and winter. Its dense, rounded form keeps the plant looking neat with minimal care. Branches are fine-textured.
▶**Uses:** Hedges, shrub beds, foundation planting, massing, planting beside patios, attracting birds, naturalizing, filling in empty corners of yards
▶**Needs:** Plant in slightly acidic soil that's moist but well drained; however, shrubs will adapt to other soils. Grow in full sun or partial shade. Resists aphids better than European cranberrybush.

VIBURNUMS

David Viburnum

Viburnum davidii

Broadleaf evergreen shrub

Viburnum davidii

▶**Hardiness:** Zones 8-10
▶**Size:** 3' high and wide
▶**Features:** Neat, broad, rounded habit; beautiful deeply creased evergreen leaves; and bright blue fruits in late summer and fall make this a prized shrub where it can be grown. Clusters of ivory flowers in early summer are a bonus.
▶**Uses:** Excellent foundation plant, lovely in the shrub or mixed border.
▶**Needs:** Best in moist soil high in organic matter. Full sun in cooler climates to part shade in warmer ones.

VIBURNUMS

Doublefile Viburnum

Viburnum plicatum tomentosum

Deciduous flowering shrub

Viburnum plicatum tomentosum

▶**Hardiness:** Zones 4-8
▶**Size:** 5'-15' tall, 10'-18' wide
▶**Features:** For horizontal layers of branches covered with lacy white spring flowers, plant doublefile viburnum. Red berries develop as the hot season fades, and scarlet foliage appears in the fall. Leaves are coarse-textured. Blooms in partial shade and full sun.
▶**Uses:** Specimen plants, seasonal accents, massing, corners of houses or yards, in front of fences, balancing vertical plants, beside patios, natural areas
▶**Needs:** Plant in fertile soil that's moist but well drained. Grow in full sun to partial shade. Water regularly.

VIBURNUMS

European Cranberrybush Viburnum

Viburnum opulus 'Roseum'

Deciduous flowering shrub

Viburnum opulus 'Roseum'

▶**Hardiness:** Zones 3-8
▶**Size:** 8'-10' tall, 10'-15' wide
▶**Features:** Grow snowballs in the spring. A blizzard of blossoms—puffy, white, and round—covers this large shrub, commanding attention in the spring. Coarse dark foliage provides background. European cranberry viburnum has an irregular to mounding form. Sometimes sold as snowball viburnum or 'Sterile.'
▶**Uses:** Specimen plants, seasonal accents, focal points, large courtyards or entries, anchoring planting beds, contrasting with evergreen backgrounds, corners of houses or yards
▶**Needs:** Plant in wet or well-drained soil. This cold-hardy plant doesn't tolerate heat well; grow in afternoon shade in hotter climates, full sun elsewhere.

VIBURNUMS

Korean Spice Viburnum

Viburnum carlesii

Deciduous flowering shrub

Viburnum carlesii

▶ ***Hardiness:*** Zones 4–8
▶ ***Size:*** 4'–6' tall, 4'–6' wide
▶ ***Features:*** This spring bloomer features fragrant flowers in late April–May. Blooms are pink to red in bud and open pure white. It grows slowly and can be pruned to maintain desired size and shape.
▶ ***Uses:*** Specimen use, foundation plantings, shrub beds, planting beside entries, walkways, patios and outdoor seating areas for fragrance
▶ ***Needs:*** Plant in full sun or part shade in acidic, moist, well-drained soil. Prune to shape shrubs after flowering.

VIBURNUMS

Laurustinus Viburnum

Viburnum tinus

Broadleaf evergreen shrub

Viburnum tinus 'Spring Bouquet'

▶ ***Hardiness:*** Zones 8–10
▶ ***Size:*** 6'–10' tall, 8'–12' wide
▶ ***Features:*** Rounded evergreen leaves and neat but vigorous growth habit make this a popular choice for massing in borders and as a screen in mild-winter zones. The white or pink-tinged flower clusters appear in early spring and are slightly fragrant.
▶ ***Uses:*** Screen, massing
▶ ***Needs:*** Best in full sun and well-drained soil in a site protected from wind. In deep, moist soils plants can be overly vigorous. Avoid fertilizing, watering, and pruning in late summer to discourage new growth that may be damaged by winter freezes.

VIBURNUMS

Mohican Viburnum

Viburnum lantana 'Mohican'

Deciduous flowering shrub

Viburnum lantana 'Mohican'

▶ ***Hardiness:*** Zones 3–8
▶ ***Size:*** 6'–8' tall, 6'–8' wide
▶ ***Features:*** With its white flowers, coarse-textured dark green foliage, and orange-red fruit, this hardy and adaptable shrub is at home about anywhere in the landscape. Flower display lasts about a week in the spring. Fruit display is effective for a month in late summer. Fall color is quite attractive. Compact plants thrive in midwestern and northeastern gardens.
▶ ***Uses:*** Shrub beds, background plantings, seasonal accents, massing, attracting birds, foundation plantings with evergreens, natural areas
▶ ***Needs:*** Plant in slightly acidic soil that's moist but well drained; however, shrubs will adapt to other soils, including clay. Grow in full sun or partial shade. Resists bacterial leaf spot.

VIBURNUMS

Sweet Viburnum

Viburnum odoratissimum

Evergreen shrub

Viburnum odoratissimum

▶ ***Hardiness:*** Zones 8–10
▶ ***Size:*** 10'–20', spread to 20'
▶ ***Features:*** Big plant with big evergreen leaves will take on big landscaping jobs. Grow it when you want to hide poor views, add privacy, or establish a background. Fragrant white flowers appear in spring; coarse-textured leaves throughout the year. Medium growth rate.
▶ ***Uses:*** Hedges, screening, privacy, skirting raised decks, providing background in large planting beds
▶ ***Needs:*** Grow in full sun or partial shade—afternoon shade in hot areas. Moist, well drained, slightly acidic soil is preferred. Water regularly, especially in sandy areas. Prune to keep plants neat and control size.

Vinca, Annual

Catharanthus spp.

Annual

Catharanthus spp.

▶ **Size:** 4"–14" tall, 4"–2' wide
▶ **Features:** Annual vinca is hard to beat for lots of carefree color in hot, dry areas. It languishes in cool weather but thrives in summer heat. Colors available are pink, magenta, salmon, and white. Recent breeding has resulted in many new colors—red, purple, and even something close to blue. Blooms summer through fall. Don't confuse this with the evergreen groundcovers called vinca or periwinkle (see below).
▶ **Uses:** Massed as a bedding plant in hot, dry locations. Performs well in containers.
▶ **Needs:** Rich, well-drained soil; full sun; light shade, especially in Zones 6–11; moderate water. It is somewhat drought tolerant. Grow as an annual in Zones 2–8; as a perennial in Zones 9–11. Plant established seedlings in spring after all danger of frost has passed. Mulch. Fertilize regularly. Cut plants back by about one-fourth to one-third in late summer to encourage new growth and flowering.
▶ **Choices:** Flowers come in pinks, whites, and purples. 'Cooler' series is good for Zones 3–4. 'Carpet' is 4" tall and 24" wide, making it excellent for baskets, window boxes, and rock gardens.

Vinca; Littleleaf Periwinkle

Vinca minor

Evergreen groundcover

Vinca minor

▶ **Hardiness:** Zones 4–8
▶ **Size:** 6"–8" tall, with indefinite spread
▶ **Features:** Fill in bare shady areas with a dense blanket of glossy green leaves. Lavender blue flowers appear each spring. This plant grows slowly in poor soil and is not for coastal areas. It may be sold as creeping myrtle. Requires little maintenance once established.
▶ **Uses:** Bare shady spots, hillsides, erosion control, beneath trees, woodland gardens, underplanting with spring bulbs
▶ **Needs:** Grow in sun or partial shade north of Zone 7; farther south, grow in full or partial shade. Plant in well-drained, moist, fertile soil high in organic matter. Mix in peat moss or composted leaves at planting time.
▶ **Choices:** 'Alba'—white flowers. 'Aureola'—leaves veined with creamy yellow; lavender blossoms.

Vinca, Large; Large Periwinkle

Vinca major

Evergreen trailing groundcover

Vinca major 'Variegata'

▶ **Hardiness:** Zones 7–11
▶ **Size:** 12"–18" tall, 24' wide
▶ **Features:** With leaves about three times the size as littleleaf vinca and big 2" flowers that appear sporadically all summer until fall, large vinca makes considerable impact in the landscape. North of Zone 7 it is best known as a container plant grown to spill gracefully out of hanging baskets and window boxes.
▶ **Uses:** Evergreen groundcover in the South; container plant farther north.
▶ **Needs:** Bright open shade of tall trees is ideal. Plant 12"–24" apart in spring in moist, well-drained soil high in organic matter. Keep soil moist. Shear back hard in early spring to keep plants neat.
▶ **Choices:** 'Maculata' has pale blue flowers and variegated yellow and green leaves. 'Variegata' has white edges on the leaves.

Viola, Violet

see Pansy

Virginia Bluebells

Mertensia virginica

Perennial

Mertensia virginica

▶ **Hardiness:** Zones 3–7
▶ **Size:** 12"–18" tall, 8"–10" wide
▶ **Features:** Upright plants with large tongue-shape leaves bear big clusters of blue tubular flowers with a pink cast to them in early to midspring. The plants are spring ephemerals, meaning that after bloom is over the leaves yellow and disappear by midsummer. In moist woodlands they often self-sow to form large stands.
▶ **Uses:** Lovely in the woodland garden as well as the mixed border where other plants can grow over the dying foliage in summer.
▶ **Needs:** Full sun to light shade in Zones 3–6 and Pacific Northwest; light to full shade in hot summer regions in Zones 7–8. Rich, moist, neutral to acidic soil. Ample moisture during spring bloom, then only moderate moisture. Plant established plants outdoors in spring. Mulch to keep soil cool and moist. However, mulching inhibits any desired spreading, because plants self-seed well in ideal conditions. Fertilize by applying 1"–2" of compost each spring. Plants go dormant after blooming. Overplant with ferns to cover bare spots. No division is needed. To move plants, dig deeply to get at deep roots.
▶ **Choices:** Flowers come in blues, pinks, purples, and white.

Virginia Creeper
Parthenocissus quinquefolia

Deciduous vine

Parthenocissus quinquefolia

▶ ***Hardiness:*** Zones 4–9
▶ ***Size:*** 20' or more in all directions
▶ ***Features:*** This five-leaved native vine is easy to grow. Plant where it can climb on solid surfaces. This plant is often mistaken for poison ivy. The old saying—leaves of three let it be, leaves of five let it thrive—applies to this handsome plant. Rapid growth rate. Leaves turn bright red in autumn. Tolerates a variety of soil conditions.
▶ ***Uses:*** Natural areas, seaside gardens, masonry or stone walls, fences or buildings, hiding blank walls, adding coarse texture, backgrounds, seasonal accents, groundcover for erosion control
▶ ***Needs:*** Grow in any soil, from alkaline to acidic, dry to moist. Rocky soil is fine. Plant in full sun or partial shade. More sun yields brighter fall color. Tolerates heat, drought, and salt spray.
▶ ***Choices:*** Also try *P. q. var. Englemannii;* it boasts burgundy fall color and is hardy to Zone 3.

Vitex agnus-castus
see Chaste Tree; Lilac Chaste Tree

Vriesea splendens
see Bromeliads: Flaming Sword

Wake-Robin
see Trillium

Wall Rockcress
see Rockcress, Wall

Wandering Jew
Tradescantia zebrina

Tropical evergreen trailing perennial

Tradescantia zebrina

▶ ***Size:*** Grows trailing stems several feet long unless tips are pinched.
▶ ***Features:*** This easy-to-grow trailing plant has beautiful striped, slightly shimmering 2"–4" leaves in deep greens, burgundies, pinks, yellows, creams, and silvers. Excellent in a hanging basket.
▶ ***Uses:*** As a houseplant, in hanging baskets
▶ ***Needs:*** Bright light and even some direct light are important to keep the rich color of the leaves and to prevent plants from getting leggy. Keep soil very moist during most of the year; keep slightly drier in winter. Average household warmth. Setting pots on a tray with pebbles and water is beneficial. Fertilize three times in summer. Pinch ends of stems to control size and encourage a bushier, lusher plant.
▶ ***Choices:*** May be sold under a variety of botanical names, such as *T. albiflora* or *T. fluminensis* or zebrina. 'Quicksilver' is green and silvery-white striped. 'Tricolor' is white and pink striped.

Washingtonia robusta
see Palms: Mexican Fan Palm

Watermelon
Citrullus lanatus

Warm-season annual fruit

Watermelon 'Sugar Baby'

▶ ***Size:*** Grows a few inches tall, 2'–6' wide depending on the type
▶ ***Features:*** Juicy fruits growing on sprawling vines in mid- to late summer
▶ ***Uses:*** In the vegetable garden
▶ ***Needs:*** Full sun. well-drained, well-warmed soil high in organic matter with a pH above 6.0. Ample moisture until fruit begins to ripen, then less. Does best in the South with its warm, wet, long growing season. Plant seeds 1" deep or established seedlings two weeks after your region's last frost date. (In Zones 5–6, plant established seedlings to gain growing time.) Plant in raised beds or hills (2' wide; 4" tall mounds) to assure faster-warming soil. Space plants 2'–4' apart, depending on the type. Check the package or label. Mulch to conserve moisture and keep developing fruits clean. Determining exactly when a watermelon is ripe is a fine art. Clues are that the skin is dull, the tendril on the stem turns brown and dry, and the portion touching the ground changes from white to creamy pale yellow.
▶ ***Choices:*** In Zones 5–6, choose the smaller, faster-maturing types such as 'Garden Baby' and 'Sugar Baby' to accommodate the shorter growing season. Look for short-vine or bush types that use less space, some as little as 3 square feet. Small types bear fruits 5–10 pounds; large types can bear fruit that is easily 25 pounds, and, as with 'Carolina Cross', up to 100 pounds.

Water Hyssop
see Bacopa

Wax Myrtle, Pacific

Myrica cerifera

Evergreen tree

Myrica cerifera

▶***Hardiness:*** Zones 7–9
▶***Size:*** 10'–15' tall, 10'–15' wide
▶***Features:*** Got a black thumb? Plant wax myrtle; it'll turn your thumb green no matter where you plant it. Add a little water and fertilizer, and wax myrtle will soar along with your gardening ego. The dense canopy of this little tree shows its glossy, olive-green leaves year-round, unless hit with a blast of cold temperatures. Trees take pruning well; easy to trim to expose multiple trunks and develop as small tree. Can also be grown as large shrubs. Thin canopies in ice-prone areas to prevent trees from splitting. Tolerates harsh growing conditions. Fast-growing, pest- and problem-free.
▶***Uses:*** Screening, privacy, poolside, parking areas, patios, along walkways, city conditions, seaside landscapes, berms, or areas surrounded by paving, small specimen tree in planting beds
▶***Needs:*** Plant in wet or dry soil, including poor, sandy soils. Grow in full sun or partial shade. Tolerates heat, salt spray, and high humidity. Trees will perform best with regular watering and fertilization. Prune lower limbs to develop tree form.
▶***Choices:*** 'Fairfax'—dwarf selection, 6' to 8' tall.

Wax Plant

see Hoya

Weigela

Weigela florida

Deciduous flowering shrub

Weigela florida

▶***Hardiness:*** Zones 4–9
▶***Size:*** 6'–9' tall, 9'–12' wide
▶***Features:*** Arching sprays of colorful tubular flowers cover this large shrub in early summer, and often again in fall. New cultivars with colorful summer foliage extend the blooming season to nearly all summer. This is an easy, practically foolproof shrub for the low-maintenance landscape.
▶***Uses:*** In the shrub border, as a specimen
▶***Needs:*** Full sun to light shade. Rich, well-drained, neutral to alkaline soil; tolerates poor soil. Moderate moisture, but will tolerate drought. Plant in spring or fall. Work a few spadefuls of compost into the planting hole; further fertilizing not needed in most conditions. Mulch to conserve moisture. Prune right after flowering each year or every few years. To prune remove branches at ground level that have flowered to keep shrub blooming and maintain shape. It is usually problem free.
▶***Choices:*** Flowers are pink, red, or white. Most types grow large, but 'Java Red', 'Variegata Nana', 'Minuet', and 'Tango' grow 4' tall or shorter. 'Fine Wine' is one of the new burgundy-leaved varieties with deep red flowers.

Western Red Cedar

see Arborvitae

White Bird-of-Paradise

see Bird-of-Paradise, White

White Birch, European

see Birches

White Forsythia

see Forsythia, White

White Gaura

see Gaura, White

Whitespire Birch

see Birches

Wild Blue Phlox

see Phlox: Woodland Phlox

Willow, Desert

see Desert Willow

WILLOWS

Salix spp.

The willow tribe is a diverse bunch of trees and shrubs, ranging from dwarf, ground-covering shrubs hardy on the arctic tundra to immense weeping trees suitable for large parks and golf courses. Some are grown for their curious contorted branches, or for their large flowers called catkins that are fun to force indoors in late winter, or for their colorful twigs in winter. All are fast-growing, relatively short-lived plants with weak wood that constantly drop branches in every wind storm. And most are large plants whose ultimate size one needs to treat with respect, and plan for. Keep these water-lovers away from sewer lines and septic tanks or their roots will clog and damage them.

WILLOWS

Coral Embers Willow

Salix alba 'Britzensis'

Deciduous shrub

Salix alba 'Britzensis'

▶***Hardiness:*** Zones 2–8
▶***Size:*** 8'–10' tall, 5'–10' wide
▶***Features:*** The new stems on this shrub are bright red and are most effective during winter months after the leaves fall. Stems covered in snow

W

Plant encyclopedia

add winter interest. Coral embers willow grows in any well-drained soil as well as moist locations. Trim plants back severely in late winter to encourage vigorous new growth. Rapid growth fills planting areas quickly. Useful around ponds and streams.
▶ ***Uses:*** Shrub beds, mass planting against evergreen backgrounds, wet locations, around ponds and streams
▶ ***Needs:*** Plant in full sun in moist, well-drained soil. Tolerates wet soil. The red stem color is most prominent on young wood; prune all stems to within a few inches of the ground in early spring before new growth begins.

WILLOWS

Corkscrew Willow

Salix matsudana 'Torulosa'

Deciduous tree

Salix matsudana 'Torulosa'

▶ ***Hardiness:*** Zones 4–8
▶ ***Size:*** 12'–15' tall, 12'–15' wide
▶ ***Features:*** Known for their twisty, contorted branches and curled foliage, corkscrew willows add interest to winter scenes when limbs are bare and exposed. 'Golden Curls' contributes brightly colored twigs too. Great for growing in moist locations near water. May be sold as 'Erythroflexuosa'. Young stems are twisted and yellow-orange. Corkscrew willow has a graceful, arching form. Grows quickly and tolerates cold winters.
▶ ***Uses:*** Specimen use, accent, winter interest, natural areas
▶ ***Needs:*** Tolerates most soils, though moist, well-drained soils are best. Trees won't thrive in shallow, alkaline soil. Grow in full sun to partial shade. Cut plants back early each spring to encourage the growth of stems with bright winter color.
▶ ***Choices:*** *S. matsudana* 'Golden Curls'—contorted branches, 50' tall by 25' wide, with yellow twigs; 'Scarlet Curls'—contorted stems are reddish; leaves are curled on the contorted branches.

WILLOWS

French Pussy Willow

Salix caprea 'Kilmarnock'

Deciduous flowering shrub

Salix caprea 'Kilmarnock'

▶ ***Hardiness:*** Zones 4–8
▶ ***Size:*** 5'–6' tall, 5'–6' wide
▶ ***Features:*** If there's a place in your yard that stays wet, you've got the perfect location for French pussy willow. Decorative, furry buds cover stems in early spring before the leaves emerge. 'Kilmarnock' is a male form that produces abundant buds. The fuzzy buds are actually the male catkins or flowers. Plants may also be sold as *S. caprea* 'Pendula' or as goat willow. Rapid growth rate. Grows fast to form an interesting ornamental.
▶ ***Uses:*** Wet, boggy areas; planting beside streams, ponds, or downspouts; seasonal specimens; forcing cut branches indoors in spring arrangements
▶ ***Needs:*** Plant in any kind of soil—damp or wet soils are best. Grow in full sun. Prune immediately after bloom to control size if necessary. Pruning at this time will not destroy next year's show.

WILLOWS

Golden Weeping Willow

Salix alba 'Tristis'

Deciduous tree

Salix alba 'Tristis'

▶ ***Hardiness:*** Zones 3–8
▶ ***Size:*** 60'–75' tall, 60'–75' wide
▶ ***Features:*** With its large, rounded form and golden, weeping branches, this tree has a dramatic impact on the landscape. Plant near water to mirror the scene. Roots are invasive; avoid planting this tree near water lines, drain lines, or septic fields. Also sold as *S. ×sepulcralis* var. *chrysocoma*. Rapid growth rate. Pendulous branches sweep the ground. Yellow-gold foliage during warm months. Grows quickly; suitable for wet sites.
▶ ***Uses:*** Specimen use, planting beside ponds or streams, wet areas, hillsides, large spaces
▶ ***Needs:*** Grow in moist or wet soil in full sun. Tolerates a wide range of soil pH. Can withstand cold winter temperatures. Wood is weak and limbs break apart easily. Plan on gathering fallen limbs and small branches regularly.

WILLOWS

Weeping Willow

Salix babylonica

Deciduous tree

Salix babylonica

▶ ***Hardiness:*** Zones 4–9
▶ ***Size:*** 30'–40' tall; 30'–40' wide
▶ ***Features:*** If you have a large pond, you need a weeping willow to reflect on the water's surface. Streamerlike stems dangle to the water; roots love the soggy soil. Roots are invasive; don't plant this tree near water lines, swimming pools, drain lines, or septic fields. Though they grow quickly, trees may be short-lived. Leaves, twigs, and branches drop frequently resulting in the need for constant cleanup. Pendulous branches sweep the ground. Grows quickly to provide screening.
▶ ***Uses:*** Specimen trees; beside ponds or streams; damp, boggy areas; hillsides; large spaces
▶ ***Needs:*** Plant in soil that's wet or dry, fertile, or poor. Lush, fast growth occurs when grown in moist locations. Grow in full sun. Leaves will shed prematurely during droughts.
▶ ***Choices:*** 'Niobe'—golden bark.

Windflower

Anemone spp.

Spring-blooming bulb

Anemone coronaria 'De Caen' hybrids

▶ ***Hardiness:*** Varies according to type
▶ ***Size:*** 10" tall, 10" wide for poppy anemones; 4"–6" tall and wide for Greek anemones
▶ ***Features:*** Poppy anemones have big 4" flowers on 10" stems that are single or semidouble in blue, purple, pink, red, and white; these hybrids are the most common anemone sold as cut flowers. Greek anemones have smaller, more daisylike flowers 2" wide. They tends to naturalize and spread about the garden where their needs are met.
▶ ***Uses:*** Plant poppy anemones in mixed beds with ranunculus and early annual poppies, such as Iceland poppies. Naturalize Greek anemones in woodland gardens under deciduous trees where they're hardy.
▶ ***Needs:*** Full sun to light shade, preferably dappled with no midday sun in Zones 6–9. Rich, extremely well-drained soil. Ample moisture during spring; drier summer through fall. In Zones 4–5 plant tubers 3"–4" deep in spring a few weeks before the last frost date. In Zones 6–9 plant in October or November. Soak tubers in water overnight first. In fall, in Zone 4, provide winter mulch for *Anemone blanda.*
▶ ***Choices:*** Flowers available in blues, whites, pinks, and reds. Greek anemone *(A. blanda)* is hardy in Zones 4–8. Poppy anemone *(A.coronaria)* is hardy in Zones 6–9 and includes the popular 'De Caen' hybrids.

Winter Heath

see Heath

Winter Squash

see Squash

Winterberry

see Hollies

Wintercreeper

see Euonymus

Wintergreen

Gaultheria procumbens

Evergreen perennial

Gaultheria procumbens

▶ ***Hardiness:*** Zones 3–8
▶ ***Size:*** 3"–6" tall, 3'–4' or more wide
▶ ***Features:*** This groundcover is famous for its fragrance, delicate white or pale pink flowers in summer, and edible red winter berries. Though this plant is a little picky about where it grows, wintergreen requires only minor maintenance if the situation is right.
▶ ***Uses:*** Woodland areas, planting beneath acid-loving shrubs and trees, wintergreen fragrance, locating between stepping stones
▶ ***Needs:*** Plant in fertile, well-drained soil that's moist and acidic. Increase soil acidity by adding peat moss or composted oak leaves to the soil at planting time. Mulch with pine products to help conserve moisture. Wintergreen grows best in partial shade—plants in full sun need extra water.

Wishbone Flower

Torenia fournieri

Annual

Torenia fournieri

▶ ***Size:*** 9'–15" tall, 6"–24" wide
▶ ***Features:*** Other than impatiens and begonias, annuals for the shade are few. This Vietnam native has pansy-colored flowers that are tubular and small, but newer cultivars have showier, bigger blooms. Trailing forms are wonderful in hanging baskets. Blooms spring to frost.
▶ ***Uses:*** Massed in groups as a bedding or edging plant, or planted in containers and hanging baskets
▶ ***Needs:*** Light to medium shade, but full sun in cool-summer areas where temperatures are not above 75°F/24°C. Humus-rich, well-drained soil. Abundant moisture. Plant established plants in spring after danger of frost has passed. Work ample compost into soil. Plant in groups of a dozen or more for best effect. Mulch to conserve moisture. Fertilize occasionally, every 4–6 weeks, or work in a slow-release fertilizer at planting time. Root rot is a problem in wet, poorly drained soil.
▶ ***Choices:*** Flowers have markings in blues, purples, pinks, and white. 'Clown' series is one of the most popular cultivars.

Wisteria, Evergreen

Millettia reticulata

Evergreen or semievergreen flowering vine

Millettia reticulata

▶ ***Hardiness:*** Zones 9–10
▶ ***Size:*** 3"–6" tall, 20' wide
▶ ***Features:*** Evergreen wisteria is a good choice for covering outdoor structures and chain-link fences quickly. Reddish-purple flowers peep from behind lush, shiny leaves in summer and fall. Flowers are fragrant. Heat tolerant even in full sun.
▶ ***Uses:*** Covering arbors and trellises, hiding chain-link fences, adding texture to walls, planting in cutouts in paving
▶ ***Needs:*** Plant in any well-drained soil that receives full sun. Water regularly. Provide support—trellis, fencing, or string—for vines to climb. Prune as needed to thin out excess growth and control size.

Wisteria

Wisteria spp.

Deciduous flowering vine

Wisteria floribunda

▶***Hardiness:*** Zones 5-9
▶***Size:*** 30' or more tall, 12'-15' wide
▶***Features:*** If you can keep this strong, fast-growing vine within bounds, you'll enjoy years of drooping spring flowers, summer shade, and sculptural stems. Purple flowers dangle like grapes. Leaves cast cooling shade in summer. Aged stems appear muscular and strong. Keep wisteria out of trees, away from eaves, and off delicate arbors.
▶***Uses:*** Growing on walls, sturdy fences, or arbors; shading sitting areas; adding texture to backgrounds
▶***Needs:*** Plant in fertile, moist, well-drained soil. Grow in full sun or partial shade. Plant near well-anchored, sturdy supports. Use a bloom-booster fertilizer for abundant blooms. Prune after flowering to control size or mow over vines spreading on the ground. Prune wisteria after it has grown as big as you want it to be. After it has reached its desired size, promote flowering by thinning vines at least three times a year. If you only prune once a year, the vine will grow excessively thick foliage but yield few flowers. Start by cutting new growth when wisteria is dormant. You'll be able to identify new growth, even in winter, because the shoots at the end of vine tips are thinner than older branches. Locate the second bud on new growth; trim about half the shoots back to this point. In spring, remove all young branches that are leafless. Cut all side branches, leaving two or three buds and allowing nubby spurs to remain; the grapelike flowers will dangle from these. Follow up with summer pruning to reduce the size of branches growing to the sides by one-half. If your vine isn't flowering, it needs a little tough love. Use a shovel to sever roots about 18" around the base to a depth of 8"-10". Severing the roots will stimulate root growth and shock the plant into a flowering cycle.
Choices: Japanese wisteria *(Wisteria floribunda)* and Chinese wisteria *(Wisteria chinensis)* are both commonly offered; both have purple, pink, and white cultivars.

WITCH HAZELS

Hamamelis spp.

These elegant large shrubs or small trees bear spicy-scented blooms at unusual times of the year. The North American native, common witch hazel, bears its yellow flowers when late fall approaches winter. Chinese witch hazel and its hybrids with Japanese witch hazel *(H. ×intermedia)* bear their flowers as late winter turns into early spring. All witch hazels have flowers that are able to survive temperatures below freezing because of some amazing properties: the straplike petals curl into a protective ball as the temperature drops, then open again every time it goes above freezing to release their spicy scent. In addition to these welcome off-season flowers (which are fragrant delights to force indoors at the dead of winter), witch hazels have clean, attractive foliage that turns blazing colors in the fall. Scratch at the bark or a twig, crush a leaf, or sniff a flower—all parts of the plant have that characteristic astringent, spicy fragrance.

WITCH HAZELS

Chinese Witch Hazel

Hamamelis mollis

Deciduous flowering shrub

Hamamelis mollis

▶***Hardiness:*** Zones 6-9
▶***Size:*** 25' tall, 30' wide
▶***Features:*** Fragrant yellow flowers in late winter and early spring. Bright yellow fall foliage.
▶***Uses:*** A specimen in the woodland garden under tall, mature deciduous trees, or at edge of woods
▶***Needs:*** Best in moist, acidic soil that is well drained and high in organic matter. Plant in full sun to part shade. Little bothered by pests and diseases. Be sure to give this large shrub room to grow.

WITCH HAZELS

Common Witch Hazel

Hamamelis virginiana

Deciduous flowering shrub

Hamamelis virginiana

▶***Hardiness:*** Zones 4-9
▶***Size:*** 20'-30' tall, 15'-20' wide
▶***Features:*** Add flower fragrance to the scents experienced in autumn by planting common witch hazel. The flowers open in fall from October to November. Green summer foliage turns a spectacular golden-yellow in fall. Plants grown in full sun have a rounded shape while those grown in shade are more open and irregular. It can be used as a small tree or large shrub in the landscape. Medium growth rate. Disease and pest free; low maintenance.
▶***Uses:*** Shrub borders, large foundation plantings or massing, naturalized areas, fragrance; in shade
▶***Needs:*** Plant in full sun or partial shade in well-drained, fertile soil. It will not thrive in dry soils. Tolerant of city conditions. This shrub will get big; give it room to grow. Prune in late winter or early spring to remove dead or damaged wood.

WITCH HAZELS

Hybrid Witch Hazel

Hamamelis ×intermedia

Deciduous flowering shrub

Hamamelis ×intermedia

▶ ***Hardiness:*** Zones 5-8
▶ ***Size:*** 15'-20' tall, 15'-20' wide
▶ ***Features:*** Beautiful yellow, bronze, or deep red flowers appear in late winter and early spring when the rest of the garden is asleep. Flowers have a spicy fragrance, and are delightful to force indoors during winter for an early breath of spring. Foliage turns electric shades of red, orange, and yellow in fall. Beautiful when underplanted with late-winter blooming Christmas and Lenten roses *(Helleborus* spp.).
▶ ***Uses:*** Excellent for the naturalized woodland, or as a specimen next to a window to provide a glimpse of spring. If you have room, pair it with cornelian cherry dogwood *(Cornus mas)* which has yellow blooms that open a bit later.
▶ ***Needs:*** Plant in deep, rich soil with an abundant supply of moisture in full sun to partial shade. Pest free. Needs occasional deep watering during drought. Prune only to remove dead wood; the natural shape of this plant is beautiful and worth leaving alone.
▶ ***Choices:*** 'Arnold Promise' is a yellow-blooming form; 'Jelena' has yellow flowers that are suffused with copper, orange, and red. 'Diane' has deep red flowers and superb, rich, red fall color.

Woadwaxen
see Brooms

Woodruff
see Sweet Woodruff

Wormwood
see Artemisia

Yarrow
Achillea spp.
Perennial

Achillea spp.

▶ ***Hardiness:*** Zones 3-9
▶ ***Size:*** 2'-5' tall, 2'-3' wide
▶ ***Features:*** These long-lasting summer flowers are easy and undemanding to grow. The flat, big clusters of flowers appear in early to midsummer and usually last to late summer. The foliage is ferny and attractive, in some varieties gray or silver. Beautiful in combination with Russian sage and purple coneflower.
▶ ***Uses:*** In the mixed border or planted in large groups with ornamental grasses.
▶ ***Needs:*** Thrives in average to sandy soil; gets leggy if soil is too rich, wet, or heavy. It likes dry conditions and otherwise can be prone to fungal diseases. Plant established plants in spring or fall. Mulch to prevent weeds. Fertilize lightly if at all. This plant needs to be divided every 2-3 years. Common yarrow can sometimes be invasive.
▶ ***Choices:*** Flowers come in yellows, creams, reds, pinks, and apricots. Fern-leaf yarrow *(A. filipendulina)* and common yarrows *(A. millefolium)* do well in Zones 3-9; *A. ageratum* 'Moonshine' is hardy in Zones 3-8.

Yaupon
see Hollies

Yellow Jessamine
see Jasmines; Jessamines

Yellow Loosestrife
see Loosestrifes

Yellowwood, American
Cladrastis kentukea
Deciduous flowering tree

Cladrastis kentukea

▶ ***Hardiness:*** Zones 6-8
▶ ***Size:*** 30'-50' tall, 40'-55' wide
▶ ***Features:*** Fragrant blossoms appear to drip like white rain when this tree blooms in late spring and early summer. Coarse-textured foliage emerges a bright yellow-green in the spring and provides a nice contrast with the dark green leaves of maples and oaks. Fall color is yellow, though not as outstanding as maple. Gray-colored bark is smooth and looks like beech bark. Try the cultivar 'Rosea' if you prefer pink flowers. Medium growth rate. Upright form with spreading lower limbs.
▶ ***Uses:*** Single specimen use or as a shade tree for small yards. Group several together for a grove of bloom. Plant near outdoor seating areas to enjoy the fragrance of flowers.
▶ ***Needs:*** Plant in fertile, well-drained soil. Alkaline soils are ideal but not required. Shelter the tree from hot sun by planting in partial shade. This tree is not drought tolerant and requires adequate moisture throughout the growing season. Protect from strong winds. Prune in the summer to reduce bleeding sap.

YEWS
Taxus spp.

Yews are workhorses in the garden, providing evergreen foliage of fine texture and deep, rich dark green color. They take shearing well and make good hedges, topiary, and other formally shaped shrubs. The smaller forms are favorite foundation plants, but beware their ultimate size; many a gardener has been overwhelmed with a neglected plant that grew too big for its space.

YEWS

Anglo-Japanese Yew
Taxus ×media 'Densiformis'
Evergreen shrub

Taxus ×media 'Densiformis'

▶ ***Hardiness:*** Zones 4-7
▶ ***Size:*** 3'-4' tall, 4'-6' wide
▶ ***Features:*** Here's a dense, shrubby plant that fills a variety of landscaping needs. Fluffy needlelike foliage stays bright green year-round. Plants grow twice as wide as they will tall and thrive in the growing conditions found in the Midwest and Northeast. Many cultivars and forms are available. May also be sold as English-Japanese yew or as spreading yew.
▶ ***Uses:*** Foundation plantings, low hedges, informal or formal gardens, massing, providing background in perennial and shrub beds, parking areas, planting beside patios and driveways, adding winter interest
▶ ***Needs:*** Plant in soil that's acidic to neutral and moist but well drained. Shrubs won't thrive in soggy soil. Grows well in full sun, partial or dense shade. Easily transplanted and grown.

YEWS

Hick's Upright Yew

Taxus ×media 'Hicksii'

Evergreen shrub

Taxus ×media 'Hicksii'

▶***Hardiness:*** Zones 4–7
▶***Size:*** 20'–25' tall, 6'–10' wide
▶***Features:*** This is a perfect shrub to screen a fence or patio in a small yard. Its upright, narrow growth forms a dense screen without using up a lot of horizontal area. Plants add a formal touch wherever they are planted. Very low maintenance. Slow growth rate. Plants are upright and columnar in form. Leaves remain deep green year-round. Easy to grow and requires little care.
▶***Uses:*** Hedges, screens, specimen use; adding formal accent to entrances; forming a living fence
▶***Needs:*** Plant in sun or shade in moist, sandy, acidic soil. Soil must be well drained. Add composted leaves or peat moss to soil at planting time to boost soil acidity. Prune to shape the shrub during summer or early fall.

YEWS

Plum Yew

Cephalotaxus harringtonia

Evergreen shrub

Cephalotaxus harringtonia

▶***Hardiness:*** Zones 6–9
▶***Size:*** 5'–15' tall, 5'–15' wide
▶***Features:*** Many consider this yew relative the best substitute for *Taxus* in the South. It's quite similar in appearance with somewhat longer evergreen leaves and larger plumlike fruits on female plants, but with much greater heat and drought tolerance.
▶***Uses:*** While the species can grow to be a small tree 20' tall, there are an increasing number of cultivars available that are good for the shady border and foundation plantings.
▶***Needs:*** Best in shade but will tolerate sun. Well-drained soil is essential. Adequate water is best but plants tolerate drought well. Slow-growing.
▶***Choices:*** Many cultivars are available. 'Fastigiata' is a rounded columnar form that reaches 10' tall and 8' wide. 'Prostrata' grows 2'–3' high and as wide.

Yew Pine

see *Podocarpus*

Yucca

Yucca spp.

Evergreen perennial

Yucca filamentosa

▶***Hardiness:*** Zones 4–10
▶***Size:*** 3' tall, 3' wide, 6'–7' tall in bloom
▶***Features:*** This plant may look exotic, as if it belongs in the desert south of the border, but it's very hardy and dependable over much of the United States and Canada. The rosettes of sword-shape leaves reminiscent of agave or aloe have needle-sharp tips, and often serrated edges. In early to midsummer, an enormous flower spike arises to tower above the foliage with a candelabra of fragrant ivory bell-shape blooms. An unforgettable sight, these magnificent flower stalks can last for weeks. This plant is excellent with other easy-care plants such as low-growing junipers, ornamental grasses, Russian sage, and brooms.
▶***Uses:*** Integrate yuccas into beds with other low-maintenance plants. Plant them singly as specimens or group them into dramatic clusters.
▶***Needs:*** Full sun. Average to sandy, well-drained soil. Drought tolerant. Plant established plants in spring or fall, spacing as label directs. Use gloves to handle large plants because leaves can be sharp. Avoid fertilizing. Trim off spent flower stalks after blooming. To get more plants, in spring separate small plants that crop up around the base and transplant. It is prone to root rot in wet sites.
▶***Choices:*** Flowers are white. There are many species of yucca, some growing as modest-size perennials and some soaring to the size of trees. The most commonly grown for the flower garden is Adam's needle (*Y. filamentosa)* It has foliage 2'–3' tall and flower stalks 5'–7' tall. Hardy in Zones 4–11.

Yucca, Spineless

Yucca elephantipes

Subtropical evergreen perennial

Yucca elephantipes

▶ ***Hardiness:*** Zones 9–10
▶ ***Size:*** Grows 3'-5' tall and about 1'-2' wide
▶ ***Features:*** Sometimes referred to as a false palm, this plant sends out long, leathery leaves from a woody trunk. A good choice for a large hall or other large space, especially since the sharp leaves of other yucca species can be uncomfortable to brush against.
▶ ***Uses:*** As a houseplant, though used as a landscape plant or small tree in the warmest regions of the United States
▶ ***Needs:*** Direct light. Needs a deep, well-drained container and does best if can be moved outdoors in summer. Does fine in regular household warmth in summer but needs a cool spot (50°F/10°C to 60°F/16°C) in winter. Keep soil moist most of year; allow to dry out considerably between waterings in winter. Fertilize once a year in summer.
▶ ***Choices:*** *Y. aloifolia* is similar but is also known as Spanish bayonet because of its sharp leaves.

Zantadeschia spp.

see Calla Lily

Zebra Grass

see Grasses, Ornamental; Silver Grass

Zebra Haworthia

see Cactus and Succulents

Zebra Plant

Aphelandra squarrosa

Tropical evergreen shrub

Aphelandra squarrosa

▶ ***Size:*** grows to 3' or 4' in ideal conditions with a large container
▶ ***Features:*** Beautiful 8" glossy leaves with silvery veins. Often will send out cone-shape 4"-6" showy golden yellow flowerlike bracts.
▶ ***Uses:*** As a houseplant
▶ ***Needs:*** Bright light but not direct sun. Keep soil evenly moist but not soggy. Water with room-temperature soft water or rainwater. Good humidity important; put on a tray of pebbles and water or double-pot (see page 275) with peat moss kept wet. Does fine in average warmth of home but will not tolerate cold drafts. A rather difficult plant to grow; if not kept in evenly moist soil, high humidity, and away from cold, the plants start to drop leaves and are slow to recover, if ever.
▶ ***Choices:*** *A. squarrosa* 'Louisae' grows just 18"-24". *A. aurantiaca* has orange-red bracts.

Zelkova, Japanese

Zelkova serrata

Deciduous tree

Zelkova serrata

▶ ***Hardiness:*** Zones 5–9
▶ ***Size:*** 50'-80' tall, 50'-80' tall
▶ ***Features:*** Consider this tree as a replacement for the disease-prone American elm. Leafy shade, upright branches, and sturdy trunks are similar to elms and make it perfect for patios, yards, or lining streets. Tree trunks exfoliate in old age, revealing colorful inner bark. Plants are resistant to many of the insects and diseases that plague elms. Medium to rapid growth rate.
▶ ***Uses:*** Street, shade, and lawn tree use; lining walkways or drives; beside decks, entries, or patios
▶ ***Needs:*** Plant in fertile soil that's moist but well drained. Trees grow in acidic or alkaline soils. They tolerate wind and drought once established, as well as reflected heat from paving and pollution. Prune as needed to keep limbs overhead.

Zinnia

Zinnia elegans

Annual

Zinnia elegans

▶ ***Size:*** 12"-24" tall, 6"-15" wide
▶ ***Features:*** These large, round double flowers in hot colors are classics for the cut flower garden. They grow on erect, bushy plants. Easy to start from seed and easy to grow, they are rugged and durable, producing blooms all summer to frost.
▶ ***Uses:*** Use the lower-growing, more compact hybrids as a bedding plant for summer color. The taller varieties are best grown in the cutting garden where they can be staked and monitored to prevent mildew. All zinnias are good subjects for container gardening.
▶ ***Needs:*** Full sun in Zones 2-8; light shade in hot-summer climates in Zones 9-11. Fertile, well-drained, neutral to acidic soil. Moderate moisture to drought tolerant, depending on type. Plant established plants in spring after all danger of frost, pinching ends to encourage fuller plants. Or plant seeds directly in prepared soil outdoors after all danger of frost. Thin according to package directions. Mulch to prevent disease. Fertilize occasionally, every 4-6 weeks. Trim spent blooms to promote further flowering. This plant is mildew prone; avoid wetting leaves when watering, and select mildew-resistant cultivars, especially in the humid Midwest and South.
▶ ***Choices:*** Narrowleaf zinnia *(Z. angustifolia)* is a low-growing, mounding plant with fine-textured leaves that are covered with small single golden yellow-orange flowers all summer. It is resistant to mildew. Hybrids between this species and *Z. elegans* have recently been introduced that are low-growing with small flowers and mildew-resistant such as narrowleaf zinnia, with fully double flowers in the elegant hot colors of *Z. elegans*.

Zucchini

see Squash, Summer

A Gardening Glossary

A

acid soil: Sometimes also called sour soil. The opposite of alkaline, sometimes called sweet, soil. Acid soil is a soil with a pH lower than 7.0. A soil pH higher than 7.0 is alkaline. Neutral soil is in the middle of this range. Some garden plants thrive only in acid soil, others only in alkaline. The vast majority thrive in neutral soil.

aerate: Loosening the soil to increase water and air penetration.

alkaline soil: A soil with a pH higher than 7.0 is an alkaline soil. See also "acid soil."

annuals: Plants whose life cycle is completed in one year or less—germinating from seed, growing, flowering, setting seed and dying.

Many annuals make excellent container plants.

B

balled and burlapped: Trees and shrubs dug out of the ground and sold with burlap or a similar material wrapped around the roots instead of a pot.

bareroot plants: Plants being sold with all the soil removed from their roots. Usually sold with the tops protruding from boxes or bags and the roots packed in damp sawdust.

bedding plants: Plants—usually annuals—that are sold already well-established and ready to plant for quick growth and color.

biennial: A plant that usually lives two years. The first year it usually grows just foliage. The second year, usually, it flowers.

bolting: Usually refers to vegetables, such as lettuce, that quickly go to flower rather than producing a quality food crop. Usually caused by warm weather.

botanical name: The scientific or Latin name of a plant, usually made up of at least one word (the genus) but also often the species (the second word).

bract: Modified leaves growing just below the true flower. In some flowers the bracts are more showy than the true flowers.

bud: A flower or plant growth (usually a flower or leaf) in its early stage of development.

bud union: The point on a rose, right above the roots, where the top portion of the rose has been grafted onto the roots to produce a superior plant.

bulb: A true bulb is the thickened underground storage system of certain perennials, such as lilies. Also used casually to refer to everything from daffodils to dahlias to irises.

C

cold frame: A structure, usually box-like, that serves as a minigreenhouse to protect plants from cold.

A cold frame is handy for starting seeds early.

complete fertilizer: A plant food which contains all three of the main elements for plant growth: nitrogen, phosphorus and potassium.

compost: The black, crumbly, soil-like material created by decomposing organic matter, such as leaves, weeds, egg shells, clipped grass, and other organic matter.

conifer: A tree or shrub that bears cones and has needlelike leaves.

corm: A thickened underground stem. When planted, an entire plant grows from the corm. A crocus is the most commonly known type of corm.

cover crop: A crop, usually an annual such as rye or a legume, planted in order to capture nitrogen from the air and transmit it into the soil. Usually plowed into the soil for maximum enrichment of the soil. Often planted in the fall and allowed to die before being worked into the soil in spring.

crown: The point, usually at the soil level, at which a plant's roots and top meet.

cultivate: Process of breaking up the soil surface for the purpose of removing weeds, and preparing for planting.

cuttings, taking: Cutting off sections of stems, roots, or leaves to plant and thereby multiply the plant.

D

damping off: A fungal disease that strikes new seedlings. The plants topple over when the stem withers right at soil level. Prevent by using a special seed-starting potting mix, avoiding overwatering, and by running a fan near indoor seeds.

deciduous: Refers to a plant that loses its leaves once a year, usually in the fall.

deadhead: Pinching or cutting off spent flowers to tidy plants and promote longer bloom.

This *Hosta tardiflora* was lifted from the ground and split in two with a spade.

dethatching: The process of removing dead grass stems from the lawn to stimulate better growth.

dividing: Digging up and splitting mature plants. Can be done because the plant is overgrown or has a dead center or is flopping for no other apparent reason. Can also be done simply to get more plants.

dormant: Part of the cycle of a plant when it stops growing. The top of the plant may or may not die back.

double digging: Preparing a bed or border for planting by digging to a depth of two shovelheads. Usually the bottom soil is brought to the top and the top is put at the bottom.

drip line: The imaginary circle below the tips of the outermost branches of a tree or plant. An indicator of how far the roots reach out.

E

espalier: The training of a tree, shrub, or vine so its branches grow in a flat pattern, usually against a wall, fence, or other structure. Especially popular with fruit trees.

evergreen: A plant that keeps its leaves all year. May be a needle-leaved tree, such as a pine, or may be a broad-leafed evergreen, such as a rhododendron. Some perennials, such as moss phlox, are also evergreen and don't die back in winter.

eye: An undeveloped bud that will produce new growth.

F

fertilizer: Any material used to feed a plant. May be dry or liquid and different formulations are used for different plants to encourage different processes (foliar growth vs. blooming vs. root development). One function of compost is to fertilize plants.

foliar feeding: Fertilizer applied in liquid form as a spray so plants can take up the nutrients through their leaves.

forcing: Speeding along a plant's growth or bloom, usually to be able to appreciate them out of their usual season, as in forcing tulips for winter bloom.

frond: The branch and leaf structure of a fern or palm.

frost: Conditions that occur when temperatures drop below freezing. A light frost occurs when temperatures dip just below freezing for a short time. A light frost may injure some tender plants but won't kill them. A hard frost, sometimes called a killing frost, occurs when temperatures dip even lower and all tender plants are killed.

Sweet Woodruff makes a tidy groundcover.

G

germinate: The process of the sprouting of a seed.

girdling: A problem created when a wire or other material chokes a plant, usually a tree. This usually happens when ties to a stake or support haven't been removed.

grafting: Attaching a short length of stem of one plant onto the root stock of a different plant. Grafting is usually done to produce a more hardy or otherwise superior plant.

groundcover: Low-growing plants that are planted in groups to cover a ground in a uniform manner.

growing season: The number of days between the last killing frost in spring and the first killing frost in fall. Colder northern regions have shorter growing seasons; warm southern climates have long and even year-round growing seasons.

H

hardening off: Gradually acclimatizing indoor-grown plants to outdoor conditions of sun, wind, cold, and heat.

hardpan: A layer of soil or clay lying beneath the topsoil. Depending on the type, it can be very difficult if not impossible to dig through.

hardy: Often mistakenly called "hearty." Refers to a plant's ability to withstand cold. Used interchangeably with "cold hardy."

heeling in: Temporarily putting a plant, often at an angle, in a trench and covering the roots with soil to keep them moist and live until they can be planted in their permanent spot. Usually a plant is heeled in for just a week or two.

herbaceous: A plant with soft rather than woody stems.

humus: The dark, rich organic part of the soil that results from leaves and other natural materials decomposing. Black, well-decomposed compost sometimes is called humus.

hybrid: The offspring of two plants of different species or varieties of plants, usually with bigger and better traits.

L

leaching: The removal of salts or nutrients from soil by water moving through it. Leaching occurs in areas with high rainfall or in very sandy soils, where water moves through it very quickly.

leaflet: A smallish, leafy growth off the side of the stem or leaf

leaf mold: Partially decomposed leaves. An excellent soil amendment.

leaf margins: The edges of a leaf.

loam: An ideal garden soil made up of clay, sand, and organic matter.

Queen Anne's lace and poppies from a wildflower seed mix *naturalize* in this corner of a garden.

manure: Animal excrement worked into the soil to enrich it. Fresh manure can burn plants, but well-rotted (the same as composted) manure that has been allowed to set for a few months will not.

M

microclimate: Variations of the climate within a certain area. A microclimate can be as large as a valley or hillside or as small as a portion of your yard.

micronutrients: Mineral elements that are needed by some plants in very small quantities. If the plants you are growing require specific 'trace elements' and they are not available in the soil, they must be added.

mulch: A material, either loose or solid, placed over the soil. Most mulch is used to suppress weeds and conserve moisture, but it can also be used, as in the case of plastic, to heat soil.

N

native plant: A plant that has grown naturally, without human intervention, before the arrival of European and other immigrants.

naturalize: Planting for natural effect. In some cases, plants are naturalized by planting them in a minimally cultivated area and letting them spread. In other cases, most commonly with daffodils, the bulbs are planted in naturalistic clusters in a lawn or minimally cultivated area.

node: The part of a stem from which a leaf or new branch grows.

O

organic gardening: A method of gardening that does not use chemicals.

organic material: In gardening, refers to any material that started out as part of a living thing and will eventually break down, as in wood chips, compost, pine needles, etc. Non-organic materials would include stone, plastic, metal, etc.

P

pathogen: An organism that causes disease. Includes fungi, bacteria, and viruses.

peat moss: The partially decomposed remains of moss. Peat can come from a bog or fell and can vary in quality. Sphagnum peat moss is harvested from Canadian bogs and is the best quality.

perennial: A plant that grows for more than two years.

perlite: A mineral, heated to explode in a manner not unlike popcorn. Is added to potting mixes to improve moisture retention and drainage.

pinching back: Pinching off the tip of a plant with fingers to encourage branching and fullness.

potting soil: A soil mix used for pots and other containers. Can be blended at home but usually purchased premixed in a bag.

potting medium: Can also be called growing medium. The material in which plants grow. Can include potting soil (see above), but also soilless potting mixes and barks used to grow things like orchids.

propagation: Any method used to increase the supply of a plant, be it division, seed starting, layering, taking cuttings, or others.

pruning: Removing plant parts to improve overall plant health or shape.

Pruning a tree limb with a pruning saw

R

rhizome: A modified plant stem, such as that of an iris, that grows horizontally, under the surface of the soil.

root ball: The cluster of roots, with soil attached, of a plant.

rootbound: A condition that occurs when a potted plant outgrows the pot. Roots are tangled, matted, and too large for the plant. If the plant isn't repotted, it will start to wilt and fail to thrive.

rooting hormone: A liquid growth hormone powder into which the cut end of cuttings are dipped to promote root development.

runner: A stem growing out from the base a plants which ends in a new plant. Can be aboveground or underground.

S

staking: Supporting a plant with a straight stake (and usually also ties) or with a specially made support, including grow-through grid-types.

sucker: A growth, nearly always undesirable, sprouting from the roots of a plant.

systemic: A chemical taken up by the entire plant. Can be an herbicide, which kills the whole plant, including the roots, or an insecticide that will kill insects that feed on any part of the plant.

T

tap root: A single root growing straight down, and usually fairly deeply, into the soil.

tender plants: Plants unable to withstand any extreme cold, especially freezing temperatures.

tendril: A slender growth a vine uses to attach itself to a support.

thinning: Plucking out or otherwise removing plants from a thickly planted stand, as in thinning out carrot seedlings. Thinning can also refer to thinning out selected branches from a shrub or tree.

topsoil: The top layer of soil, usually of a higher quality, in undisturbed ground. Also refers to planting-quality (as opposed to fill dirt) soil sold by landscaping companies.

transplanting: Digging up a plant and moving it to another spot.

tuber: A flat underground stem. Potatoes and dahlias are two examples.

Hosta 'Frances Williams' has variegated leaves with a creamy white edge.

V

variegated: Multiple colors, usually on a leaf but sometimes on a flower petal.

W

woody ornamental: A plant that has woody, rather than soft, stems that is grown for ornamental (rather than food or practical) purposes. Most trees and shrubs would be classified as woody ornamentals.

Resources

Plant and Gardening Organizations

African Violet Society of America
2375 North Street
Beaumont, TX 77702
Phone: 409-839-4725
Email: avsa@earthlink.net
http://www.avsa.org

American Bamboo Society
http://www.americanbamboo.org
Email: help@americanbamboo.org

American Boxwood Society
P.O. Box 85
Boyce, VA 22620-0085
Email: info@boxwoodsociety.org
http://www.boxwoodsociety.org

American Camellia Society
Massee Lane Gardens
100 Massee Lane
Fort Valley GA 31030
Email: ask@camellias-acs.com
Phone: 478-967-2358
http://www.camellias-acs.com

American Clivia Society
10606 N. 166th E. Ave.
Owasso, OK 74055
Email: AmericanCliviaSociety@yahoo.com
Phone: 918-272-4623
http://www.AmericanCliviaSociety.org

American Community Gardening Association
Phone: 877-ASK-ACGA (877-275-2242)
http://www.communitygarden.org

Crocus **hybrids**

American Conifer Society
P.O. Box 3422
Crofton, MD 21114-0422
Email: conifersociety@aol.com
Phone: 410-721-6611
http://www.conifersociety.org

American Daffodil Society
http://www.daffodilusa.org

American Fuchsia Society
San Francisco County Fair Building
Ninth Ave. and Lincoln Way
San Francisco, CA 94122
www.americanfuchsiasociety.org

American Hemerocallis Society
http://www.daylilies.org

American Horticultural Society
George Washington's River Farm
7931 East Boulevard Drive
Alexandria, VA 22308
Email: sdick@ahs.org
Phone: 703-768-5700
http://www.ahs.org

American Hosta Society
Email: webmaster@casscats.com
For Hosta questions email
Giboshiman@aol.com
Phone: 402-298-8884
http://www.hosta.org

American Iris Society
http://www.irises.org

American Orchid Society
16700 AOS Lane
Delray Beach, FL 33446-4351
Phone: 561-404-2000
Email: TheAOS@aos.org
http://www.aos.org

American Rose Society
P.O. Box 30,000
Shreveport, LA 71130
Email: ars@ars-hq.org
Phone: 800-637-6534
http://www.ars.org

North American Native Plant Society
Box 84, Station D
Etobicoke, Ontario
Canada M9A 4X1
Email: nativeplantsoc@yahoo.ca
Phone: 416-631-4438
www.nanps.org

North American Water Garden Society
P.O. Box 175
Batavia, IL 60510
Phone: 630-326-1844
http://www.nawgs.com

National Gardening Association
1100 Dorset Street
South Burlington, VT 05403
Phone: 802-863-5251
http://www.garden.org

Dahlia **hybrid**

Soil Testing Facilities

Check with your local state university to see if they provide local or regional low-cost soil testing. To find one near you with the help of your computer's browser, type the name off your state followed by "soil testing." Non-university-based facilities include:

Wallace Laboratories
365 Coral Circle
El Segundo, CA 90245
Phone: 310-615-0116
http://www.bettersoils.com

Timberleaf Soil Testing
39648 Old Spring Rd.
Murrieta, CA 92563-5566
Email: tmbrlfsoiltest@murrieta.net
Phone: 951-677-7510

Online Pest, Disease, and Weed Indentification and Control Sites

Weed Identification
University of Illinois at Urbana Champagne's Weed Identification Site
Fill out a short on-line form that describes the weed and the site identifies it for you
http://web.aces.uiuc.edu/weedid/

Vegetable Garden Pest Identification
Texas A&M's Department of Entomology
A gallery of color photos of various vegetable garden pests along with methods of control.
http://vegipm.tamu.edu/imageindex.html

Insect Pests of Ornamental Plants
Insect Identification Laboratory of Virginia Tech.
A photographic slide show of ornamental insect and mite pests. A brief description accompanies each slide photograph.
http://www.ext.vt.edu/departments/entomology/ornamentals/slidepage.html

Weed Identification Guide
Virginia Tech Plant Pathology, Physiology, and Weed Science
Color photographs and text descriptions of several broadleaf weeds and grasses are presented. Weeds are indexed by common name. Scientific names are also provided.
http://www.ppws.vt.edu/scott/weed_id/rightsid.htm

Plant Disease Facts
Pennsylvania State University.
Color photographs and fact sheet information for diseases of landscape plants including flowering and foliage plants and woody ornamentals. Indexed by disease name and by host plant. Disease management information is included.
http://www.ppath.cas.psu.edu/extension/plant_disease

Online Weather Information

Weather.com
Daily and longer-term forecasts, as well as a special home and garden section.
http://www.weather.com

U.S. National Oceanic and Atmospheric Administration
Climate information displayed in lots of maps on rainfall, drought, heat, cold, and more.
http://www.noaa.gov/climate.html
(Go to the middle of the web page and click on the section labeled "climate")

Other sites of interest:

University of Illinois at Urbana-Champaign Veterinary Medicine
Lists of plants toxic to animals
http://www.library.uiuc.edu/vex/vetdocs/toxic.htm

Chicago Botanic Gardens
A tour of "the enabling garden" a garden designed especially for people with disabilities or those who use wheelchairs at the Chicago Botanic Gardens
http://www.chicago-botanic.org/explore/GardenEnable.html

Locating Your Local Horticulture Cooperative Extension Service and Master Gardener Classes
Whether you want a plant list of native plants for your area, want to find out about a pesky insect that's been plaguing your lawn, or you're interested in taking a Master Gardener class, your free local horticulture cooperative extension service can be of help.

The easiest way is online. Just type in "horticulture extension" followed by your state or city. Also check government pages (horticulture extension is part of the U.S. Department of Agriculture and administered locally by state universities) in your phone book.

Also be sure to check out your state's (and perhaps even your county's) horticulture extension website. It is sure to be loaded with highly regional, excellent gardening information, as well as highly localized recommended plant lists and growing information.

If none of these are of help, check with your local Home Depot garden center associate for extension and Master Gardener contact information.

Index

Page numbers in *italic type* refer to photographs, illustrations, and information in captions. Page numbers for plants listed in tables are followed by "t." Plants are listed under their common names. For plant descriptions see the Plant Encyclopedia (pages 292–537) where individual plants are listed alphabetically. Plants listed in the Plant Encyclopedia are not listed in this index.

A

B

C

F

G

H

I

J

K

L

M

N

O

P

Index

R

Index

S

Index

T

Index

U

V

Index

W

Y

Gardening 1-2-3®
Project Editor: Michael McKinley
Writer: Veronica Lorson Fowler
Graphic Designer: Ernie Shelton
Director of Photography: Kate Carter Frederick
Photographers: Marty Baldwin, Scott Little, Blaine Moats, Jason Wilde,
Primary Contributing Photographers: Doug Hetherington, Jerry Pavia
Contributing Photographers: David Cavagnero, Dr. Nick E. Christians, Alan & Linda Detrick Photography LLC, Catriona Tudor Erler, Derek Fell, David R. Frazier, John Glover, Bill Johnson, David Liebman, Tommy Miyasaki, Richard Shiell, Joseph G. Strauch, Jr.
Photo Researcher: Susan Ferguson
Copy Chief: Terri Fredrickson
Contributing Copy Editors: Barbara Feller-Roth, Fran Gardner
Contributing Proofreaders: Thomas E. Blackett, Stacie J. Gaylor, Jodie Littleton
Indexer: Ellen Sherron
Publishing Operations Manager: Karen Schirm
Senior Editor, Asset and Information Manager: Phillip Morgan
Edit and Design Coordinator: Mary Lee Gavin
Editorial and Design Assistant: Renee E. McAtee
Book Production Managers: Pam Kvitne, Marjorie J. Schenkelberg, Rick von Holdt, Mark Weaver

Additional Editorial Contributions from Art Rep Services
Director: Chip Nadeau
Illustrator: Rick Hanson

Thanks to: Janet Anderson, Staci Bailey, Mary Irene Swartz, Diane Witosky, Beckett Corporation, and Harvey's Greenhouses of Adel, IA

Meredith® Books
Executive Director, Editorial: Gregory H. Kayko
Executive Director, Design: Matt Strelecki
Managing Editor: Amy Tincher-Durik
Executive Editor: Benjamin W. Allen
Senior Associate Design Director: Tom Wegner
Marketing Product Manager: Brent Wiersma

Publisher and Editor in Chief: James D. Blume
Editorial Director: Linda Raglan Cunningham
Executive Director, New Business Development: Todd M. Davis
Director, Sales—Home Depot: Robb Morris
Executive Director, Sales: Ken Zagor
Director, Operations: George A. Susral
Director, Production: Douglas M. Johnston
Director, Marketing: Amy Nichols
Business Director: Jim Leonard

Vice President and General Manager: Douglas J. Guendel

Meredith Publishing Group
President: Jack Griffin
Senior Vice President: Bob Mate

Meredith Corporation
Chairman and Chief Executive Officer: William T. Kerr
President and Chief Operating Officer: Stephen M. Lacy

In Memoriam: E.T. Meredith III (1933-2003)

The Home Depot®
Marketing Manager: Tom Sattler

Library of Congress Control Number: 2005929391
ISBN: 0-696-22425-9

Distributed by Meredith Corporation.
Meredith Corporation is not affiliated with The Home Depot®.

Note to the Reader: Due to differing conditions, tools, and individual skills, Meredith Corporation and The Home Depot® assume no responsibility for any damages, injuries suffered, or losses incurred as a result of following the information published in this book. Before beginning any project, review the instructions carefully, and if any doubts or questions remain, consult local experts or authorities. Because codes and regulations vary greatly, you always should check with authorities to ensure that your project complies with all applicable local codes and regulations. Always read and observe all of the safety precautions provided by any tool or equipment manufacturer, and follow all accepted safety procedures.

We are dedicated to providing accurate and helpful do-it-yourself information. We welcome your comments about improving this book and ideas for other books we might offer to gardening enthusiasts. Contact us by any of these methods:
Leave a voice message at: 800/678-2093
Write to: Meredith Books, Home Depot Books
1716 Locust St.
Des Moines, IA 50309-3023
Send email to: hi123@mdp.com.

Craig A. Allen
Athens, GA

Robert Andersen
Issaquah, WA

Jason Awtrey
Kennesaw, GA

Mike Bamford
Huntington Beach, CA

Larry Baumgartner
Lake Forest, CA

Patrick Boucher
Marlborough, MA

Carmela Carrasco
Huntington Beach, CA

Mario Corona
Fullerton, CA

Tom Del Hotal
Lemon Grove, CA

Mark Edelbrock
Gig Harbor, MA

Steven J. Esguerra
San Diego, CA

Mike Etheridge
Anaheim Hills, CA

Deanna Frender
Silverdale, WA

Jennifer Fuller
Shrewsbury, MA

Ron Gascoyne, Jr.
Port Orchard, WA

Dawnya Goode
Anaheim Hills, CA

Many thanks to the employees of The Home Depot® whose "wisdom of the aisles" has made *Gardening 1-2-3®* the most useful book of its kind.

Russell Hattaway
Buford, GA

Chet Haus
Silverdale, WA

Rebecca Johnson
Woodstock, GA

Lucy Kutil
Snellville, GA

Ronald A. Lafontaine
Saugus, MA

June McNew
Snellville, GA

Richard T. Morrison
Waterville, ME

Pamela H. Neumann-Mckinney
Puyallup, WA

Dale North
Escondido, CA

Lorn Patterson
San Marcos, CA

Tom Sattler
Atlanta, GA

Jennifer Scott
North Kingstown, RI

Jeffery B. Slaughter
Seattle, WA

Georgia Lee Thieben
Garden Grove, CA

Scott R. Tubbs
Acworth, GA

Janet Wadden
Waltham, MA

Charlice Wiley
Tacoma, WA